The Globalization of World Politics

THE GLOBALIZATION OF WORLD POLITICS

An introduction to international relations

Fifth edition

John Baylis · Steve Smith · Patricia Owens

OXFORD
UNIVERSITY PRESS

OXFORD
UNIVERSITY PRESS

Great Clarendon Street, Oxford OX2 6DP

Oxford University Press is a department of the University of Oxford.
It furthers the University's objective of excellence in research, scholarship,
and education by publishing worldwide in

Oxford New York

Auckland Cape Town Dar es Salaam Hong Kong Karachi
Kuala Lumpur Madrid Melbourne Mexico City Nairobi
New Delhi Shanghai Taipei Toronto

With offices in

Argentina Austria Brazil Chile Czech Republic France Greece
Guatemala Hungary Italy Japan Poland Portugal Singapore
South Korea Switzerland Thailand Turkey Ukraine Vietnam

Oxford is a registered trade mark of Oxford University Press
in the UK and in certain other countries

Published in the United States
by Oxford University Press Inc., New York

British Library Cataloguing in Publication Data
Data available

Library of Congress Cataloging in Publication Data
Data available

Typeset by Sparks—www.sparkspublishing.com
Printed in Italy
on acid-free paper by
L.E.G.O. S.p.A.—Lavis TN

ISBN 978-0-19-956909-0

3 5 7 9 10 8 6 4 2

To Marion, Jeannie, and Bille

New to this edition

- New chapters on postcolonialism and poststructuralism.
- Increased emphasis on the global financial crisis, forced migration, diplomacy, and religion.
- Additional case studies for lecturers.
- Interactive library of links to journal articles, blogs, and video content.

Preface

We have tried in this new edition of *The Globalization of World Politics* to follow much the same format as the previous four editions, which have proved so successful. However, a number of improvements have been made. Oxford University Press commissioned over twenty reviews of the fourth edition, and we gained enormously from their comments. They told us what worked and what didn't, and all the existing chapters have been revised accordingly. We have also been contacted by many of the teachers of International Relations around the world who use the book on a regular basis. Together, all these comments have helped us identify a number of additional areas that should be covered. We think that one of the strengths of this book is the diversity of theoretical perspectives offered, and we have tried in this edition to consolidate this strength by commissioning two new theory chapters, on poststructuralism and on postcolonialism.

We want to end these comments by paying both a personal and a professional tribute to Caroline Thomas, author of the chapter on Poverty, Development, and Hunger in the previous four editions of the book. She died, aged 49, on 20 October 2008 after a long illness. Caroline was a great scholar, a wonderful teacher, and one of the most ethical and empathetic individuals we have ever met. We all miss her greatly.

More praise for *The Globalization of World Politics*:

The Globalization of World Politics is superb. The volume has a succinct and lucid style, but also manages to cover a whole range of schools of thought and policy issues. If you are asked to choose one textbook in the area of international relations this is it.

Takashi Inoguchi, University of Tokyo

The preeminent introduction to International Relations just got even better. The empirical and theoretical updates in the new edition demonstrate the authors' continuing commitment to excellence.

Malena Rosén Sundström, Malmö University

An impressive array of scholars provide superb commentary on a range of topics, all of which have critical importance for the study of international relations. Student and teachers will find the volume indispensible.

J.E. Spence, OBE, Kings College London

It is difficult to imagine a more stimulating or pedagogically sophisticated introduction to international relations.

Walter Carlsnaes, Uppsala University

This hugely valuable text will be welcomed by all those working in global politics. It tackles many of the liveliest intellectual debates on the subject, as well as offering the empirical reference points that illuminate why it is so crucial to have those debates.

Rosemary Foot, University of Oxford

This volume achieves a balance between intellectual breadth and richness, and rigorous organization and clarity. No wonder the book is such a favourite with students of the subject.

Robert Patman, University of Otago

Acknowledgements

Once again we would like to thank all those who sent us (or Oxford University Press) comments on the strengths and weaknesses of the fourth edition. We hope that those who have gone to the trouble of contributing to the review process will see many of the changes they recommended reflected in the new edition. We would also like to thank our contributors for being so helpful in responding yet again to our detailed requests for revisions to the chapters that appeared in the previous volume.

However, our greatest thanks must go to Sheena Chestnut, who once again has done an excellent job in helping us with the editorial work with this new edition. As with the previous edition, but perhaps even more so, she has been untiring, extremely efficient, and conscientious in the work she has done, even as she is writing her PhD at Harvard. The book is significantly better as a result of her hard work and professionalism. We would also like to thank Clemency Wells, who has done a wonderful job providing new content for the companion website, building on Sheena's work from the previous edition and adding her own unique stamp. The editors would also like to thank Sacha Cook of Oxford University Press for her professionalism, support, and advice during the production.

John Baylis, Steve Smith, and Patricia Owens

Alex Bellamy and Nicholas Wheeler acknowledge Vincent Keating for his help in researching and preparing this chapter for publication.

Amitar Acharya would like to thank Brian Job, Andrew Mack, and Peter Wallensteen for their comments on an earlier draft of his chapter and Lotta Harbom for assistance with the Uppsala Conflict Data Base (UCDP).

Ann Tickner would like to thank Catia Confortini for her valuable research assistance for her chapter.

The publishers would be pleased to clear permission with any copyright holders that we have inadvertently failed, or been unable, to contact.

Guided tour of the textbook features

This book is enriched with a number of learning tools to help you navigate the text and reinforce your knowledge of international relations. This guided tour shows you how to get the most out of your textbook package.

Reader's Guides

Reader's guides set the scene for upcoming themes and issues to be discussed, and indicate the scope of coverage within the chapter.

Reader's Guide

This chapter reviews the [...] realism and neo-liberali[...] between these intellec[...] ed mainstream acad[...] [re]lations (IR) in [...]

an attempt by scholars to offer a better explanation for the behaviour of states and to describe the nature of international politics. Similarly, the more policy-relevant versions of these theories prescribe competing policy agendas. The next section reviews three versions of neo-realism: Waltz's structural realism; Grieco's neo-realism or modern realism, with its focus on absolute and relative gains; and what security scholars call offensive and defensive realism or neo-realism. The third section of the chapter reviews the assumptions of neo-liberal and neo-liberal institutionalist perspectives. The fourth section focuses on the 'neo-neo debate'. This is a debate that many US scholars think is the most important intellectual issue IR today. Many other scholars see it as not much of a debate at all. It is a debate about refining common assumptions and about the future role and effectiveness of international institutions and the possibilities of cooperation. However, it is not a debate between mainstream and critical perspectives. It is a debate between 'rule-makers' and it leaves out the voices on the margins, those of the 'rule-takers'. In the fifth section of the chapter, I review how neo-realists and neo-

Boxes

Throughout the book boxes provide you with extra information on particular topics to complement your understanding of the main chapter text.

Box 22.1 Types of [...]

Audrey Kurth Cronin has ou[...] groups and their historical im[...]

'There are four types of te[...] operating around the wo[...] source of motivation: [...] rorists, ethnonation[...]

Case Study Boxes

In each chapter specific case studies have been selected to demonstrate how political ideas, concepts, and issues are manifested in the real world.

Case Study The 2[...]

which a UN resolu[...] infringements of

explicitly breach sovereignty. The 1991 Security Council resolution sanctioning intervention in Iraq (S/Res/688) at

which required the destruction of Iraqi weapons of mass destruction under UN supervision, and UN Security Council Resolution 1441 of 2002, which threatened 'serious consequences' if this were not done. Yet efforts to reach a Security Council resolution in the winter of 2003 that would clearly authorize the use of force against Iraq were unsuccessful. France and Russia threatened to veto a second Security Council resolution authorizing force.

The credibility of the UN was damaged by the failure to agree on a second Security Council resolution, and by the decision of the US and British administrations, along with a small number of allies, to use force against Iraq without clear UN authorization. There are fears of an increased tendency for the USA to act without UN authorization. The Bush administration's National Security Strategy of September 2002 stated that '[W]e will be prepared to act apart when our interests and unique responsibilities require' (NSS 2002: 31).

None the less, the aftermath of the invasion and the continued difficulties in establishing security in Iraq highlight the need for international cooperation. The UN enhances the legitimacy of military action, and can also help share in global risks, burdens, and strategies for rebuilding.

Discussion Questions

1 Has the UN as an institution recovered from the war in Iraq?

In March 2003, a US-led coalition launched a highly controversial war in Iraq, which removed Saddam Hussein from power. The justification for war stressed Iraq's possession of weapons of mass destruction, in defiance of earlier UN resolutions. Unlike in Kosovo, the gross violation of human rights was not given as a main justification for the invasion until later. Yet the failure to find weapons of mass destruction in Iraq, as well as the subsequent civil war, have fuelled the claims of critics that the war was unjustified.

There was no agreement over whether the UN Security Coun-

Key Points

Each main chapter section ends with a set of key points that summarize the most important arguments developed.

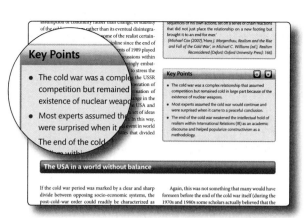

Questions

A set of carefully devised questions has been provided to help you assess your understanding of core themes, and may also be used as the basis of seminar discussion or coursework.

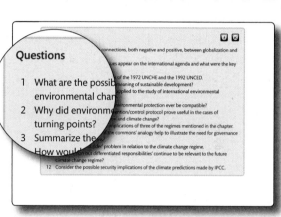

Further Reading

Take your learning further by using the reading lists at the end of chapter to find the key literature in the field, or more detailed information on a specific topic.

Glossary Terms

Key terms appear in blue in the text and are defined in a glossary at the end of the book to aid you in exam revision.

www.oxfordtextbooks.co.uk/orc/baylis5e/

The Online Resource Centre that accompanies this textbook contains many helpful additional resources for both students and lecturers.

Interactive Library

The internet can be an excellent source of information, data, and commentary on international relations—but finding the best sites isn't always easy. That's why the Online Resource Centre now includes a new interactive library, with links to interesting journal articles, blogs, audio, and video clips that relate to the book's key themes.

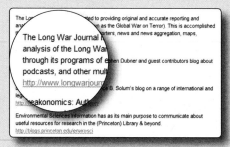

Want to hear another point of view? Up-to-date commentary on some of the latest issues and events can be found in reputable **blogs**.

Reading **journal articles** is a great way to familiarise yourself with cutting-edge research in the field.

Links to **videos** of lectures, interviews, and speeches on international relations topics have been collected together in one place so you can watch them when you choose.

The interactive library was compiled by Mikael Sundström of Lund University. Other resources were written or updated by Clemency Wells.

Student Resources

As well as the interactive library there are many other resources on the website to help you with your studies. Where we think they'll be particularly useful we've included a symbol in the book to remind you. Look out for the following icons in the textbook and then go to the Online Resource Centre to further your learning.

Extra **case studies** are included online to help you link IR theory and practice.

Test yourself with **multiple choice questions** that also provide instant feedback.

With the **flashcard glossary** you can check your knowledge of IR terminology.

The **revision guide** provides a checklist of the key points in each chapter to look back on before exams.

For each chapter key **web links** have been selected by the book's contributors.

As well as the journal articles in the interactive library we've compiled a bank of links to many IR **journal homepages**.

To direct you to the most up-to-date news in international politics **Oxford News Now** brings together regularly updated RSS feeds from a variety of news sources.

Lecturer Resources

These resources are password protected, but access is available to anyone using the book in their teaching. Please contact your local sales representative.

Case Studies

Additional case studies have been provided for lecturers to use in class discussions.

PowerPoint® slides

A suite of customizable PowerPoint® slides has been included for use in lectures or as hand-outs.

Poverty

- The monetary-based conception of poverty has been almost universalized among governments and international organizations since 1945.
- Poverty is interpreted as a condition suffered by people - the majority of whom are female - who do not earn enough money to satisfy their basic material requirements in the market place.

Test Bank

Over 450 multiple choice and true/false questions that can be downloaded to Virtual Learning Environments, or printed out, for use in assessment.

Chapter 21 - Question 09
What was termed 'the oxygen that sustains terrorism'?
- international drug-trafficking
- radical ideologies
- poverty and oppression
- media coverage

Question Bank

A selection of short answer and essay questions allow you test your students further.

Figures and Tables from the Textbook

All figures and tables in the textbook are available to download electronically.

Brief contents

Part One The historical context

Part Two Theories of world politics

Part Three Structures and processes

Part Four International issues

Part Five Globalization in the future

Detailed contents

Part One The historical context

Part Three Structures and processes

Part Four **International issues**

Part Five Globalization in the future

List of figures

List of boxes and case studies

List of tables

About the contributors

Amitav Acharya is Professor of International Relations at the American University. He has been Professor of Global Governance at the University of Bristol, UK, Professor of International Relations at Nanyang Technological University, Singapore, Professor of Political Science at York University, Toronto, and a Fellow of the John F. Kennedy School of Government at Harvard University. He is author of *Promoting Human Security: Ethical, Normative and Educational Frameworks in South-East Asia* (UNESCO, 2007) and recent articles dealing with international relations theory, norm diffusion, comparative regionalism, and Asian security in *International Organization, World Politics, International Security*, and *International Studies Quarterly*.

David Armstrong is Emeritus Professor of International Relations at the University of Exeter. His books include *Revolutionary Diplomacy* (California University Press, 1977), *The Rise of the International Organisation* (Macmillan, 1981), *Revolution and World Order* (Clarendon Press, 1993), *International Law and International Relations* (co-authored with Theo Farrell and Hélène Lambert, Cambridge University Press, 2007) and *Routledge Handbook of International Law* (editor, Routledge, 2009).

Michael Barnett is University Professor of International Affairs and Political Science at the George Washington University.

John Baylis is Emeritus Professor of Politics and International Relations and formerly Pro-Vice Chancellor at Swansea University. His PhD and DLitt are from the University of Wales. He is the author of more than twenty books, the most recent of which are *Strategy in the Contemporary World*, ed. by J. Baylis, J. Wirtz and Colin S. Gray (Oxford University Press, 3rd edn, 2010) and *The United States and Europe: Beyond the Neo-Conservative Divide?* (edited with Jon Roper, Routledge, 2006).

Alex J. Bellamy is Professor of International Relations and Executive Director of the Asia-Pacific Centre for the Responsibility to Protect at The University of Queensland, Australia. His books include Understanding Peacekeeping (with Paul D. Williams, 2nd edn 2010), *The Responsibility to Protect: The Global Effort to End Mass Atrocities* (Polity, 2009), and *Just Wars: From Cicero to Iraq* (Polity, 2007). He is currently writing *Massacres and Morality: Mass Atrocities in an Age of Non-Combatant Immunity* (Oxford) and a book on implementing the responsibility to protect (with Sara E. Davies, Routledge).

Edward Best is Professor and Head of Unit at the European Institute of Public Administration (EIPA), Maastricht. He has worked in the regional security programme of the International Institute for Strategic Studies (IISS), publishing a book on *US Policy and Regional Security in Central America* (Gower/St Martin's, 1987). He has been a consultant for the United Nations and the Inter-American Development Bank in Central America, for the European Commission in Latin America and the Helsinki Commission in the Baltic Sea region. He now specializes in EU institutions and the political aspects of European integration, as well as in comparative regionalism and the management of regional organizations. He has co-edited three books on the EU—*Rethinking the European Union: IGC 2000 and Beyond* (EIPA, 2000) with Mark Gray and Alexander Stubb, *From Luxembourg to Lisbon and Beyond: Making the Employment Strategy Work* (EIPA, 2002) with Danielle Bossaert, and *The Institutions of the Enlarged European Union* (Edward Elgar, 2008) with Thomas Christiansen and Pierpaolo Settembri—and published numerous articles on the EU and institutional arrangements for regional integration.

John Breuilly is Professor of Nationalism and Ethnicity at the London School of Economics. His major interests are in modern German and comparative European history and the historical study of nationalism. Recent publications include *Germany's Two Unifications: Anticipations, Experiences, Responses*, edited with Ronald Speirs (Palgrave, 2004), 'Introduction' to Ernest Gellner, *Nations and Nationalism* (2nd edn, Blackwell, 2006), *Nationalism, Power and Modernity in Nineteenth-Century Germany* (German Historical Institute, 2007), 'Nationalismustheorien und kritische deutsche Gesellschaftsgeschichte', in *Das Deutsche Kaiserreich in der Kontroverse*, edited by Sven Oliver Müller and Cornelius Torp (Vandenhoeck & Ruprecht, 2009), 'The Response to Napoleon and German Nationalism', in *The Bee and the Eagle: Napoleonic France and the End of the Holy Roman Empire, 1806*, edited by Alan Forrest and Peter H.Wilson (Palgrave, 2009), and 'Nationalism and the making of national pasts', in *Nations and their Histories*, edited by Susana Carvalho and François Gemenne (Palgrave, 2009).

Thomas Christiansen is Professor of European Institutional Politics at Maastricht University and Associate Professor at the European Institute for Public Administration in Maastricht. He is also Professor at the College of Europe in Bruges as well as executive editor of the Journal of European Integration. He has published widely on different aspects of the institutional politics of the European Union. Among his publications are several edited volumes, including *The Social Construction of Europe* (Sage, 2001), co-edited with Knud Erik Jørgensen and Antje Wiener, and *Informal Governance in the European Union* (Edward Elgar, 2003). *Constitutionalizing the European Union*, co-authored with Christine Reh, was published in the European Union Series at Palgrave Macmillan in 2009, and his single-authored *The Institutional Politics of the European Union* is forthcoming with Routledge.

Ian Clark is E. H. Carr Professor of International Politics at Aberystwyth University, and is the author of *Globalization and Fragmentation* (Oxford University Press, 1997) and *Globalization and International Relations Theory* (Oxford University Press, 1999). He is currently completing *Hegemony in International Society* (2011).

Michael Cox holds a Chair in International Relations at the London School of Economics, where he is also Co-Director of IDEAS—a Centre for Strategy and Diplomacy. He is the author and editor of several books on US foreign policy, world politics and the international theory of E. H. Carr, including the definitive edition of his *The Twenty Years' Crisis*, published in 2001. His latest books include *U.S. Foreign Policy: Soft Power, US Foreign Policy: Theoretical, Historical and Contemporary Perspectives*, and *The Global 1989*.

Devon Curtis is a lecturer in the Department of Politics and International Studies at the University of Cambridge and a Fellow of Emmanuel College. Her main research interests and publications deal with power-sharing and governance arrangements following conflict, UN peacebuilding, the 'transformation' of rebel movements to political parties in Africa, and critical perspectives on conflict, peacebuilding, and development.

Jack Donnelly is the Andrew Mellon Professor at the Josef Korbel School of International Studies, University of Denver. He has written extensively on the theory and practice of international human rights and on issues of international relations theory.

Tim Dunne is Dean of the new College of Social Science and International Studies at the University of Exeter. He has written and edited nine books. His most recent is the second edition of *International Relations Theories: Discipline and Diversity* (co-edited with Steve Smith and Milja Kurki), which was published in early 2010. He is an editor of the *European Journal of International Relations*.

Tony Evans is Professor of Global Politics at the University of Southampton. He has written extensively on the politics of universal human rights, including *The Politics of Human Rights: A Global Perspective* (Pluto, 2005). His most recent book, to be published in 2010, is on human rights as process within the global political economy. He is currently researching the intellectual challenge to the global neo-liberal order presented by Islamic scholarship.

Lene Hansen is Professor of International Relations at the University of Copenhagen. She is the author of *Security as Practice: Discourse Analysis and the Bosnian War* (Routledge, 2006), co-author with Barry Buzan of *The Evolution of International Security Studies* (Cambridge University Press, 2009), and the co-editor with Ole Wæver of *European Integration and National Identity: The Challenge of the Nordic States* (Routledge, 2002).

Stephen Hobden is a senior lecturer in International Politics at the University of East London, where he teaches courses on international relations theory, US foreign policy, and China's growing international role. He is currently working on a research project, together with his colleague Erika Cudworth, on complexity theory and international relations.

Darryl Howlett obtained his master's degree from Lancaster University and his PhD from Southampton University. He currently teaches courses on international security at Southampton University. His most recent publications include 'Strategic Culture' (with Jeffrey S. Lantis) in John Baylis, James J. Wirtz, and Colin S. Gray, eds, *Strategy in the Contemporary World* (Oxford University Press, 2010) and 'The Emergence of Stability: Deterrence-in-Motion and Deterrence Reconstructed' in Ian R. Kenyon and John Simpson, eds, *Deterrence and the Changing Security Environment* (Routledge, 2006).

James D. Kiras is an Associate Professor at the School of Advanced Air and Space Studies, Maxwell Air Force Base, Alabama, where he teaches on the subjects of irregular warfare and military theory. He is also a Senior Fellow of the Strategic Studies Division at the Joint Special Operations University, Hurlburt Field, Florida, and worked for a number of years in the defence policy and consulting world. Dr Kiras publishes and lectures on subjects including special operations, irregular warfare, and suicide bombing. His most recent book, co-authored with other contributors, is *Understanding Modern Warfare* (Cambridge University Press, 2008). Dr Kiras's first book was entitled *Special Operations and Strategy: From World War II to the War on Terrorism* (Routledge, 2006).

Steven L. Lamy is a Professor of International Relations in the School of International Relations at the University of Southern California. He is also the Vice Dean for Academic Programs in the College of Letters, Arts and Sciences. His latest research focuses on religion and international relations, and is funded by a grant from the Luce Foundation. A book of foreign policy case studies will be published next year.

Andrew Linklater is Woodrow Wilson Professor of International Politics at Aberystwyth University. He has published extensively on theories of international relations. His most recent book is *Critical Theory and World Politics: Sovereignty, Citizenship and Humanity* (Routledge, 2007).

Richard Little is Professor Emeritus in the Department of Politics at the University of Bristol. He is a former editor of the Review of International Studies and President of the British International Studies Association. His most recent book is *The Balance of Power: Metaphors, Myths and Models* (Cambridge University Press, 2007).

Anthony McGrew is Professor of International Relations and Head of the School of Social Sciences at Southampton University. He has written extensively on globalization and global governance. He is working on a project on new forms of global governance.

Simon W. Murden lectures in Strategic Studies and International Affairs at the Britannia Royal Naval College, Dartmouth, and the University of Plymouth. He specializes in the international security of the Middle East and Muslim world, the security architecture of globalization, war and strategy, and contemporary war and warfare. Publications include: *Emergent Regional Powers and International Relations in the Gulf 1988–91* (Ithaca Press, 1995); *Islam, the Middle East and the New Global Hegemony* (Lynne Reinner Publishers, 2002); and *The Problem of Force: Grappling with the Global Battlefield* (Lynne Reinner Publishers, 2009).

Patricia Owens is Senior Lecturer in the Department of Politics at Queen Mary, University of London. She has been a Visiting Professor at UCLA and held research positions at UC-Berkeley, Princeton, USC, and Oxford. She is author of *Between War and Politics: International Relations and the Thought of Hannah Arendt* (Oxford University Press, 2007) and *War, Security, and the Rise of the Social* (forthcoming).

Christian Reus-Smit is Professor of International Relations at the European University Institute, Florence. He is author of *American Power and World Order* (Polity Press, 2004) and *The Moral Purpose of the State* (Princeton University Press, 1999), co-author of *Theories of International Relations* (Palgrave, 2001, 2005, 2009), editor of *The Politics of International Law* (Cambridge University Press, 2004), and co-editor of *The Oxford Handbook of International Relations* (Oxford University Press, 2008), *Resolving International Crises of Legitimacy* (Special Issue, International Politics, 2007), and *Between Sovereignty and Global Governance* (Macmillan, 1998). Between 2001 and 2010 he was Head of the Department of International Relations at the Australian National University.

Brian C. Schmidt is Associate Professor of Political Science at Carleton University, Ottawa, Canada. He is the author of *The Political Discourse of Anarchy: A Disciplinary History of International Relations* (SUNY, 1998) and *Imperialism and Internationalism in the Discipline of International Relations*, co-edited with David Long (SUNY, 2005).

Len Scott is Professor of International Politics at Aberystwyth University, where he is Dean of Social Sciences. He is also Director of the Centre for Intelligence and International Security Studies. His recent publications include (with R. Gerald Hughes and Peter Jackson, eds) *Exploring Intelligence Archives: Enquiries into the Secret State* (Routledge, 2008) and *The Cuban Missile Crisis and the Threat of Nuclear War* (Continuum, 2007).

Richard Shapcott is Senior Lecturer in International Relations at the University of Queensland, Australia. He is the author of *Justice, Community and Dialogue in International Relations* (Cambridge, 2001) and *International Ethics: A Critical Introduction* (Polity Press, 2010).

Michael Sheehan is Professor of International Relations at Swansea University. He was previously Director of the Scottish Centre for International Security, University of Aberdeen. He is the author or editor of twelve books on international relations, including *The Arms Race* (Martin Robertson, 1983), *Arms Control: Theory and Practice* (Basil Blackwell, 1986), *Balance of Power: History and Theory* (Routledge, 1996), *National and International Security* (Ashgate, 2000), *Security: An Analytical Survey* (Lynne Rienner, 2005), *The International Politics of Space* (Routledge, 2007) and (with Natalie Bormann), *Securing Outer Space* (Routledge, 2009).

Steve Smith is Vice-Chancellor of the University of Exeter, and President of Universities UK from 2009 to 2011. He has held professorships of International Relations at the University of Wales, Aberystwyth and the University of East Anglia, and has also taught at the State University of New York (Albany) and Huddersfield Polytechnic. He was President of the International Studies Association for 2003–4, and was elected to be an Academician of the Social Sciences (AcSS) in 2000. He is the author or editor of fifteen books, the most recent of which are *International Relations Theories: Discipline and Diversity*, edited with Tim Dunne and Milja Kurki (Oxford University Press, 2nd edn, 2010), and *Foreign Policy: Theories, Actors, Cases*, edited with Tim Dunne and Amelia Hadfield (Oxford University Press, 2008), and of some 100 academic papers and chapters in major international journals and edited collections.

Christine Sylvester is Professor of International Relations and Development at Lancaster University, UK. She has written five books and edited two others on international relations and on post-colonial issues in Zimbabwe, and has articles on post-colonialism in *Third World Quarterly*, *Signs*, *International Feminist Journal of Politics*, and *The Geographical Journal*. Recently she edited a five-volume anthology of *Key Works in Feminist International Relations* and is the editor of a new book series on War, Politics, Experience.

Paul Taylor is Emeritus Professor of International Relations at the London School of Economics. Most recently he has published *The End of European Integration: Anti-Europeanism Examined* (Routledge, 2008), and *International Organization in the Age of Globalization* (Continuum, 2003, paperback version, June 2005). His *The Careless State: Wealth and Welfare in Britain Today* is to be published by Bloomsbury in early 2010.

Caroline Thomas was Deputy Vice Chancellor and Professor of Global Politics at the University of Southampton until her death in October 2008. She specialized in North–South relations, and published widely on the global politics of security, development, environment, and health.

J. Ann Tickner is Professor in the School of International Relations at the University of Southern California. She was President of the International Studies Association for 2006–7. She is the author of *Gender in International Relations: Feminist Perspectives on Achieving International Security* (1992) and *Gendering World Politics: Issues and Approaches in the Post-Cold War World* (2001), both published by Columbia University Press, as well as many articles and book chapters on feminist international theory and international security.

John Vogler is Professor of International Relations in the School of Politics, International Relations and Environment (SPIRE) at Keele University, UK. He is a member of the ESRC Centre for Climate Change Economics and Policy. His books include *The Global Commons: Environmental and Technological Governance* (John Wiley, 2000) and, with Charlotte Bretherton, *The European Union as a Global Actor* (Routledge, 2006). He has also edited, with Mark Imber, *The Environment and International Relations* (Routledge, 1996) and with Alan Russell, *The International Politics of Biotechnology* (Manchester University Press, 2000).

Matthew Watson is Professor of Political Economy in the Department of Politics and International Studies at the University of Warwick, UK. He is the author of some thirty articles in peer-reviewed academic journals specializing in issues of political economy and international political economics. He is also the author of two monographs, *Foundations of International Political Economy* (Macmillan, 2005) and *The Political Economy of International Capital Mobility* (Palgrave, 2007).

Nicholas J. Wheeler is Professor in the Department of International Politics at Aberystwyth University. His publications include: *The Security Dilemma: Fear, Cooperation, and Trust in World Politics*, with Ken Booth (Basingstoke: Palgrave Macmillan, 2008); *National Interest Versus Solidarity: Particular and Univeral Ethics in International Life*, edited with Jean-Marc Coicaud (United Nations University Press, 2008); *The British Origins of Nuclear Strategy 1945–55*, with Ian Clark (Clarendon Press, 1989). He has also written widely on humanitarian intervention and is the author of *Saving Strangers: Humanitarian Intervention in International Society* (Oxford University Press, 2000). He is currently researching a book provisionally entitled *Building Trust in a World of Nuclear Powers* as part of a three-year ESRC/AHRC Fellowship under RCUK's 'Global Uncertainties: Security For All in a Changing World' Programme on 'The Challenges to Trust-Building in Nuclear Worlds'. He is Director of the David Davies Memorial Institute of International Studies at Aberystwyth University, a Trustee of the Welsh Centre of International Affairs, and a member of the United Nations Association of the UK's Policy Advisory Committee.

Peter Willetts is Emeritus Professor of Global Politics at City University, London. He has written extensively on international organizations, particularly on the Non-Aligned Movement. He was a pioneer in studying the impact of NGOs on global politics, editing two early books on the subject, *Pressure Groups in the Global System* (Pinter and St Martin's, 1982) and *'The Conscience of the World': The Influence of Non-Governmental Organisations in the UN System* (Hurst and Brookings, 1996). His latest work, *Non-Governmental Organisations in World Politics* (Routledge, 2010) merges his long-standing arguments for an issue-based pluralist approach with empirical work on the expansion of the role of NGOs in diplomacy, international law, and global communications, to produce a constructivist interpretation of the contribution of NGOs to global governance.

Ngaire Woods is Professor of International Political Economy and Director of the Global Economic Governance Programme at Oxford University. Her recent books include *Networks of Influence? Developing Countries in a Networked Global Order*, with Leonardo Martinez-Diaz (Oxford University Press, 2009), *The Politics of Global Regulation*, with Walter Mattli (Oxford University Press, 2009), *The Globalizers: the IMF, the World Bank and their Borrowers* (Cornell University Press, 2006), *Exporting Good Governance: Temptations and Challenges in Canada's Aid Program*, with Jennifer Welsh (Laurier University Press, 2007), and *Making Self-Regulation Effective in Developing Countries*, with Dana Brown (Oxford University Press, 2007). She has previously published *The Political Economy of Globalization* (Macmillan, 2000), *Inequality, Globalization and World Politics*, with Andrew Hurrell (Oxford University Press, 1999), *Explaining International Relations since 1945* (Oxford University Press, 1986), and numerous articles on international institutions, globalization, and governance. Ngaire Woods has served as an adviser to the IMF Board, the UNDP's Human Development Report, and the Commonwealth Heads of Government.

Richard Wyn Jones is Director of the Wales Governance Centre at Cardiff University. He has written extensively on Welsh politics, nationalism, and security studies.

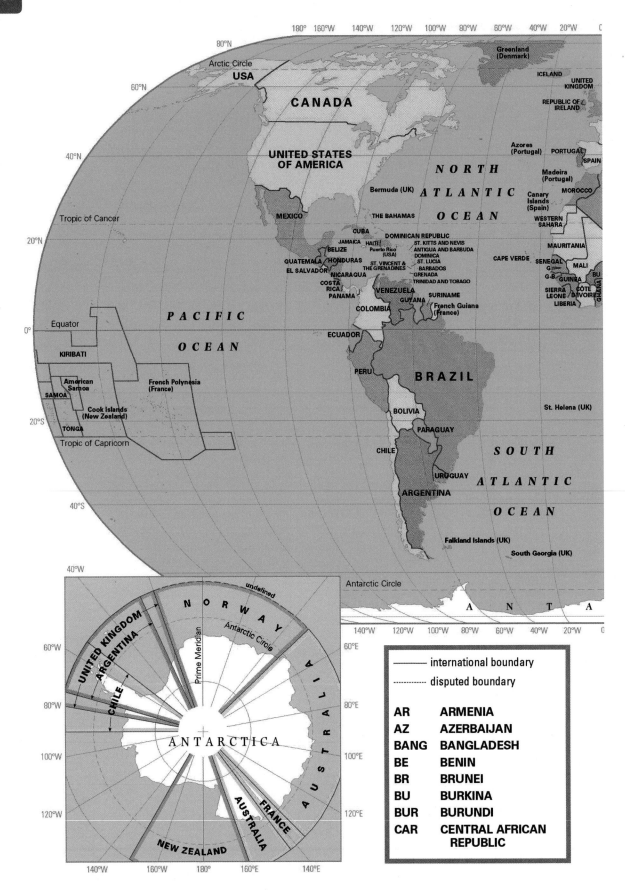

80°N
Arctic Circle
60°N
40°N
Tropic of Cancer
20°N
Equator 0°
20°S
Tropic of Capricorn
40°S

180° 160°W 140°W 120°W 100°W 80°W 60°W 40°W 20°W

Greenland (Denmark)

USA

ICELAND
UNITED KINGDOM

CANADA

REPUBLIC OF IRELAND

Azores (Portugal)   PORTUGAL
SPAIN

UNITED STATES OF AMERICA

N O R T H

Madeira (Portugal)
MOROCCO

Bermuda (UK)

A T L A N T I C

Canary Islands (Spain)

WESTERN SAHARA

MEXICO

O C E A N

THE BAHAMAS

CUBA

DOMINICAN REPUBLIC
JAMAICA   HAITI   ST. KITTS AND NEVIS
Puerto Rico (USA)   ANTIGUA AND BARBUDA
DOMINICA

MAURITANIA

BELIZE

CAPE VERDE

SENEGAL   MALI

GUATEMALA   HONDURAS   ST. VINCENT & THE GRENADINES   ST. LUCIA   BARBADOS
EL SALVADOR   GRENADA
NICARAGUA   TRINIDAD AND TOBAGO

G

BU

GUINEA

SIERRA LEONE   CÔTE D'IVOIRE

GHANA

COSTA RICA   PANAMA
VENEZUELA   SURINAME
COLOMBIA   GUYANA
French Guiana (France)

LIBERIA

P A C I F I C

ECUADOR

O C E A N

KIRIBATI

PERU

B R A Z I L

American Samoa   French Polynesia (France)

St. Helena (UK)

SAMOA   Cook Islands (New Zealand)

BOLIVIA

TONGA

PARAGUAY

CHILE

S O U T H

URUGUAY

A T L A N T I C

ARGENTINA

O C E A N

Falkland Islands (UK)

South Georgia (UK)

Antarctic Circle

A N T A

140°W 120°W 100°W 80°W 60°W 40°W 20°W

40°W
undefined
N O R W A Y
60°W
Antarctic Circle
UNITED KINGDOM
ARGENTINA
Prime Meridian
60°E
CHILE
80°W
80°E
A N T A R C T I C A
100°W
100°E
AUSTRALIA
FRANCE
120°W
120°E
AUSTRALIA
NEW ZEALAND
140°W 160°W 180° 160°E 140°E

——— international boundary
- - - - - disputed boundary

AR	ARMENIA
AZ	AZERBAIJAN
BANG	BANGLADESH
BE	BENIN
BR	BRUNEI
BU	BURKINA
BUR	BURUNDI
CAR	CENTRAL AFRICAN REPUBLIC

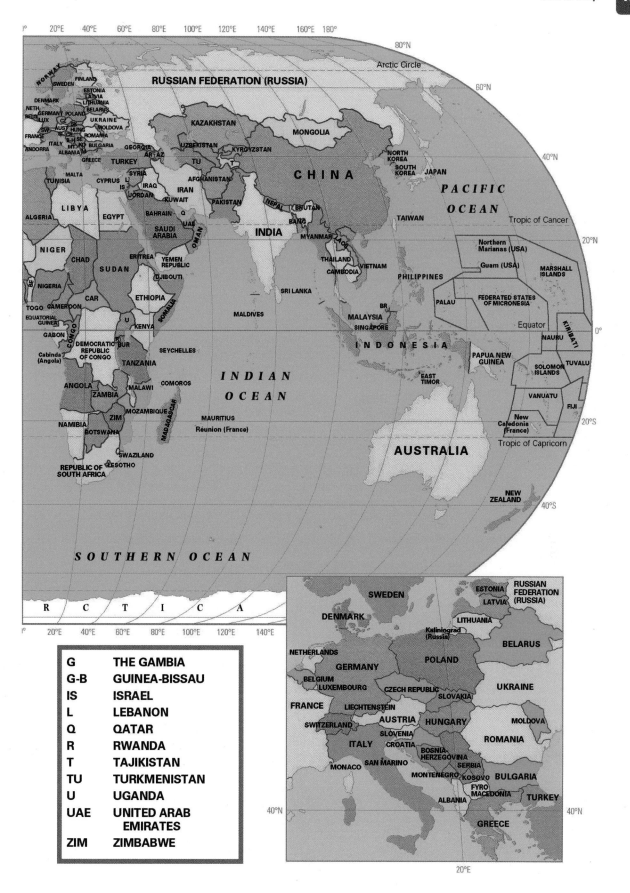

G	THE GAMBIA
G-B	GUINEA-BISSAU
IS	ISRAEL
L	LEBANON
Q	QATAR
R	RWANDA
T	TAJIKISTAN
TU	TURKMENISTAN
U	UGANDA
UAE	UNITED ARAB EMIRATES
ZIM	ZIMBABWE

Introduction

STEVE SMITH · PATRICIA OWENS · JOHN BAYLIS

The aim of this book is to provide an overview of world politics in a global era. We think that it is especially difficult to explain world politics in such an era because 'globalization', the word most often used to describe it, is a particularly controversial term. There is considerable dispute over what it means to talk of this era as one of 'globalization' and whether to do so implies that the main features of world politics are any different from those of the past. In this introduction we want to explain how we propose to deal with the concept of globalization in this book, and offer some arguments both for and against seeing it as an important new development in world politics.

Before turning to look at globalization, we want to do two things. We shall first say something about the various terms used to describe **global politics**, and then we shall spend some time looking at the main ways in which global politics has been explained. We need to do this because our aim in this introduction is definitely *not* to put forward one view of how to think about globalization somehow agreed by the editors, let alone by all the contributors to this volume. That would be impossible because there is no such agreement. Rather, we want to provide a context within which to read the chapters that follow. This means offering a variety of views on globalization and how to think about it. Our central point is that the main theoretical accounts of world politics all see globalization differently. Some treat it as nothing more than a temporary phase in human history, so we do not need fundamentally to rethink how we understand world politics. Others see it as but the latest manifestation of the growth of global **capitalism** and its processes of modernization; yet others see it as representing a fundamental transformation of world politics, one that requires new ways of understanding. The different editors and contributors to this book hold no one agreed view; they represent all the views just mentioned. Thus, for example, they would each have a different take on the global events of **9/11**, the global financial crisis that began in 2007, or the failure to reach an agreement at the 2009 global climate change talks in Copenhagen.

From what we have said so far you will gather that there are three main aims of this book:

- to offer an overview of world politics in an era that many describe as one of 'globalization';
- to summarize the main theoretical approaches available to explain contemporary world politics; and
- to provide the material necessary to answer the question of whether 'globalization' marks a fundamental transformation in world politics.

From international politics to world politics

Leaving the term 'globalization' to one side, why does the main title of this book refer to 'world politics' rather than 'international politics' or 'international relations'? These are the traditional names used to describe the kinds of interactions and processes that are the concern of this book. Indeed, you could look at the table of contents of many other introductory books and find a similar listing of main topics dealt with, yet often these books would have either 'international relations' or 'international politics' as their main title. Furthermore, the discipline that studies these issues is nearly always called International Politics, International Relations, or International Studies. Our reason for choosing the phrase 'world politics' is that we think it is more inclusive than either of the alternative terms. It is meant to signal the fact that our interest is in the politics and political patterns in the world and not only those between **nation-states** (as the terms international relations or international politics imply). Thus we are interested in relations between institutions and organizations that may or may not be states (for example, multinational corporations, terrorist groups, classes, or human rights **non-governmental organizations** (NGOs); these are sometimes known as **transnational actors**). Similarly, the term 'international relations' seems too exclusive. Of course, it often does represent a widening of concern from simply the political relations between nation-states, but it still restricts our focus to *international* relations, whereas we think that relations between, say, cities and other governments or **international organizations** can be equally important to what states and other political actors do. So we prefer to characterize the relations we are interested in as those of world politics, with the important proviso that we do not want the reader to define politics too narrowly. You will see this issue arising time and time again in the chapters that follow, since many contributors want to define politics very widely. One obvious example concerns the relationship between politics and economics; there is clearly an overlap, and a lot of bargaining power goes to the person who can persuade others that the existing distribution of resources is 'simply' an economic question rather than a political issue. We want you to think about politics very broadly for the time being, as several of the chapters will describe as 'political' features of the contemporary world that you may not have previously thought of as such. Our focus is on the patterns of political relations, defined broadly, that characterize the contemporary world. Many will be between states, but many and perhaps most will not.

Theories of world politics

The basic problem facing anyone who tries to understand contemporary world politics is that there is so much material to look at that it is difficult to know which things matter and which do not. Where on earth would you start if you wanted to explain the most important political processes? How, for example, would you explain 9/11, or the 2003 war in Iraq, the recent global financial crisis, or the failure of the climate change negotiations in Copenhagen? Why did President Barack Obama escalate the war in Afghanistan in 2010? Why was the apparent economic boom in much of the capitalist world followed by a near devastating collapse of the global financial system? As you will know, there are very different answers to questions such as these, and there seems no easy way of arriving at a definitive answer to them. Whether you are aware of it or not, whenever you are faced with such a problem you have to resort to **theories**. A theory is not simply some grand formal model with hypotheses and assumptions. Rather, **a theory is a kind of simplifying device that allows you to decide which facts matter and which do not.** A good analogy is with sunglasses with different-coloured lenses: put on the red pair and the world looks red; put on the yellow pair and it looks yellow. The world is not any different; it just looks different. So it is with theories. Shortly we shall summarize the main theoretical views that have dominated the study of world politics so that you will get an idea of which 'colours' they paint world politics. But before we do so, please note that we do not think that theory is an option. It is not as if you can say that you do not want to bother with a theory; all you want to do is to look at the 'facts'. We believe that this is simply impossible, since the only way in which you can decide which of the millions of possible facts to look at is by adhering to some simplifying device that tells you which ones matter the most. We think of theory as such a simplifying device. Note also that you may well not be aware of your theory. It may just be the view of the world that you have inherited from family, peer group, social class, or the media. It may just seem common sense to you

and not at all anything complicated like a theory. But we fervently believe that all that is happening in such a case is that your theoretical assumptions are **implicit** rather than **explicit**. We prefer to try to be as explicit as possible when it comes to thinking about world politics.

People have tried to make sense of world politics for centuries, and especially so since the separate academic discipline of International Politics was formed in 1919 when the Department of International Politics was set up at the University of Wales, Aberystwyth. Interestingly, the individual who set up that department, a Welsh industrialist called David Davies, saw its purpose as being to help prevent war. By studying international politics scientifically, it was believed, scholars could find the causes of the world's main political problems and put forward solutions to help politicians solve them. For the next twenty years, the discipline was marked by such a commitment to change the world. This is known as a **normative** position, with the task of academic study being one of making the world a better place. Its opponents characterized it as **idealism**, in that it had a view of how the world ought to be and tried to assist events to turn out that way. Many opponents of this view preferred an approach they called **realism**, which, rather unsurprisingly, stressed seeing the world as it 'really is' rather than how we would like it to be. And the 'real' world as seen by realists is not a very pleasant place; human beings are at best selfish and probably much worse. On this view, notions such as the perfectibility of human beings and the possibility of an improvement of world politics seem far-fetched. This debate between idealism and realism has continued to the present day, but it is fair to say that realism has tended to have the upper hand. This is mainly because it appears to accord more with common sense than does idealism, especially when the media bombard us daily with images of how awful human beings can be to one another. Here we would like you to think about whether such a realist view is as neutral as it is commonsensical. After all, if we teach world politics to generations of students and tell them that people are selfish, then does this not become common sense? And when they go to work in the media, for government departments or for the military, don't they simply repeat what they have been taught and act accordingly? Might realism simply be the ideology of powerful states, interested in protecting the status quo? For now, we would like to keep the issue open and simply point out that we are not convinced that realism is as objective or as non-normative as it is portrayed.

What is certainly true is that realism has been the dominant way of explaining world politics in the last one hundred years. We shall now summarize the main assumptions underlying realism, and then do the same for its main rivals as theories of world politics, **liberalism**, **Marxism**, (social) **constructivism**, **poststructuralism**, and **postcolonialism**. These theories will be discussed in much more detail in Part Two of this book, along with a chapter on **normative approaches** that seek to explain contemporary world politics. Each of these theories will also be reflected in three of the other four parts that comprise the book. In Part One we shall look at the **historical** background to the contemporary world. In Part Three we shall look at the main **structures** and processes of contemporary world politics. In Part Four we shall deal with some of the main issues in the globalized world. So although we shall not go into much depth now about these theories, we need to give you a flavour of their main themes since we want, after summarizing them, to say something about how each might think about globalization.

Realism and world politics

For realists, the main actors on the world stage are **states**, which are legally sovereign actors. **Sovereignty** means that there is no actor above the state that can compel it to act in specific ways. Other actors, such as multinational corporations or international organizations, all have to work within the framework of inter-state relations. As for what propels states to act as they do, realists see human nature as centrally important. For realists, human nature is fixed, and, crucially, it is selfish. To think otherwise is to make a mistake, and it was such a mistake that the realists accused the idealists of making. As a result, world politics (or, more accurately for realists, international politics) represents a struggle for **power** between states each trying to maximize their **national interest**. Such order as exists in world politics is the result of the workings of a mechanism known as the **balance of power**, whereby states act so as to prevent any one state

dominating. Thus world politics is all about bargaining and alliances, with **diplomacy** a key mechanism for balancing various national interests. But finally, the most important tool available for implementing states' foreign policies is military force. Ultimately, since there is no sovereign body above the states that make up the international political system, world politics is a **self-help** system in which states must rely on their own military resources to achieve their ends. Often these ends can be achieved through **cooperation**, but the potential for conflict is ever present.

In recent years, an important variant of realism, known as **neo-realism**, has developed. This view stresses the importance of the **structure** of the international political system in affecting the behaviour of all states. Thus, during the cold war two main powers dominated the **international system**. and this led to certain **rules** of behaviour; now that the cold war has ended, the structure of world politics is said to be moving towards **multipolarity** (after a phase of **unipolarity**), which for neo-realists will involve very different rules of the game.

Liberalism and world politics

Liberals have a different view of world politics, and like realists, have a long tradition. Earlier we mentioned idealism, and this was really one rather extreme version of liberalism. There are many variants of liberalism, but the main themes that run through liberal thought are that human beings are perfectible, that democracy is necessary for that perfectibility to develop, and that ideas matter. Behind all this lies a belief in *progress*. Accordingly, liberals reject the realist notion that war is the natural condition of world politics. They also question the idea that the state is the main actor on the world political stage, although they do not deny that it is important. They see multinational corporations, transnational actors such as terrorist groups, and international organizations as central actors in some issue-areas of world politics. In those issue-areas in which the state acts, they tend to think of the state not as a unitary or united actor but as a set of bureaucracies, each with its own interests. Therefore there can be no such thing as a national interest, since it merely represents the result of whatever bureaucratic organizations dominate the domestic decision-making process. In relations between states, liberals stress the possibilities for cooperation, and the key issue becomes devising international settings in which cooperation can be best achieved. The picture of world politics that results from the liberal view is of a complex system of bargaining between many different types of actor. Military force is still important but the liberal agenda is not as restricted as is the realist one. Liberals see national interests in more than just military terms, and stress the importance of economic, environmental, and technological issues. Order in world politics emerges not from a balance of power but from the interactions between many layers of governing arrangements, comprising laws, agreed **norms, international regimes**, and institutional rules. Fundamentally, liberals do not think that sovereignty is as important in practice as realists think it is in theory. States may be legally sovereign, but in practice they have to negotiate with all sorts of other actors, with the result that their freedom to act as they might wish is seriously curtailed. **Interdependence** between states is a critically important feature of world politics.

Marxist theories and world politics

The third main theoretical position we want to mention, **Marxist theory**, is also known as **historical materialism**, which immediately gives you clues as to its main assumptions. We want to point out that Marxist theory has been historically less influential than either realism or liberalism, and has less in common with either realism or liberalism than they do with each other. For Marxist theory, the most important feature of world politics is that it takes place within a world capitalist economy. In this world economy the most important actors are not states but classes, and the behaviour of all other actors is ultimately explicable by class forces. Thus states, multinational corporations, and even international organizations represent the dominant class interest in the world economic system. Marxist theorists differ over how much leeway actors such as states have, but all agree that the world economy severely constrains the freedom of manoeuvre of states. Rather than world politics being an arena of conflict between national interests or an arena with many different issue-areas, Marxist theorists conceive world politics as the setting in which **class conflicts** are played out. As for order in world politics, Marxist theorists think of it primarily in economic rather than in military terms. The key feature of the international economy is the division of the world into core, semi-periphery, and periphery areas. Within the semi-periphery and the periphery there exist cores that are tied into the capitalist world economy, while within even the core area there are peripheral economic

areas. In all of this, what matters is the dominance of the power not of states but of **global capitalism**, and it is these forces that ultimately determine the main political patterns in world politics. Sovereignty is not nearly as important for Marxist theorists as for realists since it refers to political and legal matters, whereas the most important feature of world politics is the degree of economic autonomy, and here Marxist theorists see all states as having to play by the rules of the international capitalist economy.

Social constructivism

Social constructivism is a relatively new theory about world politics, one that developed in the late 1980s and has been becoming increasingly influential since the mid-1990s. The approach arose out of a set of events in world politics, notably the disintegration of the Soviet **empire**, as symbolized most notably by the fall of the Berlin Wall in 1989. This indicated that human agency had a much greater potential role in world politics than implied by realism and liberalism. But the theoretical underpinnings of the approach are much older, and relate to a series of social-scientific and philosophical works that dispute the notion that the social world is external to the people who live in it, and is not easily changed. Realism and liberalism to different degrees stress the regularities and 'certainties' of political life (although liberalism is somewhat less adamant). By contrast, constructivism argues that we make and re-make the social world and so there is much more of a role for human agency than other theories allow. Moreover, constructivists note that those who see the world as fixed underestimate the possibilities for human progress and for the betterment of people's lives. In the words of one of the most influential constructivist theorists, Alexander Wendt, even the self-help international system portrayed by realists is something that we make and re-make: as he puts it, '**anarchy** is what states make of it' (Wendt 1992). Therefore the world that realists portray as 'natural' or 'given' is in fact far more open to change, and constructivists think that self-help is only one possible response to the anarchical structure of world politics. Even more subversively, they think that not only is the structure of world politics amenable to change, but so are the identities and interests that the other theories take as given. In other words, constructivists think that it is a fundamental mistake to think of world politics as something that we cannot change. The seemingly 'natural' structures, processes, identities, and interests of world politics could in fact be different from what they currently are, and implying otherwise is a political act.

Poststructuralism

Poststructualism has been a particularly influential theoretical development throughout the humanities and social sciences in the last thirty years. It reached international theory in the mid-1980s, but can only be said to have really arrived in the past fifteen years. None the less, in recent years it is probably as popular a theoretical approach as any discussed in this book, and overlaps with a number of them. Part of the difficulty, however, is precisely defining poststructuralism, which is also sometimes referred to as postmodernism. This is in addition to the fact, of course, that there are substantial theoretical differences within its various strands. One useful definition is by Jean-François Lyotard: 'Simplifying to the extreme, I define *post-modern* as incredulity towards metanarratives' (1984: xxiv). Incredulity simply means scepticism; 'metanarrative' means any theory that asserts it has clear foundations for making knowledge claims and involves a **foundational** epistemology. You do not need to worry too much about what this means right now. It's explained in more detail in the chapter on poststructuralism. Put simply, to have a foundational epistemology is to think that all truth claims (about some feature of the world) can be judged true or false (epistemology is the study of how we can claim to know something). Poststructuralism is essentially concerned with distrusting and exposing any account of human life that claims to have direct access to 'the truth'. Thus realism, liberalism, and Marxism are all suspect from a poststructuralist perspective because they claim to have uncovered some fundamental truth about the world. Michel Foucault, an important influence on poststructuralists in international relations, was opposed to the notion that knowledge is immune from the workings of power. Instead, he argued that power in fact produces knowledge. All power requires knowledge and all knowledge relies on and reinforces existing power relations. Thus there is no such thing as 'truth' existing outside of power. Truth is not something external to social settings, but is instead part of them. Poststructuralist international theorists have used this insight to examine the 'truths' of international relations theory to see how the concepts that dominate the discipline in fact are highly contingent on specific power relations. Poststructuralism takes apart the very concepts

and methods of our thinking, examing the conditions under which we are able to theorize about world politics in the first place.

Postcolonialism

Postcolonialism has been an important approach in cultural studies, literary theory, and anthropology for some time now, and has a long and distinguished pedigree. However, postcolonial approaches have until quite recently largely been ignored in the field of international politics. This is now changing, not least because old disciplinary boundaries are breaking down. More and more scholars working with international politics are drawing on ideas from other disciplines, including postcolonial ideas, especially those that suggest the Eurocentric character of the field. It is noteworthy that all the major theories we have discussed so far—realism, liberalism, Marxism, social constructivism, and poststructuralism—all emerged in Europe in response to specific European problems. Postcolonial scholars question whether such theories can really purport to explain *world* politics. It is more likely that they help to continue and justify the military and economic suborindation of the global South by powerful Western interests. Postcolonialism has also become more popular since the attacks of 11 September, which encouraged people to try to understand how the histories of the West and the global South have always been intertwined. For example, the identities of the colonized and colonizers are constantly in flux and mutually constituted. Postcolonial scholars argue that the dominant theories such as realism and liberalism are not neutral in terms of race, gender, and class, but have helped secure the domination of the Western world over the global South. Thus an important claim of postcolonialism is that global hierarchies of subordination and control, past and present, are made possible through the social construction of racial, gendered, and class differences. As other chapters in this volume suggest, International Relations has been slightly more comfortable with issues of class and gender. But the issue of race has been almost entirely ignored. This is even though race and racism continue to shape the contemporary theory and practice of world politics in far-reaching ways. In 1903, W. E. B. DuBois famously argued that the problem of the twentieth century would be the problem of the 'colour-line'. How will transnational racism continue to shape global politics in the twenty-first century?

Theories and globalization

The first three of these theoretical perspectives, realism, liberalism, and Marxism, have tended to be the main theories that have been used to understand world politics, with constructivism and poststructuralism becoming increasingly influential since the mid-1990s and post-colonialism gaining some influence in the 2000s. In the 1980s it became common to talk of an **inter-paradigm** debate between realism, liberalism, and Marxism; that is to say that the three theories (known as paradigms after the influential philosopher of natural science, Thomas Kuhn) were in competition and that the 'truth' about world politics lay in the debate between them. At first sight each seems to be particularly good at explaining some aspects of world politics better than the others, and an obvious temptation would be to try to combine them into some overall account. But this is not the easy option it may seem. This is because the theories are not so much different views of the same world, but are instead **six views of different worlds**. Let us explain this briefly.

While it is clear that each of the theories focuses on different aspects of world politics (realism on the power relations between states, liberalism on a much wider set of interactions between states and **non-state actors**, Marxist theory on the patterns of the world economy, constructivism on the ways in which we can develop different social structures and processes, poststructuralism on the power relationships behind all discourses about the world, and postcolonialism on the persistence of relations of hierarchy in world politics made possible by race, gender, and class subordination), each is saying more than this. Each view is claiming that it is picking out **the most important features** of world politics and that it offers a **better account** than do the rival theories. Thus the six approaches are really in competition with one another; and while you can certainly choose between them, it is not so easy to add bits from one to the others. For example, if you are a Marxist, you think that state behaviour is ultimately determined by class forces, forces that the realist does not think affect state behaviour. Similarly, constructivism suggests that actors do not face a world that is fixed, and thus it is one that they can in principle change, in direct contrast to the core beliefs of realism. In other words, these theories are really versions of what world politics is like rather than partial pictures of it. They do not agree on what the 'it' is.

Perhaps none of these theories has all the answers when it comes to explaining world politics in a global

era. In fact, each sees 'globalization' differently. We do not want to tell you which theory seems best, since the purpose of this book is to give you a variety of conceptual lenses through which you might want to look at globalization and/or question whether globalization really exists as anything more than a buzz-word. All we shall do is say a few words about how each theory might respond to what is referred to as 'globalization'. We shall then go on to say something about the possible rise of globalization and offer some ideas on its strengths and weaknesses as a description of contemporary world politics.

1 For **realists**, globalization—however its advocates define it—does not alter the most significant feature of world politics, namely the territorial division of the world into nation-states. While the increased interconnectedness between economies and societies might make them more dependent on one another, the same cannot be said about the states-system. Here, powerful states retain sovereignty, and globalization does not render obsolete the struggle for political power between those states. Nor does it undermine the importance of the threat of the use of force or the importance of the balance of power. Globalization may affect our social, economic, and cultural lives, but it does not transcend the international political system of states.

2 For **liberals**, the picture looks very different. They tend to see globalization as the end product of a long-running transformation of world politics. For them, globalization fundamentally undermines realist accounts of world politics since it shows that states are no longer such central actors as they once were. In their place are numerous actors of differing importance according to the issue-area concerned. Liberals are particularly interested in the revolution in technology and communications represented by globalization. This increased interconnectedness between societies, which is economically and technologically led, results in a very different pattern of world political relations from that which has gone before. States are no longer sealed units, if ever they were, and as a result the world looks more like a cobweb of relations than like the state model of realism or the class model of Marxist theory.

3 For **Marxists**, globalization is a bit of a sham. It is nothing particularly new, and is really only the latest stage in the development of international capitalism. It does not mark a qualitative shift in world politics,

nor does it render all our existing theories and concepts redundant. Above all, it is a Western-led capitalist phenomenon that basically simply furthers the development of global capitalism. Rather than make the world more alike, it further deepens the existing divide between the core, the semi-periphery, and the periphery.

4 For **constructivist** theorists, globalization tends to be presented as an external force acting on states, which leaders often argue is a reality that they cannot challenge. This, constructivists argue, is a very political act, since it underestimates the ability of leaders to challenge and shape globalization, and instead allows them to duck responsibility by blaming 'the way the world is'. Instead, constructivists think that we can mould globalization in a variety of ways, notably because it offers us very real chances to create cross-national **social movements** aided by modern technological forms of communication such as the Internet.

5 For **poststructuralists**, 'globalization' does not exist out there in the world. It is a discourse. Poststructuralists are sceptical of the grand claims made by realists, liberals, and Marxists about the nature of globalization and argue that any claims about the meaning of so-called 'globalization' make sense only in the context of a specific discourse that itself is a product of power. These various regimes of truth about globalization merely reflect the ways in which both power and truth develop together in a mutually sustaining relationship through history. The way to uncover the workings of power behind the discourse of 'globalization' is to undertake a detailed historical analysis of how the practices and statements about globalization are 'true' only within specific discourses.

6 **Postcolonial** scholarship on globalization is similar to much Marxist thought in that it highlights the important degree of continuity and persistence of colonial forms of power in the globalized world. For example, the level of economic and military control of Western interests in the global South is in many ways actually greater now than it was under direct control—a form of 'neo'-colonialism. So although the era of formal colonial imposition by force of arms is largely over, an important starting point for postcolonial scholarship is the issue of vast inequality on a global scale, the forms of globalizing power that make this systematic inequality possible, and the continued domination of subaltern peoples, those classes dominated under hegemony such as poor rural women in the global South.

By the end of the book we hope you will work out which of these theories (if any) best explains 'globalization'. We spend a lot of time in Part Two outlining these theories in more detail so as to give you much more of an idea of the main issues involved. The central point we want to make here is to reinforce our comment earlier that theories do not portray 'the' truth. In other words, the theories we have mentioned will see globalization differently because they have **a prior** view of what is most important in world politics.

Globalization and its precursors

The focus of this book is how to think about 'globalization', and as we have already said, our concern is with offering you an overview of world politics in a global era. **Globalization is mostly simply (or simplistically!) defined as a the process of increasing interconnectedness between societies such that events in one part of the world increasingly have effects on peoples and societies far away.** A globalized world is one in which political, economic, cultural, and social events become more and more interconnected, and also one in which they have more impact. In other words, societies are affected more and more extensively and more and more deeply by events of other societies. These events can conveniently be divided into three types, **social**, **economic,** and **political.** In each case, the world seems to be 'shrinking', and people are increasingly aware of this. The Internet is but the most graphic example of this since it allows you to sit at home and have instant communication with websites around the world. Electronic mail has also transformed communications in a way that the editors of this book would not have envisaged just a few years ago. But these are only the most obvious examples. Others would include: worldwide television communications, global newspapers, international social movements such as Amnesty International or Greenpeace, global franchises such as McDonald's, Coca-Cola, and Mac, the global economy, and global risks such as pollution, climate change, and HIV/AIDS.

There are, of course, many other examples, but you get the picture. It is these developments that seem to have changed the nature of world politics from what it was just a few years ago. The important point to stress is that it is not just that the world has changed but that the changes are qualitative and not merely quantitative; a strong case can be made that a 'new' world political system has emerged as a result of these processes.

However, what many people refer to as 'globalization' is not some entirely new phenomenon in world history. Indeed, as we shall note later on, many argue that it is merely a new name for a long-term feature. While we leave it to you to judge whether in its current manifestation it represents a new phase in world history or merely a continuation of processes that have been around for a long time, we want to note that there have been several precursors to globalization. In other words, the processes many refer to as encompassing globalization bear a marked similarity to at least nine features of world politics discussed by writers before the contemporary period. We shall now note these briefly.

First, globalization has many features in common with the **theory of modernization** (see Modelski 1972 and Morse 1976). According to these writers, industrialization brings into existence a whole new set of contacts between societies, and changes the political, economic, and social processes that characterized the pre-modernized world. Crucially, industrialization altered the nature of the state, both widening its responsibilities and weakening its control over outcomes. The result is that the old power-politics model of international relations becomes outmoded. Force becomes less usable, states have to negotiate with other actors to achieve their goals, and the very **identity** of the state as an actor is called into question. In many respects it seems that modernization is part of the globalization process, differing only in that it applied more to the developed world and involved nothing like as extensive a set of transactions.

Second, there are clear similarities with the arguments of influential writers such as Walt Rostow (1960), who argued that **economic growth** followed a pattern in all economies as they went through industrialization. Their economies developed in the shadow of more 'developed' economies until they reached the stage where they were capable of self-sustained economic growth. What this has in common with globalization is that Rostow saw a clear pattern to economic development, one marked by stages that all economies would follow as they adopted capitalist policies. In a similar vein, much globalization theory has several points in common with the infamous argument of Francis Fukuyama (1992) that the power of the economic market is resulting in liberal democracy replacing all other types of government. Although he recognizes that there are other types of political **regime** to challenge liberal democracy, he does not think that any of the alternatives, such as communism, fascism, or **Islam**, will be able to deliver the economic goods in the way that liberal democracy can. In this sense there is a direction to history, and that direction is towards the expansion of the economic market throughout the world.

Third, there was the important literature emerging out of the liberal paradigm discussed above. Specifically, there were very influential works on the nature of **economic interdependence** (Cooper 1968), the role of transnational actors (Keohane and Nye 1977), and the resulting cobweb model of world politics (Mansbach, Ferguson, and Lampert 1976). Much of this literature anticipates the main theoretical themes of globalization, although again it tends to be applied much more to the developed world than is the case with globalization.

Fourth, there are notable similarities between the picture of the world painted by globalization and that portrayed in Marshall McLuhan's (1964) influential work on the **global village**. According to McLuhan, advances in electronic communications resulted in a world where we could see in real time events that were occurring in distant parts of the world. For McLuhan, the main effects of this development were that time and space become compressed to such an extent that everything loses its traditional identity. As a result, the old groupings of political, economic, and social organization simply do not work any more. Without doubt, McLuhan's work significantly anticipates some of the main themes of globalization, although it should be noted that he was talking primarily about the communications revolution, whereas the globalization literature tends to be much more extensive.

Fifth, there are significant overlaps between some of the main themes of globalization and the work of writers such as John Burton (1972) and Hedley Bull (1977). Hedley Bull pointed to the development over the centuries of a set of agreed norms and common understandings between state leaders, such that they effectively formed a society rather than merely an international system. However, although Bull was perturbed by the emergence of what he called the 'new medievalism', in which a series of subnational and international organizations vied with the state for authority, he did not feel that the nation-state was about to be replaced by the development of a **world society**. Burton went further and spoke of the emergence of such a society; the old **state system** was becoming outmoded, as increasingly significant interactions took place between non-state actors. It was Burton who coined the term 'cobweb model' of world politics. The central message here was that the most important patterns in world politics were those created by trade, communications, language, ideology, etc., along with the more traditional focus on the political relations between states.

Sixth, in the 1960s, 1970s, and 1980s, there was the visionary work of those associated with the **World Order Models Project** (WOMP), an organization set up in 1968 to promote the development of alternatives to the inter-state system which would result in the elimination of war. What is most interesting about their many studies (see, e.g., Mendlovitz 1975 and Falk 1975, 1995*b*) is that they focused on the questions of global government that today are central to much work going on under the name of globalization. For WOMPers (as they were known), the unit of analysis is the individual, and the level of analysis is the global. Interestingly, by the mid-1990s WOMP had become much wider in its focus, concentrating on the world's most vulnerable people and the environment.

Finally, there are very marked similarities between some of the political aspects of globalization and long-standing ideas of liberal progress. These have most recently been expressed in the **liberal peace theory** of writers such as Bruce Russett (1993) and Michael Doyle (1983*a* and 1983*b*), although they go back centuries to writers such as Immanuel Kant. The main idea is that liberal democracies do not fight one another, and although of course there can be dispute as to what is a liberal democracy, adherents to this view claim quite plausibly that there is no case where two democracies have ever gone to war. The reason they claim this is that public accountability is so central in democratic systems that publics will not allow leaders easily to engage in wars with other democratic **nations**. Again the main link with globalization is the assumption that there is progress to history, and that this is making it far more difficult to start wars.

The above list incorporates some of the possible precursors to globalization. Our intention is not to suggest that we agree with any of these accounts. Many of them we certainly do not agree with. Rather it is to indicate the similarities between these precursors and the more contemporary discourse of globalization.

Globalization: myth or reality?

Our final task in this introduction is to offer you a summary of the main arguments for and against globalization as a distinct new phase in world politics. We do not expect you to decide where you stand on the issue at this stage, but we think that we should give you some of the main arguments so that you can keep them in mind as you read the rest of this book. Because the arguments for globalization as an important new phase of world politics have been rehearsed above—and also because they are most effectively summarized in the chapter that follows—we shall spend a little more time on the criticisms. The main arguments in favour of globalization comprising a new era of world politics are:

1 The pace of **economic transformation** is so great that it has created a new world politics. States are no longer closed units and they cannot control their economies. The world economy is more interdependent than ever, with trade and finances ever expanding.

2 **Communications** have fundamentally revolutionized the way we deal with the rest of the world. We now live in a world where events in one location can be immediately observed on the other side of the world. Electronic communications alter our notions of the social groups we work with and live in.

3 There is now, more than ever before, a **global culture**, so that most urban areas resemble one another. Much of the urban world shares a common culture, much of it emanating from Hollywood.

4 The world is becoming more **homogeneous.** Differences between peoples are diminishing.

5 **Time and space seem to be collapsing.** Our old ideas of geographical space and of chronological time are undermined by the speed of modern communications and media.

6 There is emerging a **global polity,** with transnational social and political movements and the beginnings of a transfer of allegiance from the state to sub-state, transnational, and international bodies.

7 A **cosmopolitan culture** is developing. People are beginning to 'think globally and act locally'.

8 A **risk culture** is emerging with people realizing both that the main risks that face them are global

(pollution and HIV/AIDS) and that states are unable to deal with the problems.

However, just as there are powerful reasons for seeing globalization as a new stage in world politics, often allied to the view that globalization is progressive, that is to say that it improves the lives of people, there are also arguments that suggest the opposite. Some of the main ones are given below.

1   One obvious objection to the globalization thesis is that globalization is merely a buzz-word to denote the latest phase of capitalism. In a very powerful critique of globalization theory, Hirst and Thompson (1996) argue that one effect of the globalization thesis is that it makes it appear as if national governments are powerless in the face of global trends. This ends up paralysing governmental attempts to subject global economic forces to control and regulation. Believing that most globalization theory lacks historical depth, they point out that it paints the current situation as **more unusual than it is,** and also as more firmly entrenched than it might in fact be. Current trends may well be reversible. Hirst and Thompson conclude that the more extreme versions of globalization are 'a myth', and they support this claim with five main conclusions from their study of the contemporary world economy (1996: 2–3). First, the present internationalized economy is not unique in history. In some respects they say it is less open than the international economy was between 1870 and 1914. Second, they find that 'genuinely' transnational companies are relatively rare; most are national companies trading internationally. There is no trend towards the development of international companies. Third, there is no shift of finance and capital from the developed to the underdeveloped world. Direct investment is highly concentrated among the countries of the developed world. Fourth, the world economy is not global; rather trade, investment, and financial flows are concentrated in and between three blocs—Europe, North America, and Japan. Finally, they argue that this group of three blocs could, if they coordinated policies, regulate global economic markets and forces. Note that Hirst and Thompson are looking only at economic theories of globalization, and many of the main accounts deal with factors such as communications and culture more than economics. None the less, theirs is a very powerful critique of one of the main planks of the more extreme globalization thesis, with their central criticism that seeing the global economy as something beyond our control both misleads us and prevents us from developing policies to control the national economy. All too often we are told that our economy must obey 'the global market'. Hirst and Thompson believe that this is a myth.

2   Another obvious objection is that globalization is very **uneven in its effects.** At times it sounds very much like a Western theory applicable only to a small part of humankind. To pretend that even a small minority of the world's population can connect to the Internet is clearly an exaggeration when in reality most people on the planet have probably never made a telephone call in their lives. In other words, globalization applies only to the developed world. In the rest of the world, there is nothing like this degree of globalization. We are in danger of overestimating the extent and the depth of globalization.

3   A related objection is that globalization may well be simply **the latest stage of Western imperialism.** It is the old modernization theory discussed above in a new guise. The forces that are being globalized are conveniently those found in the Western world. What about non-Western values? Where do they fit into this emerging global world? The worry is that they do not fit in at all, and what is being celebrated in globalization is the triumph of a Western worldview, at the expense of the worldviews of other cultures.

4   Critics have also noted that there are very considerable **losers** as the world becomes more globalized. This is because globalization represents the success of liberal capitalism in an economically divided world. Perhaps one outcome is that globalization allows the more efficient exploitation of less well-off nations, and all in the name of openness. The technologies accompanying globalization are technologies that automatically benefit the richest economies in the world, and allow their interests to override local ones. Not only is globalization imperialist; it is also exploitative.

5   We also need to make the straightforward point that not all globalized forces are necessarily good ones. Globalization makes it easier for drug cartels and terrorists to operate, and the Internet's anarchy raises crucial questions of censorship and preventing access to certain kinds of material.

6   Turning to the so-called **global governance** aspects of globalization, the main worry here is about responsibility. To whom are the transnational social movements responsible and democratically accountable?

If IBM or Shell becomes more and more powerful in the world, does this not raise the issue of how accountable it is to democratic control? David Held has made a strong case for the development of what he calls **cosmopolitan democracy** (1995), but this has clearly defined legal and democratic features. The worry is that most of the emerging powerful actors in a globalized world precisely are *not* accountable. This argument also applies to seemingly 'good' global actors such as Amnesty International and Greenpeace.

7 Finally, there seems to be a **paradox** at the heart of the globalization thesis. On the one hand, it is usually portrayed as the triumph of Western, market-led values. But how do we then explain the tremendous economic success that some national economies have had in the globalized world? Consider the so-called 'Tigers' of Asia, countries such as Singapore, Taiwan, Malaysia, and Korea, which have enjoyed some of the highest growth rates in the international economy but, according to some, subscribe to very different 'Asian' values. These nations emphatically reject certain 'Western' values, and yet they have had enormous economic success. The paradox, then, is whether these countries can continue to modernize so successfully without adopting Western values. If they can, then what does this do to one of the main themes of the globalization literature, namely the argument that globalization represents the spreading across the globe of a set of values? If these countries do continue to follow their own roads towards economic and social modernization, then we must anticipate future disputes between 'Western' and 'Asian' values over issues like human rights, **gender**, and religion.

We hope that these arguments for and against the dominant way of representing globalization will cause you to think deeply about the utility of the concept of globalization in explaining contemporary world politics. The chapters that follow do not take a common stance **for** or **against globalization.** We shall end by posing some questions that we would like you to keep in mind as you read the remaining chapters:

- Is globalization a new phenomenon in world politics?
- Which theory discussed above best explains globalization?
- Is globalization a positive or a negative development?
- Is globalization merely the latest stage of capitalist development?
- Does globalization make the state obsolete?
- Does globalization make the world more or less democratic?
- Is globalization merely Western imperialism in a new guise?
- Does globalization make war more or less likely?
- In what ways is war a globalizing force in itself?

We hope that this introduction and the chapters that follow help you to answer these questions, and that this book as a whole provides you with a good overview of the politics of the contemporary world. Whether or not you conclude that globalization is a new phase in world politics, whether you think it is a positive or a negative development, or whether you conclude that it doesn't really exist at all, we leave you to decide. But we think it important to conclude this chapter by stressing that globalization—whether a new form of world politics, merely a new name for an age-old set of features, or something else—clearly is a very complex phenomenon that is contradictory and difficult to comprehend. Not all people in the world share a view of globalization as a progressive force in world politics. It is not one thing. How we think about politics in the global era will reflect not merely the theories we accept, but our own positions in this globalized world. In this sense, how we respond to world events may itself be ultimately dependent on the social, cultural, economic, and political spaces we occupy. In other words, world politics suddenly becomes very personal: how does your economic position, your ethnicity, gender, culture, or your religion determine what globalization means to you?

Further Reading

There are several good introductory guides to the globalization debate. A comprehensive discussion is found in **A. McGrew and D. Held** (2007), *Globalization Theory: Aprroaches and Controversies* (Cambridge: Polity Press). See also **D. Held and A. McGrew** (eds) (2003), *The Global Transformations Reader*, 2nd edn (Cambridge: Polity Press). **J. A. Scholte** (2005), *Globalization: A Critical Introduction*, 2nd edn (London: Macmillan) offers a good overview of aspects of globalization. Also see **C. el-Ojeili and P. Hayden** (2006), *Critical Theories of Globalization* (Basingstoke: Palgrave Macmillan).

    A. McGrew and P. Lewis (1992), *Global Politics* (Cambridge: Polity Press) is a good collection of essays about global politics and contains some very relevant chapters on the relationship between the three theories discussed above and globalization. **R. Robertson** (1992), *Globalization: Social Theory and Global Culture* (London: Sage) is a very widely cited survey of the relations between globalization and global culture. **J. N. Rosenau and E.-D. Czempiel** (1992), *Governance without Government* (Cambridge: Cambridge University Press) is a good collection of essays dealing with the political aspects of globalization. **C. Enloe** (2007), *Globalization and Militarism: Feminists Make the Link* (Lanham, MD: Rowman & Littlefield) is a good analysis from a leading feminist of the connections between globalization and various forms of violence.

    We would also point you to other books in the same Rowman & Littlefield series on 'globalization' edited by **M. B. Steger and T. Carver,** in particular **S. Krishna** (2008), *Globalization and Postcolonialism: Hegemony and Resistance in the Twenty-first Century* and **V. M. Moghadam** (2008), *Globalization and Social Movements: Islamism, Feminism, and the Global Justice Movement.*

    Excellent critiques of the globalization thesis are **J. Rosenberg** (2002), *The Follies of Globalization Theory* (London: Verso), **D. Held and A. McGrew** (2002), *Globalization/Anti-globalization* (Cambridge: Polity Press), **B. Gills** (ed.) (2002), *Globalization and the Politics of Resistance* (Basingstoke: Palgrave Macmillan) and **B. K. Gills and W. R. Thompson** (eds) (2006), *Globalization and Global History* (London: Routledge), **Joseph Stiglitz** (2003), *Globalization and Its Discontents* (London: Penguin) and (2006) *Making Globalization Work* (New York: W. W. Norton), **R. Falk** (1999), *Predatory Globalization: A Critique* (Cambridge: Polity Press), **L. Weiss** (1998), *The Myth of the Powerless State* (Cambridge: Polity Press), **P. Hirst and G. Thompson** (1999), *Globalization in Question*, 2nd edn (Cambridge: Polity Press), **T. Barkawi** (2006), *Globalization and War* (Oxford: Rowman & Littlefield), and **R. Kiely** (2007), *The New Political Economy of Development: Globalization, Imperialism, Hegemony* (Basingstoke: Palgrave Macmillan).

Online Resource Centre

Visit the Online Resource Centre that accompanies this book to access more learning resources on this chapter topic at www.oxfordtextbooks.co.uk/orc/baylis5e/

Chapter 1

Globalization and global politics

ANTHONY MCGREW

Reader's Guide

This chapter provides an account of globalization and its consequences for our understanding of world politics. Globalization is a long-term historical process that denotes the growing intensity of worldwide interconnectedness: in short, a 'shrinking world'. It is, however, a highly uneven process such that far from creating a more cooperative world it is also a significant source of global friction, instability, enmity, and conflict. Whilst it has important consequences for the power and autonomy of national governments, it by no means prefigures, as many have argued or desired, the demise of the nation-state or of geopolitics. Rather, globalization is associated with significant transformations in world politics, the most significant of which are the focus of this chapter. In particular the chapter concludes that a conceptual shift in our thinking is required to grasp fully the nature of these transformations. This conceptual shift involves embracing the idea of global politics: the politics of an embryonic global society in which domestic and world politics, even if conceptually distinct, are practically inseparable. It also requires rethinking many of the traditional organizing assumptions and institutions of modern political life—from sovereignty to democracy—since in a globalized world, power is no longer simply organized according to a national or territorial logic. This chapter has two key objectives: to elucidate and elaborate the concept of globalization; and to explore its consequences for our understanding of world politics.

Introduction

Globalization—simply the widening, deepening, and speeding up of worldwide interconnectedness—is a contentious issue in the study of world politics. Some—the hyperglobalists—argue that it is bringing about the demise of the sovereign **nation-state** as global forces undermine the ability of governments to control their own economies and societies (Ohmae 1995; Scholte 2000). By contrast, the sceptics reject the idea of globalization as so much 'globaloney.' They argue that states and geopolitics remain the principal agents and forces shaping **world order** (Krasner 1999; Gilpin 2001). This chapter takes a rather different approach—a transformationalist perspective—arguing that both the hyperglobalists and sceptics alike exaggerate their arguments, thereby producing misleading interpretations of contemporary world politics. This transformationalist perspective acknowledges that far from leading to the demise of the sovereign state, globalization is associated with the emergence of a conspicuously **global politics** in which the traditional distinction between domestic and international affairs is no longer very meaningful. Under these conditions,

'politics everywhere, it would seem, are related to politics everywhere else', such that the orthodox approaches to international relations—which are constructed upon this very distinction—provide at best only a partial insight into the forces shaping the contemporary world (Rosenau in Mansbach, Ferguson, and Lampert 1976: 22).

Since it is such a 'slippery' and overused concept, it is hardly surprising that globalization should engender such intense debate. Accordingly, this chapter begins by reviewing the concept of globalization before exploring its implications for the study of world politics. The chapter is organized into two main sections: the first will address several interrelated questions, namely: what is globalization? How is it best conceptualized and defined? How is it manifest today, most especially given the events of **9/11** and the 2008–9 global financial crisis? Is it really all that new? The second section will explore the ways in which globalization is producing a form of global politics that is highly skewed in favour of the most powerful to the exclusion of the majority of humankind.

Making sense of globalization

Over the last three decades the sheer scale and scope of global interconnectedness has become increasingly evident in every sphere, from the economic to the cultural.

Worldwide economic integration has intensified as the expansion of global commerce, finance, and production binds together the economic fortunes of **nations**, communities, and households across the world's major trading regions and beyond within an emerging global market economy. As the credit crunch of 2008 illustrates, the integration of the world economy is such that no national economy is able to insulate itself from the contagion effect of turmoil in the world's financial markets. Instability in one region, whether the collapse of the Argentinean economy in 2002 or the East Asian recession of 1997, very rapidly takes its toll on jobs, production, savings, and investment many thousands of miles away, while a collapse of confidence in US banks is felt everywhere from Birmingham to Bangkok.

Every day over $2 trillion flows across the world's foreign exchange markets. No government, even the most powerful, has the resources to resist sustained speculation against its currency and thereby the credibility of its economic policy (see Ch. 27). Furthermore, governments have to borrow significant sums in world bond markets. Their creditworthiness determines the availability and cost of such borrowing. In the aftermath of the 2008–9 financial crises, many governments, including the UK and USA, confront real reductions in public spending in order to protect their creditworthiness in world bond markets.

Transnational corporations now account for between 25 and 33 per cent of world output, 70 per cent of world trade, and 80 per cent of international investment, while overseas production by these firms considerably exceeds the level of world exports, making them key players in the global economy controlling the location and distribution of economic and technological resources.

New modes and infrastructures of global communication have made it possible to organize and mobilize like-minded people across the globe in virtual real time, as expressed in coordinated worldwide protests in early 2003 against military intervention in Iraq and the 45,000 international **non-governmental organizations** (NGOs), from Greenpeace to the Climate Action Network, not to mention the activities of transnational criminal and terrorist networks, from drugs cartels to Al Qaeda.

With a global communications infrastructure has also come the transnational spread of ideas, cultures, and information, from Madonna to Muhammad, both among like-minded peoples and between different cultural groups—reinforcing simultaneous tendencies towards both an expanded sense of global solidarity among the like-minded and difference, if not outright hostility, between different cultures, nations, and ethnic groupings.

People—with their cultures—are also on the move in their tens of millions—whether legally or illegally— with global migration almost on a scale of the great nineteenth-century movements but transcending all continents, from south to north and east to west, while over 600 million tourists are on the move every year.

As globalization has proceeded, so has the recognition of transnational problems requiring global regulation, from climate change to the proliferation of weapons of mass destruction. Dealing with these transnational issues has led to an explosive growth of transnational and global forms of rule-making and regulation from **G20** summits in 2009 responding to the global financial crisis to the 2009 Copenhagen Climate Change Conference. This is evident in both the expanding jurisdiction of established **international organizations**, such as the **International Monetary Fund** or the International Civil Aviation Organization, and the literally thousands of informal networks of **cooperation** between parallel government agencies in different countries, from the Financial Action Task Force (which brings together government experts on money-laundering from different countries) and the Dublin Group (which brings together drug enforcement agencies from the European Union, the USA, and other countries).

With the recognition of global problems and global interconnectedness has come a growing awareness of

the multiple ways in which the security and prosperity of communities in different regions of the world are bound together. A single terrorist bombing in Bali has repercussions for public perceptions of security in Europe and the USA, while agricultural subsidies in the USA and the EU have significant consequences for the livelihoods of farmers in Africa, Latin America, and the Caribbean.

We inhabit a world in which the most distant events can rapidly, if not almost instantaneously, come to have very profound consequences for our individual and collective prosperity and perceptions of security. For those of a sceptical persuasion, however, this is neither far from a novel condition nor is it necessarily evidence of globalization if that term means something more than simply international **interdependence**, that is linkages between countries.

What, then, distinguishes the concept of globalization from notions of internationalization or interdependence? What, in other words, is globalization?

Box 1.1 Definitions of globalization

Globalization is variously defined in the literature as:

1 'The intensification of worldwide social relations which link distant localities in such a way that local happenings are shaped by events occurring many miles away and vice versa.'
   (Giddens 1990: 21)

2 'The integration of the world-economy.'
   (Gilpin 2001: 364)

3 'De-territorialization—or . . . the growth of supraterritorial relations between people.'
   (Scholte 2000: 46)

4 'time-space compression'.
   (Harvey 1989)

Key Points

Over the last three decades the sheer scale, scope, and acceleration of global interconnectedness has become increasingly evident in every sphere from the economic to the cultural. Sceptics do not regard this as evidence of globalization if that term means something more than simply international interdependence, i.e. linkages between countries. The key issue becomes what we understand by the term 'globalization'.

Conceptualizing globalization

Initially, it might be helpful to think of globalization as a process characterized by:

- a *stretching* of social, political, and economic activities across political frontiers so that events, decisions, and activities in one region of the world come to have significance for individuals and communities in distant regions of the globe. Civil wars and conflict in the world's poorest regions, for instance, increase the flow of asylum seekers and illegal migrants into the world's affluent countries;
- the intensification, or the growing *magnitude*, of interconnectedness, in almost every sphere of social existence from the economic to the ecological, from the activities of Microsoft to the spread of harmful microbes, such as the SARS virus, from the intensification of world trade to the spread of weapons of mass destruction;
- the *accelerating pace* of global interactions and processes as the evolution of worldwide systems of transport and communication increases the rapidity or velocity with which ideas, news, goods, information, capital, and technology move around the world. Routine telephone banking transactions in the UK are dealt with by call centres in India in real time, whilst at the outset of the recent financial crisis stock markets across the globe displayed a synchronized collapse within hours rather than in weeks as in the Great Crash of 1929;
- the growing *extensity*, *intensity*, and *velocity* of global interactions is associated with a deepening enmeshment of the local and global in so far as local events may come to have global consequences and global events can have serious local consequences, creating a growing collective awareness or consciousness of the world as a shared social space, that is globality or **globalism.** This is expressed, among other ways, in the worldwide diffusion of the very idea of globalization itself as it becomes incorporated into the world's many languages, from Mandarin to Gaelic.

As this brief description suggests, there is more to the concept of globalization than simply interconnectedness. It implies that the cumulative scale, scope, velocity, and depth of contemporary interconnectedness is dissolving the significance of the borders and boundaries that separate the world into its many constituent states or national economic and political spaces (Rosenau 1997).

Rather than growing interdependence between discrete bounded national states, or internationalization, as the sceptics refer to it, the concept of globalization seeks to capture the dramatic shift that is under way in the organization of human affairs: from a world of discrete but interdependent national states to the world as a shared social space. The concept of globalization therefore carries with it the implication of an unfolding process of structural change in the scale of human social and economic organization. Rather than social, economic, and political activities being organized solely on a local or national scale today, they are also increasingly organized on a transnational or global scale. Globalization therefore denotes a significant shift in the scale of social organization, in every sphere from economics to security, transcending the world's major regions and continents.

Central to this structural change are contemporary informatics technologies and infrastructures of communication and transportation. These have greatly facilitated new forms and possibilities of virtual real-time worldwide organization and **coordination,** from the operations of multinational corporations to the worldwide mobilization and demonstrations of the anti-globalization movement. Although geography and distance still matter, it is nevertheless the case that globalization is synonymous with a process of **time–space compression**—literally a shrinking world—in which the sources of even very local developments, from unemployment to ethnic conflict, may be traced to distant conditions or decisions. In this respect globalization embodies a process of **deterritorialization**: as social, political, and economic activities are increasingly 'stretched' across the globe, they become in a significant sense no longer organized solely according to a strictly territorial logic. Terrorist and criminal networks, for instance, operate both locally and globally. National economic space, under conditions of globalization, is no longer coterminous with national territorial space since, for example, many of the UK's largest companies have their headquarters abroad and many domestic companies now outsource their production to China and East Asia, among other locations. This is not to argue that territory and borders are now irrelevant, but rather to acknowledge that under conditions of globalization their *relative significance*, as constraints upon social action and the exercise of power, is declining. In an era of instantaneous real-time global communication and organization, the distinction

Case Study 1 Global production and the iPod

Take just one component of the iPod nano, the central microchip provided by the US company PortalPlayer. The core technology of the chip is licensed from British firm ARM and is modified by PortalPlayer's programmers in California, Washington State, and Hyderabad. PortalPlayer then works with microchip design companies in California that send the finished design to a 'foundry' in Taiwan (China) that produces 'wafers' (thin metal disks) imprinted with thousands of chips. The capital costs of these foundries can be more than $2.5 million. These wafers are then cut up into individual disks and sent elsewhere in Taiwan (China), where each one is tested. The chips are then encased in plastic and readied for assembly by Silicon-Ware in Taiwan (China) and Amkor in the Republic of Korea. The finished microchip is then warehoused in Hong Kong (China) before being transported to mainland China where the iPod is assembled.

Working conditions and wages in China are low relative to Western standards and levels. Many workers live in dormitories and work long hours. It is suggested that overtime is compulsory. Nevertheless, wages are higher than the average of the region in which the assembly plants are located and allow for substantial transfers to rural areas and hence contribute to declining rural poverty. PortalPlayer was only established in 1999 but had revenues in excess of $225 million in 2005. PortalPlayer's chief executive officer has argued that the outsourcing to countries such as India and Taiwan (China) of 'non-critical aspects of your business' has been crucial to the development of the firm and its innovation: 'it allows you to become nimbler and spend R&D dollars on core strengths'.

Since 2003, soon after the iPod was launched, the share price of Apple, the company that produces and sells the iPod, has risen from just over $6 to over $60. Those who own shares in Apple have benefited from the globalization of the iPod.

Sources: C. Joseph, 'The iPod's Incredible Journey',
Mail on Sunday, 15 July 2006;
'Meet the iPod's "Intel"', Business Trends, 32(4) (April), 2006;
World Bank (2006), Global Economic Prospects 2007:
Managing the Next Wave of Globalization
(Washington, DC: World Bank): 11.

between the domestic and the international, inside and outside the state, breaks down. Territorial borders no longer demarcate the boundaries of national economic or political space.

A 'shrinking world' implies that sites of power and the subjects of power quite literally may be continents apart. As the world financial crisis of 2008 illustrates, the key sites and agencies of decision-making, whether in Washington, Beijing, New York, or London, quite literally are oceans apart from the local communities whose livelihoods are affected by their actions. In this respect globalization denotes the idea that power (whether economic, political, cultural, or military) is increasingly organized and exercised at a distance (or has the potential to be so). As such the concept of globalization denotes the relative denationalization of power in so far as, in an increasingly interconnected global system, power is organized and exercised on a transregional, transnational, or transcontinental basis while—see the discussion of political globalization—many other actors, from international organizations to criminal networks, exercise power within, across, and against states. States no longer have a monopoly of power resources, whether economic, coercive, or political.

To summarize: globalization is a process that involves a great deal more than simply growing connections or interdependence between states. It can be defined as:

> A historical process involving a fundamental shift or transformation in the spatial scale of human social organization that links distant communities and expands the reach of power relations across regions and continents.

Such a definition enables us to distinguish globalization from more spatially delimited processes such as **internationalization** and **regionalization**. Whereas internationalization refers to growing interdependence between states, the very idea of internationalization presumes that they remain discrete national units with clearly demarcated borders. By contrast, globalization refers to a process in which the very distinction between the domestic and the external breaks down. Distance and time are collapsed, so that events many thousands of miles away can come to have almost immediate local consequences while the impacts of even more localized developments may be diffused rapidly around the globe.

Box 1.2 Globalization at risk? The financial crisis of 2008

Whilst the causes of the financial crisis of 2008 remain hotly debated, there is a general consensus that both in terms of its scale and severity the crisis posed the greatest risk to the effective functioning of the entire world economy since the Great Depression of the 1930s. Without unprecedented internationally coordinated intervention by the governments of the world's major economies, confirmed at the 2009 G20 summits in London and Pittsburgh, the crisis could have degenerated into an economic catastrophe much worse than that of 1929. As the crisis unfolded throughout 2008 and 2009, it precipitated an unprecedented contraction in global economic transactions from international bank lending to foreign investment, trade in commodities and manufactures and transnational production. Whether this contraction prefigures a significant trend of economic deglobalization or is simply a temporary adjustment to the current global market downturn has yet to be established definitively. The 'great correction' of 2008 has put economic globalization at risk. Paradoxically, in doing so it has reinforced tendencies towards political globalization as governments seek to coordinate their economic strategies to prevent a slide into a global depression or towards protectionism. Moreover, for emerging powers, such as China, India, and Brazil, economic globalization remains essential to sustaining economic growth and national prosperity. Whilst economic globalization is at risk as a consequence of the 'great correction' of 2008, the outcome may be more of a moderation of its pace and intensity, by comparison with more recent historical trends, as opposed to a process of deglobalization, i.e. a reversal of such trends.

If globalization refers to transcontinental or trans-regional networks, flows, or interconnectedness, then regionalization can be conceived as the intensification of patterns of interconnectedness and integration among states that have common borders or are geographically proximate, as in the European Union (see Ch. 26). Accordingly, whereas flows of trade and finance between the world's three major economic blocs—North America, Asia Pacific, and Europe—constitute globalization, by contrast, such flows within these blocs are best described as regionalization.

Key Points

- Globalization denotes a tendency towards the growing extensity, intensity, velocity, and deepening impact of worldwide interconnectedness.
- Globalization is associated with a shift in the scale of social organization, the emergence of the world as a shared social space, the relative deterritorialization of social, economic, and political activity, and the relative denationalization of power.
- Globalization can be conceptualized as a fundamental shift or transformation in the spatial scale of human social organization that links distant communities and expands the reach of power relations across regions and continents.
- Globalization is to be distinguished from internationalization and regionalization.

Contemporary globalization

According to John Gray, the cataclysmic attacks on the United States on 11 September 2001 heralded a new epoch in world affairs, 'The era of globalization is over' (Naím 2002). In response to the perceived threat of globalized terrorism, governments sought to seal their borders. Moreover, in response to the global financial crisis many governments have become more interventionist, protecting key national industries from foreign and trade competition. As a consequence, the intensity of economic globalization (whether measured in terms of trade, financial, or investment flows) has undoubtedly diminished by comparison with its peak at the turn of this century. This has been seized upon by those of a sceptical persuasion (see Box 1.3) as confirmation of their argument (Hirst and Thompson 2003). Sceptics conclude that not only has globalization been highly exaggerated but also that it is a myth or 'conceptual folly'

that conceals the reality of a world which is much less interdependent than it was in the nineteenth century, and one that remains dominated by geopolitics and Western capitalism (Hirst and Thompson 1999; Gilpin 2002; Rosenberg 2000, 2005). By contrast, for many of a more globalist persuasion, the very events of 9/11 and the financial crisis are indicative of just how globalized the world has become in the twenty-first century. What is at issue here, at least in part, are differing (theoretical and historical) interpretations of globalization.

One of the weaknesses of the sceptical argument is that it tends to conflate globalization solely with economic trends: it sometimes invokes a form of economic reductionism. As such it overlooks non-economic trends and tendencies or treats them as insignificant. However, contemporary globalization is not a singular process: it is manifest within all aspects of social life, from politics

Box 1.3 The sceptical view of globalization

Sceptical accounts of globalization tend to dismiss its significance for the study of world politics. They do so on the grounds that:

1   By comparison with the period 1870 to 1914, the world is much less globalized economically, politically, and culturally.

2   The contemporary world is marked by intensifying geopolitics, regionalization, and internationalization, rather than by globalization.

3   The vast bulk of international economic and political activity is concentrated within the group of OECD states.

4   By comparison with the heyday of European global empires, the majority of the world's population and countries in the South are now much less integrated into the global system.

5   Geopolitics, state power, nationalism, and territorial boundaries are of growing, not less, significance in world politics.

6   Globalization is at best a self-serving myth or conceptual folly (according to Rosenberg) that conceals the significance of Western capitalism and US hegemony in shaping contemporary world politics.

7   Responses to the financial crisis demonstrate the centrality of hegemonic and national power to the effective functioning of the world economy.

(Hirst and Thompson 1999, 2003; Hay 2000; Hoogvelt 2001; Gilpin 2002; Rosenberg 2005)

Box 1.4 Patterns of contemporary globalization

Globalization, to varying degrees, is evident in all the principal sectors of social interaction:

Economic: in the economic sphere, patterns of worldwide trade, finance, and production are creating global markets and, in the process, a single global capitalist economy—what Castells (2000) calls 'global informational capitalism'. Multinational corporations organize production and marketing on a global basis while the operation of global financial markets determines which countries get credit and upon what terms.

Military: in the military domain the global arms trade, the proliferation of weapons of mass destruction, the growth of transnational terrorism, the growing significance of transnational military corporations, and the discourse of global insecurity point to the existence of a global military order.

Legal: the expansion of transnational and international law from trade to human rights alongside the creation of new world legal institutions such as the International Criminal Court is indicative of an emerging global legal order.

Ecological: a shared ecology involves shared environmental problems, from global warming to species protection, alongside the creation of multilateral responses and regimes of global environmental governance.

Cultural: involves a complex mix of homogenization and increased heterogeneity given the global diffusion of popular culture, global media corporations, communications networks, etc., simultaneously with the reassertion of nationalism, ethnicity, and difference. But few cultures are hermetically sealed off from cultural interaction.

Social: shifting patterns of migration from South to North and East to West have turned migration into a major global issue as movements come close to the record levels of the great nineteenth-century movements of people.

to production, culture to crime, and economics to education. It is implicated directly and indirectly in many aspects of our daily lives, from the clothes we wear, the food we eat, the knowledge we accumulate, through to our individual and collective sense of security in an uncertain world. Evidence of globalization is all around us: universities are literally global institutions, from the recruitment of students to the dissemination of academic research. To understand contemporary globalization therefore requires a mapping of the distinctive patterns of worldwide interconnectedness in all the key sectors of social activity, from the economic and the political through to the military, the cultural, and the ecological.

As Box 1.4 illustrates, globalization is occurring, albeit with varying intensity and at a varying pace, in every domain of social activity. Of course it is more advanced in some domains than others. For instance, economic globalization is much more extensive and intensive than is cultural or military globalization. To this extent contemporary globalization is highly uneven. Making sense

of it requires asking: the globalization of what? Contrary to the sceptics, it is crucial to appreciate that globalization is a complex *multidimensional process*: patterns of economic globalization and cultural globalization are neither identical nor reducible to one another. In this respect, drawing general conclusions about globalizing tendencies simply from one domain produces a somewhat partial and inaccurate interpretation. As noted, in the aftermath of 9/11 and the financial crisis of 2008 the slowdown in economic globalization was heralded by sceptics as evidence of the end of globalization. This interpretation ignores the accelerating pace of globalization in the military, technological, and cultural domains. Moreover, what is highly distinctive about contemporary globalization is the confluence of globalizing tendencies across all the key domains of social interaction. Significantly, these tendencies have proved remarkably robust in the face of global instability and military conflicts.

If patterns of contemporary globalization are uneven, they are also highly *asymmetrical*. It is a common misconception that globalization implies universality: that the 'global' in globalization implies that all regions or countries must be similarly enmeshed in worldwide processes. This is plainly not the case, for it very markedly involves differential patterns of enmeshment, giving it what Castells calls its 'variable geometry' (Castells 2000). The rich OECD countries are much more globalized than many of the poorest sub-Saharan African states. Globalization is not uniformly experienced across all regions, countries, or even communities since it is inevitably a highly differentiated process. Among OECD and sub-Saharan African states, elites are in the vanguard of globalization while the poorest in these countries find themselves largely excluded from its benefits. Globalization exhibits a distinctive geography of inclusion and exclusion, resulting in clear winners and losers not just between countries but within and across them. For the most affluent it may very well entail a shrinking world—jet travel, global television and the World Wide Web—but for the largest slice of humanity it tends to be associated with a profound sense of disempowerment. Inequality is deeply inscribed in the very processes of contemporary globalization such that it is more accurately described as **asymmetrical globalization**.

Given such asymmetries, it should not be surprising to learn that globalization does not prefigure the emergence of a harmonious global community or an ethic of global cooperation. On the contrary, as 9/11 tragically demonstrated, the more the world becomes a shared social space, the greater the sense of division, difference, and enmity it may create. Historically, violence has always been central to globalization, whether in the form of the 'New Imperialism' of the 1890s or the current 'war on global terror'. Beyond the OECD core globalization is frequently perceived as Western globalization, stoking fears of a new **imperialism** and significant counter-tendencies, from the protests of the anti-globalization movement to forms of economic or cultural protectionism as different ethnic or national communities seek to protect their indigenous culture and ways of life. Rather than a more cooperative world order, contemporary globalization, in many respects, has exacerbated existing tensions and conflicts, generating new divisions and insecurities, creating a potentially more unruly world. More recently it is associated with a historic power shift in world politics since it has been the critical factor in propelling China, India, and Brazil to the rank of major economic powers. This power transition is eroding several centuries of Western dominance of the global order. The emergence of the G20, as opposed to the **G8**, as the key global arena in which global responses to the 2008 financial crisis were coordinated, attests to the dramatic redistribution of economic power consequent upon the most recent phase of globalization.

By comparison with previous periods, contemporary globalization combines a remarkable confluence of dense patterns of global interconnectedness, alongside their unprecedented **institutionalization** through new global and regional infrastructures of control and communication, from the **World Trade Organization** (WTO) to transnational corporations. In nearly all domains contemporary patterns of globalization have not only surpassed those of earlier epochs, but also displayed unparalleled qualitative differences—that is in terms of how globalization is organized and managed. The existence of new real-time global communications infrastructures, in which the world literally is transformed into a single social space, distinguishes very clearly contemporary globalization from that of the past. In these respects it is best described as a thick form of globalization or globalism (Held, McGrew *et al.* 1999; Keohane and Nye 2003).

As such, thick globalization delineates the set of constraints and opportunities that confront governments, conditioning their freedom of action or autonomy, most especially in the economic realm. For instance, the unprecedented scale of global financial flows at over $2 trillion per day imposes a significant discipline on any government, even the most economically powerful, in

---

Box 1.5 The engines of globalization

Explanations of globalization tend to focus on three interrelated factors: technics (technological change and social organization); economics (markets and capitalism); and politics (power, interests, and institutions).

Technics is central to any account of globalization since it is a truism that without modern communications infrastructures, in particular, a global system or worldwide economy would not be possible.

Economics—crucial as technology is, so too is its specifically economic logic. Capitalism's insatiable requirement for new markets and profits leads inevitably to the globalization of economic activity.

Politics—shorthand here for ideas, interests, and power—constitutes the third logic of globalization. If technology provides the physical infrastructure of globalization, politics provides its normative infrastructure. Governments, such as those of the USA and the UK, have been critical actors in nurturing the process of globalization.

Box 1.6 The three waves of globalization

Globalization is not a novel phenomenon. Viewed as a secular historical process by which human civilizations have come to form a single world system, it has occurred in three distinct waves.

In the first wave, the age of discovery (1450–1850), globalization was decisively shaped by European expansion and conquest.

The second wave (1850–1945) evidenced a major expansion in the spread and entrenchment of European empires.

By comparison, contemporary globalization (1960 on) marks a new epoch in human affairs. Just as the Industrial Revolution and the expansion of the West in the nineteenth century defined a new age in world history, so today the microchip and the satellite are icons of a globalized world order. It is also associated with a shift in economic power from the West to the East with the rise of China and India.

the conduct of national economic policy. Thick globalization embodies a powerful systemic logic that constitutes the circumstances in which states operate and thereby the limits to state power. It therefore has significant consequences for how we understand world politics.

Key Points

- Economic globalization may be at risk as a result of the 2008 financial crisis, but the contemporary phase of globalization has proved more robust than the sceptics recognize.
- Contemporary globalization is a multidimensional, uneven, and asymmetrical process.
- Contemporary globalization is best described as a thick form of globalization or globalism.

A world transformed: globalization and distorted global politics

Consider a political map of the world: its most striking feature is the division of the entire earth's surface into almost 200 neatly defined territorial units, namely sovereign states. To a student of politics in the Middle Ages a map of the world dominated by borders and boundaries would make little sense. Historically, borders are a relatively recent invention, as is the idea that states are sovereign, self-governing, territorially delimited political communities or polities. Although today a convenient fiction, this presumption remains central to orthodox state-centric conceptions of world politics as the pursuit of power and interests between sovereign states. Globalization, however, calls this state-centric conception of world politics into question. Taking globalization seriously therefore requires a conceptual shift in the way we think about world politics.

The Westphalian Constitution of world order

The Peace Treaties of Westphalia and Osnabruck (1648) established the legal basis of modern statehood and by implication the fundamental rules or constitution of modern world politics. Although Pope Innocent referred to the Westphalian settlement at the time as 'null, reprobate and devoid of meaning for all time', in the course of the subsequent four centuries it has formed the **normative structure** or constitution of the modern

world order. At the heart of the Westphalian settlement was agreement among Europe's rulers to recognize each other's right to rule their own territories free from outside interference. This was codified over time in the doctrine of sovereign statehood. But it was only in the twentieth century, as global empires collapsed, that sovereign statehood and with it national **self-determination** finally acquired the status of universal organizing principles of world order. Contrary to Pope Innocent's desires, the Westphalian Constitution by then had come to colonize the entire planet.

Constitutions are important because they establish the location of legitimate political authority within a

Box 1.7 The Westphalian Constitution of world politics

1 **Territoriality**: humankind is organized principally into exclusive territorial (political) communities with fixed borders.

2 **Sovereignty**: within its borders the state or government has an entitlement to supreme, unqualified, and exclusive political and legal authority.

3 **Autonomy**: the principle of self-determination or self-governance constitutes countries as autonomous containers of political, social, and economic activity in that fixed borders separate the domestic sphere from the world outside.

polity and the rules that inform the exercise and limits of political power. In codifying and legitimating the principle of sovereign statehood, the Westphalian Constitution gave birth to the modern states-system. It welded the idea of **territoriality** with the notion of legitimate sovereign rule. Westphalian sovereignty located supreme legal and political authority within territorially delimited states. Sovereignty involved the rightful entitlement to exclusive, unqualified, and supreme rule within a delimited territory. It was exclusive in so far as no ruler had the right to intervene in the sovereign affairs of other nations; unqualified in that within their territories rulers had complete authority over their subjects; and supreme in that there was no legal or political authority beyond the state. Of course for many, especially weak states, sovereignty—as the legitimate claim to rule—has not always translated into effective control within their territories. As Krasner recognizes, the Westphalian system has for many states been little more than a form of 'organized hypocrisy' (Krasner 1999). Nevertheless this never fundamentally compromised its influence upon the developmental trajectory of world politics. Although the UN Charter and the Universal Declaration of Human Rights modified aspects of the Westphalian Constitution, in qualifying aspects of **state sovereignty**, it remains the founding covenant of world politics. However, many argue that contemporary globalization presents a fundamental challenge to the Westphalian ideal of sovereign statehood and in so doing is transforming world order.

From (state-centric) geopolitics to (geocentric) global politics

As globalization has intensified over the last five decades, it has become increasingly difficult to maintain the popular fiction of the 'great divide': treating political life as having two quite separate spheres of action, the domestic and the international, which operate according to different logics with different rules, actors, and agendas. There is a growing recognition that, as former President Clinton described it:

> the once bright line between domestic and foreign policy is blurring. If I could do anything to change the speech patterns of those of us in public life, I would like almost to stop hearing people talk about foreign policy and domestic policy, and instead start discussing economic policy, security policy, environmental policy.
>
> *(Quoted in Cusimano 2000: 6)*

Box 1.8 The post-Westphalian order

Territoriality

Borders and territory still remain politically significant, not least for administrative purposes. Under conditions of globalization, however, a new geography of political organization and political power (from transgovernmental networks to regional and global bodies) is emerging that transcends territories and borders.

State sovereignty

The sovereign power and authority of national government—the entitlement of states to rule within their own territorial space—is being transformed but not necessarily eroded. Sovereignty today is increasingly understood as the shared exercise of public power and authority between national, regional, and global authorities.

State autonomy

In a more interdependent world, simply to achieve domestic objectives national governments are forced to engage in extensive multilateral collaboration and co-operation. But in becoming more embedded in systems of global and regional governance, states confront a real dilemma: in return for more effective public policy and meeting their citizens' demands, whether in relation to transnational terrorism, the drugs trade or the financial crisis, their capacity for self-governance—that is state autonomy—is compromised.

As the substantive issues of political life consistently ignore the artificial foreign/domestic divide, from the worldwide coordination of anti-globalization protests to national courts enforcing the rulings of the World Trade Organization, the Westphalian Constitution appears increasingly anachronistic. A post-Westphalian world order is emerging, and with it a distinctive form of **global politics**.

To talk of global politics is to recognize that politics itself is being globalized, with the consequence that there is much more to the study of world politics than conflict and cooperation between states, even if this remains crucial. In other words, globalization challenges the one-dimensionality of orthodox accounts of world politics that conceive it principally in state-centric terms of geopolitics and the struggle for power between states. By contrast, the concept of global politics focuses our attention upon the global structures and processes of rule-making, problem-solving, the maintenance of security and order in the world system (Brown 1992). It acknowledges the continuing centrality of states and geopolitics, but does not *a priori* privilege either in understanding and explaining contemporary world affairs. For under conditions of political globalization, states

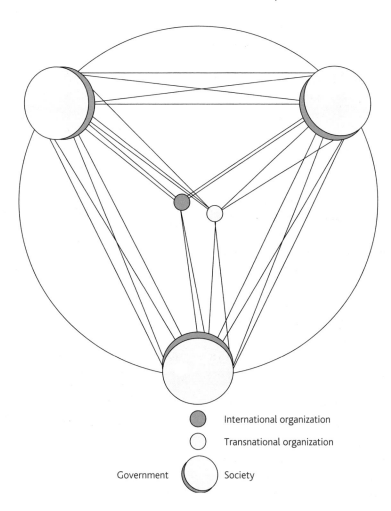

International organization

Transnational organization

Government   Society

Figure 1.1 The World Wide Web

are increasingly embedded in thickening and overlapping worldwide webs of: multilateral institutions and multilateral politics from **NATO** and the World Bank to the G20; transnational associations and networks, from the International Chamber of Commerce to the World Muslim Congress; **global policy networks** of officials, corporate and non-governmental actors, dealing with global issues, such as the Global AIDS Fund and the Roll Back Malaria Initiative; and those formal and informal (transgovernmental) networks of government officials dealing with shared global problems, including the Basle Committee of central bankers and the Financial Action Task Force on money-laundering (Fig. 1.1).

Global politics directs our attention to the emergence of a fragile **global polity** within which 'interests are articulated and aggregated, decisions are made, values allocated and policies conducted through international

or transnational political processes' (Ougaard 2004: 5). In other words, to how the global order is, or fails to be, governed.

Since the UN's creation in 1945, a vast nexus of global and regional institutions has developed, increasingly linked to a proliferation of non-governmental agencies and networks seeking to influence the governance of global affairs. While **world government** remains a fanciful idea, an evolving **global governance** complex exists—embracing states, international institutions, transnational networks and agencies (both public and private)—that functions, with variable effect, to promote, regulate, or intervene in the common affairs of humanity (Fig. 1.2). Over the last five decades, its scope and impact have expanded dramatically, with the result that its activities have become significantly politicized, as the G20 London Summit and recent Copenhagen Summit on Climate Change attest.

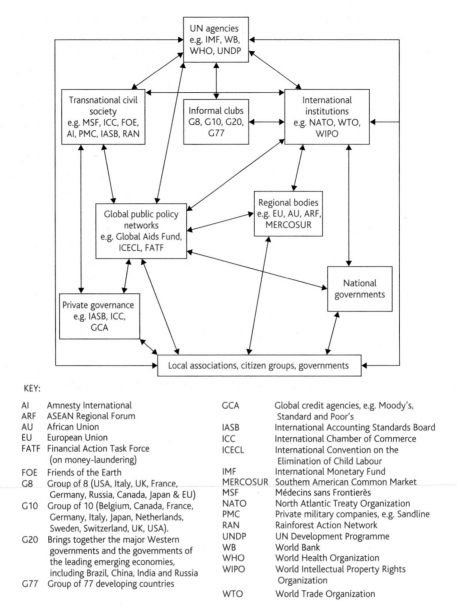

Figure 1.2 The global governance complex

KEY:

AI	Amnesty International	GCA	Global credit agencies, e.g. Moody's, Standard and Poor's
ARF	ASEAN Regional Forum		
AU	African Union	IASB	International Accounting Standards Board
EU	European Union	ICC	International Chamber of Commerce
FATF	Financial Action Task Force (on money-laundering)	ICECL	International Convention on the Elimination of Child Labour
FOE	Friends of the Earth	IMF	International Monetary Fund
G8	Group of 8 (USA, Italy, UK, France, Germany, Russia, Canada, Japan & EU)	MERCOSUR	Southern American Common Market
		MSF	Médecins sans Frontierès
G10	Group of 10 (Belgium, Canada, France, Germany, Italy, Japan, Netherlands, Sweden, Switzerland, UK, USA).	NATO	North Atlantic Treaty Organization
		PMC	Private military companies, e.g. Sandline
		RAN	Rainforest Action Network
G20	Brings together the major Western governments and the governments of the leading emerging economies, including Brazil, China, India and Russia	UNDP	UN Development Programme
		WB	World Bank
		WHO	World Health Organization
		WIPO	World Intellectual Property Rights Organization
G77	Group of 77 developing countries	WTO	World Trade Organization

This evolving global governance complex comprises the multitude of formal and informal structures of political coordination among governments, intergovernmental and transnational agencies—public and private—designed to realize common purposes or collectively agreed goals through the making or implementing of global or transnational rules, and the regulation of transborder problems. A good illustration of this is the creation of international labour codes to protect vulnerable workers. The International Convention on the Elimination of Child Labour (ICECL), for instance, was the product of a complex politics involving public and private actors from trade unions, industrial

associations, humanitarian groups, governments, legal experts, not forgetting officials and experts within the International Labour Organization (ILO).

Within this global governance complex, private or non-governmental agencies have become increasingly influential in the formulation and implementation of global public policy. The International Accounting Standards Board establishes global accounting rules, while the major credit-rating agencies, such as Moody's and Standard and Poor's, determine the credit status of governments and corporations around the globe. This is a form of private global governance in which private organizations regulate, often in the shadow of global public authorities, aspects of global economic and social affairs. In those realms in which it has become highly significant, mainly the economic and the technological, this private global governance involves a relocation of authority from states and multilateral bodies to non-governmental organizations and private agencies.

Coextensive with the global governance complex is an embryonic **transnational civil society**. In recent decades a plethora of NGOs, transnational organizations (from the International Chamber of Commerce, international trade unions, and the Rainforest Network to the Catholic Church), advocacy networks (from the women's movement to Nazis on the net), and citizens' groups have come to play a significant role in mobilizing, organizing, and exercising political power across national boundaries. This has been facilitated by the speed and ease of modern global communications and a growing awareness of common interests between groups in different countries and regions of the world. At the 2006 Ministerial Meeting of the WTO in Hong Kong, the representatives of environmental, corporate, and other interested parties outnumbered the formal

representatives of government. Of course, not all the members of transnational civil society are either civil or representative; some seek to further dubious, reactionary, or even criminal causes while many lack effective accountability. Furthermore, there are considerable inequalities between the agencies of transnational civil society in terms of resources, influence, and access to key centres of global decision-making. Multinational corporations, like Rupert Murdoch's News International, have much greater access to centres of power, and capacity to shape the global agenda, than does the Rainforest Action Network.

If global politics involves a diversity of actors and institutions, it is also marked by a diversity of political concerns. The agenda of global politics is anchored not just in traditional geopolitical concerns but also in a proliferation of economic, social, cultural, and ecological questions. Pollution, drugs, human rights, and terrorism are among an increasing number of transnational policy issues that, because of globalization, transcend territorial borders and existing political jurisdictions, and thereby require international cooperation for their effective

---

Case Study 2 Security and violence in global politics

Paradoxically, the same global infrastructures that make it possible to organize production on a worldwide basis can also be exploited to lethal effect. National security increasingly begins abroad, not at the border, since borders are as much carriers as barriers to transnational organized violence. This has become increasingly evident in relation to 'new wars'—complex irregular warfare in the global South. Inter-state war has been almost entirely supplanted by intra-state and trans-state conflict located in the global South, or on the perimeters of the West. These so-called 'new wars' are primarily located in weak states and rooted in identity politics, local conflicts, and rivalries. They involve complex irregular war-

fare between military, para-military, criminal, and private forces that rages through, but often around and across, state borders with little discrimination between civilians and combatants. The United Nations estimates, for instance, that thirty-five people die every hour across the globe as a consequence of irregular armed conflict. These 'new wars', whether in Bosnia, Darfur, or Venezuela, are curiously modern since they are sustained largely by the capacity of combatants to exploit global networks to provide finance, arms, émigré support, or aid, as well as to facilitate profiteering, racketeering, and shadow economies, such as the diamond or drugs trade, which pays for arms and influence. Despite their apparently localized quality, 'new wars' are in fact a manifestation of the contemporary globalization of organized violence. Disorder in one part of the world (as in Darfur in 2006, or in Kosovo and Somalia in the 1990s) combines with global media coverage and the speed of travel to feed insecurity, creating overlapping global security complexes. These complexes bind together the security of societies across the North–South divide. They also highlight a major disjuncture between the distribution of formal military power and the distribution of effective coercive power in the world today. Al Qaeda, the Triads, private military companies, drug cartels, narco-terrorism, and the illicit global arms trade are all examples of the growth of informal organized violence or post-international violence. They pose, as Keohane starkly notes, a profound challenge since 'States no longer have a monopoly on the means of mass destruction: more people died in the attacks on the World Trade Center and the Pentagon than in the Japanese attack on Pearl Harbor in 1941'.

(Keohane 2002: 284)

resolution. Politics today is marked by a proliferation of new types of 'boundary problem'. In the past, of course, nation-states principally resolved their differences over boundary matters by pursuing reasons of state backed by diplomatic initiatives and, ultimately, by coercive means. But this militaristic logic appears singularly inadequate and inappropriate to resolve the many complex issues, from economic regulation to resource depletion and environmental degradation to chemical weapons proliferation, which engender—at seemingly ever greater speeds—an intermeshing of 'national fortunes'.

This is not to argue that the sovereign state is in decline. The sovereign power and authority of national government—the entitlement of states to rule within their own territorial space—is being transformed but by no means eroded. Locked into systems of global and regional governance, states now assert their sovereignty less in the form of a legal claim to supreme power than as a bargaining tool, in the context of transnational systems of rule-making, with other agencies and social forces. Sovereignty is bartered, shared, and divided among the agencies of public power at different levels, from the local to the global. The Westphalian conception of sovereignty as an indivisible, territorially exclusive form of public power is being displaced by a new sovereignty regime, in which sovereignty is understood as the shared exercise of public power and authority. In this respect we are witnessing the emergence of a post-Westphalian world order.

Furthermore, far from globalization leading to 'the end of the state', it elicits a more activist state. This is because, in a world of global enmeshment, simply to achieve domestic objectives national governments are forced to engage in extensive multilateral **collaboration** and **cooperation**. But in becoming more embedded in frameworks of global and regional governance, states confront a real dilemma: in return for more effective public policy and meeting their citizens' demands, their capacity for self-governance—that is, **state autonomy**—is compromised. Today, a difficult trade-off is posed between effective governance and self-governance. In this respect, the Westphalian image of the monolithic, unitary state is being displaced by the image of the **disaggregated state** in which its constituent agencies increasingly interact with their counterparts abroad, international agencies, and NGOs in the management of common and global affairs (Slaughter 2004) (Fig. 1.3).

Global politics is a term that acknowledges that the scale of political life has altered fundamentally: politics understood as that set of activities concerned primarily with the achievement of order and justice is not confined within territorial boundaries. It questions the utility of the distinction between the domestic and the foreign, inside and outside the **territorial state**, the national and the international since decisions and actions taken in one region affect the welfare of communities in distant parts of the globe, with the result that domestic politics is internationalized and world politics

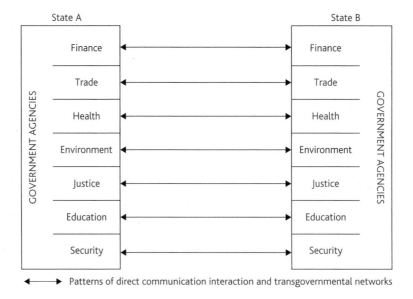

Figure 1.3 The disaggregated state

becomes domesticated. It acknowledges that power in the global system is not the sole preserve of states but is distributed (unevenly) among a diverse array of public and private actors and networks (from international agencies, through corporations to NGOs), with important consequences for who gets what, how, when, and where. It recognizes that political authority has been diffused not only upwards to supra-state bodies, such as the European Union, but also downwards to sub-state bodies, such as regional assemblies, and beyond the state to private agencies, such as the International Accounting Standards Board. It accepts that sovereignty remains a principal juridical attribute of states but concludes that it is increasingly divided and shared between local, national, regional, and global authorities. Finally, it affirms that, in an age of globalization, national polities no longer function as closed systems. On the contrary, it asserts that all politics—understood as the pursuit of order and justice—are played out in a global context.

However, as with globalization, inequality and exclusion are endemic features of contemporary global politics. There are many reasons for this, but three factors in particular are crucial: first, enormous inequalities of power between states; second, global governance is shaped by an unwritten constitution that tends to privilege the interests and agenda of global capitalism; third, the technocratic nature of much global decision-making, from health to security, tends to exclude many with a legitimate stake in the outcomes.

These three factors produce cumulative inequalities of power and exclusion—reflecting the inequalities of power between North and South—with the result that contemporary global politics is more accurately described as distorted global politics: 'distorted' in the sense that inevitably those states and groups with greater power resources and access to key sites of global decision-making tend to have the greatest control or influence over the agenda and outcomes of global politics. In short, global politics has few democratic qualities. This sits in tension with a world in which democracy is generally valued. Whether a more democratic or just global politics is imaginable and what it might look like is the concern of normative theorists and is the subject of later chapters in this volume (see Chs 12 and 32).

Key Points

- Globalization is transforming but not burying the Westphalian ideal of sovereign statehood. It is producing the disaggregated state.

- Globalization requires a conceptual shift in our thinking about world politics from a principally state-centric perspective to the perspective of geocentric or global politics—the politics of worldwide social relations.

- Global politics is more accurately described as distorted global politics because it is afflicted by significant power asymmetries.

Conclusion

This chapter has sought to elucidate the concept of globalization and identify its implications for the study of world politics. It has argued that globalization reconstructs the world as a shared social space. It does so, however, in a far from uniform manner: contemporary globalization is highly uneven—it varies in its intensity and extensity between different spheres of activity; it is highly asymmetrical; and it embodies a highly unequal geography of global inclusion and exclusion. In doing so it is as much a source of conflict and violence as of cooperation and harmony in world affairs.

In focusing upon the consequences of globalization for the study of international relations, this chapter has argued that it engenders a fundamental shift in the constitution of world politics. A post-Westphalian world order is in the making as sovereign statehood is transformed by the dynamics of globalization. A conceptual shift in our thinking is therefore required: from international (inter-state) politics to global politics—the politics of state and non-state actors within a shared global social space. Global politics is imbued with deep inequalities of power such that in its current configuration it is more accurately described as distorted global politics: a politics of domination, contestation, and competition between powerful states and transnational social forces.

Questions

1   Distinguish the concept of globalization from that of regionalization and internationalization.
2   What do you understand by the Westphalian Constitution of world order?
3   Why is global politics today more accurately described as distorted global politics?
4   Outline the principal causes of globalization.
5   Review the sceptical argument and critically evaluate it.
6   What are the principal characteristics of the post-Westphalian order?
7   Identify some of the key elements of political globalization.
8   What do you understand by the term 'global governance complex'?
9   Distinguish the concept of global politics from that of geopolitics and international (inter-state) politics.
10   Is the state being eclipsed by the forces of globalization and global governance?
11   Why is globalization associated with the rise of new powers such as China and India?

Further Reading

Castells, M. (2000), *The Rise of the Network Society* (Oxford: Blackwell). This is a now contemporary classic account of the political economy of globalization that is comprehensive in its analysis of the new global informational capitalism.

Duffield, M. (2001), *Global Governance and the New Wars* (London: Zed). A very readable account of how globalization is leading to the fusion of the development and security agendas within the global governance complex.

Gilpin, R. (2001), *Global Political Economy* (Princeton, NJ: Princeton University Press). A more sceptical view of economic globalization that, although taking it seriously, conceives it as an expression of Americanization or American hegemony.

Held, D., and McGrew, A. (2007), *Globalization/Anti-Globalization: Beyond the Great Divide*, 2nd edn (Cambridge: Polity Press). A short introduction to all aspects of the current globalization debate and its implications for the study for world politics.

Hirst, P., and Thompson, G. (2009), *Globalization in Question*, 3rd edn (Cambridge: Polity Press). An excellent and sober critique of the hyperglobalist argument, which is thoroughly sceptical about the globalization thesis, viewing it as a return to the *belle époque* and heavily shaped by states.

Holton, R. (2005), *Making Globalization* (Basingstoke: Palgrave Macmillan). A comprehensive overview of globalization and its implications for the study of the social sciences written from a sociological perspective.

James, H. (2009), *Creation and Destruction of Value* (Boston, MA: Harvard University Press). The first serious study from a renowned economic historian to explore the comparisons between the collapse of globalization and world order in the 1930s and the prospects for globalization in the aftermath of the 2008 global financial crisis.

Kennedy, P., et al. (2002), *Global Trends and Global Governance* (London: Pluto Press). A good introduction to how globalization is reshaping world politics and the nature of global governance.

Rosenberg, J. (2005) 'Globalization Theory: A Post Mortem'. *International Politics* **42**(2): 2–74. A very influential essay that delivers a substantive Marxist critique of the transformationalist account of globalization.

Scholte, J. A. (2005), *Globalization—A Critical Introduction*, 2nd edn (Basingstoke: Palgrave Macmillan). An excellent introduction to the globalization debate from its causes to its consequences for the global political economy from within a critical political-economy perspective.

Online Resource Centre

 Visit the Online Resource Centre that accompanies this book to access more learning resources on this chapter topic at www.oxfordtextbooks.co.uk/orc/baylis5e/

Part One

The historical context

In this part of the book, we want to provide a historical context within which to make sense of globalization. We have two main aims: **first**, we want to introduce you to the most important aspects of international history, and we shall do this by giving you a more chronologically concentrated set of chapters. We start with an overview of international society from its origins in ancient Greece through to the beginning of the twenty-first century. We think that you need to have some basic understanding of the main developments in the history of world politics, as well as some kind of context for thinking about the contemporary period of world history. This is followed by a chapter that looks at the main themes of twentieth-century history until the end of the cold war. The final chapter

of this part of the book looks at developments within international history since 1990. These chapters give you a great deal of historical information that will be of interest in its own right. Our **second** aim is to draw to your attention the main themes of international history so that you can develop a deeper understanding of the issues, both theoretical and empirical, that are dealt with in the remaining four parts of this book. We hope that an overview of international history will give you a context within which to begin thinking about globalization: is it a new phenomenon that fundamentally changes the main patterns of international history, or are there precedents for it that make it seem less revolutionary?

ORC in the spotlight: key points

Visit www.oxfordtextbooks.co.uk/orc/baylis5e/ for the online revision guide, flashcard glossary, and podcasts to get to grips with the key points from each chapter and apply them in your exams and essays.

Chapter 2

The evolution of international society

DAVID ARMSTRONG

Reader's Guide

This chapter discusses the idea of international society and some of its historical manifestations. 'International society' refers to the rules, institutions, and shared practices that different groups of political communities have developed in the course of their interaction. It has taken many forms over 5,000 years, but today's international society is composed of interconnected but independent sovereign states. It faces a complex range of challenges in the era of globalization.

Introduction: the idea of international society

There are many different ways of characterizing the overall structure and pattern of relations among distinct political communities. At one hypothetical extreme we might imagine an unrestrained struggle of all against all, in which war, conquest, and the slaughter or enslavement of the defeated constituted the sole forms of contact between the communities. At the other extreme we might conceive a world government in which the individual societies retained distinctions based on such features as language, culture, or religion, but their political and legal independence was no greater than that of the constituent parts of the USA. Between these extremes we find the many forms of interaction that have emerged in different times and places throughout world history. These range from **empires**, which can themselves be loosely or tightly organized, more or less centralized and relatively formal or informal, to **international systems** organized on the basis of the independence of individual units—or their **sovereignty**—with various kinds of **international hierarchical** orders in between.

In the broadest sense, the term **international society** may be applied to any of these modes of interaction that are governed to some degree by common rules and practices. However, the term has come to be applied more narrowly to a particular historical narrative and to a theoretical perspective derived, in part, from this historical narrative. The narrative concerns the emergence of the European **state system**, with its key principles of sovereignty and **non-intervention**, from the complex medieval order that preceded it. In one version of these events, the European states formed an association referred to as the 'family of nations' or the 'international society'. This was seen as founded both on their determination to safeguard their sovereign status and on a set of values, or a 'standard of civilization', that marked out the members of this inner circle from those outside. Within the club, relations were to be governed by the principles of **sovereign equality** and non-intervention and the rules of **international law** (see Ch. 17). Outside it, those societies deemed 'uncivilized' could be subject to various means of control or domination, ranging from the 'unequal treaties' that were used to carve out Western spheres of influence in China to outright colonization elsewhere.

The theoretical perspective that draws upon this experience is known as the international society approach or the **English school** of International Relations,

the most systematic and comprehensive presentation of whose ideas came from Hedley Bull (see Box 2.1). His starting point is that, as states accept no higher power than themselves, they exist in a condition of international **anarchy** (absence of government). Unlike realists, who emphasize the inevitability of power struggles that can only be constrained by a **balance of power**, he sees order in world politics as also potentially deriving from the existence of an international society. Historical examples of such international societies had a common culture encompassing linguistic, ethical, religious, and artistic elements, which assisted the degree of communication and mutual understanding required for common rules and institutions to emerge.

Both the English school and the much older historical narrative on which it draws have been attacked for helping to legitimize what was, in reality, an oppressive and exploitative colonial order. Although the notion of a Christian international society pre-dated Columbus, it was used in a more systematic way to justify the European seizure of land from the indigenous peoples of America and elsewhere (Keal 2003). Similarly, the idea of the 'standard of civilization' was employed to rationalize nineteenth-century imperialism and the unequal treatment of nations like China and the Ottoman Empire. Some would argue that, from this perspective, the use today of terms such as 'the international community' merely masks the same old reality: one dominated by the great powers.

Such criticisms of the international society tradition may have much validity, but it is also important to remain aware of the insights into world politics that a more nuanced and balanced understanding of international society can yield. The interactions among states and other international actors can be fully comprehended only if we can appreciate the larger context within which these interactions take place. There are, of course, many

---

Box 2.1 Bull on international society

A society of states (or international society) exists when a group of states, conscious of certain common interests and common values, forms a society in the sense that they conceive themselves to be bound by a common set of rules in their relations with one another, and share in the working of common institutions.

(Bull 1977: 13)

ways of conceptualizing this larger context, each of which gives rise to its own distinct perspective and findings. An emphasis on the world economic structure might interpret events in terms of the development of capitalism. A stress on the power relativities among states might see the world in terms of an ongoing struggle to contain attempts by one great power to achieve preponderance through a balance of power. An interpretation of world history in terms of the clash between different structures of ideas might perceive developments as part of an inevitable dialectic between modernity and reaction. Yet, while major transitions might have been driven by various deep-seated economic, power-political, or cultural factors, human agency has always played the key role in determining the underlying rules, norms, and institutions that shape the relations among international actors at any given time. The term 'international society' is, in essence, a shorthand way of depicting the overall structure constituted by such norms, rules, and institutions. In this sense, far from being a purely European invention, it has been present in different forms throughout world history.

Key Points

- 'International society' is any association of distinct political communities that accept some common values, rules, and institutions.

- It is the central concept of the 'English School' of International Relations.

- Although originally coined to refer to relations among European states, the term may be applied to many different sets of political arrangements among distinct political communities.

Ancient worlds

Contemporary international society comprises the norms, rules, established practices, and institutions governing the relations among sovereign states: communities occupying a defined territory within which they exercise juridical independence. Its essential principles, such as non-intervention and legal equality in international relations, reflect the common interest underpinning such an association, namely protecting and legitimizing sovereignty itself and excluding other contenders for legal authority within the state.

No early international society resembles this model, mainly because none puts unambiguous emphasis on sovereign equality: the equal status in international law of all states that characterizes contemporary international society. In some cases, one powerful state would deal with others only on the basis of an acknowledgement of its own superior standing. In others, such as early Islam and medieval Europe, different forms of **supranational** religious authority (the caliphate and the papacy) coexisted in a sometimes uneasy relationship with their secular, usually monarchical, counterparts. Medieval Europe was also marked by a complex mosaic of **subnational** and **transnational** entities, all of which claimed various entitlements and frequently possessed some independent military capacity. These included barons, dukes, bishops, chivalric orders like the Knights Templar, and associations of trading cities, like the Hanseatic League.

The term 'international society' may, however, still be used in all of these cases since they all engaged in regular interaction that was, at least sometimes, non-violent and was also characterized by rules and shared values, or at least similar underlying normative assumptions. Such characteristics were in evidence even when the earliest communities began to settle in fixed territorial areas and consequently to develop more complex hierarchical social orders and more varied economies than their hunter-gatherer ancestors had enjoyed, as well as more comprehensive structures of religious beliefs (Buzan and Little 2000). Territorial possession needed to be defined, defended, and, if possible, accepted by outside groups. Growing economic complexity and diversity gave rise to increasing trade relations with other communities, which in turn produced the need for mutual understanding and, ideally, rules about such issues as the rights of 'foreigners' to travel through or reside in other lands. As rulers extended their authority over ever-larger areas, they were increasingly drawn to less violent (and therefore cheaper and safer) means of consolidating and legitimizing their positions. **Diplomatic envoys, treaties,** and careful definition of the rights and duties of lesser kings all played their part in such endeavours. Finally, as primitive religious beliefs evolved into comprehensive ideologies, embracing complex notions of right and wrong and divine reward and retribution, so the relations among early societies acquired common normative assumptions.

Box 2.2 Chronology

551–479 BCE	Life of Confucius	**1789**	French Revolution begins
490–480	Greeks victorious against Persia	**1815**	Napoleon defeated at Waterloo. Beginning of Concert of Europe
Circa 250	Kautilya writes *Arthasastra*	**1856**	End of Crimean War. Ottoman Empire formally accepted as a member of the European international society
200	Idea of war crimes mentioned in Hindu code of Manu		
146	Rome destroys Carthage, its great historical enemy	**1863**	Formation of the International Committee of the Red Cross in Geneva, followed by the first Geneva Convention on the laws of war in 1864
395 CE	Permanent division of Roman Empire	**1919**	Establishment of the League of Nations
570–632	Life of Muhammad, founder of Islam	**1945**	Establishment of the United Nations
1414–18	Council of Constance	**1948**	United Nations Universal Declaration of Human Rights
1453	Ottoman Empire captures Constantinople	**1949**	Four new Geneva Conventions
1553	Ottoman–French Treaty against Habsburgs	**1960**	UN General Assembly resolution condemns colonialism as a denial of fundamental human rights
1583–1645	Life of Grotius, 'father of international law'	**1979**	Islamic Revolution in Iran
1648	Peace of Westphalia ends Thirty Years War	**1989**	Fall of Berlin Wall symbolizes end of the cold war
1683	Defeat of Ottomans at Vienna	**2001**	9/11 attack on USA
1713	Treaty of Utrecht formally recognizes balance of power as basis of order in European society of states	**2003**	Start of American-led war in Iraq
		2007	Start of global economic crisis
1776	American War of Independence begins		

It is probable that some variant of these processes was apparent wherever tribes began to establish settled communities or city-states. In the ancient Middle East, treaties between the 'great kings' and their vassals concerned matters such as borders, trade, grazing rights, inter-marriage, extradition, defence, and the rights and duties of citizens of one state visiting or residing in another. Treaties were accompanied by ceremonies and rituals, and generally contained clauses invoking divine sanctions upon treaty-breakers. They were often negotiated by diplomatic envoys, who did not enjoy the equivalent of diplomatic immunity characteristic of modern international society: they could be punished and held hostage, and in several cases were actually killed. However, like ancient treaties, the institution of diplomacy was invested with religious solemnity.

The fragmentary written evidence from this period offers tantalizing glimpses of the normative underpinnings of the relations among the major states. One postwar treaty between Egypt and the Hittites (*c.* 1300 BCE) pledged permanent alliance, freedom of commerce, and extradition of criminals, subject to the surprisingly humane provision that neither they nor their close relatives should be subjected to extreme punishment. However, the elements of international society that we can discern were almost certainly marginal aspects of a world in which the frequently brutal struggle for survival in economic conditions of bare subsistence constituted the central reality. As economic circumstances improved and settled communities became less vulnerable to marauding nomadic tribes who were outside and impervious to any conception of international rules, so more refined international systems began to appear. In the period from about 700 BCE to the beginnings of Roman domination in the first century BCE the three most notable examples of such systems were to be found in China, India, and Greece.

In all three cases, the countries were divided for much of the period into separate polities but, alongside often fierce competition and conflict, they also retained a sense of their cultural unity. In Greece, the city-states had a common language and religion, together with institutions like the Olympic Games and the Delphic Oracle, which were designed to emphasize this unity.

All city-states placed a high value on their independence, which enabled them to unite against the threat of Persian hegemony.

Their common Greek identity did not prevent several bids at hegemony, sometimes accompanied by brutal warfare. This cautions against exaggerating the degree to which the Greeks constituted a highly developed international society. None the less, other aspects of inter-city relations suggest that an authentic and well-established international society was also a genuine element in their affairs. There was a rudimentary institutional basis of international society in the form of the **Amphyctionic Council**: a religious institution whose concern was to provide some protection for shrines such as the Delphic Oracle and to enable Greeks to engage in religious rituals even during times of war. It also occasionally played a limited role in helping to bring war to an end. **Arbitration** helped settle certain inter-city disputes, especially those involving territory where the land in question had a particular religious, strategic, or economic significance. Finally, the *proxenia* was essentially an ancient version of the modern institution of the consulate, in which a *proxenos* (lit. 'for the foreigner') was appointed to represent the interests of the foreign communities in the larger states.

Greek international society was also underpinned by shared moral understandings about rightful international conduct that were ultimately derived from religious norms. These concerned areas such as diplomacy, the sanctity of treaties, entry into war, and the treatment of enemy dead. Although violations in all these areas certainly occurred, there were also various forms of sanction, including incurring a reputation for unreliability or dishonesty and being punished following a subsequent arbitration.

Ancient India similarly had numerous religious norms that—in principle if not always in practice—applied to international relations. This was especially true of warfare, where India had a much wider and more complex set of norms than any of the other ancient societies. These ranged from conceptions of what constituted a **just war** through various rituals to be observed at the outbreak of war to numerous prohibitions on certain forms of conduct during and after war. The concept of *dharma*, a multifaceted term signifying natural and eternal laws, provided the underlying moral foundation for these injunctions. Kautilya's *Arthasastra* urged the necessity for humane conduct in war as a requirement of prudent statecraft rather than simply of morality. As with Greece and the earlier Near-Eastern societies, treaties in India were regarded as having a sacred quality, although additional securities against the breaking of a treaty, such as hostages, were sometimes insisted on.

In the case of China during the five hundred years before its separate kingdoms were unified under the Chin dynasty in 221 BCE, international relations, as with India and Greece, took place in a context of cultural and intellectual richness and dynamism. This produced a complex range of contending schools of thought that, inevitably, touched upon questions of war and peace and other international issues. As is the case with Greece and India, it is hard to determine with any precision the degree to which the principles of conduct elaborated by Confucius and other thinkers influenced the actual practice of the contending states. In the earlier 'Spring and Autumn' period (722–481 BCE) the frequent wars that characterized the constant struggle for hegemony were sometimes fought in an almost formalistic manner, with rules of chivalry strictly observed. During the later 'Warring States' period (403–221 BCE), however, great improvements in the techniques of warfare produced a fierce and brutal struggle for dominance that was eventually won by the Chin state. The new Imperial China was to last in different forms and with varying degrees of unity for more than 2,000 years. It came to adopt the formal position that its civilization was so superior to all the others that relations with foreigners— 'outer barbarians'—were possible only on the basis of an acknowledgement by the foreigners of China's higher status, including the payment of tribute to the emperor. The Chinese identified themselves—at least in Confucian theory—essentially in cultural terms and saw their place in the world as at the top of a culturally determined hierarchy.

Our final ancient society, Rome, was obliged during its Republican period to deal with rival powers, such as Carthage, on a basis of equality. Such relationships were based on principles relating to treaties and diplomacy similar to those found in Greece and India. Rome, however, developed a more extensive legal terminology than any other ancient society, and some of this was carried over into its international relations. Republican Rome often sought legal means of settling certain kinds of disputes with other states, and also required various religious rituals to be gone through before a war could be declared just, and therefore legal. Rome also acknowledged a set of norms known as *ius gentium* (**law of nations**). As Rome's power grew from the first century BCE, its need to deal with other states on a basis of equality declined.

Key Points

- Elements of international society may be found from the time of the first organized human communities.

- Early forms of diplomacy and treaties existed in the ancient Middle East.

- Relations among the city-states of ancient Greece were characterized by more developed societal characteristics, such as arbitration.

- Ancient China, India, and Rome all had their own distinctive international societies.

The Christian and Islamic orders

Rome left a long shadow on Europe even after the formal division of the empire into eastern and western parts in AD 395. Indeed, the eastern, Byzantine Empire, with its capital at Constantinople (modern Istanbul), survived for nearly a thousand years, although faced with constant pressure from the rising power of Islam, whose forces finally overthrew it in 1453. Byzantium, which also became the centre of Orthodox Christianity, made up for its relative military weakness *vis-à-vis* the Islamic world by building up a highly effective intelligence network and using policies of divide and rule among its enemies, aided by the most organized and well-trained (if also the most duplicitous) diplomatic corps to have appeared in world politics up to that point.

In the West, the papacy long maintained its claim to have inherited Rome's **supranational** authority over medieval Europe. The Pope's role was usually conceptualized in terms of its 'authority' rather than its 'power', and specific papal edicts were frequently ignored by secular rulers. None the less, the Catholic Church was an important unifying element in medieval Europe's international society. The Church's comprehensive moral and ethical code touched upon international relations in several key respects. There were, for example, prohibitions against dealing with Muslim or other non-Christian states. In reality, neither the papal code nor the similar Islamic doctrine prevented either trade or alliance with non-believers, but it needed to be taken into account, if only because violations might need to be justified later. To back up its religious doctrines, the Church constructed an elaborate legal order, comprising a system of sanctions, the use of arbitration, formal legal hearings, and numerous specific rules called **canon law**. The Church laid down rules on the safe conduct of diplomats and on many aspects of treaties, including injunctions against their violation and the grounds on which they could be annulled. The Church's main sanction was the threat of

excommunication, but it could also order lesser punishments, such as fines or public penance. The structure as a whole was maintained by the priesthood: a 'massive international bureaucracy', in Martin Wight's words (1977: 22).

The Church also elaborated the most systematic doctrine to date of 'just war': the norms to be observed in embarking upon a war in the first place and in the actual conduct and conclusion of war (see Ch. 12). The specific problem confronting Augustine, Aquinas, and other Christian thinkers was how to reconcile war—which might be necessary to defend Christian lands from their enemies—with fundamental Christian doctrines such as 'turning the other cheek' to enemies. Their attempted resolution of this conundrum, through requirements for war to have a just cause, use proportionate force, be declared by a proper authority, have a fair prospect of success, and be waged with the right intention, failed more often than not. The requirements were seldom, if ever, observed fully in practice. However, they entered the international discourse and stayed there to the present day. They also influenced later attempts to devise international conventions aimed at limiting the horrors of war.

The other great religion of this period, Islam, also had profound implications for international politics. First, the dramatic and rapid expansion of the Arab peoples in the century after the death of Muhammad in AD 632 across the Middle East and into Africa, Asia, and Europe created a dynamic new force that soon found itself at odds with both Roman and Byzantine Christianity. Second, Islam was originally conceived as creating a single unifying social identity for all Muslims—the *umma* or community of believers—that overrode other kinds of social identity, such as tribe, race, or state. In its early stages, the ideal of the *umma* was to some extent realized in practice through the institution of the caliphate. The great schism between *sunni* and *shia* branches of the faith, together with the urge to independence of the numerous local leaders, brought an end to the caliphate as an effective central political institution, although the adoption of Islam by the nomadic Turks brought a new impetus. The Turks established the Ottoman Empire (1299–1922), which, at its peak, dominated much of southern Europe, the Middle East, and North Africa. It did not suffer a major defeat in Europe until the battle of Vienna in 1683, after which it gradually declined in significance.

In early Islamic theory, the world was divided into the *dâr al-harb* (the abode of war) and the *dâr al-Islam* (the abode of Islam). A permanent state of war existed between the two abodes, although truces, lasting up to a maximum of ten years, were possible. Muslims were theoretically obliged to wage **jihad** (struggle by heart, words, hand, and sword) until the *dâr al-harb* had embraced Islam. The sole exception were the 'peoples of the book' (Christians and Jews, although the designation was sometimes pragmatically extended to other religions), who were permitted to continue their religions, albeit at the price of paying a poll tax and accepting fewer rights than Muslims. The periods of truce between the two abodes required treaties: once signed, these were to be strictly observed by Muslims. Indeed, Islamic doctrine on honouring treaty commitments was rather stricter than its Catholic equivalent. Islam also laid down various moral principles to be observed in the course of war. Although, as with Christian just-war ideas, these were frequently disregarded, there were occasions when military leaders attempted to observe them.

These doctrines were developed by Muslim jurists during Islam's initial, dramatic expansion. Inevitably, as Islam's internal unity broke down and various nations successfully resisted the advance, the Islamic world had to accept the necessity of **peaceful coexistence** with unbelievers for rather longer than the ten-year truce. Close commercial links between the two 'abodes' developed and in some cases Christian rulers were allowed to set up settlements with some **extraterritorial** privileges in Muslim countries. The heads of these settlements were called 'consuls'. By the sixteenth century, the Ottoman Empire had also become an important player in the great power politics of Europe. In a noted treaty of 1535 between Sultan Sulayman and Francis I, King of France, the Ottomans lined up with one Christian king against the most powerful Christian force of the time, the Habsburg Empire.

> ### Key Points
>
> - Medieval Europe's international society was a complex mixture of supranational, transnational, national, and subnational structures.
> - The Catholic Church played a key role in elaborating the normative basis of medieval international society.
> - Islam developed its own distinctive understanding of international society.

The emergence of the modern international society

Contemporary international society is based upon a conception of the state as an independent actor that enjoys legal supremacy over all non-state actors (or that is sovereign). Logical corollaries of this include, first, the legal equality of all states, since any other system would be **hierarchical**, **hegemonial**, or **imperial**. The second corollary is the principle of non-intervention by outside forces in the domestic affairs of states, since acknowledgement of a right by outsiders to intervene would implicitly give some other actor superior authority. The three central institutions of an international society based on these principles derive from its essential attributes. First, formal communication between states was carried on by diplomats who, because they stood for their sovereign masters, should have the same immunity as their master had from the laws of the land they were based in. Second, rules given the status of international law could not be binding upon states without their consent. Third, given that order in international affairs could not be maintained—as in domestic societies— by a higher authority vested with adequate means of enforcement, such international order as was possible could emerge only from the ongoing struggle among states to prevent any of their number from achieving preponderance, or, more precisely, from the balance of power that such a struggle might produce. By the eighteenth century, the balance of power had come to be seen not just as a fortuitous occurrence in international relations but as a fundamental institution and even as part of international law.

These constituent ingredients of European international society took hundreds of years to take shape.

The key development was the emergence of the modern state, which began with the assertion of monarchical power against other contenders such as the Pope or local barons. At the same time the power struggles among the royal houses as well as the external threat from the Ottomans pushed them constantly to refine what were to become the familiar tools of statecraft. These included, most crucially, the establishment of centralized and efficient military power; but three other elements were also of great importance: a professional diplomatic service; an ability to manipulate the balance of power; and the evolution of treaties from essentially interpersonal contracts between monarchs sanctioned by religion to agreements between states that had the status of 'law'.

It is impossible to allocate a precise date to any of these developments since, in reality, they were taking place in a random manner across Europe over centuries. The Byzantines had taken diplomacy and intelligence-gathering to a higher level. Even before the Italian Renaissance, Venice had learnt this new craft from its own interaction with Byzantium and issued the first set of formal rules relating to diplomacy in the thirteenth century. The jealous rivalry among the Italian city-states led them to set up the first system of **resident ambassadors** in order to keep a watchful eye on each other. The Italian states also engaged in a constant balance-of-power game, including frequent wars. Other European states absorbed Italian ideas about international relations so that permanent embassies, together with agreed rules about **diplomatic immunity** and other ambassadorial privileges, became an established part of European international society. Fourteenth-century Italy also saw an early statement of one of the key doctrines of the sovereignty principle: 'the king is emperor in his own kingdom'.

Three key developments from the end of the fifteenth century played a crucial role in shaping the post-medieval European international society. First, the larger, more powerful states, such as France and the Habsburg Empire, were increasingly dominating some of the smaller states. Second, the Protestant Reformation of the sixteenth century dealt a devastating blow to the Catholic Church's claim to supreme authority, thus indirectly enhancing the counter-claim of state sovereignty. Finally, Columbus's voyage to the New World in 1492, followed by Vasco da Gama's discovery of a sea route to India in 1498 (thus enabling the dangerous and Muslim-controlled land route to be bypassed), had enormous consequences for European international relations. These included a new spatial awareness and interest in cartography, leading to a much stronger emphasis on territory and strictly defined boundaries.

Two parallel developments need to be borne in mind in evaluating the significance of all this for international society. The first is the struggle for power in Europe, which experienced 450 more years of increasingly violent and widespread war before it reached something resembling a final resolution of the tensions unleashed by these forces. History increasingly unfolded globally rather than regionally as the rest of the world was drawn into Europe's conflicts, first through colonization, then in the two world wars of the twentieth century, finally through the many consequences of decolonization. But the trend towards a uniform politico-legal entity, namely the sovereign state, was unstoppable, first in Europe and eventually in the rest of the world.

Second, there was an ongoing attempt further to develop the few ordering devices permitted by a society of sovereign states. The voyages of discovery gave a huge impetus both to the study of international law and to its use in treaties designed to clarify and define more precisely the various entitlements and responsibilities to which the age of discovery had given rise. In addition, the balance of power came to be increasingly recognized as the most effective instrument against would-be hegemonial powers, making its mastery one of the supreme objects of statecraft. Finally, several of the major wars were followed by systematic attempts to refine and improve upon such means of pursuing international order.

Box 2.3 The Council of Constance

An important legal controversy that may be seen as anticipating modern doctrines of international society occurred at the Council of Constance (1414–18). One issue before the Council concerned Poland's alliance with the non-Christian state of Lithuania against the Teutonic Order, which had been authorized to spread Christianity by force. The alliance contradicted the prevailing doctrine that pagan communities had no legal rights and war against them was, therefore, justified. The Polish defence of their alliance argued that the question whether a community had rights under the law of nations depended entirely on whether they exercised effective jurisdiction over a given territory, not on their religious beliefs: a revolutionary doctrine at the time but one that gradually became established orthodoxy.

(Alexandrowicz, C. H. (1963), 'Paulus Vladimiri and the Development of the Doctrine of Coexistence of Christian and Non-Christian countries', British Yearbook of International Law, 441–48)

The first sixteenth-century writings on international law came mainly from Spanish jurists, such as Francisco de Vitoria (*c.* 1480–1546), who considered the thorny issue of whether the indigenous inhabitants of the Americas possessed any legal rights. Traditional Catholic theory denied them any such rights, but Vitoria, though supporting the Spanish *conquista*, advanced a complex counter-argument, to the effect that the Indians did have some (albeit limited) rights under natural law. In doing so, however, he also went some way towards shifting the location of legitimate authority from the Pope to the emerging sovereign states. This argument, given the extreme inequality of power between the indigenous populations and the Spanish, has been criticized more recently as advancing an early use of the sovereignty doctrine as a justification for imperial exploitation and oppression (Anghie 1996).

Later writers on international law attempted to define the rights and duties owed by sovereign states towards each other, the nature of the international society within which sovereign states existed, and the role of the balance of power in this international society, as well as setting down a host of specific rules relating to such matters as diplomacy, treaties, commerce, the law of the sea, and, most of all, war. Their works, especially those of Grotius and Vattel, were of considerable influence, being carefully scrutinized by, among others, the governments of China and Japan in the nineteenth century, when they came under strong pressure from Europeans to grant what the Europeans were claiming as legal 'rights'—for example, to trade.

The Thirty Years War (1618–48) is often seen as Europe's last religious war, but in fact it was not just a struggle for power but a conflict over legitimate authority among several different kinds of contenders. The Papacy was certainly one of these, but one of its chief supporters, the Habsburg Empire, stood for a kind of dynastic hegemony, while the Holy Roman Emperor was less concerned with his traditional religious dimension than with his continuing hold over the many German states, which, in their turn, stood for the new doctrine of sovereign independence. Holland's struggle (which had been proceeding ever since Philip II of Spain had declared a death sentence on all its inhabitants for heresy in 1568) may be regarded as an early example of a struggle to establish a state based on what was to become the dominating element of nationality.

The **Peace of Westphalia** (1648), which ended the Thirty Years War, is regarded by many as the key event ushering in the contemporary international system. The Peace established the right of the German states that constituted the Holy Roman Empire to conduct their own diplomatic relations: a very clear acknowledgement of their sovereignty. They were also formally stated to enjoy 'an exact and reciprocal Equality': the first formal acceptance of sovereign equality for a significant number of states. More generally, the Peace may be seen as encapsulating the very idea of a society of states. The participants very clearly and explicitly took over from the Papacy the right to confer international legitimacy upon individual rulers and states and to insist that states observe religious toleration in their internal policies (Armstrong 1993: 30–8). The balance of power was formally incorporated in the **Treaty of Utrecht** (1713), which ended the War of the Spanish Succession (1701–14), when a 'just equilibrium of power' was formally declared to be the 'best and most solid basis of mutual friendship and durable harmony'.

The period from 1648 to 1776 saw the international society that had been taking shape over the previous two hundred years come to fruition. Wars were frequent, if lacking the ideological intensity of the Thirty Years War. Some states, notably the Ottoman Empire, slowly declined; others, such as Britain and Russia, rose. Hundreds of mini-states still existed but it was the interaction among no more than ten key players that determined the course of events. Yet despite constant change and many wars, European writers from de Callière in 1716 to Heeren in 1809 were unanimous in their view that Europe in its entirety constituted a kind of 'republic' (Whyte 1919; Heeren 1971). Some pointed to religious and cultural similarities in seeking to explain this phenomenon, but the central elements that all were agreed on were a determination by all states to preserve their freedom, a mutual recognition of each other's right to an independent existence, and above all a reliance on the balance of power. Diplomacy and international law were seen as the other two key institutions of international society, so long as the latter was based clearly on state consent.

It should be noted that some scholars have disputed this interpretation of eighteenth-century international society. The French historian, Albert Sorel, dismissed the notion of an eighteenth-century 'Christian republic' as 'an august abstraction', arguing that ruthless self-interest was the only principle that mattered (Cobban and Hunt 1969). Indeed, even some, such as Edmund Burke, who believed that there was a true European international society, were appalled by the dismemberment of Poland from 1772 onwards, which Burke saw as a first move away from a system founded on 'treaties, alliances, common interest and public faith' towards a Hobbesian state of nature (Stanlis 1953). More recently, Stephen Krasner (1999) has argued more generally that sovereignty was never more than a legal fiction—or an 'organized hypocrisy'—that disguised the extent to which powerful states were able to pursue their own interests without hindrance. Such viewpoints, at the very least, caution against the more idealistic formulations of an international society whose foundation stone was undoubtedly the self-interest of its members.

The American and French revolutions were to have profound consequences for international society. In the case of the USA, these stemmed mainly from its emergence as a global superpower in the twentieth century. The consequences of the French Revolution were more immediate. First, the revolutionary insistence that sovereignty was vested in 'the nation' rather than the rulers—especially dynastic imperial rulers like the Habsburgs—gave a crucial impetus to the idea of 'national self-determination'. This was the principle that was increasingly to dominate international politics in the nineteenth and twentieth centuries, and to endanger imperial systems that were seen as denying the rights of **nations** (people defined by linguistic, ethnic, and cultural bonds) to become sovereign states themselves.

The second consequence of the French Revolution stemmed from the response to it of the main European powers. After the defeat of Napoleon, the leading states increasingly set themselves apart from the smaller ones as a kind of great powers' club. This system, known as the 'Concert of Europe', lasted until the First World War. It was characterized by regular meetings of the club that had the aims of maintaining the European balance of power drawn up at the end of the Napoleonic Wars and reaching collective decisions on various potentially divisive issues. The leading dynastic powers, Austria and Russia, wanted the Concert to give itself the formal right to intervene in any revolution. This was strongly resisted by Britain, which was the least threatened by revolution, on the grounds that such a move would violate the key principle of non-intervention. However, the Concert unquestionably marked a shift away from the free-for-all and highly decentralized system of eighteenth-century international society towards a more managed, hierarchical system. This affected all three of the key institutional underpinnings of the Westphalian international society: the balance of power, diplomacy, and international law. In 1814 the powers had already formally declared their intention to create a 'system of real and permanent balance of power in Europe', and in 1815 they carefully redrew the map of Europe to implement this system. The main diplomatic development was the greatly increased use of conferences to consider and sometimes settle matters of general interest. In a few technical areas, such as international postal services, telegraphy, and sanitation, permanent international organizations were set up. In international law, the powers sought to draft what Clark (1980: 91) terms 'a procedure of international legitimation of change', especially in the area of territorial change. There were attempts by the great powers collectively to guarantee various treaties, such as those defining the status of Switzerland, Belgium, and Luxembourg. A great many treaties laid down rules in various technical and economic areas as well as over a few humanitarian issues, notably slavery and the treatment of those wounded in war. It should be noted, however, that, while the Concert did help to bring some measure of peace and order to Europe, elsewhere it was one of the mechanisms whereby the European powers legitimized their increasing domination of Asia and Africa. For example, the Congress of Berlin of 1885 helped to prevent a major war over rival claims in Africa but it also set out the rules governing 'new acts of occupation'. Pious sentiments about bringing the 'benefits of civilization' to Africa meant little.

The First World War brought an abrupt and permanent end to the Concert of Europe. New powers, notably the USA and Japan, had appeared and there were increasing demands for national liberation in India and other parts of the European empires. Moreover, existing smaller states were less willing to be dictated to by the great powers' club, as was apparent in the deliberations to set up the world's first multipurpose, universal international organization, the **League of Nations**, in 1919. This may be seen as the first comprehensive attempt to establish a formal organizational foundation for international society that would enshrine all its key rules and norms.

If nineteenth-century Europe's international society had taken the form of a joint **hegemony** by the great powers' club, the League represented a significant departure from this in two important respects. First, in line with the belief of the highly influential American President, Woodrow Wilson, that the balance-of-power system itself had been a major cause of the war, the League was based on a new principle of **collective security** rather than a balance of power. The central notion here was that all states would agree in advance to unite against any act of aggression. This, it was hoped, would deter any potential aggressor. Second, League membership was worldwide, not merely European.

The League represented an ambitious attempt to construct a more highly organized **international society** capable of bringing order across a whole range of issues. The **international system**, however, remained firmly based on the sovereignty principle and hence still reliant upon a balance of power among the major states. The reality of the post-war period was that one power, the USA, had refused to join the League and was pursuing a policy of non-involvement in European international relations. By the 1930s, four of the remaining powers, Germany, Italy, Japan, and Russia, all had governments characterized by extremist ideologies and expansionist tendencies that threatened the interests of other great powers, with only Britain and France committed to the status quo. In other words, there was a serious *imbalance* of power.

> ### Key Points
>
> - The main ingredients of contemporary international society are the principles of sovereignty and non-intervention, and the institutions of diplomacy, the balance of power, and international law.
> - These took centuries to develop, although the Peace of Westphalia (1648) was a key event in their establishment throughout Europe.
> - The Napoleonic Wars were followed by a shift to a more managed, hierarchical, international society within Europe and an imperial structure in Europe's relations with much of the rest of the world.
> - The League of Nations was an attempt to place international society on a more secure organizational foundation.

The globalization of international society

A significant cause of the League's weakness had been the refusal of the American Senate to ratify the post-war **Versailles Peace Treaty** (including the League Covenant), and it was largely American determination not to make the same mistake in 1945 that led to a considerably stronger new version of the League in the shape of the United Nations (also see Ch. 19). In practice, however, the UN was very seldom able to play the leading role envisioned for it in the post-war international society, largely because the **cold war** prevented agreement between the two most important members of the Security Council, the USA and the Soviet Union. Indeed, the cold war meant, effectively, the division of the world into two contending hegemonial international societies.

Although Soviet–American competition affected all aspects of world politics, the rough balance of power between the two superpowers did help to secure a degree of order, especially in Europe, where the military confrontation was greatest. There were also many relatively non-contentious areas where the two were able to agree to further development of international law. Elsewhere, decolonization brought about what amounted to the globalization of European international society as the newly free colonies unanimously opted for state sovereignty and for an international society based on the various corollaries of sovereignty that had emerged in European

international society: mutual recognition, non-intervention, diplomacy, and consensual international law. Successive leaders in the developing countries attempted to promote alternatives, such as pan-Africanism, pan-Arabism and pan-Islam, but to no avail.

The collapse of the Soviet Union from 1989 completed the globalization of international society. Although in some respects resembling a traditional European empire, the Soviets had also stood for an alternative, transnational conception of international society: one based on the notion that the working classes of all countries enjoyed a solidarity that cut across state boundaries. After the 1979 Iranian Revolution, the Ayatollah Khomeini made a similar call on Muslims to see their religion rather than their state as the central focus of their loyalties.

> ### Key Points
>
> - The United Nations was intended to be a much-improved League of Nations but the cold war prevented it from functioning as such.
> - Decolonization led to the worldwide spread of the European model of international society.
> - The collapse of the Soviet Union completed this process.

Case Study The Iranian Revolution, 1979

Since 1941 Iran had been governed by Shah Mohammad Reza Pahlavi, who liked to portray himself as heir to the great Persian emperors. He allied himself closely with the USA and pursued modernization along Western lines, but as his regime came increasingly to be seen as corrupt, brutal, and wasteful of its huge oil wealth, the USA was associated with his growing unpopularity. Opposition to his rule came from many groups, including liberals and leftists, but after the Iranian Revolution of 1979 the country was increasing dominated by conservative Muslim clerics, led by Ayatollah Khomeini, and declared itself an Islamic Republic.

Khomeini challenged not just American power but the prevailing conceptions of international society. He believed that the problems of the Middle East and other Muslim countries were caused by their disregard of Islamic religious principles and called for the overthrow of 'the illegitimate political powers that now rule the entire Islamic world' and their replacement by religious governments. More generally, he argued that not only were earthly governments illegitimate, but the state itself and the concept of nationality were equally invalid. In opposition to the Westphalian division of the world into sovereign states, each defined by territorial boundaries ('the product of a deficient human mind'), Khomeini insisted that the only important social identity for Muslims was their membership of the community of believers, or *umma*.

If Khomeini had little time for the state itself, he had even less for the notion of a society of states with rules, norms of behaviour, and institutions to which Iran was supposed to adhere. For Khomeini, the correct approach to international relations, as to everything else, was determined by Islam: 'the relations between nations should be based on spiritual grounds'. These placed the transnational bonds of the *umma* above unnatural territorial boundaries that served merely to divide Muslims from each other. Relations with non-Muslim societies were also to be conducted according to traditional Islamic principles. As interpreted by Khomeini, these included, in the words of the Iranian Constitution, support for 'the just struggle of the oppressed and deprived in every corner of the globe'. International institutions like the UN were merely part of the superpowers' structure of oppression, while international law should be observed only if it accorded with the Koran. Similarly, Khomeini supported the seizure of the American embassy in Tehran and the holding hostage of many diplomats there for more than a year.

Although Iran espouses the minority, Shia, branch of Islam, which is strongly opposed by many adherents of the majority, Sunni, branch, the Iranian Revolution, particularly its anti-American and Islamist aspects, had many admirers in the Muslim world and may be seen as a key event in the rise of radical Islamist movements around the world. However in Iran itself the theocratic regime came under increasingly virulent challenge following the disputed Presidential election of June 2009, which returned the fundamentalist Mahmoud Ahmadinejad to power.

(Armstrong 1993: 188–97)

Conclusion: problems of global international society

As we have seen, in most earlier international societies some measure of independence coexisted with clear hegemonial or imperial elements. International society after the cold war was the first occasion when sovereign equality was—in practice as well as theory—the central legal norm for the whole world. At the start of the new millennium, all 192 UN members had formally agreed to what Jackson terms a **global covenant** (see Box 2.4) enshrining the core values of independence, non-intervention, and, generally, 'the sanctity, integrity and inviolability of all existing states, regardless of their level of development, form of government, political ideology, pattern of culture or any other domestic characteristic or condition' (Jackson and Owens 2001: 58). They had also agreed to severe constraints on their right to go to war and to promote respect for human rights for all. However, this conception of international society raises several major questions.

Box 2.4 Robert Jackson on freedom and international society

'[*The Global Covenant*] can be read as an extended essay on international freedom. Modern international society is a very important sphere of human freedom; it affords people the political latitude to live together within their own independent country, according to their own domestic ideas and beliefs, under a government made up of people drawn from their own ranks: international freedom based on state sovereignty.'

(Jackson 2000: vii)

First, globalization itself is serving to dissolve traditional social identities as countless 'virtual communities' emerge and as the global financial markets limit states' freedom to control their own economic policies. Some argue that globalization is bringing in its wake a new cosmopolitan culture, in which the central norms revolve around the rights of individuals rather than those of states. They point to the growing importance of 'global civil society' in the form of non-governmental organizations like Amnesty or Greenpeace as a key aspect of this process (see Ch. 20). Others use examples of 'humanitarian intervention' to argue that a more 'solidarist' international society is emerging in which a strict principle of non-intervention can be qualified in the event of serious humanitarian emergencies (Wheeler and Dunne 1998). Similarly, some suggest that, as the world becomes ever more closely integrated, so we have moved from a conception of international law as a minimum set of rules of **coexistence** to one enabling greater **cooperation**.

Second, the post-cold-war order has produced an increasing number of collapsed, failed or fragmenting states, especially in Africa. Sovereign equality implies an ability not just to participate as an equal on the international stage but to maintain orderly government within the state. One consequence of the inability of some governments to perform these functions is a new set of serious security problems *within* rather than *between* states, with which international society—because of the principle of non-intervention—is poorly equipped to deal.

Third, American military power is currently greater than that of the next ten most powerful states combined, which some saw as producing a situation without precedent in international history: a 'unipolar moment'. After **9/11**, the USA showed a willingness to employ its power—unilaterally if necessary—to defend what it saw as its vital interest. However, its experiences in both Iraq and Afghanistan appeared to demonstrate serious limitations on the capacity of military power to achieve

complex political objectives such as promoting democracy. Similarly, the global financial crisis from 2007 indicated that the balance of economic power was shifting away from the USA, as major holders of the dollar as a reserve currency, especially China, showed an increasing reluctance to continue, in effect, to underpin the American economy. Given the fundamental American role in promoting and giving shape to globalization—in the Internet, culture, finance, and underlying normative elements—a weakened USA has obvious implications for the future evolution of a globalized international society.

Fourth, earlier European international societies were underpinned by a common culture and shared values. Although all states have signed up to human rights norms and most declare their support of democracy, these are often interpreted very differently by different societies. Moreover, there is a growing tendency in developing states to see such values as part of a hypocritical Western strategy of imperialism. Radical Islamist movements have been at the forefront of this kind of resistance. One might also point to the evident disinclination of the emerging superpower, China, to let human rights considerations override its economic or political self-interest in its dealings with oppressive regimes in some developing countries.

Fifth, two issues—the environment and severe poverty (Chs 21 and 28)—are at the same time increasing in importance and are difficult to accommodate within a sovereignty-based international society. Tackling global poverty might require sustained and far-reaching involvement by richer states in the poorer states' domestic affairs, together with constraints on economic freedom in the leading economies. Dealing with climate change—a problem that does not observe national boundaries—may need not just extensive international legislation but enforcement mechanisms that also severely curtail states' freedom. As the December 2009 Copenhagen Conference on Climate Change demonstrated, states are further than ever from agreement on such constraints on their power.

All these issues revolve, in different ways, around two central questions: can an international society founded on the principle of sovereignty endure? And should it? English School theorists, like Bull, have always argued the need for international society to have a foundation of agreed ideas and values, which may mean much greater absorption of non-Western elements if it is to become genuinely universal. One possible future—that of a **clash of civilizations** (Huntington 1996)—starts from the assumption that Western and non-Western values are simply incompatible. What is envisaged here is essentially the existence of two or more distinct international societies in contention with each other, much as Christendom and Islam interacted in the Middle Ages. Another argues for a more assertive Westernism, including the imposition of Western values, if necessary: a return, in some respects, to the nineteenth century's international society, albeit with more altruistic intentions. A third emphasizes the need to develop 'globally institutionalized political processes by which norms and rules can be negotiated on the basis of dialogue and consent, rather than simply imposed by the most powerful' (Hurrell 2006: 213). In this formulation, sovereignty would remain the cornerstone of international society but with more inclusive, responsive, and effective collective decision-making processes.

Sovereignty has always shown itself capable of evolving to meet different circumstances. Dynastic sovereignty gave way to popular sovereignty and states have accepted increasing limitations on their freedom to do as they choose, including on their right to go to war. In the twentieth century the term came to be indelibly linked to the concept of national self-determination, bringing an end to the European powers' ability to insist on respect for all their sovereign rights, while simultaneously denying these to their colonies. Peoples who have only won independence in the last few decades are unlikely to wish to relinquish it in favour of a more truly cosmopolitan order, so international society is likely to remain firmly based on the sovereignty principle. Whether such an international society will be able to deal with the new challenges it faces will depend on its capacity to evolve again as it has in the past.

Box 2.5 Andrew Hurrell on the future of international society

All stable societies have to find some agreed process and procedure by which moral conflicts can be adjudicated and managed, if not resolved. Within world politics the challenge is still more daunting given the diversity and divisiveness of sentiments, attachments, languages, cultures and ways-of-living, combined with the massive inequalities of power, wealth and capacity. A global moral community in which claims about justice can both secure authority and be genuinely accessible to a broad swathe of humanity will be one that is built around some minimal notion of just process, that prioritizes institutions that embed procedural fairness, and that cultivates the shared political culture and the habits of argumentation and deliberation on which such institutions necessarily depend.

(Hurrell 2006: 213)

Key Points

- Globalization poses serious problems for a sovereignty-based international society.
- These include the challenges emanating from new forms of community, failing states in Africa, American hyperpower, growing resistance to Western ideas, and global poverty and environmental issues.

Questions

1 Discuss and evaluate Hedley Bull's concept of international society.
2 Compare and contrast medieval Christian and Islamic conceptions of international society.
3 Why has the balance of power been such a central institution of a society of sovereign states?
4 Critically evaluate the general view of the Peace of Westphalia as the founding moment of modern international society.
5 Was nineteenth-century European international society merely a means of legitimizing imperialism?
6 Why has an originally European society of states become the general norm around the world?
7 Why did the 1979 Iranian Revolution pose such a challenge to the accepted understanding of international society?
8 Can an international society of sovereign states resolve such problems as extreme poverty and climate change?

9. How might international society be affected by the rising power of China?
10. Does the rise of radical Islamism demonstrate the validity of Huntington's 'clash of civilizations' thesis?

Further Reading

Bellamy, A. J. (2005), *International Society and Its Critics* (Oxford: Oxford University Press). Useful recent collection of essays using several theoretical perspectives to look at the English School's contemporary relevance.

Bull, H. (2002), *The Anarchical Society: A Study of Order in World Politics* (Basingstoke: Palgrave Macmillan). The third edition of this classic statement of the English School approach to international society, with valuable Forewords by Andrew Hurrell and Stanley Hoffmann.

Bull, H., and Watson, A. (eds) (1984), *The Expansion of International Society* (Oxford: Clarendon Press). Edited collection of essays (including five by Bull and Watson) on different aspects of the historical expansion of European international society to the rest of the world.

Buzan, B. (2004), *From International to World Society? English School Theory and the Social Structure of Globalisation* (Cambridge: Cambridge University Press). An important study that attempts to develop more rigorous conceptualizations of English School theory, particularly in the context of globalization.

Buzan, B., and Little, R. (2000), *International Systems in World History* (Oxford: Oxford University Press). A theoretically informed and wide-ranging discussion of the development of different kinds of international systems over five thousand years.

Clark, I. (2005), *Legitimacy in International Society* (Oxford: Oxford University Press). A historical and theoretical discussion of the notion of international legitimacy, conclusively demonstrating its centrality to the concept of an international society.

Jackson, R. (2000), *The Global Covenant: Human Conduct in a World of States* (Oxford: Oxford University Press). A richly textured re-examination of the underlying pluralist norms of classical international society theory in the contemporary world.

Keal, P. (2003), *European Conquest and the Rights of Indigenous Peoples: The Moral Backwardness of International Society* (Cambridge: Cambridge University Press). A challenging recent study of the contribution of international society to the destruction and dispossession of indigenous peoples.

Keene, E. (2002), *Beyond the Anarchical Society: Grotius, Colonialism and Order in World Politics* (Cambridge: Cambridge University Press). A valuable discussion of the dualistic nature of classical notions of international society: pluralistic toleration of difference alongside promotion of the 'standard of civilization'.

Little, R., and Williams, J. (eds) (2006), *The Anarchical Society in a Globalized World* (Basingstoke: Palgrave Macmillan). A recent collection of essays considering Bull's classic work after thirty years.

Watson, A. (1992), *The Evolution of International Society* (London: Routledge). A general historical account of international society since the earliest times, with a particular focus on hegemony.

Online Resource Centre

 Visit the Online Resource Centre that accompanies this book to access more learning resources on this chapter topic at www.oxfordtextbooks.co.uk/orc/baylis5e/

Chapter 3

International history 1900–90

LEN SCOTT

Reader's Guide

This chapter examines some of the principal developments in world politics from 1900 to 1990: the development of total war, the onset of the cold war, the advent of nuclear weapons, and the end of European imperialism. The dominance of, and conflict between, European states in the first half of the twentieth century was replaced as the key dynamic in world affairs by the confrontation between the United States of America and the Union of Soviet Socialist Republics (USSR). The cold war encompassed ideological, political, and military interests of the two states (and their allies), and extended around the globe. How far, and in what ways, global conflict was promoted or prevented by the cold war are central questions. Similarly, how decolonization became entangled with East–West conflicts is central to understanding many struggles in the 'Third World'. Finally, how dangerous was the nuclear confrontation between East and West? The chapter explores the role of nuclear weapons in specific phases of the cold war, notably in *détente*, and then with the deterioration of Soviet–American relations in the 1980s.

Introduction

The First World War (also known as the Great War) began between European states on European battlefields, but extended across the globe. It was the first modern, industrialized **total war**, as the belligerents mobilized their populations and economies as well as their armies, and as they endured enormous casualties over many years. The Second World War was even more total in nature and global in scope, and helped bring about fundamental changes in world politics. Before 1939, Europe had been the arbiter of world affairs, when both the USSR and the USA remained, for different reasons, preoccupied with internal development at the expense of a significant global role. The Second World War brought the Soviets and the Americans militarily and politically deep into Europe, and helped transform their relations with each other. This transformation was soon reflected in their relations outside Europe, where various confrontations developed. Like the Second World War, the cold war had its origins in Europe, but quickly spread, with enormous consequences for countries and peoples around the world.

The Great War brought the demise of four European empires: Russian, German, Austro-Hungarian, and Ottoman (in Turkey). After 1945, European power was in eclipse. The economic plight of the wartime belligerents, including those who emerged as victors, was increasingly apparent, as was growing realization of the military and economic potential of the USA and the USSR. Both emerged as 'superpowers', combining global political ambition with military capabilities that included weapons of mass destruction. European political, economic, and military weakness contrasted with the appearance of Soviet strength and the growing Western perception of malign Soviet intent. The onset of the cold war in Europe marked the collapse of the wartime alliance between the UK, the USSR, and the USA. Whether this was inevitable after 1945 remains contentious. The most tangible legacy of the Second World War was the atomic bomb, built at enormous cost, and driven by fear that Nazi Germany might win this first nuclear arms race. After 1945, nuclear weapons posed unprecedented challenges to world politics and to the leaders responsible for conducting post-war diplomacy. The cold war provided context and pretext for the growth of nuclear arsenals that threatened the very existence of humankind, and which have continued (and continue to spread) beyond the end of the cold war and the East–West confrontation.

Since 1900 world politics has been transformed in a variety of ways, reflecting political, technological, and ideological developments, of which three are examined in this chapter: (1) the transition from European crises to modern, industrialized total war; (2) the end of empire and the withdrawal of European countries from their imperial acquisitions; and (3) the cold war: the political, military, and nuclear confrontation between the USA and the Soviet Union. There have, of course, been other important changes, and indeed equally important continuities, which are explored in other chapters. Nevertheless, the three principal changes outlined above provide a framework for exploring events and trends that have shaped international politics and the world we now inhabit.

Modern total war

The origins of the Great War have long been debated. For the victorious allies, the question of how the First World War began became a question of how far the Germans and their allies should be held responsible. At Versailles, the victors imposed a statement of German war guilt in the final settlement, primarily to justify the reparations they demanded. Debates among historians about the war's origins focused on political, military, and systemic factors. Some suggested that responsibility for the war was diffuse, as its origins lay in complex dynamics of the respective alliances and their military imperatives.

One of the more influential post-war interpretations, however, came from the West German historian, Fritz Fischer, who in his 1967 book, *Germany's Aims in the First World War*, argued that German aggression, motivated by the internal political needs of an autocratic elite, was responsible for the war.

However complex or contested the origins of the war were in retrospect, the motivations of those who fought were more explicable. The masses of the belligerent nations shared nationalist beliefs and patriotic values. As they marched off to fight, most thought war would be short, victorious, and, in many cases, glorious. The reality of the European battlefield and the advent of trench warfare was otherwise. Defensive military technologies, symbolized by the machine gun, triumphed over the tactics and strategy of attrition, although by November 1918 the allied offensive finally achieved the rapid advances that helped bring an end to the fighting. It was total war in the sense that whole societies and economies were mobilized: men were conscripted into armies and women went to work in factories. The western and eastern fronts remained the crucibles of the fighting, although conflict spread to various parts of the globe, for example when Japan went to war in 1914 as an ally of Britain. Most importantly, the USA entered the war in 1917 under President Woodrow Wilson, whose vision of international society, articulated in his **Fourteen Points**, was to drive the agenda of the Paris Peace Conference in 1919. The overthrow of the Tsar and the seizure of power by Lenin's Bolsheviks in November 1917 soon led Russia, now the USSR, to negotiate withdrawal from the war. Germany no longer fought on two fronts, but soon faced a new threat as the resources of the USA were mobilized. With the failure of its last great military offensive in the West in 1918, and with an increasingly effective British naval blockade, Germany agreed to an armistice.

The **Versailles Peace Treaty** augured both a new framework for European security and a new international order. Neither objective was achieved. There were crucial differences between the victorious powers over policies towards Germany and principles governing the international order. The treaty failed to tackle what was for some the central problem of European security after 1870—a united and frustrated Germany—and precipitated German revanchism by creating new states and devising contested borders. For some scholars, 1914–45 represented a thirty-year war. Others saw the period 1919 to 1939 as a twenty-year crisis. Economic factors were also crucial. The effects of the **Great Depression**, triggered in part by the Wall Street Crash of 1929, weakened liberal democracy in many areas and strengthened the appeal of communist, fascist, and Nazi parties. The effect on German society was particularly significant. All modernized states suffered mass unemployment, but in Germany inflation was acute. Economic and political instability provided the ground in which support for the Nazis took root. By 1933, Adolf Hitler had achieved power, and the transformation of the German state began. There remain debates about how far Hitler's ambitions were carefully thought through and how far he seized opportunities. A controversial analysis was

provided by A. J. P. Taylor in his 1961 book, *Origins of the Second World War*, in which he argued that Hitler was no different from other German political leaders. What was different was the particular philosophy of Nazism and ideas of racial supremacy and imperial expansion. British and French attempts to negotiate with Hitler culminated in the Munich Agreement of 1938. Hitler's territorial claims over the Sudetenland in Czechoslovakia were accepted as the price for peace, but within months Germany had seized the rest of Czechoslovakia and was preparing for war on Poland. Recent debates about **appeasement** have focused on whether there were realistic alternatives to negotiation, given the lack of military preparedness with which to confront Hitler.

By 1939, the defensive military technologies of the Great War gave way to armoured warfare and air power, as the German blitzkrieg brought speedy victories over Poland, and in the west. Hitler was also drawn into the Balkans in support of his Italian ally, Mussolini, and into North Africa. With the invasion of the Soviet Union in June 1941, the scale of fighting and scope of Hitler's aims were apparent. Massive early victories on the eastern front gave way to winter stalemate, and the mobilization of Soviet peoples and armies. German treatment of civilian populations and Soviet prisoners of war reflected Nazi ideas of racial supremacy, and resulted in the deaths of millions. German anti-Semitism and the development of concentration camps gained new momentum after a decision on the 'Final Solution of the Jewish Question' in 1942. The term **holocaust** entered the political lexicon of the twentieth century, as the Nazis attempted the genocide of the Jewish people and other minorities, such as the Roma, in Europe.

The rise and fall of Japan

After 1919, international attempts to provide collective security were pursued through the League of Nations. The US Senate prevented American participation in the League, however, and Japanese aggression against Manchuria in 1931, the Italian invasion of Abyssinia in 1935, and German involvement in the Spanish Civil War 1936–9 were met with ineffective international responses. In 1868, Japan had emerged from several centuries of isolationism to pursue industrial and military modernization, and then imperial expansion. In 1937, China, already embroiled in civil war between communists and nationalists, was invaded by Japan. Tokyo's ambitions, however, could only be realized at the expense of European empires and American interests. President

Table 3.1 Second World War estimated casualties

Hiroshima (6 August 1945): 70,000–80,000 'prompt'; 140,000 by end 1945; 200,000 by 1950
Nagasaki: (9 August 1945): 30,000–40,000 'prompt'; 70,000 by end 1945; 140,000 by 1950
Tokyo (9 March 1945): 100,000 +
Dresden (13–15 February 1945): 24,000–35,000+
Coventry (14 November 1940): 568
Leningrad (siege 1941–4): 1,000,000 +

Roosevelt increasingly sought to engage the USA in the European war, against strong isolationist sentiments, and by 1941, German submarines and American warships were in an undeclared war. The imposition of American economic sanctions on Japan precipitated Japanese military preparations for a surprise attack on the US fleet at Pearl Harbor on 7 December 1941. When Germany and Italy declared war on the USA in support of their Japanese ally, Roosevelt decided to prioritize the European over the Pacific theatre. After a combined strategic bombing offensive with the British against German cities, the allies launched a 'second front' in France, for which the Soviets had been pressing.

Defeat of Germany in May 1945 came before the atomic bomb was ready. The destruction of the Japanese cities, Hiroshima and Nagasaki, remains a controversy. Aside from moral objections to attacking civilian populations, their destruction generated fierce debate, particularly among American historians, about why the bomb was dropped. Gar Alperovitz, in his 1965 book *Atomic Diplomacy*, argued that, as President Truman knew Japan was defeated, his real motive was to coerce Moscow

in pursuit of post-war American interests in Europe and Asia. Such claims generated angry and dismissive responses from other historians. Ensuing scholarship has benefited from more historical evidence, although debate persists over how far Truman dropped the bomb simply to end the war, and how far other factors, including coercion of the Soviet Union in post-war affairs, entered his calculations.

Key Points

- Debates about the origins of the First World War focus on whether responsibility should rest with the German government or whether war came because of more complex systemic factors.

- The Paris Peace settlement failed to address the central problems of European security, and in restructuring the European state system created new sources of grievance and instability. The principles of self-determination espoused in particular by Woodrow Wilson did not extend to the empires of the European colonial powers.

- The rise of Hitler posed challenges that European political leaders lacked the ability and will to meet.

- The German attack on the Soviet Union extended the scope and barbarity of the war from short and limited campaigns to extended, large-scale, and barbaric confrontation, fought for total victory.

- The Japanese attack on Pearl Harbor brought the USA into the war in Europe and eventually led Germany into war on two fronts (again).

- Debate persists about whether the atomic bomb should have been used in 1945, and about the effect that this had on the cold war.

End of empire

The demise of imperialism in the twentieth century marked a fundamental change in world politics. It reflected, and contributed to, the decreasing importance of Europe as the arbiter of world affairs. The belief that national **self-determination** should be a guiding principle in international politics marked a transformation of attitudes and values. During the age of imperialism political status accrued to imperial powers. After 1945, imperialism became a term of opprobrium. Colonialism and the United Nations Charter were increasingly recognized as incompatible, although independence was often slow and sometimes marked by prolonged and armed struggle. The cold war often complicated and

hindered the transition to independence. Various factors influenced the process of decolonization: the attitude of the colonial power; the ideology and strategy of the anti-imperialist forces; and the role of external powers. Political, economic, and military factors played various roles in shaping the transfer of power. Different imperial powers and newly emerging independent states had different experiences of withdrawal from empire.

Britain

In 1945, the British Empire extended across the globe. Between 1947 and 1980, 49 territories were granted

Table 3.2 Principal acts of European decolonization, 1945–80

Country	Colonial state	Year of independence
India	Britain	1947
Pakistan	Britain	1947
Burma	Britain	1948
Sri Lanka	Britain	1948
Indonesia	Holland	1949
Ghana	Britain	1957
Malaya	Britain	1957
French African colonies*	France	1960
Zaïre	Britain	1960
Nigeria	Britain	1960
Sierra Leone	Britain	1961
Tanganyika	Britain	1961
Uganda	Britain	1962
Algeria	Britain	1962
Rwanda	Belgium	1962
Kenya	Britain	1963
Guinea-Bissau	Portugal	1974
Mozambique	Portugal	1975
Cape Verde	Portugal	1975
São Tomé	Portugal	1975
Angola	Portugal	1975
Zimbabwe	Britain	1980

*including Cameroon, Central African Republic, Chad, Gabon, Ivory Coast, Madagascar, Mali, Mauritania, Niger, Senegal, and Upper Volta.

apartheid, after 1948, the South Africans engaged in what many saw as the internal equivalent of imperialism. South Africa also conducted more traditional imperialist practices in its occupation of Namibia. It also exercised an important influence in post-colonial/cold war struggles in Angola and Mozambique after the last European empire in Africa—that of Portugal—collapsed when the military dictatorship was overthrown in Lisbon.

France

The British experience of decolonization stood in contrast to that of the French. France had been occupied during the Second World War, and successive governments sought to preserve French international prestige by maintaining its imperial status. In Indo-China after 1945, Paris attempted to preserve colonial rule, withdrawing only after prolonged guerrilla war and military defeat at the hands of Vietnamese revolutionary forces, the Viet Minh, led by Ho Chi Minh. In Africa, the picture was different. The wind of change also blew through French Africa, and under President Charles de Gaulle, France withdrew from empire, while attempting to preserve its influence. In Algeria, however, the French refused to leave. Algeria was regarded by many French people as part of France itself. The resulting war, from 1954 to 1962, led to hundreds of thousands of deaths, and France itself was brought to the edge of civil war.

independence. In 1947, the independence of India, the 'Jewel in the Crown' of the empire, paved the way for the creation of the world's largest democracy, although the creation of India and Pakistan led to intercommunal ethnic cleansing and hundreds of thousands of deaths. Indian independence was largely an exception in the early post-war years, as successive British governments were reluctant to rush towards decolonization. End of empire in Africa came towards the end of the 1950s and early 1960s, symbolized by Prime Minister Harold Macmillan's speech in South Africa in February 1960 when he warned his hosts of the 'wind of change' blowing through their continent.

British withdrawal from Africa was relatively peaceful, save for conflicts with indigenous revolutionaries, notably in Kenya (1952–6) and Malaya (1948–60). In Rhodesia/Zimbabwe, however, the transition to 'one person one vote' and black majority rule was prevented by a white minority prepared to disregard both the British government and world opinion. This minority was aided and abetted by the South African government. Under

Legacies and consequences: nationalism or communism?

From the perspective of the former colonies, the principles of self-determination that underpinned the new global order were slow to be implemented, and required political, ideological, and in some cases military mobilization. The pattern of decolonization in Africa was thus diverse, reflecting attitudes of colonial powers, the nature of local nationalist or revolutionary movements, and in some cases the involvement of external states, including cold war protagonists. Tribal factors were also an ingredient in many cases. How far tribal divisions were created or exacerbated by the imperial powers is an important question in examining the political stability of the newly independent states. Equally important is how capable the new political leaderships in these societies were in tackling their political and formidable economic problems of poverty and under-development.

In Asia, the relationship between **nationalism** and revolutionary **Marxism** was a potent force. In Malaya, the British defeated an insurgent communist movement (1948–60). In Indo-China (1946–54) the French failed to do likewise. For the Vietnamese, centuries of foreign oppression—Chinese, Japanese, and French—soon focused on a new adversary, the USA. For Washington, early reluctance to support European imperialism gave way to incremental and covert commitments, and, from 1965, open involvement with the newly created state of South Vietnam. American leaders spoke of a domino theory, in which if one state fell to communism, the next would be at risk. Chinese and Soviet support provided additional cold war contexts. Washington failed, however, to coordinate limited war objectives with an effective political strategy, and once victory was no longer possible, sought to disengage through 'peace with honor'. The *Tet* (Vietnamese New Year) offensive of the 'Viet Cong' guerrillas in 1968 marked a decisive moment, convincing many Americans that the war would not be won, although it was not until 1973 that American forces finally withdrew, two years before South Vietnam was defeated.

The global trend towards decolonization was a key development in the twentieth century, though one frequently offset by local circumstances. Yet, while imperialism withered, other forms of domination or **hegemony** took shape. The notion of hegemony has been used as criticism of the behaviour of the superpowers, most notably with Soviet hegemony in Eastern Europe, and American hegemony in Central America.

Key Points

- The First World War preciptated the collapse of four European empires (the Russian, German, Austro-Hungarian, and the Ottoman Empire in Turkey).

- Different European powers had different attitudes to decolonization after 1945: some, such as the British, decided to leave, while others sought to preserve their empires, in part (the French) or whole (the Portuguese).

- European powers adopted different attitudes to different regions/countries. For example, British withdrawal from Asia came much more quickly than from Africa after 1945.

- The process of decolonization was relatively peaceful in many cases; it led to revolutionary wars in others (Algeria, Malaya, and Angola), whose scale and ferocity reflected the attitudes of the colonial power and the nationalist movements.

- The struggle for independence/national liberation became embroiled in cold war conflicts when the superpowers and/or their allies became involved, for example in Vietnam. Whether decolonization was judged successful depends, in part, on whose perspective you adopt—that of the European power, the independence movement, or the people themselves.

Cold war

The rise of the USA as a world power after 1945 was of paramount importance in international politics. Its conflict with the Soviet Union provided one of the crucial dynamics in world affairs, and one that affected—directly or indirectly—every part of the globe. In the West, historians have debated with vigour and acrimony who was responsible for the collapse of the wartime relationship between Moscow and Washington. The rise of the USSR as a global power after 1945 is equally crucial in this period. Relations between Moscow and its Eastern European 'allies', with the People's Republic of China (PRC), and with revolutionary forces in the Third World, have been vital issues in world politics, as well as key factors in Soviet–American affairs.

Some historians date the origins of the cold war to the 'Russian revolution' of 1917, while most focus on events between 1945 and 1950. Whether the cold war was inevitable, whether it was the consequence of mistakes and misperceptions, or whether it reflected the response of courageous Western leaders to malign and aggressive Soviet intent, are central questions in debates about the origins and dynamics of the cold war. Hitherto, these debates have drawn from Western archives and sources, and reflect Western assumptions and perceptions. With the end of the cold war, greater evidence has emerged of Soviet motivations and understanding.

1945–53: onset of the cold war

The onset of the cold war in Europe reflected failure to implement the principles agreed at the wartime conferences of Yalta and Potsdam. The future of Germany, and of various Central and Eastern European countries, notably Poland, were issues of growing tension between the former wartime allies. Reconciling principles of national self-determination with national security was a formidable task. In the West, there was growing feeling that Soviet policy towards Eastern Europe was guided not by historic concern with security but by ideological expansion. In March 1947, the Truman administration sought to justify limited aid to Turkey and Greece with rhetoric designed to arouse awareness of Soviet ambitions, and a declaration that the USA would support those threatened by Soviet subversion or expansion. The **Truman doctrine** and the associated policy of **containment** expressed the self-image of the USA as inherently defensive, and were underpinned by the **Marshall Plan** for European economic recovery, proclaimed in June 1947, which was essential to the economic rebuilding of Western Europe. In Eastern Europe, democratic socialist and other anti-communist forces were undermined and eliminated as Marxist–Leninist regimes, loyal to Moscow, were installed. The only exception was in Yugoslavia, where the Marxist leader, Marshal Tito, consolidated his position while maintaining independence from Moscow. Subsequently, Tito's Yugoslavia was to play an important role in the Third World Non-Aligned Movement.

The first major confrontation of the cold war took place over Berlin in 1948. The former German capital was left deep in the heart of the Soviet zone of occupation, and in June 1948 Stalin sought to resolve its status by severing road and rail communications. West Berlin's population and political autonomy were kept alive by a massive airlift. Stalin ended the blockade in May 1949. The crisis saw the deployment of American long-range bombers in Britain, officially described as 'atomic-capable', although none were actually armed with nuclear weapons. US military deployment was followed by political commitment enshrined in the **North Atlantic Treaty Organization** (NATO) treaty signed in April 1949. The key article of the treaty—that an attack on one member would be treated as an attack on all—accorded with the principle of collective self-defence enshrined in Article 51 of the UN Charter. In practice, the cornerstone of the alliance was the commitment of the USA to defend Western Europe. In reality, this soon meant the willingness of the USA to use nuclear weapons to deter Soviet 'aggression'. For the Soviet Union 'political encirclement' soon entailed a growing military, and specifically nuclear, threat.

While the origins of the cold war were in Europe, events and conflicts in Asia and elsewhere were also crucial. In 1949, the thirty-year-long Chinese civil war ended in victory for the communists under Mao Zedong. This had a major impact on Asian affairs and on perceptions in both Moscow and Washington. In June 1950, the North Korean attack on South Korea was interpreted as part of a general communist strategy, and a test case

for American resolve, and the will of the United Nations to withstand aggression. The resulting American and UN commitment, followed in October 1950 by Chinese involvement, led to a war lasting three years, in which over 3 million people died before pre-war borders were restored. North and South Korea themselves remained locked in seemingly perpetual hostility, even after the end of the cold war.

Assessing the impact of the cold war on the Middle East is more difficult. The founding of the state of Israel in 1948 reflected the legacy of the Nazi genocide and the failure of British colonial policy. The complexities of politics, diplomacy, and armed conflict in the years immediately after 1945 cannot be readily understood through the prism of Soviet–American ideological or geo-strategic conflict. Both the Soviet Union and the USA helped the creation of a Jewish state in previously Arab lands, although in the 1950s Soviet foreign policy supported Arab nationalism. The pan-Arabism of the charismatic Egyptian leader, Gamal Abdel Nasser, embraced a form of socialism, but was far removed from Marxism–Leninism. The state of Israel was created by force, and owed its survival to a continuing capacity to defend itself against adversaries who did not recognize the legitimacy if its existence. Israel developed relations with the British and the French, culminating in their secret agreement to attack Egypt in 1956. Over time, a more crucial relationship developed with the USA, with whom a de facto strategic alliance emerged. Yet Britain, France, and the USA also developed a complex of relationships with Arab states, reflecting historical, strategic, and economic interests.

1953–69: conflict, confrontation, and compromise

One consequence of the Korean War was the build-up of American forces in Western Europe, lest communist aggression in Asia distract from the real intent in Europe. The idea that communism was a monolithic political entity controlled from Moscow became an enduring American fixation, not shared in London or elsewhere. Western Europeans nevertheless depended on the USA for military security, and this dependence deepened as the cold war confrontation in Europe was consolidated. The rearmament of the Federal Republic of Germany in 1954 precipitated the creation of the **Warsaw Pact** in 1955. The military build-up continued apace, with unprecedented concentrations of conventional and, moreover, nuclear forces. As the Soviet Union developed its ability to strike the USA with nuclear weapons, the credibility of 'extended deterrence' was questioned as the USA's willingness to risk 'Chicago for Hamburg' was called into doubt. The problem was exacerbated as NATO strategy continued to depend on the willingness of the USA not just to fight, but to *initiate*, nuclear war on Europe's behalf. By the 1960s, there were some 7,000 nuclear weapons in Western Europe alone. NATO deployed nuclear weapons to offset Soviet conventional superiority, while Soviet 'theatre nuclear' forces in Europe compensated for overall American nuclear superiority.

The death of Stalin in 1953 portended significant consequences for the USSR at home and abroad. Stalin's eventual successor, Nikita Khrushchev, strove to modernize Soviet society, but helped unleash reformist forces in Eastern Europe. While Poland was controlled, the situation in Hungary threatened Soviet hegemony, and in 1956 the intervention of the Red Army brought bloodshed to the streets of Budapest and international condemnation on Moscow. Soviet intervention coincided with an attack on Egypt by Britain, France, and Israel, precipitated by Colonel Nasser's seizure of the Suez Canal. The British government's actions provoked fierce domestic and international criticism, and the most serious rift in the 'special relationship' between Britain and the USA. President Eisenhower was strongly opposed to his allies, and in the face of what were effectively American economic sanctions, the British abandoned the operation (and their support for the French and Israelis). International opprobrium at the Soviet action in Budapest was lessened and deflected by what many saw as the final spasms of European imperialism.

Khrushchev's policy towards the West mixed a search for political coexistence with the pursuit of ideological confrontation. Soviet support for movements of national liberation aroused fears in the West of a global communist challenge. American commitment to liberal democracy and national self-determination was often subordinated to cold war perspectives, as well as American economic and political interests. The cold war saw the growth of large permanent intelligence organizations, whose roles ranged from estimating intentions and capabilities of adversaries to covert intervention in

Case Study The Cuban missile crisis

In October 1962, the USA discovered that, contrary to private and public assurances, the Soviet leadership was secretly deploying nuclear missiles in Cuba. President Kennedy responded with a naval blockade of the island, and American nuclear forces moved to unprecedented states of alert. The superpowers stood 'eyeball to eyeball', and most historians believe this was the moment in the cold war when the risk of nuclear war was greatest. Evidence from Soviet archives and sources, together with Western records, suggests that as the crisis reached its climax on 26–28 October, both Kennedy and Khrushchev were increasingly anxious to reach a diplomatic settlement, including by political concessions. The USA possessed overwhelming nuclear superiority at this time, but both leaders recognized the risk of escalation to nuclear war would be a global, national, and personal disaster. Nevertheless, recent evidence suggests that the risk of inadvertent nuclear war—arising from a concatenation of misperception, the actions of subordinates, and organizational failure—was much greater than was realized by political leaders then or by historians later.

The diplomatic impasse was resolved six days after Kennedy announced the blockade, when Nikita Khrushchev undertook to withdraw the missiles in return for assurances that the USA would not invade Cuba. It has also now emerged that President Kennedy provided a secret undertaking to remove equivalent NATO nuclear missiles from Europe. While much of the literature has focused on the Soviet–American confrontation, greater attention has been given to the Cuban side. It is now clear that one of Khrushchev's primary objectives was to deter an American attack on Cuba that both Moscow and Havana anticipated. Fidel Castro's role has also received closer scrutiny. As the crisis reached its climax, he cabled Khrushchev, who interpreted the message as advocating a pre-emptive nuclear attack on the USA. Castro also later stated that he would have wanted to use the tactical nuclear weapons which the Soviets had sent to fight an American invasion. Castro's message to Khrushchev reinforced the Soviet leader's determination to strike a deal with Kennedy, which he did without consulting the Cubans.

In the aftermath of the crisis, important progress was made towards negotiation of the Partial Test Ban Treaty in 1963, which banned the testing of nuclear weapons in the atmosphere. There was recognition that crises were to be avoided, and no further attempts were made by Moscow to coerce the West over Berlin. Nevertheless, both sides continued the build-up of their nuclear arsenals.

Table 3.3 Cold war crises

1948-9	Berlin	USSR/USA/UK
1954-5	Taiwan straits	USA/PRC
1961	Berlin	USSR/USA/NATO
1962	Cuba	USSR/USA/Cuba
1973	Arab-Israeli war	Egypt/Israel/Syria/Jordan/ USA/USSR
1983	Exercise *Able Archer*	USSR/USA/NATO

Table 3.4 Revolutionary upheavals in the Third World, 1974-80

Ethiopia	Overthrow of Haile Selassie	Sept. 1974
Cambodia	Khmer Rouge takes Phnom Penh	April 1975
Vietnam	North Vietnam/'Viet Cong' take Saigon	April 1975
Laos	Pathet Lao takes over state	May 1975
Guinea-Bissau	Independence from Portugal	Sept. 1974
Mozambique	Independence from Portugal	June 1975
Cape Verde	Independence from Portugal	June 1975
São Tomé	Independence from Portugal	June 1975
Angola	Independence from Portugal	Nov. 1975
Afghanistan	Military coup in Afghanistan	April 1978
Iran	Ayatollah Khomeini installed in power	Feb. 1979
Grenada	New Jewel Movement takes power	March 1979
Nicaragua	Sandinistas take Managua	July 1979
Zimbabwe	Independence from Britain	April 1980

Source: Halliday F. (1986), *The Making of the Second Cold War* (London: Verso): 92.

the affairs of other states. Crises over Berlin in 1961 and Cuba in 1962 (see Case Study) marked the most dangerous moments of the cold war. In both, there was a risk of direct military confrontation and, certainly in October 1962, the possibility of nuclear war. How close the world came to Armageddon during the Cuban missile crisis and exactly why peace was preserved remain matters of debate among historians and surviving officials.

The events of 1962 were followed by a more stable period of coexistence and competition. Nuclear arsenals, nevertheless, continued to grow. Whether this is best characterized as an arms race, or whether internal political and bureaucratic pressures drove the growth of nuclear arsenals, is open to interpretation. For Washington, commitments to NATO allies also provided pressures and opportunities to develop and deploy shorter-range ('tactical' and 'theatre') nuclear weapons. The global nuclear dimension increased with the emergence of other nuclear weapon states: Britain in 1952, France in 1960, and China in 1964. Growing concern at the spread or proliferation of nuclear weapons led to the negotiation of the Nuclear Non-Proliferation Treaty (NPT) in 1968, wherein states that had nuclear weapons committed themselves to halt the arms race, while those who did not promised not to develop them. Despite successes of the NPT, by 1990 several states had developed or were developing nuclear weapons, notably Israel, India, Pakistan, and apartheid South Africa.

1969-79: the rise and fall of détente

As America's commitment in Vietnam was deepening, Soviet–Chinese relations were deteriorating. Indeed, by 1969 the PRC and the USSR fought a minor border war over a territorial dispute. Despite (or because of) these tensions, the foundations for what became known as **détente** were laid between the USSR and the USA, and for what became known as **rapprochement** between China and the USA. Détente in Europe had its origins in the **Ostpolitik** of the German Socialist Chancellor, Willy

Brandt, and resulted in agreements that recognized the peculiar status of Berlin, and the sovereignty of East Germany. Soviet–American détente had its roots in mutual recognition of the need to avoid nuclear crises, and in the economic and military incentives in avoiding an unconstrained arms race. Both Washington and Moscow also looked towards Beijing when making their bilateral calculations.

In the West, détente was associated with the political leadership of President Richard Nixon and his adviser Henry Kissinger, who were also instrumental in Sino–American *rapprochement*. This new phase in Soviet–American relations did not mark an end to political conflict, as each side pursued political goals, some of which were increasingly incompatible with the aspirations of the other superpower. Both sides supported friendly regimes and movements, and subverted adversaries. All this came as various political upheavals were taking place in the Third World (see Table 3.4). The question of how far the superpowers could control their friends, and how far they were entangled by their commitments, was underlined in 1973 when the Arab–Israeli war embroiled both the USA and the USSR in what became a potentially dangerous confrontation. Getting the superpowers involved in the war—whether by design or serendipity—helped create the political conditions for Egyptian–Israeli *rapprochement*. Diplomatic and strategic relations were transformed as Egypt switched its allegiance from Moscow to Washington. In the short term, Egypt was isolated in the Arab world. For Israel, fear of a war of annihilation fought on two fronts was lifted. Yet continuing political violence and terrorism, and the enduring enmity between Israel and other Arab states, proved insurmountable obstacles to a more permanent regional settlement.

Soviet support for revolutionary movements in the Third World reflected Moscow's self-confidence as a 'superpower' and its analysis that the Third World was turning toward socialism. Ideological competition ensued with the West and with China. In the USA, this was viewed as evidence of duplicity. Some Americans claim that Moscow's support for revolutionary forces in Ethiopia in 1975 killed détente. Others cite the Soviet role in Angola in 1978. Furthermore, the perception that the USSR was using arms control agreements to gain military advantage was linked to Soviet behaviour in the Third World. Growing Soviet military superiority was reflected in growing Soviet influence, it was argued. Critics claimed the SALT (Strategic Arms Limitation Talks) process enabled the Soviets to deploy multiple independently targetable warheads on their large intercontinental ballistic missiles (ICBMs), threatening key American forces. The USA faced a 'window of vulnerability', it was claimed. The view from Moscow was different, reflecting various assumptions about the scope and purpose of détente, and the nature of nuclear deterrence. Other events were also seen to weaken American influence. The overthrow of the Shah of Iran in 1979 resulted in the loss of an important Western ally in the region, although the ensuing militant Islamic government was hostile to both superpowers.

December 1979 marked a point of transition in East–West affairs. NATO agreed to deploy land-based Cruise and Pershing II missiles in Europe if negotiations with the Soviets did not reduce what NATO saw as a serious imbalance. Later in the month, Soviet armed forces intervened in Afghanistan to support their revolutionary allies. The USSR was bitterly condemned in the West and in the Third World for its actions, and soon became committed to a protracted and bloody struggle that many compared to the American war in Vietnam. In Washington, President Carter's image of the Soviet Union fundamentally changed. Nevertheless, Republicans increasingly used foreign and defence policy to attack the Carter presidency. Perceptions of American weakness abroad permeated domestic politics, and in 1980, Ronald Reagan was elected President. He was committed to a more confrontational approach with the Soviets

on arms control, Third World conflicts, and East–West relations in general.

1979–86: 'the second cold war'

In the West, critics of *détente* and arms control argued that the Soviets were acquiring nuclear superiority. Some suggested that the USA should pursue policies and strategies based on the idea that victory in nuclear war was possible. The election of Ronald Reagan in 1980 was a watershed in Soviet–American relations. One issue that Reagan inherited, and which loomed large in the breakdown of relations between East and West, was nuclear missiles in Europe. Changes in the strategic and European nuclear 'balances' had generated new anxieties in the West about the credibility of extended deterrence. NATO's resulting decision to deploy land-based missiles capable of striking Soviet territory precipitated a period of great tension in relations between NATO and the USSR, and political friction within NATO. Reagan's own incautious public remarks reinforced perceptions that he was as ill informed as he was dangerous in matters nuclear, although key arms policies were consistent with those of his predecessor, Jimmy Carter. On arms control, Reagan was uninterested in agreements that would freeze the status quo for the sake of getting agreement, and Soviet and American negotiators proved unable to make progress in talks on long-range and intermediate-range weapons. One particular idea had significant consequences for arms control and for Washington's relations with its allies and its adversaries. The Strategic Defense Initiative (SDI), quickly dubbed 'Star Wars', was a research programme designed to explore the feasibility of space-based defences against ballistic missiles. The Soviets appeared to take SDI very seriously, and claimed that Reagan's real purpose was to regain the nuclear monopoly of the 1950s. Reagan, himself, retained an idiosyncratic attachment to SDI, which he believed could make nuclear weapons impotent and obsolete. However, the technological advances claimed by SDI proponents did not materialize and the programme was eventually reduced and marginalized.

The resulting period of tension and confrontation between the superpowers has been described as the **second cold war** and compared to the early period of confrontation and tension between 1946 and 1953. In Western Europe and the Soviet Union, there was real fear of nuclear war. Much of this was a reaction to the rhetoric and policies of the Reagan administration. American statements on nuclear weapons and military intervention in

Grenada in 1983, and against Libya in 1986, were seen as evidence of a new belligerence. Reagan's policy towards Central America, and support for the rebel *Contras* in Nicaragua, were sources of controversy within the USA and internationally. In 1986, the International Court of Justice found the USA guilty of violating international law for the Central Intelligence Agency's (CIA's) covert attacks on Nicaraguan harbours.

The Reagan administration's use of military power was none the less limited: rhetoric and perception were at variance with reality. Some operations ended in humiliating failure, notably in Lebanon in 1983. Nevertheless, there is evidence that some in the Soviet leadership took very seriously the words (and deeds) of the Reagan administration and were anxious that Washington might be planning a nuclear first strike. In 1983, Soviet air defences shot down a South Korean civilian airliner in Soviet airspace. The American reaction, and the imminent deployment of American nuclear missiles in Europe, created a climate of great tension in East–West relations. And in November 1983 Soviet intelligence misinterpreted a NATO training exercise (codenamed *Able Archer*) and may have believed that NATO was preparing to attack them. How close the world came to a serious nuclear confrontation in 1983 is not yet clear. Emerging evidence from Soviet sources suggests that the risk of inadvertent nuclear war in this period could have been significant.

Throughout the early 1980s, the Soviets were handicapped by a succession of ageing political leaders (Brezhnev, Andropov, and Chernenko), whose ill-health further inhibited Soviet responses to the American challenge and the American threat. This changed dramatically after Mikhail Gorbachev became President in 1985. Gorbachev's 'new thinking' in foreign policy, and his domestic reforms, created a revolution, both in the USSR's foreign relations and within Soviet society. At home, **glasnost** (or openness) and **perestroika** (or restructuring) unleashed nationalist and other forces that, to Gorbachev's dismay, were to destroy the Union of Soviet Socialist Republics.

Gorbachev's aim in foreign policy was to transform international relations, most importantly with the USA. His domestic agenda was also a catalyst for change in Eastern Europe, although, unlike Khrushchev, he was not prepared to react with force or coercion. When

Table 3.5 Principal nuclear weapons states: nuclear arsenals, 1945–90

	1945	1950	1955	1960	1965	1970	1975	1980	1985	1990
USA	6	369	3,057	20,434	31,982	26,662	27,826	24,304	24,327	21,004
USSR	–	5	200	1,605	6,129	11,643	19,055	30,062	39,197	37,000
UK	–	–	10	30	310	280	350	350	300	300
France	–	–	–	–	32	36	188	250	360	505
PRC	–	–	–	–	5	75	185	280	425	430
Total	6	374	3,267	22,069	38,458	38,696	47,604	55,246	64,609	59,239

Source: Norris, R. S. and Kristensen, H. (2006), 'Nuclear notebook', *Bulletin of the Atomic Scientists*, 62(4) (July/Aug.): 66.

Table 3.6 Principal arms control and disarmament agreements

Treaty	Purpose of agreement	Signed	Parties
Geneva protocol	Chemical weapons: bans use	1925	100 +
Partial Test Ban Treaty	Bans atmospheric, underwater, outer-space nuclear tests	1963	100 +
Nuclear Non-Proliferation Treaty	Limits spread of nuclear weapons	1968	100 +
Biological Weapons Convention	Bans production/use	1972	80 +
SALT I Treaty	Limits strategic arms*	1972	USA/USSR
ABM Treaty	Limits anti-ballistic missiles	1972	USA/USSR
SALT II Treaty	Limits strategic arms*	1979	USA/USSR
INF Treaty	Bans two categories of land-based missiles	1987	USA/USSR
START 1 Treaty	Reduces strategic arms*	1990	USA/USSR

*Strategic arms are long-range weapons.
Source: adapted from Harvard Nuclear Study Group (1985), 'Arms Control and Disarmament: What Can and Can't be Done', in F. Holroyd (ed.), *Thinking About Nuclear Weapons* (Buckingham: Open University): 96.

confronted with revolt in Eastern Europe, Gorbachev's foreign ministry invoked Frank Sinatra's song, 'I did it my way', to mark the end of the **Brezhnev doctrine** that had limited Eastern European sovereignty and political development. The **Sinatra doctrine** meant that Eastern Europeans were now allowed to 'do it their way'. Throughout Eastern Europe, Moscow-aligned regimes gave way to democracies, in what was for the most part a peaceful as well as speedy transition (see Ch. 4). Most dramatically, Germany was united and East Germany (the German Democratic Republic) disappeared.

Gorbachev paved the way for agreements on nuclear and conventional forces that helped ease the tensions that had characterized the early 1980s. In 1987, he travelled to Washington to sign the Intermediate Nuclear Forces (INF) Treaty, banning intermediate-range nuclear missiles, including Cruise and Pershing II. This agreement was heralded as a triumph for the Soviet President, but NATO leaders, including Margaret Thatcher and Ronald Reagan, argued that it was vindication of the policies pursued by NATO since 1979. The INF Treaty was concluded more quickly than a new agreement on cutting strategic nuclear weapons, in part because of continuing Soviet opposition to the SDI. And it was Reagan's successor, George Bush, who concluded a Strategic Arms Reduction Treaty (START) agreement that reduced long-range nuclear weapons (though only back to the level at which they had been in the early 1980s). Gorbachev used agreements on nuclear weapons as a means of building trust, and demonstrated the serious and radical nature of his purpose. However, despite similar radical agreements on conventional forces in Europe (culminating in the Paris agreement of 1990), the end of the cold war marked success in nuclear *arms control* rather than nuclear *disarmament*. The histories of the cold war and of the bomb are very closely connected, but while the cold war is now over, nuclear weapons are still very much in existence.

Key Points

- There are disagreements about when and why the cold war began, and who was responsible. Distinct phases can be seen in East–West relations, during which tension and the risk of direct confrontation grew and receded.

- Some civil and regional wars were intensified and prolonged by superpower involvement; others may have been prevented or shortened.

- Nuclear weapons were an important factor in the cold war. How far the arms race had a momentum of its own is a matter of debate. Agreements on limiting and controlling the growth of nuclear arsenals played an important role in Soviet–American (and East–West) relations.

- The end of the cold war has not resulted in the abolition of nuclear weapons.

- Various international crises occurred in which there was the risk of nuclear war. How close we came to nuclear war at these times remains open to speculation and debate.

Conclusion

The changes that took place in twentieth-century politics were enormous. Assessing their significance raises many complex issues about the nature of international history and international relations. How did war come in 1914? What accounts for the rise of Hitler? Who won the cold war, how, and with what consequences? These are questions that have generated robust debate and fierce controversy. Several points are emphasized in this conclusion concerning the relationship between the three aspects explored in the chapter (total war, end of empire, and cold war). However war came in 1914, the transformation of warfare into industrialized total war reflected a combination of technological, political, and social forces. Political leaders proved incapable of restoring peace and stability, and attempts to reconstruct the European state system after 1919 failed to address enduring problems and created new obstacles to a stable order. The rise of Nazi Germany brought a new conflagration and new methods of fighting and killing. The scale of carnage and suffering was unprecedented. Nazi ideas of racial supremacy brought brutality and mass murder across Europe and culminated in genocide against the Jews. One consequence was the creation of Israel in 1948, which helped set in motion conflicts and events that continue to have global repercussions. The rise of an aggressive military regime in

Tokyo likewise portended protracted and brutal war across the Pacific.

The period since 1945 has witnessed the end of European empires constructed before, and in the early part of, the twentieth century, and has also witnessed the rise and fall of the cold war. The relationship between the end of empire and cold war conflicts in the Third World is a close, though complex, one. In some cases, the involvement of the superpowers helped bring about change. In others, direct superpower involvement resulted in escalation and prolongation of the conflict. Marxist ideology in various forms provided inspiration to many Third World liberation movements, but provocation to the USA (and others). The example of Vietnam is most obvious in these respects, but in a range of anti-colonial struggles the cold war played a major part. Precisely how the cold war influenced decolonization is best assessed on a case-by-case basis. One key issue is how far the values and objectives of revolutionary leaders and their movements were nationalist rather than Marxist. It is claimed that both Ho Chi Minh in Vietnam and Fidel Castro in Cuba were primarily nationalists, who turned to Moscow and to communism only in the face of American and Western hostility. The divisions between the Soviet Union and the People's Republic of China also demonstrate the diverging trends within the practice of Marxism. In several instances, conflict between communists became as bitter as conflict between communists and capitalists. In other areas, notably the Middle East, Marxism faced the challenge of radical political ideas (pan-Arabism, revolutionary Islam) that held greater attraction for the peoples involved. The role of the superpowers was nevertheless apparent, even if their involvement was more complex and diffuse. In moments of crisis it was nevertheless significant.

Similarly, the relationship between the cold war and the history of nuclear weapons is a close, though problematic, one. Some historians contend that the use of atomic weapons by the USA played a decisive part in the origins of the cold war. Others would see the paranoia generated by the threat of total annihilation as central to understanding Soviet defence and foreign policy:

the unprecedented threat of devastation is crucial to understanding the mutual hostility and fear of leaders in the nuclear age. It is also argued that without nuclear weapons direct Soviet–American conflict would have been much more likely, and that had nuclear weapons not acted as a deterrent, then war in Europe would have been much more likely. On the other hand, there are those who contend that nuclear weapons played a limited role in East–West relations, and that their importance is exaggerated.

Nuclear weapons have been a focus for political agreement, and during *détente*, nuclear arms agreements acted as the currency of international politics. Yet how close we came to nuclear war in 1961 (Berlin), or 1962 (Cuba), or 1973 (Arab–Israeli war), or 1983 (Exercise *Able Archer*), and what lessons might be learned from these events, are crucial questions for historians and policy-makers alike. One central issue is how far cold war perspectives and the involvement of nuclear-armed superpowers imposed stability in regions where previous instability had led to war and conflict. The cold war may have led to unprecedented concentrations of military and nuclear forces in Europe, but this was a period characterized by stability and great economic prosperity, certainly in the West.

Both the cold war and the age of empire are over, although across the globe their legacies, good and bad, seen and unseen, persist. The age of 'the bomb', and of other weapons of mass destruction (chemical and biological), continues. How far the clash of communist and liberal/capitalist ideologies helped facilitate or retard globalization is a matter for reflection. Despite the limitations of the human imagination, the global consequences of nuclear war remain all too real. The accident at the Soviet nuclear reactor at Chernobyl in 1986 showed that radioactivity knows no boundaries. In the 1980s, scientists suggested that if only a fraction of the world's nuclear weapons exploded over a fraction of the world's cities, it could bring an end to life itself in the northern hemisphere. While the threat of strategic nuclear war has receded, the global problem of nuclear weapons remains a common and urgent concern for humanity in the twenty-first century.

Questions

1 How far was Germany responsible for the outbreak of war in 1914?
2 In what ways was the Versailles Treaty a contributory factor to European political instability in the period 1919–39?
3 Were there effective alternatives to the appeasement of Hitler?
4 Why were atomic bombs dropped on Hiroshima and Nagasaki?
5 Why did the USA become involved in wars in Asia after 1945? Illustrate your answer by reference to either the Korean or Vietnam wars.
6 Compare and contrast American and Soviet objectives during *détente*.
7 Why did France try to remain an imperial power in Indo-China and Algeria?
8 Were the British successful at decolonization after 1945?
9 Compare and contrast the end of empire in Africa with that in Asia after 1945.
10 Did nuclear weapons keep the peace in Europe after 1945?
11 How close did we come to nuclear war during either the Berlin crisis (1961) or the Cuban missile crisis (1962)?
12 What role did nuclear weapons play in Soviet–American relations during the 1980s?

Further Reading

Best, A., Hanhimäki, J. M., Maiolo, J. A., and Schulze, K. E. (2004), *International History of the Twentieth Century* (London: Routledge). A comprehensive and authoritative account of twentieth-century history.

Betts, R. (1998), *Decolonization* (London: Routledge). This book provides an introductory theoretical overview that examines the forces that drove decolonization, and explores interpretations of post-colonial legacies.

Chamberlain, M. E. (1999), *Decolonization: The Fall of the European Empires* (Oxford: Blackwell). An analysis of the end of British, French, and smaller European empires on a region-by-region basis.

Halliday, F. (1986), *The Making of the Second Cold War*, 2nd edn (London: Verso). This book explores the phase in the cold war of Soviet–American antagonism, 1979–85, and places this within a broader thematic and critical analysis of the cold war.

Keylor, W. R. (2006), *The Twentieth Century World and Beyond: An International History since 1900* (Oxford: Oxford University Press). A comprehensive and balanced assessment of twentieth-century international history.

Mueller, J. (1990), *Retreat From Doomsday: The Obsolescence of Major War* (New York: Basic Books). A distinctive perspective on twentieth-century warfare and the importance (or otherwise) of nuclear weapons in international politics.

Newhouse, J. (1989), *The Nuclear Age* (London: Michael Joseph). An accomplished history of nuclear weapons that examines the technological and political aspects of the arms race, from Hiroshima to debates on nuclear strategy in the 1980s.

Reynolds, D. (2000), *One World Divisible: A Global History since 1945* (New York: W. W. Norton). A highly authoritative, comprehensive, and nuanced analysis of world politics since 1945.

Young, J., and Kent. J. (2003), *International Relations since 1945* (Oxford: Oxford University Press). A comprehensive survey of the impact of the cold war on world politics since 1945, providing an analysis of war in the Middle East, the development of European integration, and the demise of the European empires in Africa and Asia.

Online Resource Centre

 Visit the Online Resource Centre that accompanies this book to access more learning resources on this chapter topic at www.oxfordtextbooks.co.uk/orc/baylis5e/

Chapter 4

From the cold war to the world economic crisis

MICHAEL COX

Reader's Guide

This chapter provides a broad overview of the two decades following the end of cold war in 1989. The chapter is divided into three main sections. The first section begins with the unexpected end of the cold war itself. The second section goes on to discuss some—though by no means all—of the main trends of the 1990s, with a special focus on the USA, Europe, Russia, and East Asia. The remainder of the chapter then looks at the so-called 'war on terror' (including the reasons for the war in Iraq), followed by a discussion of the longer-term geopolitical implications of the world economic crisis.

Introduction

Three broad theses will be advanced in this chapter. The first is that even if we speak of the world after 1989 as being 'post cold war', we should never understate the extent to which this world was shaped by the way the cold war ended and the many problems and opportunities it left behind. The second relates to US primacy and notes that even though one of the more obvious structural features of the post-cold-war international system has been a renewed US hegemony—some have even talked of a new American empire—this new position of strength has not easily translated into a coherent foreign policy for the post-cold-war world. The third thesis is that new challenges to the status quo—and there are several, from

terrorism, the spread of nuclear weapons, and growing instability in the Middle East—still look unlikely to have a major impact on the underlying dynamics driving globalization. However, one thing might: the economic crisis that tore through the world's financial system in 2009 leaving several long-term problems in its wake. The longer-term consequences of the first major crisis of capitalism since the 1930s remain to be seen. But even the most optimistic of analysts concede that we have turned an important geopolitical corner as a result, and that the world over the next ten years is likely to be a good deal more disturbed than it was during the last ten. Interesting times lie ahead.

The end of the cold war

When major wars end, they invariably pose enormous problems for those whose task it is to make the peace. This was true following the First World War in 1919. It was more obviously the case in 1945 when the Second World War concluded (see Ch. 3). And it was true once again when the last of the great 'wars' of the twentieth century—the **cold war**—finally wound down in 1989. But what was the cold war and how did its end impact on the international system?

The cold war was the by-product of the Second World War that left the international order divided between two great **superpowers**, both with formidable capabilities—the USA much more so than the USSR—and both representing rival social systems, one socialist, the other capitalist. This rivalry began in Europe when the USSR refused to withdraw from those countries it had originally liberated from Nazism. However, it soon assumed a global character as it shifted to Asia and the wider **Third World**. Here the real costs of the competition were felt most acutely in terms of lives lost (nearly twenty-five million), development strategies thwarted, and democratic aspirations compromised. Elsewhere the results were quite different. Indeed, among the great capitalist powers themselves, the cold war created a degree of unity and cohesion that the world had not witnessed for at least two generations. For this reason many came to view the bipolar system after 1947 as not merely the expression of a given international reality, but something that might be viewed as desirable too.

Certainly realists like Kenneth Waltz came to regard the new international system, in which there were two coherent blocs under the tutelage of a single great power, and two superpowers balancing the imperial aspirations of the other, as more likely to produce stability and order than any of the possible theoretical alternatives.

The cold war should thus be regarded less as a war in the conventional sense—significantly the USSR and the USA never directly engaged in armed hostilities —and more a managed rivalry. This in the main is how policy-makers came to view the relationship; indeed, many came to accept in private (even if it could not be said in public) that their rival had legitimate security concerns that the other should recognize. This in turn helps explain why the cold war remained 'cold'. It also helps explain why the superpowers acted with such caution for the greater part of the cold war era. In fact, given the very real fear of outright nuclear war, the shared aim of the two superpowers was not so much to destroy the other—though a few on both sides occasionally talked in such terms—but more to maintain the peace by containing the ambitions of the other.

All systems operate by rules, and the cold war was no different. One can thus imagine the enormous shock waves produced by the collapse of this system in 1989. Hardly anybody had predicted such a development. Even fewer believed it could ever happen peacefully. Nor had most policy-makers or academics planned for it. Indeed, many in the field of International Relations viewed 1989 as a serious challenge to the so-called scientific status of a discipline that took it for granted that an upheaval on this scale was almost inconceivable. IR scholars may have later done much to help explain why the old order collapsed. However, there was no hiding the fact that the discipline's assumption of continuity rather than change, of stability of the cold war system rather than its eventual disintegration, did much to undermine some of the realist certainties that had helped define the discipline since the end of the Second World War. Indeed, the events of 1989 played a major role in shaping many of the discussions within the field during the 1990s, with an increasingly embattled group of realists (see Ch. 5) continuing to stress the importance of material factors in compelling the USSR towards the negotiating table, and a rising generation of constructivists insisting that the big transformation of the late 1980s was less the by-product of a change in the relative capabilities of either the USSR or the USA and more the result of Gorbachev's adoption of a set of ideas that undermined the logic of confrontation. In this way, a major discussion concerning one critical event in world politics helped to define the great debates that divided scholars of IR in the years thereafter.

> **Box 4.1** The end of an era
>
> 'Gorbachev may have earlier vowed that he would redefine the East–West relationship. In reality he did much more, and whether as a result of Soviet economic decline, a shift in ideas, imperial overstretch, or a simple failure to understand the consequences of his own actions, set off a series of chain reactions that did not just place the relationship on a new footing but brought it to an end for ever.'
>
> *(Michael Cox (2007), 'Hans J. Morgenthau, Realism and the Rise and Fall of the Cold War', in Michael C. Williams (ed.), Realism Reconsidered (Oxford: Oxford University Press): 166)*

> **Key Points**
>
> - The cold war was a complex relationship that assumed competition but remained cold in large part because of the existence of nuclear weapons.
> - Most experts assumed the cold war would continue and were surprised when it came to a peaceful conclusion.
> - The end of the cold war weakened the intellectual hold of realism within International Relations (IR) as an academic discourse and helped popularize constructivism as a methodology.

The USA in a world without balance

If the cold war period was marked by a clear and sharp divide between opposing socio-economic systems, the post-cold-war order could readily be characterized as one where states were compelled to play by a single set of rules within an increasingly integrated world economy. The term most frequently used to describe this new order was **globalization**, a notion that had barely been used before 1989, but now came be to employed more regularly to define an apparently new system of international relations where, according to one reading, markets would come to matter more than states (a much exaggerated thesis), and boundaries and frontiers rendered increasingly porous—almost meaningless—by the sheer volume of cross-border activity (see Part Five). Globalization, however, was not the only obvious by-product of communism's collapse and the opening up of previously closed planned economies. In terms of the distribution of power, the most significant consequence was what appeared to some as the triumph of the USA over its main rival and the emergence of what came to be defined as a new 'unipolar' world system.

Again, this was not something that many would have foreseen before the end of the cold war itself (during the 1970s and 1980s some scholars actually believed that the USA was in decline). Nor at first did academics view this as the most likely outcome of 1989. However, as events began to unfold—most notably following the USA's stunning military victory over Iraq and the collapse of the USSR in 1991—it soon became obvious that the **new world order** that was unfolding was one in which the USA held an especially privileged position. Certainly, as the 1990s unfolded all of the most obvious indicators of power—hard and soft—all seemed to point to only one conclusion: there was now only one serious global player left standing internationally. Indeed, by the turn of the century the popular view was that the USA had been transformed from a mere superpower (its designation until 1989) into what the French foreign minister Hubert Vedrine in 1998 termed a 'hyperpower'.

This new global conjuncture raised a series of important questions. The most central was: how long could this position of primacy actually endure? There was no easy answer. Most realists, unsurprisingly, took it as read that other great powers would in time emerge to balance the USA. Others believed that because it enjoyed special advantage in nearly every sphere, the new US **hegemony** would last well into the twenty-first century. This in turn fed into a second debate concerning the exercise of US power under conditions of **unipolarity**. American liberals tended to advise restraint and the embedding of US power into international institutions as the most effective and acceptable way of exercising global hegemony. Others, of a more nationalist persuasion, argued against such constraint. The USA, they insisted, had the power. It had always used it wisely in the past. And there was no reason to suspect it would not use it wisely again in the future.

For a period, however, the inclination of most US foreign-policy-makers (especially during the Clinton years) was towards restraint. In fact, in spite of its great power advantage, there was no clear indication during the 1990s that the USA was especially enthusiastic to project its power with any serious purpose; indeed,

according to some commentators, it was difficult to know what its purpose was any longer, other than to spread democracy and promote globalization. The USA may have possessed vast **capabilities**, and various American writers may have waxed lyrical about this new 'Rome on the Potomac'. But there appeared to be no real desire in a post-cold-war environment of expending American blood and treasure in foreign adventures. The USA after the cold war was thus a most curious **hegemon**. On the one hand, its power seemed to be unrivalled; on the other, it seemed to have very little idea about how to use this power or whether it really had to. The end of the cold war and the disappearance of the Soviet threat may have rendered the USA more powerful. But it also made it a very reluctant warrior. In a very important sense, the USA during the 1990s remained a superpower without a mission.

Box 4.2 The paradox of power

'There is a paradox between the magnitude of American power and Washington's inability to use that power to always get what it wants in international politics ... hegemony is not omnipotence.'

(Christopher Layne (2006), 'Impotent Power', cited in The National Interest, Sep./Oct. 41–2)

Key Points

- In terms of the balance of power, the end of the cold war, followed by the collapse of the USSR, dramatically increased the USA's weight in the international system.

- By 2000, the popular view was that the USA was more 'hyperpower', than mere 'superpower'.

- The disappearance of a 'clear and present danger' in the form of the USSR and communism made Americans reluctant to use US forces abroad.

- The USA after the cold war might best be described as a 'superpower without a mission'.

Europe: a work in progress

If for the USA the biggest post-cold-war problem was how to develop a coherent global policy in a world where there was no single major threat to its interests, then for Europeans the main issue was how to manage the new enlarged space that had been created as a result of the events in 1989. Indeed, while more triumphant Americans would continue to proclaim that it was they who had actually won the cold war in Europe, it was Europeans who were the real beneficiaries of what had taken place in the late 1980s. There were sound reasons for thinking thus. First, a continent that had once been divided was now whole again. Germany had also been peacefully united. The states of Eastern Europe had achieved one of the most important of international rights: the right of self-determination. Finally, the threat

of serious war with potentially devastating consequences for Europe had been eliminated. Naturally, the transition from one order to another was not going to happen without certain costs being borne, most notably by those who would now have to face up to life under competitive capitalism. Nor was the collapse of communism in some countries an entirely bloodless affair, as events in former Yugoslavia (1990–9) revealed only too tragically. That said, Europe—an enlarged Europe—still had much to look forward to.

But what kind of Europe would it be? To this there was more than one kind of answer, with some, especially the French, believing it should now develop its own specific European security arrangements (an optimism that soon foundered on the killing fields of Bosnia), and others that it should remain closely tied to the USA—a view most forcefully expressed by the new elites of Central Europe themselves. Europeans could not agree either about what kind of Europe they preferred. There were genuine federalists who sought an ever-deeper union that would fulfil the European dream while being able to balance the powerhouses of the USA and Japan. There were others who feared such a development and, marching under the traditional banner of **sovereignty**, managed to play the Eurosceptic card with some success among ordinary Europeans, who seemed more critical of the European project than the elites in Brussels themselves. Finally, Europeans divided over economics, with a clear line being drawn between *dirigistes*, who favoured greater state involvement in the management of a specifically European social model, and free marketers—led by the British—who argued that under conditions of global competition such a protected system was simply not sustainable and that thoroughgoing economic reform was essential.

While many in 'old' Europe debated Europe's future, policy-makers themselves were confronted with the more concrete issue of how to bring the 'East' back into the 'West', a process that went under the general heading of enlargement. In terms of policy outcome, the strategy scored some notable successes. Indeed, by 2007 the European Union had grown to become 27 members (and NATO to 26). In the process, the two bodies also changed their club-like character, much to the consternation of some older members, who found the new entrants to be as much trouble as asset. In fact, according to critics, enlargement had proceeded so rapidly that the essential core meaning of both organizations had been lost. The EU in particular, it was now argued by some, had been so keen to enlarge that it had lost the will to integrate. Still, it was difficult not to be impressed by the capacity of institutions that had helped shape part of Europe during the cold war being employed now in quite new roles to help manage the relatively successful (though never easy) transition from one kind of European order to another. For those realists who had earlier disparaged the part institutions might play in preventing anarchy in Europe, the important roles played by the EU and NATO seemed to prove that institutions were essential.

Institutions alone, though, did not provide a ready answer to what Europe ought or ought not be doing in a world system. Here again there was more than one European view. Hence several analysts continued to feel that Europe was bound to remain a largely 'civilian power', spreading its own values and acting as example,

but should not become a serious military actor. Others took a more robust view. Europe's growing weight in the world economy, they felt, its inability to act as a united organization in former Yugoslavia, not to mention the great capabilities gap that was rapidly opening up between itself and the USA, all compelled Europe to think more seriously about hard power. The result was the birth of the European Security and Defence Policy in 1998, followed by a series of other moves that culminated with the publication of the *European Security Strategy* (*ESS*) in 2003 (EC 2003). Viewing security in broadly globalist terms, where open borders and disturbing events in far-away places—especially poor ones—were bound to spew up their consequences on Europe's shores, Europe, it argued, was compelled by the logic of interdependence to engage far more seriously with international affairs.

Defining a new international role for the EU, however, did not by itself create the instruments or the capabilities for fulfilling this role. Europeans may have wished for a stronger Europe—though by no means all Europeans thought in this way. However, there was marked reluctance by most states to hand over serious security powers to Brussels. Even the final passage of the Lisbon Treaty in late 2009, which advocated (amongst other things) the creation of new posts that would give the EU more voice on the world stage, only passed after much controversy; even then, it was still not clear whether the new foreign policy positions would make for a stronger European role in world affairs. Europe may have travelled a long way since the end of the cold war in 1989. As its many supporters pointed out, how could one judge a project to have been a failure or in crisis when by the end of the first decade of the twenty-first century it had more members than ever, its own functioning currency, and a greater presence abroad than ever before. However, there were still many obstacles to be overcome before Europe could finally (if ever) realize its full global potential. It remained, as it had been since the end of the cold war, a 'work in progress'.

Box 4.3 Europe's mid-life crisis?

'The future of the EU is hard to predict. Over the next decade it could undergo a bout of further integration; it could fall apart into opposing camps of those who would go forward or those who would go back; or perhaps most likely, it could just muddle through.'

(Cited in The Economist, 17–23 March 2007, 'Special Report on the European Union', p. 20)

Key Points

- In spite of the break-up of former Yugoslavia, Europe benefited as much from the end of the cold war as the USA.

- Europeans after the cold war were divided over a series of key issues, most notably the degree of European integration, economic strategy, and the foreign policy aspirations of the European Union.

- The *European Security Strategy* of 2003 was one of the first serious efforts by the EU to think about its international role under conditions of globalization.

- The Lisbon Treaty was finally ratified in 2009 but did not solve the question of Europe's future foreign policy.

Russia: from Yeltsin to Putin and Medvedev

One of the many problems facing the West after the cold war was how to define its relationship with post-communist Russia, a country confronting several degrees of stress after 1991 as it began to travel the road that would one day move it (it was hoped) from what it had once been—a superpower with a planned economy and a formal Marxist ideology (see Ch. 8)—to what it might one day become—democratic, liberal, and market-oriented. As even the most sanguine of Europeans accepted, none of this was ever going to be easy for a state that had had the same system for nearly three-quarters of a century. And so it proved during the 1990s, an especially painful decade during which Russia moved from being what it had once been before—a superpower that could effectively challenge the USA—to a declining power with diminishing economic and ideological assets. Nor was there much by way of economic compensation. On the contrary, as a result of its speedy adoption of Western-style privatization, Russia experienced something close to a 1930s-style depression, with industrial production plummeting, living standards falling, and whole regions once devoted to cold war military production experiencing free fall. President Boris Yeltsin's foreign policy, meanwhile, did little to reassure many Russians. Indeed, his decision to get close to Russia's old capitalist enemies gave the distinct impression that he was selling out to the West. This may have made him a hero outside Russia. However, to many ordinary Russians it seemed as if he (like his predecessor Gorbachev) was conceding everything and getting very little in return. Nationalists (see Ch. 24) and old communists, of whom there were still a significant number, were especially scathing. Yeltsin and his team, they argued, had not only given away Russia's assets at knock-down prices to a new class of oligarchs, but he was also trying to turn Russia into a Western dependency. In short, he was not standing up for Russia's **national interest**.

Whether his successor Vladimir Putin had a clear vision for Russia when he took over the presidency mattered less than the fact that, having assumed office, he began to stake out very different positions. These included a greater nationalism at home, a much clearer recognition that the interests of Russia and those of the West would not always be one and the same, and what turned into a persistent drive to ensure that the Russian economy—and Russia's huge natural resources—served the purposes of the state and not just the new rich and their Western friends. Putin also redefined the notion of democracy and gave it what he saw as a distinctly Russian or sovereign character in which the outward form of democracy remained intact while its inner content in terms of an independent parliament and equal access to a free media was gradually hollowed out. Nor did he (or his successor Medvedev) win many friends in the liberal West with their brutal policies towards break-away Chechnya and apparent indifference towards human rights more generally. Nor was Russia's image problem helped by the brutal murder of several journalists within Russia itself—Anna Politkovskaya being perhaps the most famous—and the even more bizarre killing of former Russian official and dissident in London, Alexander Litvinenko, in 2006.

These shifts inside Russia produced much confusion in the West. At first the Americans and the Europeans turned something of a blind eye to these developments on the realist assumption that it was important to work closely with Russia, partly for economic reasons—trade was rising—partly because of its geographical proximity to Europe, and partly because Russia was, after all, a permanent member of the UN Security Council and a nuclear weapons state. However, the cumulative impact of Putin's policies could not but damage Russia's relationship with the West. Taken together, they did not lead to what some at the time persisted in calling—very loosely—a 'new' cold war. What it did mean, though, was that the West could no longer regard Russia as for ever being what it had earlier hoped it would become some years before: a 'strategic partner' engaged in a more or less smooth transition towards 'normal' liberal democracy.

Still, the West had much less to fear now than it had during the cold war proper. Russia, after all, was not the same geographical entity as the USSR. Economic reform meanwhile had made it dependent on Western markets. And ideologically the new Russia hardly represented a serious global rival. To this degree there was much less for the West to be concerned about. In fact, according to many Russians, it was not the West that should fear Russia, but rather Russia that should be worried about the machinations of the West in general and the USA in particular, as both tried to extend their economic and strategic ties into what Moscow continued to view as its own backyard. It had 'lost' the three Baltic republics to the West in the 1990s; it was therefore determined to make sure it did not now lose Ukraine or Georgia. On this there would be no compromise. The scene was thus set for further conflict. In Ukraine this took the form of growing economic pressure. Towards Georgia the policy was more aggressive still, especially following the election of American-linked and pro-NATO President Mikheil Saakashvili. By 2006 relations had become distinctly tense; by 2007 extremely bad; and by 2008 altogether poisonous—reaching a tragic impasse in August of the same year when Russia and Georgia finally went

to war with one another. Given Russia's overwhelming military superiority, the outcome of the conflict was a foregone conclusion. Equally predictable was the negative impact the war had on Western and American opinion. Indeed, in the USA especially, many Americans regarded Russia's war of aggression against tiny (though not entirely blameless) Georgia as a major turning-point that signalled the beginning of a long-drawn-out competition between the democratic West on the one hand and authoritarian Russia on the other.

Thus nearly twenty years after the USSR's disintegration, and a decade or more after Yeltsin had passed from office, the outlook looked grim. Admittedly President Obama did seek to 'reset the button' on the Russia–USA relationship when he assumed office in 2009. There were also important areas where the two countries would continue to find common purpose, most notably over controlling the spread of nuclear weapons. However, no amount of fine diplomacy or soothing words could completely restore the trust that had been lost. A problematic future therefore beckoned.

Key Points

- The first Russian President, Boris Yeltsin, sought a new partnership with the West but was often accused by his domestic enemies of not defending the Russian national interest.
- Vladimir Putin and his successor Medvedev have pursued more authoritarian policies at home, brought Russia's economic assets back under state control, and pursued a more nationalist foreign policy abroad.
- A new cold war between the West and Russia is unlikely because of the important economic and political changes that have occurred in Russia since the collapse of the USSR in 1991.
- The war in Georgia in August 2008 saw a near collapse in Russia's relations with the USA and the West.

East Asia: primed for rivalry?

If history continues to play a crucial role in shaping modern Western images of post-Soviet Russia—and Russian images of the West—then the past also plays a part in defining the international relations of East Asia; and a most bloody past it had been since the Second World War, punctuated by several devastating wars (in China, Korea, and Vietnam), revolutionary insurgencies (in the Philippines, Malaya, and Indonesia),

authoritarian rule (nearly everywhere), and revolutionary extremism (most tragically in Cambodia). The contrast with the post-war European experience could not have been more pronounced. In fact, scholars of International Relations have been much taken with the comparison, pointing out that whereas Europe managed to form a new liberal security community during the cold war, East Asia did not (see Ch. 26). In part this was the result of the formation of the EU and the creation of NATO (organizations of which there were no equivalent in Asia). But it was also because Germany managed to effect a serious reconciliation with its immediate neighbours while Japan (for largely internal reasons) did not. Nor did the end of the cold war do much to bring about a speedy resolution of these various issues. In fact, whereas the end of the cold war in Europe transformed the continent dramatically, this was much less true in East Asia, where powerful communist parties continued to rule—in China, North Korea, and Vietnam—and at least two outstanding territorial disputes (one less important one between Japan and Russia, and a potentially far more dangerous one between China and Taiwan) continued to threaten the security of the region.

For all these reasons, one very influential American scholar, Aaron Friedberg, argued in an equally influential article in 1993 that, far from being 'primed for peace', East Asia was still ripe for new rivalries. Indeed, according to Aaron Friedberg, Europe's very bloody past between 1914 and 1945 could easily turn into Asia's future. This was not a view shared by every commentator, however. In fact, as events unfolded, this uncompromisingly tough-minded realist perspective came under sustained criticism. This did not deny the possibility of future disturbances; how could one argue otherwise, given Korean division, North Korea's nuclear programme, and China's claim to Taiwan? But it did suggest that the region was not quite the powder-keg painted by Friedberg. There were several reasons why.

The first and most important reason was the great economic success experienced by the region itself. The sources of this have been much debated, with some suggesting that the underlying reasons were cultural (Asian values—see Ch. 25), others that it was directly economic (cheap labour plus plentiful capital), and a few that it was the by-product of the application of a non-liberal model of development employing the strong state to drive through rapid economic development from above. Some have also argued that the USA played a crucial role by opening its market to East Asian goods while providing the region with critical security on the cheap. Whatever the cause or combination of causes, the simple fact remains that East Asia by the end of the twentieth century had become the third powerhouse in the global economy, accounting for nearly 25 per cent of world GDP.

Second, although many states in East Asia might have had powerful memories of past conflicts, these were beginning to be overridden in the 1990s by a growth in regional trade and investment. Indeed, although East Asia carried much historical baggage (some of this deliberately exploited by political elites in search of legitimacy), economic pressures and material self-interest appeared to be driving countries in the region together rather than apart. The process of East Asian economic integration may have been slow to develop (**ASEAN** was formed only in 1967). Nor was integration accompanied by the formation of anything like the European Union. However, once regionalism began to take off during the 1990s, it showed no signs of slowing down.

A third reason for optimism lay with Japan. Here, in spite of an apparent inability unambiguously to apologize for past misdeeds and atrocities—a failure that cost it dear in terms of soft power **influence** in the region— its policies could hardly be characterized as disturbing. On the contrary, having adopted its famous peace constitution in the 1950s and renounced the possibility of ever acquiring nuclear weapons (see Ch. 23) (Japan was one the strongest upholders of the original Non-Proliferation Treaty), Japan demonstrated no interest at all in upsetting its suspicious neighbours by acting in anything other than a benign manner. Furthermore, by spreading its not inconsiderable largesse in the form of aid and large-scale investment, it went some of the way to foster better international relations in the region. Even its old rival China was a significant beneficiary, and by 2003 over 5,000 Japanese companies were operating on the Chinese mainland.

This leads us to China itself. Much has been written about 'rising China', especially by realists who argue— in classical fashion—that when new powerful states emerge on to the international stage they are bound to disturb the peace. China may look benign now, they agree. That, however, is not how things will look in a few years' time—once it has risen. Again, though, there may be more cause for guarded optimism than for pessimism, largely because China itself has adopted policies (both economic and military) whose purpose is clearly to reassure its neighbours that it can rise peacefully and thus effectively prove the realists wrong. It has also translated these reassuring words into concrete policies by supporting regional integration, exporting its not inconsiderable capital to other countries in East Asia, and working as a responsible state rather than as a spoiler inside regional multilateral institutions. Certainly, such policies are beginning to bear fruit, with once-sceptical neighbours—even possibly Japan—increasingly now

Box 4.5 The China challenge

'The task of creating more effective institutions to deal with short-term threats to regional stability is made all the more urgent because in the long run there is a very real structural transformation taking place that could alter the relatively benign constellation of factors currently at play: namely the rise of China.'

(Thomas Berger (2000), 'Set for Stability? Prospects for Conflict and Cooperation in East Asia', Review of International Studies, 26: 427–8)

viewing China as a benign instrument of development rather than of threat.

In the end, though, all strategic roads in China (and in East Asia as a whole) lead to the one state whose presence in the region remains critical: the USA. Although theoretically opposed to a unipolar world in which there is only one significant global player, the new Chinese leadership has pursued a most cautious policy towards the USA. No doubt some Americans will continue to be wary of a state run by the Communist Party whose human rights record (see Ch. 30) can hardly be described as exemplary. However, so long as China continues to act in a cooperative fashion, of bandwagonning rather than balancing, there is every chance that relations will continue to prosper. But there is no guaranteeing the long-term outcome. With growth rates running at something like 10 per cent per annum, with its apparently insatiable demand for overseas raw materials, and enormous dollar reserves at

its disposal, China has already changed the terms of the debate about the future of international politics. For some time to come, it may well remain what one observer has called a 'colossus with feet of clay', overly dependent on foreign investment and still militarily light-years behind the USA. But even such a colossus presents a set of challenges that simply did not exist in the much simpler days of the cold war. Indeed, one of the great ironies of international history may be that China as a rising capitalist power playing by the rules of the market may turn out to be more of a problem for the West than China the communist power in those far-off days when it denounced the imperialists across the ocean and called upon Asians to drive the Yankees out of the region.

Key Points

- Compared to Europe after 1945, the international relations of East Asia during the cold war were highly volatile, marked by revolutions, wars, and insurgencies.

- The end of the cold war left many issues in its wake and led Aaron Friedberg (1993) to conclude that Asia was primed for further rivalry.

- Friedberg's thesis has been challenged as being too pessimistic: economic growth, regional integration, the USA's presence, and Japan's peaceful foreign policy continue to make the region less dangerous than he suggested.

- One of the big questions now facing the region and the USA is 'rising China'. Realists insist it will challenge the status quo. Others believe it can rise peacefully.

The war on terror: from 9/11 to Iraq

If the end of the cold war marked one of the great turning-points of the late twentieth century, **11 September 2001** was a reminder that the international order that had come into being as a result was not one that found ready acceptance everywhere. Bin Laden was no doubt motivated by far more than a distaste for globalization and American primacy. As his many would-be analysts have pointed out, his vision was one that pointed back to a golden age of Islam rather than forward to something modern. That said, his chosen method of attacking the USA using four planes, his use of video to communicate with followers, his employment of the global financial system to fund operations, and his primary goal of driving the USA out of the Middle East (whose control by the West was essential to the continued working of

the modern international economy) could hardly be described as medieval. US policy-makers certainly did not regard him as some odd thro back to earlier times. Indeed, the fact that he threatened to use the most modern and dangerous weapons—namely **weapons of mass destruction**—to achieve his objectives made him a very modern threat, but one that could not be dealt with by the kind of traditional means developed during the cold war. As the Bush administration constantly reiterated, this new danger meant that old methods, such as containment and deterrence, were no longer relevant. If this was the beginning of a 'new' cold war, as some argued at the time, then it was one unlikely to be fought using policies and methods learned between 1947 and 1989.

The very peculiar character of this new non-state threat led by a man whose various pronouncements owed more to holy texts than anything else made it difficult for some in the West to understand the true character of radical Islamic terrorism. A few believed that the threat was more existential than serious, more functionally useful for the USA in its quest for global pre-eminence than actually genuine. Furthermore, as the controversial **war on terror** unfolded—first in Afghanistan and then in other parts of the world—a few critics of a more radical persuasion began to wonder where the real danger actually lay. Indeed, as the USA began to flex its not inconsiderable military muscle and widened the war on terror to include Iraq, North Korea, and Iran, some began to turn their critical attention away from the original threat posed by radical Islamism towards the USA itself. In this way the original target of **9/11** was transformed from the early status of victim into the imperial source of most of the world's unfolding problems (see Ch. 22).

The various controversies surrounding the Bush administration's responses to international **terrorism** should not, however, obscure one simple fact: the impact that 9/11 was to have upon both the USA and US foreign policy more generally. Most obviously, the new threat environment provided the USA with a fixed point of reference around which to organize its international affairs; and organize it did, in the shape of building close relations with those many states—Russia, India, and China perhaps being the more important—that were now prepared to join it in waging a global war against terror. The events of 9/11 also compelled the USA to act in a far more assertive fashion abroad. Indeed, some of Bush's more conservative supporters believed that one of the reasons for the attack on the USA in the first place was that it had not been assertive enough in the 1990s. Finally, in what some saw as a near revolution in US foreign policy, the Bush team seemed to abandon the defence of the status quo in the Middle East. The events of 9/11, they argued, had changed the original formula whereby the USA turned a blind eye to autocratic regimes that existed in the region in exchange for cheap oil and stability. This was no longer enough, especially when it involved the USA doing deals with states such as Saudi Arabia that produced the dangerous ideologies that had inspired those who had flown those planes on 9/11, or who directly or indirectly had given (and were still giving) aid and comfort to terrorists around the world.

In this way the intellectual ground was prepared for the war against Iraq in 2003. The war, though, remains something of a conundrum. After all, Iraq had not been involved in 9/11, the regime itself was secular, and it shared the same goal as the USA in at least one respect: of seeking to contain the geopolitical ambitions of Islamic Iran. For all these reasons, different analysts have identified rather different factors to explain the war, ranging from the ideological influence exercised by the 'neo-cons' on President Bush, the USA's close relationship with Israel, and its desire to control Iraq's oil. No doubt all these things fed in to the final decision. However, one is left with more questions than easy answers, with possibly the most credible answer being the less conspiratorial one that the USA went to war partly because it thought it would win fairly easily, partly because it got its intelligence wrong, and partly because it thought—rather unwisely—that building a new regime in Iraq would be just as easy as getting rid of the old one.

Whatever the original calculations made by those who planned this least realist of all modern wars, it is by now clear that this so-called 'war of choice' was a strategic blunder that neither delivered stable democracy to Iraq nor inspired others in the region to undertake serious political reform. It has also had the doubly dangerous consequence of disturbing the whole of the Middle East, while making it possible for Iran to gain even greater influence in the region. Finally, as result of its action in Iraq, the USA and its allies have provided radical Islamists around the world with a rallying point that they appear to have exploited with some skill. The bombings in London and Madrid were no doubt the result of many factors; however, few now believe they were entirely unconnected to what had been happening in the Middle East since 2003.

With or without Iraq, however, the West still confronted a challenge in the form of violent radical Islam,

---

Box 4.6 End the crusade

'The debacle that is Iraq reaffirms the lesson that there is no such thing as a good crusade. This was true a thousand years ago when those European Christian knights tried to impose their faith and way of life on the holy Land—and is equally true today.... Divine missions and sensible foreign policy just don't go together.'

(Dimitri K. Simes (2007), 'End the Crusade', in The National Interest, 87 (Jan. – Feb.): 5)

Case Study The Iraq War and its origins

International relations as a field has always been concerned to understand the origins of wars. Long-term changes in the balance of power, fear of encirclement, imperial ambition—not to mention misperception and ideology—have all been employed at one time or another to explain why states engage in military action. The Iraq War presents a useful, and possibly difficult, test case for various theories of war origins. Several competing explanations have been advanced so far to explain the US decision to go to war against Iraq in 2003. These include, among others, the official argument that Iraq represented a serious and potentially rising threat to a critically important region; the more material-

ist thesis that the USA was determined to secure direct control of Iraq's massive reserves of oil; and the popular claim that the war was the product of pressures arising from within the USA itself—here identified as the Israel lobby, the ideologically inclined neo-conservatives, and their various supporters on the Christian Right. The student of world politics, however, is left with a number of unanswered questions. First, would the war have happened without the quite unexpected election of George W. Bush in late 2000? In other words, didn't the individual make a huge difference to the decision taken? Second, could Bush have then taken the USA to war without the profound shock created by the equally unexpected attack of 9/11? To this extent, wasn't the war largely the by-product of fear and insecurity as much as anything else? Third, what role did British Prime Minister Tony Blair play? Indeed, was this a war made possible by an alliance with a middle-range power? Fourth, would it have been feasible at all if various American writers had not thought the USA so powerful that it could more or less do anything in the world? To what extent, in other words, did the notion of the 'unipolar moment' contribute to the final decision to go to war? Furthermore, were the intellectual grounds for the war not also laid by those during the post-cold-war period who thought it wise to promote democracy and encouraged others to intervene into the internal affairs of sovereign states for humanitarian purposes? Finally, to what extent could one argue that the Iraq War was in the US national interest; and if it was, then why did so many realists oppose the war?

one that not only fed off Western blunders and policies (especially American ones in the Middle East), but a set of cultural values, state practices, and historical grievances that made it almost impossible to deal with effectively—without compromising what it meant to be part of the West. Herein, though, lay another problem: how precisely to define this conflict. It was certainly not fashionable among some to characterize it as one between two different 'civilizations' (a term originally made popular by the American writer Samuel Huntington back in 1993). Nevertheless, there was something distinctly uncompromising about a conflict between those who on the one side supported democracy, pluralism, individualism, and a separation between state and church, and those on the other who preached intolerance and supported **theocracy** while calling for armed struggle and *jihad* against the unbeliever, the Zionists and their supporters in the West. Nor did there seem to any end in sight to this particular conflict. Motivated by a sense of the injustices done to Moslems around the

world—most visibly the Palestinians—and spurred on by a vision of paradise in which there would always be a hallowed place for those who had died in the name of their faith, there would always be enough martyrs in the world to carry on the struggle against the enemy from Pakistan to the streets of Bradford, from Jakarta to the skies over Detroit.

Key Points

- September 11 effectively brought the post-cold war era to an end and in the process transformed US foreign policy.

- The war to remove Saddam Hussein was sold as part of the war on terror; very few analysts, however, saw a connection between Iraq and 9/11.

- The reasons for going to war in Iraq have been much disputed, although most people now believe it was a strategic error.

- The struggle between violent *jihad* and the West shows no signs of abating.

The world economic crisis

In the midst of this ongoing 'war' against global terror, two things happened that appeared to change world politics for ever: one was internal to the USA and involved the critical transition from one president who had been defined by 9/11 to a new leader who sought to change the terms of the debate about the USA's role in the world; and the other was very directly linked to another great event in world politics—the near meltdown of the world's financial system in 2007 and 2008. These apparently unrelated events were, in fact, very closely connected. Thus as the USA began to grow weary of fighting an ethically problematic and highly costly war against a hydra-headed enemy abroad, it turned to one of the few serious American politicians who had been most vocal in his opposition to the way in which the 'war' had been conducted (Barack Obama had voted against the Iraq war and had for a long time called for the USA to abandon some of the more morally dubious means it had employed in combating terrorism). Then, as it confronted what looked like an economic catastrophe in the autumn of 2008, Americans in their majority transferred their support away from one party (the Republicans), who had hitherto seen 'government' as the problem, to another (the Democrats), who accepted that if the USA were to avoid another great depression it would have to adopt a set of radical policies that did not shy away ideologically from using the state to save the market from itself. Barack Obama may have been no radical. However, he did promise a new start to a nation facing a very real and measurable crisis. Indeed, when Americans voted for the first black President in late 2008—and did so in very large numbers—they did so less so out of confidence and more out of fear in the hope that he would restore the USA's diminished standing abroad and bring back some sense of economic normality at home.

In large part Barack Obama succeeded in fulfilling his early and immediate promise. Thus within a year of his election the prestige of the USA had never been higher (especially in Europe). On the home front, meanwhile, the financial system did at last begin to acquire some degree of stability (although only after the most unorthodox economic measures had been adopted). Still, there was no hiding the damage that had been done. Nor did there seem to any quick 'Obama fix' to any one of the several problems still confronting the world's most significant power. Indeed, in one area in particular—the

Middle East—things seemed to get worse, in spite of Obama's efforts to engage Iran, talk to the Palestinians and Israelis together, withdraw from Iraq, and build bridges to the Muslim public opinion. Moreover, like all inspirational leaders who promise reform, he found that it was easier to talk change than to bring it about. Indeed, one of the great problems he faced during his first year in office was that many of the promises he made in the field of foreign policy all came close to foundering—without crashing completely—on the rocks of hard reality. Obama was undoubtedly talented and committed to doing international relations in a very different way from his predecessor. Yet, even a leader as capable and articulate as Obama could not bring about a new agreement covering global climate change (note here the failure at Copenhagen in December 2009), or compel the Russians to become more sensitive to Western positions, or induce his allies in NATO to commit many more active troops to fighting on the ground in the escalating war in Afghanistan (what he termed a war of 'necessity' as distinct from the war of 'choice' in Iraq. Election promises were one thing; making the world a better or more secure place was something else altogether.

Nor could Obama's elevated rhetoric alter something that was fast becoming obvious to most observers in the second decade of the twenty-first century: the economic crisis itself had brought about a profound shift in the international order. Twenty years previously, in 1989, communism had collapsed and American-style liberal capitalism had triumphed, creating the conditions for a new world order (see Ch. 7). This had not made the 1990s perfectly peaceful. Nor had it eliminated danger. But it had provided the most stunning answer possible as to where the future might lie—namely with the West and the kind of economic system for so long associated with and championed by the USA. Now, with the unfolding of a crisis that was very much 'made in America' by an American economic system that celebrated the hidden hand of the market over regulation and government direction, a corner had been turned, one that weakened both the global attractiveness of the American economic model as well as its capacity to act and solve global problems alone. This may have produced the necessary impetus leading to the election of a president of hope in the shape of Barack Obama. On the other hand, it could not but make the world a less stable place and the USA's position within it less secure.

Key Points

- Barack Obama was elected in 2008 in the midst of the deepest financial crisis in the USA since the 1930s.

- His foreign policy aimed to correct many of the errors committed by the Bush administration—notably in the Middle East

- His comprehensive approach to world affairs raised US standing but by itself could not solve the many challenges facing the USA.

- The economic crisis has left the USA in a weakened international position.

Conclusion

Thus, nearly twenty years after the end of a cold war that had produced such high expectations—some of them illusory—the world seemed to be facing a more uncertain future. One should not exaggerate, of course. In Europe, peace reigned. Great power war was not about to destroy the structure of the international system. The actual numbers being killed in wars around the world was on the decline. Globalization meanwhile continued to benefit more people than it disadvantaged. Still, in spite of these many obvious and positive features, the future contained many uncertainties, especially perhaps for the USA, a hegemon by any measure but one that seemed fast to be losing its capacity either to lead others or to solve the many challenges confronting it. It may be too soon to talk—as some are already beginning to—of the end of the American era, or (more dramatically) of the collapse of what some of late have been calling a 'new' American empire. It is certainly premature to predict somebody else's century replacing that of the USA. But only a few years after the collapse of its main ideological foe in the shape of the USSR, the USA no longer looked or sounded as self-confident as it once did when it appeared to be riding high during the glory days of the 1990s. Pundits have predicted the decline of the USA before—and been proved wrong. This time some believe they may be right. Perhaps another world order beckons.

Questions

1 How have scholars of International Relations attempted to explain the end of the cold war?
2 Why did liberal theorists assume that the world would become a more stable place after the end of the cold war, and why did realists disagree with them?
3 If the USA won the cold war, why did it have such problems defining a grand strategy for itself after 1989 and before 9/11?
4 What is new about globalization?
5 How successfully has Europe adapted to the challenges facing it since the end of the cold war?
6 Is the West facing a new cold war with post-communist Russia?
7 Is China's rise bound to lead to conflict with the USA?
8 Can East Asia avoid new conflicts in the future?
9 What do you understand by the term 'war on terror'?
10 Why did the USA go to war against Iraq?
11 What are the main foreign policy problems facing the administration of President Barack Obama?
12 Is globalization under threat because of the world economic crisis?

Further Reading

Bisley, N. (2006), *Rethinking Globalization* (Basingstoke: Palgrave). The best single volume on the subject.

Booth, K., and Dunne, T. (eds) (2002), *Worlds in Collision* (Basingstoke: Palgrave). This is a collection of short, well-written essays on the world after 9/11.

Cox, M., Booth, K., and Dunne, T. (eds) (1999), *The Interregnum: Controversies in World Politics, 1989–1999* (Cambridge: Cambridge University Press). A wide-ranging survey of most of the key issues facing the world after 1989.

Cox, M., Ikenberry, G. J., and Inoguchi, T. (eds) (2000), *American Democracy Promotion: Impulses, Strategies, and Impacts* (Oxford: Oxford University Press). This book looks at a critically important and neglected facet of US foreign policy.

Cox, M. and Stokes D. (eds) (2008), *US Foreign Policy* (Oxford University Press). A comprehensive survey.

Held, D. et al. (2005), *Debating Globalization* (Cambridge: Polity Press). A useful collection of opposing views.

Leonard, M. (2005), *Why Europe will Run the 21st Century* (London: Fourth Estate). A now unfashionably optimistic perspective on the future of Europe.

O'Meara, P., Mehlinger, H. D., and Krain, M. (eds) (2000), *Globalization and the Challenges of a New Century* (Bloomington, IN: Indiana University Press). This is a very useful collection of many well-known essays about global order and disorder.

Ruthven, M. (2002), *A Fury for God: The Islamist Attack on America* (London: Granta Books). This is a fine analysis of the ideology of radical Islamism.

Sifry, M. L., and Cerf, C. (eds) (2003), *The Iraq Reader* (New York: Touchstone Books). The best collection on the debate to go to war.

Zakaria, F. (2008) *The post-American World* (New York: W.W. Norton). Influential study of the emerging new world order after Bush.

Online Resource Centre

 Visit the Online Resource Centre that accompanies this book to access more learning resources on this chapter topic at www.oxfordtextbooks.co.uk/orc/baylis5e/

Part Two
Theories of world politics

In this part of the book we introduce you to the main theories that try to explain world politics. We have two main aims: **first**, we want you to be able to grasp the main themes of the theories that have been most influential in explaining world politics. To this end, we have included in this part chapters on the six main theoretical perspectives on world politics: realism, liberalism, Marxism, social constructivism, poststructuralism and postcolonialism. Of these, realism has been by far the most influential theory but, as we mentioned in the Introduction, it has also attracted fierce criticism for being an ideology masquerading as an objective theory. Most of the history of International Relations theory has seen a dispute between realism and its liberal and Marxist rivals, with the debate between realism and liberalism being the most long-standing and well developed. For this reason we have a chapter on contemporary mainstream debates between neo-realists and neo-liberals. This is followed by a chapter on the increasingly important approach of social constructivism. We then introduce you to other recent theoretical work in world politics, in two new chapters.

These focus on poststructuralism and postcolonialism. Given the growing importance of explicitly normative approaches to world politics, the section ends with a chapter on international ethics. So, by the end of this part we hope that you will be able to understand the main themes of the various theories and be able to assess their comparative strengths and weaknesses.

Our **second** aim is to give you the overview of theory that you need to be able to assess the significance of globalization for an understanding of world politics. After reading these chapters on theory, we hope that you will be in a better position to see how these theories of world politics might interpret globalization in different ways. We feel that you should then be able to decide for yourself both which interpretation you find most convincing and what kind of evidence you might find in the remaining parts of the book to enable you to be able to work out just how much globalization marks a new distinct stage in world politics, requiring new theories, or whether it is simply a fad or fashion that might alter the surface of world politics but not its main underlying features.

ORC in the spotlight: key terms

Glossary

Absolute gains: all states seek to gain more power and influence in the system to secure their national interests. This is absolute gain. Offensive neo-realists are also concerned with increasing power relative to other states. One must have enough power to secure interests and more power than any other state in the system—friend or foe.
Abuse: states justify self-interested wars by reference to humanitarian principles.
Agent-structure problem: the problem is how to think about the relationship between agents and structures. One view is that agents are born with already formed identities and interests and then treat other actors and the broad structure that their interactions produce as a constraint on their interests. But this suggests that actors are pre-social to the extent that there is little interest in their identities or possibility that they might change their interests through their interactions with others. Another view is to treat the structure not as a constraint but rather as constituting the actors themselves. Yet this might treat agents as cultural dupes because they are nothing more than artefacts of that structure. The pro-

synonymous with a craven collapse before the demands of dictators—encouraging, not disarming, their aggressive designs.
ASEAN (Association of Southeast Asian Nations): a geopolitical and economic organization of several countries located in Southeast Asia. Initially formed as a display of solidarity against Communism, its aims now have been redefined and broadened to include the acceleration of economic growth and the promotion of regional peace. By 2005 the ASEAN countries had a combined GDP of about $884 billion.
Asian financial crisis: the severe disruption to the economies of Thailand, South Korea, Malaysia, the Philippines and Indonesia in 1997/1998, starting as huge international speculation against the prevailing price of those five countries' currencies and then spreading to intense balance sheet problems for their banking sectors.
Asymmetrical globalization: describes the way in which contemporary globalization is unequally experienced across the world and among different social groups in such a way that it produces a distinctive geography of

Not sure of the difference between unipolarity and multipolarity? Struggle to define INGOs and GDL? Visit www.oxfordtextbooks. co.uk/orc/baylis5e/ for flashcard glossaries and multiple choice questions to learn and memorize all of the key terms.

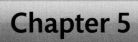

Chapter 5

Realism

TIM DUNNE · BRIAN C. SCHMIDT

Reader's Guide

Realism is the dominant theory of International Relations. Why? Because it provides the most powerful explanation for the state of war that is the regular condition of life in the international system. This is the bold claim made by realists in defence of their tradition, a claim that will be critically examined in this chapter. The second section will ask whether there is one realism or a variety of realisms. The argument presented below suggests that despite important differences, particularly between classical and structural realism, it is possible to identify a shared core set of assumptions and ideas. The third section outlines these common elements, which we identify as self-help, statism, and survival. In the final section, we return to the question of how far realism is relevant for explaining or understanding the globalization of world politics. Although there are many voices claiming that a new set of forces is challenging the Westphalian state system, realists are generally sceptical of these claims, arguing that the same basic patterns that have shaped international politics in the past remain just as relevant today.

Introduction: the timeless wisdom of realism

The story of **realism** most often begins with a mythical tale of the idealist or utopian writers of the inter-war period (1919–39). Writing in the aftermath of the First World War, the 'idealists', a term that realist writers have retrospectively imposed on the inter-war scholars, focused much of their attention on understanding the cause of war so as to find a remedy for its existence. Yet, according to the **realists**, the inter-war scholars' approach was flawed in a number of respects. For example, they ignored the role of power, overestimated the degree to which human beings were rational, mistakenly believed that **nation-states** shared a set of interests, and were overly optimistic that humankind could overcome the scourge of war. The outbreak of the Second World War in 1939 confirmed, for the realists at least, the inadequacies of the idealists' approach to studying international politics.

A new approach, one based on the timeless insights of realism, replaced the discredited idealist approach.[1] Histories of the academic field of International Relations describe a Great Debate that took place in the late 1930s and early 1940s between the inter-war idealists and a new generation of realist writers, which included E. H. Carr, Hans J. Morgenthau, Reinhold Niebuhr, and others, who all emphasized the ubiquity of power and the competitive nature of politics among nations. The standard account of the Great Debate is that the realists emerged victorious, and the rest of the International Relations story is, in many respects, a footnote to realism. It is important to note, however, that at its inception, there was a need for realism to define itself against an alleged 'idealist' position. From 1939 to the present, leading theorists and policy-makers have continued to view the world through realist lenses. Realism taught American leaders to focus on interests rather than on ideology, to seek peace through strength, and to recognize that great powers can coexist even if they have antithetical values and beliefs. The fact that realism offers something of a 'manual' for maximizing the interests of the **state** in a hostile environment explains in part why it remains the dominant tradition in the study of world politics. The theory of realism that prevailed after the Second World War is often claimed to rest on an older, classical tradition of thought. Indeed, many contemporary realist writers often claim to be part of an ancient tradition of thought that includes such illustrious figures as Thucydides (c.

460–406 BC), Niccolò Machiavelli (1469–1527), Thomas Hobbes (1588–1679), and Jean-Jacques Rousseau (1712–78). The insights that these realists offered into the way in which state leaders should conduct themselves in the realm of international politics are often grouped under the doctrine of *raison d'état*, or **reason of state**. Together, writers associated with *raison d'état* are seen as providing a set of maxims to leaders on how to conduct their foreign affairs so as to ensure the security of the state.

According to the historian Friedrich Meinecke, *raison d'état* is the fundamental principle of international conduct, the **state**'s First Law of Motion. 'It tells the statesman what he must do to preserve the health and strength of the State' (1957: 1). Most importantly, the state, which is identified as the key actor in international politics, must pursue power, and it is the duty of the statesperson to calculate rationally the most appropriate steps that should be taken so as to perpetuate the life of the state in a hostile and threatening environment. For realists of all stripes, the survival of the state can never be guaranteed, because the use of force culminating in war is a legitimate instrument of statecraft. As we shall see, the assumption that the state is the principal actor, coupled with the view that the environment that states inhabit is a perilous place, helps to define the essential core of realism. There is, however, one issue in particular that theorists associated with *raison d'état*, and classical realism more generally, were concerned with: the role, if any, that morals and ethics occupy in international politics.

Realists are sceptical of the idea that universal moral principles exist and, therefore, warn state leaders against sacrificing their own self-interests in order to adhere to some indeterminate notion of 'ethical' conduct. Moreover, realists argue that the need for survival requires state leaders to distance themselves from traditional morality, which attaches a positive value to caution, piety, and the greater good of humankind as a whole. Machiavelli argued that these principles were positively harmful if adhered to by state leaders. It was imperative that state leaders learned a different kind of morality, which accorded not with traditional Christian virtues but with political necessity and prudence. Proponents of *raison d'état* often speak of a **dual moral standard**: one moral standard for individual citizens living inside the state and a different standard for the state in its external relations with other states. Justification for the two moral standards stems from the fact that the conditions of international politics often make it necessary for state leaders to act in a manner (for example, cheating, lying, killing) that would be entirely unacceptable for the individual. But before we reach the conclusion that realism is completely immoral, it is important to add that proponents of *raison d'état* argue that the state itself represents a moral force, for it is the existence of the state that creates the possibility for an ethical **political community** to exist domestically. Preserving the life of the state and the ethical community it envelops becomes a moral duty of the statesperson. Thus it is not the case that realists are unethical; rather they find that sometimes 'it is kind to be cruel' (Desch 2003).

Although the advanced student might be able to detect some subtle differences, it is fair to say that there is a significant degree of continuity between classical realism and modern variants. Indeed, the three core elements that we identify with realism—**statism**, **survival**, and **self-help**—are present in the work of a classical realist such as Thucydides and structural realists such as Kenneth Waltz.

Realism identifies the group as the fundamental unit of political analysis. When Thucydides and Machiavelli were writing, the basic unit was the *polis* or city-state, but since the Peace of Westphalia (1648) realists consider the sovereign state as the principal actor in international politics. This is often referred to as the state-centric assumption of realism. **Statism** is the term given to the idea of the state as the legitimate representative of the collective will of the people. The legitimacy of the state is what enables it to exercise authority within its domestic borders. Yet outside the boundaries of the state, realists argue that a condition of **anarchy** exists. By anarchy what is most often meant is that international politics takes place in an arena that has no overarching central authority above the individual collection of sovereign states. Thus, rather than necessarily denoting complete chaos and lawlessness, the concept of anarchy is used by realists to emphasize the point that the international realm is distinguished by the lack of a central authority.

Following from this, realists draw a sharp distinction between domestic and international politics. Thus, while Hans J. Morgenthau argues that 'international politics, like all politics, is a struggle for power', he goes to great lengths to illustrate the qualitatively different result this struggle has on international politics as compared to domestic politics ([1948] 1955: 25). A prominent explanation that realists provide for this difference in behaviour relates to the different organizational **structure** of domestic and international politics. Realists argue that the basic structure of international politics is one of anarchy in that each of the independent sovereign states considers itself to be its own highest authority and does not recognize a higher power. Conversely, domestic politics is often described as a hierarchical structure in which different political actors stand in various relations of super- and subordination.

It is largely on the basis of how realists depict the international environment that they conclude that the first priority for state leaders is to ensure the survival of their state. Under anarchy, the survival of the state cannot be guaranteed. Realists correctly assume that all states wish to perpetuate their existence. Looking back at history, however, realists note that the actions of some states resulted in other states losing their existence (for example, Poland has experienced this fate four times in the past three centuries). This is partly explained in light of the power differentials of states. Intuitively, states with more power stand a better chance of surviving than states with less power. **Power** is crucial to the realist lexicon and has traditionally been defined narrowly in military strategic terms. Yet irrespective of how much power a state may possess, the core **national interest** of all states must be survival. Like the pursuit of power, the promotion of the national interest is, according to realists, an iron law of necessity.

Self-help is the principle of action in an anarchical system where there is no global government. According to realism, each state actor is responsible for ensuring its own well-being and survival. Realists do not believe it is prudent for a state to entrust its safety and survival on another actor or international institution, such as the United Nations. States, in short, should not depend on other states to ensure their own security. Unlike in domestic politics, there is no emergency number that states can dial when they are in mortal danger.

You may at this point be asking what options are available to states to ensure their own security. Consistent with the principle of self-help, if a state feels threatened, it should seek to augment its own power **capabilities** by engaging, for example, in a military arms build-up. Yet this may prove to be insufficient for a number of smaller states who feel threatened by a much larger state. This brings us to one of the crucial mechanisms that realists throughout the ages have considered to be essential to preserving the liberty of states—the **balance of power**. Although various meanings have been attributed to the concept of the balance of power, the most common definition holds that if the survival of a state or a number of weaker states is threatened by a hegemonic state or coalition of stronger states, they should join forces, establish a formal alliance, and seek to preserve their own independence by checking the power of the opposing side. The mechanism of the balance of power seeks to ensure an equilibrium of power in which case no one state or coalition of states is in a position to dominate all the others. The **cold war** competition between the East and West, as institutionalized through the formal alliance system of the **Warsaw Pact** and the **North Atlantic Treaty Organization** (NATO), provides a prominent example of the balance of power mechanism in action.

The peaceful conclusion of the cold war caught many realists off guard. Given that many realists claim a scientific basis to their causal account of the world, it is not surprising that their inability to foresee the dynamics that led to the end of the bipolar cold war system sparked the publication of several powerful critiques of realist theory. Critics also maintained that realism was unable to provide a persuasive account of new developments such as regional **integration**, humanitarian intervention, the emergence of a **security community** in Western Europe, and the growing incidence of intra-state war wracking the global South. In addition,

proponents of globalization argued that realism's privileged actor, the state, was in decline relative to **non-state actors** such as **transnational corporations** and powerful regional institutions. Critics also contend that realism is unable to explain the increasing incidence of intra-state wars plaguing the global South. As Box 5.1 discusses, realists claim that their theory does indeed explain the incidence of intra-state conflicts. The cumulative weight of these criticisms led many to question the analytical and moral adequacy of realist thought.

By way of a response to the critics, it is worth reminding them that the death-knell of realism has been sounded a number of times already, by the scientific approach in the 1960s and **transnationalism** in the 1970s, only to see the resurgence of a robust form of structural realism in the 1980s. In this respect realism shares with conservatism (its ideological godfather) the recognition that a theory without the means to change is without the means of its own preservation. The question of realism's resilience touches upon one of its central claims, namely, that it is the embodiment of laws of international politics that remain true across time (history) and space (geopolitics). Thus while political conditions have changed since the end of the cold war, realists believe that the world continues to operate according to the logic of realism. The question whether realism does embody 'timeless truths' about politics will be returned to in the conclusion of the chapter.

Box 5.1 Realism and intra-state war

Since the end of the cold war, intra-state war (internal conflicts in one state) have become more prevalent than inter-state war. Since realists generally focus on the latter type of conflict, critics contend that realism is irrelevant to the predicament of the global South that has been wracked by nationalist and ethnic wars. But this is not the case, and realists have turned their attention to analysing the causes of intra-state war and recommending solutions.

Structural realists maintain that when the sovereign authority of the state collapses, such as in Somalia and Haiti, internal wars happen for many of the same reasons that wars between states happen. In a fundamental sense, the dichotomy between domestic order and international disorder breaks down when the state loses the legitimate authority to rule. The resulting anarchy inside the state is analogous to the anarchy among states. In such a situation, realist theory contends that the different groups inside the state will vie for power in an attempt to gain a sense of security. Barry Posen (1993) has applied the key realist concept of the **security dilemma** to explain the political dynamics that result when different ethnic, religious, and cultural groups suddenly

find themselves responsible for their own security. He argues that it is natural to expect that security will be their first priority and that they will seek the means to perpetuate their own existence. Yet, just as in the case of states, one group's attempt to enhance its security will create uncertainty in the minds of rival groups, which will in turn seek to augment their own power. Realists argue that this revolving spiral of distrust and uncertainty leads to intense security competition and often to military conflict among the various independent groups who were earlier subject to the sovereign power of the state.

In addition to analysing the cause of intra-state wars, realists have prescribed solutions. Unlike many liberal solutions to civil and ethnic wars that rest on power-sharing agreements and the creation of multi-ethnic states, realists have advocated separation or partition. For realists, anarchy can be eliminated by creating a central government. And while the creation of multi-ethnic states might be a noble endeavour, realists argue that they do not have a very good success rate. Ethnically homogeneous states are held by realists to be more stable and less dependent on outside military occupation.

Key Points

- Realism has been the dominant theory of world politics since the beginning of academic International Relations.

- Outside the academy, realism has a much longer history in the work of classical political theorists such as Thucydides, Machiavelli, Hobbes, and Rousseau.

- The unifying theme around which all realist thinking

converges is that states find themselves in the shadow of anarchy such that their security cannot be taken for granted.

- At the start of the new millennium, realism continues to attract academicians and inform policy-makers, although in the period since the end of the cold we have seen heightened criticism of realist assumptions.

One realism, or many?

The intellectual exercise of articulating a unified theory of realism has been criticized by writers who are both sympathetic and critical of the tradition (M. J. Smith 1986; Doyle 1997). The belief that there is not one realism, but many, leads logically to a delineation of different types of realism. A number of thematic classifications have been offered to differentiate realism into a variety of distinct categories. The most simple distinction is a form of periodization that differentiates realism into three historical periods: classical realism (up to the twentieth century), which is frequently depicted as beginning with Thucydides' text on the Peloponnesian War between Athens and Sparta and incorporating the ideas of many of those included in the classic canon of Western political thought; modern realism (1939–79), which typically takes the so-called First Great Debate between the scholars of the inter-war period and a new wave of scholars who began to enter the field immediately before and after the Second World War as its point of departure; and structural or neo-realism (1979 onwards), which officially entered the picture following the publication of Kenneth Waltz's landmark text *Theory of International Politics* (1979). While these different periods suggest a neat historical sequence, they are problematic in so far as they close down the important question about divergence within each historical phase. Rather than opt for the neat but intellectually unsatisfactory system of historical periodization, we outline below our own representation of realisms that makes important connections with existing categories deployed by other thinkers in the field. A summary of the varieties of realism outlined below is contained in Table 5.1.

Classical realism

The classical realist lineage begins with Thucydides' representation of power politics as a law of human behaviour. The drive for power and the will to dominate are held to be fundamental aspects of human nature. The behaviour of the state as a self-seeking egoist is understood to be merely a reflection of the characteristics of the people that comprise the state. It is human nature that explains why international politics is necessarily power politics. This reduction of realism to a condition of human nature is one that frequently reappears in the leading works of the realist canon, most famously in the work of the high priest of post-war realism, Hans J. Morgenthau. Classical realists argue that it is from the nature of man that the essential features of international politics, such as competition, fear, and war, can be explained. Morgenthau notes, 'politics, like society in general, is governed by objective laws that have their roots in human nature' (Morgenthau [1948] 1955: 4). The important point for Morgenthau is, first, to recognize that these laws exist and, second, to devise the most appropriate policies that are consistent with the basic fact that human beings are flawed creatures. For both Thucydides and Morgenthau, the essential continuity of the power-seeking behaviour of states is rooted in the biological drives of human beings.

Another distinguishing characteristic of classical realism is its adherents' belief in the primordial character of power and ethics. Classical realism is fundamentally about the struggle for belonging, a struggle that is often violent. Patriotic virtue is required in order for communities to survive in this historic battle between good and evil, a virtue that long predates the emergence of **sovereignty**-based notions of community in the mid-seventeenth century. Classical realists therefore differ from contemporary realists in the sense that they engaged with moral philosophy and sought to reconstruct an understanding of virtue in light of practice and historical circumstance. Two classical realists who

Table 5.1 A taxonomy of realisms

Type of realism	Key thinkers	Key texts	'Big idea'
Classical realism (Human nature)	Thucydides (c. 430–406 BC)	The Peloponnesian War	International politics is driven by an endless struggle for power, which has its roots in human nature. Justice, law, and society have either no place or are circumscribed.
	Machiavelli (1532)	The Prince	Political realism recognizes that principles are subordinated to policies; the ultimate skill of the state leader is to accept, and adapt to, the changing power political configurations in world politics.
	Morgenthau (1948)	Politics among Nations	Politics is governed by laws that are created by human nature. The mechanism we use to understand international politics is the concept of interests, defined in terms of power.
Structural realism (international system)	Rousseau (c. 1750)	The State of War	It is not human nature but the anarchical system that fosters fear, jealousy, suspicion, and insecurity.
	Waltz (1979)	Theory of International Politics	Anarchy leads to a logic of self-help in which states seek to maximize their security. The most stable distribution of power in the system is bipolarity.
	Mearsheimer (2001)	Tragedy of Great Power Politics	The anarchical, self-help system compels states to maximize their relative power position.
Neoclassical realism	Zakaria (1998)	From Wealth to Power	The systemic account of world politics provided by structural realism is incomplete. It needs to be supplemented with better accounts of unit-level variables such as how power is perceived, and how leadership is exercised.

wrestled with the degree to which state leaders could be guided by ethical considerations were Thucydides and Machiavelli.

Thucydides was the historian of the Peloponnesian War, a conflict between two great powers in the ancient Greek world, Athens and Sparta. Thucydides' work has been admired by subsequent generations of realists for the insights he raised about many of the perennial issues of international politics. Thucydides' explanation of the underlying cause of the war was 'the growth of Athenian power and the fear which this caused in Sparta' (1.23). This is considered to be a classic example of the impact that the anarchical structure of international politics has on the behaviour of state actors. On this reading, Thucydides makes it clear that Sparta's **national interest**, like that of all states, was survival, and the changing distribution of power represented a direct threat to its existence. Sparta was, therefore, compelled by necessity to go to war in order to forestall being vanquished by Athens. Thucydides also makes it clear that Athens felt equally compelled to pursue power in order to preserve the **empire** it had acquired. The famous Athenian leader, Pericles, claimed to be acting on the basis of the most

fundamental of human motivations: ambition, fear, and self-interest. (See our case study, The Melian dialogue.)

Later classical realists—notably Machiavelli and Morgenthau—would concur with Thucydides' suggestion that the logic of power politics has universal applicability. Instead of Athens and Melos, we could just as easily substitute the vulnerability of Machiavelli's beloved Florence to the expansionist policies of external great powers. In Morgenthau's era, there were many examples where the innate drive for more power and **territory** seemed to confirm the realist iron law: for example, Nazi Germany and Czechoslovakia in 1939, and the Soviet Union and Hungary in 1956. The seemingly endless cycle of war and conflict confirmed in the minds of twentieth-century classical realists the essentially aggressive impulses in human nature. How is a leader supposed to act in a world animated by such dark forces? The answer given by Machiavelli is that all obligations and treaties with other states must be disregarded if the security of the community is under threat. Moreover, imperial expansion is legitimate as it is a means of gaining greater security. Other classical realists, however, advocate a more temperate understanding

Case Study The Melian dialogue—realism and the preparation for war

One of the significant episodes of the war between Athens and Sparta is known as the 'Melian dialogue', and represents a fascinating illustration of a number of key realist principles. The Case Study reconstructs the dialogue between the Athenian leaders who arrived on the island of Melos to assert their right of conquest over the islanders and the response this provoked. In short, what the Athenians are asserting over the Melians is the logic of power politics. Because of their vastly superior military force, they are able to present a *fait accompli* to the Melians: either submit peacefully or be exterminated. The Melians for their part try to buck the logic of power politics, appealing in turn with arguments grounded in justice, God, and their allies the Spartans. As the dialogue makes clear, the Melians were forced to submit to the realist iron law that power politics prevails in human affairs.

A short excerpt from the Dialogue appears below (Thucydides 1954/1972: 401–7). Note that the symbol [...] indicates where words have been omitted from the original text.

ATHENIANS. Then we on our side will use no fine phrases saying, for example, that we have a right to our empire because we defeated the Persians. [...] you know as well as we do that, when these matters are discussed by practical people, the standard of justice depends on the equality of power to compel and that in fact the strong do what they have the power to do and the weak accept what they have to accept.

MELIANS. [...] you should not destroy a principle that is to the general good of all men—namely, that in the case of all who fall into danger there should be such a thing as fair play and just dealing [...]

ATHENIANS. This is no fair fight, with honour on one side and shame on the other. It is rather a question of saving your lives and not resisting those who are far too strong for you.

MELIANS. It is difficult [...] for us to oppose your power and fortune [...] Nevertheless we trust that the gods will give us fortune as good as yours [...]

ATHENIANS. Our opinion of the gods and our knowledge of men lead us to conclude that it is a general and necessary law of nature to rule whatever one can. This is not a law that we made ourselves, nor were we the first to act upon it when it was made. We found it already in existence, and we shall leave it to exist forever among those who come after us. We are merely acting in accordance with it, and we know that you or anybody else with the same power as ours would be acting in precisely the same way. [...] You seem to forget that if one follows one's self-interest one wants to be safe, whereas the path of justice and honour involves one in danger. [...] This is the safe rule—to stand up to one's equals, to behave with deference to one's superiors, and to treat one's inferiors with moderation.

MELIANS. Our decision, Athenians, is just the same as it was at first. We are not prepared to give up in a short moment the liberty which our city has enjoyed from its foundation for 700 years.

ATHENIANS. [...] you seem to us [...] to see uncertainties as realities, simply because you would like them to be so.

of moral conduct. Mid-twentieth-century realists such as Butterfield, Carr, Morgenthau, and Wolfers believed that anarchy could be mitigated by wise leadership and the pursuit of the national interest in ways that are compatible with **international order**. Taking their lead from Thucydides, they recognized that acting purely on the basis of power and self-interest without any consideration of moral and ethical principles frequently results in self-defeating policies. After all, as Thucydides showed, Athens suffered an epic defeat while following the realist tenet of self-interest.

Structural realism

Structural realists concur that international politics is essentially a struggle for power but they do not endorse the classical realist assumption that this is a result of human nature. Instead, structural realists attribute security competition and inter-state conflict to the lack of an overarching authority above states and the relative distribution of power in the international system. Waltz defined the structure of the international system in terms of three elements—organizing principle, differentiation of units, and distribution of capabilities. Waltz identifies two different organizing principles: anarchy, which corresponds to the decentralized realm of international politics; and hierarchy, which is the basis of domestic order. He argues that the units of the international system are functionally similar sovereign states; hence unit-level variation is irrelevant in explaining international outcomes. It is the third tier, the distribution of capabilities across units, that is, according to Waltz, of fundamental importance to understanding crucial international outcomes. According to structural realists, the relative distribution of power in the international system is the key independent variable in understanding important international outcomes such as war and peace, alliance politics, and the balance of power. Structural realists are interested in providing a rank-ordering of states so as to be able to differentiate and count the number of great powers that exist at any particular point in time. The number of great powers, in turn, determines the structure of the international system. For example, during the cold war from 1945 to 1989 there were two great powers—the USA and the Soviet Union—that constituted the bipolar international system.

How does the international distribution of power impact the behaviour of states, particularly their power-seeking behaviour? In the most general sense, Waltz argues that states, especially the great powers, have to be sensitive to the capabilities of other states. The possibility that any state may use force to advance its interests results in all states being worried about their survival. According to Waltz, power is a means to the end of security. In a significant passage, Waltz writes 'because power is a possibly useful means, sensible statesmen try to have an appropriate amount of it'. He adds, 'in crucial situations, however, the ultimate concern of states is not for power but for security' (Waltz 1989: 40). In other words, rather than being power maximizers, states, according to Waltz, are security maximizers. Waltz argues that power maximization often proves to be dysfunctional because it triggers a counter-balancing coalition of states.

A different account of the power dynamics that operate in the **anarchic system** is provided by John Mearsheimer's theory of **offensive realism**, which is another variant of structural realism. While sharing many of the basic assumptions of Waltz's structural realist theory, which is frequently termed **defensive realism**, Mearsheimer differs from Waltz when it comes to describing the behaviour of states. Most fundamentally, 'offensive realism parts company with defensive realism over the question of how much power states want' (Mearsheimer 2001: 21). According to Mearsheimer, the structure of the international system compels states to maximize their relative power position. Under anarchy, he agrees that self-help is the basic principle of action. Yet he also argues that not only do all states possess some offensive military capability, but there is a great deal of uncertainty about the intentions of other states. Consequently, Mearsheimer concludes that there are no satisfied or status quo states; rather, all states are continuously searching for opportunities to gain power at the expense of other states. Contrary to Waltz, Mearsheimer argues that states recognize that the best path to peace is to accumulate more power than anyone else. Indeed, the ideal position, although one that Mearsheimer argues is virtually impossible to achieve, is to be the global hegemon of the **international system**. Yet because Mearsheimer believes that global **hegemony** is impossible, he concludes that the world is condemned to perpetual great power competition.

Contemporary realist challenges to structural realism

While offensive realism makes an important contribution to realism, some contemporary realists are sceptical of the notion that the international distribution of power alone can explain the behaviour of states. Since the end of the cold war a group of scholars have attempted to move beyond the parsimonious assumptions of structural realism and incorporated a number of additional factors located at the individual and domestic level into their explanation of international politics. While systemic factors are recognized to be an important influence on the behaviour of states, so are factors such as the perceptions of state leaders, state–society relationships, and the motivation of states. In attempting to build a bridge between structural and unit-level factors (which many classical realists emphasized), this group of scholars has been characterized by Gideon Rose (1998) as 'neoclassical realists'. According to Stephen Walt, the causal logic of **neoclassical realism** 'places domestic politics as an intervening variable between the distribution of power and foreign policy behavior' (Walt 2002: 211).

One important intervening variable is leaders themselves, namely how they perceive the international distribution of power. There is no objective, independent reading of the distribution of power; rather, what matters is how state leaders derive an understanding of the distribution of power. While structural realists assume that all states have a similar set of interests, neoclassical realists such as Randall Schweller (1996) argue that historically this is not the case. He argues that, with respect to Waltz, the assumption that all states have an interest in security results in neo-realism exhibiting a profoundly status quo basis. Schweller returns to the writings of realists such as Morgenthau and Kissinger to remind us of the key distinction that they made between status quo and revisionist states. Neoclassical realists would argue that the fact that Germany was a revisionist state in the 1930s and a status quo state since the end of the Second World War is of fundamental importance to understanding its role in the international system. Not only do states differ in terms of their interests; they also differ in terms of their ability to extract and direct resources from the societies they rule. Fareed Zakaria (1998) introduces the intervening variable of state strength into his theory of state-centred realism. State strength is defined as the ability of a state to mobilize and direct the resources at its disposal in the pursuit of particular interests. Neoclassical realists argue that different types of state possess different capacities to translate the various elements of national power into state power. Thus, contrary to Waltz, all states cannot be treated as 'like units'.

Given the varieties of realism that exist, it is hardly surprising that the overall coherence of the realist tradition of enquiry has been questioned. The answer to the question of 'coherence' is, of course, contingent upon how strict the criteria are for judging the continuities that underpin a particular theory. Here it is perhaps a mistake to understand traditions as a single stream of

thought, handed down in a neatly wrapped package from one generation of realists to another. Instead, it is preferable to think of living traditions like realism as the embodiment of both continuities and conflicts. Despite the different strands running through the tradition, there is a sense in which all realists have a common set of propositions.

> ### Key Points
>
> - There is a lack of consensus in the literature as to whether we can meaningfully speak about realism as a single coherent theory.
> - There are good reasons for delineating different types of realism.
> - Structural realism divides into two camps: those who argue that states are security maximizers (defensive realism), and those who argue that states are power maximizers (offensive realism).
> - Neoclassical realists bring individual and unit variation back into the theory.

The essential realism

The previous paragraphs have argued that realism is a theoretically broad church, embracing a variety of authors and texts. Despite the numerous denominations, we argue that all realists subscribe to the following 'three ss': statism, survival, self-help. Each of these elements is considered in more detail in the subsections below.

Statism

For realists, the state is the main actor and sovereignty is its distinguishing trait. The meaning of the sovereign state is inextricably bound up with the use of force. In terms of its internal dimension, to illustrate this relationship between violence and the state we need look no further than Max Weber's famous definition of the state as 'the monopoly of the legitimate use of physical force within a given territory' (M. J. Smith 1986: 23).[2] Within this territorial space, **sovereignty** means that the state has supreme authority to make and enforce laws. This is the basis of the unwritten contract between individuals and the state. According to Hobbes, for example, we trade our liberty in return for a guarantee of security. Once security has been established, **civil society** can begin. But in the absence of security, there can be no art,

no culture, no society. The first move for the realist, then, is to organize power domestically. Only after power has been organized can community begin.

Realist international theory appears to operate according to the assumption that, domestically, the problem of order and security is solved. However, on the 'outside', in the relations among independent sovereign states, insecurities, dangers, and threats to the very existence of the state loom large. Realists largely explain this on the basis that the very condition for order and security—namely, the existence of a sovereign—is missing from the international realm.

Realists claim that, in anarchy, states compete with other states for power and security. The nature of the competition is viewed in zero-sum terms; in other words, more for one actor means less for another. This competitive logic of power politics makes agreement on universal principles difficult, apart from the principle of non-intervention in the internal affairs of other sovereign states. But even this principle, designed to facilitate **coexistence**, is suspended by realists, who argue that in practice non-intervention does not apply in relations between great powers and their 'near abroad'. As evidenced by the most recent behaviour of the USA in

Afghanistan and Iraq, powerful states are able to overturn the non-intervention principle on the grounds of national security and international order.

Given that the first move of the state is to organize power domestically, and the second is to accumulate **power** internationally, it is self-evidently important to consider in more depth what realists mean by their ubiquitous fusion of politics with power. It is one thing to say that international politics is a struggle for power, but this merely begs the question of what realists mean by power. Morgenthau offers the following definition of power: 'man's control over the minds and actions of other men' ([1948] 1955: 26). There are two important points that realists make about the elusive concept of power. First, power is a relational concept: one does not exercise power in a vacuum, but in relation to another entity. Second, power is a relative concept: calculations need to be made not only about one's own power capabilities, but about the power that other state actors possess. Yet the task of accurately assessing the power of states is infinitely complex, and is often reduced to counting the number of troops, tanks, aircraft, and naval ships a country possesses in the belief that this translates into the ability to get other actors to do something they would not otherwise do.

A number of criticisms have been made as to how realists define and measure power, many of which are discussed in later chapters. Critics argue that realism has been purchased at a discount precisely because its currency, power, has remained under-theorized and inconsistently used. Simply asserting that states seek power provides no answer to crucial questions. Why do states struggle for power? Surely power is a means to an end rather than an end in itself? Is there not a difference between the mere possession of power and the ability to change the behaviour of others?

Structural realists have attempted to bring more conceptual clarity to bear on the meaning of power. Waltz tries to overcome the problem by shifting the focus from power to capabilities. He suggests that capabilities can be ranked according to their strength in the following areas: 'size of population and territory, resource endowment, economic capability, military strength, political stability and competence' (1979: 131). The difficulty here is that resource strength does not always lead to military victory. For example, in the 1967 Six Day War between Israel and Egypt, Jordan, and Syria, the distribution of resources clearly favoured the Arab coalition and yet the supposedly weaker side annihilated its enemies' forces and seized their territory. The definition of power as capabilities is even less successful at explaining the relative economic success of Japan over China. A more sophisticated understanding of power would focus on the ability of a state to control or influence its environment in situations that are not necessarily conflictual.

An additional weakness of the realist treatment of power concerns its exclusive focus upon state power. For realists, states are the only actors that really 'count'. **Transnational corporations**, **international organizations**, and ideologically driven terrorist **networks**, such as Al Qaeda, rise and fall but the state is the one permanent feature in the landscape of modern global politics. Yet many today question the adequacy of the state-centric assumption of realism.

Survival

The second principle that unites realists is the assertion that, in international politics, the pre-eminent goal is survival. Although there is ambiguity in the works of the realists as to whether the accumulation of power is an end in itself, one would think that there is no dissenting from the argument that the ultimate concern of states is security. Survival is held to be a precondition for attaining all other goals, whether these involve conquest or merely independence. According to Waltz, 'beyond the survival motive, the aims of states may be endlessly varied' (1979: 91). Yet, as we mentioned in the previous section, a recent controversy among structural realists has arisen over the question of whether states are in fact principally security or power maximizers. Defensive realists such as Waltz argue that states have security as their principal interest and therefore seek only the requisite amount of power to ensure their own survival. According to this view, states are profoundly defensive actors and will not seek to gain greater amounts of power if that means jeopardizing their own security. Offensive realists such as Mearsheimer argue that the ultimate goal of all states is to achieve a hegemonic position in the international system. States, according to this view, always desire more power and are willing, if the opportunity arises, to alter the existing distribution of power even if such an action may jeopardize their own security. In terms of survival, defensive realists hold that the existence of status quo powers lessens the competition for power, while offensive realists argue that the competition is always keen because revisionist states and aspiring hegemons are always willing to take risks with the aim of improving their position in the international system.

Niccolò Machiavelli tried to make a 'science' out of his reflections on the art of survival. His short and engaging book, *The Prince*, was written with the explicit intention of codifying a set of maxims that would enable leaders to maintain their hold on power. In important respects, we find two related Machiavellian themes recurring in the writings of modern realists, both of which derive from the idea that the realm of international politics requires different moral and political rules from those that apply in domestic politics. The task of understanding the real nature of international politics, and the need to protect the state at all costs (even if this may mean the sacrifice of one's own citizens), places a heavy burden on the shoulders of state leaders. In the words of Henry Kissinger, the academic realist who became Secretary of State during the Nixon Presidency, 'a nation's survival is its first and ultimate responsibility; it cannot be compromised or put to risk' (1977: 204). Their guide must be an **ethic of responsibility**: the careful weighing up of consequences; the realization that individual acts of an immoral kind might have to be performed for the greater good. By way of an example, think of the ways in which governments frequently suspend the legal and political rights of 'suspected terrorists' in view of the threat they pose to **national security**. The principal difficulty with the realist formulation of an 'ethics of responsibility' is that, while instructing leaders to consider the consequences of their actions, it does not provide a guide as to how state leaders should weigh the consequences (M. J. Smith 1986: 51).

Not only does realism provide an alternative moral code for state leaders; it suggests a wider objection to the whole enterprise of bringing ethics into international politics. Starting from the assumption that each state has its own particular values and beliefs, realists argue that the state is the supreme good and there can be no community beyond borders. This moral relativism has generated a substantial body of criticism, particularly from liberal theorists who endorse the notion of universal human rights. For a fuller discussion see Chapter 6.

Self-help

Waltz's *Theory of International Politics* (1979) brought to the realist tradition a deeper understanding of the international system within which states coexist. Unlike many other realists, Waltz argued that international politics was not unique because of the regularity of war and conflict, since this was also familiar in domestic politics. The key difference between domestic and international orders lies in their structure. In the domestic polity,

citizens do not have to defend themselves. In the international system, there is no higher authority to prevent and counter the use of force. Security can therefore only be realized through self-help. In an anarchic structure, 'self-help is necessarily the principle of action' (Waltz 1979: 111). But in the course of providing for one's own security, the state in question will automatically be fuelling the insecurity of other states.

The term given to this spiral of insecurity is the **security dilemma**. According to Wheeler and Booth, security dilemmas exist 'when the military preparations of one state create an unresolvable uncertainty in the mind of another as to whether those preparations are for "defensive" purposes only (to enhance its security in an uncertain world) or whether they are for offensive purposes (to change the status quo to its advantage)' (1992: 30). This scenario suggests that one state's quest for security is often another state's source of insecurity. States find it very difficult to trust one another and often view the intentions of others in a negative light. Thus the military preparations of one state are likely to be matched by those of neighbouring states. The irony is that, at the end of the day, states often feel no more secure than before they undertook measures to enhance their own security.

In a self-help system, structural realists argue that the balance of power will emerge even in the absence of a conscious policy to maintain the balance (i.e. prudent statecraft). Waltz argues that balances of power result irrespective of the intentions of any particular state. In an anarchic system populated by states that seek to perpetuate themselves, alliances will be formed that seek to check and balance the power against threatening states. Classical realists, however, are more likely to emphasize the crucial role that state leaders and diplomats play in maintaining the balance of power. In other words, the balance of power is not natural or inevitable; it must be constructed.

There is a lively debate among realists concerning the stability of the balance of power system. This is especially the case today, in that many argue that the balance of power has been replaced by **unipolarity**. It is questionable whether other countries will actively attempt to balance against the USA, as structural realism would predict. Whether it is the contrived balance of the Concert of Europe in the early nineteenth century, or the more fortuitous balance of the cold war, balances of power are broken—either through war or through peaceful change—and new balances emerge. What the perennial collapsing of the balance of power demonstrates is that states are at best able to mitigate the worst consequences of the security dilemma but are not able to escape it. The reason for this terminal condition is the absence of trust in international relations.

Historically, realists have illustrated the lack of trust among states by reference to the parable of the 'stag hunt'. In *Man, the State and War*, Kenneth Waltz revisits Rousseau's parable:

> Assume that five men who have acquired a rudimentary ability to speak and to understand each other happen to come together at a time when all of them suffer from hunger. The hunger of each will be satisfied by the fifth part of a stag, so they 'agree' to cooperate in a project to trap one. But also the hunger of any one of them will be satisfied by a hare, so, as a hare comes within reach, one of them grabs it. The defector obtains the means of satisfying his hunger but in doing so permits the stag to escape. His immediate interest prevails over consideration for his fellows.

> *(1959: 167–8)*

Waltz argues that the metaphor of the stag hunt provides a basis for understanding the problem of coordinating the interests of the individual versus the interests of the common good, and the pay-off between short-term interests and long-term interests. In the self-help system of international politics, the logic of self-interest militates against the provision of collective goods, such as 'security' or 'free trade'. In the case of the latter, according to the theory of comparative advantage, all states would be wealthier in a world that allowed free movement of goods and services across borders. But individual states, or groups of states like the European Union, can increase their wealth by pursuing protectionist policies providing other states do not respond in kind. Of course the logical outcome is for the remaining states to become protectionist; international trade collapses, and a world recession reduces the wealth of each state. Thus the question is not whether all will be better off through **cooperation**, but rather who is likely to gain more than another. It is because of this concern with **relative gains** issues that realists argue that cooperation is difficult to achieve in a self-help system.

Key Points

- **Statism** is the centrepiece of realism. This involves two claims. First, for the theorist, the state is the pre-eminent actor and all other actors in world politics are of lesser significance. Second, state 'sovereignty' signifies the existence of an independent political community, one that has juridical authority over its territory.

- **Key criticism**: statism is flawed on both empirical (challenges to state power from 'above' and 'below') and normative grounds (the inability of sovereign states to respond to collective global problems such as famine, environmental degradation, and human rights abuses).

- **Survival**: the primary objective of all states is survival; this is the supreme national interest to which all political leaders must adhere.

- **Key criticism**: are there no limits to what actions a state can take in the name of necessity?

- **Self-help**: no other state or institution can be relied upon to guarantee your survival.

- **Key criticism**: self-help is not an inevitable consequence of the absence of a world government; it is a logic that states have selected. Moreover, there are historical and contemporary examples where states have preferred collective security systems, or forms of regional security communities, in preference to self-help.

Conclusion: realism and the globalization of world politics

The chapter opened by considering the often repeated realist claim that the pattern of international politics—wars interrupted by periods characterized by the preparation for future wars—have remained constant over the preceding twenty-five centuries. Realists have consistently held that the continuities in international relations are more important than the changes, but many find this to be increasingly problematic in the present age of globalization. But the importance of realism has not been diminished by the dynamics of globalization. It is not clear that economic **interdependence** has made war less likely. The state continues to be the dominant unit in world politics. And globalization should not be seen as a process that is disconnected from the distribution of power in the international system. In this sense, this current phase of globalization is fundamentally tied to Westernization and, to be even more specific, Americanization.

Not surprisingly, realist thinkers have been quick to seize on the apparent convergence between our post-

9/11 experience and the cycle of violence predicted by the theory. There were, however, some apparent contradictions in the realist account of the conflict. To begin with, the attacks on the US homeland were committed by a non-state actor. Not only was the enemy a global network of Al Qaeda operatives; their goal was unconventional in that they did not seek to conquer territory but challenge by force the ideological supremacy of the West. Set against these anomalies, the leading states in the system were quick to identify the network with certain territorial states—the Taliban government of Afghanistan being the most immediate example, but also other pariah states that allegedly harboured terrorists. The USA rushed to link the overthrow of Saddam Hussein's Iraq with its global **war on terror**. Moreover, rather than identifying the terrorists as transnational criminals and using police enforcement methods to counter their threat, the USA and its allies defined them as enemies of the state that had to be targeted and defeated using conventional military means.

For realists such as Colin Gray and Kenneth Waltz, 9/11 was not the beginning of a new era in world politics so much as a case of 'business as usual' (see their essays in Booth and Dunne 2002). For Waltz, the Iraq War illustrated the tendency for states with overwhelming power to misuse it. While neoconservatives in the Bush administration championed the virtues of American hegemony, the pre-emptive use of military force, and democracy promotion, realists viewed this as a recipe for disaster (Schmidt and Williams 2008). The liberal crusading aspect of post-9/11 American foreign policy has resulted in a number of scholars returning to the insights of classical realists such as Morgenthau and Kennan, who had earlier warned of the dangers that follow when states neglect their core national interests. Most realists argued that the Iraq War was not in the American national interest, and were public in their condemnation (see Box 5.2). Iraq, they argued, could have been deterred from threatening both the security of the USA and its neighbours in the Middle East. It is now obvious that the costly military intervention and lengthy occupation of Iraq has weakened the USA's ability to contain the rising threat from China.

Realists do not have to situate their theory of world politics in opposition to globalization *per se*; rather, what they offer is a very different conceptualization of the process. Their analysis is a stark rejoinder to the more idealist defenders of globalization who see a new pacific world order emerging out of the ashes of the previous order. What is important about a realist view

> ### Box 5.2 Realism against wars: an unlikely alliance?
>
> Realists are often portrayed as advocates of an aggressive foreign policy. Such a representation has always lacked credibility. Hans Morgenthau opposed the US war against the North Vietnamese on the grounds that it defied a rational understanding of the national interest. He believed that US goals were not attainable 'without unreasonable moral liabilities and military risks' (M. J. Smith 1986: 158). The US-led war against Iraq in 2003 is the most recent example of realism's council against the use of force. As the intense round of negotiations were under way in the Security Council, in the autumn of 2002, 34 leading realist thinkers co-signed an advertisement in the *New York Times* entitled 'War with Iraq is *Not* in America's National Interest' (Art *et al.*,original emphasis). John J. Mearsheimer and Stephen M. Walt developed this position further in early 2004. Why, they asked, had the USA given up on the policy of deterrence, which proved to be successful during the cold war? They end the article with a bold, and some might say prescient, conclusion:
>
> > This war would be one the Bush administration chose to fight but did not have to fight. Even if such a war goes well and has positive long-range consequences, it will still have been unnecessary. And if it goes badly—whether in the form of high U.S. casualties, significant civilian deaths, a heightened risk of terrorism, or increased hatred of the United States in the Arab and Islamic world—then its architects will have even more to answer for.
> >
> > *(Mearsheimer and Walt 2003: 59)*

of globalization is the claim that rudimentary transnational governance is possible, but at the same time it is entirely dependent on the distribution of power. Given the preponderance of power that the USA holds, it should not be a surprise that it has been one of the foremost proponents of globalization. The core values of globalization—liberalism, capitalism, and consumerism—are exactly those espoused by the USA. At a deeper cultural level, realists argue that modernity is not, as liberals hope, dissolving the boundaries of difference among the peoples of the world. From classical realists such as Rousseau to structural realists such as Waltz, protagonists have argued that interdependence is as likely to breed 'mutual vulnerability' as peace and prosperity. And while questioning the extent to which the world has become any more interdependent in relative terms, realists insist that the state is not going to be eclipsed by global forces operating either below or above the nation-state. Nationalism, realists have continuously reminded us, remains a potent force in world politics.

There are good reasons for thinking that the twenty-first century will be a realist century. Despite efforts of federalists to rekindle the idealist flame, Europe continues to be as divided by different national interests as it is united by a common good. As Jacques Chirac put it in 2000, a 'united Europe of states' was much more likely than a 'United States of Europe'. Outside Europe and North America, many of the assumptions that underpinned the post-war international order, particularly those associated with human rights, are increasingly being seen as nothing more than a Western idea backed by economic dollars and military 'divisions'. If China continues its rate of economic growth, it will be more economically powerful than the USA by 2020 (Mearsheimer 1990: 398). By then, realism leads us to predict that Western norms of individual rights and responsibilities will be under threat. Rather than transforming global politics in its own image, as liberalism has sought to do in the twentieth century, realism may need to assert itself in the West in order for Western traditions and values to survive the twenty-first.

Questions

1   How does the Melian dialogue represent key concepts such as self-interest, the balance of power, alliances, capabilities, empires, and justice?
2   Do you think there is one realism, or many?
3   Do you know more about international relations now than an Athenian student did during the Peloponnesian War?
4   Do realists confuse a *description* of war and conflict for an *explanation* of why they occur?
5   Is realism anything more than the ideology of powerful, satisfied states?
6   How would a realist explain the war on terror?
7   Will the West have to learn to be more realist, and not less, if its civilization is to survive in the twenty-first century?
8   What is at stake in the debate between defensive and offensive realism?
9   Is structural realism sufficient to account for the variation in the behaviour of states?
10 Can realism help us to understand the globalization of world politics?

Further Reading

For a general survey of the realist tradition

Guzzini, S. (1998), *Realism in International Relations and International Political Economy* (London: Routledge). Provides an understanding of the evolution of the realist tradition.

Smith, M. J. (1986), *Realist Thought from Weber to Kissinger* (Baton Rouge, LA: Louisiana State University Press). An excellent discussion of many of the seminal realist thinkers.

Walt, S. M. (2002), 'The Enduring Relevance of the Realist Tradition', in **I. Katznelson and H. V. Milner** (eds), *Political Science: The State of the Discipline* (New York: W. W. Norton). A state-of-the-art exposition of the realist tradition.

Twentieth-century classical realism

Carr, E. H. (2001), *The Twenty Years' Crisis 1919–1939: An Introduction to the Study of International Relations* (London: Palgrave). An important critique of liberal idealism.

Morgenthau, H. J. (1948), *Politics among Nations: The Struggle for Power and Peace* (New York: Alfred A. Knopf). A foundational text for the discipline of International Relations.

Structural realism

Keohane, R. (ed.) (1986), *Neorealism and its Critics* (New York: Columbia University Press). This collection of essays includes key chapters by Waltz, an interesting defence of realism by Robert Gilpin, and powerful critiques by Richard Ashley, Robert Cox, and J. G. Ruggie.

Mearsheimer, J. (2001), *The Tragedy of Great Power Politics* (New York: W. W. Norton). This is the definitive account of offensive realism.

Waltz, K. (1979), *Theory of International Politics* (Reading, MA: Addison-Wesley). This the exemplar for structural realism.

Neoclassical realism

Rose, G. (1998), 'Neoclassical Realism and Theories of Foreign Policy', *World Politics*, 51: 144–72. An important review article that is credited with coining the term 'neoclassical realism'.

Lobell, S. E., Ripsman, N. M., and Taliaferro, J. W. (eds) (2009), *Neoclassical Realism, the State, and Foreign Policy* (Cambridge: Cambridge University Press). A comprehensive survey of neoclassical realism.

Zakaria, F. (1998), *From Wealth to Power: The Unusual Origins of America's World Role* (Princeton, NJ: Princeton University Press). Puts forth his theory of state-centric realism.

Online Resource Centre

 Visit the Online Resource Centre that accompanies this book to access more learning resources on this chapter topic at www.oxfordtextbooks.co.uk/orc/baylis5e/

Notes

1   A number of critical histories of the field of International Relations have recently challenged the notion that the inter-war period was essentially 'idealist' in character. Both Peter Wilson (1998) and Brian C. Schmidt (1998) argue that it is simply a myth that an idealist paradigm dominated the study of international relations during the inter-war period of the field's history.

2   Weber is rightly regarded by Smith as the theorist who has shaped twentieth-century realist thought, principally because of his fusion of politics with power.

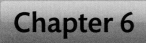

Chapter 6

Liberalism

TIM DUNNE

Reader's Guide

The practice of international relations has not been accommodating to liberalism. Whereas the domestic political realm in many states has witnessed an impressive degree of progress, with institutions providing for order *and* justice, the international realm in the era of the modern states-system has been characterized by a precarious order and the *absence* of justice. The introductory section of the chapter will address this dilemma before providing a definition of liberalism and its component parts. The second section considers the core concepts of liberalism, beginning with the visionary internationalism of the Enlightenment, through to the idealism of the inter-war period, and the institutionalism that became dominant in the second half of the twentieth century. The third and final section considers liberalism in an era of globalization: in particular, it contrasts a status quo reading of the liberal project with a radicalized version that seeks to promote and extend cosmopolitan values and institutions.

Introduction

Although **realism** is regarded as the dominant theory of international relations, **liberalism** has a strong claim to being the historic alternative. In the twentieth century, liberal thinking influenced policy-making elites and public opinion in a number of Western states after the First World War, an era often referred to in academic international relations as **idealism**. There was a brief resurgence of liberal sentiment at the end of the Second World War with the birth of the United Nations, although this beacon of hope was soon extinguished by the return of **cold war** power politics. In the 1990s, liberalism appeared resurgent as Western state leaders proclaimed a **new world order** and intellectuals provided theoretical justifications for the inherent supremacy of their liberal ideas over all other competing ideologies. After **9/11**, the pendulum has once again swung towards the realist pole as the USA and its allies have sought to consolidate their power and punish those whom they define as terrorists and the states that provide them with shelter.

How do we explain the divergent fortunes of liberalism in the domestic and international domains? While liberal values and institutions have become deeply embedded in Europe and North America, the same values and institutions lack legitimacy worldwide. To invoke the famous phrase of Stanley Hoffmann's, 'international affairs have been the nemesis of Liberalism'. 'The essence of Liberalism', Hoffmann continues, 'is self-restraint, moderation, compromise and peace' whereas 'the essence of international politics is exactly the opposite: troubled peace, at best, or the **state of war**' (Hoffmann 1987: 396). This explanation comes as no surprise to realists, who argue that there can be no progress, no law, and no justice, where there is no common power. Despite the weight of this realist argument, those who believe in the liberal project have not conceded defeat. Liberals argue that power politics itself is the product of ideas, and, crucially, ideas can change. Therefore, even if the world has been inhospitable to liberalism, this does not mean that it cannot be re-made in its image.

While the belief in the possibility of progress is one identifier of a liberal approach to politics (Clark 1989: 49–66), there are other general propositions that define the broad tradition of liberalism. Perhaps the appropriate way to begin this discussion is with a four-dimensional definition (Doyle 1997: 207). First, all citizens are juridically equal and possess certain basic rights to education,

access to a free press, and religious toleration. Second, the legislative assembly of the state possesses only the authority invested in it by the people, whose basic rights it is not permitted to abuse. Third, a key dimension of the liberty of the individual is the right to own property, including productive forces. Fourth, liberalism contends that the most effective system of economic exchange is one that is largely market driven and not one that is subordinate to bureaucratic regulation and control, either domestically or internationally. When these propositions are taken together, we see a stark contrast between liberal values of **individualism**, tolerance, freedom, and constitutionalism; and conservatism, which places a higher value on order and authority and is willing to sacrifice the liberty of the individual for the stability of the **community**.

Although many writers have tended to view liberalism as a theory of government, what is becoming increasingly apparent is the explicit connection between liberalism as a political and economic theory and liberalism as an international theory. Properly conceived, liberal thought on a global scale rests on the application of an analogy from the character of a political actor to its international conduct. Like individuals, states have different characteristics—some are bellicose and warprone, others are tolerant and peaceful: in short, the **identity** of the state determines its outward orientation. Liberals see a further parallel between individuals and sovereign states. Although the character of states may differ, all states are accorded certain 'natural' rights, such as the generalized right to non-intervention in their domestic affairs. On another level, the domestic analogy refers to the extension of ideas that originated inside liberal states to the international realm, such as the coordinating role played by institutions and the centrality of the rule of law to the idea of a just **order**. In a sense, the historical project of liberalism is the domestication of the international.

Liberals concede that we have far to go before this goal has been reached. Historically, liberals have agreed with realists that war is a recurring feature of the **anarchic system**. But unlike realists, they do not identify **anarchy** as the cause of war. How, then, do liberals explain war? As Box 6.1 demonstrates, certain strands of liberalism see the causes of war located in **imperialism**, others in the failure of the **balance of power**, and still others in the problem of undemocratic **regimes**. And

Box 6.1 Liberalism and the causes of war, determinants of peace

One of the most useful analytical tools for thinking about differences between individual thinkers or particular variations on a broad theme such as liberalism is to differentiate between levels of analysis. For example, Kenneth Waltz's *Man, the State and War* (1959) examined the causes of conflict operating at the level of the individual, the state, and the international system itself. The table below turns Waltz on his head, as it were, in order to show how different liberal thinkers have provided competing explanations (across the three levels of analysis) for the causes of war and the determinants of peace.

Images of liberalism	Public figure/period	Causes of conflict	Determinants of peace
First image (Human nature)	Richard Cobden (mid-19th century)	Interventions by governments domestically and internationally disturbing the natural order	Individual liberty, free trade, prosperity, interdependence
Second image (The state)	Woodrow Wilson (early 20th century)	Undemocratic nature of international politics, especially foreign policy and the balance of power	National self-determination; open governments responsive to public opinion; collective security
Third image (The structure of the system)	J. A. Hobson (early 20th century)	The balance of power system	A world government, with powers to mediate and enforce decisions

ought this to be remedied through **collective security**, commerce, or world government? While it can be productive to think about the various strands of liberal thought and their differing prescriptions (Doyle 1997: 205–300), given the limited space permitted to deal with a broad and complex tradition, the emphasis below will be on the core concepts of international liberalism and the way in which these relate to the goals of order and justice on a global scale.[2]

At the end of the chapter, the discussion will return to a tension that lies in the heart of the liberal theory of politics. As can be seen from a critical appraisal of the four-fold definition presented above, liberalism pulls in two directions: its commitment to freedom in the economic and social spheres leans in the direction of a minimalist role for governing institutions, while the democratic political culture required for basic freedoms to be safeguarded requires robust and interventionist institutions. This has variously been interpreted as a tension between different liberal goals, or more broadly as a sign of rival and incompatible conceptions of liberalism. Should a liberal polity—no matter what the size or scale—preserve the right of individuals to retain property and privilege, or should liberalism elevate equality over liberty so that resources are redistributed from the strong to the weak? When we are looking at politics on a global scale, it is clear that inequalities are far greater while at the same time our institutional capacity to do something about them is that much less. As writers on **globalization** remind us, the intensification of global flows in trade, resources, and people has weakened the state's capacity to govern. Closing this gap requires nothing short of a radical reconfiguration of the relationship between **territoriality** and governance.

Key Points

- Liberalism is a theory of both government within states and good governance between states and peoples worldwide. Unlike realism, which regards the 'international' as an anarchic realm, liberalism seeks to project values of order, liberty, justice, and toleration into international relations.

- The high-water mark of liberal thinking in international relations was reached in the inter-war period in the work of idealists, who believed that warfare was an unnecessary and outmoded way of settling disputes between states.

- Domestic and international institutions are required to protect and nurture these values.

- Liberals disagree on fundamental issues such as the causes of war and what kind of institutions are required to deliver liberal values in a decentralized, multicultural international system.

- An important cleavage within liberalism, which has become more pronounced in our globalized world, is between those operating with a positive conception of liberalism, who advocate interventionist foreign policies and stronger international institutions, and those who incline towards a negative conception, which places a priority on toleration and non-intervention.

Core ideas in liberal thinking on international relations

Immanuel Kant and Jeremy Bentham were two of the leading liberals of the **Enlightenment**. Both were reacting to the barbarity of international relations, or what Kant graphically described as 'the lawless state of savagery', at a time when domestic politics was at the cusp of a new age of rights, **citizenship**, and constitutionalism. Their abhorrence of the lawless state of savagery led them individually to elaborate plans for 'perpetual peace'. Although written over two centuries ago, these manifestos contain the seeds of core liberal ideas, in particular the belief that reason could deliver freedom and justice in international relations. For Kant the imperative to achieve perpetual peace required the transformation of individual consciousness, republican constitutionalism,

and a federal contract between states to abolish war (rather than to regulate it, as earlier international lawyers had argued). This federation can be likened to a permanent peace treaty, rather than a 'superstate' actor or world government. The three components of Kant's hypothetical treaty for a permanent peace are outlined in Box 6.2.

Kant's claim that liberal states are pacific in their international relations with other liberal states was revived in the 1980s. In a much-cited article, Michael Doyle argued that liberal states have created a 'separate peace' (1986: 1151). According to Doyle, there are two elements to the Kantian legacy: restraint among liberal states and 'international imprudence' in relations with non-liberal states. Although the empirical evidence seems to support the **democratic peace** thesis, it is important to bear in mind the limitations of the argument. In the first instance, for the theory to be compelling, believers in the thesis need to provide an explanation as to why war has become unthinkable between liberal states. Kant had argued that if the decision to use force were taken by the people, rather than by the prince, then the frequency of conflicts would be drastically reduced. But logically, this argument implies a lower frequency of conflicts between liberal and non-liberal states, and this has proven to be contrary to the historical evidence. An alternative explanation for the democratic peace thesis might be that liberal states tend to be wealthy, and therefore have less to gain (and more to lose) by engaging in conflicts than poorer authoritarian states. Perhaps the most convincing explanation of all is the simple fact that liberal states tend to be in relations of amity with other liberal states. War between Canada and the USA is unthinkable, perhaps not because of their liberal democratic constitutions, but because they are friends (Wendt 1999: 298–9), with a high degree of convergence in economic and political matters. Indeed, war between states with contrasting political and economic systems may also be unthinkable because they have a history of friendly relations. An example here is Mexico and Cuba, which maintain close bilateral relations despite their history of divergent economic ideologies.

Irrespective of the scholarly search for an answer to the reasons why liberal democratic states are more peaceful, it is important to note the political consequences of this hypothesis. In 1989 Francis Fukuyama wrote an article entitled '**The End of History**' which celebrated

---

Box 6.2 Immanuel Kant's 'Perpetual Peace: A Philosophical Sketch'

First Definitive Article: *The Civil Constitution of Every State shall be Republican*

'If, as is inevitably the case under this constitution, the consent of the citizens is required to decide whether or not war is to be declared, it is very natural that they will have great hesitation in embarking on so dangerous an enterprise ...'

(Kant 1991: 99–102)

Second Definitive Article: *The Right of Nations shall be based on a Federation of Free States*

'Each nation, for the sake of its own security, can and ought to demand of the others that they should enter along with it into a constitution, similar to a civil one, within which the rights of each could be secured ... *But peace can neither* be inaugurated nor secured without a general agreement between the nations; thus a particular kind of league, which we will call a pacific federation is required. It would be different from a peace treaty in that the latter terminates one war, whereas the former would seek to end all wars for good ... It can be shown that this idea of federalism, extending gradually to encompass all states and thus leading to perpetual peace, is practicable and has objective reality.'

(Kant 1991: 102–5)

Third Definitive Article: *Cosmopolitan Right shall be limited to Conditions of Universal Hospitality*

'The peoples of the earth have thus entered in varying degrees into a universal community, and it has developed to the point where a violation of rights in one part of the world is felt everywhere. The idea of a cosmopolitan right is therefore not fantastic and overstrained; it is a necessary complement to the unwritten code of political and international right, transforming it into a universal right of humanity.'

(Kant 1991: 105–8)

the triumph of liberalism over all other ideologies, contending that liberal states were more stable internally and more peaceful in their international relations (1989: 3–18). Other defenders of the democratic peace thesis were more circumspect. As Doyle recognized, liberal democracies are as aggressive as any other type of state in their relations with authoritarian regimes and stateless peoples (1995*b*: 100). How, then, should states inside the liberal zone of peace conduct their relations with non-liberal regimes? How can the positive Kantian legacy of restraint triumph over the historical legacy of international imprudence on the part of liberal states? These are fascinating and timely questions that will be taken up in the final section of the chapter.

Two centuries after Kant first called for a 'pacific federation', the validity of the idea that democracies are more pacific continues to attract a great deal of scholarly interest. The claim has also found its way into the public discourse of Western states' foreign policy, appearing in speeches made by US presidents as diverse as Ronald Reagan, William Jefferson Clinton, and George W. Bush. Less crusading voices within the liberal tradition believe that a legal and institutional framework must be established that includes states with different cultures and traditions. Such a belief in the power of law to solve the problem of war was advocated by Jeremy Bentham at the end of the eighteenth century: 'Establish a common tribunal' and 'the necessity for war no longer follows from a difference of opinion' (Luard 1992: 416). Like many liberal thinkers after him, Bentham showed that federal states such as the German Diet, the American Confederation, and the Swiss League were able to transform their identity from one based on conflicting interests to a more peaceful federation. As Bentham famously argued, 'between the interests of nations there is nowhere any real conflict'.

Cobden's belief that **free trade** would create a more peaceful world order is a core idea of nineteenth-century liberalism. Trade brings mutual gains to all the players, irrespective of their size or the nature of their economies. It is perhaps not surprising that it was in Britain that this argument found its most vocal supporters. The supposed universal value of free trade brought disproportionate gains to the hegemonic power. There was never an admission that free trade among countries at different stages of **development** would lead to relations of dominance and subservience.

The idea of a natural **harmony of interests** in international political and economic relations came under challenge in the early part of the twentieth century. The

fact that Britain and Germany had highly interdependent economies before the Great War (1914–18) seemed to confirm the fatal flaw in the association of economic interdependence with peace. From the turn of the century, the contradictions within European civilization, of progress and exemplarism on the one hand and the harnessing of industrial power for military purposes on the other, could no longer be contained. Europe stumbled into a horrific war, killing 15 million people. The war not only brought an end to three **empires** but also was a contributing factor to the Russian Revolution of 1917.

The First World War shifted liberal thinking towards a recognition that peace is not a natural condition but is one that must be constructed. In a powerful critique of the idea that peace and prosperity were part of a latent natural order, the publicist and author Leonard Woolf argued that peace and prosperity required 'consciously devised machinery' (Luard 1992: 465). But perhaps the most famous advocate of an international authority for the management of international relations was Woodrow Wilson. According to this US president, peace could only be secured with the creation of an **international organization** to regulate international anarchy. Security could not be left to secret bilateral diplomatic deals and a blind faith in the balance of power. Just as peace had to be enforced in domestic society, the international domain had to have a system of regulation for coping with disputes and an international force that could be mobilized if non-violent conflict resolution failed. In this sense, more than any other strand of liberalism, idealism rests on the **domestic analogy** (Suganami 1989: 94–113).

In his famous '**Fourteen Points**' speech, addressed to Congress in January 1918, Wilson argued that 'a general association of nations must be formed' to preserve the coming peace—the **League of Nations** was to be that general association. For the League to be effective, it had to have the military power to deter aggression and, when necessary, to use a preponderance of power to enforce its will. This was the idea behind the **collective security** system that was central to the League of Nations. Collective security refers to an arrangement where 'each state in the system accepts that the security of one is the concern of all, and agrees to join in a collective response to aggression' (Roberts and Kingsbury 1993: 30). It can be contrasted with an alliance system of security, where a number of states join together usually as a response to a specific external threat (sometimes known as collective defence). In the case of the League of Nations, Article 16 of the League's Charter noted the obligation that, in the event of war, all member states must cease normal relations with the offending state, impose sanctions, and, if necessary, commit their armed forces to the disposal of the League Council should the use of force be required to restore the status quo.

The League's constitution also called for the **self-determination** of all nations, another founding characteristic of liberal idealist thinking on international relations. Going back to the mid-nineteenth century, self-determination movements in Greece, Hungary, and Italy received support among liberal powers and public opinion. Yet the default support for self-determination masked a host of practical and moral problems that were laid bare after Woodrow Wilson issued his proclamation. What would happen to newly created minorities who felt no allegiance to the self-determining state? Could a democratic process adequately deal with questions of identity—who was to decide what constituency was to participate in a ballot? And what if a newly self-determined state rejected liberal democratic norms?

The experience of the League of Nations was a disaster. While the moral rhetoric at the creation of the League was decidedly idealist, in practice states remained imprisoned by self-interest. There is no better example of this than the USA's decision not to join the institution it had created. With the Soviet Union outside the system for ideological reasons, the League of Nations quickly became a talking shop for the 'satisfied' powers. Hitler's decision in March 1936 to reoccupy the Rhineland, a designated demilitarized zone according to the terms of the **Treaty of Versailles**, effectively pulled the plug on the League's life-support system (it had been put on the 'critical' list following the Manchurian crisis in 1931 and the Ethiopian crisis in 1935).

According to the history of the discipline of International Relations, the collapse of the League of Nations dealt a fatal blow to idealism. There is no doubt that the language of liberalism after 1945 was more pragmatic; how could anyone living in the shadow of the Holocaust be optimistic? Yet familiar core ideas of liberalism remained. Even in the early 1940s, there was recognition of the need to replace the League with another international institution with responsibility for international peace and security. Only this time, in the case of the United Nations there was an awareness among the framers of the Charter of the need for a consensus between the great powers in order for enforcement action to be taken; hence the veto system (Article 27 of the UN Charter), which allowed any of the five permanent members of the Security Council the power of veto.

This revision constituted an important modification to the classical model of collective security (Roberts 1996: 315). With the ideological polarity of the cold war, the UN procedures for collective security were still-born (as either of the **superpowers** and their allies would veto any action proposed by the other). It was not until the end of the cold war that a collective security system was put into operation, following the invasion of Kuwait by Iraq on 2 August 1990 (see Case Study).

An important argument advanced by liberals in the early post-war period concerned the state's inability to cope with modernization. David Mitrany (1943), a pioneer **integration** theorist, argued that transnational **cooperation** was required in order to resolve common problems. His core concept was ramification, meaning the likelihood that cooperation in one sector would lead governments to extend the range of **collaboration** across other sectors. As states become more embedded in an integration process, the 'cost' of withdrawing from cooperative ventures increases.

This argument about the positive benefits from transnational cooperation is one that informed a new generation of scholars (particularly in the USA) in the 1960s and 1970s. Their argument was not simply about the mutual gains from trade, but that other **transnational actors** were beginning to challenge the dominance of sovereign states. World politics, according to pluralists (as they are often referred to) was no longer an exclusive arena for states, as it had been for the first three hundred years of the Westphalian states-system. In one of the central texts of this genre, Robert Keohane and Joseph Nye (1972) argued that the centrality of other actors, such as interest groups, **transnational corporations**, and **international non-governmental organizations** (INGOs), had to be taken into consideration. Here the overriding image of international relations is one of a cobweb of diverse actors linked through multiple channels of interaction.

Although the phenomenon of transnationalism was an important addition to the IR theorists' vocabulary, it remained underdeveloped as a theoretical concept. Perhaps the most important contribution of **pluralism** was its elaboration of **interdependence**. Due to the expansion of **capitalism** and the emergence of a global culture, pluralists recognized a growing interconnectedness in which 'changes in one part of the system have direct and indirect consequences for the rest of the system' (Little 1996: 77). Absolute **state autonomy**, so keenly entrenched in the minds of state leaders, was being circumscribed by interdependence. Such a development

Case Study The 1990–1 Gulf War and collective security

Iraq had always argued that the sovereign state of Kuwait was an artificial creation of the imperial powers. When this political motive was allied to an economic imperative, caused primarily by the accumulated war debts following the eight-year war with Iran, the annexation of Kuwait seemed to be a solution to Iraq's problems. The Iraqi President, Saddam Hussein, also assumed that the West would not use force to defend Kuwait, a miscalcu-

lation fuelled by the memory of the support the West had given Iraq during the Iran–Iraq War (the so-called 'fundamentalism' of Iran was considered to be a graver threat to international order than the extreme nationalism of the Iraqi regime).

The invasion of Kuwait on 2 August 1990 led to a series of UN resolutions calling for Iraq to withdraw unconditionally. Economic sanctions were applied while the US-led coalition of international forces gathered in Saudi Arabia. Operation 'Desert Storm' crushed the Iraqi resistance in a matter of six weeks (16 January to 28 February 1991). The 1990–1 Gulf War had certainly revived the UN doctrine of collective security, although a number of doubts remained about the underlying motivations for the war and the way in which it was fought (for instance, the coalition of national armies was controlled by the USA rather than by a UN military command as envisaged in the Charter). President George H. Bush declared that the war was about more than one small country, it was about a 'big idea; a **new world order**'. The content of this new world order was 'peaceful settlement of disputes, solidarity against aggression, reduced and controlled arsenals, and just treatment of all peoples'.

brought with it enhanced potential for cooperation as well as increased levels of vulnerability.

In his 1979 work, *Theory of International Politics*, the neo-realist Kenneth Waltz attacked the pluralist argument about the decline of the state. He argued that the degree of interdependence internationally was far lower than the constituent parts in a national political system. Moreover, the level of economic interdependence—especially between great powers—was less than that which existed in the early part of the twentieth century. Waltz concludes: 'if one is thinking of the international–political world, it is odd in the extreme that "interdependence" has become the word commonly used to describe it' (1979: 144). In the course of their engagement with Waltz and other neo-realists, early pluralists modified their position. Neo-liberals,[4] as they came to be known, conceded that the core assumptions of **neo-realism** were indeed correct: the anarchic international structure, the centrality of states, and a rationalist approach to social scientific enquiry. Where they differed was apparent primarily in the argument that anarchy does not mean that durable patterns of cooperation are impossible: the creation of **international regimes** matters here as they facilitate cooperation by sharing information, reinforcing **reciprocity**, and making defection from norms easier to punish (see Ch. 17). Moreover, in what was to become the most important difference between neo-realists and neo-liberals (developed further

in Ch. 7), the latter argued that actors would enter into cooperative agreements if the gains were evenly shared. Neo-realists dispute this hypothesis: what matters is a question not so much of mutual gains as of **relative gains**: in other words, a neo-realist state has to be sure that it has more to gain than its rivals from a particular bargain or regime.

There are two important arguments that set neo-liberalism apart from democratic peace liberalism and the liberal idealists of the inter-war period. First, academic enquiry should be guided by a commitment to a scientific approach to theory building. Whatever deeply held personal values scholars maintain, their task must be to observe regularities, formulate hypotheses as to why that relationship holds, and subject these to critical scrutiny. This separation of fact and value puts neo-liberals on the positivist side of the methodological divide. Second, writers such as Keohane are critical of the naïve assumption of nineteenth-century liberals that commerce breeds peace. A free-trade system, according to Keohane, provides incentives for cooperation but does not guarantee it. Here he is making an important distinction between cooperation and harmony. 'Co-operation is not automatic', Keohane argues, 'but requires planning and negotiation' (1986b: 11). In the following section we see how contemporary liberal thinking maintains that the institutions of world politics after 1945 successfully embedded all states into a cooperative order.

Key Points

- Early liberal thought on international relations took the view that the natural order had been corrupted by undemocratic state leaders and outdated policies such as the balance of power. Enlightenment liberals believed that a latent cosmopolitan morality could be achieved through the exercise of reason and through the creation of constitutional states. In addition, the unfettered movement of people and goods could further facilitate more peaceful international relations.

- Although there are important continuities between

Enlightenment liberal thought and twentieth-century ideas, such as the belief in the power of world public opinion to tame the interests of states, liberal idealism was more programmatic. For idealists, persuasion was more important than abstract moral reasoning.

- Liberal thought at the end of the twentieth century became grounded in social scientific theories of state behaviour. Cooperation among rational egoists was possible to achieve if properly coordinated by regimes and institutions.

Liberalism and globalization

When applying liberal ideas to international relations today, we find two clusters of responses to the problems and possibilities posed by globalization.

The first alternative is that of the **liberalism of privilege** (Richardson 1997: 18). According to this perspective, the problems of globalization need to be addressed by a combination of strong democratic states in the core of the international system, robust regimes, and open markets and institutions. For an example of the working out of such a strategy in practice, we need to look no further than the success of the liberal **hegemony** of the post-1945 era. The US writer, G. John Ikenberry, is an articulate defender of this liberal order. In the aftermath of the Second World War, the USA took the opportunity to 'embed' certain fundamental liberal principles into the regulatory rules and institutions of international society. Most importantly, and contrary to realist thinking, the USA chose to forsake short-run gains in return for a durable settlement that benefited all states. According to Ikenberry, the USA signalled the cooperative basis of its power in a number of ways. First, in common with liberal democratic principles, the USA was an example to other members of international society in so far as its political system is open and allows different voices to be heard. Foreign policy, like domestic policy, is closely scrutinized by the media, public opinion, and political committees and opposition parties. Second, the USA advocated a global free-trade regime in accordance with the idea that free trade brings benefits to all participants (it also has the added advantage, from the hegemon's point of view, of being cheap to manage). Third, the USA appeared to its allies at least as a reluctant hegemon that would not seek to exploit its significant power-political advantage. Fourth, and most importantly, the USA created and participated in a range of important international institutions that constrained its actions. The Bretton Woods system of economic and financial accords and the **NATO** security alliance are the best examples of the highly institutionalized character of American power in the post-1945 period.

Box 6.3 G. John Ikenberry and the crisis of the liberal order

In a recent article (2009a), Ikenberry claims that the liberal order of the post-1945 world is in crisis. He usefully contrasts three phases in the development of liberalism in international politics. 'Liberal internationalism 1.0' is identified with the League of Nations, and the attendant commitments to liberal principles of free trade, national self-determination, and collective security. The second phase–'Liberal Internationalism 2.0'–refers to the 1945-era of embedded liberalism. A third phase of this order–'3.0'–is associated with the globalization of liberalism alongside the hollowing out of state capacities and institutional authority.

Ikenberry believes that the institutional architecture of the contemporary order is in crisis. The origins of the crisis lie in the confluence of the following tends: the increased difficulty in realizing common interests among the major powers now that the bipolar nuclear threat has dissipated; a disjuncture between concentrations of power in the system and reluctance by the majority of states to allow leading states and their institutions to 'rule'; the erosion of sovereignty norms without a clear and shared set of agreements about where local and global responsibilities begin and end; new threats emanating from state failure; and the emergence of global powers (such as India and China) whose ownership of, and participation in, the institutional order cannot be taken for granted. These factors add up to a single and fundamental claim: 'there is an authority crisis in today's liberal order' (2009b: 80). Critics argue that this kind of crisis narrative is a convenient trigger for *more* liberal ordering. It also risks misrepresenting liberalism in terms of great powers in the driving seat of global public policy, when governance is multi-level and action is driven by private and public actors (Koivisto and Dunne, 2010).

Advocates of this liberal hegemonic order note wryly that it was so successful that allies were more worried about abandonment than about domination.

The post-1945 system of regulatory regimes and institutions has been successful in part due to the fact that they exist. In other words, once one set of institutional arrangements becomes embedded, it is very difficult for alternatives to make inroads. There are two implications that need to be teased out here. One is the narrow historical 'window' that exists for new institutional design; the other is the durability of existing institutions. 'In terms of American hegemony, this means that, short of a major war or a global economic collapse, it is very difficult to envisage the type of historical breakpoint needed to replace the existing order' (Ikenberry 1999: 137). One of the problems, Ikenberry would argue, with the liberal order of the twenty-first century is precisely that there has not been a breakpoint that has enabled a reordering of world politics, such that new global powers such as China and India—and old unfulfilled ones such as Russia—feel satisfied with the balance of power and advantage in the world today.

Let us accept for a moment that the post-1945 **international order** has been successful and durable because US hegemony has been of a liberal character. The logic of this position is one in which the interests of all are identified with the interests of the USA and its Western allies. The challenge of managing international relations therefore becomes one where powerful states, and the institutions they dominate, are able to claim special rights and privileges over other members of international society. At the other end of the spectrum, the current order is highly unresponsive to the needs of weaker states and peoples. According to the United Nations Development Programme, the resulting global inequality is 'grotesque'. One statistic is particularly graphic: the richest 20 per cent of the world's population receives three-quarters of the world's income, while the poorest 20 per cent receive only 1.5 per cent.

Given that liberalism has produced such unequal gains for the West and the rest, it is perhaps surprising that contemporary US-based liberal scholars have become obsessed with the question of preserving the current order rather than reconstituting it according to more just distributive principles. Rather than seeing reform as a task that wealthy Western countries have a responsibility to undertake, the use of Western power is more often equated with extending control of institutions, protecting markets and security access to precious resources. When this hegemonic liberal order comes under challenge, as

it did on 9/11, the response is uncompromising. It is noticeable in this respect that former President George W. Bush mobilized the language of liberalism against Al Qaeda, the Taliban, and also Iraq. He referred to the 2003 war against Iraq as 'freedom's war'.

The potential for liberalism to embrace **imperialism** is a tendency that has a long history (Doyle 1986: 1151–69). We find in Machiavelli a number of arguments for the necessity for republics to expand. Liberty increases wealth and the concomitant drive for new markets; soldiers who are at the same time citizens are better fighters than slaves or mercenaries; and expansion is often the best means to promote a state's security. In this sense, contemporary US foreign policy is no different from the great expansionist republican states of the pre-modern period such as Athens and Rome. Few liberals today would openly advocate territorial expansion along the lines of nineteenth-century European colonial powers; at the same time, many have been drawn to consider the virtues of empire as a way of delivering liberty in an insecure world. Even when empire is rejected by liberals such as Michael Doyle, their defence of interventionism in the affairs of non-liberal states suggests that the line between internationalism and imperialism is a very fine one. Doyle's defence of democracy promotion by a policy mix of forcible and non-forcible instruments is featured in Box 6.4.

This strategy of preserving and extending liberal institutions is open to a number of criticisms. For the sake of simplicity, these will be gathered up into an alternative to the liberalism of privilege that we shall call **radical liberalism**. An opening objection made by proponents of the latter concerns the understanding of liberalism embodied in the neo-liberal defence of international institutions. The liberal character of those institutions is assumed rather than subjected to critical scrutiny. As a result, the incoherence of the purposes underpinning these institutions is often overlooked. The kind of economic **liberalization** advocated by Western financial institutions, particularly in economically impoverished countries, frequently comes into conflict with the norms of democracy and human rights. Three examples illustrate this dilemma. First, the more the West becomes involved in the organization of developing states' political and economic infrastructure, the less those states are able to be accountable to their domestic constituencies, thereby cutting through the link between the government and the people that is so central to modern liberal forms of representative democracy (Hurrell and Woods 1995: 463). Second, in order to qualify for Western aid and loans, states are often

Box 6.4 Defending and extending the liberal zone of peace

As we have seen, advocates of the democratic peace thesis believe that liberal states act peacefully towards one another. Yet this empirical law does not tell liberal states how to behave towards non-liberal states. Should they try to convert them, thereby bringing them into the zone of peace, or should they pursue a more defensive strategy? The former has not been successful in the past, and in a world of many nuclear weapons states, crusading could be suicidal. For this reason, Michael Doyle suggests a dual-track approach.

- The first track preserves the liberal community, which means forging strong alliances with other like-minded states and defending itself against illiberal regimes. This may require liberal states to include in their foreign policy strategies such as the balance of power in order to contain authoritarian states.

- The second track is more expansionist and aims to extend the liberal zone by a variety of economic and diplomatic instruments. Doyle categorizes these in terms of 'inspiration' (hoping that peoples living in non-democratic regimes will struggle for their liberty), 'instigation' (peace building and economic restructuring), and 'intervention' (legitimate if the majority of a polity is demonstrating widespread disaffection with their government and/or their basic rights are being systematically violated).

Doyle concludes with the warning that the march of liberalism will not necessarily continue unabated. It is in our hands, he argues, whether the international system becomes more pacific and stable, or whether antagonisms deepen. We must be willing to pay the price—in institutional costs and development aid—to increase the prospects for a peaceful future. This might be cheap when compared with the alternative of dealing with hostile and unstable authoritarian states.

(Doyle 1999)

required to meet harsh economic criteria requiring cuts in many welfare programmes; the example of the poorest children in parts of Africa having to pay for primary school education (Booth and Dunne 1999: 310)—which is their right according to the Universal Declaration of Human Rights—is a stark reminder of the fact that economic liberty and political equality are frequently opposed. Third, the inflexible response of international financial institutions to various crises in the world economy has contributed to a backlash against liberalism per se. Richard Falk puts this dilemma starkly: there is, he argues, a tension between 'the ethical imperatives of the global neighbourhood and the dynamics of economic globalisation' (1995a: 573). Radical liberals argue that the hegemonic institutional order has fallen prey to the neo-liberal consensus, which minimizes the role of the public sector in providing for welfare, and elevates the market as the appropriate mechanism for allocating resources, investment, and employment opportunities.

A second line of critique pursued by radical liberals concerns not so much the contradictory outcomes but the illiberal nature of the regimes and institutions. To put the point bluntly, there is a massive **democratic deficit** at the global level. Issues of international peace and security are determined by only 15 members of international society, of whom only five can exercise a power of veto. In other words, it is hypothetically possible for up to 200 states in the world to believe that military action ought to be taken but such an action would contravene the UN Charter if one of the permanent members were to cast a veto. If we take the area of political economy, the power exerted by the West and its international financial institutions perpetuates structural inequality. A good example here is the issue of free trade, which the West has pushed in areas where it gains from an open policy (such as in manufactured goods and financial services) but resisted in areas in which it stands to lose (agriculture and textiles). At a deeper level, radical liberals worry that *all* statist models of governance are undemocratic as elites are notoriously self-serving.

These sentiments underpin the approach to globalization taken by writers such as Danielle Archibugi, David Held, Mary Kaldor, and Jan Aart Scholte, among others, who believe that **global politics** must be democratized (Held and McGrew 2002). Held's argument is illustrative of the analytical and prescriptive character of radical liberalism in an era of globalization. His diagnosis begins by revealing the inadequacies of the 'Westphalian order' (or the modern states-system, conventionally dated from the middle of the seventeenth century). During the latter stages of this period, we have witnessed rapid democratization in a number of states, but this has not been accompanied by democratization of the **society of states** (Held 1993). This task is increasingly urgent given the current levels of interconnectedness, since 'national' governments are no longer in control of the forces that shape their citizens' lives (for example, the decision by one state to permit deforestation has environmental consequences for all states). After 1945, the UN Charter set limits to the **sovereignty** of states by recognizing the rights of individuals in a whole series of human rights conventions. But even if the UN had lived up to its Charter in the post-1945 period, it would still have left the building blocks of the Westphalian order largely intact, namely: the hierarchy between great powers and the rest (symbolized by the permanent membership of the Security Council); massive inequalities of wealth between states; and a minimal role for **non-state actors** to **influence** decision-making in international relations.

In place of the Westphalian and UN models, Held outlines a **cosmopolitan model of democracy**. This requires, in the first instance, the creation of regional parliaments and the extension of the authority of such regional bodies (like the European Union) that are already in existence. Second, human rights conventions must be entrenched in national parliaments and monitored by a new International Court of Human Rights. Third, reform or replacement of the UN with a genuinely democratic and accountable global parliament will be required. Without appearing to be too sanguine about the prospects for the realization of the cosmopolitan model of democracy, Held is nevertheless adamant that if democracy is to thrive, it must penetrate the institutions and regimes that manage global politics.

Radical liberals place great importance on the civilizing capacity of global society. While the rule of law and the democratization of international institutions is a core component of the liberal project, it is also vital that citizens' **networks** are broadened and deepened to monitor and cajole these institutions. These groups form a linkage between individuals, states, and global institutions. It is easy to portray radical liberal thinking as 'utopian', but we should not forget the many achievements of global civil society so far. The evolution of international humanitarian law, and the extent to which these laws are complied with, is largely down to the millions of individuals who are active supporters of human rights groups like Amnesty International and Human Rights Watch (Falk 1995b: 164). Similarly, global protest movements have been responsible for the heightened sensitivity to environmental degradation everywhere.

This emphasis on what Richard Falk calls 'globalization from below' is an important antidote to neo-liberalism's somewhat status-quo-oriented worldview. But just as imperialism can emerge from a complacent liberalism of privilege, the danger for radical liberals is naïvety. How

is it that global institutions can be reformed in such a way that the voices of ordinary people will be heard? And what if the views of 'peoples' rather than 'states' turn out to be similarly indifferent to global injustice? There is a sense in which radical liberal thought wants to turn back the clock of globalization to an era in which markets were places where local producers exchanged products grown from their small-holdings or made by human labour. It is not clear that such a lifestyle is preferable to a world in which relatively inexpensive goods are produced in mechanized factories and bought in multinational supermarkets. Perhaps the least plausible aspect of the radical liberal project is the injunction to reform global capitalism. Just how much of a civilizing effect is global civil society able to exert upon the juggernaut of capitalism? And can this movement bridge the globalization divide in which democratic institutions are territorially located while forces of production and destruction are global?

Key Points

- The victor states in the wartime alliance against Nazi Germany pushed for a new international institution to be created: the United Nations Charter was signed in San Francisco in June 1945 by 50 states. It represented a departure from the League in two important respects. Membership was near universal and the great powers were able to prevent any enforcement action from taking place that might be contrary to their interests

- In the late twentieth century, the embedded liberalism of the post-1945 order has come under challenge. The ability of the USA to steer world order is diminishing, rising powers are wanting a greater share of the spoils, and new security challenges (**weapons of mass destruction** (WMD), climate change) have heightened the vulnerability of all peoples.

- In the context of globalization, there is merit in contrasting a liberalism of privilege with radical liberalism. The former seeks to restore the authority of Western states and the privileges they enjoy, while the latter believes that the liberal order can be sustainable only if it responds to the just demands of the excluded and the impoverished.

Conclusion

The euphoria with which liberals greeted the end of the cold war in 1989 has been dissipated to a large extent by **9/11** and the **war on terror**. The pattern of conflict and insecurity that we have seen at the beginning of the twenty-first century suggests that liberal democracy remains at best an incomplete project. Images and narratives from countries in every continent—Afghanistan,

Liberia, Chechnya, Colombia, Burundi, the Democratic Republic of Congo, Iraq, Myanmar, Zimbabwe, and so on—remind us that in many parts of the world, anti-liberal values of warlordism, torture, intolerance, and injustice are expressed daily. Moreover, the reasons why these states have failed can to some extent be laid at the door of liberalism, particularly in terms of its promotion of often irreconcilable norms of sovereignty, democracy, national self-determination, and human rights (Hoffmann 1995–6: 169).

One response to the argument that liberalism is incomplete or under threat is to call for more liberalism. This is certainly the approach taken by G. John Ikenberry and his co-author Daniel Deudney (2009*a*, 2009*b*). They believe that there is only one path to modernization, and that illiberal voices will be drowned out by the imperatives to open markets and hold governments accountable. A deeper reason for the crisis in liberalism is that it is bound up with an increasingly discredited Enlightenment view of the world. Contrary to the hopes of Bentham, Hume, Kant, Mill, and Paine, the application of reason and science to politics has not brought communities together. Indeed, it has arguably shown the fragmented nature of the **political community**, which is regularly expressed in terms of ethnic, linguistic, or religious differences. Critics of liberalism argue that the universalizing mission of liberal values, such as democracy, capitalism, and secularism, undermines the traditions and practices of non-Western cultures (Gray 1995: 146). When it comes to doing intercultural politics, somehow liberals just don't seem to take 'no' for an answer. The Marxist writer Immanuel Wallerstein has a nice way of expressing the dilemma over universalism. Liberals view it as 'a "gift" of the powerful to the weak'

that places them in a double bind: 'to refuse the gift is to lose; to accept the gift is to lose' (in Brown 1999).

At the outset, the chapter pointed to a tension within liberalism. The emphasis on personal liberty, unfettered trade, and the accumulation of property can contribute to a society riven with inequality, suspicion, and rivalry. Pulling in the opposite direction, liberalism contains within it a set of values that seek to provide for the conditions of a just society through democratic institutions and welfare-oriented economies. Projecting this tension on to a global stage leads to two possibilities for liberalism in an era of globalization. One variant is that relatively weak institutions try to respond to the challenge of coordinating the behaviour of states in a decentralized international order. In this world economic growth is unevenly distributed. As a consequence, preventive military action remains an ever-present possibility in order to deal with chaos and violence produced by dispossessed communities and networks. The more progressive model, advocated by radical liberals, seeks to heighten regulation through the strengthening of international institutions. This is to be done by making institutions more democratic and accountable for the negative consequences of globalization. The charge of utopianism is one that is easy to make against this position and hard to refute. In so doing, liberals of a radical persuasion should invoke Kant's axiom that 'ought' must imply 'can'.

Questions

1   Do you agree with Stanley Hoffmann that international affairs are 'inhospitable' to liberalism?

2   What arguments might one draw upon to support or refute this proposition?

3   Was the language of international morality, used by liberal idealists in the inter-war period, a way of masking the interests of Britain and France in maintaining their dominance of the international system after the First World War?

4   Should liberal states promote their values abroad? Is force a legitimate instrument in securing this goal?

5   How much progress (if any) has there been in liberal thinking on international relations since Kant?

6   Are democratic peace theorists right, but for the wrong reasons?

7   Which strategy of dealing with globalization do you find more convincing: the one that holds that states and institutions should maintain the current order or the one that supports reform driven by global civil society?

8   Is there a fundamental tension at the heart of liberalism between liberty and democracy? If so, how is this tension played out in the international domain?

9   Are liberal values and institutions in the contemporary international system as deeply embedded as neo-liberals claim?

10   Is the liberal order in crisis today, as G. John Ikenberry argues? Are emerging global powers a threat to the liberal order?

Further Reading

Liberalism in International Relations

Brown, C., Nartin, T., and Rengger, N. (eds) (2002), *International Relations in Political Thought: Texts from the Ancient Greeks to the First World War* (Cambridge: Cambridge University Press). See especially the readings from classical liberal thought in sections 7, 8, and 9.

Doyle, M. (1997), *Ways of War and Peace* (New York: W. W. Norton). Doyle classifies liberalism into the following strands: liberal pacifism, liberal imperialism, and liberal internationalism. See also, in a shorter and modified form, his article: Doyle, M. (1986), 'Liberalism and World Politics', *American Political Science Review*, 80(4): 1151–69.

Hoffmann, S. (1987), *Janus and Minerva* (Boulder, CO: Westview Press): 394–436. An excellent account of liberalism and its troubled relationship to international relations.

Richardson, J. L. (1997), 'Contending Liberalisms: Past and Present', *European Journal of International Relations*, 3(1): 5–33. A thorough overview of liberalism in political thought and in IR. Parts of the argument in this chapter mirror Richardson's article.

Smith, M. J. (1992), 'Liberalism and International Reform', in **T. Nardin and D. Mapel** (eds), *Traditions of International Ethics* (Cambridge: Cambridge University Press): 201–24. A comprehensive piece that draws out the premises of liberalism and in particular the belief in international organization.

Walt, S. (1998), 'International Relations: One World, Many Theories', *Foreign Policy*, 110: 29–46. Not only does this contain a useful short overview of liberalism; it highlights the imperfect application of liberal theory in practice.

Liberalism in American and British foreign policy

Cox, M., Ikenberry, G. J., and Inoguchi, T. (eds) (2000), *American Democracy Promotion: Impulses, Strategies and Impacts* (Oxford: Oxford University Press): 1–17. See especially the introduction, which puts US democracy promotion in context.

— **Booth, K., and Dunne, T.** (eds) (1999), *The Interregnum: Controversies in World Politics 1989–1999* (Cambridge: Cambridge University Press). Contains a range of perspectives on the pattern of world power in the 1990s.

Held, D., and McGrew, A. (eds) (2002), *The Global Transformation Reader*, 2nd edn (Cambridge: Polity Press). A useful collection of essays with many contributors who represent radical liberalism.

Paul, T. V., and Hall, J. A. (eds) (1999), *International Order and the Future of World Politics* (Cambridge: Cambridge University Press). See especially the essay on the role of liberal institutions by G. John Ikenberry, 'Liberal Hegemony and the Future of American Post-war Order', 123–45.

Ikenberry, G. J. (2009), 'Liberal Internationalism 3.0: America and the Dilemmas of Liberal World Order', *Perspectives in Politics*, 71(1): 71–87. A pivotal case for the reform of the post-1945 order, by an influential liberal thinker.

Online Resource Centre

 Visit the Online Resource Centre that accompanies this book to access more learning resources on this chapter topic at www.oxfordtextbooks.co.uk/orc/baylis5e/

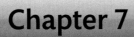

Chapter 7

Contemporary mainstream approaches: neo-realism and neo-liberalism

STEVEN L. LAMY

Reader's Guide

This chapter reviews the core assumptions of neo-realism and neo-liberalism and explores the debate between these intellectual siblings that has dominated mainstream academic scholarship in International Relations (IR) in the USA. Realism and neo-realism, and to some extent neo-liberalism, have also had a profound impact on US foreign policy. Neo-realists dominate the world of security studies and neo-liberals focus on political economy and more recently on issues such as human rights and the environment. These theories do not offer starkly contrasting images of the world. Neo-realists state that they are concerned with issues of survival. They claim that neo-liberals are too optimistic about the possibilities for cooperation among states. Neo-liberals counter with claims that all states have mutual interests and can gain from cooperation. Both are normative theories of a sort, biased towards the state, the capitalist market, and the status quo. The processes of globalization have forced neo-realists and neo-liberals to consider similar issues and address new challenges to international order. In the introduction, I discuss the various versions of neo-liberalism and neo-realism, and ask the reader to consider how theory shapes our image of the world. Each theory represents an attempt by scholars to offer a better explanation for the behaviour of states and to describe the nature of international politics. Similarly, the more policy-relevant versions of these theories prescribe competing policy agendas. The next section reviews three versions of neo-realism: Waltz's structural realism; Grieco's neo-realism or modern realism, with its focus on absolute and relative gains; and what security scholars call offensive and defensive realism or neo-realism. The third section of the chapter reviews the assumptions of neo-liberal institutionalist perspectives. The fourth section focuses on the 'neo-neo debate'. This is a debate that many US scholars think is the most important intellectual issue in IR today. Many other scholars see it as not much of a debate at all. It is a debate about refining common assumptions and about the future role and effectiveness of international institutions and the possibilities of cooperation. However, it is not a debate between mainstream and critical perspectives. It is a debate between 'rule-makers' and it leaves out the voices on the margins, those of the 'rule-takers'. In the fifth section of the chapter, I review how neo-realists and neo-liberal thinkers react to the processes of globalization. The chapter concludes with a suggestion that we are only seeing part of the world if we limit our studies to the neo-perspectives and the neo–neo debate.

Introduction

The debate between neo-realists and neo-liberals has dominated mainstream international relations scholarship in the USA since the mid-1980s. Two of the major US journals in the field, *International Organization* and *International Security*, are dominated by articles that address the relative merits of each theory and its value in explaining the world of international politics. **Neo-realism** and neo-liberalism are the progeny of **realism** and **liberalism** respectively. They are more than theories; they are paradigms or conceptual frameworks that define a field of study, and define an agenda for research and policy-making. As previous chapters on liberalism (Ch. 6) and realism (Ch. 5) have suggested, there are many versions and interpretations of each paradigm or theory. Some realists are more 'hard-line' on issues such as defence or participation in international agreements, while other realists take more accommodating positions on these same issues. The previous chapter on liberalism provides a useful description of the varieties of this theory, and this chapter will explore those that have the greatest impact on academic discourse in the USA and on the people who develop US foreign policy. This chapter will also show the considerable differences in how the scholarly and policy world define and use the labels neo-realism and neo-liberalism.

For most academics, neo-realism refers to Kenneth Waltz's Theory of International Politics (1979). Waltz's theory emphasizes the importance of the **structure** of the **international system** and its role as the primary determinant of **state** behaviour. Yet most scholars and policy-makers use neo-realism to describe a recent or updated version of realism. Recently, in the area of security studies, some scholars use the terms **offensive** and **defensive realism** when discussing the current version of realism; or neo-realism (see Ch. 5).

In the academic world, neo-liberal generally refers to neo-liberal institutionalism, or what is now called institutional theory by those writing in this theoretical domain. However, in the policy world, neo-liberalism means something different. A neo-liberal foreign policy promotes free trade or open markets and Western democratic values and institutions. Most of the leading Western states have joined the US-led chorus, calling for the 'enlargement' of the **community** of democratic and capitalist **nation-states**. There is no other game in town; the financial and political institutions created after the Second World War have survived, and these provide the foundation for current political and economic **power** arrangements.

In reality, neo-liberal foreign policies tend not to be as wedded to the ideals of **democratic peace**, free trade, and open borders. **National interests** take precedence over morality and universal ideals, and, much to the dismay of traditional realists, economic interests are given priority over geopolitical ones.

For students beginning their study of International Relations (IR), these labels and contending definitions can be confusing and frustrating. Yet, as you have learned in reading previous chapters in this volume, understanding these perspectives and theories is the only way you can hope to understand and explain how leaders and citizens alike see the world and respond to issues and events. This understanding may be more important when discussing neo-realism and neo-liberalism because they represent dominant perspectives in the policy world and in the US academic community.

There are clear differences between neo-realism and neo-liberalism; however, these differences should not be exaggerated. Robert Keohane (in Baldwin 1993), a neo-liberal institutionalist, has stated that neo-liberal institutionalism borrows equally from realism and liberalism. Both theories represent status-quo perspectives and are what Robert Cox calls problem-solving theories (see Ch. 10). This means that both neo-realism and neo-liberalism address issues and problems that could disrupt the status quo, namely, the issues of **security**, conflict, and **cooperation**.

Neither theory advances prescriptions for major reform or radical transformation of the international system. Rather, they are system maintainer theories, meaning that adherents are generally satisfied with the current international system and its actors, values, and power arrangements. These theories address different sets of issues. In general, neo-realist theory focuses on issues of military security and war. Neo-liberal theorists focus on issues of cooperation, international political economy, and, most recently, the environment. For neo-liberal institutionalists, the core question for research is how to promote and support cooperation in an anarchic and competitive international system. For neo-realists, the core research question is how to survive in this system.

A review of the assumptions of each theory and an analysis of the contending positions in the so-called neo–neo debate and a discussion of how neo-liberals and neo-realists react to the processes of **globalization** follows.

Neo-realism

Kenneth Waltz's theory of **structural realism** is only one version of neo-realism. A second group of neo-realists, represented by the scholarly contributions of Joseph Grieco (1988a and 1988b), have integrated Waltz's ideas with the ideas of more traditional realists, such as Hans Morgenthau, Raymond Aron, Stanley Hoffmann, and Robert Gilpin, to construct a contemporary or **modern realist** profile. A third version of neo-realism is found in security studies. Here scholars talk about offensive and defensive realists. These versions of neo-realism are briefly reviewed in the next few pages.

Structural realism

Waltz's neo-realism is distinctive from traditional or classical realism in a number of ways. First, realism is primarily an inductive theory. For example, Hans Morgenthau would explain international politics by looking at the actions and interactions of the states in the system. Thus, the decision by Pakistan and India to test nuclear weapons could be explained by looking at the influence of military leaders in both states and the long-standing differences compounded by their geographic proximity. All these explanations are unit or bottom-up explanations. Neo-realists, such as Waltz, do not deny the importance of unit-level explanations; however, they believe that the effects of structure must be considered. According to Waltz, structure is defined by the ordering principle of the international system, which is **anarchy**, and the distribution of **capabilities** across units, which are states. Waltz also assumes that there is no differentiation of function between different units.

The structure of the international system shapes all foreign policy choices. For a neo-realist, a better explanation for India and Pakistan's nuclear testing would be anarchy or the lack of a common power or central authority to enforce **rules** and maintain **order** in the system. In a competitive system, this condition creates a need for weapons to survive. Additionally, in an **anarchic system**, states with greater power tend to have greater influence.

A second difference between traditional realists and Waltz's neo-realism is found in their view of power. To realists, power is an end in itself. States use power to gain more power and thus increase their influence and ability to secure their national interests. Although traditional realists recognize different elements of power (for example, economic resources and technology), military power is considered the most obvious element of a state's power. Waltz would not agree with those who say that military force is not as essential as it once was as a tool of statecraft. As recent conflicts in Russia, Iraq, Afghanistan, Sudan, Lebanon, and Sri Lanka suggest, many leaders still believe that they can resolve their differences by force.

For neo-realists, power is more than the accumulation of military resources and the ability to use this power to coerce and control other states in the system. Waltz and other neo-realists see power as the combined capabilities of a state. States are differentiated in the system by their power and not by their function. Power gives a state a place or position in the international system and that shapes the state's behaviour. During the **cold war**, the USA and the USSR were positioned as the only two **superpowers**. Neo-realists would say that such positioning explains the similarities in their behaviour. The distribution of power and any dramatic changes in that distribution of power help to explain the structure of the international system. Specifically, states will seek to maintain their position or placement in the system. The end of the cold war and the disintegration of the Soviet Empire upset the **balance of power** and, in the eyes of many neo-realists, increased uncertainty and instability in the international system. Waltz concurs with traditional realists when he states that the central mechanism for order in the system is balance of power. The renewed emphasis on the importance of the United Nations and **NATO** and their interventions in crisis areas around the world may be indicative of the major

powers' current search for order in the international system. Waltz would challenge neo-liberal institutionalists who believe that we can manage the processes of globalization merely by building effective international institutions (see Case Study). He would argue that their effectiveness depends on the support of major powers.

A third difference between realism and Waltz's neo-realism is each one's view on how states react to the condition of anarchy. To realists, anarchy is a condition of the system, and states react to it according to their size, location, domestic politics, and leadership qualities. In contrast, neo-realists suggest that anarchy defines the system. Further, all states are functionally similar units, meaning that they all experience the same constraints presented by anarchy and strive to maintain

---

Case Study 1 'The underbelly of globalization': toxic waste dumping in the global South

Families in several villages near Abidjan, Ivory Coast awoke one summer morning to a horrible smell of rotten eggs, and many were suffering with burning eyes and nosebleeds. Eventually, ten people died, thousands sought medical care and children developed sores and blisters. The number of people seeking medical care overwhelmed the health care system in this region and demonstrations against the government led to arrests and the resignation of key political officials. This is the kind of human security problem that we will see more of as the industrialized North dumps its waste and worn-out computers and cellphones on the poor South. What was the cause of this problem and are there not laws or treaties aimed at addressing these kinds of issues?

The source of this environmental and medical crisis was a 'stinking slick of black sludge' that had been illegally dumped in eighteen areas around Abidjan by tanker trucks hired by a local company with no experience in properly disposing of toxic materials. A Swiss oil and metals trading corporation that also leased the ship hired this local company. The *Probo Koala* had brought this deadly mix to the Ivory Coast from Amsterdam. Trafigura, the global trading firm, planned on properly disposing the petrochemical wastes in Amsterdam. But once fumes overcame workers cleaning the ship in Amsterdam, the Dutch disposal company stopped the process, ordered an analysis of the wastes and alerted Dutch government authorities. An early analysis of the toxic waste showed

concentrations of chemicals that could paralyse a person's nervous system and could kill. When the Amsterdam waste disposal company raised its price because of this danger, the *Probo Koala* was allowed to take back its waste and sailed for Estonia to pick up Russian oil products and then continue to Western Africa.

Officials from Trafigura notified Ivorian officials that the ship was carrying toxic wastes, but they were still allowed to land in Abidjan. Both company officials and the government of the Ivory Coast were well aware that there were no facilities in Abidjan for properly disposing of this waste. The Ivorian company, Tommy, hired tanker trucks that were loaded with the toxic wastes from the *Probo Koala*. During the night, the tankers dumped their loads in eighteen areas around the city of Abidjan.

The disposal and dumping of toxic wastes is a global problem. As environmental regulations in the North become more stringent, corporations move to the South for dumping. Wastes follow the path of least resistance—global corporations look for countries with weak laws and without the capacity or will to enforce any national or international laws aimed at regulating the waste disposal market. Who is responsible for this problem? How should it be managed? *Neoliberal institutionalists* believe that we can establish regimes or governing arrangements to manage trade in toxic wastes and prevent illegal dumping. In fact, a previous dumping incident in Koko, Nigeria, was a catalyst for a conference and treaty to govern the transnational movement of toxic wastes. At the Basel convention in 1989, the global South wanted an absolute ban on all toxic waste trade and the global North lobbied for a much weaker treaty. The first version of this treaty was ratified in 1992 and revisions in 1994 and 1998 have essentially banned the export of hazardous waste from North to South. Yet enforcement depends on the cooperation of citizens, global corporations, and governments at all levels. At the time this was considered a victory for the poor and advocates for environmental justice and human security for all. Unfortunately, the Ivory Coast case shows how difficult it is to manage the processes of globalization and to control those individuals who place profits over the well-being of people.

(For more information: Basel Action Network, <www.ban.org>)

their position in the system. Neo-realists explain any differences in policy by differences in power or capabilities. Both Belgium and China recognize that one of the constraints of anarchy is the need for security to protect their national interests. Leaders in these countries may select different policy paths to achieve that security. A small country such as Belgium, with limited resources, responds to anarchy and the resulting **security dilemma** by joining alliances and taking an activist role in regional and international organizations, seeking to control the arms race. China, a major power and a large country, would most likely pursue a unilateral strategy of increasing military strength to protect and secure its interests.

Relative and absolute gains

Joseph Grieco (1988*a*) is one of several realist/neo-realist scholars who focuses on the concepts of **relative** and **absolute gains.** Grieco claims that states are interested in increasing their power and influence (absolute gains) and, thus, will cooperate with other states or actors in the system to increase their capabilities. However, Grieco claims that states are also concerned with how much power and influence other states might achieve (relative gains) in any cooperative endeavour. This situation can be used to show a key difference between neo-liberals and neo-realists. Neo-liberals claim that cooperation does not work when states fail to follow the rules and 'cheat' to secure their national interests. Neo-realists claim that there are two barriers to international cooperation: cheating and the relative gains of other actors. Further, when states fail to comply with rules that encourage cooperation, other states may abandon multilateral activity and act unilaterally.

The likelihood of states abandoning international cooperative efforts is increased if participants see other states gaining more from the arrangement. If states agree to a ban on the production and use of landmines, all the signatories to the treaty will be concerned about compliance. Institutions will be established to enforce the treaty. Neo-realists argue that leaders must be vigilant for cheaters and must focus on those states that could gain a military advantage when this weapons system is removed. In some security situations, landmines may be the only effective deterrent against a neighbouring state with superior land forces. In this situation, the relative gains issue is one of survival. In a world of uncertainty and competition, the fundamental question, according to Grieco and others who share his view of neo-realism, is not whether all parties gain from the cooperation, but who will gain more if we cooperate?

Security studies and neo-realism

Recently, security studies scholars, primarily in the USA, have suggested a more nuanced version of a realism that reflects their interests in understanding the nature of the security threats presented by the international system and the strategy options that states must pursue to survive and prosper in the system. These two versions of neo-realism, offensive and defensive realism (many scholars in this area prefer to be called modern realists and not neo-realists), are more policy-relevant than Waltz and Grieco's version of neo-realism, and thus may be seen as more prescriptive than the other versions (Jervis 1999).

Offensive neo-realists appear to accept most of Waltz's ideas and a good portion of the assumptions of traditional realism. Defensive neo-realists suggest that our assumptions of relations with other states depend on whether they are friends or enemies. When dealing with friends such as the European Union, the assumptions governing US leaders are more akin to those promoted by neo-liberals. However, there is little difference between defensive and offensive neo-realists when they are dealing with expansionary or pariah states, or traditional enemies.

John Mearsheimer (1990, 1994/5), an offensive realist in security studies, suggests that relative power and not absolute power is most important to states. He suggests that leaders of countries should pursue security policies that weaken their potential enemies and increase their power relative to all others. In this era of globalization, the incompatibility of states' goals and interests enhances the competitive nature of an anarchic system and makes conflict as inevitable as cooperation. Thus

---

Box 7.1 Core assumptions of neo-realists

- States and other actors interact in an anarchic environment. This means that there is no central authority to enforce rules and norms or protect the interests of the larger global community.

- The structure of the system is a major determinant of actor behaviour.

- States are self-interest-oriented, and an anarchic and competitive system pushes them to favour self-help over cooperative behaviour.

- States are rational actors, selecting strategies to maximize benefits and minimize losses.

- The most critical problem presented by anarchy is survival.

- States see all other states as potential enemies and threats to their national security. This distrust and fear creates a security dilemma, and this motivates the policies of most states.

talk of reducing military budgets at the end of the cold war was considered by offensive neo-realists to be pure folly. Leaders must always be prepared for an expansionary state that will challenge the global order. Moreover, if the major powers begin a campaign of disarmament and reduce their power relative to other states, they are simply inviting these expansionary states to attack.

John Mearsheimer and Stephen Walt (2003) were critical of the decision by George W. Bush to go to war in Iraq. They argue that the Bush administration 'inflated the threat' by misleading the world about Iraq's **weapons of mass destruction** (WMD) and its links to terrorists who might attack the USA in the future.

More importantly for security neo-realists, this war was unnecessary because the **containment** of Iraq was working effectively and there was no 'compelling strategic rationale' for this war. The war with Iraq will cost the USA billions of dollars, and it has already required a tremendous commitment of US military forces. With Iraq, Afghanistan, and the global war on **terrorism**, the US military is over-extended. The unilateralism of the Bush administration concerned both offensive and defensive neo-realists because it hurts the absolute and relative power of the USA.

Defensive neo-realists Robert Jervis (1999) and Jack Snyder (1991) claim that most leaders understand that the costs of war clearly outweigh the benefits. The use of military force for conquest and expansion is a security strategy that most leaders reject in this age of **complex interdependence** and globalization. War remains a tool of statecraft for some; however, most wars are seen by citizens and leaders alike to be caused by irrational or dysfunctional forces within a society, such as excessive militarism or ethnonationalism.

Defensive neo-realists are often confused with neo-liberals. Although they have some sympathy for the neo-liberal argument that war can be avoided by creating security institutions (for example, alliances or arms control treaties) that diminish the security dilemma and provide mutual security for participating states, they do not see institutions as the most effective way to prevent all wars. Most believe that conflict is simply unavoidable in some situations. First, aggressive and expansionary states do exist and they challenge **world order** and, second, simply in pursuit of their national interests, some states may make conflict with others unavoidable.

Defensive neo-realists are more optimistic than are offensive neo-realists. However, they are considerably less optimistic than neo-liberals for several reasons (Jervis 1999). First, defensive neo-realists see conflict as unnecessary only in a subset of situations (for example, economic relations). Second, leaders can never be certain that an aggressive move by a state (for example, support for a revolutionary movement in a neighbouring state) is an expansionary action intended to challenge the existing order or simply a preventive policy aimed at protecting their security. Third, defensive realists challenge the neo-liberal view that it is relatively easy to find areas where national interests might converge and become the basis for cooperation and institution building. Although they recognize that areas of common or mutual interests exist, defensive neo-realists are concerned about non-compliance or cheating by states, especially in security policy areas.

Key Points

- Kenneth Waltz's structural realism has had a major impact on scholars in International Relations. Waltz claims that the structure of the international system is the key factor in shaping the behaviour of states. Waltz's neo-realism also expands our view of power and capabilities. However, he agrees with traditional realists when he states that major powers still determine the nature of the international system.

- Structural realists minimize the importance of national attributes as determinants of a state's foreign policy behaviour. To these neo-realists, all states are functionally similar units, experiencing the same constraints presented by anarchy.

- Structural realists accept many assumptions of traditional realism. They believe that force remains an important and effective tool of statecraft, and balance of power is still the central mechanism for order in the system.

- Joseph Grieco represents a group of neo-realists or modern realists who are critical of neo-liberal institutionalists who claim that states are mainly interested in absolute gains. Grieco claims that all states are interested in both absolute and relative gains. How gains are distributed is an important issue. Thus there are two barriers to international cooperation: fear of those who might not follow the rules and the relative gains of others.

- Scholars in security studies present two versions of neo-realism or modern realism. Offensive neo-realists emphasize the importance of relative power. Like traditional realists, they believe that conflict is inevitable in the international system and leaders must always be wary of expansionary powers. Defensive realists are often confused with neo-liberal institutionalists. They recognize the costs of war and assume that it usually results from irrational forces in a society. However, they admit that expansionary states willing to use military force make it impossible to live in a world without weapons. Cooperation is possible, but it is more likely to succeed in relations with friendly states.

Neo-liberalism

As the previous chapter on liberalism indicates, there are a number of versions of the theory and all have their progeny in contemporary neo-liberal debates. David Baldwin (1993) identified four varieties of liberalism that influence contemporary international relations: commercial, republican, sociological, and liberal institutionalism.

The first, **commercial liberalism,** advocates free trade and a market or capitalist economy as the way towards peace and prosperity. Today, this view is promoted by global financial institutions, most of the major trading states, and multinational corporations. The **neo-liberal orthodoxy** is championed by popular authors like Thomas Friedman (2005), and argues that free trade, private property rights, and free markets will lead to a richer, more innovative, and more tolerant world. **Republican liberalism** states that democratic states are more inclined to respect the rights of their citizens and are less likely to go to war with their democratic neighbours. In current scholarship, this view is presented as democratic peace theory. These two forms of liberalism, commercial and republican, have been combined to form the core foreign policy goals of many of the world's major powers.

In **sociological liberalism**, the notion of community and the process of interdependence are important elements. As transnational activities increase, people in distant lands are linked and their governments become more interdependent. As a result, it becomes more difficult and more costly for states to act unilaterally and to avoid cooperation with neighbours. The cost of war or other deviant behaviour increases for all states and, eventually, a peaceful international community is built. Many of the assumptions of sociological liberalism are represented in the current globalization literature dealing with popular culture and **civil society**.

Liberal institutionalism or **neo-liberal institutionalism** is considered by many scholars to present the most convincing challenge to realist and neo-realist thinking. The roots of this version of neo-liberalism are found in the functional **integration** scholarship of the 1940s and the 1950s, and regional integration studies of the 1960s. These studies suggest that the way towards peace and prosperity is to have independent states pool their resources and even surrender some of their **sovereignty** to create integrated communities to promote economic growth or respond to regional problems (see Ch. 26). The European Union is one such institution that began

as a regional community for encouraging multilateral cooperation in the production of coal and steel. Proponents of integration and community building were motivated to challenge dominant realist thinking because of the experiences of the two world wars. Rooted in liberal thinking, integration theories promoted after the Second World War were less idealistic and more pragmatic than the liberal internationalism that dominated policy debates after the First World War.

The third generation of liberal institutional scholarship was the transnationalism and complex interdependence of the 1970s (Keohane and Nye 1972, 1977). Theorists in these camps presented arguments that suggested that the world had become more pluralistic in terms of actors involved in international interactions and that these actors had become more dependent on each other. Complex interdependence presented a world with four characteristics: (1) increasing linkages among states and **non-state actors**; (2) a new agenda of international issues with no distinction between low and high politics; (3) a recognition of multiple channels for interaction among actors across national boundaries; and (4) the decline of the efficacy of military force as a tool of statecraft. Complex interdependence scholars would suggest that globalization represents an increase in linkages and channels for interaction, as well as in the number of interconnections.

Neo-liberal institutionalism or institutional theory shares many of the assumptions of neo-realism. However, its adherents claim that neo-realists focus excessively on conflict and competition, and minimize the chances for cooperation even in an anarchic international system. Neo-liberal institutionalists see 'institutions' as the mediator and the means to achieve cooperation among actors in the system. Currently, neo-liberal institutionalists are focusing their research on issues of **global governance** and the creation and maintenance of institutions associated with managing the processes of globalization.

For neo-liberal institutionalists, the focus on mutual interests extends beyond trade and **development** issues. With the end of the cold war, states were forced to address new security concerns like the threat of terrorism, the proliferation of **weapons of mass destruction**, and an increasing number of internal conflicts that threatened regional and global security. Graham Allison (2000) states that one of the consequences of the globalization of security concerns such as terrorism, drug trafficking, and pandemics like HIV/AIDS is the realization that threats to any country's security cannot be addressed unilaterally. Successful responses to security threats require the creation of regional and global **regimes** that promote cooperation among states and the **coordination** of policy responses to these new security threats.

Robert Keohane (2002*b*) suggests that one result of the **9/11** terrorist attacks on the USA was the creation of a very broad coalition against terrorism, involving a large number of states and key global and regional institutions. Neo-liberals support cooperative **multilateralism** and are generally critical of the pre-emptive and unilateral use of force previously condoned in the 2002 Bush doctrine. Still in the policy world, the Obama administration has made it a priority to re-establish US leadership in reforming institutions of global governance. This administration places an emphasis on multilateralism and sees the USA as a builder of world order and as a partner in global problem solving. The priority given to global cooperation and multilateralism was evident in President Obama's work with the **G20** to address the global economic crisis and his diplomatic efforts to reach an agreement at the climate talks in Copenhagen. The President's commitment to regional and global institutions was clearly expressed in Obama's Nobel Peace Prize acceptance speech:

> Peace requires responsibility. Peace entails sacrifice. That is why NATO continues to be indispensable. That is why we must strengthen UN and regional peacekeeping, and not leave the task to a few countries. (http://nobelprize.org)

Most neo-liberals would believe that the US-led war with Iraq did more to undermine the legitimacy and influence of global and regional security institutions that operated so successfully in the first Gulf War (1990–1) and continue to work effectively in Afghanistan. The Obama administration has made it clear that the USA cannot and will not act alone.

The core assumptions of neo-liberal institutionalists include:

- States are key actors in international relations, but not the only significant actors. States are rational or instrumental actors, always seeking to maximize their interests in all issue-areas.
- In this competitive environment, states seek to maximize absolute gains through cooperation. Rational

behaviour leads states to see value in cooperative behaviour. States are less concerned with gains or advantages achieved by other states in cooperative arrangements.

- The greatest obstacle to successful cooperation is non-compliance or cheating by states.
- Cooperation is never without problems, but states will shift **loyalty** and resources to institutions if these are seen as mutually beneficial and if they provide states with increasing opportunities to secure their international interests.

The neo-liberal institutional perspective is more relevant in issue-areas where states have mutual interests. For example, most world leaders believe that we shall all benefit from an open trade system, and many support trade rules that protect the environment. Institutions have been created to manage international behaviour in both areas. The neo-liberal view may have less relevance in areas in which states have no mutual interests. Thus cooperation in military or national security areas, where someone's gain is perceived as someone else's loss (**a zero-sum perspective**), may be more difficult to achieve.

Key Points

- Contemporary neo-liberalism has been shaped by the assumptions of commercial, republican, sociological, and institutional liberalism.

- Commercial and republican liberalism provide the foundation for current neo-liberal thinking in Western governments. These countries promote free trade and democracy in their foreign policy programmes.

- Neo-liberal institutionalism, the other side of the neo-neo debate, is rooted in the functional integration theoretical work of the 1950s and 1960s, and the complex interdependence and transnational studies literature of the 1970s and 1980s.

- Neo-liberal institutionalists see institutions as the mediator and the means to achieve cooperation in the international system. Regimes and institutions help govern a competitive and anarchic international system, and they encourage, and at times require, multilateralism and cooperation as a means of securing national interests.

- Neo-liberal institutionalists recognize that cooperation may be harder to achieve in areas where leaders perceive they have no mutual interests.

- Neo-liberals believe that states cooperate to achieve absolute gains, and the greatest obstacle to cooperation is 'cheating' or non-compliance by other states.

The neo–neo debate

By now it should be clear that the neo–neo debate is not particularly contentious, nor is the intellectual difference between the two theories significant. As was suggested earlier in the chapter, neo-realists and neo-liberals share an epistemology; they focus on similar questions and agree on a number of assumptions about man, the state, and the international system. A summary of the major points of contention is presented in Box 7.2.

Box 7.2 The main features of the neo-realist/neo-liberal debate

1 Both agree that the international system is anarchic. Neo-realists say that anarchy puts more constraints on foreign policy and that neo-liberals minimize the importance of survival as the goal of each state. Neo-liberals claim that neo-realists minimize the importance of international interdependence, globalization, and the regimes created to manage these interactions.

2 Neo-realists believe that international cooperation will not happen unless states make it happen. They feel that it is hard to achieve, difficult to maintain, and dependent on state power. Neo-liberals believe that cooperation is easy to achieve in areas where states have mutual interests.

3 Neo-liberals think that actors with common interests try to maximize absolute gains. Neo-realists claim that neo-liberals overlook the importance of relative gains. Neo-liberals want to maximize the total amount of gains for all parties involved, whereas neo-realists believe that the fundamental goal of states in cooperative relationships is to prevent others from gaining more.

4 Neo-realists state that anarchy requires states to be preoccupied with relative power, security, and survival in a competitive international system. Neo-liberals are more concerned with economic welfare or international political economy issues and other non-military issue areas such as international environmental concerns.

5 Neo-realists emphasize the capabilities (power) of states over the intentions and interests of states. Capabilities are essential for security and independence. Neo-realists claim that uncertainty about the intentions of other states forces states to focus on their capabilities. Neo-liberals emphasize intentions and preferences.

6 Neo-liberals see institutions and regimes as significant forces in international relations. Neo-realists state that neo-liberals exaggerate the impact of regimes and institutions on state behaviour. Neo-liberals claim that they facilitate cooperation, and neo-realists say that they do not mitigate the constraining effects of anarchy on cooperation.

(Adapted from Baldwin 1993: 4–8)

If anything, the current neo-liberal institutionalist literature appears to try hard to prove that its adherents are a part of the neo-realist/realist family. As Robert Jervis (1999: 43) states, there is not much of a gap between the two theories. As evidence of this, he quotes Robert Keohane and Lisa Martin (1999: 3): 'for better or worse institutional theory is a half-sibling of neo-realism'.

The following section reviews key aspects of this debate. With regard to anarchy, the theories share several assumptions. First, they agree that anarchy means that there is no common authority to enforce any rules or laws constraining the behaviour of states or other actors. Neo-liberal institutionalists and neo-realists agree that anarchy encourages states to act unilaterally and to promote **self-help** behaviour. The condition of anarchy also makes cooperation more difficult to achieve. However, neo-realists tend to be more pessimistic and to see the world as much more competitive and conflictive. Neo-realists see international relations as a struggle for survival, and in every interaction there is a chance of a loss of power to a future competitor or enemy. Neo-liberal institutionalists recognize the competitive nature of international relations. However, the opportunities for cooperation in areas of mutual interest may mitigate the effects of anarchy.

Some scholars suggest that the real difference between the neos is that they study different worlds. The neo-liberal institutionalists focus their scholarship on political economy, the environment, and human rights issues. Neo-liberals work in what we once called the low politics arena, issues related to human security and the good life. Their assumptions work better in these issue-areas.

Neo-realists tend to dominate the security studies area. Neo-realist scholars study issues of international security or what was once called high politics issues. Many neo-realists assume that what distinguishes the study of international relations from political science is the emphasis on issues of survival.

For neo-liberal institutionalists, foreign policy is now about managing complex interdependence and the various processes of globalization. It is also about responding to problems that threaten the economic well-being, if not the survival, of people around the world. Foreign policy leaders must find ways to manage financial markets so that the gap between rich and poor does not become insurmountable. These same leaders must find ways to deal with toxic waste dumping that threatens clean water supplies in developing states. The anodyne for neo-liberal institutionalists is to create institutions to manage issue-areas where states have mutual interests. Creating, maintaining, and further empowering these institutions is the future of foreign policy for neo-liberal institutionalists.

Neo-realists take a more state-centric view of foreign policy. They recognize international relations as a world of cooperation and conflict. However, close to their traditional realist roots, neo-realists see foreign policy as dominated by issues of national security and survival. The most effective tool of statecraft is still force or the threat of force and, even in these times of globalization, states must continue to look after their own interests. All states, in the language of the neo-realists, are **egoistic value maximizers**.

Neo-realists accept the existence of institutions and regimes, and recognize their role as tools or instruments of statecraft. From a neo-realist view, states work to establish these regimes and institutions if they serve their interests (absolute gain), and they continue to support these same regimes and institutions if the cooperative activities promoted by the institution do not unfairly advantage other states (relative gains). Neo-realists also would agree that institutions can shape the content and direction of foreign policy in certain issue-areas and when the issue at hand is not central to the security interests of a given state.

Neo-liberals agree that, once established, institutions can do more than shape or influence the foreign policy of states. Institutions can promote a foreign policy agenda by providing critical information and expertise. Institutions also may facilitate policy-making and encourage more cooperation at local, national, and international levels. They often serve as a catalyst for coalition building among state and non-state actors. Recent work on environmental institutions suggests that they can promote changes in national policies and actually encourage both national and international policies that address environmental problems (Haas, Keohane, and Levy 1993).

A major issue of contention in the debate is the notion that institutions have become significant in international relations. Further, they can make a difference by helping to resolve global and regional problems and encourage cooperation rather than conflict. Neo-liberal institutionalists expect an increase in the number of institutions and an increase in cooperative behaviour. They predict that these institutions will have a greater role in managing the processes of globalization and that states will come to the point where they realize that acting unilaterally or limiting cooperative behaviour will not lead to the resolution or management of critical global problems. Ultimately, neo-liberal institutionalists claim that the significance of these institutions as players in the game of international politics will increase substantially.

Neo-realists recognize that these institutions are likely to become more significant in areas of mutual interest, where national security interests are not at stake. However, the emphasis that states place on relative gains will limit the growth of institutions and will always make cooperation difficult. For neo-realists, the important question is not: will we all gain from this cooperation, but who will gain more?

What is left out of the debate?

One could argue that the neo–neo debate leaves out a great number of issues. Perhaps with a purpose, it narrows the agenda of international relations. It is not a debate about some of the most critical questions, such as 'Why war?' or 'Why inequality in the international system?' Remember that this is a debate that occurs within the mainstream of International Relations (IR) scholarship. Neo-realists and neo-liberal institutionalists agree on the questions; they simply offer different responses. Some important issues are left out and assumptions about international politics may be overlooked. As a student of IR, you should be able to identify the strengths and weaknesses of a theory. Let us consider three possible areas for discussion: the role of domestic politics, learning, and political globalization.

Both theories assume that states are value maximizers and that anarchy constrains the behaviour of states. But what about domestic forces that might promote a more cooperative strategy to address moral or ethical issues? Neo-realist assumptions suggest a sameness in foreign policy that may not be true. How do we account for the moral dimensions of foreign policy such as development assistance given to poor states that have no strategic or economic value to the donor? Or how do we explain domestic interests that promote isolationist policies in the USA at a time when system changes would suggest that international activism might result in both absolute and relative gains? We may need to challenge Waltz and ask if the internal make-up of a state matters. All politics is now *glocal* (global and local) and neo-realists especially, but also neo-liberals, must pay attention to what goes on inside a state. Issues of political culture, **identity**, and domestic political games must be considered.

We must assume that leaders and citizens alike learn something from their experiences. The lessons of two world wars prompted Europeans to set aside issues of sovereignty and nationalism and build an economic community. Although some neo-liberal institutionalists recognize the importance of learning, in general neither theory explores the possibility that states will learn and may shift from a traditional self-interest perspective to an emphasis on common interests. There may be a momentum to cooperation and institution building that both theories underestimate. Can we assume that institutions and cooperation have had some impact on conditions of anarchy?

Both neo-realists and neo-liberals neglect the possibility that political activities may be shifting away from the state. A number of scholars have suggested that one of the most significant outcomes of globalization is the emergence of global or transnational political advocacy **networks** (Keck and Sikkink 1998). Institutions promoted primarily by these advocacy networks have had a major impact on human rights and human security issues.

Key Points

- The neo–neo debate is not a debate between two polar opposite worldviews. They share an epistemology, focus on similar questions, and agree on a number of assumptions about international politics. This is an intra-paradigm debate.

- Neo-liberal institutionalists and neo-realists study different worlds of international politics. Neo-realists focus on security and military issues. Neo-liberal institutionalists focus on political economy, environmental issues, and, lately, human rights issues.

- Neo-realists explain that all states must be concerned with the absolute and relative gains that result from international agreements and cooperative efforts. Neo-liberal institutionalists are less concerned about relative gains and consider that all will benefit from absolute gains.

- Neo-realists are more cautious about cooperation and remind us that the world is still a competitive place where self-interest rules.

- Neo-liberal institutionalists believe that states and other actors can be persuaded to cooperate if they are convinced that all states will comply with rules, and that cooperation will result in absolute gains.

- This debate does not discuss many important issues that challenge some of the core assumptions of each theory. For example, neo-realism cannot explain foreign policy behaviour that challenges the norm of national interest over human interests.

- Globalization has contributed to a shift in political activity away from the state. Transnational social movements have forced states to address critical international issues and in several situations have supported the establishment of institutions that promote further cooperation, and fundamentally challenge the power of states.

Neo-liberals and neo-realists on globalization

As I suggested earlier in this chapter, most neo-realists do not think that globalization changes the game of international politics much at all. States might require more resources and expertise to maintain their sovereignty, but neo-realists think most evidence suggests that states are increasing their expenditures and their jurisdictions over a wide variety of areas. Ultimately, we still all look to the state to solve the problems we face, and the state still has a monopoly over the legal use of coercive power. Most neo-realists assume that conditions of anarchy and competition accentuate the concerns for absolute and relative gains. As Waltz suggested in a recent article on the topic, '[t]he terms of political, economic and military competition are set by the larger units of the international political system' (Waltz 2000:

53). Waltz recognizes that globalization presents new policy challenges for nation-states but he denies that the state is being pushed aside by new global actors. The state remains the primary force in international relations and has expanded its power to effectively manage the processes of globalization.

What neo-realists are most concerned with are the new security challenges presented by globalization. Two examples follow.

Neo-realists are concerned with the uneven nature of economic globalization. Inequality in the international system may be the greatest security threat in the future. People without food are inclined to seek change, and often that change will be violent. Economic globalization can also accentuate existing differences in societies, creating instability in strategic regions, thereby challenging world order.

Most neo-realists would claim that forces of globalization challenge sovereignty. However, states have not lost their authority and control. Yet globalization has had a significant impact on domestic politics and the existing power structures. **Transnational social movements** (TSMOS) and global advocacy networks have successfully shifted many political issues away from the state. For example, some neo-realists are concerned that the power and security of the state are being undermined by political movements seeking to force states to make new rules that control the use of nuclear and conventional weapons. These movements deftly use the press, the Internet, and activist networks to challenge many of the core assumptions of the dominant realist/neo-realist policy perspective. Realists and neo-realists tend to favour elitist models of decision-making, especially in security areas. Some neo-realists have expressed concern that globalization might contribute to an unwanted democratization of politics in critical security areas (see Chs 14 and 22). Their concern is that expertise will be overwhelmed by public emotions.

Most of the discussion of globalization among neo-liberals falls into two categories: (1) a free-market commercial neo-liberalism that dominates policy circles throughout the world; and (2) academic neo-liberal institutionalism that promotes regimes and institutions as the most effective means of managing the globalization process.

The end of the cold war was the end of the Soviet experiment in command economics, and it left capitalism and free-market ideas with few challengers in international economic institutions and national governments. Free-market neo-liberals believe that governments should not fight globalization or attempt to slow it down. These neo-liberals want minimal government interference in the national or global market. From this perspective, institutions should promote rules and norms that keep the market open and discourage states that attempt to interfere with market forces. Other more social democratic neo-liberals support institutions and regimes that manage the economic processes of globalization as a means to prevent the uneven flow of capital and other resources that might widen the gap between rich and poor states.

Box 7.3 Neo-liberalism and its current critics

Critical voices

'Free trade theorists claimed that the *rising tide will lift all boats, providing broad,* economic benefits to all levels of society. The evidence so far clearly shows that it lifts only yachts.'
(Barker and Mander 1999: 4)

After twenty years of carefully following international economic rules such as free trade, price deregulation, and privatization as promoted by the neo-liberal **Washington consensus**, several Latin American countries have elected new governments that are more concerned about uneven economic growth and greater inequalities within their countries. Venezuela, Bolivia, and Ecuador have new leaders who are hostile to privatization schemes and who are not afraid of nationalizing foreign corporations to address much-needed social programmes in their countries. Many of these 'socialist' governments are supported by native peoples or indigenous groups who are concerned with the foreign ownership of natural resources like coal, oil, and gas. Dani Rodrik (1997) argues that globalization raises the mobility of capital, making it very difficult for governments to tax profit. Thus profits from energy resources are not available for social programmes like health, education, and poverty reduction. The leader of this twenty-first-century socialist revolution is Hugo Chavez, the President of Venezuela. He is building a Latin American coalition to challenge US military and political hegemony and neo-liberal orthodoxy in the Latin American region and the world.

Neo-liberal defenders

The benefits of globalization are clear to neo-liberal free-market advocates, and these advocates believe that those who fight against these processes suffer from globalphobia and neglect to appreciate key benefits of a global economy. First, the more global the economy, the more manufacturers or producers in a given country can take advantage of commodities, production processes, and markets in other countries. Second, globalization encourages the diffusion of knowledge and technology, which increases the opportunities for economic growth worldwide. Third, the rich countries and corporations in the global North have capital that they will lend to developing states for economic growth if these states accept the rules of the neo-liberal economic system. Fourth and finally, if trade barriers are minimal and government takes a minor role in trying to manage the economy, the chances for government corruption and political interference are greatly reduced. Most neo-liberals have sound faith in the market and believe that globalization will encourage further economic integration among public and private actors in the economy. Private forms of economic integration are increasing across the world. Banks, investment firms, and industries are merging, linking Europe with the USA, China with Africa, and Russia with Colorado. Neo-liberals predict that the globalization momentum will increase due to the declining costs of transportation, technology, and communications. Distance is disappearing.
(Adapted from Burtless et al. 1998)

Recent demonstrations against global economic institutions in the USA and Europe suggest that there are many who feel that the market is anything but fair. People marching in the streets of London and Seattle called for global institutions that provide economic well-being for all and for reformed institutions that promote social justice, ecological balance, and human rights (see Box 7.3). The critics of economic globalization state that governments will have to extend their jurisdictions and intervene more extensively in the market to address these concerns, as well as open the market and all its opportunities to those people now left out. Given the current neo-liberal thinking, this kind of radical change is unlikely.

Key Points

- Neo-realists think that states are still the principal actors in international politics. Globalization challenges some areas of state authority and control, but politics is still international.

- Neo-realists are concerned about new security challenges resulting from uneven globalization, namely inequality and conflict.

- Globalization provides opportunities and resources for transnational social movements that challenge the authority of states in various policy areas. Neo-realists are not supportive of any movement that seeks to open critical security issues to public debate.

- Free-market neo-liberals believe globalization is a positive force. Eventually, all states will benefit from the economic growth promoted by the forces of globalization. They believe that states should not fight globalization or attempt to control it with unwanted political interventions.

- Some neo-liberals believe that states should intervene to promote capitalism with a human face or a market that is more sensitive to the needs and interests of all the people. New institutions can be created and older ones reformed to prevent the uneven flow of capital, promote environmental sustainability, and protect the rights of citizens.

Conclusion: narrowing the agenda of international relations

Neo-realism and neo-liberal institutionalism are status quo rationalist theories. They are theories firmly embraced by mainstream scholars and by key decision-makers in many countries. There are some differences between these theories; however, these differences are minor compared to the issues that divide reflectivist and rationalist theories and critical and problem-solving theories (see Ch. 10).

In scholarly communities, neo-realism generally represents an attempt to make realism more theoretically rigorous. Waltz's emphasis on system structure and its impact on the behaviour of states leads one to conclude that international relations is not explained by looking inside the state. Neo-realists who reduce international politics to microeconomic rational choice or instrumental thinking also minimize the idiosyncratic attributes of individual decision-makers and the different cultural and historical factors that shape politics within a state. These more scientific and parsimonious versions of neo-realism offer researchers some powerful explanations of state behaviour. However, do these explanations offer a complete picture of a given event or a policy choice? Does neo-realist scholarship narrow the research agenda? Recently, neo-realist scholars have been criticized for their inability to explain the end of the cold war and other major transformations in the international system. Neo-realists minimize the importance of culture, traditions, and identity—all factors that shaped the emergence of new communities that helped to transform the Soviet empire.

Contributions by neo-realists in security studies have had a significant impact on the policy community. Both defensive and offensive neo-realists claim that the world remains competitive and uncertain, and the structure of the international system makes power politics the dominant policy paradigm. This fits with the interests and belief systems of most military strategists and foreign policy decision-makers in positions of power in the world today. It continues the realist tradition that has dominated international politics for centuries and it suggests that the criticisms of the realist/neo-realist tradition may be limited to the academic world. However, critical perspectives, inside and outside the academic world, are causing some realists/neo-realists to re-examine their assumptions about how this world works. Certainly, defensive neo-realists represent a group of scholars and potential policy advisers who understand the importance of multilateralism and the need to build effective institutions to prevent arms races that might lead to war. There is some change, but the agenda remains state-centric and focused on military security issues.

Neo-liberalism, whether the policy variety or the academic neo-liberal institutionalism, is a rejection of the more utopian or cosmopolitan versions of liberalism. US foreign policy since the end of the cold war has involved a careful use of power to spread an American version of liberal democracy: peace through trade, investment, and commerce. In the last few years, US foreign policy has promoted business and markets over human rights, the environment, and social justice. Washington's brand of neo-liberalism has been endorsed by many of the world's major powers and smaller trading states. The dominant philosophy of statecraft has become a form of 'pragmatic meliorism', with markets and Western democratic institutions as the chosen means for improving our lives. Again, we see a narrowing of choices and a narrowing of the issues and ideas that define our study of international politics.

Neo-liberal institutionalism, with its focus on cooperation, institutions, and regimes, may offer the broadest agenda of issues and ideas for scholars and policy-makers. Neo-liberal institutionalists are now asking if institutions matter in a variety of issue-areas. Scholars are asking important questions about the impact of **international regimes** and institutions on domestic politics and the ability of institutions to promote rules and norms that encourage environmental sustainability, human rights, and economic development. It is interesting that many neo-liberal institutionalists in the USA find it necessary to emphasize their intellectual relationship with neo-realists and ignore their connections with the English School and more cosmopolitan versions of liberalism (see Ch. 6). The emphasis on the shared assumptions with neo-realism presents a further narrowing of the agenda of international politics. A neo-liberal institutional perspective that focuses on the nature of international society or community and the importance of institutions as promoters of norms and values may be more appropriate for understanding and explaining contemporary international politics.

Every theory leaves something out. No theory can claim to offer a picture of the world that is complete. No theory has exclusive claims to the truth. Theories in international politics offer insights into the behaviour of states. Realists and neo-realists give great insights into power, conflict, and the politics of survival. However, neo-realism does not help us understand the impact of economic interdependence on state behaviour or the potential effects of institutions and regimes on domestic politics. Here is where neo-liberal institutionalism helps us construct a picture of international politics. Theories empower some actors and policy strategies and dismiss others. Neo-realism and neo-liberal institutionalism are theories that address status quo issues and consider questions about how to keep the system operating. These theories do not raise questions about the dominant belief system or the distribution of power and how these may be connected to conditions of **poverty** and violence. As you continue your studies in international politics, be critical of the theories being presented. Which theories explain the most? Which theory helps you make sense of this world? What does your theory leave out? Who or what perspective does the theory empower? Who or what view of the world is left out?

Questions

1 What are the similarities between traditional realism and neo-realism?
2 What are the intellectual foundations of neo-liberal institutionalism?
3 What assumptions about international politics are shared by neo-liberals and neo-realists? What are the significant differences between these two theories?
4 How do you react to those who say that the neo–neo debate is not much of a debate at all? Is this merely an academic debate or has this discussion had any influence on foreign policy?
5 Do you think globalization will have any impact on neo-realist and neo-liberal thinking? Is either theory useful in trying to explain and understand the globalization process?
6 What do defensive and offensive neo-realists believe? How important are their theories to military strategists?
7 What is the difference between relative and absolute gains? What role do these concepts play in neo-realist thinking? In neo-liberal thinking?

8 How might the proliferation of institutions in various policy areas influence the foreign policy process in major, middle-ranking, and small states? Do you think these institutions will mitigate the effects of anarchy as neo-liberals claim?

9 Why do you think neo-realism and neo-liberalism maintain such dominance in US International Relations scholarship?

10 If we study international politics as defined by neo-realists and neo-liberal institutionalists, what are the issues and controversies we would focus on? What is left out of our study of international politics?

Further Reading

General surveys with excellent coverage of the neo-realist and neo-liberal perspectives

Doyle, M. (1997), *Ways of War and Peace* (New York: W. W. Norton). Discusses the antecedents to neo-realism and neo-liberalism. Excellent sections on Hobbes and structural realism, and varieties of liberalism.

Mandelbaum, M. (2002), *The Ideas that Conquered the World* (New York: Public Affairs). An excellent review of the core ideas of peace, democracy, and free-market capitalism. Liberalism is discussed as the sole surviving ideology as the cold war ended.

For more information on the neo-liberal/neo-realist debate

Baldwin, D. (ed.) (1993), *Neo-realism and Neo-liberalism: The Contemporary Debate* (New York: Columbia University Press). Includes reflections on the debate section with articles by Grieco and Keohane.

Doyle, M., and Ikenberry, G. J. (eds) (1997), *New Thinking in International Relations Theory* (Boulder, CO: Westview Press). The chapters by Grieco on realism and world politics and Weber on institutions and change are very useful.

Security and neo-realism

Mearsheimer, J. (2003), *The Tragedy of Great Power Politics* (New York: W. W. Norton). The author presents the basics of his offensive realist theory of world politics and uses historical evidence to support his position that all states seek to survive by maximizing their power.

—— and Walt, S. (2003), 'An Unnecessary War', *Foreign Policy* (Jan.–Feb.): 51–9. The article raises several serious concerns about how the Bush administration distorted the facts to justify the war with Iraq.

Neo-liberalism and neo-liberal institutionalism

Haas, P., Keohane, R., and Levy, M. (eds) (1993), *Institutions for the Earth* (Cambridge, MA: MIT Press). An excellent collection of case studies asking if institutions have any impact on international, regional, and domestic environmental policies.

Nye, J., and Donahue, J. (eds) (2000), *Governance in a Globalizing World* (Washington, DC: Brookings Institution Press). Explores the meaning of globalization, its impact on nation-states, and how globalization might be managed to solve global problems and serve the interests of humankind.

Online Resource Centre

 Visit the Online Resource Centre that accompanies this book to access more learning resources on this chapter topic at www.oxfordtextbooks.co.uk/orc/baylis5e/

Chapter 8

Marxist theories of international relations

STEPHEN HOBDEN · RICHARD WYN JONES

Reader's Guide

This chapter will introduce, outline, and assess the Marxist contribution to the study of International Relations. Having identified a number of core features common to Marxist approaches, the chapter discusses how Marx's ideas were internationalized by Lenin and subsequently writers within the world-system framework. It then examines how Frankfurt School Critical Theory, and Gramsci and his various followers, introduced an analysis of culture into Marxist analysis, and how, more recently new (or orthodox) Marxists have sought a more profound re-engagement with Marx's original writings. The chapter argues that no analysis of globalization is complete without an input from Marxist theory. Indeed, Marx was arguably the first theorist of globalization, and from the perspective of Marxism, the features often pointed to as evidence of globalization are hardly novel, but are rather the modern manifestations of long-term tendencies within the development of capitalism.

Introduction: the continuing relevance of Marxism

With the end of the **cold war** and the global triumph of 'free market' capitalism, it became commonplace to assume that the ideas of Marx, and his numerous disciples, could be safely consigned to the dustbin of history. The 'great experiment' had failed. While Communist Parties retained **power** in China, Vietnam, and Cuba, they did not now constitute a threat to the **hegemony** of the global capitalist system. Rather, in order to try to retain power, these parties were themselves being forced to submit to the apparently unassailable logic of 'the market' by aping many of the central features of contemporary capitalist societies. One of the key lessons of the twentieth century, therefore, would appear to be that Marxist thought leads only to a historical dead end. The future is liberal and capitalist.

Yet despite this, Marx and Marxist thought more generally refuse to go away. The end of the Soviet experiment and the apparent lack of a credible alternative to capitalism may have led to a crisis in Marxism, but two decades later there appears to be something of a renaissance. There are probably two reasons why this renaissance is occurring, and why Marxists walk with a renewed spring in their step.

First, for many Marxists the communist experiment in the Soviet Union had become a major embarrassment. In the decades immediately after the October Revolution, most had felt an allegiance to the Soviet Union as the first 'Workers' State'. Subsequently, however, this loyalty had been stretched beyond breaking point by the depravities of Stalinism, and by Soviet behaviour in its post-Second World War satellites in Eastern Europe. What was sometimes termed 'actually existing socialism' was plainly not the communist utopia that many dreamed of and that Marx had apparently promised. Some Marxists were openly critical of the Soviet Union. Others just kept quiet and hoped that the situation, and the human rights record, would improve.

The break-up of the Soviet bloc has, in a sense, wiped the slate clean. This event reopened the possibility of arguing in favour of Marx's ideas without having to defend the actions of governments that justify their behaviour with reference to them. Moreover, the disappearance of the Soviet Union has encouraged an appreciation of Marx's work less encumbered by the baggage of Marxism–Leninism as a state ideology. The significance of this is underlined when it is realized that many of the concepts and practices that are often taken as axiomatic

of Marxism do not in fact figure in Marx's writings: these include the 'vanguard party', 'democratic centralism', and the centrally directed 'command economy'.

Second, and perhaps more importantly, Marx's social theory retains formidable analytical purchase on the world we inhabit. The vast bulk of his theoretical efforts consisted of a painstaking analysis of **capitalism** as a mode of production, and the basic elements of his account have not been bettered. Indeed, with the ever-increasing penetration of the market mechanism into all aspects of life, it is arguable that Marx's forensic examination of both the extraordinary dynamism and the inherent contradictions of capitalism are even more relevant now than in his own time. A particular strength of Marx's work is his analysis of crisis. Liberal accounts of capitalism suggest that free markets will move towards equilibrium and will be inherently stable. Our day-to-day lived experience suggests otherwise. The 1987 stock-market crash, the **Asian financial crisis** of the late 1990s, and the '**credit crunch**' of 2008–9 all demonstrate that global capitalism continues to be rocked by massive convulsions that have enormous implications for the lives of individuals around the globe. On Marx's account, such convulsions, and their baleful human consequences, are an inherent and inescapable part of the very system itself.

Compared to **realism** and **liberalism** (see Chs 5, 6, and 7), Marxist thought presents a rather unfamiliar view of international relations. While the former portray world politics in ways that resonate with those presented in the foreign news pages of our newspapers and magazines, Marxist theories aim to expose a deeper, underlying—indeed hidden—truth. This is that the familiar events of world politics—wars, treaties, international aid operations, etc.—all occur within structures that have an enormous influence on those events. These are the structures of a global capitalist system. Any attempt to understand world politics must be based on a broader understanding of the processes operating within global capitalism.

In addition to presenting an unfamiliar view of world politics, Marxist theories are also discomfiting, for they argue that the effects of global capitalism are to ensure that the powerful and wealthy continue to prosper at the expense of the powerless and the poor. We are all aware that there is gross inequality in the world. Statistics concerning the human costs of **poverty** are truly numbing in their awfulness (the issue of global poverty is further discussed in Ch. 28). Marxist theorists argue that the relative prosperity of the few is dependent on the destitution of the many. In Marx's own words, 'Accumulation of wealth at one pole is, therefore, at the same time accumulation of misery, agony of toil, slavery, ignorance, brutality at the opposite pole.'

In the next section we shall outline some of the central features of the Marxist approach—or historical **materialism,** as it is often known. Following on from this, subsequent sections will explore some of the most important strands in contemporary Marx-inspired thinking about world politics. We should note, however, that given the richness and variety of Marxist thinking about world politics, the account that follows is inevitably destined to be partial and to some extent arbitrary.

Our aim in the following is to provide a route map that we hope will encourage readers to explore further the work of Marx and of those who have built on the foundations he laid.

Key Points

- Marx's work retains its relevance despite the collapse of Communist Party rule in the former Soviet Union.
- Of particular importance is Marx's analysis of capitalism, which has yet to be bettered.
- Marxist analyses of international relations aim to reveal the hidden workings of global capitalism. These hidden workings provide the context in which international events occur.

The essential elements of Marxist theories of world politics

In his inaugural address to the Working Men's International Association in London in 1864, Karl Marx told his audience that history had 'taught the working classes the duty to master [for] themselves the mysteries of international politics'. However, despite the fact that Marx himself wrote copiously about international affairs, most of this writing was journalistic in character. He did not incorporate the international dimension into his theoretical mapping of the contours of capitalism. This 'omission' should perhaps not surprise us. The sheer scale of the theoretical enterprise in which he was engaged, as well as the nature of his own methodology, inevitably meant that Marx's work would be contingent and unfinished.

Marx was an enormously prolific writer, and his ideas developed and changed over time. Hence it is not surprising that his legacy has been open to numerous interpretations. In addition, real-world developments have also led to the revision of his ideas in the light of experience. A variety of schools of thought has emerged, which claim Marx as a direct inspiration, or whose work can be linked to Marx's legacy. Before we discuss what is distinctive about these approaches, it is important that we examine the essential elements of commonality that lie between them.

First, all the theorists discussed in this chapter share with Marx the view that the social world should be analysed as a totality. The academic division of the social world into different areas of enquiry—history, philosophy, economics, political science, sociology, international relations, etc.—is both arbitrary and unhelpful. None can be understood without knowledge of the others: the social world has to be studied as a whole. Given the scale and complexity of the social world, this entreaty clearly makes great demands of the analyst. None the less, for Marxist theorists, the disciplinary boundaries that characterize the contemporary social sciences need to be transcended if we are to generate a proper understanding of the dynamics of world politics.

Another key element of Marxist thought, which serves further to underline this concern with interconnection and context, is the materialist conception of history. The central contention here is that processes of historical change are ultimately a reflection of the economic development of society. That is, economic development is effectively the motor of history. The central dynamic that Marx identifies is tension between the **means of production** and **relations of production** that together form the economic base of a given society. As the means of production develop, for example through technological advancement, previous relations of production become outmoded, and indeed become fetters restricting the most effective utilization of the new productive capacity. This in turn leads to a process of social change whereby relations of production are transformed in order to better accommodate the new configuration of means. Developments in the economic base act as a catalyst for the broader transformation of society as a whole. This is because, as Marx argues in the Preface to his *Contribution to the Critique of Political Economy*, 'the mode of production of material life conditions the social, political and intellectual life process in general'. Thus the legal, political, and cultural **institutions** and practices of a given society reflect and reinforce—in a more or less mediated form—the pattern of power and control in the economy. It follows logically, therefore, that change in the economic base ultimately leads to change in the 'legal and political superstructure'. (For a diagrammatical representation of the base–superstructure model, see Fig. 8.1.) The relationship between the base and superstructure is one of the key areas of discussion within Marxism, and for critics of Marxist approaches. A key contribution to this debate has been the work of Historical Sociologists inspired by the work of Max Weber (see Box 8.1).

Class plays a key role in Marxist analysis. In contrast to liberals, who believe that there is an essential harmony of interest between various social groups, Marxists hold that society is systematically prone to class conflict. Indeed, in the *Communist Manifesto*, which Marx co-authored with Engels, it is argued that 'the history of all hitherto existing societies is the history of class struggle' (Marx and Engels 1967). In capitalist society, the main

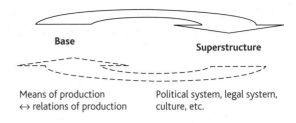

Base   **Superstructure**

Means of production   Political system, legal system,
↔ relations of production   culture, etc.

Figure 8.1 The base–superstructure model

axis of conflict is between the bourgeoisie (the capitalists) and the proletariat (the workers).

Despite his commitment to rigorous scholarship, Marx did not think it either possible or desirable for the analyst to remain a detached or neutral observer of this great clash between capital and labour. He argued that 'philosophers have only interpreted the world in various ways; the point, however, is to change it'. Marx was committed to the cause of **emancipation**. He was not interested in developing an understanding of the dynamics of capitalist society simply for the sake of it. Rather, he expected such an understanding to make it easier to overthrow the prevailing order and replace

---

Box 8.1 Historical Sociology

As we have seen, one of the key debates in Marxism concerns the relationship between the base and superstructure. Traditionally Marxists have focused attention on the base, seeing the elements of the superstructure as a reflection of economic relations. At its most forceful, this is often viewed as 'economic determinism'—the view that social relations (e.g. law, politics) can be directly correlated from the underlying mode of production. Frankfurt School critical theorists and neo-Gramscian scholars have relaxed this view, focusing their analysis on the superstructure, and its role in maintaining the economic base.

Another way of thinking about these issues is to consider the work of Historical Sociologists. The term 'historical sociology' is somewhat daunting and potentially misleading. In essence it means an approach to the study of the social world that draws upon history as the main source of evidence. Historical Sociologists are interested in the ways in which social life changes over time, and attempt to provide explanations for those changes. As an example, Theda Skocpol's book *States and Social Revolution* (1979) attempted to develop a theory of revolution, and then drew upon the examples of the French, Russian, and Chinese revolutions to confirm her analysis.

Historical Sociology comes in many different forms (see Hobden and Hobson 2002), one of which is Marxism itself, having as it does a theory of history. However, in International Relations, the term has become synonymous with the work of what are termed neo-Weberian scholars. These writers came to the attention of International Relations theorists because of their interest in international relations; their analysis of social change, in particular state formation, provided a more nuanced account than that suggested by realism. For example, part of Skocpol's theoretical analysis argues that it was inter-state relations (e.g. involvement in war) that contributed to a revolutionary outcome, and influenced the outcome of revolutions. Likewise Charles Tilly (1975; see also Tilly, 1992) in his analysis of state development, drew a direct link between war and statemaking with his claim that 'war made the state and the state made war'.

Perhaps the most influential of the neo-Weberians has been Michael Mann. His major work, *The Sources of Social Power* (1986, 1993), attempts a rewriting a global history through the lens of a multi-causal approach to social change. Whereas Marxists see the main explanation of social change at an economic level, Mann argues that there are four types of social power: ideology, economic, military, and political (often shortened to IEMP). Rather than arguing that one source of social power is more significant (as Marxists do), Mann argues that different sources of social power have been more significant in different historical epochs. For example, Mann argues that in recent centuries economic power has been significant, whereas in the past ideological power (particularly religion) has been more important. Furthermore, the sources of social power can amalgamate to give different combinations. Pre-guessing Mann, one might argue that, given the increasing significance of religion in international politics, economics and ideology are the leading sources of social power in the current era.

it with a communist society—a society in which wage labour and private property are abolished and social relations transformed.

It is important to emphasize that the essential elements of Marxist thought, all too briefly discussed in this section, are also essentially contested. That is, they are subject to much discussion and disagreement even among those contemporary writers who have been influenced by Marxist writings. There is disagreement as to how these ideas and concepts should be interpreted and how they should be put into operation. Analysts also differ over which elements of Marxist thought are most relevant, which have been proven to be mistaken, and which should now be considered as outmoded or in need of radical overhaul. Moreover, there are substantial differences between them in terms of their attitudes to the legacy of Marx's ideas. The work of the

new Marxists draws far more directly on Marx's original ideas than does the work of the **critical theorists**. Indeed, the latter would probably be more comfortable being viewed as post-Marxists than as straightforward Marxists. But even for them, as the very term post-Marxism suggests, the ideas of Marx remain a basic point of departure.

Key Points

- Marx himself provided little in terms of a theoretical analysis of international relations.
- His ideas have been interpreted and appropriated in a number of different and contradictory ways, resulting in a number of competing schools of Marxism.
- Underlying these different schools are several common elements that can be traced back to Marx's writings.

Marx internationalized: from *Imperialism* to world-systems theory

Although Marx was clearly aware of the international and expansive character of capitalism (a point that we shall return to in the conclusion), as we have already intimated, his key work *Capital* focuses on the development and characteristics of nineteenth-century British capitalism. At the start of the twentieth century a number of writers took on the task of developing analyses that incorporated the implications of capitalism's trans-border characteristics, in particular **imperialism** (see Brewer 1990). At the forefront of such studies was Trotsky's discussion of combined and uneven development, and Luxemburg's discussions of the relations between more and less advanced capitalist states. Trotsky argued that the level of development of any particular state (and his interest was in pre-revolutionary Russia) would be affected by its relations with others. Development would be 'combined' because no state could develop independently within a capitalist system of states. It would be 'uneven' because the rates of development of state would not follow a uniform pattern; some would necessarily develop faster than others.

In her *The Accumulation of Capital* Rosa Luxemburg also extended the analysis of a specific national economy developed by Marx. Her argument was that capitalism as a mode of production in Western Europe had emerged within and alongside pre-capitalist sets of relations. Furthermore, capitalism actually depended for its continued growth on pre-capitalist societies. These provided

markets for goods from advanced capitalist countries, and sources of cheap labour.

The best-known and most influential work to emerge from this debate, though, is the pamphlet written by Lenin, and published in 1917, called *Imperialism, the Highest Stage of Capitalism*. Lenin accepted much of Marx's basic thesis, but argued that the character of capitalism had changed since Marx published the first volume of *Capital* in 1867. Capitalism had entered a new stage—its highest and final stage—with the development of monopoly capitalism. Under monopoly capitalism, a two-tier structure had developed within the world economy, with a dominant core exploiting a less-developed periphery. With the development of a core and periphery, there was no longer an automatic **harmony of interests** between all workers posited by Marx. The bourgeoisie in the core countries could use profits derived from exploiting the periphery to improve the lot of their own proletariat. In other words, the capitalists of the core could pacify their own working class through the further exploitation of the periphery.

Lenin's views were developed by the Latin American Dependency School, adherents of which developed the notion of core and periphery in greater depth. In particular, Raul Prebisch argued that countries in the periphery were suffering as a result of what he called 'the declining terms of trade'. He suggested that the price of manufactured goods increased more rapidly than that of raw materials. So, for example, year by year it requires more tons of coffee to pay for a refrigerator. As a result of their reliance on primary goods, countries of the periphery become poorer relative to the core. Other writers, in particular André Gunder Frank and Henrique Fernando Cardoso developed this analysis further to show how the development of less industrialized countries was directly 'dependent' on the more advanced capitalist societies. It is from the framework developed by such writers that contemporary world-systems theory emerged.

World-systems theory is particularly associated with the work of Immanuel Wallerstein. For Wallerstein, global history has been marked by the rise and demise of a series of world systems. The modern world system emerged in Europe at around the turn of the sixteenth century. It subsequently expanded to encompass the entire globe. The driving force behind this seemingly relentless process of expansion and incorporation has been capitalism, defined by Wallerstein as 'a system of production for sale in a market for profit and appropriation of this profit on the basis of individual or collective ownership' (1979: 66). Within the context of this system, all the institutions of the social world are continually being created and re-created. Furthermore, and crucially, it is not only the elements within the system that change. The system itself is historically bounded. It had a beginning, has a middle, and will have an end.

In terms of the geography of the modern world system, in addition to a core–periphery distinction, Wallerstein added an intermediate semi-periphery, which displays certain features characteristic of the core and others characteristic of the periphery. Although dominated by core economic interests, the semi-periphery has its own relatively vibrant indigenously owned industrial base (see Fig. 8.2). Because of this hybrid nature, the semi-periphery plays important economic and political roles within the modern world system. In particular, it provides a source of labour that counteracts any upward pressure on wages in the core and also provides a new home for those industries that can no longer function profitably in the core (for example, car assembly and textiles). The semi-periphery also plays a vital role in stabilizing the political structure of the world system.

According to world-systems theorists, the three zones of the world economy are linked together in an exploitative relationship in which wealth is drained away from the periphery to the centre. As a consequence, the relative positions of the zones become ever more deeply entrenched: the rich get richer while the poor become poorer.

Together, the core, semi-periphery, and periphery make up the geographic dimension of the world economy. However, described in isolation they provide a rather static portrayal of the world system. A key component of Wallerstein's analysis has been to describe how world systems have a distinctive life cycle: a beginning, a middle, and an end. In this sense, the capitalist world system is no different from any other system that has preceded it. Controversially, Wallerstein argues that the end of the **cold war**, rather than marking a triumph for liberalism, indicates that the current system has entered its 'end' phase; a period of crisis that will end only when it is replaced by another system (Wallerstein 1995). On Wallerstein's reading, such a period of crisis is also a time of opportunity. When a system is operating smoothly, behaviour is very much determined by its structure. In a time of crisis, however, actors have far greater agency to determine the character of the replacement structure. Much of Wallerstein's recent work has been an attempt to develop a political programme to promote a new world system that is more equitable and just than the current one (Wallerstein 1998, 1999, 2006). From this perspective, to focus on **globalization** is to ignore what is truly novel about the contemporary era. Indeed, for Wallerstein, current globalization discourse represents a 'gigantic misreading of current reality' (Wallerstein 2003: 45). Those phenomena evoked

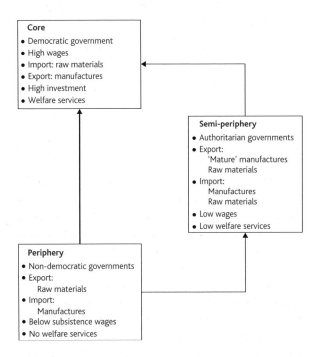

Figure 8.2 Interrelationships in the world economy

by 'globalization' are manifestations of a world system that emerged in **Europe** during the sixteenth century to incorporate the entire globe: a world system now in terminal decline.

Various writers have built on or amended the framework established by Wallerstein (Denemark *et al.* 2000). Christopher Chase-Dunn, for example, lays much more emphasis on the role of the inter-state system than Wallerstein. He argues that the capitalist mode of production has a single logic in which both politico-military and exploitative economic relations play key roles. In a sense he attempts to bridge the gap between Wallerstein's work and that of the new Marxists (discussed below), by placing much more of an emphasis on production in the world economy and how this influences its development and future trajectory (see Chase-Dunn 1998).

André Gunder Frank (one of the most significant Dependency School writers) has launched a significant critique of Wallerstein's work, and of Western social theory in general. He argues not only that the world system is far older than suggested by Wallerstein (Frank and Gills 1996); it is also an offshoot of a system that originated in Asia (Frank 1998). His work builds on that of Janet Abu-Lughod. She has challenged Wallerstein's account of the emergence of the modern world system in the sixteenth century, arguing that, during the medieval period, Europe was a peripheral area to a world economy centred on the Middle East (Abu-Lughod 1989). Frank concurs, arguing that Europe was not the birthplace of the current capitalist world economy, but rather that the rise of Europe occurred within the context of an existing world system. Hence social theory, including Marxism, which tries to examine 'Western exceptionalism', is making the mistake of looking for the causes of that rise to dominance in the wrong place, Europe, rather than within the wider, global context.

Feminist Marxists have also played a significant role in theorizing the development of an international capitalist system. A particular concern of feminist writers (often drawing their inspiration from Engels's 1884 work *The Origin of the Family, Private Property, and the State*) has been the role of women both in the workplace and as the providers of domestic labour necessary for the reproduction of capitalism. Mies (1998 [1986]), for example, argued that women play a central role in the maintenance of capitalist relations. There is, she argues, a sexual division of labour: first, in the developed world as housewives, whose labour is unpaid, but vital in maintaining and reproducing the labour force; and second, in the developing world as a source of cheap labour. Women, she later argued, were the 'last colony' (Mies *et al.* 1988), a view that can be traced back to Luxemburg's claim regarding the role of the colonies in international capitalism.

Key Points

- Marxist theorists have consistently developed an analysis of the global aspects of international capitalism—an aspect acknowledged by Marx, but not developed in *Capital*.

- World-systems theory can be seen as a direct development of Lenin's work on imperialism and the Latin American Dependency School.

- Feminist writers have contributed to the analysis of international capitalism by focusing on the specific role of women.

Gramscianism

In this section we discuss the strand of Marxist theory that has emerged from the work of the Italian Marxist Antonio Gramsci. Gramsci's work has become particularly influential in the study of international political economy, where a neo-Gramscian or 'Italian' school is flourishing. Here we shall discuss Gramsci's legacy, and the work of Robert W. Cox, a contemporary theorist who has been instrumental in introducing his work to an international relations audience.

Antonio Gramsci (1891–1937) was a Sardinian and one of the founding members of the Italian Communist Party. He was jailed in 1926 for his political activities, and spent the remainder of his life in prison. Although he is regarded by many as the most creative Marxist thinker of the twentieth century, he produced no single, integrated theoretical treatise. Rather, his intellectual legacy has been transmitted primarily through his remarkable *Prison Notebooks* (Gramsci 1971). The key question that animated Gramsci's theoretical work was: why had it proven to be so difficult to promote revolution in Western Europe? Marx, after all, had predicted that revolution, and the **transition** to socialism, would occur first in the most advanced capitalist societies. But, in the event, it was the Bolsheviks of comparatively backward Russia that had made the first 'breakthrough', while all the subsequent efforts by putative revolutionaries in Western and Central Europe to emulate their success ended in failure. The history of the early twentieth century seemed to suggest, therefore, that there was a flaw in classical Marxist analysis. But where had they gone wrong?

Gramsci's answer revolves around his use of the concept of **hegemony**, his understanding of which reflects his broader conceptualization of power. Gramsci develops Machiavelli's view of power as a centaur, half beast, half man: a mixture of coercion and consent. In understanding how the prevailing order was maintained, Marxists had concentrated almost exclusively on the coercive practices and **capabilities** of the state. On this understanding, it was simply coercion, or the fear of coercion, that kept the exploited and alienated majority in society from rising up and overthrowing the system that was the cause of their suffering. Gramsci recognized that while this characterization may have held true in less developed societies, such as pre-revolutionary Russia, it was not the case in the more developed countries of the West. Here the system was also maintained through consent.

Consent, on Gramsci's reading, is created and re-created by the hegemony of the ruling class in society. It is this hegemony that allows the moral, political, and cultural values of the dominant group to become widely dispersed throughout society and to be accepted by subordinate groups and classes as their own. This takes place through the institutions of **civil society:** the **network** of institutions and practices that enjoy some autonomy from the state, and through which groups and individuals organize, represent, and express themselves to each other and to the state (for example, the media, the education system, churches, voluntary organizations, etc.).

Several important implications flow from this analysis. The first is that Marxist theory needs to take superstructural phenomena seriously, because while the structure of society may ultimately be a reflection of social relations of production in the economic base, the nature of relations in the superstructure is of great relevance in determining how susceptible that society is to change and transformation. Gramsci used the term 'historic bloc' to describe the mutually reinforcing and reciprocal relationships between the socio-economic relations (base) and political and cultural practices (superstructure) that together underpin a given order. For Gramsci and Gramscians, to reduce analysis to the narrow consideration of economic relationships, on the

one hand, or solely to politics and ideas, on the other, is deeply mistaken. It is the interaction that matters.

Gramsci's argument also has crucial implications for political practice. If the hegemony of the ruling class is a key element in the perpetuation of its dominance, then society can only be transformed if that hegemonic position is successfully challenged. This entails a counter-hegemonic struggle in civil society, in which the prevailing hegemony is undermined, allowing an alternative historic bloc to be constructed.

Gramsci's writing reflects a particular time and a particular, and in many ways unique, set of circumstances. This has led several writers to question the broader applicability of his ideas (see Burnham 1991; Germain and Kenny 1998). But the most important test, of course, is how useful ideas and concepts derived from Gramsci's work prove to be when they are removed from their original context and applied to other **issues** and problems. It is to this that we now turn.

Robert Cox—the analysis of 'world order'

The person who has done most to introduce Gramsci to the study of world politics is the Canadian scholar Robert W. Cox. He has developed a Gramscian approach that involves both a critique of prevailing theories of International Relations and International Political Economy, and the development of an alternative framework for the analysis of world politics.

To explain Cox's ideas, we begin by focusing on one particular sentence in his seminal 1981 article 'Social Forces, States, and World Orders: Beyond International Relations Theory'. The sentence, which has become one of the most often-quoted lines in all of contemporary International Relations theory, reads as follows: 'Theory is always *for* some one, and *for* some purpose' (1981: 128). It expresses a worldview that follows logically from the Gramscian, and broader Marxist, position that has been explored in this chapter. If ideas and values are (ultimately) a reflection of a particular set of social relations, and are transformed as those relations are themselves transformed, then this suggests that all knowledge (of the social world at least) must reflect a certain context, a certain time, a certain space. Knowledge, in other words, cannot be objective and timeless in the sense that some contemporary realists, for example, would like to claim.

One key implication of this is that there can be no simple separation between facts and values. Whether consciously or not, all theorists inevitably bring their values to bear on their analysis. This leads Cox to suggest that we need to look closely at each of those theories, those ideas, those analyses that claim to be objective or value-free, and ask who or what is it for, and what purpose does it serve? He subjects **realism**, and in particular its contemporary variant **neo-realism,** to thoroughgoing critique on these grounds. According to Cox, these theories are for—or serve the interests of—those who prosper under the prevailing order, that is the inhabitants of the developed states, and in particular the ruling elites. Their purpose, whether consciously or not, is to reinforce and legitimate the status quo. They do this by making the current configuration of International Relations appear natural and immutable. When realists (falsely) claim to be describing the world as it is, as it has been, and as it always will be, what they are in fact doing is reinforcing the ruling hegemony in the current world order.

Cox contrasts problem-solving theory, that is theory that accepts the parameters of the present order, and thus helps legitimate an unjust and deeply iniquitous system, with critical theory. Critical theory attempts to challenge the prevailing order by seeking out, analysing, and, where possible, assisting social processes that can potentially lead to emancipatory change.

One way in which theory can contribute to these emancipatory goals is by developing a theoretical understanding of world orders that grasps both the sources of stability in a given system, and also the dynamics of processes of transformation. In this context, Cox draws upon Gramsci's notion of hegemony and transposes it to the international realm, arguing that hegemony is as important for maintaining stability and continuity here as it is at the domestic level. According to Cox, successive dominant powers in the international system have shaped a world order that suits their interests, and have

---

Case Study The politics of neo-liberalism

A good example of the hegemonic power of the USA, many Marxists would argue, is the success that it has had in getting neo-liberal policies accepted as the norm throughout the world. The set of policies most closely associated with the neo-liberal project are, revealingly, known as the **Washington consensus**. Many would argue that these are 'common-sense' policies and that those Third World countries that have adopted them have merely realized that such economic policies best reflect their interests. However, Marxists would argue that an analysis of the self-interest of the hegemon, and the use of coercive power, provide a more convincing explanation of why such policies have been adopted.

The adoption of neo-liberal policies by Third World countries has had a number of implications. Spending on health and education has been reduced, they have been forced to rely more on the export of raw materials, and their markets have been saturated with manufactured goods from the industrialized world. It does not take a conspiracy theorist to suggest that these neo-liberal policies are in the interests of capitalists in the developed world.

First, there is the area of free trade. It is clear that it will always be in the interest of the hegemon to promote free trade—this is because, assuming it is the most efficient producer, its goods will be the cheapest anywhere in the world. It is only if countries put up barriers to trade that the hegemon's products will be more expensive than theirs. Second, there is the area of raw materials. If Third World countries are going to compete in a free trade situation, the usual result is that they become more reliant on the export of raw materials. Again this is in the interest of the hegemon, as increases in the supply of raw material exports mean that the price falls. Additionally, where Third World countries have devalued their currency as part of a neo-liberal package, the price of their exported raw materials is also reduced. Finally, when Third World governments have privatized industries, investors from North America and Europe have frequently been able to snap up airlines, telecommunications companies, and oil industries at bargain prices.

If neo-liberal policies appear to have such negative results for Third World countries, why have they been so widely adopted? Pressure from the core, or in other words, coercion, is a key factor. Throughout the 1970s and 1980s and continuing to today there has been a major debt crisis between the Third World and the West. Third World countries turned to the major global financial institutions such as the International Monetary Fund for assistance. For Third World countries, the price of getting that assistance was that they would implement neo-liberal policies.

Hence Marxists would argue that a deeper analysis of the adoption of neo-liberal policies is required. Such an analysis would suggest that the global acceptance of neo-liberalism is very much in the interests of the developed world and has involved a large degree of coercion. That such policies seem 'natural' and 'common-sense' is an indication of the hegemonic power of the USA.

done so not only as a result of their coercive capabilities, but also because they have managed to generate broad consent for that order even among those who are disadvantaged by it.

For the two hegemons that Cox analyses (the UK and the USA), the ruling, hegemonic idea has been 'free trade'. The claim that this system benefits everybody has been so widely accepted that it has attained 'common-sense' status. Yet the reality is that while 'free trade' is very much in the interests of the hegemon (which, as the most efficient producer in the global economy, can produce goods which are competitive in all markets, so long as they have access to them), its benefits for peripheral states and regions are far less apparent. Indeed, many would argue that 'free trade' is a hindrance to their economic and social development. The degree to which a state can successfully produce and reproduce its hegemony is an indication of the extent of its power. The success of the USA in gaining worldwide acceptance for neo-liberalism suggests just how dominant the current hegemon has become (see Case Study).

But despite the dominance of the present world order, Cox does not expect it to remain unchallenged. Rather, he maintains Marx's view that capitalism is an inherently unstable system, riven by inescapable contradictions. Inevitable economic crises will act as a catalyst for the emergence of counter-hegemonic movements. The success of such movements is, however, far from assured. In this sense, thinkers like Cox face the future on the basis of a dictum popularized by Gramsci, that is, combining 'pessimism of the intellect' with 'optimism of the will'.

Recent Gramscian writing

More recent Gramsican writing, including notable contributions by Mark Rupert (1995, 2000; Rupert and Solomon, 2005) and W. I. Robinson (1996, 2004), continue to display this characteristically Gramscian combination of pessimism and optimism—in their case, a search for plausible alternative futures within a capitalist system that both regard as increasingly globalized—as well as a central focus on the question of hegemony. Robinson's more recent work (2004) posits the formation of a transnational capitalist class and traces the emergence of a 'transnational state', existing alongside more traditional 'nation-states', a state-form that the author considers increasingly anachronistic. Indeed, on Robinson's reading, and in contrast with Cox's analysis of earlier periods, in the twenty-first century it is increasingly this transnational capitalist class, rather than any particular **nation-state,** that wields hegemonic power.

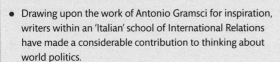

Key Points

- Drawing upon the work of Antonio Gramsci for inspiration, writers within an 'Italian' school of International Relations have made a considerable contribution to thinking about world politics.

- Gramsci shifted the focus of Marxist analysis more towards superstructural phenomena. In particular, he explored the processes by which consent for a particular social and political system was produced and reproduced through the operation of hegemony. Hegemony allows the ideas and ideologies of the ruling stratum to become widely dispersed, and widely accepted, throughout society.

- Thinkers such as Robert W. Cox have attempted to 'internationalize' Gramsci's thought by transposing several of his key concepts, most notably hegemony, to the global context.

Critical theory

There are, without doubt, many overlaps between **critical theory** and Gramscian approaches to the study of world politics. As we saw in the previous section, Robert W. Cox refers to his own Gramsci-influenced approach as critical theory. Moreover, both Gramscianism and critical theory have their roots in Western Europe of the 1920s and 1930s—a place and a time in which Marxism was forced to come to terms not only with the failure of a series of attempted revolutionary uprisings, but also with the rise of fascism. Nevertheless, there are differences between them. Contemporary critical theory and Gramscian thoughts about international relations draw upon the ideas of different thinkers, with differing intellectual concerns. In addition, there is a clear difference in focus between the two strands, with those influenced by Gramsci tending to be much more concerned with issues relating to the subfield of international political economy than critical theorists. Critical theorists, on the other hand, have involved themselves with questions concerning **international society**, international ethics, and **security**. In this section we introduce critical theory and the thought of one of its main proponents in the field of International Relations, Andrew Linklater. In addition, we will briefly introduce Critical Security Studies, an approach to the study of security that draws on both critical theory and Gramscian influences.

Critical theory developed out of the work of the **Frankfurt School**. This was an extraordinarily talented group of thinkers who began to work with each other in the 1920s and 1930s. As left-wing German Jews, the members of the school were forced into exile by the Nazis' rise to power in the early 1930s, and much of their most creative work was produced in the USA. The leading lights of the first generation of the Frankfurt School included Max Horkheimer, Theodor Adorno, and Herbert Marcuse. A subsequent generation has taken up the legacy of these thinkers and developed it in important and innovative ways. The best known is Jürgen Habermas, who is regarded by many as the most influential of all contemporary social theorists. Given the vast scope of critical theory writing, we can do no more here than introduce some of the key features.

The first point to note is that their intellectual concerns are rather different from those of most other Marxists in that they have not been much interested in the further development of analysis of the economic base of society. They have instead concentrated on questions relating to culture, bureaucracy, the social basis and nature of authoritarianism, the structure of the family, and on exploring such concepts as reason and **rationality** as well as theories of knowledge. Frankfurt School theorists have been particularly innovative in terms of their analysis of the role of the media, and what they have famously termed the 'culture industry'. In other words, in classical Marxist terms, the focus of critical theory is almost entirely superstructural.

Another key feature is that critical theorists have been highly dubious as to whether the proletariat in contemporary society does in fact embody the potential for emancipatory transformation in the way that Marx had believed. Rather, with the rise of mass culture and the increasing commodification of every element of social life, Frankfurt School thinkers have argued that the working class has simply been absorbed by the system and no longer represents a threat to it. This, to use Marcuse's famous phrase, is a one-dimensional society to which the vast majority simply cannot begin to conceive an alternative.

Finally, critical theorists have made some of their most important contributions through their explorations of the meaning of **emancipation**. Emancipation, as we have seen, is a key concern of Marxist thinkers, but the meaning that they give to the term is often very unclear and deeply ambiguous. Moreover, the historical record is unfortunately replete with examples of unspeakably barbaric behaviour being justified in the name of emancipation, of which imperialism and Stalinism are but two. Traditionally, Marxists have equated emancipation with the process of humanity gaining ever greater mastery over nature through the development of ever-more sophisticated technology, and its use for the benefit of all. But early critical theorists argued that humanity's increased domination over nature had been bought at too high a price, claiming that the kind of mind-set that is required for conquering nature slips all too easily into the domination of other human beings. In contrast, they argued that emancipation had to be conceived in terms of a reconciliation with nature—an evocative if admittedly vague vision. By contrast, Habermas's understanding of emancipation is more concerned with communication than with our relationship with the natural world. Setting aside the various twists and turns of his argument, Habermas's central political point is that the route to emancipation lies through radical democracy, that is, through a system in which the widest possible participation is encouraged not only in word (as is the case in many Western democracies) but also in deed, by actively identifying barriers to participation—be they social, economic, or cultural—and overcoming them. For Habermas and his many followers, participation is not to be confined within the borders of a particular sovereign state. Rights and obligations extend beyond state frontiers. This, of course, leads him directly to the concerns of International Relations, and it is striking that Habermas's recent writings have begun to focus on the international realm. However, thus far, the most systematic attempt to think through some of the key issues in world politics from a recognizably Habermasian perspective has been made by Andrew Linklater.

Andrew Linklater has used some of the key principles and precepts developed in Habermas's work in order to argue that emancipation in the realm of international relations should be understood in terms of the expansion of the moral boundaries of a **political community** (see Ch. 31). In other words, he equates emancipation with a process in which the borders of the sovereign state lose their ethical and moral significance. At present, state borders denote the furthest extent of our sense of duty and obligation, or at best, the point where our sense of duty and obligation is radically transformed, only proceeding in a very attenuated form. For critical theorists, this situation is simply indefensible. The goal is therefore to move towards a situation in which citizens share the same duties and obligations towards non-citizens as they do towards their fellow citizens.

To arrive at such a situation would, of course, entail a wholesale transformation of the present institutions of governance. But an important element of the critical theory method is to identify—and, if possible, nurture—tendencies that exist within the present conjuncture that point in the direction of emancipation. On this basis, Linklater identifies the development of the European Union as representing a progressive or emancipatory tendency in contemporary world politics. If true, this suggests that an important part of the international system is entering an era in which the sovereign state, which has for so long claimed an exclusive hold on its citizens, is beginning to lose some of its pre-eminence. Given the notorious pessimism of the thinkers of the Frankfurt School, the guarded optimism of Linklater in this context is indeed striking.

Critical Security Studies

Critical Security Studies (CSS) is the name given to a trend in the study of security issues that has gained prominence in recent years (in particular through the work of Keith Krause and Mike Williams (1997), Ken Booth (1991, 2004, 2007) and Richard Wyn Jones (1995, 1999)). CSS combines influences from Gramscianism and critical theory with aspects of peace research and the so-called 'alternative defence thinking'. In contrast to much mainstream security thinking (in the West at least), CSS refuses to accept the state as the 'natural' object of analysis, arguing that, for much of the world's population, states are part of the security problem rather than a provider of security. Instead, proponents of CSS tend to argue that it is beholden on security analysts to place individual human beings at the centre of their analysis. Like Linklater, they regard their work as supporting and nurturing emancipatory tendencies, for it is only through emancipation that security can ultimately be assured.

Key Points

- Critical theory has its roots in the work of the Frankfurt School.

- Habermas has argued that emancipatory potential lies in the realm of communication and that radical democracy is the way in which that potential can be unlocked.

- Andrew Linklater has developed critical theory themes to argue in favour of the expansion of the moral boundaries of the political community, and has pointed to the European Union as an example of a post-Westphalian institution of governance.

New Marxism

In this section we examine the work of writers who derive their ideas more directly from Marx's own writings. These new Marxists have returned to the fundamental tenets of Marxist thought and sought to reappropriate ideas that they regard as having been neglected or somehow misinterpreted by subsequent generations. On this basis they have sought both to criticize other developments within Marxism, and to make their own original theoretical contributions to the understanding of contemporary trends. In this section we shall introduce the work of two writers associated with this strand of Marxist thought: Justin Rosenberg and Benno Teschke, who have used key elements of Marx's writings to critique other theoretical approaches to international relations and globalization theory.

Justin Rosenberg—capitalism and global social relations

The focus of Rosenberg's analysis is the character of the international system and its relationship to the changing character of social relations. His starting point is a critique of realist International Relations theory. In particular, Rosenberg challenges realism's claim to provide an ahistorical, essentially timeless account of international relations by analyses of the differences in the character of international relations between the Greek and Italian city-states. A touchstone of realist theory is the similarity between these two historical cases. Rosenberg, however, describes the alleged resemblances between these two eras as a 'gigantic optical illusion'. Instead, his analysis suggests that the character of the international system in each period was completely different. In addition, he charges that attempts to provide an explanation of historical outcomes during these periods, working purely from the inter-state level, is not feasible (as, for example, in realist accounts of the Peloponnesian War). Finally, Rosenberg argues that realist attempts to portray international systems as autonomous, entirely political realms founder because in the Greek and Italian examples this external autonomy was based on the character of internal—and in each case different—sets of social relations.

As an alternative, Rosenberg argues for the development of a theory of international relations that is sensitive to the changing character of world politics. This theory must also recognize that international relations are part of a broader pattern of social relations. His starting point is Marx's observation:

> It is always the direct relationship of the owners of the conditions of production to the direct producers . . . which reveals the innermost secret, the hidden basis of the entire social structure, and with it the political form of the relation of sovereignty and dependence, in short, the corresponding specific form of the state. (Rosenberg 1994: 51)

In other words, the character of the relations of production permeate the whole of society—right up to, *and including*, relations between states. The form of the state will be different under different modes of production, and as a result the characteristics of inter-state relations will also vary. Hence, if we want to understand the way that international relations operate in any particular era, our starting point must be an examination of the mode of production, and in particular the relations of production.

In his more recent work Rosenberg has turned his critical attention to 'globalization theory' (Rosenberg 2000, 2006). He argues that globalization is a descriptive category denoting 'the geographical extension of social processes'. That such social processes have become a global phenomenon is beyond dispute, and a 'theory of globalization' is needed to explain what and why this is happening. Such a theory, for Rosenberg, should be rooted in classical social theory. But instead of this, a body of 'globalization theory' has emerged premised on the claim that the supposed compression of time and space that typifies globalization requires a whole new social theory in order to explain contemporary developments. But on Rosenberg's reading, this body of theory has produced

little in terms of explaining the processes. Moreover, the events of the early twenty-first century were not those predicted by 'globalization theory'. As a result, such theorizing is best understood as a product of changes that occurred in the last years of the twentieth century, and in particular the political and economic vacuum created by the collapse of the Soviet Union, rather than an adequate explanation of them. A proper explanation, rooted in classical social theory, would examine the underlying social relations that have led to the capitalist system becoming dominant throughout the globe.

Benno Teschke—social property relations

In a major contribution to the Marxist literature on international relations, Benno Teschke (2003) provides not only a critique of existing International Relations theory, but also, through the concept of social property relations, a means of analysing changes in the constitution and practices of actors in the international system. Teschke's work can be seen as building on Rosenberg's observation that social relations provide the indispensable starting point for an analysis of international relations, in particular by presenting an analysis of how system transformation occurs, and describing the major transitions of the past millennium.

A social property approach examines the way in which class relations, forms of exploitation, and control of the means of production have changed in different historical epochs. Teschke argues that such an approach is 'applicable to all geopolitical orders' (2003: 47). A major claim of his analysis is that rather than one major change between the feudal and modern international systems, there have been two major transformations—between feudal and early modern (dominated by absolutist monarchies) and between early modern and modern (capitalist states). Both these periods of change were gradual periods of transformation during which the international system comprised more than one type of actor: during the former transition a mixture of feudal and absolutist states; during the latter absolutist and capitalist states.

The practice of international relations was different during each of these three periods, reflecting the character of social property relations dominant in each epoch. Such an analysis leads to the claim that the significance of the **Treaties of Westphalia,** seen by most International Relations theorists as the major transition to modernity, has been overstated. Instead, Westphalia constitutes the point at which absolutist rather than capitalist states became the key actors of the international system. The modern international system started to emerge only with the appearance of the first capitalist state (Britain). This capitalist state form reflected the development of capitalist property relations. Since the seventeenth century, the capitalist state has become the prominent state form. As a result, the practices of international relations have changed, reflecting, Teschke argues, developments in the character of social property relations.

Key Points

- New Marxism is characterized by a direct (re)appropriation of the concepts and categories developed by Marx.

- Rosenberg uses Marx's ideas to criticize realist theories of international relations, and globalization theory. He seeks to develop an alternative approach that understands historical change in world politics as a reflection of transformations in the prevailing relations of production.

- For Benno Teschke, the study of social property relations provides the means for analysing the key elements of international relations, and the transitions between one international system and another.

Conclusion: Marxist theories of international relations and globalization

As outlined in the first chapter of this book, globalization is the name given to the process whereby social transactions of all kinds increasingly take place without accounting for national or state boundaries, with the result that the world has become 'one relatively borderless social sphere'. The particular trends pointed to as typifying globalization include: the growing **integration** of national economies; a growing awareness of ecological interdependence; the proliferation of companies, **social movements**, and intergovernmental agencies operating on a global scale; and a communications revolution that has aided the development of a global consciousness.

Marxist theorists would certainly not seek to deny that these developments are taking place, nor would they deny their importance, but they would reject any notion that they are somehow novel. Rather, in the words of Chase-Dunn, they are 'continuations of trends that have long accompanied the expansion of capitalism' (1994: 97). Marx and Engels were clearly aware not only of the global scope of capitalism, but also of its potential for social transformation. In a particularly prescient section of the *Communist Manifesto* (Marx and Engels 1967: 83–4), for example, they argue:

The bourgeoisie has through its exploitation of the world market given a cosmopolitan character to production and consumption in every country. . . . All old-established national industries have been destroyed or are daily being destroyed. They are dislodged by new industries, whose introduction becomes a life and death question for all civilized nations, by industries that no longer work up indigenous raw material, but raw material drawn from the remotest zones; industries whose products are consumed, not only at home, but in every quarter of the globe. . . .

According to Marxist theorists, the globe has long been dominated by a single integrated economic and political entity—a global capitalist system—that has gradually incorporated all of humanity within its grasp. Within this system, all elements have always been interrelated and interdependent. 'National economies' have long been integrated to such an extent that their very nature has been dependent on their position within a capitalist world economy. The only thing 'new' is an increased awareness of these linkages. Similarly, ecological processes have always ignored state boundaries, even if it is only recently that growing environmental degradation has finally allowed this fact to permeate public consciousness.

The growth of **multinational corporations** certainly does not signify any major change in the structure of the modern capitalist system. Rather, they form part of a long-term trend towards the further integration of the global economy. Neither is international contact between those movements that oppose the prevailing political and economic order a new development. In fact, as even the most cursory examination of the historical record will amply attest, such movements, be they socialist, nationalist, or ecological in character, have always drawn inspiration from, and forged links with, similar groups in other countries. Finally, the much-vaunted communications revolution is the latest manifestation of a long-term trend.

While the intensity of cross-border flows may be increasing, this does not necessarily signify the fundamental change in the nature of world politics proclaimed by so many of those who argue that we have entered an era of globalization. Marxist theorists insist that the only way to discover how significant contemporary developments really are is to view them in the context of the deeper structural processes at work. When this is done, we may well discover indications that important changes are afoot. Many Marxists, for example, regard the delegitimation of the sovereign state as a very important contemporary development. However, the essential first step in generating any understanding of those trends regarded as evidence of globalization must be to map the contours of global capitalism itself. If we fail to do so, we shall inevitably fail to gauge the real significance of the changes that are occurring.

Another danger of adopting an ahistoric and uncritical attitude to globalization is that it can blind us to the way in which reference to globalization is increasingly becoming part of the ideological armoury of elites within the contemporary world. 'Globalization' is now regularly cited as a reason to promote measures to reduce workers' rights and lessen other constraints on business. Such ideological justifications for policies that favour the interests of business can only be countered through a broader understanding of the relationship between the political and economic structures of capitalism. As we have seen, the understanding proffered by the Marxist theorists suggests that there is nothing natural or inevitable about a world order based on a global market. Rather than accept the inevitability of the present order, the task facing us is to lay the foundations for a new way of organizing society—a global society that is more just and more humane than our own.

Questions

1 How would you account for the continuing vitality of Marxist thought?

2 How did Lenin's approach to international relations differ from that of Marx?

3 How useful is Wallerstein's notion of a semi-periphery?

4 Why has Wallerstein's world-systems theory been criticized for its alleged Euro-centrism? Do you agree with this critique?

5 Evaluate Rosenberg's critique of 'globalization theory'.

6 In what ways does Gramsci's notion of hegemony differ from that employed by realist international relations writers?

7 How has Linklater developed critical theory for an international relations audience?

8 In what ways might it be argued that Marx and Engels were the original theorists of globalization?

9 What do you regard as the main contribution of Marxist theory to our understanding of world politics?

10 How useful is the notion of emancipation used by critical theorists?

11 Do you agree with Cox's distinction between 'problem-solving theory' and 'critical theory'?

12 Assess Wallerstein's claim that the power of the USA is in decline.

Further Reading

Cox, R. W. (1981), 'Social Forces, States and World Orders: Beyond International Relations Theory', *Millennium* 10(2): 126–55. Cox's much-quoted essay continues to inspire.

Derlurguian, G. M. (2005), *Bourdieu's Secret Admirer in the Caucasus: A World-System Biography* (Chicago, IL: University of Chicago Press). This unconventional book is a dazzling display of the insights generated by the world-system approach.

Hobden, S., and Hobson, J. M. (2002), *Historical Sociology of International Relations* (Cambridge: Cambridge University Press). A manifesto for the use of historical sociology in the study of international relations.

Lenin, V. I. (1916), *Imperialism: The Highest Stage of Capitalism* (multiple editions available). While of limited contemporary relevance, it is still worth reading this once- influential pamphlet.

Linklater, A. (2007), *Critical Theory and World Politics: Sovereignty, Citizenship and Humanity* (London: Routledge). The most recent contribution by this influential critical theorist.

Marx, K., and Engels, F. (1848), *The Communist Manifesto* (multiple editions available). The best introduction to Marx's thinking. It remains essential reading even after one hundred and fifty years.

Megill, A. (2002), *Karl Marx: The Burden of Reason (Why Marx Rejected Politics and the Market)* (Lanham, MD: Rowman & Littlefield). For those with a serious interest in the subject, this scholarly, sympathetic, yet ultimately highly critical evaluation of Marx's thought is a must-read.

Morton, A. (2007), *Unravelling Gramsci: Hegemony and Passive Revolution in the Global Political Economy* (London: Pluto Press). A clear discussion of the contemporary relevance of Gramsci.

Teschke, B. (2003), *The Myth of 1648: Class, Geopolitics and the Making of Modern International Relations* (London: Verso). A powerful alternative reading of the development of International Relations.

Wallerstein, I. (2004), *World-Systems Analysis: An Introduction* (Durham, NC: Duke University Press). A summary of Wallerstein's life-work.

Wyn Jones, R. (1999), *Security, Strategy and Critical Theory* (Boulder, CO: Lynne Rienner). The first three chapters provide an introduction to some of the key intellectual concerns of the Frankfurt School while the remainder outline Critical Security Studies.

Online Resource Centre

 Visit the Online Resource Centre that accompnaies this book to access more learning resource on this chapter topic at www.oxfordtextbooks.co.uk/orc/baylis5e/

Chapter 9

Social constructivism

MICHAEL BARNETT

Reader's Guide

This chapter provides an overview of constructivist approaches to International Relations (IR) theory. Constructivism's antecedents are located in the 1980s and in a series of critical reactions to mainstream international relations theory in the USA, namely neo-realism and neo-liberal institutionalism. These theories emphasized the distribution of power and the unwavering pursuit by states of power and wealth, and minimized the power of ideas. Constructivism countered by highlighting how ideas define and can transform the organization of world politics, shape the identities and interests of states, and determine what counts as legitimate action. Although initially given a cold reception, Constructivism quickly gained credibility and popularity in the 1990s due to the end of the cold war, the enduring insights of sociological and critical theory, and the ability to generate novel accounts of world politics. Although there are important differences among constructivists, they share several commitments that generate a distinctive approach for understanding how the world is made and re-made through human action.

Introduction

Constructivism rose very quickly from rather humble beginnings to become one of the leading schools in International Relations (IR). Twenty years ago constructivism did not exist. Twelve years ago the leading American journal of IR, *International Organization*, proclaimed that the next great debate in the discipline would be between rationalism and constructivism. Today constructivism is widely recognized for its ability to capture important features of global politics and viewed as an important theory of international relations.

This chapter explores constructivism's origins, its fight for disciplinary acceptability, its core commitments, and features of its research agenda as it relates to global change. I shall highlight two factors surrounding its birth, one theoretical and the other sociological. The midwives of constructivism are an unlikely pairing: neo-realism and neo-liberal institutionalism, on the one hand, and sociological and critical theory, on the other. The 1980s were dominated by the 'neos', as recalled in Chapter 7. Notwithstanding their substantive differences, they assumed that states have innate and fixed interests such as power and wealth, and are constrained in their ability to further those interests because of material forces such as geography, technology, and the distribution of power. Critics drew from sociological and critical theory to argue that social forces such as ideas, knowledge, **norms**, and **rules** influence states' identities and interests, and the very organization of world politics. These claims later became part of constructivism's intellectual oeuvre.

The American context influenced constructivism's evolution. I do not mean that Americans created constructivism. Indeed, as with the development of realism in the USA, most of its leading figures came from outside the USA. Nor do I mean that constructivism's ideas are quintessentially American. Indeed, many of constructivism's core beliefs, including the claim that societies shape the identities, interests, and capacities of individuals, hail from European social and political thought and run counter to the American culture that emphasizes **individualism**. Nor is constructivism alone concerned with international norms and conceptualizing international politics not as a system but as a society. Various theories pre-dated constructivism, some of which are included in this volume, that made similar claims, including feminist approaches to international relations and the English School and its recognition of the **society of states**, as discussed in Chapters 2 and 10.

Instead, my emphasis on the American context is intended to highlight how constructivism's conceptual contours and research agenda have been profoundly shaped by its struggle for acceptance in an American disciplinary context. In order to prove itself, constructivism had to produce workmanlike empirical research that mattered to neo-liberal institutionalist and neo-realist scholars; eventually constructivists succeeded in convincing them that constructivism had to be taken seriously.

Although there are various versions of constructivism, they have a common concern with how ideas define the international **structure**; how this structure shapes the identities, interests, and foreign policies of states; and how state and **non-state actors** reproduce that structure—and at times transform it. The concern with the making and re-making of world politics underscores constructivism's strong interest in global change. Although constructivism has investigated various features of global change, in this chapter I shall focus on two: the convergence by states around similar ways for organizing their domestic and international life; and how norms become internationalized and institutionalized, that is, globally accepted to the point that they constrain what states and non-state actors do and influence their ideas of what is legitimate behaviour. Constructivist arguments, thus, help us understand some elementary features of the globalization of world politics.

In the beginning . . .

Constructivism's origins can be traced to the 1980s, when neo-realism and neo-liberal institutionalism dominated American international relations theory. Waltz aspired to make realism more rigorous, scientific, and amenable to hypothesis testing. He did so by specifying the nature of the units and their preferences, and how the structure of the **international system** constrains those preferences. The most important actors are states.

Although Waltz was unclear whether they pursued survival, security, or power, and whether they maximized or satisfied, he was very clear that these interests suffocated any possibility that ideas, norms, or values might shape state behaviour. He argued that the structure of the international system had three elements: **anarchy** (the absence of a supranational authority); functional non-differentiation of the units (because anarchy created a **self-help** system, all states had to be self-reliant and safeguard their security); and the distribution of power. But because the world has always been an anarchy and states have always been obsessed about their survival, to understand enduring tendencies in world politics required scholars to focus only on the position of the state in international hierarchy and the distribution of power. Waltz depicted a dreary world in which states were suspicious, misanthropic, and aggressive, not necessarily because they were born that way but because the environment punished anything else (see Ch. 7).

Neo-liberal institutionalism responded to neo-realism's pessimistic view of international politics by demonstrating that states had the capacity to cooperate on a range of issues. States did not always have conflicting interests; they often had convergent interests and desired to cooperate to improve their lives. A primary obstacle to cooperation was the fact that states did not trust each other to abide by their agreements. In order to encourage cooperation in the absence of trust, states constructed international institutions that can perform various functions, including monitoring and publicizing cheating.

Neo-realism and neo-liberal institutionalism dominated international relations theory in the USA during the 1990s. As recounted in Chapter 7, these camps disagreed over the effects of anarchy, whether state interests varied, whether states sought absolute or **relative gain**, whether institutions can shape state behaviour, and whether and how cooperation was possible. Yet they shared a commitment to individualism and **materialism**. Individualism is the view that actors have fixed interests and that the structure that constrains their behaviour derives from the aggregation of the properties of the actors. Although neo-realists and neo-liberals differ because the former believe that the pursuit of security is primary while the latter can envision other goals such as the pursuit of wealth, for empirical and theoretical reasons they assume that state interests are hard-wired and unmalleable. Materialism is the view that the structure that constrains behaviour is defined by distribution of power, technology, and geography. Neo-realism denies

that ideas and norms can trump interests. Neo-liberal institutionalism, though, recognizes that states might willingly construct norms and institutions to regulate their behaviour because doing so will enhance their long-term interests. Although both approaches allow for the possibility that ideas and norms can constrain how states pursue their interests, neither contemplates the possibility that ideas and norms might define their interests.

The 1980s were characterized not only by the dominance of neo-realism and neo-liberal institutionalism, but also by a growing interest in social theory, that is, how to conceptualize the structure and its organizing principles, the actors and the rules that regulate their relations, and the relationship between the structure and the actors. Specifically, they challenged neo-realism's and neo-liberal institutionalism's individualism and materialism. The critiques came from many schools. Some drew from sociological theory, emphasizing how structures constrain and constitute (or construct) the identities and interests of actors. Others drew from critical theory and the desire to uncover the power behind seemingly value-neutral concepts such as sovereignty and recovering the meanings that actors give to their activities. Nor were the protagonists conspiring to promote any single research programme. Instead, they were daring international relations to imagine how the structure of international politics constructs the identities and interests of states and to consider how self-reflective states can transform the very structure of world politics.

There were many important contributions in the 1980s, but arguably four were most influential for establishing constructivism's theoretical orientation and conceptual vocabulary. John Ruggie's review essay (1983) of Kenneth Waltz's *Theory of International Politics* helped to establish a countermovement. He attacked the centrepoint of Waltz's conceptual architecture: structure. As already discussed, Waltz conceives the international structure as having three elements: anarchy; functional non-differentiation between states; and the distribution of power. Any genuine transformation in the structure, in his view, required a movement from anarchy to hierarchy. But, according to Waltz, this has never happened, nor is it likely to. Ruggie, though, argued that we should pay more attention to the second element, differentiation. The states-system, he observed, has been organized according to alternative principles. For instance, and perhaps most critically, the modern international system begins with the end of feudalism and the emergence of sovereignty, that is, with a shift from heteronomy and overlapping authorities to **state sovereignty** and the centralization of authority in the modern state. In short, Waltz inexplicably neglected sovereignty, the defining organizing principle of the modern states-system. Bringing sovereignty back in allowed Ruggie, and others who followed in his footsteps, to highlight the importance of societal and transnational processes for understanding changes in world politics.

The following year Richard Ashley (1984) published an immensely influential critique of neo-realism. Drawing from **poststructural** and **critical theory**, he levelled a variety of charges. In his view, neo-realism is so fixated on the state that it cannot see a world populated by non-state actors. It treats states as having fixed interests and thus cannot see how their interests are created, constructed, and transformed by global-historical forces. It is so committed to individualism that it cannot see how societies shape individuals and how global-historical forces create the identities, interests, and capacities of states. It is so committed to materialism that it constructs an artificial view of society that is completely devoid of ideas, beliefs, and rules. It treats basic concepts of international relations, such as sovereignty, as if they are natural and thus fails to recognize how they are socially and culturally produced within a historical context. Ashley's devastating critique of the underpinnings of neo-realism revealed not only its limitations but also the power of poststructural and critical theory (see Ch. 10).

In 1987 Alexander Wendt introduced the **agent-structure problem** to international relations scholars: how to conceptualize the relationship between agents (states) and structures (the international structure)? Waltz's approach, he observed, began with states, examined the aggregate properties of states' **capabilities** to determine a structure defined by the international distribution of military power, and then posited that this structure constrains what states can do and generates inter-state patterns. The problem, Wendt argued, is that structures do more than constrain agents; they also construct or constitute their identities and interests. An alternative formulation is offered by Immanuel Wallerstein's world-systems theory, which claims that there is a structure to the world system that is defined by **capitalism**, and that the structure determines what states are and what they do. While the virtue of this approach is that it recognizes that structures can define who the actors are, the vice is that it envisions that actors will mechanically reproduce that structure. Moreover, while these theories offer alternative understandings of the relationship between agents and structures, both treated structures in strictly material terms—for Waltz it was the distribution of military power and for Wallerstein it was capitalism. Yet structures are also defined by ideas, norms, and rules; in other words, structures contain normative *and* material elements. The challenge, therefore, is to recognize that normative structures shape who are the central actors in world politics, their identities and interests, and their role in reproducing and possibly transforming those structures.

Employing Anthony Giddens's concept of **structuration**, Wendt argued that an international normative structure shapes the identities and interests of states, and through their interactions states re-create that very structure. This approach, he claimed, generates a more complete understanding of the relationship between states (actors) and the international system (normative structure). The norms that are part of any structure do not operate behind the back of actors; instead, actors determine what they are. Frequently actors reproduce these norms without much thought because of taken-for-granted knowledge, habits, and routines. Yet at other times they self-consciously attempt to construct new norms that might affect not only the incentives for certain behaviour but also the very structure itself. Actors are constrained by the underlying structure and must overcome resistance by other actors who either have a vested interest in the underlying rules, a preferred alternative, or just cannot imagine anything else. Yet no structure is so suffocating that it eliminates the possibility that actors might reflect critically on their actions and work to transform their world.

Drawing from legal, sociological, and linguistic theories, Friedrich Kratochwil (1991) offered one of the first systematic treatments of rules and norms in international relations. He introduced international relations scholars to the distinction between regulative and constitutive rules. **Regulative rules** regulate already existing activities. Rules for the road determine how to drive. The World Trade Organization's rules regulate trade. **Constitutive rules** create the very possibility for these activities. The rules of rugby not only prohibit blocking but also help to define the very game (and distinguish it from American football); after all, if forwards began to block for backs, not only would this be a penalty but it would change the game itself. The rules of sovereignty not only regulate state practices but also make possible the very idea of a sovereign state. Furthermore, rules are not static but rather are revised through practice, reflection, and arguments by actors regarding how they should be applied to new situations. In order to best understand the **meanings** that rules have for actors, and the basis on which they are defended and revised,

Kratochwil insisted that scholars adopt interpretive methods. We cannot know the meanings of rules from the outside looking in but rather need to see the world as it is understood by the participants.

By drawing from critical and sociological theory to demonstrate the limitations of neo-realism and neo-liberal institutionalism, these and other scholars were opening space for an alternative research programme. These ideas were not warmly received in all quarters. To some extent this is how the intellectual elite always treat challengers. The critics did not always help their cause, though. They frequently belittled the theories and research agendas of the mainstream. They could write in highly alienating ways, hardly encouraging a wide readership or a sympathetic reading. Moreover, the critiques were long on erudition but short on empirical analysis. Those asked to learn a second language

rather late in life understandably wanted evidence that doing so would help them better understand the world. Ultimately, if constructivism were to become accepted, it had to demonstrate that it could back up its bark with some empirical bite.

> ### Key Points
>
> - International relations theory in the 1980s was dominated by neo-realism and neo-liberal institutionalism; both theories ascribed to materialism and individualism.
> - Various scholars critical of neo-realism and neo-liberalism drew from critical and sociological theory to demonstrate the effect of normative structures on world politics.
> - The mainstream responded coolly to these challenges, demanding that critics demonstrate the superiority of these alternative claims through empirical research.

The rise of constructivism

Constructivism, a term coined by Nicholas Onuf in his important book, *The World of Our Making* (1989), met that challenge. Four background factors sponsored its meteoric rise in the 1990s. One was the end of the cold war. Although only a handful of scholars had ever imagined that the cold war might end with a whimper and not a bang, neo-realists and neo-liberal institutionalists were especially hard pressed to explain this outcome. Their commitment to **individualism** and **materialism** meant that they could not grasp what appeared to reside at the heart of this stunning development: the revolutionary impact of ideas to transform the organization of world politics. Constructivism was tailor-made for understanding what had been unthinkable to most scholars. Nor did these approaches provide insight into what might come next. The USA was enjoying a unipolar moment, but the distribution of power could not determine whether it would aspire to become a global hegemon or work through multilateral institutions. Moreover, across the world the end of the cold war triggered national debates over what was the national interest, debates that frequently involved a consideration of their national identity, which presupposed a discussion of critical similarities and differences. In other words, states were actively debating their national **identity**—who are 'we' and where do 'we' belong?—in order to determine their interests and the desired regional and international order. To understand the dissolution and creation of new international orders required, so

it seemed, a constructivist sensibility. Finally, the end of the cold war clipped the prominence of traditional security themes, neo-realism's comparative advantage, and raised the importance of transnationalism, human rights, and other subjects that played to constructivism's strengths.

Constructivists also convinced the mainstream in the USA that they were committed to 'science'. At first, many mainstream scholars dismissively labelled constructivism as 'anti-science' and postmodern—a remarkable claim that only revealed their commitment to a very narrow conception of social science that was defined by positivism and the search for timeless laws. In response, constructivists worked to widen and modernize the concept of social science as they demonstrated a commitment to the logic of enquiry in the quest to better explain world politics. Over time the relations between constructivists and the mainstream improved. The same could not be said for relations between constructivists and those subscribing to poststructural and critical theory (see Ch. 10). After all, constructivists had gained considerable intellectual insights from these approaches, but unlike poststructural and critical theorists who dismissed the idea of explanatory theory, were committed to social science (Adler 2000).

Constructivism's reliance on sociological theory also furthered its rise to respectability. The discussions in international relations regarding how to conceptualize the relationship between states and the international system had been played (and replayed) in sociology for over a century as it debated how to conceptualize the relationship between the individual and society. Max Weber wrote against individualism and claimed that sociology was concerned with how culture shaped the meanings and significance that actors gave to their actions. George Herbert Mead wrote of the role of symbols in mediating the interactions of individuals. Talcott Parsons slammed individualism and argued that the beliefs, commitments, and ideas that individuals have in their heads come from society. Constructivists resurrected these arguments and applied them to their own debates with neo-realists and neo-liberals; the latter could not easily dismiss the ideas of such eminent sociologists that had influenced various areas of political science.

Ultimately, constructivism's success derived from its ability to further an understanding of issues of central concern to neo-realism and neo-liberal institutionalism. The **epistemic community** literature carefully explored how expert groupings help states discover both their interests and ways for producing durable cooperation. Peter Katzenstein's *The Culture of National Security* (1996) challenged standard neo-realist claims in a series of critical

areas—including alliance patterns, military intervention, arms racing, Great Power transformation—and demonstrated how identity and norms shape state interests and must be incorporated to generate superior explanations. The growing literature on sovereignty investigated its origins, its spread from the West to the global South, and the historical and regional variation in its meaning. By the end of the 1990s constructivism was no longer a fad or something attributed to the wild innocence of youth but instead was an accepted form of analysis.

Key Points

- The end of the cold war meant that there was a new intellectual space for scholars to challenge existing theories of international politics.
- Constructivists drew from established sociological theory to demonstrate how social science could help international relations scholars understand the importance of identity and norms in world politics.
- Constructivists demonstrated how attention to norms and states' identities could help uncover important issues neglected by neo-realism and neo-liberalism.

Constructivism

Before proceeding to identify constructivism's tenets, two caveats are in order. Constructivism is a social theory and not a substantive theory of international politics. Social theory is broadly concerned with how to conceptualize the relationship between agents and structures; for instance, how should we think about the relationship between states and the structure of international politics? Substantive theory offers specific claims and hypotheses about patterns in world politics; for instance, how do we explain why democratic states tend not to wage war on one another? In this way constructivism is best compared with **rational choice**. Rational choice is social theory that offers a framework for understanding how actors operate with fixed preferences that they attempt to maximize under a set of constraints. It makes no claims about the content of those preferences; they could be wealth or religious salvation. Nor does it assume anything about the content of these constraints; they could be guns or ideas. Rational choice offers no claims about the actual patterns of world politics. For instance, neo-realism and neo-liberalism subscribe to rational choice, but they arrive at rival claims about patterns of conflict and cooperation in world politics because they

make different assumptions about the effects of anarchy. Like rational choice, constructivism is a social theory that is broadly concerned with the relationship between agents and structures, but it is not a substantive theory. Constructivists, for instance, have different arguments regarding the rise of sovereignty and the impact of human rights norms on states. In order to generate substantive claims, scholars must delineate who are the principal actors, what are their interests and capacities, and what is the content of the normative structures.

Also, there are many different kinds of constructivists. Some draw from the insights of James March, John Meyer, and organizational theory, and others from Michel Foucault and discourse analysis. Some prioritize agents and others structures. Some focus on inter-state politics and others on transnationalism. There are differences over the possibility of social science. Different empirical puzzles drive different approaches. These fault-lines have spawned a proliferating number of labels. Neoclassical. Modernist. Postmodern. Naturalistic. Thick. Thin. Linguistic. Narrative. Weak. Strong. Systemic. Holistic. This development should not be surprising. All schools have internal rivalries.

Still, there is unity within such diversity. 'Constructivism is about human consciousness and its role in international life' (Ruggie 1998: 856). This focus on human consciousness suggests a commitment to idealism and holism, which, according to Wendt (1999), represent the core of constructivism. **Idealism** demands that we take seriously the role of ideas in world politics. The world is defined by material and ideational forces. But these ideas are not akin to beliefs or psychological states that reside inside our heads. Instead, these ideas are social. Our mental maps are shaped by collectively held ideas such as knowledge, symbols, language, and rules. Idealism does not reject material reality but instead observes that the meaning and construction of that material reality is dependent on ideas and interpretation. The **balance of power** does not objectively exist out there waiting to be discovered; instead states debate what is the balance of power, what is its meaning, and how they should respond. Constructivism also accepts some form of **holism** or structuralism. The world is irreducibly social and cannot be decomposed into the properties of already existing actors. The emphasis on holism does not deny agency but instead recognizes that agents have some autonomy and their interactions help to construct, reproduce, and transform those structures. Although the structure of the cold war seemingly locked the USA and the Soviet Union into a fight to the death, leaders on both sides creatively transformed their relations and, with it, the very structure of global politics.

This commitment to idealism and holism has important implications for how we think about and study world politics. But in order to appreciate its insights, we must learn more about its conceptual vocabulary, and in order to demonstrate the value of learning this 'second language', I shall contrast constructivism's vocabulary with that of rational choice. The core observation is the **social construction of reality**. This has a number of related elements. One is the emphasis on the socially constructed nature of actors and their identities and interests. Actors are not born outside of and prior to society, as individualism claims. Instead, actors are produced and created by their cultural environment. Nurture, not nature. For instance, what makes an Arab state an *Arab* state is not the fact that the populations speak Arabic but rather that there are rules associated with Arabism that shape the Arab states' identity, interests, and foreign policies that are deemed legitimate and illegitimate. Another element is how knowledge, that is, symbols, rules, concepts, and categories, shapes how individuals construct and interpret their world. Reality does not exist out there waiting to be discovered; instead, historically

produced and culturally bound knowledge enables individuals to construct and give meaning to reality. In other words, existing categories help us to understand, define, and make sense of the world. There are lots of ways to understand collective violence, and one of the unfortunate features of a bloody twentieth century is that we have more categories to discriminate between forms of violence, from civil war to ethnic cleansing, to crimes against humanity, to genocide.

This constructed reality frequently appears to us an objective reality, which relates to the concept of **social facts**. There are those things whose existence is dependent on human agreement and those things whose existence is not. Brute facts such as rocks, flowers, gravity, and oceans exist independent of human agreement and will continue to exist even if humans disappear or deny their existence. Social facts are dependent on human agreement and are taken for granted. Money, refugees, terrorism, human rights, and sovereignty are social facts. Their existence depends on human agreement, they will only exist so long as that agreement exists, and their existence shapes how we categorize the world and what we do.

The social construction of reality also shapes what is viewed as legitimate action. Do we choose only the most efficient action? Do the ends justify the means? Or, is certain action just unacceptable? The earlier distinction between constitutive and regulative rules parallels the conceptual distinction between the **logic of consequences** and the **logic of appropriateness**. The logic of consequences attributes action to the anticipated costs and benefits, mindful that other actors are doing just the same. The logic of appropriateness, however, highlights how actors are rule-following, worrying about whether their actions are legitimate. The two logics are not necessarily distinct or competing. What is viewed as appropriate and legitimate can affect the possible costs of different actions; the more illegitimate a possible course of action appears to be, the higher the potential cost for those who proceed on their own. The USA's decision to go into Iraq without the blessing of the UN Security Council meant that other states viewed the USA's actions as illegitimate, were less willing to support them, and thus raised the costs to the USA when it went ahead.

By emphasizing the social construction of reality, we also are questioning what is frequently taken for granted. This points to several issues. One is a concern with the origins of those social constructs that now appear to us as natural and are now part of our social vocabulary. Sovereignty did not always exist; it was a product of historical forces and human interactions that generated new distinctions regarding where political authority resided. The category of weapons of mass destruction is a modern invention. Although individuals have been forced to flee their homes ever since Adam and Eve were exiled from Eden, the political and legal category of 'refugees' is only a century old (see Box 9. 1).

To understand the origins of these concepts requires attention to the interplay between existing ideas and institutions, the political calculations by leaders who had ulterior motives, and morally minded actors who were attempting to improve humanity. Also of concern are alternative pathways. Although history is path dependent, there are contingencies, historical accidents, the conjunction of material and ideational forces, and human intervention that can force history to change course. The events of **11 September 2001** and the response by the Bush administration arguably transformed the direction of world politics. This interest in possible and counterfactual worlds works against historical determinism. Alexander Wendt's (1992) claim that 'anarchy is what states make of it' calls attention to how different beliefs

and practices will generate divergent patterns and organization of world politics (see Box 9.2).

A world of Mahatma Gandhis will be very different from a world of Osama bin Ladens.

Constructivists also examine how actors make their activities meaningful. Following Max Weber's (1949: 81) insight that 'we are cultural beings with the capacity and the will to take a deliberate attitude toward the world and to lend it *significance*', constructivists attempt to recover the **meanings** that actors give to their practices and the objects that they construct. These derive not from private beliefs but rather from culture. In contrast to the rationalist presumption that culture, at most, constrains action, constructivists argue that culture informs the meanings that people give to their action. Sometimes constructivists have presumed that such meanings derive from a hardened culture. But because culture is fractured and because society comprises different interpretations of what is meaningful activity, scholars need to consider these cultural fault-lines and treat the fixing of meanings as an accomplishment that is the essence of

---

Box 9.1 Social construction of refugees

Who is a refugee, why does this category matter, and how has it changed? There are many ways to categorize people who leave their homes, including migrants, temporary workers, displaced peoples, and refugees. Before the twentieth century refugee as a legal category did not exist, and it was not until the First World War that states recognized peoples as refugees and gave them rights. Who was a refugee? Although many were displaced by the First World War, Western states limited their compassion to Russians who were fleeing the Bolsheviks (it was easier to accuse a rival state of persecuting its people); only they were entitled to assistance from states and the new refugee agency, the High Commissioner for Refugees. However, the High Commissioner took his mandate and the category and began to apply it to others in Europe who also had fled their country and needed assistance. Although states frequently permitted him to expand into other regions and provide more assistance, states also pushed back and refused to give international recognition or assistance to many in need—most

notably when Jews were fleeing Nazi Germany. After the Second World War and as a consequence of mass displacement, states re-examined who could be called a refugee and what assistance they could receive. Because Western states were worried about having obligations to millions of people around the world, they defined a refugee as an individual 'outside the country of his origin owing to a well-founded fear of persecution' as a consequence of events that occurred in Europe before 1951. In other words, their definition excluded those outside Europe who were displaced because of war or natural disasters because of events after 1951. Objecting to this arbitrary definition that excluded so many, the new refugee agency, the United Nations High Commissioner for Refugees, working with aid agencies and permissive states, seized on events outside Europe and argued that there was no principled reason to deny to them what was given to Europeans.

Over time the political meaning of refugee came to include anyone who was forced to flee their home and crossed an international border, and eventually states changed the international legal meaning to reflect the new political realities. Now, in the contemporary era, we are likely to call someone a refugee if they are forced to flee their homes because of man-made circumstances and do not worry if they have crossed an international border. To capture these peoples, we now have a term 'internally displaced peoples'. One reason why states wanted to differentiate 'statutory' refugees from internally-displaced peoples is because they have little interest in extending their international legal obligations to millions of people and do not want to become too involved in the domestic affairs of states. Still, the concept of refugees has expanded impressively over the last 100 years, and the result is that there are millions of peoples who are now entitled to forms of assistance that are a matter of life and death.

Box 9.2 Alexander Wendt on the three cultures of anarchy

[T]he deep structure of anarchy [is] cultural or ideational rather than material ... [O]nce understood this way, we can see that the logic of anarchy can vary ... [D]ifferent cultures of anarchy are based on different kinds of roles in terms of which states represent Self and Other. [T]here are three roles, enemy, rival, and friend ... that are constituted by, and constitute, three distinct macro-level cultures of international politics, Hobbesian, Lockean, and Kantian, respectively. These cultures have different rules of engagement, interaction logics, and systemic tendencies ...The logic of the Hobbesian anarchy is well known: 'the war of all against all ...' This is the true self-help system ... where actors cannot count on each other for help of even to observe basic-self-restraint ... Survival depends solely on military power ... Security is deeply competitive, a zero-sum affair ... Even if what states really want is security rather than power, their collective beliefs force them to *act* as if they are power-seeking ... The Lockean culture has a different logic ... because it is based on a different role structure, rivalry rather than enmity ... Like enemies, rivals are constituted by representations about Self and Other with respect to violence, but these representations are less threatening: unlike enemies, rivals expect each other to act as if they recognize their sovereignty, their life and liberty, as a *right*, and therefore not to try to conquer or dominate them ... Unlike friends, however, the recognition among rivals does not extend to the right to be free from violence in disputes. The Kantian culture is based on a role structure of friendship ... within which states expect each other to observe two simple rules: (1) disputes will be settled without war or the threat of war (the rule of non-violence); and (2) they will fight as a team if the security of any one is threatened by a third party.

(Wendt, 1999: 43, 279, 251, 298–9)

politics. Some of the most important debates in world politics are about how to define particular activities. Development, human rights, security, humanitarian intervention, sovereignty are all important orienting concepts that can have any number of meanings. States and non-state actors have rival interpretations of the meanings of these concepts and will fight to try to have their preferred meaning collectively accepted.

The very fact that these meanings are fixed through politics, and that once these meanings are fixed they have consequences for the ability of people to determine their fates, suggests an alternative way of thinking about **power**. Most international relations theorists treat power as the ability of one state to compel another state to do what it otherwise would not and tend to focus on the material technologies, such as military firepower and economic statecraft, which have this persuasive effect. Constructivists have offered two important additions to this view of power. The forces of power go beyond material; they also can be ideational. Consider the issue of **legitimacy**. States, including great powers, crave legitimacy, the belief that they are acting according to and pursuing the values of the broader international community. There is a direct relationship between their legitimacy and the costs of a course of action: the greater the legitimacy, the easier time they will have convincing others to cooperate with their policies; the lesser the legitimacy, the more costly the action. This means, then, that even great powers will frequently feel the need to alter their policies in order to be viewed as legitimate—or bear the consequences. Further evidence of the constraining power of legitimacy is offered by the tactic of 'naming and shaming' by human rights activists. If states did not care about the reputation and the perception that they were acting in a manner consistent with prevailing international standards, then such a tactic would have little visible impact; it is only because law-breaking governments want to be perceived as acting in a manner consistent with international norms that they can be taunted into changing their conduct.

Moreover, the effects of power go beyond the ability to change behaviour. Power also includes how knowledge, the fixing of meanings, and the construction of identities allocate differential rewards and capacities. If development is defined as per capita income, then some actors, namely states, and some activities, namely industrialization, are privileged; however, if development is defined as basic needs, then other actors, namely peasants and women, gain voice, and other activities, namely small-scale agricultural initiatives and cottage industries, are visible. International humanitarian law tends to assume that 'combatants' are men and 'civilians' are women, children, and the elderly; consequently, as Box 9.3 relates, men and women might be differentially protected by the laws of war.

Although there is tremendous debate among constructivists over whether and how they are committed to social science, there is some common ground. To begin, they reject the unity of science thesis, that is, that the methods of the natural sciences are appropriate for understanding the social world. Instead, they argue that the objects of the natural world and the social world are different in one crucial respect: in the social world the subject knows herself through reflection upon her actions as a subject not simply of experience but of intentional action as well. Humans reflect on their experiences and use these experiences to inform their reasons for their behaviour. Atoms do not. What necessitates

> **Box 9.3** Charli Carpenter on the effects of gender on the lives of individuals in war-torn societies
>
> International agencies mandated with the protection of war-affected civilians generally aim to provide protection in a neutral manner, but when necessary they prioritize the protection of the 'especially vulnerable.' According to professional standards recently articulated by the International Committee for the Red Cross, 'special attention by organizations for specific groups should be determined on the basis of an assessment of their needs and vulnerability as well as the risks to which they are exposed.' If adult men are most likely to lose their lives directly as a result of the fall of a besieged town, one would expect that, given these standards, such agencies would emphasize protection of civilian men in areas under siege by armed forces. Nonetheless, in places where civilians have been evacuated from besieged areas in an effort to save lives, it is typically women, children, and the elderly who have composed the evacuee population . . . While in principle all civilians are to be protected on the basis of their actions and social roles, in practice only certain categories of population (women, elderly, sick, and disabled) are presumed to be civilians regardless of context . . . Thus . . . gender is encoded within the parameters of the immunity norm: while in principle the 'innocent civilian' may include other groups, such as adult men, the presumption that women and children are innocents, whereas adult men may not be means that 'women and children' signifies 'civilian' in a way that 'unarmed adult male' does not . . . Similarly, gender beliefs are embedded in . . . the concept of 'especially vulnerable populations' . . . In this context it never would have occurred to protection agencies to evacuate men and boys first, even if they had had the chance.
>
> *(Carpenter 2003: 662, 671, 673–4)*

a human science, therefore, is the need to understand how individuals give significance and meaning to their actions. Only then will we be able to explain human action. Consequently, the human sciences require methods that can capture the interpretations that actors bring to their activities. Max Weber, a founding figure of this approach, advocated that scholars employ *verstehen* to recreate how people understand and interpret the world. To do so, scholars need to exhibit empathy, to locate the practice within the collectivity so that one knows how this practice or activity counts, and to unify these individual experiences into objectively, though time-bound, explanations (Ruggie 1998: 860).

Most constructivists remain committed to causality and explanation, but insist on a definition of causality and explanation that is frequently accepted by many IR scholars. A highly popular view of causality is that independent and dependent variables are unrelated and that a cause exists when the movement of one variable precedes and is responsible for the movement of another. Constructivists, though, add that structures can have a causal impact because they make possible certain kinds of behaviour and thus generate certain tendencies in the international system. Sovereignty does not cause states with certain capacities; instead, it produces them and invests them with capacities that make possible certain kinds of behaviours. Being a sovereign state, after all, means that states have certain rights and privileges that other actors in world politics do not. States are permitted to use violence (though within defined limits) while non-state actors that use violence are, by definition, terrorists. Knowing something about the structure, therefore, does important causal work. Constructivists also are committed to explanatory theory, but reject the

idea that explanation requires the discovery of timeless laws. In fact, it is virtually impossible to find such laws in international politics. The reason for their absence is not because of some odd characteristic of international politics. Instead, this elusiveness exists for all the human sciences. As Karl Popper observed, the search for timeless laws in the human sciences will be forever elusive because of the ability of humans to accumulate knowledge of their activities, to reflect on their practices and acquire new knowledge, and to change their practices as a consequence. Accordingly, constructivists reject the search for laws in favour of contingent generalizations (Price and Reus-Smit 1998).

Constructivists use a variety of methods. They adopt ethnographic and interpretive techniques in order to re-create the meanings that actors bring to their practices and how these practices relate to social worlds. They employ large-*n* quantitative studies in order to demonstrate the emergence of a world culture that spreads specific practices, values, and models. They use genealogical methods to identify the contingent factors that produced the categories of world politics that are subsequently taken for granted. They utilize structured, focused comparisons in order better to understand the conditions under which norms diffuse from one context to another. They even use computer simulations to model the emergent properties of world politics.

Throughout, though, constructivists have attempted to interpret evidence as it relates to alternative explanations. Although they have largely positioned their claims against neo-realism and neo-liberal institutionalism, they have clarified the differences by contrasting constructivism with rational choice. The presumption, then, is that these are rival social theories. In many ways, they are. Rational choice treats actors as pre-social; constructivism as social. Rational choice treats interests as fixed; constructivism as constructed by the environment and interactions. Rational choice holds that the only effect of the environment is to constrain and regulate the actions of already constituted actors; constructivism adds that it also can construct the actors' identities and interests. Rational choice uses the logic of consequences to understand behaviour; constructivism adds the logic of appropriateness.

Given that rationalists and constructivists adopt such different frameworks for thinking about world politics, some scholars argue that these social theories are incommensurable; that is, they cannot be combined or reconciled because they contain opposing assumptions and capture different features of reality. Consequently, the only kind of possible relationship is some form of pluralism and any attempt at a grand synthesis, the mother of all social theories, will produce either a theoretic mutant or theoretical imperialism. For much the same reason, other scholars ridicule gladiatorial, winner-take-all, competition.

Other scholars look for points of connection and evaluate the relative strengths of each approach in order to see when they might be combined to enrich our understanding of the world. One possibility is strategic social construction (Finnemore and Sikkink 1998). Actors attempt to change the norms that subsequently guide and constitute state identities and interests. Human rights activists, for instance, try to encourage compliance with human rights norms not only by naming and shaming those who violate these norms, but also by encouraging states to identify with these norms because it is the right thing to do. Another possibility is to consider the relationship between the normative structure and strategic behaviour. Some use constructivism to identify how identity shapes the state's interests and then turn to rational choice for understanding strategic behaviour. In this view, the American identity shapes **national interests**, and then the structure of the international system informs its strategies for pursuing those interests. Yet some scholars go further and argue that the cultural context shapes not only identities and interests of actors but also the very strategies they can use as they pursue their interests. In other words, while 'game' metaphors are most closely associated with game theory and rational choice, some constructivists also argue that the normative structure shapes important features of the game—including the identity of the players to the strategies that are appropriate. Not all is fair in love,

war, or any other social endeavour. For decades Arab nationalism shaped the identities and interests of Arab states, contained norms that guided how Arab leaders could play the game of Arab politics, and encouraged Arab leaders to draw from the symbols of Arab politics to try to manoeuvre around their Arab rivals and further their own interests. How Arab leaders played out their regional games was structured by the norms of Arab politics. They had very intense rivalries and as they vied for prestige and status they frequently accused each other of being a traitor to the Arab nation or harming the cause of Arabism. But rarely did they use military force. Until the late 1970s the idea of relations with Israel was a virtual 'taboo', violated by Egyptian Anwar Sadat's trip to Jerusalem in 1977 and separate peace treaty in 1979. Arab states did not respond through military action but rather by evicting Egypt from the Arab League, and then Sadat paid the ultimate price for his heresy when he was assassinated in 1981.

In general, these examples of the possible connections between constructivism and rational choice remind us that we should be open to and utilize as many approaches as possible as we try to enrich our understanding of how the world works.

Key Points

- Constructivists are concerned with human consciousness, treat ideas as structural factors, consider the dynamic relationship between ideas and material forces as a consequence of how actors interpret their material reality, and are interested in how agents produce structures and how structures produce agents.

- Knowledge shapes how actors interpret and construct their social reality.

- The normative structure shapes the identity and interests of actors such as states.

- Although the meanings that actors bring to their activities are shaped by the underlying culture, meanings are not always fixed and the fixing of meaning is a central feature of politics.

- Social rules are regulative, regulating already existing activities, and constitutive, making possible and defining those very activities.

- Social construction denaturalizes what is taken for granted, asks questions about the origins of what is now accepted as a fact of life, and considers the alternative pathways that might have produced and can produce alternative worlds.

- Power is not only the ability of one actor to get another actor to do what they would not do otherwise, but also as the production of identities, interests, and meanings that limit the ability of actors to control their fate.

Constructivism and global change

Constructivism's focus on how the world hangs together, how normative structures construct the identities and interests of actors, and how actors are rule-following, might seem ideal for explaining why things stay the same but useless for explaining why things change. This is hardly true. Constructivism claims that what exists need not have existed and need not—inviting us to think of alternative worlds and the conditions that make them more or less possible. Indeed, constructivism scolded neo-realism and neo-liberal institutionalism for their failure to explain contemporary global transformations. The **Peace of Westphalia** helped to establish sovereignty and the norm of non-interference, but in recent decades various processes have worked against the principle of non-interference and suggested how state sovereignty is conditional on how states treat their populations, best known as a responsibility to protect. **World orders** are created and sustained not only by Great Power preferences but also by changing understandings of what constitutes a legitimate international order. Until the Second World War the idea of a world organized around **empires** was hardly illegitimate; now it is. One of today's most pressing and impressive issues concerning global change is the 'end of history' and the apparent homogenization of world politics—that is, the tendency of states to organize their domestic and international lives in similar ways and the growing acceptance of certain international norms for defining the good life and how to get there. Below I explore three concepts that figure centrally in such discussions—diffusion, socialization, and the **internationalization and institutionalization of norms**.

A central theme in any discussion of global change is diffusion. Stories about **diffusion** concern how particular models, practices, norms, strategies, or beliefs spread within a population. Constructivists have highlighted two important issues. One is **institutional isomorphism**, which observes that those organizations that share the same environment will, over time, resemble each other. In other words, if once there was a diversity of models within the population, over time that diversity yields to conformity and convergence around a single model. There used to be various ways to organize state structures, economic activity, free-trade agreements, and on and on. But now the world is organized around the **nation-state**, states favour democratic forms of governance and market economies, and most international organizations have a multilateral form. It is possible that the reason for this convergence is that states now realize that some institutions are just superior to others. An additional possibility is that states look alike because they want acceptance, legitimacy, and status. For instance, one explanation for the recent wave of democratization and elections is that states now accept that democratic elections are a more efficient and superior way to organize politics; it also could be, though, that lots of states have decided to turn democratic and run elections not because they were persuaded that it would be more efficient but rather because they wanted to be viewed as part of the 'modern world' and receive the benefits associated with being a legitimate state.

How do things diffuse? Why are they accepted in new places? One factor is coercion. Colonialism and Great Power imposition figured centrally in the spread of capitalism. Another factor is strategic competition. Heated rivals are likely to adopt similar weapons systems in order to try to stay even on the military battlefield. States also will adopt similar ideas and organizations for at least four other reasons. Formal and informal pressures can cause states to adopt similar ideas because doing so will bring them needed resources. States want resources and in order to attract these resources they will adopt and reform their institutions in order to signal to various communities that they are part of the club and are utilizing 'modern' techniques. In other words, they value these new institutions not because they truly believe that they are superior but rather because they are symbols that will attract resources. Eastern European countries seeking entry into the European Union adopted various reforms not only because they believed that they are superior but also because they are the price of admission.

Also, during periods of uncertainty, when states are unsure of how to address existing challenges, they are likely to adopt those models that are perceived as successful or legitimate. Political candidates in newly democratizing countries reorganize their party and campaign organizations in order to increase their prospects of electoral victory. To that end, they draw from those models of success, largely from the American context, not necessarily because they have evidence that the American campaign model is truly better but rather because it appears modern, sophisticated, and superior. Furthermore, frequently states adopt particular models because of their symbolic standing. Many Third World governments have acquired very expensive weapons systems that have very little military value because they convey to others that they are sophisticates and are a part of the 'club'. Iran's nuclear ambitions might owe to its desire for regional dominance, but it also could be that it wants to own this ultimate status symbol. Finally, professional associations and expert communities also diffuse organizational models. Most associations have established techniques, codes of conduct, and methodologies for determining how to confront challenges in their area of expertise. They learn these techniques through informal interactions and in formal settings such as in universities. Once these standards are established, they become the 'industry standard' and the accepted way of addressing problems in an area. Part of the job of professional associations and expert networks is to communicate these standards to others; doing so makes them agents of diffusion. Economists, lawyers, military officials, arms control experts and others diffuse practices, standards, and models through networks and associations. If the American way of campaigning is becoming increasingly accepted around the world, it is in part due to a new class of professional campaign consultants that have converged around a set of accepted techniques and are ready to peddle their wares to willing customers.

In their discussion of changing identities and interests, constructivists have also employed the concept of socialization. How can we explain how states change so that they come to identify with the identities, interests, and manners of the existing members of the club, and, accordingly, change their behaviour so that it is consistent with those of the group? According to Alistair Iain Johnston (2008), the place to look is the intimate relations between states within international institutions and organizations. Specifically, he explores the possibility that China changed its security policies over the last two decades because of socialization processes contained in various multilateral forums. Furthermore, he argues that socialization can be produced by several mechanisms: by mimicking, when state officials face tremendous uncertainty and decide that the best way to proceed is to adopt the practices that seem to have served others well; social influence, when state officials aspire to status within the existing group and are sensitive to signs of approval and disapproval; and persuasion, when state officials are convinced by the superiority of new ways of thinking about the world. Consistent with the earlier comment that we should look for ways in which

constructivism and rational choice are both competing and complementary explanations of state behaviour, Johnston argues that some paths to socialization are closer to what rationalists have in mind, especially as they emphasize the costs and benefits of action, and some are closer to what constructivists have in mind, especially as they emphasize the desire to be accepted by the broader community and to show the ability to learn.

Discussions of diffusion and socialization also draw attention to the **internationalization of norms**. Norms are standards of appropriate behaviour for actors with a given identity. Norms of humanitarianism, **citizenship**, military intervention, human rights, trade, arms control, and the environment not only regulate what states do; they can also be connected to their identities and thus expressive of how they define themselves and their interests. Norms constrain behaviour because actors are worried about costs and because of a sense of self. 'Civilized' states are expected to avoid settling their difference through violence not because war might not pay but rather because it violates how 'civilized' states are expected to act. Human rights activists aspire to reduce human rights violations not only by 'naming and shaming' those who violate these rights but also by persuading potential violators that the observation of human rights is tied to their identity as a modern, responsible state. The domestic debates on the USA's treatment of 'enemy combatants' concerned not only whether torture worked but also whether it is a legitimate practice for civilized states.

These expectations of what constitutes proper behaviour can diffuse across the population to the point that they are taken for granted. Norms, therefore, do not simply erupt but rather evolve through a political process. A central issue, therefore, is the internationalization and institutionalization of norms, or what is now called the **life cycle of norms** (see Box 9.4).

Although many international norms have a taken-for-granted quality, they have to come from somewhere and their path to acceptance is nearly always rough and rocky. Although most states now recognize that prisoners of war have certain rights and cannot be subjected to summary executions on the battlefield, this was not always the case. These rights originated with the emergence of international humanitarian law in the late nineteenth century, and then slowly spread and became increasingly accepted over the next several decades in response to considerable debate regarding how to minimize the horrors of war. Now most states accept that prisoners of war have rights, even if those rights are

Box 9.4 Finnemore and Sikkink on the three stages of the life cycle of norms

Norm emergence

'This stage is typified by persuasion by norm entrepreneurs [who] attempt to convince a critical mass of states ... to embrace new norms. Norm entrepreneurs call attention to issues or even "create" issues by using language that names, interprets, and dramatizes them.' Norm entrepreneurs attempt to establish 'frames ... that resonate with broader public understandings and are adopted as new ways of talking about and understanding issues'. Norm entrepreneurs need a launching pad to promote their norms, and will frequently work from non-governmental organizations and with international organizations and states. 'In most cases for an emergent norm to reach a threshold and move toward the second stage, it must become institutionalized in specific sets of international rules and organizations ... After norm entrepreneurs have persuaded a critical mass of states to become norm leaders and adopt new norms ... the norm reaches a critical threshold or tipping point.'

Norm cascade

'The second stage is characterized more by a dynamic of imitation as the norm leaders attempt to socialize other states to become norm followers. The exact motivation for this second stage where the norm "cascades" through the rest of the population (in this case, states) may vary, but ... a combination of pressure for conformity, desire to enhance international legitimation, and the desire of state leaders to enhance their self-esteem facilitate norm cascades.' These processes can be likened to socialization. 'To the degree that states and state elites fashion a political self or identity in relationship to the international community, the concept of socialization suggests that the cumulative effect of many countries in a region adopting new norms' is akin to peer pressure.'

Norm internalization

The third stage is 'norm internalization ... Norms acquire a taken-for-granted quality and are no longer a matter of ... debate' and thus are automatically honoured. 'For example, few people today discuss whether women should be allowed to vote, whether slavery is useful, or whether medical personnel should be granted immunity during war.'

(Adapted from Finnemore and Sikkink 1998: 894–905)

not fully observed. Several decades ago many scholars and jurists objected to the very idea of humanitarian intervention because it violated sovereignty's principle of non-interference and allowed great powers to try to become sheep in wolf's clothing. Over the last fifteen years, though, there is a growing acceptance of humanitarian intervention and a 'responsibility to protect'—when states are unable or unwilling to protect their citizens, then the international community inherits that responsibility. This revolutionary concept emerged through fits and starts and in response to tragedies such as Rwanda and propelled by various states and humanitarian organizations.

Among the various consequences of institutional isomorphism and the internationalization of norms, three are noteworthy. There used to be a myriad of ways to organize human activities, but that diversity has slowly but impressively yielded to conformity. Yet just because states look alike does not mean that they act alike. After all, many states gravitate towards particular models not because they really think that the model is better but in order to improve their legitimacy. These states, then, can be expected to act in ways that are inconsistent with the expectations of the model. For instance, if governments adopt democratic forms of governance and elections solely for symbolic reasons, then we should expect the presence of democratic institutions to exist alongside authoritarian and illiberal practices. There also is a deepening sense of an 'international community'. The internationalization of norms suggests that actors are increasingly accepting standards of behaviour because they are connected to a sense of self that is tied to the international community. These norms, in other words, are bound up with the values of that community. To the extent that these values are shared, it becomes possible to speak of an international community. A third consequence is the presence of power even within an international community. Whose vision of international community is being constructed? Diffusion rarely goes from the Third World to the West; instead, it travels from the West to the Third World. The international society of states began as a European society and then expanded outward; the internationalization of this society and its norms shaped the identities and foreign policy practices of new members. In other words, the convergence on similar models, the internationalization of norms, and the possible emergence of an international community should not be mistaken for a world without power and hierarchy. In general, the constructivist concern with international diffusion and the internationalization of norms touches centrally on global change because of the interest in a world in motion and transformation.

Key Points

- The recognition that the world is socially constructed means that constructivists can investigate global change and transformation.

- A key issue in any study of global change is diffusion, captured by the concern with institutional isomorphism and the life cycle of norms.

- Although diffusion sometimes occurs because of the view that the model is superior, frequently actors adopt a model either because of external pressures or because of its symbolic legitimacy.

- Institutional isomorphism and the internationalization of norms raise issues of growing homogeneity in world politics, a deepening international community, and socialization processes.

- Relations among the city-states of ancient Greece were characterized by more developed societal characteristics, such as arbitration.

- Ancient China, India, and Rome all had their own distinctive international societies.

Box 9.5 Key concepts of constructivism

Agent–structure problem: the problem is how to think about the relationship between agents and structures. One view is that agents are born with already formed identities and interests and then treat other actors and the broad structure that their interactions produce as a constraint on their interests. But this suggests that actors are pre-social to the extent that there is little interest in their identities or possibility that they might change their interests through their interactions with others. Another view is to treat the structure not as a constraint but rather as constituting the actors themselves. Yet this might treat agents as cultural dupes because they are nothing more than artefacts of that structure. The proposed solution to the agent–structure problem is to try and find a way to understand how agents and structures constitute each other.

Constructivism: an approach to international politics that concerns itself with the centrality of ideas and human consciousness; stresses a holistic and Idealist view of structures; and how the structure constructs the actors' identities and interests, how their interaction is organized and constrained by that structure, and how their very interaction serves to either reproduce or transform that structure.

Holism: the view that structures cannot be decomposed into the individual units and their interactions because structures are more than the sum of their parts and are irreducibly social. The effects of structures, moreover, go beyond merely constraining the actors but also construct them.

Idealism: although often associated with the claim that it is possible to create a world of peace, idealism as a social theory argues that the most fundamental feature of society is social consciousness. Ideas shape how we see ourselves and our interests, the knowledge that we use to categorize and understand the world, the beliefs we have of others, and the possible and impossible solutions to challenges and threats. Idealism does not disregard material forces such as technology, but instead claims that the meanings and consequences of these material forces are not given by nature but rather driven by human interpretations.

Identity: the understanding of the self in relationship to an 'other'. Identities are social and thus are always formed in relationship to others. Constructivists generally hold that identities shape interests; we cannot know what we want unless we know who we are. Because identities are social and are produced through interactions they can change.

Individualism: the view that structures can be reduced to the aggregation of individuals and their interactions. International relations theories that subscribe to individualism assume that the nature of the units and their interests, usually states and the pursuit of power or wealth, and then examine how the broad structure, usually the distribution of power, constrains how states can act and generates certain patterns in international politics. Individualism stands in contrast to holism.

Materialism: the view that material forces, including technology, are the bedrock of society is the organization of material forces. For international relations scholars, this leads to forms of technological determinism or the distribution of military power for understanding the state's foreign policy and patterns of international politics.

Normative structure: international relations theory traditionally defines structure in material terms, such as the distribution of power, and then treats structure as a constraint on actors. In contrast to a materialist structure, a normative structure includes the collectively held ideas such as knowledge, rules, beliefs, and norms that not only constrain actors—they also construct categories of meaning, constitute their identities and interests, and define standards of appropriate conduct. Critical here is the concept of a norm, a standard of appropriate behaviour for actors with a given identity. Actors adhere to norms not only because of benefits and costs for doing so, but also because they are related to a sense of self.

Rational choice: an approach that emphasizes how actors attempt to maximize their interests, how they attempt to select the most efficient means to achieve those interests, and endeavours to explain collective outcomes by virtue of the attempt by actors to maximize their preferences under a set of actors to maximize their preferences under a set of constraints. Deriving largely from economic theorizing, the rational-choice approach to politics and international politics has been immensely influential and applied to a range of issues.

Conclusion

This chapter surveyed the global-historical, intellectual, and disciplinary forces that made constructivism a particularly attractive way of thinking about international politics, whose continuities and transformations it invites students to imagine. It explores why the world is organized the way it is, considers the different factors that shape the durable forms of world politics, and seeks alternative worlds. In doing so, it challenges received wisdoms and opens up new lines of enquiry. Although many in the discipline treated as strange the claim that ideas can shape how the world works, in fact what is strange is a view of a world devoid of ideas. After all, is it even possible to imagine such a world? What would it look like? Is it even possible to imagine a world driven only by materialist forces? What would it look like?

Constructivism challenged the discipline's mainstream on its own terms and on issues that were at the heart of its research agenda. Its success has sometimes led to the false impression that constructivism is a substantive theory and not the social theory that it is. As such, it is much more and much less than meets the eye. It is much less because it is not properly a theory that can be viewed as a rival to many of the theories in this volume. It offers no predictions about enduring regularities or tendencies in world politics. Instead, it suggests how to investigate them. Consequently, it is much more than meets the eye because it offers alternative ways of thinking about a range of concepts and issues, including power, alliance formation, war termination, military intervention, the liberal peace, and international organizations.

What of the future of constructivism? It depends on which version of constructivism we are discussing. Constructivists generally accept certain commitments, including idealism, holism, and an interest in the relationship between agents and structures. They also accept certain basic claims, such as the social construction of reality, the existence and importance of social facts, the constitution of actors' identities, interests, and subjectivities, and the importance of recovering the meaning that actors give to their activities. But they also exhibit tremendous differences. Although sometimes these disagreements can appear to derive from academic posturing, the search for status, and the narcissism of minor differences, in fact there also can be much at stake, as suggested in Chapter 10. These differences will exist as long as constructivism exists. This is healthy because it will guard against complacency and enrich our understanding of the world.

Questions

1 What were the silences of neo-realism and neo-liberal institutionalism?
2 How did international relations scholars use critical and sociological theory to address important issues overlooked by neo-realism and neo-liberal institutionalism?
3 What is the core of constructivism?
4 Do you find constructivism a useful approach for thinking about world politics?
5 Do you agree that we should try to understand how actors make meaningful their behaviour in world politics? Or is it enough to examine behaviour?
6 How are meanings fixed in world politics?
7 Do you think that constructivism adds richness and complexity at the expense of our desire to understand patterns in world politics?
8 What sort of relationship can exist between rational choice and constructivism?
9 What do you think are the core issues for the study of global change, and how does constructivism help you address those issues? Alternatively, how does a constructivist framework help you identify new issues that you had not previously considered?

10 What sorts of questions are opened up by thinking about socialization in world politics?

11 How does the concept of diffusion help you understand why and how the world has changed?

12 In what way do you think that socialization of individuals looks like socialization of states?

Further Reading

Adler, E. (2003), 'Constructivism', in Walter Carlneas, Beth Simmons, and Thomas Risse (eds), *Handbook of International Relations* (Thousand Oaks, CA: Sage). A terrific overview of the origins and fundamentals of constructivism and its relationship to existing theories of international politics.

Barnett, M. (1998), *Dialogues in Arab Politics: Negotiations in Regional Order* (New York: Columbia University Press). Examines how Arab leaders played the game of Arab politics and, in doing so, transformed the very nature of Arab politics. An example of how constructivists might think about how strategic action is shaped by a normative structure.

Carpenter, C. (2003), ' "Women and Children First": Gender, Norms, and Humanitarian Evacuation in the Balkans 1991–1995', *International Organization*, 57(4) (Fall): 661–94.

Fearon, J., and Wendt, A. (2003), 'Rationalism vs. Constructivism', in Walter Carlneas, Beth Simmons, and Thomas Risse (eds), *Handbook of International Relations* (Thousand Oaks, CA: Sage). A very useful exposition of how rational choice and constructivism overlap, written by two of the leading proponents of each approach in international relations.

Finnemore, M., and Sikkink, K. (2001), 'Taking Stock: The Constructivist Research Program in International Relations and Comparative Politics', *Annual Review of Political Science*, 4: 391–416. A highly insightful account of constructivism's insights and future directions of research.

—— —— (1999), 'International Norms and Political Change', in P. Katzenstein *et al.* (eds), *Explorations and Controversies in World Politics* (Cambridge, MA: MIT Press).

Hollis, M., and Smith, S. (1990), *Explaining and Understanding International Relations* (New York: Oxford University Press). Explains in an exceptionally clear fashion the contrast between a conception of world politics driven by self-interested action and a conception informed by rules and interpretive methods.

Johnston, A. I. (2008), *Social States: China in International Institutions, 1980–2000* (Princeton, NJ: Princeton University Press).

Katzenstein, P. (ed.) (1996), *The Culture of National Security* (New York: Columbia University Press). An edited collection that clearly identifies why we need to examine how identities and norms shape state interests, and explores those claims in a range of critical security areas.

Wendt, A. (1999), *A Social Theory of International Politics* (Cambridge: Cambridge University Press). The seminal text that explains the central elements and dissects the important controversies of constructivism.

Online Resource Centre

 Visit the Online Resource Centre that accompanies this book to access more learning resources on this chapter topic at www.oxfordtextbooks.co.uk/orc/baylis5e/

Chapter 10

Poststructuralism

LENE HANSEN

Reader's Guide

This chapter focuses on poststructuralism, one of the International Relations (IR) perspectives furthest away from the neo-realist and neo-liberal mainstream. Poststructuralists in IR draw upon a larger body of philosophical texts known as poststructuralism. They argue that the state stands at the centre of world politics and that we should understand it as a particular form of political community. This challenges neo-realism's and neo-liberalism's conception of the state as a rational actor driven by self-help and relative or absolute gains. The mainstream's conception is, argues poststructuralism, ahistorical and it marginalizes non- and trans-state actors, stateless people, and those persecuted by 'their own' states. Poststructuralists hold that foreign policies always imply a particular representation of ours and others' identities and that identities have no fixed meaning, but are constituted in language.

Introduction

Like **constructivism**, poststructuralism became part of International Relations (IR) in the 1980s (see Ch. 9). As constructivists, poststructuralists in IR were influenced by social and philosophical theory that had played a major role in the humanities since the 1970s. Politically, the early and mid-1980s were dominated by the **second cold war,** and this context made an impact on poststructuralists, who feared that the two blocs would destroy each other in a nuclear **holocaust** (see Ch. 3). Poststructuralists held that the key to the **cold war** lay in the enemy constructions that both East and West promoted. The cold war is of course now long gone, but poststructuralism is still very much focused on **high politics** (those themes high on the foreign policy agenda, such as war, security, and the military), and it maintains a concern with states' constructions of threats and enemies.

Poststructuralists bring a critical perspective to the study of world politics in two important respects. They are critical of the way that most states conduct their foreign policies and they are critical of how most IR theories tell us to study what states do. Poststructuralists disagree with **realism** (see Ch. 5) that we should see the state as a **self-help** actor or as a unit that stays the same through history. Rather, the state is a particular way of understanding **political community**, that is, whom we can trust and whom we feel we have something in common with (see also Chs 24 and 32). Likewise, if the **international system** is **anarchic**, it is because states and other actors reproduce this system, not because it is given once and for all. Poststructuralism wants us to take seriously what is excluded and marginalized by existing policies and theories, and it tells us to think critically of how we construct the world. To poststructuralists there is no objective yardstick that we can use to define threats, dangers, enemies, or, say, underdevelopment. We need to investigate how constructions of the world, and those people and places that inhabit it, make particular polices seem natural and therefore legitimate. Poststructuralism tells us to take the state and **power** very seriously, but it does so in a manner that sets it aside from the other theories of world politics that you have encountered so far (see Chs 5–9).

Studying the social world

Because poststructuralism adopts a critical attitude to world politics, it raises questions about **ontology** (what is in the world) and **epistemology** (how we can study the world). As you have learned from previous chapters, there has never been an ontological consensus in IR. Realists have held that the self-help state is the essential core and that the drive for power or security makes it impossible to move beyond the risk of war (see Ch. 5). Liberalists (see Ch. 6) have disagreed, arguing that states can build a more cooperative and peaceful system. Both realism and liberalism agree, though, that the state is the main building block.

Although ontological assumptions are absolutely central for how we think about the world, scholars and students often go about studying world politics without giving ontology much thought. That is because ontological assumptions come into view only when theories with different ontological assumptions clash. As long as one works within the same **paradigm,** there is no need to discuss one's basic assumptions, and energy can be devoted to testing competing hypotheses, comparing old explanations with new ones, or compiling sets of data. One of the strengths of poststructuralism has been to call attention to how much the ontological assumptions we make about the state actually matter.

Poststructuralism also brings epistemology to the fore and it argues in favour of a constitutive, post-positivist, **anti-foundationalist** position. As a consequence, it is seen as one of the most alternative approaches in IR (see Fig. 10.1 and Chs 11 and 16).

As argued in Chapter 7, mainstream approaches adopt a positivist epistemology. They strive to find the causal relations that 'rule' world politics and they work with dependent and independent variables. In the case of **democratic peace** theory, for example, this implies a research agenda where the impact of state-type (democratic/non-democratic) on foreign policy behaviour (going to war or not) can be tested (see also Chs 6 and 14). Post-positivists argue that the social world is so far removed from the hard sciences where casual epistemologies originate that it is unhelpful to understand it through causal cause–effect relationships. Compared to

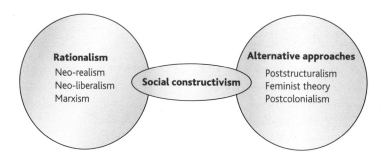

Figure 10.1 International theory at the beginning of the twenty-first century

constructivists (Ch. 9), who adopt a concept of causality as structural pressure, poststructuralists hold that causality as such is inappropriate, not because there are no such things as **structures**, but because these structures are constituted through human action. Structures cannot therefore be independent variables. As you will see from the rest of this chapter, **constitutive theories** are still *theories*, not just descriptions or stories about the world. Thus it is not easier or less rigorous to develop non-causal, constitutive theories; it is just different.

The distinction between causal and non-causal theories is also captured by the distinction between **explanatory theories** and constitutive theories. As you read through the literature on world politics, you will encounter other labels that point to much the same things, with causal–constitutive and **foundationalist–anti-foundationalist** being the most common ones. These distinctions are not completely identical, but there is a certain convergence between them in that causal, explanatory, positivist theories are usually foundationalist; and constitutive, non-causal, and non-positivist theories are usually anti-foundationalist (see Box 10.1).

You should note that epistemological differences cannot simply be resolved through reference to 'facts'. Different epistemologies lead you to select different kinds of 'facts' and to treat them differently. To take the example of ethnic war, realist and liberal scholars look for the factors that explain why ethnic wars occur. Here the relevant facts are the number of ethnic wars, where and when they took place, and facts we hypothesize

might explain them: for instance forms of government or economic **capabilities**. Poststructuralists by contrast ask what calling something an 'ethnic war' implies for our understanding of the war and the policies that could be used to stop it. Here the facts come from texts that document different actors' use of 'war labels'.

Box 10.1 Epistemological distinctions

- Foundationalism: holds that all truth claims can be judged true or false; usually against empirical 'facts'.
- Anti-foundationalism: holds that each theory poses different questions; hence what counts as 'facts' and 'truths' differs from theory to theory.
- Explanatory theory: makes causal statement about relations between dependent and independent variables.
- Constitutive theory: theorizes the relationship between 'variables' as mutually constituting each other; hence 'variables' cannot be said to stand in a causal relationship to one another.

Key Points

- Poststructuralists raise questions about ontology and epistemology.
- Poststructuralism is critical of statism and of taking the anarchical system for granted.
- Poststructuralism adopts a constitutive epistemology.
- What count as facts depends on the ontological and epistemologies assumptions a theory makes.

Poststructuralism as a political philosophy

As mentioned in the Introduction, IR poststructuralists bring philosophical ideas and concepts to the study of world politics. These can be quite complex and hard to explain, but let us begin with four concepts that have been particularly influential: discourse, deconstruction, genealogy, and intertextuality.

Discourse

Poststructuralism holds that language is essential to how we make sense of the world. Language is social because we cannot make our thoughts understandable to others without a set of shared codes. This is captured by the concept of **discourse,** which the prominent French philosopher Michel Foucault defined as a linguistic system that orders statements and concepts. Politically, language is significant because politicians—and other actors relevant to world politics—must legitimate their foreign polices to audiences at home and abroad. The words we use to describe something are not neutral, and the choice of one term over another has political implications. To take an example, if what happens in Darfur, Sudan is described as 'a **genocide**', there is a strong moral pressure on the **international community** to 'do something', but not if what happens is described as '**tribal**' warfare'.

As you can see from this example, poststructuralism understands language not as a neutral transmitter, but as *producing* meaning. Things do not have an objective meaning independently of how we constitute them in language. You may recall from Chapter 9 that constructivists make a distinction between **social facts** and **brute facts**, and poststructuralists hold that even brute facts are socially constructed. This does not mean that things do not happen in the real world—such as if you fire an armed gun at someone they will get hurt—but it does mean that there is no given essence to 'a thing' or 'an event': is the shooting an accident, an attack, or divine retribution for something bad you did? What possible meanings can be assigned to a specific event thus depends on the discourses that are available. For example, we might attribute an illness like a heart attack to either our lifestyle (how we eat, live, drink, and exercise), or to our genes (which we cannot do much about), or divine punishment. Using the concept of discourse, we can say that heart attacks are constituted differently within a 'lifestyle discourse', a 'genetic discourse', and a 'religious discourse'. Each discourse provides different views of the body, what can be done to prevent disease, and thus what policies of disease prevention should be adopted. Poststructuralists stress that discourses are not the same as ideas, and that materiality or 'the real world' is not abandoned (see Box 10.2). To take materiality seriously means for example that advances in health technologies can change the way that discourses construct those afflicted by heart attacks or other diseases such as cancer or HIV/AIDS.

> **Box 10.2** Ernesto Laclau and Chantal Mouffe on the materiality of discourse
>
> 'The fact that every object is constituted as an object of discourse has *nothing to do* with whether there is a world external to thought, or with the realism/idealism opposition. An earthquake or the falling of a brick is an event that certainly exists, in the sense that it occurs here and now, independently of my will. But whether their specificity as objects is constructed in terms of "natural phenomena" or "expressions of the wrath of God", depends upon the structuring of a discursive field. What is denied is not that such objects exist externally to thought, but the rather different assertion that they could constitute themselves as objects outside any discursive condition of emergence .... We will affirm the *material* character of every discursive structure. To argue the opposite is to accept the very classical dichotomy between an objective field constituted outside of any discursive intervention, and a discourse consisting of the pure expression of thought.'
>
> (Laclau and Mouffe 1985: 108)

Deconstruction

To see language as a set of codes means that words (or signs) make sense only in relation to other words. We cannot know what 'horse' means unless that word is connected to other words: 'animal', 'furry', 'hoofed', and 'fast'. Moreover, we know what something is only by comparing it to something it is not. A 'horse' is *not* 'human', 'feathered', 'legless', and 'slow'. To see language as connected signs underscores the *structural* side of post-*structuralism* (see Box 10.3).

What sets *post*-structuralism aside from structuralism (or more precisely structural linguistics) is that poststructuralism sees sign structures as unstable because

> **Box 10.3** 'Postmodernism' and 'poststructuralism'
>
> 'Poststructuralism does not mean "anti-structuralism", but a philosophical position that developed out of structuralism ..., a position which in many ways shares more with structuralism than with its opponents.'
>
> (Wæver 2002: 23)
>
> Postmodernism refers to a historical period (usually after the Second World War), a direction in art, literature and architecture, and is used to describe new empirical phenomena such as 'postmodern war' (see Ch. 13). Poststructuralism refers to a body of thought that is not confined to a specific historical period. Poststructuralism and postmodernism are often conflated by non-poststructuralists in International Relations (Campbell 2007: 211–12).

connections between words are never given once and for all. To take the 'horse', it might be 'an animal', but in many situations, it is seen as more 'human' than 'real animals' such as 'pigs' or 'worms'. Its 'animalness' is itself unstable and given through other signs at a given time and place. This might at first seem quite far removed from world politics, but it tells us that the way we describe events, places, peoples, and states are neither neutral nor given by the things themselves. For example, in 2002, when President George W. Bush spoke about an '**axis of evil**' threatening the Western world, this implied a radical difference between the USA and the countries (Iraq, Iran, and North Korea) that were part of this axis.

The French philosopher Jacques Derrida's theory of **deconstruction** adds that language is made up by dichotomies, for instance between the developed and the underdeveloped, the modern and the pre-modern, the civilized and the barbaric. These dichotomies are not 'neutral', because one term is superior to the other. There is a clear hierarchy between the developed–modern–civilized on the one hand and the underdeveloped–pre-modern–barbaric on the other. Deconstruction shows how such dichotomies make something, for instance of how developed a country is, look like an objective description although it is in fact a structured set of values. Poststructuralists disagree on whether one might describe deconstruction as a methodology (see Box 10.4), but agree that a central goal is to problematize dichotomies, show how they work, and thereby open up alternative ways to understand world politics.

Box 10.4 Views on poststructuralist methodology

Poststructuralists differ in their assessment of whether a poststructuralist methodology is possible and desirable.

Lene Hansen holds that 'Many of the methodological questions that poststructuralist discourse analysis confronts are those that face all academic work: what should be the focus of analysis?, how should a research design be built around it?, and how is a body of material and data selected that facilitates a qualitatively and quantitatively reliable answer? Poststructuralism's focus on discourses as articulated in written and spoken text calls in addition for particular attention to the methodology of reading (how are identities identified within foreign policy texts and how should the relationship between opposing discourses be studied?) and the methodology of textual selection (which forums and types of text should be chosen and how many should be included?)' (Hansen 2006: 2).

Others, including Rita Floyd, are more sceptical, holding that 'Derrida would have been fundamentally opposed to even the possibility' (Floyd 2007: 216).

Genealogy

Genealogy is another of Foucault's concepts, defined as a 'history of the present'. It starts from something contemporary, say climate change (see also Ch. 21), and asks two questions: what political practices have formed the present and which alternative understandings and discourses have been marginalized and often forgotten? A genealogy of climate change might start by asking who are allowed to speak and make decisions at events such as the Copenhagen climate summit in 2009. Then it asks what constructions of 'the climate' and '**global responsibility**' are dominant and how these constructions relate to past discourses. By looking into the past we see alternative ways to conceptualize humans' relationship with 'the climate' and gain an understanding of the discursive and material structures that underpin the present.

The concept of power

The concepts of genealogy and discourse point us towards Foucault's conception of power. Power to Foucault is 'productive': it comes about when discourses constitute particular subject positions as the 'natural' ones. 'Actors' therefore do not exist outside discourse; they are produced through discourse. When states and **institutions** manage to establish themselves as having the knowledge to govern a particular issue, this is also an instance of power. Knowledge is not opposed to power—as in the classical phrase 'speaking truth to power'—but is integral to power itself. As a concrete example, take the way Western scholars have 'gained knowledge' about non-Western peoples by describing them as inferior, backward, underdeveloped, and sometimes threatening. This takes for granted that a foreign **identity** exists and that it can be studied (see also Ch. 11). More broadly, to speak from a position of knowledge is to exercise authority over a given issue. Poststructuralists in IR have also picked up one of Foucault's more specific conceptualizations of power, namely that of biopower. Biopower works at two levels: at the individual level we are told to discipline and control our bodies, and at the collective level we find that governments and other institutions seek to manage whole populations. A good example of biopolitics is that of population control, where states have promoted such 'body-disciplining' practices as abstinence before marriage and contraceptives in the attempt to reduce the number of births or prevent particular groups of women from getting pregnant. Practices targeted at the individual are built around the idea that

Case Study 1 Discourses on HIV/AIDS

HIV/AIDS has been situated right at the heart of discussions of **globalization** since the disease was discovered in the 1980s (see also Box 29.3). Some states have tried to prevent themselves from exposure to the virus by excluding people with HIV/AIDS from entering and staying. The USA, for example, adopted a travel ban in 1987 which was in place until January 2010. The Joint United Nations Programme on HIV/AIDS (UNAIDS) has fought such policies because in the words of Executive Director Michel Sidibé, 'Such discrimination has no place in today's highly mobile world' (UNAIDS 2010).

From a poststructuralist perspective, policies on HIV/AIDS are not simply seeking to solve a material problem—HIV/AIDS—but constitute the disease and those who are affected by it in specific ways. The policies that ban people with HIV/AIDS from entering a country invoke a discourse of danger: those who enter are a

risk to those who already live there, that is, the 'home population' (see also Epstein 2007). But why are those with HIV/AIDS a danger? Obviously, there are those who might be dangerous because they act irresponsibly by having unprotected sex or sharing needles, but even those who do not are also banned from entering. Adopting the concept of biopolitics, we might say that the danger stems from the 'infected' body itself, that bodies have 'a life'—and an untrustworthiness—independently of how disciplined a manner its 'owner' behaves (Elbe 2009). And if the individual cannot discipline 'its' body, states are justified in 'controlling' a whole group of 'infected people'. Here we see that biopolitics and a traditional state-centric discourse come together to legitimize the view that states have the right to close their borders to individuals from other states. The opposing discourse, that of 'rights of travel', implies a very different representation of those living with the virus. Rather than being threats to 'home populations', they have the same rights as other human beings, including those of travel. By focusing on human rights rather than on dangers, this discourse adopts a normative position that breaks with a state-centric way of thinking (see Chs 5, 12, and 30).

Discussion Questions

- How do you think HIV/AIDS affects the social construction of different continents and countries?
- HIV/AIDS has been constructed as a matter of development as well as one of security—how do the two discourses differ and what might be the effects in terms of the policies that are adopted to prevent HIV/AIDS?

there is 'a' population that can be studied and steered in a particular direction (see Case Study 1 for a further discussion of how the concepts of discourse and biopolitics can be used to understand global politics on HIV/AIDS). It is clear that poststructuralism's concept of power goes beyond that of realism, which defines power as material capabilities (see Ch. 5). Compared to constructivism, which also includes knowledge and identities (see Ch. 9), poststructuralism looks more critically at how actors get to be constituted as actors in the first place.

Intertextuality

The theory on **intertextuality** is developed by the semiotic theorist Julia Kristeva. It argues that we can understand the social world as comprised of texts. This is because texts form an intertext; that is, they are connected to texts that came before them. In some situations this is self-evident. Take for example declarations made by international institutions like the **North Atlantic Treaty Organization** (NATO), the **European Union**

(EU) and the United Nations, which quote previous declarations and perhaps statements by member countries. But intertextual relations are also made in more abstract ways. For example, to say that 'the Balkans' is filled with 'ancient hatred' is to draw on a body of texts that constitutes 'the Balkans' as pre-modern and barbaric. Intertextuality might also involve images, or interpreting events that are not exclusively written or spoken. For instance, when presidents meet in front of the television cameras expressing their commitment to solve the financial crisis, we look not just at what is said but what having such a meeting signifies. The presidential press conference is in other words an important 'sign' within the larger text that defines **diplomacy**. Intertextuality also implies that certain things are taken for granted because previous texts have made the point so many times that there is no need to state it again. If you read through NATO documents from the cold war, you will find that they might not necessarily mention the Soviet Union all that much. That is because everyone at the time knew that NATO's main

purpose was to deter the Soviet Union from attacking members of NATO. Working with intertextuality, we should therefore ask ourselves what a given text does not mention either because it is taken for granted or because it is too dangerous to say.

At the same time as intertextuality points to the way in which texts always 'quote' past texts, it also holds that individual texts are unique. No text is a complete reproduction of an earlier one. Even when one text incorporates another by quoting it in full, the new context modifies the older text. This is of significance to the study of world politics because it underscores that meaning changes when texts are quoted by other texts. Take the Muhammad Cartoons that were printed by the Danish newspaper *Jyllands-Posten* in September 2005. They have now been reproduced by many other newspapers and on the Internet, and many different readings have been offered. If you look at the cartoons today, you cannot therefore 'read' them in the same way as you could when they were first published.

Popular culture

The argument that we should understand world politics through the lens of intertextuality has led poststructuralists to look at forms of text that are not normally discussed by IR theories. James Der Derian has studied the intertext of popular spy novels, journalism, and academic analysis (Der Derian 1992). Others, including Michael J. Shapiro (1988, 1997) and Cynthia Weber (2006), analyse television shows, film, and photography. Poststructuralists hold that there are several reasons why we should pay attention to **popular culture**. For one thing, states actually take popular culture seriously, even if it is 'just fiction'. In 2006, the Kazakh government launched an advertising campaign in the USA because they wanted to correct the picture of Kazakhstan given in the movie *Borat*, and in 2010 a Turkish television

drama's depiction of Israeli security forces led the Israeli Foreign Ministry to protest to the Turkish ambassador. Another reason why we should take popular culture seriously—and why states do so too—is that film, television, music, and video are watched and listened to by many people across the world. As the world has become increasingly globalized, popular culture has spread quickly from one place to another and new media technologies, such as cellphones, have fundamentally changed who can produce the 'texts' of world politics. Think for example of soldiers' videos of the wars in Iraq and Afghanistan that are uploaded to the Internet, and the photos from Abu Ghraib. Finally, popular culture might foreshadow events in the real world and provide us with complex, critical, and thought-provoking visions of world politics.

Key Points

- Four concepts from poststructuralist philosophy have been used to produce new knowledge about world politics: discourse, deconstruction, genealogy, and intertextuality.
- To look at world politics as discourse is to study those linguistic structures through which materiality is given meaning.
- Deconstruction argues that language is a system of unstable dichotomies where one term is valued as superior.
- Genealogy asks which political practices have formed the present and which alternative understandings and discourses have been marginalized and forgotten.
- Intertextuality holds that we can see world politics as made up by texts. All texts refer to other texts, yet each is unique. Intertextuality calls attention to silences and taken-for-granted assumptions.
- Popular culture plays an important role in the constitution of world politics.

Deconstructing state sovereignty

Poststructuralists use the four key concepts (discourse, deconstruction, genealogy, and intertextuality) to answer the 'big questions' of IR: what is the status of the state? Is the international system doomed to recurring conflicts and power politics, as realism holds? Or is it possible to move towards more cooperative arrangements, as argued by liberalism?

The inside-outside distinction

Poststructuralists agree with realists that the state is absolutely central to world politics. Yet in contrast to realists, who take the state for granted, poststructuralists deconstruct the role the state plays in world politics as well as in the academic field of IR. Arguing that the

state is not 'a unit' that has the same essence across time and space, R. B. J. Walker (1990) holds that the state is a particular way to organize political community (see also Ch. 32). The question of political community is of utmost importance to national as well as international politics because it tells us why the forms of governance that are in place are legitimate, whom we can trust, whom we have something in common with, and whom we should help if they are under attack, suffering or hungry (see also Ch. 24). The sovereign, territorial state has an unrivalled position as *the* political community, but it only came to have this position as a result of a series of events and processes that began with the **Treaties of Westphalia** (see Ch. 2).

Walker tells us that we can learn something important about the transition from the medieval to the modern state system because this shows us two different ways of organizing political community. In the medieval world there were so-called overlapping authorities. This means that religious and political authorities—the Pope and the Emperors and those below them—were interwoven and that there was no single institution that could make sovereign decisions. As described in Chapter 2, with the Treaties of Westphalia this changed as states became the sovereign authorities within their own territories and in relations with each other. In terms of how we think about relations between people, the medieval world worked according to what Walker calls a principle of 'hierarchical subordination'. Hierarchical subordination assigns each individual to a particular position within society. At the top was the Emperor and the Pope, next came the bishops and the kings, then the priests and local nobility, and at the bottom were those who owned nothing and who had no rights. The Treaties of Westphalia began a process whereby people became more closely linked to states, and after the French Revolution each citizen had the same status. This did not mean that all individuals were citizens or that all citizens had the same amount of money, wealth, education, or property, but there was no longer anything in a person's nature, as with the principle of hierarchical subordination, that made him or her inherently superior or inferior.

State sovereignty implies, in Walker's words, a division of the world into an 'inside' the state (where there is **order**, trust, **loyalty**, and progress) and an 'outside' (where there is conflict, suspicion, self-help, and anarchy). Walker then uses the principle of deconstruction to show that the national–international distinction is not simply an objective account of how the 'real world works'. The distinction is not maintained by something outside itself, but by the way in which the two sides of the dichotomy reinforce each other: we know the international only by what it is not (national), and likewise the national only by what it is not (the international). The world 'inside' states is not only different from the international realm 'outside'; the two are constituted as each other's opposition. The inside–outside dichotomy is stabilized by a long series of other dichotomies, including those of peace and war, reason and power, and order and anarchy.

Poststructuralists have shown how the inside–outside dichotomy, which like all dichotomies is inherently unstable, is held in place by being reproduced again and again. States reproduce state sovereignty, but so do academic texts. Richard K. Ashley points for example to realism's 'double move' (Ashley 1987: 413–18). The first move is to assume that we can only understand '**community**' in one way and that is the one we know from domestic politics. When we think of 'international community', it is built on what we know from the state. The second move consists of arguing that such a community is possible only within the territorial state. The harmony, reason, and **justice** that are possible within states cannot be extended to the international sphere, as this is fraught with anarchy, repetition, and power politics. The realist scholar must therefore educate governments not to incorporate ethics and justice in their foreign policies. If you remember Box 5.2 from Chapter 5, this told us about realists opposed to the war with Iraq in 2003. Their opposition was based on an assessment of the American **national interest**, not moral concerns.

The strength of state sovereignty

We should note that when poststructuralists write about the inside–outside dichotomy, they are not making the claim that the world works neatly that way. There are plenty of states where domestic politics does not follow the description of the 'inside' as one of progress, reason, and justice, yet the national–international dichotomy still manages to govern much of world politics. More critically, we might say that the success of the inside–outside dichotomy is shown by how well it silences numerous 'facts' and 'events' that should in fact undermine it. We can for example see the national–international dichotomy at work when states choose not to intervene in other states that are prosecuting their 'own' citizens. Or think of countries where children of refused asylum seekers are deported with their parents even if they are born in the country where asylum was sought.

Case Study 2 Territoriality, identity, and sex trafficking

NGOs, the media, states, and international institutions such as the EU are giving sex trafficking increasing attention. 'Trafficking' defines a movement across state borders and 'trafficked' women are taken from one country to another, not moved within a state. They cross territorial boundaries illegally, either because they are smuggled into a country, or because they enter under false pretences (on tourist visas or to do domestic work, for instance). Trafficking implies a transgression of the territorial boundary, but trafficked women also have a political visibility that women who are doing the same kind of 'work' within a country do not get.

Trafficked women are defined as victims. The *Report of the Experts Group on Trafficking in Human Beings*, published by the European Commission in 2004, states:

> The core elements of trafficking, as defined in the [UN] Protocol, are coercion, abuse and deceit. The definition covers all forms of trafficking into sexual exploitation, slavery, forced labour and servitude. Furthermore, it makes a clear distinction between trafficking and prostitution as such …, leaving it to individual States how to address prostitution in their respective domestic laws. (*Ibid.*: 6).

This quote shows how a political boundary is drawn between what states should cooperate on (namely trafficking) and what they should not (prostitution). It also shows that the trafficked woman is one who has been 'coerced' and 'deceived', not someone who 'knows' and 'acts'. Poststructuralist feminists point out that the dichotomies between 'deception' and 'knowledge' and between 'victim' and 'agent' are problematic. Many trafficked women describe themselves in ways that do not fit these dichotomies: they have some knowledge and are not forced. But 'admitting' this puts them into the category of 'sex workers' and 'illegal immigrants' who are not worthy of the same kind of protection as 'the victims' (Aradau 2008 and Penttinen 2008).

Discussion Questions

- What does sex trafficking say about sovereignty, boundaries, and the construction of identity?

- Trafficking discourse involves not only gender identities, but those of race and development. How are those employed, and what does this tell us about globalization?

- How do you see the role of trafficked women in local and global responses to trafficking?

One of the strengths of poststructuralism is that it points to how state sovereignty is often both questioned and supported. Chapter 5 described how the attacks of 9/11 and the **war on terror** undermined state sovereignty at the same time as Western states saw them through the lens of state-based territoriality: 'American soil' was attacked and the Taliban regime in Afghanistan was held responsible for what happened on 'its' **territory**. Or, consider Somali pirates who 'work' in a way that escapes the control of the Somali state. In response, Western states have tried to bring order back by sending NATO warships to patrol the waters off the Somali coast. As the pirates transgress state sovereignty, we also see states respond by protecting 'their' ships from being attacked. Before we declare the inside–outside distinction dead and gone, we should therefore take its flexibility and resilience into account (see also Case Study 2).

Universal alternatives

Poststructuralists warn that although our deconstruction of state sovereignty makes it look less like an objective fact, it is not easy to transcend; nor can it be replaced by a '**global community**'. As R. B. J. Walker puts it, 'The state is a political category in a way that the world, or the globe, or the planet, or humanity is not' (Walker 1997: 72). The way to engage a dichotomy is not simply to reverse the hierarchy between the terms (that is replace 'the state' with 'the global'), but to rethink all the complex dichotomies around which it revolves. If we leave the state in favour of the global, a crucial question becomes how we prevent a return to the model we know from the medieval world, that is, one of a global community where individuals are ranked and given different value. Poststructuralists hold that claims to 'global', 'universal' solutions always imply that something else is

different and 'particular'. And that which is different is almost always in danger of being forced to change to become like the universal. Poststructuralists are therefore sceptical of idealists or liberals who advocate universal principles, but who overlook the power involved in defining what is 'the universally' good and right (see also Chs 30 and 32).

The dangers—and power—of universal discourse are brought out by the discourse of Western governments with troops in Iraq and Afghanistan in the mid- and late 2000s (see also Ch. 6). Within this discourse, 'fighting **terrorism**' took place to defend 'freedom', 'liberty', 'security', and 'democracy'. Although this might at first sound unproblematic—even appealing—the problem is that this set of universally good categories is spoken and defined not by a truly global voice, but by a particular set of states. The good 'universal' categories were aimed at those who were not—yet or ever—part of that universal project, and the universal discourse reinforced 'the West' as the one that could define 'real' universalism. To many, and not only poststructuralists (see Ch. 11 on postcolonialism), this echoes the time when the colonial West had the power, right, and 'obligation' to define what was good for the rest of the world.

Poststructuralism's critique of universalism shows that although poststructuralists are critical of realism, they agree with realists that we should take power and the state seriously. Many poststructuralists see much of value in classical realism because it is historically sensitive and concerned with the big political and normative questions of world politics. **Neo-realism,** on the other hand, is criticized for its ahistorical view of the state, its reification of the international structure, and its positivist epistemology.

Key Points

- State sovereignty is a practice that constitutes identity and authority in a particular manner.
- Poststructuralists deconstruct the distinction between the national and the international by showing that the two terms stabilize each other and depend upon a long series of other dichotomies.
- The global is not a political category like the state, and therefore cannot replace it.
- Poststructuralists warn against the danger of universal discourse because it is always defined from a particular position of power.

Identity and foreign policy

Poststructuralists have also moved from the general study of state sovereignty to ask how we should understand foreign policy. In traditional foreign policy analysis, foreign policies are designed to defend the state (security policies), help it financially (economic policies), or make it do good in the world (development policies). Poststructuralists hold by contrast that there is no stable object—the state—from which foreign policies are drawn, but that foreign policies rely upon and produce particular understandings of the state. Foreign policies constitute the identity of the Self through the construction of threats, dangers, and challenges, that is, its Other(s). As Michael J. Shapiro puts it, this means that the politics of representation is absolutely crucial. How we represent others affects the representation of our selves, and this representation is decisive for which foreign policies we choose (Shapiro 1988). For example, debates within the EU over whether Turkey should be accepted as a new member centre on whether Turkey is a European country and whether it is possible to be European and Muslim at the same time. The way in which

EU countries answer these questions has implications not only for the construction of Turkey's identity, but for that of **Europe**'s. Foreign policies are thus not protecting an identity that is already given and in place, but discourses through which identities are (re)produced.

Identity as performative

In theoretical terms, this implies that poststructuralism conceptualizes identity as relational and performative. The concept of performativity comes from Judith Butler, and holds that identities have no objective existence, but that they depend on discursive practices (Campbell 1992). Identities are socially 'real', but they cannot maintain their 'realness' if we do not reproduce them. Because identities have no existence independently of the foreign policies that produce them, we cannot say that identities cause foreign policy. To take the example of the EU and Turkey, there is no objective European identity that causes a decision on Turkish membership. Rather, it is through debates over Turkey's membership

application that European identity is being defined. Does this mean, then, that foreign policies cause identities? No, because foreign policies are also at the same time made with reference to understandings of identity that are to some extent already in place. In the case of the EU, the discourse on Turkey does not start from scratch, but with historically powerful constructions of Europe as white, Christian, civilized, and modern. Identities are in short simultaneously a product of and the justification for foreign policies. If we go back to the discussion of epistemology at the beginning of this chapter, we see that we cannot theorize the relationship between identity and foreign policy in causal terms, but that this is a constitutive relationship. This also means that poststructuralism theorizes identity differently from liberalism. As you may recall from Chapter 6, liberalists incorporate identity, but hold that it might determine states' outward orientation. In other words, identity has a causal impact on foreign policy.

Probably the most important development of a performative theory of identity and foreign policy is David Campbell's *Writing Security: United States Foreign Policy and the Politics of Identity*, first published in 1992. Campbell takes a broad view of what foreign policy is and distinguishes between 'Foreign Policy' (the policies undertaken by states in the international arena), and 'foreign policy' (all those discursive practices that constitute something as 'foreign' in relation to the Self). 'Foreign policy' might just as well take place within states as between them. It might for instance involve **gender** and **sexual relations,** as when women are deemed unfit to participate in the military because they lack the proper 'mindset' (and thus would be dangerous for male soldiers to fight alongside), or when homosexuals are described as alien to the national sense of self. By looking not only at Foreign Policy, but also at 'foreign policy', poststructuralism casts light on the symbolic boundaries that are constituted within and across states.

Much of the concern in poststructuralism has been with what Campbell calls the discourses of danger. Because such discourses work with very clear dichotomies, it is easy to see how the Other defines the Self. Yet poststructuralism also investigates those identities that are not so radically different from the Self. When we go beyond the simple Self–radical Other construction, we find more complex identity constellations that can involve several Others. Such Others might threaten each other rather than the Self and be constituted by different kinds of otherness. One case that highlights such more complex constellations is the war in Bosnia in the 1990s where one Other (Bosnian Muslims) was threatened by another Other (Bosnian Serbs). This challenged the international community to undertake a **humanitarian intervention** (Ch. 30) and poststructuralists have shown that this was legitimized within a discourse that split the Other into 'innocent civilians' and 'Balkan governments' (Campbell 1998). As Western responsibility was extended only to the 'innocent civilians', a full—and more political—understanding of Western involvement was avoided.

Subject positions

When poststructuralists write about **identities** as constituted in discourse, they usually use the term subjectivities or subject positions to underscore that identity is not something that someone has, but that it is a position that one is constructed as having. Individuals and institutions navigate between different subject positions and might identify with the positions they are given by others to a greater or lesser extent. Think for example about the way the subject position of 'the Muslim' has come to be used in Western Europe. Some 'Muslims' embrace this subject position and seek to give it a positive status by showing, for example, that Muslim organizations are as democratic as, say, 'normal' French, Danish, or Austrian ones. Other 'Muslims' protest that they do not see themselves as Muslim at all, but rather as women, Swedes, or athletes. As you can see, it is crucial which subject positions are defined as important, because they set the context for the 'identity landscape' that we have to operate within (see Box 10.5). We need to ask not only what constructions of 'the Muslim' are available, but why 'the Muslim' has become such an important identity to construct.

Obviously, some subject positions are more desirable than others because they provide a superior position compared to other identities. Take 'the Muslim' in Western discourses. Here the starting point is that the Muslim is inferior to the European, Western, or Danish subject. Thus when institutions and individuals try to present a more positive view of Muslims, this happens in critical response to a reigning discourse of 'the Muslims' as not quite as good as the 'real' European. A superior subject position also usually provides the subject with more room for agency. If you recall poststructuralism's view of power as productive, you see that power is very much involved in the construction of subject positions.

Poststructuralism's critical take on subjectivity makes it ask '*who* can speak within this discourse?' and '*how*

Box 10.5 Subject positions and images

Subject positions are also constituted through images. These are two different representations of 'the Muslim'. What are the differences and similarities?

Muslim business woman

Pakistan: the Prophet's birthday

states. Because Palestine is not recognized as a state, it is allowed access only as an observer. To the extent that a state-centric discourse rules world politics, **non-state actors** and **stateless** individuals have severe difficulties gaining a voice. Another example of the 'who can speak and how' is that of development discourse where those who receive aid are constituted as less knowledgeable than the Western donors. As a consequence, the development subject is not qualified to say what kind of aid it wants, but should listen and learn.

As we explained in the presentation of the concept of discourse above, discourses are also material. The constitution of subjectivity happens therefore not only as a linguistic process, but as we engage our physical surroundings. Poststructuralists such as Charlotte Epstein (2007) and Mark Salter (2006) have studied how biometric passports, visa restrictions, and the way entry is regulated at airports 'govern' who gains access, and how one should look and act. Material technologies—the incorporation of chips into passports, on-line applications for entry into a country, large data systems containing huge amounts of information—work together with discourses and policies to have effects on everyday life.

Key Points

- In keeping with the non-foundationalist ontology that poststructuralism adopts, there are no natural or objective identities, 'only' those that are produced in discourse.
- The term 'subjectivities' or 'subject positions' underscores that identity is not something that someone has, but a position that one is constructed as having.
- The relationship between identity and foreign policy is performative and mutually constitutive.
- Poststructuralism asks 'who and how can the subject speak?' What are the silences and marginalization produced by the reigning constitution of subjectivity?

can the subject speak?' These questions also imply attention to those who cannot speak or who can speak only with limited authority and agency. One example of how discourses exclude and marginalize is that of statism within the UN system. Consider the United Nations General Assembly, which has 192 members, all of them

Conclusion

This chapter has introduced you to the main thoughts and concepts of poststructuralism. Poststructuralism might be particularly good at drawing your attention to the fact that actors, entities, and 'things' we assume are given actually depend on how we construct them. Academic perspectives play an important role in the reproduction of particular visions of world politics: if

we are told over and over again that the state is concerned only with its national interest, power politics and **survival**, then we act according to that picture of the state. Poststructuralists also warn that there are no easy solutions to state sovereignty and that liberal calls for universal human rights, freedom, liberty, and democracy inevitably involve constructions of power and exclusions. While sympathetic to much in critical theory's account of the structures that produce global inequalities, poststructuralists are also sceptical that emancipation can tackle power and avoid the pitfalls of universalist discourse (see Ch. 8).

Poststructuralism might not offer grand solutions, but it has a critical impact on world politics. For one thing, deconstructions of policy discourses and the dominant **neo-neo** position force us to reconsider what basic ontological assumptions guide our way of thinking. Moreover, poststructuralists have always been keen to point to the ways in which responsibility is constructed. More recently, poststructuralists including David Campbell, James Der Derian, and Cynthia Weber have turned to documentary film-making and photography exhibitions as ways to engage a larger audience in different ways than through the academic text.

As all other theories of International Relations, poststructuralism has of course also been the subject of criticism. Critics have held that poststructuralists use such dense philosophical vocabulary that it borders on the incomprehensible or that once one cuts through the fancy language there is not all that much substance. Others argue that poststructuralism fails to adequately account for material processes and hence for much of what actually happens 'outside of discourse'. Another line of critique centres on epistemological and methodological differences. Those, like most of the US mainstream, who hold that theories should make causal claims simply do not accept poststructuralists' embrace of constitutive epistemologies. As in the case of the other theoretical perspectives in this book, we advise you to think critically about poststructuralism too.

Questions

1 Do you think all theories should make causal claims?
2 How do you see material facts and technology influencing discourses, for example in discussions of climate change?
3 How would a genealogy of the financial crisis differ from a liberal or realist study thereof?
4 Do you agree that it is a good idea to incorporate popular culture in the study of world politics?
5 Do you think that images are important to world politics? Is poststructuralism a better framework for studying images than other International Relations theories and why (not)?
6 What are the signs that state sovereignty might still be in place and what points to its erosion?
7 What alternative forms of political community do you think could replace the state?
8 Discuss how realism, liberalism, Marxism, constructivism, and poststructuralism would analyse 9/11. What are the differences and similarities?
9 Could 'terrorism' be replaced by another identity in Western discourse, and what would the political consequences be?
10 Which subject positions are central in the discourses on hunger? Who can speak and how? What are the consequences for international policy making?

Further Reading

Campbell, D. (1992, 2nd edn 1998), *Writing Security: United States Foreign Policy and the Politics of Identity* (Manchester: Manchester University Press). Theorizes the importance of otherness for states foreign policy and provides a thorough analysis of the USA.

Der Derian, J. (1992), *Antidiplomacy: Spies, Terror, Speed, and War* (Cambridge, MA and Oxford: Blackwell). Uses multiple forms of text to explore how diplomatic interactions take place in many settings, including computer simulations and real-time media coverage.

Der Derian, J. and Shapiro, M. J. (1989), *International/Intertextual Relations: Postmodern Readings of World Politics* (Lexington, MA: Lexington Books). Early application of the theory of intertextuality to world politics with contributions by R. K. Ashley, W. E. Connolly, B. S. Klein, R. B. J. Walker, and others.

Hansen, L. (2006), *Security as Practice: Discourse Analysis and the Bosnian War* (London: Routledge). Presents a theory of non-radical otherness and a poststructuralist methodology.

Hansen, L. and Wæver, O. (eds) (2002), *European Integration and National Identity: The Challenge of the Nordic States* (London: Routledge). Offers a poststructuralist framework for analysing discourses on European integration and applies it to the Nordic states.

Klein, B. S. (1994), *Strategic Studies and World Order: The Global Politics of Deterrence* (Cambridge: Cambridge University Press). Brings Michel Foucault to the discipline of Strategic Studies, nuclear deterrence and NATO.

Lisle, D. (2006), *The Global Politics of Contemporary Travel Writing* (Cambridge: Cambridge University Press). Demonstrates how poststructuralism can be used in an analysis of travel writing.

Shapiro, M. J. (1988,) *The Politics of Representation: Writing Practices in Biography, Photography, and Policy Analysis* (Madison, WI: The University of Wisconsin Press). Shows that foreign policy relies upon representations of identity and takes place across multiple genres.

Walker, R. B. J. (1993), *Inside/Outside: International Relations as Political Theory* (Cambridge: Cambridge University Press). Explains how state sovereignty relies upon particular understandings of identity, community, authority, order, and power.

Weber, C. (2006), *Imagining America at War: Morality, Politics, and Film* (London: Routledge). A study of the way in which films engage national identity and foreign policy after 9/11.

Online Resource Centre

Visit the Online Resource Centre that accompanies this book to access more learning resources on this chapter topic at www.oxfordtextbooks.co.uk/orc/baylis5e/

Chapter 11

Post-colonialism

CHRISTINE SYLVESTER

Reader's Guide

This chapter considers a new stream of analysis that brings colonial, postcolonial, and the current era of post-colonial history into International Relations (IR). It does so through the presentation and analysis of everyday people and their experiences in countries that were once colonies, and through theories that respond to European and North American versions of history that focus on Great Power states and their interactions. Drawing on the humanities fields of social history, literary studies, philosophy, and psychoanalysis for inspiration, post-colonial analysis endeavours to fill the many gaps in Eurocentric constructions of the world so that people and ideas associated with former colonies can be visible, audible, and influential today. Its recent theories of hybrid identity and postcolonial epochal trends in the international system also address hierarchies of inter-state and transnational relations that still prevail in globalized IR and that provide opportunities for people to combine into new political and identity groupings.

Introduction: post-colonial thinking comes to International Relations

Post-colonialism is a relatively new approach to the study of International Relations (IR). It entered the field only in the 1990s, slightly later than feminist and poststructuralist approaches (see Chs 10 and 16). As in the case of those theories, the timing of the post-colonial entrée to IR relates to the failure of the field to predict some of the major events of the twentieth century, such as the struggles to decolonize and, later, the fall of the Berlin Wall, the demise of the Soviet Union, and the end of the **cold war**. Until the 1990s, IR relied on just a few key theories, mainly realism (Ch. 5), liberalism (Chs 6 and 7) and Marxism (Ch. 8). These were not attuned to what has been termed people power, the efforts of ordinary people to end colonial rule or cold war divisions that kept East and West Berliners apart. With IR weakened by the inadequacies of its reigning theories, approaches that had been denied legitimacy were able to gain influence in the field. The new entrants stretched the field by refusing the idea that **nation-states** are always the key actors in IR—Great Powers in particular—and emphasizing the many locations and relations that could be considered as IR. Post-colonial analysis is one of these new entrants.

The main contributions of post-colonial analysis have been threefold: to bring historical relations of colonial powers with colonies into the study of IR; to provide views and theories of those relations from the perspectives of colonized peoples rather than from the perspectives of Great Powers alone; and to encourage the use of novels, poetry, diaries, and testimonials as sources of valuable information on the nature of colonialism and post-colonialism. There is also a fourth contribution of post-colonialism: when we remove the hyphen, the changed form indicates that the global era of our time is postcolonial. The use of the term 'postcolonial' signifies

lingering colonial hierarchies of race, class, and gender despite the winding down of the formal colonial period, and the tendency of IR (and many people in the West) to pay more attention to the foreign policies of the USA and European countries than to those of most former colonies, such as Zambia, Botswana, Jamaica, Bangladesh, the Philippines, or Bolivia. The chapter traces the development of post-colonial thought and ends by using the more current term, postcolonial studies, to refer to the discipline in the present era. 'Post-colonial' is used throughout this chapter to refer to the analysis of colonialism and anti-colonialism. 'Postcolonial' is used to indicate a turn since the 1990s towards analysing the current era of IR as the postcolonial era. Although the two terms are often used interchangeably, it is more common today to see the unhyphenated term. It is used to think about and theorize the many ways that colonial conditions of the past, such as race, class, and gender biases, linger on into the present and interact with today's international relations of globalization, war, empire, migration, and identity politics.

Key Points

- Post-colonialism is a new approach in IR that provides a bottom-up rather than state-down approach to the study of international relations.

- Among other more traditional sources, it uses fiction and personal testimonials as sources of information about colonial and post-colonial people and situations relevant to international relations.

- It is broad enough to include specific colonial and post-colonial relations as well as the notion that our era in international relations is 'postcolonial'.

Former colonies face International Relations

International Relations has not traditionally been interested in investigating relations of dominance and subordination in the world. The field developed around the study of sovereign states and their interactions. Colonies, by definition, were not independent and sovereign, and many had to struggle violently or non-violently to cut the reins of their colonial power and gain sovereign independence. They then faced the challenge of fulfilling

the responsibilities of duly constituted states to protect national populations, oversee economic development, and provide social services such as education. The later the colonization and independence occurred, the greater the struggles and challenges of post-colonial governance. Colonial overlords of earlier eras became less powerful as time went on but they were also unwilling to give up the colonies that gave them some prestige and considerable economic advantage. The poorest countries of the world today were recent colonies, and many wars and conditions of civil unrest and underdevelopment overshadow them. Yet IR, with its longstanding preoccupation with relations of Great Powers, did not have the interest or the tools to broaden its scope to groups, cultures, movements, knowledges, locations, and relations that would encompass the peoples of former colonies. Implicitly, the worldview of IR was European and North American. To include relations of gender, race, culture, inequality, exploitation, and colonialization as international relations, the field had to develop an interest in historical relations of states and groups, instead of burying those in quick background sketches in their research.

It can seem in hindsight as if the neglect of colonial history and social relations as international relations required remarkable stubbornness or blindness. From the end of the Second World War onwards, considerable activity in international relations revolved around **decolonization** (moving to end colonial rule). More than 60 colonies achieved independence as states and members of the United Nations by the mid-1960s, 50 in Africa alone. The timing of that wave of independence coincided with the cold war, when the two superpowers competed for ideological, economic, and technological dominance. Some new states became battlegrounds in the cold war (Vietnam, Korea) and others posed the prospect of new allies for the superpowers if modernized quickly—and armed militarily—so that they could withstand the blandishments of the opposing bloc (see Ch. 3).

That order of priorities was symptomatic of the hierarchies of power and knowledge in the world, and entirely unacceptable to radical leaders in Cuba, China, and Indonesia, who believed that former colonies should carve out their own destinies. In 1955, 29 mostly Asian and African countries created the beginnings of a post-colonial, non-aligned, Third World bloc of international relations at the **Bandung Conference** in Indonesia. Although more favourable to socialism than capitalism, the bloc sought to draw resources from each superpower, rather than choose a side in the cold war. All foreign aid would then be put in the service of plans and policies set by the new states themselves, not by the superpowers and their agendas. That trend intensified at the 1966 **Tricontinental Conference**, held in Havana, Cuba, with 500 delegates from independent and decolonizing states of Latin America, the Caribbean, Asia, and Africa. One of the main speakers was Che Guevara, the militant theorist and practitioner of national liberation

through armed struggle. He used the occasion to expound his theory of guerrilla warfare as the best method for the remaining colonies to employ in their struggles for independence from recalcitrant Europeans. He also advocated popular armed struggles wherever corrupt Latin American regimes were propped up by a **neo-colonial** USA, whose only concern in the region was to keep anti-communist and pro-business leaders in power at all costs. The model for the Third World was China and Cuba; the latter was where guerrilla warfare had driven the corrupt regime of Battista out of Cuba in the 1950s and had facilitated Fidel Castro's rise to power 90 miles off the coast of Florida.

Influenced strongly by cold war foreign policies of the West, International Relations was largely complicit in the American effort to isolate tricontinental thinkers as dangerous pro-communist, anti-American agitators. Even the far more moderate Bandung Conference had drawn the attention of students of IR only by introducing the non-aligned movement and popularizing the concept of a Third World positioned strategically between, yet drawing resources from, the First World West and the Second World Soviet bloc. By contrast, post-colonial studies remembers that the Tricontinental Conference gave birth to the short-lived journal *Tricontinental*, which was one of the first outlets for works by thinkers who were influential in Third World politics and would become the backbone of early post-colonial thinking—people like Franz Fanon and Ho Chi Minh. The journal contributors were from different continents, cultures, and experiences, and yet they commonly wrote about the dominance of Euro-American politics, history, and power in ways that distorted or erased other knowledges from the history books. The determination of some of these thinkers to turn the violent methods perpetrated on their societies against intransigent colonists themselves reflected fury at the automatic subordination that their countries, peoples, and ideas experienced in colonial and then also in post-colonial cold war international relations.

Franz Fanon is one of the early analysts who advocated the violent overthrow of colonialism and dominance-subordination relations in new states. A psychologist trained in Martinique and France, Fanon experienced a level of racism during and following medical training that impelled him to resign from a prominent position in the Caribbean to join the Algerian anti-colonial struggle against France. Fanon's *Black Skin, White Masks* (1952) and *The Wretched of the Earth* (1963) initiated an ongoing discussion in fledgling post-colonial studies about mechanisms of colonial control. Unlike the emphasis in IR on objective power relations (which would point out that France is more powerful than its colony of Algeria in military, economic, and cultural terms), the stress in Fanon's work is on the power of colonial discourses to colonize the minds of all involved. This meant that European colonizers would see their exercise of dominating power as justified, and colonized societies would come to accept and internalize the diminished and subordinate statuses imposed on them. The vehicle of such status differentiation is not the force of the gun but the force of language—words, racial epithets, and daily insults thrown at people. Thus Fanon drew on works of anti-colonial poets and writers as he discussed the importance of building a national consciousness that does not mimic European ways.

The Wretched of the Earth details the steps by which violence becomes the only tool that can drive out those insulting messages and free the colonized to achieve

self-defined identity and national consciousness. Yet that freedom often remains elusive even after independence, as local elites—native intellectuals—play the class and power cards they acquired from Europe and work only for their own interests. The struggle for national consciousness, therefore, is complex culturally and politically, and extends long past the immediate post-colonial moment of a country. Yet whose national consciousness Fanon is talking about is an open question, for it is the men in his accounts who are posed as the 'natural' ringleaders of resistance. Fanon praises women in their role in nationalist struggles, but he gives them a back seat to the men, who plan the actions and later assume positions of national power.

As these early writings came out, the field of IR, as Arlene Tickner (2003: 296) puts it, carried on its 'lack of correspondence between standard IR terminology, categories, and theories, and third world realities'. Focused on established state relations and the organizations these created, IR approached the phenomenon of new states in the 1960s and 1970s not through the work of Third World intellectuals but often through an analysis of radical North–South politics that were emerging in international relations. That politics came in several forms. A voting bloc known as the **Group of 77** formed in the United Nations to encourage Third World solidarity in raising or responding to issues. The **Organization of Petroleum Exporting Countries** (OPEC) began to take control of natural resources like oil that were valued by the West. Demands were also made in the United Nations for a **New International Economic Order** (NIEO) that would be more favourable to the circumstances of post-colonial societies, offering preferential terms of trade, aid, and resource allocation in a system where all states would be equal partners in global economic governance. Wars and conflicts that engaged the cold war protagonists put the spotlight on countries of Southeast Asia and Central America, and on foreign aid issues. We might say that IR researchers began paying more attention to post-colonial states in the 1970s, but did so by narrowly framing research around threats posed to an established world order managed by developed states.

Whether agendas for Third World countries were being forged by superpowers and academics of IR living in the West, or by leaders and intellectuals from post-colonial societies, the direction of knowledge was from the top down. Society might be spoken about in their various missives, but everyday lives were not explored in ways that could yield fuller pictures of colonial experiences and post-colonial proclivities. Bottom-up initiatives

Box 11.1 Franz Fanon, a call to repudiate European ways

'The new day which is already at hand must find us firm, prudent, and resolute. We must leave our dreams and abandon our old beliefs and friendships from the time before life began. Let us waste no time in sterile litanies and nauseating mimicry. Leave this Europe where they are never done talking of Man, yet murder men everywhere they find them, at the corner of every one of their own streets, in all the corners of the globe. For centuries they have stifled almost the whole of humanity in the name of a so-called spiritual experience. Look at them today swaying between atomic and spiritual disintegration. And yet it may be said that Europe has been successful in as much as everything that she has attempted has succeeded. Europe undertook the leadership of the world with ardor, cynicism, and violence. Look at how the shadow of her palaces stretches out ever further! Every one of her movements has burst the bounds of space and thought. Europe has declined all humility and all modesty; but she has also set her face against all solicitude and all tenderness. She has only shown herself parsimonious and niggardly where men are concerned; it is only men that she has killed and devoured. So, my brothers, how is it that we do not understand that we have better things to do than to follow that same Europe? That same Europe where they were never done talking of Man, and where they never stopped proclaiming that they were only anxious for the welfare of Man: today we know with what sufferings humanity has paid for every one of their triumphs of the mind. Come, then, comrades, the European game has finally ended; we must find something different. We today can do everything, so long as we do not imitate Europe, so long as we are not obsessed by the desire to catch up with Europe.'

(Fanon 1963: 311–12)

were not the order of the day; vanguard politics was. Also, the notables associated with early post-colonial thinking and with responses to it in Europe and North America were predominantly men, who assumed that post-colonial states needed what men at the top needed or could arrange. It was only when post-colonial studies developed as a named academic field in the 1980s that the early writings and activities of anti-colonial thinkers could be put into a larger context of local resistance, disruption, and opportunities created by empire-building; reciprocal flows of knowledge and culture to and from colonies; and the lives and politics of everyday people in post-colonial settings, particularly women's lives. Until then, both IR and anti-colonial thinking focused on states rather than on people, and both were influenced by ideological currents in the cold war period.

> **Key Points**
>
> - IR showed some interest in colonial and post-colonial relations, but only from the perspective of Great Power interests.
> - The cold war period saw Great Powers competing over influence in newly independent countries.
> - Unwilling to choose between Western and Soviet bloc patronage, some post-colonial state regimes met at conferences and formed the non-aligned movement to create a Third World bloc.
> - The Third World was able to show some power over the Great Powers through OPEC and by demanding an NIEO.
> - But the agendas of and for the Third World did not take into account the lives of average people in post-colonial settings.

Revising history, filling gaps

Post-colonialism as an academic field was also heavily influenced by research trends in India, where a group of historians were developing social histories that they referred to as **subaltern studies**. Not content to study India through the eyes of its former colonial power or local leaders, these scholars started studying the history and culture of people at the lowest levels of Indian society, the subalterns. That term was coined in the early twentieth century by the Italian Marxist Antonio Gramsci to denote groups so subordinated and even despised in their national societies that they had been cast out from nationalist activities and all national histories, local and international (see Ch. 8). The subaltern studies group endeavoured to turn around the position of the subaltern in knowledge, from being the lowest in a chain of influence starting with colonial powers and ending with the post-colonial state and its leaders to being the most relevant for building the kind of knowledge that could respond to tales of colonial power, glory, and individual or national (European) heroism. The subaltern studies group, which included Ranajit Guha, Dipesh Chakrabarty, and Gayatri Spivak, also had an activist interest in reversing the marginal and oppressive conditions of lower-class existence. Like feminist analysts who dared to begin their study of international relations with the lives of women rather than elite men or states (see Enloe 1990), subaltern analysis focused on people who up to that point were seen—if seen at all—as victims of history or quaint examples of local culture. The key question for

these scholars was: what does history and contemporary life look like when it starts from subaltern points of view, from the bottom up instead of from the top down? It was a question that would soon be taken up and refined in post-colonial contexts far from South Asia.

To try to answer it was to enter uncultivated terrain. There were scant or no historical 'data' on subaltern people. The subaltern studies group had to think of ways of working with neglected groups and learning about their lives. One avenue was to analyse colonial and post-colonial fictional literatures, travelogues, and diaries. These portrayed the fabric of ordinary life under colonization as well as the changes brought about by nationalist rejections of colonialism and post-colonial state efforts to build national identity. Post-colonial literary analysis became a central methodology of post-colonial studies. Graeme Turner (1993:1), an Australian scholar, argued that local stories are 'ultimately produced by the culture; thus, they generate meanings, take on significances, and assume forms that are articulations of the values, beliefs—the ideology—of the culture'. Chenjerai Hove, a Zimbabwean poet and novelist whose fiction, *Bones*, won a Commonwealth prize, puts this another way: 'I don't want to keep fiction and reality apart. Human beings are very complex animals. Our decisions, feelings and experiences are determined by our wishes, legends and the past. I believe … that people themselves are bits of imagination. We are invented. We are invented by other people' (Hove 1994: 15). We invent ourselves too, in ways that can mimic what we read, view, and hear or that resist portrayal by others. The Kenyan novelist Ngugi wa Thiong'o (1986: 16) writes: 'how people perceive themselves affects how they look at their culture, at their politics and at the social production of wealth, at their entire relationship to nature and to other human beings.'

One of the most influential post-colonialist writers, Edward Said, used imaginative literatures extensively in his writings. In fact, it has been argued that the field might have remained focused on anti-colonial militancy and Marxist approaches to subaltern studies in India and elsewhere had Said not introduced a key cultural component into the discussions. Said (1935–2003) was a Christian Palestinian by birth, but his family moved to Cairo from Jerusalem when the first Arab–Israeli war began, and then moved about between Jerusalem, Cairo, and other Middle East locations. Said settled in the USA for university and PhD training, and rose to the position of Professor of English and Comparative Literature at Columbia, which he held at his death. He is best known for his work on **Orientalism** and a book by that name published in 1978 that became so prominent that some credit it and not subaltern studies with the beginning of post-colonial studies. *Orientalism* considers the ways that the Middle East and Asia are represented in Western novels, biographies, and artworks. Commonly, these depict places lost in times past, inclined towards despotic rule, and prone to 'odd' cultural rituals that can be both pleasurable and symptomatic of weakness. The Orient was invented as a place that Western men could praise as gentle, sensuous, and alluringly feminine, where men and women would luxuriate and indulge themselves in modes considered degenerate by European *mores*. For instance, it was commonly noted that Oriental women covered their faces but wore flimsy apparel and mesmerized men with sexualized dances that held the promise of uncomplicated heterosexual pleasure. The men appeared sapped by the culture of pleasure and easy to conquer; or they appeared irrationally cruel. That Orient was a powerfully pictured but vague location that the Westerner believes he can control and enjoy, penetrate and possess, and hide in to escape Victorian morality.

That picture continues to exert an exaggerated influence on Western thought and international relations. The Orient of travel writings and imaginative literatures that fascinated Said is so different from the West that it cannot be incorporated into frameworks of Great Power international relations, even though many of the areas deemed oriental have had extensive imperial and state-building histories of their own. To Said, the perceived oddities of Oriental culture gain far more significance than would usually be the case in international relations. The curiosities of the 'Orient' were worth crossing deserts to see, but the combination of attraction and distrust kept the orientalized Middle East and Asia impossibly distant from European and Christian moralities and logics. The journey to the Orient, therefore, would not be based on respect for the achievements and contributions to knowledge and international relations of an area; indeed, Said notes that Orientalists showed little interest in imaginative literatures by Oriental writers. The implicit goal, which repeats across time in politics, media, and the popular imagination, was to reaffirm cultural difference and render things 'Oriental' marginal to the West and subordinate to Western international relations. These invented representations that go back two centuries shape Western views of Arab, Muslim, and Confucian countries today, as shown by common media representations of Middle Eastern Muslims as backward and yet cunningly dangerous to the Western world (Porter 2009).

Said's work is canonical in post-colonial studies, but it has also come in for criticism. One concern is that it represents colonized people through stories written by Western men. Said's construction of colonial and Orientalist discourse is so beholden to Western masculine fantasy that it cannot accommodate the views of Western women, who were also physically present in Middle Eastern and Asian countries, and whose writings can call into question the dominant masculine representations. Said also neglects women in Middle Eastern countries who defy Western images of passivity and sexual availability. And, although he embraced humanism, *Orientalism* draws stark dividing lines between colonized and colonizer, as though the flow of knowledge and power were all in one direction only.

Research that draws on fiction is still not prominent in the field of IR. Fiction lies outside usual social-science standards of correct 'data' that is, information gathered from factual sources that is evaluated using approved methods, such as statistical analysis of secondary data on, say, indices of development in Third World countries. In addition, because IR has specialized in abstract theories and studies that focus on concepts such as the state, state system, power, markets, international organizations, and foreign policy, it has not imagined ways in which daily aspects of life can shape and be shaped by international relations; what attracts the field is the extraordinary event, like war. Fiction, by contrast, can weave stories about producers for international markets, consumers of international products, travellers, migrants, or refugees,

Box 11.2 New postcolonial literature

Recent postcolonial theorizing presents more nuanced and updated aspects of societies operating in a globalized time. Power is multifaceted and it flows in a number of directions for and against societies of the Third World. Some of it continues to draw on postcolonial imaginative literatures. Indeed, there is now a large stable of writers whose works take the broad sweeps of colonial to post-colonial moments as occasions needing exploration, texture, and daily lives to understand. Among the most firmly established and lauded fiction writers who have mostly resided in former colonies, are Arundhati Roy, Chinua Achebe, Yvonne Vera, Jean Rhys, Aime Cesaire, Ngugi wa Thiong'o and Tsitsi Dangarembga. Other post-colonial writers live in the West and are known to write about hyphenated lives that exist between the cultures of their birth or their parents' birth in post-colonial places and circumstances of their present lives in the West. The many distinguished novelists and poets in this second group include Jamaica Kincaid, VS Naipaul, Salman Rushdie, and Hanif Kureishi. Although literary scholars study their works, as one might expect, some social science-based academics do too. The anthropologist Veena Das (2007: 39) is one of those and for her, 'some realities need to be fictionalized before they can be apprehended'. In her study of the violence accompanying women's displacement during the partition period in South Asia, Das presents scenes that use the words of fiction to help her define the research she needs to do.

employees of embassies or businesses catering to tourists. It can help researchers to understand cultural difference and how it affects international relations. Culture is another topic that IR has had difficulty apprehending. During the cold war years, culture was synonymous with ideology, politics, and economics, rather than with literatures, religious beliefs, language, and history. Afterwards, Francis Fukuyama (1989) treated countries that brought aspects of their cultures to bear on international relations as operating in the past. Samuel Huntington (1996) could identify seven or eight active culture clusters or civilizations in the world, and noted that many of these were hostile to the West. In the post-cold-war era, he said, clashes between civilizations rather than states would cause the greatest problems in international relations. His 'civilizations' and Fukuyama's anachronistic 'cultures' loomed as totalities that had no internal differences of class, race, or gender, or intercultural influences that came from international migrations. Even very recently, when Robert Kagan (2003) discusses fissures in European and American international relations, his concern is with diverging 'strategic cultures', the sense that (all) Europeans and (all) Americans hold opposing views of the challenges facing the world.

People living in former colonies were as invisible to IR as other people in the world, except that their invisibility was born of colonial disregard and Orientalist notions. People from former colonies appeared in IR in cameo roles as exotic guerrillas, terrorists, and mass victims or mass celebrators of outcomes they did not determine through 'normal' democratic politics. They were people who needed to be killed or rescued, fates that suggested they were some 'kind of degeneration of God's original perfection' (Inayatullah and Blaney 2004: viii). Post-colonial scholarship within IR has helped to challenge those 'rules', in part by applying literary, critical, interpretive, and culturally oriented concerns to the study of IR. Some researchers have considered how imaginative literatures, knowledges, and researched voices from post-colonial areas of the world could change IR theorizing (Sylvester 1994). Others have been addressing core research topics of IR, such as security, war, and aspects of international political economy, through fieldwork with groups that have rarely if ever been considered salient to the discipline. Bina D'Costa (2006) has interviewed women survivors of rape during the Bangladesh Independence War. Swati Parashar (2009) considers alternative ways of thinking about war and gender drawn from interviews with women militants in Kashmir and Sri Lanka. Megan MacKenzie (2009) has interviewed former women combatants in the Sierra Leone war, and others, like Katharine Moon (1997) and Christine Chin (1998), have shed light on international gender and economic relations by considering sex workers at Korean military bases and Malaysian domestic workers in international political economy. Not all of these researchers might think of themselves as actively engaged in post-colonial analysis as opposed to feminist analysis of international relations. Many of them, however, acknowledge how trying it can be—methodologically and personally—to listen to difficult stories and painful emotions relayed by women living in post-colonial settings, whose experiences are often magnified by the poverty around them and by cultural rigidities about what women may and may not do. Das (2007: 38) notes how elusive are the 'languages of pain through which social sciences could gaze at, touch or become textual bodies on which this pain is written'.

The eminent post-colonial scholar, feminist, and literary analyst Gayatri Spivak (1988) has raised the related question of whether the subaltern can even speak to social science interviewers from the West. Is it possible, she asks, for that Western researcher, or the local researcher from another class than subaltern—which includes most members of the subaltern studies group and later post-colonial analysts—to hear the subaltern without putting her words and experiences into familiar Western frameworks? Ironically, even well-intentioned researchers can reinforce neo-colonial patterns of domination, exploitation, and social erasure for the very groups they seek to free of those conditions. Those who live outside the societies they study, in North America or Europe, for example, can represent subalterns in post-colonial societies through the lenses of privilege. They might lump together economically dispossessed people into 'a' subaltern category, as if social differenti-ation would not characterize subalterns as much as other economic groups. The researcher might think she or he is being attentive to the subaltern but, in fact, it might be impossible to escape making the West and its ways of understanding others the real (though hidden) subject of a subaltern study.

Spivak raises crucially important questions about interacting across cultures and differences of class, race, gender, generation, language, and the like, and her con-cerns have elicited strong debate in post-colonial studies circles. Consider the possibility, though, that the subal-tern can speak and the researcher can listen under certain conditions. **World-travelling** is a post-colonial method-ology associated with feminist scholars of Latin American background—Maria Lugones (1990), Norma Alarcon (1990), Gloria Anzaldua (1990)—and with Christine Sylvester (1995, 2002) in International Relations. The world-traveller strives to achieve a space of mutual un-derstanding using the tool of empathy, which is the ability to enter into the spirit of a different experience and find in it an echo of some part of oneself. World-travellers might never physically travel away from home, but they can learn to travel knowingly within their own repertory of identities and experiences. It is a skill that many sub-alterns have already had to learn by virtue of operating in contexts where knowing the colonizer—their language,

say, or cultural styles of behaviour—is crucial for mak-ing a living, buying and selling goods, dealing with state bureaucracies, or journeying by bus to relatives. A post-colonial interviewer, by contrast, will probably be less practised in skills she does not have to hone to get through the challenges of the day. She must work to recall facets of her background and self-identity that resonate with peo-ple she interacts with in post-colonial contexts. Alarcon (1990: 363) says the Western world-traveller must also 'learn to become unintrusive, unimportant, patient to the point of tears, while at the same time open to learning any possible lessons'—lessons that help her connect with others rather than maintain pristine distance from them. Then the subaltern can speak—and gradually the words can help shape International Relations to be more inclu-sive of the world and well rounded in its sense of groups that have been historically neglected as participants in international relations.

Key Points

- Post-colonial studies started with an interest in the lives and knowledges of people of subaltern statuses in India.
- With little information on subaltern life, early post-colonial writers turned to post-colonial fiction for insight.
- Fiction as a data source that highlights life within particular cultures is something the field of International Relations has conventionally eschewed.
- Groups within International Relations, however, have brought post-colonial fiction and culture to their work. It is very prominent in feminist International Relations.
- It is important to bear in mind Gayatri Spivak's question of whether the subaltern can speak or whether the Western researcher ends up putting that speech into dominant Western frameworks.
- World-travelling methods encourage researchers and subalterns to find common meeting points that bring the Western researcher closer to the subaltern world, rather than vice versa.

Becoming post-colonial

Post-colonial theorizing was taking several directions by the 1990s. One steady path was literary analysis, an original interest that expanded to include Western works set in colonial situations. Joseph Conrad's tale of Western men defeated by Africa and Africans in *Heart of Darkness* has been of interest, as has Charlotte Bronte's *Jane Eyre*, which features a Jamaican Creole woman kept in the attic by a British man whose small

fortune came from marrying her, but who seeks to deny the marriage so that he can marry Jane. In that stream of post-colonial analysis, researchers ask whether the stories harbour a subtext of imperial exploitation or offer a critique of colonialism. In addition, such works demonstrate the limited choices women face in all societies, whether they are with Western partners or not.

A second direction takes up robust theorizing of the present moment in history. Where IR scholarship places us in the era of globalization, it is also possible to argue that the current era of international relations is postcolonial (minus the hyphen). It is a time of the present and that extends into the future; yet it is a time when colonial patterns of trade, governance, and social relations persist. Homi Bhabha's work straddles concerns with the post-colonial and the postcolonial. Like Said, Bhabha has addressed how colonial discourses constructed the colonized, which we recognize as a central question of power in post-colonialism. Bhabha argues that colonialism was never fully successful in defining and restricting the lives of colonial and post-colonial subjects. Drawing more on psychoanalysis (an echo of Fanon's approach) than on literary theory, Bhabha maintains that colonial discourse was always ambivalent about the people it colonized. They are alternately portrayed as passive and conquerable, and irrational and untamed by modern moral codes. That the colonial subject cannot be pinned down leads to repeated stereotyping to mask the ambivalence. This anxious repetition, as Bhabha calls it, is accompanied by efforts to train some 'natives' to speak European languages and aspire to European values and culture. Bhabha points out that such individuals do not necessarily behave like trained parrots that mimic their owners' speech. Rather, they develop **hybrid identities**—partly local and partly Western—that increase colonial anxieties and confound efforts to put natives in their place. Colonials intensify the stereotyping in the hopes of commanding people to remain where colonialism has assigned them, but that breeds resistance to rather than complacency with the colonial venture and runs against the trends of our time: hybridity opens new directions of history, identity and politics.

Bhabha's theory of identity formation in colonial contexts 'contest[s] genealogies of "origin" that lead to claims for cultural supremacy and historical priority' (1994: 157). It becomes difficult to maintain the notion that the West is entirely different from, and above, the former colonial areas of the world, when its knowledge is taken on in hybrid ways by those who have been thought of as conquerable or passive. As the challenging title of a book by Dipesh Charkrabarty suggests, those once said to be subordinated to Western knowledge can gain the power to turn the game around and begin *Provincializing Europe* (2000). An example of this from international relations could be the emergence of a powerful OPEC, most members of which are former colonies that gained control of oil production in their countries and

> **Box 11.3** Anne McClintock on problems raised by the term 'post-colonialism'
>
> 'Can most of the world's countries be said, in any meaningful or theoretically rigorous sense, to share a single "common past", or a single common "condition", called the "post-colonial condition", or "post-coloniality"? The histories of African colonization are certainly, in part, the histories of the collisions between European and Arab empires, and the myriad African lineage states and cultures. Can these countries now best be understood as shaped exclusively around the "common" experience of European colonization? Indeed, many contemporary African, Latin American, Caribbean and Asian cultures, while profoundly affected by colonization, are not necessarily *primarily* preoccupied with their erstwhile contact with Europe. On the other hand, the term "post-colonialism" is, in many cases, prematurely celebratory. Ireland may, at a pinch, be "post-colonial", but for the inhabitants of British-occupied Northern Ireland, not to mention the Palestinian inhabitants of the Israeli Occupied Territories and the West Bank, there may be nothing "post" about colonialism at all ... [and] no "post-colonial" state anywhere has granted women and men equal access to the rights and resources of the nation-state ... Rather, a proliferation of historically nuanced theories and strategies is called for, which may enable us to engage more effectively in the politics of affiliation ... [or] face being becalmed in an historically empty space in which our sole direction is found by gazing back, spellbound at the epoch behind us, in the perpetual present marked only as a "post".'
>
> *(McClintock 1992: 4, 8, 13)*

now sell it to a petrochemical-dependent West on their own terms. Bhabha (1994) also has ideas that relate to the world-travelling methodology of politics described earlier. He talks, for example, of **dissemiNations** that occur when people with hybrid identities and cultures become **diasporic**, travelling physically from South to North to live, thereby undercutting an idea closely associated with international relations that nations are coherent, fixed, and territorial locations of identity and power. Ideas can also travel through the various channels of the information revolution, intersecting directly or via film, fashion, books, art, and the like. So many hyphenations emerge that it can be difficult to conceive of one majority identity that could dominate any other anywhere. Simultaneously disruptive and empowering processes propel us into 'Third Spaces', which Bhabha says are neither colonial nor post-colonial—and are not necessarily Third World. They are, rather, postcolonial dissemiNations.

By focusing on the contemporary period, a shift occurs that is bigger than the minor change in spelling from **post-colonial** to **postcolonial**. Instead of identifying people by the territorial place they once occupied in a colonially imagined hierarchy, the physical movement of peoples and information across the globe means that no group is confined to one location or ruled over, as during the colonial era. A **Global South** exists in various forms within and across former colonial powers, as well as in former colonies associated with the southern hemisphere. People of the South migrate in great numbers to northern countries now, which reverses the pattern of the colonial period. Information flows more easily to the South and cultures interpenetrate, so that it becomes difficult to identify a cluster of traits that clearly demarcates one culture from another. Yet minus the hyphen, postcolonialism also denotes a time in history that is still beholden in important ways to colonial-style hierarchies. Think of the early twenty-first-century wars that feature powerful Western states unleashing profound military technologies on starkly poorer countries, like Afghanistan and Iraq. Older imperial ventures were often led by European militaries and those of today gain a similar influence over local politics, which raises the spectre of a democratic empire advancing on states and populations that 'need to be controlled'. At the same time, discontinuities with the past loom: Bhabha thinks the world is deconstructing itself as people and ideas appear where they are not expected to be and would not have been in earlier eras (see Ch. 10). These trends complicate international relations and challenge International Relations to develop theories and methodologies that tap into contradictions of our time.

Postcolonial thinking has other signposts. It expands the spatial reach of the post-colonial to regions of the world that have vastly differing temporal relationships with colonialism. Some colonized countries were politically independent by the early 1800s (Canada and much of Latin America), and other countries experienced colonialism from the 1800s on (Australia, New Zealand, most of Africa and Asia); in the case of Australia and Canada, strong ties to the mother country are still celebrated rather than rejected. It is also important to bear in mind that some countries were not colonized by the West: Japan colonized Korea. Postcolonial perspectives also consider within-country conflicts with indigenous groups over land and rights, and lingering colonial situations that do not entirely make sense within a postcolonial tradition, such as British Northern Ireland and a Hong Kong where contemporary livelihoods, cityscapes, and lifestyles are rooted in and yet surpass the colonial era of British oversight.

Postcolonial analysis as a way of studying international relations has been recognized in a number of books by scholars of IR (Ling 2002; Sylvester 2002; Chowdhry and Nair 2003; Inayatullah and Blaney 2004), in regular articles in journals like *Alternatives*, *Feminist International Journal of Politics*, and *Borderlands*, and in periodic discussions elsewhere, such as a section on Said's influence in the journal *Millennium* (2008). Along with the most famous of the postcolonial writers discussed earlier, the still early study of international relations as postcolonial relations draws on the work of other leading thinkers of postcolonialism. Arjun Appadurai (1996), a social–cultural anthropologist, has converted globalization into postcolonial language and processes. He writes about five types of cultural flows of imagination: ethnoscapes, mediascapes, technoscapes, financescapes, and ideoscapes, all of which operate globally and beyond the absolute control of states; perhaps they will replace states in the future. Trinh Minh-ha, a Vietnamese-American film maker, has also been influential. In *Women, Native, Other* (1989: 1–2), she depicts the strengths of village diplomacy in an unnamed Third World setting, where 'there is no need for a linear progression which gives the comforting illusion that one knows where one goes'. Chandra Mohanty (1988) usefully warns Western feminists not to talk about Third World women as *the* Third World woman, a one-size-fits-all image that can inhibit transnational feminist linkages. Ien Ang (1995: 57) declares herself a feminist but she does not want to be part of a Western-identified project to create 'a natural political destination for all women, no matter how multicultural'. All these postcolonial thinkers have had an influence on International Relations scholarship, particularly on poststructuralist agendas (Ch. 10) and feminist International Relations (Ch. 16).

Key Points

- Some post-colonial work builds theory that follows up and expands ideas on colonization and resistance developed by anti-colonial intellectuals like Frantz Fanon.
- Edward Said is an important influence on theory building through his analysis of Orientalism.
- Homi Bhabha, another important figure in the field, argues that colonials constructed the Orient from their own fantasies and desires but could not capture or control hybrid colonial identities and dissemiNations.
- Contemporary theorists remove the hyphen from the term post-colonial to indicate that the current era is postcolonial and has continuities and discontinuities with colonialism.

Conclusions: post-colonialism in International Relations

Post-colonialism/postcolonialism did not start as a branch of IR or even as a companion to it. Its alternative histories, subaltern explorations, and theoretical moves from post-colonial to postcolonial thinking have been shaped through borrowings from many academic disciplines, from literary studies to social history to French philosophy to psychoanalysis. It has not, however, drawn on or been shaped by the field of IR; nor, until fairly recently, has it been taken into that discipline as a subfield of its knowledge. The neglect of topics now identified as postcolonial reveals a field's shallow interest historically in politics outside Great Power states. Great Powers held colonies, but those colonies were not studied as centres of power and agency unless they caused difficulties for individual Great Powers. The histories and peoples and cultures of what are known as Third World countries (or countries of the South or underdeveloped countries) were all but invisible to International Relations until the 1980s. Post-colonial/postcolonial studies has provided ways to fill large gaps in IR knowledge and has put the state in its place as one of many sites of politics and relations in the field. In those tasks it has been joined by feminist analysis and poststructuralism, assisted by a post-cold war human rights agenda and diasporic movements that reverse the usual direction taken during the colonial period (North to South).

Postcolonialism highlights the international relations of colonial actions in the Third World, the continuities of that past and the present, and the ways ordinary people can be involved in and shape transnational flows of knowledge, culture, identity, and imagination in the future. And it does so with a mission that still includes the liberation of subaltern statuses in today's world-time, a phenomenon that would surely be the ultimate answer to discourses and deeds that uphold global relations of dominance and subordination. Engaging and persuasive when not overly complex and notoriously difficult to read, postcolonialism none the less has many critics. They charge, among other things, that most of the analysis looks back at colonialism rather than forward, attacks the West instead of also attacking poor governance in Third World states today, and is so preoccupied with language and identity that it leaves questions of whether the subaltern can eat for Western agencies of development to resolve (Sylvester 1999). That is to say, postcolonialism can seem esoteric, too literary, and strangely devoid of urgency to help those it defends abstractly. Indeed, in *Critique of Postcolonial Reason* (1999), Gayatri Spivak rejects aspects of post-colonialism as a form of reason that has been preoccupied with past issues and post-colonial nationalisms. It is time, she thinks, to focus more practically on contemporary issues, such as domination by World Bank and International Monetary Fund policies. She is also sensitive to the failure of so many Third World states to improve life for women, peasants, and working-class citizens, a

---

Case Study Zimbabwe: a post-colonial dilemma in International Relations

What happens when a post-colonial state starts terrorizing the very population it sought to liberate from colonialism? What, if anything, can and should the international or post-colonial community do? In the case of Iraq, the USA and the UK determined that

a post-colonial country was ruled by a dangerous tyrant, Saddam Hussein, who had to be forcefully removed. Hussein had used poison gas, a weapon of mass destruction, against an ethnic group living within its own borders, the Kurds, and was said to have a large arsenal of similar weapons that could be unleashed on the West. He was also accused of working with Al Qaeda in the days leading up to the attack on the World Trade Center on 11 September 2001. A coalition of the willing intervened militarily, ousted Hussein and overturned his authoritarian government, although the outcome of that controversial effort remains to be seen.

Compare this with the international community's lack of response to Robert Mugabe, the leader of post-colonial Zimbabwe in Southern Africa, who has been tyrannizing and nearly starving his population since the early 2000s in order to control them. Elected to power in 1980, when the colony of Southern Rhodesia gained independence from Britain after a decade-long armed struggle, Mugabe alternated between proclaiming Marxist intentions for the country, following a liberal–capitalist pragmatism that carried forward important elements of the colonial political economy acceptable to international trade partners, and unleashing authoritarian tendencies that showed intolerance of democratic politics, racist tendencies, and willingness to foist brutal military and police reprisals on groups and individuals that opposed him or were depicted as opposing him. Over the years, the Marxist elements of Mugabe's ideology dropped out of sight and it seemed that Zimbabwe was heading towards a solid liberal, capitalist, and mostly democratic post-colonial future. Zimbabwe was even called the Pride of Africa by many of its neighbours for reconciling with white colonial settlers (the Rhodesians), who owned and farmed the best agricultural land in the country, and for embracing liberal principles of economic growth with equity. For a while, Mugabe was the leader of the non-aligned nations, the group whose history figures so prominently in post-colonial analysis.

Mugabe is still in power today but his reputation lies in ruins, as does much of the once-prosperous country. Starting in 2000, as his popularity waned and his determination to remain in power strengthened, Mugabe turned his back on the economy and on most Zimbabweans, and moved steadily towards vengeful and callous authoritarian rule, policed by the army and by young thugs who terrorized the population into silence. The economy ground to a halt and Zimbabwe experienced the highest inflation in the world, one of the highest rates of HIV, 80 per cent unemployment, life expectancy under 40 years, rampant corruption, and human rights violations that have included assaults on opponents and a racial strategy to drive out white farmers without compensating them for their seized farms. His government has been forced to share power with the opposition Movement for Democratic Change (MDC), headed by Morgan Tsvangirai, but Mugabe has been singularly uncooperative in this arrangement. The United Nations expresses repeated concerns about starvation and undernourishment in a country that once exported food while farms go to government officials who do not know how to farm nor wish to learn. Mugabe justifies his actions by arguing that he is trying to remedy the conditions Zimbabwe inherited from British colonialism, when the best agricultural lands went to white settlers and established black farmers were forced into areas of poorer soils. Mugabe constantly proclaims that Zimbabwe will never be a colony again, that it will do things its own way.

Without a doubt, Mugabe's anti-colonial posture has been turned against the country's own population. Yet the international and regional response to Mugabe has been muted. In part, this is because Mugabe is seen across Africa as the original independence leader of the country, one of the few still alive. His fight against the colonial order is deemed of such historic importance that neighbouring states show extraordinary patience in dealing with him, despite a steady stream of Zimbabwean refugees crossing into their states. Sensitive to the recent colonial history of Southern Africa, the West does not want to be seen as re-enacting colonial invasion and insisting on regime change. And as cynics point out, Zimbabwe is a landlocked country that does not have oil. The result is that no country has reacted to Mugabe the way some reacted to Hussein. The USA has frozen government assets held in American banks and investment firms, and the European Union refuses to let Mugabe and his entourage into Europe. Neither of these international punishments seems to worry Mugabe, who has simply switched his investments and leisure pursuits to places like Hong Kong.

This difficult issue of international relations is treated in fascinating works by researchers associated with post-colonial theorizing and analysis, such as Stephen Chan (2003), who writes about the high stakes and calculated steps Mugabe has taken to stay in power. Imaginative literature written by the latest generation of Zimbabweans reveals the daily implications of Mugabe's reign in Zimbabwe on ordinary people; Petina Gappah (2009) has an excellent collection of stories about life in contemporary Zimbabwe.

Questions
- Can you think of ways to apply early post-colonial or later postcolonial ideas to situations like Zimbabwe?
- Drawing on post-colonial/postcolonial thinking, consider how a leader like Mugabe can feel no remorse about turning against his own people and against his own earlier achievements.

point she shares with analysts like Robert Young, Arif Dirlik, and Aijaz Ahmad.

But all subfields or streams of thinking in International Relations are constantly critiqued. The strength of the field today is that it has given room to newer concerns about daily international relations rather than remaining focused on heroic or tragic episodes alone. By insisting that states and people who have spent time in colonial circumstances have much to contribute to knowledge and contemporary history, postcolonial analysis does a great service for International Relations. It responds to a field that has had its own history of myopic imperial sight.

Questions

1   What is post-colonial analysis?
2   How does post-colonial analysis differ from postcolonial analysis?
3   How has International Relations studied colonies and the colonial era in the past?
4   Frantz Fanon and Edward Said are both important thinkers in the post-colonial/postcolonial field. Why?

5 How is post-colonial thinking tied to the idea of the subaltern?

6 Do you think the subaltern can speak or that Westerners are always overdubbing them with their preoccupations?

7 Do you think it makes sense to change the focus from post-colonial analysis to postcolonialism? What is gained and lost in that shift?

8 What do you think of Homi Bhabha's ideas on hybrid identity in a postcolonial era? Is your identity hybrid? How?

9 Can one use post-colonial/postcolonial analysis to understand terrorism?

10 What are some of the continuities and discontinuities in the world between the colonial period and the present?

11 Why do feminists and poststructuralists in international relations find post-colonial/ postcolonial thinking so useful?

Further Reading

Chan, S. (2009), *The End of Certainty: Towards a New Internationalism* (London: Zed Books). Argues that fusing different strands of Western, Eastern, religious and philosophical thought is required to understand and move forward amidst the many changes and uncertainties of contemporary international relations.

Fanon, F. (1963) *Wretched of the Earth* (New York: Grove Press). A riveting theory of colonial and anti-colonial violence and the social attitudes on which each is based.

Hardt, M., and Negri, A. (2000), *Empire* (Cambridge, MA: Harvard University Press). A Marxian argument that contemporary international relations is characterized by new forms of power and empire that postcolonial analysis has not yet grasped.

Krishna, S. (2009), *Globalization and Postcolonialism: Hegemony and Resistance in the Twenty-First Century* (Lanham, MD: Rowman & Littlefield). Compares and contrasts economic globalization with postcolonialism as a stream of thinking and politics that opposes inequalities.

Loomba, A. (2005), *Colonialism/Postcolonialism*, 2nd edn (London: Routledge). This introduction to postcolonial thinkers places their ideas in a wider network that makes it impossible to think in either/or terms about the West and the non-West.

Said, E. (1978), *Orientalism* (Harmondsworth: Penguin). One of the key texts in post-colonial studies.

Sylvester, C. (2006), 'Bare Life as a Development/Postcolonial Problematic', *The Geographical Journal* 172(1): 66–77. Notes differences between international development and postcolonial analyses, and draws on postcolonial fiction as one way to discover mutuality.

Williams, P., and Chrisman, L. (eds) (1994), *Colonial Discourse and Post-Colonial Theory: A Reader* (New York: Columbia University Press). An anthology of some of the most important pieces of early post-colonial/postcolonial thought.

Young, R. J. C. (2003), *Postcolonialism: A Very Short Introduction* (Oxford: Oxford University Press). An innovative introduction that starts with subaltern experiences and then talks about theories.

Online Resource Centre

 Visit the Online Resource Centre that accompanies this book to access more learning resources on this chapter topic at www.oxfordtextbooks.co.uk/orc/baylis5e/

Chapter 12

International ethics

RICHARD SHAPCOTT

Reader's Guide

Ethics is the evaluative study of what actors ought to do, rather than the descriptive study of what they have done, or are doing. International ethics is central to international politics because it refers to the ultimate purposes of our studies and guides the actions we might take in light of our knowledge. Globalization increases not only the scope and intensity of human political and economic relationships, but also of our ethical obligations. Globalization makes it harder to draw clear ethical distinctions between insiders and outsiders and, consequently, raises the idea of a cosmopolitan community of humankind. How then should we think about ethics and what principles ought to guide the policies of states, non-governmental organizations (NGOs), corporations, and individuals in their relations with everybody else? This chapter examines how these questions have been answered by different thinkers and actors in world politics and discusses the three most significant and difficult ethical issues facing the world in the age of globalization.

Introduction

Ever since human beings gathered into social groups they have been confronted by the issue of how to treat outsiders. Most communities have drawn significant moral distinctions between insiders and outsiders, applying different standards accordingly. It is also the case that many communities, and individuals, have not made these distinctions into an absolute moral standard and have offered hospitality, aid, and charity to strangers with whom they come into contact.

According to the *Oxford English Dictionary*, the field of ethics is 'the science of morals; the department of study concerned with the principles of human duty'. International ethics addresses the nature of duties across community boundaries and how members of political communities, mostly nation-states, ought to treat 'outsiders' and 'strangers' and whether it is right to make such a distinction. Two questions therefore lie at the heart of international ethics as field of study. The first is whether outsiders ought to be treated according to the same principles as insiders are (in other words, ought outsiders to be treated as moral equals?). The second question refers to how this can be done in a world characterized by two conditions: the existence of international anarchy and moral pluralism. The first of these is often seen as a practical challenge because anarchy makes it harder to get things done and reinforces self-interested, rather than altruistic, tendencies of individuals and states. The second presents both a practical and an ethical challenge. Not only is it harder to get things done when there is no agreement, but deciding which, or whose, ethics should apply, and whether there are any universal rules is itself an ethical problem.

The advent of globalization provokes a re-examination of these challenges and prompts us to ask whether human beings ought to be considered, first, as one single moral community with some rules that apply to all (cosmopolitanism); second, as a collection of separate communities each with their own standards and no common morality (realism); or, third, as a collection of separate communities with some minimally shared standards (pluralism**).**

The ethical significance of boundaries: cosmopolitanism and its alternatives

Most academic debate on international ethical issues draws from Western traditions of moral theory. In particular, **deontological** and **consequentialist** ethics, and especially Kantianism and **utilitarianism** have been important. Deontology refers to the nature of human duty or obligation. Deontological approaches spell out rules that are always right for everyone to follow, in contrast to rules that might produce a good outcome for an individual, or their society. For deontologists, rules ought to be followed because they are right in themselves and not because of the consequences they may produce. Kantian approaches emphasize rules that are right because they can be, in principle, agreed upon by everyone (universalizability) and are the most important traditions of deontological ethics in the international sphere.

In contrast, consequentialist accounts judge actions by the desirability of their outcomes. Realism (see Ch. 5), for instance, judges a statesperson's actions as right or wrong depending on whether they serve the state's interests. Utilitarianism, on the other hand, judges acts by their expected outcomes in terms of human welfare and the 'greatest good of the greatest number'. These ethical theories provide different ways of assessing action and deciding what is in fact ethical and are largely drawn from the European heritage of secular reason and natural law. Of course not all ethical codes are derived from these traditions; religion and culture arguably provide most of the world's moral guidance. However, most everyday ethics, including religious ethics, are a mixture of both deontological and consequential considerations.

While understanding these distinctions is important, what matters more in international ethics is the conclusions drawn about the ethical significance of borders. A more relevant distinction exists between cosmopolitan, or universalist, positions and anti-cosmopolitan, sometimes referred to as communitarianism or particularism. Cosmopolitans, including deontologists and utilitarians, argue that morality itself is universal: a truly moral rule or code will be applicable to everyone. National borders are therefore 'morally irrelevant'. Many religious ethics are cosmopolitan in scope; both Christianity and Islam preach the moral unity of humankind.

In contrast, anti-cosmopolitans argue that national boundaries provide important ethical constraints. They tend to fall into two different streams: realism and pluralism. Realism (see Ch. 5) claims that the facts of international anarchy and sovereignty mean that the only viable ethics are those of self-interest and survival. Pluralism argues that anarchy does not prevent states from agreeing to a minimal core of standards for coexistence. Both realism and pluralism begin from the premise that morality is 'local' to particular cultures, times, and places. Because ethics is local, our morality has meaning only in the specific—what Michael Walzer calls 'thick'—culture to which we belong. Different cultures have their own ethics and it is impossible to claim access to one single account of morality. A single universal morality is a cultural product with no global legitimacy. Realists and pluralists claim that cosmopolitanism is both impossible (impractical) and undesirable because of the international state of nature, and because profound cultural pluralism means that there is a lack of agreement about whose ethics should apply universally. Cosmopolitanism, realism, and pluralism are reflected in current practices of states and other actors. For instance, since the end of the Second World War many international actors have used the universalist vocabulary of human rights to claim that there are cosmopolitan standards of treatment that all people can claim and that all states recognize. In contrast, others have claimed that threats to national security require states to do 'unthinkable' things, like torture or carpet bombing (see Case Study 2), which override conventional ethics. Alternatively, it is also argued that because there is no real agreement on comprehensive standards, it is indefensible to enforce them against those, like certain Asian or African states, who do not share the cultural assumptions underpinning these laws. Thus, while it is true that a common apparently universal language of human rights exists, there is no clear agreement about what this entails.

Globalization brings these different ethical positions into greater relief and, for many, provides the strongest reason for applying universal standards. Because globalization increases interconnections between communities, it also increases the variety of ways in which communities can harm each other, either intentionally or not. For instance, globalization makes it harder to ignore the impact of day-to-day actions, such as driving a car or buying new clothes, on the global environment and in the global economy. The more intense governance of the global economy also raises ethical issues of fairness associated with the rules of international institutional structures. Globalization exacerbates and intensifies these ethical dilemmas by increasing the effects that different communities and individuals have on each other. It especially allows for a far greater awareness of the suffering of 'distant strangers'. Under these conditions,

---

Box 12.1 Cosmopolitanism, realism, and pluralism

Cosmopolitanism

'We should recognize humanity wherever it occurs, and give its fundamental ingredients, reason and moral capacity, our first allegiance.'

(Martha Nussbaum 1996: 7)

Liberal cosmopolitanism: 'First, individualism: ultimate units are human beings, or persons ... Second, universality: the status of ultimate unit of concern attaches to every living human being equally, not merely to some subset ...Third, generality: .... persons are the ultimate unit of concern for everyone—not only for their compatriots, fellow religionists, or such like.'

(Thomas Pogge 1994: 9)

'The key point is that it is wrong to promote the interest of our own society or our own personal advantage by exporting suffering to others, colluding in their suffering, or benefiting from the ways in which others exploit the weakness of the vulnerable.'

(Andrew Linklater 2002: 145)

Communitarianism

'Humanity has members but no memory, so it has no history and no culture, no customary practices, no familiar life-ways, no festivals, no shared understanding of social goods.'

(Michael Walzer 1994a: 8)

'Justice is rooted in the distinct understanding of places, honours, jobs, things of all sorts, that constitute a shared way of life. To override those understandings is (always) to act unjustly.'

(Michael Walzer 1983: 314)

Realism

'The appeal to moral principles in the international sphere has no concrete universal meaning .... that could provide rational guidance for political action, ...it will be nothing but the reflection of the moral preconceptions of a particular nation ...'

'a foreign policy guided by universal moral principles .... is under contemporary conditions .... a policy of national suicide.'

(Hans Morgenthau 1952: 10)

Pluralism

'a world of diversity in which the variety of national cultures finds expression in different sets of citizenship rights, and different schemes of social justice, in each community'.

(David Miller 2002: 976)

the ethical framework associated with Westphalian sovereignty—which gives only minor moral significance to the suffering of outsiders—seems less adequate. In a globalized world, communities are challenged to develop new principles or refine old ones to govern these interactions. However, the lack of any single standard of fairness and justice between states makes this task more difficult because it raises the question of whose principles should apply. Therefore, in a world that is being globalized, one ethical challenge is to ask 'Is it possible to define some principles that everyone might be able to agree upon?'

Cosmopolitanism

Even though our world may be characterized by high levels of interdependence, we still tend to live morally 'constrained' lives, in which national borders have significant ethical status. Cosmopolitans, however, argue that despite this division of humanity into separate historically constituted communities, it remains possible to identify with, and have a moral concern for, humanity. Cosmopolitanism refers to the idea that humanity is to be treated as a single moral community that has moral priority over our national (or subnational) communities.

The first part of the cosmopolitan claim is that there are no good reasons for ruling any person out of ethical consideration. The second dimension of cosmopolitan thought is the attempt to define exactly what obligations and rules ought to govern the universal community. The attempt to give inclusion substantive content is usually associated with deontological and Kantian thought in particular. Deontologists argue that not only should we consider outsiders as morally equal, but also that, as a consequence, we are morally obliged to do certain things and refrain from others.

One of the common arguments of liberal cosmopolitanism is that treating everyone as equal requires 'impartial consideration of the claims of each person' (Beitz 1992: 125). Because there are no morally significant differences between people as people, everyone's interests should be judged from a disinterested position. Impartiality requires that particular affiliations, like national identity, must be assessed from the position of the good of the whole—because they are not in themselves necessarily just or defensible. Impartiality arguments are usually deployed in terms of defending the idea of global distributive justice (see below). For the most ambitious liberal cosmopolitans, impartiality leads inevitably to the claim that the political institutions of the planet should guarantee global equality of rights and goods.

Most cosmopolitans agree that national membership and the borders between nations are defensible only in so far as they serve individuals' needs, by providing them with a sense of belonging, identity, and stability that is necessary to be a fully functioning human being. This has led some to argue that national favouritism, or 'compatriot priority', can be defended from an impartial position. In other words, impartiality does not necessarily lead to a cosmopolitan account of global justice (Goodin 1988). However, cosmopolitans still maintain that our fundamental moral claims derive from our status as human beings and therefore national loyalties have at best a derivative moral status.

Kant and cosmopolitanism

Long before the existence of modern states and telecommunications, the Stoic philosopher Diogenes claimed he was a 'citizen of the world'. However, in modern times, the source of greatest inspiration for cosmopolitanism was the German Enlightenment philosopher Immanuel Kant. For Kant, the most important philosophical and political problem facing humankind was the eradication of war and the realization of a universal community governed by a rational cosmopolitan law. The central concept of Kant's thought, and the lynchpin upon which his project for a perpetual peace (see Ch. 6) between states rested, is the principle of the categorical imperative (CI).

Specifically, one should 'Act only on that maxim through which you can at the same time will that it shall become a universal law' (Kant, quoted in Linklater 1990a: 100). This means that, to act morally, a rational person must act upon a principle that anybody could wish everybody else to obey in respect of everybody else. For Kant, the most important expression of this imperative was the principle that humans should be treated as ends in themselves: 'Act in such a way that you always treat humanity, whether in your own person or in the person of any other, never simply as a means, but always at the same time as an end' (Kant, quoted in *ibid.*: 101). The effect of the CI is to grant every individual equal moral standing in relation to each other. Most Kantian thought focuses on the nature of the obligations that accompany the belief in human equality and freedom. This principle directly and indirectly underpins much of contemporary international ethics, especially discussions about global justice. However, the more basic argument is that treating people as ends in themselves requires us to think universally. Restricting moral concern to members of one's own state or nation renders any belief in equality incomplete.

Box 12.2 The categorical imperative

The categorical imperative states that for a rational being to act morally, it must act according to universal laws. Specifically one should 'Act only on that maxim through which you can at the same time will that it shall become a universal law' (quoted in Linklater 1990a: 100). This means that, to act morally, a rational person must act upon a principle that anybody could wish everybody else to obey in respect of everybody else. For Kant, the most important expression of this imperative was the principle that humans should be treated as ends in themselves: 'Act in such a way that you always treat humanity, whether in your own person or in the person of any other, never simply as a means, but always at the same time as an end' (quoted in *ibid.*: 101). An example is slavery, because slaves are humans who are reduced to the status of the property of others. They have no rights and their interests are not taken into account in regard to decisions that affect them. Warfare between states is likewise another violation, because it reduces both citizens and non-citizens alike to means of achieving (the states') ends. For Kant, this is a moral law that results from the nature of reason itself, but also from human nature, understood as both self-interested and reasonable, that is our capacity to be 'rational devils'.

Kantian thought has given rise to a number of different approaches. A common distinction is made between moral and institutional cosmopolitanism, where the first refers to the acts required of individuals, and the second to the rules that govern societies. Cosmopolitan duties to recognize individual equality apply to individuals, as well as to the global institutional/legal order.

In sum, the major tasks of cosmopolitanism are to defend moral universalism, to explore what it might mean to follow the CI in a world divided into separate states, and to develop an account of an alternative political order based on Kant's work (see Chs 1 and 31). Most discussion of international ethics refers to the dilemmas states and other actors face in seeking to decide, interpret, and act according to these obligations in their policies.

This account of global cosmopolitan duties emphasizes both individual and institutional obligations without either claiming the need for a world state or denying national identity. A cosmopolitan commitment to avoiding harm involves only the idea that one's national identity and well-being should not come at the expense of outsiders. Obligations to friends, neighbours, and fellow countrymen must be balanced with obligations to strangers and to humanity.

Key Points

- Globalization lends support to cosmopolitan ethical theory.
- Cosmopolitanism advances the idea of a universal human community in which everybody is treated as equal.
- The most important cosmopolitan thinker is Immanuel Kant.
- Cosmopolitanism has both moral and political meaning.
- Cosmopolitanism does not require a world state.
- Cosmopolitans emphasize both positive and negative duties, usually expressed in terms of responsibilities not to harm and responsibilities to provide humanitarian assistance or hospitality.

Anti-cosmopolitanism: realism and pluralism

While cosmopolitanism in one form or another tends to predominate in academic debate on international ethics, anti-cosmopolitan arguments tend to be more persuasive in the practices of states. Anti-cosmopolitans also provide powerful criticism of some of the assumptions and blindspots of cosmopolitan thought. They also help us to understand why cosmopolitanism has only limited applicability in the contemporary international order.

Realist ethics

For realists, the facts of anarchy and statehood mean that the only viable ethics are those of self-interest. Many people have characterized realist ethics as Machiavellian at worst and amoral at best. Realist ethics seems to contradict universal ethics such as human rights. But realists, such as Hans Morgenthau and George F. Kennan, often argue that underlying this toughness is a different, more pragmatic, morality. The statesperson's duty is to ensure the survival of their state in the uncertain conditions of international anarchy. To do otherwise would be to risk the lives and interests of their own people. Thus self-help is a moral duty and not just a practical necessity. Realists therefore advise states to focus on material and strategic outcomes rather than on the morality, conventionally understood, of their actions. For instance, a realist like Henry Kissinger may advise bombing a neutral state, such as Laos, if it will serve the military goals of defeating the enemy, North Vietnam. Alternatively, this approach may also involve having friendly relations and showing support for governments with poor human rights records, such as Chile under the military rule of Augusto Pinochet, or arguably Pakistan today, in order to secure an advantage against a military foe, such as the USSR or Al Qaeda. While the critics say that this can slip into opportunism, justifying almost any actions on ethical grounds, realists maintain that statespeople have a duty to their own people first and that ignoring these realities in the name of some Kantian ideal would be a dereliction of that duty (Morgenthau 1948).

Many realists proclaim such self-interested ethics as virtuous and agree with E. H. Carr's (1939) scepticism towards those individuals and states who claim to be acting in the name of universal morality. Thus contemporary realists, like John Mearsheimer, are sceptical about former US President George W. Bush's aims of spreading democracy in the Middle East and the claim in the National Security Strategy of the USA (NSS 2001: 5) that 'American values are universal values'. Realists believe that such statements are usually either a cynical mask or a self-interested delusion. In reality, there are no such universal values, and even if there were, anarchy would prevent states from acting in accordance with them.

Realists are vulnerable to the observation that not every choice that states face is between survival and destruction, rather than, say, advantage or disadvantage. It does not stand to reason that seeking advantage allows the statesperson to opt out of conventional morality in the same way that survival might. It is a limitation of most realist writers that they simply favour the national interest over the interests of outsiders. In other words, realists display a preference for the status quo, the states-system and nationalism, which is not fully defensible. This favouritism reminds us that realism is as much prescriptive and normative as it is descriptive and explanatory.

Pluralist ethics of coexistence

The other main expression of communitarian assumptions is pluralism. Because communitarians value community and diversity, they recognize that the many ways in which individuals are formed in different cultures is a good thing in itself. Therefore they argue that the best ethics is one that preserves diversity over homogeneity.

Pluralism recognizes that states have different ethics but can agree upon a framework whereby they tolerate each other, do not impose their own views on others, and agree on certain, limited, harm principles. These duties are best expressed through an ethics of tolerance and coexistence between political communities. States have different ethics but can agree upon a framework, sometimes likened to an egg-box, whereby they tolerate and do not impose their own views on each other. This allows them to feel reasonably secure and to go about their business in relative peace. In this view, sovereignty is an ethical principle that allows states and the different cultures they harbour to exist alongside each other.

For pluralists, we have greater and more specific duties to our 'own kind' than we do to outsiders. Any duties to humanity are at best attenuated and mediated by states. Pluralism is distinguished from **solidarism,** which argues that states have duties to act against other states when basic human values are denied by practices like genocide. Pluralists resist attempts to develop a more solidarist world in which humanitarian intervention, for instance, is institutionalized: 'The general function of international society is to separate and cushion, not to act' (Vincent 1986: 123).

Pluralists are sceptical about the use of human rights in diplomacy as it gives some states the opportunity to deny others their sovereignty (Bull 1977; Jackson 2000). Likewise, pluralists do not believe in universal distributive justice, either as a practical possibility or as a moral good in itself, because it requires the imposition of a specific, usually liberal, account of justice on other cultures. They see the imposition of any specific values or ethics on others as a harmful thing both for that community and for international order as a whole (Walzer 1994a; Jackson 2000; Miller 2002). The primary ethical responsibility of the statesperson is to maintain order and peace between states, not to develop a global account of justice.

The most developed account of a pluralist ethics is John Rawls's *The Law of Peoples* (1999). According to Rawls, liberal states have no cosmopolitan duties to globalize their own conception of distributive justice. Instead, societies are to be understood as if they have only minimal impact upon each other. For Rawls, the conditions required for global distributive justice are not present. Therefore the best that can be hoped for is a 'law of peoples', which covers rules of self-determination, just war, mutual recognition (sovereignty), non-intervention, and mutual aid.

Box 12.3 Rawls's 'law of peoples'

1 People are free and independent, and their freedom and independence are to be respected by other peoples.

2 Peoples are to observe treaties and undertakings.

3 Peoples are to observe a duty of non-intervention.

4 Peoples have the right of self-defense but no right to instigate war for reasons other than self-defense.

5 Peoples are to honor human rights.

6 People are to observe certain specified restrictions in the conduct of war.

7 Peoples have a duty to assist other people living under unfavorable conditions that prevent their having a just or decent political and social regime (Mutual Aid).

(Rawls 1999)

However, pluralists invoke a universal principle that it is wrong for people to impose harms on others. More importantly, cosmopolitans ask whether 'eggbox' ethics is enough under conditions of globalization. Cosmopolitans argue that a strict ethics of coexistence is simply out of date when the scope for intercommunity harm has increased exponentially.

Key Points

- Realism and pluralism are the two most common objections to cosmopolitan ethics and the possibility of moral universalism.

- Realists argue that necessity demands a statist ethics, restricting moral obligations to the nation-state.

- Pluralism is an 'ethics of coexistence' based on sovereignty.

Duties of justice and natural duties: humanitarianism and harm

Another way of looking at the differences between cosmopolitans and anti-cosmopolitans is in terms of a distinction between duties of justice and natural or humanitarian duties. Looking at it this way reveals a higher degree of convergence on basic cosmopolitan principles.

The most common way in which cosmopolitan obligations are discussed is in terms of either positive or negative duties. Positive duties are duties to act, to do something, including duties to create a just social order, or duties of assistance. Humanitarianism, or mutual aid, involves a positive duty to aid those in dire need or who are suffering unnecessarily, wherever they may be and regardless of cause. This includes aid to the victims of famine and natural disasters, but also to those who suffer during wartime such as non-combatants and soldiers retired from the field. These are not charity provisions but moral duties that it would be not only bad but morally *wrong* to ignore. The idea of a positive duty underlies the recent UN Report on the international **responsibility to protect** (see Ch. 31), which spells out the responsibilities of states to uphold human rights within their own borders and abroad. The responsibility to protect argument also emphasizes that states' rights are dependent on their fulfilling this duty.

Negative duties are duties to stop doing something, usually duties to avoid unnecessarily harming others. States have traditionally recognized a negative duty of non-intervention that requires them to refrain from certain actions.

Cosmopolitans emphasize extensive positive (i.e. justice and aid) and negative (i.e. non-harming) duties across borders. Anti-cosmopolitans argue that compatriot priority means that we have only limited, largely negative, duties to those outside our own community. This does involve a commitment to a sort of cosmopolitan 'basic moral minimum' of two types, so-called natural duties (Rawls 1972), including mutual aid; and basic human rights (Shue 1981). Of the natural duties, mutual aid, the positive duty to offer assistance in times of need, such as *temporary* famine relief or humanitarian emergency aid, and the negative duty not to harm or inflict unnecessary suffering are the most important. In the public eye, positive duties, such as aid to victims of tsunamis or ethnic cleansing, take a higher profile and demand more attention, but in academic contexts at least as much attention is given to negative duties, and in particular duties not to harm others.

Andrew Linklater argues that cosmopolitan duties to do no harm generally fall into three categories. First, bilateral relationships: what 'we' do to 'them' and vice versa. Second, third-party relationships: what they do to each other. Third, global relationships: what we all do to each other (Linklater 2002, 2005). Examples of the first are cases where one community 'exports' damaging practices, goods, or by-products to another. In this case, states have a duty to consider the negative effects they have on each other, as well as a duty to prevent and punish harmful actions of **non-state actors** and individuals for whom they are directly responsible. For instance, some states have laws that punish citizens who engage in 'sex tourism' abroad. Thus states should not pursue their own national advantage without considering the harm this may cause others. An example of the second is when a state is involved in harming either members of its own community or its neighbour's, such as in cases of genocide. Third-party states and the **international community** also have duties to prevent, stop, or punish the perpetrators of these harms. The third relationship refers to practices or harms to which many communities contribute, often in different proportions, such as in the case of global warming (see Case Study 1). States have

a negative duty not to export harms to the world as a whole and a positive duty to contribute to the resolution of issues arising from such harms.

Problems arise in the discussion of negative duties because they rely on a fairly clear line of causation: if a state is harming another one, then it should cease doing so. Additionally, sometimes the effects of our actions are diffuse, or more than one party may be engaged in a harmful practice, as in the case of global warming (see Case Study 1). A negative duty to cease harming implies only a cessation of action; however, some argue that there is also a positive duty to prevent other harms occurring, as well as duties of compensation or redress.

This account of global duties emphasizes both individual and institutional obligations without either claiming the need for a world state or denying national

Global warming (GW) raises truly global ethical questions because it potentially affects every person on the planet. The environment, and the atmosphere in particular, are considered commons (see Ch. 21) because they are shared by all. The ethics of the global commons are explicitly cosmopolitan in the sense that they refer to the earth's environment as a single biological community that creates a human community of interdependence. This ethics emphasizes that national gains or advantages need to be sacrificed or moderated if the environmental problems are to be solved and the 'tragedy of the commons' is to be avoided.

GW is a good example of both positive and negative duties. At face value it seems reasonably clear that there are negative duties for those countries that have contributed most to GW, and that will do so in the future, to cease doing so. Most people would agree that we should all take responsibility for harming someone else, especially if we have benefited from it. In the case of GW this would mean that there is a proportionate responsibility on the part of the advanced industrial countries, especially the USA, Europe, Japan, and Canada, to reduce their greenhouse gas emissions (GHGE) and to take financial responsibility for the harms that their past and future emissions will cause others. There are also positive duties on the part of the richer states to aid those with the least capacity to adjust to the costs involved in GW. This is

regardless of the rich countries' role in causing the problem. That is, there are positive duties to aid the poorest states and populations, who will be disproportionately affected and who have done the least to contribute to GW. We can think, for instance, of counties like Bangladesh, mostly at or below sea level, or Pacific island states, which are barely industrialized but which are likely to be the first to disappear. It seems clear that on both positive and negative grounds there is a responsibility to help for those who can do so. In addition, there is also a positive duty that is arguably generated by the negative duty. If we have harmed someone, we ought to help them overcome the harm we have caused them, especially if they are unable to do so unassisted. That is, there is not only a negative duty to cease or reduce GHGE, but also a positive duty to redress the damage done. This is an issue of redistributive justice—a duty to aid those most affected by one's harms.

These arguments are buttressed by further points regarding the capacity of rich states to pay and by the two different types of cost that are likely to be faced by all countries. One is the cost of reducing GHGE and the other is the cost of dealing with the likely impacts of rising sea levels and other environmental consequences. Poorer countries are at a disadvantage in both regards. This issue is of course complicated by the fact that the production of GHGE is so central to economic growth, especially in industrializing countries. Any attempt to curtail their output implies a restriction on the prospects for economic growth in those countries that perhaps need it most. Indeed, there is even an argument that the 'people in the developing world need to increase their emissions in order to attain a minimally decent standard of living for themselves and their families' (Singer and Gregg 2004: 57). The overall cost to rich states of addressing GW are proportionally lower than for poor states. In addition, the costs that might be incurred by the rich states are likely to be of a qualitatively different nature. For rich states, dealing with climate change might only affect the *luxury* or non-necessary end of their quality of life, whereas for poor states reducing emissions will more probably affect the basic necessities of life and survival.

identity. A commitment to avoiding harm involves only the idea that one's national identity and well-being should not come at the expense of outsiders and recognizes that obligations to friends, neighbours, and fellow countrymen must be balanced with obligations to strangers and to humanity.

Global ethical issues

The following sections discuss two important international ethical issues, one new and the other older, that are exacerbated under conditions of globalization. The just war tradition has provided one of the most enduring sets of ethical standards for states and their servants in their conduct with outsiders. In contrast, the topic of global distributive justice has been taken seriously only in the last forty years or so. Both issues highlight the nature of the ethical challenges that face states in a world in which the effects of their actions are capable of being globalized.

Just war tradition

The just war tradition (JWT) (often erroneously referred to as just war theory) is a set of guidelines for determining and judging whether and when a state may have recourse to war and how it may fight that war. The JWT is concerned with applying moral limits to states' recourse to war and to limiting harms that states can commit against other states, military forces, and civilians. It consists of two parts: the *jus ad bellum* (or justice of war) and the *jus in bello* (the justice in war). Where *jus ad bellum* refers to the occasion of going to war, *jus in bello* refers to the means, the weapons, and tactics employed by the military in warfare (see Box 12.4 and Case Study 2).

The aim of JWT is not a just world. Nor is the idea of just war (JW) to be confused with holy wars or crusading, which are wars designed to spread a particular faith or political system. The JWT aims only to limit wars by restricting the types of justification that are acceptable. The European JWT has its origins in the works of Christian theologians, and especially St Augustine. Just war thinking is also important in Islam and is often incorrectly associated entirely with the idea of **jihad**.

JWT has both cosmopolitan and pluralist elements. Broadly speaking, the *jus ad bellum* tradition is generally associated with pluralism, or what Michael Walzer calls the legalist tradition. In this view, what is acceptable or

---

Box 12.4 The just war

Jus ad bellum

- Just cause: this usually means self-defence or defence of a third party.
- Right authority: only states can wage legitimate war. Criminals, corporations, and individuals are illegitimate.
- Right intention: the state leader must be attempting to address an injustice or an aggression, rather than seeking glory, expansion, or loot.
- Last resort: the leaders must have exhausted all other reasonable avenues of resolution or have no choice because of imminent attack.
- Reasonable hope of success: states should not begin wars they cannot reasonably expect to win.
- Restoration of peace: it is just to wage a war if the purpose is to restore the peace or return the situation to the status quo.
- Proportionality of means and ends: the means of war, including the war itself, must be proportionate to the ends being sought. States must use minimal force in order to achieve their objectives. It is not justifiable to completely destroy enemy forces or their civilian populations in order to remove them from your territory.

Jus in bello

- Proportionality of means: states must use minimal, or proportionate, force and weaponry. Thus it is not justifiable to completely destroy the enemy's forces if you can use enough force to merely defeat them. For example, a state should not use a nuclear weapon when a conventional one might do.
- Non-combatant immunity: states should not directly target non-combatants, including soldiers retired from the field, or civilians and civilian infrastructure not required for the war effort. Non-combatant immunity is central to just war theory, 'since without it that theory loses much of its coherence. How can a theory that claims to regard wars as an instrument of justice countenance the injustice involved in the systematic suppression of the rights of non-combatants?' (Coates 1997: 263).
- The law of double effect: actions may incur non-combatant losses if these are unintended (but foreseeable) consequences, for example civilians living adjacent to an arms factory. However, the real issue is whether deaths can really be unintended if they are foreseeable. The dilemma facing just war theorists is whether to be responsible for those deaths in the same way as for intended deaths.

Case Study 2 *Jus in bello*: saturation bombing

One example that illustrates many of the issues of *jus in bello* is the use of 'saturation' or 'area' city bombing during the Second World War. During the war, both the allied and axis powers targeted each other's cities with large-scale bombing raids. In pursuance of their war against Hitler, the British targeted massive bombing runs against Germany, destroying many cities and killing hundreds of thousands of civilians. The most famous of these was the bombing of the German city of Dresden. Dresden was especially controversial because it had no military significance at all. In the firestorm that was created by the allies, at least 100,000 people died. Likewise, the Americans, during the closing stages of the war against Japan, repeatedly bombed Tokyo and other major Japanese cities in raids that targeted cities rather than military sites. The main argument used to defend these clear breaches of the discrimination principle was that it was necessary to break the will of the people to continue fighting. Other arguments were that it was no longer possible to discriminate between civilians and non-civilians because of the advent of 'total war'. Others claimed that the war against Hitler was a 'supreme emergency' in which the survival of Britain was at stake. In most of these arguments, except the first, strategists refer to the doctrine of double effect: the death of civilians was foreseeable but unintentional.

However, British military planners had developed the tactic of saturation bombing before the war began, as part of an overall strategic plan. In addition, the campaigns lasted well beyond the immediate danger to Britain's survival that existed during the Battle of Britain. So it is clear that civilian deaths were both anticipated and planned as part of a war-fighting strategy. On these grounds, most authors now agree that this practice constituted a fundamental violation of just war principles.

---

unacceptable are rules about and for states, concerning what states owe each other. The rules it lays down refer to times when it is legitimate for states to wage war. The justifications for war are given not to God or humanity, but to other states. The only acceptable justifications are the defence of individual state sovereignty and, arguably, the defence of the principle of a society of states itself.

We can compare this with the more cosmopolitan elements of *jus in bello*, which refer explicitly to civilians and to what is owed to them in terms of harm minimization. The *jus in bello* principle informs, and has been codified in, international humanitarian law, such as the Geneva Conventions, as well as a number of other treaties limiting the use and deployment of certain weapons, including chemical weapons, landmines, and weapons of mass destruction (WMD). The ultimate referent is humanity, and the rules about proportionality, noncombatant immunity, and discrimination all refer to the rights of individuals to be exempt from harm.

From the position of the realist, the JWT imposes unjustifiable limits upon statecraft. International politics is the realm of necessity and in warfare any means must be used to achieve the end of the state. Necessity overrides ethics when it is a matter of state survival or when military forces are at risk. The state must judge for itself when it is most prudent to wage war and what is necessary for victory. From the position of the pacifist, the core doctrine of the JWT encourages war only by providing the tools to justify it. For pacifists and other critics, not only is killing always wrong; the JWT is unethical because it provides war with a veneer of legitimacy.

Box 12.5 Islamic just war tradition

The ethics of war are central to Islam. The prophet Muhammad himself led troops into battle in the name of Islam. It is clear from both the Koran and the teachings (*hadith*) of Muhammad that at (limited) times it is incumbent upon Muslims to wage war. For this reason it is often said that while Islam's ultimate purpose is to bring peace through universal submission to Allah, there is no 'pacifist' tradition within Islam. At times some Muslim authorities have argued that there is a duty to spread the realm of Islam through war, as happened in the centuries after Muhammad's death, with the establishment of the caliphate. Others, the majority, argue that the Koran sanctions war only in self-defence. Fundamentalist groups like Al Qaeda use this to justify their campaigns against the USA and its allies, both in the USA and in Iraq and Afghanistan. However, most Islamic authorities reject both Al Qaeda's interpretation of 'defence' and its strategy of attacking civilian targets outside the 'occupied' or threatened territory of the 'Dar al Islam' as illegitimate interpretations. Most interpreters argue that there are Islamic equivalents of the just cause clause, right authority, right intent, and some *jus in bello* clauses, including civilian immunity.

Global justice, poverty, and starvation

The globalizing of the world economy, especially since the Second World War, has undoubtedly given rise to large global inequalities. It has also been responsible for an increase in the number and proportion of the human population suffering from absolute poverty and starvation (see Ch. 28). At the same time, cosmopolitans like Pogge point out that globalization also means that there is now the capacity to end global poverty, relatively quickly and cheaply. Globalization raises the issue of universal distributive justice and the nature of the moral duties owed to the world's poor by the world's rich. The existence of both significant inequality and of massive hunger and starvation raises the question of whose responsibility it is either to reduce inequality or to end absolute starvation, especially in the presence of extreme wealth. Global poverty thus provides support for the cosmopolitan argument for an account of global distributive justice.

The Singer solution

According to Peter Singer, 'globalization means that we should value equality between societies, and at the global level, as much as we value political equality within one society' (2002: 190). Singer argues that an impartial and universalist (and utilitarian) conception of morality requires that those who can help, ought to, regardless of any causal relationship with poverty. He argues for a comprehensive mutual aid principle where 'if it is in our power to prevent something bad from happening, without thereby sacrificing anything of comparable moral importance we ought, morally, to do it' (1985: 231). People in affluent countries, and in affluent sections of poor countries, are morally obligated to help those who are in danger of losing their lives from poverty-related causes.

In order to justify this claim, Singer asks us to consider the following situation: 'if I am walking past a water pond and see a child drowning in it, I ought to wade in and pull the child out. This will mean getting

---

Box 12.6 Peter Singer on distributive justice

'Each one of us with wealth surplus to his or her essential needs should be giving most of it to help people suffering from poverty so dire as to be life-threatening. That's right: I'm saying that you shouldn't buy that new car, take that cruise, redecorate the house or get that pricey new suit. After all, a $1,000 suit could save five children's lives.'

(Singer 1999)

---

my clothes muddy, but this is insignificant, while the death of the child would presumably be a very bad thing' (1985: 231).

Persistent global hunger and dire poverty present us with the same moral choice. If we think it wrong to let a child die for fear of muddying our trousers, then we ought also to think it is wrong to let a child, or millions of other people, die from hunger and poverty when it is in our capacity to prevent it without incurring a significant loss. Therefore we, who are able to help, have a positive duty to aid those in need.

According to Singer and Peter Unger, people in well-off countries ought to give all the money left over after paying for necessities to alleviate Third World poverty. This is a moral duty and not an issue of charity; that is, we ought to consider ourselves to be doing something *wrong* if we do not help. In Kantian terms, we are not treating the world's poor as ends in themselves, because we are in effect placing less value on their lives than on our own material pleasure.

Liberal institutional cosmopolitanism

Liberal institutional cosmopolitans, like Charles Beitz, Darrel Moellendorf, and Thomas Pogge, argue that global interdependence generates a duty to create a globally just institutional scheme. For Beitz and Moellendorf, John Rawls's substantive account of justice can provide the criteria for justice globally.

Rawls (1971) argued that justice begins with the 'basic structure' of society, by which he meant 'the way in which the major social institutions distribute fundamental rights and duties and determine the division of advantages from social cooperation' (Rawls 1971: 7). To be just, society must have just basic assumptions about who has rights, or equal moral standing, and duties, and who benefits materially from the production of goods and services. Rawls's theory of justice is both a procedural account of justice and a substantive one, concerned with distribution of wealth and advantage (see Box 12.7). Rawls, as noted above, rejected the possibility of global distributive justice modelled on his theory. However, most Rawlsians argue that Rawls's conclusions do not follow from his own premises.

Cosmopolitans concerned with global justice are predominantly, but not exclusively, concerned with the basic structure of global society, that is, with the ways in which the rules of global order distribute rights, duties, and the benefits of social cooperation. The basic structure of international order should be governed by cosmopolitan principles focused on the inequalities

Box 12.7 Rawls and the 'original position'

Rawls's social contract is the result of an experiment in which members of a closed society have been told they must design its basic rules. The catch is: no individual can know where they may end up within this society. They may be wealthy, poor, black, white, male, female, talented, intelligent, etc. All they know about themselves is that they have a capacity to conceive of 'the good', to think rationally about ends, and possess certain basic physical needs. Rawls describes this as decision-making behind 'a veil of ignorance'. Rawls thinks rational contractors constrained like this would choose a society in which each person would have 'an equal right to the most extensive scheme of equal basic liberties compatible with a similar scheme of liberties for others' (1971: 60). He also thinks there would be a form of equality of outcome, as well as opportunity. This he refers to as the difference principle, where inequality is unjust except in so far as it is a necessary means to improving the position of the worst-off members of society. For the international realm, a second contracting session takes place between the representatives of peoples. The conclusion of this round is a contract that resembles the traditional rules of international society: self-determination, just war, mutual recognition, and non-intervention; in other words, rules of coexistence, not of justice. Cosmopolitan interpreters of Rawls reject this conclusion and the necessity of the second contracting session.

Box 12.8 Thomas Pogge on international order

'The affluent countries and their citizens continue to impose a global economic order under which millions avoidably die each year from poverty-related causes. We would regard it as a grave injustice, if such an economic order were imposed within a national society.'

(Pogge 2001b: 44)

between individuals rather than states. What ultimately matters is how poor or badly off someone is in the world, not just in their own country.

Thus, while Beitz and Moellendorf have some differences over the exact mechanisms for addressing inequalities, they none the less agree with Thomas Pogge's claim that the difference principle that 'the terms of international cooperation … should … be designed so that the social inequalities … tend to optimize the worst representative individual share' (Pogge 1989: 251) should apply globally. In practice, this comes down to a claim that the global original position might entail the redistribution of wealth to counter natural resources inequality and some compensation 'for the uneven distribution of natural resources or to rectify past injustices … and a portion of the global product actually attributable to global (as opposed to domestic) social cooperation should be redistributed' (Beitz 1979: 169).

Pogge's solution

Unlike Singer and Beitz, Thomas Pogge emphasizes the causal relationship between the wealth of the rich and the poverty of the poor. Pogge argues that the rules of the system and basic structure of international society

actively damage or disadvantage certain sectors of the economy, thus directly contradicting Rawlsian principles of justice. The rich have a duty to help the poor because the international order, which they largely created, is a major cause of world poverty. Indeed, Pogge argues that the rich countries are collectively responsible for about 18 million deaths from poverty annually.

Most importantly, Pogge argues that our negative duties not to harm others give rise to positive duties to aid them. Therefore we who gain most from the current order have an obligation to change the order and to change it in such a way that the most needy benefit. The structure of international trade and economic interdependence should ensure that, despite an unequal distribution of material resources worldwide, no one should be unable to meet their basic requirements, nor should they suffer disproportionately from the lack of material resources. Finally, pluralist objections do not cancel out this obligation: 'There is an injustice in the economic scheme, which it would be wrong for more affluent participants to perpetuate. And that is so quite independently of whether we and the starving are united by a communal bond' (Pogge 1994: 97).

Key Points

- There are two components of the just war tradition: *jus ad bellum* and *jus in bello*.
- Just war is different from holy war.
- The just war tradition contains elements of cosmopolitanism and communitarianism.
- Discussions of global justice are dominated by utilitarian and Rawlsian theories.
- It is not always agreed that inequality is itself a moral problem.
- Cosmopolitans argue that there is a responsibility of the rich to help the poor stemming from positive and negative duties.

Conclusion

This chapter outlined some of the main approaches to international ethics and some of the most important ethical issues that characterize globalization. Ethical issues confront all actors in the international realm and especially states that have a large capacity to aid or harm others. The biggest challenge facing states and other actors stems from the existence of moral pluralism and political anarchy in the international realm. These challenges make our decisions harder and our reasoning more complex, but they do not remove our obligations to outsiders. In the context of globalization, cosmopolitanism challenges realists and pluralists on two grounds. First, they ask: is it possible any longer to defend not acting to help others when we can without harming ourselves? Second, and more problematically, they ask: is it possible any longer to resist the duty to create a world in which unnecessary suffering is minimized and the equality of everyone is realized in political institutions? Most thinkers on international ethics therefore reject either a thoroughgoing realism or a strict pluralism. Instead, for most writers, given the scope of interdependence occurring under globalization, the question is not whether, but *how*, to be ethical in the international realm.

Cosmopolitanism, perhaps more so than ever before in human history, is present in both the words and deeds of many states, international institutions, and individuals, including the Universal Declaration of Human Rights (UDHR) and the International Criminal Court (ICC). A cosmopolitan commitment to prevent unnecessary harm is present in the Geneva Conventions and the treaties banning the use of anti-personnel landmines. The presence of a global civil society made of individuals and non-governmental organizations (NGOs), which calls states to account for their action or inaction on pressing issues such as global poverty (e.g. the 'Make Poverty History' campaign, led by Bob Geldof and Bono), is testament to the cosmopolitan idea of world citizenship. Many of these actors work in the belief that all humans ought to be treated equally. They invoke basic conceptions of what humans are due as humans, including basic rights to food, shelter, and freedom from unnecessary suffering.

While there are elements of cosmopolitanism present in the international order, most state practice and most people continue to give priority to their fellow nationals. State practice continues to favour insiders over outsiders, especially in relation to issues like global warming where core activities are put in question. The advent of the war on terror has exacerbated this tension in recent years. Fearing for their security, states have focused their attention on security issues to the detriment of human rights issues in particular. Likewise, the failure of the Doha round of World Trade Organization negotiations in July 2006 was evidence of the inability of states to address effectively the concerns of the poorest states and to cease harming them through maintaining unfair trade rules. While even basic ethical obligations remain unfulfilled for many people, the cosmopolitan ethics underpinning this agreement also raise the possibility of more advanced duties. While disagreement remains, there is none the less significant agreement about basic rights, freedom from poverty and starvation, and the idea that national boundaries should not prevent us from treating all others with respect.

Questions

1 What is the core idea of cosmopolitanism?
2 What are the ethical implications of globalization?
3 What are the main objections to cosmopolitanism?
4 How ethically significant should national borders be considered?
5 In what ways does globalization challenge communitarian ethics?
6 Are principles of justice universal?
7 Is there a responsibility for the rich countries to end global poverty?
8 Are positive or negative duties most helpful in addressing global and international ethical issues?
9 Does humanitarianism exhaust our international ethical obligations, or do we also have an obligation of justice to the world?
10 Can cosmopolitanism and anti-cosmopolitan positions find common ground on humanitarianism and harm?

Further Reading

Beitz, C. (1979), *Political Theory and International Relations* (Princeton, NJ: Princeton University Press). The first cosmopolitan reading of John Rawls's *Theory of Justice* (1971).

Dower, N. (1998), *World Ethics: The New Agenda* (Edinburgh: Edinburgh University Press). A useful overview of the ethical agenda under globalization.

Hashmi, S. H. (ed.), (2002), *Islamic Political Ethics*: *Civil Society, Pluralism, and Conflict* (Princeton, NJ: Princeton University Press). An insightful collection of essays exploring the domestic and international ethics of Islam.

Hayden, P. (2005), *Cosmopolitan Global Politics* (Aldershot: Ashgate). A systematic cosmopolitan treatment of the ethical and political issues surrounding globalization.

Miller, D. (2007), *National Responsibility and Global Justice* (Oxford: Oxford University Press). A systematic treatment of liberal nationalist anti-cosmopolitanism.

Moellendorf, D. (2002), *Cosmopolitan Justice* (Boulder, CO: Westview Press). A more recent application of a Rawlsian approach.

Nardin, T. and Mapel, D. (eds) (1992), *Traditions of International Ethics* (Cambridge: Cambridge University Press). The most comprehensive account of the ways in which people have thought about international ethics.

Pogge, T. (2002), *World Poverty and Human Rights: Cosmopolitan Responsibilities and Reforms* (Cambridge: Polity Press). Develops the most detailed and rigorous argument in favour of cosmopolitan principles of distributive justice based on negative obligations generated by rich countries' complicity in global poverty.

Rawls, J. (1999), *The Law of Peoples* (Cambridge, MA: Harvard University Press). Rawls's own contribution to international ethics develops something like an ethics of coexistence between 'reasonable peoples'.

Singer, P. (2002), *One World: The Ethics of Globalisation* (Melbourne: Text Publishing). The most important utilitarian argument in favour of positive duties to redistribute wealth from the rich to the poor. It also examines the ethics of global trade and global warming.

Shapcott, R. (2010), *International Ethics: A Critical Introductio* (Cambridge, Polity). A detailed examination of the differences between cosmopolitanism and its critics exploring their ramifications in the areas of migration, aid, war, and poverty.

Walzer, M. (2000), *Just and Unjust Wars: A Moral Argument with Historical Illustrations* (New York: Basic Books). A classic philosophical and historical study on the just war tradition and ethics of war more generally.

Online Resource Centre

 Visit the Online Resource Centre that accompanies this book to access more learning resources on this chapter topic at www.oxfordtextbooks.co.uk/orc/baylis5e/

Part Three

Structures and processes

In this part of the book we want to introduce you to the main underlying structures and processes in contemporary world politics. There will obviously be some overlap between this part and the next, since the division between structures and processes, and international issues is largely one of perspective. For us, the difference is that by structures and processes we mean relatively stable features of world politics that are more enduring and constant than are the issues dealt with in the next part. Again, we have two aims in this part: **first**, we want to provide a good overview of some of the most important structures and processes in world politics at the beginning of the twenty-first century. We have therefore chosen a series of ways of thinking about world politics that draw attention to these underlying features. Again, we realize that what

is a structure and what is a process is largely a matter of debate, but it may help to say that together these provide the setting in which the issues dealt with in the next part of the book will be played out. All the features examined in this part will be important for the resolution of the issues we deal with in the next part, since they comprise both the main structures of world politics that these issues have to face and the main processes that will determine their fate. Our **second** aim is that these structures and processes will help you to think about globalization by forcing you to ask again whether or not it is a qualitatively different form of world politics than hitherto. Does globalization require or represent an overthrow of the structures and processes that have been central in world politics to date?

ORC in the spotlight: case study

If you like to learn theory by application why not visit www.oxfordtextbooks.co.uk/orc/baylis5e/ where you will find extra case studies and weblinks to useful articles and organizations. These are a great way to supplement the case studies in the book.

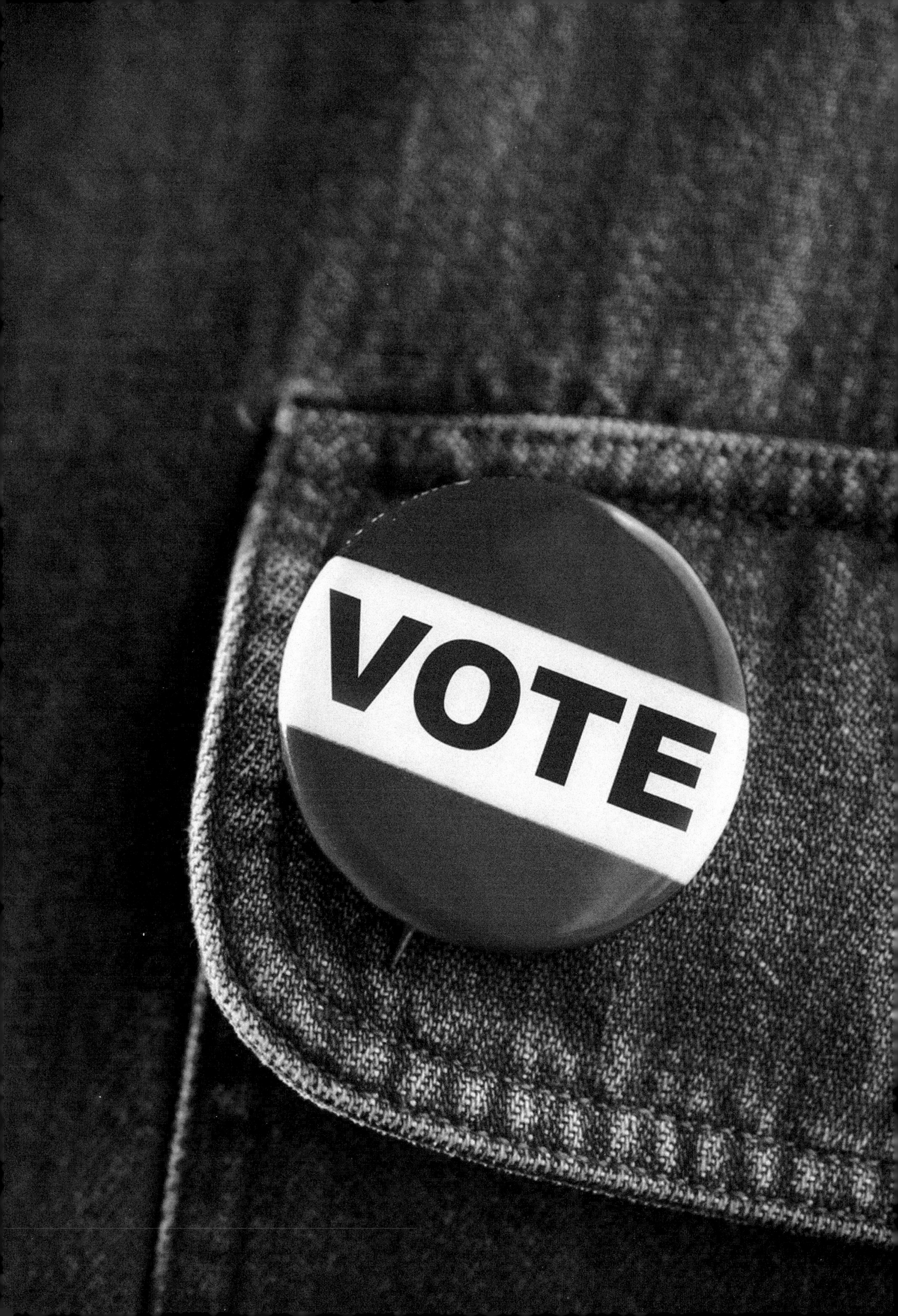
VOTE

Chapter 13

The changing character of war

MICHAEL SHEEHAN

Reader's Guide

War has been one of the key institutions of the practice of international relations, and has always been a central focus of the study of international relations. In the post-cold war period, many observers have suggested that the nature of war is undergoing fundamental changes, or even that in some parts of the world at least, it has become obsolete. With the advance of economic interdependence through globalization, and the spread of democracy, some groups of states seem to have formed security communities where war between them is no longer a possibility.

Elsewhere, however, war has continued to exist, and to take a number of different forms. For some countries such as the USA the use of advanced technology to achieve dramatic victories against conventional armies has led to suggestions that a **revolution in military affairs** is under way. Other parts of the world, however, have been characterized by warfare in which non-state actors have been prominent, the military technology employed has been relatively unsophisticated, and atrocities have been commonplace. Such 'new wars', it is argued by many, are a direct result of the process of globalization.

Introduction

The British strategic thinker Basil Liddell Hart once wrote that 'if you want peace, understand war', while the revolutionary Marxist Leon Trotsky declared confidently that 'you may not be interested in war, but war is interested in you'. This advice remains appropriate in the contemporary world. Around 14,400 wars have occurred throughout recorded history, claiming the lives of some 3.5 billion people. Since 1815 there have been between 224 and 559 wars, depending on the definition of war that is used (Mingst, 2004: 198). War has not disappeared as a form of social behaviour and shows no signs of doing so, though it is not necessarily an inevitable form of human behaviour. Since the end of the cold war, the annual number of wars, the number of battle deaths, and the number of war-related massacres have all declined sharply compared with the cold war period. Between 1989 and 1992 nearly one hundred wars came to an end, and in terms of battle deaths, the 1990s were the least violent decade since the end of the Second World War (*Human Security Report 2005*: 17). Despite the overall decline in the incidence of war, however, in many regions it is very much present and is displaying some novel features in comparison to those typical of the cold war period (see Ch. 4).

Box 13.1 The obsolescence of war

A striking feature of war in some parts of the contemporary world is its absence. The North Atlantic region has been described as a 'security community', a group of states for whom war has disappeared as a means of resolving mutual disputes, although they may continue to use war against opponents outside the security community. One common characteristic of these states is that they are democracies, and it has been suggested that while democracies will go to war, they are not prepared to fight against a fellow democracy. The assumption of this 'democratic peace' argument is that where groups of democracies inhabit a region, war will become extinct in that region, and that as democracy spreads throughout the world, war will decline. However, there is a danger that some wars will occur as democracies attempt to overthrow non-democratic regimes to spread the 'democratic zone of peace', so that wars will be fought in the name of peace. In addition, for some observers, even non-democracies will be averse to fighting wars when both they and their Great Power rivals are armed with nuclear weapons. John Mueller and Charles Mosko have both argued that while war as such will not disappear, a 'warless society' will exist, embracing the superpowers and major European powers in their relations with each other.

The utility of warfare

In the contemporary world, powerful pressures are producing changes to national economies and societies. Some of these can be seen to reflect the impact of **globalization**, others are the result of the broader effects of postmodernity, but their cumulative effect has been to bring about significant political and social changes, which have in turn been reflected in changed perceptions of the nature of threats coming from the external environment. This is turn has influenced beliefs regarding the utility of force as an instrument of policy, and the forms and functions of war. In the past two centuries, the 'modern' era of history, war has traditionally been seen as a brutal form of politics, a way in which **states** sought to resolve certain issues in international relations, and an outcome of their willingness to amass military power for defence and deterrence, and to project it in support of their foreign and defence policies. The two 'world wars' of the twentieth century typified this approach to the instrumentality of war. However, in the post-cold war period, the kinds of threats that have driven the accumulation of military power in the developed world have not taken the form of traditional state-to-state military rivalry, but have been a response to rather more amorphous and less predictable threats such as **terrorism** (see Ch. 22), insurgencies, and internal crises in other countries that seem to demand the projection of military force to resolve them.

The nineteenth-century strategist Carl von Clausewitz argued that the fundamental nature of war as the use of violence in pursuit of political goals is immutable. The nature of war refers to the constant, universal, and inherent qualities that ultimately shape war as a political instrument throughout the ages, such as violence, chance, and uncertainty. The forms of war relate to the impermanent, circumstantial, and adaptive features that war develops, and that account for the different periods of warfare throughout history, each displaying attributes determined by socio-political and historical preconditions, while also influencing those conditions. Clausewitz also distinguished between the *objective* and *subjective* nature of war, the former comprising the elements common to all wars, and the latter consisting of those features that make each war unique. The characteristics or *form* of war typical in any particular age might change, but the essential *nature* of war could not. For Clausewitz, the novel characteristics of war were not the result of new inventions, but of new ideas and social conditions. It would not be surprising, therefore, to see that the processes of postmodernity and **globalization** of an international system characterized by constant and even accelerating change should be marked by changes in the forms of warfare being waged in the system. Wars are a socially constructed form of large-scale human group behaviour, and must be understood within the wider contexts of their political and cultural environments.

In an era of unprecedented communications technologies, new fields of warfare have emerged. **Non-state actors** in the post-cold war period have moved to transform both cyberspace and the global media into crucial battlegrounds, alongside terrestrial military and terrorist operations, so that war is now fought on a number of different planes of reality simultaneously, and reality itself is subverted in the cause of war through sophisticated strategies of informational and electronic deception. The battlefield of the past has now become the **'battlespace'**, and it is three-dimensional in the sense of including air-power and the use of space satellites, and in some senses is non-dimensional, in that it also embraces cyberspace and communications wavebands (Box 13.2).

At the same time, the tangible capacity for war-making has also been developing.

Military technology, with enormous destructive capacity, is becoming available to more and more states. This is important not just because the technology to produce and deliver weapons of mass destruction is spreading, but also because highly advanced 'conventional' military technology is becoming more widely available.

Box 13.2 Cyberwarfare

As states become more dependent on complex information-gathering and weapons-targeting technologies and command systems, they become vulnerable to cyber warfare. Cyberspace is 'the total interconnectedness of human beings through computers and telecommunications'. Cyber warfare therefore relates to a state's ability to attack another state's computer and information networks in cyberspace and to protect its own capabilities from attacks by adversaries. This is critical in contemporary high-technology warfare, where the USA, for example, seeks to dominate the information domain so totally in wartime that it can conduct its military operations without effective opposition. Such attacks can be limited to purely military targets or can be directed against the adversary's economic and political system more generally. A large number of states such as India and Cuba are believed to be developing cyber warfare capabilities and several, including the USA, Russia, China, and the UK, have incorporated cyber warfare into their military doctrines.

One of the effects of the end of the cold war has been a massive process of disarmament by the former cold war enemies. This surplus weaponry flooded onto the global arms market, much of it highly advanced equipment being sold off comparatively cheaply.

Key Points

- 'War has been a central feature of human history.
- Since the end of the cold war, both the frequency and lethality of war have shown a sharp decline.
- War between the great powers in particular has become much more unlikely than in previous eras.
- Changes in the international system may be changing the character of war.

Definitions

In order to evaluate how war might be changing, it is first of all necessary to say what it is. Because war is a fluid concept, it has generated a large number of sometimes contradictory definitions. Some have seen it as any form of armed and organized physical conflict, while for Quincy Wright war was 'a violent contact of distinct but similar entities' (Freedman 1994: 69). General descriptions of this sort are not particularly helpful for understanding contemporary war, the first because it is insufficiently specific and could equally describe

gang warfare, the latter because it makes an unreasonable assumption about the nature of the combatants. Violent crime is an important aspect of global human insecurity, killing more people each year than war and terrorism combined, but it is not war. More useful is Clausewitz's statement that war is 'an act of force intended to compel our opponents to fulfil our will', and 'a continuation of political intercourse with a mixture of other means'. In Clausewitz's work, the meaning is clarified in the context by the assumption that the reader understands that he is talking about large-scale military confrontations between the representatives of states. Webster's Dictionary reinforces this position by defining war as 'a state of usually open and declared armed hostile conflict between states or nations'. Unfortunately, in the current era, that is not something that can simply be assumed, because non-state groups have become prominent actors in contemporary warfare. A more useful definition in this sense is Hedley Bull's, that it is 'organised violence carried on by political units against each other' (Bull 1977: 184). Bull goes on to insist that violence is not war unless it is both carried out by a political unit, and directed against another political unit.

It is possible to argue that war is simply any form of armed violence between groups of people, but it is valid to ask what sorts of goals are involved and how much violence is required for an armed clash to be called a 'war'. Is a clash between two street gangs in which several people are killed really the same phenomenon as a military conflict between two or more states in which millions are deliberately killed? However, choosing a particular threshold can also seem arbitrary, as with the influential Singer and Small definition, which requires a war to involve at least 1,000 battle deaths per year. By this token, the 1982 Falklands/Malvinas War between Argentina and the UK would barely qualify, although few would argue that that conflict was not a war. Some sense of scale is clearly needed, but perhaps Quincy Wright's less specific formulation is still reasonable, that war is 'a conflict among political groups, especially sovereign states, carried on by armed forces of considerable magnitude, for a considerable period of time' (Wright 1968: 453).

Key Points

- War in the contemporary era is not always easy to define.
- War is a brutal form of politics.

The nature of war

If, as some have argued, war has indeed taken on new forms in the post-cold war era, or perhaps has even seen an evolution in its essential nature, then it is necessary to compare these recent examples with traditional forms and interpretations of war in order to determine what, if anything, has changed, and what are simply contemporary manifestations of an ancient phenomenon. This is not as straightforward an exercise as it might at first appear. War is a form of organized human violence, and when conducted by states using significant quantities of personnel, materiel and firepower, it is comparatively easy to recognize. But at the lower end of the spectrum of violence it begins to overlap with other forms of conflict such as **terrorism**, insurgency, and criminal violence, and clear distinctions and definitions become harder to maintain (see Ch. 22). War always involves violence, but not all violence can be described as war. Violence is a necessary, but not a sufficient, requirement for a conflict to be defined as a war.

Wars are fought for reasons. The Western understanding of war, following Clausewitz, sees it as instrumental, a means to an end. Wars in this perspective are not random violence; they reflect a conscious decision to engage in them for a rational political purpose.

Box 13.3 Thucydides on war

In some ways wars have changed little over the ages. As long as 2,500 years ago the Greek historian Thucydides observed:

'That war is an evil is something we all know, and it would be pointless to go on cataloguing all the disadvantages involved in it. No one is forced into war by ignorance, nor, if he thinks he will gain by it, is he kept out of it by fear. The fact is that one side thinks that the profits to be won outweigh the risks to be incurred, and the other side is ready to face danger rather than accept an immediate loss.'

(Thucydides, History of the Peloponnesian War, Book IV)

War and society

War is a form of social and political behaviour. This was one of the central arguments of Clausewitz. It remains true at the start of the twenty-first century, but only if we operate with a broad and flexible understanding of what constitutes politics. As our understanding of politics, and the forms it can take, has evolved in the postmodern era, we should expect the same to be true of the character of war, since that is itself a form of politics.

The political nature of war has been evolving in recent decades under the impact of globalization, which has increasingly eroded the economic, political, and cultural autonomy of the state. Contemporary warfare takes place in a local context, but it is also played out in wider fields and influenced by **non-governmental organizations, intergovernmental organizations** (see Ch. 20), regional and global media, and users of the Internet. In many ways, contemporary wars are partly fought on television, and the media therefore have a powerful role in providing a framework of understanding for the viewers of the conflict.

War is an extremely paradoxical activity. Human beings are simultaneously the most violent and the most cooperative species that has inhabited the earth. In one sense war is very clearly 'made up of acts of enmity rather than co-operation, of imposition rather than negotiation, of summary killing rather than due process, of destruction rather than creation' (Francis 2004: 42). Yet in another sense, war is clearly a profoundly social activity, an example of humanity's 'enormous capacity for friendly co-operation' (Bigelow 1969: 3). Michel Foucault called the institution of war 'the military dimension of society' (Foucault 1996: 415). This is because the conduct of war requires a society to cooperate in performing complex tasks on a large scale. Societies can fight wars because they are able to cooperate at the internal level. On the other hand, they feel themselves compelled to fight other societies because they often find it difficult to cooperate at the external level. The very act of fighting outsiders may make it easier to cooperate internally. Unless a war is highly unpopular domestically, there is a sense in which a state at war is also a state at peace.

War is both a highly organized and a highly *organizing* phenomenon. In the words of the sociologist Charles Tilly, 'war made the state, and the state made war'. The machinery of the state derived historically from the organizational demands of warfare, and modern states owe their origins and development to a large degree to the effects of earlier wars. The modern state was born during the Renaissance, a time of unprecedented violence. The intensity of armed conflict during this period triggered an early **revolution in military affairs**, in which the size of armies, their associated firepower, and the costs of warfare all increased dramatically. The need to survive in such a competitive and violent era favoured larger, more centralized political units that were able to control extensive tracts of territory, master complex military technologies, and mobilize the immense human resources required for success in battle.

Modernity and warfare

The high point of this evolution was the Thirty Years War, which racked Europe from 1618 to 1648 (see Ch. 2). By the end of that conflict Europe was entering a new phase of historical development, **modernity**, which would come to dominate international history for the next three hundred years before giving way to **post-modernity** in the late twentieth century. Modernity had many features and, as Clausewitz noted, each age has its own dominant characteristic form of war, which reflects the era in which it occurs, although there will also be other forms reflecting cultural and geographical realities. There was therefore a form of warfare that was typical of modernity.

The period of modernity was characterized by the rise of nationalism and increasingly centralized and bureaucratic states with rapidly rising populations, by the scientific and industrial revolutions, and by the growth of secular ideologies with messianic visions and an intolerance of opposing **metanarratives**, broad overarching ideologies such as **Marxism.** The warfare that was characteristic of the period reflected the forces of modernity, and its enormous transformational effects. States mobilized mass armies through centralized bureaucracies and the power of nationalism. They armed and equipped them with the products of industrialization and expected their populations to sacrifice themselves for the state, and to show no mercy to the opposing population that was being called upon to make the same self-sacrifice for its own motherland. The result was industrialized warfare on a massive scale, in which civilian populations as much as enemy soldiers were seen as legitimate targets, a process that culminated in the nuclear attacks on Japan in 1945.

At the same time, another feature of warfare during the modern period was that, at least in the conflicts between the developed states, it was governed by **rules.** An entire body of **international law** was developed to constrain and regulate the use of violence in wartime (see Ch. 17). Quincy Wright argues that war always involves a legal relationship, which distinguishes it from mere fighting, even organized fighting. It is 'a condition of time in which special rules permitting and regulating violence between governments prevails' (Wright 1965: 2). This is an important feature distinguishing war from other forms of violence. It is a particular *kind* of relationship between politically motivated groups.

War and change

The intensity of war often unleashes or accelerates numerous forces for change, transforming industry, society, and government in ways that are fundamental and permanent. By weakening or destroying traditional structures, or by compelling internal reforms, war may create conditions conducive to social change and political modernization. The requirement to defeat the opponent's forces may lead to advances in technologies such as transportation, food manufacture and storage, communications, and so on that have applications well beyond the military sphere. It was in this sense that for the ancient Greek thinker Heraclitus, war was 'the father of all and the king of all'.

Historically, during the period of modernity, the conduct of war compelled governments to centralize power in order to mobilize the resources necessary for victory. Bureaucracies and tax burdens increased in size

to support the war effort. But the strains involved in preparing for and engaging in war can also lead to the weakening or disintegration of the state.

Nevertheless, war, in terms of both preparation and actual conduct, may be a powerful catalyst for change, but technological or even political modernization does not necessarily imply moral progress. Evolution in war, including its contemporary forms, may involve change that is morally problematic, as indeed is the case with the forces of globalization more generally (see Ch. 12). War is a profound agent of historical change, but it is not the fundamental driving force of history.

Key Points

- Contemporary warfare is being influenced by globalization.
- War requires highly organized societies.
- War can be a powerful catalyst for change.
- The nature of war remains constant, but its form reflects the particular era and environment in which it occurs.

The revolution in military affairs

Although many observers have suggested that the character of war is changing significantly, their reasons for coming to this conclusion are often quite different. One school of thought focuses on the so-called **revolution in military affairs** (RMA). The concept of the revolution in military affairs became popular after the dramatic American victory in the 1991 Gulf War. The manner in which superior technology and doctrine appeared to give the USA an almost effortless victory suggested that future conflicts would be decided by the possession of technological advantages such as advanced guided weapons and space satellites. However, the subsequent popularity of the RMA concept has not produced a clear consensus on what exactly the RMA is, or what its implications might be. Although analysts agree that the RMA involves a radical change or some form of discontinuity in the history of warfare, there is disagreement regarding how and when these changes or discontinuities take place, or what causes them.

The former US Secretary of Defense, William Cohen, defined an RMA as 'when a nation's military seizes an opportunity to transform its strategy, military doctrine,

training, education, organization, equipment, operations and tactics to achieve decisive military results in fundamentally new ways' (Gray 2002: 1).

RMA proponents argue that recent breakthroughs and likely future advances in military technology mean that military operations will be conducted with such speed, precision, and selective destruction that the whole character of war will change and this will profoundly affect the way that military/political affairs are conducted in the next few decades. Most of the RMA literature focuses on the implications of developments in technology. In the conflicts in Kuwait (1991), Serbia (1999), and Iraq (2003), American technology proved vastly superior to that of its opponent. In particular, computing and space technology allowed the US forces to acquire information about the enemy to a degree never before seen in warfare, and allowed precision targeting of weapon systems. Advanced communications allowed generals to exercise detailed and instant control over the developing battle and to respond quickly to developments. The speed, power, and accuracy of the weapons employed enabled them to be carefully targeted so as to destroy vital objectives without inflicting unnecessary casualties on civilian populations. Opponents lacking counters to these technologies found themselves helpless in the face of overwhelming American superiority. It was historically significant that at the outset of the American invasion of Iraq in 2003, the Iraqi forces initiated anti-satellite warfare by attempting to jam the US military satellite signals. Such attacks will be a feature of future inter-state wars, where the information systems and processes of the opponent's armed forces will become crucial targets. However, the RMA emphasis on military technology and tactics, while understandable, risks producing an over-simplistic picture of what is an extremely complex phenomenon, in which non-technological factors can play a crucial part in the outcome.

Military responses to the RMA

In addition, most of the literature and debate on the RMA has been American and has tended to take for granted the dominance conferred by technological superiority. The current RMA is based upon a particularly Western concept of war fighting and may well be of utility only in certain well-defined situations. There has been far less discussion of how the opponents of a technologically advanced state might use unconventional or asymmetric responses to fight effectively against a more technologically sophisticated opponent (see Box 13.4). Asymmetric conflicts since 1990 have been fought by US-led 'coalitions of the willing' against Iraq (1991 and 2003), Yugoslavia, and Afghanistan. Because of the extreme superiority in combat power of the coalition, the battle phases of these asymmetric conflicts have been fairly brief and have produced relatively few combat deaths compared to the cold war period. However, in the post-conventional insurgency phases in Iraq and Afghanistan, the asymmetry has produced guerrilla-style conflict against the technological superiority of the coalition forces. This is a significant dimension of contemporary asymmetric warfare. Techniques such as guerrilla warfare and terrorism, which in earlier historical periods were employed as minor elements of a larger conventional strategy, are now being used as strategies in their own right.

A skilful opponent will always seek to capitalize on its own strengths while minimizing those of the enemy. In any war the outcome will be largely determined by the relative power of the combatants, which will influence

> **Box 13.4** Asymmetric warfare
>
> Asymmetric warfare exists 'when two combatants are so different in their characters, and in their areas of comparative strategic advantage, that a confrontation between them comes to turn on one side's ability to force the other side to fight on their own terms ... The strategies that the weak have consistently adopted against the strong often involve targeting the enemy's domestic political base as much as his forward military capabilities. Essentially such strategies involve inflicting pain over time without suffering unbearable retaliation in return'.
>
> (L. Freedman, 'Britain and the Revolution in Military Affairs', *Defense Analysis*, 14 (1998): 58)

the methods they use to fight the war. Some combatants may not even be trying to defeat the enemy armed forces as such, but simply to manipulate violence in order to demoralize the opponent and lead them to make concessions. RMA authors also tend to work within a Westphalian state-centric model that overemphasizes the traditional state-to-state confrontation, and may not be particularly relevant in the intra-state insurgency warfare that has been prevalent since 1991.

The conflict in Iraq from 2003 onwards (see Case Study) raised major questions about the pattern of warfare likely after the RMA. Who are the most likely future opponents of states capable of adopting the RMA technologies? Does the RMA influence all forms of war or simply large-scale, conventional inter-state war? What about urban warfare or nuclear weapons? What is the likely response of opponents such as terrorists, insurgents, and armed forces unable to acquire RMA technology themselves?

Technology and the RMA

The danger in the emphasis on technological aspects that is central to the RMA literature is that it can lead to an underestimation of the political and social dimensions of war. The outcomes of wars are influenced by a wide range of factors in addition to technology, and in most parts of the contemporary world, the current and potential wars are not being influenced by the RMA technology, which is possessed by only a handful of states. However, some conflicts are being influenced by elements of the RMA, such as specific technologies. The conventional fighting between India and Pakistan in the late 1990s involved highly advanced weapon systems and the use by India of satellite technology.

Case Study The Iraq War, 2003–10

On 20 March 2003, US-led coalition forces invaded Iraq with the proclaimed objective of locating and disarming suspected Iraqi weapons of mass destruction. The coalition forces conducted a swift and overwhelmingly successful campaign, leading to the capture of Baghdad and the collapse and surrender of the Iraqi armed forces. President George W. Bush proclaimed the official end of major combat operations on 2 May 2003. While casualties during this conventional phase of fighting were historically low for a major modern war, the fighting quickly evolved into an insurgency in which guerrilla and terrorist attacks on the coalition forces and Iraqi civilian population were the norm. By the end of 2009 the coalition forces had suffered nearly 4,700 deaths and 32,000 wounded. More than 9,000 Iraqi soldiers and police were killed in the same period along with some 55,000 insurgents. Estimates of Iraqi civilian deaths are disputed, and range from 100,000 to 600,000. By July 2009 all the original coalition allies had withdrawn their forces in the face of an apparently endless insurgency, leaving only US forces to continue operations.

The Iraq War illustrates a number of the themes that have been prominent in discussions of the possible future development of war. The rapid coalition victory saw the Iraqi armed forces shattered by the technological superiority of the advanced weapons and information systems of the US forces, suggesting that a revolution in military affairs was under way.

The doctrine employed by the American forces was also vital. The allied success was the result not just of technological supe-riority, but also of a superior manoeuvre-oriented operational doctrine. The swift and comparatively bloodless victory for the American-led forces reinforced the view that in the post-cold war strategic environment, there were few inhibitions on the use of force by the USA. With the trauma of Vietnam apparently laid to rest, war had become swift, decisive, and affordable for the USA, and the end of the cold war removed the threat of regional conflict escalating into a nuclear war with another superpower.

A central feature of the conflict was the American dominance of information warfare, both in the military sense of the ability to use satellite and other systems for reconnaissance, communications, and weapons targeting, and in the postmodern sense of the manipulation of the civilian communications and global media images of the war to produce an international understanding of the fighting that reflected what the US administration wished the watching world to perceive.

However, the conflict did not end with the surrender of the regular Iraqi forces, confirming, in turn, some of the arguments of the proponents of the 'postmodern' and 'new war' theses. The ability to operate using complex informal military networks allowed the insurgents to conduct effective asymmetric warfare, despite the overwhelming superiority of the US military technology. In addition, the insurgents were able to use the global media to manipulate perceptions of the character and implications of the strategy terrorism and destabilization. The techniques used by the insurgents were brutal, ruthless and targeted against the civilian population, in a campaign supported by outside forces and finance, and sustained by an overtly identity-based campaign, again reflecting features of the 'postmodern' and 'new wars' conceptions.

Discussion questions

1 Which tells us more about the future of war—the rapid allied conventional victory, or the long insurgency that followed?

2 What can we learn from the Iraq insurgency about the nature and utility of 'asymmetric' warfare?

3 The 1991 US–Iraq war laid to rest America's 'Vietnam syndrome'. Has the 2003 war brought it back?

While some authors have questioned the existence of a true RMA (see Box 13.5), there are arguments for seeing it as an inevitable outcome of the era of globalization and postmodernity. Alvin and Heidi Toffler (1993) argue that the way a society makes war reflects the way it makes wealth. Starting with the very invention of agriculture, every revolution in the system for creating wealth triggered a corresponding revolution in the system for making war. Therefore, to the extent that a new 'information economy' is emerging, this will bring with it a parallel revolution in warfare. In the 'information age', information is the central resource for wealth production and power, and the RMA is the inevitable outgrowth of basic changes in the form of economic production (see Ch. 15).

A major part of the appeal of the RMA concept in Western societies is that it suggests the possibility of using so-called smart weapons to achieve quick, clean victory in war. The RMA technologies allow the battlefield to be controlled in a way that was not possible in previous eras, so that the tempo of battle can be orchestrated and wars won without massive loss of life. To the extent that such an RMA is occurring, for the foreseeable future it is very much an American-led RMA, and reflects

Box 13.5 The revolution in military affairs: a cautionary note

Benjamin Lambeth warns that '"a revolution in military affairs" cannot be spawned merely by platforms, munitions, information systems and hardware equities. These necessary but insufficient preconditions must be supported by an important set of intangibles that have determined war results since the days of Alexander the Great—namely, clarity of goals backed by proficiency and boldness in execution. In the so-called "RMA debate", too much attention has been devoted to technological magic at the expense of the organisational, conceptual and other human imputs needed to convert the magic from lifeless hardware into combat outcomes.'

(B. S. Lambeth, 'The Technology Revolution in Air warfare', Survival, 39 (1997): 75)

strength of the USA to minimize casualties. Yet the reality of war is that it is never clean or bloodless. In conflicts such as the 1991 Iraq War and the 1999 Kosovo War, 'smart' weapons often proved inaccurate or were delivered against the wrong targets. Even in the age of computer-guided weapons and space technology, war remains a brutal and bloody undertaking, where political objectives are achieved through the deliberate infliction of human suffering on a major scale.

Key Points

- Dramatic technological advances mean that a revolution in military affairs may be under way.
- Few states currently possess such technology.
- The 'information age' is increasingly reflected in 'information warfare'.
- Opponents with little or no access to RMA technology are likely to use 'asymmetric warfare' to fight the war on their own terms.

American understandings of how and why military affairs are conducted. The American approach has been to attempt to win wars quickly by applying overwhelming force, and to use the industrial and technological

Postmodern war

Global society is moving from the modern to the postmodern age. This is a process that has been under way for several decades and is the result of a wide range of economic, cultural, social, and political changes that are altering the meaning of the '**state**' and the '**nation**'. As this happens, it will affect the character of war. In some parts of the world the state is deliberately transferring functions, including military functions, to private authorities and businesses. In other areas, these functions are being seized from the state by other political actors. At the same time, globalization has weakened the 'national' forms of identity that have dominated international relations in the past two centuries, and reinvigorated earlier forms of political identity and organization, such as religious, ethnic, and clan loyalties.

The greatly increased role of the media is one feature of this evolution. The media have become far more important in terms of shaping or even constructing understandings of particular wars. Media warfare has made war more transparent. Each side now goes to great lengths to manipulate media images of the conflict, and journalists have effectively been transformed from observers into active participants, facing most of the same dangers as the soldiers and helping to shape the course of the war through their reporting. Just as 'modernity' and its wars

were based on the mode of production, so 'postmodernity' and its wars reflect the mode of information.

Another postmodern development has been the increasing 'outsourcing' of war. Over the past decade, more and more states have contracted out key military services to private corporations. Privatized military companies (PMCs) sell a wide range of war-related services to states. Hundreds of PMCs have operated in more than fifty countries since the end of the cold war. The growth of PMCs reflects a broader global trend towards the privatization of public assets. Through the provision of training and equipment, PMCs have influenced the outcomes of several recent wars, including those in Angola, Croatia, Ethiopia, and Sierra Leone. PMCs played a significant role in the 2003 US-led invasion of Iraq.

The twentieth century saw the advent of **total war**, which involved the complete mobilization of the human, economic, and military resources of the state in the pursuit of victory, and which recognized few if any moral restraints in terms of who could be targeted if their destruction would bring victory closer. The effects of the Industrial Revolution, along with the advent of popular democracy and modern bureaucracy, had combined to 'nationalize' war to involve the whole of society. Raymond Aron called this **hyperbolic war**, where the growing scale and intensity of war are driven by the pressure of industrial and technological advances.

However, it is noticeable that while the Second World War ended with a nuclear strike against Japan, nuclear weapons have never been used in a subsequent conflict. Nina Tannenwald argues that 'a powerful **nuclear taboo** against the use of nuclear weapons has developed in the global system' (2007: 2). This is a significant development. Because of their long ranges and widespread effects, the nuclear arsenals of the major powers are examples of **military globalization**, and this has been reflected in nuclear proliferation (see Ch. 23). Yet, paradoxically, these most powerful of weapons to date have delivered no value to their possessors as instruments of warfare, as distinct from their deterrent role. This in turn has emphasized the utility of both conventional and unconventional warfighting capabilities.

The brutality and ethnic cleansing characteristic of many contemporary wars are not only not historically novel, but are in many ways a variant of the same totalizing mentality that dominated Western war fighting during the era of modernity. In modern Western inter-state war, as Foucault noted, wars 'are waged on behalf of the existence of everyone; entire populations are mobilied for the purpose of wholesale slaughter in the name of life necessity; massacres have become vital' (Foucault 1990: 137). Martin Shaw uses the term 'degenerate wars' to capture the continuity of contemporary wars with the genocidal total wars of the twentieth century.

New wars

Mary Kaldor has suggested that a category of 'new wars' has emerged since the mid-1980s. The driving force behind these new wars is globalization (see Box 13.6), 'a contradictory process involving both integration and fragmentation, homogenisation and diversification, globalisation and localisation' (Kaldor 1999: 3). These conflicts are typically based around the disintegration of states and subsequent struggles for control of the state by opposing groups, which are simultaneously attempting to impose their own definition of the national identity of the state and its population. Just as earlier wars were linked to the emergence and creation of states, the 'new wars' are related to the disintegration and collapse of states, and much of the pressure on such states has come from the effects of globalization on the international system. In the past decade, 95 per cent of armed conflicts have taken place within states, rather than between them.

The 'new wars' occur in situations where the economy of the state is performing extremely poorly, or even collapsing, so that the tax revenues and power of the state decline dramatically, producing an increase in corruption and criminality. As the state loses control, access to weapons and the ability to resort to violence are increasingly privatized, and paramilitary groups proliferate, organized crime grows, and political legitimacy collapses. One of the effects of these developments is that the traditional distinction between the 'soldier' and the 'civilian' becomes blurred or disappears altogether. At the same time, however, the 'new wars' are often characterized not by conventional conflict between opposing soldiers, but rather by the use of violence by an army against an unarmed civilian population, either to 'ethnically cleanse' an area, or to extort economic and sexual resources.

For Kaldor, a significant feature of these conflicts is the combatants focus on questions of **identity**, which she sees as being a result of the pressures produced by globalization. In the postmodern world there has been a breakdown of traditional cleavages based on class and ideology, and a greater emphasis on identity and culture

Box 13.6 Globalization and war

'The impact of globalisation is visible in many of the new wars. The global presence in these wars can include international reporters, mercenary troops and military advisers, diaspora volunteers as well as a veritable "army" of international agencies ranging from non-governmental organisations (NGO's) like Oxfam, Save the Children, Médecin sans Frontières, Human Rights Watch and the International Red Cross, to international institutions like the United Nations High Commissioner for Refugees (UNHCR), the European Union (EU), the United Nations Children's Fund (UNICEF), the Organisation for Security and Cooperation in Europe (OSCE), the Organisation for African Unity (OAU) and the United Nations itself, including peacekeeping troops.'

(M. Kaldor, New and Old Wars: Organised Violence in a Global Era (Cambridge: Polity, 1999): 4)

(see Ch. 25). To the extent that war is a continuation of politics, therefore, war has become increasingly driven by questions of culture and identity.

The relationship between identity and war is also shifting in terms of the gender and age of the combatants. The 'feminization' of war has grown as women have come to play increasingly visible and important roles, from auxiliaries in the late modern period, to direct front-line roles in the postmodern period, from uniformed military personnel to female suicide bombers. But war has been 'feminized' in a darker sense also. The majority of the violence of the 'new wars' is directed against women. The genocide in Rwanda in 1994 also saw more than a quarter of a million rapes (Munkler 2005: 20). Children have also become more visible as participants, rather than non-combatants, in war. In the civil war in Sierra Leone, nearly 70 per cent of the combatants were under the age of eighteen. Children fight in around three-quarters of today's armed conflicts, and may make up 10 per cent of armed combatants (Brocklehurst 2007: 373). Nearly one-third of the militaries that use child soldiers include girls in their ranks. The use of child soldiers is made easier by the fact that the 'new wars' are dominated by the use of light weapons, small enough to be used by youths and children.

Post-Westphalian warfare

Mark Duffield (1998) argues that the non-state dimension of much contemporary warfare is striking, and that describing such conflicts as 'internal' or 'intra-state' is misleading, since the combatants often are not attempting to impose a political authority in the traditional sense. Sub-state threats do not trigger the full mobilization of the states military and other resources in the way that an inter-state threat would. Because they often blur political and military threats, they are more difficult to counter within the traditional state-to-state strategic approach.

The assumption that 'war' is something that takes place between states is based on an acceptance of the 'Westphalian' **state system** as the **norm**. War was an armed conflict between opposing states, fought by uniformed, organized bodies of men. They were regulated by formal acts including declarations of war, laws of neutrality, and peace treaties. As the state system evolves in response to postmodernity and globalization, typical forms of warfare can be expected to evolve also. Thus it is not surprising that commentators should speak of '**post-Westphalian war**'. The sub-state features of many wars are prominent, as they are increasingly fought by militias, paramilitaries, warlord armies, criminal gangs, private security firms, and tribal groupings, so that the Westphalian state's monopoly of violence is increasingly challenged from both outside and inside. This has been notable in conflicts such as those in the Democratic Republic of Congo, Sudan and Bosnia. 'Paramilitaries' include armed police, border guards, internal security forces, riot squads, militias, and privatized armies. They are usually more heavily armed than police forces, but less well equipped than regular soldiers. Because of this, they can be quickly raised, equipped, and trained, making them particularly prominent in recent conflicts.

These complex interrelationships of non-traditional actors are not limited to insurgents or criminal gangs. Because of the prevalence of **humanitarian intervention** and the belief that economic **development** acts as a deterrent to war, aid organizations, UN agencies, armed forces, and private security firms are increasingly networked in areas such as the Balkans, Africa, and the Middle East (see Ch. 31). The causes of internal conflict are often related to poverty and underdevelopment, so that issues of **poverty**, stability, development, and peace have been increasingly seen as linked in an overall pattern of insecurity (see Ch. 28). This has meant a greater willingness by developed states to see war as in many ways an issue of underdevelopment and political insecurity, and the presence of such social and economic insecurity as being in itself a justification for wars of intervention, or what Ulrich Beck has called the 'new military humanism' (Chomsky 1999: 4).

Many of the features of the 'new wars' are not new in the sense that they have been common in earlier periods of history—ethnic and religious wars, for example, or conflicts conducted with great brutality. Looting and plunder have been a feature of most wars in history. Low-intensity conflicts have in fact been the most common form of armed conflict since the late 1950s. However, it can be argued that the initiators of the 'new wars' have been empowered by the new conditions produced by globalization that have weakened states and created parallel economies and privatized protection. Such conflicts will typically occur in **failed states**, countries where the government has lost control of significant parts of the national territory and lacks the resources to re-impose control. Steven Metz has termed the countries falling

Box 13.7 'Third-tier' states

Steven Metz groups the world's states into three 'tiers' for the purpose of predicting likely forms of conflict. Those of the first tier are the states that have effective functioning economies and political systems, and exhibit high degrees of internal stability and external law-abiding behaviour. The democracies of the North Atlantic region are typical of this group. Second-tier states exhibit periodic instability, and may have areas within their territory where the government does not exercise internal **sovereignty**. However, the state is not in danger of collapse. Third-tier states are marked by crisis. There are considerable areas where the central government has lost control and non-governmental armed forces are operating. In such areas the 'warlords' or other groupings neither exercise full control over the areas they dominate,

nor contribute to the stability of the country as a whole, which is therefore essentially ungovernable. War in such areas will typically 'involve substate groups fighting for the personal glory of the leader, or wealth, resources, land, ethnic security or even revenge for real or perceived past injustices'. Such conflicts may involve groups representing different ethnic or communal groupings and 'the fighting will usually be undertaken with low-technology weapons but fought with such intensity that the casualty rates may be higher than in conventional warfare, especially among civilians caught up in the fighting'.

(Craig Snyder and J. Johan Malik, 'Developments in Modern Warfare', in Craig Snyder (ed.), Contemporary Security and Strategy (London: Macmillan, 1999): 204)

into this category as the **'third tier'** states of the global political system (Box 13.7).

This weakness of the state makes a significant difference in the economic support for the 'new wars' compared to their 'modern' predecessors. The 'new war' economies are decentralized, and highly reliant on external assets. Participation in the war by the general population is usually low. Unemployment is generally high, providing a source of recruits seeking an income. The fighting units therefore finance themselves through plunder and the black market, or through external assistance, not through state taxation as in the 'old' wars. Criminal activities such as hostage-taking, trafficking of weapons, drugs, and people, and money laundering are also used to support the war effort. This merging of a regional war zone with international criminal networks produces what Herfried Munkler calls 'an **open war economy**' sustained by the forces of globalization (2005: 96). Where foreign aid is reaching the conflict zone, theft or extortion of the aid will also fund the fighting. Globalization also means that the combatants do not produce their own weaponry, as

was typical in 'modern' war, but acquire it directly or indirectly through intermediaries on the global arms market, or through the disintegration of the state structures, as in Moldova and Chechnya.

For some observers, the economic rationale, rather than politics, is what drives the 'new wars', so that war has become a continuation of economics by other means. It is the pursuit of personal wealth, rather than political power, that is the motivation of the combatants. In some conflicts, therefore, war has become the end rather than the means.

Key Points

- 'New wars', following state collapse, are often conflicts over identity as much as over territory.
- The 'new wars' in fact follow a pattern of warfare that has been typical since the late 1950s.
- Such conflicts typically occur in countries where development is lacking and there is significant economic insecurity.

Conclusions

The end of the cold war has not significantly altered the dominant patterns of war that have been in place for the past fifty years. The 'new' forms of conflict are for the most part not new as such, but have received more Western attention since the end of the cold war. While they are often characterized by great brutality, the absence of heavy weaponry and superpower support means that casualty

levels are markedly lower than during the cold war. RMA technologies have dramatic potential, but have so far had little impact outside US operations. While war is less common and less deadly than in the 1945–92 period, it remains a brutal and inhumane form of politics. The forms of warfare that are most prevalent currently are directly linked to the globalized international economy.

Questions

1 To what extent is globalization a cause of war?
2 In what ways are wars examples of cooperative behaviour?
3 Why do some authors believe that war between the current great powers is highly unlikely?
4 What is the distinction between the *nature* and the *character* (or form) of war?
5 To what extent is a 'revolution in military affairs' taking place?
6 What is 'asymmetric warfare'?
7 How important is gender in understanding war?
8 What do you understand by the term, the 'new wars'?
9 What is the relationship between children and contemporary war?
10 Has war become more brutal since the end of the cold war?

Further Reading

Biddle, S., *Military Power: Explaining Victory and Defeat in Modern Battle* (Princeton, NJ: Princeton University Press, 2004). An interesting and stimulating study of warfare since 1900, analysing the techniques and technologies that have aided the offence and defence to achieve victory in modern wars.

Blank, S. J., 'Preparing for the Next War: Reflections on the Revolution in Military Affairs', *Strategic Review*, 24 (1996): 17–25. An analysis of the post-1990 revolution in military affairs, which argues cogently that in order to benefit from the technological advantages of the RMA, states must embrace necessary organizational and doctrinal changes.

Brocklehurst, H., *Who's Afraid of Children? Children, Conflict and International Relations* (Aldershot: Ashgate, 2006). A ground-breaking study of the place of children in modern warfare, exploring their roles as warriors, as victims and as witnesses. The book raises searching questions about the meaning of 'childhood' and 'child' in the light of contemporary conflict.

Cohen, E. A., 'Change and Transformation in Military Affairs', *The Journal of Strategic Studies*, 27 (3) (2004): 395–407. An engaging article in which the author argues that the changes in the structures of military forces and the nature of battle mean that there has been a fundamental change in the character of war in the past two decades.

Coker, C., *Humane Warfare* (London: Routledge, 2001). A challenging book that argues that the horrors of twentieth-century warfare have led Western democracies to seek to fight 'humane wars', characterized by minimal military and civilian casualties on both sides.

Duyvestyn, I., and Angstrom, J. (eds), *Rethinking the Nature of War* (London: Frank Cass, 2005). A collection of excellent essays debating the changing character of war in the post-cold-war era.

Gray, C. S., *Strategy for Chaos: Revolutions in military affairs and the evidence of history* (London: Frank Cass, 2002). A very good introduction to the RMA debates with useful historical case studies of earlier RMAs.

Ignatieff, M., *The Warrior's Honor: Ethnic War and the Modern Conscience* (New York: Henry Holt, 1997). An examination of the motivations of 'moral interventionists', such as aid workers, journalists, and peacekeepers, and those of the ethnic warriors with whom they engage in postmodern war zones.

Kaldor, M., *New and Old Wars: Organised Violence in a Global Era* (Cambridge: Polity, 1999). A controversial study of the 'new wars', focusing on the 'identity' dimension of the conflicts. Usefully read in tandem with Munkler's study.

Munkler, H., *The New Wars* (Cambridge: Polity, 2005). An extremely stimulating and thoughtful study of the dominant forms of post-cold-war conflict, both the new wars, which Munkler analyses though the prism of the globalized economy, and international terrorism.

Van Creveld, M., *The Transformation of War* (New York: The Free Press, 1991). Another stimulating and controversial set of arguments. Van Crefeld is particularly strong in bringing out the socio-economic demands of modern warfare.

von Clausewitz, C., *On War*, edited and translated by Michael Howard and Peter Paret (Princeton, NJ: Princeton University Press, 1989). It is always better to read Clausewitz himself rather than authors discussing his ideas. Still absolutely essential reading for the serious student of war.

Online Resource Centre

 Visit the Online Resource Centre that accompanies this book to access more learning resources on this chapter topic at www.oxfordtextbooks.co.uk/orc/baylis5e/

Chapter 14

International and global security

JOHN BAYLIS

Reader's Guide

This chapter focuses on the effects of the end of the cold war on global security. In particular, it looks at the question of whether international relations, especially in an era of increasing globalization, are likely to be as violent in the future as they have been in the past. The chapter begins by looking at disagreements that exist about the causes of war and whether violence is always likely to be with us. It then turns to traditional/classical realist and more contemporary neo-realist perspectives on international security, before considering alternative approaches. The chapter ends by looking at the continuing tension between national and international security, and suggests that, despite the important changes associated with the processes of globalization, there seem few signs that a fundamentally different, more peaceful, paradigm of international politics is emerging, or that it is possible for such a transformation to occur.

Introduction

Students of international politics deal with some of the most profound questions it is possible to consider. Among the most important of these is whether it is possible to achieve international security in the kind of world in which we live. For much of the intellectual history of the subject a debate has raged about the causes of war. For some writers, especially historians, the causes of war are unique to each case. Other writers believe that it is possible to provide a wider, more generalized explanation. Some analysts, for example, see the causes lying in human nature, others in the outcome of the internal organization of states, and yet others in international **anarchy**. In a major work on the causes of war, Kenneth Waltz considers what he calls the three 'images' of war (man, the state, and the international system) in terms of what thinkers have said about the origins of conflict throughout the history of Western civilization (Waltz 1954). Waltz himself puts particular emphasis on the nature of international anarchy ('wars occur because there is nothing to stop them from occurring') but he also recognizes that a comprehensive explanation requires an understanding of all three. In his words: 'The third image describes the framework of world politics, but without the first and second images there can be no knowledge of the forces that determine policy, the first and second images describe the forces in world politics, but without the third image it is impossible to assess their importance or predict their result' (Waltz 1954: 238).

In this ongoing debate, as Waltz points out, there is a fundamental difference between political philosophers over whether conflict can be transcended or mitigated. In particular, there has been a difference between **realist** and **idealist** thinkers, who have been respectively pessimistic and optimistic in their response to this central question in the international politics field (see Ch. 5). In the post-First World War period, idealism claimed widespread support as the League of Nations seemed to offer some hope for greater international order. In contrast, during the cold war, which developed after 1945, realism became the dominant school of thought. War and violent conflict were seen as perennial features of inter-state relations stretching back through human history. With the end of the cold war, however, the debate began again. For some, the end of the intense ideological confrontation between East and West was a major turning point in international history, ushering in a new paradigm in which inter-state violence would gradually become a thing of the past and new cosmopolitan values would bring greater cooperation between individuals and human collectivities of various kinds (including states). This reflected more optimistic views about the development of a peaceful global society. For others, however, realism remained the best approach to thinking about international security. In their view, very little of substance had changed as a result of the events of 1989. Although the end of the cold war initially brought into existence a new, more cooperative era between the superpowers, realists argued that this more harmonious phase in international relations was only temporary.

This chapter focuses on this debate in an era of increasing globalization, highlighting the different strands of thinking within these two optimistic and pessimistic schools of thought. Before this can be done, however, it is necessary to consider what is meant by 'security' and to probe the relationship between national security and international security. Attention will then shift to traditional ways of thinking about national security and the influence that these ideas have had on contemporary thinking. This will be followed by a survey of alternative ideas and approaches that have emerged in the literature in recent years. The conclusion will then provide an assessment of these ideas before returning to the central question of whether or not greater international security is more, or less, likely in the contemporary era.

What is meant by the concept of security?

Most writers agree that security is a 'contested concept'. There is a consensus that it implies freedom from threats to core values (for both individuals and groups), but there is a major disagreement about whether the main focus of inquiry should be on 'individual', 'national', 'international', or 'global' security. For much of the cold war period most writing on the subject was dominated by the idea of national security, which was largely defined in militarized terms. The main area of interest for both academics and statesmen tended to be on the military capabilities that their own states should develop to deal with the threats that faced them. More recently, however, this idea of security has been criticized for being ethnocentric (culturally biased) and too narrowly defined. Instead a number of contemporary writers have argued for an expanded conception of security outward from the limits of parochial national security to include a range of other considerations. Barry Buzan, in his study, *People, States and Fear* (1983), argues for a view of security that includes political, economic, societal, environmental as well as military aspects, and that is also defined in broader international terms. Buzan's work raises interesting and important questions about whether national and international

security considerations can be compatible and whether states, given the nature of the international system, are capable of thinking in more cooperative international and global terms.

This focus on the tension between national and international security is not accepted by all writers on security. There are those who argue that the emphasis on state and inter-state relations ignores the fundamental changes that have been taking place in world politics, especially in the aftermath of the cold war. For some, the dual processes of integration and fragmentation associated with globalization that characterize the contemporary world mean that much more attention should be given to 'societal security'. According to this view, growing integration in regions like Europe is undermining the classical political order based on nation-states, leaving nations exposed within larger political frameworks (like the EU). At the same time, the fragmentation of various states, like the Soviet Union and Yugoslavia, has created new problems of boundaries, minorities, and organizing ideologies that are causing increasing regional instability (Waever *et al.* 1993: 196). This has led to the argument that ethno-national groups, rather than states, should become the centre of attention for security analysts.

At the same time, other commentators argue that the stress on national and international security is less appropriate because of the emergence of an embryonic global society in the post-cold war era. Like the 'societal security' theorists, they point to the fragmentation of the nation-state but they argue that more attention should be given, not to society at the ethno-national level, but to global society. These writers argue that one of the most important contemporary trends is the broad process of globalization that is taking place. They accept that this process brings new risks and dangers. These include the risks associated with such things as international terrorism, a breakdown of the global monetary system, global warming, and the dangers of nuclear accidents. These threats to security, on a planetary level, are viewed as being largely outside the control of nation-states. Only the development of a global community, they believe, can deal with this adequately.

At the same time, other writers on globalization stress the transformation of the state (rather than its

Box 14.1 Notions of 'security'

'A nation is secure to the extent to which it is not in danger of having to sacrifice core values if it wishes to avoid war, and is able, if challenged, to maintain them by victory in such a war.'
(Walter Lippmann)

'Security, in any objective sense, measures the absence of threats to acquired values and in a subjective sense, the absence of fear that such values will be attacked.'
(Arnold Wolfers)

'In the case of security, the discussion is about the pursuit of freedom from threat. When this discussion is in the context of the international system, security is about the ability of states and societies to maintain their independent identity and their functional integrity.'
(Barry Buzan)

'Stable security can only be achieved by people and groups if they do not deprive others of it; this can be achieved if security is conceived as a process of emancipation.'
(Booth and Wheeler)

demise) and the new security agenda in the early years of the new century. In the aftermath of what has become known as '9/11' in September 2001 and the new era of violence that followed it, Jonathan Friedman argues that we are living in a world 'where polarization, both vertical and horizontal, both class and ethnic, has become rampant, and where violence has become more globalized and fragmented at the same time, and is no longer a question of wars between states but of sub-state conflicts, globally networked and financed, in which states have become one actor, increasingly privatized, amongst others' (2003: ix). For many of those who feel like this, the post-9/11 era is a new and extremely dangerous period in world history. Whether the world is so different today than in the past is a matter of much contemporary discussion. In order to consider this issue we need to begin by looking at the way 'security' has been traditionally conceived.

> ### Key Points
>
> - Security is a 'contested concept'.
> - The meaning of security has been broadened to include political, economic, societal, and environmental, as well as military, aspects.
> - Differing arguments exist about the tension between national and international security.
> - Different views have also emerged about the significance of globalization for the future of international security.

The traditional approach to national security

As Chapter 2 has shown, from the **Treaties of Westphalia** in 1648 onwards, states have been regarded as by far the most powerful actors in the international system. They have been 'the universal standard of political legitimacy', with no higher authority to regulate their relations with each other. This has meant that security has been seen as the priority obligation of state governments. They have taken the view that there is no alternative but to seek their own protection in what has been described as a **self-help** world.

In the historical debate about how best to achieve national security, writers like Hobbes, Machiavelli, and Rousseau tended to paint a rather pessimistic picture of the implications of state sovereignty. The international system was viewed as a rather brutal arena in which states would seek to achieve their own security at the expense of their neighbours. Inter-state relations were seen as a struggle for power, as states constantly attempted to take advantage of each other. According to this view, permanent peace was unlikely to be achieved. All that states could do was to try to balance the power of other states to prevent any one from achieving overall **hegemony**. This was a view shared by writers such as E. H. Carr and Hans Morgenthau, who developed what became known as the **realist** (or **'classical' realist**) school of thought in the aftermath of the Second World War. More recent attempts to update these ideas can be seen in the works of Alastair J. H. Murray, Thomas Christensen, Randall Schweller, William Wohlforth, and Fareed Zakaria. Their work is sometimes referred to as **neoclassical realism.** Alastair J. H. Murray, and Anatol Lieven and John Hulsman have also developed what has become known as 'ethical realism'. According to Lieven and Hulsman,

> Ethical realism ... embodies a strong sense of the fundamentally tragic nature of the human condition. Its vision is not purely tragic, however, because it also believes in the ability of men and nations to transcend in spirit their circumstances and to strive toward the good, though never fully to achieve it. In this, ethical realism differs from much of the 'traditional' or 'classical' realism, whose exponents also have a tragic sense but too often ignore both moral factors and the possibility of domestic progress, and believe that in the end, states, and the relative power of states, are the only really important imperatives on the international scene.
>
> (Lieven and Hulsman 2006: 58)

The realist, pessimistic view of international relations is shared by other writers, such as Kenneth Waltz and John Mearsheimer. The pessimism of these **neo-realists** rests on a number of key assumptions they make about the way the international system works (see Ch. 7).

Key neo-realist assumptions

- The international system is anarchic. By this they do not mean that it is necessarily chaotic. Rather, anarchy implies that there is no central authority capable of controlling state behaviour.
- States claiming sovereignty will inevitably develop offensive military capabilities to defend themselves and extend their power. As such they are potentially dangerous to each other.
- Uncertainty, leading to a lack of trust, is inherent in the international system. States can never be sure of the intentions of their neighbours and, therefore, must always be on their guard.
- States will want to maintain their independence and sovereignty, and, as a result, survival will be the most basic driving force influencing their behaviour.
- Although states are rational, there will always be room for miscalculation. In a world of imperfect information, potential antagonists will always have an incentive to misrepresent their own capabilities to keep their opponents guessing. This may lead to mistakes about 'real' state interests.

Taken together, these assumptions, neo-realists argue, produce a tendency for states to act aggressively towards each other.

According to this view, national security, or insecurity, is largely the result of the **structure** of the international system (this is why these writers are sometimes called 'structural realists'). The structure of anarchy is seen as highly durable. The implication of this is that international politics in the future is likely to be as violent as international politics in the past. In an important article entitled 'Back to the Future', written in 1990, John

Mearsheimer argued that the end of the cold war was likely to usher in a return to the traditional multilateral **balance of power** politics of the past, in which extreme nationalism and ethnic rivalries would lead to widespread instability and conflict. Mearsheimer viewed the cold war as a period of peace and stability brought about by the bipolar structure of power that prevailed. With the collapse of this system, he argued that there would be a return to the kind of great power rivalries that had blighted international relations since the seventeenth century.

For neo-realist writers like Mearsheimer, international politics may not be characterized by constant wars but nevertheless a relentless security competition takes place, with war, like rain, always a possibility. It is accepted that cooperation among states can and does occur, but such cooperation has its limits. It is 'constrained by the dominating logic of security competition, which no amount of co-operation can eliminate' (Mearsheimer 1994/5: 9). Genuine long-lasting peace, or a world where states do not compete for power, therefore, is very unlikely to be achieved. For neo-realists the post-cold war unipolar structure of power, with US pre-eminence, is likely to give way to a new international structure, with the rise of states such as China, India, and Brazil.

Key Points

- Debates about security have traditionally focused on the role of the state in international relations.
- Realists and neo-realists emphasize the perennial problem of insecurity.
- The 'security dilemma' is seen by some writers as the essential source of conflict between states.

The difficulties of cooperation between states

Neo-realist writers point to the Gulf War in 1991, the violent disintegration of the former Yugoslavia and parts of the former Soviet Union, continuing violence in the Middle East, the Iraq War and the war in Afghanistan, to illustrate that we continue to live in a world of mistrust and constant security competition. Cooperation between states occurs, but it is difficult to achieve and even more difficult to sustain. There are two main factors, it is suggested, that continue to make

cooperation difficult, even after the changes of 1989. The first is the prospect of cheating; the second is the concern that states have about what are called relative gains.

The problem of cheating

Despite some differences between them (see Ch. 7), writers like Waltz and Mearsheimer argue that there are distinct limits to cooperation between states because states have always been, and remain, fearful that others will cheat on any agreements reached and attempt to gain advantages over them. This risk is regarded as particularly important, given the nature of modern military technology, which can bring about very rapid shifts in the balance of power between states. 'Such a development', Mearsheimer has argued, 'could create a window of opportunity for the cheating side to inflict a decisive defeat on the victim state' (1994/5: 20). States realize that this is the case and, although they join alliances and sign arms control agreements, they remain cautious and aware of the need to provide for their own national security in the last resort.

The problem of relative gains

Cooperation is also inhibited, according to many neo-realist writers, because states tend to be concerned with 'relative gains', rather than '**absolute gains**'. Instead of being interested in cooperation because it will benefit both partners, states, they suggest, always have to be aware of how much they are gaining compared with the state they are cooperating with. Because all states will be attempting

to maximize their gains in a competitive, mistrustful, and uncertain international environment, cooperation will always be very difficult to achieve and hard to maintain.

Such a view of the problems of cooperation in the post-cold war world is not, however, shared by all writers. There is a wide body of opinion among scholars (and politicians) that the neo-realist view of international relations should be modified or even replaced. Opposition to neo-realism takes a wide variety of forms. To illustrate alternative ways of thinking about contemporary international security, six different approaches will be considered. Despite the differences between writers in these fields, many of them hold a common view that greater international and global security in the future is possible.

Key Points

- Trust is often difficult between states, according to realists and neo-realists, because of the problem of cheating.

- Realists and neo-realists also point out the problem of 'relative gains', where states compare their gains with those of other states when making their decisions about security.

The opportunity for cooperation between states

Liberal institutionalism

One of the main characteristics of the neo-realist approach to international security is the belief that international institutions do not have a very important part to play in the prevention of war. Institutions are seen as the product of state interests and the constraints imposed by the international system itself. It is these interests and constraints that shape the decisions on whether to cooperate or compete, rather than the institutions to which they belong.

Such views have been challenged by both statesmen and a number of international relations specialists, particularly following the end of the cold war. When he was British Foreign Secretary, Douglas Hurd, for example, made the case in June 1992 that institutions themselves had played, and continued to play, a crucial role in enhancing security, particularly in Europe. He argued that the West had developed 'a set of international institutions which have proved

their worth for one set of problems'. He went on to argue that the great challenge of the post-cold war era was to adapt these institutions to deal with the new circumstances that prevailed (Hurd, quoted in Mearsheimer 1994/5).

This view reflected a belief, widely shared among Western statesmen, that a framework of complementary, mutually reinforcing institutions—the EU, NATO, WEU, and the Organization for Security and Co-operation in Europe (OSCE)—could be developed to promote a more durable and stable European security system for the post-cold war era. It is a view also shared by a distinctive group of academic writers that developed since the 1980s and early 1990s. These writers share a conviction that the developing pattern of institutionalized cooperation between states opens up unprecedented opportunities to achieve greater international security in the years ahead. Although the past may have been characterized by constant wars and conflict, important changes are taking place in international relations at the beginning

---

Box 14.2 Democratic peace theory

Another 'liberal' approach to international security has gathered momentum in the post-cold-war world. This centres on the argument that democratic states tend not to fight other democratic states. Democracy, therefore, is seen as a major source of peace (see Ch. 8). As with 'liberal institutionalism', this is a notion that has received wide support in Western political and academic circles. In his State of the Union Address in 1994, President Bill Clinton went out of his way to point to the absence of war between democracies as a justification for American policies of promoting a process of democratization. Support for this view can be seen in the Western policy of promoting democracy in Eastern and Central Europe following the end of the cold war and opening up the possibility of these states joining the European Union.

Democratic peace theory has been largely associated with the writings of Michael Doyle and Bruce Russett. In the same way that contemporary realists have been influenced by the work of Hobbes, Rousseau, and Machiavelli, Doyle points to the importance of the insights contained in Immanuel Kant's 1795 essay, *Perpetual Peace*. Doyle contends that democratic representation, an ideological commitment to human rights, and transnational interdependence provide an explanation for the 'peace-prone' tendencies of democratic states (1995a: 180–4). Equally, the absence of these attributes, he argues, provides a reason why non-democratic states tend to be 'war-prone'. Without these domestic values and restraints, the logic of power replaces the liberal logic of accommodation.

---

of the twenty-first century that create the opportunity to dampen down the traditional security competition between states.

This approach, known as liberal institutionalism or **neo-liberalism**, operates largely within the realist framework, but argues that international institutions are much more important in helping to achieve cooperation and stability than 'structural realists' realize (see Ch. 7). According to Keohane and Martin (1995: 42), 'institutions can provide information, reduce transaction costs, make commitments more credible, establish focal points for coordination and, in general, facilitate the operation of reciprocity'. Supporters of these ideas point to the importance of European economic and political institutions in overcoming the traditional hostility of European states.

As such, it is suggested that in a world constrained by state power and divergent interests, international institutions operating on the basis of reciprocity will at least be a component of any lasting peace. In other words, international institutions themselves are unlikely to eradicate war from the international system, but they can play a part in helping to achieve greater cooperation between states.

Key Points

- Neo-realists reject the significance of international institutions in helping many to achieve peace and security.

- Contemporary politicians and academics, however, who write under the label of liberal institutionalism or **neo-liberalism**, see institutions as an important mechanism for achieving international security.

- Liberal institutionalists accept many of the assumptions of realism about the continuing importance of military power in international relations but argue that institutions can provide a framework for cooperation that can help to overcome the dangers of security competition between states.

Alternative approaches

'Constructivist' theory

The notion that international relations are not only affected by power politics but also by ideas is shared by writers who describe themselves as 'constructivist theorists'. According to this view, the fundamental structures of international politics are social rather than strictly material. This leads **social constructivists** to argue that changes in the nature of social interaction between states can bring a fundamental shift towards greater international security (see Ch. 9).

At one level, many constructivists, like Alexander Wendt, share a number of the major realist assumptions about international politics. For example, some accept that states are the key referent in the study of international politics and international security; that international politics is anarchic; that states often have offensive capabilities; that states cannot be absolutely certain of the intentions of other states; that states have a fundamental wish to survive; and that states attempt to behave rationally. Some, such as Wendt, also see themselves as structuralists; that is, they believe that the interests of

Box 14.3 Key concepts

'A **security community** is a group of people which has become "integrated". By integration we mean the attainment, within a territory, of a "sense of community" and of institutions and practices strong enough and widespread enough to assure . . . dependable expectations of "peaceful change" among its population. By a "sense of community" we mean a belief . . . that common social problems must and can be resolved by processes of "peaceful change".'

(Karl Deutsch)

'**Security regimes** occur when a group of states co-operate to manage their disputes and avoid war by seeking to mute the security dilemma both by their own actions and by their assumptions about the behaviour of others.'

(Robert Jervis)

'Acceptance of **common security** as the organizing principle for efforts to reduce the risk of war, limit arms, and move towards disarmament, means, in principle, that co-operation will replace confrontation in resolving conflicts of interest. This is not to say that differences among nations should be expected to disappear . . . The task is only to ensure that these conflicts do not come to be expressed in acts of war, or in preparations for war. It means that nations must come to understand that the maintenance of world peace must be given a higher priority than the assertion of their own ideological or political positions.'

(Palme Report 1992)

individual states are, in an important sense, constructed by the structure of the international system.

However, constructivists think about international politics in a very different way from neo-realists. The latter tend to view structure as made up only of a distribution of material capabilities. Constructivists view structure as the product of social relationships. Social structures are made possible by shared understandings, expectations, and knowledge. As an example of this, Wendt argues that the security dilemma is a social structure composed of inter-subjective understandings in which states are so distrustful that they make worst-case assumptions about each other's intentions, and, as a result, define their interests in 'self-help' terms. In contrast, a **security community** (like NATO) is a rather different social structure, composed of shared knowledge in which states trust one another to resolve disputes without war.

The emphasis on the structure of shared knowledge is important in constructivist thinking. Social structures include material things, like tanks and economic resources, but these only acquire meaning through the shared knowledge in which they are embedded. The idea of power politics, or realpolitik, has meaning to the extent that states accept the idea as a basic rule of international politics.

According to social constructivist writers, power politics is an idea that affects the way states behave, but it does not describe all inter-state behaviour. States are also influenced by other ideas, such as the rule of law and the importance of institutional cooperation and restraint. In his study, 'Anarchy is What States Make of It', Wendt argued that security dilemmas and wars can be seen, in part, as the outcome of self-fulfilling prophecies. The 'logic of reciprocity' means that states acquire a shared knowledge about the meaning of power and act accordingly. Equally, he argues, policies of reassurance can also help to bring about a structure of shared knowledge that can help to move states towards a more peaceful security community (see Wendt 1999).

Although constructivists argue that security dilemmas are not acts of God, they differ over whether they can be escaped. For some, the fact that structures are socially constructed does not necessarily mean that they can be changed. This is reflected in Wendt's comment that 'sometimes social structures so constrain action that transformative strategies are impossible' (1995: 80). Many constructivist writers, however, are more optimistic. They point to the changes in ideas introduced by Gorbachev during the second half of the 1980s, which led to a shared knowledge about the end of the cold war. Once both sides accepted that the cold war was over, it really was over. According to this view, understanding the crucial role of social structure is important in developing policies and processes of interaction that will lead to cooperation rather than conflict. For the optimists, there is sufficient 'slack' in the international system to allow states to pursue policies of peaceful social change rather than engage in a perpetual competitive struggle for power.

Key Points

- Constructivist thinkers base their ideas on two main assumptions: (1) that the fundamental structures of international politics are socially constructed and (2) that changing the way we think about international relations can help to bring about greater international security.

- Some constructivist thinkers accept many of the assumptions of neo-realism, but they reject the view that 'structure' consists only of material capabilities. They stress the importance of social structure defined in terms of shared knowledge and practices as well as material capabilities.

- Constructivists argue that material things acquire meaning only through the structure of shared knowledge in which they are embedded.

- The power politics and realpolitik practices emphasized by realists are seen as derived from shared knowledge, which can be self-fulfilling.

Critical, feminist, and discursive security studies

Despite the differences between constructivists and realists about the relationship between ideas and material factors, they agree on the central role of the state in debates about international security. Other theorists, however, believe that the state has been given too much prominence. Keith Krause and Michael Williams have defined critical security studies in the following terms: 'Contemporary debates over the nature of security often float on a sea of unvoiced assumptions and deeper theoretical issues concerning to what and to whom the term *security* refers … What most contributions to the debate thus share are two inter-related concerns: what security is and how we study it' (1997: 34). What they also share is a wish to de-emphasize the role of the state and the need to re-conceptualize security in a different way. Critical security studies, however, includes a number of different approaches. These include critical theory, 'feminist' approaches, and 'poststructuralist' approaches (see Buzan and Hansen 2009). Given that these are dealt with in other chapters, they are dealt with only briefly here.

Robert Cox draws a distinction between problem-solving theories and critical theories. Problem-solving theorists work within the prevailing system. They take the existing social and political relations and institutions as starting points for analysis and then see how the problems rising from these can be solved and ameliorated. In contrast, critical theorists focus their attention on the way these existing relationships and institutions emerged and what might be done to change them (see Chs 8 and 10). For critical security theorists, states should not be the centre of analysis because they are not only extremely diverse in character but they are also often part of the problem of insecurity in the international system. They can be providers of security, but they can also be a source of threat to their own people. According to this view, therefore, attention should be focused on the individual rather than on the state. This has led to greater attention being given to what has been called human security (see Ch. 29) and has resulted in a further broadening of the conception of 'security' to include areas such as health security (McInnes and Lee 2006).

Feminist writers also challenge the traditional emphasis on the central role of the state in studies of international security. While there are significant differences between feminist theorists, all share the view that works on international politics in general, and international security in particular, have been written from a 'masculine' point of view (see Ch. 16). In her work, Tickner argues that women have seldom been recognized by the security literature despite the fact that conflicts affect women as much as, if not more than, men. The vast majority of casualties and refugees in war are women and children and, as the recent war in Bosnia confirms, the rape of women is often used as a tool of war (Tickner 1992).

In a major feminist study of security, *Bananas, Beaches and Bombs*, Cynthia Enloe points to the patriarchal structure of privilege and control at all levels that, in her view, effectively legitimizes all forms of violence. She highlights the traditional exclusion of women from international relations, suggesting 'that they are in fact crucial to it in practice and that nowhere is the state more gendered in the sense of how power is dispersed than in the security apparatus' (Terriff *et al.* 1999: 91). She also challenges the concept of 'national security', arguing that the use of such terms is often designed to preserve the prevailing male-dominated order rather than protect the state from external attack.

Feminist writers argue that if gender is brought more explicitly into the study of security, not only will new issues and alternative perspectives be added to the security agenda, but the result will be a fundamentally different view of the nature of international security. According to Jill Steans, 'Rethinking security involves thinking about militarism and patriarchy, mal-development and environmental degradation. It involves thinking about the relationship between poverty, debt and population growth. It involves thinking about resources and how they are distributed' (Steans 1998. See also Smith 2000).

Recent years have seen the emergence of poststructuralist approaches to international relations, which have produced a somewhat distinctive perspective towards international security (see Ch. 10). Poststructuralist writers share the view that ideas, discourse, and 'the logic of interpretation' are crucial in understanding international politics and security. Like other writers who adopt a 'critical security studies' approach, poststructuralists see 'realism' as one of the central problems of international insecurity. This is because realism is a discourse of power and rule that has been dominant in international politics in the past and has encouraged security competition between states. Power politics is seen as an image of the world that encourages behaviour that helps bring about war. As such, the attempt to balance power is itself part of the very behaviour that leads to war. According to this view, alliances do not produce peace, but lead to war. The aim, for many poststructuralists, therefore, is to replace the discourse of realism or power with a different discourse and alternative interpretations of threats to 'national security'. The idea is that once the 'software' programme of realism that people carry around in their heads has been replaced by a new 'software' program based on cooperative norms, individuals, states, and regions will learn to work with each other and global politics will become more peaceful.

Box 14.4 Securitization theory

Securitization theory argues that 'security' is a *speech act*. This is summed up by one writer who argues that 'A securitizing actor by stating that a particular *referent object* is threatened in its existence claims a right to extraordinary measures to ensure the referent objects survival. The issue is then moved out of the sphere of normal politics into the realm of emergency politics, where it can be dealt with swiftly and without normal (demo-cratic) rules and regulations of policy making. For the content of security this means that it has no longer any given meaning but that it can be anything a securitizing actor says it is. Secu-rity—understood in this way—is a social construction, with the meaning of security dependent on what is done with it.'

(Taureck 2006)

Key Points

- Critical security theorists argue that most approaches put too much emphasis on the state.

- Some critical security theorists wish to shift the main referent to the individual and suggest that 'emancipation' is the key to greater domestic and international security.

- Feminist writers argue that gender tends to be left out of the literature on international security, despite the impact of war on women.

- Feminist writers also argue that bringing gender issues back in will result in a reconceptualization of the study of international security.

- Poststructuralists try to reconceptualize the debate about global security by looking at new questions that have been ignored by traditional approaches.

- There is a belief among poststructuralist writers that the nature of international politics can be changed by altering the way we think and talk about security.

Global society and international security

The opportunity to pursue changes in the international system is shared by scholars who point to new trends already taking place in world politics. Writers from the global society school of thought argue that the process of globalization (which has been developing for centuries) has accelerated to the point 'where the clear outlines of a global society' are now evident. The emergence of a global economic system, global communications, and the elements of a global culture have helped to provide a wide network of social relationships that transcends state frontiers and encompasses people all over the world. This has led to the growing obsolescence of terri-torial wars between the great powers. At the same time, so the argument goes, new risks associated with the environment, poverty, and weapons of mass destruction are facing humanity, just at a time when the nation-state is in crisis.

Supporters of the 'global society' school accept that globalization is an uneven and contradictory process. The end of the cold war has been characterized not only by an increasing global awareness and the creation of a range of global social movements, but also by the frag-mentation of nation-states. This has been most obvious among the former communist states, especially the So-viet Union, Yugoslavia, and Czechoslovakia. The result

of this 'fracture of statehood' has been a movement away from conflicts between the Great Powers to new forms of insecurity caused by nationalistic, ethnic, and religious rivalries within states and across state boundaries. This has been reflected in the brutal civil wars that have been fought in Bosnia, Russia, Somalia, Rwanda, Yemen, and Kosovo during the 1990s (see Ch. 13). Mary Kaldor has described these conflicts as 'new wars' that can only be understood in the context of globalization. The inten-sification of interconnectedness, she argues, 'has meant that ideological and/or territorial cleavages of an earlier era have increasingly been supplanted by an emerging political cleavage between … cosmopolitanism, based on inclusive, multicultural values and the politics of particularist identities' (Kaldor 1999: 6). The cleavage between those who are part of the global processes and those who are excluded gives rise to wars characterized by 'population expulsion through various means such as mass killing, forcible resettlement, as well as a range of political, psychological and economic techniques of intimidation' (*ibid.*: 8).

Such conflicts pose a critical problem for the interna-tional community of whether to intervene in the domes-tic affairs of sovereign states to safeguard minority rights and individual human rights (see Chs 30 and 31). This dilemma, according to global society theorists, reflects the historic transformation of human society that is currently taking place. Although states continue to limp along, many global theorists argue that it is now increasingly necessary to think of the security of individuals and of groups within the emergent global society (see Ch. 29).

Not all writers on globalization, however, agree with this view. Some argue that while the state is being transformed (from both within and without) by the processes of globalization, it remains a key referent in the contemporary debate about security. This is one of the central arguments in Ian Clark's study of *Globalization and International Relations Theory*. Clark argues that 'What globalization can bring to bear on the topic of security is an awareness of widespread systemic developments without any resulting need to downplay the

role of the state, or assume its obsolescence' (1999: 125). What is interesting for Clark is the way that security is being reshaped by globalization and the changes that this is creating for the security agenda of states. In particular, as states become less able to provide what they have traditionally provided, he argues that domestic bargains about what citizens are prepared to sacrifice for the state are being renegotiated. This is reflected in the type of security activities in which what he describes as globalized states are prepared to engage, and in the extent to which they are prepared to pursue them unilaterally. According to this view of globalization, states are not withering away but are being transformed as they struggle to deal with the range of new challenges (including those of security) that face them (see Ch. 33 and Box 14.6).

Case Study Insecurity in the post-cold war world: the Democratic Republic of the Congo

Events in the Democratic Republic of the Congo since the end of the cold war provide a good illustration of the complexities of contemporary conflict and the dangers of providing simple explanations of why wars occur. Between 1996 and 2009, in this 'forgotten war' (sometimes called 'Africa's World War'), it is estimated that 5.4 million people have lost their lives as a result of ethnic strife, civil war, and foreign intervention, as well as starvation and disease. The key events are as follows.

In 1996 the conflict and genocide in neighbouring Rwanda (in which 800,000 people died) spilled over into the Congo (named Zaire at the time). Rwandan Hutu forces, who fled after a Tutsi-led government came to power, set up bases in the eastern part of the country to launch attacks on Rwanda. This resulted in Rwandan forces invading the Congo with the aim of ousting the existing government of Mobutu Sese-Soko and putting in power their own government under Laurent-Désiré Kabila. This was achieved in May 1997. Kabila soon fell out with his backers in August 1998, however, and Rwanda and Uganda inspired a rebellion designed to overthrow him. This led to further intervention, this time by Zimbabwe, Angola, Namibia, Chad, and Sudan in support of the Kabila government. Although a ceasefire was signed in 1999, fighting continued in the eastern part of the country. In January 2001 Kabila was assassinated and replaced by his son, Joseph Kabila. Fighting continued until 2003, partly due to ethnic divisions (the DRC is a country of 250 ethnic groups and 242 different languages) but also because of the continuing occupation of foreign troops (often engaged in illegal mining of minerals and diamonds). These foreign troops often formed alliances with local militias to fight their enemies on DRC soil. Negotiations designed to broker a peace agreement eventually led to the Pretoria Accord in April 2003. As a result, some of the foreign troops left but hostilities and massacres continued, especially in the east of the country as rival militias backed by Rwanda

and Uganda continued to fight and plunder the resources of the DRC.

On 18 July 2003, the Transitional Government was set up as a result of what was known as the Global and All-inclusive Agreement. The Agreement required parties to help reunify the country, disarm and integrate the warring parties, and hold elections. Continued instability, however, meant that the elections did not take place until 2006. Even after these elections, however, peace remained elusive. Conflict continued among foreign troops and numerous militia groups on the Rwandan and Ugandan borders, causing serious refugee crises and civilian deaths. In 2009 the death rate was an estimated 45,000 a month from widespread disease and famine, as well as the continuing fighting.

This conflict in the DRC highlights the utility of a broader definition of 'security' and the importance of new ideas relating to 'human' and 'societal' security. It also illustrates the relative shift from inter-state wars to intra-state conflicts, involving ethnic militias, in what are sometimes called 'failed states'. Nevertheless, the war also highlights the continuing importance of conflict across state boundaries and traditional regional balance of power rivalries.

Key Points

- Supporters of the 'global society school' argue that the end of the twentieth century witnessed an accelerating process of globalization.

- Globalization can be seen in the fields of economic development, communications, and culture. Global social movements are also a response to new risks associated with the environment, poverty, and weapons of mass destruction.

- The 'fracture of statehood' is giving rise to new kinds of conflict within states rather than between states, which the state system cannot deal with. This has helped encourage an emerging politics of global responsibility.

- There are disputes about whether globalization will contribute to the weakening of the state or simply to its transformation, and over whether a global society can be created that will usher in a new period of peace and security.

Conclusion: the continuing tensions between national, international, and global security

At the centre of the contemporary debate about global and international security dealt with above is the issue of continuity and change, as well as different ways of thinking about 'security'. This involves questions about how the past is to be interpreted and whether international politics is in fact undergoing a dramatic change as a result of the processes of globalization, especially after 9/11. There is no doubt that national security is being challenged by the forces of globalization, some of which have a positive effect, bringing states into greater contact with each other, while others have a more malign effect. Bretherton and Ponton have argued that the intensification of global connectedness associated with economic globalization, ecological interdependence, and the threats posed by weapons of mass destruction means that 'co-operation between states is more than ever necessary' (1996: 100–1). It has also been argued that the increased need for interdependence caused by globalization will help 'to facilitate dialogue at the elite level between states, providing significant gains for global security' (Lawler 1995: 56–7). At the same time, however, globalization also appears to be having negative effects on international security. It is often associated with fragmentation, rapid social change, increased economic inequality, terrorism, and challenges to cultural and religious identities that contribute to conflicts within, and between, states (see Ch. 22). Globalization has also facilitated the proliferation of weapons technologies, including those associated with weapons of mass destruction, which remain a major potential source of international insecurity. This ambivalent effect of globalization, in turn, reinforces the search for national security and unilateralism for some states, while at the same time encouraging other states to seek greater multilateral and global solutions as they are less able to provide security for their citizens.

In the first part of the twenty-first century, therefore, despite important changes taking place in world politics, the traditional ambiguity about international security remains. In some ways the world is a much safer place to live in as a result of the end of the cold war and the removal of nuclear confrontation as a central element in East–West relations. It can be argued that some of

Box 14.5 Observations on 9/ 11

'Global security was changed dramatically by the events of 11 September 2001. The definition of security has … once again been narrowed. The concern is very much national security in a globalized world, in which direct attacks are now, as they were during the Cold War, seen as the primary and most imminent challenge. … issues such as the promotion of democratization, respect for human rights, and problems with environmental degredation appear, at least for the moment, to have been put on the back-burner.'

(Stubbs 2002: 178–9)

'If "the post-Cold War security bubble finally burst" on September 11, what also shattered along with it was a series of cosy assumptions about the world within which we happen to live—one of the most influential of which was that under conditions of globalization the propensity for international conflict would more likely diminish than increase. As the terrorist attacks on New York and Washington revealed only too graphically, Globalization not only appeared to have many determined enemies as well-meaning friends, but enemies of a quite novel (and undeterrable) character. What it also revealed—again to the discomfort of those who assumed the world was becoming a better safer place—was that the worst sometimes happens.'

(Michael Cox, in Booth and Dunne 2002: 152)

the processes of globalization and the generally cooperative effects of international institutions have played an important part in dampening down some of the competitive aspects of the security dilemma between states. These trends, however, are offset to a significant extent, as the continuing turmoil in the Middle East, the wars in Afghanistan and Iraq, and the subsequent 'war on terror', demonstrate. It is evident that military force continues to be an important arbiter of disputes both between and particularly within states, as well as a weapon used by terrorist movements who reject the status quo. Also, conventional arms races continue in different regions of the world. Nuclear, chemical, and biological weapons still exert a powerful influence on the security calculations of many states; crazy and ambitious politicians remain at the head of some governments; and cultural differences, as well as diverse values and the tensions inherent in globalization itself, prevent the emergence of global agreement on a wide range of important issues. Water resources, food, and energy are potential sources of conflict, and it remains unclear how great power relations will develop in the years ahead, as geo-political and geo-strategic changes unfold. At a time of uncertainty and anxiety, individual and societal insecurity is increasingly evident as the forces of fragmentation and integration associated with globalization destabilize traditional identities and thereby complicate relationships within and between states.

As a result, it would be difficult to conclude that a paradigmatic shift towards a more peaceful world is taking place in international politics and global security in the aftermath of the cold war, or indeed that such a permanent shift is possible. The empirical historical evidence as well as contemporary events suggest caution. Periods of more cooperative inter-state (and inter-group) relations have often in the past led to a false dawn and an unwarranted euphoria that 'perpetual peace' was about to break out. The structure of the international system, particular kinds of political systems, human nature, and the forces of globalization impose important constraints on the way that individuals, states, or international institutions behave. So does the continuing predominance of realist attitudes towards international and global security among many of the world's political leaders (see Ch. 5).

Box 14.6 The impact of globalization on security

'Under conditions of Globalization, the traditional focus of security and the nation-state begins to become problematic: the security state is no longer at the centre of security concerns, as it loses the ability to exclusively provide insurance against contingency, as both the scope of security issues changes (from the strictly national level to include the global and the local), and the functions of the state are integrated into institutions at other levels. The consequences of this for the structure of international or world order are important, as functional aspects of states are further integrated on the international and global scale.'

(Mabee 2009: 145)

This is not to argue that there is no room for peaceful change or that new ideas and discourses about world politics are unimportant in helping us to understand the complexities of contemporary global security and insecurity. Opportunities to develop greater international and global security will always exist. It is noteworthy that the potential for considerable conflict in the aftermath of the global financial crisis of 2008/9, at least at the time of writing, has not materialized, partly, at least, because of the cooperative efforts of world leaders. In a broader sense, however, the crisis created very considerable insecurity and the potential for social, political, and economic unrest. Similarly, in 2010 there were encouraging signs of attempts to marginalize nuclear weapons in world politics. Whether they will be enough to reverse the trend towards greater nuclear proliferation and off-set the dangers of nuclear terrorism, however, remains far from clear.

In a world of continuing diversity, mistrust, and uncertainty, it is likely that the search for a more cooperative global society will remain in conflict with the powerful pressures that exist for states, and other political communities, to look after what they perceive to be their own sectional, religious, national, or regional security against threats from without and within. This seems particularly apparent given the level of violence that has occurred since 9/11. Whether and how greater international and global security can be achieved still remains, as Herbert Butterfield once argued, 'the hardest nut of all' for students and practitioners of international politics to crack. This is what makes the study of global security such a fascinating and important activity.

Questions

1 Why is security a 'contested concept'?
2 Why do traditional realist writers focus on national security?
3 What do neo-realist writers mean by 'structure'?
4 Why do wars occur?
5 Why do states find it difficult to cooperate?
6 Do you find 'liberal institutionalism' convincing?
7 Why might democratic states be more peaceful?
8 What is distinctive about 'constructivist' views of international security?
9 How do 'critical security' theory, 'feminist' views and poststructuralist views about international security differ from those of 'neo-realists'?
10 Has increasing globalization brought more or less global security?
11 Is the tension between national and global security resolvable?
12 Has international security changed since 9/11?

Further Reading

K. N. Waltz's study, *Man, the State and War* (New York: Columbia University Press, 1954), is one of the best sources for the study of the causes of war.

J. C. Garnett, 'The Causes of War and the Conditions of Peace', in J. Baylis, J. Wirtz, and C. S. Gray (eds), *Strategy in the Contemporary World* (Oxford: Oxford University Press, 3rd edn, 2010) provides a more up-to-date approach to the causes of war.

B. Buzan's *People, States and Fear* (London: Harvester, 1983) provides a broader approach to 'security' and is an excellent starting point for the study of national and international security.

B. Buzan and I. Hansen, *The Evolution of International Security Studies* (Cambridge: Cambridge University Press, 2009) provides a very good account of the intellectual history of the development of international security studies from the early cold war rather narrow definitions of security associated with the confrontation between the superpowers to the current diverse understandings of environmental, economic, human, and other securities.

M. J. Smith, *Realist Thought from Weber to Kissinger* (Baton Rouge, LA: Louisiana State University Press, 1986) covers the development of what has been described as classical realism and discusses some of the major thinkers in the field.

A. Wendt, 'Anarchy is What States Make of It: The Social Construction of Power Politics', in *International Organization*, 46 (2) (1992) gives a very useful analysis of the 'Constructivist' perspective. See also **Alexander Wendt**, *Social Theory of International Politics* (Cambridge: Cambridge University Press, 1999).

O. Waever, B. Buzan, M. Kelstrup, and P. Lemaitre, *Identity, Migration and the New Security Agenda in Europe* (London: Pinter, 1993) provides an original perspective for studying the kind of non-state aspects of security which have affected Europe in the post-cold war period.

Very useful discussions about the changing nature of security can be found in
C. Bretherton and G. Ponton (eds), *Global Politics: An Introduction* (Oxford: Blackwell, 1996);
  T. Terriff, S. Croft, L. James, and P. Morgan, *Security Studies Today* (Cambridge: Polity
  Press, 1999); K. Krause and M. C. Williams (eds), *Critical Security Studies: Concepts and
  Cases* (London: UCL Press, 1997); and S. Lawson (ed.), *The New Agenda for Global Security:
  Cooperating for Peace and Beyond* (St Leonard's: Allen and Unwin, 1995).
B. Mabee, *The Globalization of Security* (London: Palgrave, 2009) provides an interesting up-to-
  date approach to security from a historical sociology perspective.

Online Resource Centre

Visit the Online Resource Centre that accompanies this book to access more learning
resources on this chapter topic at www.oxfordtextbooks.co.uk/orc/baylis5e/

Chapter 15

International political economy in an age of globalization

NGAIRE WOODS

Reader's Guide

In 2008 the world economy faced melt-down. A financial crisis began in the USA and soon spread around the world. These events highlighted the tensions between states and markets, the challenges of globalization, and the role of institutions in the global economy. This chapter examines what drives actors and explains events in the international economy. The first section outlines how international economic relations and institutions were created and shaped in the post-war economy. The second section outlines three traditional approaches to **international political economy** (IPE) that help to identify key actors, processes, and levels of analysis. These are the **liberal**, **mercantilist**, and **Marxist** traditions. More modern approaches have built on '**rational choice**' analysis. What 'rational choice' means and the argument about how it should be used are both explored. These perspectives and tools for studying IPE are then applied to help us to make sense of globalization and its impact on the world economy. What is globalization and what challenges does it pose for all states (and other actors) in the world economy? It is often assumed that international institutions and organizations will manage these challenges. In the final section of the chapter we return to the theories of IPE in order to answer the question: what role can we expect institutions to play in managing globalization?

Introduction

International political economy (IPE) is about the interplay of economics and politics in world affairs. The core question of IPE is: what drives and explains events in the world economy? For some people, this comes down to a battle of 'states versus markets'. However, this is misleading. The 'markets' of the world economy are not like local street bazaars in which all items can be openly and competitively traded and exchanged. Equally, politicians cannot rule the global economy. World markets and countries, local firms, and multinational corporations that trade and invest within them are all shaped by layers of **rules**, **norms**, laws, organizations, and even habits. Political scientists like to call all these features of the system **institutions**. International political economy tries to explain what creates and perpetuates institutions and what impact institutions have on the world economy.

In 2008 a global economic crisis began when a major US financial firm failed (see Case Study). The crash of Lehman Brothers exposed the degree to which some banks had excessively leveraged themselves, spiralling into a dizzyingly profitable but—as it turned out—catastrophically risky way. All too few institutions prevented them. As a result, prominent economists declared that the world was facing a 'Great Depression' of a kind not seen since the 1930s. Governments in the USA and the UK were forced to bail out banks, and to pump money into the wider economy to prevent jobs, sales, and markets from drying up. Other countries were also affected. In Europe, those whose financial systems were connected to the USA and the UK, such as Ukraine, Hungary, Iceland, and Latvia, were soon seeking emergency assistance from the IMF (International Monetary Fund). Elsewhere in the world a wider 'development emergency' soon emerged as the collapse in demand for commodities, goods, and services in the world's largest richest economies affected all those countries that supplied them. The global dimensions of the problem were recognized by leaders who created a new forum—the **G20**—comprising the leaders of the world's largest economies so as to coordinate responses to the crisis.

The economic shocks of 2008 brought into sharp focus perennial themes of international political economy. The relationship between states and markets was highlighted by the fact that some (but not all) states failed to restrain their financial markets. They let their banks make massive profits at the expense of societies (and other countries), which ended up paying the costs when the banks failed. Globalization and who benefits most from it was revisited in the wake of the crisis, particularly by countries that benefited little from financial liberalization but were harshly affected by the crisis. The primacy of the US economic model came under renewed scrutiny as emerging economies trumpeted the success of their more state-centric policies in weathering the crisis. Relations between the so-called '**North**' (industrialized countries) and '**South**' (developing countries) were transformed as emerging economies carved out a new position for themselves in international institutions, including in the new G20, while other developing countries remained marginalized. Perhaps surprisingly, the international economic institutions used to manage the crisis were those created in the aftermath of the Second World War, in spite of widespread agreement that they needed updating.

The post-war world economy

The institutions and framework of the world economy have their roots in the planning for a new economic order that took place during the last phase of the Second World War. In 1944, policy-makers gathered at **Bretton Woods** in the USA to consider how to resolve two very serious problems. First, they needed to ensure that the **Great Depression** of the 1930s would not happen again. In other words, they had to find ways to ensure a stable global monetary system and an open world trading system (see Box 15.1). Second, they needed to rebuild the war-torn economies of Europe.

At Bretton Woods three institutions were planned in order to promote a **new world economic order** (see Boxes 15.2 and 15.4). The **International Monetary Fund** was created to ensure a stable exchange rate regime and the provision of emergency assistance to countries facing a temporary crisis in their balance of payments regime. The **International Bank for Reconstruction and**

Box 15.1 Planning the post-war economy and avoiding another Great Depression

The Great Depression had been greatly exacerbated, if not caused, by 'beggar-thy-neighbour' economic policies. In the late 1920s and 1930s, governments all over the world tried to protect themselves from economic crisis by putting up trade barriers and devaluing their currencies. Each country believed that by doing this they would somehow manage to keep their economy afloat while all around them neighbouring economies sank. The Great Depression demonstrated that this did not work. At the end of the Second World War, the challenge was to create a system which would prevent this, in particular by ensuring:

- a stable exchange rate system;
- a reserve asset or unit of account (such as the gold standard);
- control of international capital flows;
- the availability of short-term loans to countries facing a temporary balance of payments crisis;
- rules to keep economies open to trade.

Box 15.2 The Bretton Woods institutions: the IMF and the World Bank

Both the International Monetary Fund and the World Bank were established in 1946 after wartime negotiations held at Bretton Woods in the USA with headquarters (opposite one another) in Washington, DC. The **IMF** was created to promote international monetary cooperation and resolve the inter-war economic problems (see Box 15.1), although several of these functions ended when the Bretton Woods system broke down in 1971 (see Box 15.3). The IMF now has a membership of 185 countries, each of whom contributes a quota of resources to the organization (proportionate to the size of their economy), which also determines their percentage of voting rights and the amount of resources to which they can have automatic access. Since the 1980s, the IMF has become an institution offering financial and technical assistance to developing and transitional economies. The terms on which countries receive assistance include the government having to commit to undertake specific 'conditions' or policy reforms, called **conditionality** (see www.imf.org).

What we now call the **World Bank** started out as the International Bank for Reconstruction and Development (IBRD), an agency to foster reconstruction in war-torn Europe as well as development in the rest of the world. It has since become the world's largest source of development assistance, providing nearly $16 billion in loans annually to eligible member countries, through the IBRD, the International Development Association (IDA), the International Finance Corporation (IFC), and the Multilateral Guarantee Agency (MIGA). As with the IMF, the World Bank requires members to whom it lends to undertake specific reforms within their economy. Most recently, this has included requiring borrowing governments to demonstrate their commitment to reducing poverty within their countries. With the exception of IDA (which is funded by donations), the World Bank's resources come from its issue of bonds in the capital markets. These bonds are backed up by guarantees provided by the governments who belong to the institution (see www.worldbank.org).

Development (IBRD, later called the **World Bank**) was created to facilitate private investment and reconstruction in Europe. The Bank was also charged with assisting **development** in other countries, a mandate that later became the main reason for its existence. Finally, the **General Agreement on Tariffs and Trade** (GATT) was signed in 1947 and became a forum for negotiations on trade **liberalization**.

The 1944 plans for the world economy, however, were soon postponed when in 1945 the USA made its first priority the **containment** of the Soviet Union. Fearing the rise of communism in war-ravaged Europe, the USA took a far more direct role than planned in reconstructing Europe and managing the world economy. In 1947 the USA announced the **Marshall Plan**, which directed massive financial aid to Europe and permitted the USA to set conditions on it. The planned gold standard was replaced by the **dollar standard** which the USA managed directly, backing the dollar with gold. Unsurprisingly, by the time the IMF, the World Bank, and the GATT began to function in the 1950s, they were distinctly **Western bloc organizations** that depended heavily on the USA.

US support for the Bretton Woods system began to change when weaknesses emerged in the US economy. After 1965 the USA widened its costly military involvement in Vietnam, and also started to spend more money on public education and urban redevelopment programmes at home (President Johnson's 'Great Society' programmes), and all this without raising taxes. The damage was dramatic. As prices rose within the US economy,

the **competitiveness** of US goods and services in the world economy dropped. Likewise, confidence in the US dollar plummeted. Firms and countries turned away from the dollar and the US capacity to back its currency with gold was brought into question. Meanwhile, other countries in the world economy were enhancing their position. European allies were benefiting from the growing and deepening economic **integration** in Europe. By the late 1960s, the development of the European Economic Community (EEC) provided a springboard for European policy-makers to diverge from US positions, such as over **NATO**, military exercises, and support for the gold standard. In Asia, the phenomenal success of **export-led growth** in Japan and in newly industrializing countries such as South Korea and Taiwan created a new challenge to US trade competitiveness, and a new agenda for trade negotiations.

Box 15.3 The 'Bretton Woods system' and its breakdown

What was the 'Bretton Woods system'?
At the Bretton Woods Conference in 1944 it was agreed that all countries' currencies would be fixed at a certain value. They became fixed to the dollar, and the US government promised to convert all dollars to gold at $35 per ounce. In other words, exchange rates were anchored to a dollar–gold standard. In the Bretton Woods system, any country wanting to change the value of its currency had to apply to the IMF for permission. The result was very stable and unchanging exchange rates.

What was the 'breakdown' of the system?
In August 1971 the US government announced that it was suspending the convertibility of the dollar to gold at $35 per ounce. This removed gold from the dollar–gold standard and paved the way for major currencies to 'float' instead of staying at fixed values. The USA also announced in August 1971 that it was adding a 10 per cent surcharge on import duties (to improve trade balance by curtailing imports that were flooding into the USA, and to try to stem the outflow of dollars to the rest of the world), hence also turning back the Bretton Woods ideal of maintaining open trade in times of economic difficulty.

Was this a sign of declining US hegemony?
Over a decade after the breakdown of the Bretton Woods system, leading academics debated whether the change reflected a loss in US power, or was indeed an exercise of its power. For some, the breakdown of the system was an exercise of US leadership: the US hegemon smashed the BW system in order to increase its own freedom of economic and political action (Gowa 1983). Others argued that the USA had lost its capacity to maintain the system, but explained that a regime could nevertheless survive without the hegemon (Keohane 1984). At the heart of the debate was a disagreement about whether cooperation in the international political economy depends upon one state being both capable and willing to set and enforce the rules of the game, with powers to abrogate and adjust those same rules. This debate about the nature of cooperation continues today in competing explanations of international institutions (see last section of this chapter).

Facing these pressures, the USA changed the rules of the international monetary system in 1971. The government announced that it would no longer convert dollars to gold at $35 per ounce, and that it was imposing a 10 per cent surcharge on import duties (to improve its trade balance by curtailing imports which were flooding into the USA, and to try to stem the outflow of dollars to the rest of the world). These actions broke the Bretton Woods system. This was not the only change in the world economy during this period.

In the 1970s, the period of high growth enjoyed after the Second World War came to an abrupt end, leaving very high inflation. Further compounding the problem, the first oil crisis in 1973 plunged the world economy into **stagflation** (a combination of economic stagnation or low growth and high inflation). In the monetary system, the role of the IMF collapsed when the Bretton Woods system broke down in 1971 and the major industrialized countries failed to find a way to coordinate their exchange rate policies within the IMF framework. Instead, the major currencies floated and industrialized countries began to discuss monetary issues among themselves in groups such as the Group of Seven (or **G7**, comprising the USA, Japan, Germany, the UK, France, Italy, and Canada), which first met in 1975.

In the trading system, **cooperation** had steadily grown in negotiations under the auspices of the GATT (see Box 15.4). However, in the 1970s, the gains that had been made in reducing tariff barriers, especially among industrialized countries, were reversed by policies of **new protectionism.** As each country grappled with stagflation, many introduced new forms of barriers (or 'non-tariff barriers'), in particular to keep out the new competitive imports from successful developing countries. An egregious example of the new protectionism was the Multifiber Arrangement of 1973, which placed restrictions on all textile and apparel imports from developing countries, blatantly violating the GATT principle of **non-discrimination**.

The new protectionism in industrialized countries further fuelled the anger of developing countries, which in the 1970s launched a concerted campaign in the United Nations General Assembly for a **New International Economic Order** (NIEO). The determination of developing countries to alter the rules of the game was further bolstered by the success of OPEC oil-producing developing countries in raising oil prices in 1973. The agenda of the NIEO covered trade, aid, investment, the international monetary and financial system, and institutional reform. Developing countries sought better representation in international economic institutions, a fairer trading system, more aid, the regulation of foreign investment, the protection of economic **sovereignty**, and reforms to ensure a more stable and equitable financial and **monetary system**.

A kind of **summit diplomacy**, which also took place in the 1970s, was that between North (the industrialized countries) and South (developing countries). These negotiations were underpinned by a different kind of thinking and scholarship about IPE. The developing countries'

Box 15.4 The post-war trading system, the GATT, and the WTO

The General Agreement on Tariffs and Trade (GATT) was an interim agreement signed in 1947 in the expectation that it would be superseded by an international trade organization. A permanent trade organization was not created until 1994, and so for four decades the interim GATT continued to exist as an arrangement among 'contracting parties' backed up by a very small secretariat based in Geneva and a minuscule budget. In essence, the GATT was a forum for trade negotiations, with numerous rounds of talks culminating in the very successful Kennedy Round of 1962–7, where breakthroughs were made in the reduction of trade barriers among industrialized countries. However, when protectionism flourished in the 1970s, the GATT proved powerless to restrain powerful members such as the USA and European countries from restricting trade (e.g. the Multifiber Arrangement 1974 restricting textile imports) and abusing the many exceptions and safeguards written into the agreement. The GATT also functioned as a forum for dispute settlement (i.e. upholding trade rules). However, it was both slow and impotent in this regard, constrained by the need for consensus on any decision regarding disputes. The GATT was replaced by the World Trade Organization (WTO) as a result of agreements forged in the last round of GATT talks, the Uruguay Round (1986–94). Established on 1 January 1995, the WTO's functions include: administering WTO trade agreements; being a forum for trade negotiations; handling trade disputes; monitoring national trade policies; supplying technical assistance and training for developing countries; and cooperating with other international organizations. It is located in Geneva with a secretariat staff of 500 (see www.wto.org).

push for reform of the international economic system reflected **dependency theory** and structuralist theories of international economic relations that highlighted negative aspects of **interdependence**. In particular, these theorists were concerned to identify aspects of the international economy and institutions that impeded the possibilities of development in the South. Their central concern was to answer why so many countries within the world economy remained underdeveloped, in spite of the promises of modernization and global growth. The most sympathetic official 'Northern' answer to these concerns was voiced in the **Brandt Report** in 1980, the findings of a group of high-level policy-makers who had been asked to examine how and why the international community should respond to the challenges of interdependence and development.

The NIEO campaign was unsuccessful for several reasons. The United Nations General Assembly (UNGA) was an obvious institution for developing countries to choose in making their case since, unlike the IMF or World Bank, it offers every country one vote. However, the UNGA had no power to implement the agenda of the developing countries. Furthermore, although many industrialized countries were sympathetic to the developing countries' case in the 1970s, these governments did not act on the agenda in the 1970s and by the 1980s a new set of governments with a distinctly less sympathetic ideology had come to power in the USA, the UK, and Western Germany.

The 1980s opened with a shift in US economic policy. In 1979 the US Federal Reserve dramatically raised interest rates. This action was taken to stem inflation by contracting economic activity in the USA. However, the reverberations in the rest of the world economy were immediate and extensive. During the 1960s and 1970s, US and European policies had facilitated the rapid growth of **global capital markets** and financial flows. In the 1970s these flows were further buoyed by the investments of oil producers who needed to find outlets for the vast profits made from the oil price rise of 1973. The money found its way to governments in developing countries, which were offered loans at knock-down prices. The rise in interest rates in 1979 was an abrupt wake-up call to both borrowers and creditors (many of whom were US-based banks), who suddenly realized that many of the loans could not be repaid. The IMF was immediately called in to prevent any developing country defaulting on these loans, since it was feared that such a default would causes a **global financial crisis**.

The **debt crisis** meant that the IMF's role in the world economy became largely that of ensuring that indebted countries undertook 'structural adjustment' in their economies. **Structural adjustment** meant immediate measures to reduce inflation, government expenditure, and the role of the government in the economy, including **trade liberalization**, **privatization**, and **deregulation**. These 'neo-liberal' policies were in marked contrast to the Keynesian analysis that had prevailed until the 1980s, during the decades of growth in the world economy. **Keynesians** (named after economist John Maynard Keynes) believe that governments should play an active and interventionist role in the economy in order to ensure both growth and equity. By contrast, the new 'neo-liberalism' sought to roll back the state and the role of government, leaving decisions about allocation, production, and distribution in the economy to the market. By the late 1980s the term **Washington consensus** was being used, sometimes pejoratively, to imply that these policies were mainly a reflection of US interests.

The 1990s brought the end of the cold war, and the challenge of how to integrate Central and Eastern European countries and the former Soviet Union into the global economy. The IMF and World Bank became deeply involved but the Washington Consensus was not broad enough for the purpose. Both institutions began to embrace a broader and deeper view of conditionality aimed at promoting 'good governance' in member countries. But many thought conditionality had gone too far when, in the wake of the **East Asian financial crisis** in 1997, the IMF imposed far-reaching and overly draconian conditions on countries such as Korea. The impact would be felt in subsequent years as the IMF's lending role waned in most emerging market economies. Over this time, the World Bank sought to broaden its appeal through enhanced relations with governments as well as with **non-governmental organizations** (NGOs). Its legitimacy seemed less tarnished. At the same time, the newly established **World Trade Organization** (WTO) began operations in 1995, opening up a new forum within which a broad range of international issues would be negotiated, including not just traditional trade issues but such things as **intellectual property rights**, trade-related investment measures, and food safety standards.

In the first decade of the twenty-first century, a shift in global economic power was emerging. In September 2003, during global trade negotiations in Mexico, a group of 20 countries including Brazil, South Africa, India, and China, resisted the powerful USA and European Union and refused to engage unless some of their terms were heeded. In the IMF and World Bank in 2006 a shift in voting power was conceded in favour of China, Mexico, Turkey, and Korea. Yet few believed this would be enough fully to engage these countries in the institutions. Several emerging countries—with China in the lead—became donors in their own right. As world energy consumption grew, so too did the power of countries supplying energy resources. In Venezuela, this led to a rhetoric of renewed Third Worldism not seen since the 1970s. Meanwhile, across most industrialized countries, calls for greater efforts to reduce climate-changing emissions became ever stronger. For scholars of international relations, the twenty-first century brought serious questions about how international institutions might assist not only in managing new challenges in the global economy, but equally in managing a shift in power among the states that make up—and make work—the existing institutions. This questioning was greatly accelerated by the financial crisis that began in 2008.

Key Points

- Immediately after the Second World War international institutions were created to facilitate cooperation in the world economy.

- The onset of the **cold war** postponed the operation of these institutions, as the USA stepped in directly to manage the reconstruction of Europe and the international monetary system based on the dollar.

- The Bretton Woods system of managed exchange rates and capital flows operated until its breakdown in 1971, when the USA announced it would no longer convert the dollar to gold.

- The 1970s were marked by a lack of international economic cooperation among the industrialized countries, which floated their exchange rates and indulged in new forms of trade protectionism.

- Developing countries' dissatisfaction with the international system came to a head in the 1970s when they pushed unsuccessfully for a new international economic order.

- Trade negotiations were broadened to include many new areas, but this led to later resistance from emerging economies.

- In 2007 a power shift became more obvious in the global economy, with emerging economies such as China and India playing a more prominent role in negotiations in trade, finance, and development assistance, and in the G20 formed after the 2008 financial crisis.

Traditional and new approaches to IPE

Traditional approaches to IPE: liberal, mercantilist, and Marxian

There are several competing explanations for the nature of the institutions and system described above. A slightly old-fashioned way to describe the competing approaches to IPE is to divide the subject into liberal, mercantilist, and Marxist traditions. These labels still usefully describe different economic traditions, each of which has a particular moral and analytical slant on global economic relations.

The liberal tradition

The liberal tradition is the **free market** one in which the role of voluntary exchange and markets is emphasized both as efficient and as morally desirable. The assumption is that free trade and the free movement of capital will ensure that investment flows to where it is most profitable to invest (hence, for example, flowing into underdeveloped areas where maximal gains might be made). Free trade is crucial, for it permits countries to benefit from their comparative advantages. In other words, each country can exploit its own natural advantages, resources, and endowments, and gain from specialization. The economy is oiled by freely exchangeable currencies and open markets that create a global system of prices, which, like an **invisible hand**, ensures an efficient and equitable distribution of goods and services across the world economy. Order in the global economy is a fairly minimal one. The optimal role of governments and institutions is to ensure the smooth and relatively unfettered operation of markets. It is assumed that governments face a wide range of choices in the world system and likewise vis-à-vis their own societies and populations. This means that governments that fail to pursue 'good' economic policies do so because decision-makers are either too corrupt or too ignorant of the correct economic choices they might make.

The mercantilist tradition

The mercantilist tradition stands in stark contrast to the liberal one. Mercantilists share the presumptions of **realists** in international relations. They do not focus on individual policy-makers and their policy choices, but rather assume that the world economy is an arena of **competition among states** seeking to maximize relative strength and power. Simply put, the **international system** is like a jungle in which each state has to do what it can to survive. For this reason, the aim of every state must be to maximize its wealth and independence. States will seek to do this by ensuring their self-sufficiency in key strategic industries and commodities, and by using trade protectionism (tariffs and other limits on exports and imports), subsidies, and selective investments in the domestic economy. Obviously, within this system some states have more power and capability than others. The most powerful states define the rules and limits of the system: through **hegemony**, alliances, and **balances of power**. Indeed, stability and order will be achieved only where one state can play the role of hegemon, or in other words, is willing and able to create, maintain, and enforce basic rules. Amid this, the economic policies of any one government will always be subservient to its quest to secure the external and internal sovereignty of the state.

The Marxian tradition

The Marxian tradition also sees the world economy as an arena of competition, but not among states. **Capitalism** is the driving force in the world economy. Using Marx's language, this means that world-economic relations are best conceived as a **class struggle** between the 'oppressor and the oppressed'. The oppressors or capitalists are those who own the **means of production** (trade and industry). The oppressed are the working class. The struggle between the two arises because capitalists seek to increase their profits and this requires them to exploit the working class ever more harshly. In international relations this description of 'class relations' within a capitalist system has been applied to describe relations between the **core** (industrialized countries) and **periphery** (developing countries), and the unequal exchange that occurs between the two. **Dependency theorists** (who have focused mainly on Latin America) describe the ways classes and groups in the 'core' link to the 'periphery'. Underdevelopment and poverty in so many countries is explained as the result of economic, social, and political structures within countries that have been deeply influenced by their international economic relations. The global capitalist order within which these societies have emerged is, after all, a global capitalist order that reflects the interests of those who own the means of production.

Box 15.5 Traditional perspectives on IPE

Liberal	Mercantilist	Marxist
The world economy has the potential to be a seamless global marketplace in which free trade and the free movement of capital shape the policies of governments and economic actors. Order would be achieved by the 'invisible hand' of competition in the global market place.	As an arena of inter-state competition, the world economy is one in which states seek to maximize their wealth and independence vis-à-vis other states. Order is achieved only where there is a balance of power or hegemony.	The world economy is best described as an arena of capitalist competition in which classes (capitalists and workers) and social groups are in constant conflict. Capitalists (and the states they are based in) are driven by the search for profits, and order is achieved only where they succeed in exacting the submission of all others.

It becomes clear in contrasting these traditions of thinking about international economic relations that each focuses on different actors and driving forces in the world economy, and that each has a different conception of what 'order' means and what is necessary to achieve it.

Comparing the different traditions also highlights three different levels of analysis: the structure of the international system (be that international capitalism or the configuration of power among states in the system); the nature of a particular government or competition within its institutions; and the role of interest groups and societal forces within a country. At each of these levels of analysis we need to ask: what drives the actors concerned and therefore how might we explain their preferences, actions, and the outcomes that result? In answering this question we enter into more methodological preoccupations that today divide the study of IPE.

New approaches to IPE

International political economy is divided by the different normative concerns and analytical questions highlighted by the traditions outlined above. Equally, the discipline is now subject to a lively **methodological debate** about how scholars might best explain policies and outcomes in IPE. In essence, this debate is about whether you can assume what states' (and other actors') preferences and interests are. If you can, then rational choice (or 'neo-utilitarian') approaches to IPE make sense. However, if you open up the question as to why and how states and other actors come to have particular preferences, then you are pushed towards approaches now often labelled '**social constructivism**' (see Ch. 9).

Political economy: the application of rational choice to groups within the state

In the USA, the study of IPE has become dominated by a 'rational choice' or neo-utilitarian approach. This borrows economic concepts to explain politics. Instead of exploring the ideas, personalities, ideologies, or historical traditions that lie behind policies and institutions, rational choice focuses on the **incentive structure** faced by those making decisions. It is assumed that actors' interests and preferences are known or fixed, and that actors can make strategic choices as to how best to promote their interests. The term 'rational choice' is a useful one to describe this approach since it proposes that even though a particular policy may seem stupid or wrong, it may well once have been rational. 'Rational' in

this sense means that for the actor or group concerned, this was the optimal choice given the specific incentives and institutional constraints and opportunities that existed at the time.

Rational choice has been applied to interest groups and their influence on IPE in what has been called a **political economy approach**. This approach has its roots in explanations of trade policy which focus on interest groups. More recent applications have attempted to explain why countries adapt in particular ways to changes in the world economy. The analysis proceeds on the assumption that governments and their policies are important but that the policies and preferences of governments reflect the actions of specific interest groups within the economy. These groups may emerge along class or sectoral lines. Indeed, the assumptions of rational choice are applied to explain how particular groups within the economy emerge and what their goals and policy preferences are. Furthermore, rational choice provides a framework for understanding the coalitions into which these groups enter and their interactions with other institutions. For example in explaining why banks were able to expose the public to such risks through their excessively leveraged activities, some scholars focus on the ways the financial sector 'captured' the regulatory system. The private financial sector had greater information, far more resources and lobbying power than other stakeholders, and regulators had little incentive, institutional or personal, robustly to apply regulation (Mattli and Woods 2009).

Institutionalism: the application of rational choice to states

A different application of rational choice lies in the **institutionalist approach** to IPE (about which more is said in the last section). This approach applies the assumptions of rational choice to states in their interaction with other states. Drawing on theories of **delegation and agency**, it offers an explanation as to why institutions exist and for what purposes. The core assumption is that states create international institutions and delegate power to them in order to maximize utility within the constraints of world markets and world politics. Frequently, this comes down to the need to resolve collective-action problems. For example, states realize that they cannot achieve their goals in areas such as trade or environment unless all other states also embark upon a particular course of action. Hence institutions are created to ensure that there is no defection or free-riding, and the collective goal is achieved.

Box 15.6 Examples of new approaches to IPE

Institutionalist	Political economy	Constructivist
Institutionalists regard the world economy as an arena of inter-state cooperation. They see the core actors as governments and the institutions to whom they delegate power, and the key driving forces as rational choice at the level of the state, motivated by the potential gains from cooperation. For institutionalists, the key condition for order is the existence of international institutions, which permit cooperation to continue.	For political economists, the world economy is characterized by competition among vested interests within different kinds of states, and the core actors are interest groups formed within the domestic economies of the states. The key driving force is rational choice at the level of groups within the domestic economy responding to changes in the international economy. Political economists are not concerned with theorizing about the conditions necessary for international order.	Constructivists focus on the ideas, knowledge, and historical circumstances that shape identity and preferences in the global economy and the boundaries within which international economic relations take place. The concept of **hegemony** is used by those who probe the interests and ideas embodied in the rules and norms of the system. Neo-Gramscians highlight that the dominant power within the system will achieve goals not just through coercion but equally by ensuring the consent of other actors within the system. This means that dominant powers will promulgate institutions, ideologies, and ideas, all of which help to persuade other actors that their best interests converge with those of the dominant power.

Social constructivism

In contrast to rational choice analysis, other approaches to international political economy assume that policies within the world economy are affected by **historical** and **sociological factors**. Much more attention is paid to the ways in which actors formulate preferences, as well as to the processes by which decisions are made and implemented. In other words, rather than assuming that a state or decision-maker's preferences reflect rational choices within given constraints and opportunities, analysts in a broader tradition of IPE examine the beliefs, roles, traditions, ideologies, and patterns of **influence** that shape preferences, behaviour, and outcomes.

Interests, actions, and behaviour in the world economy are conceived as taking place within a structure of ideas, culture, and knowledge. We cannot simply assume that the preferences of actors within the system reflect objectively definable competing 'interests'. Rather, the way actors understand their own preferences will depend heavily upon prevailing beliefs and patterns of thinking in the world economy, many of which are embodied in institutions. The question this poses is: whose interests and ideas are embodied in the rules and norms of the system?

For some, the answer to the question 'in whose interest?' lies in hegemony. The dominant power within the system will achieve goals not just through coercion but equally by ensuring the consent of other actors within the system. This means that dominant powers will promulgate institutions, ideologies, and ideas, all of which help to persuade other actors that their best interests converge with those of the dominant power. For example, **neo-Gramscians** interpret the dominance

of market liberalism from the 1980s at least through until 2008 as a reflection of US interests in the global economy, successfully projected through structures of knowledge (it became the dominant paradigm in top research universities), through institutions (such as the IMF, which became forceful proponents of neo-liberal policy prescriptions), and through broader cultural beliefs and understandings (the very language of 'free' market contrasting with restricted or repressive regimes).

New approaches to IPE highlight a powerful debate within the subject about whether we should treat states' interests and preferences as given or fixed. We return to this question in the final section of this chapter. There we shall examine why states form institutions and what role such institutions might play in managing **globalization**. First, though, we need to establish what is globalization in the world economy and what are its implications.

Key Points

- Rational choice explains outcomes in IPE as the result of actors' choices, which are assumed always to be rationally power or utility maximizing within given particular incentives and institutional constraints.

- Institutionalists apply rational choice to states in their interactions with other states in order to explain international cooperation in economic affairs.

- Constructivist approaches pay more attention to how governments, states, and other actors construct their preferences, highlighting the role of identities, beliefs, traditions, and values in this process.

- Neo-Gramscians highlight that actors define and pursue their interests within a structure of ideas, culture, and knowledge, which itself is shaped by hegemonic powers.

The globalization debate in IPE

The nature and impact of globalization is the subject of profound debate within IPE (as within other areas of international relations discussed in this book). The term globalization is used to refer to at least four different sets of forces or processes in the world economy. **Internationalization** describes the increase in economic transactions across borders that has been taking place since the turn of the century but that some argue has undergone a quantitative leap in recent decades. The **technological revolution** describes the effect of new electronic communication, which permits firms and other actors to operate globally with much less regard for location, distance, and borders. One effect of the technological revolution is to speed up **deterritorialization**, or the extent to which territorial distances, borders, and places influence the way people collectively identify themselves and act, and seek political voice or recognition. In the decade before the 2008 crisis, there was much talk of footloose banks becoming deterritorialized and global. Their nationality was no longer relevant. However, in the wake of the crisis, it became clear that banks may 'live globally', but they die nationally, with their national governments picking up the costs of bailing them out. Finally, **liberalization** describes the policies undertaken by states that have made a new global economy possible. This includes changes in rules and institutions, which facilitated a new scale of transnational economic activity in certain sectors (but by no means all) of the world economy, including the liberalizing of trade, investment, and production.

In IPE several competing claims are made about globalization. For example, while some scholars argue that globalization is nothing new, others posit that globalization is dramatically diminishing the role of the state (see Ch. 1). Still others claim that globalization is exacerbating inequalities and giving rise to a more unequal and unjust world. To make sense of these different arguments, and the evidence adduced to support them, it is worth thinking about the approaches to IPE covered in previous sections, for they help to identify key differences in emphasis that give rise to conflicting interpretations of globalization. For example, sceptics who deny that globalization is transforming world politics tend to focus on the 'internationalization' element of globalization (see Box 15.7). They can then draw upon evidence that throws into doubt whether the number of transactions taking place among states has indeed risen (UNDP 1997), and make the argument that there is 'nothing new' in the growing interdependence of states. By contrast, **liberal enthusiasts** of globalization focus on technological innovation and the non-political 'objective' forces that are shrinking the world economy. They argue that this is creating a less political, more efficient, more unified world order. Those who focus on deterritorialization highlight that there is also a negative side to globalization. Just as technological innovation permits a more active global civil society, so too it permits the growth of an uncivil one. Terrorist **networks** and the growth of transnational crime grow easily and are harder to combat in an era of globalization. This puts an important caveat on a final argument about globalization—one that prioritizes the role powerful states play in shaping the process. Focusing on liberalization, several analysts highlight the role of powerful states, and the USA especially, in setting the rules of the new globalized international economy, and predict their increasing influence over other states. Yet the 2008 crisis demonstrated some limits to this. The post-war order and institutions were created by the USA, which was at

---

Box 15.7   Four aspects of globalization

- **Internationalization** describes the increase in transactions among states reflected in flows of trade, investment, and capital, facilitated by inter-state agreements on trade, investment, and capital, and by domestic policies permitting the private sector to transact abroad.

- The **technological revolution** refers to the way modern communications (Internet, satellite communications, high-tech computers) have made distance and location less important factors not just for government (including at local and regional levels) but equally in the calculations of other actors, such as firms' investment decisions or in the activities of **social movements**.

- **Deterritorialization** is accelerated by the technological revolution and refers to the diminution of influence of territorial places, distances, and boundaries over the way people collectively identify themselves or seek political recognition. This permits transnational political and economic activity, both positive and negative.

- **Liberalization** describes government policies that reduce the role of the state in the economy, such as through the dismantling of trade tariffs and barriers, the deregulation and opening of the financial sector to foreign investors, and the privatization of state enterprises.

Case Study The international financial crisis of 2008

In September 2008, a large US investment bank called Lehman Brothers defaulted, catalysing a major financial crisis. The government of the USA was soon forced to rescue the largest US insurance company, American International Group (AIG) while the UK and other European governments were forced to intervene to rescue other institutions. The total costs of cleaning up after the crisis were estimated one year later at US$11.9 trillion and, in the fourth quarter of 2008, industrialized countries were experiencing an unprecedented economic decline of 7.5 per cent.

In wealthy industrialized countries, the financial crisis exposed failures in corporate governance, in credit-rating agencies, and in regulation. Poor corporate governance led to excessive risk-taking by some providers of financial services. Poorly designed incentives, such as pay and bonuses, favoured short-term risk-taking. Credit-rating agencies who should have signalled fragilities in some institutions had little incentive so to do. Most of all, the financial crisis exposed the enormous and costly implicit guarantee that governments give to financial services firms because they are simply 'too big to fail'.

In poorer developing countries, the crisis provoked what the IMF and World Bank would describe in 2009 as a 'development emergency'. Trade slumped as demand from the rich countries fell, and even as the world economy recovered in 2010, the IMF was still predicting a further 16 per cent drop in low-income countries' exports of goods and services. Remittances, or money sent back home by workers in foreign countries, plummeted and

were set to fall by a further 10 per cent in 2010. Flows of foreign direct investment dried up. Aid flows became yet more unpredictable and never reached the levels donors had promised. In short, for developing countries, the crisis revealed that participation in an interdependent global economy carries great risks due to unregulated global finance (from which most developing countries benefit little).

National and international policy-makers alike have agreed on the primacy of state authorities in regulation to restrict excessive risk. They have also agreed that national regulators must harmonize their policies in order to achieve global financial stability.

the time the world's largest creditor; and had much to gain from the liberalization of trade in certain sectors and the liberalization of global finance. However, in 2008 the USA was the world's largest debtor. Emerging economies such as China, Brazil, and India had to be engaged in a coordinated solution. In these countries the government plays a stronger role in the economy than in the USA. At the same time, as these economies internationalize in more sectors, they too will acquire an interest in global liberalization.

International institutions in the globalizing world economy

Globalization increases interdependence among states and increases the need for governments to coordinate. Financial crises in the 1990s, including in East Asia, led some policy-makers to call for stronger, more effective international institutions, including a capacity to ensure better information and monitoring, deeper cooperation, and regulation in the world economy. At the same time, critics argued that the crisis revealed the problems and flaws of existing international institutions and the bias or interests that they reflect. These positions echo a larger debate in IPE about the nature and impact of institutions in the world economy. This debate is important in helping us to determine what role international

institutions might play in managing the new problems and challenges arising from globalization.

Competing accounts of institutions echo the differences in approaches to IPE already discussed. Institutionalists (or neo-liberal institutionalists (see Ch. 7)) tell us that states will create institutions in order better to achieve gains through policy **coordination** and cooperation. However, several conditions are necessary for this to occur. Under certain conditions, institutionalists argue that states will agree to be bound by certain rules, norms, or decisions of **international organizations**. This does not mean that the most powerful states in the system will always obey the rules. Rather, institutions affect

Table 15.1 The debate about institutions

	Institutionalist (or 'neo-liberal Institutionalist')	Realist (or 'neo-realist')	Constructivist
Under what conditions will states create international institutions?	For mutual gains (rationally calculated by states).	Only where relative position vis-à-vis other states is not adversely affected.	Institutions arise as a reflection of the identities and interests of states and groups that are themselves forged through interaction.
What impact do institutions have on international relations?	Expand the possible gains to be made from cooperation.	Facilitate the coordination of policies and actions but only in so far as this does not alter the balance of power among states.	Reinforce particular patterns of interaction, and reflect new ones.
The implications for globalization	Institutions can manage globalization to ensure a transition to a more 'liberal' economy (see Box 15.5).	Institutions will 'manage' globalization in the interests of dominant and powerful states.	Changing patterns of interaction and discourse will be reflected in institutional responses to globalization.

international politics because they open up new reasons to cooperate, they permit states to define their interests in a more cooperative way, and they foster negotiations among states as well as compliance with mutually agreed rules and standards.

The institutionalist account offers reasons for a certain kind of optimism about the role international institutions will play in managing globalization. Institutions will smooth over many gaps and failures in the operation of markets, and serve to ensure that states make genuinely rational and optimizing decisions to cooperate. Globalization will be managed by existing institutions and organizations and, indeed, new institutions will probably also emerge. Globalization managed in this way will ensure that the world economy moves more towards the **liberal** model and that both strong and weak states benefit. Although the financial crisis of 2008 highlights serious gaps in financial regulation (see Case Study), these can be remedied so as to permit countries to harness the advantages of free trade and free movements of capital in the world economy.

Realists (and neo-realists in particular) disagree with institutionalists (see Chs 5 and 7). Realists reject the idea that institutions emerge primarily as a solution to universal problems or market failures. They argue that international institutions and organizations will always reflect the interests of dominant states within the system. When these states wish to coordinate policies with others, they will create institutions. Once created, however, these institutions will not (as the institutionalists argue)

transform the way states define and pursue their interests. Institutions will be effective only for as long as they do not diminish the power of dominant states *vis-à-vis* other states.

Let us consider what this means in practice. Take a state deciding whether to sign up to a new trade agreement or support the decision of an international organization. The institutionalists argue that policy-makers will consider the **absolute gains** to be made from the agreement, including the potential longer-term gains, such as advancing a more stable and credible system of rules. The neo-realists, by contrast, argue that policy-makers will primarily be concerned with **relative gains**. In other words, they will ask, 'do we gain more from this than other states?' (rather than 'do we gain from this?'). If other states stand to gain more, then the advantages of signing up are outweighed by the fact that the power of the state will be diminished vis-à-vis other states. For realists, cooperation and institutions are heavily constrained by underlying calculations about power. Having signed an agreement or created an international organization, a powerful state will not necessarily be bound by it. Indeed, if it got in the way of the state's interests (defined in realist terms), a powerful state will simply sweep the institution aside. The implications for globalization and its impact on weak states are rather grim. International institutions, including organizations such as the IMF, the World Bank, the WTO, the G8 and the EU, will manage globalization, but in the interests of their most powerful members. Institutions will only accommodate the needs and interests of weaker states when in so doing they do not diminish the dominant position of powerful states. From a realist perspective, it follows that critics who argue that the international institutions do not work for the interests of poor and developing countries are correct. However, the realists are equally certain that those protesting about this will have little impact.

This interpretation of international institutions is rebutted not only by institutionalists, but by those who delve into the ways ideas, beliefs, and interactions shape the behaviour of states. In an earlier section, we mentioned constructivists.

Constructivists reject the idea that institutions reflect the 'rational' calculations of states either within inter-state competition (realists) or as part of a calculation of longer-term economic advantage and benefits from cooperation (institutionalists). In fact, what constructivists reject is the idea that states' interests are objectively definable and fixed. Instead, they argue that any one state's interests are affected by its **identity** as a state and that both its interests and identity are influenced by a **social structure of interactions**, **normative ideas**, and beliefs. If we cannot assume that states have a particular identity or interest prior to their interactions, then the institutionalists are wrong to assume that institutions emerge as rational responses to the needs of markets, trade, finance, and the like. Equally, the realists are wrong to assume that institutions can only be reflections of power politics. To quote constructivist Alex Wendt, 'anarchy is what states make of it' (1992). In other words, identities and interests are more fluid and changing than realists permit. Through their interactions and discourse, states change and these changes can reflect in institutions.

Constructivism and the neo-Gramscian approach highlight actors and processes involved in globalization that are neglected in realist and institutionalist accounts,

and have important ramifications for institutions. For example, when transnational groups protect against the WTO, the IMF, and the World Bank, they are part of an ongoing dialogue that affects states in several ways. The international attention to these issues places them on the agenda of international meetings and organizations. It also puts pressures on political leaders and encourages interest groups and pressures to form within the state. As a result, the beliefs, ideas, and conceptions of interest in international relations change and this can shift the attention, nature, and functions of international institutions. On this view, globalization is not just a process affecting and managed by states. Several other actors are involved, both within and across societies, including international institutions, which play a dynamic role. The governance or management of globalization is shaped by a mixture of interests, beliefs, and values about how the world works and how it ought to be. The existing institutions doubtless reflect the interests of powerful states. However, these interests are the products of the way states interact and are subject to reinterpretation and change.

Key Points

- Institutionalists argue that international institutions will play an important and positive role in ensuring that globalization results in widely spread benefits in the world economy.

- Realists and neo-realists reject the institutionalist argument on the grounds that it does not account for the unwillingness of states ever to sacrifice power relative to other states.

- Constructivists pay more attention to how governments, states, and other actors construct their preferences, highlighting the role that state identities, dominant beliefs, and ongoing debates and contestation plays in this process.

Conclusion

Globalization increases the challenges faced by all actors in the world economy: states, firms, **transnational actors**, and international organizations. Strong states are trying to shape institutions to manage financial crises, powerful NGOs, and globalizing firms. Weak states are trying to survive increasingly precarious and changeable economic circumstances. Common to all states is the search for greater stability and

predictability, although governments disagree over how and where this should be achieved. One layer of governance this chapter has not examined is that of regional organizations and institutions (see Ch. 26). The fact that in recent years virtually every state in the world has joined at least one regional trade grouping underscores the search for new ways to manage globalization. At the same time, **regionalism** highlights the scepticism of many states about international institutions, and their fears that institutions are too dominated by powerful states, or unlikely to constrain them. The result is an emerging multi-layered governance in the world economy. At each level (international, regional, and state) the core issues debated in this chapter arise. These include: whose interests are served by the institution? What forces are shaping it? Who has access to it? Whose values does it reflect? Globalization casts a spotlight on these arrangements since the transformations occurring in the world economy are being powerfully shaped by them.

Questions

1   In what ways did the Bretton Woods framework for the post-war economy try to avoid the economic problems of the inter-war years?
2   What was the 'breakdown in the Bretton Woods system'?
3   Did a loss of US hegemony cause the breakdown of the Bretton Woods system?
4   Are there any issues on which mercantilists agree with liberals?
5   What is different about the Marxian and mercantilist depictions of power in the international economy?
6   Does rational choice theory explain more about outcomes than actors' preferences?
7   In what way do neo-Gramscians invoke structure in their explanation of IPE?
8   Why do sceptics doubt that globalization is transforming IPE?
9   What vulnerabilities faced by states in the globalizing economy did the Asian financial crisis demonstrate?
10   How can we explain the different impact globalization has on different states?
11   How and why do institutionalists argue that institutions change the behaviour of states?
12   For whom might the realist account of institutions and globalization be cheerful reading?

Further Reading

Abdelal, R., Parsons, C., and Blythe, M. (2010), *Constructing the International Economy* (Cornell University Press). A selection of constructivist analyses of international political economy.

Cohen, B. (2007), 'The Transatlantic Divide: Why are American and British IPE so Different?', *Review of International Political Economy*, 14 (2)

Frieden, J., and Lake, D. A. (eds) (2000), *International Political Economy: Perspectives on Global Power and Wealth* (New York: St Martin's Press). Introduces core texts from each approach to international political economy with useful editors' introductions.

Held, D., McGrew, A., Goldblatt, D., and Perrator, J. (1999), *Global Transformations: Politics, Economics and Culture* (Cambridge: Polity Press). A resource book on the empirical evidence of globalization in all aspects of international relations.

Katzenstein, P., Keohane, R., and Krasner, S. (1998), 'International Organization and the State of World Politics', *International Organization*, 52(4): 645–85. A review article of key developments in the study of international relations and international political economy.

Mattli, W., and Woods, N. (2009), *The Politics of Global Regulation* (Princeton, NJ: Princeton University Press). A theory of why global regulation is more effective in some areas than others, with a framing theoretical chapter and several case studies.

Oatley, T., and Silver, M. (2003), *International Political Economy: Interests and Institutions in the Global Economy* (Harlow: Pearson). A public or rational choice approach to international political economy.

Stiglitz, Joseph (2010) *Free fall: Free markets and the sinking of the global economy* (New York: Allen Lane). An account of the causes of the 2008 financial crisis by a Nobel-Prize winning economist who long-predicted a crisis.

Woods, N. (2006), *The Globalizers: The IMF, the World Bank, and their Borrowers* (Ithaca, NY: Cornell University Press). A study of how geo-politics, economics, and bureaucracy shape what the IMF and World Bank do.

Online Resource Centre

Visit the Online Resource Centre that accompanies this book to access more learning resources on this chapter topic at www.oxfordtextbooks.co.uk/orc/baylis5e/

Chapter 16

Gender in world politics

J. ANN TICKNER

Reader's Guide

This chapter introduces you to the way in which gender helps to structure world politics. It does so using feminist perspectives on international relations. It begins with an overview of feminist theories more generally and offers a feminist definition of gender. Feminists define gender as an unequal structural relationship of power. Building on a variety of the International Relations (IR) theoretical perspectives discussed in Part Two of this book, IR feminists use gender, defined in this way, to help them understand why women are disadvantaged relative to men in all societies. The chapter focuses on feminist perspec-

tives on security and the global economy. It examines the masculinity of war and national security, suggesting that states' national security policies are often legitimated in terms of masculine characteristics. This helps us understand why women have been so under-represented in powerful positions in the international policy world and in militaries. Feminists consider the security of individuals to be as important as the security of states. We shall see how gendered economic structures of inequality, associated with a global gendered division of labour, can help us explain why the majority of the world's poor are women. The chapter concludes by outlining some policy practices that are helping to lessen gender inequality.

Introduction

Feminist perspectives entered the International Relations discipline at the end of the 1980s, at about the same time as the end of the **cold war**. This was not a coincidence. During the previous forty years, the conflict between the USA and the Soviet Union had dominated the agenda of International Relations (see Ch. 3). The decade after the end of the cold war (1989–2000) was one of relative peace between the major powers (see Ch. 4). Many new issues appeared on the International Relations' agenda. More attention was paid to economic relations. There were lively debates between proponents of economic globalization and those who claimed that it was not helping to reduce world poverty. The meaning of security was expanded to include human as well as state security (see Ch. 29). International Relations began to pay more attention to ethno-national conflicts and to the high number of civilians killed or injured in these conflicts (see Ch. 13). More attention was also paid to **international organizations**, **social movements**, and **non-state actors** (see Ch. 20). As the globalization theme of this book makes clear, international politics is about much more than inter-state relations.

This broad set of issues seems the most compatible with feminist approaches. Feminists are not satisfied with framing international politics solely in terms of inter-state politics. While women have always been players in international politics, their participation has more often taken place in non-governmental settings such as social movements rather than in inter-state policy-making. Women also participate in international politics as diplomats' wives, as nannies going abroad to find work to support their families, and as sex workers trafficked across international boundaries. Women's voices have rarely been heard in the halls of state power or in the leadership of militaries. Nevertheless, women are deeply affected by decisions that their leaders make. Civilian casualties constitute about 90 per cent of the casualties in today's wars, and women and children make up the majority of these casualties. Women are the majority of the world's poorest population. Economic policies, constructed in distant centres of power, affect how resources are distributed in local communities. Broader global frameworks are more suited to investigating these issues.

Before examining how gender is at work in these global issues, we begin with a brief introduction to feminist theory and a definition of what feminists mean by the term **gender**.

Feminist theories

Feminism as an academic discipline grew out of the feminist movement of the 1960s and 1970s—a movement dedicated to achieving political, social, and economic equality for women. Many feminists link constructing knowledge to political practice. This form of knowledge-building is called emancipatory knowledge. It means producing knowledge that can help inform practices to improve women's lives. The most important goal for feminist theory is to explain women's subordination, which exists to varying degrees in all societies, and to seek ways to end it. However, feminists disagree on the reasons for this subordination and, thus, how to overcome it.

There are many different types of feminist theory. They all give us different reasons for women's subordination. They include liberal, Marxist, socialist, post-colonial, and poststructural (see various chapters in Part Two). Liberal feminists believe that removing legal obstacles can overcome women's subordination. However, all the other approaches—which we shall call post-liberal—see deeply rooted structures of **patriarchy** in all societies, which cannot be overcome by legal remedies alone. Marxist and socialist feminists look for explanations of women's subordination in the labour market, which offers greater rewards and prestige for paid work in the public sphere than for unpaid work in the household. (Women do most of the unpaid work, even when they work for wages; this imposes what feminists call a **double burden**.) Postcolonial and poststructural feminists believe that we cannot generalize about all women. Women experience subordination differently because they are differently placed in and among societies depending on their class and race, as well as on their gender. All these post-liberal feminist theories use gender as an important category of analysis.

Feminists define gender

In everyday usage, gender denotes the biological sex of individuals. However, feminists define gender differently—as a set of socially and culturally constructed characteristics that vary across time and place. When we think of characteristics such as power, autonomy, rationality, and public, we associate them with masculinity or what it means to be a 'real man'. Opposite characteristics, such as weakness, dependence/connection, emotionality, and private, are associated with femininity. Studies have shown that both women and men assign a more positive value to masculine characteristics. These definitions of masculinity and femininity are relational, which means that they depend on each other for their meaning. In other words, what it means to be a 'real man' is not to display 'womanly' weaknesses. Since these characteristics are social constructions, not biological ones, it is quite possible for women, particularly those in powerful positions like former US Secretary of State Condoleezza Rice or former British Prime Minister Margaret Thatcher, to appear to act like 'real men'. In fact, certain feminists have argued that such behaviour is necessary for both women and men to succeed in the tough world of international policy-making (Cohn 1993: 230–1, 237–8).

Sometimes gender is thought to be synonymous with women. But feminists believe that gender is as much about men and masculinity as it is about women. Since, at the top level, international politics is a masculine world, it is particularly important to pay attention to various forms of masculinity that are often used to legitimate states' foreign and military policies. For example,

characteristics such as power, autonomy, and rationality, which we have identified as masculine, are characteristics that are most valued in states' foreign policies.

But gender is about more than personal characteristics. Since, as we have seen, gender characteristics are generally unequal—meaning that people of both sexes ascribe more positive value to the masculine ones—gender is also a structure of meaning that signifies power relationships. If gender characteristics denote inequality, gender becomes a mechanism for the unequal distribution of social benefits and costs. Therefore gender is crucial for analysing global politics and economics, particularly with respect to issues of inequality, insecurity, and social justice. Feminists believe we need to make unequal gender structures visible in order to move beyond them.

We have shown that gender is an analytical tool, not just a descriptive category. Now that we have examined feminist theory and defined gender, let us look at how IR feminists use gender as a category of analysis.

> ### Key Points
>
> - Feminists define gender as a set of socially constructed characteristics that define what we mean by masculinity and femininity.
> - Gender is a system of social hierarchy in which masculine characteristics are more valued than feminine ones.
> - Gender is a structure that signifies unequal power relationships between women and men.

Putting a gender lens on global politics

IR feminists use gender analysis to help them answer questions about global politics. V. Spike Peterson and Anne Sisson Runyan call this putting on our gender-sensitive lenses. Let us see what kind of questions we might ask when we put on our gender-sensitive lenses.

Some feminist questions

As of 2008, less than 9 per cent of the world's heads of state were women and most of the world's military personnel were men. In order to understand the lack of women in high places we might begin by asking 'Where

are the women?' Cynthia Enloe (1989: 8) suggests that we need to look in unconventional places, not normally considered within the boundaries of global politics, to answer this question. She asks us to consider whether women's roles, as secretaries, clerical workers, domestic servants, and diplomats' wives, are relevant to the business of international politics. She shows us how vital women in these various roles are to states' foreign policies and to the functioning of the global economy.

But making women visible does not explain why they are disproportionately situated in low-paid or non-remunerated occupations far from the halls of power. To

Box 16.1 Gender-sensitive lenses

'[A gender-sensitive lens] focuses our attention selectively...
   Lenses simplify our thinking by focusing our attention on what seems most relevant. They "order" what we see and provide direction for subsequent actions. In this sense, lenses are like maps: ... Like maps, lenses enable us to make sense of where we are, what to expect next, and how to proceed ... [W]e choose the lens we assume is most appropriate for a particular context—a lens that we expect will enable us to make sense of and act appropriately in that context.'

(Peterson and Runyan 2010: 38–9)

Box 16.2 Women leaders

- World percentage of women in parliaments (2009): 18.6%
- Percentage of women in Upper House or Senate (2009): 17.6%
- Percentage of women in Single House or Lower House of Parliament (2009): 18.8%

explain this we must put on our gender-sensitive lenses and think about women's places within gendered global structures and processes that constrain their security and their economic opportunities. We might want to ask some further questions. How are the types of power necessary to keep unequal gender structures in place perpetuated? Does it make any difference to states' policy practices that their foreign and security policies are often legitimated through appeals to various types of masculinity? Does it make a difference that it is predominantly men who fight wars? Answering these questions may help us to see that what is so often taken for granted in how the world is organized is, in fact, keeping in place certain social arrangements and institutional structures that contribute to the subordination of women and other disadvantaged groups.

To help them answer these questions, IR feminists use a number of different theoretical approaches that build on feminist theory more generally. Let us look at some examples.

Liberal feminism

Liberal feminists document various aspects of women's subordination. They have investigated problems of refugee women, income inequalities between women and men, and the kinds of human rights violations incurred disproportionately by women, such as trafficking and rape in war. They look for women in the institutions and practices of global politics and observe how their presence (or absence) affects and is affected by international policy-making. They ask what a world with more women in positions of power might look like. Liberal feminists believe that women's equality can be achieved by removing legal and other obstacles that have denied them the same rights and opportunities as men.

Many IR feminists disagree with liberal feminism. As we noted earlier, post-liberal feminists emphasize that

gender inequalities continue to exist in societies that have long since achieved formal legal equality. They suggest that we must look more deeply at gender hierarchies in order to explain these inequalities. Post-liberal feminists draw on, but go beyond, a variety of IR approaches discussed in Part Two, such as critical theory, social constructivism and poststructuralism. What is unique to these feminist approaches is that they use gender as a category of analysis. Let us look at some examples of each.

Feminist critical theory

Feminist critical theory has roots in Gramscian Marxism (see Ch. 8). It explores both the ideational and material manifestations of gendered **identities** and gendered power in global politics. Sandra Whitworth is a feminist critical theorist. In her book, *Feminism and International Relations* (1994), she claims that understanding gender depends only in part on the material conditions of women and men in particular circumstances. She suggests that gender is also constituted by the meaning given to that reality—in other words, *ideas* that men and women have about their relationships to one another. Whitworth examines the different ways gender was understood over time in the International Planned Parenthood Federation (IPPF) and the International Labour Organization (ILO). She shows that changes in the meaning of gender had differing effects on these institutions' population policies at various times in their history.

Feminist social constructivism

Feminist constructivism builds on social constructivism (see Ch. 9). Feminist constructivists study the processes whereby ideas about gender influence global politics as well as the ways that global politics shape ideas about gender. Elisabeth Prügl is a feminist constructivist. Her book, *The Global Construction of Gender* (1999), uses feminist constructivism to analyse the treatment of home-based work in international law. Since most home-based workers are women, the debate about regulating this type of employment is an important one for feminists. Low wages and poor working conditions are often justified on the grounds that home-based work is not 'real work' since it takes place in the private reproductive sphere of the household rather than in the more valued public sphere of waged-based production. Prügl shows how ideas about femininity have contributed to the international community's debates about institutionalizing these home-based workers' rights, a debate that finally culminated in the passage of the ILO's Homework Convention in 1996 (see Case Study 2 below).

Feminist poststructuralism

Poststructuralists focus on meaning as it is codified in language (see Ch. 10). They claim that we understand reality through our use of language. They are particularly concerned with the relationship between knowledge and power—meaning that those who construct meaning and create knowledge gain a great deal of power by so doing. Feminist poststructuralists point out that men have generally been seen as the knowers and that what has counted as knowledge has generally been based on men's lives in the public sphere. Women have generally not been seen as knowers or as the subjects of knowledge.

Charlotte Hooper's book *Manly States* (2001) is an example of poststructural textual analysis. Hooper claims that we cannot understand international relations unless we understand the implications of the fact that it is conducted mostly by men. She asks how might international relations shape men as much as men shape international relations. Hooper sets about answering this question through an analysis of masculinity, together with a textual analysis of *The Economist*, a prestigious British

weekly newspaper that covers business and politics. She concludes that *The Economist* is saturated with signifiers of masculinity and that gendered messages are encoded in the magazine regardless of the intentions of its publishers or authors. This is one example of how gender politics pervades our understanding of world politics.

Postcolonial feminism

Postcolonialists focus on colonial relations of domination and subordination, established under European **imperialism** in the eighteenth and nineteenth centuries (see Ch. 11). Postcolonialists claim that these dominance relationships persist, and that they are built into the way Western knowledge portrays people and countries in the South today. Postcolonial feminism makes similar claims about the way Western feminism has constructed knowledge about non-Western women. Just as feminists in general have criticized Western knowledge for being knowledge constructed mainly from men's lives, postcolonial feminists see similar problems arising from feminist knowledge that is based largely on the experiences of relatively privileged Western women. Chandra Mohanty (1988) suggests that women's subordinations must be addressed within their own cultural context, rather than through some universal understanding of women's needs. She criticizes Western feminists' portrayal of **Third World** women as poor, under-educated, victimized, and lacking in agency.

We have examined some writings of IR feminists who have put on their gender-sensitive lenses in order to understand why women are disadvantaged relative to men and what difference this makes to global politics. Let us now look through our gender-sensitive lenses at two important realms of global politics—security and economic globalization.

Key Points

- IR feminists use gender-sensitive lenses to help them answer questions about why women often play subordinate roles in global politics.

- Liberal feminists believe that women's equality can be achieved by removing legal obstacles that deny women the same opportunities as men.

- Post-liberal feminists argue that we must look more deeply at unequal gendered structures in order to understand women's subordination.

- Feminist critical theorists show how both ideas and material structures shape people's lives and how changes

- in the meaning of gender have changed the practices of international organizations over time.

- Feminist constructivists show us the various ways in which ideas about gender shape and are shaped by global politics.

- Poststructural feminists claim that there is a link between knowledge and power. Since men have generally been seen as knowers and as subjects of knowledge, this influences how we see global politics.

- Postcolonial feminists suggest that women's subordination must be differentially understood in terms of race, class, and geographical location.

Gendering security

Challenging the myth of protection

We often think of men as protectors and women and children as people who need protection. One of the stories that has been told throughout history is that men fight wars to protect women and children. The high number of civilian casualties in contemporary wars, about 90 per cent of total casualties, suggests that we should be questioning this story. A large proportion of these casualties are women and children. Women and children constitute the majority of the world's refugee population.[1] When women, often acting as heads of households, are forced into refugee camps, their vulnerability, and that of their children, increases. In wartime, women are particularly subject to rape and prostitution (see Box 16.3). Rape is not just an accident of war but often a systematic military strategy. It is estimated that 20,000 to 35,000 women were raped during the war in Bosnia and Herzegovina. In Bosnia, rape was associated with a policy of ethnic cleansing. The strategy included forced pregnancies to make Bosnia a Serbian state by implanting Serbian babies in Bosnian Muslim mothers (Pettman 1996: 101).

These stories about women in conflict situations severely challenge the **protection myth**. Yet such myths have been important in upholding the legitimacy of war. Using our gender-sensitive lenses to look at the effects of war on women helps us to gain a better understanding of the unequal **gender relations**, such as the protector/

Box 16.3 Military prostitution as a security issue

Around many army bases, women are kidnapped and sold into prostitution. Katharine Moon has written an account of military prostitution around US military bases in South Korea in the 1970s. As part of an attempt to provide a more hospitable environment for American troops, the South Korean government undertook a policy of policing sexual health and work conduct of prostitutes. Moon's account shows us how military prostitution interacted with US–Korean security policies at the highest level. In the name of national security, the Korean state promoted policies that exploited these women's lives. Stories like Moon's shed light on the lives of women in places not normally considered relevant to global politics. By linking their experiences to wider processes, they show how national security can translate into personal insecurity for certain individuals.

(Adapted from Moon 1997)

---

protected relationship that legitimates military activities and hides some of the negative effects of war on civilians. Let us now look more deeply into how these gendered constructions can help us understand national and international security.

Gendering war

Gender-sensitive lenses help us to see the association between war and masculinity. Militaries work hard to turn men into soldiers who must go into combat. Military training depends on the denigration of anything considered feminine—to act like a soldier is to be not 'womanly'. This image of a soldier is related to the protection myth—the soldier as a just warrior, self-sacrificially protecting women, children, and other vulnerable people. The idea that young men fight wars to protect these vulnerable groups who cannot be expected to protect themselves has been an important motivator for the recruitment of military forces. It has also helped sustain support for war by both women and men. In wartime, the just warrior who displays heroic masculine characteristics is often contrasted with an enemy who is portrayed as dangerous often through the use of feminized and sometimes racialized characteristics. This serves as further support for the need for protection. For example, entry into the US-led war in Afghanistan was partially justified as a heroic intervention on behalf of presumably helpless Afghani women. The Taliban response was also shaped by gendered justifications of protecting 'their' women from outside influence. Both sides in the conflict further justified their positions through the use of feminized imagery of the other (Tickner 2002).

These images of the masculinity of war depend on rendering women's role in war invisible, or as the patriotic and supportive mother, wife, or daughter. Even in exceptional circumstances, such as in the Second World War when women took over factory jobs vacated by men who went off to war, women were expected to return to traditional roles when the war was over. But now that women are being accepted into the armed forces of certain states in ever-larger numbers, the picture is more complicated. The presence of women in militaries stirs deep currents, particularly with respect to their role in combat. Placing women in combat is in strong tension with our culturally embedded view of what it means to be a warrior and who the people in need of protection actually are. In certain cases, it has been strongly resisted by the military itself, with claims of its negative effect on combat readiness. It is a controversial issue for feminists. Most feminists believe that equality dictates that women should be allowed to serve in militaries. However, some feminists believe that women should reject fighting in men's wars.

It is interesting to note the degree to which the importance of militarized masculinity varies over time and place, and how these variations affect international policy-making. During the 1990s—a time of relative peace, at least in the North—we were becoming more accustomed to less militarized models of masculinity. Global businessmen conquering the world with brief-cases rather than bullets became our new heroes. Bill Gates, the chairman of Microsoft Corporation, a bourgeois hero who looks distinctly unwarrior-like, amasses dollars rather than weapons. And, in 1992, Bill Clinton was elected President of the USA after having refused to serve in the Vietnam War.

In the USA, these softer images of masculinity ended abruptly on **11 September 2001**. Post-9/11, militarized masculinity came back in vogue. After the attacks on the World Trade Center, firefighters and police officers in New York became the new male heroes. Women disappeared from television news broadcasts as male experts briefed Americans about 'America's New War'. However, this new form of warfare, the **war on terror**, as it was called, came with multiple gendered images. Americans saw new enemies in the form of young Muslim men, who were subjected to ethnic, as well as gender, profiling on the excuse that the USA was 'at war'. Militarized masculinity influenced the 2004 US presidential campaign, when both Republican George W. Bush and Democrat John Kerry emphasized their military or National Guard service as qualifications for the office of President. Clearly, this puts female candidates for high office in the USA at a disadvantage. While the 2006 mid-term elections saw Congresswoman Nancy Pelosi become the first woman House Majority Leader, only one out of the Democratic Party's top eleven women candidates to the US House of Representatives in the 2006 election was successful. Nine out of eleven of their male counterparts won. Many of them emphasized their toughness and ability to stand up to security threats during their campaigns.[2] These trends suggest that, in

times of war, US voters, women and men alike, show greater support for leaders who demonstrate a more obviously militarized masculinity. The election of US President Barack Obama in 2008 suggests that, in the USA, this image of militarized masculinity may have softened somewhat.

We have seen that, in spite of the myth of protection, civilians are not being protected in today's wars. We have also seen that, in certain cases, such as military prostitution camps, individuals' security may be sacrificed to national security. Qualifications for leadership positions in foreign policy are often tied up with what it means to be a 'real man'. This may help us understand why there are relatively few women in these top positions and in militaries. We conclude this section by thinking how we might redefine security using our gender-sensitive lenses.

Feminist definitions of security

Since, as we have seen, **national security** can be in tension with individual security, feminists prefer to define security broadly—as the diminution of all forms of violence, including physical, economic, and ecological. They suggest that we think about security from the bottom up instead of from the top down, meaning that we start with the security of individual or **community** rather than with that of the **state** or the **international system**. This allows us to examine critically the role of states as adequate security providers. In certain states torn by conflict, the more the government is preoccupied with national security, the less its citizens, especially women, experience physical security. While state violence is a particular problem in certain states, many states formally at peace sustain huge military budgets at the same time that social spending, on which women depend more than men, is being cut.

We have seen how the security-seeking behaviour of states is legitimated by its association with certain types of masculinity. This narrows the range of permissible ways for states to act and may actually reduce the likelihood of achieving a peaceful solution to a conflict. Conciliatory gestures are often seen as weak and not in the **national interest**. This can also contribute to the perceived inauthenticity of women's voices in matters of policy-making.

We have also seen how most war casualties today are civilians—often women and children. But it is important not to see women only as victims. If we are to define security more broadly, we must begin to see women, as well as men, as security providers. As civilian war casualties increase, women's responsibilities rise. When men go off to fight, women are left behind as mothers, family providers, and caregivers. Instead of a warrior patriot, we might begin to think about a citizen defender as a definition of a security provider that could include us all, civilians and soldiers alike. It could also provide a less militarized notion of security.

As we said at the beginning of this section, feminist definitions of security also include economic security. Let us now turn to an examination of economic security, as well as some broader issues of gender in the global economy.

Key Points

- Traditional stories about war, which portray men as protectors and women and children as being protected, are severely challenged by today's wars, in which women and children are being killed and injured in large numbers.

- War's association with masculinity and the image of a soldier as a heroic male are challenged by an increasing number of women in militaries around the world.

- Militarized masculinity is popular when states are preoccupied with national security threats; consequently conciliatory options in policy-making tend to get discounted and it is difficult for women's voices to be regarded as legitimate, particularly in matters of security policy.

- Feminists define security broadly to include the diminution of all forms of violence, physical, economic, and ecological.

Gender in the global economy

There are enormous differences in the socio-economic status of women, depending on their race, class, nationality, and geographic location. Nevertheless, women are disproportionately located at the bottom of the socio-economic scale in all societies. On average, women earn two-thirds of men's earnings[3] even though they work longer hours, many of which are spent in unremunerated reproductive and caring tasks. Even when women do rise to the top, they almost always earn less than men.

We cannot explain the disproportionate numbers of women in marginal under-rewarded economic activities by attributing them to legal restrictions and economic barriers alone. Women do not do as well as men in societies where legal restrictions on employment and earnings have long since been removed. Putting on our gender-sensitive lenses, we might ask to what extent these disturbing figures are attributable to unequal gendered structures in the global economy. Feminists call these structures the **gendered division of labour**.

The historical foundations of the gendered division of labour

We can trace the origins of the contemporary gendered division of labour back to seventeenth-century Europe. At that time, definitions of male and female were becoming polarized in ways that were suited to the growing division between work and home required by early **capitalism**. Industrialization and the increase in waged labour, largely performed by men, shifted work from home to factory. The term housewife, which began to be used to describe women's work in the private domestic sphere, reinforced the gender dimensions of this split. Gendered constructs, such as **breadwinner** and 'housewife', have been central to modern Western definitions of masculinity, femininity, and capitalism. Even though many women do work outside the home for wages, the association of women with domestic roles, such as housewife and caregiver, has become institutionalized and even naturalized. This means that it is seen as **natural** for women to do the domestic work. Putting the burden of household labour on women reduces their autonomy and economic security.

As a result of these role expectations, when women do enter the workforce, they are disproportionately represented in the caring professions, such as nursing, social services, and primary education, or in **light industry** (performed with light machinery). Women choose these occupations not on the basis of market rationality and profit maximization alone, but also because of values and expectations about mothers and caregivers that are emphasized in the socialization of young girls. Occupations that are disproportionately populated by women tend to be the most poorly paid. Assumptions about appropriate gender roles mean that women are often characterized as supplemental wage earners to the male head of household. But estimates suggest that one-third of all households worldwide are headed by women, a fact frequently obscured by role expectations that derive from the notion of male breadwinners and female housewives.

Consequences of the gendered division of labour

Gender expectations about appropriate roles for women contribute to low wages and double burdens. Women's cheap labour is particularly predominant in textiles and electronics. These industries favour hiring young unmarried women who can achieve a high level of productivity at low wages. Frequently, they are fired if they get married or pregnant. Because of expectations associated with traditional gender roles, there is a belief that women possess 'nimble fingers', have patience for tedious jobs, and are 'naturally' good sewers. When women are seen as naturally good at these tasks, it means that these kinds of work are not seen as skilled and are remunerated accordingly. Moreover, political activity does not go with female respectability. Employers hire women on the assumption that they will provide a 'docile' labour force unlikely to organize for better conditions.

Gender expectations about suitable roles for women enter into another global labour issue, that of home-based work. As companies have moved towards a more **flexible labour** force (less benefits and job security) in all parts of the world, cost-saving has included hiring home-based workers who are easily hired and fired. This leads to increased economic vulnerability in times of economic crisis such as the one that started in 2008. Exempt from any national labour standards that may exist in the worker's home country, home-based workers are generally paid lower wages than factory workers and are not paid at all when there is no work. Since women, often of necessity, prefer work that more easily accommodates

family responsibilities, home-based workers are predominantly women. The gendered division of labour that defines women as housewives, a category with expectations that labour is free, legitimizes wages at below-subsistence levels (Prügl 1999: 198).

Even when women do enter the workforce, they continue to suffer from a double burden. This means that, in addition to their paid work, women usually carry most of the responsibility for household labour. We are accustomed to think that women are not 'working' when they engage in household labour. In actual fact, such tasks are crucial for reproducing and caring for those who perform waged work. However, these tasks often constrain women's opportunities for paid work, and the narrow definition of work, as work in the waged economy, tends to render invisible many of the contributions women *do* make to the global economy.

The gendered division of labour also affects women's work in agriculture, a role that is significant, particularly in many parts of Africa. While women do undertake cash crop production, frequently they work as unpaid family labour in small units that produce independently or on contract. Consequently, men are more likely to gain access to money, new skills, and technology. When agricultural production moves into the monetarized economy, women tend to get left behind in the **subsistence** (not for wages) sector, producing for family needs.

In this section we have seen how women are disadvantaged relative to men by the gendered division of labour. Women's relative lack of economic opportunities is not caused by market forces alone but by processes that result from gendered expectations about the kinds of work for which women are believed to be best suited. Nevertheless, when women do work for wages, this undermines the legitimacy of men's domination that occurs because of men's traditional role as family providers. For women, having a job can be better than no work at all and extra cash significantly enhances the

---

Box 16.4 Challenging gender expectations: women workers organize

In the early 1980s, US athletic shoe manufacturers sought to increase profits by subcontracting to male entrepreneurs setting up factories in South Korea and Taiwan where labour costs were low. The companies took advantage of a political climate that suppressed labour rights and played on women's cultural socialization to work hard for low wages in order to serve their country, their husbands, and their fathers. Defying their docile reputation, South Korean women began to organize labour unions and fight for their rights to unionize, to better working conditions, and to fair wages. As women's efforts were successful, the shoe companies withdrew their contracts and renegotiated with companies in China, Indonesia, and Thailand. In these new locations, companies were able to maintain higher profit margins by exploiting women workers who had fewer rights and thus were more acquiescent. This story shows us how companies take advantage of cultural expectations about women in order to increase profits. Now, women are organizing across borders, trying to overcome the employment insecurities fostered by mobile companies.

(Adapted from Enloe 2004)

Case Study 1 Microcredit: empowering women through investment

In 1976, a Bangladeshi economist, Muhammad Yunus, founded the Grameen Bank. The Bank is a lending programme that provides its largely female clientele with small loans for business investment. These small loans, which are called microcredit, are directed towards women because women have a better record for investment and repayment than men. Women are more likely to invest the loans rather than spend the money on themselves, and they are more likely to repay. Loan repayment rates fluctuate between 96 per cent and 100 per cent. Loans directed towards women are also seen as a method of empowerment that gives women access to resources, economic security, and higher status in the household. Up to 5 per cent of borrowers per year rise out of poverty. Borrowers also increase the educational and nutritional standards within their families.

In Bangladesh in 2009, Grameen Bank reported 7.94 million borrowers in 84,787 villages, 97 per cent of whom were women. In addition to financing small enterprises, home-building and education, the Bank encourages women's empowerment through fostering entrepreneurialism and encouraging family planning. Borrowers now own 90 per cent of the Bank, with the other 10 per cent owned by the government. The Bank earns a profit, and since 1995, has been self-sufficient. Since the 1970s, the microcredit lending model has been replicated in 40 countries. Organizations participating in the microcredit model number in the thousands, and the Grameen Bank and its founder were jointly awarded the 2006 Nobel Peace Prize.

Microcredit is widely publicized as a successful model for development *and* the empowerment of women. To a large extent this has proved to be correct. However, there are critics who argue that gender-based money lending can actually reinforce

gendered social hierarchies. Critics suggest that, while women get access to *micro* credit, men continue to dominate the *real* credit market. And, while women are the actual borrowers, in certain cases men retain control. Moreover, the financial crisis that started in 2008 is likely to affect the microcredit sector, with the risk of reversing much of the progress made in achieving the economic empowerment of women.

Case Study 1 Microcredit: Discussion questions

1 What do you think might be the gender assumptions behind microcredit lending?

2 Do you agree or disagree with critics that gender-based lending could worsen gendered social hierarchies?

---

income of poor families. It also increases women's financial independence.

We can see that it is difficult to generalize about the gender consequences of economic globalization. Nevertheless, the claim that we live in a world characterized by gendered boundaries of economic inequality is undisputed. The global economy operates not only according to market forces but also according to gendered divisions of labour that value women's work lower than men's. In addition, much of women's non-monetarized labour contributes to the global economy, but remains invisible. In our earlier discussion of security, we saw how masculine values influence states' national security policy and how this can be detrimental to women's political opportunities. When we discussed feminist theory, we saw that one of the goals of feminism is to produce knowledge that can help improve women's lives. We now look at some of the improvements that are being made by, and on behalf of, women throughout the world.

Key Points

- A gender-sensitive perspective helps us see how women's relative disadvantage to men in terms of material well-being is due to the gendered division of labour.

- The gendered division of labour dates back to seventeenth-century Europe and the subsequent separation of paid work in the public sphere from unpaid work in the private sphere, a separation that has an effect on the kind of work that women do in the public sphere.

- Women are disproportionately clustered in low-paying jobs in garment industries, services, and home-based work or in subsistence agriculture.

- In addition to paid work, women perform most of the unpaid reproductive and caring labour in the private sphere, labour that is invisible in economic analysis. This constrains women's choices in the public sphere.

- Since waged work can be empowering for women, even when they are paid less than men, we must not overgeneralize about the negative effects of the gendered division of labour.

Using knowledge to inform policy practice

Now that we understand how structures of gender inequality contribute to women's subordination, let us examine some of the efforts women are making to diminish the negative effects of these gendered structures in both the political and economic realms. Many of the improvements in women's lives can be attributed to women themselves working in **non-governmental organizations** (NGOs) and in social movements. Frequently, their actions are informed by feminist emancipatory knowledge. (It may be helpful for you to refer to the earlier discussion on emancipatory knowledge.)

The United Nations (UN) held its first official conference on women in Mexico City in 1975. This conference launched the UN Decade for Women (1976–85). It was the first in a series of official intergovernmental women's conferences, sponsored by the UN. It is largely due to women organizing worldwide that the UN has put women's issues on its agenda. At the beginning of the UN Decade, women from the North took the lead in organizing. Economic issues having to do with employment and wages took precedence. By the end of the Decade, women from the South began to organize around the impact of the economic crisis of the 1970s caused by high prices for food and oil on the international market and a downturn in the global economy. Their work led to the establishment of a network of Southern women known as Development Alternatives with Women for

a New Era (DAWN). DAWN is not only engaged in political advocacy. Using feminist knowledge, it also publishes analyses of the impact of global economic policy on Southern countries, focusing on Southern women.

Parallel NGO conferences have been held at each of the official UN Conferences on Women. Attendance at these conferences increased from 5,000 in Mexico City in 1975 to an estimated 25,000 in Beijing in 1995 (Jaquette 2003: 336). Pressure from women's groups was important in getting the United Nations to disaggregate its data, such as its quality of life indicators, by sex. The availability of data is important in getting issues on policy agendas. Adoption of the Gender Development Index (GDI) by the UN Human Development Programme in 1995 was an important step in helping to formulate policies to improve women's well-being. Another important step towards gender equality was the adoption by the UN and other international **intergovernmental organizations** of a policy called gender mainstreaming. Gender mainstreaming requires organizations that adopt it to evaluate the gendered effects of all aspects of their institutional decision-making (see Box 16.6).

In 1996, the International Labour Organization adopted a convention that set international standards for the type of home-based work we discussed earlier. Pressure for adoption began with the organizing and lobbying efforts of the Self-Employed Women's Association (SEWA), a trade union based in India composed of

Box 16.5 Milestones in women's organizing

1975	First United Nations World Conference on Women, Mexico City, Mexico
1976–85	UN Decade for Women
1979	The Convention on the Elimination of All Forms of Discrimination against Women (CEDAW) adopted by the UN General Assembly
1980	Second UN World Conference on Women, Copenhagen, Denmark
1985	UN World Conference to Review and Appraise the Achievements of the UN Decade for Women, Nairobi, Kenya
1995	Fourth UN World Conference on Women, Beijing, China
1996	Gender mainstreaming adopted as official UN policy by the UN General Assembly
2000	Women 2000: Gender Equality, Development and Peace for the 21st Century, also known as 'Beijing+5'. Held at UN headquarters, New York, USA
2005	Review and Appraisal of the 1995 World Conference on Women in Beijing and Beijing+5, Commission on the Status of Women (CSW), 49th Session, United Nations, New York, USA

Box 16.6 Gender Development Index and gender mainstreaming

The Gender Development Index (GDI) measures states' development using the Human Development Index (HDI) indicators: literacy, life expectancy, school enrolment, and income disaggregated by gender, to illustrate a state's development, adjusted for degrees of gender inequality. This index takes as its central assumption that the larger the degree of gender inequality, the more this has a negative effect on states' quality of development. The GDI also shows that states high on the HDI may have low degrees of gender inequality.

Gender mainstreaming was established as a global strategy for achieving gender equality in the 1995 Beijing Platform for Action ratified by all UN member states. It has been adopted as the official policy of the United Nations, the European Union, the Organization of American States and a number of other governmental and intergovernmental organizations. Gender mainstreaming prescribes the review and revision of policy processes in all sectors of government, with an eye towards eliminating gender-based disparities in policy formulation and implementation.

(True 2003)

Case Study 2 The self-employed women's movement

The Self-Employed Women's Association (SEWA) is a women's labour union founded in 1972 in the city of Ahmedabad, India. It has grown into a community-based movement organizing self-employed women in 13 Indian states into labour unions, a lending cooperative, education, and other community-based empowerment initiatives. It has also advocated for and achieved policy changes in national and international forums.

SEWA was founded by labour organizer Ela Bhatt as a response to the large number of women workers in the informal market who were not recognized as workers by the state or by society. Over 90 per cent of working Indian women were and are employed in the informal sector. These self-employed and home-based workers are especially susceptible to exploitation by contractors and middlemen, job insecurity, and police harassment. SEWA women began to organize themselves in order to achieve recognition and establish their rights and protections as workers. For example, women banded together to stop police extortion of vegetable vendors in Ahmedabad.

The movement expanded to include broader empowerment initiatives. In 1974, SEWA instituted a member-funded and -directed microcredit bank that gives poor women access

to capital and at the same time managerial and organizational experience. The SEWA Bank is member-owned and -directed, in keeping with the grass-roots strategy of the movement.

As the SEWA Bank expanded and SEWA success grew, the movement extended its influence further into the policy realm and into organizing in rural areas. In 1986, SEWA succeeded in instituting a national commission to analyse and advise on issues of self-employed women. At the international level, SEWA was instrumental in getting the International Labour Organization to adopt home-based work as a policy issue in 1991, and in contributing to a global alliance of home-based workers called the HomeNet Organization in 1994. In 1996, this resulted in the ILO Homework Convention, legislation designed to protect home-based workers' rights.

SEWA, faithful to the movement's philosophy of using member-driven strategies, developed contextually specific objectives for poor women in rural areas. For example, when SEWA organizers in rural regions encountered opposition from employers, SEWA focused on increasing work opportunities through cooperative enterprises in order to increase women's employment alternatives. These agricultural and crafts cooperatives give women more access to and control over resources. Liberal feminists often cite SEWA as an example of successfully integrating women into the market economy. Postcolonial feminists cite it as an example of local voices speaking for themselves and achieving culturally and contextually specific empowerment.

Case Study 2 The self-employed women's movement: discussion questions

1 Compare SEWA's and Grameen's (Case Study 1) approaches to poverty alleviation. Which do you think is more successful in challenging gender hierarchies? Why?

2 Do you think SEWA's model could be used in other parts of the world, including where you live? Do you know of similar organizations in your local area?

women engaged in small-scale trade and home-based work (see Case Study 2).

The work of women's caucuses at various UN conferences has resulted in feminist agendas based on some of the ideas we have discussed. Women's activism has challenged the hierarchical political structures, evident at intergovernmental UN conferences, and NGO forums have practised forms of participatory democracy and moved feminist ideas into the policy mainstream of various international organizations. Women in NGOs and social movements, informed by feminist knowledge, are playing an important role in pressuring international organizations and national governments to adopt policies that will further women's equality.

Key Points

- Much of the success in moving towards gender equality is due to women's organizing in NGOs and social movements. This has resulted in getting women's issues on the policy agendas of the United Nations and other intergovernmental organizations.

- Feminists believe that feminist knowledge should be useful for improving women's lives, and many feminist social movements are informed by feminist knowledge.

- Data disaggregated by sex are vital for identifying women's problems and lobbying for change. The adoption of the Gender Development Index by the United Nations has helped us to see where problems are most acute and to track evidence of improvement.

- Gender mainstreaming, which has been adopted by certain international organizations and national governments, is a policy that evaluates legislation in terms of whether it is likely to increase or reduce gender equality.

Conclusion

Using a number of different feminist approaches, this chapter has introduced you to some of the ways gender structures world politics. We began by situating IR feminist approaches in feminist theory more generally and by offering a feminist definition of gender. IR feminists have drawn on a variety of feminist theories to help them understand why women have not been visible in global politics and why they are economically disadvantaged relative to men in all societies. They also examine broader questions about how gender shapes and is shaped by global politics. When we are sensitive to gender as a category of analysis, we can see how characteristics we associate with masculinity are particularly valued in global politics, especially in matters of national security. Feminists define security more broadly—not just in terms of the security of the state, but also in terms of the physical and economic security of individuals. Evidence suggests that women as a group suffer certain economic insecurities by virtue of being women. To explain this, IR feminists point to a gendered division of labour. Differing expectations about what is meant by women's and men's work lead to problems when women end up in lower-paying jobs and with a larger share of unremunerated work in the household.

We have seen that IR feminism can tell us some new things about global policy-making and about the workings of the global economy that other approaches do not. This does not mean that feminism can tell us *everything* we need to know about global politics. However, it is important to note that since all global actors have a gender identity, gender is present in all global processes. For this reason, it is hard to separate feminist approaches from other IR approaches in the same way that we can separate **realism** from **liberalism** or from **Marxism**. We have seen that IR feminism is grounded in different IR theoretical approaches, such as liberalism, constructivism and poststructuralism. One further question we might think about is how our gender-sensitive lenses might help us to see these other approaches in new ways.

Questions

1 Feminists define gender as a social construction. What does this mean? What kinds of questions does IR feminism try to answer using gender as a category of analysis?

2 Women's participation at the highest levels of international and national policy-making has been extremely limited. Do you think this is important for understanding global politics?

3 Do you think women's roles, as diplomats' and soldiers' wives, domestic servants, sex workers, homemakers, and home-based workers, are relevant to the business of international politics? If so, how?

4 Why is the myth that wars are fought to protect women and children problematic from a feminist perspective? What would be a feminist approach to understanding state violence?

5 Does women's participation in military combat undermine or reinforce militarized masculinity? Consider how different feminist perspectives would answer this question.

6 How do feminists define security? Why do some of them believe that national security may undermine personal security? Do you agree or disagree with this claim?

7 How and why does the gendered division of labour contribute to women's subordination relative to men? How does it contribute to men's relative success?

8 Do you see potential for feminist activism/feminist IR to change conventional masculinist practices of international relations?

9 Can men be feminists? Why or why not?

10 Since feminist approaches draw from different IR perspectives, does feminism belong in one chapter of this book? How might gender-sensitive lenses see theories in other chapters?

Further Reading

Ackerly, B. A., Stern, M., and True, J. (eds) (2006), *Feminist Methodologies for International Relations* (Cambridge: Cambridge University Press). A good introduction to feminist methods and methodologies for IR feminist scholarship.

Enloe, C. (2004), *The Curious Feminist: Searching for Women in a New Age of Empire* (Berkeley, CA: University of California Press). A collection of essays exploring the unrecognized ways that women participate in international politics, including security, war, and the global political economy.

Marchand, M. H., and Runyan, A. S. (eds) (2000), *Gender and Global Restructuring: Sightings, Sites, and Resistances* (New York: Routledge). This book addresses gender in the global economy, going beyond conventional approaches to globalization to reveal the complexities of global restructuring based on economic and social disparities.

Peterson, V. S., and Runyan, A. S. (2010), *Global Gender Issues in the New Millennium*, 3rd edn (Boulder, CO: Westview Press). A comprehensive introduction to the subject matter of feminist IR.

Tickner, J. A. (2001), *Gendering World Politics: Issues and Approaches in the Post-Cold War Era* (New York: Columbia University Press). A survey and synthesis of feminist scholarship in the major subfields of International Relations, and a set of visions for the future of feminist IR.

Online Resource Centre

 Visit the Online Resource Centre that accompanies this book to access more learning resources on this chapter topic at www.oxfordtextbooks.co.uk/orc/baylis5e/

Notes

1 Females make up approximately half of the world's total displaced persons. Children under age 18 make up 44 per cent of refugees and asylum seekers. Approximately one out of ten refugees, asylum seekers or internally displaced persons are children under the age of 5. (United Nations High Commissioner for Refugees (2009), *2008 Global Trends: Refugees, Asylum-seekers, Returnees, Internally Displaced and Stateless Persons*. Available online at: http://www.unhcr.org/4a375c426.html.)

2 This phenomenon was reported in Lizza, R. (2007), 'The Invasion of the Alpha Male Democrat', *New York Times*, 7 January.

3 This worldwide average was approximated. See ILO (n.d.), 'Facts on Women at Work', available online at: www.ilo.org/public/english/region/eurpro/budapest/download/womenwork.pdf.

Chapter 17

International law

CHRISTIAN REUS-SMIT

Reader's Guide

This chapter introduces students to the practice of modern international law and to debates surrounding its nature and efficacy. It begins by exploring the reasons why international societies construct institutions, and why different sorts of institutions have emerged in different historical contexts. It then considers the nature and origins of the modern institution of international law, its close connection with the practice of multilateralism, and the recent cosmopolitanization of the global legal order. After a brief discussion of the laws of war, we conclude with a survey of different theoretical approaches to international law.

Introduction: the paradox of international law

As students of International Relations, our default position is to assume that international law matters little to the cut and thrust of international politics. The power and interests of states are what matters, and law is either a servant of the powerful or an irrelevant curiosity. Widespread as this scepticism is, it is confounded by much state behaviour. If international law doesn't matter, why do states and other actors devote so much effort to negotiating new legal regimes and augmenting existing ones? Why does so much international debate revolve around the legality of state behaviour, around the applicability of legal rules, and around the legal obligations incumbent on states? And why is compliance with international law so high, even by domestic standards?

This chapter introduces students to the practice of modern international law and to debates surrounding its nature and efficacy. It is written primarily for students of international politics, but should also be of interest to law students curious about the political foundations of international law. Our starting point is the idea that international law is best understood as a core international institution, a set of norms, rules, and practices created by states and other actors to facilitate diverse social goals, from order and coexistence to justice and human development. It is, however, an institution with distinctive historical roots, and understanding these roots is essential to grasping its unique institutional features.

Order and institutions

Realists portray international relations as a struggle for power, a realm in which states are 'continuously preparing for, actively involved in, or recovering from organised violence in the form of war' (Morgenthau 1985: 52). While war has certainly been a recurrent feature of international life, it is a crude and deeply dysfunctional way for states to ensure their security or realize their interests. Because of this, states have devoted as much, if not more, effort to liberating themselves from the condition of war than to embroiling themselves in violent conflict. Creating some modicum of international order has been an abiding common interest of most states, most of the time (Bull 1977: 8).

To achieve international order, states have created international institutions. People often confuse institutions and organizations, incorrectly using the two terms interchangeably. International institutions are commonly defined as complexes of norms, rules, and practices that 'prescribe behavioral roles, constrain activity, and shape expectations' (Keohane 1989a: 3). International organizations, like the United Nations, are physical entities that have staff, head offices, and letterheads. International institutions can exist without any organizational structure—the 1997 Ottawa Convention banning landmines is an institution, but there is no landmines head office. Many institutions have organizational dimensions, though. The World Trade Organization (formerly the General Agreement on Tariffs and Trade) is an institution with a very strong organizational structure. While institutions can exist without an organizational dimension, international organizations cannot exist without an institutional framework, as their very existence presupposes a prior set of norms, rules, and principles that empower them to act and which they are charged to uphold. If states had never negotiated the Charter of the United Nations, the organization simply could not exist, let alone function.

In modern **international society**, states have created three levels of institutions (see Box 17.1). There are deep constitutional institutions, such as the principle of **sovereignty**, which define the terms of legitimate statehood. Without the institution of sovereignty, the world of independent states, and the international politics it engenders, would simply not exist. States have also created fundamental institutions, like international law and multilateralism, which provide the basic rules and practices that shape how states solve cooperation and coordination problems. These are the institutional norms, techniques, and structures that states and other actors invoke and employ when they have common ends they want to achieve or clashing interests they want to contain. Lastly, states have developed issue-specific institutions or regimes, such as the Nuclear Non-Proliferation Treaty (NPT), which enact fundamental institutional practices in particular realms of inter-state relations. The NPT is a concrete

Box 17.1 Levels of international institutions

Constitutional institutions

Constitutional institutions comprise the primary rules and norms of international society, without which society among sovereign states could not exist. The most commonly recognized of these is the norm of sovereignty, which holds that within the state, power and authority are centralized and hierarchical, and outside the state no higher authority exists. The norm of sovereignty is supported by a range of auxiliary norms, such as the right to self-determination and the norm of non-intervention.

Fundamental institutions

Fundamental institutions rest on the foundation provided by constitutional institutions. They represent the basic norms and practices that sovereign states employ to facilitate coexistence and cooperation under conditions of international anarchy. They are the rudimentary practices states reach for when seeking to collaborate or coordinate their behaviour. Fundamental institu-

tions have varied from one historical system of states to another, but in the modern international system the fundamental institutional practices of contractual international law and multilateralism have been the most important.

Issue-specific institutions or 'regimes'

Issue-specific institutions or 'regimes' are the most visible or palpable of all international institutions. They are the sets of rules, norms, and **decision-making procedures** that states formulate to define who constitute legitimate actors and what constitutes legitimate action in a given domain of international life. Examples of regimes are the Nuclear Non-Proliferation Treaty, the Framework Convention on Global Climate Change, the Ottawa Convention on Anti-Personnel Landmines, and the International Covenant on Civil and Political Rights. Importantly, issue-specific institutions or regimes are concrete enactments in specific issue-areas of fundamental institutional practices, such as international law and multilateralism.

---

expression of the practices of international law and multilateralism in the field of arms control.

We are concerned here with the middle strata of fundamental institutions. 'Fundamental institutions are the elementary rules of practice that states formulate to solve the coordination and collaboration problems associated with coexistence under anarchy' (Reus-Smit 1999: 14). In modern international society, a range of such institutions exists, including international law, multilateralism, bilateralism, diplomacy, and management by the Great Powers. Since the middle of the nineteenth century, however, the first two of these have provided the basic framework for international cooperation and the pursuit of order.

Key Points

- States have strong incentives to free themselves from the insecurities of international anarchy.

- States face common coordination and collaboration problems, yet cooperation remains difficult under anarchy.

- To facilitate cooperation, states create international institutions, of which three levels exist in modern international society: constitutional institutions, fundamental institutions, and issue-specific institutions or 'regimes'.

- We are concerned with fundamental institutions, of which international law is one of the most important.

The modern institution of international law

Historical roots

The contemporary international legal system is a historical artefact. Not in the sense of being irrelevant to present circumstances, but in the sense of being deeply structured by the social and political conditions of modernity. Like most present-day institutions, it bears the imprint of the revolutions in social thought and practice that from the eighteenth century onwards transformed the political landscape of Europe and then much of the world. Great thinkers such as Hugo Grotius (1583–1645) and Emerich de Vattel (1714–67) are often cast as the

'fathers' of international law, and the Treaties of Augsburg (1555), Westphalia (1648), and Utrecht (1713) are seen as landmarks in the development of international public law. Yet despite the importance of these historical figures and moments, the modern international legal system acquired many of its distinctive characteristics as late as the nineteenth century.

The present international system has its roots in Europe, and before the nineteenth century the vast majority of European states were monarchies. The kings and queens who ruled these states justified their power by appealing to the doctrine of divine right, to the idea that monarchs were ordained with authority directly from God (Bodin 1967: 40). At this time law was generally understood as the command of a legitimate superior—humanity in general, including monarchs, was subject to God's law and natural law, both of which embodied the command of God. The subjects of particular states were also ruled by municipal law, which was the command of monarchs, who stood above such law. These ideas about divinity, authority, and law had a profound influence on early international law. Derived from the law of nature, international law was understood as a set of divinely ordained principles of state conduct, accessible to all endowed with right reason. European monarchs were obliged to observe international law not because they had reached a contractual agreement with one another, or at least not primarily, but because of fealty to God (Grotius 1925: 121).

In the late eighteenth and early nineteenth centuries, the legitimacy of the absolutist state was challenged by the principles of liberalism and nationalism. By the second half of the nineteenth century, European states underwent dramatic internal transformations, as the principles of constitutionalism and popular sovereignty weakened monarchs' authority, empowered parliamentary institutions, and extended the franchise. With this transformation came a new conception of law—law as reciprocal accord. Law was deemed legitimate to the extent that it was authored by those subject to the law, or their representatives, and it applied equally to all citizens in all like circumstances. Once this ideal was firmly established within the major European states, it started to filter into relations between states, leading to the rise of contractual international law, or what is often termed 'positive' law. International law was now seen as the product of negotiations between sovereign states, not the command of God, and states were obliged to observe such law, not because of fealty, but because they had entered into reciprocally binding agreements with other states—because international law represents the 'mutual *will* of the nations concerned' (Von Martens 1795: 47–8).

Box 17.2 Key constitutive legal treaties

Over the past five centuries, the nature and scope of international society has been conditioned by a series of international legal instruments that have defined the nature of legitimate statehood, the scope of sovereign authority, and the bounds of rightful state action, international and domestic. Some of the more important of these are as follows.

The Treaties of Westphalia, 1648
The Treaties of Osnabruck and Münster, which together form the 'Peace of Westphalia', ended the Thirty Years War and were crucial in delimiting the political rights and authority of European monarchs. Among other things, the Treaties granted monarchs rights to maintain standing armies, build fortifications, and levy taxes.

The Treaties of Utrecht, 1713
The Treaties of Utrecht, which brought an end to the Wars of Spanish Succession, consolidated the move to territorial sovereignty in Europe. The Treaties of Westphalia did little to define the territorial scope of sovereign rights, the geographical domain over which such rights could extend. By establishing that fixed territorial boundaries, rather than the reach of family ties, should define the reach of sovereign authority, the Treaties of Utrecht were crucial in establishing the present link between sovereign authority and territorial boundaries.

The Treaty of Paris, 1814
The Treaty of Paris ended the Napoleonic Wars and paved the way for the Congress of Vienna (1814–15). The Congress of Vienna, in turn, defined the nature of the post-Napoleonic War settlement, and ultimately led to the Concert of Europe. The Concert has often been credited with successfully limiting Great Power warfare for a good part of the nineteenth century, but it is also noteworthy as an institution for upholding monarchical authority and combating liberal and nationalist movements in Europe.

The Peace Treaty of Versailles, 1919
The Treaty of Versailles formally ended the First World War (1914–18). The Treaty established the League of Nations, specified the rights and obligations of the victorious and defeated powers (including the notorious regime of reparations on Germany), and created the 'Mandatories' system under which 'advanced nations' were given legal tutelage over colonial peoples.

The Charter of the United Nations, 1945
The Charter of the United Nations is the legal regime that created the United Nations as the world's only 'supranational' organization. The Charter defines the structure of the United Nations, the powers of its constitutive agencies, and the rights and obligations of sovereign states party to the Charter. Among other things, the Charter is the key legal document limiting the use of force to instances of self-defence and collective peace enforcement endorsed by the United Nations Security Council.

The Declaration on Granting Independence to Colonial Countries and Peoples, 1960
Though not a legally binding document, General Assembly Resolution 1514 (XV) signalled the normative delegitimation of European colonialism, and was critical in establishing the right to self-determination, which in turn facilitated the wholesale decolonization of the European empires.

Conditioned by these historical forces, the modern institution of international law has developed four distinctive characteristics: a multilateral form of legislation; a consent-based form of legal obligation; a peculiar language of reasoning and argument; and a strong discourse of institutional autonomy.

Multilateral legislation

If we define legislation broadly, as the formulation and enactment of legally binding norms or rules, then the legislation of international law takes place formally and informally. New norms and rules evolve constantly through the informal arguments, social learning, and repeated practices of states and non-state actors. For instance, there is now considerable debate about whether new legal norms are evolving to qualify state sovereignty and permit humanitarian intervention. If such norms are evolving, these processes are far from complete. If they do consolidate, however, it will have been less the result of formal legal codification than persistent normative debate and the reinterpretation of existing legal norms. Informal processes such as these are crucially important, as they are one of the principal means by which customary norms of international law evolve. Customary norms are a special category of international law; they have such high normative standing in the community of states that they are considered binding upon all states irrespective of whether they have consented. Many of the rules governing territorial jurisdiction, freedom of the seas, and the diplomatic immunities of states are customary, and most of these evolved through informal processes (Byers 1999: 3).

In addition to these informal modes of law-making, states have also developed more formal methods of legislation, the most distinctive being the practice of multilateralism. Before the Napoleonic Wars, multilateralism was a relatively marginal institutional practice. States certainly engaged in cooperative practices involving three or more states, but these were often aggregations of bilateral arrangements (such as the Peaces of Westphalia and Utrecht), and were seldom based on reciprocally binding rules of conduct (a mark of true multilateralism (Ruggie 1993)). It was only in the nineteenth century, as liberalism began transforming the internal constitutions of leading European powers, that multilateralism became the preferred mode of international legislation. If law was legitimate only if those subject to it authored it, and only if it applied equally to all subjects in all like circumstances, then an international means of legislation had to be found that could meet such standards. It was in this context that multilateralism rose to prominence. New ideas of international law are thus deeply entwined with the rise of multilateralism, and it is not surprising that the nineteenth and twentieth centuries saw a dramatic proliferation of multilateral treaties.

Consent and legal obligation

Grotius wrote that states are obliged to obey the law of nations—along with the laws of nature and God—'even though they have made no promise' (1925: 121). Fealty to God was the ultimate root of all legal obligations in the Age of Absolutism, and consent constituted a secondary, if still important, source of obligation. This contrasts dramatically with the situation today, in which consent is treated as the primary source of international legal obligation (Henkin 1995: 27). This emphasis on consent is integral to much contemporary discourse on international law. Leaders of states will often use the fact of their consent, or the lack of such, to display their sovereign rights. And critics use evidence of state consent to criticize governments for failing to live up to their obligations under international law.

The status of consent as the principal source of modern international legal obligation is complicated, however, by two things. To begin with, we have already noted that states are, in reality, bound by rules to which they have not formally consented, principally those of customary international law. In determining whether a norm constitutes customary law, scholars and jurists look for general observance of the norm and *opinio juris*, the recognition by states that they are observing the norm because it constitutes law (Price 2004: 107). Both of these are thought to be indicators of tacit consent, but as critics of liberalism have long argued, tacit consent is not the same as actual consent, and extrapolating tacit consent from norm-consistent behaviour is fraught with difficulties. Second, the idea that consent is the principal source of international legal obligation is philosophically highly problematic (Reus-Smit 2003). As the celebrated legal theorist H. L. A. Hart observed, consent can only be obligating if there exists a prior rule that specifies that promises to observe legal rules are binding. But because this rule would be what gives consent its normative standing, consent cannot be the source of that prior rule's obligatory force (1994: 225).

Language and practice of justification

In addition to its distinctive forms of legislation and legal obligation, the modern institution of international law is characterized by a peculiar language and practice of justification. If we consider the role that international law plays in global life, we see that it operates as more than a pristine set of rules calmly and logically applied to clear-cut situations by authoritative juridical interpreters. International law is alive in the central political debates of international society; it structures arguments about right and wrong, about the bounds of legitimate action, about authority and membership, and about the full spectrum of international issues, from the management of fisheries to the use of force. On close inspection, though, we see that this argument and debate takes a distinctive form.

First, international legal argument is rhetorical. It is tempting to believe that legal argument is strictly logical, that it is concerned with the straightforward, objective application of a rule to a situation. But this ignores the central and inevitable role that interpretation plays in determining which rules apply, their meaning, and the nature of the case at hand. In reality, legal argument appears as rhetorical as it is logical. As Friedrich Kratochwil argues:

> Legal arguments deal with the finding and interpretation of the applicable norms and procedures, and with the presentation of the relevant facts and their evaluations. Both questions turn on the issue of whether a particular interpretation of a fact-pattern is acceptable rather than 'true'; consequently strict logic plays a minor role in this process of finding the law.
>
> (1989: 42)

Second, international legal argument is analogical: it is concerned 'to establish similarities among different cases or objects in the face of (striking) dissimilarities' (Kratochwil 1989: 223). International actors reason with analogies in three different ways. They use them to interpret a given rule (rule A was interpreted in a particular way, and given the logic applied, rule B should be interpreted the same way). They draw similarities between one class of action and another to claim that the former is, or is not, rule-governed (case C was rule-governed, and given the similarities with case D, case D should be rule-governed as well). And they invoke analogies to establish the status of one rule with reference to other rules (rule E has customary status, and since the same levels of assent and dissent are evident in the case of rule F, rule F should be accorded customary status as well).

The discourse of institutional autonomy

The final distinctive characteristic of the modern institution of international law is its strong discourse of institutional autonomy. As students of international relations, we are accustomed to think of politics and law as separate social domains, as realms of human action with distinct logics and practices. One of the most interesting insights of recent studies is that political actors regularly speak and act as if at some point in a negotiation, at some stage in a crisis, action moved from the political to the legal realm, a realm in which different types of argument and practice prevail. In the political realm, claims of self-interest and barely veiled coercive practices are

---

Box 17.3 Features of the modern institution of international law

Multilateral legislation

The principal mechanism modern states employ to 'legislate' international law is multilateral diplomacy, which is commonly defined as cooperation between three or more states based on, or with a view to formulating, reciprocally binding rules of conduct.

Consent and legal obligation

It is a norm of the modern international legal system that states are obliged to observe legal rules because they have consented to those rules. A state that has not consented to the rules of a particular legal treaty is not bound by those rules. The only exception to this concerns rules of customary international law, and even then implied or tacit consent plays an important role in the determination of which rules have customary status.

Language and practice of justification

Modern international law is characterized by a distinctive form or argument, justification, or reasoning. As accompanying text explains, this practice is both rhetorical and analogical.

The discourse of institutional autonomy

In many historical periods, and in many social and cultural settings, the political and legal realms have been entwined. For instance, the Absolutist conception of sovereignty bound the two realms together in the figure of the sovereign. In the modern era, by contrast, the political and legal realms are thought to be radically different, with their own logics and institutional settings. Domestically, this informs ideas about the constitutional separation of powers; internationally, it has encouraged the view that international politics and law are separate spheres of social action. This has not only affected how the academic disciplines of international relations and law have evolved, but also how state practice has evolved.

considered legitimate if distasteful, but in the legal realm legal reasoning and argument become the legitimate form of action. Compare, for instance, US strategies on Iraq within the confines of the UN Security Council in 2003, where Washington's arguments were constrained by available legal justifications, with its practices outside the Council, where its claims were more self-interested and its practices more openly coercive.

Two things should be noted about this discourse of institutional autonomy. First, imagining the political and legal realms as separate and distinct is a modern phenomenon. In the age of absolute monarchies in Europe, politics and law were joined in the figure of the sovereign. One of the features of modern, particularly liberal, thought is the idea that political and legal powers need to be separated by quarantining politics to the executive and legislative realms, and legal interpretation and application to the judicial realm. This is what lies behind the modern constitutional idea of a 'separation of powers'. Second, imagining separate political and legal realms in international relations contributes to international order, and is thus politically functional for states. Perception of a legal realm, recognition that a spectrum of issues, practices, and processes are governed by legal rules and procedures, and mutual understanding that certain forms of action are empowered or foreclosed within the legal realm, brings a certain discipline, structure, and predictability to international relations that would be missing in conditions of pure anarchy.

Key Points

- Modern international law is a historical artefact, a product of the revolutions in thought and practice that transformed the governance of European states after the French Revolution (1789).

- Before the French Revolution, in the 'Age of Absolutism', law was understood principally as the command of a legitimate superior, and international law was seen as a command of God, derived from natural law. In the modern period law has come to be seen as something contracted between legal subjects, or their representatives, and international law has been seen as the expression of the mutual will of nations.

- Because of its historical roots, the modern institution of international law has a number of distinctive characteristics, informed largely by the values of political liberalism.

- The most distinctive characteristics of the modern institution of international law are its multilateral form of legislation, its consent-based form of legal obligation, its language and practice of justification, and its discourse of institutional autonomy.

From international to supranational law?

So long as international law was designed primarily to facilitate international order—to protect the negative liberties of sovereign states—it remained a relatively circumscribed, if essential, institution. This was apparent in four characteristics of international law, at least until developments of the last three decades. First, states were the primary *subjects* of international law, the principal bearers of rights and obligations. 'The classic view has been that international law applies only to states' (Higgins 1994: 40). The 1933 Montevideo Convention on the Rights and Duties of States establishes the 'state as a person of international law', defines what constitutes a state, and lays down the principal rights and obligations enjoyed by states (Weston *et al.* 1990: 12). Second, and related to the above, states were the primary *agents* of international law, the only actors empowered to formulate, enact, and enforce international law. International law was thus viewed as an artefact of state practice, not the legislation of a community of humankind. Third,

international law was concerned with the regulation of inter-state relations. How states interacted with one another fell within the purview of international law; how they operated within their territorial boundaries did not, a distinction enshrined in the twin international norms of self-determination and non-intervention. Finally, the scope of international law was confined— or attempted to be confined—to questions of order not justice. The principal objective of international law was the maintenance of peace and stability based on mutual respect for each state's territorial integrity and domestic jurisdiction; issues of distributive justice and the protection of basic human rights lay outside its brief.

In recent decades states have sought to move beyond the simple pursuit of international order towards the ambitious yet amorphous objective of global governance, and international law has begun to change in fascinating ways. First, although states are 'still at the heart of the international legal system' (Higgins 1994: 39), individuals,

Case Study   Is international law an expression of Western dominance?

From one perspective, international law is easily cast as a Western, even imperial, institution. As we have seen, its roots lie in the European intellectual movements of the sixteenth and seventeenth centuries. Ideas propagated at that time not only drew on ideas of natural law, which could be traced back to ancient Greek and Roman thought; they also drew a clear distinction between international laws that were appropriate among Christian peoples and those that should govern how Christians related to peoples in the Muslim world, the Americas, and later Asia. The former were based on assumptions of the inherent equality of Christian peoples, the latter on the inherent superiority of Christians over non-Christians.

Further evidence of this Western bias can be found in the 'standard of civilization' that European powers codified in international law during the nineteenth century (Gong 1984). According to this standard, non-Western polities were granted sovereign recognition only if they exhibited certain domestic political characteristics and only if they were willing and able to participate in the prevailing diplomatic practices. The standard was heavily biased towards Western political and legal institutions as the accepted model. On the basis of the standard, European power divided the world's peoples into 'civilized', 'barbarian', and 'savage' societies, a division they used to justify various degrees of Western tutelage.

Many claim that Western bias still characterizes the international legal order. Cited here is the Anglo-European dominance of peak legal institutions, most notably the United Nations Security Council, and international human rights law, which is said to impose a set of Western values about the rights of the individual on non-Western societies where such ideas are alien. These biases are seen as coming together around the issue of humanitarian intervention. Western powers are accused of using their privileged position on the Security Council, and of brandishing human rights norms, to intervene in the domestic politics of weak, developing countries.

All these criticisms have validity. However, the nature and role of international law in contemporary world politics is more complex than at first appears. To begin with, at the heart of the modern international legal system lies a set of customary norms that uphold the legal equality of all sovereign states, as well as their rights to self-determination and non-intervention. Non-Western states have been the most vigorous proponents and defenders

of these cardinal legal norms, and their survival as independent political entities depends on the continued salience of such principles. Second, non-Western peoples were more centrally involved in the development of the international human rights regime than is commonly acknowledged. The Universal Declaration of Human Rights was the product of a deliberate and systematic process of intercultural dialogue, a dialogue involving representatives of the world's major cultures (Glendon 2002). And the International Covenant on Civil and Political Rights, which is often portrayed as a reflection of Western values, was shaped in critical ways by newly independent postcolonial states (Reus-Smit 2001a). What is more, international human rights law has been an important resource in the struggles of many subject peoples against repressive governments and against institutions such as colonialism.

groups, and organizations are increasingly becoming recognized subjects of international law. The development of an expansive body of international human rights law, supported by evolving mechanisms of enforcement, has given individuals, as well as some collectivities, such as minority groups or indigenous peoples, clear rights under international law. And recent moves to hold individuals criminally responsible for violations of those rights—evident in the war crimes tribunals for Rwanda and the former Yugoslavia, the creation of a new International Criminal Court, and the arrest in London of Augusto Pinochet, the former Chilean dictator, for

crimes against humanity—indicate the clear obligations individuals bear to observe basic human rights. Second, non-state actors are becoming important agents in the international legal process. While such actors cannot formally enact international law, and their practices do not contribute to the development of customary international law, they often play a crucial role in shaping the normative environment in which states are moved to codify specific legal rules, in providing information to national governments that encourages the redefinition of state interests and the convergence of policies across different states, and, finally, in actually drafting international treaties and conventions. This last role was first seen in how the International Committee of the Red Cross drafted the 1864 Geneva Convention (Finnemore 1996b: 69–88), and more recently in the role that non-state actors played in the development of the Ottawa Convention on Anti-Personnel Landmines (Price 1998) and in the creation of the International Criminal Court.

Third, international law is increasingly concerned with global, not merely international, regulation. Where the principles of self-determination and non-intervention once erected a fundamental boundary between the international and domestic legal realms, this boundary is now being breached by the development of international rules that regulate how states should behave within their territories. Notable here is international trade law, the growing corpus of international environmental law, as well as the previously mentioned body of international human rights law. The penetration of these laws through the boundaries of the sovereign state is facilitated by the growing tendency of national courts to draw on precepts of international law in their rulings. Finally, the rules, norms, and principles of international law are no longer confined to maintaining international order, narrowly defined. Not only does the development of international humanitarian law indicate a broadening of international law to address questions of global justice, but recent decisions by the United Nations Security Council, which warrant international interventions in places like East Timor, have seen gross violations of human rights by sovereign states treated as threats to international peace and security, thus legitimating action under Chapter 7 of the UN Charter. In doing so, the Security Council implies that international order is dependent upon the maintenance of at least minimum standards of global justice.

Because of these changes, it has been suggested that international law may be gradually transforming into a system of supranational law. Once states are no longer the only subjects and agents of international law, once international law is involved in global regulation, and once its scope has been extended to encompass issues of justice as well as order, it has broken the bounds of both its initial intent and original practice. While these changes have not yet prompted the rewriting of international legal texts, and both international lawyers and international relations scholars are responding cautiously, current developments have injected new excitement and energy into the field of international law, which many previously regarded as moribund, and have caused International Relations scholars to look afresh at the role of legal norms in shaping world politics, something often dismissed as idealism.

Key Points

- So long as international law was designed to facilitate international order, it was circumscribed in key ways: states were the principal subjects and agents of international law; international law was concerned with the regulation of inter-state relations; and the scope of international law was confined to questions of order.

- The quest for global governance is pushing international law into new areas, raising questions about whether international law is transforming into a form of supranational law.

- Individuals, and to some extent collectivities, are gradually acquiring rights and responsibilities under international law, establishing their status as both subjects and agents under international law.

- Non-governmental actors are becoming increasingly important in the development and codification of international legal norms.

- International law is increasingly affecting domestic legal regimes and practices, and the rules of the international legal system are no longer confined to issues of order. As international humanitarian law evolves, issues of global justice are permeating the international legal order.

The laws of war

International law governing the use of force is rightly considered the core of the modern international legal system. Traditionally, such law has divided into two types: *jus ad bellum*, the law governing when states may use force or wage war, and *jus in bello*, the law governing the conduct of war once launched. Two things should be noted about these dimensions of the laws of war. First, from their earliest articulations, they have always been entwined. For instance, Grotius's three-volume *The Law of War and Peace* devoted one volume to *jus ad bellum* and one to *jus in bello*. Second, the content of *jus ad bellum* and *jus in bello* has undergone significant change, with what were once cardinal norms being, in some cases, completely reversed. The laws of war have thus been an evolving project, responding over time to the profound social and technological changes that have transformed the international system over the last five centuries.

The most dramatic change has occurred in the central precepts of *jus ad bellum*. Early writings on just war stressed the importance of just cause, the idea that waging war was justified, morally as well as legally, if a state was responding to an unwarranted attack or seeking reparations for damages. This was greatly complicated, however, by norms that appeared to cut in the opposite direction. For instance, it was widely believed that sovereign rights could be secured through conquest. In others words, if a ruler succeeded in establishing control over a territory and its people, he or she was the sovereign authority. During the nineteenth century, the idea that just cause established just war gave way to the much more permissive notion that war was justified if it served a state's vital national interests, interests that the state itself had the sole right to define. This was the heyday of the principle that the right to wage war was a fundamental sovereign right, a privilege that defined the very essence of sovereignty. The dire consequences of this principle were evident in the First and Second World Wars, and after 1945 the scope of legally justifiable war was dramatically circumscribed. The Charter of the United Nations confines the legitimate use of force to two situations: the use of force in self-defence (Chapter 7, Article 51), which remained an unqualified sovereign right, and the use of force as part of a Security Council sanctioned peace enforcement action (Chapter 7, Article 42).

Parallel to these changes, the precepts of *jus in bello* have evolved as well. Here the trend has been less one of radical change in core principles than a gradual expansion of the scope of international legal constraints on permissible conduct in war. Three areas of constraint are particularly noteworthy. The first relates to the kind of weaponry that is legally permitted. The Hague Conferences of 1899 and 1907 were landmarks in this regard, establishing conventions prohibiting the use of expanding bullets, the dropping of bombs from balloons, and the use of projectiles that diffused gases. Since then legally binding treaties have come into force proscribing a range of weaponry, including the use and deployment of landmines and the manufacture and use of chemical weapons. The second area of constraint relates to how military combatants must be treated. Of central importance here are the four Geneva Conventions of 1864, 1906, 1929, and 1949 respectively, along with their three additional protocols of 1977 (the first two) and 2005 (the third). The third area concerns the treatment

of non-combatants, for which the Geneva Conventions were also crucially important. The deliberate targeting of non-combatants has long been proscribed, but in recent years attempts have been made to tighten these proscriptions further. Worth noting here is the successful move to codify rape in war as an international crime.

The evolution of the laws of war is one of the clearest examples of the aforementioned shift from international to supranational law. This is particularly apparent in the development since the end of the cold war of, first, the international criminal tribunals for the former Yugoslavia and Rwanda (ICTY and ICTR) and, second, the International Criminal Court (ICC). The last of these is the most ambitious international judicial experiment since the end of the Second World War, established to prosecute the crimes of genocide, crimes against humanity, war crimes, and the crime of aggression (as yet undefined by the Court).

Since 2001 the laws of war have come under sustained challenge, as the USA's conduct in the 'war on terror' has pushed the limits of both *jus ad bellum* and *jus in bello*. The Bush administration's invasion of Afghanistan was widely seen as a legitimate act of self-defence, the Taliban government having openly harboured the Al Qaeda terrorist organization responsible for the 9/11 attacks on New York and Washington. The subsequent invasion of Iraq, however, was roundly criticized as a violation of international law. The administration's attempt to establish a new right of 'preventive' self-defence was unsuccessful, and it was unable to persuade a majority of Security Council members that the threat posed by Saddam Hussein was sufficient to justify an international peace enforcement action. A persistent aura of illegality has thus surrounded the Iraq conflict, an aura exacerbated by perceived abuses of *jus in bello* in the war on terror. Most notable here has been the treatment of suspected terrorist combatants. The Bush administration drew major international criticism for its imprisonment of suspects at Guantanamo Bay without the protections of the 1949 Geneva Convention or normal judicial processes within the USA. It was also widely criticized for its practice of 'extraordinary rendition', the CIA's abduction of suspects overseas and their purported transfer to third countries known to practise torture. Over the past decade, therefore, fears have grown that the established framework of international law is crumbling, unable to deal with the 'revisionist' practices of a unilateralist lone superpower (for an excellent overview, see Steiner *et al.* 2008). This perception has been accentuated by other notable challenges to the laws of war, challenges that appeared to have the tacit consent of Washington. Israel's invasion of Gaza stands out here, an invasion criticized for grave breaches of the Fourth Geneva Convention by the Goldstone *Report of the United Nations Fact Finding Mission on the Gaza Conflict* (United Nations 2009). Soon after his election, President Obama moved quickly to bring American practice closer in line with established precepts of international law, issuing an Executive Order to close the Guantanomo detention centre, banning rendition for purposes of torture, mandating that the Red Cross be given access to anyone detained in conflict, and re-engaging multilateral processes on the use of force.

Key Points

- Placing limits on the legitimate use of force is one of the key challenges of the international community, and the laws of war have evolved to meet this challenge.

- The laws of war have traditionally been divided into those governing when the use of force is legitimate, *jus ad bellum*, and how war may be conducted, *jus in bello*.

- Laws governing when war is legally permitted have changed dramatically over the history of the international system, the most notable difference being between the nineteenth-century view that to wage war was a sovereign right to the post-1945 view that war was only justified in self-defence or as part of a UN mandated international peace enforcement action.

- Laws governing how war may be conducted divide, broadly, into three categories: those governing weaponry, combatants, and non-combatants.

- Since 2001 both *jus ad bellum* and *jus in bello* have come under challenge as the Bush administration sought to conduct the war on terror without the constraints of established principles of international law, a practice that the Obama administration has sought to reverse.

Theoretical approaches to international law

Like most aspects of international relations, several theoretical perspectives have been formulated to explain the nature, function, and salience of international law. What follows is a brief survey of the most prominent theoretical perspectives on international law, focusing on those approaches that together constitute the principal axes of contemporary debate.

Realism

Realists are great sceptics about international law, and they are deeply hostile to the liberal–idealist notion of 'peace through law'. George Kennan, the renowned realist diplomat–scholar, argued that this 'undoubtedly represents in part an attempt to transpose the Anglo-Saxon concept of individual law into the international field and to make it applicable to governments as it is applicable here at home to individuals' (1996: 102). The absence of a central authority to legislate, adjudicate, and enforce international law leads realists to doubt whether international law is really law at all. At best, Morgenthau claimed, it is a form of 'primitive law', akin to that of 'preliterate societies, such as the Australian aborigines and the Yurok of northern California' (1985: 295). For realists, international legal obligation is weak at best. Within the state, citizens are obliged to obey the law because sanctions exist to punish illegal behaviour. Yet sanctions are few in international relations, and enforcement mechanisms are rudimentary. To speak of states having strong international legal obligations is thus nonsensical for realists. (For a more detailed discussion of realism, see Ch. 5).

Neo-liberal institutionalism

Until recently, neo-liberals shied away from directly discussing international law, even though their concept of 'regimes' bore a close affinity (see Chs 6 and 7). This was partly because much of their inspiration came from economic theory rather than from law, and partly because in the realist-dominated field of cold war international relations it was less provocative to speak the language of regimes and institutions than that of international law. Since the end of the cold war, however, neo-liberals have been at the forefront of calls for a more productive dialogue between international relations and international law. Not surprisingly, though, their understanding of this dialogue, and the initiatives they have taken to foster it, have been heavily influenced by their rationalist theoretical commitments (see Chs 9 and 10 for criticisms). States are treated as rational egoists, law is seen as an intervening variable between the goals of states and political outcomes, and law is seen as a regulatory institution, not a constitutive one that conditions states' identities and interests (see Goldstein *et al.* 2000).

Constructivism

As explained in Chapter 9, constructivists argue that normative and ideational structures are as important as, if not more important than, material structures; they hold that understanding how actors' identities shape their interests and strategies is essential to understanding their behaviour; and they believe that social structures are sustained only through routinized human practices (see Ch. 9). These ideas provide clear openings for the study of international law, and it is not surprising that constructivists have found considerable common ground with legal theorists. By broadening our understanding of politics to include issues of identity and purpose as well as strategy; by treating rules, norms, and ideas as constitutive, not just constraining; and by stressing the importance of discourse, communication, and socialization in framing actors' behaviour, constructivists offer resources for understanding the politics of international law lacking in realist and neo-liberal thought.

The new liberalism

The 'new liberalism' in international relations (which draws on strands of liberal thought discussed in Chs 6 and 7) seeks to reformulate liberalism as a positive social scientific paradigm, in a 'nonideological and nonutopian form appropriate to empirical social science' (Moravcsik 1997: 513). The theory rests on three core assumptions. The first holds that the 'fundamental actors in international politics are individuals and private groups, who are on average rational and risk-averse' (*ibid.*: 516). The second proposes that '[s]tates (or other political institutions) represent some subset of domestic society, on the basis of whose interests state officials define state preferences and act purposively in world politics' (*ibid.*: 518). The third and final assumption is that, in the arena of international relations, the 'configuration of interdependent state preferences determines state behavior' (*ibid.*: 520). In sum, the new liberalism is a 'second image' theory that gives analytical priority to the domestic sources of international relations.

Building on Moravcsik's three core assumptions, Anne-Marie Slaughter has proposed a three-tiered conception of international law. It is important to note,

however, that her departure from the idea of the state as a unitary actor is more radical than Moravcsik's. Where he simply emphasizes the primacy of individuals and private groups, the most prominent of which shape state preferences, Slaughter disaggregates the state itself, stressing the transnational linkages between the executive, legislative, administrative, and judicial parts of different states. Her three tiers of international law thus consist of the following: the voluntary law of individuals and groups in transnational society; the law of transnational governmental institutions; and the law of inter-state relations (Slaughter 1995). The influence of liberal thought on Slaughter's theory does not stop at the schematic level, though. Because liberal theory stresses the primacy of individuals and private groups in shaping political and legal outcomes, the traditional ordering of international law, which privileges the international public law of inter-state relations, is turned on its head, with law that directly regulates individuals and groups (the first two tiers) taking precedence. Furthermore, within international public law, law that most directly affects individual–state relations is given priority, thus placing human rights law at the 'core' of international law (Slaughter 2000).

Critical legal studies

To this point we have considered a number of theories bearing the mark of political liberalism. During the 1980s a body of critical international legal theory emerged to challenge the inherent liberalism of modern international legal thought and practice. Often termed 'critical legal studies' or the 'new stream', its proponents argue that liberalism is stultifying international legal theory, pushing it between the equally barren extremes of 'apology'—the rationalization of established sovereign order—and 'utopia'—the naïve imagining that international law can civilize the world of states (Koskenniemi 1989). Their critique of liberalism in international law incorporates four propositions (see Purvis 1991). First, they argue that the underlying logic of liberalism in international law is incoherent. Such liberalism denies that there can be any objective values beyond the particularistic values of individual states, and yet it imagines that international conflicts can be resolved on the basis of objective and neutral rules. Second, critical legal scholars claim that international legal thought operates within a confined intellectual structure. The twin pillars of this structure are liberal ideology and public international legal argument. The former works to naturalize the sovereign order, to place beyond critical reflection the principles of sovereignty and sovereign equality. The latter confines legitimate legal argument within certain confines. '[T]raditional international legal argument', Nigel Purvis contends, 'must be understood as a recurring self-referential search for origins, authority, and coherence' (1991: 105). Third, critical legal scholars challenge the purported determinacy of international legal rules. Legal positivism holds that a rule has a singular and objective meaning—hence the idea of 'finding the law'. For the critics, this is patently false: 'any international legal doctrine can justify multiple and competing outcomes in any legal debate' (*ibid.*: 108). Finally, critical legal scholars argue that the authority of international law can only ever be self-validating; it is only through its own internal rituals that it can attain the legitimacy needed to attract state compliance and engagement (*ibid.*: 109–13).

Key Points

- Realists argue that international law is only important when it serves the interests of powerful states.

- Neo-liberals explain how self-interested states come to construct dense networks of international legal regimes.

- Constructivists treat international law as part of the normative structures that condition state and non-state agency in international relations. Like other social norms, they emphasize the way in which law constitutes actors' identities, interests, and strategies.

- New liberals emphasize the domestic origins of state preferences and, in turn, international law. Within international law, they stress the need to disaggregate the state to understand transnational legal integration and interaction, and they prioritize international humanitarian law.

- Critical legal studies concentrates on the way in which the inherent liberalism of international law seriously curtails its radical potential.

Conclusion

This chapter opened by noting the 'paradox' of international law, the fact that while scholars often downplay the value and efficacy of international law, sovereign states devote enormous amounts of time and energy to constructing ever more elaborate legal regimes. We then considered the role that institutions play in facilitating coexistence and cooperation among states, and how the modern institution of international law arose historically. It was argued that international law was both functional to the needs of an increasingly complex international system, but also deeply grounded in ideas about legitimate rule that accompanied the rise of political liberalism. After considering trends that may be transforming international law into a form of supranational, or transnational law, we concluded by surveying the principal theories about the nature and efficacy of international law, each of which presents a different set of viewpoints on the 'paradox' of international law.

Questions

1   Can you think of other factors, in addition to those listed in the chapter, that contributed to the rise of modern international law in the last two centuries?

2   Is the 'paradox of international law' really a paradox?

3   Do you find persuasive the argument that states create institutions to sustain international order?

4   Can you think of other distinctive characteristics of the modern institution of international law not raised in the chapter?

5   Which of the theories of international law surveyed do you find most persuasive, and why?

6   If you were asked to predict the future of international law, how would you use the theories surveyed to construct an answer?

7   What do you think are the strengths and weaknesses of the international legal system?
8   What evidence do you see that international law is transforming into a form of supranational law?
9   What are the implications of the rise of supranational law for the sovereignty of states?
10 How should we think about the relationship between international law and justice and ethics in international relations?

Further Reading

Armstrong, D., Farrell, T., and Lambert, H. (2007), *International Law and International Relations* (Cambridge: Cambridge University Press). An excellent introduction to international law written for students of International Relations.

Byers, M. (2000), *The Role of Law in International Politics* (Oxford: Oxford University Press). A comprehensive collection of advanced essays on the politics of international law.

Cassese, A. (2005), *International Law*, 2nd edn (Oxford: Oxford University Press). An outstanding international legal text by a leading scholar and jurist.

Goldsmith, J. L., and Posner, E. A. (2006), *The Limits of International Law* (New York: Oxford University Press). A vigorous critique of the institution of international law and its capacity to produce substantial goods for international society.

Guzman, A. (2008), *How International Law Works: A Rational Choice Theory* (Oxford: Oxford University Press). One of the clearest statements of a rational choice theory of international law that is fruitfully compared with Kratochwil (1989) and Reus-Smit (2004).

Higgins, R. (1995), *Problems and Process: International Law and How We Use It* (Oxford: Oxford University Press). A very good introduction to international law by a justice of the International Court of Justice.

Kratochwil, F. (1989), *Rules, Norms, and Decisions* (Cambridge: Cambridge University Press). The most sustained and advanced constructivist work on international legal reasoning. Compare with Guzman (2008).

Reus-Smit, C. (ed.) (2004), *The Politics of International Law* (Cambridge: Cambridge University Press). An edited collection that presents a constructivist perspective on international law, illustrated by a range of contemporary case studies. Compare with Guzman (2008).

Shaw, M. (2008), *International Law* (Cambridge: Cambridge University Press). One of the most popular textbooks on international law.

Simmons, B., and Steinberg, R. H. (eds) (2007), *International Law and International Relations* (Cambridge: Cambridge University Press). A collection of advanced essays on the politics of international law drawn from the premier journal *International Organization*.

Online Resource Centre

Visit the Online Resource Centre that accompanies this book to access more learning resources on this chapter topic at www.oxfordtextbooks.co.uk/orc/baylis5e/

Chapter 18

International regimes

RICHARD LITTLE

Reader's Guide

Liberal institutionalists and realists are engaged in a major debate about the role played by regimes—delineated areas of rule-governed activity—in the international system. Both schools acknowledge that although the international system is anarchic (without a ruler) in structure, it has never been anomic (without rules). Interest in regimes surfaced in the 1970s along with concern about the ability of the USA to sustain the economic regimes formed after the Second World War. What are the essential features of regimes? There is no straightforward answer to this question, and the chapter uses a definition, typology, and examples to reveal their complex character. Under what circumstances do regimes come into existence? This question forms the nub of the debate. Although liberal institutionalists and realists use very similar tools of analysis—drawing on microeconomics and game theory—they arrive at very different conclusions. Are the conclusions compatible? The question remains contested.

Introduction

An important dimension of globalization has been the establishment of worldwide **regimes**—rule-governed activity within the **international system**. Although international rules pre-date the emergence of the modern **state**, it was during the twentieth century that regimes became a global phenomenon, with states enmeshed in increasingly complex sets of rules and institutions that regulated international relations around the world. There is now no area of international intercourse devoid of regimes, where states are not circumscribed by the existence of mutually accepted sets of rules. Indeed, many regimes are so firmly embedded in the system that they are almost taken for granted. Most people do not consider it at all surprising, for example, that we can put a letter in a post-box, and be confident that it will be delivered anywhere in the world from the Antarctic to Zimbabwe, or that we can get on an aeroplane and expect to fly unmolested to our destination at any point across the globe. Only when something goes drastically wrong, as, for example, in 1983, when the Soviet Defence Forces shot down the civilian South Korean airliner KAL 007, killing all 269 persons on board, is our attention drawn to the fact that international relations are, in practice, extensively regulated by complex regimes negotiated and policed by states. International terrorism is, as a consequence, particularly disturbing because terrorists do not consider themselves bound by regimes.

It may seem unremarkable, at first sight, that states have established regimes to ensure that mail gets delivered anywhere in the world and that aircraft can fly safely from one country to another. The advantages of such regimes appear so obvious that it would be more remarkable if such regimes had not been put in place. However, the existence of these regimes becomes rather more surprising when it is acknowledged how much controversy can surround the formation of regimes, how contentious established regimes can prove to be, and how frequently attempts to form regimes can fail. It is because the use of regimes to promote everything from arms control to the enhancement of global economic welfare seems to be so self-evidently beneficial that the difficulty of securing regimes requires some explanation. Sadly, there is no agreed answer. Although few doubt that regimes are an important feature of the contemporary international system, as this chapter aims to demonstrate, theorists in the field of International Relations (IR) are deeply divided about how and why regimes are formed and maintained.

From the 1970s onwards a series of global developments, to be discussed below, have encouraged theorists in IR to focus on the rapid expansion of regimes in the international system. The new breed of regime theorists has spawned an enormous literature (Levy *et al.* 1995), with increasingly complex and diverse research now being conducted across the globe (Rittberger 1993).

It is argued in this chapter that regime theorists are located within two broad schools of thought: **realism** and **liberalism** (see Chs 5 and 6). Although Hasenclever, Mayer, and Rittberger (1997; Hasenclever 2000) see this division as an oversimplification, it does allow us to trace the broad parameters of the debate precipitated by the attempts to understand regimes. The chapter also aims to illustrate that, in the attempt to accommodate the growth of regimes, both realists and liberals have had to extend their frames of reference.

Realists are often sceptical of or uninterested in **international law**, and yet they have developed an important position on regimes. At the same time, regime theorists in the liberal camp, identified as liberal institutionalists, have accepted key assumptions made by neo-realists, and these, along with their social science credentials, move them beyond the established liberal tradition (see Ch. 6). But despite the shared theoretical assumptions, liberal institutionalists and realists adhere to very different assessments of regimes (see Box 18.1). Liberal institionalists focus on the way that regimes allow states to overcome the obstacles to **collaboration** imposed by the anarchic structure of the international system. Realists, by contrast, are interested in the way that states use their power capabilities in situations requiring **coordination** to influence the nature of regimes and the way that the costs and benefits derived from regime formation are divided up. Collaboration and coordination are seen to constitute different approaches to **cooperation**.

Although there are important differences between these two schools of thought, there are also important similarities (see Ch. 7). In particular, both consider regimes to be the product of rational self-interested actors. As a consequence, they approach the establishment of rules from a very different perspective to social constructivists, who assume that the existence of rules can

Box 18.1 Liberal institutionalist v. realist approaches to the analysis of regimes

Common assumptions

1 States operate in an anarchic international system.

2 States are rational and unitary actors.

3 States are the units responsible for establishing regimes.

4 Regimes are established on the basis of cooperation in the international system.

5 Regimes promote international order.

Liberal institutionalists

1 Regimes enable states to collaborate.

2 Regimes promote the common good.

3 Regimes flourish best when promoted and maintained by a benign hegemon.

4 Regimes promote globalization and a liberal world order.

Realists

1 Regimes enable states to coordinate.

2 Regimes generate differential benefits for states.

3 Power is the central feature of regime formation and survival.

4 The nature of world order depends on the underlying principles and norms of regimes.

help to shape how actors define their identity and interests and demonstrate that they share a common view of the world (see Chs 9 and 17. Although the literature on regimes is still dominated by rationalists, critics of this perspective are now starting to focus on regimes that are more difficult to explain from a rationalist perspective, such as the international protection of minority rights (Cronin 2003).

Why did IR theorists focus on regime formation in the 1970s? One factor was the growing awareness that, outside of the Soviet sphere, the USA had played the role of **hegemon** after the Second World War. The term derives from the Greek, meaning leader, and the USA could play this role because of its preponderance of power in the international system. During this era, the USA, because of its hegemonic position, had been able to establish and maintain a complex array of economic regimes in the West. These regimes played a vital role in the growing prosperity after the Second World War. By the 1970s, however, partly because of the economic success in Europe and Japan, and partly because of the

disastrous policy in Vietnam, the capacity of the USA to maintain its hegemonic status was in doubt. It is unsurprising that an interest in regimes coincided with this development.

Liberal institutionalists and realists reacted to this development in very different ways. Liberal institutionalists were concerned because while the need for regimes was becoming increasingly urgent, they believed that the loss of hegemonic status by the USA made it increasingly difficult to establish these regimes. Realists argued, by contrast, that if the USA did lose its hegemonic status, then with the shift in the balance of power the liberal principles governing these regimes established by the USA would be challenged by Third World states wanting new regimes established on the basis of different **norms** and principles. Although their analyses pointed in different directions, both liberal institutionalists and realists acknowledged the need for a more sophisticated theoretical understanding of regimes.

After the **cold war**, the USA became even more hegemonic than in the past, but concern also began to grow that the USA was losing interest in the formation of new **international regimes**. For example, in 2004 President Bush withdrew US support for the Kyoto Protocol to the UN Framework Convention on Climate Change, which was by then ratified or acceded to by over 120 states. By 2009, however, although the USA under Preseident Obama was eager to get universal agreement at the Copenhagen Climate Change Conference, its hegemonic position was now being challenged by the growing power of China and the determination of the G77 not to be bullied into accepting a deal favoured by the developed world. As a result, the possibility of establishing an international regime with universal acceptance began to look increasingly remote.

As we shall see in this chapter, the liberal explanation for this problem focuses on the loss of American power and the inability of the USA to forge a consensus around an optimum set of solutions to the problem of climate change. Realists, on the other hand, focus on the growing conflict of interest that exists between the developed and developing world. The developing world argues that the problem has been precipitated by the developed world and that, as a consequence, the developed world must shoulder most of the costs for resolving the problem. With China now endorsing this position, the developed world is operating on a new and a very different playing field. These two theoretical positions are not incompatible, and together they begin to provide a powerful explanation for why it is proving increasingly difficult to formulate effective regimes.

The chapter also suggests that the need for a theoretical understanding of international regimes is now more important than ever.

Key Points

- Regimes represent an important feature of globalization.
- A growing number of global regimes is being formed.
- The term regimes, and social science approaches to them, are recent but fit into a long-standing tradition of thought about international law.

- The onset of détente, the loss of hegemonic status by the USA, and the growing awareness of environmental problems sensitized social scientists to the need for a theory of regimes.
- Liberal institutionalists and realists have developed competing approaches to the analysis of regimes.

The nature of regimes

Before presenting the theoretical approaches developed by the liberal institutionalists and the realists, this section discusses in more detail their conceptualization of an international regime and then uses some of the major areas of world politics, now regulated by regimes, to illustrate the concept.

Conceptualizing regimes

Although it may be helpful in the first instance to think of regimes as rule-governed behaviour, a more complex conceptualization has been developed by theorists working in the field of IR. This conceptualization is captured by a definition and typology of regimes.

Defining regimes

There are many definitions of a regime, but the one formulated in the early 1980s by Stephen Krasner remains the standard formulation and it very effectively encapsulates the complexity of the phenomenon (see Box 18.2). Krasner's definition reveals that a regime is more than a set of rules; it presupposes quite a high level of **institutionalization**. Indeed, regime theorists have been criticized for doing no more than introducing new terminology to characterize the familiar idea of an international organization. Regime theorists acknowledge that international organizations can be embraced by regime theory, but they insist that their approach encompasses much more. Reus-Smit's (Ch. 17) distinction between institutions and organizations establishes the same

point. The parameters of a regime can be illustrated by means of a typology.

Classifying regimes

One simple but useful classification establishes a typology of regimes along two dimensions (Levy *et al.* 1995). The vertical dimension highlights the formality of a regime (see Table 18.1). A regime can be associated with a highly formalized agreement or even the emergence of an international organization. But, at the other extreme, a regime can come into existence in the absence of any formal agreements. Historically, informal agreements between states have been established on the basis of precedence. The horizontal axis then focuses on the extent to which states expect or anticipate that their behaviour will be constrained by their accession to an implicit or explicit set of agreements.

If there are no formal agreements, and no convergence in the expectation that rules will be adhered to, then it is clear that there is *no regime* in existence. On the other hand, even in the absence of formal rules, there can be an expectation that informal rules will be observed, suggesting the existence of a *tacit regime*. By contrast, it is also possible to identify situations where formal rules have been brought into existence without any expectation that they will be observed, indicating the existence of **a dead-letter regime**. Finally, there are *full-blown regimes*, where there is a high expectation that formal rules will be observed (see Table 18.1). Examples of these different types of regimes will be given in the next section.

Box 18.2 Defining regimes

Regimes are identified by Krasner (1983: 2) as 'sets of implicit or explicit principles, norms, rules, and decision-making procedures around which actors' expectations converge in a given area of international relations'.

An example of a regime

This is a complex definition and it needs to be unpacked. Krasner has done this, by drawing on the **General Agreement on Tariffs and Trade** (GATT) for illustrative purposes. The GATT was initially an agreement drawn up in 1947 and reflected the belief of its signatories that it was necessary to establish an organization that would be responsible for the regulation of international trade. In fact, it proved impossible to establish such an organization at that time, and the GATT acted as a substitute. It was given a secretariat and a general director responsible for carrying out the preparatory work for a series of conferences at which the signatories of the GATT met and reached agreements intended to foster international trade. In 1994, after the Uruguay Round of negotiations, it was agreed that it was now time to move beyond the GATT and establish a formal World Trade Organization, as originally intended. Krasner was writing before this development took place, but it does not affect the validity of the GATT as an illustration of what is meant by a regime.

The four defining elements of a regime

1 **Principles** are represented by coherent bodies of theoretical statements about how the world works. The GATT operated on the basis of liberal principles which assert that global welfare will be maximized by free trade.

2 **Norms** specify general standards of behaviour, and identify the rights and obligations of states. So, in the case of the GATT, the basic norm is that tariffs and non-tariff barriers should be reduced and eventually eliminated. Together, norms and principles define the essential character of a regime and these cannot be changed without transforming the nature of the regime.

3 **Rules** operate at a lower level of generality than principles and norms, and they are often designed to reconcile conflicts which may exist between the principles and norms. Third World states, for example, wanted rules which differentiated between developed and underdeveloped countries.

4 **Decision-making procedures** identify specific prescriptions for behaviour, the system of voting, for example, which will regularly change as a regime is consolidated and extended. The rules and procedures governing the GATT, for example, underwent substantial modification during its history. Indeed, the purpose of the successive conferences was to change the rules and decision-making procedures.

(Krasner 1985: 4–5)

Table 18.1 A typology of regimes

Convergence of expectations		Formality
Low	High	
No regimes	Tacit regimes	Low
Dead-letter regimes	Full-blown regimes	High

(Adapted from Levy et al. 1995)

Globalization and international regimes

As we move into the twenty-first century it becomes increasingly clear that not every aspect of the globalization of world politics is beneficial. Technology makes it possible to see and talk to people on the other side of the globe and to fill the supermarkets—at least those in the wealthy sectors of the global economy—with increasingly exotic commodities from all round the world. But it has also made it possible to build weapons with the potential to wreak global devastation and to pollute the atmosphere irreversibly. It is becoming increasingly apparent that if we are all to benefit rather than suffer from globalization, it is essential to manage the process. No one thinks that this task will be easy; pessimists doubt that it is even possible. Regime theorists, on the other hand, see grounds for optimism. They believe that **survival** depends upon our capacity to regulate global activity by means of regimes; and, as we demonstrate in this section, although not in any comprehensive fashion, the evidence indicates that states can establish regimes across a wide range of activities.

Security regimes

Although **security regimes** are primarily a twentieth-century phenomenon, permitting states to escape from the security dilemma (see Ch. 14), it is possible to identify earlier examples. The Concert of Europe, for instance, constitutes a regime formed by the conservative states of post-Napoleonic Europe to counter future revolution and conflict. At the same time, on the other side of the Atlantic, the British and Americans established the Rush–Bagot agreement in 1817 to demilitarize the Great Lakes. But whereas the tacit regional regime in Europe began to decay soon after it was formed, the full-blown bilateral regime in North America became steadily stronger until, eventually, the long border between Canada and the USA was permanently demilitarized.

Regular attempts to establish full-blown security regimes, however, only started to proliferate during the twentieth century, particularly after the onset of the cold war. But the effectiveness of these regimes has often been questioned. Jervis (1983b), for example, argues that some of the major regimes, such as SALT 1 (1972) and SALT 2 (1979), designed to bring the arms race between the USA and the Soviet Union under control, were effectively dead-letter regimes. Despite the prolonged negotiations and detailed agreements, there was no evidence that they brought the arms race under control, because neither **superpower** expected the other to desist from developing new weapons technology. Nevertheless, arms control agreements can establish fragile security regimes and, for example, the Partial Test Ban Agreement of 1963 has undoubtedly encouraged a prohibition of atmospheric testing. Even the fragile nuclear non-proliferation regime is seen to have helped to deter many states from crossing the nuclear threshold despite the prevailing assumption in the twentieth century that many of them would do so (Rublee 2009).

Environmental regimes

As scientists have become increasingly aware of the damage being done to the global environment, so the importance attached to environmental regimes has steadily risen (see Ch. 21). Oil pollution, global warming, and damage to the ozone layer are the issues that have attracted most public attention, but regimes have been established in a wide range of areas in the attempt to protect the global environment. For example, international conventions to save endangered plant and animal species can be traced back to the 1970s, and a comprehensive Convention on Biological Diversity came into force in December 1993. There have also been attempts since the mid-1980s to regulate the international movement of hazardous waste material, with the Basle Convention establishing a complete ban in March 1993 on the shipping of hazardous waste from countries in the developed world to countries

in the underdeveloped world (Breitmeier, Young, and Zurn 2007). At the same time, however, there is now a growing sense that governments are doing too little, too late. This was the general reaction to the outcome of the climate change summit held at the end of 2009 in Copenhagen, It proved impossible to transcend the complex of competing interests on display at the conference. At the very end of the conference, a deal brokered by the USA with China, Brazil, India, and South Africa to attempt to limit global warming to no more than 2 °C was regarded as nothing more than a face-saving exercise by the participating states. The theoretical sections of this chapter will endeavour to explain why it is so difficult to make progress in this crucial area.

Economic regimes

It is often argued that the regimes in the economic arena are more firmly entrenched than those in any other. As already noted, however, the international economy could not function in the absence of the infrastructure provided by the communication regimes. The two sets of regimes are inextricably linked. Indeed, over the last decade, as the regimes governing the international economy have become ever more firmly established, the underlying liberal principles governing these regimes have started to impinge on the communication regimes. This development is reflected in the growing attempts to open postal services, telecommunications, and national airlines to greater competition. This development is leading to a modification of the basic principle underlying these regimes that in the past has always favoured state control over the rules regulating these activities (Zacher, with Sutton 1996).

It is not possible to provide even a brief survey of the complex economic regimes established in the era after the Second World War. But it is worth noting that they reflect the determined effort made by the USA, in particular, to consolidate a set of regimes built upon liberal principles. In particular, the USA wished to establish a trading regime established on free trade principles and, as we have seen, the GATT, now the **World Trade Organization** (WTO), was established to achieve this goal. At the same time, however, the USA also recognized that, to flourish, trade requires stable domestic economies and a stable monetary system. A range of international organizations, such as the **International Monetary Fund** and the International Bank for Reconstruction and Development, was established after 1945 to promote an environment where trade could flourish. Although there were fears that the economic regimes established by the USA would collapse as weaknesses in its own economy became apparent in the late 1960s, the economic regimes brought into existence after 1945 have proved surprisingly resilient The financial crisis that erupted in 2008 tested some of these regimes to the limit but, so far, the world economy has survived intact. Nevertheless, new regimes need to be brought into play to improve the regulation of existing financial institutions, and this chapter indicates why this will prove problematic (see Ch. 15).

Key Points

- Regime theory is an attempt initiated in the 1970s by social scientists to account for the existence of rule-governed behaviour in the anarchic international system.

- Regimes have been defined by principles, norms, rules, and decision-making procedures.

- Regimes can be classified in terms of the formality of the underlying agreements and the degree of expectation that the agreements will be observed. Full-blown, tacit, and dead-letter regimes can be identified.

- Regimes now help to regulate international relations in many spheres of activity.

Competing theories of regime formation

Both liberal institutionalists and realists acknowledge that regimes are an important feature of contemporary international relations, and they also start from the same theoretical premise that a regime represents the response of rational actors operating within the anarchic structure of the international system (see Ch. 7). But despite this common starting point, realists and liberal institutionalists develop very different theoretical assessments of regimes.

The liberal institutional approach

For liberal institutionalists, regimes help to overcome the problem of **anarchy**. They draw on theoretical ideas developed outside international relations to explain why anarchy inhibits collaboration and how to promote regime formation.

Impediments to regime formation

To explain why anarchy impedes regime formation, liberal institutionalists turn to **microeconomics** and **game theory**. Microeconomists study economic units operating under the conditions of perfect competition found, in theory, within the marketplace, and liberal institutionalists then draw an analogy between the economic market and the international system because both are constituted by anarchic structures. For microeconomists, the absence of centralized institutions constitutes an important asset of the marketplace. Unrestrained by external interference, rational economic units pursue competitive and self-interested strategies that result in

goods being bought and sold at what microeconomic theory demonstrates is the optimum price.

This benign image of the economic market might seem to generate very little insight for liberal institutionalists. But the microeconomic approach becomes more relevant when attention is turned to the concept of **market failure**. Although microeconomists insist that an unrestrained market provides the most effective mechanism for the production of economic goods, it is accepted that the market is not effective when it comes to the production of **public goods** such as roads and hospitals, and, indeed, there are circumstances when unrestrained competition produces **public bads**, the obvious example being pollution. Microeconomists argue that the underprovision of public goods or the proliferation of public bads occurs because sometimes economic actors need to collaborate rather than compete. The principal mechanism to promote collaboration, often only accepted with reluctance, takes the form of state intervention. The state can, when necessary, intervene in the marketplace and require economic actors to collaborate. So, for example, if rivers have become polluted as the result of industrial waste, the state can pass legislation that requires all the economic actors involved to produce alternative outlets for the industrial waste. Here, the anarchic structure of the market gives way to the hierarchical structure of the state.

Within the international system, of course, no global equivalent of the state exists to enact legislation compelling sovereign states to subscribe to a common policy. As a consequence, the widespread evidence of global problems persisting because of sovereign states failing to collaborate is unsurprising. Global pollution, resource depletion, arms races, and trade barriers are all evidence of market failure—where states have preferred to compete rather than to collaborate. Nevertheless, the existence of regimes indicates that collaboration is certainly possible within the anarchic arena. Anarchy does not preclude collaboration; it simply makes it difficult to achieve, and game theory helps to explain why.

Game theorists are mathematicians interested in non-zero-sum games that focus on the strategic interaction between rational actors who can pursue either competitive or collaborative strategies. The interaction produces a much more complex situation than is found in the purely competitive market setting. Liberal institutionalists, while generally avoiding the mathematics, have drawn on some of the conceptual apparatus developed by game theorists in order to enhance their theoretical appreciation of why anarchy inhibits collaboration. Theory building requires a distillation of the essential elements of the situation under scrutiny, and

game theory is particularly parsimonious. It focuses on the interaction between two actors, each with only two possible strategies—one cooperative and the other competitive—and so strategic interaction involves four possible outcomes. On the basis of this very simple conceptual apparatus it becomes possible to model a wide range of social situations. By stripping away the detail, it becomes easier to understand the underlying dynamics of the situation. So, for example, it is argued that all instances of market failure can be modelled by the game known as **Prisoner's Dilemma** (see Box 18.3).

The logic associated with the Prisoner's Dilemma is seen by liberal institutionalists to account for why a wide range of irrational outcomes in the international arena can be explained in rational terms. It explains why states have persisted in overfishing the seas, in polluting the atmosphere, in selling arms to undesirable regimes, and in promoting policies that inhibit trade. All represent cases of market failure, with states choosing to pursue competitive rather than collaborative strategies. They fail to pursue collaborative strategies because they

---

Box 18.3 The game of Prisoner's Dilemma

The Prisoner's Dilemma scenario

The governor of a prison once had two prisoners whom he could not hang without a voluntary confession of at least one. Accordingly, he summoned one prisoner and offered him his freedom and a sum of money if he would confess at least a day before the second prisoner did so, so that an indictment could be prepared and so that the second prisoner could be hanged. If the latter should confess at least a day before him, however, the first prisoner was told, then the prisoner would be freed and rewarded and he would be hanged. 'And what if we both should confess on the same day, your Excellency?', asked the first prisoner. 'Then you each will keep your life but will get ten years in prison.' 'And if neither of us should confess, your Excellency?' 'Then both of you will be set free—without any reward, of course. But will you bet your neck that your fellow prisoner—that crook—will not hurry to confess and pocket the reward? Now go back to your solitary cell and think about your answer until tomorrow.' The second prisoner in his interview was told the same, and each man spent the night alone considering his dilemma (Deutsch 1968: 120).

The two actors are confronted with two possible strategies, generating a situation with four possible outcomes. Being rational, the prisoners can place these outcomes on a preference ranking. The matrix below reveals the preference rankings for the two prisoners. Both prisoners will pursue the strategy that will optimize their position in the light of the strategies available to the other prisoner. To avoid being hanged, both prisoners will confess and end up in prison for ten years, thereby demonstrating how individual **rationality** leads to collective irrationality. The sub-optimal outcome could only be avoided if the two prisoners possessed a mechanism that allowed them to collaborate.

In this figure, cell numerals refer to ordinally ranked preferences: 4 = best, 1 = worst. The first number in each cell refers to A's preference and the second number refers to B's preference.

Key

*   Dominant strategy: both players have dominant rather than contingent strategies. A strategy becomes dominant if it is preferable to the alternative strategy no matter which strategy the other player adopts.

†   Denotes an equilibrium outcome.

‡   A Pareto-optimal outcome: Vilfredo Pareto (1848–1923) was an Italian sociologist and economist who developed a criterion for identifying when an exchange between two parties has reached its most efficient or optimal point. He argued, in essence, that the point is reached when one party is better off and the other party is no worse off than before the exchange took place. An implication of this optimum is discussed later.

expect the other members of the **anarchic system** to pursue competitive strategies. It would be irrational for one state to require its fishing industry to observe a fishing quota, for example, if it is believed that the fishing industries in other states are intending to disregard the quota. As a consequence, states avoid a Pareto-optimal outcome and are driven by rational calculation to pursue a strategy that, through strategic interaction, leads to a suboptimal outcome.

If the Prisoner's Dilemma game does accurately map this situation, however, then it not only explains why anarchy inhibits collaboration, but also indicates that states acknowledge the advantages of collaboration. They are only inhibited from moving to collaborative strategies by their expectation that other states will defect. The Prisoner's Dilemma demonstrates the importance of identifying a mechanism that will convince all the actors that there is no danger of defection. Liberal institutionalists believe that the establishment of regimes provides evidence that mechanisms of this kind must exist.

The facilitation of regime formation

Liberal institutionalists have followed two different routes in their attempt to explain the emergence of regimes. First, they have drawn on the work of microeconomists, who have insisted that state intervention is not the only mechanism available to produce public goods. It is suggested that if there is a dominant or hegemonic actor operating within the market, then that actor may well be prepared to sustain the cost of producing a public good (Olson 1965). Liberal institutionalists have had no difficulty extending this line of argument to the international arena. During the course of the nineteenth century, for example, a regime was established that outlawed the international traffic of slaves. States agreed to observe the humanitarian principle underpinning this regime because they expected other states to do so. The expectation emerged because it was recognized that Great Britain intended to police the regime and possessed the naval capacity to do so. The regime was consolidated, therefore, because of Britain's hegemonic status within the international system.

As already indicated, it is widely accepted that the economic regimes established after the Second World War owe their existence to the presence of the USA as a hegemonic power. But when liberal institutionalists examined the consequences of hegemonic decline, they concluded that established regimes would persist. Although the Prisoner's Dilemma indicated that market failures occur because in an anarchic system there is an

expectation that states will compete rather than collaborate, once states have moved away from the sub-optimal outcome resulting from mutually competitive strategies, then there is no incentive to defect from the mutually collaborative strategies and return to the sub-optimal outcome. Even in the absence of a hegemon, therefore, liberal institutionalists argue that established regimes will survive (Keohane 1984).

A second route explored by the liberal institutionalists reinforces this conclusion. It is argued that if the Prisoner's Dilemma is played only once, then the game exaggerates the difficulty of generating collaboration. It is more realistic, however, to see the game being played repeatedly. The **shadow of the future** then looms over the players, affecting their strategic calculations. Because the game will be played on future occasions, it becomes worthwhile taking a risk and pursuing a collaborative strategy in order to produce the optimal outcome. If all states can be persuaded to do the same, then there will be little incentive to defect in the future, because if one state defects, then, 'tit for tat', all the others will follow. The major mechanism for establishing and maintaining a regime is not, then, the existence of a hegemon, but the principle of **reciprocity**. Liberal institutionalists have increasingly come to focus on factors that will strengthen reciprocity within the system. Inspection and surveillance facilities become very important for ensuing that states are operating within the parameters of a regime. The establishment of satellite surveillance, for example, was a significant factor in encouraging the USA and the Soviet Union to reach arms control agreements. Attention has also been drawn to the importance of scientific knowledge. States are unwilling to restrict their activities on the basis of speculation, and respond much more effectively when scientists start to agree about the significance of their findings. With states becoming ever more open and scientific understanding constantly expanding, so the international environment will become increasingly 'information rich'. It is this trend, liberal institutionalists argue, that will do most to facilitate regime building in the future (Keohane 1984).

The realist approach

Unsurprisingly, realists contest the liberal institutional approach. First, they attack the comparison drawn between a hegemon providing public goods in the international system and the state dealing with domestic cases of market failure. Second, realists deny that regimes emerge as the result of states endeavouring to overcome the pressure to compete under conditions of anarchy. Regimes form, realists argue, in situations when uncoordinated strategies interact to produce sub-optimal outcomes.

Power and regimes

Despite being aware in the 1970s and 1980s that the hegemonic status of the USA was being questioned, realists did not conclude that this development might lead to an anomic world. Instead, they focused on Third World demands for a new set of principles and norms to underpin the regimes associated with the world economy. Existing regimes were seen to work against the interests of Third World states, opening them up to unfair competition and malign economic forces. Realists took seriously the case presented by the Third World, but argued that the principles and norms demanded by the Third World would only come into operation if the balance of power moved against the West (Tucker 1977; Krasner 1985). This assessment runs directly counter to the liberal institutionalist image of the USA as a benign benefactor, underwriting a set of regimes that allowed the members of the anarchic international system to escape from a sub-optimal outcome and into a position of Pareto optimality. Instead, the USA was a hegemon that used its power to sustain a regime that promoted its own long-term interests. Liberal institutionalists ignore the contested status of liberal norms and principles.

From the realist perspective, therefore, the USA helped to ensure that regimes were underpinned by a particular set of principles and norms. But a full appreciation of the realist's position also requires the recognition that a hegemon can effectively veto the formation of a regime. For example, in 1972, when the USA launched its first remote-sensing satellite, the event caused concern among a large range of countries. These satellites have the capacity to gather important and sensitive commercial and strategic data about countries all around the world. Not only can the satellites identify where military equipment is located: they can also identify the size of a crop yield and the location of minerals. There were several attempts to establish a regime that would limit the right of states to acquire data without the permission of the state under surveillance (Brown *et al.* 1977). Many states have considered that they would benefit from such a regime. But because the balance of power was tilted in favour of states that possessed these satellites and they were clear that such a regime would not work to their benefit, they vetoed the proposed regime.

Regimes and coordination

The realist account of regimes, however, must also explain why states adhere to the principles and norms underlying a regime that they oppose. In accounting for this phenomenon, realists, like liberal institutionalists, resort to game theory. They argue that states wishing to form a regime confront the problem of coordination, as illustrated by the **Battle of the Sexes** (see Box 18.4), not collaboration, as illustrated by the Prisoner's Dilemma. Here the problem is not associated with the danger of defection to a competitive strategy, but the possibility of failing to coordinate strategies, with the consequence that a mutually desired goal is unintentionally missed.

Coordination problems are very familiar to strategic thinkers. Schelling (1960) illustrates the problem with the example of a couple becoming separated in a department store. Both wish to get back together again, but there is a danger that they will wait for each other in different places; situations of this kind generate a coordination problem. In the absence of communication, solving coordination problems can be difficult, even impossible. But with the aid of communication, a solution can be very straightforward and uncontroversial. For example, while communication between an aircraft and an air traffic control centre can occur in any mutually agreed language, it is obviously unacceptable for the pilot and the air traffic controller not to be able to speak a common language. Under the rules of the International Civil Aviation Organization, every international pilot and some personnel in every air traffic control centre must be able to speak English. This is a highly stable equilibrium and the rule undoubtedly contributes to air safety. But it is only one of a large body of rules forming the regime that regulates international civil aviation. It has major training implications and it is not an issue that can be constantly renegotiated. It needs to be embodied in a stable regime that all the involved parties can treat as a constant.

The decision to choose English under these circumstances may have been relatively uncontroversial, but it does not follow that a common aversion to certain outcomes (a pilot speaking only German and the air traffic controller speaking only Japanese) will necessarily generate a common interest in a particular outcome (everyone speaking English). And this is the main lesson to be learned from the Battle of the Sexes game—there can be more than one outcome reflecting a Pareto optimum. Indeed, there can be many positions that represent a Pareto optimum, and they can then be located on

Box 18.4 The Battle of the Sexes and Pareto's frontier

The Battle of the Sexes

The scenario of this game envisages a couple who have just fallen in love and decide to go on holiday together. The problem is that one wants to go hiking in the mountains and the other wants to visit art galleries and museums in the city. But both much prefer to be with their partner than to go on holiday alone. When mapped on to a matrix, two stable equilibriums emerge from the scenario.

A (male)

	Holiday in city	Holiday in mountains
B (female) Holiday in city	4, 3†	4, 1
Holiday in mountains	1, 4	2, 2†

In this figure, cell numerals refer to ordinally ranked preferences: 4 = best, 1 = worst. The first number in each cell refers to A's preference and the second number refers to B's preference.

* Denotes an equilibrium outcome and a Pareto-optimal strategy.

The Pareto frontier

Wishing to reach a compromise, the couple might decide to split their week's holiday, spending time in the city and in the mountains. Since the two extreme positions represent a Pareto optimum, so too must all the possible combinations; these can be mapped to form a Pareto frontier.

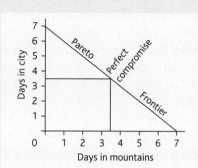

what is referred to as the Pareto frontier (see Box 18.4). So in the context of civil aviation, every spoken language can be located on the frontier because, in principle, any language can be chosen, provided that everyone speaks it. And the use of any common language is preferable to the alternative that would arise in the event of a failure to coordinate and identify a common language.

Realists argue that this line of analysis helps us to understand why states might conform to a regime while wishing to change the underlying principles. The explanation is that the states are already operating on the Pareto frontier. They observe the regime because they are operating in a coordination situation, and a failure to coordinate will move them into a less advantageous situation. The French can rail against the use of English in the civil aviation context, but they have no alternative but to persist with the policy. The same argument applies to Third World states: they wish to trade with the West, while preferring to do so on more advantageous terms. The application of new trade principles would represent another point on the Pareto frontier. But, as yet, because the balance of power continues to favour the West, there are few signs of new economic principles emerging that are more favourable to the Third World.

The situation is somewhat different in the area of communication regimes. All forms of electronic communication use electromagnetic waves that are emitted along an electromagnetic spectrum. Coordination here is essential, because interference occurs if more than one user adopts the same frequency of the spectrum at the same time over the same area. It is not possible, therefore, for states to operate on a unilateral basis, so the establishment of a regime was essential. Moreover, because the electromagnetic spectrum is a limited resource, principles and rules for partitioning the resource had to be determined. In the first instance, states agreed that the spectrum should be allocated on the basis of need. But by 1980 this principle had resulted in the Soviet Union and the USA claiming half of the available frequencies, and 90 per cent of the spectrum was allocated to provide benefits for 10 per cent of the world's population (Krasner 1985). It is unsurprising to find this outcome being challenged by developing states, which argued that part of the spectrum should be reserved for future use. More surprisingly, this new principle has been accepted. But realists argue that this is not the result of altruism on the part of the developed world. It is a consequence of the fact that developing states can interfere with the signals of neighbouring countries. This gave them access to a power lever, which they otherwise would not have possessed (Krasner 1991).

Key Points

- The market is used by liberal institutionalists as an analogy for the anarchic international system.
- In a market/international setting, public goods get underproduced and public bads get overproduced.
- Liberal institutionalists draw on the Prisoner's Dilemma game to account for the structural impediments to regime formation.

- A hegemon, 'the shadow of the future', and an information-rich environment promote collaboration and an escape route from the Prisoner's Dilemma.
- Realists argue that liberal institutionalists ignore the importance of power when examining regimes.
- Realists draw on the Battle of the Sexes to illuminate the nature of coordination and its link to power in an anarchic setting.

Conclusion

Although liberal institutionalists and realists acknowledge that regimes are an important feature of the international system, and draw on similar tools of analysis, they reach very different conclusions about the circumstances in which regimes emerge. For liberal institutionalists, regimes arise because there is always a danger in the anarchic international system that competitive strategies will trump cooperative strategies. By contrast, realists link the emergence of regimes to situations where there is a mutual desire to cooperate, but where anarchy generates a problem of coordination.

The implications of power for the two approaches also diverge. For liberal institutionalists, power may be used by a hegemon to pressure other states to collaborate and conform to a regime. But it is also acknowledged that states can establish and maintain regimes in the absence of hegemonic power. Collaborative strategies are pursued and maintained because of the 'shadow of the future'—a mutual recognition that if any state defects from a regime, it will result in mass defection on a 'tit for tat' basis and states moving from an optimal to a suboptimal outcome. For realists, on the other hand, power is seen to play a crucial role, not as a threat to discipline states caught defecting from a collaborative agreement, but in the bargaining process—to determine the shape of a regime around which all states will coordinate their actions.

Stein (1983), who introduced the distinction between collaborative and coordination games into the regime literature, never assumed, however, that they represented mutually incompatible approaches to regime formation. In practice, the two games discussed in this chapter that capture the distinction simply distil different aspects of the complex processes associated with regime formation. The case study on the international whaling moratorium illustrates the complexity that surrounds regime analysis.

In the first instance, the 15 major whaling nations established the regime because they acknowledged the need to regulate the whaling industry. The Prisoner's Dilemma game helps us to understand the kind of problems that they wished to overcome. These problems revolved around the uncertainty about what the other states were going to do. Once they agreed to collaborate, establishing quotas proved to be relatively straightforward because they recognized that if they went over their quota, the regime would collapse.

With the passage of time, however, problems arose not because of difficulties associated with policing the regime, but because differences emerged among the members about its fundamental goal. Initially, the International Whaling Commission (IWC) members all agreed that the goal was to eliminate the danger of harvesting too many whales each year. But by the 1970s, this goal began to be questioned by environmentalists, who believed that there was no satisfactory justification for continuing to catch whales because there are more efficient and humane ways of feeding people. Because of these competing positions, the issue has now become highly politicized, and the difficulty of maintaining the regime at this juncture is much more effectively captured by the Battle of the Sexes game: one camp wants a regime that ensures that whaling is effectively regulated and the other camp wants a regime that outlaws whaling.

The whaling moratorium came into force, at least in part, because of the hegemonic status of the USA. New members with no vested interest in whaling chose to

Case Study International whaling moratorium

In 1986, the International Whaling Commission (IWC) established a total moratorium on commercial whaling that remains in place today. The IWC is an international regulatory body established in 1946 by the 15 major whaling nations that agreed, on a voluntary basis, to establish and maintain a whaling regime. Commercial whaling was, as a consequence, regulated by quotas for the next four decades. But by the 1970s there were growing concerns among environmentalists that many species of whales could soon become extinct.

The 1986 moratorium was controversial from the start, however, because the IWC was, by then, split into pro-whaling and anti-whaling camps. On the one hand, some long-established whaling nations, such as Britain and the USA, were now no longer interested in maintaining whaling fleets. At the same time, powerful environmental lobbies, like Greenpeace, had raised the spectre of species extinction and promoted the image of whale hunting as barbaric. On the other hand, in states like Norway, Iceland, and Japan, whaling was portrayed as in-

tegral to national identity as well as crucial to the way of life of aboriginal peoples.

As the IWC fractured, however, new states were joining, often siding with the USA in the anti-whaling camp, thereby shifting the balance of power against pro-whalers, and the anti-whalers eventually secured the necessary three-quarters majority in favour of a moratorium; it passed on a 25–7 vote with 5 abstentions. Unsurprisingly, states in the pro-whaling camp have never accepted the need for a moratorium, questioning the validity of the scientific evidence and insisting on the viability of quotas. Nevertheless, only Iceland withdrew from the IWC, in 1992, although it was permitted to rejoin in 2002, despite its reservations about the moratorium.

Japan has spearheaded the resistance to the moratorium, making the most of the exemptions on scientific and aboriginal whaling. In 2007, for example, Japan planned to catch 1,300 whales for scientific research (more than were caught in the final year of commercial whaling). The whales were subsequently sold for commercial use. The research reveals that there is now no need for a moratorium and that the growing population of whales consumes five times more fish than humans—scientific evidence that anti-whalers vigorously dispute (see Heazle 2006).

But Japan is now the major aid donor in the world, and some of its aid recipients, with no historical interest in whaling, have been encouraged to join the IWC; new members include states from West Africa and Central America, as well as micro-states in the Pacific and the Caribbean. As membership, mainly from the Third World, has steadily increased to over 70 states, so the balance of power has tipped once again in favour of the pro-whalers. In 2006, an IWC vote calling for an end to the moratorium was passed by 33 to 32 votes, not enough to overturn the moratorium, but enough to destabilize the whaling regime.

vote with the USA, thereby bolstering the anti-whaling camp. But ever since the moratorium came into force, Japan has endeavoured to challenge the US-backed policy, thereby risking US resentment, and indeed international opprobrium, as well as prolonging a dispute that has become the source of escalating bitterness. The unremitting determination of Japan to overturn the moratorium is often considered surprising because the consumption of whale meat by the Japanese has plummeted and whale meat is no longer a significant element in their diet. But opposition to the moratorium has become an issue of principle, and there is an unwillingness to bow to pressures that from the Japanese perspective are not validated by science and are dictated primarily by emotion.

Third world states with no established interests in whaling have been the unexpected beneficiaries of the dispute, as Japan, unwilling to withdraw from the whaling regime, has drawn on its influence on Third World states in an attempt to wrest control from the anti-whaling camp. Because of the continuing hegemonic influence of the USA, the Japanese are unlikely to overturn the moratorium (McNeill 2006), but the stalemate that emerged in 2006 is sufficient to threaten the survival of the regime. None of the key actors wishes to see this happen and the Battle of the Sexes game predicts that a compromise formula will be sought and eventually found, but three years on, agreement has yet to be reached, revealing how difficult it can often be to establish international regimes.

Questions

1 What are the defining elements of a regime?
2 Is a regime the same as an organization?
3 Why did the study of international regimes develop in the 1970s?
4 What characteristic features do the realist and liberal institutionalist approaches to regime analysis share?
5 How has microeconomics influenced the liberal institutionalist approach to regimes?
6 What are the main implications of strategic interaction?
7 What are the implications of the Prisoner's Dilemma game for regime analysis?
8 What major mechanisms do liberal institutionalists advance to promote regime formation?
9 How does the realist approach to regime analysis differ from the liberal institutional approach?
10 What does the Battle of the Sexes game tell us about the role of power in regime formation?
11 What does operating at the Pareto frontier mean in the context of regime theory?
12 Are realist and liberal institutionalist approaches to regime analysis compatible?

Further Reading

Brown, S. et al. (1997), *Regimes for the Ocean, Outer Space and the Weather* (Washington, DC: Brookings Institution). An early attempt to examine areas that need to be regulated by regimes.

Cronin, B. (2003), *Institutions for the Common Good: International Protection Regimes in International Society* (Cambridge: Cambridge University Press). An important counter to rationalist-based accounts of regimes.

Gruber, L. (2000), *Ruling the World: Power Politics and the Rise of Supranational Institutions* (Princeton, NJ: Princeton University Press). Associates great powers in supranational institutions with go-it-alone power that requires other states to follow suit.

Hasenclever, A., Mayer, P., and Rittberger, V. (1997), *Theories of International Regimes* (Cambridge: Cambridge University Press). Argues that in addition to realism, which focuses on power, and neo-liberalism, which focuses on interests, cognitivism, focusing on ideas, now forms a third school of thought in the regime literature.

Keohane, R. O. (1984), *After Hegemony: Cooperation and Discord in the World Political Economy* (Princeton, NJ: Princeton University Press). One of the most influential liberal institutional texts on the theory underlying regime formation.

—— **and Nye, J. S.** (1977), *Power and Interdependence* (Boston, MA: Little Brown). Examines the role of regimes in an interdependent world, advancing four models to account for regime change.

Krasner, S. D. (ed.) (1983), *International Regimes* (Ithaca, NY: Cornell University Press). A seminal text setting out the main theoretical issues.

—— (1985), *Structural Conflict: The Third World against Global Liberalism* (Berkeley, CA: University of California Press). This is one of the major realist texts. It explores North–South disputes over regimes.

Oye, K. A. (ed.) (1986), *Cooperation under Anarchy* (Princeton, NJ: Princeton University Press). An influential set of theoretical essays on how cooperation takes place under anarchic conditions.

Rittberger, V. (ed.) (1993), *Regime Theory and International Relations* (Oxford: Clarendon Press). This important book examines regime theory from European and American perspectives.

Zacher, M. W., with Sutton, B. A. (1996), *Governing Global Networks: International Regimes for Transportation and Communications* (Cambridge: Cambridge University Press). A liberal institutionalist account of regimes, arguing that they are based on mutual interests, and not on the dictates of the most powerful states.

Online Resource Centre

 Visit the Online Resource Centre that accompanies this book to access more learning resources on this chapter topic at www.oxfordtextbooks.co.uk/orc/baylis5e/

Chapter 19

The United Nations

PAUL TAYLOR · DEVON CURTIS

Reader's Guide

This chapter focuses on the development of the United Nations (UN) and the changes and challenges that it has faced since its establishment in 1945. The UN is a grouping of states, and is therefore premised on the notion that states are the primary units in the international system. The institutions of the UN reflect an uneasy hybrid between traditions of great power consensus and traditions of universalism that stress the equality of states. Furthermore, while the UN was established as a grouping of sovereign states, the chapter argues that UN institutions have taken on an increasing range of functions, and have become much more involved within states. Justice for individuals is increasingly seen as a concomitant of international order. Serious deficiencies in human rights, or in economic welfare, can lead to international tensions. This development has led to challenges to traditional views about intervention within states. It has also led to the expansion of UN institutions to address an increased number of economic and social questions, and the search for better ways to coordinate these activities.

Introduction

The United Nations (UN) is made up of a group of international **institutions**, which include the central system located in New York, the **Specialized Agencies**, such as the World Health Organization (WHO) and the International Labour Organization (ILO), and the **Programmes and Funds**, such as the United Nations Children's Fund (UNICEF) and the United Nations Development Programme (UNDP). When created more than half a century ago in the aftermath of the Second World War, the United Nations reflected the hope for a just and peaceful global **community**. It is the only global institution with the legitimacy that derives from universal membership, and a mandate that encompasses security, economic and social development, the protection of human rights, and the protection of the environment. Yet the UN was created by **states** for states, and the relationship between **state sovereignty** and the protection of the needs and interests of people has not been fully resolved. Questions about the meaning of sovereignty and the limits of UN action have remained key issues. Since the founding of the UN, there has been an expansion of UN activities to address conditions within states, an improvement in

UN capacity in its economic and social work, and an increased tendency to accord the UN a moral status. Threats to global security addressed by the UN now include inter-state conflict, threats by **non-state actors**, as well as political, economic, and social conditions within states. Despite the growth in UN activities, however, there are some questions about the relevance and effectiveness of the UN. The failure by the USA and the UK to get clear UN Security Council authorization for the war in Iraq in 2003 led to well-publicized criticism of the UN and a crisis in international relations. Yet the troubled aftermath of the invasion and persistent questions about the legitimacy of a war that was not sanctioned by the UN show that the UN has acquired important moral status in **international society**.

After describing the main organs of the UN, this chapter will look at the changing role of the UN in addressing matters of peace and security, and then matters of economic and social development. It will focus on how the UN's role has evolved in response to changes in the global political context, and on some of the problems that it still faces.

A brief history of the United Nations and its principal organs

The United Nations was established on 24 October 1945 by 51 countries, as a result of initiatives taken by the governments of the states that had led the war against Germany and Japan. By 2010, 192 countries were members of the United Nations, nearly every state in the world. When joining, member states agreed to accept the obligations of the **United Nations Charter**, an international treaty that sets out basic principles of international relations. According to the Charter, the UN had four purposes: to maintain international peace and security; to develop friendly relations among nations; to cooperate in solving international problems and in promoting respect for human rights; and to be a centre for harmonizing the actions of nations. At the UN, all the member states—large and small, rich and poor, with differing political views and social systems—had a voice and a vote in this process. Interestingly, while the United Nations was clearly created as a grouping of states, the Charter referred to the needs and interests of peoples as well as those of states (see Box 19.1).

In many ways, the United Nations was set up to correct the problems of its predecessor, the **League of Nations**. The League of Nations had been established after the First World War, and was intended to make future wars impossible, but a major problem was the League's lack of effective power. There was no clear division of responsibility between the main executive committee (the League Council) and the League Assembly, which included all member states. Both the League Assembly and the League Council could only make recommendations, not binding resolutions, and these recommendations had to be unanimous. Any government was free to reject any recommendation. Furthermore, in the League, there was no mechanism for coordinating military or economic actions against miscreant states, which further contributed to the League's weakness. Key states, such as the USA, were not members of the League. By the Second World War, the League had already failed to address a number of acts of aggression.

Box 19.1 Selected Articles of the UN Charter

The UN Charter contains references to both the rights of states and the rights of people.

The Preamble of the UN Charter asserts that 'We the peoples of the United Nations [are] determined [...] to reaffirm faith in fundamental human rights, in the dignity and worth of the human person, in the equal rights of men and women and of nations large and small'.

Article 1(2) states that the purpose of the UN is to develop 'friendly relations among nations based on respect for the principle of equal rights and self-determination of peoples and to take other appropriate measures to strengthen universal peace'.

Article 2(7) states that 'Nothing contained in the present Charter shall authorize the United Nations to intervene in matters which are essentially within the domestic jurisdiction of any state'.

Chapter VI deals with the 'Pacific Settlement of Disputes'.

Article 33 states that 'The parties to any dispute, the continuance of which is likely to endanger the maintenance of international peace and security, shall, first of all, seek a solution by negotiation, enquiry, mediation, conciliation, arbitration, judicial settlement, resort to regional agencies or arrangements, or other peaceful means of their own choice'.

Chapter VII deals with 'Action with Respect to Threats to the Peace, Breaches of the Peace, and Acts of Aggression'.

Article 42 states that the Security Council 'may take such action by air, sea, or land forces as may be necessary to maintain or restore international peace and security'. The Security Council has sometimes authorized member states to use 'all necessary means', and this has been accepted as a legitimate application of Chapter VII powers.

Article 99 authorizes the Secretary-General to 'bring to the attention of the Security Council any matter which in his opinion may threaten the maintenance of international peace and security'.

The structure of the United Nations was intended to avoid some of the problems faced by the League of Nations. The UN has six main organs: the Security Council, the General Assembly, the Secretariat, the Economic and Social Council, the Trusteeship Council, and the International Court of Justice (see Fig. 19.1).

The Security Council

In contrast to the League of Nations, the United Nations recognized great power prerogatives in the Security Council. The UN Security Council was given the main responsibility for maintaining international peace and security. It was made up initially of 11 states, and then, after 1965, of 15 states. It includes five permanent members, namely the USA, Britain, France, Russia (previously the Soviet Union), and China, as well as ten non-permanent members. Unlike those of the League, the decisions of the Security Council are binding, and must only be passed by a majority of nine out of the 15 members, as well as each of the five permanent members. These five permanent members therefore have **veto power** over all Security Council decisions. The convention emerged that abstention by a permanent member is not regarded as a veto.

The five permanent members of the Security Council were seen as the major powers when the UN was founded, and they were granted a veto on the view that if the great powers were not given a privileged position, the UN would not work. This view stems from realist theory. Indeed, this tension between the recognition of power politics through the Security Council veto, and the universal ideals underlying the United Nations, is a defining feature of the organization. There have been widespread and frequent calls for the reform of the Security Council, but this is very difficult (see Box 19.2).

When the Security Council considers a threat to international peace, it first explores ways to settle the dispute peacefully under the terms of **Chapter VI** of the UN Charter (see Box 19.1). It may suggest principles for a settlement or may suggest mediation. In the event of fighting, the Security Council tries to secure a ceasefire. It may send a **peacekeeping** mission to help the parties maintain the truce and to keep opposing forces apart (see the discussion of peacekeeping below). The Council can also take measures to enforce its decisions under **Chapter VII** of the Charter. It can, for instance, impose economic sanctions or order an arms embargo. On rare occasions, the Security Council has authorized member states to use **all necessary means**, including collective military action, to see that its decisions are carried out.

The Council also makes recommendations to the General Assembly on the appointment of a new Secretary-General and on the admission of new members to the UN.

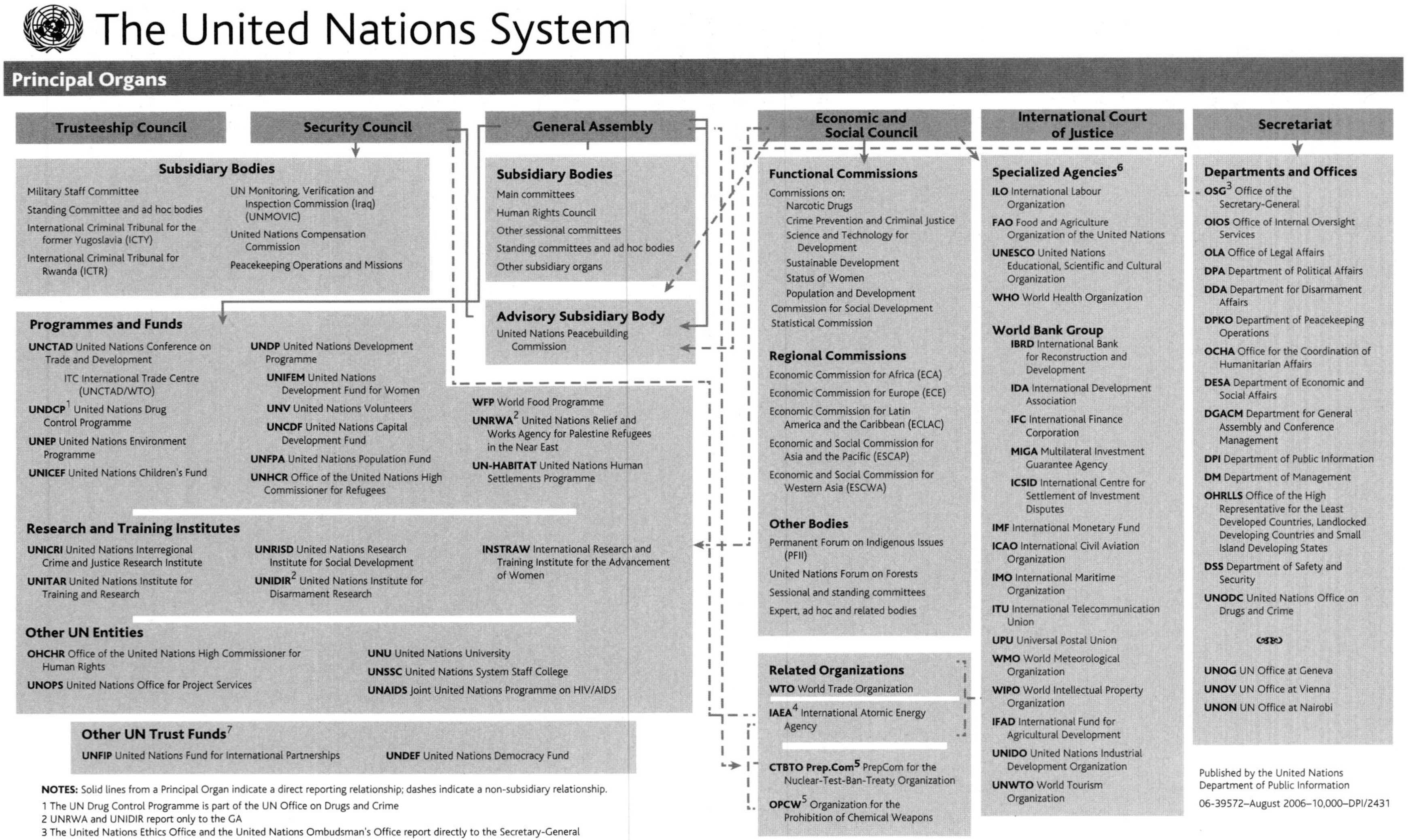

The United Nations System

Principal Organs

Trusteeship Council

Security Council

General Assembly

Economic and Social Council

International Court of Justice

Secretariat

Subsidiary Bodies

Military Staff Committee
Standing Committee and ad hoc bodies
International Criminal Tribunal for the former Yugoslavia (ICTY)
International Criminal Tribunal for Rwanda (ICTR)

UN Monitoring, Verification and Inspection Commission (Iraq) (UNMOVIC)
United Nations Compensation Commission
Peacekeeping Operations and Missions

Subsidiary Bodies

Main committees
Human Rights Council
Other sessional committees
Standing committees and ad hoc bodies
Other subsidiary organs

Advisory Subsidiary Body

United Nations Peacebuilding Commission

Functional Commissions

Commissions on:
Narcotic Drugs
Crime Prevention and Criminal Justice
Science and Technology for Development
Sustainable Development
Status of Women
Population and Development
Commission for Social Development
Statistical Commission

Regional Commissions

Economic Commission for Africa (ECA)
Economic Commission for Europe (ECE)
Economic Commission for Latin America and the Caribbean (ECLAC)
Economic and Social Commission for Asia and the Pacific (ESCAP)
Economic and Social Commission for Western Asia (ESCWA)

Other Bodies

Permanent Forum on Indigenous Issues (PFII)
United Nations Forum on Forests
Sessional and standing committees
Expert, ad hoc and related bodies

Specialized Agencies[6]

ILO International Labour Organization
FAO Food and Agriculture Organization of the United Nations
UNESCO United Nations Educational, Scientific and Cultural Organization
WHO World Health Organization

World Bank Group
IBRD International Bank for Reconstruction and Development
IDA International Development Association
IFC International Finance Corporation
MIGA Multilateral Investment Guarantee Agency
ICSID International Centre for Settlement of Investment Disputes

IMF International Monetary Fund
ICAO International Civil Aviation Organization
IMO International Maritime Organization
ITU International Telecommunication Union
UPU Universal Postal Union
WMO World Meteorological Organization
WIPO World Intellectual Property Organization
IFAD International Fund for Agricultural Development
UNIDO United Nations Industrial Development Organization
UNWTO World Tourism Organization

Departments and Offices

OSG[3] Office of the Secretary-General
OIOS Office of Internal Oversight Services
OLA Office of Legal Affairs
DPA Department of Political Affairs
DDA Department for Disarmament Affairs
DPKO Department of Peacekeeping Operations
OCHA Office for the Coordination of Humanitarian Affairs
DESA Department of Economic and Social Affairs
DGACM Department for General Assembly and Conference Management
DPI Department of Public Information
DM Department of Management
OHRLLS Office of the High Representative for the Least Developed Countries, Landlocked Developing Countries and Small Island Developing States
DSS Department of Safety and Security
UNODC United Nations Office on Drugs and Crime

UNOG UN Office at Geneva
UNOV UN Office at Vienna
UNON UN Office at Nairobi

Programmes and Funds

UNCTAD United Nations Conference on Trade and Development
  ITC International Trade Centre (UNCTAD/WTO)
UNDCP[1] United Nations Drug Control Programme
UNEP United Nations Environment Programme
UNICEF United Nations Children's Fund

UNDP United Nations Development Programme
  UNIFEM United Nations Development Fund for Women
  UNV United Nations Volunteers
UNCDF United Nations Capital Development Fund
UNFPA United Nations Population Fund
UNHCR Office of the United Nations High Commissioner for Refugees

WFP World Food Programme
UNRWA[2] United Nations Relief and Works Agency for Palestine Refugees in the Near East
UN-HABITAT United Nations Human Settlements Programme

Research and Training Institutes

UNICRI United Nations Interregional Crime and Justice Research Institute
UNITAR United Nations Institute for Training and Research

UNRISD United Nations Research Institute for Social Development
UNIDIR[2] United Nations Institute for Disarmament Research

INSTRAW International Research and Training Institute for the Advancement of Women

Other UN Entities

OHCHR Office of the United Nations High Commissioner for Human Rights
UNOPS United Nations Office for Project Services

UNU United Nations University
UNSSC United Nations System Staff College
UNAIDS Joint United Nations Programme on HIV/AIDS

Other UN Trust Funds[7]

UNFIP United Nations Fund for International Partnerships
UNDEF United Nations Democracy Fund

Related Organizations

WTO World Trade Organization
IAEA[4] International Atomic Energy Agency
CTBTO Prep.Com[5] PrepCom for the Nuclear-Test-Ban-Treaty Organization
OPCW[5] Organization for the Prohibition of Chemical Weapons

Published by the United Nations
Department of Public Information
06-39572—August 2006—10,000—DPI/2431

NOTES: Solid lines from a Principal Organ indicate a direct reporting relationship; dashes indicate a non-subsidiary relationship.

1 The UN Drug Control Programme is part of the UN Office on Drugs and Crime
2 UNRWA and UNIDIR report only to the GA
3 The United Nations Ethics Office and the United Nations Ombudsman's Office report directly to the Secretary-General
4 IAEA reports to the Security Council and the General Assembly (GA)
5 The CTBTO Prep.Com and OPCW report to the GA
6 Specialized Agencies are autonomous organizations working with the UN and each other through the coordinating machinery of the ECOSOC at the intergovernmental level, and through the Chief Executives Board for coordination (CEB) at the inter-secretariat level
7 UNFIP is an autonomous trust fund operating under the leadership of the United Nations Deputy Secretary-General. UNDEF's advisory board recommends funding proposals for approval by the Secretary-General.

Figure 19.1 The structure of the United Nations system

Box 19.2 The reform of the Security Council

Since the Security Council is the main executive body within the United Nations with primary responsibility for maintaining international peace and security, it is not surprising that many discussions of UN reform have focused on the Security Council.

The founders of the UN deliberately established a universal General Assembly and a restricted Security Council that required unanimity among the great powers. Granting permanent seats and the right to a veto to the great powers of the time, the USA, the Soviet Union (now Russia), France, the United Kingdom, and China, was an essential feature of the deal.

The composition and decision-making procedures of the Security Council were increasingly challenged as membership of the United Nations grew, particularly after decolonization. Yet the only significant reform of the Security Council occurred in 1965, when the Council was enlarged from 11 to 15 members and the required majority from seven to nine votes. Nonetheless, the veto power of the permanent five (P-5) members was left intact.

The Security Council does not reflect today's distribution of military or economic power, and does not reflect a geographic balance. Germany and Japan have made strong cases for permanent membership. Developing countries have demanded more representation on the Security Council, with countries such as South Africa, India, Egypt, Brazil, and Nigeria making particular claims. However, it has proved to be impossible to reach agreement on new permanent members. Should the European Union be represented instead of the United Kingdom, France, and Germany individually? How would Pakistan view India's candidacy? How would South Africa react to a Nigerian seat? What about representation by an Islamic country? These issues are not easy to resolve. Likewise, it is very unlikely that the P-5 countries will relinquish their veto.

None the less, while large-scale reform has proved impossible, there have been changes in Security Council working procedures that have made it more transparent and accountable.

The General Assembly

The recognition of power politics through veto power in the Security Council can be contrasted with the universalist principles underlying the other organs of the United Nations. All UN member states are represented in the General Assembly—a 'parliament of nations'—which meets to consider the world's most pressing problems. Each member state has one vote. A two-thirds majority in the General Assembly is required for decisions on key issues such as international peace and security, the admission of new members, and the UN budget. A simple majority is required for other matters. However, the decisions reached by the General Assembly have only the status of recommendations, rather than binding decisions. One of the few exceptions is the General Assembly's Fifth Committee, which makes decisions on the budget that are binding on members.

The General Assembly can consider any matter within the scope of the UN Charter. There were 172 items on the agenda of the sixty-fourth session of the General Assembly (2009–10), including topics such as the role of diamonds in fuelling conflict, the situation in the Middle East, international **cooperation** in the peaceful uses of outer space, peacekeeping operations, women in development, and the illicit trade in small arms and light weapons. Since General Assembly resolutions are non-binding, they cannot force action by any state, but its recommendations are important indications of world opinion and represent the moral authority of the community of nations.

The Secretariat

The Secretariat carries out the substantive and administrative work of the United Nations as directed by the General Assembly, the Security Council, and the other organs. It is led by the Secretary-General, who provides overall administrative guidance. In December 2006, Ban Ki-Moon from South Korea was sworn in as the eighth Secretary-General. The Secretariat consists of departments and offices with a total staff of 40,000 around the world (A/64/352).

On the recommendation of the other bodies, the Secretariat also carries out a number of research functions and some quasi-management functions. Yet the role of the Secretariat remains primarily bureaucratic and it lacks the political power and the right of initiative of, for instance, the Commission of the European Union. The one exception to this is the power of the Secretary-General under Article 99 of the Charter, to bring situations that are likely to lead to a breakdown of international peace and security to the attention of the Security Council (see Box 19.1). This Article, which may appear innocuous at first, was the legal basis for the remarkable expansion of the diplomatic role of the Secretary-General, compared with its League predecessor. Due to this, the Secretary-General is empowered to become involved in a large range of areas that can be loosely interpreted as threats to peace, including economic and social problems, and humanitarian crises.

The Economic and Social Council

The Economic and Social Council (ECOSOC), under the overall authority of the General Assembly, is intended to coordinate the economic and social work of the United Nations and the UN family of organizations. It also consults with **non-governmental organizations** (NGOs), thereby maintaining a vital link between the United Nations and **civil society**. ECOSOC's subsidiary bodies include: Functional Commissions, such as the Commission on the Status of Women; Regional Commissions, such as the Economic Commission for Africa; and other bodies (see Fig. 19.1).

Along with the Secretariat and the General Assembly, ECOSOC is responsible for overseeing the activities of a large number of other institutions known as the United Nations system. This includes the Specialized Agencies and the Programmes and Funds (see Fig. 19.1). The Specialized Agencies, such as the World Health Organization (WHO) and the International Labour Organization (ILO), have their own constitutions, regularly assessed budgets, executive heads, and assemblies of state representatives. They are self-contained constitutionally, financially, and politically, and not subject to the management of the central system.

The Programmes and Funds are much closer to the central system in the sense that their management arrangements are subject to direct General Assembly supervision, can be modified by Assembly resolution, and are largely funded on a voluntary basis. Since the establishment of the United Nations in 1945, a number of new issues have come onto the international agenda, such as the rights and interests of women, climate change, resource depletion, population growth, **terrorism**, and the spread of HIV/AIDS. Frequently, those issues led to a new organization in the Programmes and Funds. Examples of Programmes and Funds include the United Nations Development Programme (UNDP), and the United Nations Children's Fund (UNICEF).

Whereas the League of Nations attributed responsibility for economic and social questions to the League Assembly, the Charter of the United Nations established ECOSOC to oversee economic and social institutions. This change was a consequence of thinking in more **functionalist** terms. Organizations were set up to deal with specific economic and social problems. However, ECOSOC was not given the necessary management powers. It can only issue recommendations and receive reports from the Specialized Agencies. In consequence, the UN's economic and social organizations have continuously searched for better ways of achieving effective management (see discussion of the reform process below).

The Trusteeship Council

When the United Nations was created, the Trusteeship Council was established to provide international supervision for 11 Trust Territories administered by seven member states and to ensure that adequate steps were taken to prepare the territories for self-government or independence. By 1994, all Trust Territories had attained self-government or independence, either as separate states or by joining neighbouring independent countries. The last to do so was the Trust Territory of the Pacific Islands, Palau, which had been previously administered by the United States. Its work completed, the Trusteeship Council now consists of the five permanent members of the Security Council. It has amended its rules of procedure to allow it to meet when necessary.

The International Court of Justice

The International Court of Justice is the main judicial organ of the UN. Consisting of 15 judges elected jointly by the General Assembly and the Security Council, the Court decides disputes between countries. Participation by states in a proceeding is voluntary, but if a state agrees to participate, it is obligated to comply with the Court's decision. The Court also provides advisory opinions to other UN organs and Specialized Agencies upon request.

Key Points

- The United Nations was established to preserve peace between states after the Second World War.

- In a number of ways, the institutions of the United Nations reflected lessons learned from its predecessor, the League of Nations.

- The institutions and mechanisms of the United Nations reflect both the demands of great power politics (i.e. Security Council veto) and universalism. They also reflect demands to address the needs and interests of people, as well as the needs and interests of states. The tensions between these various demands are a key feature of UN development.

The United Nations and the maintenance of international peace and security

The performance of the United Nations in questions of peace and security has been shaped by the global political context. Clearly, there have been changes in international society since the UN was founded in 1945 that have had an impact on the UN system. The cold war between the USA and the Soviet Union hampered the functioning of the UN Security Council, since the veto could be used whenever the major interests of the USA or Soviet Union were threatened. From 1945 to 1990, 193 substantive vetoes were invoked in the Security Council, compared to only 23 substantive vetoes from 1990 to 2010. Furthermore, while the UN Charter provided for a standing army to be set up by agreement between the Security Council and consenting states, the East–West cold war rivalry made this impossible to implement. The end result was that the UN Security Council could not function in the way in which the UN founders had expected.

Since member states could not agree upon the arrangements laid out in Chapter VII of the Charter, especially with regard to setting up a UN army, there followed a series of improvisations to address matters of peace and security. First, a procedure was established under which the Security Council agreed to a mandate for an agent to act on its behalf. This occurred in the Korean conflict in 1950, and the Gulf War in 1990, when action was undertaken principally by the USA and its allies.

Second, there have been many instances of classical peacekeeping. No reference to peacekeeping exists in the UN Charter, but classical peacekeeping mandates and mechanisms are based on Chapter VI of the UN Charter. Classical peacekeeping involves the establishment of a UN force under UN command to be placed between the parties to a dispute after a ceasefire. Such a force only uses its weapons in self-defence, is established with the consent of the host state, and does not include forces from the major powers. This mechanism was first used in 1956, when a UN force was sent to Egypt to facilitate the exodus of the British and French forces from the Suez canal area, and then to stand between Egyptian and Israeli forces. Since the Suez crisis, there have been a number of classical peacekeeping missions, for instance, monitoring the Green Line in Cyprus, and in the Golan Heights.

Third, there has been a new kind of peacekeeping, sometimes called multidimensional peacekeeping or **peace enforcement**, which emerged after the end of the cold war. These missions are more likely to use force to achieve humanitarian ends. The new peacekeeping mandates are sometimes based on Chapter VII of the UN Charter. Such forces have been used when order has collapsed within states, and therefore address civil wars as well as international conflict. A key problem has been that UN peacekeepers have found it increasingly difficult to maintain a neutral position and have been targeted by belligerents. Examples include the intervention in Somalia in the early 1990s and intervention in the former Yugoslavia in the mid-1990s. In the Democratic Republic of the Congo (DRC) in 2009, UN peacekeepers assisted the Congolese national army in a military offensive against rebels, leading to violent reprisals.

UN peacekeeping went through a rapid expansion in the early 1990s. In 1994, UN peacekeeping operations involved nearly 80,000 military personnel around the world, seven times the figure for 1990 (Pugh 2001: 115). In late 2009, the total number of peacekeeping personnel (military and police) in the UN's 19 ongoing peacekeeping missions was just over 98,000.

Increased attention to conditions within states

The new peacekeeping was the product of a greater preparedness to intervene within states. This challenged the traditional belief that diplomats should ignore the internal affairs of states in order to preserve international stability. An increasing number of people believed that the international community, working through the UN, should address individual political and civil rights, as well as the right to basic provisions like food, water, health care, and accommodation. Under this view, violations of individuals' rights were a major cause of disturbances in relations between states: a lack of internal justice risked international disorder. The UN reinforced this new perception that pursuing justice for individuals, or ensuring **human security**, was an aspect of **national interest**.

In the past, however, the United Nations had helped promote the traditional view of the primacy of international order between states over justice for individuals, so the new focus on individual rights was a significant change. What accounts for this change?

First, the international environment had changed. The cold war stand-off between the East and the West had meant that member states did not want to question the conditions of the sovereignty of states. Jean Kirkpatrick's (1979) notorious essay, which recommended tolerating abhorrent dictatorships in Latin America in order to fight communism, was a reasonable report of the situation at that time: unsavoury right-wing regimes in Latin America were tolerated because they were anti-Soviet, and interfering in the other's sphere risked escalation of conflict (Forsythe 1988: 259–60).

Second, the process of decolonization had privileged statehood over justice. The UN reflected the claims of colonies to become states, and had elevated the right to statehood above any tests of viability, such as the existence of a nation, adequate economic performance, defensibility, or a prospect for achieving justice for citizens. This unconditional right to independence was enunciated in the General Assembly Declaration on the Granting of Independence to Colonial Countries and Peoples in 1960. There emerged a convention that the claims of elites in the putative states could be a sufficient indication of popular enthusiasm, even when the elites were unrepresentative and the claims misleading.

Charles Beitz was one of the first to question this when he concluded that statehood should not be unconditional: attention had to be given to the situation of individuals after independence (Beitz 1979). Michael Walzer and Terry Nardin produced arguments leading to similar conclusions: states were conditional entities in that their right to exist should be dependent on a criterion of performance with regard to the interests of their citizens (Walzer 1977; Nardin 1983). Such writings helped alter the moral content of **diplomacy**.

The new relationship between order and justice was, therefore, a product of particular circumstances. After the cold war, it was felt that threats to international peace and security did not only emanate from aggression between states. Rather, global peace was threatened by civil conflict (including refugee flows and regional instability), humanitarian emergencies, violations of global standards of human rights, and problems such as poverty and inequality. In 1992, then Secretary-General Boutros Boutros-Ghali outlined a new ambitious UN agenda for peace and security in a report called *An Agenda for Peace* (see Box 19.3).

More recently, other types of non-state-based threats, such as terrorism and the proliferation of small arms and weapons of mass destruction, have an increasingly

---

Box 19.3 An agenda for peace

In the early 1990s after the end of the cold war, the UN agenda for peace and security expanded quickly. Then Secretary-General Boutros Boutros-Ghali outlined the more ambitious role for the UN in his seminal report, *An Agenda for Peace* (1992). The report described interconnected roles for the UN to maintain peace and security in the post-cold war context. These included:

- **Preventive diplomacy:** involving confidence-building measures, fact-finding, and preventive deployment of UN authorized forces.
- **Peacemaking:** designed to bring hostile parties to agreement, essentially through peaceful means. However, when all peaceful means have failed, **peace enforcement** authorized under Chapter VII of the Charter may be necessary. Peace enforcement may occur without the consent of the parties.
- **Peacekeeping:** the deployment of a UN presence in the field with the consent of all parties (this refers to classical peacekeeping).
- **Post-conflict peacebuilding:** to develop the social, political, and economic infrastructure to prevent further violence and to consolidate peace.

---

prominent place on the UN security agenda. Partly due to the terrorist attacks in the USA in 2001 as well as the impasse reached in the UN Security Council over Iraq in 2003, then Secretary-General Kofi Annan named a high-level panel to examine the major threats and challenges to global peace. The 2004 final report emphasized the interconnected nature of security threats, and presented development, security, and human rights as mutually reinforcing. Many of the report's recommendations were not implemented, but some were, notably the establishment of a new UN Peacebuilding Commission (see Box 19.4).

Key Points

- The cold war and the decolonization process had discouraged more active involvement by the United Nations within states.
- After the cold war, it became more difficult for states and diplomats to accept that what happened within states was of no concern to outsiders.
- By the mid-1990s the UN had become involved in maintaining international peace and security by resisting aggression between states, by attempting to resolve disputes within states (civil wars), and by focusing on conditions within states, including economic, social, and political conditions.

Box 19.4 The UN Peacebuilding Commission

The UN Peacebuilding Commission was established in December 2005 as an intergovernmental advisory subsidiary body of the General Assembly and the Security Council. It was first proposed by the Secretary-General's High Level Panel on Threats, Challenges and Change in December 2004, and again in the Secretary-General's Report *In Larger Freedom* in March 2005 (UN 2005). Existing mechanisms at the UN were thought to be insufficient in responding to the particular needs of countries emerging from conflict. Many countries, such as Liberia, Haiti, and Somalia in the 1990s, had signed peace agreements and hosted UN peacekeeping missions, but reverted to violent conflict. The Peacebuilding Commission provides targeted support to countries in the volatile post-conflict phase to help prevent the recurrence of conflict. It proposes integrated strategies and priorities for post-conflict recovery, in order to improve coordination among the myriad of actors involved in post-conflict activities. The establishment of the Peacebuilding Commission is indicative of a growing trend at the UN to coordinate security and development programming.

The organizational committee of the Peacebuilding Commission is made up of 31 member states, and the first session was held in June 2006. There are also country-specific meetings to look at the post-conflict strategies, priorities, and programming for specific countries. The first four countries on the agenda of the Peacebuilding Commission are Burundi, Sierra Leone, Guinea-Bissau, and Central African Republic. The Peacebuilding Support Fund, with a target of $250 million, is designed to provide support during the early stages of a peacebuilding process. It supports countries that are on the Peacebuilding Commission's agenda as well as countries in similar circumstances designated by the Secretary-General.

The United Nations and intervention within states

As issues of peace and security were increasingly understood to include **human security** and justice, the UN was expected to take on a stronger role in maintaining standards for individuals within states. A difficulty with carrying out the new tasks was that it seemed to run against the doctrine of non-intervention. Intervention was traditionally defined as a deliberate incursion into a state without its consent by some outside agency, in order to change the functioning, policies, and goals of its government and achieve effects that favour the intervening agency (Vincent 1974) (see Ch. 31).

At the founding of the UN, sovereignty was regarded as central to the system of states. States were equal members of international society, and were equal with regard to international law. Sovereignty also implied that states recognized no higher authority than themselves, and that there was no superior jurisdiction. The governments of states had exclusive jurisdiction within their own frontiers, a principle enshrined in Article 2(7) of the United Nations Charter.

In earlier periods, however, states had intervened in each other's business and thought that they had a right to do so. The USA refused to accept any curtailment of their right to intervene in the internal affairs of other states in their hemisphere until 1933, when they conceded the point at the seventh International Conference of American States. The US position was very similar to the **Brezhnev doctrine** of the 1970s, which held that the Soviet Union had the right to intervene in the member states of the socialist commonwealth to protect the principles of socialism.

Much earlier, the British had insisted on the abolition of slavery in their relations with other states. They stopped ships on the high seas, and imposed the abolition of slavery as a condition in treaties (Bethell 1970). There were also occasions when states tried to bind other states to respect certain principles in their internal affairs. A number of states in Eastern Europe, such as Hungary and Bulgaria, were bound to respect the rights of minorities within their frontiers based on agreements made at the Berlin Conference of 1878 by the great powers. In practice, then, intervention was a common feature of international politics, sometimes for good cause.

By the 1990s, some people believed that there should be a return to this earlier period where intervention was justified, but it was felt that a wider range of instruments should be used to protect generally accepted standards. They insisted on a key role for the United Nations in granting a licence to intervene. It was pointed out that the UN Charter did not assert merely the rights of states, but also the rights of peoples: statehood could be interpreted as conditional upon respect for such rights. There was ample evidence in the UN Charter to justify the view that extreme transgressions of human rights could be a justification for intervention by the international community.

The major pronouncements of the UN General Assembly referred to the primary responsibility of states for dealing with complex crises within their frontiers. A 1991

General Assembly resolution implied some relaxation of this principle when it held that 'The sovereignty, territorial integrity and national unity of States must be fully respected in accordance with the Charter of the United Nations. In this context, humanitarian assistance should be provided with the consent of the affected country and in principle on the basis of an appeal by the affected country' (A/RES/46/182). The use of the phrase 'in principle', and the term 'should', implied that there could be occasions where intervention was necessary even when consent in the target state was not possible. In the Outcome Document of the 2005 World Summit, the General Assembly said that if national authorities are 'manifestly failing to protect their populations from genocide, war crimes, ethnic cleansing and crimes against humanity', and if peaceful means are inadequate, the international community could take collective action through the UN Security Council according to Chapter VII of the Charter (A/RES/60/1, paras 138 and 139). This document echoes recommendations from the *Responsibility to Protect*, the 2001 final report of the International Commission on Intervention and State Sovereignty (see Ch. 31).

Yet the number of occasions on which a UN resolution justified intervention due to gross infringements of the rights of individuals has remained limited. Kosovo was arguably the first occasion on which international forces were used in defiance of a sovereign state in order to protect humanitarian standards. NATO launched the air campaign in March 1999 in Kosovo against the Republic of Yugoslavia without a mandate from the Security Council, since Russia had declared that it would veto such action. None the less, NATO states noted that by intervening to stop ethnic cleansing and crimes against humanity in Kosovo they were acting in accordance with the principles of the UN Charter.

The Iraq War in 2003 was questionably another case, although the legality of intervention under existing Security Council resolutions is contested, especially in view of the failure to obtain a second UN Security Council resolution to give an explicit mandate for the action (see Case Study). The US action against Afghanistan in 2001 is an exceptional case in which the UN Security Council acknowledged the right of a state which had been attacked—referring to the events of 11 September 2001 in the USA—to respond in its own defence.

Arguably, earlier instances of intervention did not explicitly breach sovereignty. The 1991 Security Council resolution sanctioning intervention in Iraq (S/Res/688) at

---

Case Study The 2003 intervention in Iraq

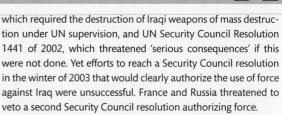

In March 2003, a US-led coalition launched a highly controversial war in Iraq, which removed Saddam Hussein from power. The justification for war stressed Iraq's possession of weapons of mass destruction, in defiance of earlier UN resolutions. Unlike in Kosovo, the gross violation of human rights was not given as a main justification for the invasion until later. Yet the failure to find weapons of mass destruction in Iraq, as well as the subsequent civil war, have fuelled the claims of critics that the war was unjustified.

There was no agreement over whether the UN Security Council authorized military action in Iraq. American and British diplomats pointed to UN Security Council Resolution 687 of 1991, which required the destruction of Iraqi weapons of mass destruction under UN supervision, and UN Security Council Resolution 1441 of 2002, which threatened 'serious consequences' if this were not done. Yet efforts to reach a Security Council resolution in the winter of 2003 that would clearly authorize the use of force against Iraq were unsuccessful. France and Russia threatened to veto a second Security Council resolution authorizing force.

The credibility of the UN was damaged by the failure to agree on a second Security Council resolution, and by the decision of the US and British administrations, along with a small number of allies, to use force against Iraq without clear UN authorization. There are fears of an increased tendency for the USA to act without UN authorization. The Bush administration's National Security Strategy of September 2002 stated that '[W]e will be prepared to act apart when our interests and unique responsibilities require' (NSS 2002: 31).

Nonetheless, the aftermath of the invasion and the continued difficulties in establishing security in Iraq highlight the need for international cooperation. The UN enhances the legitimacy of military action, and can also help share in global risks, burdens, and strategies for rebuilding.

Discussion Questions

1 Has the UN as an institution recovered from the war in Iraq?

2 What lessons about the future of the UN might be drawn from the experience of the war in Iraq?

the end of the Gulf War did not breach Iraqi sovereignty in so far as its implementation depended on Saddam Hussein's consent. The 1992 Security Council resolution (S/Res/733) that first sanctioned UN involvement in Somalia was based on a request by Somalia. A later resolution for Somalia (S/Res/794) authorizing the USA to intervene did not mention the consent of Somali authorities, but by that time a central Somali government did not exist.

The difficulty in relaxing the principle of non-intervention should not be underestimated. For instance, the UN was reluctant to send peacekeepers to Darfur without the consent of the Sudanese government. After intensive international diplomacy and negotiations about the nature of the force, Sudan consented and the force was formally established in July 2007 (S/Res/1769).

Some fear a slippery slope whereby a relaxation of the non-intervention principle by the UN will lead to military action by individual states without UN approval. It could be argued that the action against Iraq in 2003 illustrates the danger (see Case Study).

In summary, an increasing readiness by the UN to intervene within states in order to promote internal justice for individuals would indicate a movement towards **global governance** and away from unconditional sovereignty. There have been some signs of movement in this direction, but principles of state sovereignty and non-intervention remain important. There is still some support for the view that Article 2(7) of the UN Charter should be interpreted strictly: there can be no intervention within a state without the express consent of the government of that state. Others believe that intervention within a country to promote human rights is justifiable only on the basis of a threat to international peace and security, such as the appearance of significant numbers of refugees, or the judgement that other states might intervene militarily. Some liberals argue that this condition is flexible enough to justify intervention to defend human rights whenever possible.

Overall, the UN's record on the maintenance of international peace and security has been mixed. On the one hand, there has been a stronger assertion of the responsibility of international society, represented by the United Nations, for gross offences against populations. None the less, the practice has been patchy. Intimations of a new world order in the aftermath of the Gulf War in 1991 quickly gave way to despondency with what were seen as failures in Somalia, Rwanda, other parts of Africa, and the former Yugoslavia, and increasing disagreement about the proper role of the UN in Kosovo and Iraq. Compared to the enthusiasm about the potential for the UN in the early 1990s, the debates and disagreements at the time of the war in Iraq in 2003 were striking. Debates about which institutions and actors are most effective in conducting peace operations have been reinvigorated, and a variety of non-UN actors, including regional organizations and ad hoc coalitions, have been involved in some recent military operations.

Box 19.5 Selected documents related to the changing role of the United Nations system

Development of the economic and social organizations
A/32/197, Dec. 1977. The first major General Assembly resolution on reform of the economic and social organizations.
A/48/162, Dec. 1993. A major step towards reform of the economic and social organization of the United Nations, especially ECOSOC.

Development of the UN's role in maintaining international peace and security
SC Res. 678, Nov. 1990, sanctioned the use of force against Saddam Hussein.
SC Res. 816, Apr. 1993, enforced the no-fly zone over Bosnia in that it permitted NATO war planes to intercept Bosnian Serb planes in the zones.
SC Res. 1160, 1199, and 1203 contained arguments relevant to the action on Kosovo. SC Res. 1244 contained the agreement at the end of the bombing.

Development of humanitarian action through the UN
SC Res. 688, Apr. 1991, sanctioned intervention at the end of the Gulf War to protect the Kurds in northern Iraq.
SC Res. 733, Jan. 1992, sanctioned UN involvement in Somalia. **A/46/182, Apr. 1992,** is the major document on the development of the machinery for humanitarian assistance.
SC Res. 794, Dec. 1992, sanctioned American intervention in Somalia under Chapter VII of the UN Charter. The government of Somalia had ceased to exist in the eyes of the member states of the Security Council.
SC Res. 1441, Nov. 2002, resolution on Iraq, which threatened serious consequences if Saddam Hussein failed to reveal his weapons of mass destruction to the team of UN inspectors.
SC Res. 1769, July 2007, established an African Union/UN Hybrid operation in Darfur, Sudan.

Key Points

- New justifications for intervention in states were being considered by the 1990s.
- Most operations of the United Nations were justified in the traditional way: as a response to a threat to international peace and security.
- The United Nations does not have a monopoly on peace operations. While the UN often provides legitimation, operations are sometimes conducted by regional organizations, ad hoc coalitions, or hybrid arrangements involving the UN with non-UN actors.

The United Nations and economic and social questions

As described above, there has been an increased tendency to view threats to peace and security in terms of traditional threats such as aggression between states, but also civil conflict within states, threats emanating from non-state actors, and threats relating to economic and social conditions within states. Holders of this view believe that conditions within states, including human rights, justice, development, and equality, have a bearing on global peace. The more integrated global context has meant that economic and social problems in one part of the world may affect other areas. In addition, promoting social and economic development is an important UN goal in itself. The preamble to the UN Charter talks of promoting 'social progress and better standards of life in larger freedom', and the need to 'employ international machinery for the promotion of the economic and social advancement of all peoples'.

The number of institutions within the UN system that address economic and social issues has significantly increased since the founding of the UN. None the less, the main contributor states have been giving less and less to economic and social institutions. By the mid-1990s, there was a crippling financial crisis in the regular Assessed Budget for the UN, and in the budget for peacekeeping operations. This was only mitigated when the USA agreed, under certain conditions, to repay what it owed the UN and when it returned to full funding in December 2002.

Paradoxically, despite the shortage of funds, the UN has acquired skills and resources with regard to key economic and social problems. During the 1990s, a number of new issues were brought on to the international agenda. Several global conferences were convened to discuss pressing problems, such as environmental issues at a conference in Rio de Janeiro (1992), human rights at a conference in Vienna (1993), population questions at a conference in Cairo (1994), and women's issues at a conference in Beijing (1995). These conferences each spawned a commission to carry forward the programme. Such conferences represented a growing sense of interdependence and the globalization of human concerns. They also stimulated a renewed interest in translating broad socio-economic concerns into more specific manageable programmes (see Box 19.6). Follow-up conferences were held ten years later to take stock of progress.

In 2000, the UN convened a Millennium Summit, where heads of state committed themselves to a series of measurable goals and targets, known as the Millennium Development Goals (MDGs). These goals, to be achieved by 2015, include reducing by half the number of people living on less than a dollar a day, achieving universal primary education, and reversing the spread of HIV/AIDS and malaria (A/55/L.2). Since 2000, the UN has been integrating the MDGs into all aspects of its work at the country level, but progress on reaching the MDGs has been very uneven.

Box 19.6 The United Nations Climate Change Conference in Copenhagen: COP15

The United Nations Climate Change Conference in Copenhagen was the most recent UN Global Conference focusing on environmental issues. The first UN Conference on the Human Environment took place in Stockholm in 1972, stimulated the creation of national environment ministries around the world, and established the United Nations Environment Programme (UNEP).

Twenty years later, the UN Conference on Environment and Development, the Earth Summit, was held in Rio de Janeiro. The United Nations Framework Convention on Climate Change (UNFCCC) was one of three conventions signed by many governments at the 1992 Earth Summit. The Kyoto Protocol of 1997 was an addition to the UNFCCC, which set binding targets for reducing greenhouse gas emissions.

There was a series of intergovernmental meetings at the highest level to discuss progress on the limitation of greenhouse gases and to agree a successor agreement to the Kyoto Protocol. The climax of the series was the meeting in December 2009 at Copenhagen of the representatives of 192 countries to agree a new set of binding agreements on the limitation of greenhouse gases. This meeting was referred to as COP15, since it was the fifteenth meeting of the Committee of the Parties to the Kyoto Protocol. The diplomacy leading up to it was highly complicated, but high hopes were attached to its outcome. The participating states could not, however, agree to a legally binding set of targets for the reduction of gas emissions, and it was still unclear what would happen when the Kyoto Protocol expired in 2012.

Several aspects of the COP15 are interesting. It marked a new level of multilateral cooperation among African states, which opposed legally binding limits in the absence of sufficient financial transfers from the developed world. The conference was thus consistent with a long tradition of UN conferences in agreeing on principles, but rejecting legally binding agreements, as with the World Population Conference of 1974. The Conference made clear that environmental issues remained prominent on the UN agenda, and demonstrated the importance of the United Nations as a framework for moving towards global agreement. Yet it stopped short of the detail, of legal commitment, and of specific arrangements for monitoring its application. The Chinese, in particular, strongly opposed any attempt to introduce international monitors of compliance within China.

Key Points

- The number of institutions within the UN system that address economic and social issues has significantly increased. Several Programmes and Funds were created in response to global conferences.

- Despite a shortage of funds and coordination problems, the UN has done important work in key economic and social areas.

- The Millennium Development Goals have focused attention on measurable socio-economic targets and have further integrated the work of the UN at the country level, but progress towards reaching the goals has been uneven.

The reform process in the economic and social arrangements of the United Nations

In the mid-to-late 1990s, alongside growing UN involvement in development issues, the UN economic and social arrangements underwent reform at two levels: first, reforms concerned with operations at the country (field) level; and second, reforms at the general or headquarters level.

framework has also helped country field staff achieve a more coherent approach to development. This can be contrasted to earlier arrangements whereby the various agencies would work separately on distinct projects, often in ignorance of each other's presence in the same country.

Country level

The continuing complaints of NGOs about poor UN performance in the field served as a powerful stimulus for reform. A key feature of the reforms at the country (field) level was the adoption of Country Strategy Notes. These were statements about the overall development process tailored to the specific needs of individual countries. They were written on the basis of discussions between the Specialized Agencies, Programmes and Funds, donors, and the host country, and described the plans of the various institutions and donors in a particular country. The merit of the Country Strategy Notes is that they clearly set out targets, roles, and priorities.

Another reform at the country level was the strengthening of the Resident Coordinator, usually an employee of the United Nations Development Programme (UNDP). He or she became the responsible officer at the country level, and was provided with more training to fulfil this role. Field-level officers were also given enhanced authority, so that they could make decisions about the redeployment of funds within a programme without referring to headquarters. There was also an effort to introduce improved communication facilities and information-sharing. The activities of the various UN organizations were brought together in single locations or 'UN houses', which facilitated inter-agency communication and collegiality. The new country-level approach was called an Integrated Programmes approach. The adoption of the Millennium Development Goals

Headquarters level

If the UN role in economic and social affairs at the country level was to be effective, reform was also required at the headquarters level. The United Nations family of economic and social organizations has always been a polycentric system. Historically, there was no organization or agent within the system capable of managing the wide range of economic and social activities under the UN umbrella. Reform efforts in the 1990s focused on the reorganization and rationalization of the Economic and Social Council (ECOSOC).

In the UN Charter, the powers given to the General Assembly and ECOSOC were modest. ECOSOC could only issue recommendations and receive reports. By contrast, UN reform in the mid-to-late 1990s allowed ECOSOC to become more assertive and to take a leading role in the coordination of the UN system. ECOSOC was to ensure that General Assembly policies were appropriately implemented on a system-wide basis. ECOSOC was given the power to take final decisions on the activities of its subsidiary bodies and on other matters relating to system-wide coordination in economic, social, and related fields (A/50/227, para. 37).

One of ECOSOC's responsibilities was to review common themes in the work of the nine Functional Commissions, such as the Commission on Narcotic Drugs, the Commission on Sustainable Development, and the Commission on the Status of Women (see Fig. 19.1). The reform effort aimed to eliminate duplication and overlap in the work of the Functional Commissions. ECOSOC would integrate the work of its Functional Commissions and provide input to the General Assembly, which was responsible for establishing the broader economic and social policy framework.

Overall, economic and social reorganization meant that the two poles of the system were better coordinated: the pole where intentions are defined through global conferences and agendas, and the pole where programmes are implemented. Programmes at the field level were better integrated and field officers were given enhanced discretion. The reform of ECOSOC sharpened its capacity to shape broad agreements into cross-sectoral programmes with well-defined objectives. At the same time, ECOSOC acquired greater capacity to act as a conduit through which the results of field-level monitoring could be conveyed upwards to the Functional Commissions. These new processes had the effect of strengthening the **norms** of a multilateral system.

Key Points

- In the mid-to-late 1990s, under the leadership of then Secretary-General Kofi Annan, the UN embarked on an overarching reform effort.
- Reform of the economic and social arrangements of the UN aimed at improving coordination, eliminating duplication, and clarifying spheres of responsibility.
- These efforts strengthened the norms of the multilateral system.

Conclusion

Changes in the role of the UN reflect the changes in perceptions of international society and the nature of sovereign states. Over the past sixty years, the rules governing the **international system** have become increasingly numerous and specific, covering a large range of the activities of relations between states. Concerns have expanded to include not only the protection of the rights of states, but also the rights of individuals. Yet obtaining the agreement of governments to principles of individual rights is only a first step in building a more orderly and just world. It is also necessary to have consistent and reliable instruments to trigger action when standards are breached.

The United Nations Security Council is the instrument that comes closest to meeting these aims. Despite the flaws of the Security Council, it is striking that even the largest states prefer to get authorization from the Security Council for any action they propose. In Kosovo, the states that participated in the NATO intervention wanted to demonstrate that they were acting according to the UN Charter and the relevant Security Council resolutions. In Iraq, the US and UK governments invested considerable diplomatic energy in getting a second Security Council resolution in support of military action. The effort failed, but nevertheless it was attempted.

Participation in the United Nations gives governments status in the international system. Membership and success in the UN has come to be regarded as legitimizing **state autonomy.** Hence holding office, taking the initiative, providing personnel, and policing norms are seen to have value because they add to the self-esteem as well as to the power of the state. The UN has become the essential club for states.

The capacity of the UN in its economic and social work, its development work, and its management of peacekeeping and post-conflict peacebuilding has expanded since the 1990s. None the less, the predominance of US military power, the possibility that the USA will act again without clear UN authorization, the heightened concern over terrorism and weapons of mass destruction, the inability to respond effectively to crises in the eastern Democratic Republic of the Congo, Somalia, and Darfur, and the pervasiveness of inequality and injustice across the world, signal that further changes and adaptations within the UN system will be necessary.

Questions

1. How does the United Nations try to maintain international order?
2. Why have more states decided to support the work of the United Nations?
3. What are some of the barriers to UN Security Council reform?
4. Does increased UN activity undermine the sovereignty of states?

5 How far have traditional restraints been relaxed with regard to intervention within states?

6 How have definitions of threats to peace and security changed in the post-cold war period?

7 How has UN peacekeeping evolved?

8 Has reform of the economic and social arrangements of the UN been effective?

9 Why was there greater opposition to developing the international accountability of states during the cold war?

10 Has the UN outlived its usefulness?

Further Reading

Adebajo, A. (ed.) (2009), *From Global Apartheid to Global Village: Africa and the United Nations* (Scottsville: University of Kwazulu-Natal Press). A collection of views from African scholars and practitioners on the influence of the UN in Africa.

Archer, C. (2001), *International Organisations*, 3rd edn (London: Routledge). A succinct survey of the range of international institutions and their main purposes.

Berdal, M., and Economides, S. (eds) (2007), *United Nations Interventionism, 1991–2004* (Cambridge: Cambridge University Press). Includes case studies of eight UN operations, and discusses the impact of the 'new interventionism' on international order.

Claude, I. L. Jr. (1971, 1984), *Swords into Plowshares: The Progress and Problems of International Organization*, 4th edn (New York: Random House). A classic text on the history of international institutions, particularly concerned with their role in war and peace. Useful for the history of the UN.

Dodds, F. (ed.) (1997), *The Way Forward: Beyond Agenda 21* (London: Earthscan). An account of the involvement of the UN system in the issues raised in the Functional Commissions, such as social development, the status of women, and environmental protection.

Karns, M., and Mingst, K. (2004), *International Organizations: The Politics and Processes of Global Governance* (Boulder, CO: Lynne Rienner). A comprehensive overview of the main actors and processes of global governance.

Malone, D. (ed.) (2004), *The UN Security Council: From the Cold War to the 21st Century* (Boulder, CO: Lynne Rienner). Discusses the history of the UN Security Council and major UN operations.

Roberts, A., and Kingsbury, B. (eds) (1993), *United Nations, Divided World: The UN's Roles in International Relations*, 2nd edn (Oxford: Clarendon Press). An important collection of readings by practitioners and academics.

Taylor, P., and Groom, A. J. R. (eds) (2000), *The United Nations at the Millennium* (London: Continuum). A detailed account of the institutions of the central UN system.

Thakur, R. (2006), *The United Nations, Peace and Security* (Cambridge: Cambridge University Press). Discusses the changing role of the UN peace operations.

Weiss, T., and Daws, S. (eds) (2007), *The Oxford Handbook on the United Nations* (Oxford: Oxford Univeristy Press). A comprehensive collection on the history of the UN and key topics and debates relating to the institution.

Online Resource Centre

 Visit the Online Resource Centre that accompanies this book to access more learning resources on this chapter topic at www.oxfordtextbooks.co.uk/orc/baylis5e/

Chapter 20

Transnational actors and international organizations in global politics

PETER WILLETTS

Reader's Guide

The subject of International Relations originally covered simply the relations between states. Economic bodies and social groups, such as banks, industrial companies, students, environmentalists, and women's organizations, were given secondary status as non-state actors. This two-tier approach has been challenged, particularly by the effects of globalization. First, ambiguities in the meaning given to 'a state', and its mismatch with the contemporary world, result in it not being a useful concept. Greater clarity is obtained by analysing intergovernmental and inter-society relations, with no presumption that one sector is more important than the other. Second, we can recognize governments are losing sovereignty when faced with the economic activities of transnational companies and the violent threat from criminals, terrorists, and guerrillas. Third, non-governmental organizations (NGOs) engage in such a web of global relations, including participation in diplomacy, that governments have lost their political independence. We conclude that events in any area of global policy-making have to be understood in terms of complex systems, containing governments, companies, and NGOs interacting in a variety of international organizations.

Introduction

In **diplomacy**, **international law**, journalism, and academic analysis, it is widely assumed that international relations consist of the relations between coherent units called **states**. This chapter will argue that better understanding of political change is obtained by analysing the relations between governments and many other actors from each country. **Global politics** also includes companies and **non-governmental organizations** (NGOs). Thus the five main categories of political actors in the global system are:

- nearly 200 governments, including 192 members of the UN;
- 82,100 **transnational companies** (TNCs), such as ExxonMobil, Shell, Wal-Mart, Mitsubishi, Volkswagen, General Electric, Hewlett-Packard, ArcelorMittal, Vodaphone, Microsoft, or Nestlé, with these parent companies having 807,400 foreign affiliates;
- around 9,500 single-country non-governmental organizations, such as Population Concern (UK) or the Sierra Club (USA), which engage in significant international activities;
- 240 **intergovernmental organizations** (IGOs), such as the UN, NATO, the European Union, or the International Coffee Organization, plus some 2,500 regular autonomous conferences and treaty review bodies; and
- 7,600 international non-governmental organizations (INGOs), such as Amnesty International, the Baptist World Alliance, or the International Chamber of Shipping, plus a similar number of less well-established international caucuses and **networks** of NGOs.

All these actors play a regular part in global politics and each government interacts with a range of **non-state actors**. Sometimes guerrilla groups challenge the authority of particular governments. In addition, even though they are considered not to be legitimate participants in the system, terrorists and other criminal gangs have an impact, often minor, but sometimes in a major way. Very many more companies and NGOs operate only in a single country, but have the potential to expand into other countries. (For data on TNCs, see UNCTAD 2009: 228–30; and for data on IGOs and NGOs, see UIA 2008: Vol. 5, Figure 0.1.)

Nobody can deny the proliferation of these organizations and the range of their activities. The controversial questions are whether the non-state world has significance in its own right and whether it makes any difference to the analysis of inter-state relations. It is possible to *define* international relations as covering the relations between states. This is known as the state-centric approach, or **realism**. Then it is only a tautology (true by definition) to say that non-state actors are of secondary importance. A more open-ended approach, known as **pluralism**, is based on the assumption that all types of actor can affect political outcomes. The very phrase 'non-state' actors implies that states are dominant and other actors are secondary. An alternative phrase, **transnational actors**, has been coined by academics in order to assert forcefully that international relations are not limited to governments, and other actors operate across country boundaries. This chapter will first consider how assumptions made about 'states' inhibit analysis of transnational actors and **international organizations**. Then the nature of the different types of actor will be outlined. Finally, the case will be argued for always considering the activities of a range of political actors.

Problems with the state-centric approach

The great advantage of the state-centric approach is that the bewildering complexity of world politics is reduced to the relative simplicity of the interactions of fewer than 200 supposedly similar units. However, there are four major problems that suggest that the benefits of simplification have been gained at the cost of the picture becoming distorted and blurred.

Confusion over three meanings of 'state'

Writers who refer to the state often fail to use the term consistently and lack intellectual rigour by merging three concepts. The **state** as a legal person is a highly abstract fiction. This is easily confused with the concrete concept of a **country**, with a distinct political system of people with common values. Then there is a very dissimilar concept of a state as the apparatus of **government**. Unfortunately, no standard method exists to handle the ambiguity. From now on, this chapter will use the word 'state' to indicate the abstract legal concept, while country and government will be used to analyse political behaviour.

Within traditional International Relations scholarship, **civil society** is understood to be *part of the state*, whereas for philosophers and sociologists, focusing on the state as government, civil society is *separate from the state*. Thus, in international law or when the state means the whole country, there is very little room to acknowledge the existence of distinct transnational actors. Alternatively, when the 'state' means the 'government' and does not encompass civil society, we can investigate both intergovernmental relations and the inter-society relations of transnational actors.

The lack of similarity between countries

The second problem is that giving all 'states' the same legal status implies that they are all essentially the same type of unit, when in fact they are not remotely similar. Orthodox analysis acknowledges differences in size between the '**superpowers**' and middle and small 'powers'. Nevertheless, this does not suggest that, in 2008, despite the relative decline of the USA, its economy was bigger than the economies of Japan, China, Brazil, Russia, and India combined, nor that it was 30 times Saudi Arabia's, 536 times Ethiopia's and over 73,000 times greater than Kiribati's. In terms of population, the divergences are even greater. China's population in 2008 was larger than the 159 smallest UN members combined. The European 'city states' and small island countries of the Caribbean and the Pacific, in the UN, with populations measured in tens of thousands, are not comparable entities to ordinary small countries (economic and population data from World Bank 2009: 378–89). Alternatively, comparing the governments of the world reveals a range of democracies, feudal regimes, ethnic oligarchies, economic oligarchies, populist regimes, theocracies, military dictatorships, and idiosyncratic combinations. The only thing that the countries have in common is the general recognition of their right to have their own government. They are legally equal and politically very different.

The consequence of admitting the differences in size is to make it obvious that the largest transnational actors are considerably larger than many of the countries.

In 2008, the 50 largest transnational industrial companies, by global sales, each had annual revenues greater than the GNP of 125 members of the United Nations (UNCTAD 2009: Table A.I.10; and World Bank 2009: 378–89). Using people as the measure, many NGOs, particularly trade unions, churches, and campaigning groups in the fields of human rights, women's rights, and the environment, have their membership measured in millions, whereas 41 of the 192 countries in the UN had populations of less than one million, of which 13 were less than 100,000 (World Bank *ibid.*). There is also great variation in the complexity and diversity of the economies and the societies of different countries, and hence the extent to which they are each involved in transnational relations.

State systems and international systems

Third, there is an underlying analytical inconsistency in supposing that 'states' are located in an **anarchic international system**. Whether it means a legal entity, a country, or a government, the 'state' is seen as a coherent unit, acting with common purpose and existing as something more than the sum of its parts (the individual people). At the same time, most advocates of the state-centric approach deny the possibility of such collective entities existing at the global level. The phrase 'international system' is denied its full technical meaning of a collectivity in which the component elements (the individual 'states') lose some of their independence. No philosophical argument has been put forward to explain this inconsistency in the assumptions made about the different levels of analysis. By exaggerating the coherence of 'states' and downplaying the coherence of global politics, both transnational relations and intergovernmental relations are underestimated.

The difference between state and nation

Fourth, there is a behavioural assumption that politics within 'states' is significantly different from politics between 'states'. This is based on the idea that people's loyalty to their **nation** is more intense than other loyalties. Clearly, it cannot be denied that **nationalism** and national **identity** invoke powerful emotions for most people, but various caveats must be made about their political relevance. Communal identities form a hierarchy from the local through the nation to wider groupings. Thus, both local communities and intergovernmental bodies, such as the European Community, can also make claims on a person's loyalty.

There has been a long-standing linguistic conjuring trick whereby national loyalty is made to appear as if it is focused on the **nation-state**. Both inter*national* relations and trans*national* relations cover relations across 'state' boundaries, although logically the words refer to relations between national groups, such as the Scots and the Welsh. In the real world, only a few countries, such as Iceland, Poland, and Japan, can make a reasonable claim that their people are from a single nation, and in all such cases there are significant numbers of the national group resident in other countries, often in the USA. Most countries are multinational and many national groups are present in several countries. Thus national loyalty is actually quite different from loyalty to a country.

Key Points

- The concept of the 'state' has three very different meanings: a legal person, a political community, and a government.

- The countries and governments around the world may be equal in law, but have few political similarities. Many governments control fewer resources than many transnational actors.

- It cannot be assumed that all country-based political systems are more coherent than global systems, particularly as national loyalties do not match country boundaries.

- By abandoning the language of 'states' and 'non-state' actors, we can admit the possibility of theorizing about many types of actor in global politics. By distinguishing government from society and nation from country, we can ask whether private groups, companies, and national minorities in each country engage in transnational relations.

Transnational companies as political actors

All companies that import or export are engaging in transnational economic activities. If they lobby foreign governments about trade, they become transnational political actors. However, they are not known as **transnational companies** (TNCs) until they have branches or subsidiaries outside their home country. In 2008, among the 100 TNCs with the highest levels of assets outside their home country, 57 were from twelve Western European countries, 19 from the USA, four with dual headquarters in Western countries, ten from Japan, three from South Korea and one each from Australia, Canada, China, Malaya, Mexico, Singapore, and Hong Kong. Only developed countries, East and South-East Asia, a few Latin American countries, India, and South Africa host large TNCs. Nevertheless, there are now transnational companies based in as many as 131 UN

Box 20.1 Transnational corporations from developing countries

The classical image of a TNC is a large company from the USA that has expanded production and sales overseas, dominating a global market and exploiting cheap labour in developing countries. In contrast to this, in the twenty-first century, TNCs from developing countries have become increasingly important.

- More than one quarter of all TNCs now have their headquarters in developing countries.

- The top 100 developing country TNCs in 2007 were from 16 countries: China, Hong Kong, Taiwan, India, Malaysia, Singapore, Korea, the Philippines, Thailand, Brazil, Mexico, Venezuela, South Africa, Kuwait, Qatar, and Turkey. These TNCs are expanding faster, both in their home country and in other countries, than the major developed country TNCs. However, the world's three biggest TNCs together had more foreign assets than all of these 100 companies.

- Most developing-country TNCs are small, but some are becoming major players in particular industries, such as cars, electronics, steel, and container shipping. The Chinese

TNC, Lenovo, now owns the IBM PC brand, while the Indian TNC, Tata, has taken over Corus, the major European steel manufacturer.

- Developing-country TNCs are more likely to invest in neighbouring countries, but they are increasingly investing in the developed world as well. They own more than 500 affiliates in the USA and a similar number in Britain.

- In the USA, opposition in Congress to developing country TNCs has been strong enough to block a Chinese takeover of the US oil company, UNOCAL, and to force Dubai Ports World to divest itself of six US ports.

Two examples illustrate this new world of successful developing country TNCs: Marcopolo, a Brazilian company, manufactures buses in several South American countries and sells them in more than 80 countries; and Hikma Pharmaceuticals, a Jordanian company, manufactures in two other Arab countries and in Portugal, having strong sales in West Asia and North Africa, along with recent expansion in Europe and the USA.

(UNCTAD, World Investment Report 2006 and 2009)

member countries—39 European, North American, and other developed countries and 92 from China and other developing and transition countries, including 30 African countries—plus seven other territories (UNCTAD 2009: Table A.I.8).

Financial flows and loss of sovereignty

The consequences of the extensive transnationalization of major companies are profound. It is no longer possible to regard each country as having its own separate economy. Two of the most fundamental attributes of **sovereignty**, control over the currency and control over foreign trade, have been diminished substantially. These two factors mean that governments have lost control of financial flows. The successive crises in the 1980s and the 1990s for the dollar, the pound, the French franc, and the yen established that the governments with the greatest financial resources are helpless against the transnational banks and other speculators. Then, from 2007 onwards, with the global credit crunch, we have seen that even the combined might of the **G20** cannot control the global financial system.

The effects of trade on finance are less obvious. When goods move physically across frontiers, it is usually seen as being trade between the relevant countries, but it may also be **intra-firm trade**. As the logic of intra-firm trade is quite different from that of inter-country trade, governments cannot have clear expectations of the effects of their financial and fiscal policies on TNCs. A company may respond to higher tax rates by changing its **transfer prices** to reduce its tax bill. Several other motives might induce a company to distort transfer prices, including evasion of controls on the cross-border movements of profits or capital.

Triangulation of trade and loss of sovereignty

Governments have great difficulty regulating international transactions. Even the US administration was unable to prevent its citizens visiting communist Cuba during the cold war. It may be possible to prevent the *direct* import or export of goods. However, there is no guaranteed method of preventing *indirect* trade from one country to another. This is known as **triangulation**. Only if a UN Security Council resolution obliges all the countries of the world to impose sanctions is there a reasonable prospect of a determined government preventing TNCs from evading sanctions. However, in such a situation sovereignty over the relevant trade then lies with the Security Council and not with the individual governments.

Regulatory arbitrage and loss of sovereignty

It is difficult for governments to regulate the commercial activities of companies within their country, because companies may choose to engage in **regulatory arbitrage**. If a company objects to one government's policy, it may threaten to limit or close down its local production and increase production in another country. The government that imposes the least demanding health, safety, welfare, or environmental standards will offer competitive advantages to less socially responsible companies. There is also a strong global trend towards the reduction of corporation taxes. It thus becomes difficult for any government to set high standards and maintain taxes. In the case of banking, the political dangers inherent in the risks of a bank collapsing through imprudent or criminal behaviour are so great that the major governments have set common capital standards, under the Basle Committee rules. Whatever control is achieved does not represent the successful exercise of sovereignty over companies: it is the partial surrender of sovereignty to an intergovernmental body.

Extraterritoriality and sovereignty

In addition, transnational companies generate clashes of sovereignty between different governments. Let us consider the example of a company that has its headquarters in the USA and a subsidiary company that it owns in the UK. Three lines of authority exist. The US government can control the main company and the UK government can control the subsidiary. Each process would be the standard exercise of a government's sovereignty over its internal affairs. In addition, both governments would accept that the TNC can, within certain limits, control its own policies on purchasing, production, and sales. Under normal circumstances these three lines of authority can be exercised simultaneously and in harmony. However, when the US government decisions cover the global operations of the TNC, there is a clash of sovereignty. Does the subsidiary obey the UK government or the orders of the US government issued via its headquarters? This problem of **extraterritoriality** is inherent in the structure of all TNCs.

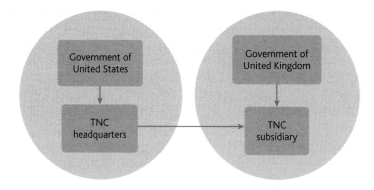

Figure 20.1 Who controls the UK subsidiary of a US TNC?

As a matter of routine policy implementation, clashes now have to be resolved between different decisions in different jurisdictions on competition policy, mergers and acquisitions, accounting procedures, and anti-corruption measures. Will US accounting standards apply to European companies, because some of their operations are in the USA? Can the directors of parent TNCs be prosecuted for the payment of bribes by their overseas branches? The long-term trend is for such questions to be resolved by global standardization of domestic policy. For example, the OECD has developed a Convention on Combating Bribery of Foreign Public Officials in International Business Transactions.

From domestic deregulation to global re-regulation

For most companies most of the time, their interests will be in accord with the government's policy of increasing employment and promoting economic growth. Conflicts will arise over the regulation of markets to avoid the risks of **market failures** or externalization of social and environmental costs of production. Domestic deregulation and **globalization** of economic activity mean that regulation is now occurring at the global level rather than within individual countries. Three factors involving TNCs push towards the globalization of politics. First, governments can reassert control only by acting collectively. Second, consumer pressures are leading to

global codes of conduct being accepted by companies and implemented in collaboration with NGOs. A third push is for global companies to submit to social and environmental auditing. These factors are coming together in the collaboration between governments, NGOs, and the UN Secretariat to recruit the major TNCs as voluntary partners in a Global Compact, to implement ten principles of corporate social responsibility on human rights, labour standards, the environment, and anti-corruption.

Key Points

- The ability of TNCs to change transfer prices means that they can evade taxation or government controls on their international financial transactions.

- The ability of TNCs to use triangulation means that individual governments cannot control their country's international trade.

- The ability of TNCs to move production from one country to another means that individual governments are constrained in regulating and taxing companies.

- The structure of authority over TNCs generates the potential for intense conflict between governments, when the legal authority of one government has extraterritorial impact on the sovereignty of another government.

- In some areas of economic policy, governments have lost sovereignty and regulation now has to be exercised at the global level rather than by governments acting independently.

Non-legitimate groups and liberation movements as political actors

A variety of groups engage in violent and/or criminal behaviour on a transnational basis. A distinction can be made between activity that is considered criminal

around the world, such as theft, fraud, personal violence, piracy, or drug trafficking, and activity that is claimed by those undertaking it to have legitimate political motives.

In reality, the distinction may sometimes be blurred, for example when criminals claim political motives or political groups are responsible for acts such as terrorism, torture, or involving children in violence. For all governments, neither criminal activity nor political violence can be legitimate within their own jurisdiction and generally not in other countries.

Transnational criminals and their political impact

Politically, the most important criminal industries are illicit trading in arms and in drugs. They have been estimated to be the two most valuable commodities in world trade. Other criminal trading of lesser value has also occurred in diamonds, computer chips, tropical hard woods, ivory, and endangered species of birds and mammals. As travel has increased, trafficking in people has become easier and has increased significantly in recent years. There is a new slave trade, mainly for sexual exploitation of young women. TNCs are most concerned to prevent trade in counterfeit goods and theft of intellectual property, particularly of music, films, and computer software.

Criminals may be seen as local gangs, dominating particular areas of large cities, but they are also organized into networks nationally and transnationally, in order to engage in illicit trade. Both the supply of drugs and the demand for weapons come primarily from 'failed states' and other areas that are not under effective control of a central government. Sometimes the remoteness of the terrain and the ease of heroin or cocaine production has led poor people in developing countries to move into the drugs trade. Sometimes it is the leaders of a political rebellion who promote drugs cultivation as a means of funding their revolt. Whatever the origins, in such situations the drug barons and war lords can establish effective control over a large area and even take on some of the functions of governments. NGOs were important in initiating global political cooperation to limit illicit diamond trading through the Kimberley Process and the ivory trade through the Convention on Trade in Endangered Species. Very little has been achieved against the drug barons, not least because the demand for drugs and the supply of arms from the developed countries have not been controlled.

The same four sovereignty problems arise with tackling criminals as with regulating TNCs. First, criminal financial flows can be massive and money-laundering threatens the integrity of banking and other financial institutions. Second, criminal trade has been so extensively diversified through triangulation that no government could confidently claim that their country is not a transit route for drugs or arms. Third, as with regulatory arbitrage by TNCs, police action in one country may displace well-organized gangs to another country, rather than stop their activities. Fourth, illicit drugs and money-laundering involve questions of extraterritorial jurisdiction. However, in contrast to the regulation of TNCs, transnational police activities involve high levels of cooperation.

Terrorists, guerrillas, and national liberation movements

The concept of a terrorist is deeply controversial. The term 'terrorist' has generally been used, as one of abuse against groups who engage in violent behaviour, by people who oppose the goals of the group. US law has defined terrorism in a more precise, abstract manner, as 'the unlawful use of force or violence against persons or property to intimidate or coerce a government, the civilian population, or any segment thereof, in furtherance of political or social objectives' (FBI 1999: i). The definition fails to resolve whether terrorism includes attacks by governments on civilians or excludes the use of force by dissidents against military targets.

Political violence has been adopted by a variety of different groups. Violence is most common when broadly based nationalist movements or ethnic minorities reject the legitimacy of a government. These groups are often called **terrorists** to express disapproval, **guerrillas** by those who are more neutral, or **national liberation movements** by their supporters. Political violence is more likely to be considered legitimate when a group appears to have widespread support; when political channels have been closed to them; when the target government is exceptionally oppressive; and when the violence is limited to 'military targets'. Groups that fail to match these four characteristics obtain only very limited transnational support.

Since **11 September 2001**, the political balance has changed substantially. The scale of the destruction wrought by Al Qaeda organizing 19 hijackers simultaneously taking control of four passenger aircraft and using these as weapons against New York and Washington did much to delegitimize *all* groups who use violence for political purposes. Historically, terrorism has mainly been an instrument of internal conflict within a single society, but Al Qaeda suddenly presented the world with a new threat of a transnational **global network**. Within a few years they staged attacks in Kenya, Tanzania, Yemen, Saudi Arabia, the USA, Tunisia, Indonesia,

Turkey, Spain, and Britain. Despite this, it is an analytical mistake to treat contemporary terrorism as a single phenomenon. The Palestinian, Kashmiri, and Chechnya disputes clearly have roots that are totally independent of each other, and started well before Al Qaeda existed. There are different transnational processes for different conflicts generating terrorism. Even Al Qaeda itself is a disparate coalition of anti-American fundamentalist groups rather than a coherent disciplined organization. In Chapter 22, there is a full discussion of the non-religious basis of other contemporary terrorist groups.

Extensive political violence used by governments against their citizens was commonplace and immune from diplomatic criticism, as recently as the 1970s. Because of a widespread desire to end the impunity of individual government leaders, soldiers, and officials responsible for the horrors of large-scale political violence at the end of the twentieth century, a revolution has occurred in international law. First of all, temporary tribunals were established to cover atrocities in Yugoslavia and Rwanda. Then a new permanent International Criminal Court (ICC) was created in July 2002 to prosecute those who commit genocide, war crimes, or crimes against humanity. The ICC is a modification of the inter-state system, because it was created by political campaigning of human rights NGOs, because bitter opposition from the sole 'superpower' was defeated and because the sovereign responsibility to prosecute criminals can be assumed by a global court. In September 2005, the United Nations went further, replacing state sovereignty with a collective 'responsibility to protect', when national authorities are manifestly failing (UNGA Res. 60/1).

The significance of criminals, terrorists, and guerrillas

Before September 2001, analysis of transnational criminals and guerrillas did not present a challenge to orthodox state-centric theory. However, globalization has changed the nature of sovereignty and the processes of government. The operations of criminals and other non-legitimate groups have become more complex, spread over a wider geographical area, and increased in scale, because the improvements in communications have made it so much easier to transfer people, money, weapons, and ideas on a transnational basis. Government attempts to control such activities have become correspondingly more difficult. The legal concept of sovereignty may nominally still exist, but political practice has become significantly different. Now virtually every government feels it has to mobilize external support to exercise 'domestic jurisdiction' over criminals. Defeat of Al Qaeda will not be achieved by military counter-terrorism, but by global political change that delegitimizes **fundamentalism** and violence. Oppressive action by governments is subject to extensive review under global human rights mechanisms and, in some situations, may be subject to prosecution at the ICC.

Key Points

- Effective action against transnational criminals by individual governments is difficult for the same reasons as control of TNCs is difficult.

- Groups using violence to achieve political goals generally do not achieve legitimacy, but in exceptional circumstances they may be recognized as national liberation movements and take part in diplomacy.

- The transnational activities of criminals and guerrillas shift problems of the domestic policy of countries into the realm of global politics.

- Terrorism may be particular to individual countries, have transnational aspects, or be carried out by groups in a transnational network, but it is not a single political force.

- Governments cannot act as independent sovereign actors in response to terrorism, nor in using violence themselves.

Non-governmental organizations as political actors

The politics of an individual country cannot be understood without knowing what groups lobby the government and what debate there has been in the media. Similarly, international diplomacy does not operate on some separate planet, cut off from global civil society.

Consultative status at the UN for NGOs

As a result of pressure, primarily from American groups, the United Nations Charter contains Article 71, providing for the Economic and Social Council (ECOSOC) to consult with NGOs. In 1950, the Council formally

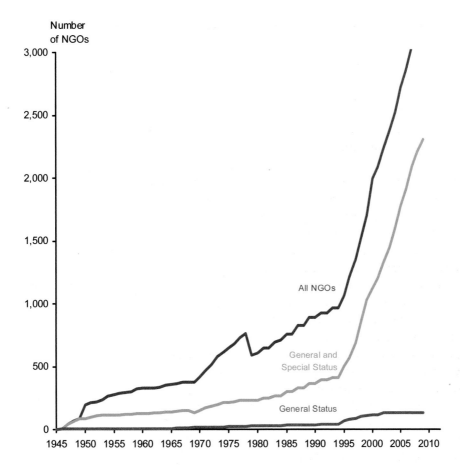

Figure 20.2 The growth of NGOs at the UN
General Status: having a large membership and working on most ECOSOC questions
Special Status: large regional/national NGOs or specialist NGOs of high status
All NGOs: including also the ECOSOC Roster of small or very specialist NGOs

codified its practice, in a statute for NGOs. It recognized *three categories* of groups: (1) a small number of high-status NGOs, concerned with most of the Council's work; (2) specialist NGOs, concerned with a few fields of activity and having a high reputation in those fields; and (3) a Roster of other NGOs that are expected to make occasional contributions to the Council (UN, ECOSOC 1950). Since then the term NGO has, for diplomats, been synonymous with a group that is eligible for ECOSOC consultative status.

The UN definition of an acceptable NGO

The ECOSOC statute and the way it has been applied embodies six principles:

1 An NGO should support the aims and the work of the UN. However, it is very rare that objections are made to the political purposes of NGOs.

2 Officially, an NGO should be a representative body, with identifiable headquarters, and officers who are responsible to a democratic policy-making conference. In practice many highly prestigious NGOs, particularly development and environment NGOs, are not membership organizations.

3 An NGO cannot be a profit-making body. Individual companies cannot gain consultative status, but trade federations of commercial interests are recognized as NGOs.

4 An NGO cannot use or advocate violence.

5 An NGO must respect the norm of 'non-interference in the internal affairs of states'. This means an NGO cannot be a political party, but parties can, like companies, form international federations. Also, NGOs concerned with human rights should not restrict their activities to a particular group, nationality, or country.

6   An international NGO is one that is not established by intergovernmental agreement.

Many NGO activists believe the UN should be more restrictive and only accept groups that are 'true' NGOs, contributing to 'progressive' **social movements**. Environmentalists are often upset that business federations are accepted and the whole NGO community at the UN agonized over the National Rifle Association being admitted to the Roster in November 1996.

NGOs and globalization

The creation of a complex global economy has had effects way beyond the international trade in goods and services. Most companies, in each distinct area of activity, have formed organizations to facilitate communication, to harmonize standards, and to manage adaptation to complex change. Equally the employees have found that they face common problems in different countries and so trade unions and professional bodies have developed their own transnational links. Any form of **international regime** to formulate policy for an industry, whether it is non-governmental or intergovernmental, will encourage the strengthening of the global links among the NGOs concerned with its activities.

NGOs have also made their own contribution to globalization, by developing access to the Internet, the communication system that underpins all globalization processes. They took the new technology being used by universities and governments and made it available to the public (Willetts 2010). In the 1980s—years before the existence of the web—peace, development, human rights, and environmental activists made e-mail, libraries of documents, and electronic discussion forums available to NGOs and to individuals, by establishing the first Internet service providers. Both the UN and the World Bank first went on the Internet by using NGO servers. After the web became available in 1993, NGOs were also pioneers in the development of websites. These changes in communications constitute a fundamental change in the structure of world politics. Governments have lost sovereignty over the transnational relations of their citizens. They may attempt to monitor or control transboundary communications, but closing the border is no longer technologically possible.

NGOs structures for global cooperation

When NGOs cooperate transnationally, they may use one of four different types of **structure**. In the past, a formal joint organization, known as an INGO (an international NGO) was usually established, with a permanent headquarters, a secretariat, and a regular programme of meetings. With the advent of the Internet it is now just as likely that a looser **network** will be formed, often with a single NGO providing the technical support for e-mail communications and a joint website. The most famous networks, such as Jubilee 2000, the Coalition for an International Criminal Court, and the International Campaign to Ban Landmines, have united around a single policy domain, brought together hundreds of NGOs from all around the world, and achieved major policy changes against the opposition of leading governments. These are known as advocacy networks (Keck and Sikkink 1998). At the meetings of intergovernmental organizations, NGOs may combine in a caucus. This is a temporary network formed solely for the purpose of lobbying on the agenda items at the particular meeting. Finally, there are governance networks, formed by NGOs to maintain and enhance the participation rights of NGOs in intergovernmental meetings. They differ from advocacy networks and caucuses in not having common political goals, other than their common interest in being allowed access to the policy-making process.

Key Points

- Most transnational actors can expect to gain recognition as NGOs by the UN, provided they are not individual companies, criminals, or violent groups and they do not exist solely to oppose an individual government.

- The ECOSOC statute provides an authoritative statement that NGOs have a legitimate place in intergovernmental diplomacy.

- The creation of a global economy leads to the globalization of unions, commercial bodies, the professions, and scientists in international NGOs.

- NGOs made the Internet a public global communications system.

- Governments can no longer control the flow of information across the borders of their country.

- NGOs from each country may combine in four ways: as international NGOs; as advocacy networks; as caucuses; and as governance networks.

International organizations as structures of global politics

International organizations provide the focus for global politics. The new physical infrastructure of global communications makes it easier for them to operate. In addition, when the sessions of the organizations take place, they become distinct structures for political communication. Face-to-face meetings produce different outcomes from telephone or written communications. Multilateral discussion produces different outcomes from interactions in networks of bilateral communications.

International organizations as systems

It was argued earlier that it inconsistent to see 'states' as coherent entities, while asserting that anarchy exists at the global level. We can be consistent by accepting the existence of systems at all levels of world politics. Thus international organizations of all types transcend country boundaries and have a major impact on the governmental actors and transnational actors composing them. For a system to exist, there must be a sufficient density of interactions, involving each of its elements, at a sufficient intensity to result both in the emergence of properties for the system as a whole and in some consistent effect on the behaviour of the elements. Generally, international organizations will have founding documents defining their goals, rules of procedure constraining the modes of behaviour, secretariats committed to the status and identity of the organization (or at least committed to their own careers), past decisions that provide norms for future policy, and interaction processes that socialize new participants. All these features at the systemic level will be part of the explanation of the behaviour of the members and thus the political outcomes will not be determined solely by the initial goals of the members. The statement that international organizations form systems implies that they are politically significant and that global politics cannot be reduced to 'inter-state' relations.

The intergovernmental versus non-governmental distinction

Normally a sharp distinction is made between **intergovernmental organizations** and **international non-governmental organizations**. This conveys the impression that inter-state diplomacy and transnational relations are separate from each other. In practice there is another category of **hybrid international organizations**, in which governments work with NGOs. Among the most important hybrids are the International Red Cross, the World Conservation Union (IUCN), the International Council of Scientific Unions, the International Air Transport Association, and other economic bodies combining companies and governments. In order to be regarded as a hybrid, the organization must admit as full members *both* NGOs, parties, or companies *and* governments or governmental agencies. Both types of member must have full rights of participation in policy-making, including the right to vote on the final decisions. When the principle of formal equality of NGOs and governments is acknowledged by both sides in such a manner, the assumption that governments can dominate must be abandoned.

> **Key Points**
>
> - International organizations are structures for political communication. They are systems that constrain the behaviour of their members.
>
> - Governments form intergovernmental organizations and transnational actors form international non-governmental organizations. In addition, governments and transnational actors accord each other equal status by jointly creating hybrid international organizations.
>
> - International organizations are more than the collective will of their members. They have a distinct impact upon other global actors.

Conclusion: issues and policy systems in global politics

State-centric writers accommodate transnational activity by distinguishing the high politics of peace and security, taking place in military alliances and UN diplomacy, from the low politics of other policy questions, debated in specialist UN bodies, other IGOs and INGOs. Then, by asserting that it is more important to analyse peace and war, actors in low politics are defined out of the analysis. In practice it is not so simple. Scientists, the Red Cross, religious groups, and other NGOs are involved in arms control negotiations; economic events may be treated as crises; social policy can concern matters of life and death; and heads of government do at times make the environment a top priority. It is useful to analyse global politics in terms of a variety of dimensions describing each **policy domain** and the actors within it, but the different dimensions do not correlate. A single high/low classification does not work.

The move from a state-centric to a pluralist model depends on rejecting a static unidimensional concept of **power**. Contrary to the realist view, **capabilities** alone do not determine influence. Explaining outcomes requires examining whether the resources of actors are relevant to

the goals being pursued, describing the degree of divergence between the goals of the different actors, and analysing how they are changed by the interaction processes.

Increasingly, the impact of NGOs is explained from a constructivist perspective (see Ch. 9). In terms of Finnemore and Sikkink (1998), NGOs are **norm entrepreneurs**, initiating and sustaining change in global political debates that determine policy-making. NGOs have the ability to communicate in a manner that commands the attention and respect of other actors. If power is seen solely in military terms, governments are expected to be dominant. If power is seen solely in economic

---

Case Study   The baby milk advocacy network

The prototype for global campaigning by NGOs has been the International Baby Foods Action Network, which challenges the marketing of dried milk powder, by the major food and pharmaceutical TNCs. In the early 1970s, medical staff in developing countries gradually became aware that the death rate for babies was rising, because of reduced breast feeding. If the family was poor and used insufficient milk powder, the baby was undernourished. If the water or the bottle was not sterile, the baby developed gastric diseases. Bottle feeding today causes around one and a half million deaths a year.

The question was first taken up by the New Internationalist magazine and War on Want (WoW) in Britain in 1973-4. A Swiss NGO, the Third World Action Group (AgDW), then published a revised translation of WoW's report, under the title Nestlé Kills Babies. When Nestlé sued for libel, AgDW mobilized groups from around the world to supply evidence for their defence. The Swiss court found AgDW guilty in December 1976 on one of Nestlés four original counts, on the technical basis that Nestlé was only indirectly responsible for the deaths.

The question moved to the USA, when religious groups involved in Latin America fought another court case against Bristol-Meyers. Increased awareness led to a new group, the Infant Formula Action Coalition, organizing a boycott of Nestlé's products that spread to many countries. In the hope of defusing the increasing pressure, the International Council of Infant Food Industries accepted a proposal by Senator Kennedy for the World

Health Organization and UNICEF to hold a meeting on infant feeding in October 1979. Rather than depoliticizing the question, the companies found they were facing demands to limit their marketing. The meeting also taught a group of NGOs how much they could benefit from working together with a common political strategy. They decided to continue to cooperate by forming IBFAN, as a global advocacy network.

The new network was able to mobilize a diverse coalition of medical professionals, religious groups, development activists, women's groups, community organizations, consumer lobbies, and the boycott campaigners. Against intense opposition from the TNCs and the US administration, IBFAN succeeded in achieving the adoption of an International Code of Marketing of Breast-Milk Substitutes, by WHO's Assembly in May 1981. The key provisions of the Code were that 'there should be no advertising or other form of promotion to the general public' nor any provision of free samples to mothers.

As of 2009, 30 countries had implemented the Code by means of a comprehensive law, another 33 countries had implemented many, but not all, provisions as law, and a further 87 countries had weak legal provisions or voluntary policies. While many countries have strengthened their laws in the last decade, IBFAN downgraded its classification for all but one of the EU countries from medium to weak compliance, after a new European Union Directive in 2006 failed to meet the Code's minimum standards. IBFAN's work continues along two tracks. It monitors and reports violations of the Code by companies, including in countries where marketing is now illegal; and it also seeks to upgrade the law in countries that are only partially implementing the Code.

(This account is based upon Chetley (1986) and information on www.ibfan.org, the IBFAN website.)

Discussion Questions

1 Identify the actors involved in the global politics of baby foods and classify them into the following categories: governments, NGOs, TNCs, IGOs, INGOs, and networks.

2 How was it possible for a global campaign by NGOs to achieve success against the combined opposition of major TNCs and the US Reagan administration?

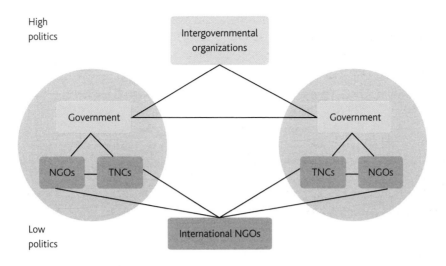

Figure 20.3 The orthodox view of international relations

terms, TNCs are expected to be dominant. However, if power includes possession of status, information, and communication skills, then it is possible for NGOs and international organizations to mobilize support for their values and to exercise influence over governments.

Thus the governments, the TNCs, the NGOs, the intergovernmental organizations, and the international NGOs that have the ability to exercise influence will vary according to the **issues** invoked by a policy problem. Table 20.1 illustrates the point that there is not a single international system of nearly 200 'states', but a variety of **policy domains**, each involving their own distinct actors. Governments have a special role, linking the different domains, because membership of the UN obliges governments to form policy and vote on most issues.

In practice, they are less centralized and cohesive than it appears in the UN, because different departments of government handle the different policy questions. The transnational actors and international organizations generally are more specialist and involved in a limited range of policy questions. Amnesty International rarely has significance in environmental politics and Greenpeace is rarely concerned with human rights, but each is central to its own domain. Being a specialist generates high status, provides command over information, and enhances communication skills. These capabilities enable a challenge to be made to the governments that control military and economic resources.

Within both domestic and global politics, civil society is the source of change. The European empires were

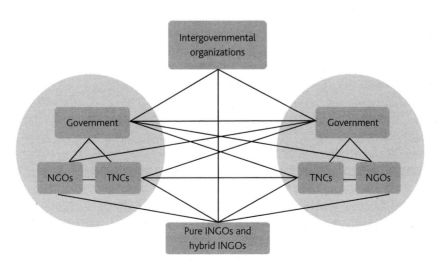

Figure 20.4 The full range of international connections

Table 20.1 The variety of political actors involved in different policy domains

	Apartheid in South Africa	Human rights	Population planning	Environment
Main governments involved	South Africa, UK, USA versus African governments	Democratic versus authoritarian governments	All types of governments	Those who feel threatened by problems versus those who do not
Transnational companies	Wide range, but especially mining and oil	Any working with oppressive governments	Medical, pharmaceutical, and food	Mainly industrial, energy, and transport
Guerrillas	ANC, PAC, and SWAPO	Any taking hostages	Any in control of territory	Generally not concerned
Grass-roots NGOs	Anti-Apartheid Movement	Human rights groups and the oppressed	Religious, women's, and health groups	Friends of the Earth, WWF, Greenpeace etc.
UN intergovernmental policy forum	Committee Against Apartheid and Security Council	Human Rights Council	Commission on Population and Development	Commission on Sustainable Development
UN Secretariat	Centre Against Apartheid	Office … for Human Rights	UNICEF, UN Pop. Fund	UNDP, UNEP
Other IGOs	Organization of African Unity	Council of Europe, OAS, and AU	WHO World Bank	World Bank
International NGOs	Many involved, with a secondary concern	Amnesty International and others	International Planned Parenthood Federation	Environment Liaison Centre International and other networks
Hybrid INGOs	Those concerned with trade	ILO	None	World Conservation Union (IUCN)

dismembered by nationalist movements, with support from lawyers, journalists, unions, and the churches. Democracy and human rights have been extended by women's groups, ethnic minorities, and dissident groups. The environment has moved up the agenda in response to grass-roots anger at the loss of natural beauty, protests against threats to health, and warnings from scientists about ecosystems being at risk of collapse. The right to have access to family planning supplies, sexual information, and reproductive health services was established by women being prepared to go to jail to challenge repressive laws. The start of the cold war was not simply the formation of military alliances; it was a political struggle of communism as a transnational movement against the transnational appeal of democracy, the Catholic Church, and nationalism. The arms race and the process of **détente** included conflict between arms manufacturers and peace movements, with scientists being crucial to both sides. The end of the cold war was driven by economic failure within communist countries and the political failure in response to demands from unions, human rights dissidents, the churches, and environmentalists. The response to refugee crises has been dominated by the media, the UN, and NGOs. The shift from seeing development as increasing a country's GNP to meeting ordinary people's basic needs and using resources in a sustainable manner was driven by development NGOs and the environmental movement. The international relations of the twentieth century have all occurred within complex, pluralist political systems.

Key Points

- The high politics/low politics distinction is used to marginalize transnational actors. It is invalid because politics does not reduce to these two categories.

- A simple concept of power will not explain outcomes. Military and economic resources are not the only capabilities: communication facilities, information, authority, and status are also important political assets.

- Different policy domains contain different actors, depending upon the salience of the issues being debated.

- TNCs gain influence through the control of economic resources. NGOs gain influence through possessing information, gaining high status, and communicating effectively. TNCs and NGOs have been the main source of economic and political change in global politics.

Questions

1   Outline three meanings of the concept of a 'state' and explain the implications of each for the study of transnational actors.
2   What are the different types of transnational actor? Give examples of each type.
3   What is a nation? How does the concept differ from that of a state?
4   How do transnational companies affect the sovereignty of governments?
5   What measures could you use to compare the size of countries, TNCs, NGOs, and international organizations? Are countries always larger than transnational actors?
6   What types of NGO are, and what types are not, eligible to obtain consultative status with the Economic and Social Council of the United Nations?
7   What is a hybrid international organization?
8   How is it possible for NGOs to exercise influence in global politics? (Note: this question can be answered both in theoretical terms and in practical empirical terms.)
9   What contribution did NGOs in the Coalition for an International Criminal Court make to the creation of the Court?
10 Explain the difference between analysing international relations as a single international system and as the global politics of many different policy domains.

Further Reading

Case study materials

Edwards, M. and J. Gaventa, *Global Citizen Action: Lessons and Challenges* (Boulder, CO: Lynne Rienner, 2001): focuses on broadly based campaigning networks, with six case studies on civil society interaction with the international financial institutions and seven case studies on environment, human rights, and development campaigns.

Keck, M. E. and K. Sikkink, *Activists Beyond Borders: Advocacy Networks in International Politics* (Ithaca, NY: Cornell University Press, 1998): a major contribution to the literature on the nature of modern transnational advocacy networks, with case studies on Latin America, the environment, and violence against women.

Risse-Kappen, T. (ed.), *Bringing Transnational Relations Back In* (Cambridge: Cambridge University Press, 1995): provides a set of six case studies around the theme that transnational influence depends upon the structures of governance for an issue-area at both the domestic level and in international institutions.

Weiss, T. G., and Gordenker, L. (eds.), *NGOs, the UN and Global Governance* (Boulder, CO: Lynne Rienner, 1996): six studies of NGO activity and three chapters addressing cross-cutting themes, set within a pluralist approach.

Willetts, P. (ed.), *'The Conscience of the World'. The Influence of Non-Governmental Organizations in the UN System* (London: Hurst and Co., 1996): defines what is an NGO, gives the history of the League and the UN consultative arrangements, and offers seven case studies of the influence of NGOs in the UN system.

Willetts, P., *Non-Governmental Organizations in World Politics. The Construction of Global Governance* (London: Routledge, 2010): outlines the access of NGOs to UN policy-making, demonstrates their enhanced status in international law, establishes their role in creating the Internet and assesses their impact on global governance.

UN materials

Kaul, I., et al., *Human Development Report 1993* (New York: Oxford University Press, 1993): an official UN annual report, which in this edition concentrates on the contribution made by NGOs to development.

UNCTAD, Division on Transnational Corporations and Investment, *World Investment Report* (New York: UN, 1991 and each year thereafter): an official UN annual report, which assesses the scale of TNC participation in global production, investment and trade.

Online Resource Centre

 Visit the Online Resource Centre that accompanies this book to access more learning resources on this chapter topic at www.oxfordtextbooks.co.uk/orc/baylis5e/

Part Four

International issues

In this part of the book we want to give you an overview of the main issues in contemporary world politics. The previous three parts have been designed to give you a comprehensive foundation for the study of contemporary international issues. As with the other sections, this one also has two aims: **first**, we want to give you an understanding of some of the more important problems that appear every day in the media headlines and that, directly and indirectly, affect the lives of each of us. These issues are the stuff of globalization, and they take a number of different forms. Some, like the environment and nuclear proliferation, pose dangers of global catastrophe. Others, like nationalism, cultural differences, and humanitarian intervention, together with regionalism and integration, raise important questions and dilemmas about the twin processes of fragmentation and unification that characterize the world in which we live. Yet other issues, such as terrorism, global trade and finance, human rights, human security, poverty, development, and hunger, are fundamentally intertwined with globalization. Our **second** aim, of course, is that by providing overviews of these issues we are posing questions about the nature of globalization. Is it new? Is it beneficial? Is it unavoidable? Does it serve specific interests? Does it make it more or less easy to deal with the problems covered in these chapters? The picture that emerges from these chapters is that the process of globalization is a highly complex one, with major disagreements existing about its significance and its impact. Some contributors see opportunities for greater cooperation because of globalization, while others see dangers of increased levels of conflict at the beginning of the twenty-first century. What do you think?

ORC in the spotlight: questions

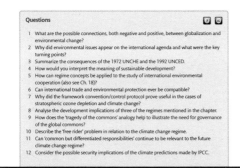

Prepare for exams by testing your knowledge thoroughly. Use the questions at the end of each chapter alongside our handy online resources. Visit www.oxfordtextbooks.co.uk/orc/baylis5e/ for multiple choice questions and a revision guide that will help you learn all of the key points.

Environmental issues

JOHN VOGLER

Reader's Guide

As environmental problems transcend national boundaries they come to be a feature of international politics. This chapter indicates that environmental issues have become increasingly prominent on the international agenda over the last fifty years, assisted by the effects of globalization. It shows how this has prompted attempts to arrange cooperation between states and surveys the form and function of such activity with reference to some of the main international environmental regimes. Because climate change has become a problem of such enormous significance, a separate section is devoted to the efforts to create an international climate regime. This is followed by a brief consideration of how some of the theoretical parts of this book relate to international environmental politics.

Introduction

Although humankind as a whole now appears to be living well above earth's carrying capacity, the **ecological footprints** of individual states vary to an extraordinary extent. See, for example, the unusual map of the world (Fig. 21.1), where the size of countries is proportionate to their carbon emissions. Indeed, if everyone were to enjoy the current lifestyle of the developed countries, more than three additional planets would be required.

This situation is rendered all the more unsustainable by the process of **globalization**, even though the precise relationship between environmental degradation and the over-use of resources, on the one hand, and globalization, on the other, is complex and sometimes contradictory. Globalization has stimulated the relocation of industry, population movement away from the land, and ever-rising levels of consumption, along with associated emissions of effluents and waste gases. While often generating greater income for poorer countries exporting basic goods to developed-country markets, ever freer trade can also have adverse environmental consequences, by disrupting local ecologies and livelihoods.

On the other hand, there is little evidence that globalization has stimulated a 'race to the bottom' in environmental standards, and it has even been argued that increasing levels of affluence have brought about local environmental improvements, just as birth rates tend to fall as populations become wealthier. Economists claim that globalization's opening up of markets can increase efficiency and reduce pollution, provided that the environmental and social damage associated with production of a good is properly factored into its market price. Similarly, globalization has promoted the sharing of knowledge and the influential presence of **non-governmental organizations** (NGOs) in global environmental politics. Whatever the ecological balance sheet of globalization, the resources upon which human beings depend for survival, such as fresh water, a clean atmosphere, and a stable climate, are now under serious threat.

Global problems may need global solutions and pose a fundamental requirement for **global environmental governance**, yet local or regional action remains a vital aspect of responses to many problems; one of the defining characteristics of environmental politics is the awareness of such interconnections and of the need to 'think globally—act locally'. NGOs have been very active in this respect, as shown in Chapter 20 of this book.

Despite the global dimensions of environmental change, an effective response still has to depend upon a fragmented international political system of over 190 sovereign **states**. Global environmental governance

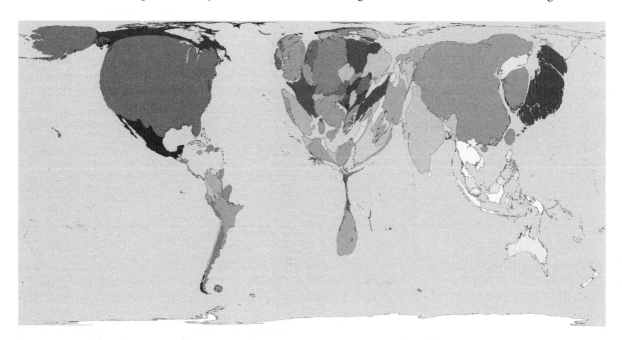

Figure 21.1 Map of world in proportion to carbon emissions

consequently involves bringing to bear inter-state relations, **international law**, and **international organizations** in addressing shared environmental problems. Using the term 'governance'—as distinct from government—implies that regulation and control have to be exercised in the absence of central government, delivering the kinds of service that a world government would provide if it were to exist. You should refer to Chapter 18 for the essential concepts employed in **regime** analysis, which is commonly applied in the study of international governance.

> ## Key Points
>
> - The current use and degradation of the earth's resources is unsustainable and closely connected in sometimes contradictory ways to the processes of globalization.
>
> - There are vast inequalities between rich and poor in their use of the earth's resources and the ecological shadow or footprint that they impose on it.
>
> - The response at the international level is to attempt to provide global environmental governance. In a system of sovereign states this involves international cooperation.

Environmental issues on the international agenda: a brief history

Before the era of globalization there were two traditional environmental concerns: conservation of natural resources and the damage caused by pollution. Neither pollution nor wildlife respect international boundaries, and action to mitigate or conserve sometimes had to involve more than one state. There were also numerous, mostly unsuccessful, attempts to regulate exploitation of maritime resources lying beyond national jurisdiction, including several multilateral fisheries commissions. The 1946 International Convention for the Regulation of Whaling and its International Whaling Commission (IWC) show an interesting move away from the original goal of conserving the whaling industry by regulating catches, towards the preservation of the great whales *per se* through declaring an international moratorium on whaling. This shift still generates bitter confrontation between NGOs, most IWC members, and the small number of nations—Japan, Norway, and Iceland—that wish to resume commercial whaling.

Post-Second World War global economic recovery brought with it evidence of damaging pollution of the atmosphere, of watercourses, and of the sea, notably the Mediterranean, leading to international agreements in the 1950s and 1960s covering such matters as discharges from oil tankers. This worthy activity was, though, hardly the stuff of great power politics. Such 'apolitical' matters were the domain of new United Nations **Specialized Agencies**, like the Food and Agriculture Organization, but were hardly central to diplomacy at the UN General Assembly (UNGA) in New York. This neglect was reflected in academic writing at the time, as exemplified by Hans J. Morgenthau's famous text, *Politics among Nations* (1955), which mentions the natural environment

only as a fixed contextual factor or a constituent of national power.

However, the salience of environmental issues grew in the 1960s, and in 1968 the UNGA accepted a Swedish proposal for what became the 1972 UN Conference on the Human Environment (UNCHE) 'to focus governments' attention and public opinion on the importance and urgency of the question'. This Conference led to the creation of the United Nations Environment Programme (UNEP) and the establishment of environment departments by many governments. Yet it was already clear that, for the countries of the South, constituting the majority in the UNGA, environmental questions could not be separated from their demands for development, aid, and the restructuring of international economic relations. This was the political context surrounding the emergence of the concept of **sustainable development** (also see Ch. 28) but before this was formulated by the Brundtland Commission in 1987 (WCED 1987), the environment had been pushed to the periphery of the international agenda by the global economic downturn of the 1970s and then the onset of the second cold war (see Ch. 3).

Environmental degradation continued none the less. Awareness of new forms of transnational pollution, such as 'acid rain', joined existing concerns over point-source pollution (when the pollutant comes from a definite source), followed by a dawning scientific realization that some environmental problems—the thinning of the stratospheric ozone layer and the possibility of climate change—were truly global in scale. The attendant popular concern over such issues and the relaxation of East–West tension created the opportunity for a second great UN conference, for which the connection between

Box 21.1 Chronology

1946	International Convention for the Regulation of Whaling
1955	UK Clean Air Act to combat 'smog' in British cities
1958	International Convention for the Prevention of Pollution of the Sea by Oil
1959	Antarctic Treaty
1962	Rachel Carson publishes Silent Spring
1967	Torrey Canyon oil tanker disaster
1969	Greenpeace founded
1971	At the Founex Meeting in Switzerland, Southern experts formulated a link between environment and development
1972	United Nations Conference on the Human Environment (UNCHE) in Stockholm
	Establishment of the United Nations Environment Programme (UNEP)
1973	MARPOL Convention on oil pollution from ships
	Convention on International Trade in Endangered Species (CITES)
1979	Long Range Transboundary Air Pollution Convention (LRTAP)
1980	Convention on the Conservation of Antarctic Marine Living Resources
1982	UN Law of the Sea Convention (enters into force in 1994)
1984	Bhopal chemical plant disaster
1985	Vienna Convention for the Protection of the Ozone Layer. The Antarctic 'ozone hole' confirmed
1986	Chernobyl nuclear disaster
1987	Brundtland Commission Report
	Montreal Protocol on Substances that Deplete the Ozone Layer
1988	Establishment of the Intergovernmental Panel on Climate Change (IPCC)
1989	Basel Convention on the Transboundary Movement of Hazardous Wastes
1991	Madrid Protocol (to the Antarctic Treaty) on Environmental Protection
1992	United Nations Conference on Environment and Development (UNCED) held at Rio de Janeiro. Publication of the Rio Declaration and Agenda 21. United Nations Conventions on Climate Change (UNFCCC) and Biological Diversity (CBD) both signed. Establishment of the Commission on Sustainable Development (CSD)
1995	World Trade Organization (WTO) founded
1997	Kyoto Protocol to the UNFCCC
1998	Rotterdam Convention on Hazardous Chemicals and Pesticides
	Aarhus Convention on Access to Information, Public Participation in Decision-making and Access to Justice in Environmental Matters
2000	Cartagena Protocol on Biosafety
	Millennium Development Goals set out
2001	US President Bush revokes signature of the Kyoto Protocol
2002	World Summit on Sustainable Development (WSSD), Johannesburg. Johannesburg Plan of Implementation
2005	Entry into force of the Kyoto Protocol and introduction of the first international emissions trading system by the European Union
2006	International discussions commenced on the climate change regime after 2012
2007	Fourth Assessment Report of the IPCC, Bali CoP produces a 'road map' for climate negotiations
2009	Copenhagen climate CoP fails to provide a new international agreement

environment and development had been explicitly drawn through the Brundtland Commission's notion of sustainable development. Though subject to many subsequent interpretations, its political essence remains an accommodation between the environmental concerns of developed states and the development demands of the South, without which there could have been no Earth Summit and no Rio process.

The 1992 UN Conference on Environment and Development (UNCED) or 'Earth Summit' was the largest international conference held so far, raising the profile of the environment as an international issue while concluding several significant documents and agreements, such as *Agenda 21* and international conventions on climate change and the preservation of biodiversity. The event's underlying politics were captured in its title—a conference on 'environment and development'—where the most serious arguments concerned aid pledges to finance the environmental improvements under discussion. A process was created at the UN to review the implementation of the Rio agreements, including meetings of the new Commission on Sustainable Development (CSD) and a Special Session of the UNGA in 1997.

On UNCED's tenth anniversary in 2002, the World Summit on Sustainable Development (WSSD) was held in Johannesburg. The change of wording indicated how

Box 21.2 Sustainable development

Over 50 separate definitions of sustainable development have been counted. Its classic statement was provided by the 1987 Brundtland Commission Report:

Sustainable development is development that meets the needs of the present without compromising the ability of future generations to meet their own needs.

(Brundtland et al. 1987: 43)

Behind it lay an explicit recognition of limitations to future growth that were social, technological, and environmental. In addressing them, emphasis was placed upon needs, and the highest priority was given to those needs experienced by the world's poor. Central to the concept was the idea of fairness between generations as well as between the rich and poor currently inhabiting the planet.

By the time of the 2002 World Summit the concept had been subtly altered:

to ensure a balance between economic development, social development and environmental protection as interdependent and mutually reinforcing components of sustainable development.

(UNGA, A/57/532/add.1, 12 December 2002)

Ensuring environmental sustainability, by integrating sustainable development principles into national decision-making, was the seventh of eight UN Millennium Development Goals agreed in 2000.

---

of the environment has responded to the issue-attention cycle in developed countries, peaking at certain moments and then declining. The causes are complex and during the 1960s reflected the counter-cultural and radical movements of the time along with wider public reactions to a series of trends and events. The most totemic of these was Rachel Carson's hugely influential book *Silent Spring* (1962), which powerfully conjoined the conservationist and anti-pollution agendas by highlighting the damage inflicted upon bird-life by industrial pesticides like DDT. Well-publicized environmental disasters, such as the 1959 mercury poisoning at Minimata in Japan and the 1967 wreck of the *Torrey Canyon* oil tanker close to Cornish beaches, fed public concern. The failure of established political parties to embrace these issues effectively encouraged the birth of several new high-profile NGOs—Friends of the Earth, Greenpeace, and the World Wildlife Fund for Nature—alongside more established pressure groups such as the US Sierra Club and the British Royal Society for the Protection of Birds. The interest in environmental action at the international level and, indeed, most of the NGOs exerting pressure to this end were an almost exclusively developed world phenomenon. Public attention then receded until the ending of the second cold war coincided with a new concern over global environmental problems, providing the political impetus for the 1992 Earth Summit. Interest waned again during the ensuing decade, although by 2005–6 public alarm over the impact of climate change again propelled environmental issues up the political agenda. The demand was, of course, for international action and governance, but what exactly did this mean? The next section attempts to answer this question by reviewing the functions of international environmental cooperation.

---

conceptions of environment and development had shifted since the 1970s. Now discussion was embedded in recognition of the importance of globalization and of the dire state of the African continent. **Poverty** eradication was clearly emphasized, along with practical progress in providing clean water, sanitation, and agricultural improvements. One controversial element was the role to be played in such provision by private–public sector partnerships.

While the UN conferences marked the stages by which the environment entered the international political mainstream, they also reflected underlying changes in the scope and perception of environmental problems. As scientific understanding expanded, it was becoming a commonplace, by the 1980s, to speak in terms of global environmental change, as most graphically represented by the discovery of the 'ozone hole' and the creeping realization that human activities might be dangerously altering the global climate itself.

Alongside actual environmental degradation and advances in scientific knowledge, the international politics

Key Points

- In the late nineteenth and early twentieth centuries international environmental politics was strictly limited, but from around 1960 its scope expanded as environmental problems acquired a transnational and then a global dimension.

- The process was reflected in and stimulated by the three great UN conferences of 1972, 1992, and 2002, whose most important role was to make the connection between the international environmental and development agendas, as expressed in the important concept of sustainable development.

- International environmental politics reflected the issue-attention cycle in developed countries and relied heavily on increasing scientific knowledge.

The functions of international environmental cooperation

International cooperation establishes governance regimes to regulate transboundary environmental problems and sustain the global commons. Regimes encompass more than formal agreements between states, although these are very important (see Ch. 18). Moreover, there are other functions and consequences of international cooperation beyond regime formation.

The pursuit of **power**, status, and wealth is rarely absent from international deliberations. This is often neglected in discussions of international environmental cooperation, even though many of the great international gatherings and even some of the more mundane ones clearly reflect struggles for national and organizational advantage. Organizations seek to maintain their financial and staff resources as well as their place within the UN system. UNEP, for example, despite extensive debates over granting it the higher and more autonomous status of a UN Specialized Agency, remains a mere programme. Some suspect that much of the activity at international environmental meetings is simply to issue declarations convincing domestic publics that something is being done, even if environmental conditions continue to deteriorate.

Transboundary trade and pollution control

When animals, fish, water, or pollution cross national frontiers, the need for international cooperation arises and the regulation of transboundary environmental problems is the longest-established function of international cooperation, reflected in hundreds of multilateral, regional, and bilateral agreements providing for joint efforts to manage resources and control pollution. Prominent examples of multilateral environmental agreements (MEAs) include the 1979 Long Range Transboundary Air Pollution convention and its various protocols and conventions governing such things as the cross-border movement of hazardous waste and chemicals.

Controlling, taxing, and even promoting trade has always been one of the more important functions of the state, and trade restrictions can also be used as an instrument for nature conservation, as in the 1973 Convention on International Trade in Endangered Species (CITES). The use of trade penalties and restrictions by MEAs has been a vexed issue when the objective of environmental protection has come into conflict with the rules of the GATT/World Trade Organization (WTO) trade regime (see Ch. 15). Such a problem arose when the international community attempted to address the controversial question of the new biotechnology and genetically modified organisms (GMOs) by developing the 2000 Cartagena Protocol to the UN Convention on Biodiversity. Opponents argued that attempts to regulate the movement of GMOs was an attempt to disguise protectionism rather than to safeguard the environment and human health. Whether the WTO trade rules should take precedence over the emerging biosafety rules was debated at length until the parties agreed to avoid the issue by providing that the two sets of rules should be 'mutually supportive'. The background to such arguments is a wider debate about the relationship between trade and the environment.

Box 21.3 Trade and the environment

The issue of the relationship between trade and environmental degradation is much broader than disputes over the relationship between the World Trade Organization (WTO) and particular multilateral environmental agreements (MEAs). Globalization is partly shaped by the efforts of the GATT/WTO to open up protected markets and expand world trade. Many green activists argue that trade itself damages the environment by destroying local sustainable agriculture and by encouraging the environmentally damaging long-range transport of goods. The rearrangement of patterns of production and consumption has indeed been one of the hallmarks of globalization. Liberal economists and apologists for the WTO claim that if the 'externalities', such as the pollution caused, can be factored into the price of a product, then trade can be beneficial to the environment through allowing the most efficient allocation of resources. In this view, using trade restrictions as a weapon to promote good environmental behaviour would be unacceptable and, indeed, the rules of the WTO allow only very limited restrictions to trade on environmental grounds (GATT XXg) and certainly not on the basis of 'process and production methods'. A number of trade dispute cases have largely confirmed that import controls cannot be used to promote more sustainable or ethical production abroad, including the famous 1991 GATT Tuna–Dolphin case which upheld Mexican and EC complaints against US measures blocking imports of tuna caught with the methods that kill dolphins as by-catch. Developing-country governments remain resistant to green trade restrictions as a disguised form of protection for developed world markets.

Norm creation

The development of international environmental law and associated **norms** of acceptable behaviour has been both rapid and innovative over the last thirty years. Some are in the form of quite technical policy concepts that have been widely disseminated and adopted as a result of international discussion. The precautionary principle has gained increasing but not uncritical currency. Originally coined by German policy-makers, this principle states that where there is a likelihood of environmental damage, banning an activity should not require full and definitive scientific proof. (This was a critical issue in the discussions on GMOs mentioned above.) Another norm is that governments should give 'prior informed consent' to potentially damaging imports.

The UN Earth Summits were important in establishing environmental norms. The 1972 Stockholm Conference produced its 'Principle 21', which combines **sovereignty** over national resources with state responsibility for external pollution. This should not be confused with *Agenda 21*, issued by the 1992 Rio Earth Summit, a complex 40-chapter document of some 400 pages that took two years to negotiate in UNCED's Preparatory Committee. *Agenda 21* was frequently derided, not least because of its non-binding character, but this internationally agreed compendium of environmental 'best practice' subsequently had a wide impact and remains a point of reference. For example, many local authorities have produced their own 'local Agenda 21s'. Under the Aarhus Convention (1998), North American and European governments agreed to guarantee to their publics a number of environmental rights, including the right to obtain environmental information held by governments, to participate in policy decisions, and to have access to judicial processes.

Capacity building

Although not a specific norm of the type dealt with above, **sustainable development** provides a normative framework reflecting an underlying deal between developed and developing worlds. Frequent North–South arguments since Rio about the levels of aid and technology transfer that would allow developing countries to achieve sustainable development have seen many disappointments and unfulfilled pledges. In 1991, UNEP, UNDP, and the World Bank created the Global Environmental Facility (GEF) as an international mechanism specifically for funding environmental projects in developing countries. In 2003–6 it attracted donations of around US$3 billion. Most environmental conventions now aim at **capacity building** through arrangements for the transfer of funds, technology, and expertise, because most of their member states simply lack the resources to participate fully in international agreements. The stratospheric ozone and climate change regimes aim to build capacity and could not exist in their current form without providing for this function.

Scientific understanding

International environmental cooperation relies upon shared scientific understanding, as reflected in the form of some important contemporary environmental regimes. An initial framework **convention** will signal concern and establish mechanisms for developing and sharing new scientific data, thereby providing the basis for taking action in a control protocol. Generating and sharing scientific information has long been a function of international cooperation in such public bodies as the World Meteorological Organization (WMO) and myriad academic organizations such as the International Council for the Exploration of the Seas (ICES) and the International Union for the Conservation of Nature (IUCN). Disseminating scientific information on an international basis makes sense, but it needs funding from governments because, except in areas like pharmaceutical research, the private sector has no incentive to do the work. International environmental regimes usually have standing scientific committees and subsidiary bodies to support their work. Perhaps the greatest international effort to generate new and authoritative scientific knowledge has been in the area of climate change, through the Intergovernmental Panel on Climate Change (IPCC) (see Box 21.6 below).

Governing the commons

The global commons are usually understood as areas and resources that do not fall under sovereign jurisdiction—they are not owned by anybody. The high seas and the deep ocean floor come within this category (beyond the 200-mile exclusive economic zone), as does Antarctica (based upon the 1959 Antarctic Treaty). Outer space is another highly important common, its use being vital to modern telecommunications, broadcasting, navigation, and surveillance. Finally, there is the global atmosphere.

The commons all have an environmental dimension, as resources but also as 'sinks' that have been

Box 21.4 The tragedy of the commons—local and global

Many writers, including Garrett Hardin (1968), who coined the term 'tragedy of the commons', have observed an inherent conflict between individual and collective interest and **rationality** in the use of property that is held in common. Hardin argued that individual actions in exploiting an 'open access' resource will often bring collective disaster as the pasture, fish stock (common pool), or river (common sink) concerned suffers ecological collapse through over-exploitation. Of course, no problem will be perceived if the 'carrying capacity' of the common is sufficient for all to take as much as they require, but this is rarely now the case due to the intensity of modern exploitation and production practices, and recent scientific advances have sharpened humankind's appreciation of the full extent of the damage imposed on the earth's ecosystems. Hardin's solution to the dilemma—enclosure of the commons through privatization or nationalization—has only limited applicability in the case of the global commons, for two main reasons: it is physically or politically impossible to enclose them; and there is no central world government to regulate their use.

increasingly degraded. The fish and whale stocks of the high seas have been relentlessly over-exploited to the point where some species have been wiped out and long-term protein sources for human beings are imperilled. The ocean environment has been polluted by land-based effluent and oil, and other discharges from ships. It has been a struggle to maintain the unique wilderness of the Antarctic in the face of increasing pressure from human beings, and even outer space now faces an environmental problem in the form of increasing amounts of orbital debris left by decades of satellite launches. Similarly, the global atmosphere has been degraded in a number of highly threatening ways, through damage to the stratospheric ozone layer and, most importantly, by the enhanced greenhouse effect now firmly associated with changes to the earth's climate. This is often characterized as a 'tragedy of the commons'. Where there is unrestricted access to a resource owned by no one, there will be an incentive for individuals to grab as much as they can and, if the resource is finite, there will come a time when it is ruined by over-exploitation as the short-term interests of individual users overwhelm the longer-run collective interest in sustaining the resource.

Within the jurisdiction of governments it may be possible to solve the problem by turning the common into

private property or nationalizing it, but for the global commons such a solution is, by definition, unavailable. Therefore the function of international cooperation in this context is the very necessary one of providing a substitute for **world government** to ensure that global commons are not misused and subject to tragic collapse. This has been done through creating regimes for the governance of the global commons, which have enjoyed varying degrees of effectiveness. Many of the functions discussed above can be found in the global commons regimes, but their central contribution is a framework of rules to ensure mutual agreement between users about acceptable standards of behaviour and levels of exploitation, consistent with sustaining the ecology of the commons.

Enforcement poses difficult challenges due to the incentives for users to 'free ride' on these arrangements by taking more than a fair share, or refusing to be bound by the collective arrangements. This can potentially destroy regimes because other parties will then see no reason to restrain themselves either. In local commons regimes, inquisitive neighbours might deter rule-breaking, and a similar role at the international level can be performed by NGOs. However, it is very difficult to enforce compliance with an agreement on the part of sovereign states, even when they have undertaken to comply—a fundamental difficulty for international law and hardly unique to environmental regimes (see Ch. 17). Mechanisms have been developed to cope with this problem, but how effective they, and the environmental regimes to which they apply, can be is hard to judge, as this involves determining the extent to which governments are in legal and technical **compliance** with their international obligations. Moreover, it also involves estimating the extent to which state behaviour has actually been changed as a result of the international regime concerned. Naturally, the ultimate and most demanding test of the effectiveness of global commons regimes is whether or not the resources or ecologies concerned are sustained or even improved.

For the Antarctic, a remarkably well-developed set of rules designed to preserve the ecological integrity of this last great wilderness has been devised within the framework of the 1959 Treaty. The Antarctic regime is a rather exclusive club: the Treaty's 'Consultative Parties' include the states that had originally claimed sovereignty over parts of the area, while new members

Box 21.5 The Montreal Protocol and stratospheric ozone regime

The consequences of the thinning of stratospheric ozone layer include excessive exposure to UV/B radiation resulting in increased rates of skin cancer for human beings and damage to immune systems. Stratospheric ozone depletion arose from a previously unsuspected source—artificial chemicals containing fluorine, chlorine, and bromine, which were involved in chemical reaction with ozone molecules at high altitudes. Most significant were the CFCs (chlorofluorocarbons), which had been developed in the 1920s as 'safe' inert industrial gases and which had been blithely produced and used over the next fifty years for a whole variety of purposes from refrigeration to air-conditioning and as propellants for hair spray. There was no universal agreement on the dangers posed by these chemicals and production and use continued—except, significantly, where the US Congress decided to ban some non-essential uses. This meant that the US chemical industry found itself under a costly obligation to find alternatives. As evidence on the problem began to mount, UNEP acted to convene an international conference in Vienna. It produced a 'framework convention'—the 1985 Vienna Convention on substances that deplete the stratospheric ozone layer—agreeing that international action might be required and that the parties should continue to communicate and develop and exchange scientific findings. These proved to be very persuasive, particularly with the added public impetus provided by the dramatic discovery of the Antarctic 'ozone hole'.

Within two years the Montreal Protocol was negotiated. In it the parties agreed to a regime under which the production and trading of CFCs and other ozone-depleting substances would be progressively phased out. The developed countries achieved this for CFCs by 1996 and Meetings of the Parties (**MoP**) have continued to work on the elimination of other substances since that time. There was some initial resistance from European chemical producers, but the US side had a real incentive to ensure international agreement because otherwise its chemical industry would remain at a commercial disadvantage. The other problem faced by the negotiators involved the developing countries, which themselves were manufacturing CFC products. As the Indian delegate put it, it was the developed countries' mess and their responsibility to clear it up! Why should developing countries be forced to change over to higher cost CFC alternatives? There were two responses to this. The first was an article in the Protocol giving the developing countries a period of grace. The second was a fund, set up in 1990, to finance the provision of alternative non-CFC technologies for the developing world.

Illegal production and smuggling of CFCs was evident in the 1990s. This tested the monitoring and compliance systems of the Protocol (which included a possible use of trade sanctions against offenders). None the less, the regime has generally proved to be effective and has continually widened the scope of its activities to deal with further classes of ozone-depleting chemicals. The damage to the ozone layer will not be repaired until the latter part of the twenty-first century, given the long atmospheric lifetimes of the chemicals involved. However, human behaviour has been significantly altered to the extent that the scientific subsidiary body of the Montreal Protocol has been able to report a measurable reduction in the atmospheric concentration of CFCs.

---

of the club have to demonstrate their involvement in scientific research on the frozen continent. Antarctic science was crucial to the discovery of a problem that resulted in what is perhaps the best example of effective international action to govern the commons. In 1985, a British Antarctic Survey balloon provided definitive evidence of serious thinning of the stratospheric ozone layer. A diminishing ozone layer is a global problem *par excellence*, because it protects the earth and its inhabitants from the damaging effects of the sun's UV/B radiation. A framework convention was signed about the issue in 1985, followed in 1987 by the Montreal Protocol, imposing international controls over ozone-depleting chemicals. The further evolution of the ozone layer regime offers the paramount example of how international cooperation can achieve an effective solution to a global environmental problem. The problem's causes were isolated, international support was mobilized, compensatory action was taken to ensure that developing countries participated, and a set of rules and procedures was developed that proved to be effective, at least in reducing the concentration of the offending chemicals in the atmosphere, if not yet fully restoring the stratospheric ozone layer.

Key Points

- International environmental meetings serve several political objectives alongside environmental aims.
- A key function of international cooperation is transboundary regulation but attempts at environmental action may conflict with the rules of the world trade regime.
- International action is needed to promote environmental norms, develop scientific understanding, and assist the participation of developing countries.
- International cooperation is necessary to provide governance regimes for the global commons.

Climate change

Unlike the ozone layer problem, climate change and the enhanced greenhouse effect had long been debated among scientists, but only in the late 1980s did sufficient international consensus emerge to stimulate action. There were still serious disagreements over the likelihood that human-induced changes in mean temperatures were altering the global climate system. The greenhouse effect is essential to life on earth. Greenhouse gases (GHGs) in the atmosphere (see Fig. 21.2) insulate the earth's surface by trapping solar radiation. Before the Industrial Revolution, carbon dioxide concentrations in the atmosphere were around 280 parts per million, and have since grown exponentially (to a 2005 figure of 379 ppm) due to burning of fossil fuels and reductions in some of the 'sinks' for carbon dioxide—notably forests. Methane emissions have also risen with the growth of agriculture (IPCC 2007: 11). The best predictions of the IPCC are that, if nothing is done to curb intensive fossil fuel emissions, there will be a likely rise in mean temperatures of the order of 2.4–6.4 °C by 2099. The exact consequences of this are difficult to predict on the basis of current climate modelling, but sea-level rises and turbulent weather are generally expected. According to the EU, to avoid climate catastrophe, it would be necessary to hold temperature increases below 2 °C by keeping atmospheric CO_2 concentrations below 550 ppm. These figures remain subject to international disagreement with small island states, threatened with inundation, demanding a lower threshold. In the first decade of the twenty-first century, unusual weather patterns, storm events, and the melting of polar ice sheets have added a dimension of public concern to the fears expressed by the scientific community.

As a commons problem, climate change is on a quite different scale from anything that the international system has previously encountered. Climate change is really not a 'normal' international environmental problem—it threatens huge changes in living conditions and challenges existing patterns of energy use and security. There is almost no dimension of international relations that it does not actually or potentially affect, and it has already become the subject of 'high politics', discussed at **G8** summits and in high-level meetings between political leaders.

One way of examining the dimensions of the problem and the steps taken at the international level to respond to the threat is to make a comparison with the stratospheric ozone problem discussed in the previous section. There are, of course, some similarities. CFCs (chlorofluorocarbons) are in themselves greenhouse gases and the international legal texts on climate change make it clear that controlling them is the responsibility of the Montreal Protocol. The experience with stratospheric ozone and other recent conventions has clearly influenced efforts to build a climate change regime based on a framework convention followed by a protocol.

The UN Framework Convention on Climate Change (UNFCCC) was signed at the Rio Earth Summit in 1992. It envisaged the reduction of greenhouse gas emissions and their removal by sinks, hoping that a start could be made by including a commitment from the developed nations to cut their emissions back to 1990 levels by 2000. In a US election year this proved to be impossible

Box 21.6 The Intergovernmental Panel on Climate Change

Set up in 1988 under the auspices of the World Meteorological Organization (WMO) and UNEP, the Intergovernmental Panel on Climate Charge (IPCC) brings together the majority of the world's climate change scientists in three working groups: on climate science, impacts, and economic and social dimensions. They have produced assessment reports in 1990, 1995, and 2001, which are regarded as the authoritative scientific statements on climate change. The reports are carefully and cautiously drafted with the involvement of government representatives and represent a consensus view.

The Fourth Assessment Report, published in February 2007, concluded that 'warming of the climate system is unequivocal, as is now evident from observations of increases in global average air and ocean temperatures, widespread melting of snow and ice and rising global sea level' (IPCC 2007: 4). Most of the temperature increase 'is *very likely* due to the observed increase in anthropogenic greenhouse gas concentrations' (*ibid.*: 8, original italics). The use of words is significant here for the IPCC defines '*very likely*' as being more than 90 per cent certain. This represents a change from the previous report which had only estimated that human activity was '*likely*' or more than 66 per cent certain to be responsible for temperature increases.

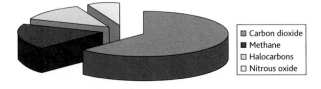

■ Carbon dioxide
■ Methane
□ Halocarbons
□ Nitrous oxide

Figure 21.2 Greenhouse gas contributions to global warming

and the parties had to be content with a non-binding declaration that an attempt would be made. There was a binding commitment, however, for parties to draw up national inventories of sources and sinks. As this included the developing nations, many of whom were ill equipped to fulfil this obligation, there was also funding for capacity building. Most importantly, the convention locked the parties into holding a continuing series of annual conferences—the **CoPs**—to consider possible actions and review the adequacy of existing commitments, supported by regular meetings of the subsidiary scientific and implementation bodies. By the second CoP in Kyoto in 1997, the parties agreed a 'control' measure—the Kyoto Protocol involving emissions reductions be developed countries facilitated by 'flexibility mechanisms'.

The problem faced by the framers of the Kyoto Protocol was vastly more complex and demanding than that which their counterparts at Montreal had confronted

---

Box 21.7 The Kyoto Protocol

The 1997 Kyoto Protocol to the UN Framework Convention on Climate Change commits the developed countries to make an average of a 5.2 per cent cut in their greenhouse gas emissions from a 1990 baseline. Within this, different national targets were negotiated: for example, 7 per cent for the USA and 8 per cent for the European Union (EU). These were to be achieved by the first commitment period—2008–12.

The Kyoto mechanisms
In order to provide flexible ways of achieving these targets, three mechanisms were also agreed:

1 **Emissions Trading**. This envisages a system where a market in rights to pollute is created. For example, efficient power plants can sell their permits to emit carbon dioxide to others and a long-term reduction in the number of permits available will mean that the price of carbon rises, alternative power sources become more competitive, and the overall amount of carbon dioxide emitted is reduced.

2 **Joint Implementation (JI)**. Under this mechanism a developed country can receive credits against its own emissions reduction target by financing projects in another developed country. The argument is that a given amount of money is best spent where it can achieve the greatest reduction in world emissions of greenhouse gases. Countries with very efficient power plants will have an incentive to use this scheme.

3 **The Clean Development Mechanism (CDM)**. Applies the same principle to relations between developed and developing countries. This has already stimulated a good deal of interest in China and elsewhere because it is a source of new funds and technology transfer.

---

so successfully in 1987. Instead of controlling a single set of industrial gases for which substitutes were available, reducing greenhouse gas emissions would involve energy, transport, and agriculture—the fundamentals of life in modern societies. Whether this must involve real sacrifices in living standards and 'impossible' political choices is a tough question for governments, although there are potential economic benefits from cutting emissions through the development of alternative energy technologies.

A second key difference from the ozone regime experience was that, despite the unprecedented international scientific effort of the IPCC, there was no scientific consensus of the kind that had promoted agreement on CFCs. Scientific disagreement over the significance of human activities and projections of future change have since narrowed dramatically, but there are still those who have an interest in denying or misrepresenting the science. Mistakes by the IPCC and its contributors have also damaged its authority. There is a further problem in that, even though the effects of climate change are not fully understood, there is enough evidence for some nations to calculate that there might be benefits to them from climatic alterations. Regions of Russia, for example, might become more temperate with rises in mean temperature and more suitable for agricultural production (although one could equally well argue the extremely damaging effects of melting permafrost in Siberia). One generalization that could be made with certainty is that it is the developing nations, with limited infrastructure and major populations located at sea level, that are most vulnerable. In recognition of this and on the understanding that a certain level of warming is now inevitable, international attention has begun to shift towards the problem of adaptation to the inevitable effects of climate change as well as mitigation of its causes. Once again, the comparative simplicity of the stratospheric ozone problem is evident—the effects of ozone depletion were spread across the globe and affected North Europeans as well as those living in the southern hemisphere.

At the heart of the international politics of climate change as a global environmental problem is the structural divide between North and South (see Chs 8 and 28). For the Montreal Protocol there was a solution available at an acceptable price, delivered through the Multilateral Ozone Fund. Once again, climate change is different. One of the most significant **principles** set out in the UNFCCC was that of common but differentiated responsibilities. That is to say that, while climate change was the 'common concern' of all, it had been produced

Case Study   Common but differentiated responsibilities?

A key principle of the climate change regime, written into the 1992 UNFCCC, was the notion of 'common but differentiated responsibilities'. This, in effect, meant that although all nations had to accept responsibility for the world's changing climate, it was developed nations that were immediately responsible because they had benefited from the industrialization which was generally regarded as the source of the excess carbon dioxide emissions that had caused mean temperature increases (refer to Fig. 21.1).

Consider the relationship between national carbon dioxide emissions and share of global population in the 1990s. The USA emitted around 25 per cent of the global total but has only 4.5 per cent of global population. Chinese figures were 14 per cent but with over 20 per cent of the world's population while the 35 least developed nations emitted under 1 per cent and account for over 10 per cent of the world's population.

Accordingly, the developed countries were listed in Annex I of the Convention and it was agreed that they, rather than develop-

ing countries, would have to lead the way in making emissions reductions.

This approach was followed in the Kyoto Protocol, where only developed-country parties are committed to make reductions. Even before the Protocol was agreed, the US Senate passed the Byrd–Hagel Resolution making it clear that it would not ratify any agreement where developing nations, who were now economic competitors of the USA, did not also have to make emissions reductions.

The future of the climate change regime
In 2004 the International Energy Agency estimated that emissions would rise by 62 per cent by 2030 but, most significantly, that at some point in the 2020s developing-world emissions would overtake those of the developed OECD countries. It therefore became clear that to have any chance of success, the future climate change regime would have to include emissions reductions by countries such as China and India. The situation is complicated by the fact that although China's emissions may now exceed those of the USA, its share of accumulated emissions is much less and, in any case, under globalization, a substantial part of its total is accounted for by industrial production displaced from developed countries. The fundamental question is: on what basis should countries be asked to reduce their emissions? The most radical and equitable answer would be to give each individual a fixed carbon allowance, probably allowing rich people to maintain something of their lifestyle by buying the allowances of the poor. A more likely alternative is to find ways of creating and then raising a global carbon price such that utilizing alternatives to fossil fuel becomes an economically attractive development path.

as a consequence of the development of the old industrialized nations and it was their responsibility to take the lead in cutting emissions.

The achievement at Kyoto was to bind most of the developed nations to a set of emissions cuts that varied (see Box 21.7). This achieved at least part of the objectives of the European Union, but it was soon seen to be wholly inadequate in terms of the projected scale of the global warming problem. In return, the European Union accepted the US proposal for the Kyoto mechanisms and has since become their enthusiastic champion. When the Bush administration renounced the Kyoto Protocol in 2001, declaring adherence impossibly damaging to the US economy, much of the burden of ensuring that Kyoto eventually entered into force fell upon the EU and tested the diplomatic capabilities of this new type of international actor and its component member states. The EU also pioneered the world's first international emissions trading system, both to achieve the EU's Kyoto target of an 8 per cent reduction in

emissions by 2012 and to encourage other countries to join the scheme.

The climate regime has been afflicted by the 'free rider' problem. If some countries join together and agree to make cuts that are costly, then others who do not can enjoy the environmental benefits of such action without paying. Thus, proceeding without the USA has been very difficult, not only because it produces around one-quarter of global carbon dioxide emissions, but also because its failure to be involved affects the willingness of others to participate, and particularly the fast-developing economies of the South.

In 2007, at the Bali CoP, the problem of US participation was addressed by a 'road map' in which parallel negotiations were set up on the future of the Convention and the Protocol, with the USA absent from the latter. The intention was to achieve a new agreement by the 2009 Copenhagen CoP, and the EU and other developed countries made pledges of future emissions reductions. Hopes were raised by the arrival of President Obama and his commitment to climate legislation in the USA, although not to the Kyoto Protocol. Developing countries continued to demand the retention of Kyoto and substantial financial aid to assist them with mitigation and adaptation, while China and India offered more efficient use of fossil fuels but not actual reductions in their projected emissions. No new binding climate treaty was agreed. Instead, the Conference noted the Copenhagen Accord, agreed at the last minute by the USA and the large developing countries. The Accord recognizes the need to hold mean temperature increases below 2° C. It does not represent an extension of Kyoto, although its Parties agree to 'strengthen emissions reductions initiated under the Protocol'. The Annex I countries made a series of pledges to cut emissions by 2020: the EU 20 per cent or 30 per cent (conditional), Japan 25 per cent, both against a 1990 baseline: the USA and Canada, 17 per cent against a 2005 baseline. For the developing non-Annex I countries there were voluntary pledges. China and India promised to attempt to reduce the carbon intensity of their rising emissions by 40–45 per cent and 20–25 per cent respectively. Two positive aspects were agreement on a scheme to reduce emissions from the destruction and degradation of forests (REDD) and a related move to set up a large climate fund with contributions from Annex I countries rising to $100 billion per annum. Its purpose would be to assist the developing countries with mitigation of their emissions and adaptation to the effects of climate change. The Copenhagen Accord, which will be reviewed in 2015, sets an agenda for the development of the climate regime. There is probably no more urgent or important task for international cooperation.

Key Points

- Climate change, because of its all-embracing nature and its roots in essential human activities, poses an enormous challenge for international cooperation.

- A limited start was made with the Kyoto regime, but this was undermined by the absence of the USA. Although the 2009 Copenhagen Conference was a disappointment to climate activists, a start was made in involving the major economies of the South in a new regime.

The environment and International Relations theory

The academic study of the international relations of the environment has naturally tried to understand the circumstances under which potentially effective international cooperation can occur. The preceding discussion of climate change shows that this question remains important. Most scholars have used the concept of regime as explained in Chapter 18. Note, for instance, how the defining characteristics of regimes—principles, norms, **rules** and **decision-making procedures**—can be applied to the environmental cases mentioned in this chapter (see also Ch. 9). Those who try to explain the record of environmental regimes tend to adopt a liberal institutionalist stance, stressing as a key motivating factor the joint gains arising from cooperative solutions to the problem of providing public goods such as a clean atmosphere (see Chs and 7). One important addition to the regime literature, made by scholars of environmental politics, reflects the importance of scientific knowledge and the roles of NGOs in this area. Whereas orthodox regime approaches assume that behaviour is based on the pursuit of power or interest, students of international environmental cooperation have noted the independent role played by changes in knowledge (particularly scientific understanding). This cognitive approach is reflected in studies of the ways in which transnationally organized groups of scientists and policy-makers—often referred to as **epistemic communities**—have influenced the development of environmental regimes (see Ch. 9).

Liberal institutionalist analysis of regime creation may still be the predominant IR approach to global environmental change, but it is not the only one. It makes the important, but often unspoken, assumption that the problem to be solved is how to obtain global governance in a fragmented system of sovereign states. Marxist and Gramscian writers would reject this formulation (see Ch. 8). For them, the **state system** is part of the problem rather than the solution, and the proper object of study is the way in which global **capitalism** reproduces relationships that are profoundly damaging to the environment. The global spread of neo-liberal policies accelerates those features of globalization—consumerism, the relocation of production to the South, and the thoughtless squandering of resources—driving the global ecological crisis (see Ch. 28). Proponents of this view also highlight the incapacity of the state to do anything other than assist such processes. It follows that the international cooperation efforts described here at worst legitimize this state of affairs and at best provide some marginal improvements to the devastation wrought by global capitalism. For example, they would point to how free market concepts are now routinely embedded in discussions of sustainable development and how the WTO rules tend to subordinate attempts to provide environmental regulation of GMOs. This argument is part of a broader debate among political theorists concerning whether the state can ever be 'greened'. The opposing view would be that within any time frame that is relevant to coping with a threat of the immediacy and magnitude of climate change, the state and international cooperation remain the only plausible mechanisms for providing the necessary global governance, and we shall simply have to do the best we can with existing state and international organizational structures.

The other theoretical connection that must be made is to the pre-eminent concern of orthodox IR—**security** (see Ch. 14). This link can be thought of in two ways. First, it is argued that environmental change contributes to the incidence of both internal conflict and even inter-state war, even though the causal connections are complex and involve many factors. It is already evident that desertification and the degradation of other vital resources are intimately bound up with cycles of poverty, destitution, and war in Africa. However, if we consider such predicted consequences of climate change as mass migrations of populations across international boundaries and acute scarcity of water and other resources, the outlines of potential future conflicts come into sharper focus (see Chs 28 and 29).

The link between environmental change and armed conflict is essentially an extension of traditional thinking about security, defined in terms of collective violence and attacks upon the state. A more intriguing question is whether we should now redefine the idea of security to encompass environmental threats as well as those stemming from **terrorism** and war (see Ch. 14). As the public becomes more sharply aware of the full magnitude of the climate problem, political discourse begins to 'securitize' the environment, that is, to characterize the environment as a security problem. Because governments usually prioritize security matters, people wishing to mobilize political attention and resources, and encourage potentially painful societal adaptation, will be tempted to stretch traditional definitions of security.

Key Points

- The environment has been a growth area for IR scholars interested in identifying the conditions under which effective international cooperation can emerge.

- Scholars differ in the importance that they attach to various kinds of explanatory factors in their analyses of international environmental regime-building activities—crude calculations of the power and interests of key actors such as states, cognitive factors such as shared scientific knowledge, the impact of non-governmental actors, and even the extent to which the system of states is itself part of the problem.

- IR scholars are also interested in the extent to which the environment in general and particular environmental problems are now being seen as security issues in academic, political, and popular discourse, and whether this securitization of the environment is something to be welcomed.

Conclusion

This chapter has shown, briefly, how environmental issues have moved from the margins to an increasingly central place on the international agenda. Climate change is now widely perceived to be at least the equal of any other issue and arguably the most important faced by humankind. The rise to prominence of environmental issues is intimately associated with globalization due to the strain that this places on the earth's carrying capacity in terms consumption levels, resource depletion, and rising greenhouse gas emissions. Globalization has also facilitated the growth

of transnational green politics and interventions by NGOs to raise public awareness, influence international conferences, and even monitor the implementation of agreements by states.

At every stage, two distinctive aspects of international environmental politics have played a central role. The first is the complex relationship between scientific understanding of the biosphere, politics, and policy, as exemplified by the interplay between the IPCC and the actions of governments building the climate regime. The second is the connection between environment and development, which has been expressed in the shifting meanings given to the concept of sustainable development and whose acknowledgement has been a precondition for international action on a whole range of environmental issues. Nowhere is this more evident than in debates about the future direction of the climate regime.

The international response to environmental change has been in the form of attempts to arrange global environmental governance through extensive cooperation between governments. This chapter has attempted to provide some insight into the range and functions of such regime-creating activities, which provide a basis upon which the international community is attempting to grapple with the climate problem. The academic community has generally followed this enterprise by concentrating upon the question of how regimes may be formed and sustained. More critical theorists will take a different view of the meaning of international cooperation (see Chs 8 and 10). Furthermore, the challenges posed to international theory by the global environmental predicament will undoubtedly involve the need to think through the connections between security, climate change, and globalization.

Questions

1 What are the possible connections, both negative and positive, between globalization and environmental change?
2 Why did environmental issues appear on the international agenda and what were the key turning points?
3 Summarize the consequences of the 1972 UNCHE and the 1992 UNCED.
4 How would you interpret the meaning of sustainable development?
5 How can regime concepts be applied to the study of international environmental cooperation (also see Ch. 18)?
6 Can international trade and environmental protection ever be compatible?
7 Why did the framework convention/control protocol prove useful in the cases of stratospheric ozone depletion and climate change?
8 Analyse the development implications of three of the regimes mentioned in the chapter.
9 How does the 'tragedy of the commons' analogy help to illustrate the need for governance of the global commons?
10 Describe the 'free rider' problem in relation to the climate change regime.
11 Can 'common but differentiated responsibilities' continue to be relevant to the future climate change regime?
12 Consider the possible security implications of the climate predictions made by IPCC.

Further Reading

Barnett, J. (2001), *The Meaning of Environmental Security: Ecological Politics and Policy in the New Security Era* (London: Zed Books). This lively and critical book is for readers who wish to explore the growing connections between environmental and security issues.

Barry, J., and Eckersley, R. (eds) (2005), *The State and the Global Ecological Crisis* (Cambridge, MA: MIT Press). A provocative set of essays on the continuing relevance of the state, long forsaken by green activists, but still the fundamental unit of global environmental governance.

Birnie, P., and Boyle, A. (2002), *International Law and the Environment* (Oxford: Oxford University Press). An invaluable source of detailed information on formal aspects of international environmental cooperation.

Brenton, T. (1994), *The Greening of Machiavelli: The Evolution of International Environmental Politics* (London: Earthscan). A diplomatic participant's account of the international politics of the environment up to and including the Rio Earth Summit.

Dauvergne, P. (ed.) (2005), *Handbook of Global Environmental Politics* (Cheltenham: Edward Elgar). This very extensive collection of 30 essays covering states' governance and security, capitalism, trade and corporations, civil societies, knowledge, and ethics will provide the reader with a more 'advanced' view of current concerns and controversies in the field.

de Sombre, B. (2006), *Global Environmental Institutions* (Abingdon: Routledge). Provides a concise introduction within a series on global governance.

Elliott, L. (2004), *The Global Politics of the Environment* (Basingstoke: Palgrave). This comprehensive and up-to-date text provides detailed and wide-ranging coverage of the field and of the key international agreements.

Lipschutz, R. D. (2004), *Global Environmental Politics: Power Perspectives and Practice* (Washington, DC: CQ Press). Makes innovative and critical connections between global environmental politics and a broad array of relevant political thought and practice.

O'Neill, K. (2009) *The Environment and International Relations* (Cambridge: Cambridge University Press). An excellent and comprehensive review of the theoretical literature in the field.

Paterson, M. (2001), *Understanding Global Environmental Politics: Domination, Accumulation, Resistance* (Basingstoke: Palgrave). As the title suggests, this book provides an alternative critical view of global environmental politics, investigating such problems as the political economy of car use.

Vogler, J. (2000), *The Global Commons: Environmental and Technological Governance* (Chichester: John Wiley). Uses regime analysis to compare and account for the various international arrangements for the ocean, Antarctic, space, and atmospheric commons.

Online Resource Centre

 Visit the Online Resource Centre that accompanies this book to access more learning resources on this chapter topic at www.oxfordtextbooks.co.uk/orc/baylis5e/

Chapter 22

Terrorism and globalization

JAMES D. KIRAS

Reader's Guide

Globalization has contributed to the growth of terrorism from a regional phenomenon into a global one. Precisely how it has contributed, however, is hard to determine. The difficulty lies in the complex nature of terrorism and disagreements on what constitutes globalization. Global terrorism has been explained in cultural, economic, and religious terms linked to globalization. Such terms are necessary, but ultimately are not sufficient, to explain the relationship. Technology associated with globalization has enabled terrorist groups to conduct operations that are deadlier, more distributed, and more difficult to combat than they were in the past. Technological advantage, however, is not one-sided, and states can use technology to diminish the global impact of terrorism.

Introduction

The relationship between **terrorism** and globalization is difficult to describe accurately. Each phenomenon is complicated in its own right and defies simple characterization. It is inaccurate to suggest that globalization is responsible for terrorism, but technologies associated with globalization have been exploited by terrorists. In particular, technologies have improved the ability of terrorist groups to work together, share information, and reach out to previously unavailable audiences. Technology, however, cannot change the character of the terrorist message or the nature of the struggle. Terrorism is a weapon of the weak conducted by a minority of individuals who promote an extremist ideology—it often fails to create political change. The global community is not powerless in the face of such violence. In order to succeed, the global community must utilize the resources at its disposal collaboratively to diminish support for terrorism and demonstrate the illegitimacy of terrorist messages and aspirations.

Definitions

Terrorism and globalization have at least one thing in common—both are complex phenomena open to subjective interpretation. Definitions of terrorism vary widely, but they start from a common point of departure. Terrorism is characterized, first and foremost, by the use of violence. This tactic of violence takes many forms and often indiscriminately targets non-combatants. The purpose for which violence is used, and its root causes, is where most of the disagreements about terrorism begin. Historically, the term 'terrorism' described state violence against citizens during the French Revolution. Over the past half-century, however, terrorism has come to mean the use of violence by small groups to achieve political change. Terrorism differs from criminal violence in its degree of political legitimacy. Those sympathetic to terrorist causes suggest that violence is the only remaining option that can draw attention to the plight of the aggrieved. Such causes have included ideological, ethnic, and religious exclusion or persecution.

Defining terrorism can be difficult as groups often espouse multiple grievances and compete with one another for resources and support. In addition, the relative importance of these grievances within groups can change over time. Those targeted by terrorists are less inclined to see any justification, much less legitimacy, behind attacks that are designed to spread fear by killing and maiming civilians. As a result, the term 'terrorist' has a pejorative value that is useful in delegitimizing those who commit such acts.

Reaching consensus on what constitutes terrorism is difficult. The legitimacy of terrorist means and methods is the foremost reason for disagreement. Some view terrorist acts as legitimate only if they meet the criteria associated with the 'just war' tradition. These criteria, which apply to all applications of force, have been expanded to include a just cause, proportional use of violence, and the use of force as a last resort. Realists suggest that the political violence used by terrorist groups is illegitimate on the basis that states alone have a monopoly on the legitimate use of physical force.

Yet even with the use of violence by states, there is disagreement on what constitutes the legitimate application of armed force. For example, during the 1980s

Box 22.1 Types of terrorist groups

Audrey Kurth Cronin has outlined different types of terrorist groups and their historical importance in the following way:

'There are four types of terrorist organizations currently operating around the world, categorized mainly by their source of motivation: left-wing terrorists, right-wing terrorists, ethnonationalist/separatist terrorists, and religious or "sacred" terrorists. All four types have enjoyed periods of relative prominence in the modern era, with left-wing terrorism intertwined with the Communist movement, right-wing terrorism drawing its inspiration from Fascism, and the bulk of ethnonationalist/separatist terrorism accompanying the wave of decolonization especially in the immediate post-World War II years. Currently, "sacred" terrorism is becoming more significant ... Of course, these categories are not perfect, as many groups have a mix of motivating ideologies some ethnonationalist groups, for example, have religious characteristics or agendas—but usually one ideology or motivation dominates.'

(Cronin 2002/3: 39)

Box 22.2 Legitimacy

Martha Crenshaw provides an analytic, albeit subjective approach to determine the legitimacy of terrorist acts of violence:

'The value of the normative approach (to terrorism) is that it confronts squarely a critical problem in the analysis of terrorism, and indeed any form of political violence: the issue of legitimacy. Terrorists of the left deny the legitimacy of the state and claim that the use of violence against it is morally justified. Terrorists of the right deny the legitimacy of the opposition and hold that the violence in the service of order is sanctioned by the values of the status quo ... the need for scholarly objectivity and abstraction does not excuse use from the obligation to judge the morality of the use of force, whether by the state or against.'

She adds that morality can be judged in two ways:

'morality of the ends and the morality of the means. First, are the goals of the terrorists democratic or nondemocratic? That is, is their aim to create or perpetuate a regime of privilege and inequality, to deny liberty to other people, or to further the ends of justice, freedom, and equality ... Terrorism must not, as the terrorists can foresee, result in *worse* injustice than the condition the terrorists oppose ... The morality of the means of terrorism is also open to judgment. The targets of terrorism are morally significant; witness the difference between material objects and human casualties.'

(Crenshaw 1983: 2–4)

Libya sponsored terrorist acts as an indirect method of attacking the USA, France, and the United Kingdom. Those states, in turn, condemned Libyan sponsorship as contravening international norms and responded with sanctions, international court cases, and occasional uses of force. Disagreement associated with the invasion of Iraq in 2003, led by the USA, relates to interpretations over whether or not the conditions for 'just war' were met prior to commencement of military operations. Some suggest that the conditions were not met, and that actions by the coalition should be considered as an 'act of terrorism' conducted by states. Leaders in the USA and the United Kingdom dismiss the charge on the basis that a greater evil was removed. Violating international norms in the pursuit of terrorists runs the risk of playing into perceptions that the state itself is a terrorist threat. Critics suggest that US policy towards terrorist detainees and 'extraordinary renditions' damages the nation's credibility as a global champion for individual rights and freedoms.

As with other forms of irregular warfare, terrorism is designed to achieve political change for the purposes of obtaining power in order to right a perceived wrong. Terrorism, however, is the weakest form of irregular warfare with which to alter the political landscape. The reason for this weakness is that terrorist groups rarely possess the broader support of the population that characterizes insurgency and revolution. Terrorist groups often lack broader support for their objectives because their goals for change are based on radical ideas that do not have widespread appeal. In order to influence change, terrorists must provoke drastic responses that act as a catalyst for change or weaken their opponent's moral resolve. In a few cases, terrorist acts have achieved relatively rapid change. The bombings in Madrid in 2004, for example, influenced the outcome of elections in Spain in a dramatic fashion, and anecdotal evidence suggests that the attack was designed with just such a purpose in mind. Many terrorist leaders hope that their actions will lead to disproportionate reactions by a state that in turn disaffect public or international opinion and increase support for their cause. Some suggest, for example, that Al Qaeda goaded the USA into invading and 'occupying' Iraq, which has bolstered terrorist recruiting. Terrorist campaigns, however, often take years or decades to achieve meaningful results, and the amount and nature of force used can be problematic. Terrorist groups risk fading into obscurity if they do not cow the public or conduct newsworthy attacks. However, as the recent violence in Iraq suggests, attacks by terrorists that are so horrific, such as publicized beheadings, puts support for terrorist causes at risk. Therefore terrorism is defined here as 'the use of violence by sub-state groups to inspire fear, by attacking civilians and/or symbolic targets, for purposes such as drawing widespread attention to a grievance, provoking a severe response, or wearing down their opponent's moral resolve, to effect political change'.

As with definitions of terrorism, there is general agreement on at least one aspect of globalization. Technologies allow the transfer of goods, services, and information almost anywhere quickly and efficiently. In the case of information, the transfer can be secure and is nearly instantaneous. The extent of social, cultural, and political change brought on by globalization, including increasing interconnectedness and homogeneity in the international system, remain the subject of much disagreement and debate, as other chapters in this volume have outlined. These disagreements, in turn, influence discussion of the extent to which globalization has contributed to the rise of modern terrorism. There is little doubt that the technologies associated with globalization have been used to improve the effectiveness and reach of terrorist groups. The relationship between globalization and terrorism is best understood as the next step in the evolution of political violence since terrorism became a transnational phenomenon in the 1960s. In order to understand the changes perceived in terrorism globally, it is useful to understand the evolution of terrorism from a transnational to a global phenomenon.

Key Points

- Agreement on what constitutes terrorism continues to be difficult, given the range of potential acts involving violence.
- Terrorism, or acts of violence by sub-state groups, has been separated from criminal acts on the basis of the purpose for which violence is applied, namely political change.

- Terrorist groups succeed when their motivations or grievances are perceived to be legitimate by a wider audience. Disproportionate or heavy-handed responses by states to acts of terrorism serve to legitimize terrorist groups.
- The definition of globalization, as with terrorism, is open to subjective interpretation, but the technologies associated with globalization have improved terrorist capabilities.

Terrorism: from transnational to global phenomenon (1968–2001)

Historically, terrorists have used readily available means to permit small numbers of individuals to spread fear as widely as possible. In the late nineteenth and early twentieth centuries, anarchists relied upon revolvers and dynamite. Yet terrorists and acts of terrorism rarely had an impact beyond national borders. Three factors led to the birth of transnational terrorism in 1968: the expansion of commercial air travel; the availability of televised news coverage; and broad political and ideological interests among extremists that intersected around a common cause. As a result, terrorism grew from a local to a transnational threat. Air travel gave terrorists unprecedented mobility. For example, the Japanese Red Army trained in one country and attacked in another, such as the 1972 Lod Airport massacre in Israel. Air travel appealed to terrorists for other reasons. Airport security measures, including passport control, were almost non-existent when terrorists began hijacking airlines. These **skyjackings** suited terrorist purposes well. Hijacked airlines offered a degree of mobility, and therefore security, for the terrorists involved. States also acquiesced to terrorist demands, which encouraged further incidents. The success of this tactic spurred other terrorist groups, as well as criminals and political refugees, to follow suit. As a result, incidents of hijacking skyrocketed from five in 1966 to 94 in 1969. Shared political ideologies stimulated cooperation and limited exchanges between groups as diverse as the Irish Republican Army (IRA) and the Basque separatist Euzkadi Ta Askatasuna (ETA). Besides sharing techniques and technical experience, groups demanded the release of imprisoned 'fellow revolutionaries' in different countries, giving the impression of a coordinated global terrorist network. The reality was that groups formed relationships of convenience, based around weapons, capabilities, and money, to advance local political objectives.

Televised news coverage also played a role in expanding the audience who could witness the theatre of terrorism in their own homes. Individuals who had never heard of 'the plight of the Palestinians' became notionally aware of the issue after incidents such as the live coverage of the hostage taking conducted by Black September during the 1972 Munich Olympics. Although media coverage was termed the oxygen that sustains terrorism, terrorists discovered that reporters and audiences lost interest in repeat performances over time. In order to sustain viewer interest and compete for coverage, terrorist groups undertook increasingly spectacular attacks, such as the seizure of Organization of Petroleum Exporting Countries (OPEC) delegates by 'Carlos the Jackal' in Austria in December 1975. Terrorism experts speculated that terrorist leaders understood that horrific, mass casualty attacks might cross a threshold of violence. This may explain why few terrorist groups attempted to acquire or use weapons of mass destruction (WMD), including nuclear, chemical, and biological weapons.

The Iranian 'Islamic Revolution' of 1979 was a watershed event in transnational terrorism. Although Israeli interests remained primary targets for attack, due to continued sympathy for the Palestinian cause, a number of groups began to target citizens and other symbols of the USA. The decade of terrorism (1980–90) included incidents such as suicide bombings (Lebanon, 1983) and hijackings (TWA Flight 847, 1985). During this decade three disturbing trends emerged: fewer attacks that were more deadly and indiscriminate; the increasing sophistication of attacks; and a greater willingness to perform suicide attacks.

Transnational Marxist–Leninist groups discovered that their source of support disappeared at the end of the cold war. In addition, state law enforcement and paramilitary forces were increasingly effective in combating terrorism. Other terrorist groups discovered that transnational attacks were counter-productive in achieving local aims. For example, ETA and the IRA sought negotiations but still used terrorist attacks as

a bargaining ploy and to remain visible domestically. Although Marxist–Leninist, transnational terrorism was decreasing in scale and intensity, militant Islamic terrorism, symbolized by the group Al Qaeda and enabled by globalization, was growing into a global phenomenon.

Key Points

- The majority of transnational terrorist attacks from 1979 onwards targeted American citizens and symbols.
- Trends in terrorism since 1968 include greater casualties, increasing sophistication, and suicide attacks.
- Transnational Marxist-Leninist groups have replaced by global militant Islamic terrorist groups.

Terrorism: the impact of globalization

Al Qaeda, or 'The Base', received global recognition as a result of its attacks conducted in New York and Washington on 11 September 2001. But what exactly is Al Qaeda? Is it a global terrorist group that threatens Western civilization and values, a sub-state financial and resource provider to like-minded terrorist groups, or merely a group acting as the purveyors of an extremist set of beliefs that justifies political violence to fulfil militant Islamic myths? Experts continue to debate what Al Qaeda is, what it represents, and the actual threat that it poses. Part of the reason for the disagreement stems from the fact that Al Qaeda, as the standard-bearer for militant Islam, has evolved considerably since the invasion of Afghanistan. Immediately after **9/11**, Al Qaeda was depicted as the centre of a global nexus of terrorism connected to almost all terrorist groups. More recently, however, Al Qaeda has appeared less as a group and more as a global movement that markets and exploits its own form of militant Islam in a loose network of 'franchised' cells and groups. Regardless of how one views Al Qaeda, one cannot dispute the influence and appeal of its message across national boundaries. Efforts to explain the vitality of global terrorism in general—and Al Qaeda in particular—focus on three areas linked to aspects of globalization: culture, economics, and religion.

Cultural explanations

Culture is one way to explain why militant Islam's call for armed struggle has been successful in underdeveloped

countries. In particular, violence is the only method to preserve traditions and values against a cultural tsunami of Western products and materialism. Once sought after as an entry method to economic prosperity, Western secular, materialist values are increasingly rejected by those seeking to regain or preserve their own unique cultural identity. The social changes associated with globalization and the spread of free market capitalism appear to overwhelm the identity or values of groups who perceive themselves as the losers in the new international system. In an attempt to preserve their threatened identity and values, groups actively distinguish themselves from despised 'others'. At the local level, this cultural friction may translate into conflicts divided along religious or ethnic lines to safeguard identity.

According to one explanation, however, the number of distinct civilizations is limited globally. They include Western, Confucian, Japanese, Islamic, Hindu, Slavic-Orthodox, and Latin American (Huntington 1993: 25). Geography and relative cultural stability limit abrasion between some of the civilizations. Where individuals perceive their own civilization to be weak, insecure, or stagnant, and interaction is high between weak and strong civilizations, conflict may be inevitable. Samuel Huntington suggests that a major fault-line exists between the liberal Western civilization and an Islamic one, 'humiliated and resentful of the West's military presence in the Persian Gulf, the West's overwhelming military dominance, and . . . [unable] to shape their own destiny' (1993: 32).

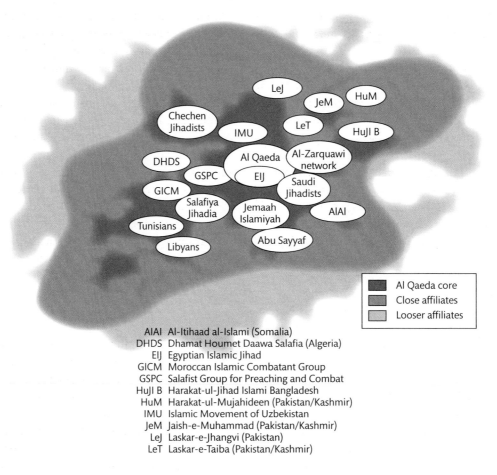

AIAI Al-Itihaad al-Islami (Somalia)
DHDS Dhamat Houmet Daawa Salafia (Algeria)
EIJ Egyptian Islamic Jihad
GICM Moroccan Islamic Combatant Group
GSPC Salafist Group for Preaching and Combat
HuJI B Harakat-ul-Jihad Islami Bangladesh
HuM Harakat-ul-Mujahideen (Pakistan/Kashmir)
IMU Islamic Movement of Uzbekistan
JeM Jaish-e-Muhammad (Pakistan/Kashmir)
LeJ Laskar-e-Jhangvi (Pakistan)
LeT Laskar-e-Taiba (Pakistan/Kashmir)

Figure 22. 1 The Terrorist Nebula and Regional Clusters
Derived from *Beyond al-Qaeda: Part 1, The Global Jihadist Movement,* p. 80

Critics of Huntington suggest, among other things, that he assumes a degree of homogeneity within the Islamic world that simply does not exist (also see Ch. 25). Theologically and socially, the Islamic 'civilization' contains a number of deep fault-lines that impede the cooperation required to challenge the West. The extremely bloody sectarian violence between Sunni and Shi'a in Iraq is only one example of these very real fissures. Militant Islamic calls to kill non-combatants and fellow Muslims represent another internal fault-line. Non-believers fall into the categories of infidels (those of different religion) and apostates (those Muslims who do not share their interpretation of the Koran). As a result, Osama bin Laden's unequivocal sanction to Abu Musab al-Zarqawi to kill Muslim Shi'a in Iraq in 2005 calls into question the morality of the means, and therefore the legitimacy of bin Laden and militant Islam as the champions of Muslim values among the wider and moderate Islamic community.

Economic explanations

Not everyone agrees that defence of culture or identity is the primary motivation for globalized terrorist violence. Others see economic aspects as the crucial motivating factor in the use of violence to effect political change. Although globalization provides access to a world market for goods and services, the net result has also been perceived as a form of Western economic imperialism. The USA and the post-industrial states of Western Europe form the global North or economic 'core' that dominates international economic institutions such as the World Bank, sets exchange rates, and determines fiscal policies. The actions and policies can be unfavourable to the underdeveloped countries, or global South, that comprise the periphery or gap. Political decisions by the leaders of underdeveloped countries to deregulate or privatize industries to be competitive globally may lead to significant social and economic upheaval. The citizenry may shift loyalties to illegal activities such as terrorism if the state breaks its social contract with them (Junaid 2005: 143–4).

Wealth is also linked to personal security and violence. With little possible opportunity to obtain wealth locally, individuals will leave to pursue opportunities elsewhere. The result is emigration and/or the rapid growth of burgeoning urban centres that act as regional hubs for the flow of global resources. Movement, however, is no guarantee that individual aspirations will be realized. In that case, individuals may turn to violence for criminal (i.e. personal gain) or political (i.e. to change the existing political system through insurgency or terrorism) reasons. Paradoxically, rising standards of living and greater access to educational opportunities associated with globalization may lead to increased expectations. If those expectations are unrealized, individuals can turn to extreme political views and action against 'the system' that denies them the opportunity to realize their ambitions. A prominent study suggests that a sense of alienation and lack of opportunity among some Muslim males is a contributing factor to their decision to turn to violence globally (Sageman 2004: 95–6).

Other views offer a broader explanation. In particular, the writings of revolutionary Franz Fanon provide insights in the use of political violence to right economic wrongs (Onwudiwe 2001: 52–6). In the 1960s, Fanon suggested that the end of colonialism would not end conflict between the West and the oppressed. This struggle would be replaced by another until the economic and power imbalances were removed (Fanon 1990: 74). Terrorist violence is motivated by inequalities of the global economy. Therefore terrorist attacks against the World Trade Center in 1993 and 2001 were not reactions against the policies of the USA *per se*, but rather a blow against an icon of global capitalism. Statements by fringe groups, including neo-Nazis, anarchists, and the 'New, New Left', are additional evidence that globalization might be a stimulus for political violence (Rabasa, Chalk, *et al.* 2006: 86–93).

The explanation that recent terrorist violence is a reaction to economic globalization is flawed for a number of reasons. These reasons include the personal wealth and social upbringing of a number of members of global terrorist groups, as well as trends in regional patterns of terrorist recruitment. Many former leaders and members of transnational terrorist groups, including the German Red Army Faction and the Italian Red Brigades, came from respectable families. The same holds true for a number of modern-day anti-globalization anarchists.

Within militant Islamic groups, most of their leaders and senior operatives attended graduate schools around the globe in fields as diverse as engineering and theology, and were neither poor nor downtrodden (Sageman 2004: 73–4).

The links between terrorism and poverty also vary considerably between regions. Many militant Islamic terrorists in Europe have employment rates and salaries that are close to EU averages for their age group (Bakker 2006: 41, 52). One might expect that the poorest region globally would account for a high percentage of terrorists, but this is not the case. Despite conditions that favour the outbreak of terrorist violence in sub-Saharan Africa against economic imperialism and global capitalism, the region has not proved a breeding ground for terrorism.

Religion and 'new' terrorism

In the decade prior to 9/11, a number of scholars and experts perceived that fundamental changes were taking place in the character of terrorism. The use of violence for political purposes, to change state ideology or the representation of ethnic minority groups, had failed in its purpose and a new trend was emerging. **Postmodern** or **'new' terrorism** was conducted for different reasons altogether. Motivated by promises of rewards in the afterlife, some terrorists are driven by religious reasons to kill as many of the non-believers and unfaithful as possible (Laqueur 1996: 32–3). Although suicide tactics had been observed in Lebanon as early as 1983, militant Islam had previously been viewed as a **state-sponsored**, regional phenomenon (Wright 1986: 19–21).

New terrorism, which some authors use to explain the global **jihad**, is seen as a reaction to the perceived oppression of Muslims worldwide and the spiritual bankruptcy of the West. As globalization spreads and societies become increasingly interconnected, Muslims have a choice: accept Western beliefs to better integrate or preserve their spiritual purity by rebelling. Believers in the global *jihad* view the rulers of 'Islamic' countries such as Pakistan, Saudi Arabia, or Iraq as apostates who have compromised their values in the pursuit and maintenance of secular, state-based power. The only possible response is to fight against such influences through *jihad*. *Jihad* is understood by most Islamic scholars and imams to mean the internal struggle for purity spiritually, although it has also been interpreted historically as a method to establish the basis for just war. Extremists who espouse militant Islam, including Osama bin Laden and Ayman al-Zawahiri, understand *jihad* in a different way. For the *jihadi* terrorist, there can be no compromise with either infidels or apostates.

The difference in value structures between secular and religious terrorists makes the responses to the latter difficult. Religious terrorists will kill themselves and others to secure rewards in the afterlife. Differences in value structures make the deterrence of religious terrorism difficult if not impossible, as secular states cannot credibly threaten materially that which terrorists value spiritually. Secular terrorism has had as its goal the pursuit of power in order to correct flaws within society but retain the overarching system. Religious terrorists, in contrast, do not seek to modify but rather replace the normative structure of society (Cronin 2002/3: 41).

The use of religion, as a reaction to and an explanation for the phenomenon of global terrorism, contains some of the same incongruities as those focused on cultural and economic aspects. For Western observers, religious reasons appear to explain how individual terrorists are convinced to take their own lives and kill others. Personal motivations can include promises of financial rewards for family members, achieving fame within a community, taking revenge for some grievance, or simply achieving a form of self-actualizing. Yet few religious terrorist leaders, planners, and coordinators martyr themselves. Religion provides terrorist groups with a crucial advantage: the mandate and sanction of the divine to commit otherwise illegal or immoral acts. There is a substantial difference between religious motivation as the single driving factor for individuals to commit acts of terrorism and the ultimate purpose for which violence is being used. Scholars disagree on the ultimate political purpose of religiously inspired suicide violence. Such purposes can include competing with other terrorist groups for popular support in a process of 'outbidding' (Bloom 2005: 77–9) or for self-determination, to convince foreign occupiers to withdraw their forces (Pape 2005: 45–6). A common theme among *jihadi* statements is another political purpose: overthrowing apostate regimes and assuming political power. Political power, in turn, is necessary to impose the militant Islamic form of Sharia law within a state and restore the just and pure society of the caliphate.

Key Points

- Cultural, economic, and religious aspects provide necessary, but insufficient, explanations for globalized terrorist violence individually.

- The current wave of terrorist violence uses religion as a motivator and to provide the justification to kill non-combatants.

- The ultimate purpose for modern militant Islamic violence is obtaining political power in order to conduct political, social, economic, and religious reform according to Sharia law.

Globalization, technology, and terrorism

Few challenge the point that terrorism has become much more pervasive worldwide due to the processes and technologies of globalization. The technological advances associated with globalization have improved the capabilities of terrorist groups to plan and conduct operations with far more devastation and coordination than their predecessors could have imagined. In particular, technologies have improved the capability of groups and cells in the following areas: proselytizing, coordination, security, mobility, and lethality.

Proselytizing

Terrorist groups have traditionally sought sympathy and support within national boundaries or in neighbouring countries as a means to sustain their efforts. Sustaining terrorist causes has traditionally been more difficult as terrorist messages, goals, and grievances tend to be extreme, and therefore less appealing, than those of insurgents. For example, land reform, government corruption, or foreign occupation motivates larger numbers of individuals to support or join insurgencies, whereas the radical political ideology espoused by groups such as the Japanese Red Army and the Weather Underground had little appeal in largely prosperous and stable democratic societies. States traditionally have had an advantage in their ability to control information flows and use their resources to win the battle of hearts and minds against terrorist groups. Terrorist leaders understand how the Internet has changed this dynamic: 'we are in a battle, and that more than half of this battle is taking place in the battlefield of the media. And that we are in a media battle in a race for the hearts and minds of our Umma' (Office of the Director of National Intelligence 2005: 10).

The continued expansion of the number of Internet service providers, especially in states with relaxed or ambivalent content policies or laws, combined with capable and cheap computers, software, peripherals, and wireless technologies, has empowered individuals and groups with the ability to post tracts on or send messages throughout the World Wide Web. One form of empowerment is the virtual presence that individuals have. Although prominent *jihadi* terrorists' physical presence can be removed through imprisonment or death, their virtual presence and influence is immortalized on the World Wide Web, as the case of Mustafa Setmariam Nasar suggests.

Another form of empowerment for terrorist groups brought on by globalization is the volume, range, and sophistication of propaganda materials. Terrorist groups were once limited to mimeographed manifestos and typed communiqués. Terrorist supporters and sympathizers now build their own websites. An early example was a website sympathetic to the Tupac Amaru Revolutionary Movement. This website posted the group's communiqués and videos during the seizure of the Japanese embassy in Lima in 1997. Webmasters sympathetic to terrorist groups also control the content and connotation of the material posted on their websites. The website of the Liberation Tigers of Tamil Eelam, for example, posts items that cast the group as an internationally 'accepted' organization committed to conflict resolution. Messages, files, and polemics can be dispatched to almost anywhere on the globe via the Internet or text messaging almost instantaneously.

For the purposes of spreading messages to the widest possible audience for those without Internet or text-messaging capabilities, and where speed of communication is not a requirement or a possibility for security reasons,

---

Case Study 1 Three generations of militant Islamic terrorists

The first generation of militant Islamic terrorists closely affiliated with Al Qaeda shared a number of traits. Some fought in Afghanistan against the Soviet Union and aligned with Osama bin Laden over disagreements in 1994 about who to fight next. Bin Laden believed it was necessary to fight the 'far' enemy, the USA (and by extension, the West) which was responsible for a number of perceived injustices against Islam. Others advocated the overthrow of 'near' enemies who ruled over secular Islamic states. To fight the far enemy, bin Laden moved to Afghanistan in 1998 and established numerous training camps, research facilities, and a support bureaucracy. One of those who migrated to Afghanistan at this time was Mustafa Setmariam Nasar.

Nasar is better known as 'Abu Musab al-Suri' or 'The Syrian'. Like many first-generation jihadists, he played a role in the fight against the Soviets in Afghanistan. He also supported local jihadist groups in Spain, Algeria, and elsewhere. Prior to 9/11, Nasar ran a training camp in Afghanistan tied to Bin Laden. Like his peers, Nasar is well educated and this is apparent in his writings. His

works are numerous and include various interviews, pamphlets, as well as a massive 1,600-page tract and detailed training manual entitled 'Global Islamic Resistance Call'. In addition, Nasar videotaped a number of his lectures based upon the manual. What sets Nasar apart from his other first-generation colleagues is his ability to look critically at Al Qaeda's successes and failures. In particular, Nasar foresaw the effectiveness of US and partner nation efforts against the traditional hierarchical organization of Al Qaeda, and decried the 'Tora Bora mentality' of fighting fixed battles against forces that dominate air and space. Nasar argued to move to something more secure, elusive, and difficult to defeat: a system of jihad comprising 'a method of secret guerrilla war consisting of unconnected cells, numerous and different types of cells' rather than a first-generation organization (or *tanzim*) (Lia 2008: 315). He transferred his knowledge and skills to next-generation militant Islamic terrorists virtually. Both the manual and the videos are available online despite Nasar's capture in Pakistan in November 2005, realizing part of his ambition.

Younis Tsouli represents the new generation of militant Islamic terrorism with different skills from his predecessors and the system envisioned by Nasar. Tsouli's identity was unknown to authorities until just before his arrest. The same cannot be said for Tsouli's virtual persona, '*Irhabi* 007' ('Terrorist 007'). Irhabi 007 achieved notoriety in jihadist discussion forums for his technical acumen for hacking websites, circumventing online surveillance techniques, and posting militant Islamic training and propaganda videos. Law enforcement officials suspected that Irhabi 007 was in the USA given his use of websites and servers based there. Cooperation between British and American officials led to Tsouli's eventual discovery and arrest at a flat in West London in late 2005. His reputation in online jihadist circles was built in a year.

terrorists need not rely exclusively on virtual methods. Any computer of modest capabilities can be used by members of terrorist groups and their sympathizers to create propaganda leaflets and posters at very low cost in large quantities. Whereas offset printing machines and photocopiers are difficult to move, a laptop computer and printer can be packed in a suitcase, increasing the mobility of the terrorist cell generating the material and making them more difficult to locate.

Terrorist groups in Chechnya and the Middle East have also made increasing use of video cameras to record the preparations for and results of attacks, including successful roadside bombings and the downing of helicopters. With the right software and a little knowledge, individuals or small groups can download or obtain digital footage and music, and produce videos that appeal to specific groups. Video footage is useful in inspiring potential recruits and seeking donations by support elements within the organization. For example, videos of sniper and other attacks against coalition forces in Iraq, produced by Al-Furquan and As-Sahab, have been distributed by terrorist recruiters. The competition between global news outlets ensures that the images of successful and/or dramatic attacks reach the widest audience possible. These outlets have a ready source of material via sites such as press-release.blogosphere.com. Its front page lists statements and videos (some as large as 300Mb) from groups such as Ansar al-Sunna, the Islamic State of Iraq, and Al-Qaeda Organization in the Islamic Maghreb.

Coordination

During the era of transnational terrorism, groups planned and conducted individual attacks or mounted multiple attacks from a single staging base. The technologies associated with globalization have enabled terrorist cells and groups to mount coordinated attacks in different countries. Indeed, a hallmark of militant Islamic groups is their ability to conduct multiple attacks in different locations. The simultaneous bombings of the US embassies in Kenya and Tanzania in 1998 are one example. Other examples include the synchronized detonation of ten of 13 bombs on packed commuter trains in Madrid in March 2004 and three of the four July 2005 London Underground bombings.

The technologies associated with globalization, including commercially available handheld radios and phones, have allowed terrorist cell members and groups to operate independently at substantial distances from one another and network together. The Global System for Mobile Communications (GSM) standard, for example, ensures that any compliant phone will work anywhere in the world where a GSM network has been established. E-mail and cellphone contact among geographically separated group members allows them to conduct their attacks in separate locations or converge on a specific target area. For example, the 9/11 hijackers utilized cheap and readily available pre-paid phone cards to communicate between cell leaders and senior leadership and, according to at least one press account, coordinated final attack authorization before the jets took off from different locations.

Terrorist groups under pressure from aggressive counter-measures have utilized technologies and other innovations to maintain their activities tactically and strategically. On a tactical level, IRA and Al Qaeda bomb manufacturers have demonstrated the ability to respond rapidly to electronic counter-measures. More recently, press reports suggest that Shi'ite groups within Iraq were able to intercept and download Predator drone video feeds using commercially available software. At the strategic level, Al Qaeda has continued to evolve despite losing its sanctuary and training camps in Afghanistan since December 2001. Instead of a hierarchical organization with fixed training bases, what has developed in its stead is a virtual global militant Islamic 'community of practice' characterized by individuals exchanging information and discussing the best ways to coordinate and conduct attacks. Some Western analysts have labelled the current decentralized version of global terrorism as 'Al Qaeda 2.0', which is neither centrally planned nor controlled. Cells form around individuals sympathetic to militant Islamic goals accessible via webcast or online *jihadi* discussion forums. At present, law enforcement officials believe that there are more than 5,000 active militant Islamic discussion sites along the lines of the now-defunct Muntada al-Ansar al-Islami. The watchword for such violence can be thought of as a variation on the activist motto 'think globally, act locally', which reinforces the perception of militant Islam's global depth, power, and reach.

Security

Terrorist cells without adequate security precautions are vulnerable to discovery and detection. Translations of captured Al Qaeda manuals, for example, demonstrate the high value its writers place on security, including surveillance and counter-surveillance techniques. The technological enablers of globalization assist terrorist cells and leaders in preserving security in a number of ways, including distributing elements in a coordinated network, remaining mobile (see below), and utilizing clandestine and/or encrypted communications.

The security of terrorist organizations has historically been preserved by limiting communication and information exchanges between cells. This ensures that if one cell is compromised, its members only know each other's identities and not those of other cells. Therefore the damage done to the organization is minimized. Security is even more important to clandestine cells operating on their own without central direction. The use of specific codes and ciphers, known only to a few individuals, is one way of preserving the security of an organization. Although codes and ciphers have inevitably been broken, and information obtained through interrogation, such activities take time. During that time, terrorist groups adjust their location and operating methods in an attempt to stay ahead of counter-terrorist forces. Technological advances, including faster processing speeds and software developments, now mean that those sympathetic to terrorist causes can contribute to the cause virtually, through servers located hundreds or thousands of miles away.

Terrorist groups have been able to leverage technological developments designed to shield a user's identity from unauthorized commercial or private exploitation (Gunaratna 2002: 35). Concerns about infringements on civil liberties and privacy during the early years of the Internet led to the development of 64 and 128-bit encryption freeware that is extremely costly and time-consuming to crack. In addition, access to hardware such as cell phones, personal data assistants, and computers can be restricted via the use of passwords. The use of Internet protocol address generators, anonymity protection programs, and rerouted communications, as well as private chat rooms where password-protected or encrypted files can be shared, also provide a degree of security. Within the virtual *jihadist* community, youth sympathetic to the militant Islamic cause, post information in discussion groups on ways to circumvent electronic surveillance through awareness of phishing and mobile phone monitoring techniques and the use of electronic 'dead letters'—saving draft messages in shared third-party email accounts, such as Hotmail, without sending anything that could be intercepted.

Mobility

The reduced size and increased capabilities of personal electronics also give terrorists mobility advantages. Mobility has always been a crucial consideration for terrorists and insurgents alike, given the superior resources that states have been able to bring to bear against them. In open societies that have well-developed infrastructures, terrorists have been able to move rapidly within and between borders, and this complicates efforts to track them. The globalization of commerce has also improved terrorist mobility. The expansion in the volume of air travel and goods that pass through ports has increased exponentially through globalization. Between states, measures have been taken to ease the flow of goods, services, and ideas in a less restrictive fashion to improve efficiency and lower costs. One example is the European Schengen Agreement, in which border security measures between EU member states have been relaxed to speed deliveries. Market demands for efficiencies of supply, manufacture, delivery, and cost have complicated efforts of states to prevent members of terrorist groups from exploiting gaps in security measures designed to deter or prevent illicit activities. Additional mobility also allows terrorist groups to transfer expertise, as the arrest of three members of the IRA suspected of training counterparts in the Fuerzas Armadas Revolucionarias de Colombia (FARC) in Bogota in August 2001 appears to demonstrate.

The use of air travel by terrorists before 9/11 has been well documented. Mohammed Atta, for example, travelled extensively between Egypt, Germany, and the Middle East beforehand. In this respect, the latest generation of terrorists, including Umar Farouk Abdulmutallab, resembles their transnational predecessors in exploiting travel methods for attacks. Terrorist use of transportation need not necessarily be overt in nature, as the volume of goods transported in support of a globalized economy is staggering and difficult to monitor effectively. For example, customs officials cannot inspect all the vehicles or containers passing through border points or ports. To illustrate the scale of the problem, the USA receives 10 million containers per year and one port, Los Angeles, processes the equivalent of 12,000 twenty-foot containers daily. Western government officials fear that terrorist groups will use containers as a convenient and cheap means to ship WMD. Incidents in Italy in 2001 and Israel in 2004 confirm that terrorist groups are aware of the convenience and cheapness of globalized shipping to improve their mobility.

Case study 2 Umar Farouk Abdulmutallab

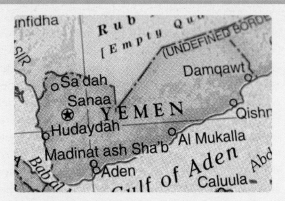

Umar Farouk Abdulmutallab provides the portrait of a globally mobile citizen turned terrorist. He is a 23-year-old Nigerian citizen and the privileged son of a wealthy and successful African banker. Abdulmutallab had every advantage growing up, including schooling at the British International School (Nigeria), University College London, the San'a Institute for the Arabic Language (Yemen), and the University of Wollongong (United Arab Emirates). Despite his material comforts, Abdulmutallab blogged about his sense of loneliness and isolation. His travel put him into contact with Anwar al-Awlaki, a Yemeni imam linked to a number of global terrorists including the Fort Hood gunman, Nidal Malik Hasan. At some point, Abdulmutallab received a specialized two-stage bomb manufactured in Yemen sewn into an undergarment. He tried unsuccessfully to detonate the device on Northwest Flight 253 after purchasing a ticket in Ghana and travelling from Lagos to Amsterdam to Detroit on 25 December 2009.

Lethality

Globalization has undoubtedly had a troubling influence on terrorism, but the one element that concerns counter-terrorism experts and practitioners the most is future catastrophic attacks using WMD. During the transnational era, terrorists could obtain advanced weapons to conduct more lethal attacks, including rudimentary WMD, but they largely did not. Few tried to acquire them and fewer still, including the Weather Underground, threatened their use. The precise reasons why terrorists did not acquire and use such weapons during this era are unclear. Experts speculated, however, that terrorist leaders understood that the more lethal their attacks were, the greater the likelihood that a state or the international community would focus their entire efforts on hunting them down and eradicating them.

Since the end of the cold war, however, some terrorist leaders have expressed both the desire and will to use WMD. Evidence that US troops recovered in Afghanistan in 2001 outlined plans by Al Qaeda to produce and test biological and chemical weapons under a plan code-named *zabadi* (curdled milk). A raid on a suspected Al Qaeda flat in London (2004) revealed quantities of ricin, a toxin, and in 2004 and 2007 Al Qaeda affiliated groups used or planned to use chlorine gas in attacks in Jordan and Iraq. Militant Islamic statements have mentioned, and one *fatwa* supports, the use of any means, including WMD, to kill as many infidels and apostates as possible. Globalized media, ironically, may have played a role in shaping terrorist plans. Al Qaeda leaders are alleged to have conjured up mass casualty attacks as a result of spectacular special effects contained in Hollywood blockbuster movies.

In the absence of WMD, globalization has facilitated access to weapons, resources, and proficiency required to conduct smaller, but more lethal, attacks. Terrorist groups from Chechnya to Sri Lanka have shared their expertise in the manufacturing of lethal bombs triggered by increasingly sophisticated and globally available remote control devices. Within Iraq since 2003, and increasingly in Afghanistan, insurgent and terrorist groups have been able to obtain the knowledge and resources required to build sophisticated homemade bombs called 'improvised explosive devices' (IEDs). Such IEDs range in lethality and complexity. The USA, for example, claims that Iran supports terrorist violence in Iraq through the supply of specific IED technology. State sponsorship, however, may no longer be necessary in a globalized world. Digital videos suggests that terrorists are already conducting distance learning through a 'virtual *jihad* academy' in which prospective terrorists study everything from conducting ambush attacks to making and using IEDs, in order to increase their effectiveness and lethality.

Key Points

- Elements of globalization that permit the rapid exchange of ideas and goods can also be leveraged and exploited by terrorist groups.

- The technologies associated with globalization allow terrorists to operate in a highly distributed global 'network' that shares information and allows small cells to conduct highly coordinated, lethal attacks.

- Globalization may allow some terrorist groups to acquire, manufacture, and use weapons of mass of destruction in order to conduct catastrophic attacks.

Combating terrorism

States plagued by transnational terrorism responded individually and collectively to combat the phenomenon during the cold war. These responses ranged in scope and effectiveness, and included passing anti-terrorism laws, taking preventive security measures at airports, and creating special operations counter-terrorism forces such as the West German Grenzschutzgruppe–9 (GSG–9). Successful rescues in Entebbe (1976), Mogadishu (1977), and Prince's Gate, London (1980) demonstrated that national counter-terrorism forces could respond effectively both domestically and abroad. A normative approach to tackling the problem, founded on the principles of international law and collective action, was less successful. Attempts to define and proscribe transnational terrorism in the United Nations bogged down in the General Assembly over semantics but other cooperative initiatives were successfully implemented. These included the conventions adopted through the International Civil Aviation Organization (ICAO) to improve information sharing and legal cooperation, such as the Hague Convention for the Suppression of Unlawful Seizure of Aircraft (1970). Another collective response to improve information sharing and collaborative action was the creation of the Public Safety and Terrorism Sub-Directorate within Interpol in 1985. However, most initiatives and responses throughout this decade were largely unilateral, regional, or *ad hoc* in nature.

State leaders disagree on how best to deal with the current form of global terrorist violence. Much of the controversy relates to the nature of the threat and the approach that should be taken to deal with it. Some national leaders view the form of militant Islam as an intractable problem in which there can be no negotiation. The leaders of the USA, Great Britain, and Australia have suggested that all states should cooperate in a global war on terror to deal with the threat. The stakes in 'the Long War' consist of the preservation of basic freedoms and a way of life. In order to defeat terrorism, individual states have a responsibility to protect civilian populations while dealing with terrorist cells, supporters, and sympathizers within their own borders. Given the global, elusive, and adaptive character of the militant Islamic threat, the best approach for dealing with global terrorism is to pool resources together in a coalition of the willing, in which forces from the global North are seeking to improve the capabilities of specific partner states in the global South. The end result will be the

development of a Global Counter-terrorism Network (GCTN) of states able to detect, track, and eliminate terrorist threats while non-military efforts address the root causes of terrorism. One example of globalization in practice has been the use by the USA of unarmed and armed Global Hawk, Predator, and Reaper drones to conduct surveillance and strikes against terrorist targets. The drones are flown remotely from bases in the USA, their video feeds are disseminated to operations centers and users locally, regionally, and globally, and attacks are authorized, conducted, and monitored without US forces having to engage in direct combat, leading to claims of 'virtual or push-button warfare'.

Other national leaders are less comfortable with the concept of 'war' against terrorism. In their view, actions by the military can only lead to terrorist reprisals or, worse, the return of terrorism to its original connotation, the sanctioned use of terror by the state to repress its own citizenry. In their eyes, terrorism is a crime that is best dealt with through law enforcement methods. By dealing with terrorism as a police problem, states uphold the rule of law, maintain the high moral ground, preserve democratic principles, and prevent the establishment of martial law. Military force should only be used in extreme circumstances and even then its use may have negative consequences. Terrorism is best dealt with inside state borders and through cooperative international law enforcement efforts to arrest suspects and provide them with due process. The law enforcement approach to terrorism must balance taking enough measures against terrorist groups without crossing over into the realm of ' "political justice," where the rules and rights enshrined in the principle of due process are either willfully misinterpreted or completely disregarded' (Chalk 1996: 98). To do little against domestic or global terrorism, in the name of upholding the rule of law, risks offering terrorist groups a sanctuary and the security of rights and laws.

The virtual opinion of a number of non-governmental organizations (NGOs), members of blogs, and webmasters has also been critical of the 'war' on terrorism. Those suspicious of the motives of the political elite of the USA range widely in their opinions. Conspiracy theorists online suggest that the war in Iraq, Afghanistan, and elsewhere is the first stage in the establishment of an Orwellian system that is constantly in conflict with the terrorist 'other' to justify continued violation of personal privacy.

More objective communities of practice and NGOs, such as Human Rights Watch, routinely provide monitoring and online reporting of suspected government human rights and civil liberties abuses. One example is the persistent attention paid to the status of terrorist detainees held in US custody at Guantanamo Bay.

Although disagreements still exist over how best to deal with terrorism philosophically, pragmatically the largest problems reside in locating terrorists and isolating them from their means of support. Locating and identifying terrorists is a tedious and time-consuming process that requires collecting, assessing, and analysing information collected from a range of sources. Information technologies associated with globalization have been useful in assisting this process. Such technologies allow identification of terrorist patterns before and after attacks, with systems capable of performing calculations measured in the trillions per second (floating point operations, or flops). Terrorist finances and organizations are evaluated through link analysis to construct a more comprehensive picture of the how terrorist elements interact. In addition, huge volumes of information can be reduced and exchanged electronically between departments, agencies, and other governments, or made available on secure servers whose capacities are measured in terabytes. Discovering terrorist cells, however, has much to do with luck and pursuing non-technical leads. States bureaucracies can impede or negate technical and resources advantages over terrorist groups.

In order to deal with global terrorism, the international community must address its most problematic modern aspects: the appeal of messages that inspire terrorists to commit horrific acts of violence. Killing or capturing individuals does little to halt the spread of extremist viewpoints that occur under the guise of discussion and education. In the case of Islam, for example, radical mullahs and imams twist the tenets of the religion into a doctrine of action and hatred, where spiritual achievement occurs through destruction rather than personal enlightenment. In other words, suicide attacks offer the promise of private goods (spiritual reward) rather than public good (positive contributions to the community over a lifetime). Precisely how the processes and technologies of globalization can assist in delegitimizing the pedagogy that incites terrorists will remain one of the most vexing challenges for the international community for years to come.

Key Points

- States, individually and collectively, have political, military, legal, economic, and technological advantages in the struggle against terrorist groups.
- Differences between states over the nature and scope of the current terrorist threat, and the most appropriate responses to combat it, reflect subjective characterizations based on national biases and experiences.

Conclusion

Terrorism remains a complex phenomenon in which violence is used to obtain political power to redress grievances that may have become more acute through the process of globalization. Globalization has improved the technical capabilities of terrorists and given them global reach, but has not altered the fundamental fact that terrorism represents the extreme views of a minority of the global population. In other words, globalization has changed the scope of terrorism but not its nature. The benefits that globalization provides terrorists is neither one-sided nor absolute. The same technologies and processes also enable more effective means of states to combat them. Global terrorists can only succeed through popular uprising or the psychological or physical collapse of their state-based adversary. Neither outcome is likely given the limitations of terrorist messages and capabilities. Terrorist and counter-terrorist campaigns are characterized by prolonged struggle to maintain advantages in legitimacy domestically and internationally. The challenge for the global community will be in utilizing its advantages to win the war of ideas that motivates and sustains those responsible for the current wave of terrorist violence.

Questions

1 Why is linking terrorism with globalization so difficult to do theoretically?
2 When did terrorism become a truly global phenomenon and what enabled it to do so?
3 In what ways are the technologies and processes associated with globalization more beneficial to states or terrorists?
4 Given that terrorism has been both a transnational and a global phenomenon, why has it not been more successful in effecting change?
5 Of all of the factors that motivate terrorists, is any one more important than others, and, if so, why?
6 What has changed in terrorism over the past half-century, and have any factors remained the same? If so, what are they and why have they remained constant?
7 What role does technology play in terrorism and will it change how terrorists operate in the future? If so, how?
8 What are the dilemmas that terrorist groups face with respect to WMD?
9 What is the primary challenge that individual states and the international community as a whole face in confronting terrorism?
10 How has the concept of security, in personal, societal, and international terms, changed as a result of globalized terrorism—and how will it change in the future?

Further Reading

Ganor, B. (2005), *The Counter-Terrorism Puzzle: A Guide for Decision Makers* (New Brunswick, NJ: Transaction). Emphasizes the dilemmas and practical difficulties associated with various counter-terrorism policy options.

Hoffman, B. (2006), *Inside Terrorism*, revised and expanded edition (New York: Columbia University Press). The best single-volume work on the development of terrorism, its evolution over time, and current and future prospects for defeating it.

Juergensmeyer, M. (2000), *Terror in the Mind of God: The Global Rise of Religious Violence* (Berkeley, CA: University of California Press). Highlights similarities between religious leaders across faiths and sects at how they justify killing non-combatants.

Lia, B. (2008), *Architect of Global Jihad: The Life of Al-Qaida Strategist Abu Mus'ab al-Suri* (New York: Columbia University Press). Provides a study on al-Suri and assesses his significance to Al Qaeda. Noteworthy for a translation of key excerpts of al-Suri's 'Global Islamic Resistance Cal'l.

Rabasa, A., Chalk, P., et al. (2006), *Beyond al-Qaeda. Part 1: The Global Jihadist Movement and Part 2: The Outer Rings of the Terrorist Universe* (Santa Monica, CA: RAND). This two-part report provides a comprehensive survey of current militant Islamic terrorist groups, the impact of Iraq on the global *jihad*, and the linkages between terrorism and organized crime. Available for downloading at: www.rand.org/pubs/monographs/2006/RAND_MG429.pdf (Part 1) and www.rand.org/pubs/monographs/2006/RAND_MG430.pdf (Part 2).

Roy, O. (2004), *Globalized Islam: The Search for the New Ummah* (New York: Columbia University Press). A provocative work that challenges many of the assumptions about and explanations for the rise of militant Islam.

Sageman, M. (2004), *Understanding Terror Networks* (Philadelphia, PA: University of Pennsylvania Press). Analyses Al Qaeda members based on information gathered from open sources that arrives at thought-provoking conclusions about the formation of the militant global *jihad* network.

Schmid, A. P., Jongman, A. J., et al. (1988), *Political Terrorism: A New Guide to Actors, Authors, Concepts, Data Bases, Theories, and Literature* (New Brunswick, NJ: Transaction). A still useful, if at times overwhelming, reference work that highlights the problems associated with defining and studying terrorism.

Online Resource Centre

 Visit the Online Resource Centre that accompanies this book to access more learning resources on this chapter topic at www.oxfordtextbooks.co.uk/orc/baylis5e/

Chapter 23

Nuclear proliferation

DARRYL HOWLETT

Reader's Guide

This chapter identifies those factors that have made nuclear proliferation a global phenomenon since 1945. Over this period the nature of nuclear weapons has transformed military and political relationships, while the global diffusion of nuclear and ballistic missile technology has meant that more actors are in a position both to acquire a nuclear capability and deliver it over longer distances. This chapter also reveals the complexities associated with the globalization of the nuclear proliferation issue and some of the theoretical aspects related to it. There are difficulties in determining the motivations driving nuclear weapons acquisition and the capabilities that might be constructed once it has occurred. This complexity has been made more acute as a result of novel proliferation concerns in the last twenty years. As a result, non-proliferation efforts have focused on measures that: raise the costs of nuclear acquisition; develop standards of nuclear and missile behaviour; and create the conditions allowing for reductions in nuclear stockpiles to occur in a safe and secure manner.

Introduction

The issue of nuclear proliferation represents one of the more marked illustrations of globalization. Although only five states (China, France, Russia (Soviet Union), the United Kingdom and the USA) are acknowledged by the Treaty on the Non-Proliferation of Nuclear Weapons (NPT) as Nuclear Weapon States (NWS), others have the capability to construct nuclear devices. This was emphasized in May 1998 when India and Pakistan, previously regarded as 'threshold' or near-nuclear states, demonstrated their respective capabilities by conducting a series of nuclear tests followed by ballistic missile launches. These events highlighted another aspect of nuclear globalization: the potential emergence of a regionally differentiated world. While some regions have moved from a situation where nuclear weapons once had a high profile in strategic thinking to one where these weapons have assumed lower significance, other regions may be moving in the opposite direction. In Latin America, South Pacific, South-East Asia, Africa, and Central Asia the trend has been towards developing the region as a **Nuclear Weapons Free Zone** (NWFZ). In other regions, such as South Asia and possibly elsewhere, the trend appears to be towards a higher profile for nuclear capabilities. What is unclear is the impact that nuclearization (meaning nuclear weapons acquisition) in some regions will have on those moving towards denuclearization (meaning a process of removing nuclear weapons).

Developments stemming from the dissolution of the Soviet Union also raised novel problems. This is the only case where a previously acknowledged NWS has been subjected to political disintegration. At the time there was little understanding of what the consequences would be from such a state implosion and only in hindsight can we judge its full significance. That it was a period of unprecedented nuclear transformation requiring long-term **cooperation** between previously hostile states is not in doubt. Less obvious is the observation that this period of transition was facilitated by the foresight of policy-makers from both sides of the former cold war divide and by the framework of arms control and disarmament agreements then in place. Ensuring nuclear stability during this period might therefore have been more difficult had it not been for policies such as the Co-operative Threat Reduction Programme and agreements like the multilateral NPT and bilateral Strategic Arms Reduction Treaties (START), signed initially between the USA and the Soviet Union (and later between the USA and Russia). One debate that has sparked diverging responses is a thesis asserting that the gradual spread of nuclear weapons to additional states is to be welcomed rather than feared. The thesis is based on the proposition that just as nuclear deterrence maintained stability during the cold war, so can it induce similar stabilizing effects on other conflict situations. This argument is challenged by those who hold that more will be worse not better, and that measures to stem nuclear proliferation represent the best way forward (Sagan and Waltz 1995 and 2003).

The responses to nuclear proliferation encompass unilateral, bilateral, regional, and global measures that

---

Box 23.1 Waltz thesis

1 Nuclear weapons have spread rather than proliferated because these weapons have proliferated only vertically as the Nuclear Weapon States have increased their arsenals.

2 Nuclear weapons have spread horizontally to other states only slowly. This slowness is fortunate as rapid changes in international conditions can be unsettling.

3 The gradual spread of nuclear weapons is better than either no spread or rapid spread.

4 New nuclear states will feel the constraints that nuclear weapons impose and this will induce a sense of responsibility on the part of their possessors and a strong element of caution on their use.

5 The likelihood of war decreases as deterrent and defensive capabilities increase; nuclear weapons, responsibly used, make wars hard to start.

(Sagan and Waltz 1995)

Box 23.2 Sagan's 'proliferation pessimism' argument

1 Professional military organizations, because of common biases, inflexible routines, and parochial interests, display organizational behaviours that are likely to lead to deterrence failures and deliberate or accidental war.

2 Because future nuclear-armed states are likely to have military-run or weak civilian governments, they will lack the positive constraining mechanisms of civilian control while military biases may serve to encourage nuclear weapons use, especially during a crisis.

(Sagan and Waltz 1995)

collectively have been termed the global nuclear non-proliferation regime. Advocates of this global regime argue that it is these measures (including treaties like the NPT, export controls, international safeguards, nuclear and radiological supplier agreements, and other standard-setting arrangements) that have constrained nuclear acquisition. Conversely, there have been several criticisms of this regime and even long-term supporters acknowledge it is in need of strengthening. Among the criticisms of the emerging global regime are that it: is a product of a bygone first nuclear age (1945–90) and is not suited to the demands of the potentially more dangerous second nuclear age (1990–), where there are multiple actors and concerns include the possible proliferation of both radiological and nuclear devices; is unable to alleviate the security dilemma that many states confront and, hence, does not address the security motivation driving nuclear weapons acquisition; and is a discriminatory arrangement because the NPT only requires that the five NWS pursue nuclear disarmament in good faith (under its Article VI) while all other parties (designated as **Non-Nuclear Weapons States** (NNWS)) must forgo the acquisition of nuclear weapons. Thus there has always been a tension between whether the NPT is primarily a measure for preventing additional nuclear or radiological-armed actors emerging or a means for achieving nuclear disarmament.

A debate has also emerged concerning the worth of this emerging regime as an instrument of global nuclear policy. This is being addressed in a manner that has not been seen for decades and against an international backdrop that differs radically from earlier times. At its heart are issues relating to the future global security environment and including questions concerning the likely proliferation challenges of the coming decades, energy security, environmental change, and what the impact of the economic recession will have on these factors.

Nature of nuclear weapons and their effects

Technical basis of nuclear weapons

Unless a radiological or nuclear device (or the materials required for their manufacture) can be obtained 'off the shelf' as a result of purchase or theft, the usual route for any state or non-state actor seeking such a capability would be via the acquisition of the necessary infrastructure. The latter includes a range of radiological, nuclear, conventional, computational, and electronic technologies.

Nuclear weapons manufacture, for example, is complex and likely to remain for the foreseeable future a state-based process. Nuclear reactors and nuclear weapons differ in their management of the nuclear chain reaction and the energy produced. Whereas in a reactor energy output is achieved through a sustained and regulated process, in a nuclear weapon the objective is to attain a large explosive yield by creating a critical mass of nuclear material as a result of an uncontrolled and rapid chain reaction (Gardner 1994: 6–7). Nuclear weapons consequently derive their explosive energy from techniques designed either to split the atoms rapidly, thus creating a chain reaction (so-called fission weapons), or by using fission weapons as a primary initiator to compress and heat hydrogen atoms so that they combine or fuse (so-called thermonuclear or fusion weapons). Energy production in a nuclear reactor involves a means for regulating the chain reaction, a moderator that surrounds the fissile core for maintaining the chain reaction, and a

Box 23.3 Technology of nuclear weapons

Separate processes are required to obtain the two fissile materials needed to construct a nuclear weapon. Uranium is found in nature and comprises 99.3 per cent uranium 238 (U-238) and 0.7 per cent uranium 235 (U-235). The U-235 has the same chemical properties as the U-238 but has a different atomic weight. It is the latter isotopic form that is used in a nuclear weapon. To produce the weapon, the amount of U-235 in a quantity of natural uranium is increased to weapons grade by a process called enrichment so that eventually it becomes 90 per cent+ of the sample. Once a sufficient quantity of weapons grade U-235 has been accumulated to achieve a critical mass, defined by the International Atomic Energy Agency (IAEA) as 25 kilograms—although the amount could be smaller—then there is enough fissile material to construct one nuclear weapon.

Plutonium does not occur naturally: it is one of the end products of the irradiation of natural or only very slightly enriched (2–3 per cent) uranium in a nuclear reactor. Plutonium 239 (Pu-239) is the result of a controlled nuclear reaction process. Because the two are chemically different, it is possible to separate plutonium and uranium through a process known as reprocessing. The figure of 6 to 8 kilograms is usually the quantity quoted for one weapon although this varies with the design.

means for removing the heat produced from the reactor core by the chain reaction, which can also provide the steam to drive turbines and generate electricity.

Nuclear weapons effects

The effects of nuclear weapons can be considerable. Because of this, the United Nations Commission for Conventional Armaments in 1948 introduced a new category of **weapons of mass destruction** (WMD) to distinguish nuclear weapons from conventional forms. More recently, another concept, known as CBRN (referring to chemical, biological, radiological, and nuclear capabilities), has appeared and some analysts have argued that the term WMD should be unravelled because each of the weapons types has different effects, with nuclear weapons being the true WMD (Panofsky 1998).

A nuclear weapon produces its energy in three distinct forms: blast; heat or thermal radiation; and nuclear radiation. Experience of nuclear testing has also revealed another feature of a nuclear weapons explosion, the phenomenon known as electro-magnetic pulse (EMP). This can cause acute disruption to electronic equipment.

Extensive damage to human populations may result from a nuclear weapons detonation. Awareness of these effects stems from the two weapons dropped on Hiroshima and Nagasaki at the end of the Second World War, which remains the only time nuclear weapons have been used. What is also known is that the weapons that destroyed these Japanese cities were relatively small in comparison with the destructive forces generated by later testing of thermonuclear weapons.

Key Points

- Nuclear weapons production requires a broad-based technological infrastructure.
- Possible manufacture of radiological devices has also become a key security concern.
- Nuclear reactors and nuclear weapons differ in their management of the chain reaction, and in the nature of the energy produced.
- In 1948, the United Nations introduced the category known as WMD.
- A new category has appeared known as CBRN.
- Nuclear weapons produce energy in three forms—blast, heat and nuclear radiation—and the phenomenon known as EMP.
- Nuclear weapons were used at the end of the Second World War and have not been used in conflict since.

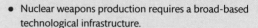

Diffusion of nuclear and missile technology

Diffusion of nuclear technology

Since 1945 nuclear technology for civil and military uses has disseminated on a global scale. Immediately after the Second World War only the USA possessed the capability to manufacture a nuclear weapon. By 1964 four other states had crossed the nuclear weapons threshold, an event traditionally understood as the testing of a nuclear explosive device (the Soviet Union (1949), the United Kingdom (1952), France (1960), and China (1964)).

Complications for the definition of a NWS contained in the NPT were raised by the detonation of nuclear devices by India and Pakistan in 1998. Neither state was party to the NPT, so they were not in breach of any international legal obligation. Yet India's and Pakistan's move from a presumed 'threshold' position to demonstrating an overt nuclear weapons capability not only questioned the NPT's definition of a NWS; it also raised the question of whether other states that had signed the Treaty might follow this path.

There are also concerns about the future of nuclear supply arrangements and the role of transnational **networks**. Today, with several nuclear suppliers, coupled with the possibility that transnational networks operating outside established controls may exist (such as the one discovered in 2004), there is the prospect that the acquisition of at least rudimentary nuclear capabilities has become easier. In response, efforts have been under way to strengthen supplier guidelines while the United Nations has made it mandatory, via Security Council Resolution 1540, for states to pass and enforce domestic legislation that criminalizes those individuals or networks engaged in transnational WMD-related activities (Bosch and Van Ham 2007).

Nuclear delivery

During the 1950s nuclear weapons required large aircraft designed to carry these weapons to their target. Thereafter, as the technology developed for manufacturing ballistic missiles and for nuclear ordnance that was compact enough to be carried by these missiles, so the possibility increased that more states would seek to deliver nuclear weapons by this means.

Ballistic missiles consequently represent the most sophisticated method of nuclear delivery and were once restricted to a few states. But just as the diffusion of nuclear technology is a global phenomenon, so the capability to deploy a ballistic missile has become more commonplace. Should these missiles be linked to the delivery of nuclear ordnance, then more states will have the capacity to hit targets over longer distances and, by implication, also widen their potential for strategic engagement. It is this aspect that brought to the fore once more the debate over the merits of deploying defences against ballistic missiles.

Following the passing of the National Missile Defense (NMD) Act in 1999, the USA embarked on a programme of ballistic missile interceptor testing and deployment. International reaction to these developments have met with concerns in Russia and China about the impact on global stability between these states, which have also involved debates in Europe about the implications of ballistic missile interceptor deployments for heightening regional tensions.

Because START 1 expired at the end of 2009, and the 2002 Strategic Offensive Reductions Treaty (SORT) will do so in 2012, the USA and Russia began negotiating a new strategic nuclear arms reduction agreement. In 2010 Presidents Obama and Medvedev, respectively, agreed to reduce their strategic delivery vehicles and the associated nuclear warheads to between 1,500 and 1,675. President Obama also announced earlier, at another venue, that the stationing of missile defences in Europe would be reconsidered such that naval-based rather than land-based systems could be the preferred option. The impact of these debates within and between different regions will therefore be a critical feature of the future global security environment.

Additional arms control and disarmament measures may also be considered in light of UN Security Resolution 1887 (2009), which resolves to 'seek a safer world for all and to create the conditions for a world without nuclear weapons, in accordance with the goals of the … NPT, in a way that promotes international stability, and based on the principle of undiminished security for all'.

Key Points

- The nature of nuclear weapons and the dissemination of the capabilities to manufacture them around the world since 1945 makes nuclear proliferation a good illustration of the globalization of world politics.

- Greater attention has been paid to theoretical aspects.

- A debate has emerged over the merits of the further proliferation/spread of nuclear weapons.

- Because of new proliferation challenges generated by what some analysts call the 'second nuclear age', a debate has begun over whether the nuclear non-proliferation regime can cope with the demands placed on it.

- A major element of the nuclear proliferation process is the acquisition of the technologies to produce fissile materials to construct either a fission (nuclear) or fusion (thermonuclear) weapon.

- The effects of nuclear weapons are manifest in the form of blast, heat, and nuclear radiation.

- Since 1945, the spread of nuclear technology for civil and military purposes has meant that states beyond the five that possess nuclear weapons now have the capacity to produce nuclear devices at relatively short notice, if they have not already done so.

- Over the same period the nature of the civil nuclear trading market has also changed, leading to proliferation concerns because there are more nuclear suppliers around.

- There has also been a diffusion of ballistic missile and space-launch technology since 1945.

- A debate over the merits of deploying defensive systems to counter ballistic missiles has emerged.

- UN Security Council Resolution 1887 has been passed and a new strategic nuclear arms control agreement has been struck between the USA and Russia.

Theorizing nuclear proliferation and non-proliferation

Conceptual issues

One question that has provoked interest is what constitutes nuclear proliferation: does it refer to a single decision to acquire a nuclear weapon or is it part of a process that may stretch over several years and consequently no one identifiable decision can be located? Research on what has been referred to as 'the proliferation puzzle' has thus embraced several conceptual issues (Meyer 1984; Davis and Frankel 1993; Lavoy 1995; Ogilvie-White 1996; Hymans 2006). Similarly, while much literature endorses the propositions derived from political realism, which asserts that in an anarchic international environment states will seek nuclear weapons to enhance their security, insights from other theoretical positions have become more commonplace (see chapters in Part Two). This has generated questions concerning what the 'level of analysis' should be in studying nuclear proliferation. Should the focus be on the individual, the organization, the cultural group, the state, the international system, or some combination of these? This may be even more complex where radiological devices are concerned.

The argument has also been advanced that norms, taboos, and epistemic communities have played an important role in the nuclear context (Adler 1992; Price and Tannenwald 1996). One viewpoint sees international norms as increasingly significant both as constraints on nuclear behaviour and in setting appropriate standards among a range of actors. Similarly, in fostering nuclear non-proliferation dialogues some analysts stress the role played by culture and **identity** factors (Krause and Williams 1997). Scholars have also drawn attention to non-governmental organizations (NGOs) and epistemic communities, referring to groups of individuals, often from different disciplines and countries, that operate as conduits for ideas on non-proliferation.

Another issue with enduring resonance concerns the question of what can explain nuclear 'non-use' since 1945. This debate started early in the nuclear calendar as authors like Bernard Brodie argued that nuclear weapons were useful only in their non-use (Brodie 1946; Gray 1996). Over the years the main explanation of non-use has centred on the notion of nuclear deterrence: states have been deterred from using nuclear weapons because of concerns of retaliation in kind by adversaries.

In looking to alternative accounts of non-use, some have focused more on the nature of the weapon and the impact this has on normative judgements. Nina Tannenwald has challenged those arguments that rely on rational cost–benefit analysis relating to power, capabilities and interests by exploring other non-material aspects, such as the constraining influence of what is termed the 'nuclear taboo' (Tannenwald 1999 and 2007). In identifying such a taboo, Barry Buzan and Eric Herring define it as 'a strategic cultural prohibition against the use of nuclear weapons … an assumption that nuclear weapons should not be used rather than a conscious cost–benefit calculation' (1998: 165). Strategic cultural predispositions towards the acquisition and potential use of nuclear weapons have also been studied (Johnson, Kartchner, and Larsen 2009).

Nuclear motivations

Traditional analysis of the motivations for nuclear proliferation has focused at the state and inter-state levels. For much of the post-Second World War period the pattern of nuclear weapons acquisition established by the five NWSs was considered to be the one most likely to be followed by any future proliferating state. Analysis of the motivational aspect consequently addressed the strategic, political, and prestige rationales that led these states to seek nuclear weapons. The strategic motivation focused on the role that nuclear weapons played in the Second World War and its immediate aftermath, when initially they were seen as war-fighting or war-winning weapons. Later, attention shifted to the role that nuclear weapons played in deterrence, leading to the assumption that one of the principal motivations for acquisition was the deterrence of other nuclear weapons-capable states. Similarly, the political and prestige benefits that nuclear weapons conferred on those states with the wherewithal to manufacture them were also deemed significant. Nuclear weapons were seen as the most modern form of weaponry and their custodians were automatically afforded a seat at the 'top table of international affairs'.

Inherent in traditional analyses was a form of technological determinism, that once a state acquired the necessary infrastructure it would then develop nuclear weapons. Supporting this assumption was the view that these states would also follow the same path as the five NWS. Thus it could be predicted that any new nuclear state would pursue a dedicated military nuclear programme, conduct an overt nuclear test, produce a stockpile of weapons, and finally acquire an effective means for delivering the weapons to their target. While this explanation of the process is still relevant, over time analyses of the dynamics of nuclear proliferation have become more complex.

It is now more difficult to explain nuclear proliferation by focusing on a single variable. Analysts have argued that it is necessary to consider a range of factors that may influence nuclear weapons acquisition. These may include: traditional technological factors, the availability of nuclear technology, and a cadre of trained nuclear scientists who encourage acquisition; domestic politics, imperatives within a political party, or the domestic political situation may propel a state towards nuclear weapons; diplomatic bargaining, that acquisition of a nuclear capability can be used to influence or bargain with both perceived allies and enemies; and non-intervention, that a nuclear capability can deter or prevent intervention by other states.

Other features of the 'proliferation puzzle' that need to be understood are the instances of nuclear restraint—why some states abandon the nuclear weapons option—and nuclear reversal—why some states relinquish their nuclear capabilities (Campbell, Einhorn, and Reiss 2004). Factors having a bearing here are: there may have been a change in strategic circumstances, such as the forging of an alliance with a NWS; technical difficulties in the construction of the nuclear weapon may have been encountered; or a perception emerges that the acquisition of such weapons would increase vulnerabilities. Developments since 1945 have thus questioned the technological determinist argument.

Further complexity is added when attention is focused at the sub-state or **transnational actor** level as the motivations of non-state actors may be different from those associated with states. In much traditional thinking, only states were considered to have the wherewithal to acquire nuclear capabilities. Nuclear commerce was conducted on a state-to-state basis and it was states that entered into international arms control and disarmament treaties. Today, states are no longer the sole focus of attention, as non-state actors have also featured.

Studies conducted during the 1970s and 1980s on nuclear terrorism indicated that there were risks associated with particular groups acquiring a nuclear device or threatening to attack nuclear installations. One study by the International Task Force on Prevention of Nuclear Terrorism concluded that it was possible for a terrorist group to build a crude nuclear device provided it had sufficient quantities of chemical high explosives

and weapons-usable fissile materials. More significantly, it was felt that such a group would be more interested in generating social disruption by making a credible nuclear threat rather than actually detonating a nuclear device and causing mass killing and destruction (Leventhal and Alexander 1987). More recent occurrences have served to alter this latter judgement.

Events in the mid-1990s, such as the first bombing of the World Trade Center in New York in 1993 and the attack against the US Government building in Oklahoma in April 1995, revealed the extent of damage and loss of life that could be caused. While both instances involved traditional methods of inflicting damage, the use of nerve agents (chemical weapons) in an underground train network in central Tokyo in March 1995 to cause both death and widespread panic has been viewed as representing a quantum change in methods. These concerns have intensified since the tragic events of 11 September 2001 when the World Trade Center this time was destroyed by a coordinated attack using civilian aircraft loaded with aviation fuel as the method of destruction. The attack not only produced mass casualties; it also changed the assumption about terrorist use of CBRN capabilities (Wilkinson 2003).

Nuclear capabilities and intentions

Paralleling the problems of analysing the motivational aspect are those associated with determining whether a state or terrorist group actually possesses a radiological or nuclear capability. The case of South Africa indicates the difficulties in this area. On 24 March 1993 the then President F. W. de Klerk announced that South

> **Box 23.4** Compliance and non-compliance
>
> Compliance with international treaty obligations has been a perennial issue in the nuclear proliferation context. It has raised complex questions related to both the nature of any violation of agreements and the type of response to it. Violations may be only minor and relate to misinterpretation of procedures: conversely, they may be major and linked to breaches of specific treaty obligations. The type of response could therefore vary depending on how the violation is judged and, as a consequence, may involve a spectrum from a procedural warning issued through an international organization like the IAEA or more stringent measures such as special inspection arrangements, sanctions, and the use of force. The issue of compliance is therefore likely to receive continuing attention in the years ahead as it is not just responses to states that will be the subject of attention but responses to non-state actors as well.

Africa had produced six nuclear devices prior to 1989 but had dismantled them before signing the NPT. While this announcement confirmed what many previously speculated—that South Africa possessed a nuclear capability during the 1980s—it also suggested that a state did not need to test a nuclear device to be in possession of a nuclear stockpile. Additionally, there are currently other industrialized states with large nuclear power programmes that could be used to produce quantities of fissile materials for military purposes if a decision were taken to do so. The main barrier to nuclear weapon acquisition in such cases may therefore be political, not technological.

The situations in the Democratic People's Republic of Korea (DPRK), Iran, and Iraq have raised important issues concerning capabilities and intentions. These instances reveal the difficulties in obtaining consensus in international forums on how to respond to non-compliance and the problems associated with verifying treaty compliance in situations where special inspection or nuclear development arrangements are agreed. In the case of Iraq, a special inspection arrangement known as UNSCOM (United Nations Special Committee) was established following the 1991 Gulf War to oversee the dismantling of the WMD programme that had come to light as a result of the conflict. By the late 1990s problems were encountered over access to particular sites and UNSCOM inspectors were withdrawn. Disagreements also surfaced among the five Permanent Members of the United Nations Security Council (P-5) concerning how to implement the UN resolutions that had been passed in connection with Iraq since 1991. These had not been resolved at the time of the intervention in Iraq that occurred in 2003 and subsequent inspections in Iraq were unable to find evidence of significant undeclared WMD.

The complexity associated with compliance has similarly featured in connection with Iran. The country became the subject of attention from the International Atomic Energy Agency (IAEA) over delays in signing an Additional Protocol to Iran's safeguards agreement

Case Study 1 The Democratic People's Republic of Korea (DPRK)

Following the attention that focused on the DPRK between 1991 and 1993, when there were fears that the country was pursuing an undeclared nuclear programme, a special nuclear arrangement was instituted in 1994. Known as the 'Agreed Framework', it provided the DPRK with light-water reactors and fuel supplies in exchange for that country's agreement that it would not produce nuclear weapons. Thereafter the Agreed Framework experienced problems prompting continued uncertainty surrounding the DPRK's nuclear intentions. The situation was exacerbated in August 1998 when the DPRK tested a missile whose trajectory took it over the territory of Japan. Tensions were heightened when the DPRK stated in January 2003 that it had withdrawn from the NPT and would continue its nuclear programme. Concomitantly, efforts began to find an appropriate response including several rounds of a forum known as the six-party talks involving China, Japan, Russia, Republic of Korea, DPRK, and the United States. On 19 September 2005, at the fourth round of these talks, the parties agreed a Joint Statement aimed at the denuclearization of the DPRK and the Korean Peninsula. The Statement included a plan of coordinated steps linking denuclearization with cooperation in economic and energy development in accordance with the principle of 'commitment for commitment'. But subsequent meetings produced little progress. Pessimism that the plan would never get implemented grew following the announcement by the DPRK in October 2006 that it had tested a nuclear weapon. The test resulted in the Security Council imposing sanctions on the DPRK and a flurry of diplomatic activity by the other five participants in the talks to find a response. A potentially significant breakthrough was achieved on 15 February 2007 following concerted negotiations. The DPRK accepted a package, based on the terms of the 2005 Statement, that it would begin a process to shut down, seal, and eventually disable the Yongbyon nuclear complex in return for energy and humanitarian aid. But in 2008 the situation again changed as the DPRK reversed the dismantlement programme, tested a Taep'o-dong-2C/3 ballistic missile and the six-party talks stalled. On 25 May the following year, the DPRK conducted a second nuclear test, which resulted in the Security Council adopting Resolution 1874 (2009) and stating its 'gravest concern' at this development. Then in September 2009 the DPRK acknowledged that it was also developing a uranium enrichment capability, which had previously been suspected, in addition to the plutonium programme. Early in 2010, the DPRK's leader Kim Jong II called for a a peace treaty to end the armistice situation on the Korean Peninsula, in place since the 1950s, and for direct talks with the United States. The concern, however, is that this could be another means for that country to buy time for further development of its nuclear and missile programmes.

that requires increased transparency on the part of a NNWS in respect of its nuclear programme. Although Iran later did sign the Protocol, speculation was fuelled because the IAEA discovered facilities capable of enriching uranium that had not been declared to it. In an effort to find a solution, a dialogue between Iran and the so-called EU-3 (France, Germany, and the United Kingdom) began in October 2003. While an agreement was reached between the parties in Paris in November 2004, the situation was not resolved. In 2006 the UN Security Council passed resolutions, under Chapter VII of the UN Charter, requiring Iran to comply with its international obligations. Further discussion between the P-5 plus Germany on how to achieve compliance followed as a result of continued uncertainty over Iran's nuclear programme and concomitant concerns over its development of a ballistic missile and satellite launch capability. Throughout this period Iran maintained that the nuclear programme was peaceful and in November 2009 stated that the country would expand its uranium enrichment capability.

Key Points

- The characterization of motivations for acquiring nuclear weapons has become more complex.
- There are difficulties in determining whether nuclear proliferation has occurred.
- A number of states have the potential to manufacture nuclear weapons if they want to, and a few embarked on military nuclear programmes before abandoning them.
- The role of non-state actors has added a further dimension to nuclear globalization.
- There is an ongoing task of ensuring the safety and security of nuclear materials around the world.
- The complexity surrounding compliance with international obligations has been a feature of debate since the early 1990s.

Evolution of global nuclear control and anti-proliferation measures

Early efforts to control nuclear weapons, 1945–70

Global efforts to constrain nuclear weapons acquisition began soon after 1945. In January 1946 the UN General Assembly passed a resolution establishing the UN Atomic Energy Commission (UNAEC). The remit of the UNAEC was to make proposals for the elimination of nuclear weapons and the use of nuclear energy for peaceful purposes under international control. Due to disagreements between the USA and the Soviet Union, these proposals were never implemented.

The issue of international atomic energy control was revisited following President Eisenhower's Atoms for Peace speech on 8 December 1953. It was stressed that Eisenhower's proposal was not a disarmament plan but an initiative to open the benefits of atomic energy to the world community. Negotiations to implement 'Atoms for Peace' culminated in the establishment of the IAEA on 29 July 1957, although it was not until the mid-1960s that this organization was able to implement a comprehensive monitoring system (or safeguards) to ensure that materials in the nuclear energy programmes were not diverted for military use.

In the late 1950s negotiations also began on a Comprehensive Test Ban Treaty (CTBT). These occurred in the context of a Soviet Union–United Kingdom–USA moratorium on nuclear testing (1958–61), and calls for the three NWSs to engage in nuclear disarmament. The negotiations did not result in an agreement, largely because the three states were unable to overcome differences concerning verification: namely, the provisions for a system that could provide assurance of detection of violation, especially for underground testing. However, in 1963 the three states did agree the Partial Test Ban Treaty (PTBT). This prohibited nuclear testing in the atmosphere, in outer space, and underwater, and meant that future testing by parties to the Treaty had to be conducted underground.

Measures to prevent the nuclearization of specific environments and geographical areas have also been agreed (Goldblat 2002). The first NWFZ applied to a populated region is the Treaty for the Prohibition of Nuclear Weapons in Latin America (the Tlatelolco Treaty), which was opened for signature in 1967. Between 1958 and 1968 the issues posed by more states acquiring nuclear weapons received international attention. In 1961 the UN General Assembly adopted the Irish Resolution, which called for limitations to prevent additional states from acquiring nuclear weapons and for all states to refrain from transfer or acquisition of such weapons. A breakthrough in the negotiation of a non-proliferation treaty came as a result of Resolution 2028, adopted by the UN General Assembly in 1965, and the tabling of a joint US–Soviet draft on 11 March 1968. Following further amendments, the latter draft was passed by the UN General Assembly on 12 June 1968, opened for signature on 1 July 1968, and the NPT formerly entered into force on 5 March 1970 (Shaker 1980).

Anti-proliferation efforts since 1970

Since 1970, anti-proliferation measures have continued to evolve. In March 1971 the IAEA negotiated its INFCIRC/153 safeguards document, which provides a model for all safeguards negotiated with parties to the NPT. Additional arrangements have been established for the conduct of international nuclear trade. In 1971 the Zangger Committee adopted guidelines or a 'trigger list' pursuant to the NPT allowing for IAEA safeguards to be applied on nuclear transfers, especially those involving the equipment or material for the processing, use, or production of special fissionable materials. But following the global expansion of nuclear power programmes, the increasing trade with non-NPT parties, and what India referred to as a 'peaceful' nuclear explosion it conducted in 1974, some nuclear suppliers decided that further export guidelines were necessary. Formed in 1975, the Nuclear Suppliers Group (NSG)

agreed that additional conditions should be attached to sensitive nuclear exports like reprocessing and uranium enrichment plants.

At the First United Nations Special Session on Disarmament (UNSSOD–1) in 1978, China, France, Soviet Union, the United Kingdom, and the USA all issued unilateral statements on so-called negative security assurances on the use or threat of use of nuclear weapons against NNWSs. These assurances embraced specific qualifications related to each state's nuclear doctrine and security arrangements, but only China's was unconditional. China stated that it would not be first to use nuclear weapons and undertook not to threaten to use nuclear weapons against any NNWS.

In 1987, seven missile technology exporters established identical export guidelines to cover the sale of nuclear-capable ballistic or cruise missiles. Known as the Missile Technology Control Regime (MTCR), this supply arrangement seeks 'to limit the risks of nuclear proliferation by controlling transfers of technology which could make a contribution to nuclear weapons delivery systems other than manned aircraft' (Karp 1995). Membership of the MTCR has expanded to include many of the major missile producers and the guidelines now embrace missile systems capable of carrying chemical and biological payloads. Over time, concerns have been expressed about the long-term

---

Case Study 2   United States–India nuclear cooperation agreement

On 1 October 2008 the US Congress approved a nuclear cooperation agreement with India, which had initially been signed between the two countries in July 2005. Before this agreement, the United States had imposed restrictions on nuclear and other technology transfers to India. India for its part had remained a non-party to the NPT and developed a civil and military nuclear capability. The 2005 agreement allowed India to acquire technology from the United States and for US companies to construct

nuclear reactors in India and provide fuel for its civil nuclear programme. In return for this technology, India agreed to: grant the IAEA access to its civil nuclear facilities (but military ones remain excluded); sign an Additional Protocol with the IAEA to allow for more intrusive safeguards inspections; continue the moratorium on nuclear testing; improve the security arrangements for its nuclear forces; and support nuclear non-proliferation measures. The agreement has met with a mixed reception domestically in the two countries and internationally. Proponents of the agreement consider that it will allow for closer collaboration in areas such as nuclear power production and non-proliferation, as well as other aspects of economic and mutual security interest. Opponents argue that it: allows India to continue developing its nuclear forces because the military facilities are not covered; allows India the possibility of diverting nuclear materials from the civil to the military programme once US transfers have begun; could weaken the NPT; and sends the wrong non-proliferation message by granting concessions to those states seeking nuclear weapons. In India critics consider the agreement allows the United States too much oversight of its nuclear programme and economic future, and that it will be detrimental to India's long-term security.

viability of the MTCR. While these acknowledge that the arrangement has fulfilled its initial purpose in slowing down missile proliferation, there are calls for new measures. Missile defences are one means for dealing with the problem, but other suggestions include global or regional ballistic test notification centres and multilateral arms limitation measures for missiles with certain ranges. Also in 2002 a new initiative, known as The Hague Code of Conduct, was launched (Smith 2002). As the name implies, the Code seeks to develop standards of appropriate behaviour in the transfer of missiles and missile parts.

At the time of the 1995 NPT Conference, expectations were high that the documents adopted by consensus then would provide the foundation for strengthening the Treaty. Events afterwards indicated that this assessment was premature as differences surfaced between the parties over how these documents should be interpreted. Similarly, in 1995 expectations were high that a CTBT would soon be agreed and implemented, but again this proved premature. Although a CTBT was opened for signature in 1996, it has not entered into force. This will only occur once a group of 44 states (including the five NWS and states such as India, Pakistan, and the DPRK) have signed and ratified the Treaty. This has meant that the success or otherwise of the CTBT is dependent on developments in several states. Significantly, also, not everyone agrees that this Treaty is a worthwhile measure. Proponents claim that the restriction on nuclear testing will limit both vertical and **horizontal proliferation**.

Box 23.5 1995 NPT Review and Extension Conference

On 11 May 1995 the NPT Review and Extension Conference extended the NPT indefinitely without a vote. This extension decision was adopted in conjunction with two other documents and a resolution which established a set of principles and objectives for nuclear non-proliferation and disarmament; outlined new procedures for strengthening the Treaty review process; and called for the establishment of a Middle East zone free of nuclear weapons and other weapons of mass destruction within the context of the Middle East peace process. However, the parties were unable to agree a consolidated text on the review of the Treaty and, as in 1980 and 1990, the Conference concluded on 12 May without a final declaration. Even then, the outcome of the 1995 NPT Conference was hailed a success. This was because the Treaty became permanent, new measures were established to strengthen future NPT review conferences, and a plan of action for non-proliferation and disarmament was outlined.

Critics of a CTBT argue that any such testing prohibition is unverifiable and will therefore be unable to constrain proliferation.

Problems have similarly been encountered over attempts to negotiate a Fissile Material Cut-off Treaty (FMCT). One issue has been whether the FMCT should prevent future production of fissile materials only or deal with this aspect in conjunction with an agreement to remove existing stockpiles. The verification provisions of any such treaty have also been the subject of differing proposals. One feature of this debate that will demand innovative thinking is how, as safely and cost effectively as possible, any excess fissile material can be disposed of, given the large quantities involved.

The document tabled at the 1995 Conference by the Arab states party to the NPT, known as the Resolution on the Middle East, calls on all states in the region to accede to the NPT. The debate over this resolution has highlighted the problems associated with the attempt to ensure universal adherence to the Treaty. For although signatories to the NPT have increased to the point where 188 states are now party, Israel, India, and Pakistan have remained non-signatories while the DPRK withdrew in 2003. The question is therefore: how, if at all, the Treaty can be made universal?

In response to evolving proliferation dynamics, new initiatives were devised. One strategy that began in the post-cold war period is counter-proliferation, which emphasizes a role for limited ballistic missile defences and a more proactive stance to prevent nuclear proliferation. Another concept known as anti-proliferation also emerged, and this was deemed to incorporate 'the traditional nonproliferation agenda as well as new elements responding to the political and military implications of the proliferation process itself' (Roberts 1993: 140).

By the end of the second decade of the twenty-first century the context of nuclear proliferation was thus undergoing change and in response a panoply of measures have been introduced to deal with the situation. These include, the Proliferation Security Initiative, the Global Initiative to Combat Nuclear Terrorism, the New Start Treaty and the Global Nuclear Energy Partnership. Additionally, in 2010 a Nuclear Security Summit was convened to enhance the security of radiological and nuclear materials around the world. President Obama's 2010 Nuclear Posture Review also gave top priority to combating nuclear proliferation. Finally, there have also been calls for a reappraisal of the prospects for creating new multilateral nuclear fuel centres (an idea that has been around for several decades). Regional safeguards organizations, such as the one established in the European Union (known as EURATOM), have similarly been the subject of attention as possible models for facilitating greater regional oversight of nuclear energy developments.

Key Points

- Nuclear control and anti-proliferation measures have been evolving since 1945.
- The IAEA has established a global safeguards system.
- Attempts to implement a CTBT and negotiate a FMCT have stalled following a period of renewed impetus after 1995.
- A number of NWFZs have been negotiated.
- The NPT now has 188 parties, although India, Israel, and Pakistan remain non-signatories.
- In 1987 the MTCR began operating and The Hague Code of Conduct was introduced in 2002.
- NPT Review Conferences have been held every five years since 1970.
- Since 1995, the NPT has encountered several challenges related to new incidences of nuclear testing, attempts to achieve universality, disposal of fissile material, compliance, and verification.
- It has been suggested that a 'second nuclear age' has emerged.
- New measures have been implemented in response to the consequences of nuclear globalization.

Conclusion

At the heart of the current debate are thus complex issues related to the future global security environment. They include questions such as: what are likely to be the main proliferation challenges of the coming decade? what would happen if the NPT weakens irreparably over time? and what the implications are of the renewed interest in nuclear power generation in the context of the debate over global warming? One response to these questions could be to develop the initiatives already under way into a comprehensive approach for long-term global nuclear governance, though ensuring it remains situated on the original treaty-based foundations. The NPT is now an old treaty with many limitations, but it also provides an international legal framework that allows for collective actions to address pressing global security issues. Such an approach might encompass: attempts to resolve disputes and build trust and confidence at the bilateral and regional levels; the strengthening of international norms; innovation in areas such as compliance, verification, safeguards, intelligence, and fissile and radiological material production, security and disposal; the involvement of non-parties to the NPT; ongoing efforts aimed at nuclear disarmament; and continuing commitment by all parties to the Treaty's objectives.

Box 23.6 Chronology

1945	United States detonates the world's first nuclear weapon.
1946/7	United States and the Soviet Union submit plans for the international control of atomic energy to the newly formed United Nations Atomic Energy Commission (UNAEC).
1949	Soviet Union tests its first nuclear weapon.
1952	United Kingdom tests its first nuclear weapon.
1953	President Eisenhower of the United States introduces his 'Atoms for Peace' proposal to the United Nations General Assembly.
1957	International Atomic Energy Agency (IAEA) inaugurated.
1958	European Atomic Energy Community (EURATOM) begins its operation within the European Community.
1960	France becomes the fourth state to test a nuclear weapon.
1961	United Nations General Assembly adopts the 'Irish Resolution' calling for measures to limit the spread of nuclear weapons to additional states.
1963	Partial Test Ban Treaty (PTBT) entered into force.
1964	China becomes the fifth state to test a nuclear weapon.
1967	Treaty for the Prohibition of Nuclear Weapons in Latin America (the Tlatelolco Treaty) was opened for signature.
1968	Treaty on the Non-Proliferation of Nuclear Weapons (the NPT) opened for signature.
1969	Tlatelolco Treaty entered into force.
1970	NPT entered into force.

1971	IAEA concludes the INFCIRC (Information Circular)/153 Safeguards Agreement and the Zangger Committee also adopted a set of nuclear export guidelines pursuant to the NPT.
1972	Anti-Ballistic Missile (ABM) Treaty is signed between the United States and the Soviet Union.
1974	India detonates a nuclear explosive device declared to be for peaceful purposes and the Nuclear Suppliers Group (NSG) is formed.
1975	First Review Conference of the NPT is held in Geneva, and by the end of the year 97 states had become party to the Treaty.
1978	First United Nations Special Session on Disarmament (UNSSOD-1) provides the forum for the five Nuclear Weapon States to issue unilateral statements on negative security assurances.
1980	Second NPT Review Conference is held in Geneva.
1983	United States announces its Strategic Defence Initiative (SDI).
1985	Third NPT Review Conference is held in Geneva.
1987	Missile Technology Control Regime (MTCR) is established.
1990	Fourth NPT Review Conference is held in Geneva.
1991	A United Nations Special Committee (UNSCOM) is established to oversee the dismantling of Iraq's undeclared nuclear weapons programme. The United States announces its Safety, Security, Dismantlement (SSD) Programme following the dissolution of the Soviet Union.
1993	South Africa announces that it had produced six nuclear devices up until 1989 and then dismantled them prior to signing the NPT. The Democratic People's Republic of Korea (DPRK) announced its intention to withdraw from the NPT following allegations concerning its nuclear programme.
1995	Review and Extension Conference of the NPT is held in New York and the then 179 parties decide to extend the NPT indefinitely and also establish a new Treaty Review Process and a set of principles and objectives for non-proliferation and disarmament.
1996	The Comprehensive Test Ban Treaty (CTBT) is opened for signature.
1997	First Preparatory Committee (PrepCom) for the new NPT Treaty Review Process convenes in Geneva.
1998	India and Pakistan conduct a series of nuclear and missile tests.
1999	United States announces its National Missile Defense (NMD) Act.
2000	Sixth NPT Review Conference is held in New York for the now 188 parties to the Treaty. The five Nuclear Weapon States reiterate the undertaking 'to accomplish the total elimination of their nuclear arsenals'.
2002	Cuba becomes the 189th party to the NPT and The Hague Code of Conduct for missile technology transfers is initiated.
2003	The issue of non-compliance and responses to it become the focus of attention as the DPRK announces its 'withdrawal' from the NPT and intervention occurs in Iraq.
2004	A transnational non-state nuclear supply network is discovered and Libya agrees unconditionally to dismantle its weapons of mass destruction infrastructure in compliance with international agreements and the United Nations Security Council passes Resolution 1540.
2005	Seventh NPT Review Conference is held in New York.
2006	DPRK announces that it has tested a nuclear weapon.
2007	Iran announces progress on its uranium enrichment programme. DPRK has successful test of Taep'o-dong-2C/3 ballistic missile.
2009	Iran successfully launches a satellite into orbit using booster based on DPRK Taep'o-dong-2C/3 ballistic missile. DPRK announces that it has conducted a second nuclear test. UN Security Council passes Resolution 1887.
2010	USA and Russia sign new strategic nuclear arms control agreement. Nuclear Security Summit convened. Eighth NPT Conference is held in New York marking 40th anniversary of the Treaty.

Questions

1 What properties make nuclear weapons different from conventional forms?
2 What are the implications of the global diffusion of nuclear and long-range delivery vehicle technology?
3 What role do norms, taboos, and epistemic communities play in the context of nuclear proliferation?
4 How have the motivations for acquiring nuclear weapons changed since 1945?
5 In what ways has it become more difficult to determine whether nuclear proliferation has actually occurred?

6   Does the non-state actor represent a new nuclear proliferation challenge?
7   What nuclear proliferation concerns have stemmed from the dissolution of the Soviet Union?
8   What are the main arguments for and against the proliferation/spread of nuclear weapons?
9   Were the early efforts to control nuclear weapons doomed to failure?
10   What initiatives are needed to ensure global nuclear governance for the twenty-first century?

Further Reading

Theoretical aspects

Buzan, B., and Herring, E. (1998), *The Arms Dynamic in World Politics* (London: Lynne Rienner). This text covers theoretical and empirical aspects associated with the arms dynamic in the context of nuclear weapons.

Campbell, K. M., Einhorn, R. J., and Reiss, M. B. (2004), *The Nuclear Tipping Point: Why States Reconsider Their Nuclear Choices* (Washington, DC: Brookings Institution Press). This volume explores the factors that lead states to reconsider their nuclear options.

Hymans, J. E. (2006), *The Psychology of Nuclear Proliferation* (Cambridge: Cambridge University Press). Using four case studies, the author draws on materials from the humanities, social sciences, and natural sciences to analyse nuclear decision-making in the states chosen for study.

Johnson, J. L., Kartchner, K. M., and Larsen, J. A. (eds) (2009), *Strategic Culture and Weapons of Mass Destruction: Culturally Based Insights into Comparative National Security Policymaking* (Basingstoke: Palgrave Macmillan). This study considers the significance of strategic culture as a means for understanding why different actors may acquire and potentially threaten to use weapons of mass destruction.

Sagan, S. D., and Waltz, K. N. (1995), *The Spread of Nuclear Weapons. A Debate* (New York and London: W. W. Norton, 2nd edn 2003). This book juxtaposes the contrasting arguments of the two authors concerning the spread of nuclear weapons.

On nuclear use and non-use

Herring, E. (ed.) (2000), *Preventing the Use of Weapons of Mass Destruction* (special issue), *Journal of Strategic Studies*, 23(1) (March). The contributors to this volume concentrate on the issues associated with preventing the use of WMD.

Lavoy, P. R., Sagan, S., and Wirtz, J. J. (eds) (2000), *Planning the Unthinkable: How New Powers Will Use Nuclear, Biological and Chemical Weapons* (Ithaca, NY: Cornell University Press). The authors compare how military threats, strategic cultures, and organizations shape the way leaders intend to employ WMD.

Tannenwald, N. (2007), *The Nuclear Taboo. The United States and the Non-Use of Nuclear Weapons Since 1945* (Cambridge: Cambridge University Press. Cambridge Studies in International Relations 87)

Non-proliferation/anti-proliferation measures

Bosch, O., and Van Ham, P. (eds) (2007), *Global Non-Proliferation and Counter-Terrorism* (Washington, DC: Brookings Institution Press). This volume assesses the impact of UN Security Resolution 1540.

Simpson, J., and Howlett, D. (eds) (1995), *The Future of the Non-Proliferation Treaty* (New York: St Martin's Press). This explores the background issues associated with the NPT in the lead up to the 1995 Review and Extension Conference.

Alternative nuclear futures
Quinlan, M. (2009), *Thinking About Nuclear Weapons. Principles, Problems, Prospects* (Oxford: Oxford University Press, 2009). This book considers the role of nuclear weapons in global security past, present and future.

Online Resource Centre

 Visit the Online Resource Centre that accompanies this book to access more learning resources on this chapter topic at www.oxfordtextbooks.co.uk/orc/baylis5e/

Nationalism

JOHN BREUILLY

Reader's Guide

In this chapter I consider the relationship between nationalism and global politics. I question the conventional view that nationalism preceded globalization and brought about a world order of nation-states that has come under threat from a more recent globalization. Instead, I argue that globalization preceded and has constantly shaped nationalism. I begin by looking at how nationalism has been defined and explained. I then outline how global politics has shaped nationalism over a number of distinct phases since 1750. The key connection between the two is the nation-state, both as nationalist objective and as the main power container of the modern world. However, nationalism, the nation-state, and relations between nation-states change in each phase. This historical perspective can help us to understand current relationships between global politics and nationalism.

Introduction: concepts and debates

A standard view of the relationship between nationalism, **nation-states**, and **global politics** goes something like this. (1) There developed in Europe from about the mid-seventeenth century an order of sovereign, **territorial states** (the 'Westphalian system') (see Ch. 2.). (2) The rise of nationalism from the late eighteenth century nationalized this state order, extending from **Europe** until the whole world was organized as a series of nation-states (see Box 24.1). International relations became relations between nation-states. (3) **Globalization** undermines this political order. It undermines the 'state' by eroding sovereign territorial **power**. It undermines the 'nation' by creating alternative identities. Before considering propositions (2) and (3), I shall outline key concepts and debates concerning nationalism and nation-state.

I define **nationalism** as the idea that the world is divided into nations that provide the overriding focus of political **identity** and loyalty, which in turn demands national **self-determination**. Let us take three key words in this definition. Nationalists think of the **nation** in different ways. The same group can be claimed by competing nationalists. (Turkish nationalists claim Kurds in Turkey as Turkish, a view Kurdish nationalists reject.) Defining nation is more difficult than defining nationalism. Some writers stress objective features such as language; some its subjective, imagined character; while others are sceptical about using the term at all. Box 24.2 provides

examples of these three views. By overriding, I mean that many people think the world is divided into nations, which are the main but not sole object of political loyalty. **Self-determination** usually means independent

Box 24.2 Definitions of nation

'[The nation] ... is an imagined political community—imagined as both inherently limited and sovereign. . . . It is imagined because the members of even the smallest nation will never know most of their fellow-members, meet them, or even hear of them, yet in the minds of each lives the image of their communion. . . . The nation is imagined as *limited* because even the largest of them encompassing perhaps a billion living human beings, has finite, if elastic boundaries, beyond which lie other nations. . . . It is imagined as sovereign because the concept was born in an age in which Enlightenment and Revolution were destroying the legitimacy of the divinely-ordained, hierarchical dynastic realm.'

(Benedict Anderson 1991: 5–6)

'let us define it [the nation] at the outset as a large social group integrated not by one but by a combination of several kinds of objective relationships (economic, political, linguistic, cultural, religious, geographical, historical), and their subjective reflection in collective consciousness. Many of these ties could be mutually substitutable—some playing a particularly important role in one nation-building process, and no more than a subidiary part in others. But among them, three stand out as irreplaceable: (1) a "memory" of some common past, treated as a "destiny" of the group—or at least of its core constituents; (2) a density of linguistic or cultural ties enabling a higher degree of social communication within the group than beyond it; (3) a conception of the equality of all members of the group organized as a civil society.'

(Miroslav Hroch 1996: esp. 79)

'Neither objective nor subjective definitions are thus satisfactory, and both are misleading. In any case, agnosticism is the best initial posture of a student in this field, and so this book assumes no *a priori* definition of what constitutes a nation. As an initial working assumption any sufficiently large body of people whose members regard themselves as members of a "nation", will be treated as such. However, whether such a body of people does so regard itself cannot be established simply by consulting writers or political spokesmen of organizations claiming the status of "nation" for it. The appearance of a group of spokesmen for some "national idea" is not insignificant, but the word "nation" is today used so widely and imprecisely that the use of the vocabulary of nationalism today may mean very little indeed.'

(Eric Hobsbawm 1990: 8–9)

Box 24.1 The development of a world of nation-states

Date	Rough number of nation(al) states*
1500	2 (England, France)
1800	6 (Britain, France, Holland, USA, Spain, Portugal)
1900	30 (including Belgium, Germany, Italy, Serbia, Romania, Greece, Brazil, Argentina, Japan, Canada)
1923	45 members of the League of Nations
1945	51 states established the United Nations
1950	60 members of UN
1960	99 members of UN
1970	127 members of UN
2006	192 members of UN

*Before 1923 this is an estimate based on historical judgement. Thereafter it is based on membership of the League of Nations and the United Nations.

statehood. However, nationalists might settle for something less, such as autonomy within a federal state.

Nationalism can be considered as ideology, as politics, as sentiments. Definitions of nationalism usually frame it as ideology, a political worldview. However, we might have ignored this ideology had it not become significant. This happened when nationalism shaped people's sense of identity: nationalism as sentiments. It happened when nationalism was taken up by movements seeking to form nation-states: nationalism as politics.

It is helpful to divide each aspect of nationalism into types. Here are some examples. Ideology can be **civic** and **ethnic**. **Civic nationalism** is commitment to a state and its values. State membership determines nationality, as in the multi-ethnic immigrant society of the USA. **Ethnic nationalism** is commitment to a group of (imagined) common descent. Nation precedes state, as in ethno-national states formed in modern Europe. There are problems with this distinction. Every nationalism invokes culture and values, and these change, often quickly. Cultural factors like religion and language cannot easily be assigned to the ethnic or civic category. There is a danger of moralizing the distinction (civic good; ethnic bad). Nevertheless, the distinction can be useful.

Nationalist sentiments can be of the elite or of the masses. Some nationalist ideas appeal only to a small stratum of the population, whereas others have popular resonance. In terms of politics, nationalism can be state-

strengthening and state-subverting. State-strengthening nationalism accepts an existing state as broadly legitimate but seeks to strengthen it, internally by 'purifying' the nation and reforming government, externally by reclaiming 'national' territory and extending power. State-subverting nationalism aims to create a new state, usually by separation from a larger state, sometimes by unifying smaller states.

The relationship of nationalism to global politics varies with these types. Mass-nationalism, using ethnic ideas to subvert an existing state, is very different from elite-nationalism, using civic ideas to strengthen an existing state.

It is generally agreed that nationalism is modern. Explanations of its origins and growth revolve round four key questions: (1) Does nationalism depend upon the prior existence of nations? (2) Are nations modern or do they extend far back in time? (3) Should we privilege culture, or economics, or politics in our explanations? And (4) What is the role played by internal factors (such as a shared culture) in relation to external factors (such as threats or support from powerful states) in shaping nationalism? Table 24.1 summarizes positions in this debate.

Sometimes there is confusion over the usage of 'nation' and 'state'. The leading **international organization** is the United Nations. The term 'Nations' here actually means 'States'. Cultural diversity can be so great as to render implausible any claim that these are ethno-national states.

Table 24.1 Debates on nationalism

Priority (nation or nationalism)	Dating (pre-modern/modern)	Type (ideology, politics, sentiment)	Key factor (culture, economy, politics)	Theory (short name)	Theorist (example)
Nation	Modern	Sentiment	Culture (belief as identity)	Primordialism	Walker Connor
Nation	Pre-modern (ethnie)	Sentiment	Culture (myths and memories)	Ethno-symbolism	Anthony Smith
Nation	Pre-modern	Sentiment	Culture (beliefs as creeds)	Perennnialism	Adrian Hastings
Nationalism	Modern	Sentiment	Economy (industry)	Modernism	Ernest Gellner
Nationalism	Modern	Sentiment	Culture (communication)	Modernism	Benedict Anderson
Nationalism	Modern	Ideology	Culture (intellectuals)	Modernism	Elie Kedourie
Nationalism	Modern	Politics	Politics (elite and modern states)	Modernism	Paul Brass Charles Tilly Michael Mann

In many states, the lack of democracy renders implausible any claim that these are civic-national states. What then does the term nation-state mean? I do not think it worth trying to identify how 'national' states are because the criteria are so fuzzy, and also because it means accepting basic nationalist assumptions. Instead, I shall treat as nation-states states that claim to be national, however nation is defined, are not confronted internally by powerful state-subverting nationalist movements, and are accepted by the international community.

Key Points

- Nationalism claims that the nation exists and should form the basis of the political order.
- Nationalism can be considered as ideology, as sentiments, and as politics.
- We can construct different typologies of nationalism, such as ethnic/civic, elite/mass, state-strengthening/state-subverting.
- The most important debates on nationalism concern whether it is cause or consequence of nation, the relative importance of culture, economics and politics, and the different roles played by internal and external factors.
- It is impossible to define a 'nation-state' in objective terms without accepting the assumptions of nationalism. Therefore nation-state will be defined largely in terms of its self-description and that of the international community.

Nationalism, nation-states, and global politics in history

We start with the historical relationship between nationalism and the global spread of nation-states. Some historians identify forms of 'globalization' far back in time. From 1500 we can trace new global connections between human beings as the Americas were brought into contact with Eurasia and Africa. Some historians also claim to trace nationalism and nation-states back at least that far. However, it is generally agreed that nationalism as politics and/or mass sentiment became significant only from around 1750. At about this time one can also identify the first significant global political conflicts between states using nationalist arguments.

Globalization has been defined in many ways, and I need to be clear what I mean by the term. My concern is with the relationship between nationalism and power, especially state-organized power, and in particular the processes leading to the nation-state emerging as the dominant form of state power, and nationalism as the dominant political ideology. Consequently I define globalization as the patterns of political interaction shaped by relations between the most powerful states that take place frequently, significantly and simultaneously in Europe, Asia, Africa, and the Americas. This is a pragmatic definition that deliberately leaves out non-state elements such as communications, transportation, economic and social interactions, although obviously these influence the patterns of state interactions.

Anglo-French rivalry, *c.* 1750–1815

Global power

In Europe and beyond, France and Britain deployed land and sea forces against each other. They used others as proxies in at least three continents (Europe, India, and North America). Both states sought to control global trading in mass commodities (cotton, tobacco, sugar) that were superimposed upon older **networks** of luxury trade. Europeans explained and justified their power as due to greater civilizational achievements than the rest of the world, which was seen as largely consisting of primitive cultures and decaying civilizations.

Global conflict and nationalism

The dominant form of nationalism within the two major powers was state-strengthening, civic, and elite. Within France and Britain, there were demands for the removal of privilege, and to make government accountable to the 'nation'. This 'civic nation' was based on the interests of an expanding middle class that was itself shaped by commercial globalization. The conflict between Britain and France provided public opinion in each state with a clear enemy. The conflict hit France harder than Britain, and precipitated revolution. From that revolution came the declaration that the state existed for the nation. Revolutionary France, when it embarked on war in Europe, appealed to other nations to rise up against their governments. Those governments deployed nationalist rhetoric in reply.

Nationalism, nation-state formation, and international relations

Nationalism became significant in British and French politics but remained mainly just an ideology elsewhere in Europe. Rebellion in the Americas freed territories from Spanish and British control, and elites used the language of civic national independence. The defeat of Napoleon left Britain the major world power.

Pax Britannica, *c.* 1815–1914

Global power

States in Europe and America were preoccupied with regional affairs. Elsewhere, Britain exerted global power. Apart from **diplomacy** to coopt or divide opponents, Britain relied upon naval supremacy and informal collaboration with local elites. Instead of combining coercive and economic power in traditional empire-state form, Britain proclaimed their separation. It abolished tariffs, ceased monopolizing overseas trade and shipping, and tied major currencies to the price of gold. This was linked to industrialization accompanied by transformations in communications (telegraph) and transportation (steam power). All this enabled huge increases in long-distance migration.

Britain attributed its success to Christianity, parliamentary institutions, and free trade. However, the coordinating nature of British power meant these could not be directly imposed, even if much violence was often used. Within Europe, the Americas, and Asia, wars in the 1860s were won by modernizing and nationalizing states that then turned their attention outwards, challenging British **hegemony**. Close links between technology and power led to state intervention; the belief that power depended upon control of overseas resources fuelled the rise of imperialist conflict.

Global conflict and nationalism

Nationalism initially imitated the civic forms projected by France and Britain, partly because success breeds imitation, partly because nationalists aimed at support from France and Britain. These nationalists projected themselves as 'historic' nations, insisting that 'non-historic' nationalities must assimilate into 'high-culture' nations. This stimulated counter-nationalism, which stressed folk culture, popular religion, and spoken language. These had little initial success but diffused nationalist ideas.

Beyond Europe there was little stimulus to nationalism, given the indirect nature of British power, which was not yet projected in nationalist forms. There were reactions against Christianity and secular modernity. Such values could be accepted (e.g. Christian conversion) or rejected. Most important were combinations, for example the 'codification' of Hinduism in India, which rejected Christianity but conferred 'Christian' features upon Hindu beliefs (see Case Study 2).

As the contradictions of British-led globalization grew, this generated new forms of nationalism. Imperialist conflict promoted popular state-strengthening nationalism in the challenger states. These combined with race ideas, which often replaced civilizational and religious claims to superiority. Although mainly projected onto the non-European world, such ideas were also used within Europe, as in modern anti-Semitism. The tightening of direct control in empires, justified in race and nationalist terms, stimulated counter-nationalisms.

Nationalism, nation-state formation, and international relations

The success of state-strengthening, elite, civic nationalism was linked to war using modern technology and organization. Nationalism became central in the new nation-states. Its liberal values were abandoned as elites confronted problems of state-building, economic development, and imperialist expansion. Ethnic, state-subverting nationalism had limited success against declining multinational states. Support from powerful states like Russia was more important than the intrinsic strength of nationalist movements. Powerful nation-states challenged British hegemony. Britain responded in like fashion. The world increasingly divided into formal and controlled spheres of **influence** after 1880. International relations were dominated by arms races based on new technology and formal alliances. Politicians appealed to public opinion and **national interests**. They then found themselves trapped by the nationalist sentiments they had helped create.

Implications for global politics

British hegemony was justified in cosmopolitan and free trade terms. Liberal nationalism developed in modernizing societies outside British zones of influence. Industrialized war enabled liberal nationalists to form new nation-states. These states established a new model. The state ruled with a bureaucratic apparatus, in conjunction with a dynamic industrial sector, over demarcated **territory**. Armed with nationalist ideas, it penetrated society in new ways: mass education and media, tariff protection, and subsidies. It projected its aggressive nationalism abroad in pursuit of **empire**. As political conflict globalized, it nationalized. Imperial powers aimed at new forms of control over other parts of the world. There was a contradiction between civilizational justifications and the reality of subordination and exploitation accompanied by race ideas. Counter-nationalism rejected imperial power, though it was often framed in broad regional terms (Pan-Africanism, Pan-Asianism, Pan-Arabism etc.). Making rejection effective became possible when global political conflict turned into world war.

The era of world war, *c.* 1914–45

Global power

Initially Eurocentric, the First World War became global (see Ch. 3). In 1917 the USA entered the war. State control over population and economy increased massively. Although the inter-war period saw military dismantling and reduced state intervention, the Second World War was more global, state intervention more extensive, war more 'total'. Radio communication and air power, large-scale economic assistance, and military **coordination** gave this war a transnational character. Military globalization was accompanied by economic de-globalization. Free trade and fixed exchange rates disappeared. Voluntary international migration decreased. Attempts to return to 'normality' in the 1920s were blown off course by the **Great Depression**. New technologies (radio, film and television, air travel, and automobiles) expanded massively. They were brought under state control, especially during war. Rather than undermining nationalism, these global processes became components of state-strengthening nationalism.

Global conflict and nationalism

In both wars the Western Allies proclaimed their cause as liberal democracy, not narrow nationalism, though liberal democracy was organized in the form of civic nation-states. However, their alliance with Russia compromised that claim, as did their failure to universalize liberal democracy after victory. Germany expressed clear-cut ethnic nationalism in 1914. Its Ottoman and Habsburg allies went to war to block state-subverting, ethno-nationalism. Victory for the Allies meant victory for the liberal democratic **principle** of 'national self-determination' embodied in Woodrow Wilson's **Fourteen Points**, but the beneficiaries were the ethno-

nationalist opponents of the defeated dynastic empires. Each new state ruled in the name of the dominant nation and regarded minorities with suspicion. Nationalists representing minorities looked to their 'own' national state for support and invoked minority rights provisions in the peace treaties. Such nationalism was inward-looking. The USA turned inwards. After a brief phase of stressing a world socialist mission, the USSR also turned inwards.

However, one distinct form of nationalism—fascism—was not insular. Fascists hated communism and **liberalism**, while rejecting old conservative elite politics. Fascists saw the nation as a supra-individual, classless collective requiring a strong state, mass mobilization, and a genius leader to assert itself in the world. The First World War gave nationalism a statist and militarist character on which fascists built. With economic depression and loss of faith in liberal democracy, fascism gained popularity. Fascist ideology was imperialist but profoundly anti-universalist. The fascist vision was of huge power blocs, each organized as a master nation/race ruling over inferior slave classes.

In the colonial world, military mobilization and attempts at economic development increased subordination and exploitation. World war made clear the divisions and fragilities of existing power structures. This promoted nationalist dreams of gaining independence, justified in liberal democratic or socialist terms.

Nationalism, nation-state formation, and international relations

Nationalism alone could not form nation-states. It succeeded only with the destruction or weakening of multinational states through war. The doctrine of national self-determination was applied after 1918 to the defeated powers, and only within Europe. International relations were transformed with the League of Nations. But the defeated powers were denied membership, and the US Senate voted against joining. The League was led by France and Britain and seen as an instrument of their interests. The League did much in pioneering concepts of **international law** and administration but failed in its ambitious objectives of creating a new peaceful **order**.

International relations became more violent and expressed in terms of competing ideologies. In each state there were strong disputes, and politics was no longer monopolized by small elites. Communist and fascist ideologies justified extreme policies that assumed that sheer willpower could overcome 'reality'. Fascism and communism did not envisage a global order of nation-

Case Study 1 Interactions between nationalism and global politics in Germany

This case shows the changing interaction between nationalism and global politics. Nationalism is diverse, but can be understood through examining the global context. Here, the changing forms of nationalism are connected to changing phases in the nature of global politics through the formation of the nation-state as in Germany.

Germany

In 1750 the German lands were fragmented and its major powers—Austria and Prussia—increasingly weak in relation to Britain, France, and Russia. The wars (1740–8, 1756–63) between Austria and Prussia were also part of the Anglo-French conflict. These two states lost heavily in wars against Napoleon up to 1809. Intellectuals took up romantic and ethnic ideas of nationalism but eventual recovery had more to do with a broad alliance against France which formed after the failure of Napoleon's invasion of Russia. After 1815 Britain was concerned that the major European powers balanced each other, leaving her free in the wider world. This included an Austria–Prussia balance in Germany. The major nationalist challenge took a liberal, constitutional form, influenced by Britain and France, but it could never develop a popular and unified appeal and was opposed by the main states.

The key shift came when liberal nationalism shifted to a state-strengthening position in support of Prussia. Early industrialization, especially in transportation (railways), communication (telegraph), and manufacturing (coal, iron, steel), had an unexpected military consequence that enabled Prussia to gain dramatic and swift victories over Austria in 1866 and France in 1870–1.

Continued rapid industrialization in Germany, mass emigration of Germans to America, and concern to challenge British hegemony led to the growth of a more populist, illiberal, and imperialist nationalism. A key moment was when Germany began building a modern battleship fleet, seen as a direct threat by Britain. That stimulated popular nationalism in Britain and alliances with Russia and France, leading to world war. German defeat spawned an extreme ethnic nationalism which, compounded by the Great Depression, brought Hitler to power. Nazism pursued race empire in Europe, and at least parity with what Hitler envisaged would be the only other two world powers in the world, the British Empire and the USA.

It required a global coalition to defeat Germany, Italy, and Japan. The result was a *de facto* partition of Germany, dividing with the cold war into a western and a communist state. Ethnic nationalism was rejected in the name of liberalism and socialism. (The third German state—Austria—declared itself neutral and not even German!) New generations in each state came to identify with that state rather than the German nation. German reunificaiton appears to contradict the rejection of nationalism. Really, however, reunification was part of the 'triumph of the West'. There was no powerful nationalist demand for unity in advance of the event itself. The collapse of communism took everyone by surprise. However, for East Germans, unification offered a fast track into the European Union and Western affluence. West Germany's liberal democratic commitment to unity with less fortunate brethren made it impossible to refuse or delay unification. Indeed, one could see reunification as the first step towards the expansion of the European Union eastwards rather than a revival of nationalism.

---

states but super-empires led by dominant races/nations or classes. Communist states eventually recognized limits, which helped them survive this era. The Third Reich pursued an escalating and ultimately self-destructive radicalism (see German case study).

In the colonial world the concern was to survive murderous conflict between the major powers. Nationalists sought to exploit these conflicts but imperial states kept control unless defeated in war. Conflict created opportunities. Nationalism could become entrenched, strong, and popular (see India case study).

Implications for global politics

World war demanded global political strategies and undermined **state sovereignty**. It reversed earlier economic globalization. Liberal democracy was threatened, reactive, and defensive, confronted by communism and fascism. In 1941 the fascist world vision seemed close to realization. However, nationalists who initially thought the fascist powers offered ways of throwing off existing imperial rule discovered that it meant exchanging one master for a worse one. Such nationalism could only succeed if old imperial power was dismantled but not replaced by new fascist power. How did this come about? In 1941–2 the USA moved out of post-1918 isolationism into world war. Its leaders were compelled to think about the war in global and integrated terms. Within two years, military victory looked likely. Global strategy turned to plotting the shape of a post-war world. Nationalism and nation-states figured centrally.

Case Study 2 Interactions between nationalism and global politics in India

This case shows the changing interaction between nationalism and global politics. Nationalism is diverse, but can be understood through examining the global context. In this case, the changing forms of nationalism and changing phases in the nature of global politics are connected by the formation of the imperial state in India.

India

Before 1750 India was enmeshed in global ties. The Mughal Empire was linked to Islamic, imperial, and long-distance trading networks that spread eastwards into China, through Asia Minor and the Middle East, into north and west Africa and, through connections with European powers, to the Americas and Southeast Asia, even north Australia. The British East India Company built on existing trading and political networks, and introduced new features, such as plantation production of tobacco, tea, coffee, opium, and cotton. There was little attempt to impose European culture or religion, or direct rule. Britain and France fought for influence and by 1815 Britain had prevailed. The following period was one of free trade and informal empire. The East India Company ruled but under public scrutiny. Christian pressures in-

creased. Reactions against Christianization promoted the codification and indigenization of Hinduism.

This broad, anti-British sentiment culminated in the great uprising of 1857 and, after its repression, the imposition of formal imperial rule. This, along with the increased exploitation of India in rivalry with other imperialist challenges, promoted nationalist ideas. The Indian National Congress, elite, civic, and at first state-strengthening, was founded in 1885. By 1914 the British had responded with communal electorates and local councils which classed Hindu and Muslim as distinct political identities.

World war brought home to many Indians that they were part of a system of global conflict. Mass-based nationalism emerged in the 1920s. Depression intensified mass discontent while the Congress Party penetrated and came to control the devolved provincial government. Britain, confronted by opponents in every part of the world, made concessions. By 1939 independence appeared just a matter of time. But with war Britain tightened control, imprisoned nationalist leaders, and courted Muslim politicians. British collapse against Japan increased nationalist expectations. Britain could not resist these once war finished but the speed of decolonization and the legacy of the wartime policies meant this took the form of partition rather than one post-colonial state.

Independent India tried to detach itself from cold war polarization by acting as leader of the non-aligned states. Congress pursued a civic territorial nationalism with much success but has been confronted by vibrant religious resistance to secularism, culminating in Hindu and Sikh nationalist challenges. Pakistan, set up as a secular but Islamic state, was unable to keep control of East Pakistan and has found Islamism increasingly important in West Pakistan.

With the end of the cold war and the latest era of globalization, India has begun to exhibit spectacular economic growth rates. The old model of India as part of the 'Third World' clearly does not work.

The era of cold war, 1945–90

Global power

The major shapers of the post-war era were the USA and the USSR (see Ch. 2). Stalin regarded Soviet expansion as providing a defensive bulwark rather than a stepping-stone to global domination. Yet that expansion, plus Communist victory in China, made communism appear a global threat. Communist power was organized as conventional territorial rule, albeit with novel institutions and ideologies. The USA envisioned hegemony differently. Sole control of nuclear weapons initially made it possible to envisage power as coordinating rather than direct (except in occupied Japan and Germany). The foundations were laid of a liberal global order based on national **sovereignty** with low tariffs, managed exchange rates, and extensive reconstruction. The first wave of decolonization in 1947–9 presaged the worldwide extension of this order.

However, the USSR soon acquired nuclear weapons and credible missile delivery systems. This intensified mutual perception of threat and made military capacity literally global. The USA retreated from its anti-imperialist stance. The nuclear umbrella handed initiatives to local states which presented themselves as valued clients of one or other **superpower**. Each had its own sphere of power. Contested zones in the Middle East, South-East Asia, and Africa were where nationalism could flourish.

US hegemony contributed to economic and cultural globalization, in such forms as mass media and consumption. US aid, private investment, low tariffs, stable exchange rates, and cheap energy produced high growth rates and integration between developed regions of the 'free world'. This world consisted of an ever-increasing number of nation-states as the decolonization process resumed from the late 1950s.

Global politics and nationalism

In Europe the focus was on stabilizing nation-states within a supranational framework (see Ch. 26). Ethnic homogenization rendered ethno-nationalism redundant and made civic nationalism easily acceptable. This ideology could accommodate US doctrines of free markets and national sovereignty. The USSR accorded formal sovereignty to its European satellites. Beyond Europe, colonial nationalists demanded territorial independence, a principle enshrined in UN **conventions** and declarations. For those who equated ethno-nationalism with nationalism, this signalled the end of nationalism. Yet independent states with poorly integrated political institutions, economies, and cultures confronted major problems. The dominant principle was that of (nation-) state sovereignty. The United Nations made no provision for minority rights, which were seen as threatening state sovereignty and encouraging ethno-nationalism. Nation-states were highly unequal and mostly located in one or other superpower bloc, but the political order was presented as one of equal sovereign nation-states.

Nationalism, nation-state formation, and international relations

The United Nations included from the outset the two major powers. The defeated powers became members. Decolonization increased membership sharply. The principle of state sovereignty was accommodated to decolonization. Anti-colonial nationalism was usually focused on gaining international legitimacy rather than violently achieving liberation. This, along with continued economic dependence, helps explain postcolonial problems like military coups, corruption, and ethnic politics: national solidarity had not been forged in the struggle for independence. These problems generated new forms of nationalism, some demanding separation, others reforms to create 'real' independence. Nationalist opposition could precipitate state collapse. However, the bipolar order and sacrosanct principle of state sovereignty prevented state collapse turning into new states. The system preferred dysfunctional states.

Implications for global politics

The nation-state was reasserted and globalized but in civic rather than ethnic form. States were legitimized by non-national values (democracy, communism), contained within blocs dominated by the USA or USSR, their sovereignty, even their 'stateness', often a fiction. Civic, state-supporting nationalism dominated. Both the USSR and USA recognized ethnic diversity, but contained within the framework of state sovereignty and civic national identity. State-subverting nationalism used civic language and demanded only devolution. Ethno-nationalism, secessionism, and irredentism would only re-emerge when the **cold war** ended.

I have gone quickly through a complex history but it is the only way to grasp the relationship between nationalism and global politics. This is not a simple relationship. There is no linear direction to the history, such as the rise of nationalism followed by the challenge of globalization. There *are* patterns and I have outlined some of these, but I leave it to you to decide if the historical record supports these suggestions. There is constantly changing interaction in which nationalism, nation-state, and global politics each take on different and related forms. With each phase, the number of nation-states increases. The ideology of nationalism becomes the principal way of justifying the existence of particular states. It combines the democratic principle (nation = people), the claim to sovereignty (national self-determination), and a sense of distinct identity. It is flexible enough to accommodate different social and political arrangements.

Nationalism is a chameleon-like idea that can adapt to changes in the global political order, matching its claims to the changing ways in which states interact. It mirrors, with its argument that the world is divided into distinct nations with particular territories, the formation of a world divided into sovereign states with sharply demarcated territories.

In this chapter I have not tried to write about 'nationalism in general': I do not think there is such a thing. If one accepts this view, it suggests that one should look at the contemporary relationship between global politics and nationalism as yet another set of different interactions. Our awareness of the history alerts us to what is new in these interactions.

Key Points

- There is no simple sequence leading either from nationalism to nation-state formation to changes in the global political order or the other way round.

- There is no single, dominant form of nationalism, but rather it can be ethnic or civic, elite or popular, and strengthen or subvert existing states.

- The best place to start is with the most important states in each historical phase.

- The political ideology of these states matters most because they have the most power and others respond to their power and ideologies.

- At the start of our history, global conflict was shifting power to extensive middle classes in Britain and France, and the national idea justified demands for reforms that challenged 'top-down' ideals of power based on religion, monarchy, and privilege.

- British victory over France popularized its liberal, constitutionalist nationalism that was taken up in imitative form by elites elswhere which were able, especially when linked to modernizing states like Prussia, Japan, and the North in the American Civil War, to form powerful nation-states.

- Those nation-states generated new forms of illiberal, imperialist nationalism to challenge British hegemony, in turn provoking colonial societies to develop counter-nationalisms.

- State-subverting nationalisms cannot on their own defeat imperial powers but are helped by the weakening of those powers in global conflict with each other.

- Therefore the ability of state-subverting nationalism to form nation-states is based on a combination of its own social base and political organization, the power and policy of the state it confronts, and a favourable international situation.

Nationalism, nation-states, and global politics today

Forms of global politics

The collapse of the USSR led to a new wave of nation-state formations. Beyond Europe the removal of the cold war freeze permitted the emergence of state-subverting nationalism. The end of managed exchange rates and deregulation of financial markets undermined state power. At the same time, the regional concentration of economic development has permitted supra-state coordination in certain regions, most notably Europe. While capital, goods, and information move freely and quickly across the world, the same does not apply to labour, especially that of unskilled people in poor countries. The digital information revolution, which has expanded massively the speed and capacity for information storage and processing, opens up the prospects of global culture, whether envisaged as homogenized culture for the masses or as a vast plurality of niche cultures, including diaspora national ones. All this opens up opportunities for new forms of nationalism.

Global politics and nationalism

At a political level the key point is that the cold war labelling and preservation of a particular set of states as civic nation-states was undermined. This enabled the rapid emergence of new forms of nationalism that were not bound to the existing state system.

First, there was state-subverting ethno-nationalism in the former Soviet Union and Yugoslavia. To counter this, the international community and the new Russian government rapidly conceded new state formations—thus turning state-subverting into state-strengthening nationalism. Furthermore, these new states were recognized as civic, territorial entities based on the federated republics of the former states. However, unlike earlier decolonization, these republics were officially based on ethnic identities. That led to conflict over ethnic minorities within the new states. This has remained fairly low-key so far as Russian speakers in the new non-Russian states are concerned, but it led to war and violent ethnic cleansing in parts of former Yugoslavia. The combination of intra-state conflict based on ethnic nationality, the lack of international support for state sovereignty but also for intervention could in some **failed states** lead to vicious ethno-nationalist violence. Rwanda was a case in point.

Second, there have been reactions against this resurgence of ethno-nationalism. One important change from the cold war phase is the increased resort to external intervention into state affairs, involving the United Nations, regional political–military organizations like **NATO**, individual states, and **non-governmental organizations** (NGOs). The justifications for these interventions are universalist—human rights, the promotion of democracy—rather than the protection of ethnic minorities. That, in turn, conditions the development of

409 Chapter 24 Nationalism

nationalism. Noting that the international community disapproves of ethno-nationalism, whether practised by the state against minorities or by minorities to subvert the state, nationalism presents itself instead as a movement for human rights, including cultural recognition, and asks for constitutional change such as devolution rather than independent statehood.

Nationalism, nation-state formation, and international relations

In the first unstable phase after 1990 there was a rapid emergence of ethno-nationalism and new nation-state formations. However, after that phase, the international community, above all the USA, has reacted against ethno-nationalism and state break-up, while at the same time enabling new forms of intervention into the internal affairs of weaker states. Nationalism has adapted accordingly and come to focus less on the classical demand for 'one state, one ethno-nation'. Instead, nationalism frequently combines sub-state and transnational connections, for example in the ways the European Union is seen to promote regional autonomy within and across individual states.

Nationalist politics is frequently represented as ethnic politics but now demanding cultural recognition and affirmative action rather than political independence. Arguably, the nation-state is ceasing to be the overwhelmingly important power-container of earlier phases of global politics. This can produce one kind of state-strengthening nationalism designed to resist the weakening of the nation-state. Here one can think of the rise of radical right nationalism, particularly concerned with the control of immigration.

Yet the very erosion of nation-state power can also promote the shift of nationalism away from either state-strengthening or state-subversion to other kinds of politics. That kind of politics can also take up connections to transnational or global political actors other than states, such as diaspora organizations. Whether we should continue to call these politics based on ethnic or culturally defined groups nationalism is a matter of debate.

The impact on global politics

The rapid emergence of new kinds of nationalism, the formation of new nation-states, and the violent conflicts with which this was sometimes associated, have altered patterns of global politics. They have stimulated new interventions by a variety of state and **non-state actors**. These interventions have been justified in universalist terms: human rights, democracy (see Ch. 30). This is new: in the era of world wars the justification was (ethno-national) minority rights and in the cold war period the principle of state sovereignty blocked intervention. All these interventions appear to undermine nation-states—culturally, politically, economically, and militarily. Obviously the impact is varied; it is greatest for the weakest states. Above all, nationalism is not the same as nation-state. It is precisely when nation-states are most threatened that nationalism, as a reaction against that, can be strongest. At the same time, the very globalization of politics can stimulate new forms of sub- and transnational politics, including that of nationalism.

> **Key Points**
>
> - The sacrosanct principle of state sovereignty was weakened with the end of the cold war, new nation-state formation, and new economic and cultural forms of globalization.
>
> - This provoked a first wave of state-subverting ethno-nationalisms, which could lead to violence and ethnic cleansing.
>
> - However, international recognition for new states as civic, territorial entities, along with new forms of intervention and pressure, put pressure on nationalism to move away from this ethnic and state-subverting character.
>
> - There is a state-strengthening nationalism that focuses on the threats globalization poses to the nation-state, and which can paradoxically get stronger the more the nation-state is weakened.
>
> - However, perhaps more important is the shift of nationalism away from a state focus towards concerns with devolution, cultural recognition, and transnational linkages.

Conclusion

Global politics has a history preceding the rise of nationalism and the formation of nation-states. Roughly, one can divide the history of global politics into its pre-

history (to *c.* 1500) when there were widespread but not worldwide political networks, its pre-national stage (*c.* 1500–1750) when such networks were worldwide but states were not yet nation-states and nationalism had not yet developed as a significant political force, and the modern period (1750 to the present) when global politics, nationalism, and the spread of the nation-state interacted with each other.

The general trend in the various historical phases from 1750 to the end of the cold war has been an increase in the number of nation-states, and—by around 1970—the acceptance, in ordinary experience but also in international politics and law, that national identity and the nation-state provide the basis of the global political order. However, it is debatable how far this can be attributed to what one might call 'the rise of nationalism'. Nationalism reflected developments in the global political order as much as it caused them. The key connecting elements between nationalism and the global political order were the formation of nation-states and their relations with each other. Furthermore, the type of nation-state and structure of international relations itself changed from one phase to the next, changes accompanied by changes in nationalism. Obviously there is an 'internal' history to nationalism, based on pre-existing sentiments and senses of identity, on struggles between social groups for power, and on changes in the way states function and relate to their societies. However, studies of nationalism tend to focus overwhelmingly on this internal history and neglect the way nationalism is shaped by—as well as shapes—the changing forms of global politics. In this chapter I have tried to focus on this aspect of the subject.

In the contemporary stage of the interaction between global politics and nationalism there remains one superpower and speeded-up forms of globalization based on open economies and new technologies of movement and communication. The unfreezing of international relations has allowed many diverse and conflicting forms of nationalism to take shape. Some of these seek to subvert and others to strengthen existing nation-states in ways that are similar to historical forms of nationalism. Thus nationalists who stress protection against immigration or the imposition of cultural homogeneity on citizens follow in the footsteps of earlier types of ethnic nationalism. Nationalists who demand expansion in the name of claiming 'national' territory do the same. So do nationalists who try to lead secessions from existing states. The language used may change, with separatist movements stressing human rights and democracy rather than ethnic identity, as that fits better the current global

political situation, but the politics is similar. There may also be more in the way of such movements, given the weakening of the commitment to the principle of state sovereignty.

More interestingly, the ways in which nation-state sovereignty is being eroded can help generate novel forms of nationalism. In other chapters in this book it has been suggested that one should think of globalization as transforming rather than either destroying or leaving untouched nation-state sovereignty. The nation-state becomes more an enabling institution in a web of international, transnational, and global networks. If this is the case, I suggest it will generate new kinds of nationalism. Some of these will see their purpose as to resist this transformation of the nation-state, for example by opposing supranational agreements on free population movement or the development of multilateral military institutions. Some will see it as their purpose to exploit these transformations in the nation-state, for example by arguing for devolution and multiculturalism, for connections between the 'same' nationality groups across state boundaries. New kinds of diaspora nationalism are emerging, using the new technologies of communications to maintain links. Notions like a 'Europe of the regions' can also underpin new kinds of national movements. What the historical perspective suggests as the most important change is that nationalism is shifting away from a focus on the independent nation-state towards other kinds of political or cultural objectives. Indeed, it is often not even calling itself nationalism. No sooner do we think we have tied down the subject than it transmutes into something else. It is only by putting it into its precise historical or contemporary context that we can grasp these transmutations.

Writers on nationalism have constantly anticipated that it is about to come to an end. The first secular creeds of modernity—liberalism and socialism—assumed that global ties would create a cosmopolitan world, whether based on free trade **capitalism** or classless communism. 'Narrow' nationalism had no place in such a globalized world. What these ideas failed to grasp was that the major power-container for managing the new global processes would be the territorial, sovereign state. This state used new technology to create superior military power, guided economic development, and increasingly shaped its population through mass schooling and control over the patterns of their interactions, and finally by providing many of the social services earlier associated with families and small communities. At the same time, the formation of a mobile, participatory society swept aside legitimations for state authority based on privilege, heredity, and religion.

Nationalism provided the new legitimation for such states. It matched the development of the sovereign state ruling over the demarcated territory with the idea that the world was divided into diverse and distinct nations. It put the nation as source of authority in place of privilege and religion. It also proved capable of generating emotional solidarity that appealed to large-scale societies made up of diverse people who were strangers to each other. This was something that liberalism and socialism had not been able to achieve on their own.

Why nationalism has managed to achieve this is a matter of fierce debate. At one extreme, nationalism is seen as an expression of a pre-existing and strong sense of solidarity (nations, ethnies, races). Only on such an existing solidarity, these writers argue, is it possible to create the modern bonds of nationalism. At the other extreme, nationalism is seen as something manipulated by modern political elites in order to secure power in the state. The second view can fit well with the view of international relations as relations between states that act fairly rationally on the basis of clear interests and calculations. The first view, by contrast, tends to see honour and emotions as playing an important part in international relations and making them unstable.

My own view is somewhat different. I have argued that nationalism is a political idea and practice that mirrors the emergence of the new order of sovereign, territorial states, and that alters its character as that order goes through different historical phases. Where there are shared values, nationalism will exploit these as expressions of national identity (e.g. making Hinduism 'Indian'), but this only works effectively in the context of modern state-formation and global political conflict. These and other approaches can be combined in a great variety of arguments, so I doubt whether the debate will ever be settled.

As nation-states espousing nationalist values—for whatever reason they have come into existence—extended their domination through the world, above all in the form of imperialist–nationalist conflict, those living in the areas brought under their domain were in turn compelled to use the nationalist idea. The nationalist idea is derivative in the sense that there is a constant imitation of the basic claims about the existence of nations and their right to have their own states. However, nationalism takes distinctive customs, histories, values, and ways of life to justify these basic claims, so it always looks very different in one place compared to another. (This is why it is pointless to argue, for example, that nationalism is opposed to religion or is combined with religion, or replaces religion. It does all three, depending on whether a 'nationalizing' of religion serves the political purposes of nationalism.) It is this that gives some plausibility to the self-perception of each nationalism that it is unique, and that it is its unique national qualities that account for its appeal and strength.

Nevertheless, one nationalism on closer inspection looks very like another. Furthermore, despite the capacity of nationalists to form organizations and even generate popular support, generally speaking, state-subverting nationalism also required a favourable international situation that weakened the resistance of the state it opposed in order to succeed. This international situation also conditioned whether nationalism presented itself in ethnic or civic forms, as that was as much about gaining support from powerful external states as it was about mobilizing popular support for the nationalist movement.

In the most recent phase of globalization, the nation-state as the basis of the global political order has arguably been called into question. But whatever we might think will happen to the nation-state, that is an issue distinct from nationalism. State-strengthening nationalism might well mobilize around the defence of a threatened nation-state. State-subverting nationalism might well exploit the new preparedness of the USA and international bodies to intervene in the affairs of states in order to demand support for claims to separate statehood. But beyond this, nationalism may well also take on new forms in which the sovereign nation-state is no longer central but rather what matters are demands such as devolution or cultural recognition, which actually weaken the concept of state sovereignty. Having established itself as such a powerful idea, sentiment, and politics, nationalism is likely to adapt to new global political patterns just as it has done constantly over more than two centuries. Where it may once have matched the formation of a global political order founded on the sovereign nation-state, it may well adapt to a new political order in which the sovereign nation-state is less central. Certainly it is too early to write the obituary of nationalism.

Questions

1 Which came first: nations or nationalism?
2 Is nationalism the major reason for the formation of nation-states?
3 Why has nationalism spread across the world in the last two centuries?
4 Is it useful to distinguish between civic and ethnic forms of nationalism?
5 How and why did nationalism develop into imperialism?
6 Why did colonial peoples take up the idea of nationalism?
7 How can changes in global politics account for changes in nationalism?
8 How has the rise of the modern state shaped the development of nationalism?
9 How has the formation of global capitalism shaped the development of nationalism?
10 Is nationalism ultimately about preserving cultural identity against global pressures towards homogenization?
11 'Nationalism is more important for strengthening than subverting the state.' Discuss.
12 'Contemporary globalization erodes nation-state sovereignty but does not undermine nationalism.' Discuss.

Further Reading

Debates on nationalism

Özkirimli, U. (2005), *Contemporary Debates on Nationalism: A Critical Engagement* (Basingstoke: Palgrave Macmillan), chapter 6, 'Nationalism and Globalization'. Deals with a number of recent debates, including the impact of globalization on nationalism.

Broad historical studies of nationalism

Breuilly, J. (1993), *Nationalism and the State*, 2nd edn (Manchester and Chicago, IL: Chicago University Press). Compares various cases, starting in Europe around 1500 and including material from twentieth-century Asia and Africa.

Hobsbawm, E. (1990), *Nations and Nationalism since 1780: Programme, Myth, Reality* (Cambridge: Cambridge University Press). Focuses on Europe in the nineteenth century and the world more broadly after 1918.

Broad historical studies of globalization and modern global history

Bayly, C. (2004), *The birth of the modern world 1780–1914* (Oxford: Blackwell). Places the formative phase of nationalism in a world-historical framework.

Darwin, J. (2007), *After Tamerlane: the global history of empire* (London: Penguin Allen Lane). Shows how empires have shaped modern nationalism and nation-states.

McNeill, J. R., and McNeill, W. H. (2003), *The Human Web: A Bird's Eye View of History* (New York: W. W. Norton). The best single-volume world history of the networks human beings form that I know.

Osterhammel, J., and Peterssen, N. P. (2005), *Globalisation: A Short History* (Princeton, NJ: Princeton University Press). A short and clear overview.

Nationalism and international relations

Mayall, J. (1990), *Nationalism and International Society* (Cambridge: Cambridge University Press). The principal general study of the subject.

Moore, M. (ed.) (1998), *National Self-Determination and Secession* (Oxford: Oxford University Press). An account of the issue of secession.

Nationalism and globalization

So far as I know there are no general studies concerned solely with this subject. However, recent handbooks and general studies devote chapters to the relationship between globalization and nationalism. Among these are: **Delanty, G., and Kumar, K.** (eds) (2006), *The Sage Handbook of Nations and Nationalism* (London: Sage), especially the chapters in Part 2, 'Nations and Nationalism in a Global Age'; **Hutchinson, J.** (2004), *Nations as Zones of Conflict* (London: Sage), especially Chapter 5, 'Nationalism and the Clash of Civilisations'.

Online Resource Centre

 Visit the Online Resource Centre that accompanies this book to access more learning resources on this chapter topic at www.oxfordtextbooks.co.uk/orc/baylis5e/

Chapter 25

Culture in world affairs

SIMON MURDEN

Reader's Guide

Referring to culture to describe and analyse world politics is among the most contested approaches in International Relations. Cultural analysis is prone to be used in rather vague and intuitive ways, and the field is riven by polemic and counter-polemic, with some critics arguing that cultural analysis is unsound or even pernicious. So, why refer to culture? Because human beings live in communities, and wherever a community forms it gives rise to a culture that informs social life and political practice. Indeed, as a new wave of globalization swept the world from the late twentieth century, the significance of culture appeared to be heightened. The West was the dominant ideological and cultural force in late twentieth-century globalization, and its cosmopolitan culture appeared to be making the world more alike, but the world of globalization was increasingly multicultural and the cultural agenda more difficult to control. As different communities and cultures came into closer contact, existing patterns of culture and social order were challenged everywhere. Culture was a dimension of international security that seemed to require more consideration.

Introduction: culture in human affairs

Wherever human beings form communities, a **culture** comes into existence. Cultures may be constructed on a number of levels: in village or city locations, or across family, clan, ethnic, national, religious, and other networks. Individual humans are almost always participants in a number of distinct but overlapping communities and cultures. Communities produce linguistic, literary, and artistic genres, as well as beliefs and practices that characterize social life and indicate how society should be run. An awareness of a common language, ethnicity, history, religion, and landscape represent the building blocks of culture. Few cultures are completely insular or unchanging but, to be recognizable, totems of identity must enjoy some consensus and persistence. Cultures also define external boundaries by inducing members of the community to believe in the distinctiveness and value of their culture. Cultures almost always embody ideas and practices that support patterns of pre-eminence or **hegemony** (see Ch. 8) within and between communities.

Cultures may refer to a variety of totems and boundaries, but religious affiliation has historically been among the most powerful. Religions transmit values about the existence of God/gods, and how such knowledge must shape human life. Religious doctrines give worshippers and worshipping communities a moral core, a community spirit, and a guide to social stability. While some religions—Judaism, Hinduism, and Sikhism—define a limited community and have little appeal to outsiders, other religions—Christianity and **Islam**—offer universal values to the community of humankind. When claims are made in societies about 'cultural authenticity', they are often made about religious totems, and by those priests, mullahs, and gurus who claim to be qualified to transmit them.

The rational and scientific foundations of Western modernity have challenged all religious faiths since the eighteenth century. The **Enlightenment** gradually allowed individuals to question the existence of God and the culture of religious community. However, religion has retained a grip on the mind of humanity to this day—a fact that events in the late twentieth century demonstrated. The Islamic revival from the 1970s was one of the great phenomena of the twentieth century. In India, the Hindu revivalist Bharatiya Janata Party (BJP) became a national political force, challenging the secular foundations of the Indian state. In China, the relaxation of communist totalitarianism led to an upsurge in religious worship and local superstitions; most unwelcome to the Chinese government was the Falun Gong movement, a synthesis of existing Asian religion and 'New Age' ideas inspired by a Chinese guru based in the USA that rapidly struck a chord with millions of Chinese in the 1990s. Across South-East Asia, Islamic, Christian, and Buddhist revivalism was evident, as was increasing inter-communal conflict. In Russia and Eastern Europe, Orthodox and other Christians retook a public space in former communist societies.

Culture writ large: the civilization

The broadest construction of cultural identity is the **civilization**. In the eighteenth and nineteenth centuries, the European notion of civilization was linked to social and intellectual accomplishment. The supposed superiority of European civilization, with its Greek and Roman heritage and its modernity expressed in the **nation-state** and science, was embodied in the term. Defining those outside civilization—the Other—made the idea more meaningful, and shaped the way in which areas and peoples of the world were regarded. As Europeans built their global empires, they imposed their culture by force. Only by the mid-twentieth century did European beliefs about their cultural superiority begin to change, although the idea that the West represented a model of progress persisted (see Ch. 2). Civilization was redefined as a descriptive term to categorize the broadest groups of people that were able to identify with a sufficiently coherent set of aesthetic, religious, philosophic, historic, and social traditions.

Box 25.1 Bhikhu Parekh on religion and the construction of identity

'However unworldly its orientation might be, every religion has a moral core, and an inescapable political dimension. If I am expected to be "my brother's keeper" or to "love my neighbour" or be an integral part of the umma (the universal Islamic community), or if I believe that everyone is created by God, it deeply matters to me how others live and are treated by their fellow humans and the state ... Religious people sincerely wish to live out their beliefs and do not see this as an exclusively private or even personal matter.'

(Parekh 1997a: 5)

Civilizations represent coherent traditions, but are dynamic over time and place. For instance, medieval Christendom drew on ancient and Eastern civilizations for many of its philosophical and technological advances; subsequently, Christendom was remoulded into a European civilization based around the nation-state and, finally, was expanded and adapted in North America and eventually redesignated as Western civilization. The process embodied both physical and conceptual reformulation, with theocratic, monarchial, and nationalist values superseded by the liberal ideal of equality, **democracy**, and free markets. However, what is important to understand about the rise of the liberal ideal as the definitive marker of Western civilization was that, even for its principal promoters in Britain and the USA, it emerged from a long process of meshing and disentangling with quite contradictory ideas and practices. In the nineteenth and twentieth centuries, Britons and Americans meshed their **liberalism** (see Ch. 6) with a concept of civilization that claimed cultural and racial superiority over non-Europeans. Liberalism ran alongside the contradictions of imperial conquest, racial enslavement, and colonial rule. In the second half of the twentieth century—with the signing of the Atlantic Charter in 1941 being an important moment of future intent—the most outrageous contradictions in Anglo-American liberalism were ironed out, and the liberal ideal became synonymous with what it was to be Western.

Today, a number of reasonably distinct civilizations exist: notably the Western, Islamic, Indian, and Chinese. Other peoples are not so easily pigeonholed, either because they are not united around sufficiently distinct or powerful cultural totems, or because they are torn between different civilizations; in this respect, the categorization of peoples in South America, Africa, and Russia is more problematic. However, today no civilization is completely distinct from the influence of others, and all have been especially affected by the influence of the West.

The problem with cultural analysis

The problem with cultural analysis is that the concept can be such an all-encompassing one that it may be very difficult to make useful generalizations, much less come to any conclusion about the extent to which cultural influences had on particular events or social phenomena. In fact, one of the principal criticisms of cultural analysis is that it fails to show how culture works: how cultural identity really affects particular human behaviour, especially at the level of world politics (Reeves 2004: 137).

But, peering through the cultural maze is no different from using other concepts and theories in social science. It requires the identification of key factors (cultural totems) and then some generalization about how they influence what the community tends to perceive, how it organizes itself, and what it decides to do. At the level of world politics, a cultural analysis may seek to trace the relative influence of key cultural beliefs, norms, and practices—in comparison to other major factors of influence such as ideology or economic imperatives—on the decision-making of actors: the way culture shapes the immanent preferences held by a community and its policy-makers; the institutional manifestations of cultural commonality, notably in the form of regional or functional organizations; and, at the sub-state level, the transnational networks that are imbued with a common cultural viewpoint.

The other problem in undertaking cultural analysis is that when it emerged in the 1990s, especially the way the field converged on Samuel Huntington's 'clash of civilizations' thesis (Huntington 1996), it became thoroughly entangled in a pejorative debate between conservatives and their critics. Cultural analysis was criticized not only as a derivation of realism (said to construct a world of conflict) but also as a discourse that stemmed from a political agenda to maintain existing patterns of community, culture, and exclusion. Few thinkers on culture can have escaped being accused of some biased or malign motive.

Yet thinking about culture is necessary. It is difficult to look at the world and not see culture, and while

---

Box 25.2 The Western account of culture

'There is the whole corpus of cultural and philosophical knowledge which provides the underpinning for the "Western cultural account" ... Primarily this account emphasises the possibility of individual and social progress through the application of universal **rationality** and empirical science, goals which involve the mastery of nature for human ends. Then there is the status of the individual human being, who is at the ontological centre of the Western idea of modernity. The significance of the individual is reflected in debates about the sources of moral and political authority in the conceptions of free will versus determinism, and in accounts seeking to explain the dynamism of market societies by reference to the purposive behaviour of rational consumers.'

(Axford 1995: 2)

culture may not be the only major influence on human behaviour, or even the most important or direct influence, it is certainly one of them. Moreover, understanding the role of culture in world politics has been given added relevance by the acceleration of cultural synthesis that has come about due to contemporary globalization. Distinct cultures do exist, but they have all had to come to terms with the emergence of a global community and a putative cosmopolitan culture. The patterns of cultural synthesis and resistance that stem from this meeting are a matter of some importance.

Key Points

- All communities produce cultures. A culture is composed of the customs, norms, and practices that inform social life. Religion remains a core influence in many cultures.

- Individuals typically participate in more than one level of community, and so humans must often reconcile competing cultural inclinations.

- Civilization is still the broadest form of cultural identity, representing a level of identity that may spread across nations and states.

Culture in the post-cold war world

During the **cold war** (see Chs 3 and 4), cultural differences ostensibly took a back seat to the global geopolitical struggle between the USA and the Soviet Union. Differences were defined in ideological and economic terms, and superimposed upon world politics regardless of local cultural characteristics. Both **superpowers** offered their model to the world for imitation, and alignment to one of the two great blocs defined the 'Other'.

The end of the cold war saw a radical reshaping of world politics, with the triumph of the West reinforced by the revolution in commmunications technologies. Cultural analysis was to be central in a number of seminal texts that sought to explain what was happening in the post-cold-war world, especially Francis Fukuyama's *End of History* (1992) (see Ch. 6), Samuel Huntington's *Clash of Civilizations* (1996) and Benjamin Barber's *Jihad vs McWorld* (1996). Above all, culture seemed to offer a way to understand the similarities and differences of the new age, where a new globalizing capitalism and cosmopolitan culture met a world of many cultures, as well as where existing communities and cultures were in closer contact with each other.

The power of globalizing capitalism and its culture looked immense. John Agnew and Stewart Corbridge perceived that a new 'deterritorialized' geopolitical order—the hegemony of 'transnational liberalism'—was emerging, and commented that 'a new ideology of the market (and of market access) [was] being embedded in and reproduced by a powerful constituency of liberal states, international **institutions,** and what might be called the "circuits of capital" themselves' (Agnew and Corbridge 1995: 166). Much of the world was increasingly brought into the global economy and indoctrinated with its values. At that time, Francis Fukuyama certainly

thought that the great debates about how societies should be run were basically over. What Fukuyama termed the liberal idea—the combination of liberal democracy and the market—had drawn a finishing line in the history of political and social development (Fukuyama 1992: 45). The liberal idea was the best that anybody was going to

Box 25.3 Francis Fukuyama on Islam in the world of universal liberalism

For Francis Fukuyama, the end of the cold war had left the 'liberal idea'—liberal democracy and market capitalism—as humankind's universal project. To Fukuyama, it seemed that there was 'no ideology with pretensions to universality that [was] in a position to challenge liberal-democracy, and no universal principle of legitimacy other than the sovereignty of the people'. Fukuyama could only see localized resistance to the liberal idea, notably in the form of Islam. Fukuyama perceived that:

'The appeal of Islam [was] potentially universal, reaching out to all men as men ... And Islam has indeed defeated liberal democracy in many parts of the Islamic world, posing a grave threat to liberal practices even in countries where it has not achieved political power directly ... Despite the power demonstrated by Islam in its current revival, however, it remains the case that this religion has virtually no appeal outside those areas that were culturally Islamic to begin with. The days of Islam's cultural conquests, it would seem, are over. It can win back lapsed adherents, but has no resonance for the young people of Berlin, Tokyo, or Moscow. And while nearly a billion are culturally Islamic—one-fifth of the world's population—they cannot challenge liberal-democracy on its own territory on the level of ideas. Indeed, the Islamic world would seem more vulnerable to liberal ideas in the long run than the reverse.'

(Fukuyama 1992: 45-6)

get, and it was superseding other political and social ideas and forms of organization.

Profound cultural change accompanied the spread of globalizing capitalism. A wave of democratization swept across large parts of the world, as did the influence of what Benjamin Barber called McWorld: the inescapable experience of consumer icons, such as Coca-Cola, McDonald's, Disney, Nike, and Sony, and the ubiquitous landscape of shopping malls, cinemas, sports stadiums, and branded restaurants. Beside the phenomenon of economic and cultural 'crowding out', liberal reformism drove the transformation of societies by drawing more women and young people into wage-earning work and consumption. Traditional forms of social hegemony were liable to be blown apart as men and women were encouraged to count value in terms of money, consumption, and entertainment rather than in terms of duty, community, and piety. 'Economic man' was disinclined to care about the socio-cultural being if that contradicted the imperatives of the marketplace. Above all, the uplifting of women in the West had been the most significant social phenomenon of the twentieth century, and one that globalization promised to extend everywhere. The cultural impact of this new globalization was felt in the West itself, but the discontinuities were often at their most stark in former communist bloc and the developing world.

The multiculturalism of globalization

Western culture was the most important influence in the world of liberalizing globalization, but the culture of the emerging global community was increasingly multicultural. The never-ending quest of capitalists to entertain and sell did much to further cultural synthesis, most obviously in the realms of dress, art, film, television, and food. Western-originated images and aspirations were absorbed by, for instance, India's Bollywood film industry or South America's soap operas, and then sent around the world. Chinese, Indian, and French culinary culture coexisted with McDonald's and Kentucky Fried Chicken almost everywhere. By the early twenty-first century, the rising giants of China and India were exerting a more direct and sustained cultural influence across the world.

Globalization fostered a cosmopolitan culture in which consumerism was a key totem, but while it was apt to make different parts of the world more alike, humanity was not about to become identical. Local ethnic and religious cultures survived alongside the cosmopolitan culture and, as people and ideas increasingly flowed around the world, they also existed in closer proximity to other cultures. The arenas for cultural mixing were the world's great cities—London, Paris, Berlin, Moscow, New York, Los Angeles, Sydney, and others—and living in such places required embracing tolerance and multiculturalism, or it meant risking inter-communal suspicion and conflict. The presence of so many Muslims in Western societies, for instance, undoubtedly changed the parameters of what Westerners could think and say about Islam. Western governments backed the transition to a more inclusive multiculturalism with new laws against inciting racial or religious distrust and conflict.

> ### Key Points
>
> - The West has been the dominant civilization in the modern age, and all other civilizations have had to deal with its influence. In the post-cold war world, the hegemony of the West and of its liberal capitalism challenged the culture and social order of most societies.
>
> - In the world of the global community, a globalizing cosmopolitan culture has emerged, and while the West was the most important influence on it, the rise of non-Western powers has meant that other cultures are increasingly influential.
>
> - Globalization has also fostered multicultural landscapes across the world. Most local cultures are in the process of changing as they meet the norms and practices of globalizing cosmopolitan culture as well as interact more closely with other existing cultures.

The counter-revolutionaries of the global age

As globalization challenged all communities and cultures, the forces of reaction gathered everywhere but were most notable in non-Western societies. The West was widely stereotyped for its arrogance, irresponsible **individualism**, and permissive sexual climate, and its free market capitalism denounced as exploitative and morally bankrupt. In the absence of a global-level theory of resistance, the opposition to liberalizing globalization was largely parochial and led by cultural conservatives, a fact reflected in the religious element in much of it.

Across the world, societies clung to the familiar by remembering religion and its associated values, for not everyone wished the freedom to question, to doubt, and to be troubled. As ever, religion helped humans deal with uncertainty and fear, clarifying the purpose of human life and regulating the behaviour of individuals, families, and groups. If religious doctrines were not taken on wholesale, then they were often translated into backward-looking moral prescriptions about such things as the role of women, the education of youth, the nature of personal responsibility, the punishment of deviancy, and the definition of the outsider.

Popular culture was at the forefront of the cultural counter-revolution. Some Muslims governments sought to contain the global tidal wave of foreign news, music videos, and pornography by banning satellite television and restricting access to the Internet. The place of women in society, and especially the issue of veiling (the *hijab*), was the key totem for Islamists. In Asia, a debate about the importance of 'Asian values' also got under way, with the state–business elite turning the 'liberal idea' on its head, and to argue that individualism and **pluralism** actually negated economic success. The application of 'Asian values' in such places as Malaysia and Singapore often meant controlling the aspirations and behaviour of youth. Even in the USA, revivalist Christians railed against the secular state, 'Hollywood social values', abortion, the teaching of evolution, and the **cosmopolitanism** of contemporary America; the contemporary Christian mission in the USA sought to mesh America's capitalism with older notions of community and morality.

Religious revivalism sometimes took the form of extreme literalism, often termed **fundamentalism**. The roots of fundamentalism varied. Messianic preachers continued to find audiences. More significantly, fundamentalism often stemmed from a wider fear that existing society was being destroyed. Many fundamentalist groups were born in opposition to the perceived evils of modernity's secularism, pluralism, social atomization, and moral emptiness.

Claiming the legitimacy of God, fundamentalists promulgated interpretations of their faith that allowed for political and social violence, and sometimes even looked forward to some apocalyptic final vision. Thus, just as the Marxist-inspired revolutionaries of the 1950s and 1960s disappeared, a new breed of religious militants became a principal cause of sub-state **terrorism** in the world (see Ch. 22). Islamic fundamentalists led the new wave of violence, shaking the stability of many

Box 25.4 Fundamentalism

'Fundamentalism is more than a political protest against the West or the prevailing establishment. It also reflects deep-seated fear of modern institutions and has paranoid visions of demonic enemies everywhere. It is alarming that so many people in so many different parts are so pessimistic about the world that they can only find hope in fantasies of apocalyptic catastrophe. Fundamentalism shows a growing sense of grievance, resentment, displacement, disorientation, and anomie that any humane, enlightened government must attempt to address.'

(Armstrong 1997: 17)

Muslim states. In India, fundamentalist Muslim and Sikh secessionists fought pitched battles with the Indian Army, while Hindu extremists provoked and attacked other communities. Extremism could also be found in Christianity. In the USA, the Waco siege and Oklahoma bombing were manifestations of a violent paranoia. Eastern religion produced the Aum Shinrikyo sect in the 1990s, a group that sought to commit mass murder on the Tokyo underground with the use of sarin nerve gas. Where religious fundamentalists struck a chord, the prospect for a peace synthesis between the global and the local was much reduced.

A clash of civilizations?

Concerns about cultural revivalism and conflict were best reflected in a debate primed by the Harvard professor Samuel Huntington. In an article entitled 'The **Clash of Civilizations**' (*Foreign Affairs*, 1993) and in a subsequent book (1996), Huntington offered a new paradigm of world politics in which the principal patterns of conflict and cooperation were shaped by culture and, ultimately, by civilization. Huntington suggested that the civilizations that would determine the future of world politics were the 'Western, Confucian, Japanese, Islamic, Hindu, Slavic-Orthodox, Latin American, and possibly African' (Huntington 1993: 25).

For Huntington, the clash of civilizations represented a historic development. Hitherto, the history of the international system had been essentially about the struggles between monarchs, nations, and ideologies within Western civilization. The end of the cold war had inaugurated a new era, in which non-Westerners were no longer the hapless recipients of Western power, but now counted among the movers of history. The rise of civilizational politics intersected four long-run processes at play in the international system:

1 The relative decline of the West.
2 The rise of the Asian economy and its associated 'cultural affirmation', with China poised to become the greatest power in human history.
3 A population explosion in the Muslim world, and the associated resurgence of Islam.
4 The impact of globalization, including the extraordinary expansion of transnational flows of commerce, information, and people.

For Huntington, behind the façade of liberalizing globalization was cultural revivalism on a grand scale. The world was becoming a smaller place, and this was raising human consciousness about cultural differences. With Western-originated ideas widely seen to have failed in much of the world, communities were moving to recreate some rooted past. Socialism and **nationalism** (see Ch. 24) were giving way to 'Islamization, Hinduization, and Russianization'. The 'liberal idea' might be presented as the foundation of globalization and some cosmopolitan culture by the West, but its individualism, secularism, pluralism, democracy, and human rights had only superficial resonance in Islamic, Sinic, Hindu, Buddhist, and Orthodox cultures. In reality, the differences between civilizations ran deep: they were about man and God, man and woman, the individual and the state, and notions of rights, authority, obligation, and justice. Culture was about the basic perceptions of life that had been constructed over centuries.

For Huntington, culture worked at the level of motivation. States remained key actors, but civilizational politics became real when states and peoples identified with each other's cultural concerns or rallied around the 'core state' of a civilization. The Orthodox, Hindu, Sinic, and Japanese civilizations were centred on powerful unitary states. The West had a closely linked core that included the USA, Britain, France, and Germany. Islam was without a clear core state, and for this reason experienced much more intra-civilizational conflict as a number of contenders—Turkey, Iran, Iraq, Egypt, Saudi Arabia—competed for influence. The fact that Islam was organizationally divided did not refute the idea that a pan-Islamic consciousness existed.

Cultural conflict could be found at a 'micro' and a 'macro' level. At the micro level, groups from different civilizations were prone to conflict across local 'fault-lines', and by means of a 'kin–country syndrome' were liable to bring in their wider brethren. Huntington observed that Islam had particularly 'bloody borders', a situation that would continue until Muslim population growth slowed in the second or third decade of the twenty-first century. At the 'macro level', a more general competition was evident, with the principal division between the dominant 'West' and, to varying degrees, the 'Rest'. According to Huntington, the West's dominance was most contested by the two most dynamic non-Western civilizations, the Sinic and the Islamic. Resistance to the West was most evident over issues such as arms control and the promotion of Western political values, which were regarded as a form of neo-imperialism.

Huntington's thesis was highly contentious, with critics pointing to conceptual and empirical problems (Murden 1999). The treatment of culture was brief, and the conclusions pessimistic. Huntington failed to tell the stories of interaction and synthesis that have always gone on between civilizations. Having lost the Soviet Union as its Other, some thought Huntington was needlessly constructing new enemies for the West, and that the *Clash of Civilizations* was purposely intended to be a self-fulfilling prophecy. Much of the criticism was based on a caricature of Huntington's work, but some criticism reflected the aforementioned difficulties involved in cultural analysis. Where Huntington could really be criticized was in his downplaying of the other factors that influence the behaviour of humans and their organizations: above all, the 'reason of states' and the imperatives of economics. The belligerence of even the keenest of civilizational warriors is usually tempered by pragmatic considerations. Huntington's paradigm may have over-extrapolated his argument about cultural revivalism and failed to sufficiently recognize that cultural–civilizational influences were counterbalanced by other powerful forces, but that did not mean that cultural activism was not a significant phenomenon in world politics, notably at the micro level of conflict. The *Clash of Civilizations* may not have told the whole story of what was happening in the post-cold war world, but it told part of it.

Key Points

- The new wave of globalization has met local resistance from cultural conservatives seeking to preserve their cultures and social orders from unbridled change.

- In the aftermath of the cold war, a major stream in the culture debate was sparked by Samuel Huntington when he suggested that cultural revivalism was producing a 'clash of civilizations', and this was about to become the principal cause of international conflict.

A counter-revolution at the civilizational level: The case of Islam

In much of the post-cold war debate about culture, it was Islam that came into the frame. Parts of the Muslim world had long struggled with modernity. An Islamic militancy that emphasized the corrupt character of the West and its modernity had also been a factor in world politics since the Iranian revolution of 1978–9. In addition, Islamic activists were locked in conflict against adjoining civilizations and secular states across the Balkans, West and East Africa, the Middle East, the Caucasus, Central Asia, India, Indonesia, and the Philippines, with their efforts to promulgate Islamic law a particularly explosive issue.

Islamic culture in the modern age

The Muslim world represents an example *par excellence* of the experience of almost all non-Western societies in the modern age. Muslim peoples have had to deal with the geopolitical and cultural hegemony of the West since the eighteenth century. The collapse of the Ottoman Empire at the end of the First World War heralded the emergence of the secular, nationalist, and authoritarian state as Muslim modernizers argued that Islam was the cause of backwardness and decline, and what was required was the imitation of Western culture and organization. In Turkey, following the seizure of power by Mustafa Kemal, the Islamic caliphate was abolished, and Western forms of law, written script, and dress were enforced. Women were forcibly unveiled. A secular and nationalist model of modernization was also to be adopted in Iran and in much of the Arab world. Muslims were divided by Turkish, Iranian, and Arab nationalisms.

However, the progress of secular modernity did not run smoothly. In some places, notably Syria and Iraq, the state was hijacked by clan and sectarian groups. The forces of Arab nationalism also foundered on their demonstrable inability to take on Israel, with the Six Day War of June 1967 being an important moment of failure. Jerusalem was lost. Although Arab nationalism retained an appeal for a time, a new force was stirring: revivalist Islam. Economic failure deepened the crisis. Rapid population growth and rural–urban migration meant that urban life for most was characterized by poor housing, strained services, and underemployment. In the 1950s and 1960s, secular elites had at least appealed to the masses with socialism and nationalism, but after the *infitah* (economic reform and opening) model was initiated in Anwar Sadat's Egypt in the 1970s, the interests, values, and lifestyles of the elites turned towards the West. The elites essentially abandoned the masses, leaving Islam as the voice of opposition not only to the ruling regimes, but also to the culture that came with *infitah*.

The Islamic revival that began in the Middle East eventually spread across the entire Muslim world. The conservative Islamic monarchies of the Gulf promoted missionary (*da'wa*) activities, but the Islamic revival was really a mass movement born in the crisis of modernization. Many young Muslims turned to Islam as a community and culture that gave the forgotten and the hopeless self-worth.

> ### Key Points
>
> - The impact of the West has been the principal issue facing Muslim peoples since the eighteenth century. Muslim modernizers sought to imitate the West, but the performance of the secular state often undermined their vision of modernity.
> - Islam remains a powerful influence in many Muslim societies. When secular states faltered, Islam was there to fill the vacuum of political and social leadership.

Islamic fundamentalism

The Islamic revival had many manifestations in Muslim societies—more men went to mosque and more young women wore the *hijab*, but it was a new political militancy that was to have the most dramatic effects. Sayyid Qutb in Egypt (d. 1966), Abu al-Ala al-Mawdudi in Pakistan (d. 1979), and Grand Ayatollah Ruhollah Khomeini in Iran (d. 1989) led an Islamic revolt that was to strike a chord across the Muslim world. The militants advocated a return to the basic texts of Islam—hence the term Islamic fundamentalists—and the re-Islamization of Muslim society by means of the implementation of *sharia* law by an Islamic state.

Militant Islam stood in opposition to Western-style modernity. Liberalism and Islam represent two different systems for understanding, appreciating, and behaving in the world. Liberalism is a vision of economic freedom, individual choice, and the removal of social restraints. Islam may be able to absorb some liberal references, but, ultimately, it is a vision of submission to God, the believer community, and a certain kind of social order. Islamic societies tend to frown on the idea of individual consciousness and choice. In the post-Enlightenment West, the idea of a better future has been a central one. In militant Islam, Muslims should look forward to a better past. The perfect Islamic polity was established in the first years of Islam, and its timeless principles recorded in the Koran and other early scripts. The Koran and *sharia* represented the perfect constitution, in which **sovereignty** ultimately resided with God, not with human beings. Many Islamists recognized the validity of community consultation (*shura*), but the idea of sovereign popular democracy was alien. For some militants, certain Islamic injunctions—such as a criminal law that conducts public executions and amputations, and the archaic regulation of women and non-Muslims—were totems of an authentic Islamic community and could not be reformed.

The Muslim Brotherhood (*Ikhwan al-Muslimin*)—a movement originally founded in Egypt by Hasan al-Banna in 1928, and spread to Syria, Palestine, Jordan, and North Africa—was behind much of the Islamic revival. Muslim Brotherhoods were both political organizations and benevolent social foundations. Much of the time, they focused on supporting Muslims in their communities, but some members turned to politics and even to violent revolution. In Egypt, the secular regime of Gamal Abdul Nasser was confronted by an element in the Muslim Brotherhood inspired by Sayyid Qutb. Qutb, who was executed by Nasser's regime in 1966, argued that foreign culture had corrupted Muslim societies to the point of *jahiliyya*, a term referring to a condition of pre-Islamic ignorance, and that it was incumbent on the few good Muslims left to form a jihadic vanguard to rid Muslim societies of such corruption and to reinstall a proper Islamic order (a *salafi* order).

Shia Muslims were moving in a separate but similar direction to militant Sunnis by the 1970s. The driving force of Shia revivalism was Grand Ayatollah Ruhollah Khomeini. Khomeini proposed a state dominated by religious scholars in which both political and religious primacy was vested in a supreme religious figure or council; the new system was termed the *velayet-e faqih* (the guardianship of the jurisconsult). The most senior Islamic expert would have the last word in ruling the state; it was a position that Khomeini was to fill himself. The Iranian Revolution that followed in 1978–9 would be about entrenching the *velayet-e faqih* in power, a process that was to take a number of years, and require the elimination of the Shia clergy's partners in the rebellion against the Shah's regime.

The Iranian Revolution itself provided great impetus to the Islamic revival. While Iran's revolution was of limited theological significance to Sunni radicals, it was an example to emulate. A populist Islamic movement had overthrown a powerful secular state, and it had also had the will to stand up to foreign corrupters and oppressors. In fact, Islamic revolution was not about to sweep across the Arab world, but during the 1970s and 1980s a crescendo of Islamic protest shook the Middle East. However, although most Islamic revivalists broadly agreed over ends—an Islamic state and *sharia* law—they tended to differ over means. The most militant wanted violent revolution, but the majority of Islamists were reluctant to engage in all-out war. Mainstream Islamists hoped to conduct a dialogue over gradually extending their values in society. For Muslim governments, keeping the mainstream away from the extremists was the central dynamic of politics. In Jordan, the mainstream Muslim Brotherhood was brought into a democratization process quite successfully. In Egypt, the state struggled to keep the mainstream Muslim Brotherhood and violent secret societies apart, but eventually ground down the violent militants. In Algeria, the secular-led army took decisions that brought mainstream and militants together in agreement over means, and produced a savage civil war. Little was resolved.

11 September 2001 and its aftermath

By the early 1990s, the Islamic revival appeared to have peaked. The grand dreams of militants about seizing the state were fading. Instead, some militants now hoped to revive Islam from the grass roots up, concentrating their efforts on proselytizing in the village or neighbourhood first. The immediate threat to the Middle Eastern state receded, but the result was chronic social violence as these grass-roots Islamists sought to take over their communities. However, just as the Islamic revival seemed blocked, the new wave of globalization that followed the end of the cold war and the Gulf War of 1991 gave it new life; the coincidence of socio-cultural pressures with real geopolitical conflict primed what happened next.

Following Iraq's defeat in 1991, the USA created a security architecture across the Middle East that included the garrisoning of US forces in Saudi Arabia. The presence of infidel troops in the land of the two Holy Cities of Mecca and Medina was so outrageous to a body of Islamic opinion that it galvanized a new phenomenon: a cadre of wealthy and well-educated Islamists in the Arabian Peninsula—Osama bin Laden was the doyen—who had the ideas, the money, and the contacts to forge

Case Study Schematic of the militant Islamic movement in the Afghan–Pakistan milieu (c. 2001)

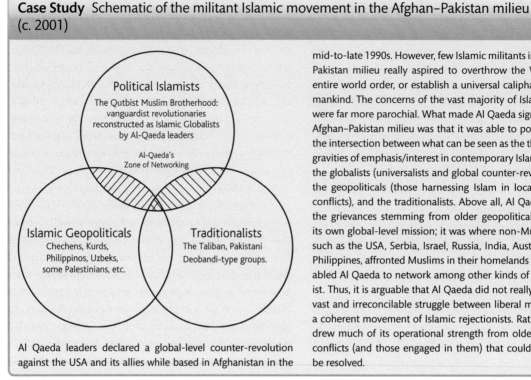

Political Islamists
The Qutbist Muslim Brotherhood: vanguardist revolutionaries reconstructed as Islamic Globalists by Al-Qaeda leaders

Al-Qaeda's Zone of Networking

Islamic Geopoliticals
Chechens, Kurds, Philippinos, Uzbeks, some Palestinians, etc.

Traditionalists
The Taliban, Pakistani Deobandi-type groups.

Al Qaeda leaders declared a global-level counter-revolution against the USA and its allies while based in Afghanistan in the mid-to-late 1990s. However, few Islamic militants in the Afghan–Pakistan milieu really aspired to overthrow the West and the entire world order, or establish a universal caliphate for all humankind. The concerns of the vast majority of Islamic militants were far more parochial. What made Al Qaeda significant in the Afghan–Pakistan milieu was that it was able to position itself at the intersection between what can be seen as the three principal gravities of emphasis/interest in contemporary Islamic militancy: the globalists (universalists and global counter-revolutionaries), the geopoliticals (those harnessing Islam in local geopolitical conflicts), and the traditionalists. Above all, Al Qaeda exploited the grievances stemming from older geopolitical conflicts for its own global-level mission; it was where non-Muslim powers, such as the USA, Serbia, Israel, Russia, India, Australia, and the Philippines, affronted Muslims in their homelands that most enabled Al Qaeda to network among other kinds of Islamic activist. Thus, it is arguable that Al Qaeda did not really reflect some vast and irreconcilable struggle between liberal modernity and a coherent movement of Islamic rejectionists. Rather, Al Qaeda drew much of its operational strength from older geopolitical conflicts (and those engaged in them) that could, in principle, be resolved.

a new global alliance of militants, dedicated to fighting the 'invasions' of the West and its version of modernity. From a refuge in Afghanistan and Pakistan, what was to become known as the Al Qaeda organization offered ideological training and financial support to various cadres of militants. Attacks on US interests in Saudi Arabia and East Africa in the latter 1990s were but a prelude to the colossal events that took place at the World Trade Center in New York and the Pentagon in Washington on **11 September 2001**.

The attacks of 9/11 not only led to the so-called global **war on terror** (see Ch. 4), but also to developments in the discourse about civilization. The US administration of George W. Bush steered its definition of civilization back towards an association with a standard of good. Of course, this standard of good was formed around an essentially American vision of freedom and democracy; it owed more to Fukuyama than to Huntington. The world was to be divided into two civilizations—not six or seven—described as the civilized and the uncivilized. The uncivilized were led by the so-called axis of evil, composed of the states of Iraq, Iran, and North Korea. Thus, in the months after 9/11, most Western leaders were keen to emphasize that the West had no fundamental quarrel with Islam itself, but only with the uncivilized stragglers of modernity, or, as Fukuyama

termed them, Islamo-fascists. Of course, the new alignment of America's strategic interests with a new mission to 'civilize' would eventually lead to the conquest of Iraq in 2003, although Fukuyama himself would later reject the very idea of undertaking such a vast socio-cultural experiment. Indeed, Iraqis would have much trouble in meshing their cultural inclinations and practices with the interests of the USA and the culture of liberalism. Iraq was to be a debacle for the Bush administration, and its mission to liberalize critical parts of the Muslim world soon fell out of favour. The USA had to be more pragmatic.

In the West itself, 9/11 and its aftermath produced a wave of alarm that fed into an existing angst about an Islamic fifth column within Western societies as well as more general concerns about the influx of immigrants and asylum seekers. The nature of multicultural society itself was questioned, with some Western leaders—notably in the United Kingdom—beginning to argue that a stable multicultural society required a bit less tolerance of difference and a bit more integration by both the main body of the community and by minorities; a 'cosmopolitan consensus' was enforced on the multicultural society. Others were more pessimistic about multiculturalism. Reflecting themes developed by Huntington, Roger Scruton argued that Western civilization was developing in a way that embodied the seeds of its own destruction. Cosmopolitan liberalism was not only devoid of any deeply held values or sense of community, but was also weakening the territorial jurisdictions that made Western-style democracy possible in the first place. Scruton urged that the nation-state be bolstered and some of the free-flowing exchanges of globalization be controlled in order to preserve the territorialized society as well as reduce the number of people that were becoming lost, disillusioned, and vengeful in these increasingly shallow communities (Scruton 2002: 159–60).

The future of Islam in the global age

The events of 9/11 and its aftermath set back the march of liberalizing globalization. Yet, while it was easy to emphasize the compatibility problems and conflicts between the Western and Islamic worlds, Muslim countries could not escape the realities of practical politics and economics. Even Islamists have had to be pragmatic, whether in opposition or in power.

The case of Iran is illuminating. The Revolution of 1978–9 promoted a missionary Islam that sought to oppose the 'forces of corruption on earth', especially the USA (see Ch. 2). The Islamic Republic neglected the realities of power, but the costs were unsustainable and by the mid-1980s the Revolution had produced its 'pragmatists'. Fences were mended, and while the Islamic Republic continued to speak up for Muslim rights everywhere, it was less prone to act on this mission. The death of Ayatollah Khomeini in 1989 and the Presidencies of Hashemi Rafsanjani and Mohammad Khatami led to a further degree political and social relaxation. The reformers realized that an Islamic insularity could not be sustained in the global age. The young, women, and the middle class wanted more freedom, although there was a powerful conservative establishment determined to stop them having it.

The reformists would suffer ups and downs in their sparring with the conservative incumbents of the theocratic institutions of the Iranian state. The fairness of parliamentary elections in February 2004 was undermined by the banning of hundreds of reformist candidates by the unelected Council of Guardians. The election of a Revolutionary revivalist, Mahmoud Ahmadinejad, as President in June 2005 was also a significant setback for those with more liberal inclinations. Following Ahmadinejad's re-election as President in questionable circumstances in June 2009, Iran's political and cultural divide would manifest itself in persistent social unrest.

By this time, the idea of the Islamic Revolution had long been harnessed by a self-serving oligarchy of public and religious officials and members of the security forces, and they would not concede the rationale for their power and privilege easily. The struggle to redefine the future of Iran would be prolonged, but the Islamic Republic held the potential for becoming a model of Islamic adaptation: a new model of Islamic democracy. The inescapable dilemma for Islamists was that they could not promote their values and practices without engaging in a world of politics and economics that was bound to affect the very nature of the Islamic community and its culture.

Finding the 'right path' was at the heart of contemporary Islamic discourse. In the Arab world, gradual change was in motion, with the Islamic idea of *shura* (consultation) acting as a touchstone for political and social reform. Morocco, Jordan, and most of the Gulf States referred to *shura* when they introduced limited forms of representative assembly. Even among the ranks of Islamic fundamentalists, there was recognition that many ordinary Muslims wanted a voice, although it was difficult to imagine that a Muslim democracy could resemble a Western democracy anytime soon. Globalization did not mean that all communities and cultures would be liberalized in the same way.

Beyond the debates about the nature of the Muslim state, all sorts of social-level activities would shape the future of Islam and its influence in the world. The Islamic world sustains a vast network of transnational contacts and **non-governmental organizations** (NGOs) that have been multiplied by the advent of the Internet. Islam has an enormous presence in cyberspace. While the cyberspace activities of violent Islamic groups are well known, the vast bulk of Islam-online is benign, with much of its content focused on trying to influence the politics and social culture of Muslim societies. Conservative forces have a substantial presence but cyberspace is also a forum for reformists, notably from the Muslim community in the West, which has more freedom to articulate innovative ideas about adapting Islam to the contemporary world. At the level of World Society (in the English School sense), the broader Islamic community is a major player.

Muslim peoples have met liberalizing globalization with various combinations of imitation, resistance, and synthesis. Thus, for all the talk about civilizational conflict in the post-cold war world, Islam's influence on international relations remains diffuse: its influence on Muslim states and their international organizations is often overmatched by the countervailing forces of national interest and capitalist economics. Islamic civilization has no rallying point. The **Islamic Conference Organization** (composed of Muslim states) is a dead-letter regime (Murden 2009: 136). While some Islamic militants do their best to rally the brethren, their grandiose dreams of a transnational Islamic revolution seem destined to be disappointed. Ultimately, and short of another event on the scale of 9/11, the likes of Al Qaeda represent only a limited threat to Muslim states, Western states, and the international order. Islam is most influential as a social ideology among Muslims, and that is the realm in which it exerts its diffuse but considerable effect in the world. The sum of these Islamic social effects is important. Islam is a brake on the capacity of liberalizing globalization to transform Muslim societies and their culture, and it does limit the extent to which Muslim societies absorb the dominant norms of globalizing politics, economics, and consumer culture.

Key Points

- Islam militants have argued that a cultural conflict with the West exists. In the 1980s, the Iranian Revolution led militant Islamism against the West. In the 1990s, the Sunni Islamists of the Al Qaeda network took up the torch.

- Islamic-inclined movements tend to be suspicious of global-level influences, but the pressures to be pragmatic are strong. The Iranian Revolution is a good example of how political and economic realities can force compromise on Islamists.

- Islam does not have a common voice. Muslims meet the forces of globalization in different ways.

Conclusion

The new wave of globalization that took place in the late twentieth century brought an unprecedented level of intercultural interaction. The speed at which many communities and cultures were changing increased markedly. Change appeared to spark a wave of cultural revivalism in the 1990s, although whether that translated itself into a reorganization of world politics along the lines suggested by Samuel Huntington was another matter. Huntington's predictions about the emergence of a world of civilizational conflict have not been vindicated in the years since. But violent resistance to social change and global-level influences has accompanied cultural revivalism, especially when religious culture is involved. Although it was unlikely that religious fundamentalists could by themselves stop the march of liberalizing globalization, the level of instability they created and the West's response to it, especially after 9/11, did begin to slow its progress. Localized rearguard actions would continue to be fought well into the twenty-first century, but the imaginings of cultural authenticity were not only those of the parochial backwater, but were an impossible dream in the age of globalization.

Questions

1 What is culture?

2 How does the influence of culture make itself felt at the level of world politics?

3 Why has religion remained such a powerful cultural influence in the world?

4 Why did Samuel Huntington argue that differences between civilizations would become the principal cause of international conflict after the end of the cold war?

5 Is the 'clash of civilizations' a credible paradigm for understanding world politics after the cold war? Are the alternative visions more plausible?

6 How many civilizations exist in the contemporary world? Does it matter?

7 What are the alternative ways in which Middle Eastern peoples have responded to the pre-eminence of the West in the modern world?

8 Can Islamic revivalism forge an alternative model of modernity?

9 How have the 9/11 attacks on the USA changed the debate about culture and globalization? Will any changes be lasting?

10 Human societies appear increasingly multicultural. Can such a world be stable?

Further Reading

Agnew, J., and Corbridge, S. (1995), *Mastering Space: Hegemony, Territory, and International Political Economy* (London: Routledge). A study on hegemony and cultural discourse since the nineteenth century that argues that globalization has created a 'deterritorialized' global hegemony.

Axford, B. (1995), *The Global System: Economics, Politics and Culture* (Cambridge: Polity Press). A study of Western modernity, and how it has been extended across the world.

Barber, B. (1996), *Jihad vs McWorld* (New York: Ballantine Books). An eloquent account of global culture and capitalism, and ways that it challenges local social systems and identities.

Buzan, B., and Gonzalez-Pelaez, A. (eds) (2009), *International Society and the Middle East* (Basingstoke: Palgrave Macmillan). An edited volume reflecting on the relationship between the Middle East and the international system from an English School perspective. Chapters by Halliday, Buzan, Bennison, Yurdusev, Gonzalez-Pelaez, Murden, Valbjorn, Hashemi, and Hinnebusch.

Fukuyama, F. (1992), *The End of History and the Last Man* (London: Penguin Books). The book that explained the power of the liberal idea, and proclaimed that the history of political development was now at an end.

—— (2004), *State Building: Governance and World Order in the Twenty-first Century* (London: Profile Books). Fukuyama's second thoughts about the progress of the liberal idea. Fukuyama is now concerned that many developing states are too weak and divided to take on liberalism without a prolonged period of state-building. Entrenching the rule of law first is more important than instituting liberal political, social, and economic freedoms.

Hashim, A. S. (2001), 'The World according to Usama Bin Laden', *Naval War College Review*, Autumn: 12–35.

Huntington, S. (1996), *The Clash of Civilizations and the Remaking of the World Order* (New York: Touchstone). The follow-up to his *Foreign Affairs* article (1993) that argued that civilizational references were becoming the driving force of international affairs.

Mosse, G. L. (1988), *The Culture of Western Europe: The Nineteenth and Twentieth Centuries*, 3rd edn (Boulder, CO: Westview Press). Examines the multifaceted development of European culture in the modern age, hightlighting the complexity of using a term that interweaves almost all aspects of social and intellectual life.

Reeves, J. (2004), *Culture and International Relations: Natives, Narratives, and Tourists* (London: Routledge). Chapter 6 especially offers a critique of contemporary cultural analysis, arguing that the attempt to use culture to explain world politics rarely works and is characterized by bad social science.

Scruton, R. (2002), *The West and the Rest: Globalization and the Terrorist Threat* (London: Continuum). An opinion piece that reflects some of the anxieties about globalization within the West following 11 September 2001. It argues that civilizations are different and that all have been damaged by liberal globalization, including the West.

Online Resource Centre

Visit the Online Resource Centre that accompanies this book to access more learning resources on this chapter topic at www.oxfordtextbooks.co.uk/orc/baylis5e/

Chapter 26

Regionalism in international affairs

EDWARD BEST · THOMAS CHRISTIANSEN

Reader's Guide

This chapter provides an overview of the different regional arrangements that have emerged around the globe over the past fifty years. Having clarified the various concepts and definitions that are being used in this respect, the chapter outlines the main driving forces that explain the rise of regionalism in recent decades. It then looks at the developments that have occurred in this regard in the Americas, in Africa, in Asia, and in the European Union, highlighting both the similarities and the differences between the various regional arrangements. The chapter argues that there is a global trend towards the establishment of regional mechanisms of cooperation and integration, and that there is no contradiction between globalization and regionalism—by contrast, regional arrangements are one way in which states in different parts of the world respond to the challenges of globalization.

Introduction

Regionalism has become a pervasive feature of international affairs. According to the **World Trade Organization** (WTO), by July 2005 only one WTO member—Mongolia—was not party to any regional trade agreement, and a total of 422 such agreements had been notified by December 2008. Regional **peacekeeping** forces have become active in some parts of the world. Regionalism has in the last decades become one of the forces challenging the traditional centrality of **states** in international relations.

That challenge comes from two directions. The word 'region' and its derivatives denote one distinguishable part of some larger geographical area. Yet they are used in different ways. On the one hand, regions are **territories** within a state, occasionally crossing state borders. On the other, regions are particular areas of the world, covering a number of different sovereign states. The issues raised for international relations have some elements in common. This chapter, however, looks only at regionalism in the international context: the range of special relationships between neighbouring countries that represent more than normal diplomatic relations but in which the component parts retain legal personality under **international law**.

The first section presents some basic concepts, dimensions, and debates. The second places regional **cooperation** in a global context and, without pretending to be exhaustive, reviews the main developments in the Americas, Africa, and Asia. The final section looks at the European Union (EU), where **integration** has, so far uniquely, gone beyond a regional organization to produce a new form of regional governance.

Regional cooperation and regional integration

Regionalism has various dimensions, and terms need to be clarified. The term **regionalization** is often used to refer to 'the growth of societal integration within a region and . . . the often undirected processes of social and economic interaction' (Hurrell 1995: 39). Such processes produce **interdependence** and may also constitute deepening perceptions of common interests and identity, including self-awareness as a region. Yet the very nature and membership of regions may be contested, and there are very different forms of interaction between the various dimensions and dynamics of regionalism. Regional agreements cover different mixtures of economic, social, political, and **security** concerns; and there are different forms of interaction between 'regionalization' and the various ways in which states may promote regional cohesion. In some cases, state-led actions have been responsible for an increase in 'real' interaction. In others, the development of ties has been more one of 'market-led integration'.

When considering the different kinds of arrangements that may be agreed between countries, a distinction is often made between 'cooperation' and 'integration'. Regional cooperation has various forms. Functional cooperation refers to limited arrangements that are agreed between states in order to work together in particular areas, for example, in transport, energy, or health. Economic cooperation refers to agreements that foresee some degree of commercial preferentialism, but with no harmonization of domestic rules nor any obligation for common action in international affairs. Political cooperation entails mutual support and commitment regarding the implementation of certain values and practices within the countries. Cooperation in foreign and security policy means that governments systematically inform and consult each other, try to adopt common positions in **international organizations**, and may even implement joint actions elsewhere. There are no necessary connections between these different areas of cooperation. And none of this has any consequence for the international status of participating countries beyond normal obligations under international law.

Formal regional integration refers to processes by which states go beyond the removal of obstacles to interaction between their countries and create a regional space subject to some distinct common rules. With regard to economic integration, several degrees of ambition are usually distinguished: free trade area, customs union, common market, economic and monetary union. From a customs union 'up', in addition to removing barriers to trade between themselves, the countries must not only adopt some measures of positive integration (i.e. harmonization of **rules**), but must also act with a single voice internationally, at the very least in tariff policy. Such processes may lead to a new level of governance above the **nation-states**, although this does not mean creation of a new 'super-state'.

While this distinction does involve some clear and fundamental choices, it should be treated with caution. Cooperation and integration are not mutually exclusive general approaches for regional governance so much as options that may be pursued for different sectors and dimensions of regional relations. All regional systems, including the EU today, contain a mixture of both.

The formal institutional arrangements of a regional system cannot be assumed to be a measure of the real depth or dynamics of a regional integration process. If regional goals are complex and long-term (e.g. to create a full common market), states may set up 'commitment institutions' in order to increase the prospects of effective compliance over time (Mattli 1999). States thus accept some pooling of **sovereignty** (i.e. the renunciation of autonomous action and/or the veto), delegation of powers to supranational bodies, and/or of 'legalization' (Moravscik 1998; Abbott *et al.* 2000). This has been mainly the case in **Europe**. The institutional **structure** of the European Community, however, has often been imitated elsewhere. In some cases, formally supranational bodies exist with little real connection with national or transnational life. Conversely, strong formal commitments may not be required to achieve important results in certain fields in certain conditions: the Nordic countries, for example, established both a Passport Union and Common Labour Market in the 1950s without any supranational arrangements (Best 2006).

Why do states decide to pursue regional integration, and what dynamics may explain the evolution of such regional arrangements? A first theme historically has been the 'management of independence': that is, the need for newly independent states to settle down in their relations (1) between themselves, (2) with the former colonial power, and (3) with other, often rival, powers. This may be summarized as the process of consolidating

international **identity** and 'actorhood': how do sets of societies want to participate in international affairs? Federal union has been the result in some cases. In others, regional organizations of one sort or another have been an important instrument for managing this often conflictual process.

A second set of issues may be grouped as the 'management of **interdependence**'. This partly refers to economic and social interaction—whether the adoption of state-led integration schemes intended to increase such interaction or of measures to ensure stability where there is market-led integration—but also to **issues** of peace and security. Regional organizations can foster 'security communities' (i.e. transnational communities in which peoples have dependable expectations of peaceful change) by promoting cooperation, establishing **norms** of behaviour, and serving as sites of socialization and learning (Adler and Barnett 1998*b*).

A third theme may be summed up as the 'management of **internationalization**', that is, the interrelationship between regional arrangements and the rest of the world. The debate about the implications of regionalism for multilateral processes of liberalization was termed the 'building-blocks-or-stumbling-blocks' question by Bhagwati (1991). Proponents of regionalism as building blocks argue that: (1) such arrangements promote internal and international dynamics that enhance the prospects for **multilateralism**; (2) regionalism can have important demonstration effects in accustoming actors to the effects of liberalization; (3) increased numbers of regional arrangements can weaken opposition to multilateral liberalization because each successive arrangement reduces the value of the margin of preference; (4) regional agreements are often more to do with strategic or political alliances than trade liberalization; and (5) regionalism has more positive than negative political effects.

Opponents of regionalism have been concerned that: (1) the net result of preferential agreements may be trade diversion; (2) there may be 'attention diversion', with participating countries losing interest in the

Box 26.1 Dynamics of regionalism	
Management of independence	Settling down by newly independent states in their relations between themselves, with the former colonial power, and with other powers
Management of interdependence	Regional mechanisms to guarantee peace and security; responses to 'regionalization'; promotion of cooperation and/or state-led integration
Management of internationalization	Regional negotiations in the multilateral system; regional/UN peacekeeping; regional responses to globalization

multilateral system, or simply an absorption of available negotiating resources; (3) competing arrangements may lock in incompatible regulatory structures and standards; (4) the creation of multiple legal frameworks and dispute settlement mechanisms may weaken discipline and efficiency; and (5) regionalism may contribute to international frictions between competing blocs (Bergsten 1997; World Bank 2005).

The historical context in which this tension plays itself out has changed considerably. In the first wave of post-war regionalism, notably in Latin America, this largely took the form of state-led efforts to reduce dependence on exports of primary commodities and to achieve industrialization through import substitution, with widespread suspicion of foreign direct investment.

The 'new regionalism' taking place since the late 1980s has been more a response to new forms of globalization, and has occurred in a more multipolar world after the end of the **cold war**. Various common features could be seen in the 1990s. Regional arrangements tended to be more open than before in terms of economic integration, and have been more comprehensive in scope. The new open regionalism, indeed, seemed to lose some of the very defining characteristics of regionalism, forming

part of 'a global structural transformation in which **non-state actors** are active and manifest themselves at several levels of the global system [and] can therefore not be understood only from the point of view of the single region' (Hettne 1999: 7–8).

Yet regionalism may also be seen as one of the few instruments that are available to states to try to manage the effects of **globalization**. If individual states no longer have the effective capacity to regulate in the face of uncontrolled movements of capital, then regionalism may be seen as a means to regain some control over global market forces—and to counter the more negative social consequences of globalization. The debate is far from over.

Key Points

- Regionalism has various dimensions and takes different forms across the world.
- Some regional integration processes are more state-led, others more market-led.
- There is a basic difference between cooperation arrangements and integration processes, but both approaches may be followed within a regional system.

Regional cooperation in a global context

Regionalism in the Americas

The American continent has been characterized by multiple, and often competing, levels of regionalism. The basic tensions date back to independence. The former British colonies in North America eventually settled down into two international actors: one federal union, the United States of America, in 1865, and one confederation, Canada, in 1867. Portuguese Brazil ended up as a federal republic in 1889. In former Spanish territories, in contrast, efforts at union failed. Two short-lived federal republics were formed: the Federal Republic of Greater Colombia (1819–31) and the Federal Republic of Central America (1823–39). Unity of Spanish America was the dream of Simon Bolívar, who in 1826 convened the Congress of Panama, proposing a 'Treaty of Union, League, and Perpetual Confederation' with a common military, a mutual defence pact, and a supranational parliamentary assembly. Bolívar's vision was not anti-American, but he preferred not to

include the USA. And like the federal republics, it soon succumbed to civil wars and rivalries between governing *caudillos*.

Latin American regionalism has thus played itself out against the background of the conflictual consolidation of current states, in which national sovereignty became a dominant feature of actorhood, and a love–hate relationship with the USA. There has been partial acceptance of a continental identity as 'America', but also a widespread perception of an identity as 'Latin America', often in opposition to the USA.

Hemispheric regionalism began with the first Pan-American Conference in Washington in 1889–90. Nine such conferences took place, leading, in the 1930s and 1940s, following decades of US interventionism, to several agreements on peace and security. The Pan-American Union became the Organization of American States (OAS) in 1948. An Inter-American System grew up, including the Inter-American Development Bank and the Inter-American Court of Human Rights.

Box 26.2 Around the world in regional organizations, 2009 (an illustrative and non-exhaustive list)

AMERICAS	Organization of American States	OAS
	North American Free Trade Agreement	NAFTA
	Central American Integration System	SICA
	Central American Common Market	CACM
	Caribbean Community	CARICOM
	Andean Community [of Nations]	CAN
	Common Market of the South	MERCOSUR
	Union of South American Nations	UNASUR
	Latin American Integration Association	LAIA
AFRICA	African Union	AU
	Arab Maghreb Union	UMA
	Community of Sahel–Saharan States	CEN–SAD
	Economic Community of West African States	ECOWAS
	West African Economic and Monetary Union	WAEMU
	Central African Monetary and Economic Community	CEMAC
	Economic Community of the Great Lakes Countries	CEPGL
	Economic Community of Central African States	ECCAS
	East African Community	EAC
	Common Market for Eastern and Southern Africa	COMESA
	Intergovernmental Authority for Development	IGAD
	Southern African Customs Union	SACU
	Southern African Development Community	SADC
ASIA	Gulf Cooperation Council	GCC
	Association of Southeast Asian Nations	ASEAN
	ASEAN Regional Forum	ARF
	South Asian Association for Regional Cooperation	SAARC
	Shanghai Cooperation Organization	SCO
	Economic Cooperation Organization	ECO
ASIA-PACIFIC	Asia Pacific Economic Cooperation	APEC
	Pacific Economic Cooperation Council	PECC
	Pacific Islands Forum	
EURASIA	Commonwealth of Independent States	CIS
	Eurasian Economic Community	EAEC
	Black Sea Economic Cooperation	BSEC
EUROPE	European Union	EU
	Council of Europe	CoE
	Nordic Council/Council of Ministers	
	Benelux Economic Union	Benelux
	Visegrad Group	V4
EURO-ATLANTIC	North Atlantic Treaty Organization	NATO
	Organization for Security and Cooperation in Europe	OSCE

During the cold war, however, it was seen with suspicion in much of the Americas as an instrument of US foreign policy.

The US policy on regional agreements changed in the later 1980s. It began in 1986 to negotiate a free trade agreement with Canada. Negotiations then began between the USA, Canada, and Mexico, leading to the establishment in 1994 of the North American Free Trade Agreement (NAFTA). This is broader in scope than most such agreements. Agriculture is covered, and

the treaty was accompanied by supplementary agreements on labour and the environment, although there are no supranational elements. A first 'Summit of the Americas' was held in Miami in 1994, with the aim of achieving a Free Trade Area of the Americas (FTAA) as well as deepening cooperation in drugs, corruption, **terrorism**, hemispheric security, **sustainable development**, and the environment. By the fourth summit in Argentina in 2005, however, the political context of Inter-Americanism had significantly changed.

Case Study Central America: a perpetual pursuit of union?

Central America can seem to present a paradox. The observer sees a number of small countries, with a common history, a relatively high degree of common identity, and apparently everything to gain from integration, but which have consistently failed, so far, to achieve the ambitious regional goals they proclaim.

Following independence, the Captaincy-General of Guatemala became the Federal Republic of Central America (1823–39), before splitting into Guatemala, El Salvador, Honduras, Nicaragua, and Costa Rica. Restoration of this Union has been a constant theme in integrationist discourse. Yet Central America was more a collection of communities than a clearly defined overarching entity, local elites elsewhere resisted leadership by Guatemala, and Costa Rica early on showed a tendency to isolationism. Nationalism grew, unionism was undermined by conflict, and outside involvement was often unhelpful. A powerful mythology of union thus coexisted with various sources of division.

A Central American Peace Conference in Washington, convened in 1907 to help end local conflicts, led to a short-lived

Central American Court of Justice (1908–18). The Organization of Central American States (ODECA) was created in 1951. The first organizations of functional cooperation emerged around this time. Some 25 such bodies now exist, covering everything from water to electrical energy, creating a complex web of regional interactions. Formal economic integration began in 1960, with the Central American Common Market (CACM). Intra-regional trade grew, but the system entered crisis at the end of 1960s. Efforts at reform in the 1970s were overtaken by political crisis and conflicts. In the 1980s, integration became associated with the Central American peace process. In this context a Central American Parliament was created as a forum for regional dialogue. In 1991, with conflicts in El Salvador and Nicaragua ended, the cold war over, and a new wave of regional integration across the world, a new period began with the Central American Integration System (SICA). This aimed to provide a global approach to integration, with four sub-systems—political, economic, social, and cultural.

The institutional system is concentrated around the Presidential summits. The Central American Parliament is directly elected but has no powers. Costa Rica never joined, while Panama moved to pull out in 2009. Similarly, as of 2009, only El Salvador, Guatemala, Honduras, and Nicaragua participated in the Central American Court of Justice. There have been repeated discussions of institutional reform. By 2008, intra-regional trade represented around 30 per cent of exports and 13 per cent of imports. Most goods originating in Central American countries enjoy free circulation. The same external tariff was being applied for 95 per cent of goods. A general Framework Convention to establish a customs union was signed in 2007. In 2009, however, El Salvador, Guatemala, and Honduras agreed to go ahead without the others. The future is being shaped also by international agreements. The Central American countries signed a free trade agreement with the USA in 2004, and began in 2007 to negotiate an association agreement with the European Union. The pursuit of union continues.

Latin American regionalism in the post-war decades was shaped by the model of state-led, import-substituting industrialization. In order to overcome dependence on exports of primary commodities, a combination of protection and planning would make it possible to reduce manufactured imports. Regional integration was a response to the limitations of this approach at the national level. This first wave produced the Central American Common Market (CACM, 1960), the Latin American Free Trade Association (LAFTA, 1961) and the Andean Pact (1969), all of which had limited success.

A wave of 'new regionalism' began in the 1980s and took off in the 1990s. The Central American Integration System (SICA) was created in 1991. The Common Market of the South (MERCOSUR) was created in 1991 by Argentina and Brazil, together with Paraguay and

Uruguay. A common market was proclaimed in 1994, although there remain exceptions. MERCOSUR has not adopted a supranational institutional system but there have been important political dimensions. In the early phases this included mutual support for the consolidation of democracy and the ending of rivalry between Argentina and Brazil.

In 1990, the Andean Presidents also re-launched their integration process. A Common External Tariff was announced in 1994. The group was renamed the Andean Community of Nations (CAN) in 1997, with the aim of consolidating a common market by 2005. The institutional system is modelled on the European Community, with elements of formal **supranationalism**: Andean norms are to be directly applicable and to enjoy primacy over national law, and they are monitored by common institutions, including a Court of Justice.

The 'new' forms of integration in the Americas were seen as fundamentally different, part of broad-based structural reforms aimed at locking in commitments in a context of unilateral and multilateral liberalization. It also seemed that there might be a new convergence of hemispheric and Latin American initiatives.

Yet developments in the 2000s have brought this into question. Proposals to bring together Andean integration and MERCOSUR began in the 1990s. The creation of a 'South American Community of Nations' was announced in 2004, becoming the 'Union of South American Nations' (UNASUR) in 2008. In 2005 CAN and MERCOSUR mutually recognized the associate membership of each other's member countries. In 2006, Venezuela, under President Chávez, left the Andean Community and applied to join MERCOSUR. All this raised a large question mark over the Free Trade Area of the Americas. Indeed, a radical alternative was proposed by Venezuela and Cuba, joined by Bolivia, Ecuador, and some Caribbean and Central American countries, known since 2009 as the Bolivarian Alliance of the Peoples of America (ALBA).

Regionalism in Africa

Contemporary regionalism in Africa emerged with the politics of anti-colonialism but often on the basis of pre-existing colonial arrangements. French West Africa was a Federation between 1904 and 1958, and a common currency known as the CFA franc was created in 1945. After several organizational transformations, Benin, Burkina Faso, Côte d'Ivoire, Guinea-Bissau, Mali, Niger, Senegal, and Togo have become members of the present West African Economic and Monetary Union (WAEMU).

In Central Africa, a monetary union guaranteed by France and a formal customs union were created in 1964. These were transformed into the Economic and Monetary Community of Central Africa (CEMAC), which took over fully in 1999. This is a monetary union using the CFA franc (now pegged to the euro) with a common monetary policy, and is formally a customs union, aiming to create a single market by 2014.

The Southern African Customs Union (SACU) was originally created in 1910. An agreement was signed in 1969 with the independent countries of Botswana, Lesotho, Swaziland, and Namibia. This has included a common external tariff and a revenue-sharing mechanism, as well as a Common Monetary Area (except for Botswana) with currencies pegged to the South African rand. A new treaty came into force in 2004.

Colonial Kenya and Uganda formed a customs union in 1917, which Tanzania (then Tanganyika) joined in 1927. After independence, cooperation continued under the East African Common Services Organization. An East African Community was created in 1967 but collapsed in 1977 as a result of political differences. Following efforts at re-integration in the 1990s, the present East Africa Community (EAC) was established in 2000. A customs union formally came into effect in 2005, and a Common Market Protocol was signed in November 2009.

In the 1970s and 1980s, a variety of other regional organizations emerged, often cutting across the previous arrangements. With Nigerian leadership, the Economic Community of West African States (ECOWAS) was created in 1975 between the francophone countries which are also members of WAEMU, and the anglophone countries of West Africa. A Preferential Trade Area cutting across eastern and southern Africa was created in 1981. This was succeeded in 1994 by the Common Market for Eastern and Southern Africa (COMESA), which in 2009 had 19 member states stretching from Libya to Madagascar. In 1983, the French Central African countries, together with the members of the Economic Community of the Great Lakes Countries, created in 1976, and São Tomé and Principe, created the Economic Community of Central African States (ECCAS). Finally, straddling the continent from Senegal to Eritrea is the Community of Sahel–Saharan States (CEN–SAD), established in 1998.

Some organizations had particular political aspects to their foundation. The aim of the Frontline States to reduce dependence on apartheid South Africa prompted the creation in 1980 of the Southern African Development Coordination Conference (SADCC). This was transformed into the Southern African Development Community (SADC) in 1992, of which post-apartheid South Africa became a member.

Other organizations have been founded with a particular special mandate that was later extended. The Intergovernmental Authority on Development (IGAD) in East Africa was founded in 1986 with a narrow mandate to deal with drought and desertification, but did little in view of tensions between its members and the situation in Somalia. In 1996 it was given a broader mandate covering conflict prevention and management.

Sub-regional cultural identity has played a particular role, for example, in the case of the Arab Maghreb Union (AMU), which came into being in 1989.

The first stage of pan-African organization was primarily political in nature. The Organization of African

Unity (OAU), created in 1963, was dedicated to the ending of colonialism and establishing of political liberation. The continental agenda has subsequently broadened. The 1991 Treaty of Abuja, coming into force in 1994, established the African Economic Community (AEC). In 2002, the OAU and AEC became the African Union (AU), formally modelled on the European Union.

There was also a move towards continental **coordination** of the multiple regional arrangements that had grown up, with a 1997 protocol formalizing relations between the AEC and 14 Regional Economic Communities (RECs)—that is, the various organizations mentioned above. The RECs have had some success in functional cooperation. However, they suffer from various institutional weaknesses, exacerbated by the multiplicity of arrangements, prompting recent initiatives for a 'rationalization'. Moreover, the factors necessary for deep integration remain elusive. There is little complementarity across economies. There are few strong regional focal points. Integration has a limited domestic constituency, in the sense of pressure from business interests or **civil society**. And there remains a general unwillingness to consider sharing sovereignty (Economic Commission for Africa and African Union 2006).

There has been a certain evolution in this respect, reflected in the New Partnership for Africa's Development (NEPAD) adopted in 2001, which includes an African Peer Review Mechanism (APRM). In addition, regional organizations have become active in conflict management. The best known is the ECOWAS Monitoring Group (ECOMOG), created in 1990 to intervene in Liberia. It also acted in Sierra Leone and Guinea-Bissau in the 1990s, before being given a formal basis in 1999. Since then, it has acted in Côte d'Ivoire in 2002 and Liberia in 2003. An AU Peace and Security Council was created in 2003. The AU has since deployed missions in Burundi, the Sudan, Somalia, and the Comoros.

Regionalism in Asia

Regionalism in Asia has followed quite different patterns. Southeast Asia is not a region with a clear historical identity. The very term 'Southeast Asia' seems to have come to prominence internationally to describe the areas south of China that were occupied by Japan in the Second World War. The first post-war organizations, notably the 1954 Southeast Asian Treaty Organization (SEATO), were US-backed bodies made up of an international range of interested powers. Malaya, the Philippines, and Indonesia briefly formed the Association of Southeast Asia (ASA, 1961) and MAPHILINDO (1963) as a means to promote regional solidarity. These were interrupted by intra-regional conflict, notably over the future of Borneo. As elsewhere, Britain had looked to federation as a means to ease its withdrawal from colonial territories. The Federation of Malaya, created in 1948, formed a new Federation of Malaysia in 1963, together with Singapore (until 1965), Sarawak, and British North Borneo (Sabah). A period of 'Confrontation' ensued between Malaysia and Indonesia, while the Philippines claimed Sabah. The Confrontation ended in 1966.

The establishment of the Association of Southeast Asian Nations (ASEAN) in 1967 between Indonesia, Malaysia, Philippines, Singapore, and Thailand was thus motivated less by a sense of common identity than by a realization that failure to prevent conflicts within the region would invite external intervention, which would in turn exacerbate intra-regional tensions. No supranational elements were foreseen. Regional cooperation was to be built by an 'ASEAN Way' based on consultation, consensual decision-making, and flexibility. Rather than starting with ambitious political commitments, ASEAN would proceed by small, informal, and voluntary steps, which could eventually become more binding and institutionalized.

Although economic cooperation was foreseen, the evolution of ASEAN was driven by political and security concerns. The first new step was taken amid the regional uncertainties following the fall of Saigon in the Vietnam War, and the communist victories in Laos and Cambodia in 1975. ASEAN leaders held their first summit in 1976, signing the Declaration of ASEAN Concord and the Treaty of Amity and Cooperation in Southeast Asia, which reaffirmed the **principles** of mutual respect, non-interference, and peaceful settlement of differences. The next turning point came at the beginning of the 1990s as ASEAN sought to affirm its identity and centrality. On the security front, in the context of the withdrawal of Vietnam from Cambodia and the end of the cold war, a succession of proposals culminated in the creation of the ASEAN Regional Forum (ARF). This came into effect in 1994, with the aim of pursuing confidence-building measures, preventive diplomacy, and eventually conflict resolution. Other steps were taken in response to the creation of the Asia Pacific Economic Cooperation (APEC).

APEC had been formed in 1989 on the principle of 'open regionalism'. It was not to involve any discrimination vis-à-vis other countries. Nor did it reflect any distinctive regional identity so much as 'the desire of the "non-Asian states" of the region to consolidate links with the "open market-oriented economies" of East Asia' (Higgott 1995: 377). In response, Malaysia under Dr Mahathir—one of the key defenders of 'Asian values' in Asian regionalism—proposed an 'East Asian Economic Caucus' excluding Australia, Canada, New Zealand, and the USA. The USA put pressure on Japan and South Korea not to participate. At the same time, it was agreed in 1992 to establish an ASEAN Free Trade Area (AFTA). The Asian financial crisis of 1997–8 provided a renewed impetus for regional cooperation and also led to a new format of cooperation with China, Japan, and South Korea as 'ASEAN plus Three' (APT), seen by some as the realization of the idea underlying the East Asian Economic Caucus.

In 2003, the member states agreed to create an ASEAN Security Community, an ASEAN Economic Community, and an ASEAN Socio-Cultural Community by 2020. The Economic Community is a 'Free Trade Area–plus', aiming at a single market but with no common external tariff, and restricted flows of labour. While it was decided not to pursue supranationalism, it was agreed to strengthen ASEAN's institutional arrangements. A new formal dispute settlement mechanism was created, and the role of the Secretariat was reinforced, together with a Development Fund and increased institutional involvement of the business sector. The development gap between old and new members (Vietnam, Myanmar/Burma, Laos, and Cambodia) also prompted new efforts to promote solidarity, through the Initiative for ASEAN Integration and the Economic Cooperation Strategy.

Asian regionalism is thus evolving on two planes. On the one hand, ASEAN continues to move towards some institutional deepening as a means to preserve its own position. The 'strengthening of ASEAN integration through the accelerated establishment of an ASEAN Community' by 2015, which was agreed at the January 2007 summit, was explicitly intended to 'reinforce ASEAN's centrality and role as the driving force in charting the evolving regional architecture' (ASEAN 2007). A new ASEAN Charter was signed in November 2007 including specific references to 'ASEAN identity'.

On the other hand, regional agreements reflect rivalries between the major powers. Comprehensive economic cooperation agreements were signed with China, Japan, and India in the course of the 2000s. China has given preference to the 'ASEAN plus Three' format, while the proposals made since 2002 by Japan for an East Asia Community have been based on 'ASEAN plus Six', also including India, Australia, and New Zealand, which has been the membership of the East Asia Summits held annually since 2005. The USA also moved in 2009 to enhance its engagement in the region, signing the ASEAN Treaty of Amity and Cooperation and participating in a first ASEAN–US Leaders' Meeting.

Eurasia and the post-Soviet states

A complex and shifting pattern of regional agreements has resulted from the efforts of the former components of the Soviet Union to settle down in a zone of cooperation and competition between Russian, Chinese, and EU influence. The Commonwealth of Independent States (CIS) was created in 1991 among all the former Soviet republics except the three Baltic states and Georgia (which joined in 1993 but withdrew following the 2008 conflict with Russia). A CIS Customs Union was proclaimed in 1995 between Russia, Belarus, and Kazakhstan. A Collective Security Treaty was signed in 1992. In 2002 this became the Collective Security Treaty Organization (CSTO), comprising Russia, Belarus, Armenia, Kazakhstan, Kyrgyzstan, and Tajikistan. Uzbekistan rejoined in 2006.

A Central Asian Commonwealth composed of all five Central Asian republics was created in 1991. A series of formations with different memberships and names led in 2006 to the Eurasian Economic Community, bringing together Central Asian Republics (other than Turkmenistan) with Russia and Belarus. Uzbekistan withdrew in 2008.

The shifting patterns of these sub-regional organizations reflect not only evolving relations between newly independent states and Russia, the former dominant power. They must also be understood against the background of rivalries between Russia and China, as well as partially shared concerns between those two powers as to the role of the USA, with its military presence in the context of operations in Afghanistan.

The 'Shanghai Five' mechanism was created by China, Russia, Kazakhstan, Kyrgyzstan, and Tajikistan in 1996. This was transformed in 2002 (with the participation of Uzbekistan) into the Shanghai Cooperation Organization (SCO), with Iran, Mongolia, India, and Pakistan as observers. It promotes confidence-building actions, and various forms of cooperation, including collaboration to counter terrorism, drug trafficking, money-laundering, and weapons smuggling. The Economic Cooperation Organization (ECO), revived by Iran, Pakistan, and Turkey in 1985, was joined by the Central Asian republics as well as Afghanistan in 1992.

In the area of Ukraine and the Caucasus, the evolution of sub-regional agreements has had more to do with support for the consolidation of democracy, as well as management of local conflicts, in the context of a certain rivalry for influence between Russia and the European Union. The GUAM Organization for Democracy and Economic Development was set up in 1997 as a forum for cooperation without Russia, and was consolidated with a new Charter in 2006. It brings together Georgia, Ukraine, Azerbaijan, and Moldova. The Community of Democratic Choice was created in Kiev in December 2005 with the stated objective of promoting 'democracy, human rights, and the rule of law'. Its members are Georgia, Macedonia, Moldova, Ukraine, as well as five EU member states—the three Baltic states, Romania, and Slovenia—with observer status for Azerbaijan, and four other EU member states (Bulgaria, the Czech Republic, Hungary, and Poland) as well as the EU as such, the USA and the Organization for Security and Cooperation in Europe (OSCE). Finally, the 1992 Black Sea Economic Cooperation (BSEC) links Armenia, Azerbaijan, Georgia, Russia, and the Ukraine to Turkey, as well as Albania, Bulgaria, Greece, Moldova, Romania, Serbia, and Montenegro.

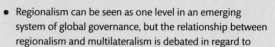

Key Points

- Regionalism can be seen as one level in an emerging system of global governance, but the relationship between regionalism and multilateralism is debated in regard to both economic liberalization and international security.

- Regionalist experiences in each continent have followed different patterns, which reflect their different historical and cultural contexts.

- The earlier waves of regionalism arose in a context of post-colonial restructuring, economic protectionism, or regional security concerns. A new wave of 'open regionalism' began around 1990 with the end of the cold war and the surge in globalization.

The process of European integration

In Europe, regionalism after 1945 has taken the form of a gradual process of integration leading to the emergence of the European Union. It was initially a purely West European creation between the 'original Six' member states born of the desire for reconciliation between France and Germany in a context of ambitious federalist plans. Yet the process has taken the form of a progressive construction of an institutional architecture, a legal framework, and a wide range of policies, which, in 2007, encompassed 27 European states.

The European Coal and Steel Community was created in 1951 (in force in 1952), followed by the European Economic Community and the European Atomic Energy Community in 1957 (in force in 1958). These treaties involved a conferral of Community competence in various areas—the supranational management of coal and steel, the creation and regulation of an internal market, and common policies in trade, competition, agriculture, and transport. Since then, powers have been extended to include new legislative competences in some fields such as the environment. Since the 1992 Treaty on European Union (the Maastricht Treaty, in force in 1993), the integration process has also involved the adoption of stronger forms of unification, notably monetary union, as well as other forms of cooperation such as non-binding coordination in economic and employment policy, or more intergovernmental cooperation in foreign and security policy.

From very limited beginnings, both in terms of membership and in terms of scope, the EU has therefore gradually developed to become an important political and economic actor whose presence has a significant impact, both internationally and domestically. This gradual process of European integration has taken place at various levels. The first is the signature and reform of the basic treaties. These are the result of Intergovernmental Conferences (IGCs), where representatives of national governments negotiate the legal framework within which the EU institutions operate. Such treaty changes require ratification in each country and can be seen as the 'grand bargains' in the evolution of the EU.

Within this framework, the institutions have been given considerable powers to adopt decisions and manage policies, although the dynamics of decision-making differ significantly across various arenas. There are important differences between the more integrated sectors of economic regulation on the one hand, and the more 'intergovernmental' areas of foreign and defence policy and internal security cooperation on the other. In some areas, a country may have to accept decisions that are

Table 26.1 Important agreements in the history of the European Union

Year (coming into force)	Treaty	Main subjects
1952	Paris Treaty	Regulation of coal and steel production in the member states, creation of supranational institutions
1958	Rome Treaties	European Economic Community—creation of a customs union (removal of all intra-union duties and creation of a common customs tariff); plans for a common market and common policies Euratom — cooperation in atomic energy
1986	Single European Act	Removal of all non-tariff barriers to the movement of persons, goods, services, and capital (the '1992 programme'); foreign policy cooperation included in the treaty provisions
1993	Maastricht Treaty	Creation of the European Union, encompassing the European Community and two parallel pillars for Common Foreign and Security Policy (CFSP) and Justice and Home Affairs; economic and monetary union (the euro)
1999	Amsterdam Treaty	Various institutional reforms, High Representative for CFSP, provisions for enhanced cooperation
2001	Nice Treaty	Reform of Commission and Council (voting weights), expansion of majority voting
2009	Lisbon Treaty	Further expansion of majority voting and of the powers of the European Parliament; creation of the post of President of the European Council; the High Representative for foreign and security policy also becoming Vice-President of the Commission, and heading a new 'European External Action Service'; European Charter of Fundamental Rights becoming legally binding

Table 26.2 Institutions of the EU

EU institution	Responsibilities	Location
European Parliament (EP)	Directly elected representatives of EU citizens, scrutinizing the operation of the other institutions, and, in many areas, sharing with the Council the power to adopt EU legislation	Strasbourg (plenary sessions); Brussels (MEP offices, committee meetings and some plenary sessions); Luxembourg (administration)
European Council	Regular summits of the leaders of the member states and the Commission, chaired by an elected President, setting the EU's broad agenda and a forum of last resort to find agreement on divisive issues (NB: distinct from the Council of Europe)	Brussels
Council of the EU	Representing the views of national governments and adopting, in many areas jointly with the EP, the ultimate shape of EU legislation	Brussels (some meetings in Luxembourg)
European Commission	Initiating, administering, and overseeing the implementation of EU policies and legislation	Brussels and Luxembourg
Court of Justice	The EU's highest court, supported by a General Court. Main competences include actions for annulment of EU acts, infringement procedures against member states for failing to comply with obligations and preliminary rulings on the validity or interpretation of EC law on request from national courts	Luxembourg
European Central Bank	Central bank responsible for setting the interest rates and controlling the money supply of the single European currency, the euro	Frankfurt am Main
Court of Auditors	The EU's audit office, responsible for auditing the revenues and the expenditure under the EU budget	Luxembourg

'imposed' on it by the (qualified) majority of member states. In other areas, it may be able to block decisions.

To understand the integration process, one needs to take account of the role played by both member states *and* by supranational institutions. Moreover, member states are not just represented by national governments, since a host of state, **non-state**, and **transnational actors** participate in the processes of domestic preference formation or direct representation of interests in Brussels. The relative openness of the European policy process means that political groups or economic interests will try to influence EU decision-making if they feel that their position is not sufficiently represented by national governments. That is one reason why the EU is increasingly seen as a system of multilevel governance, involving a plurality of actors on different territorial levels: supranational, national, and sub-state.

The complexity of the EU institutional machinery, together with continuous change over time, has spawned a lively debate among integration theorists (Rosamond 2000; Wiener and Diez 2004). Some approaches are applications of more general theories of international relations: the literature on both **realism** and interdependence has contributed to theorizing integration. Other scholars have regarded the European Union as *sui generis*—in a category of its own—and therefore in need of the development of dedicated theories of integration. The most prominent among these has been neo-functionalism, which sought to explain the evolution of integration in terms of 'spillover' from one sector to another as resources and loyalties of elites were transferred to the European level. More recently, as aspects of EU politics have come to resemble the domestic politics of states, scholars have turned to approaches drawn from comparative politics.

However, it has been the exchange between 'supranational' and 'intergovernmental' approaches that has had the greatest impact on the study of European integration. Supranational approaches regard the emergence of supranational institutions in Europe as a distinct feature and turn these into the main object of analysis. Here, the politics above the level of states is regarded as the most significant, and consequently the political actors and institutions at the European level receive most attention. Intergovernmentalist approaches, on the other hand, continue to regard states as the most important aspect of the integration process and consequently concentrate on the study of politics *between* and *within* states (see Box 26.1). But whatever one's theoretical preferences,

most scholars would agree that no analysis of the EU is complete without studying both the operation and evolution of the central institutions and the input from political actors in the member states. More recently, debate in EU studies has also centred on a wider fault-line in the social sciences: the difference between rationalist and constructivist approaches. Constructivists have challenged the implicit rationalism of much integration research until the 1990s (see Ch. 9). Their critique focused on the tendency of rationalist studies to privilege decision-making over agenda-setting, and outcomes over process. The social constructivist research agenda instead concentrates on the framing of issues *before* decisions about them are made, and therefore emphasizes the role of ideas, discourses, and social interaction in shaping interests (Christiansen, Jørgensen, and Wiener 2001).

The prospect of an ever *wider* European Union has raised serious questions about the nature and direction of the integration process. The 2004/2007 enlargement, bringing in 12 Central, East and South European countries as new members, has generally been seen as a qualitative leap for the EU, and further applications for membership are pending from Iceland, Turkey, and several successor states to the former Yugoslavia. Concerns that the enlarged Union, if not reformed substantially, would find it difficult to take decisions and maintain a reliable legal framework was one of the driving forces towards efforts of 'streamlining' the Union's institutional structure and decision-making procedures. At the beginning of the past decade, a wide-ranging institutional reform (and an ambitious shift in the language of integration) was attempted with the setting up of a Constitutional Convention in 2002 and the signing of a 'Treaty establishing a Constitution for Europe' in 2004. However, this attempt at formally recognizing and advancing the constitutional nature of the EU treaties was rejected by the voters in referendums in France and the Netherlands. After some years of 'reflection', EU leaders signed in Lisbon in 2007 a revised treaty in order to achieve many of the planned reforms—strengthening the actorhood of the Union, enhancing the powers of the European Parliament as well as of national parliaments, and increasing the efficiency of decision-making procedures through greater use of majority voting. This Lisbon Treaty came into force on 1 December 2009, and it is on the foundation of its reformed institutional structure that the EU now seeks to respond to the economic and political challenges of globalization.

Key Points

- The process of integration in post-war Europe was launched in the context of long debates about the creation of a federal system, but ultimately the choice was made in favour of a gradual path towards an 'ever closer union'.

- Integration has proceeded by conferring competence for many economic sectors to supranational institutions that can take decisions that are binding on the member states.

- Over time, more politically sensitive areas, such as monetary policy or internal and external security, have also become the domain of the European Union.

- Successive reforms of the EU treaties have sought to maintain and enhance the legitimacy and efficiency of a Union that had grown, by 2007, to 27 member states, the latest being the coming into force of the Lisbon Treaty at the end of 2009.

Conclusion

We can conclude this overview of the development of mechanisms of regional cooperation and integration with three brief observations. First, regionalism is a truly global phenomenon. It is not the case that the entire world is engulfed in a single process of globalization, or that the world is being divided along simple ideological or civilizational fault-lines. Rather, different parts of the globe are looking for different ways to accommodate themselves within the globalized **world order**, and regional arrangements are one important way of doing so. There is thus no paradox, and even less a contradiction, between regionalism and globalization. Instead, regionalism is one aspect of the process of globalization, and developments in one region inform and indeed feed into developments in others. Second, within the global trend of regionalism there are important differences in the types of organization that are being set up, ranging from rather loose and non-binding agreements to the complex institutional architecture set up by the European Union, depending on the scope and depth with which members are seeking to address issues of transnational governance. And third, there is no single or simple path of regionalism. The ways in which different regional mechanisms develop are contingent upon a multitude of factors, both internal and external to the region. Both the driving forces for more regional integration and cooperation and the obstacles that may limit those aspirations vary across the different continents. Regionalism as a global phenomenon may be here to stay, but so are the differences between the kinds of regional arrangements that are being developed in different parts of the globe.

Key Points

- The creation of regional governance structures is not a contradiction to globalization but the expression of local attempts to accommodate and respond to its challenges.

- Despite the observation of a global trend towards greater regionalism, important differences remain between the depth and the scope of regional institutions that develop in different parts of the globe.

- Regional cooperation and integration are not linear processes but depend on the varying contingencies that provide opportunities and limits in different regional contexts.

Questions

1 What have been the driving forces behind processes of regional integration and cooperation?

2 What is the relative weight of economic and political factors in explaining the emergence of regional institutions?

3 What are the dynamics behind the 'new regionalism'?

4 What role can regional organizations play in maintaining peace and security?

5 What impact have processes of regional integration and cooperation had on the Westphalian state?

6 Compare and contrast European integration with the process of regional cooperation in at least one other continent.

7   What are the main differences between supranationalist and intergovernmentalist approaches to the study of the European Union?

8   How important has the legal dimension been to the evolution of the European Union?

9   What role do the supranational institutions play in the European policy process?

10   Has the European Union been able to respond effectively to the changed circumstances of global politics?

Further Reading

Christiansen, T., Jørgensen, K. E., and Wiener, A. (eds) (2001), *The Social Construction of Europe* (London: Sage). Provides a discussion of different aspects of European integration applying insights from social constructivism, and also includes debates with critics of this approach.

De Lombaerde, P. (ed.) (2006), *Assessment and Measurement of Regional Integration* (London and New York: Routledge). An informative and innovative collection that considers from different perspectives the challenge of evaluating the actual impact of regional arrangements.

Farrell, M., Hettne, B., and Van Langenhove, L. (eds) (2005), *Global Politics of Regionalism: Theory and Practice* (London and Ann Arbor, MI: Pluto Press). A good overview of theoretical questions and key issues in regionalism, as well as the particular approaches followed in individual regions.

Hix, S. (2005), *The Political System of the European Union* (Basingstoke: Palgrave Macmillan). This advanced textbook approaches the subject from a comparative politics angle, looking in detail at the executive, legislative, and judicial politics as well as at developments in various policy areas.

Tavares, R. (2010), *Regional Security. The capacity of international organizations* (London and New York: Routledge). An overview and comparative evaluation of the experience of regional organizations across the world in maintaining peace and security.

Telò, M. (ed.) (2007), *European Union and New Regionalism. Regional Actors and Global Governance in a Post-Hegemonic Era* (Aldershot: Ashgate). This offers a good set of theoretical perspectives on regionalism in the global context, as well as examining alternative models of cooperation and the role of the EU as an international actor.

Wallace, H., Wallace, W., and Pollack, M. (eds) (2005), *Policy-making in the European Union* (Oxford: Oxford University Press). This is a wide-ranging textbook that covers all major policies and also examines ways of studying the institutional setting and the dynamics of governance in the EU.

Wiener, A., and Diez, T. (2004), *European Integration Theory* (Oxford: Oxford University Press). A comprehensive and topical reader bringing together the most important contributions to the theoretical debates in the study of European integration.

World Bank (2005), *Global Economic Prospects 2005: Trade, Regionalism and Development* (Washington, DC: World Bank). A thorough discussion of regionalism from an economic perspective, looking both at the rationales and the results of regional arrangements around the world, as well as their implications for multilateralism.

Online Resource Centre

 Visit the Online Resource Centre that accompanies this book to access more learning resources on this chapter topic at www.oxfordtextbooks.co.uk/orc/baylis5e/

Global trade and finance

MATTHEW WATSON

Reader's Guide

This chapter will introduce students to important issues in the conduct of global trade and global finance. It shows that the two spheres are regulated by different governance institutions, but that disturbances in one sphere can result in related disturbances in the other. This corresponds to one of the most widely cited definitions of economic globalization, where globalization is understood as the increased sensitivity of one part of the world economy to developments elsewhere. A brief background history is presented of important moments in the evolving regulatory structures for global trade and global finance. This highlights the increasing reluctance of governance institutions to enact regulatory restrictions on financial interests in order to facilitate growth in world trade. The consequent move towards market self-regulation means that financial markets in particular have become increasingly susceptible to moments of extreme instability, as the global banking crisis following the meltdown of sub-prime mortgage markets in 2007 illustrates particularly well.

Introduction

The 1970s was a troubled, even crisis decade for the advanced industrialized countries of the Western world. Growth rates fell quite substantially from their preceding post-Second World War plateau, with both unemployment and inflation increasing rapidly. This led to the identification of a qualitatively new economic phenomenon, **stagflation**, in which advanced industrialized economies seemed to be powerless to re-energize their economies but paid the price for attempting to do so in the form of accelerating prices.

The eventual response to the conditions of the 1970s was a turn against government intervention in the economy. National controls on the free movement of capital, money, goods, services, and people were progressively eased, and the language of 'markets' began to dominate the way in which politicians talked about their economic priorities. International institutions were also given extra authority to deprive markets of the overwhelmingly national character that they had displayed in the 1970s, and to superimpose an increasingly global character in its place.

Yet just how prevalent is the trend towards genuine economic globalization? There have certainly been large increases over the last forty years in the integration of national markets for both traded goods and financial flows, but this does not mean in itself that the ensuing market arrangements incorporate all countries of the world in any way evenly. What has been seen is the emergence of particular globalization 'hot-spots' centred on the most advanced industrialized countries, within which there has been a significant intensification of cross-border economic activity. At the same time many of the poorer countries of the world remain largely untouched by the new economic structures and appear to have little connection to these globalization hot-spots.

Partly this is an issue of development, because the organization of cross-border economic activities has tended to focus only on the most advanced sectors of the world economy. Partly it is an issue of political asymmetries within the regulatory system for global trade and global finance, with the advanced industrialized countries keeping most of the economic gains from globalization for themselves. As development issues are dealt with elsewhere in the book—see, in particular, Chapter 28—this chapter focuses instead primarily on the regulatory principles on which global trade and global finance are today grounded. The aim is to highlight the means through which the balance of power within the inter-state system is imprinted on the regulation of global trade and global finance. This will enable students to conceptualize the tendency towards economic globalization as a deeply uneven historical process.

The current regulation of global trade

When treated as a purely economic phenomenon, the most frequently cited indicator of globalization is the eye-catching intensity of the increases in world trade witnessed in the last forty years. This is demonstrated best by looking at standardized figures for the volume of world exports, because this allows for meaningful direct comparisons to be made. Taking the 2000 figure as the baseline number of 100—which itself corresponded in value terms to approximately US$8.6 trillion of world trade—this compares with standardized numbers of 22 for 1970, 37 for 1980, and 54 for 1990. In other words, the volume of world exports grew by roughly a factor of 5 between 1970 and 2000, a factor of 3 between 1980 and 2000, and a factor of 2 between 1990 and 2000 alone. This signifies an accelerating trend, and further increases in global trade after 2000 continued to be marked until the destabilizing impact of the **sub-prime crisis** of 2007/8. Between 2000 and 2006 the dollar value of global trade leapt from US$8.6 trillion to US$11.8 trillion.

The figures also show that the world economy was becoming more systematically open to global trade from the 1970s onwards. The relevant indicator here is the ratio of growth in global trade to growth in global **GDP**. If the two numbers are exactly the same, and therefore the ratio is 1:1, all increases in world export demand are fully accounted for by the fact that the world economy is becoming richer as a whole and not by the fact that it is becoming generically more open to trade. However, taking 1970–2000 as a single time period, the ratio was 1.77:1, showing that increases in global trade were almost double those of global GDP. Between 2000 and 2006 the ratio was 2.06:1, or slightly

Box 27.1 What is international trade?

Box 27.1 What is international trade?

At its most basic, international trade occurs when the citizens of one country produce a good that is subsequently consumed by the citizens of another country. There is consequently a geographical mismatch between the site of production and the site of consumption, with the good travelling across at least one national border so as to connect the producer economically with the consumer. The country producing the good for sale elsewhere in the world is the exporter; the country in which the good is eventually sold is the importer.

more than double (all figures calculated from World Trade Organization 2007).

The body that today is formally charged with overseeing the regulation of all this export activity is the **World Trade Organization** (WTO). This is a relatively new institution, having been established only in 1995. It replaced what was only ever intended as an interim body, the **General Agreement on Tariffs and Trade** (GATT), but which had regulated global trade since 1947. The GATT provided a negotiating context in which any country could extend tariff concessions agreed bilaterally to third countries. Yet by the 1990s it had become increasingly unsuited to the purpose for which it was designed (Hoekman and Kostecki 2009). As new entrants emerged within global trade patterns, the need to negotiate every third-country contract individually meant that the whole process had become almost entirely unwieldy (Mavroidis 2008).

Box 27.2 The Most Favoured Nation principle

The Most Favoured Nation (MFN) principle provided the bedrock of GATT negotiations, being formally laid down in GATT Article I. It stated that any preferential trading agreement reached with one country should be extended to other countries. The aim—which also continues to be the case under the WTO system—was to disqualify countries from using asymmetric tariffs in order to impose higher trading costs on one country than on another. The assumption underpinning the MFN principle is that a higher proportion of world GDP will be traded globally when trade takes place on a level playing field. The principle has been distorted, however, by the move towards regional trading blocs such as the European Union (EU), the North American Free Trade Agreement (NAFTA) and the Association of Southeast Asian Nations (ASEAN). Such arrangements allow countries to set lower tariffs for their in-bloc trading partners than for countries outside the bloc. This is why some globalization purists argue that regional trade agreements are an impediment to genuine economic globalization.

The WTO prides itself on being a member-based organization and, as of early 2010, it had 153 members. The majority of these members are developing countries, 32 of which have the United Nations-approved designation of Least Developed Country. The principal export goods for many developing countries are in agriculture and textiles, and these sectors are among the least comprehensively covered by the WTO's free trade agreements (McCalla and Nash 2008). This means that the incentives of membership for such countries lies less in the direct welfare gains resulting from enhanced export earnings than in other mechanisms.

Most developing countries have fragile public finances, and they depend for their continued financial viability on the capacity to tap the global financial system for flows of investment capital originating from overseas. In general, if they are to benefit from inward capital flows, such countries need to secure a positive assessment of their economic outlook in the regular country reports written by the **International Monetary Fund** (IMF). This in turn revolves around finding ways of assuring global investors that the rule of law is sufficiently established to prevent the state from appropriating overseas financial investments and to guarantee that the success of those investments will be determined solely by market mechanisms (Sinclair 2005). Membership of the WTO ensures not only that its specific free trade rules are internalized, but also that its broader market-based mindset permeates the general approach to issues of macroeconomic management. For many developing countries, then, joining the WTO is as much as anything a signalling device designed to offer assurances to global investors that any money committed to their country is likely to remain safe. Decisions about WTO membership for such countries are thereby shot through with global power relationships. The WTO is much more important to them than their membership is to the WTO.

The same is not true if we look instead at the situation of the countries of the **G7** in general and the USA and the European Union in particular. With their huge consumer markets and their ability to reposition small economies in effect as their trade captives, it would be possible for them—albeit almost certainly more time-consuming and more costly—to create exactly the same trading relationships in a series of bilateral agreements as membership of the WTO creates for them multilaterally. The export sectors of many developing countries are oriented almost solely to trade either with the USA or the EU, and if they refuse to abide by the demands of their larger trading partner, the retaliation for independently minded behaviour is likely to come at a considerable cost to their export earnings. The credibility of the USA and the EU within the global trading system arises from the power that follows their dominant position with respect to smaller trading partners, not from their membership of the WTO. The credibility of the WTO, by contrast, is wholly dependent on keeping the USA and the EU on board and engaged as active participants. This gives the USA and the EU significant hold over the policy output of the WTO.

The structure of decision-making at the WTO consequently reflects the fact that power is not distributed symmetrically among the institution's membership. The WTO is in appearance the most democratic of all the principal multilateral governance institutions, because it has legally enshrined formal provisions for a 'one member, one vote' decision-making structure (Footer 2006). In practice, however, these provisions are generally overridden by the requirement for members to agree to a package of reforms in its entirety for fear that the ongoing round of multilateral trade talks will collapse if they do not (Narlikar 2003). Votes are not taken on individual measures to build up incrementally a body of international trade law that is acceptable to a majority of WTO members. Instead, members must decide whether to accept as a whole—with no possibility of individual opt-out clauses—a package of reforms known as the **Single Undertaking**.

This package is largely agreed in advance of WTO Ministerial Meetings; the politics of the meetings themselves subsequently tend to focus on finding strategies of persuasion to secure the nominal consent for the Single Undertaking from reluctant members (Gallagher 2005). The process of pre-agreement is overwhelmingly one-way and a reflection of the prevailing global balance of power: the most developed countries have clearly defined access to the process, but the vast majority of developing countries do not. The USA and the EU hold the most prominent position in this respect, increasing the likelihood that their interests will be satisfied by the outcome of Ministerial Meetings. The politics of persuasion at those meetings is also overwhelmingly one-way: it is the most developed countries that seek the developing world's incorporation into their trade agendas, not the other way round. The USA and the EU take much larger diplomatic delegations to Ministerials than any other country in an attempt to increase the chances that other countries will sign up to the Single Undertaking. This merely multiplies the advantage they already possess in having by far the largest diplomatic missions in constant

---

Box 27.3 'The Quad' at the WTO

With over 150 members, perhaps the most important issue for the WTO is whether it embraces a decision-making structure that is effective but exclusionary or a decision-making structure that might prolong negotiations but allows each member a genuine say in their outcomes. Until now it has consistently resolved this tension by emphasizing efficiency in reaching final decisions over the democratic credentials of the decision-making process. One of the more striking images of the failed Ministerial Meeting at Seattle in 1999 was of trade delegates from developing countries standing alongside protestors outside the negotiating hall and lining up to brief the world's press about how they had been excluded from the decision-making process.

The actual decision-making process at Ministerials is typically open to at most twenty members: all the most powerful developed countries plus representatives of other groupings within the WTO. Bangladesh, for instance, often represents the whole of the 32-member Least Developing Countries grouping. Even here, these twenty members do not begin the trade negotiations from scratch. Rather, they are presented with a pre-agreed list of priorities negotiated before the Ministerial Meeting by members of the Quad. Historically, the Quad—otherwise known as the G4—consisted of the USA and the EU (the two global trade powerhouses), Japan (with its ability to bring Asian countries into agreements), and Canada (balancing EU with NAFTA interests but also representing Cairns Group concerns for agricultural liberalization). With subsequent changes in internal power structures within the WTO, however, there are now competing G4 groupings. A new Quad has emerged, comprising the USA and the EU (still the powerhouses), Brazil, and India (newly industrializing countries with huge potential consumer markets but positioned differently on the question of agricultural liberalization). Whichever G4 grouping prevails on any particular issue, most developing countries still have no access to agenda-setting power.

---

contact with the WTO at its permanent headquarters in Geneva (Koul 2005).

The impact of the global balance of power on outcomes is much more visible under the WTO system than it was under the preceding GATT system. Even though it was evident there too, the process of complex multiple bilateral negotiations of trade norms under GATT—as opposed to the Single Undertaking requirement to commit to tightly specified multilateral trade norms under the WTO—ensured that there was greater political space for developing countries to escape policies that they believed ran clearly counter to their interests. The existence of that political space was re-described by proponents of genuinely multilateral trade rules as nothing more than legal loopholes that were detrimental to the objective of global free trade. However, its subsequent eradication and the associated exposure of developing countries to other people's agenda-setting power has led to accusations from the WTO's critics of its inherent democratic deficit and to concerted opposition to its influence (Howse 2007).

The Ministerials at Seattle in 1999 and Cancún in 2003 were subjected to such high-profile protests from civil society groups that subsequent Ministerials have been scheduled for places much less accessible to such global gatherings (Jones 2004). The WTO is charged by its critics with running a wantonly asymmetrical trade system, vigorously pushing back the frontiers of free trade in areas like intellectual property rights, where developed countries benefit at developing countries' expense, but blocking free trade in areas like agriculture, where the roles would be reversed. Even if this is merely evidence of the operation of the global balance of power, it shows that the WTO is faced with a very real dilemma. While it could not survive as a credible multilateral institution without the active participation of the trading powerhouses of the USA and the EU, the practical implications of their actual participation as agenda-setters denies the WTO the status of a credibly democratic institution (Tabb 2004).

> ### Key Points
>
> - The decision to disband the GATT in favour of the law-making WTO system was an attempt to create more straightforward negotiations for global free trade.
>
> - Developing countries voluntarily sign up to become members of the WTO, but their choice to do so is often heavily influenced by the political pressures that are placed upon them to demonstrate their commitment to providing a business-friendly environment for global investors.
>
> - When they act in concert, the USA and the EU are almost always able to get their interests imprinted into WTO law, even if majority opinion among WTO members points in a different direction.

The current regulation of global finance

The regulation of global finance also suffers from civil society accusations of democratic deficit, even though this particular structure of regulation has none of the democratic pretensions associated with the WTO (Gill 2008). The contents of global financial regulation are decided largely within expert rather than political communities, and the objectives of global financial regulation are determined almost solely by the countries that finance the maintenance of the regulatory system. The two principal bodies in this respect are the International Monetary Fund and the **World Bank**, both of which date to the original **Bretton Woods** agreements of the 1940s. The formal task of the IMF is to provide short-term monetary assistance to countries struggling with financial instability, that of the World Bank to provide longer-term monetary assistance to countries seeking enhanced development prospects. Both institutions prefer to present themselves as providing purely technical help to countries in economic distress. Yet their willingness to embrace the use of **conditionalities** in return for loans immediately politicizes their activities. It produces a context in which national politicians have often had to ignore their electoral mandates and sacrifice their political legitimacy accordingly in order to satisfy the institutions' demands.

The IMF and the World Bank draw dissent from civil society activists not only because of their policy interventions in supposedly sovereign countries, but also because they are the most visible formal symbols of the institutionalized power of global finance (Porter 2005). A widespread perception exists today that this power has increased *considerably* since the 1970s (Duménil and Lévy 2004). Talk has turned increasingly to the way in which financial markets routinely discipline the political

> ### Box 27.4 Why are conditionalities politically controversial?
>
> IMF and World Bank conditionalities are so named because they ensure that countries qualify for financial assistance not on the grounds of the need within their impoverished communities, but only on condition that they follow the policy objectives laid down by the institutions. This provides IMF and World Bank officials with the power to determine policies in many developing countries, sometimes taking that power away from democratically elected governments. The Bretton Woods institutions have often been accused by their critics of selecting policy objectives drawn from within the ideological perspective of Western free market capitalism, thus destroying local economic customs and traditions and leading to the forced reconstitution of local economic lifestyles. In this way the critics allege that the institutions operate as covert agents of Western foreign economic policy, preparing developing countries for investment by Western firms.

aspirations of all political parties seeking election to government, especially those parties exhibiting specifically social democratic aspirations to defend the existing scope of welfare entitlements within society. It is almost certainly no coincidence that most social democratic parties have moved quite substantially to the right on questions of monetary policy in the intervening years, increasingly endorsing conservative monetary policies designed to hold inflation in check because this is what they believe financial markets want to hear (Notermans 2007).

The image being depicted in talk of disciplinary effects is that of a transferral of power, whereby individuals working within private financial institutions have usurped the power traditionally ascribed to governments under systems of representative democracy. The economic fate of populations is therefore not necessarily in their own hands, their choice of what policies to vote for being largely pre-empted by the ability of financial markets to override decisions to which they are opposed

Box 27.5 The Mitterrand U-turn in 1983

The single most influential instance in which financial markets appeared to override the mandate of a democratically elected G7 government occurred in the early 1980s in France. The elections in 1981 of François Mitterrand as President and Pierre Mauroy as Prime Minister, in close proximity, paved the way for a potentially decisive period of Socialist Party government. Initially, policy followed the platform on which Mitterrand was elected, choosing a course that was massively at odds with the neo-liberal programmes then being pursued in the USA under Reagan and in the UK under Thatcher. Mitterrand had promised to bring about economic recovery through large injections of government spending into the economy and to change the balance of power in the economy by nationalizing key industries. This became known as his 'Keynesianism in One Country' strategy, and Mauroy pursued it vigorously at first. However, the combination of policies produced new sources of inflation, and private financial institutions reacted by selling francs in large amounts in an attempt to destabilize the national currency and hence increase the likelihood that the government would reverse its policy course. After months of rearguard action to quell the pressure on the franc, Mitterrand bowed to the wishes of financial interests in 1983, abandoning his Keynesian strategy and adopting something much more like the neo-liberal alternative then in vogue in the USA and the UK. No G7 country has since attempted such a bold strategy in the face of the perceived power of financial markets. More than any other, the Mitterrand U-turn is the signal event that sealed in the popular imagination the intense power of global financial markets, forcing an elected government of one of the world's most advanced industrialized countries into a humiliating climb-down from its preferred policy course.

(Demmers *et al.* 2004). Private financial institutions—most prominently banks—have a vested interest in the defence of the existing price structure of financial assets, because their wealth and that of their shareholders is intimately linked to that price structure (Watson 2007). That defence typically involves the introduction of strict counter-inflationary policy in order to ensure that inflationary pressures are squeezed out of the economy as a whole. Currency traders have shown themselves to be only too willing to sell off the currencies of countries where they doubt the strength of the government's counter-inflationary commitment. These are attempts to ensure that the government moves quickly to give them a policy more to their liking.

The average daily turnover on world **currency markets** is now roughly US$2.1 trillion (Bank for International Settlements 2007). To write that out in long-hand requires the addition of eleven noughts after the '2' and the '1'. This *daily* volume compares with the *yearly* volume of all world trade of approximately US$11.8 trillion in 2006 before the onset of the sub-prime crisis. Flows of global finance consequently completely dwarf flows of global trade, with the dollar value of currency market turnover alone being approximately sixty-five times higher than the dollar value of all countries' export activities in aggregate. A large majority of the roughly US$2.1 trillion of daily turnover on world currency markets now represents currencies being bought and sold for purely speculative purposes (Kenen 1996). Such speculation represents two things. On the one hand, it is a bet placed on the power of private financial institutions to force the movement in relative currency prices that they most desire. On the other hand, it is a bet placed against governments' ability to maintain a truly autonomous policy course in the face of the disciplinary power of private financial institutions.

Speculative flows on world currency markets are such a big problem for governments because on a daily basis they are more than twice the size of the foreign currency reserves held in the central bank vaults of all IMF member states put together. This pretty much guarantees that coordinated speculative attacks will always be successful. The effects of such attacks can often be devastating, both economically and socially. During the **Asian financial crisis** of 1997/8, for instance, four of the five worst-hit countries—Thailand, South Korea, the Philippines, and Malaysia—saw the value of their currency fall 30 per cent in dollar terms (Stiglitz 2002). In other words, the people of those countries on average were able to buy only around two-thirds of the volume of goods at world prices after the crisis as had been possible before it. The fifth country, Indonesia, fared even worse. Its currency finally stabilized in 1998 at a dollar value 70 per cent below its level of twelve months previously. This meant that private financial institutions' speculation against the rupiah deprived the average Indonesian of almost three-quarters of his or her pre-crisis spending capacity (Grabel 2003). Altogether unsurprisingly in such circumstances, these five countries between them witnessed 80 million new cases of poverty between 1997 and 1998 (Thirkell-White 2005).

The IMF's response to the Asian financial crisis was much more decisive and much more in keeping with the reputation it has developed for itself as a free market ideologue than was its response to the sub-prime crisis that engulfed Western banks in 2007/8. In the latter case, it sat on the sidelines for pretty much the whole time as the crisis unfolded. It simply did not have the scale of resources at its disposal to help stabilize the beleaguered Western banks. Instead, it was left to offer verbal rather than monetary support to Western governments as they introduced interventionist programmes to keep their banks in business. This proved to be the first time since the IMF's ideological embrace of free market principles in the early 1980s that it had not come out strongly in favour of those principles when faced with examples of systematic government intervention to stabilize crisis-hit countries (Blustein 2001).

This has never been clearer than in the response to the Asian financial crisis, where stabilization assistance was made conditional upon the governments of the crisis-hit countries *not* using public debt to recapitalize their banks. The IMF's concern was that governments within the region were already too active in influencing the way that their countries' banks lent money; it wanted the banks to allocate available sources of capital more on the basis of matching supply to demand and less on the basis of political decree. The means it selected to achieve such an objective was to organize for ownership of East Asian banks to pass from Asian hands to US and EU hands (Robertson 2008). It thought that this would lead to an important demonstration effect about how to run a purely market-based financial system successfully, because the extra experience that high-level American and European managers had of working within such a system would quickly diffuse to their Asian counterparts. As a historical footnote, there is an obvious irony to explore here, given what has happened to American and European banks since.

This transfer of ownership served as a catalyst for the most noticeable change in the structure of global financial flows between the late 1990s and today. Despite the continued rise of East Asia in global trade and the emergence of China as a genuine trading powerhouse, global financial flows have not followed the same pattern. In relative terms at least, East Asia has been increasingly bypassed as global financial flows have been concentrated elsewhere within the world economy. Recent figures from the McKinsey Global Institute show that there are only three bilateral relationships in the world economy where the dollar value of annual financial investment flows amounts to more than 10 per cent of world GDP. These are the flows between the USA and the UK, the UK and Western Europe, and Western Europe and the USA (cited in Hirst, Thompson, and Bromley 2009). According to the McKinsey figures for 2007, 64 per cent of the world's US$196 trillion of financial assets was held within the USA, the UK, and Western Europe.

Global finance is therefore spatially concentrated in the North Atlantic economy. Indeed, the concentration is so marked—and intensifying—that the adjective 'global' is questionable as a description of the character of financial flows within the world economy. Perhaps more importantly for current purposes, though, the willingness of the IMF to allow governments to use public money to bail out banks following the North Atlantic financial crisis of 2007/8 but not following the Asian financial crisis of 1997/8 suggests that the heavy spatial concentration of supposedly global financial flows translates into similarly concentrated political effects.

Box 27.6 Contagious currency crises

The Asian financial crisis of 1997/8 continues to provide arguably the best example of what economists call 'contagious currency crises'. These are speculative attacks against currencies that appear to jump across borders as they affect one country and then another in very similar ways over a very short space of time. The Asian financial crisis began as the bursting of a real-estate bubble in Thailand exposed systematic over-investment throughout the economy in risky assets. Speculation then started against the Thai national currency, the baht, until its price was pushed down against the dollar as a reaction to the ultimate failure of the preceding construction boom. At that point speculation ensued against the currencies of near neighbouring and not-so-near neighbouring countries, even though those countries had no real economic connection to the Thai real-estate bubble. The famed financier George Soros (1998) likened the actions of global financial markets to those of a giant 'wrecking ball', as they moved from one Asian country to another leaving a trail of destruction in their wake.

It certainly raises the possibility that the predominance of the North Atlantic economy within global finance gives the USA, the UK, and Western Europe additional leverage in their dealings with the IMF. The same was shown to be true in the previous section with respect to the WTO, so here is one way in which the regulatory politics for global finance follow very similar contours to those for global trade.

Key Points

- The dollar value of total domestic financial assets is now considerably larger than the world economy's aggregate productive capacity, in 2007 amounting to almost four times the US$55 trillion figure for world GDP.

- The fact that speculation dominates the way in which assets are bought and sold on global financial markets places often quite exacting constraints on government autonomy over the conduct of economic policy.

- The regulatory structure over which the IMF presides operates asymmetrically, consistently favouring the interests of the most advanced industrialized countries.

A brief history of market self-regulation in trade and finance

The regulation of global trade, as has been demonstrated, takes place independently of the regulation of global finance. Yet today there are complementarities in the dominant regulatory form across the two spheres, because *in general*—see above for discussions of important exceptions—both the WTO and the IMF aspire to create systems of inter-state economic engagement that respond first and foremost to market-based signals. Market prices alone are typically used to guide economic behaviour towards particular outcomes. This is an obvious political experiment with **market self-regulation**, and there have been other similar experiments stretching back a long way into world economic history.

The first occurred in the seventeenth century. This was the era of the giant **stockholding companies**, the precursor of the modern **multinational corporation**. These were firms that raised capital to invest overseas, so that they could develop a trading infrastructure that would allow them to acquire products in the territories in which they operated for subsequent sale back home (Robins 2006). There were pretty much no legal restrictions on the activities of the giant stockholding companies, because they were typically established by royal charter. This provided them with the right to operate in distant territories at their sovereign's behest so as to appropriate wealth in the name of the nation. There were also precious few moral restrictions on the activities of

---

Box 27.7 The 'disembeddedness' of contemporary global finance

Just before the end of the Second World War, the left-wing émigré intellectual, Karl Polanyi, published a famous book of far-reaching implications on the economic causes of the European embrace of fascism in the 1930s. The book—*The Great Transformation* (Polanyi 1957 [1944])—was recognizable from the lectures he gave to the Workers' Educational Association in London as the crisis unfolded. In it, he drew an important distinction between two generic models of the market economy.

The first is when markets are 'embedded' within society. In such situations, price signals are rendered subsidiary to societal welfare. Whenever there is a trade-off between the two, policy outcomes obstruct the pure manifestation of the price mechanism and prioritize welfare-enhancing interventions instead. By contrast, 'disembedded' markets render society functional to the unimpeded operation of price signals, and any tension with societal welfare is resolved this time to preserve the purity of the price mechanism. Crucially, Polanyi suggested that society would always be minded to organize politically against the uninhibited encroachment of disembedded markets—whether to far-right ideologies as was the case in the 1930s, or to more progressive alternatives.

The original Bretton Woods agreements created a regulatory system for finance clearly consistent with Polanyian embeddedness. Elaborate structures of capital controls ensured that finance remained largely tied to the national economy, thereby serving the creation of national systems of social protection. By contrast, more modern forms of financial regulation assert globalization as their policy goal and champion the merits of disembeddedness accordingly: Polanyian disembeddedness equates to market self-regulation. As yet, a concerted societal backlash has not reversed this situation, certainly not in the direction of a more progressive political settlement, but far-right parties have recently made gains in many countries by offering avowedly nationalist alternatives to the perceived social dislocations of globalization.

Box 27.8 The East India Companies

Britain, the Netherlands, Denmark, Portugal, France, and Sweden all had their own East India Companies by the eighteenth century, allowing them to operate the trading route centred on modern-day India. As can be seen by this pattern of establishment, the giant stockholding company was a European—and pretty much a Europe-wide—phenomenon. It was a manifestation of the contemporaneous struggle amongst the European powers for territorial expansion, and as such these companies carried with them both the instinct and the physical infrastructure for colonizing faraway lands. The East India Companies sold shares within their respective 'mother countries' in order to fund both their voyages and the creation of colonial settlements through which the voyages could be turned into a commercial success. Finance flowed out of the mother country to provide the Companies with their operating capacities, but then flowed back in the opposite direction to subsequently provide the Companies' shareholders with a return on their investments. This was achieved by transporting goods from the colonies back to the mother countries where they could be sold at a profit to the new middle classes who were eager to transform their lifestyles through the consumption of exotic products. The East India Companies therefore instituted an integrated structure of global trade and global finance.

If a country was experiencing a deficit on its **balance of trade**—i.e. it was importing more for its citizens' consumption than it was exporting for other countries' citizens' consumption—gold would have to flow out of the country in order to finance the purchase of the additional exports (Gallarotti 1995). There was a strongly held belief among economists at the time that market logic alone was sufficient to ensure correct adjustment. Economic theory suggested that the outflow of gold would contract the domestic money supply and, from there, depress the general price level at home. This would reduce the level of imports coming into the domestic economy (because goods produced overseas would suddenly become less affordable compared with goods produced domestically), and at the same time increase the level of exports going out of the domestic economy (because goods produced domestically would suddenly become more affordable to overseas citizens compared with goods produced in their own countries). If the theory was correct, the global flows of finance as gold moved from one country to another should have perfectly counteracted the initial imbalance in global trade and restored balance to the world economy as a whole (Eichengreen 1996).

While the overall tendency in the regulation of global trade and global finance over the last four centuries has been towards market self-regulation of one form or another, this has by no means been a permanent feature of the world economy. Indeed, the most frequently discussed regulatory settlement within the International Relations literature—that of the Bretton Woods system of the immediate post-Second World War period—was constructed on the basis of introducing deliberate obstacles to the application of pure market logic (Helleiner 1994). The Bretton Woods system facilitated government intervention to direct flows of global trade and global finance, and the IMF and the World Bank were created under that system in order to defend the boundaries of feasible intervention. One of the ironies of the most recent reversion to a system of market self-regulation is that those same institutions now routinely discipline governments against intervention in order to promote and to sustain market logic (Harvey 2007).

The Bretton Woods Conference was held in 1944 in the New England town of that name. The Conference was attended by 44 soon-to-be victorious Allied countries from 1 to 22 July of that year. It was organized in an attempt to design a post-war governance structure for the Western world that would prevent the world

such companies, because they acted far away from any effective means of oversight, often operating as much as a year's sailing time from their country of origin. They consequently appropriated wealth in distant territories by force, setting up imperialistic governance structures and using private militias as a means of defending the efficacy of those structures. Land was seized and peoples were subjugated in order to guarantee the profitability of the companies' trading strategies (Keay 1993). Very simply, market norms were imposed by brute force.

The regulation of global trade and global finance also revolved around a system of market self-regulation in the late nineteenth and early twentieth centuries. Britain used its status as the dominant world economic power of the time to introduce a system through which market-based financial flows between two countries would correct any imbalance that developed in market-based trade flows between them. This was the **Gold Standard** system, which worked as an automatic adjustment mechanism designed to impose market logic onto the prevailing patterns of global trade and global finance (Cohen 1977).

Under the Gold Standard system, imports were paid for using gold, where each national currency was freely convertible into gold at a pre-determined and fixed rate.

economy from returning to the Great Depression that had so blighted lives and livelihoods in the preceding decade. The famous English economist, John Maynard Keynes, had argued throughout the 1930s that the Great Depression had been caused by the prevailing system of market self-regulation. He had dissented strongly from orthodox economic opinion and argued that the automatic adjustments of the Gold Standard were much more socially destructive than the entirely benign corrective mechanism depicted by economic theory (Keynes 2009 [1963]). He showed that it was output rather than prices that adjusted to global imbalances in trade, thus forcing national economies into a repetitive cycle of reduced production and job losses. The ensuing severe rises in unemployment preceded the political mobilization of many European populations to radical right-wing ideologies in the 1930s, and Keynes was determined that the structure of global trade should be stabilized in order to prevent history from repeating itself on this point.

His priority was to create a multilateral institution that would facilitate continual expansions in global trade. The proposed institution was to be called the International Trade Organization (ITO). However, concerted dissent domestically within US politics meant that President Truman did not even bother sending the final bill to Congress for ratification. It was deemed too interventionist for US politicians' tastes, for it would have introduced common conditions on things such as labour and environmental standards in order to create a genuine level playing field for the conduct of global trade (Deese 2007). An ITO without the USA, in the 1940s by far the world's largest exporter, was deemed unthinkable. The plans for its introduction were therefore hastily dropped, leading to the establishment instead of an ostensibly interim institution—the GATT—which eventually survived for 48 years before being superseded by the WTO. This was the earliest example of a single member being more important to a multilateral trade institution than the institution would have been for the member.

The failure of the ITO proposals meant that only two institutions were created at Bretton Woods: the IMF and the World Bank. Both institutions have embraced quite substantial elements of mission creep since their inception. As formally inscribed in the original Bretton Woods agreements, the priority of global economic governance at the end of the Second World War was to stimulate free market flows of traded goods rather than to stimulate free market flows of finance. Successful long-term development was assumed to be the outcome of stable trading conditions, and in an attempt to enhance such stability obstacles in the form of **capital controls** were placed upon the movement of finance between one country and another (Crotty and Epstein 1996). Market self-regulation of finance was formally disqualified in this period. The IMF was responsible for policing such a system, ensuring that capital controls remained robust and that private financial institutions were unable to circumvent them (Goodman and Pauly 1993). In effect, the IMF was initially designed as a subsidiary regulator of global trade—or, at the very least, as the regulator of heavily restrictive global financial conditions in which trade could flourish.

In the immediate post-Second World War period, then, strict limits were placed on the globalization of finance. The US Treasury Secretary of the time, Henry Morgenthau, celebrated the political curtailment of the economic liberties of private financial institutions by declaring that the goal of Bretton Woods had been to 'drive the usurious moneylenders from the temple of international finance' (cited in Gardner 1980: 76). This had echoed in discursive form Keynes's account of his desire to oversee 'the euthanasia of the rentier' (Keynes 1997 [1936]: 376). Yet the political settlement that cast finance in the role of servant to the rest of the world economy was to prove only short-lived. In a series of steps between 1971 and 1973 the Nixon administration first backed the USA away from its currency responsibilities within the Bretton Woods system and then formally reneged on them altogether (Strange 1994). The system relied on US dollars being available freely within the world economy at a fixed rate relative to the price of gold, which had the effect of fixing all exchange rates with respect to one another. Once the Nixon administration had allowed the value of the dollar to be set by global financial market activity rather than by government commitment to currency pegs, all currencies eventually floated against one another. As soon as this happened, incentives arose for the advanced industrialized countries to dismantle their capital controls in an attempt to attract flows of global finance. This they duly did, and the shackles that Bretton Woods had placed on global finance were released. The origins of today's experience of an increasingly politically powerful financial sector can be dated to this time (Posen 1993).

Key Points

- The regulation of both global trade and global finance is oriented today towards a system of market self-regulation, but as the Case Study shows, this increases the vulnerability of one sphere to shocks arising from the other.

- Under the Bretton Woods system of the immediate post-Second World War era, finance was stripped of its global

activities and generally boxed in by political decree so that it would serve the interests of stable global trade relations.

- The evolution of the regulatory system typically follows really quite closely the perceived needs of the world's most powerful economies at any particular moment of time.

Case Study The sub-prime crisis

The sub-prime crisis brought significant numbers of Western banks to the point of going out of business in 2007 and 2008 (Cohan 2009). Only public bailouts of unprecedented magnitude prevented individual crisis-hit banks from spreading their own financial woes contagiously around the whole sector and leading to mass defaults on accumulated banking debts. In many ways the sub-prime crisis was a crisis of market self-regulation. It arose because of the extent to which Western banks had misread available price signals and poured seemingly endless sums of money into making cheap mortgage credit available (Schwartz 2009). House prices rose steeply in most Western countries from the end of the 1990s, temporarily masking the difficulties that the banks were bringing upon themselves. Yet when the housing market boom first began to unravel globally in 2007, the banks discovered the full extent of their over-exposure to the so-called 'toxic assets' of mortgage-backed securities. A structure of adequate public authority over banks' activities simply did not exist to stop them from getting themselves into such deep trouble (Shiller 2008).

The sub-prime crisis has triggered a number of different cycles of political recrimination and response. Governments have tended to blame banks for creating the credit bubble that was the proximate cause of the crisis, but they have none the less still bailed them out using enormous sums of taxpayer money. Banks have tended to blame their customers in mortgage lending markets for borrowing irresponsibly at the rates made available to them, and they have significantly tightened repayment schedules

as a consequence. Voters have tended to blame their governments for having allowed banks to operate for so long in such a lightly regulated environment, although the early post-crisis patterns of anti-incumbency voting have typically rewarded parties who also favoured bank deregulation in the pre-crisis period.

Each of these three groups in their own way contributed to the manner in which the problems developed, yet this does not make them all equally culpable for the eventual mess into which the world economy descended. It is true that many people in many countries significantly over-leveraged themselves in trading up on the property ladder as house prices rose steeply in the period immediately preceding the crash. However, if the banks had not made extremely cheap credit available to them in the mortgage lending market, the option of over-leveraging would not have been available to them in the first place. Banks took to lending in this way because they were making lots of money in secondary mortgage markets from selling mortgage credit as quickly and with as little fuss as possible. Whistleblower reports subsequently emerging from within the banking sector suggest that due diligence tests on customer creditworthiness were largely suspended as the credit bubble hit its peak (Muolo and Padilla 2008). In the USA, for example, 'liar loans' temporarily became a particularly profitable niche product for many banks, so called because they required customers merely to state a level of household income to qualify for a loan rather than to demonstrate that actual earnings matched stated earnings.

This raises the question of why governments did not do more to prevent the development of the credit bubble by imposing more exacting regulations on banking activity. The dominant policy trajectory worldwide for the past four decades, of course, has been the opposite one of financial liberalization, and the liberalizing trend has had strong support from the International Monetary Fund, the World Bank, and strategically significant countries of the G7. Restrictive banking legislation therefore has not fitted with the temper of the times since the collapse of the Bretton Woods settlement in the early 1970s, especially as the banking sector has come to increased prominence in most countries in terms of its ever-greater contribution to national GDP. The liberalizing trend aside, though, there seems to be one factor specific to the recent credit bubble that appears to explain governments' reluctance to intervene against it. The credit bubble fed increases in house prices, the buoyant housing market fed enhanced feelings of wealth among the population, and these feelings in turn fed heightened consumer confidence. The resulting consumer boom created the growth dynamics that all governments treat as essential to their re-election prospects.

Conclusion

Following the downturn in the world economy in the 1970s, the move towards market self-regulation has been the most noteworthy trend in the spheres of both global trade and global finance. Economic globalization and economic theory have combined in this respect to reinforce the trend. Public discourse on the benefits of economic globalization has tended to emphasize the advantages of market arrangements; economic theory has always voiced strong support for such arrangements.

However, the complementarity of regulatory forms is not necessarily synonymous with an internally coherent regulatory system. Regulatory coherence arises only when there are overarching economic regime features that necessitate the imposition of regulatory constraints on one sphere in order to facilitate regulatory effectiveness in the other. The distinctly illiberal treatment of finance under the original Bretton Woods agreements was instrumental in maintaining the equally distinctly liberal treatment of trade. The two spheres now operate without the sort of checks and balances that symbolize a system of regulatory coherence. As a consequence, the feedback mechanisms between the two have been much enhanced, with instability in one often rebounding in different forms as instability in the other.

There has been a lot of talk following the sub-prime crisis of 2007/8 of the inadequate regulatory coordination between trade and finance under conditions of economic globalization. In particular, concern has been raised about the way in which this does not allow problems in either sphere to remain self-contained. The Director General of the WTO, Pascal Lamy, has been especially vocal in this respect, perhaps because the sub-prime crisis was a crisis originating in finance but impacting on trade. Spill-over effects from the instability caused by Western banks in 2007 and 2008 subsequently led to the largest post-Second World War year-on-year reduction in world trade in 2009: by recent historical standards the drop was a barely believable 9 per cent (World Trade Organization 2009). Despite this, the general context of market self-regulation continues to be defended by each of the multilateral governance institutions, because they claim that this is how best to promote dynamic economic conditions domestically. As a consequence, the immediate post-sub-prime crisis context looks to be one in which the dominant regulatory model trades off the hope that market self-regulation enhances domestic economic dynamism against the reality that it comes complete with an increased likelihood of crisis events.

Questions

1. What implications has the failure of the International Trade Organization had for subsequent attempts to tie trade globalization to the introduction of progressive social conditions of production?

2. Does the WTO promote genuine trade globalization or an asymmetric trade globalization favouring developed countries?

3. Assess the significance of civil society activism against the WTO at its Seattle Ministerial Meeting in 1999 for the way in which the institution now conducts its business. Did the protests make a difference?

4. To what degree is capital accumulation within financial markets now completely detached from the rest of the world economy?

5. Explain the way in which the IMF appears to have become all-powerful in its relationship with developing countries.

6. What are the mechanisms through which financial liberalization translates into enhanced disciplinary power for financial interests over government policy?

7   Do multinational corporations abuse their power when locating in developing countries today in a manner analogous to the abuses enacted by seventeenth-century stockholding companies?

8   Is there a link between the ultimate failure of the Gold Standard system in the 1920s and the Great Depression of the 1930s?

9   In so far as finance was the servant of world trade under the original Bretton Woods agreements, is it now unequivocally the master?

10 What was the role of Western banks in creating the mortgage lending conditions from which the sub-prime crisis originated?

11 Should the sub-prime crisis be viewed as the major export of the USA to the world economy of the past ten years?

12 Is a 'new Bretton Woods' necessary if regulatory coherence is once again to be introduced between the spheres of global trade and global finance?

Further Reading

Glyn, A. (2006), *Capitalism Unleashed: Finance, Globalization, and Welfare* (Oxford: Oxford University Press). A radical perspective on what has happened to societal welfare goals under the influence of financial market self-regulation.

Helleiner, E. (1994), *States and the Reemergence of Global Finance: From Bretton Woods to the 1980s* (Ithaca, NY: Cornell University Press). The best political history of the process through which governments negotiated away the capital controls of the original Bretton Woods agreements.

Narlikar, A. (2005), *The World Trade Organization: A Very Short Introduction* (Oxford: Oxford University Press). A comprehensive account of the politics of the WTO, but written specifically for the student audience.

Polanyi, K. (1957 [1944]), *The Great Transformation: The Social and Political Origins of Our Time* (Boston, MA: Beacon Press). The classic account of progressive societal struggle against disembedded financial markets and of the right-wing populism which can emerge when that struggle fails.

Scholte, J. A. (2005), *Globalization: A Critical Introduction*, 2nd edn (Basingstoke: Palgrave Macmillan). Provides students with a perspective on trade and financial globalization that consciously seeks to politicize those trends and pinpoint the potential for successful resistance.

Trebilcock, M., and Howse, R. (2005), *The Regulation of International Trade*, 3rd edn (London: Routledge). In-depth yet readable treatment of the historical evolution of the regulatory system for global trade.

Watson, M. (2005), *The Political Economy of International Capital Mobility* (Basingstoke: Palgrave Macmillan). An attempt to theorize the economics of financial market self-regulation, but from a perspective that is written to be understandable for non-economists.

Online Resource Centre

 Visit the Online Resource Centre that accompanies this book to access more learning resources on this chapter topic at www.oxfordtextbooks.co.uk/orc/baylis5e/

Chapter 28

Poverty, development, and hunger

CAROLINE THOMAS · TONY EVANS

Reader's Guide

This chapter explores and illustrates the contested nature of a number of important concepts in International Relations. It examines the orthodox mainstream understanding of poverty, development, and hunger, and contrasts this with a critical alternative approach. Consideration is given to how successful the development orthodoxy has been in incorporating and thereby neutralizing the concerns of the critical alternative. The chapter then closes with an assessment of the likelihood of globalization with a human face in the twenty-first century.

Introduction

Since 1945 we have witnessed over sixty years of unprecedented official development policies and impressive global economic growth. Yet global polarization continues to increase, with the economic gap between the richest and poorest states and people growing. While the richest 20 states increased their GDP per capita by nearly 300 per cent between the early 1960s and 2002, the poorest 20 achieved an increase of 20 per cent (World Bank Development Indicators 2009). Box 28.1 shows that as a discipline International Relations has been slow to engage with these issues of development and poverty.

Poverty, hunger, and disease remain widespread, and women and girls continue to comprise the majority of the world's poorest people. Moreover, this general situation is not confined to that part of the world that we have traditionally termed the 'South' or the **Third World**. Particularly since the 1980s and 1990s, the worldwide promotion of neo-liberal economic policies (the so-called **Washington Consensus**) by global governance institutions has been accompanied by increasing inequalities within and between states. During this period, the Second World countries of the former Eastern bloc have been incorporated into the Third World grouping of states, and millions of people previously cushioned by the state have been thrown into poverty with the transition to market economies. In the developed world, rising social inequalities characterized the social landscape of the 1980s and 1990s. Within the **Third World** countries, the adverse impact of **globalization** has been felt acutely (see Ch. 1), as countries have been forced to adopt free market policies as a condition of debt rescheduling and in the hope of attracting new investment to spur development. Gendered outcomes of these neoliberal economic policies have been noted, although the global picture is very mixed, with other factors such as class, race, and ethnicity contributing to local outcomes (Buvinic 1997: 39).

The enormity of the current challenges was recognized by the UN in 2000 with the acceptance of the **Millennium Development Goals** (www.undp.org). These set time-limited, quantifiable targets across eight areas, ranging from poverty to health, gender (see Ch. 16), education, environment, and development. The first goal was the eradication of extreme poverty and hunger, with the target of halving the proportion of people living on less than a dollar a day by 2015. Figure 28.1 shows continuing incidence of poverty at different income levels.

The attempts of the majority of governments, **intergovernmental organizations** (INGOs), and **nongovernmental organizations** (NGOs) since 1945 to address global hunger and poverty can be categorized into two very broad types, depending on the explanations they provide for the existence of these problems and the respective solutions that they prescribe. These can be identified as the dominant mainstream or orthodox approach, which provides and values a particular body of developmental knowledge, and a **critical** alternative approach, which incorporates other more marginalized understandings of the development challenge and process (see Table 28.1). Most of this chapter will be devoted

---

Box 28.1 International Relations theory and the marginalization of priority issues for the Third World

- Traditionally, the discipline focused on issues relating to inter-state conflict, and regarded human security and development as separate areas.

- Mainstream realist and liberal scholars neglected the challenges presented to human well-being by the existence of global underdevelopment.

- Dependency theorists were interested in persistent and deepening inequality and relations between North and South, but they received little attention in the discipline.

- During the 1990s, debate flourished, and several subfields developed or emerged that touched on matters of poverty, development, and hunger, albeit tangentially (e.g. global environmental politics, gender, international political economy).

- More significant in the 1990s, in raising within the discipline the concerns of the majority of humanity and states, were the contributions from post-colonial theorists, Marxist theorists (Hardt and Negri), scholars adopting a **human security** approach (Nef, Thomas), and the few concerned directly with development (Saurin, Weber).

- Interest in poverty, development, and hunger has increased with the advent of globalization.

- Most recently, social unrest in many parts of the world and the fear of terrorism have acted as a spur for greater diplomatic activity.

(Thomas and Wilkin 2004)

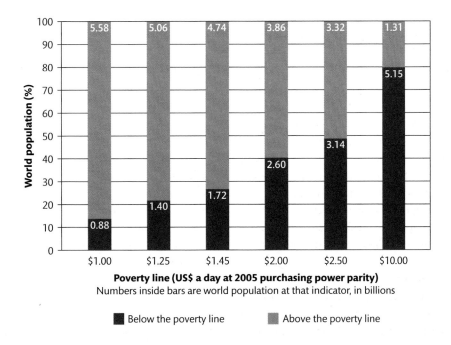

Figure 28.1 Poverty at different levels of income
Source: Progress on the Millennium Development Goals, Global Monitoring Report 2008: Goal 1 Reducing Poverty and Hunger (www.worldbank.org)

Table 28.1 Mainstream and alternative conceptions of poverty, development, and hunger

	Poverty	Development	Hunger
Mainstream approach	Unfulfilled material needs	Linear path, traditional to modern	Not enough food to go around
Critical alternative approach	Unfulfilled material and non-material needs	Diverse paths, locally driven	Enough food; the problem is distribution and entitlement

to an examination of the differences between these two approaches in relationship to the three related topics of poverty, development, and hunger, with particular emphasis on development. The chapter concludes with an assessment of whether the desperate conditions in which so many of the world's citizens find themselves today are likely to improve. Again, two contrasting approaches are outlined.

Poverty

Different conceptions of poverty underpin the mainstream and alternative views of development. There is basic agreement on the material aspects of poverty, such as lack of food, clean water, and sanitation, but disagreement on the importance of non-material aspects. Also, key differences emerge in regard to how material needs should be met, and hence about the goal of development.

Most governments, international organizations, citizens in the West, and many elsewhere adhere to the orthodox conception of poverty. This refers to a situation where people do not have the money to buy adequate food or satisfy other basic needs, and are often classified as un- or underemployed. This mainstream understanding of poverty based on money has arisen as a result of the globalization of Western culture and the attendant expansion of the market. Thus a community that provides for itself outside monetized cash transactions and wage labour, such as a hunter-gatherer group, is regarded as poor.

Since 1945, this meaning of poverty has been almost universalized. Poverty is seen as an economic condition dependent on cash transactions in the marketplace for its eradication. These transactions in turn are dependent on development defined as economic growth. An economic yardstick is used to measure and to judge all societies.

Poverty has been widely regarded as characterizing the Third World, and it has a gendered face. An approach has developed whereby it is seen as incumbent upon the developed countries to 'help' the Third World eradicate 'poverty', and increasingly to address female poverty (see World Bank, Gender Action Plan, www.worldbank.org/). The solution advocated to overcome global poverty is the further **integration** of the global economy (Thomas 2000) and of women into this process (Pearson 2000; Weber 2002). Increasingly, however, as globalization has intensified, poverty defined in such economic terms has come to characterize significant sectors of population in advanced developed countries such as the USA (see Bello 1994).

Critical, alternative views of poverty exist in other cultures where the emphasis is not simply on money, but on spiritual values, community ties, and availability of common resources. In traditional subsistence economies, a common strategy for survival is provision for oneself and one's family via community-regulated access to common water, land, and fodder. Western values that focus on individualism and consumerism are seen as destructive of nature and morally inferior. For many people in the developing world the ability to provide for oneself and one's family, including the autonomy characteristic of traditional ways of life, is highly valued. Dependence on an unpredictable market and/or an unreliable government does not, therefore, offer an attractive alternative.

Some global **institutions** have been important in promoting a conception of poverty that extends beyond material indicators. The work of the United Nations Development Programme (UNDP) since the early 1990s is significant here for distinguishing between income poverty (a material condition) and human poverty (encompassing human dignity, agency, opportunity, and choices).

The issue of poverty and the challenge of poverty alleviation moved up the global political agenda at the

close of the twentieth century, as evidenced in the UN's first Millennium Development Goal, cited earlier. Although some progress was reported in the early years of the millennium, the 2008 'credit crunch' threatens to reverse what was achieved. As UN Secretary General Ban Ki-Moon notes in the 2009 Millennium Development Goals Report, 'we face a global economic crisis whose full repercussions have yet to be felt' (www.un.org/millenniumgoals/). Whereas in 2005 it was estimated that 1.4 million people lived on less that $1.25 a day, the report estimates that in 2009 this number will increase by as much as 90 million.

Having considered the orthodox and critical alternative views of poverty, we now turn to an examination of the important topic of development. This examination will be conducted in three main parts. The first part will start by examining the orthodox view of development and will then proceed to an assessment of its effect on post-war development in the Third World. The second part will examine the critical alternative view of development and its application to subjects such as empowerment and democracy. In the third part, consideration will be given to the ways in which the orthodox approach to development has responded to some of the criticisms made of it by the critical alternative approach.

Key Points

- The monetary-based conception of poverty has been almost universalized among governments and international organizations since 1945.

- Poverty is interpreted as a condition suffered by people—the majority of whom are female—who do not earn enough money to satisfy their basic material requirements in the marketplace.

- Developed countries have regarded poverty as being something external to them and a defining feature of the Third World. This view has provided justification for the former to help 'develop' the latter by promoting further integration into the global market.

- However, such poverty is increasingly endured by significant sectors of the population in the North, as well as the Third World, hence rendering traditional categories less useful.

- A critical alternative view of poverty places more emphasis on lack of access to community-regulated common resources, community ties, and spiritual values.

- Poverty moved up the global political agenda at the start of the twenty-first century, but the 2008/9 'credit crunch' promises to reverse some of the early success.

Development

When we consider the topic of development, it is important to realize that all conceptions of development necessarily reflect a particular set of social and political values. Indeed, we can say that 'Development can be conceived only within an ideological framework' (Roberts 1984: 7).

Since the Second World War the dominant view, favoured by the majority of governments and multilateral agencies, has seen development as synonymous with economic growth within the context of a free market international economy. Economic growth is identified as necessary for combating poverty, defined as the inability of people to meet their basic material needs through cash transactions. This is seen in the influential reports of the World Bank, where countries are categorized according to their income. Those countries that have the lower national incomes per head of population are regarded as being less developed than those with higher incomes, and they are perceived as being in need of increased integration into the global marketplace.

An alternative view of development has, however, emerged from a few governments, UN agencies, grass-roots movements, NGOs, and some academics. Their concerns have centred broadly on entitlement and distribution, often expressed in the language of **human rights** (see Ch. 30). Poverty is identified as the inability to provide for one's own and one's family's material needs by subsistence or cash transactions, and by the absence of an environment conducive to human well-being broadly conceived in spiritual and community terms. These voices of opposition are growing significantly louder, as ideas polarize following the apparent universal triumph of economic **liberalism**. The language of opposition is changing to incorporate matters of **democracy** such as political empowerment, participation, meaningful **self-determination** for the majority, protection of the commons, and an emphasis on pro-poor growth. The fundamental differences between the orthodox and the alternative views of development are summarized in Box 28.2, and supplemented by Case Study 1, illustrating alternative ideas for development that take account of social and cultural values. In the following two sections we shall examine how the orthodox view of development has been applied at a global level and assess what measure of success it has achieved.

Box 28.2 Development: a contested concept

The orthodox view

- **Poverty:** a situation suffered by people who do not have the *money to buy food* and satisfy other basic *material needs*.

- **Solution:** transformation of traditional subsistence economies defined as 'backward' into industrial, commodified economies defined as 'modern'. Production for profit. Individuals sell their labour for money, rather than producing to meet their family's needs.

- **Core ideas and assumptions:** the possibility of unlimited economic growth in a free market system. Economies eventually become self-sustaining ('take-off' point). Wealth is said to trickle down to those at the bottom. All layers of society benefit through a 'trickle-down' mechanism when the superior 'Western' model is adopted.

- **Measurement:** economic growth; Gross Domestic Product (GDP) per capita: industrialization, including agriculture.

- **Process:** top-down; reliance on external 'expert knowledge', usually Western. Large capital investments in large projects; advanced technology; expansion of the private sphere.

The alternative view

- **Poverty:** a situation suffered by people who are not able to meet their *material and non-material needs* through their own effort.

- **Solution:** creation of human well-being through sustainable societies in social, cultural, political, and economic terms.

- **Core ideas and assumptions:** sufficiency. The inherent value of nature, cultural diversity, and the community-controlled commons (water, land, air, forest). Human activity in balance with nature. Self-reliance and local control through democratic inclusion, participation, and giving a voice to marginalized groups, such as women, indigenous groups.

- **Measurement:** fulfilment of basic material and non-material human needs of everyone; condition of the natural environment. Political empowerment of marginalized.

- **Process:** bottom-up; participatory; reliance on appropriate (often local) knowledge and technology; small investments in small-scale projects; protection of the commons.

Case Study 1   Taking jobs to Bangladesh's poor

The case of Hathay Bunano Proshikhan Society (HBPS) offers a good example of an alternative development model. For most Bangladeshi women living in rural districts, the opportunity to give their families a bit of extra money in the struggle against rural poverty means moving to large cities, like Dhaka or Chittagong, leaving their children and families for many months. The move from country to city strains traditional social relations and places women in an urban environment that is unfamiliar and threatening. Bangladesh's textile industry is its biggest export earner ($12.35 billion between June 2008 and 2009) and offers the best opportunity for rural women to find work. The industry is estimated to employ over 2.5 million workers in 4,200 factories. However, the poor working conditions and long hours often lead to ill health, social dislocation, and a life of misery.

In 2004 the founders of HBPS asked themselves this questions: how do you create sustainable employment free of debt without changes in the lifestyle of rural women, and while generating returns comparable with the enterprises modelled on mainstream economic limes? The answer was to create flexible employment opportunities for women in rural Bangladesh through a social business model producing knitted and crocheted children's clothes and toys.

Although working conditions are simple, often in premises rented from a villager without electricity or water, the working day provides a place where work is done in a social setting alongside friends and neighbours. Women often bring very young children to the workplace to be cared for during the day. Newly recruited workers are given training in core skills as well as basic mathematics and life skills. In this way women workers can contribute to the family economy without breaking family and village ties.

The founders of HBPS began with an investment of $500 and 12 trainees in December 2004. Today, it employs over 3,500 women at 32 sites in rural locations producing about 30,000 items a month that are exported to developed countries and fashionable shops in the USA, Europe and Australia. All profits are put back into the company and the women can earn 25 per cent more than the Bangladeshi minimum legal rate. Bringing work to the village also means that earnings are spent within the village economy rather than in distant cities, bringing benefits to the wider village community.

(www.hathaybunano.com)

Economic liberalism and the post-1945 international economic order: sixty-five years of orthodox development

During the Second World War there was a strong belief among the Allied Powers that the protectionist trade policies of the 1930s had contributed significantly to the outbreak of the war. Plans were drawn up by the USA and the UK for the creation of a stable post-war international order with the United Nations (UN), its affiliates the **International Monetary Fund** (IMF) and the **World Bank Group**, plus the **General Agreement on Tariffs and Trade** (GATT), providing the institutional bases. The latter three provided the foundations of a liberal international economic order based on the pursuit of free trade, but allowing an appropriate role for state intervention in the market in support of national security and national and global stability (Rapley 1996). This has been called embedded liberalism. The decision-making procedures of these international economic institutions favoured a small group of developed Western states. Their relationship with the UN, which in the General Assembly has more democratic procedures, has not always been an easy one.

In the immediate post-war years, attention focused on reconstructing Western Europe through the Marshall plan. As the **cold war** emerged, and both East and West sought to gain allies in the less developed and recently decolonized states, both sides offered economic support for development. The USA believed that the path of liberal economic growth would result in development, and that development would result in hostility to socialist ideals. The USSR, by contrast, attempted to sell its economic system as the most rapid means for the newly independent states to achieve industrialization and development. The process of industrialization underpinned conceptions of development in both East and West, but whereas in the capitalist sphere the market was seen as the engine of growth, in the socialist sphere central planning by the state was the preferred method.

In the early post-war and post-colonial decades, all states—whether in the West, East, or Third World—favoured an important role for the state in development.

Many Third World countries pursued a strategy of import substitution industrialization in order to try to break out of their dependent position in the world economy as peripheral producers of primary commodities for the core developed countries.

This approach, which recognized the important role of the state in development, suffered a major setback in the early 1980s. The developing countries had borrowed heavily in the 1970s in response to the rise in oil prices. The rich countries' strategy for dealing with the second oil price hike in 1979 resulted in massive rises in interest rates and steep falls in commodity prices in the early 1980s. The developing countries were unable to repay spiralling debts. Mexico threatened to default in 1982. The Group of Seven (G7) leading developed Western countries decided to deal with the debt problem on a country-by-country basis, with the goal of avoiding the collapse of the international banking system by ensuring continued repayment of debt. In this regard, the IMF and the World Bank pursued a vigorous policy of **structural adjustment lending** throughout the developing world. In applying this policy, the Fund and the Bank worked together in an unprecedented fashion to encourage developing countries to pursue market-oriented strategies based on rolling back the power of the state and opening Third World economies to foreign investment. Exports were promoted so that these countries would earn the foreign exchange necessary to keep up with their debt repayments.

With the end of the cold war and the collapse of the Eastern bloc after 1989, this neo-liberal economic and political philosophy came to dominate development thinking across the globe. The championing of unadulterated liberal economic values played an important role in accelerating the globalization process. This represented an important ideological shift. The 'embedded liberalism' of the early post-war decades gave way to the unadulterated neoclassical economic policies that favoured a minimalist state and an enhanced role for the market: the so-called **Washington Consensus**. The belief was that global welfare would be maximized by the **liberalization** of trade, finance, and investment, and by the restructuring of national economies to provide an enabling environment for capital. Such policies would also ensure the repayment of debt. The former Eastern bloc countries were now seen as in transition from centrally planned to market economies. Throughout the Third World the state was rolled back and the market given the role of major engine of growth and associated development, an approach that informed the strategies

of the IMF, the World Bank, and, through the Uruguay Round of trade discussions carried out under the auspices of GATT, the **World Trade Organization** (WTO).

By the end of the 1990s the G7 (later the **G8**) and associated international financial institutions were championing a slightly modified version of the neo-liberal economic orthodoxy, labelled the post-Washington Consensus, which stressed pro-poor growth and poverty reduction based on continued domestic policy reform and growth through trade liberalization. Henceforth, locally owned national poverty reduction strategy (PRS) papers would be the focus for funding (Cammack 2002). These papers quickly became the litmus test for funding from an increasingly integrated line-up of global financial institutions and donors.

The development achievement of the post-war international economic order: orthodox and alternative evaluations

There have been some gains for developing countries during the post-war period, as measured by the orthodox criteria for economic growth, GDP per capita, and industrialization. However, these gains have not been uniformly spread across all developing countries (Figures 28.2 and 28.3). While some Asian countries have recorded positive gains, China and India for example, African countries have fared less well (UNDP 2003). The financial crisis in the early 1980s showed marked reversals in Mexico, the East Asian states, Brazil, and Russia. While it is too early to assess the full effects of the more recent global 'credit crunch', the 2009 Millennium Development Goals Report indicates further declines (see Figure 28.4).

The orthodox liberal assessment of the past sixty years of development suggests that states that have integrated most deeply into the global economy through trade liberalization have grown the fastest, and it praises these 'new globalizers'. It acknowledges that neo-liberal economic policy has resulted in greater inequalities within and between states, but regards inequality positively as a spur to competition and the entrepreneurial spirit.

It was clear at least from the late 1970s that 'trickle-down' (the idea that overall economic growth as measured by increases in the GDP would automatically bring benefits for the poorer classes) had not worked. Despite impressive rates of growth in GDP per capita enjoyed by developing countries, this success was not reflected in their societies at large, and while a minority became

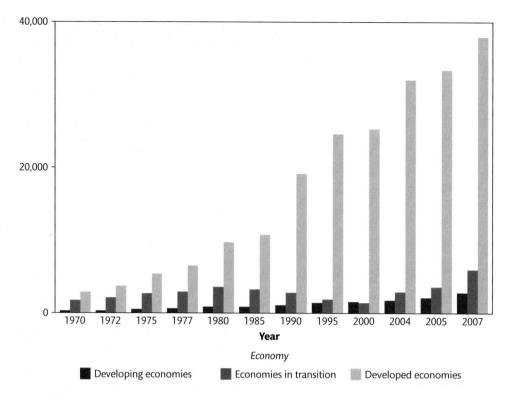

Figure 28.2 GDP for developing, transitional, and developed countries
Source: UNCTAD, *Handbook of Statistics* 2008

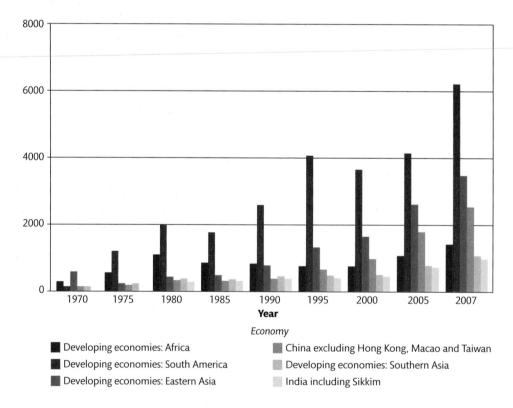

Figure 28.3 Per capita GDP for selected states and economies
Source: UNCTAD, *Handbook of Statistics* 2008

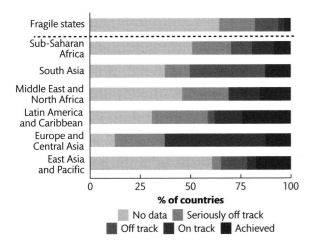

Figure 28.4 Poverty reduction: progress on the Millennium Development Goals
Source: World Bank, *Global Monitoring Report* 2009

substantially wealthier, the mass of the population saw no significant change. The even greater polarization in wealth evident in recent decades is not regarded as a problem, so long as the social and political discontent that inequality engenders is not so extensive as potentially to de-rail implementation of the liberalization project itself. According to the orthodox view, discontent will be alleviated by the development of national PRSs, which it is claimed put countries and their peoples in the driving seat of development policy, thus empowering the local community and ensuring a better distribution of benefits. Figure 28.4 shows that the much-vaunted Millennium Development Goals have so far failed to impact on the lives of those living in the poor countries.

Advocates of a critical alternative approach emphasize the pattern of distribution of gains within global society and within individual states, rather than growth. They believe that the economic liberalism that underpins the process of globalization has resulted, and continues to result, in increasing economic differentiation between and within countries, and that this is problematic. Moreover, they note that this trend has been evident over the very period when key global actors have been committed to promoting development worldwide, and indeed when there were fairly continuous world economic growth rates and positive rates of GDP growth per capita, at least until 1990 (Brown and Kane 1995).

At the beginning of the twenty-first century, exponents of a critical alternative—in contrast to their orthodox colleagues—question the value of national PRSs,

arguing that while a new focus on issues such as health and education is important, the more fundamental issue of discussion of possible links between Washington Consensus policies and poverty creation is ignored. As Glyn Roberts notes, 'GNP growth statistics might mean a good deal to an economist or to a maharajah, but they do not tell us a thing about the quality of life in a Third World fishing village' (Roberts 1984: 6).

A critical alternative view of development

Since the early 1970s, there have been numerous efforts to stimulate debate about development and to highlight its contested nature. Critical alternative ideas have been put forward that we can synthesize into an alternative approach. These have originated with various NGOs, grass-roots development organizations, individuals, UN organizations, and private foundations. Disparate **social movements** not directly related to the development agenda have contributed to the flourishing of the alternative viewpoints: for example, the women's movement, the peace movement, movements for democracy, and green movements (Thomas 2000). Noteworthy was the publication in 1975 by the Dag Hammarskjöld Foundation of *What Now: Another Development*. This alternative conception of development (see Ekins 1992: 99) argued that the process of development should be (1) need-oriented (material and non-material), (2) endogenous (coming from within a society), (3) self-reliant (in terms of human, natural, and cultural resources), (4) ecologically sound, and (5) based on structural transformations (of economy, society, gender, power relations).

Since then, various NGOs, such as the World Development Movement, have campaigned for a form of development that takes aspects of this alternative approach on board. Grass-roots movements have often grown up around specific issues, such as dams (Narmada in India) or access to common resources (the rubber tappers of the Brazilian Amazon). Such campaigns received a great impetus in the 1980s with the growth of the green movement worldwide. The two-year preparatory process before the UN Conference on Environment and Development (UNCED) in Rio, in June 1992, gave indigenous groups, women, children, and other previously voiceless groups a chance to express their views. This momentum has continued, and it has become the norm to hold alternative NGO forums, parallel to all major UN conferences.

Resistance, empowerment, and development

Democracy is at the heart of the alternative conception of development. Grass-roots movements are playing an important role in challenging entrenched structures of power in formal democratic societies. In the face of increasing globalization, with the further erosion of local community control over daily life and the further extension of the power of the market and **transnational corporations**, people express their resistance through the language of human rights (Evans 2005: Stammers 2009). They are making a case for local control and local empowerment as the heart of development. They are protecting what they identify as the immediate source of their survival—water, forest, and land. They are rejecting the dominant agenda of private and public (government-controlled) spheres and setting an alternative one. Examples include the Chiapas' uprising in Mexico, and Indian peasant protests against foreign-owned seed factories. Protests at the annual meetings of the WTO, and also the IMF and World Bank, have become routine since the late 1990s, and are indicative of an increasingly widespread discontent with the process of globalization and with the distribution of its benefits. Such protests symbolize the struggle for substantive democracy that communities across the world are working for. In this context, development is about facilitating a community's participation and lead role in deciding what sort of development is appropriate. It is not about assuming the desirability of the Western model and its associated values. This alternative conception of development therefore values diversity above universality, and is based on a different conception of rights (Evans forthcoming).

The Alternative Declaration produced by the NGO Forum at the Copenhagen Summit enshrined **principles** of community participation, empowerment, **equity**, self-reliance, and sustainability. The role of women and youth was singled out. The Declaration rejects the economic liberalism accepted by governments of North and South, seeing it as a path to aggravation rather than alleviation of the global social crisis. It called for the immediate cancellation of all debt, improved terms of trade, transparency and accountability of the IMF and World Bank, and the regulation of multinationals. An alternative view of democracy was central to its conception of development. Similar ideas emanated from the parallel NGO forums, which accompanied all the UN global conferences in the 1990s.

For some commentators, national PRSs offer the opportunity—albeit as yet unrealized—for greater community participation in development policy-making in the South. If all parties operate in the spirit intended, the PRS process could enhance representation and voice for states and peoples in the South, and it offers the best hope available for expanding national ownership of economic policy.

Now that we have looked at the critical alternative view of development, we shall look at the way in which the orthodox view has attempted to respond to the criticisms of the alternative view.

The orthodoxy incorporates criticisms

In the mainstream debate, the focus has shifted from growth to sustainable development. The concept was championed in the late 1980s by the influential Brundtland Commission (officially entitled the World Commission on Environment and Development—see Brundtland *et al.* 1987), and supported in the 1990s by a series of UN global conferences. Central to the concept of **sustainable development** is the idea that the pursuit of development by the present generation should not be at the expense of future generations. In other words, it stressed inter-generational equity as well as intra-generational equity. The importance of maintaining the environmental resource base was highlighted, and with this comes the idea that there are natural limits to growth. The Brundtland Report made clear, however, that further growth was essential; but it needed to be made environment-friendly. The Report did not address the belief, widespread among a sector of the NGO community, that the emphasis on growth had caused the environmental crisis in the first place. The World Bank accepted the concerns of the Report to some degree. When faced with an NGO spotlight on the adverse environmental implications of its projects, the Bank moved to introduce more rigorous environmental assessments of its funding activities. Similarly, concerning gender, when faced with critical NGO voices, the World Bank eventually came up with its Operational Policy 4.20 on gender (1994). The latter aimed to 'reduce gender disparities and enhance women particularly in the economic development of their countries by integrating gender considerations in its country assistance programmes' (www.worldbank.org).

With the United Nations Conference on the Environment and Development (UNCED) in June 1992, the idea that the environment and development were inextricably interlinked was taken further. However, what came out of the official inter-state process was legitimation of market-based development policies to further sustainable development, with self-regulation for transnational corporations. Official output from Rio, such as *Agenda 21*, however, recognized the huge importance of the sub-state level for addressing sustainability issues, and supported the involvement of marginalized groups. But while the groups had a role in the preparatory process, they have not been given an official role in the follow-up to UNCED. At the alternative summit, where the largest selection of non-governmental views ever expressed was aired, the viability of this strategy was challenged. For example, the possibility of structural adjustment policies being made environment-friendly was seriously questioned.

The process of incorporation has continued ever since. This is seen most recently in the language of poverty reduction being incorporated into World Bank and IMF policies: 'growth with equity' and 'pro-poor growth' are the buzzwords, yet underlying macroeconomic policy remains unchanged. An examination of the contribution of the development orthodoxy to increasing global inequality is not on the agenda. The gendered outcomes of macroeconomic policies are largely ignored. Despite promises of new funding at the UN Monterrey Conference on Financing for Development in 2002, new transfers of finance from developed to developing countries have been slow in coming. The promises made at the G8 summit of 2006 are expressed as a percentage of the donor's GDP, which, following the global downturn of 2009, will be substantially less than expected. In addition to new finance, that Summit saw commitments to write off $40 billion of debt owed by the Heavily Indebted Poor Countries (HIPCs). However, the commitment was not implemented with immediate effect, didn't cover all needy countries, and received a lukewarm reception in some G8 countries. The North–South agenda has changed little in the years since the Rio Summit, when sustainable development hit the headlines. Progress towards achieving the Millennium Development Goals in the wake of the global 'credit crunch' is acknowledged as 'sluggish' or 'negative', as 'economic growth, diminished resources, fewer trade opportunities for developing countries, and possible reductions in aid flows from donor nations threaten to reverse whatever gains have been made (Millennium Development Goals Report 2009).

An appraisal of the responses of the orthodox approach to its critics

During 2000, a series of official '+ 5' mini-conferences was held, such as Rio + 5, Copenhagen + 5, and Beijing + 5, to assess progress in specific areas since the major UN conferences five years earlier. The assessments suggested that the international community had fallen short in its efforts to operationalize conference action plans and to mainstream these concerns in **global politics**. For example, a critical reading of Beijing suggests that the conference represented a continuation of the attempts of the 1970s and 1980s to integrate women into prevailing development practice (so-called 'WID' or 'women in development'), in other words to increase their economic opportunities within the existing economic system. This stands in contrast to an attempt fundamentally to alter the social and economic power of women relative to men, which would require a transformation in prevailing development practice via the promotion of a gender and development ('GAD') approach. The World Bank's own assessment of its mainstreaming of gender, undertaken by the Social Development Task Force in 1996, concluded that gender concerns are not incorporated systematically into projects and are regarded by many as 'add-ons'.

Voices of criticism are growing in number and range. Even among supporters of the mainstream approach, voices of disquiet are heard as the maldistribution of the benefits of economic liberalism is increasingly seen to have been a threat to local, national, regional, and even global order. Moreover, the social protest that accompanies economic globalization is regarded by some as a potential obstacle to the neo-liberal project. Thus supporters of globalization are keen to temper its most unpopular effects by modification of neo-liberal policies. Small but nevertheless important changes are taking place. For example, the World Bank has guidelines on the treatment of indigenous peoples, resettlement, the environmental impact of its projects, gender, and on disclosure of information. It is implementing social safety nets when pursuing structural adjustment policies, and it is promoting microcredit as a way to empower women. With the IMF, it developed a Heavily Indebted Poor Country (HIPC) Initiative to reduce the debt burden of the poorest states. Whether these guidelines and concerns really inform policy, and whether these new policies and facilities result in practical outcomes that impact on the fundamental causes of poverty remains unclear, however.

There is a tremendously long way to go in terms of gaining credence for the core values of the alternative model of development in the corridors of power, nationally and internationally. Nevertheless, the alternative view, marginal though it is, has had some noteworthy successes in modifying orthodox development. These may not be insignificant for those whose destinies have up till now been largely determined by the attempted universal application of a selective set of local, essentially Western, values.

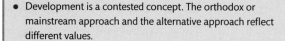

Key Points

- Development is a contested concept. The orthodox or mainstream approach and the alternative approach reflect different values.

- Development policies over the last sixty years have been dominated by the mainstream approach—embedded liberalism and, more recently, neo-liberalism—with a focus on growth.

- The last two decades of the twentieth century saw the flourishing of alternative conceptions of development based on equity, participation, empowerment, sustainability, etc., with input especially from NGOs and grass-roots movements and some parts of the UN.

- The mainstream approach has been modified slightly and has incorporated the language of its critics (e.g. pro-poor growth).

- Gains made during the last two decades may be reversed as the full consequences of the global 'credit crunch' emerge.

Hunger

Although 'the production of food to meet the needs of a burgeoning population has been one of the outstanding global achievements of the post-war period' (ICPF 1994: 104, 106), the UN Food and Agriculture Organization (FAO) estimates that over one billion people will remain hungry during 2010 (http://www.fao.org). The current

Global Hunger Index
- ≥ 30.0 extremely alarming
- 20.0–29.9 alarming
- 10.0–19.9 serious
- 1.5–9.9 low to moderate hunger
- no data
- excluded from GHI

Figure 28.5 World hunger map, 2006

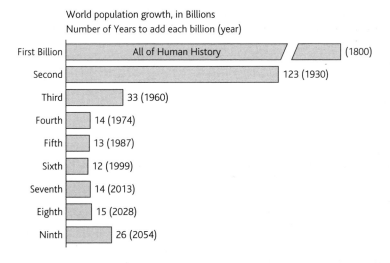

Figure 28.6 World population growth from 1800 with projections to 2050

Most populous countries, 2003

Rank	Country	Population (millions)
1	China	1,289
2	India	1,069
3	United States	292
4	Indonesia	220
5	Brazil	176
6	Pakistan	149
7	Bangladesh	147
8	Russia	146
9	Nigeria	134
10	Japan	128

Most populous countries, 2050

Rank	Country	Population (millions)
1	India	1,628
2	China	1,394
3	United States	422
4	Pakistan	349
5	Indonesia	316
6	Nigeria	307
7	Bangladesh	255
8	Brazil	221
9	Congo, Dem. Rep. of	181
10	Ethiopia	173

Figure 28.7 Most populous countries, 2003, with projections to 2050

depth of hunger across different world regions is shown in Figure 28.5. While famines may be exceptional phenomena, hunger is ongoing. Why is this so?

Broadly speaking, there are two schools of thought with regard to hunger: the orthodox, nature-focused approach, which identifies the problem largely as one of overpopulation, and the entitlement, society-focused approach, which sees the problem more in terms of distribution. Let us consider each of these two approaches in turn.

The orthodox, nature-focused explanation of hunger

The orthodox explanation of hunger, first mapped out by Thomas Robert Malthus in his *Essay on the Principle of Population in* 1798, focuses on the relationship between human population growth and the food supply. It asserts that population growth naturally outstrips the growth in food production, so that a decrease in the per capita availability of food is inevitable, until eventually a point is reached at which starvation, or some other disaster, drastically reduces the human population to a level that can be sustained by the available food supply. This approach therefore places great stress on human overpopulation as the cause of the problem, and seeks ways to reduce the fertility of the human race, or rather, that part of the human race that seems to breed faster than the rest—the poor of the 'Third World'. Supporters of this approach argue that there are natural limits to population growth—principally that of the carrying capacity of the land—and that when these limits are exceeded disaster is inevitable.

The available data on the growth of the global human population indicate that it has quintupled since the early 1800s, and is expected to grow from six billion in 1999 to ten billion in 2050. Over 50 per cent of this increase is expected to occur in seven countries: Bangladesh, Brazil, China, India, Indonesia, Nigeria, and Pakistan. Figure 28.6 provides data on world population growth from 1800, with projections through to 2050. Figure 28.7 focuses on the most populous countries—almost all of which are located in the Third World—and only 11 of them account for over half of the world's population. It is figures such as these that have convinced many adherents of the orthodox approach to hunger that it is essential that Third World countries adhere to strict family-planning policies that one way or another limit their population growth rates. Indeed, in the case of the World Bank, most women-related efforts until very recently were in the area of family planning.

The entitlement, society-focused explanation of hunger

Critics of the orthodox approach to hunger argue that it is too simplistic in its analysis and ignores the vital factor of food distribution. They point out that it fails to account for the paradox we observed at the beginning of this discussion on hunger: that despite the enormous increase in food production per capita that has occurred over the post-war period (largely due to the development of high-yielding seeds and industrial agricultural techniques), little impact has been made on the huge numbers of people in the world who experience chronic hunger. For example, the UN Food and Agriculture Organization (FAO) estimates that although there is enough grain alone to provide everyone in the world with 3,600 calories a day, even taking account of increases in population growth (i.e. 1,200 more than the UN's recommended minimum daily intake), the number of people living in hunger continues to grow.

Furthermore, critics note that the Third World, where the majority of malnourished people live, produces much of the world's food, while those who consume most of it are located in the Western world. Meat consumption tends to rise with household wealth, and a third of the

---

Case Study 2 Food shortages in Kenya

With a GDP per capita of around $1,240 (World Bank Report 2007), and a ranking of 144 out of 179 in the 2008 UNDP Human Development Report, large numbers of Kenyans suffer poverty. This is most acute in urban slums and among pastoralists and farmers living in remote and semi-arid regions. It is estimated that in 2009 5.6 million Kenyans will face food insecurity as global food prices continue to rise at unprecedented rates (World Food Programme, wfp.org/countries/Kenya). Between 2005 and 2008 global food prices have risen overall by 83 per cent. For many Kenyans the only option is to cut back on the number of meals they eat, purchase less expensive foods and consume a high-carbohydrate, less balanced and nutritious diet. Malnutrition rates are expected to increase, particularly among children.

The cause of the food crisis in Kenya is often put down to the failure of the rainy season for the three years since 2006. The consequent crop failures have undoubtedly contributed to food shortages, but so have other factors. USAID's assessment is that recurrent 'seasons of failed or poor rains, sustained high food prices, environmental degradation, outbreaks of disease, and flooding have led to deteriorating food security conditions throughout Kenya, straining coping mechanisms, exacerbating existing chronic poverty, and contributing to increased inter-ethnic conflict over access to limited land and water resources. The increasing global market in agricultural products for biofuel production is another contributing factor.'

(http://www.usaid.gov/our_work/humanitarian_assistance/ disaster_assistance/countries/kenya/template/fs_sr/fy2009/ kenya_fi_sr01_09-02-2009.pdf)

world's grain is used to fatten animals. This trend is seen in countries that have experienced rapid economic growth during the last two decades, most notably China and India, A further recent trend is the switch in land use from food production to crops for the biofuel industry (See UNCTAD report www.unctad.org/Templates/Page.asp?intItemID=4526&lang=1). The effect of this is to reduce surpluses produced by developed countries that can be sold on global markets and take fertile land out of food production for local markets. Such evidence leads opponents of the orthodox approach to argue that we need to look much more closely at the social, political, and economic factors that determine how food is distributed and why access to it is achieved by some and denied to others.

A convincing alternative to the orthodox explanation of hunger was set forward in Amartya Sen's pioneering book, *Poverty and Famines: An Essay on Entitlement and Deprivation*, which was first published in 1981 (Sen 1981, 1983). He argues that famines have often occurred when there has been no significant reduction in the level of per capita food availability and, furthermore, that some famines have occurred during years of peak food availability. Thus hunger is due to people not having enough to eat, rather than there not being enough to eat. Put another way, whether a person starves or eats depends not so much on the amount of food available, but whether or not they can establish an entitlement to that food. If there is plenty of food available in the shops, but a family does not have the money to purchase that food, and does not have the means of growing their own food, then they are likely to starve. For example, while in many parts of sub-Saharan Africa agricultural land was used traditionally to provide food for local markets, the creation of global markets has meant that more and more land is devoted to export crops to feed wealthy nations. With access to land for local production limited, little opportunity to find alternative work, and little social security arrangement in place following the austerity policies imposed by the World Bank and IMF of the 1980s (SAPs), landless rural labourers and pastoralists cannot assert their entitlement to food, even when global production increases. In short, the conditions for hunger prevail even in a world of plenty.

Globalization and hunger

It is possible to explain the contemporary occurrence of hunger by reference to the process of globalization. Globalization means that events occurring in one part of the globe can affect, and be affected by, events occurring in other, distant parts of the globe. Often, as individuals, we remain unaware of our role in this process and its ramifications. When we drink a cup of tea or coffee, or eat imported fruit and vegetables, in the developed countries, we tend not to reflect on the changes experienced at the site of production of these cash crops in the developing world. However, it is possible to look at the effect of the establishment of a global, as opposed to a local, national, or regional, system of food production. This has been done by David Goodman and Michael Redclift in their book, *Refashioning Nature: Food, Ecology and Culture* (1991).

Goodman and Redclift argue that at the beginning of the twenty-first century we are witnessing an increasingly global organization of food provision and access to food, with transnational corporations playing the major role. This has been based on the incorporation of local systems of food production into a global system of food production. In other words, local subsistence producers, who have traditionally produced to meet the needs of their family and community, may now be involved in cash-crop production for a distant market. Alternatively, they may have left the land and become involved in the process of industrialization, making them net consumers rather than producers of food in the move to urbanization.

The most important actor in the development and expansion of this global food regime has been the USA, which, at the end of the Second World War, was producing large food surpluses. These surpluses were welcomed by many developing countries, for the orthodox model of development depended on the creation of a pool of cheap wage labour to serve the industrialization process. Hence, in order to encourage people off the land and away from subsistence production, the incentive to produce for oneself and one's family had to be removed. Cheap imported food provided this incentive, while the resulting low prices paid for domestic subsistence crops made them unattractive to grow; indeed, for those who continued to produce for the local market, such as in Sudan, the consequence has been the production of food at a loss (Bennett and George 1987: 78).

Not surprisingly, therefore, the production of subsistence crops in the developing world for local consumption has drastically declined in the post-war period. Domestic production of food staples in developing countries has declined, consumer tastes have been altered by the availability of cheap imports, and the introduction of agricultural technology has displaced millions of peasants from traditional lands. Furthermore, the creation of global agri-businesses has encouraged speculative investments, adding further to price volatility. Save the Children reports that in 2006 'the volume of traded global agricultural financial products, like options and futures, increased by almost 30%' (Save the Children www.savethechildren.org.uk/en/54_5739.htm).

The increasing number of people who suffer food insecurity is often recognized by the leaders of wealthy states. It is these same leaders who also promote free market principles that create the contemporary context for hunger. However, as the 2009 World Summit demonstrated, concern does not necessarily turn into action (http://www.fao.org/wsfs/world-summit/en).

Key Points

- In recent decades global food production has burgeoned, but, paradoxically, hunger and malnourishment remain widespread.

- The orthodox explanation for the continued existence of hunger is that population growth outstrips food production.

- An alternative explanation for the continuation of hunger focuses on lack of access or entitlement to available food. Access and entitlement are affected by factors such as the North–South global divide, particular national policies, rural–urban divides, class, gender, and race.

- Globalization can simultaneously contribute to increased food production and increased hunger.

Conclusion: looking to the future—globalization with a human face?

It is clear when we consider the competing conceptions of poverty, development, and hunger explored above that there is no consensus on definitions, causes, or solutions.

We are faced with an awesome development challenge. Early indications suggest that the UN Millennium Development Goal (MDG) targets will not be met. Indeed, the 2009 Millennium Development Goals Report concludes that although 'data are not yet available to reveal the full impact of the recent economic downturn, they point to areas where progress towards the eight goals has slowed or reversed' (MDG Report 2009). The World Bank's Global Monitoring Report for 2009 offers the pessimistic assessment that the 'deepening global recession, rising unemployment, and volatile commodity prices in 2008 and 2009 are seriously affecting progress toward poverty reduction'. In particular, the Bank sees rising food prices as a central cause of 'throwing millions into extreme poverty' (http://www.worldbank.org/).

The orthodox model of development is being held up for closer scrutiny, as we become more aware of the risks as well as the opportunities that globalization and the Washington Consensus bring in their wake. The key question is: can globalization develop a human face?

The current development orthodoxy is following the reformist pathway. History will reveal whether this pathway bears the seeds of its own destruction by delivering too little, too late, to too few people. As students of International Relations, we must bring these issues in from the margins of our discipline and pursue them as central to our study.

Questions

1 What does poverty mean?
2 Explain the orthodox approach to development and outline the criteria by which it measures development.
3 Assess the critical alternative model of development.
4 How effectively has the orthodox model of development neutralized the critical, alternative view?
5 Compare and contrast the orthodox and alternative explanations of hunger.

6 What are the pros and cons of the global food regime established since the Second World War?

7 Account for the increasing gap between rich and poor states and people after fifty years of official development policies.

8 Critically explore the gendered nature of poverty.

9 Is the recent World Bank focus on poverty reduction evidence of a change of direction by the Bank?

10 Are national poverty reduction strategies contributing to national ownership of development policies in the Third World?

11 Why has the discipline of International Relations been slow to engage with issues of poverty and development?

12 Outline the consequences, for those living in poverty, of the 2008 global economic downturn.

Further Reading

General

Adams, N. B. (1993), *Worlds Apart: The North–South Divide and the International System* (London: Zed). Presents a broad economic and political history of the North–South divide, and focuses on the role of the international economic system. This book provides an effective introduction to the politics of North–South economic relations over the past half-century.

Kiely, R. (2006), *The New Political Economy of Development: Globalization, Imperialism and Hegemony* (Basingstoke: Palgrave Macmillan). An important new text that examines development in a historic and political-economic context. This is a book for ambitious students who want to take their understanding of development to a deeper level.

Rapley, J. (1996), *Understanding Development* (Boulder, CO: Lynne Rienner). Analyses the theory and practice of development in the Third World since the Second World War in a straightforward, succinct manner. It provides the reader with a firm grasp of changing development policies at the international level and their take-up over time in different states.

Thomas, C. (2000), *Global Governance, Development and Human Security* (London: Pluto). Examines the global development policies pursued by global governance institutions, especially the IMF and the World Bank, in the 1980s and 1990s. It assesses the impact of these policies on human security, and analyses different paths towards the achievement of human security for the twenty-first century.

Development

Evans, T. (2005), *The Politics of Human Rights: A Global Perspective* (London, Pluto Press). Investigates the relationship between development and claims for human rights. It focuses upon the difference between conservative and radical uses of the idea of human rights.

Rahnema, M., with Bawtree, V. (eds) (1997), *The Post Development Reader* (Dhaka: University Press, and London: Zed). Challenges the reader to think critically about the nature of development and assumptions about meanings. This is an extremely stimulating interdisciplinary reader.

Hunger

Dreze, J., Sen, A., and Hussain, A. (eds) (1995), The *Political Economy of Hunger* (Oxford: Clarendon Press). An excellent collection on the political economy of hunger.

Sen, A. (1981), *Poverty and Famines* (Oxford: Clarendon Press). Provides a ground-breaking analysis of the causes of hunger that incorporates detailed studies of a number of famines and convincingly challenges the orthodox view of the causes of hunger.

Wiesmann, D. (2006), *Global Hunger Index 2006: A Basis for Cross-country Comparisons*, Issue Brief 47 (Washington, DC: International Food Policy Research Institute). The Global Hunger Index (GHI), published by the International Food Policy Research Institute, was developed in 2006 to increase attention on the hunger problem and to mobilize the political will to address it.

Online Resource Centre

 Visit the Online Resource Centre that accompanies this book to access more learning resources on this chapter topic at www.oxfordtextbooks.co.uk/orc/baylis5e/

Human security

AMITAV ACHARYA

Reader's Guide

This chapter examines the origins of the concept of human security, debates surrounding its definition and scope, some of the threats to human security in the world today, and international efforts to promote human security. It proceeds in four parts. The section, 'What is human security?', traces the origin and evolution of the concept, and examines competing definitions offered by scholars and policy-makers. The next section reviews debates and controversies about human security, especially over the analytic and policy relevance of the notion, and the broad and narrow meanings of the concept ('freedom from fear' versus 'freedom from want'). The third section examines some of the threats to human security today. While the concept of human security encompasses a wide range of threats, due to lack of space, this section will focus on the trends in armed conflicts as well as the interrelationship between conflict and other non-violent threats to human security, such as poverty, disease, and environmental degradation. The final section analyses the international community's efforts to promote human security and concludes by identifying the major challenges to promoting the notion of human security today.

Introduction

The concept of **human security** represents a powerful, but controversial, attempt by sections of the academic and policy community to redefine and broaden the meaning of **security**. Traditionally, security meant protection of the sovereignty and territorial integrity of states from external military threats. This was the essence of the concept of national security, which dominated security analysis and policy-making during the cold war period. In the 1970s and 1980s, academic literature on security, responding to the Middle East oil crisis and the growing awareness of worldwide environmental degradation, began to think of security in broader, non-military terms. Yet the state remained the object of security, or the entity that is to be protected. The concept of human security challenges the state-centric notion of security by focusing on the individual as the main referent object of security. Human security is about security for the people, rather than for states or governments. As such, it has generated much debate. On the one hand, critics wonder whether such an approach would widen the boundaries of security studies too much, and whether 'securitizing' the individual is the best way to address the challenges facing the international community from the forces of globalization. On the other hand, advocates of human security find the concept to be an important step forward in highlighting the dangers to human safety and survival posed by poverty, disease, environmental stress, human rights abuses, as well as armed conflict. These disagreements notwithstanding, the concept of human security captures a growing realization that, in an era of rapid globalization, security must encompass a broader range of concerns and challenges than simply defending the state from external military attack.

What is human security?

The origin of the concept of human security can be traced to the publication of the *Human Development Report* of 1994, issued by the United Nations Development Programme (UNDP 1994). The Report defined the scope of human security to include seven areas:

- Economic security—an assured basic income for individuals, usually from productive and remunerative work, or, in the last resort, from some publicly financed safety net.
- Food security—ensuring that all people at all times have both physical and economic access to basic food.
- Health security—guaranteeing a minimum protection from diseases and unhealthy lifestyles.
- Environmental security—protecting people from the short- and long-term ravages of nature, man-made threats in nature, and deterioration of the natural environment.
- Personal security—protecting people from physical violence, whether from the state or external states, from violent individuals or sub-state factors, from domestic abuse, and from predatory adults.
- Community security—protecting people from the loss of traditional relationships and values, and from sectarian and ethnic violence.

- Political security—ensuring that people live in a society that honours their basic human rights and ensuring the freedom of individuals and groups from government attempts to exercise control over ideas and information.

Unlike many other efforts to redefine security where political scientists played a major role, human security was the handiwork of a group of development economists, such as the late Pakistani economist Mahabub ul Haq, who conceptualized the UNDP's *Human Development Report*. They were increasingly dissatisfied with the orthodox notion of development, which viewed it as a function of economic growth. Instead, they proposed a concept of **human development** that focuses on building human capabilities to confront and overcome poverty, illiteracy, diseases, discrimination, restrictions on political freedom, and the threat of violent conflict: 'Individual freedoms and rights matter a great deal, but people are restricted in what they can do with that freedom if they are poor, ill, illiterate, discriminated against, threatened by violent conflict or denied a political voice.' (UNDP 2005: 18–19).

Closely related to the attempt to create a broader paradigm for development was the growing concern

Box 29.1 A contested concept

'Human security can be said to have two main aspects. It means, first, safety from such chronic threats as hunger, disease and repression. And second, it means protection from sudden and hurtful disruptions in the patterns of daily life – whether in homes, in jobs or in communities. Such threats can exist at all levels of national income and development.'

(UNDP 1994)

'Human security is not a concern with weapons. It is a concern with human dignity. In the last analysis, it is a child who did not die, a disease that did not spread, an ethnic tension that did not explode, a dissident who was not silenced, a human spirit that was not crushed.'

(Mahbub ul Haq 1995)

'For Canada, human security means from pervasive threats to people's rights, safety or lives. ... Through its foreign policy, Canada has chosen to focus its human security agenda on promoting safety for people by protecting them from threats of violence.'

(Department of Foreign Affairs and International Trade (Canada) 2000)

'the concept of human security had better be confined to freedom from fear of *man-made* physical violence, also referred to as direct, personal violence. A broader understanding of human

security as freedom from structural violence will undermine the clarity of the notion and make it difficult to develop priorities and devise effective policy responses.'

(Sverre Lodgaard 2000)

'Human security may be defined as the preservation and protection of the life and dignity of individual human beings. Japan holds the view, as do many other countries, that human security can be ensured only when the individual is confident of a life free of fear and free of want.'

(Japanese Foreign Ministry Official, 2000, http://www.mofa.go.jp/policy/human_secu/speech0006.html)

'Human security can no longer be understood in purely military terms. Rather, it must encompass economic development, social justice, environmental protection, democratization, disarmament, and respect for human rights and the rule of law. ... Moreover, these pillars are interrelated; progress in one area generates progress in another.'

(Kofi Annan 2001)

'The objective of human security is to safeguard the "vital core of all human lives in ways that enhance human freedoms and human fulfilment".'

(UN Commission on Human Security 2003)

about the negative impact of defence spending on development, or the so-called 'guns versus butter' dilemma. As a global study headed by Inga Thorsson of Sweden concluded, 'the arms race and development are in a competitive relationship' (Roche 1986: 8). Drawing upon this study, a UN-sponsored International Conference on the Relationship between Disarmament and Development in 1986 in Paris sought 'to enlarge world understanding that human security demands more resources for development and fewer for arms'.

The move towards human security was also advanced by the work of several international commissions. They offered a broader view of security that looked beyond the cold war emphasis on East–West military competition. Foremost among them was the Report of the Palme Commission of 1982, which proposed the doctrine of 'common security'. The Report stressed that: 'In the Third World countries, as in all our countries, security requires economic progress as well as freedom from military fear' (Palme Commission 1982: xii). In 1987, the Report of the World Commission on Environment and Development (also known as the Brundtland Commission) highlighted the linkage between environmental degradation and conflict: 'The real sources of insecurity encompass unsustainable development, and its effects

can become intertwined with traditional forms of conflict in a manner that can extend and deepen the latter' (Brundtland *et al.* 1987: 230).

Along with attempts to broaden the notion of security to include non-military threats, there was also a growing emphasis on the individual as the central object of security. The Palme Commission's notion of common security became the conceptual basis of the Conference on Security and Cooperation in Europe (CSCE). The CSCE made East–West security cooperation conditional upon the improvement of the human rights situation in the former Soviet bloc. The North–South Roundtable on the 'Economics of Peace', held in Costa Rica in 1990, called for a shift from 'an almost exclusive concern with military security … to a broader concern for overall security of individuals from social violence, economic distress and environmental degradation' (Jolly and Ray 2006: 3).

In the post-cold-war era, the importance given to people's security has grown in salience. One reason for this is the rising incidence of civil wars and intra-state conflicts involving huge loss of life, ethnic cleansing, displacement of people within and across borders, and disease outbreaks. Traditional national security approaches have not been sufficiently sensitive towards conflicts that arise over cultural, ethnic, and religious differences, as happened in Eastern Europe, Africa, and Central Asia in the post-cold war era (Tow and Trood 2000). Another reason is the spread of democratization and the post-cold war emphasis on human rights and **humanitarian intervention.** The latter involves the principle that the international community is justified in intervening in the internal affairs of states accused of gross violation of human rights. This has led to the realization that while the concept of national security has not been rendered irrelevant, it no longer sufficiently accounts for the kinds of danger that threaten societies, states, and the international community. The notion of human security has also been brought to the fore by the crises induced by accelerating globalization. For example, the widespread poverty, unemployment, and social dislocation caused by the Asian financial crisis in 1997 underscored the vulnerability of people to the effects of economic globalization (Acharya 2004).

Key Points

- The concept of human security represents both a vertical and a horizontal expansion (or deepening and widening) of the traditional notion of national security, defined as protection of state sovereignty and territorial integrity from external military threats.

- In its broader sense, human security is distinguished by three elements: (1) its focus on the individual/people as the referent object of security; (2) its multidimensional nature; (3) its universal or global scope, applying to states and societies of the North as well as the South.

- The concept of human security has been influenced by four developments: (1) the rejection of economic growth as the main indicator of development and the accompanying notion of 'human development' as empowerment of people; (2) the rising incidence of internal conflicts; (3) the impact of globalization in spreading transnational dangers such as terrorism and pandemics; and (4) the post-cold war emphasis on human rights and humanitarian intervention.

Debates about human security

Debates over human security fall into two categories. First, believers and sceptics of the concept disagree over whether human security is a new or necessary notion and what are the costs and benefits of adopting it as an intellectual tool or a policy framework. Second, there have been debates over the scope of the concept, mainly among the believers themselves.

For critics of human security, the concept is too broad to be analytically meaningful or useful as a tool of policy-making. Roland Paris has argued: 'Existing definitions of human security tend to be extraordinarily expansive and vague, encompassing everything from physical security to psychological well-being, which provides policymakers with little guidance in the prioritization of competing policy goals and academics little sense of what, exactly, is to be studied' (Paris 2001: 88).

Another criticism is that such a concept might cause more harm than good: 'Speaking loudly about human security but carrying a Band-Aid only gives false hopes to both the victims of oppression and the international community' (Khong 2001: 3). The definition of human security is seen to be too moralistic compared to the traditional understanding of security, and hence unattainable and unrealistic (Tow and Trood 2000: 14).

A third and perhaps most powerful criticism of human security is that it neglects the role of the state as a provider of security. Buzan argues that states are a 'necessary condition for individual security because without the state it is not clear what other agency is to act on behalf of individuals' (Buzan 2001: 589). This criticism has been echoed by others, especially scholars with a realist orientation.

Advocates of human security have never totally discounted the importance of the state as a guarantor of human security. As the Report of the Commission on Human Security (UN Commission on Human Security 2003) acknowledges, 'Human security complements state security'. Nor do they claim that human and traditional security concerns are always antithetical. Weak states are often incapable of protecting the safety and dignity of their citizens. But whether traditional state security and human security conflict with each other depends very much on the nature of the regime that presides over the state. In many countries, human security as security for the people can and does get threatened by the actions of their own governments. Hence, while the 'state remains the fundamental purveyor of security . . . it often fails to fulfil its security obligations—and at times has even become a source of threat to its own people' (Mack 2004: 366). At the very least, from a human security perspective, the state cannot be regarded as the sole source of protection for the individuals (*ibid.*).

Another major debate about human security has occurred over the scope of the concept: whether it should be primarily about 'freedom from fear' or 'freedom from want'. The former view, initially articulated by the former Canadian External Affairs Minister Lloyd Axworthy, focuses on reducing the human costs of violent conflicts through measures such as a ban on landmines, using women and children in armed conflict, child soldiers, child labour, and small-arms proliferation, the formation of an International Criminal Court, and promulgating human rights and international humanitarian law (Department of Foreign Affairs and International Trade (Canada) 1999; *The Ottawa Citizen*, 28 May 1998: A18). From this perspective, the UN Charter, the Universal Declaration of Human Rights, and the Geneva Conventions are the 'core elements' of the doctrine of human security. The latter view, advocated by Japan (Director General of the Foreign Ministry of

Japan 2000), is closer to the original UNDP formulation. It stresses the ability of individuals and societies to be free from a broad range of non-military threats, such as poverty, disease, and environmental degradation (see Table 29.1).

But the differences between the two conceptions of human security can be overstated, since both regard the individual as the referent object of security, and both acknowledge the role of globalization and the changing nature of armed conflict in creating new threats to human security. Moreover, both perspectives stress safety from violence as a key objective of human security, and both call for a rethinking of state sovereignty as a necessary part of promoting human security (Hubert 2004: 351). There is considerable overlap between the two conceptions: '[D]evelopment . . .[is] a necessary condition for [human] security, just as security is a necessary condition for [human] development' (University of British Columbia, Human Security Center (hereafter *Human Security Report*) 2005: 155). Seeking freedom from fear without addressing freedom from want would amount to addressing symptoms without the cause. As the following section shows, while the deaths caused by armed conflicts have declined, other challenges to the safety and well-being of the individual have remained, and in some cases escalated.

Table 29.1 Two conceptions of human security

	Freedom from want	Freedom from fear
Original proponents	Development economists, Mahabub ul Haq, Amartya Sen	Western governments (Canada, Norway)
Main stimulus	Dissatisfaction over orthodox growth-oriented development models; guns versus butter concerns	End of the cold war; rise of complex emergencies, ethnic strife, state failure, humanitarian intervention
Type of threats addressed	Non-military and non-traditional security concerns: poverty, environmental degradation, disease, etc.	Armed conflicts, violence against individuals
Main policy goal	Promoting human development, defined as 'building human capabilities—the range of things that people can do, and what they can be. . . . The most basic capabilities for human development are leading a long and healthy life, being educated and having adequate resources for a decent standard of living . . . [and] social and political participation in society'. These capabilities are undermined by poverty, disease and ill-health, illiteracy, discrimination, threat of violent conflict, and denial of political and civil liberties. *(UNDP 2005: 18–19)*	Protecting people in conflict zones; reducing the human costs of conflict through a ban on landmines and child soldiers; protecting human rights; developing peacebuilding mechanisms.

Key Points

- The concept of human security has been criticized: (1) for being too broad to be analytically meaningful or to serve as the basis for policy-making; (2) for creating false expectations about assistance to victims of violence which the international community cannot deliver; and (3) for ignoring the role of the state in providing security to the people.

- Even among its advocates, differences exist as to whether human security is about 'freedom from fear' or 'freedom from want'. The former stresses protecting people from violent

conflicts through measures such as a ban on landmines and child soldiers. For the latter, human security is a broader notion involving the reduction of threats to the well-being of people, such as poverty and disease.

- Ultimately, however, both sides agree that human security is about security of the individuals rather than of states, and that protecting people requires going beyond traditional principles of state sovereignty.

Dimensions of human security

A pioneering report released by the Human Security Center at the University of British Columbia (2005) points to several significant trends in armed conflicts around the world (see Box 29.2 for some of the Report's main findings).

What explains the downward trend in armed conflicts around the world? (For an earlier account of conflicts in the Third World that anticipated this trend, see Acharya (1993) and Acharya (1997).) The report lists several factors: growing democratization (the

Box 29.2 Trends in conflict

- A 40% drop in armed conflicts in the world since 1991. (This counts only conflicts with at least 25 battle-related deaths where one of the parties was a state.)

- An 80% decline in the number of genocides and 'politicides'* between the high point in 1988 and 2001.

- A 70% decline in the number of international crises between 1981 and 2001.

- A 45% decrease in the number of refugees between 1992 and 2003. The number of internally displaced persons has increased, although accurate information is hard to obtain.

- A 98% decline in the average number of battle deaths per conflict per year. In 1950, an average armed conflict killed 38,000 people. In 2002, the figure was 600.**

(Source: University of British Columbia, Human Security Center (2005))

---

* The term 'politicide' describes policies that seek to destroy groups because of their political beliefs rather than religion or ethnicity (the latter being captured by the term 'genocide').
** Most of the battle deaths in the cold war period were accounted for by the Korean and Vietnam Wars. If these are excluded, the drop in battle deaths will be less dramatic.

underlying assumption here being that democracies tend to be better at peaceful resolution of conflicts); rising economic interdependence (which increases the costs of conflict); the declining economic utility of war owing to the fact that resources can be more easily bought in the international marketplace than acquired through force; the growth in the number of international institutions that can mediate in conflicts; the impact of international norms against violence, such as human sacrifice, witch-burning, slavery, duelling, war crimes, and genocide; the end of colonialism; and the end of the cold war. A specific reason identified by the Report is the dramatic increase in the UN's role in areas such as preventive diplomacy and peacemaking activities, post-conflict peacebuilding, the willingness of the UN Security Council to use military action to enforce peace agreements, the deterrent effects of war crime trials by the war crimes tribunals and the International Criminal Court (ICC), and the greater resort to reconciliation and addressing the root causes of conflict. The 80 per cent decline in the most deadly civil conflicts since the early 1990s, argued the Report, is due to the dramatic growth of international efforts at preventive diplomacy, peacemaking, and peacebuilding (*Human Security Report* 2005: Part V).

Yet the picture is not entirely positive. The decline in armed conflicts reported by the *Human Security Report* is from 1991 onwards. The number of armed conflicts had actually increased between 1960 and 1990–1, especially intra-state conflicts (which jumped from 12 in 1960 to 49 in 1991). As Figure 29.1 shows, armed conflicts in 2005 were on the same level as during the 1970s; moving higher in 2008 and markedly higher in 2004–8 period compared to the 1950s and early 1960s.

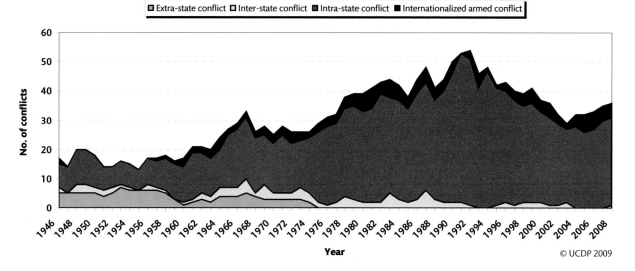

Extra-state conflict Inter-state conflict Intra-state conflict Internationalized armed conflict

© UCDP 2009

Figure 29.1 Active conflicts by type
Source: Uppsala Conflict Data Project (UCDP), Uppsala University,
available at: http://www.pcr.uu.se/research/UCDP/graphs/conflict_types_2008.gif (accessed 20 December 2009)

The findings of the 2005 *Human Security Report* were contested by others. For example, a study headed by Ziad Obermeyer relying on World Health Survey sample interviews in 13 conflict-ridden countries concluded that 'there is no evidence to support a recent decline in war deaths' (Spielmann 2009). Part of the problem is that researchers use different parameters: some (like the *Human Security Report*) count only battle deaths, others (like a study done by Milton Leitenberg of the University of Maryland) count both direct battlefield casualties as well as victims of genocide, famines that are deliberately caused, death camps and other warlike actions, to come up with a much larger number of casualties in conflict (Spielmann 2009).

And there are some horrific costs associated with these conflicts. For example, deaths directly or indirectly attributed to the conflict in the Democratic Republic of the Congo since 1998 have surpassed casualties sustained by Britain in the First World War and Second World War combined. The conflict in Sudan's Darfur region has displaced nearly 2 million people (UNDP 2005: 12). In Iraq, a team of American and Iraqi epidemiologists estimates that Iraq's mortality rate has more than doubled since the US invasion: from 5.5 deaths per 1,000 people in the year before the invasion to 13.3 deaths per 1,000 people per year in the post-invasion period. In all, some 655,000 more people have died in Iraq since the invasion in March 2003 than would have died if the invasion had not occurred (Brown 2006: A12).

The share of civilian casualties in armed conflict has increased since the Second World War. Civilians accounted for 10 per cent of the victims during the First World War and 50 per cent of the victims during the Second World War. They constitute between 80 and 85 per cent of the victims of more recent wars. Many of these victims are children, women, the sick, and the elderly (*Gendering Human Security* 2001: 18). Although death tolls from organized campaigns against civilians have declined in recent years, the number of such campaigns increased by 55 per cent between 1989 and 2005 (Univeristy of British Columbia, Human Security Center 2006: 3).

International terrorist incidents and the number of fatalities increased worldwide between 2002 and 2005. Most of the increases were associated with the war in Iraq, where the number of fatalities grew from about 1,700 in 2004 to approximately 3,400 in 2005 (National Counterterrorism Center 2005). Excluding Iraq, however, terrorist action killed fewer people worldwide in 2005—1,500 as opposed to 3,000 in 2004 (*ibid.*).

Furthermore, some of the most serious issues of human security in armed conflicts still need to be overcome, such as child soldiers and landmines. According to one study, 75 per cent of the armed conflicts today involve child soldiers (*Human Security Report* 2005: 35). Landmines and unexploded ordnance cause between 15,000 and 20,000 new casualties each year (United States Campaign to Ban Land Mines, date accessed 3

February 2007). Despite the justified optimism generated by the Ottawa Treaty (to be discussed later), there remain 80 million live mines undetected—someone steps on a landmine every 28 minutes—and 80 per cent of those killed or injured by landmines are civilians (Koehler 2007).

Finally, the decline in armed conflicts around the world is not necessarily irreversible. Some of the factors contributing to the decline of conflicts, such as democratization and the peace operations role of the UN, can suffer setbacks due to lack of support from major powers and the international community. And there remain serious possible threats to international peace and security that can cause widespread casualties, such as a conflict in the Korean peninsula, and war between China and Taiwan.

Battle deaths are not themselves an adequate indicator of threats to human security posed by armed conflict. Many armed conflicts have indirect consequences on human life and well-being. Wars are a major source of economic disruption, disease, and ecological destruction, which in turn undermine human development and thus create a vicious cycle of conflict and underdevelopment. As the *Human Development Report* (UNDP 2005: 12) puts it: 'Conflict undermines nutrition and public health, destroys education systems, devastates livelihoods and retards prospects for economic growth.' It found that out of the 52 countries that are reversing or stagnating in their attempts to reduce child mortality, 30 have experienced conflict since 1990. A British government *White Paper* on International Development notes:

> Violent conflict reverses economic growth, causes hunger, destroys roads, schools and clinics, and forces people to flee across borders. . . . Women and girls are particularly vulnerable because they suffer sexual violence and exploitation. And violent conflict and insecurity can spill over into neighbouring countries and provide cover for terrorists or organised criminal groups.
>
> *(Department for International Development 2006: 45)*

Wars also damage the environment, as happened with the US use of Agent Orange defoliant during the Vietnam War or Saddam Hussein's burning of Kuwaiti oil wells in the 1990–1 Gulf War, leading to massive air and land pollution. Similar links can be made between conflict and the outbreak of disease: '[W]ar-exacerbated disease and malnutrition kill far more people than missile, bombs and bullets' (*Human Security Report* 2005: 7). Disease accounts for most of the 3.9 million people

who have died in the conflict in the Democratic Republic of Congo (UNDP 2005: 45).

Just as wars and violent conflict have indirect consequences in causing economic disruption, ecological damage, and disease, levels of poverty and environmental degradation contribute to conflict and hence must be taken into consideration in human security research. One study shows that a country at US$250 GDP per capita has an average 15 per cent risk of experiencing a civil war in the next five years, while at a GDP per capita of $5,000, the risk of civil war is less than 1 per cent (Humphreys and Varshney 2004: 9; Department for International Development 2005: 8). While no direct link can be established between poverty and terrorism, terrorists often 'exploit poverty and exclusion in order to tap into popular discontent—taking advantage of fragile states such as Somalia, or undemocratic regimes such as in Afghanistan in the 1990s, to plan violence' (UNDP 2005: 47). Orissa in India (see case study) offers a clear example of how poverty, deprivation, and lack of economic opportunity can trigger insurgency and acts of terrorism, suggesting how freedom from fear and freedom from want are inextricably linked.

Environmental degradation, which is often linked to poverty, and climate change, are another source of conflict (Homer-Dixon 1991, 1994). Analysts have identified competition for scarce resources as a source of possible conflict between Israel and its Arab neighbours, India and Pakistan, Turkey and Syria, Egypt and Ethiopia (Rice 2006: 78). The world's poorer countries, where families often see the need for more children to compensate for a high infant mortality rate and to raise their income potential, account for a significant proportion of the growth in the world's population, which has doubled between 1950 and 1998 (*ibid.*: 80). Population growth, in turn, contributes to resource scarcity and environmental stress, often resulting in conflict. For example, South Asia, one of the poorest and most heavily populated regions of the globe, faces intensified competition and the possibility of conflict over scarce water resources. Examples include the Indo-Pakistan dispute over the Wular Barrage, the Indo-Bangladesh water dispute over the Farakka Barrage, and the Indo-Nepal dispute over the Mahakali River Treaty (*Power and Interest News Report* 2006). The potential for political upheaval or war as a consequence of environmental problems is evident in a host of poor regions around the world, including North Africa, the sub-Saharan Sahel region of Africa (including Ethiopia, Sudan, Somalia, Mali, Niger, and Chad), the island nations of the western Pacific Ocean,

Box 29.3 Key facts about disease

Those who take a broad definition of human security look not only at threats to the survival and safety of the individual from violent conflict, but also from such non-violent factors as disease, environmental degradation, and natural disasters. Below are some of the key trends in disease.

- The world has seen the appearance of at least 30 new infectious diseases, including avian flu, HIV/AIDS, Severe Acute Respiratory Syndrome, Hepatitis C, and West Nile virus, in the past three decades. Twenty diseases previously detected have re-emerged with new drug-resistant strains. (Rice 2006: 79)

- AIDS is the leading cause of death in Africa and the fourth leading cause of death worldwide. Around 40 million people worldwide are infected with HIV, 95% of whom live in developing countries. In 2004, approximately 5 million people were newly infected with the virus. HIV/AIDS killed more than 20 million people worldwide, and 3.1 million people died of AIDS-related causes in 2004. It is estimated that per capita growth in half of the countries in sub-Saharan Africa is falling by 0.5–1.2% each year as a direct result of AIDS. By 2010, per capita GDP in some of the hardest-hit countries may drop by 8% and per capita consumption may

fall even farther. (The Global Fund to Fight AIDS, Tuberculosis and Malaria, http://www.theglobalfund.org/en/about/aids/)

- Malaria causes about 350–500 million infections in humans and approximately 1–3 million deaths annually (Breman 2001: 1–11)—this would translate as about one death every 30 seconds (Greenwood et al. 2005: 1487–98). The majority, which amounts to 85–90% of malaria fatalities, occurs in sub-Saharan Africa. The economic impact of malaria has been estimated to cost Africa US$12 billion every year. (World Health Organization n.d.)

- Annually, 8 million people become ill with tuberculosis, and 2 million people die from the disease worldwide (Center for Disease Control 2005). Presently, tuberculosis is the world's greatest infectious killer of women of reproductive age and the leading cause of death among people with HIV/AIDS. (PR Newswire Europe 2002)

- A highly pathogenic H5N1 avian influenza outbreak began in South-East Asia in mid-2003 and spread to parts of Europe. Nine Asian countries reported outbreaks: the Republic of Korea, Vietnam, Japan, Thailand, Cambodia, the Lao People's Democratic Republic, Indonesia, China, and Malaysia. (World Health Organization 2006)

the Ganges River basin (principally north-eastern India and Bangladesh), and some parts of Central and South America (Petzold-Bradley, Carius, and Vincze 2001). Darfur illustrates the linkage between poverty, environmental degradation, and conflict. Traditional inter-communal conflict in Darfur over scarcity of resources and land deteriorated as a result of desertification and a shortage of rainfall. In the 1970s and 1980s, droughts in northern parts of Darfur forced its nomadic population to migrate southwards in search of water and herding grounds, and brought them into conflict with the local tribes (Environmental Degradation and Conflict in Darfur 2004).

The issue of climate change has emerged as a security concern for Western countries, although most tend to view it as a *national security* challenge, i.e. one with a potential to trigger inter-state war or violence that destabilizes international order, rather than as a *human security* concern, in which people's livelihood and well-being are compromised. But climate change can be linked to people's human security issues, such as increased poverty, state failure, food shortages, water crisis, and disease, which are authentic human security issues (Broder 2009).

Natural disasters can also affect the course of conflicts by either exacerbating or mitigating them. The December

2004 Indian Ocean tsunami changed the course of two separatist conflicts: Aceh in Indonesia and Tamil separatism in Sri Lanka. In Aceh, where the government announced a ceasefire to permit relief work, improved prospects for reconciliation followed. In contrast, the conflict in Sri Lanka, where relief supplies did not reach rebel-held territory, saw an escalation of violence, which resulted in the brutal military extermination of the Tamil Tigers by the Sri Lankan government, with considerable civilian casualties.

From the foregoing discussion, we can establish a conceptual link between the broader and narrower understandings of human security (see Figures 29.2 and 29.3).

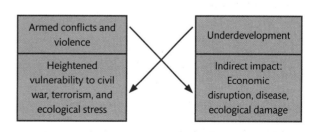

Figure 29.2 Conflict and underdevelopment: the vicious interaction

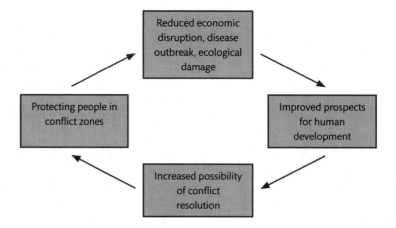

Figure 29.3 Protection and development: the virtuous interaction

Women, conflict, and human security

The relationship between gender and human security has multiple dimensions. The UN Inter-Agency Committee on Women and Gender Equality (1991: 1) notes five aspects: (1) violence against women and girls; (2) gender inequalities in control over resources; (3) gender inequalities in power and decision-making; (4) women's human rights; and (5) women (and men) as actors, not victims. Recent conflicts have shown women as victims of rape, torture, and sexual slavery. For example, between 250,000 and 500,000 women were raped during the 1994 genocide in Rwanda. Such atrocities against women are now recognized as a crime against humanity (Rehn and Sirleaf 2002: 9).

War-affected areas often see a sharp increase in domestic violence directed at women, and a growth in the number of women trafficked to become forced labourers or sex workers. Women and children comprise 73 per cent of an average population, but account for 80 per cent of the refugees in the world today, and perhaps a larger percentage as internally displaced persons. Another important aspect of the gender dimension of human security is the role of women as actors in conflicts. This involves considering the participation of women in combat. In the Eritrean war of independence, women made up 25–30 per cent of combatants. A similar proportion of women were fighting with the now-vanquished Tamil Tigers. Women play an even larger role in support functions, such as logistics, staff, and intelligence services in a conflict. It has been noted that women become targets of rape and sexual violence because they serve as a social and cultural symbol. Hence violence against them may be undertaken as a deliberate strategy by parties to a

conflict with a view to undermining the social fabric of their opponents. Similarly, securing women's participation in combat may be motivated by a desire among the parties to a conflict to increase the legitimacy of their cause. It signifies 'a broad social consensus and solidarity, both to their own population and to the outside world' (*Gendering Human Security* 2001: 18).

In recent years, there has been a growing awareness of the need to secure the greater participation of women in international peace operations. The UN Department of Peacekeeping Operations noted in a 2000 report:

> Women's presence [in peacekeeping missions] improves access and support for local women; it makes male peacekeepers more reflective and responsible; and it broadens the repertoire of skills and styles available within the mission, often with the effect of reducing conflict and confrontation. Gender mainstreaming is not just fair, it is beneficial.
>
> *(Cited in Rehn and Sirleaf 2002: 63)*

In 2000, the UN Security Council passed a resolution (Security Council Resolution 1325) mandating a review of the impact of armed conflict on women and the role of women in peace operations and conflict resolution. The review was released in 2002, entitled *Women, Peace and Security* (UN 2002). In his introduction to the report, UN Secretary General Kofi Annan noted that that 'women still form a minority of those who participate in peace and security negotiations, and receive less attention than men in post-conflict agreements, disarmament and reconstruction' (*ibid.*: ix). There is still a long way to go before the international community can fully realize the benefits of greater participation by women in UN peace operations and conflict resolution activities.

Key Points

- There has been a noticeable decline in the number of armed conflicts and battle deaths caused by conflicts. Factors contributing to this trend include rising economic interdependence among nations, the end of colonialism and the cold war, and the growing role of international institutions and the international community in peace operations.

- But the outlook is not all rosy. The world has experienced horrific acts of violence and genocide in recent years in places such as Congo, and new forms of violence may emerge. The growing number of weak or failing states, such as Iraq, Afghanistan, Burma, Nepal, Bangladesh, and Pakistan, poses a growing threat to human security.

- There is an interactive relationship between armed conflict and non-violent threats to human security such as poverty and disease. Wars and internal conflicts can lead to impoverishment, disease outbreaks, and environmental destruction. Conversely, poverty, inequality, and environmental degradation can lead to weakening and even collapse of states. Human security research should look not just at the direct and indirect consequences of conflict, but also the range of socio-economic, political, and ecological factors that contribute to conflict. Such an understanding of human security opens the way for reconciling the two conceptions of human security as freedom from fear and freedom from want.

- Women feature in armed conflicts both as victims and actors (in combat and support roles). Rape and other forms of sexual violence against them increasingly feature as an instrument of war and are now recognized as crimes against humanity. The international community is seeking ways to increase the participation of women in UN peace operations and conflict resolution functions.

Case Study Human security in Orissa, India (map: Figure 29.4)

Figure 29.4 Map of Orissa
Source: http://southasiarev.files.wordpress.com/2009/12/india-orissa-map-with-india1.jpg (accessed 15 August 2010)

Major disparities in **human security** may exist as much as *within* as *between* countries. A good example is Orissa in India.

Orissa (population: 29.7 million), located on the east coast of India, is (2008–9) the poorest state of the country. A total of 46.4 per cent of its people live below the poverty line (less than US$1 per day), compared to 27.5 per cent for the country as a whole. Life expectancy (2002–6) in Orissa is 59.6 years (the national average is 64.2), the infant mortality rate is the highest in India at 52 per 1,000 live births (2008, declining from 91 in 2001), and the literacy rate (2001) is low at 63.8 per cent (female literacy rate 50.5 per cent).

It is a paradox that Orissa remains so poor despite having an abundance of natural resources. It accounts for 32.9 per cent of India's iron ore, 50 per cent of its bauxite, 95 per cent of its nickel, 98 per cent of its chromite, and 24 per cent of its coal reserves. In 2009, Orissa had 45 steel projects representing more than US$45 billion in investment, with another US$10 billion in new aluminium projects.

Poverty in Orissa is overwhelmingly a rural phenomenon with significant regional differences *within* the state. Farmers or agricultural labourers constitute four out of five poor persons in the state. Its heavily forested interior districts remain extremely poor relative to the coastal areas.

Compared to other states of India, Orissa has not seen serious sectarian violence. Economic growth picked up during the past decade to around 10 per cent. But the interior regions of Orissa, along with the poorer regions of neighbouring states, have witnessed a Maoist (Naxalite) insurgency, inspired by extreme poverty, deprivation, and lack of economic opportunity. '[T]he Maoists claim to represent the dispossessed of Indian society, particularly the indigenous tribal groups, who suffer some of the country's highest rates of poverty, illiteracy and infant mortality' (*New York Times*, 31 October 2009) Maoists accuse the government of trying to disrupt their living and deprive them of their land in order to gain access to natural resources in the areas they inhabit. One large foreign investment scheme, a 52,000-crore steel project of South Korean multinational POSCO, faces opposition from local people who fear that it will displace them and disrupt their natural livelihood.

Human security in Orissa is also challenged by environmental degradation and recurring natural disasters. Since 1965 Orissa had experienced floods for 17 years, droughts for 19 years, and cyclones for seven years. From the early 1970s to 1996, its effective forest cover has declined from around 24 to 17 per cent.

The case of Orissa suggests, first, that **human security** needs to be studied not just at the national level, but also at subnational or local levels. Second, poverty is a major cause of conflict. Third, availability of natural resources is no guarantee of increased prosperity and stability. In the absence of measures to ensure human security, they may even enjoy an inverse relationship.

(Government of India 2009; UNDP 2004; Government of Orissa, 2007; Lepeska, 2008)

Promoting human security

The role of the international community

Because of the broad and contested nature of the idea of human security, it is difficult to evaluate policies undertaken by the international community that can be specifically regarded as human security measures. But the most important multilateral actions include the establishment of several War Crimes Tribunals, the International Criminal Court (ICC) and the Anti-Personnel Land Mines Treaty. The ICC was established on 1 July 2002 with its headquarters in The Hague, the Netherlands, although its proceedings may take place anywhere. It is a permanent institution with 'the power to exercise its jurisdiction over persons for the most serious crimes of international concern' (Rome Statute, Article 1). These crimes include genocide, crimes against humanity, war crimes, and the crime of aggression, although the Court would not exercise its jurisdiction over the crime of aggression until such time as the state parties agreed on a definition of the crime and set out the conditions under which it might be prosecuted. The ICC is a 'court of last resort'. It is 'complementary to national criminal jurisdictions', meaning that it can exercise its jurisdiction only when national courts are unwilling or unable to investigate or prosecute such crimes (Rome Statute, Article 1). The Court can only prosecute crimes that were committed on or after 1 July 2002, the date its founding treaty entered into force. Human security mechanisms such as the ICC and War Crimes Tribunals have been involved in the prosecution of some high-profile war criminals in the former Yugoslavia, Liberia, and Congo, including the former President of Yugoslavia, Slobodan Milošević (whose trial ended without a verdict after he was found dead in his cell in March 2006), and former Liberian President Charles Taylor.

The Convention on the Prohibition of the Use, Stockpiling, Production, and Transfer of Anti-Personnel Mines and on their Destruction, signed in Ottawa on 3–4 December 1997, bans the development, production, acquisition, stockpiling, transfer, and use of anti-personnel mines (Ottowa Treaty, Article 1, General Obligations, 1997). It also obliges signatories to destroy existing stockpiles. Among the countries that have yet to sign the treaty are the People's Republic of China, the Russian Federation, and the USA.

The surge in UN peacekeeping and peacebuilding operations has contributed to the decline in conflict and enhanced prospects for human security. The number of UN peacekeeping operations increased three-fold between the first forty years of the UN's founding and the twenty years since—from 13 to 47 missions (United Nations Peacekeeping website, UN n.d.). More recently, a UN Peacebuilding Commission was inaugurated in 2006. Its goal is to assist in post-conflict recovery and reconstruction, including institution-building and sustainable development, in countries emerging from conflict. The UN has also been centre stage in promoting the idea of humanitarian intervention, a central policy element of human security (see Ch. 31; see also International Commission on Intervention and State Sovereignty 2001). The concept of humanitarian intervention was endorsed by the report of the UN Secretary-General's High-Level Panel on Threats, Challenges and Change, *A More Secure World* (2004: 66, 106), the subsequent report by the Secretary General, entitled *In Larger Freedom* (UN March 2005), and finally by the UN Summit in September 2005.

UN Specialized Agencies play a crucial role in promoting human security. For example, the UN Development Programme and the World Health Organization (WHO) have been at the forefront of fighting poverty and disease respectively. Other UN agencies, such as the UN High Commissioner for Refugees (UNHCR), the UN Children's Fund (UNICEF), and the UN Development Fund for Women (UNIFEM), have played a central role in getting particular issues, such as refugees and the rights of children and women, on to the agenda for discussion, and in providing a platform for advocacy and action (MacFarlane and Khong 2006).

Non-governmental organizations contribute to human security in a number of ways: as a source of information and early warning about conflicts, providing a channel for relief operations, often being the first to do so in areas of conflict or natural disaster, and supporting government or UN-sponsored peacebuilding and rehabilitation missions. NGOs also play a central role in promoting sustainable development. A leading NGO with a human security mission is the International Committee of the Red Cross (ICRC). Established in Geneva, it has a unique authority based on the international humanitarian law of the Geneva Conventions to protect the lives and dignity of victims of war and internal violence, including the war-wounded, prisoners, refugees, civilians, and other non-combatants, and to provide them with

assistance. Other NGOs include Médecins Sans Frontières, emergency medical assistance), Save the Children
(protection of children), and Amnesty International
(human rights).

Challenges to human security promotion

Yet, whether viewed as freedom from fear or freedom
from want, the concept of human security has not
replaced national security. The *Human Development
Report* of 2005 estimates that the rich nations of the
world provide $10 to the military budget for every $1
they spend on aid. Moreover, the current global spending on HIV/AIDS, 'a disease that claims 3 million lives a
year, represents three day's worth of military spending'
(UNDP 2005: 8).

Why the continued importance of national/state security over human security? For developing countries,
state sovereignty and territorial integrity take precedence over security of the individual. Many countries in
the developing world are artificial nation-states, whose
boundaries were drawn arbitrarily by the colonial powers without regard for the actual ethnic composition or
historical linkages between peoples. State responses to
ethnic separatist movements (now conflated with terrorism), which are partly rooted in people's rejection of
colonial-imposed boundaries, have been accompanied
by the most egregious violations of human security by
governments. Moreover, many Third World states, as
well as China, remain under authoritarian rule. Human security is stymied by the lack of political space for
alternatives to state ideologies and restrictions on civil
liberties imposed by authoritarian regimes to ensure
their own survival, rather than providing security for
the their citizens.

In the developed as well as developing world, one
of the most powerful challenges to human security has
come from the war on terror (renamed by the Obama
administration as 'overseas contigency operation') led
by the USA in response to the 9/11 attacks. These have
revived the traditional emphasis of states on national
security (Suhrke 2004: 365). Although terrorists target
innocent civilians and thus threaten human security,
governments have used the war on terror to impose
restrictions on, and commit violations of, civil liberties.
The George W. Bush administration's questioning of the
applicability of the Geneva Conventions, the abandoning
of its commitments on the issue of torture in the context
of war in Iraq, and Russia's flouting of a wide range of
its international commitments (including the laws of
war, CSCE (Conference on Security and Cooperation
in Europe) and OCSE (Organization for Security and
Cooperation in Europe) commitments, as well as international and regional conventions on torture) in the
context of its war in Chechnya have further undermined
the agenda of human security.

> ## Key Points
>
> - The most important multilateral actions to date to
>   promote human security include the International
>   Criminal Court and the Anti-Personnel Land Mines Treaty.
>
> - UN agencies such as the UNHCR, UNICEF, and UNIFEM
>   have been crucial in addressing human security issues such
>   as refugees and the rights of children.
>
> - Canada and Japan are two of the leading countries that
>   have made human security a major part of their foreign
>   policy agenda. Their approach, however, shows the
>   contrast between the 'freedom from fear' and 'freedom
>   from want' conceptions of human security respectively.
>
> - Non-governmental organizations promote human security
>   by acting as a source of information and early warning
>   about conflicts, providing a channel for relief operations,
>   supporting government or UN-sponsored peacebuilding
>   and rehabilitation missions, and promoting sustainable
>   development.
>
> - The 9/11 attacks on the USA and the 'war on terror' have
>   revived the traditional state-centric approach to national
>   security at the expense of civil liberties and human
>   security, although the Obama administration has modified
>   important elements of its predecessor's strategic approach
>   to terrorism and promised greater respect for civil liberties
>   and international conventions.

Conclusion

The concept of human security reflects a number of
developments that have incrementally challenged the
traditional view of security as the protection of states
from military attack. What initially began as a rejection
of orthodox notions of economic growth in favour of
a broader notion of human development has been reinforced by new security threats such as genocides in
the Balkans and Africa, the Asian financial meltdown

of 1997, and the threat of global pandemics. The concept of human security represents an ongoing effort to put the individual at the centre of national and global security concerns while expanding our understanding of the range of challenges that can threaten individual safety and well-being, to encompass both armed conflict as well as social, economic, and ecological forces. To be sure, human security has a long way to go before being universally accepted as a conceptual framework or as a policy tool for national governments and the international community. The linkages between armed conflict, poverty, disease, and environmental stress are poorly understood and need clarification and elaboration. None the less, there can be little doubt that threats to human security, whether understood as freedom from fear or freedom from want, are real-world challenges which cannot be wished away or dismissed because of a lack of agreement over the concept and meaning of human security. Notwithstanding debates about the utility and scope of human security, there is increasing acceptance that the traditional notion of security, focusing on state sovereignty, will no longer suffice and that the international community must develop new responses to ensure the protection of people from transnational dangers in an era of globalization. The challenge for the international community is to find ways of promoting human security as a means of addressing a growing range of complex transnational dangers that have a much more destructive impact on the lives of people than conventional military threats to states.

Questions

1 What is human security? How is it different from the concept of national security?
2 Is redefining the concept of security to focus on the individual useful for analysis and for policy formulation?
3 Describe the main difference between the two conceptions of human security: 'freedom from fear' and 'freedom from want'. Are the two understandings irreconcilable?
4 Some studies show that the incidence of armed conflict in the world is in long-term decline. What are the reasons for this trend?
5 How do you link health with human security?
6 How are poverty and conflict interconnected?
7 What are the main areas of progress in the promotion of human security by the international community?
8 What are the major challenges to human security in Orissa, and what lessons do they suggest for the concept and policy application of human security?
9 What are the obstacles to human security promotion by the international community?
10 Why do we need to give special consideration to the suffering of women in conflict zones?

Further Reading

Acharya, A. (2001), 'Human Security: East Versus West', *International Journal*, 56(3): 442–60. Examines the debate between two conceptions of human security: 'freedom from fear' and 'freedom from want', with particular reference to Asia.
—— (2007), *Promoting human security: ethical, normative and educational Frameworks in South-East Asia* (Paris: UNESCO). Available from *unesdoc.unesco.org/images/0015/001518/151821E.pdf*. Pays specific attention to the human security implications of transnational threats, such as financial crises, pandemics, and natural disasters.
Burgess, P., and Taylor, O. (eds) (2004), 'What is Human Security?', *Security Dialogue*, 35 (September): 345–87. A round-table among scholars working on the area of human security who offer perspectives on the meaning, utility, and limitations of the concept.

Commission on Human Security (2003), *Human Security Now: Protecting and Empowering People* (New York: United Nations). This report, from a commission proposed by Japan and headed by Sadako Ogata of Japan and Amartya Sen of India, offers a broad conception and overview of human security, its meaning, and the challenges facing it, and recommends steps to promote human security.

Duffield, M. (2007), Development, Security and Unending War: Governing the World of Peoples (Cambridge: Polity Press). Traces the liberal genealogy of human security and cautions that a neo-liberal approach to human security amounts to empowering the state in the developmental process and perpetuating conflicts in the Third World.

Gough, I. (2004), *Insecurity and Welfare Regimes in Asia, Africa and Latin America: Social Policy in Development Contexts* (Cambridge: Cambridge University Press). A comparative study of social and economic welfare approaches to addressing human security challenges in the developing world.

Haq, M. (1995), *Reflections on Human Development* (Oxford: Oxford University Press). The book by the late Pakistani development economist, who played a pioneering role in the *Human Development Report*, outlines his thinking on human development and human security.

Matthew, R. A. (ed.) (2010), *Global Environmental Change and Human Security* (Cambridge, MA: MIT Press). A collection of essays focusing on the challenges to human security posed by environmental degradation and climate change. Issues covered include natural disasters, link between environmental change and violent conflict, equity, urban slums, sustainable development, and global health. Case studies include hurricane Katrina and Nepal and Latin America.

Tajbakhsh, S., and Chenoy, A. M. (2006), *Human Security: Concepts And Implications* (London: Routledge). A comprehensive introduction and overview, focusing on the conceptual debates and seeking to clarify the ambiguities of the concept. A valuable teaching tool.

United Nations Development Programme (1995), *Human Development Report 1994* (Oxford: Oxford University Press). The original source of the idea of human security.

Online Resource Centre

 Visit the Online Resource Centre that accompanies this book to access more learning resources on this chapter topic at www.oxfordtextbooks.co.uk/orc/baylis5e/

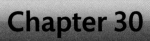
Chapter 30

Human rights

JACK DONNELLY

Reader's Guide

Thuggish dictators, like Robert Mugabe in Zimbabwe and Kim Jong-Il in North Korea, violently repressing their people and pushing many to the edge of starvation. Illegal detention, abuse, and torture of Muslims by Americans at Guantanamo Bay and in Afghanistan. Women not even allowed to drive a car, let alone vote, in Saudi Arabia. Indigenous peoples in Amazonia forced off their land to make way for mines, ranches, and farms. Men and women attacked with impunity on the streets in Brazil because of their sexual orientation. Workers with no viable choice but to labour in dangerous conditions for near-starvation wages. More than 20,000 children dying *each day* of preventable diseases. The list of gross and persistent systematic human rights violations goes on, and on, and on—and on.

Across the world, though, states and citizens regularly and forcefully speak out against such abuses. International action, as we shall see, can provide little direct help to most victims. It can, however, support local people in their struggles. Sometimes this is enough to produce real change. But even when it is not, international pressure helps to keep the issue alive and to build a foundation for future action. And, most people today agree, states and citizens have a duty not to turn a blind eye and silently tolerate systematic violations of human rights. This chapter examines the multilateral, bilateral, and transnational politics of human rights in contemporary international society, and looks at international human rights from four theoretical perspectives presented earlier in this book.

Introduction

Only seventy years ago, states throughout the world generally agreed that human rights were *not* a legitimate international concern. How a state treated its own nationals on its own territory was a protected exercise of sovereign rights, however morally repugnant those practices might be. Particular injustices that we today consider violations of human rights, such as slavery and the terms and conditions of industrial labour, were addressed internationally in the nineteenth and early twentieth centuries only as exceptional and discrete issues rather than as part of a larger set of human rights. Even the notoriously 'idealistic' Covenant of the League of Nations fails to mention human rights.

The end of the Second World War and growing awareness of the horrors of the Holocaust loosed a flood of governmental and civil society reflection and activity that culminated in the United Nations General Assembly adopting the Universal Declaration of Human Rights on 10 December 1948. (Most countries thus celebrate 10 December as Human Rights Day.) From this point on, human rights had a permanent place on international agendas, and our current global human rights regime began to emerge.

The global human rights regime

An **international regime** is conventionally defined as a set of principles, norms, rules, and decision-making procedures that states and other international actors accept as authoritative in an issue area (see Ch. 18). The global human rights regime is based on strong and widely accepted principles and norms but very weak mechanisms of international implementation. The result is a system of national implementation of international human rights.

International human rights norms

The *Charter of the United Nations*, signed in San Francisco on 26 June 1945, identified promoting respect for human rights as one of the principal objectives of the new organization. It also created a Commission on Human Rights, which became the focal point of what we today call the global human rights regime. (This role has been continued by its successor, the Human Rights Council, created by the United Nations in 2006.)

For its first two years, the principal work of the Commission was drafting the **Universal Declaration of Human Rights**, a succinct yet comprehensive list of internationally recognized human rights. **Civil and political rights** provide legal protections against abuse by the state and seek to ensure political participation for all citizens. They include rights such as equality before the law, protection against arbitrary arrest and detention, and freedoms of religion, speech, assembly, and political participation.

Economic, social, and cultural rights guarantee individuals access to essential goods and services, and seek to ensure equal social and cultural participation. Prominent examples include rights to food, housing, health care, education, and social insurance.

These two sets of rights are considered in international law to be *indivisible*. Rather than an optional list from which states may pick and choose, the Declaration holistically specifies minimum social and political conditions for a life of dignity in the contemporary world. Internationally recognized human rights are also *interdependent*. Each set strengthens the other and makes it more valuable; one without the other is much less than 'half a loaf'. International human rights are *universal* as well, applying equally to all people everywhere.

These rights have been further elaborated in a series of treaties, the most prominent of which are listed in Box 30.1. The six principal treaties (the two 1966 International Human Rights Covenants plus treaties on racial discrimination, discrimination against women, torture, and rights of the child) had, by late 2009, been ratified (accepted as legally binding) by, on average, 171 states, an impressive 87 per cent average ratification rate. Box 30.2 lists the rights recognized in the Universal Declaration and the International Human Rights Covenants, which (along with the Charter provisions on human rights) are often called the International Bill of Human Rights. For the purposes of international relations, 'human rights' means roughly this list of rights.

Box 30.1 Major international human rights treaties

	Date adopted	Entered into force	Number of parties (2009)	Supervisory committee	Individual complaints	Parties allowing complaints (2009)
International Covenant on Economic, Social and Cultural Rights	16 Dec 1966	3 Jan 1976	160	Committee on Economic, Social, and Cultural Rights	yes	not yet in force
International Covenant on Civil and Political Rights	16 Dec 1966	23 Mar 1976	165	Human Rights Committee	yes	113
International Convention on the Elimination of All Forms of Racial Discrimination	21 Dec 1965	12 Mar 1969	173	Committee on the Elimination of Racial Discrimination (CERD)	no	n.a.
Convention on the Elimination of All Forms of Discrimination against Women	18 Dec 1979	3 Sep 1981	186	Committee on the Elimination of Discrimination against Women (CEDAW)	yes	99
Convention against Torture and Other Cruel, Inhuman or Degrading Treatment or Punishment	10 Dec 1984	26 Jun 1987	146	Committee against Torture (CAT)	yes	64
Convention on the Rights of the Child	20 Nov 1989	2 Sep 1990	193	Committee on the Rights of the Child (CRC)	no	n.a.
International Convention on the Protection of the Rights of All Migrant Workers and Members of Their Families	18 Dec 1990	1 Jul 2003	42	Committee on Migrant Workers (CMW)	no	n.a.
Convention on the Rights of Persons with Disabilities	13 Dec 2006	3 May 2008	71	Committee on the Rights of Persons with Disabilities (CRPD)	yes	45
International Convention for the Protection of All Persons from Enforced Disappearance	20 Dec 2006	not yet in force	16	Committee on Enforced Disappearances (CED)	no	n.a.

Box 30.2 Rights recognized in the International Bill of Human Rights*

- Equality of rights without discrimination (Dl, D2, E2, E3, C2, C3)
- Life (D3, C6)
- Liberty and security of person (D3, C9)
- Protection against slavery (D4, C8)
- Protection against torture and cruel and inhuman punishment (D5, C7)
- Recognition as a person before the law (D6, C16)
- Equal protection of the law (D7, C14, C26)
- Access to legal remedies for rights violations (D8, C2)
- Protection against arbitrary arrest or detention (D9, C9)
- Hearing before an independent and impartial judiciary (D10, C14)
- Presumption of innocence (D11, C14)
- Protection against ex post facto laws (D11, CIS)
- Protection of privacy, family, and home (D12, C17)
- Freedom of movement and residence (D13, C12)
- Marry and found a family (D16, E10, C23)
- Freedom of thought, conscience, and religion (D18, C18)
- Freedom of opinion, expression, and the press (D19, C19)
- Freedom of assembly and association (D20, C21, C22)
- Political participation (D21, C25)
- Social security (D22, E9)

- Work, under favorable conditions (D23, E6, E7)
- Free trade unions (D23, E8, C22)
- Rest and leisure (D24, E7)
- Food, clothing, and housing (D25, E11)
- Health care and social services (D25, E12)
- Special protections for children (D25, E10, C24)
- Education (D26, E13, E14)
- Participation in cultural life (D27, E15)
- Self-determination of peoples (E1, C1)
- Seek asylum from persecution (D14)
- Nationality (D15)
- Property (D17)
- A social and international order needed to realize rights (D28)
- Humane treatment when detained or imprisoned (C10)
- Protection against debtor's prison (C11)
- Protection against arbitrary expulsion of aliens (C13)
- Protection against advocacy of racial or religious hatred (C20)
- Protection of minority culture (C27)

* The source of each right is indicated in parentheses, by document and article number. D = Universal Declaration of Human Rights. E = International Covenant on Economic, Social, and Cultural Rights. C = International Covenant on Civil and Political Rights.

Multilateral implementation mechanisms

Periodic state reports provide the principal mechanism of multilateral implementation of these international legal obligations. Supervisory committees—'treaty bodies' in the legal jargon—of independent experts receive and review state reports on national practice. Some treaties also include mechanisms for individual complaints (see Box 30.1). These multilateral 'implementation' and 'enforcement' procedures are, however, severely constrained.

State reports are publicly reviewed in a session where representatives of the reporting state address questions from the committee. Written supplemental answers and questions may ensue. Once this exchange of views and information has concluded, though, the review is complete. The treaty body has no authority to determine the extent of compliance, or even the adequacy of the state party's report or responses.

Individual complaint procedures are almost as modest. An 'opt-in' provision is required for individual complaints. Only about three-fifths of the parties to a convention typically opt in. And even when a complaint

makes it through the review process, the committee merely states its views as to whether there has been a violation. The state in question is legally free to treat those views as it sees fit.

The Human Rights Council has established a system of **universal periodic review**. Unfortunately, because the reviewers are states rather than independent experts, the typical review is both superficial and unrealistically laudatory.

More substantial work is carried out under country-specific and thematic 'special procedures'. Rapporteurs, experts, and working groups examine state practices on a wide variety of topics, including housing, arbitrary detention, education, extreme poverty, human rights defenders, contemporary forms of slavery, transnational corporations, and violence against women. Individual countries are also subject to special scrutiny. In 2009, Burundi, Cambodia, North Korea, Myanmar [Burma], the occupied Palestinian territories, Somalia, and Sudan were examined.

The International Criminal Court (ICC), created in 2002, is restricted to a very small range of rights and its activities touch few cases. As of the end of 2009, it had investigated situations in four African countries (Uganda, Democratic Republic of Congo, the Central African Republic, and Sudan), indicted fourteen people, taken five individuals into custody, and begun two trials. The symbolic value of ending of formal international legal impunity should not be underestimated. International trials can also help a country to confront and try to move beyond its past. But a guilty verdict provides only the most minimal remedy for victims—very few of whom can expect even that.

The regional multilateral picture is more varied. At one extreme, Asia lacks any regional or sub-regional human rights organization. (The Association of Southeast Asian States (ASEAN), however, is taking the first steps towards developing a sub-regional human rights mechanism.) At the other extreme, the members of the Council of Europe are subject to legally binding judgments by the very active and effective European Court of Human Rights. In between are the Inter-American regime, with a fairly strong commission and a weak court, and the African regional regime, where the African Commission on Human and Peoples' Rights is severely restricted in its powers and hamstrung by a deficient budget.

Evaluating multilateral mechanisms

Every individual helped certainly is a victory, as is every law that is modified and every administrative practice that is reformed in response to multilateral scrutiny. The aggregate enforcement impact of multilateral activities, however, is trivial when compared to the extent and range of international violations. They offer almost nothing directly to victims.

We have a system of national implementation of international human rights norms, with modest international oversight. The principal objective of most multilateral mechanisms is to develop critical yet constructive conversations that use international suasion to improve the human rights practice of particular violating states. Strong multilateral human rights procedures are a consequence, not a cause, of good national performance. Thus only in the European regional regime is there any substantial element of judicial enforcement.

Facilitating compliance

This, though, suggests that talk of 'enforcement' largely misses the nature of the multilateral contribution. Reports, reviews, complaints, and investigations aim principally to encourage, and help to facilitate, compliance with international norms. Conscientiously preparing a report to an international supervisory committee often provokes a useful review of national law and practice. And even weak international scrutiny can be of national political significance. Thus most rights-abusive regimes try to hide or deny their violations. This sense of shame, even among those whose behaviour seems shameless, is a powerful resource for human rights advocates.

States that are set on gross and systematic violations of human rights can, and regularly do, flout the global human rights regime. Multilateral actors lack the persuasive or coercive resources required to get dictators to put themselves out of business—although even the most recalcitrant regimes can sometimes be induced to make symbolic gestures that ease the suffering of at least some victims. States that are willing to improve their practices, however, can be nudged, cajoled, or induced in that direction, especially if the changes are relatively narrow and incremental. And such changes can provide modest but real benefits to thousands and sometimes even millions of people.

The impact of norms

International norms also have an independent impact.

Governments cannot legitimately deny obligations that they have voluntarily incurred by becoming parties to international human rights treaties. (If they try, they face the political costs of blatant hypocrisy.) Authoritative international human rights norms thus allow local human rights advocates to focus on how to protect and implement human rights, rather than debate whether the rights in question really are rights. They also protect local advocates from charges of being agents of alien ideologies or foreign cultural or religious traditions.

Authoritative norms similarly facilitate bilateral and transnational action. Target governments, having formally endorsed those standards themselves, are forced to rearguard efforts to deny the facts or make ad hoc appeals to 'emergency' justifications for violations.

The intrinsic force of legal norms should also be emphasized. Although 'rational actor' models have become popular in the social sciences, most states, like most people, are not simple calculators of material benefit. Rather, there is a strong, unthinking presumption of compliance, especially where international legal norms have been reproduced in national law. Ordinarily, states, like individuals, follow the law simply because it is the law.

The presumption of compliance is often overcome, typically after calculating the material benefits of violating the law. But in countries where an active civil society and democratic political participation allow for free advocacy to combat violations, there is a real possibility of forcing reluctant states back into the confines of rights-protective practices.

Key Points

- The International Bill of Human Rights provides an authoritative list of interdependent, indivisible, and universal human rights, covering a wide range of both civil and political rights and economic, social, and cultural rights. 'Human rights', for the purposes of international relations, means roughly this set of equal and inalienable universal rights.

- This extensive body of almost universally endorsed law is the most important contribution of the global human rights regime. These norms, independent of any supervisory mechanisms, help to empower human rights advocates and constrain government action.

- The global human rights regime is based on national implementation of international norms.

- Multilateral implementation mechanisms facilitate national compliance, primarily through mobilizing impartial public scrutiny that reminds states of their obligations and draws national and international attention to violations.

- Strong multilateral procedures are a consequence, not a cause, of good human rights practices.

The bilateral politics of human rights

Bilateral foreign policy—states interacting directly with other states—is the second principal mechanism of international action on behalf of human rights. Since the mid-1970s, more and more states have chosen to make human rights a regular part of their national foreign policy.

The evolution of bilateral human rights diplomacy

In the years following the adoption of the Universal Declaration, as the cold war deepened and spread, human rights were sidelined or cynically exploited for partisan political advantage by both the USA and the Soviet Union. In the mid-1970s, however, the cold war moved into a period of *détente* and human rights began to emerge again on the foreign policy agenda of the USA. Although the initial focus on emigration of Soviet Jews and the persecution of Soviet dissidents supported American cold war objectives, in 1975 the American Congress required consideration of human rights practices in making decisions to award foreign aid. In 1976, Jimmy Carter was elected President after campaigning on a promise to give human rights a significant place in American foreign policy.

The year 1977 marks a turning point in the international politics of human rights second in importance only to 1948 (the Universal Declaration) and 1989 (the end of the cold war). The Human Rights Committee, which supervises the implementation of the International Covenant on Civil and Political Rights, began its operation, symbolizing a more active multilateral embrace of human rights. Carter took office and set the USA on the path of verbally aggressive, if not always consistent or especially effective, international human rights advocacy. And Amnesty International won the Nobel Peace Prize, symbolizing the maturing of transnational human rights advocacy (the subject of the following section).

Many other countries also began explicitly including human rights among their national foreign policy objectives, beginning with the Netherlands in 1979. By the end of the cold war, human rights were explicitly included in the foreign policies of most Western states. None the less, throughout the 1970s and 1980s, stated human rights goals typically were subordinated to cold war objectives. US policy in Latin America was particularly rights-abusive (see Box 30.3).

With the collapse of the Soviet informal empire, and then the Soviet Union itself, a 'golden age' of human rights diplomacy began. Symbolic was the international response to the Tiananmen massacre in June 1989—and the continuation of significant sanctions against China over several more years (see Case Study). Increasingly aggressive international action against genocide became the signature of both bilateral and multilateral action in the 1990s, a topic considered in some detail in the following chapter. Many states also developed major programmes of civil society support, enhanced their

Box 30.3 US policy in Central and South America in the 1970s and 1980s

The Nixon and Ford administrations (1969–75, 1975–7) actively supported brutal military dictatorships in Chile, Argentina, and Uruguay. These governments, in addition to systematically violating the full range of internationally recognized human rights, perfected the practice of disappearances, the clandestine abduction of perceived opponents, who were typically tortured and often, especially in Argentina, murdered. President Jimmy Carter (1977–81) tried to put some distance between the USA and these dictatorships. The administration of Ronald Reagan (1981–9), however, reversed course and actively embraced these military *juntas* in the name of a shared struggle against communism. Only with the end of the cold war—or, in the case of Argentina, with the collapse of military rule for internal reasons in 1983—did the USA become an active and consistent supporter of democracy in the region.

In Central America as well, Carter's efforts to distance the USA from disreputable military and civilian dictatorships were reversed by the Reagan administration. In the mid-1980s, the USA provided massive military and political support to brutal governments in El Salvador and Guatemala that were butchering their own populations, at genocidal levels in Guatemala. At the same time, the USA waged a secret war and an aggressive political campaign against the democratically elected governmet of Nicaragua because of its socialist leanings.

These examples provide particularly striking evidence of the pattern of subordinating human rights to anti-communism during the cold war. Where a significant price had to be paid to pursue international human rights interests, the USA was rarely unwilling to shoulder that cost during the 1970s and 1980s, especially when cold war politics became involved. And although American hypocrisy was extreme, other Western states as well rarely made more than symbolic gestures on behalf of human rights before the end of the cold war. Non-Western states were rarely willing to do even that.

Case Study International responses to the Tiananmen Massacre

In the early morning of 4 June 1989, tanks rolled into Tiananmen Square in Beijing, putting a violent end to weeks of demonstrations that at times included over a million protestors. The ruling Communist Party, which earlier in the decade had launched a successful series of liberalizing economic reforms, proved itself willing to kill its own people on the streets in order to maintain absolute political control. (Later that autumn and winter, Eastern European governments and security forces, faced with a similar choice, chose instead to relinquish power.)

The Chinese government admits killing about two hundred unarmed civilians. Most independent estimates put the number at two to three times that in Beijing, with hundreds more killed elsewhere in the country (especially Chengdu). Tens of thousands were arrested, with many thousands more fleeing the country or going underground. Harsh treatment of detained protestors was the norm. Dozens, probably hundreds, were executed.

International responses were swift and harsh. On 5 June, the USA imposed an arms embargo, suspended high-level official contacts, and froze new aid. The European Community adopted similar sanctions on 27 June, one day after the World Bank froze $780 million in loans to China. Japan suspended its new five-year aid programme. The Group of Seven (G7) annual economic summit in Paris in July also condemned the massacre. And despite numerous small violations, sanctions were widely observed for at least a full year.

Countervailing economic and political interests, however, also played a central role. Japan and the USA illustrate the spectrum of bilateral responses.

Although most other states stopped official high-level contacts, in September 1989 a delegation from the Japanese Diet (parliament), led by Foreign Minister Ito Masayoshi, met Chinese leader Deng Xiaoping and other top officials. Three months later, Japan renewed cultural exchanges. Japanese authorities allowed Chinese embassy and consular officials to harass and intimidate Chinese students in Japan, some of whom were sent home against their will. And in July 1990, Japan unilaterally resumed foreign aid. At the end of the year, it announced a major new five-year $8 billion agreement to exchange oil and coal for technology and equipment. This not only signalled a return to business as usual but helped to buffer China from continuing Western sanctions.

The USA, by contrast, despite the growing economic and geopolitical significance of China, and the gradual erosion of international sanctions during the early 1990s, maintained major sanctions remained until May 1994. There was, however, considerable internal conflict and inconsistency. And as time wore on, it became harder and harder to justify continuing to punish China for something it did literally years earlier—particularly when such symbolic action had economic and political costs for the USA. None the less, five years of sanctions against a country as powerful as China is an unprecedented event of immense symbolic significance.

At the United Nations, China's power largely insulated it from criticism. The massacre was never the subject of a UN General

Assembly resolution. Even a mild resolution in the Commission on Human Rights was defeated in 1990. But in the early 1990s, Geneva, the home of the Commission, became the site of intensive diplomatic struggle. The fact that China engaged in an all-out diplomatic effort to avoid scrutiny of its practices suggests that we should not overly denigrate the significance of multilateral monitoring.

China lost access to billions of dollars of international aid and investment, which significantly slowed economic growth for about two years. It also responded to international pressure by making concessions on political and security issues, such as missile technology. Many individuals were released or had their conditions of detention improved in response to international pres-

sure. And the reactions of Chinese leaders and diplomats indicate that they were genuinely stung by international criticisms—which kept human rights issues alive despite the harsh crackdown in China.

In fact, China was forced to accept significant if subtle political changes. Although the government initially denied any abuses—the polite term used in China even today is 'the 4 June events'—they were soon forced to defend the facts of their behaviour, thus engaging the international human rights regime and admitting the legitimacy of human rights as an international issue. And these international responses helped to open spaces for discussion within China that began to be exploited later in the decade.

democratization initiatives, and much more closely integrated human rights into their development assistance programmes.

The events of 11 September 2001, and the ensuing American 'war on terror', marked another significant turning point. But despite overwrought American claims that 'everything changed' on 9/11, most of the progress of the 1980s and 1990s has been sustained.

War is never good for human rights. The 'war on terror' has been no exception. In a few prominent cases—Pakistan, Iraq, and Afghanistan—a dismal human rights situation has been produced by a combination of local forces and American support. But there have been as many successes as failures. For example, the democratic

norm remains robust in Latin America. Global data on human rights violations show more constancy than change and no evidence of major systematic backsliding (see Box 30.4).

There simply has not been the same wholesale sacrifice of human rights to anti-terrorism that there was to anti-communism during the cold war. The Bush administration, especially in its first term in office, did institute numerous rights-abusive practices: most notoriously, creating a concentration camp at Guantanamo to illegally hold 'enemy combatants'; secret 'renditions' of suspects to foreign countries where they were held illegally and tortured; and abuse and torture of detainees in American custody. All these practices, however, were

Box 30.4 Impact of the 'war on terror': Freedom House ratings of civil and political rights

Freedom House, a New-York-based NGO, publishes an annual *Freedom in the World* report. This provides the best and most consistent time series of data on civil and political rights, the rights that have been most directly affected by the 'war on terror.' Countries are rated as either 'free', 'partly free', or 'not free'.

The data indicate a clear progressive trend toward greater

freedom through the 1990s. But there has been no decline since 2001. Instances of backsliding have been counterbalanced by instances of progress. Although these gross evaluations may mask increased violations of particular rights, these data suggest no broad negative impact of the 'war on terror' on human rights at the global level.

	Free		Partly free		Not free	
1975 [158 countries]	40	25%	53	34%	65	41%
1985 [167 countries]	56	34%	56	34%	55	33%
1995 [191 countries]	76	40%	62	32%	53	28%
2001 [192 countries]	**85**	**44%**	**59**	**31%**	**48**	**25%**
2002 [192 countries]	89	46%	55	29%	48	25%
2003 [192 countries]	88	46%	55	29%	49	25%
2004 [192 countries]	89	46%	54	28%	49	26%
2005 [192 countries]	89	46%	58	30%	45	24%
2006 [193 countries]	90	47%	58	30%	45	23%
2007 [193 countries]	90	47%	60	31%	43	22%
2008 [193 countries]	89	46%	62	32%	42	22%

Source: http://www.freedomhouse.org/uploads/fiw09/CompHistData/CountryStatus&RatingsOverview1973-2009.pdf

dramatically curtailed, in response to both sustained internal political pressure and near-universal international opposition. And the Obama administration, in its first year of office, went a long way towards putting a definitive end to them (although Guantanamo remains open and new questions have been raised about detainees in Afghanistan).

Furthermore, except for traditional allies like Saudi Arabia and Pakistan, even the Bush administration was reluctant to embrace brutal dictators. Most notably, the USA sustained its sharp criticism of Uzbekistan following the massacre of several hundred civilians in Andijan in May 2005. The USA even accepted expulsion from Uzbekistan's Karshi-Khanabad air base later that year rather than mute its criticism. (By contrast, China, India, and Russia supported the violent crackdown on dissent.) The American response was particularly significant because Karshi-Khanabad was the principal support base for American operations in Afghanistan.

Human rights diplomacy thus enters the second decade of the twenty-first century in a relatively strong position. Human rights is almost universally embraced as not merely a legitimate but important—in some cases even essential—element of national foreign policy, in most Western and a growing number of non-Western countries. And as the early excesses of the 'war on terror' are increasingly recognized as such, there are considerable opportunities for continued modest progress.

Assessing bilateral action

Both the strengths and the weaknesses of bilateral action arise largely from the power and international political position of states.

Powerful states possess far more resources than multilateral human rights institutions. Although generally

prohibited from using force, states possess a considerable range of foreign policy options that at least some use more regularly and more aggressively than multilateral actors. Even many middle powers have the material and political resources necessary to effect significant change in a small number of targeted countries. The Netherlands, for example, has had a major impact on human rights in its former South American colony of Suriname.

Human rights, however, is but one of many national interests. Human rights are thus often sidelined in favour of other national interests. Sometimes they are even corrupted into a tool of partisan politics deployed to realize other ends. Multilateral actors are also subject to partisan inconsistency. Selective partisan attention, however, is a more severe problem among states.

Key Points

- In the mid-1970s, human rights began to emerge from its cold war slumber as an active concern of national foreign policies.

- In the 1990s, with human rights firmly entrenched on national foreign policy agendas and the cold war no longer interfering with the more consistent and aggressive pursuit of human rights objectives, more and more countries developed increasingly robust international human rights policies.

- The post-9/11 world has seen some prominent setbacks for both human rights and international human rights policies. In general, however, the progress of the 1980s and 1990s has been sustained.

- States often have more resources to bring to bear than multilateral actors. They also can act unilaterally, without the need for a wide-ranging consensus.

- States, however, are more constrained by competing foreign policy interests and much more likely to use human rights for narrow partisan purposes.

The non-governmental politics of human rights

States have been our focus so far, either directly in their bilateral foreign policy or collectively in international organizations. Non-state actors, however, are also important players in the international politics of human rights. Especially important has been the work of non-commercial groups that in IR are usually called non-governmental organizations (NGOs) (see Ch. 20).

NGOs as human rights advocates

Along with individuals, NGOs make up the sphere of 'civil society', the public political space that is neither the market nor the state. Civil society actors can operate either nationally or transnationally. ('Transnational' action is a label conventionally used for non-state actors, including businesses, operating across state boundaries.)

Transnational human rights NGOs, which go back at least to anti-slavery campaigners in the nineteenth century, have been especially important in spreading knowledge of human rights norms, especially to ordinary citizens, and publicizing the rights-abusive behaviour of states. National and transnational NGOs played an important role in getting human rights into the UN Charter. Since then, they have been a powerful force in spreading awareness of international human rights norms. Today, they are a central feature of the politics of human rights.

The best-known international human rights NGO is Amnesty International (AI), a London-based organization founded in 1961. Amnesty has over 2 million members and subscribers internationally, in over 150 countries. AI, however, is only the tip of the transnational human rights NGO iceberg. Prominent colleagues include Human Rights Watch, a New-York based research and advocacy organization; the Fédération internationale des droits de l'homme, founded in 1922, which serves as an umbrella organization for 155 human rights NGOs from all regions of the world; the International Commission of Jurists, a Geneva-based organization of legal advocates; London-based Minority Rights Group, the leading global advocate for disadvantaged ethnic, national, religious, linguistic, or cultural minorities worldwide; and ILGA, The International Lesbian, Gay, Bisexual, Trans and Intersex Association, a Brussels-based umbrella organization, founded in 1978, with nearly 700 national member groups. In addition, many transnational NGOs in related areas have included human rights centrally within their mission. Leading examples include British-based Oxfam International, whose work focuses on hunger; Médecins sans frontières, which provides health care in emergency situations; and US-based Catholic Relief Services, which is but one of many humanitarian aid and development organizations that has come to see its work in human rights terms.

Transnational human rights NGOs are dwarfed in number by tens of thousands of national groups. Like their transnational counterparts, some address human rights generally, others focus on particular rights, and still others incorporate human rights within broader mandates. Any attempt at an illustrative list, though, would be arbitrary and unrepresentative of the substantive diversity and geographical spread of such organizations.

The principal resources of NGO advocacy, both nationally and transnationally, are information and the energy of ordinary people. Traditional strategies have emphasized 'name and shame', the uncovering and dissemination of information about violations. (Amnesty's letter-writing campaigns are the iconic example.) The aim is both to embarrass offending governments and to mobilize citizens to pressure their own governments for external action on behalf of victims.

Leading NGOs have also developed sophisticated and effective lobbying operations. The case of the Netherlands is particularly striking. The Dutch section of Amnesty International has a membership of 300,000, out of a population of about 16.5 million (about 1.8 per cent of the population). This is roughly the same membership as the second of the two large Dutch trade union confederations (CNV), and one-quarter the membership of the largest labour confederation (FNV). This gives human rights advocates a powerful voice in influencing Dutch foreign policy. (For comparison, the National Rifle Association, which is often considered the most powerful lobbying group in the USA, has a membership of about 4.3 million, or about 1.4 per cent of the American population.)

Civil society advocacy, however, is deeply embedded in the system of sovereign states. Because implementation and enforcement of human rights is a state responsibility, NGOs, no less than states and international organizations, must usually act through, rather than around, states. Sometimes this means targeting rights-abusive states directly. Often the aim is to get foreign states to pressure target states. Increasingly, the approach involves a pincer movement of external and internal pressure.

When the target state has a relatively good human rights record and is subject to democratic accountability, or when the violations are especially egregious and the state feels vulnerable, such concerted national, transnational, and international action can have a significant impact. The overthrow of the dictatorial regime of Ferdinand Marcos in the Philippines in 1986, in a self-described exercise of 'people power' backed by international support, is a good example. More recently, we have seen a wave of civil-society-based 'coloured revolutions': the Rose Revolution in Georgia in 2003, the Orange Revolution in Ukraine in 2004, the Cedar Revolution in Lebanon, and the Tulip Revolution in Kyrgyzstan in 2005, and the Green protests in Iran in following the 2009 presidential election.

Assessing NGO advocacy

We should not idealize human rights NGOs. Some are largely ineffective expressions of good intentions. There are serious issues of political and financial account-ability. NGOs also lack both the power of states and the diplomatic stature of international organizations. And it must be admitted that the power of public opinion is limited and hard to pin down.

But NGOs have no other interests to distract them from advocacy. The best have developed reputations for accuracy and impartiality that serve as a major 'power' resource. Combined with the energy of interested individuals, the results often can be surprising. The single-minded non-partisan advocacy of human rights NGOs is an important check on the tendency of states to allow competing national interests and considerations of diplomatic discretion to mute human rights criticism. National and transnational NGOs have also been a major mechanism for spreading awareness of international

human rights norms and for mobilizing both elite and mass opinion.

> ### Key Points
>
> - NGOs, operating both nationally and transnationally, are the third major type of actor in the international politics of human rights.
> - Lacking the material power resources of states, NGOs are able to mobilize the political energies of civil society and, by acting with a single-minded focus on human rights, achieve results well beyond what one might expect from their modest material resources.
> - Especially effective are concerted efforts by civil society actors, states, and international organizations to pressure states both from inside and outside, in a variety of venues.

Human rights and IR theory

This section turns to four theoretical approaches examined in Part Two of this book, examining what these theories can tell us about human rights—and what human rights can tell us about IR theory.

Liberalism and human rights

Human rights—'natural rights'; 'the rights of man'—were first articulated by European liberals in the seventeenth and eighteenth centuries. Liberal natural rights played an important role in justifying revolutions in England, America, and France in 1689, 1776, and 1789. In the nineteenth century, many liberals, especially in Britain, rejected human rights in favour of utilitarianism, which defined social progress in terms of the greatest good for the greatest number rather than maximizing the enjoyment of individual rights. For the past century, though, most liberals have strongly endorsed human rights as the best mechanism for providing a life of autonomy, equality, and dignity for all citizens.

Chapter 6 presents liberalism as rooted in commitments to individual rights, popular or democratic sovereignty, property, and the market economy. If liberalism is defined in this way, internationally recognized human rights represent a critique of a 'liberal' overemphasis on property and markets, in favour of a broad and robust conception of economic and social rights, provided by a combination of market and state mechanisms. But the development of internationally recognized human rights is better understood as reflecting the changing character of liberalism.

In most countries liberals were central figures in introducing into national law and practice the economic and social rights that later came to be expressed in the Universal Declaration. Today most liberals reject the 'classical liberal' emphasis on property as reflective of partisan political views of an earlier era. And the Universal Declaration implicitly presents a model of politics that we typically call the liberal democratic welfare state; that is, a state based on individual rights, democratic accountability, and a mixed economy that provides a broad range of economic and social rights.

The historical role of liberalism, however, gives liberals no monopoly on human rights. Socialists have been major human rights advocates since the mid-nineteenth century. Even many conservatives supported the development of European welfare states, beginning with Chancellor Otto von Bismarck's crucial role in the early formation of the German welfare state. And today the human rights vision of a life of equality, autonomy, and dignity is justified and endorsed from a great variety of philosophical and political perspectives, both secular and religious. We thus have an international 'overlapping consensus' on human rights that is moral and cross-cultural, not merely legal.

Realism and human rights

Classical political realism (see Ch. 5) often stresses 'the national interest defined in terms of power', understood as a universal law of international politics. Human rights clearly reveals this notion to be a deeply problematic political prescription.

The national interest is whatever the nation is interested in. Rarely, if ever, is it reducible to power alone. And in fact many countries have decided that they are interested in devoting at least some small part of their attention and resources to the human rights of foreign nationals living abroad.

Just forty or fifty years ago, human rights was indeed typically considered to be a 'merely moral' concern; at best, a secondary 'add-on' to which decision-makers might turn after they had done the hard work of calculating 'real' interests. Over the past two or three decades, though, human rights have become no more or less real national interests than, say, economic interests or alliance interests in the foreign policy of a growing number of states. And such interests have become embedded in foreign policy with no more (or less) difficulty than other substantive policy interests.

Realism does usefully draw our attention to the fact that states in their foreign policies are principally concerned with the *national* interest. We expect foreign policy decision-makers to give the interests of their nationals special, usually even overriding, attention and consideration.

Furthermore, international human rights is but one of many foreign policy interests. Human rights advocates thus should not be surprised, and in some cases not even particularly critical, when human rights are subordinated to other foreign policy interests. Realists often provide useful reminders of the dangers of moralism and legalism in foreign policy.

Realism also usefully reminds us of the strong tendency of states to define their interests in narrowly egoistic and material terms. But once a state has decided to include human rights among its foreign policy objectives, the real work of balancing competing interests begins. What place should human rights have in the hierarchy of foreign policy objectives? How much is it worth to us to pursue this human rights objective here now? These are questions about which realism, or any other theory of international relations, has little to say. They are instead matters of inescapably contentious ethical and political judgement.

Social constructivism and human rights

Chapter 9 introduced social constructivism. We might describe the picture just offered as an account of the social construction of the national interest. The constructed nature of international human rights deserves emphasis. For example, the list of internationally recognized human rights has taken one of many possible forms. The same is true of the system of national rather than national implementation.

In the process, international society has been modestly but significantly reshaped. In particular, sovereignty and human rights have come to co-constitute one another.

Sovereignty has been a central practice of modern international society for more then three hundred years. The particular rights of sovereigns, however, have varied significantly, even dramatically. For example, at the turn of the twentieth century, states had an unquestioned and unlimited sovereign 'right of war.' After the Second World War, however, aggressive war came to be effectively outlawed. Today, control over borders is often seen as central to sovereignty. But just a hundred and fifty years ago, people moved freely across international borders without even the need for a passport.

States have long been prohibited by the rights of other sovereigns from certain mistreatments of foreign nationals temporarily on their territory. The law of war has for more than a century prohibited certain abuses of foreign nationals abroad. Over the past half-century, international human rights has imposed similar, and more extensive, restrictions on how states may treat their own nationals. The terms in which states and individuals interact has thus been reformulated, with significant implications for both national and international politics.

No less significantly, though, international human rights have been shaped by state sovereignty. We saw this above most strikingly in the principle of national implementation.

Particular processes of construction can also be seen in the lines we draw between human rights and related concepts and practices. Consider forcible humanitarian intervention against genocide. It is treated separately in the following chapter not only because of its substantive importance in post-cold-war international relations but because genocide is governed by a separate body of international law. The Universal Declaration and the International Human Rights Covenants do not mention genocide, which is instead addressed in a separate treaty (adopted by the UN General Assembly the day before the Universal Declaration). Genocide, war crimes, and human rights violations have been constructed as separate violations, each of which is associated with particular social, political, and legal practices.

More generally, it is crucial that we recognize that human rights do not provide a comprehensive account of justice or morality. And not all good things are matters of human rights. Consider security (see Ch. 14) and development. People who enjoy their human rights will be more secure, and perhaps more developed, than those who do not. But human rights are primarily about human *dignity*. (As the Covenants put it, 'these rights derive from the inherent dignity of the human person'.) Security and development fall far short of dignity—and, at the same time, extend well beyond human rights and human dignity.

Finally, human rights are not just abstract values but particular social practices to realize those values. Human rights *entitle* individuals to certain goods, services, opportunities, and protections, and authorize right-holders to claim—if necessary, to demand—those rights against society and the state. Human rights empower individuals to act, separately and collectively, on behalf of their rights. They make, and are the tools of, active citizens (rather than passive recipients of the beneficence of society or the state). And the embedding of human rights in the normative structure of contemporary international society contributes modestly but significantly to the ongoing project of making a world that more closely approximates the ideal of equal and active citizens making lives of dignity for themselves, their families, and their communities.

Critical perspectives on human rights

By whom and for whom have international human rights been constructed? These questions are posed by critical theory (see Ch. 8) and various poststructural and postcolonial approaches (see Chs 10 and 11).

Critical perspectives typically emphasize Western (or liberal, or market) hegemony, understood as a form of oppressive domination principally through ideas and values, backed secondarily by force. The standard critical story of human rights is that they were constructed by Western states and elites to spread Western economic and political power (and/or to reinforce the marginalization of women, minorities of all sorts, and the poor, both at home and abroad).

Western states have indeed been leading international proponents and domestic practitioners of internationally recognized human rights. But how much of the international spread of human rights reflects Western pressure

from above and how much reflects voluntary endorsement by Africans, Asians, and Latin Americans?

The spread of international human rights seems to have much more to do with voluntary demand from below than coercive imposition from above. Human rights have indeed often been forced on reluctant non-Western governments. But when people in Asia, Africa, and Latin America have been given the choice, they have consistently chosen human rights. And in country after country, citizens, believing themselves to hold universal human rights have demanded that their government respect those rights.

None the less, we need to be sensitive to the possibility that particular formulations of internationally recognized human rights may reflect Western or market bias. I actually doubt that there are more than a couple instances in the Universal Declaration. But whatever the answer, this question deserves careful and extensive investigation. The dangers of ideological self-delusion are real—and the tragic consequences are well illustrated by the (often apparently sincere) humanitarian justifications of the savageries of Western imperialism.

In addition, cultural arrogance and ignorance are evident in the human rights diplomacy of many states, especially the USA. For example, President Bill Clinton saw no problem in condemning Singapore for caning a young American who had vandalized hundreds of thousands of dollars of property while defending not merely capital punishment but the execution of juveniles and the mentally disabled in the USA.

Whatever the answers, the critical questions of how, by whom, and for whom international human rights have been constructed undeniably merit the most careful attention.

Key Points

- Human rights have been constructed internationally in a particular way, covering a particular range of recognized rights, distinguished in a particular way from related concepts and practices, with particular mechanisms of implementation and enforcement.

- These constructions reflect, like all social constructions, a particular perspective that privileges certain interests and values over others.

- Most states in the contemporary world have come to understand their national interest to include the fate of foreign nationals living abroad who are suffering gross and persistent systematic violations of their human rights.

Conclusion

A distinctive feature of contemporary international society—in sharp contrast to before the end of the Second World War—is the extensive body of international human rights law. How states treat their own citizens on their own territory is today unquestionably a legitimate matter of international concern.

The pursuit of such international human rights, however, continues to be restricted by rules on the use of force. Furthermore, the strong system of international norms is associated with a very weak system of international implementation. States retain near-exclusive rights and responsibilities for implementing internationally recognized human rights. Contemporary international society has constructed a system of national implementation of international human rights norms.

In this system, states continue to play a central, although by no means exclusive, role. International norms are constructed, largely consensually, in international and regional organizations. Transnational action helps to facilitate the spread of international human rights norms, mobilize external pressure on rights-abusive regimes, and support local human rights advocates. But international society, rather than world society, is the central reality in the international politics of human rights in the early twenty-first century. And globalization has only modestly strengthened the well-established pattern of combined multilateral, bilateral, and transnational action, which goes back to the very creation of human rights as an international issue area more than sixty years ago.

Questions

1 Is the system of national implementation of international human rights, all things considered, such a bad thing? Is there a *practical* alternative that might be more attractive?

2 What are the gaps in the global human rights regime? Is there a substantial dark side?

3 That something is socially constructed does not mean that it can be intentionally remade in a different way. In fact, the more deeply constructed a social practice is, the less likely it can be intentionally changed. How deep is the contemporary construction of international human rights? Where are the most likely sites for change?

4 In what ways has the world become a better place as a result of human rights having been introduced into the mainstream of international politics? In what ways worse?

5 States have traditionally been the sole duty-bearers of internationally recognized human rights. What are the attractions and shortcomings of assigning direct human rights responsibilities to businesses? Should transnational businesses be treated differently than national businesses?

6 If states are the principal mechanism by which citizens actually enjoy their human rights, and if, as many argue, globalization is undermining the state, is that likely to be a good or a bad thing for human rights? How can human rights be effectively implemented if the rights and powers of states are being eroded?

7 Are there major unexploited opportunities for regional action on behalf of human rights? Is there any other region ready to try to emulate Europe's system of regional enforcement of human rights?

8 This chapter has emphasized the independent *power* of norms. Is this emphasis warranted? What are the relative weights of normative and material power—authority and force—in international relations in general and the international relations of human rights in particular?

9 The chapter lists, in declining order of importance, 1948, 1989, 1977, and 2001 as major turning points in the international relations of human rights. Do you agree with this ranking? Are there other dates that deserve to be added to the list?

Further Reading

Brysk, A. (2009), *Global Good Samaritans: Human Rights as Foreign Policy* (Oxford: Oxford University Press). An up-to-date examination of the international human rights policies of 'caring' 'middle powers' Sweden, Canada, Costa Rica, the Netherlands, Japan, and South Africa.

Donnelly, J. (2003), *Universal Human Rights in Theory and Practice.* 2nd edn (Ithaca, NY: Cornell University Press). The standard scholarly work in the field, providing strong coverage of theoretical issues and debates over universality and relativity, with topical applications to issues of democracy, development, group rights, sexual minorities, and genocide.

Foot, R. (2000), *Rights Beyond Borders: The Global Community and the Struggle over Human Rights in China* (Oxford: Oxford University Press). A superb study of the full range of international reactions to the Tiananmen massacre.

Forsythe, D. P. (ed.) (2000), *Human Rights and Comparative Foreign Policy* (Tokyo: United Nations University Press). Although becoming a bit dated, the best comparative study of bilateral human rights politics, including especially good chapters on India, the Netherlands, the USA, and the UK.

—— (2006), *Human Rights in International Relations.* 2nd edn (Cambridge: Cambridge University Press). The best introductory book-length text available, covering the full range of international actors, with especially strong discussions of regional regimes, non-governmental organizations, and transnational corporations and human rights.

Hopgood, S. (2006), *Keepers of the Flame: Understanding Amnesty International* (Ithaca, NY: Cornell University Press). A thorough and absorbing history and analysis of the world's best-known human rights NGO.

Kennedy, D. (2004), *The Dark Sides of Virtue: Reassessing International Humanitarianism* (Princeton, NJ: Princeton University Press). A critical look at conceptual and practical shortcomings of human rights advocacy, focusing on adverse unintended consequences of well-meaning but often thoughtless advocates.

Liang-Fenton, D. (ed.) (2004), *Implementing U. S. Human Rights Policy: Agendas, Policies, and Practices* (Washington, DC: United States Institute of Peace Press). An excellent and wide-ranging set of case studies of US human rights policy towards Rwanda, Kenya, South Africa, China, Pakistan, South Korea, Bosnia, the USSR, El Salvador and Guatemala, Chile, Colombia, Turkey, and Egypt.

Sikkink, K. (2007), *Mixed Signals: U.S. Human Rights Policy and Latin America* (Ithaca, NY: Cornell University Press). An engaging study of the longest-running, and probably most fraught, regional human rights relationship, covering the entire post-Second World War period.

Walldorf, C. W. Jr (2008), *Just Politics: Human Rights and the Foreign Policy of Great Powers* (Ithaca, NY: Cornell University Press). Arguing against the conventional wisdom that human rights almost always lose out to power considerations, examines British and American decisions to break relations with rights-abusive allies.

Online Resource Centre

Visit the Online Resource Centre that accompanies this book to access more learning resources on this chapter topic at www.oxfordtextbooks.co.uk/orc/baylis5e/

Chapter 31

Humanitarian intervention in world politics

ALEX J. BELLAMY · NICHOLAS J. WHEELER

Reader's Guide

Non-intervention is commonly understood as the norm in international society, but should military intervention be permissible when governments massively violate the human rights of their citizens, are unable to prevent such violations, or if states have collapsed into civil war and anarchy? This is the guiding question addressed in this chapter. International law forbids the use of force except for purposes of self-defence and collective enforcement action authorized by the UN Security Council (UNSC). The challenge posed by humanitarian intervention is whether it also should be exempted from the general ban on the use of force. This chapter examines arguments for and against forcible humanitarian intervention and considers humanitarian intervention in the 1990s, the impact of the war on terror and the responsibility to protect.

Introduction

Humanitarian intervention poses a hard test for an international society built on principles of **sovereignty**, **non-intervention**, and the non-use of force. Immediately after the **Holocaust**, the **society of states** established laws prohibiting genocide, forbidding the mistreatment of civilians, and recognizing basic human rights. These humanitarian principles often conflict with principles of sovereignty and non-intervention. Sovereign **states** are expected to act as guardians of their citizens' **security**, but what happens if states behave as criminals towards their own people, treating sovereignty as a licence to kill? Should **tyrannical states** (Hoffmann 1995–6: 31) be recognized as legitimate members of **international society** and accorded the protection afforded by the non-intervention principle? Or, should states forfeit their sovereign rights and be exposed to legitimate intervention if they actively abuse or fail to protect their citizens? Related to this, what responsibilities do other states or **institutions** have to enforce human rights **norms** against governments that massively violate them?

Armed humanitarian intervention was not a legitimate practice during the **cold war** because states placed more value on sovereignty and **order** than on the enforcement of human rights. There was a significant shift of attitudes during the 1990s, especially among liberal democratic states, which led the way in pressing new humanitarian claims within international society. The UN Secretary General noted the extent of this change in a speech to the General Assembly in September 1999. Kofi Annan declared that there was a 'developing international norm' to forcibly protect civilians who were at risk from genocide and mass killing. The new norm was a weak one, however. At no time did the UN Security Council (UNSC) authorize forcible intervention against a fully functioning sovereign state, and intervention without UNSC authority remained controversial. States in the **global South** especially continued to worry that humanitarian intervention was a 'Trojan horse': rhetoric designed to legitimate the interference of the strong in the affairs of the weak.

At the same time, a group of liberal democratic states and **non-governmental organizations** (NGOs) attempted to build a consensus around the principle of the **responsibility to protect**. The responsibility to protect insists that states have primary responsibility for protecting their own citizens. However, if they are unwilling or unable to do so, the responsibility to end atrocities and mass killing is transferred to the wider 'international community'. The responsibility to protect was adopted by the UN General Assembly in a formal declaration at the **2005 UN World Summit**. Its advocates argue that it will play an important role in building consensus about humanitarian action while making it harder for states to **abuse** humanitarian justifications.

This chapter is divided into five sections. The first sets out the arguments for both a legal right and a moral duty of humanitarian intervention. The second section outlines objections to humanitarian intervention, including **realist**, legal, and moral objections. Next we consider the evolution of state practice during the 1990s, and in the post-**9/11** era. The final section focuses on the responsibility to protect.

The case for humanitarian intervention

In the first part, we explore the **legal** case for a right of humanitarian intervention, commonly labelled **counter-restrictionist**, and in the second part we discuss the **moral justification** for it.

The legal argument

The 'counter-restrictionist' case for a legal right of individual and collective humanitarian intervention rests on two claims: first, the **UN Charter** (1945) commits states to protecting fundamental human rights, and second, there is a right of humanitarian intervention in customary **international law**. Counter-restrictionists argue that human rights are just as important as peace and security in the UN Charter. The Charter's preamble and Articles 1(3), 55, and 56 all highlight the importance of human rights. Indeed, Article 1(3) identifies the protection of human rights as one of the principal purposes of the UN system. This has led counter-restrictionists to read a humanitarian exception to the ban on the use of force in the UN Charter. Michael Reisman (1985: 279–85) argued that given the human rights principles in the Charter, the UNSC should have taken armed action during the cold war against states that committed genocide and mass murder. The ongoing failure of the UNSC to fulfil this legal responsibility led him to assert that a legal exception to the ban on the use of force in Article 2(4) of the Charter should be created that would permit individual states to use force on humanitarian grounds. Likewise, some international lawyers (e.g. Damrosch 1991: 219) have argued that humanitarian intervention does not breach Article 2(4) because the article prohibits the use of force only against the 'political independence' and 'territorial integrity' of states, and humanitarian intervention does neither of these things.

Other counter-restrictionists admit that there is no legal basis for **unilateral humanitarian intervention** in the UN Charter, but argue that it is permitted by customary international law. For a **rule** to count as customary international law, states must claim that the practice has the status of law and actually engage in the activity. International lawyers describe this as *opinio juris*. Counter-restrictionists contend that the customary right to humanitarian intervention preceded the UN Charter, evidenced by the legal arguments offered to justify the British, French, and Russian intervention in Greece (1827) and US intervention in Cuba (1898). They also point to British and French references to customary international law to justify the creation of safe havens in Iraq (1991) and Kofi Annan's insistence that even unilateral intervention to halt the 1994 genocide in Rwanda would have been legitimate.

Critics say that these arguments exaggerate the extent of consensus about the rules governing the use of force, and their reading of the textual provisions of the UN Charter runs contrary to both majority international legal opinion (e.g. Brownlie 1974; Chesterman 2001) and the opinions expressed by its architects at the end of the Second World War.

The moral case

Many writers argue that, irrespective of what the law says, there is a moral duty to intervene to protect civilians from genocide and mass killing. They argue that **sovereignty** derives from a state's responsibility to protect its citizens; therefore when a state fails in its duty, it loses its sovereign rights (Tesón 2003: 93). Some point to the idea of **common humanity** to argue that all individuals have basic human rights and duties to uphold the rights of others (Caney 1997: 34). Others argue that today's globalized world is so integrated that massive human rights violations in one part of the world have an effect on every other part, creating moral obligations (Blair 1999). Some advocates of **just war theory** argue that the duty to offer charity to those in need is universal (Ramsey 2002: 35–6). A further variety of this argument insists that there is moral agreement between the world's major religions and ethical systems about a duty to prevent mass killing and punish the perpetrators (Lepard 2002).

There are problems with this perspective too. Granting states a moral permit to intervene opens the door to potential abuse: the use of humanitarian arguments to justify wars that are anything but. Furthermore, those who advance moral justifications for intervention run up against the problem of how bad a humanitarian crisis has to be before force can be used, and there is also the thorny issue of whether force should be used to prevent a humanitarian emergency from developing in the first place.

> ### Key Points
>
>
> - Counter-restrictionists argue in favour of a legal right of humanitarian intervention based on interpretations of the UN Charter and customary international law.
> - The claims for a moral duty of humanitarian intervention stem from the basic proposition that all individuals are entitled to a minimum level of protection from harm by virtue of their common humanity.

The case against humanitarian intervention

Seven key objections to humanitarian intervention have been advanced at various times by scholars, international lawyers, and policy-makers. These objections are not mutually exclusive, and can be found in the writings of realists, liberals, feminists, post-colonial theorists, and others, although these different theories afford different weight to each of the objections.

No basis for humanitarian intervention in international law

Restrictionist international lawyers insist that the common good is best preserved by maintaining a ban on any use of force not authorized by the UNSC. They argue that aside from the right of individual and collective self-defence enshrined in Article 51 of the UN Charter, there are no exceptions to Article 2(4). They also point to the fact that when states have acted unilaterally, they have chosen not to articulate a general right of humanitarian intervention. Interveners have typically claimed to be acting in self-defence (for instance, India's 1971 intervention in East Pakistan and Vietnam's 1978 intervention in Cambodia), have pointed to the 'implied authorization' of UNSC resolutions (for instance, the UK's justification for the 1999 intervention in Kosovo, and the US, UK and Australian justification for the 2003 invasion of Iraq), or have refrained from making legal arguments at all (for instance, the US justification for the Kosovo intervention).

States do not intervene for primarily humanitarian reasons

States almost always have mixed motives for intervening and are rarely prepared to sacrifice their own soldiers overseas unless they have self-interested reasons for doing so. For **realists** this means that genuine humanitarian intervention is imprudent because it does not serve the **national interest**. For other critics, it suggests that the powerful only intervene when it suits them to do so and that strategies of **intervention** are more likely to be guided by calculations of national interest than by what is best for the victims in whose name the intervention is ostensibly being carried out.

States are not allowed to risk the lives of their soldiers to save strangers

Realists not only argue that states do not intervene for humanitarian purposes; their **statist** paradigm also asserts that states *should not* behave in this way. Political leaders do not have the moral right to shed the blood of their own citizens on behalf of suffering foreigners. Bhikhu Parekh (1997: 56) encapsulates this position: 'citizens are the exclusive responsibility of their state, and their state is entirely their own business'. If a civil authority has broken down or is behaving in an appalling way towards its citizens, this is the responsibility of that state's citizens, and crucially of its political leaders.

The problem of abuse

In the absence of an impartial mechanism for deciding when humanitarian intervention is permissible, states might espouse humanitarian motives as a pretext to cover the pursuit of national self-interest (Franck and Rodley 1973). The classic case of **abuse** was Hitler's argument that it was necessary to invade Czechoslovakia to protect the 'life and liberty' of that country's German population. Creating a right of humanitarian intervention would only make it easier for the powerful to justify interfering in the affairs of the weak. Critics argue that a right to intervention would not create more 'genuine' humanitarian action because self-interest not sovereignty has traditionally been the main barrier to intervention. However, it would make the world a more dangerous place by giving states more ways of justifying force (Chesterman 2001).

Selectivity of response

States always apply principles of humanitarian intervention selectively, resulting in an inconsistency in policy. Because state behaviour is governed by what governments judge to be in their interest, they are selective about when they choose to intervene. The problem of selectivity arises when an agreed moral principle is at stake in more than one situation, but national interest dictates a divergence of responses. A good example of the **selectivity** of response is the argument that **NATO's** intervention in Kosovo could not have been driven by humanitarian concerns because the Alliance has done little to address the very much larger humanitarian catastrophe in Darfur. Selectivity of response is the problem of failing to treat like cases alike.

Disagreement about moral principles

Pluralist international society theory identifies an additional objection to humanitarian intervention, the problem of how to reach a consensus on what moral principles should underpin it. **Pluralism** is sensitive to human rights concerns but argues that humanitarian intervention should not be permitted in the face of disagreement about what constitutes extreme human rights violations. The concern is that in the absence of consensus on what principles should govern a right of humanitarian intervention, the most powerful states would be free to impose their own culturally determined moral values on weaker members of international society.

Intervention does not work

A final set of criticisms suggests that humanitarian intervention should be avoided because it is impossible for outsiders to impose human rights. Some **liberals** argue that states are established by the informed consent of their citizens. Thus, one of the foremost nineteenth-century liberal thinkers, John Stuart Mill (1973: 377–8), argued that **democracy** could be established only by a domestic struggle for liberty. Human rights cannot take root if they are imposed or enforced by outsiders. Mill argued that oppressed peoples should themselves overthrow tyrannical government. Others argue that humanitarian intervention can actually cause mass atrocities by encouraging dissatisfied groups to launch rebellions in the hope of provoking a disproportionate response from governments that will trigger external military intervention (Kuperman 2005, 2008). However, the validity of this theory has been seriously challenged (Western 2005).

Key Points

- States will not intervene for primarily humanitarian purposes.
- States should not place their citizens in harm's way in order to protect foreigners.
- A legal right of humanitarian intervention would be vulnerable to abuse as states employ humanitarian claims to cloak the pursuit of self-interest.
- States will apply principles of humanitarian intervention selectively.
- In the absence of consensus about what principles should guide humanitarian intervention, a right of humanitarian intervention would undermine international order.
- Humanitarian intervention will always be based on the cultural preferences of the powerful.

The 1990s: a golden era of humanitarian activism?

It has become common to describe the immediate post-cold war period as something of a 'golden era' for humanitarian activism (e.g. Weiss 2004: 136). There is no doubt that during the 1990s states began to contemplate intervention to protect imperilled strangers in distant lands. But the 1990s also saw the world stand aside in the face of mass atrocities in Rwanda and Srebrenica. This section tries to make sense of these developments. The analysis is divided into three parts: the place of humanitarian impulses in decisions to intervene; the legality and legitimacy of the interventions; and the effectiveness of these military interventions.

The role of humanitarian sentiments in decisions to intervene

In the case of northern Iraq in April 1991 and Somalia in December 1992, domestic public opinion played an important role in pressurizing policy-makers into using force for humanitarian purposes. With regard to the former, in the face of a massive refugee crisis caused by Saddam Hussein's oppression of the Kurds in the aftermath of the 1991 Gulf War, US, British, French, and Dutch military forces intervened to create protected 'safe havens' for the Kurdish people. Similarly, the US military intervention in Somalia in December 1992 was a response to sentiments of compassion on the part of US citizens. However, this sense of solidarity disappeared once the USA began sustaining casualties, indicating how capricious public opinion is.

By contrast, the French intervention in Rwanda in July 1994 seems to be an example of **abuse**. The French government emphasized the strictly humanitarian character of the operation, but this interpretation lacks credibility given the evidence that they were covertly pursuing national self-interest. France had propped up the one-party Hutu state for twenty years. The French were reportedly anxious to restore waning French influence in Africa, and were fearful that a Rwandan Patriotic Front (RPF) victory in French-speaking Rwanda would bring the country under the influence of anglophones. France therefore did not intervene until the latter stages of the genocide, which was ended primarily by the RPF's military victory, and gave safe passage to genocidaires into the neighbouring Democratic Republic of the Congo. French leaders may have been partly motivated by humanitarian sentiments, but this is a case of a state abusing the concept of humanitarian intervention since the primary purpose of the intervention was to protect French interests.

The moral question raised by French intervention is why international society failed to intervene when the genocide began in early April 1994. French intervention might have saved some lives, but it came far too late to halt the genocide, which killed some 800,000 people in a mere hundred days. There was no intervention for the simple reason that those with the military capability to stop the genocide were unwilling to sacrifice troops and resources to protect Rwandans. International solidarity in the face of genocide was limited to moral outrage and the provision of humanitarian aid.

If the French intervention in Rwanda can be criticized for being too little, too late, NATO's intervention in Kosovo in 1999 was criticized for being too much, too soon. At the beginning of the war, NATO said it was intervening to prevent a humanitarian catastrophe. Two arguments were adduced to support NATO's claim that the resort to force was justifiable. First, that Serbian actions in Kosovo had created a humanitarian emergency and breached international legal commitments. Second, that the Serbs were committing crimes against humanity and challenging **common humanity**. Closer analysis of the justifications articulated by Western leaders suggests that while humanitarianism may have provided the primary impulse for action, it was by no means the exclusive impulse, and the complexity of the motives of the interveners coloured the character of the intervention. Indeed, NATO was propelled into action by a mixture of humanitarian concern and self-interest gathered around three sets of issues. First, a fear that, left unchecked, Milošević's military and paramilitary forces would replicate the carnage of Bosnia. Second, a concern that protracted conflict in the southern Balkans would create a massive refugee crisis in Europe. Third, NATO governments were worried that if they failed to contain the crisis, it could spread and engulf the region (Bellamy 2002: 3). This supports the proposition that humanitarian intervention is nearly always prompted by mixed motives. However, this becomes a problem only if the non-humanitarian motives undermine the chances of achieving the humanitarian purposes.

How legal and legitimate were the interventions?

In contrast with state practice during the cold war, the interventions in northern Iraq, Somalia, Rwanda, and Kosovo were all justified in humanitarian terms by the intervening states. Justifying the use of force on humanitarian grounds remained hotly contested, with China, Russia, and members of the Non-Aligned Movement (NAM) defending a traditional interpretation of **state sovereignty**. However, this position became less tenable as the 1990s progressed, and by the end of the decade most states were prepared to accept that the UNSC was entitled to authorize armed humanitarian intervention. Thus many **peacekeeping** mandates passed by the UNSC since 2000 contain an instruction for international soldiers to protect endangered civilians, using force if necessary and prudent. Chapter VII of the Charter enables the UNSC to authorize military enforcement action only in cases where it finds a threat to 'international peace and security', first controversially employed for humanitarian intervention in northern Iraq (1991) and Somalia (1992). Since the early 1990s, the UNSC has expanded its list of what counts as a threat to the peace to include human suffering, the overthrow of democratic government, state failure, refugee movements, and ethnic cleansing (Wheeler 2000, 2003: 32–41).

NATO's intervention in Kosovo raised the question of how international society should treat intervention when a state, or in this case a group of states, decides to use force to alleviate human suffering without the explicit authorization of the Security Council. Although the UN did not expressly sanction NATO's use of force, the UNSC also chose not to condemn it. Russia tabled a draft UNSC resolution on 26 March 1999 condemning NATO's use of force and demanding an immediate halt to the bombing. Surprisingly, only Russia, China, and Namibia voted in favour, leading to a resounding defeat of the resolution. The UNSC's response to NATO's breach of the UN Charter's rules governing the use of force suggested that while it was not prepared to endorse unilateral humanitarian intervention, it was not necessarily going to condemn it either.

What emerges from post-cold war state practice is that Western states took the lead in advancing a new norm of armed humanitarian intervention. Although some states, notably Russia, China, India, and some members of the NAM remained very uneasy with this development, they reluctantly came to accept that military intervention authorized by the UNSC was justifiable in cases of genocide and mass killing. The best illustration of this is the fact that no member of the UNSC tried to oppose intervention in Rwanda to end the genocide on the grounds that this violated its sovereignty. Instead, the barrier to intervention was the lack of political will on the part of states to incur the costs and risks of armed intervention to save Rwandans. There were also important limits to the emerging norm: intervention outside the UN remained very controversial; the UNSC refrained from authorizing intervention against fully functioning states; and although it is inconceivable that any state would have complained about intervention in Rwanda, this was a uniquely horrible case with a rate of killing higher than that of the Holocaust.

Were the interventions successful?

Does the record of post-cold war interventions lend support to the proposition that the use of force can promote humanitarian values? Humanitarian outcomes might usefully be divided into short- and long-term outcomes. The former refer to the immediate alleviation of human suffering through the termination of genocide or mass murder and/or the delivery of humanitarian aid to civilians trapped in war zones. Long-term humanitarian outcomes focus on how far intervention addresses the underlying causes of human suffering by facilitating conflict resolution and the construction of viable polities.

'Operation Provide Comfort' in northern Iraq enjoyed initial success in dealing with the displacement problem and clearly saved lives. However, as the media spotlight began to shift elsewhere and public interest waned, so did the commitment of Western governments to protect the Kurds. While Western air forces continued to police a 'no-fly zone' over northern Iraq, the intervening states quickly handed over the running of the safe havens to what they knew was an ill-equipped and badly supported UN relief operation. This faced enormous problems owing to Iraqi hostility towards its Kurdish minority. Nevertheless, the Kurds were able to fashion a significant degree of autonomy in the 1990s, which has persisted since the 2003 US-led invasion.

Some commentators identify the initial US intervention in Somalia in the period between December 1992 and May 1993 as a successful humanitarian intervention. In terms of short-term success, the USA claims that it saved thousands of Somalis from starvation, although this is disputed (Weiss 1999: 82–7). What is not disputed is that the mission ended in disaster. This can be traced to the attempt by UNOSOM II (this UN force took over from the USA in May 1993 but its military missions were principally controlled by US commanders) to go beyond the initial US mission of famine relief to the disarmament of the warring factions and the provision of law and order. Suffering always has political causes, and the rationale behind the expanded mandate of UNOSOM II was to try to put in place a framework of political civility that would prevent a return to civil war and famine. However, this attempt to convert a short-term humanitarian outcome (famine relief) into the longer-term one of conflict resolution and reconstruction proved a failure.

The jury remains out on whether the international community can succeed in building a new multi-ethnic state in newly independent Kosovo. On the one hand, an improved security situation has enabled a marked decrease in the number of international soldiers and police deployed there, and there have been a number of successful elections and transitions of power. On the other hand, ethnic violence remains a feature of life, there is high unemployment, and Kosovo has become a haven for organized crime. Looking back, the NATO-led force that entered Kosovo at the end of Operation Allied Force succeeded in returning Kosovar Albanian refugees to their homes but failed to protect the Serbian community from reprisal attacks.

The conclusion that emerges from this brief overview is that forcible intervention in humanitarian crises is most likely to be a short-term palliative that does little to address the underlying political causes of the violence and suffering. It is for this reason that the International Commission on Intervention and State Sovereignty (ICISS) insisted that intervention was only one of three international responsibilities, the other two involving prevention and rebuilding.

Key Points

- The 1990s were described as a golden era of humanitarian activism because of a dramatic increase in the number of humanitarian interventions.

- Although some interventions were motivated by humanitarian concerns, others were not. Most interventions were prompted by mixed motives.

- The legality and legitimacy of humanitarian intervention remain hotly contested, but a norm of intervention authorized by the Security Council emerged in the 1990s.

- Interventions tended to be more successful in stopping immediate killing and less successful in building long-term peace.

Humanitarian intervention and the war on terror

What effect did the terrorist attacks on **11 September 2001** have on humanitarian intervention? Has the war on terror made it less likely that powerful states will use their militaries to save strangers by encouraging them to prioritize strategic advantage over human rights? There are two prominent perspectives on these questions.

The first is a sceptical position. It holds that since the 'war on terror' began, the USA and its allies have placed their own strategic interests ahead of concern for human rights, both overseas and at home. They became more willing to align themselves with repressive governments, such as Tajikistan and Sudan, that supported their anti-terror strategy (Ignatieff 2002). Moreover, commitments in Afghanistan and Iraq have stretched Western militaries, making governments less inclined to place additional burdens on their forces by adding new humanitarian missions. According to this view, the West has become less interested in supporting humanitarian endeavours (Bellamy and Williams 2009). Just as worrying is the fear that the USA and its allies are actually undermining the consensus on humanitarian intervention by abusing humanitarian principles in justifying their use of force.

The second perspective is more positive. It springs from the core premise that Western states will militarily intervene in humanitarian emergencies only if they believe that vital security interests are at stake. Afghanistan seemed to show that there is often a critical linkage between **failed states** and **terrorism**. Therefore some writers suggested that the war on terror provided the necessary strategic interests to motivate intervention that is defensible on grounds of both human rights and national security (Chesterman 2004). The Afghanistan experience might be seen as supporting this viewpoint, although important questions can be raised over whether military means have been properly calibrated to humanitarian ends since the intervention in October 2001 (Wheeler and Morris 2006). Moreover, the more recent experiences in relation to Iraq and Darfur suggest not only that the war on terror has fractured the fragile consensus over humanitarian intervention, but also that the problem of political will continues to bedevil effective humanitarian intervention, as it did over Rwanda.

Afghanistan

Although the US-led intervention in Afghanistan was a war of self-defence, the US President nevertheless felt the need to make a humanitarian argument to support his case. He told Afghans that 'the oppressed people of Afghanistan will know the generosity of America and its allies. As we strike military targets, we'll also drop food, medicine and supplies to the starving and suffering men and women and children of Afghanistan' (Bush 2001). The USA took steps to minimize non-combatant suffering in Afghanistan but at least two operational choices undermined the humanitarian credentials of the war. The first was the decision to rely heavily on intelligence provided by different Afghan factions for the identification of military targets. This reflected the US determination to reduce the risks to its own armed forces. But this decision left US forces open to manipulation by Afghans eager to settle scores with their rivals, resulting in a number of attacks where innocent civilians were killed. The second failure was Washington's refusal to contribute ground troops to the UN-mandated International Security Assistance Force (ISAF) and make a sustained contribution to rebuilding Afghanistan. The ISAF was initially confined to operating in Kabul and, even though it was later expanded, only relatively small 'reconstruction teams' were dispatched to other regional centres. In 2005, ISAF became primarily engaged with combating a resurgent Taliban. The relative neglect of post-intervention Afghanistan can be measured by the amount of resources committed to it. In 2004, the USA committed $18.4 billion of development spending to Iraq and a mere $1.77 billion to Afghanistan.

The fact that the USA and its allies felt it necessary to employ humanitarian arguments in this case highlights the extent to which this justification has become a legitimating basis for military intervention in the post-cold war world. However, the use of humanitarian language did not presage a new Western commitment to protecting civilians in need. In Afghanistan, the humanitarian impulse has been less important than political and strategic considerations, the protection of allied soldiers has been prioritized over the security of Afghans, and there has been insufficient commitment to post-conflict reconstruction (Wheeler 2003; Wheeler and Morris

2006). This lends credence to the sceptical view about humanitarian intervention in a post-9/11 world.

Iraq

The use of humanitarian arguments by the USA, the UK, and Australia to justify the invasion and occupation of Iraq posed a crucial challenge to the legitimacy of humanitarian intervention in international society. The Iraq War was primarily justified as one necessitated by the danger posed by Saddam Hussein's **weapons of mass destruction** (WMD). However, as the offending weapons became more elusive, those justifying the use of force to remove Saddam Hussein relied increasingly on humanitarian rationales. As criticism of the war mounted, President Bush and British Prime Minister Tony Blair frequently retorted that, regardless of WMD, the war was justifiable because 'Iraq is a better place'

without Saddam (see Cushman 2005). There are two important issues that stem from this. First, was the war in Iraq a legitimate humanitarian intervention? We cover the arguments for and against this proposition in the Case Study. Second, how was Iraq perceived by the **society of states**, and what effect has this case had on the emerging norm of humanitarian intervention?

Many commentators and politicians believe that the use of humanitarian justifications in relation to Iraq damaged the emerging norm of humanitarian intervention by highlighting the potential for the norm to be abused by the powerful to justify interfering in the affairs of the weak. Of course, many states were deeply sceptical about humanitarian intervention before Iraq, but there is evidence that some states that were initially supportive of humanitarian intervention have become less so as a result of the perceived misuse of humanitarian rationales over Iraq (Bellamy 2005: 39). A more subtle

Case Study Iraq—a humanitarian intervention?

The case for

The case for seeing Iraq as a legitimate humanitarian intervention came from a variety of sources, including liberals, neo-conservatives, and the left. We shall focus only on the **liberal** case, as put forward by Fernando Tesón (2005: 1–20; see also Cushman 2005). Tesón's case was predicated on four claims. First, the invasion of Iraq had as its purpose the ending of tyranny. According to Tesón, humanitarian intervention requires humanitarian intent, not humanitarian motive (like realists, Tesón believes that states will never act out of purely humanitarian motives). Even though the US-led coalition was not motivated by humanitarian impulses, it still had humanitarian intentions because only by overcoming tyranny and installing democracy would the threat posed by Iraq be removed. Second, Tesón insisted that the abuse of civilians by the Iraqi government was severe enough to warrant intervention, saying that it makes no sense to argue that intervention should be reserved for mass killing because that rule would prevent intervention in cases where oppression has become routine and exists over many years. Third, Tesón pointed to the fact that the

overwhelming majority of Iraqis welcomed the intervention as providing an important source of legitimacy. Finally, he argued that although UN authorization is preferable, the doctrine of humanitarian intervention permits unauthorized intervention, as in the case of Kosovo.

The case against

Opposition to this case came from an equally diverse range of people. Even some people who defend an expansive right to humanitarian intervention rejected the humanitarian case for invading Iraq. We shall focus on Terry Nardin's response to Tesón's argument (Nardin 2005: 21; see also Evans 2004; Wheeler and Morris 2006). Nardin argued that Tesón's case involved 'significant revision' of the traditional doctrine of humanitarian intervention. First, according to the traditional doctrine, intervention is permitted only by the commission of particular crimes (genocide, mass killing), not by the 'character' of the regime. As Nardin put it, 'humanitarian intervention aims to rescue the potential victims of massacre or some other crime against humanity by thwarting the violence against them' (2005: 22). Second, Nardin argued that Tesón's position overlooked international society's strong predisposition towards non-intervention. Third, he claimed that humanitarian intervention could only be justified if it was calculated to cause more good than harm. Iraq's current woes were foreseen. Finally, Nardin argues that Tesón's account misunderstood the place of humanitarian intervention in international society. Nardin argued that international society is based on rules of **coexistence** and that humanitarian intervention is a carefully calibrated exception to those rules. Tesón understands world politics as being based 'not on rules of coexistence but solely and directly on universal principles of morality and human rights' (2005: 23).

variant on this argument holds that while Iraq may not have damaged the norm itself, it has damaged the status of the USA and the UK as norm carriers, weakening the extent to which they are able to persuade others to agree to action in humanitarian crises (Bellamy 2005; Wheeler and Morris 2006). As Kenneth Roth of Human Rights Watch grimly predicted, as a consequence of the use of humanitarian justifications in relation to Iraq, 'it will be more difficult next time for us to call on military action when we need it to save potentially hundreds of thousands of lives' (Roth 2004: 2–3). Sadly, Roth's prediction was proved correct by the world's response to the humanitarian catastrophe in Darfur.

Darfur

In 2003–4, the Sudanese government and its 'janjaweed' militia embarked on what the UN has described as a 'reign of terror' in Darfur. At least 250,000 people have died and over two million people have been forced from their homes. Whilst the rate of killing declined significantly after 2004, largely because the perpetrators had achieved their goals, sporadic attacks on the civilian population persist and little progress has been made in returning the displaced. Despite this toll of human suffering, the world's response was limited to deploying an understaffed and underfunded African Union (AU) mission (AMIS) that proved incapable of protecting civilians from harm. This mission was replaced at the end of 2007 with a UN–AU hybrid operation (UNAMID), comprising mainly former AMIS personnel, which remains understaffed and lacks key equipment such as transport helicopters.

Why has the world's response been so tepid? Three sets of factors are at work. The first, which is emphasized by the British and US governments, is the lack of prudent options for military intervention to protect Darfurians. The Sudanese government has steadfastly refused to contemplate any non-African deployments in Darfur, so any armed intervention might be strongly resisted. In addition, intervention might make the Sudanese government close its ports to aid agencies, making it difficult to get life-saving assistance to the refugees. There are also worries that firm action in Darfur might ruin a peace settlement for Sudan's other civil war, which claimed two million lives over more than a decade. The second set of factors relates to persistent doubts about the legitimacy of humanitarian intervention. The idea of forcible Western intervention in Darfur is strongly opposed by Russia, China, the AU, and the NAM. Since the invasion of Iraq, many states have been keen to reaffirm the principle of

state sovereignty and are less willing than before to contemplate actions that violate this. Finally, the reluctance to act in Darfur demonstrates the continuing relevance of **statism**. Just as in Rwanda, Western governments do not want to sacrifice troops and treasure to stop one group of Africans killing another group—a consideration made more acute by the West's military overstretch caused by the war on terror. Furthermore, several of the great powers have self-interested reasons for not upsetting the Sudanese government: China has significant interests in Sudanese oil; Russia has a smaller oil interest but also sells arms to Sudan; and the USA is reluctant to weaken a potential ally in the war on terror. The enduring logic of statism means that these powers afford more weight to their interests than they do to the lives of Darfurians.

Overall, the sceptical position has proven more accurate than the optimistic one in relation to humanitarian intervention after 9/11. Humanitarian justifications are being used with greater frequency to justify a wide range of military operations, but the developing consensus on a new norm charted in the previous section has been set back by the perceived abuse of humanitarian claims in relation to Afghanistan and especially Iraq. Many governments, especially in the NAM, have reacted to this by reaffirming state sovereignty. This worrying development was manifested in international society's failure to prevent or end the humanitarian catastrophe in Darfur. Yet at the same time, the inroads that humanitarian concerns have made into the sovereign prerogatives of states can be seen in the agreement at the 2005 UN World Summit to the idea of the 'responsibility to protect'. The next section will explore how far this offers the basis for a new global consensus on the use of force to protect endangered peoples.

Key Points

- Optimists argued that 9/11 injected self-interest into humanitarian endeavours, making states more likely to intervene to halt human suffering.

- Sceptics worried that the war on terror would 'crowd out' humanitarianism and encourage powerful states to cloak self-interest with the veneer of humanitarian concern.

- There was a major debate about whether or not the war in Iraq could be justified as a legitimate humanitarian intervention.

- Iraq has made many states more wary of embracing a humanitarian exception to the rule of non-intervention.

- A combination of prudence and statism has contributed towards inactivity in the face of the humanitarian catastrophe in Darfur.

The Responsibility to Protect

The Responsibility to Protect, the 2001 report of the International Commission on Intervention and State Sovereignty (ICISS), attempted to resolve the tension between the competing claims of sovereignty and human rights by building a new consensus around the principles that should govern the protection of endangered peoples (see Evans 2008). The principle of responsibility to protect (R2P) was adopted by the UN General Assembly at the 2005 World Summit, a move described as a 'revolution ... in international affairs' by one commentator (Lindberg 2005). But what is R2P, how was it adopted, and what does it mean for the future of humanitarian intervention?

The Commission argued that states have the primary responsibility to protect their citizens. When they are unable or unwilling to do so, or when they deliberately terrorize their citizens, the 'the principle of non-intervention yields to the international responsibility to protect' (ICISS 2001: xi). The report broadens this responsibility to encompass not only the responsibility to react to humanitarian crises but also the responsibility to prevent such crises and the 'responsibility to rebuild' failed and tyrannical states. This reframing of the debate away from the question of whether states have a right of intervention towards the question of where responsibility rests for protecting endangered peoples formed the basis of an attempt to generate a new international political consensus supporting what the ICISS report calls 'intervention for human protection purposes' (*ibid.*: xiii).

To build an international consensus that would help prevent future Kosovos, the ICISS needed to make it more difficult for members of the UNSC to use the veto capriciously, but also make it harder for states to abuse humanitarian justifications. The principal device for achieving this goal was a set of criteria that governments and other observers could use to evaluate whether military intervention would be legitimate on humanitarian grounds. These criteria comprised 'just cause thresholds' (there must be large scale loss of life or ethnic cleansing, actual or apprehended), 'precautionary principles' (right intention, last resort, proportional means, reasonable prospects), 'right authority' (interventions should ideally be authorized by the UNSC, but if that is not possible interveners should seek a mandate from the UN General Assembly and, failing that, regional organizations),

and 'operational principles' (including, clear objectives, common approach, limited force, appropriate rules of engagement, and coordination with humanitarian agencies) (ICISS 2001: xii–xiii). The ICISS argued that if states committed to these principles, it would make it easier to build consensus on how to respond to humanitarian emergencies. On the one hand, it would be harder for states like China and Russia to oppose genuine humanitarian intervention because they would have committed themselves to the responsibility to protect in cases of large-scale killing and ethnic cleansing (the **thresholds** established by the ICISS that justify military intervention). On the other hand, it would be harder for states to abuse humanitarian justifications because it would be very difficult to satisfy these criteria in cases where there was not a compelling humanitarian rationale to act.

According to the ICISS, the UNSC has the primary responsibility to act during a humanitarian crisis. The report argued that if it failed to live up to this responsibility, there would be a danger that other states might choose to take the law into their own hands, with negative consequences for both order and justice. In cases where there is majority support for intervention in the UNSC (a resolution supporting intervention for humanitarian purposes has secured nine votes or more), but collective action is blocked by a veto, the ICISS suggested that states seek political support from the General Assembly. If it was not possible to secure a two-thirds majority in that body recommending military action (the legal basis of which would be highly dubious), the report even more tentatively suggested that intervention might still be justifiable if authorized by a relevant regional organizations (ICISS 2001: 75). This suggests a hierarchy of where responsibility lies, starting with the host state, then the UNSC, the General Assembly, regional organizations, coalitions of the willing, and finally individual states.

How, though, are we to persuade governments to abandon the statism that caused the world to stand aside in Rwanda and, more recently, Darfur? The ICISS had an answer to this, too. A commitment to **just cause thresholds** would create expectations among domestic publics about when their governments ought to act to save imperilled people. Thus, in cases of mass killing and ethnic cleansing, governments would be put under pressure to act because they had already committed in principle to doing so.

Although the ICISS marked a bold and important step towards building consensus, there are at least three important problems with the logic that it employed.

Agreement on criteria does not guarantee agreement on action in real cases

States might agree on what criteria to use in making judgements about humanitarian intervention, but the application of the criteria to real cases is always open to interpretation. Skilled lawyers and diplomats will use the criteria to make convincing arguments both for and against particular interventions, as they did in the recent case of Darfur (Bellamy 2005). In 2005, UNSC members argued about whether or not the Sudanese government had indeed proven itself 'unable and unwilling' to protect its people. Without an authoritative judge to determine such matters, the criteria can only provide a language for argument and discussion. They cannot resolve differences of opinion.

The criteria are open to manipulation by powerful actors

Although criteria reduce the dangers of abuse by establishing the parameters within which justifying arguments have to be framed, the way the facts are interpreted and the arguments presented are inevitably shaped by power politics. Moreover, the interpretations of powerful states with the capacity to reward and punish others are likely to carry more weight in the deliberations of governments than the arguments of those who lack such sticks and carrots.

Assumes that governments can be persuaded to act

Translating R2P from the ideal into reality rests on the notion that governments can be shamed into acting to end genocide, mass killing, and large-scale ethnic cleansing by moral pressure from other governments, their own citizens, and wider world public opinion. There are reasons to doubt that these pressures can really be so effective. Imagine if there had been an ICISS report in early 1994. Would New Zealand, as President of the UNSC for April (the presidency rotates each month between the members of the UNSC), have been able to 'shame' the Clinton administration into intervening in Rwanda? If this logic holds, why were major public campaigns such as the Save Darfur Coalition unable to persuade their

governments to act more effectively? Public opinion can only galvanize action when governments themselves are already predisposed towards taking it. Sadly, few citizens change the way they vote because their government chooses not to intervene to save foreigners.

R2P Adopted by World Governments

In 2005, the UN World Summit adopted a declaration committing all 191 member states to the principle of the responsibility to protect (R2P) (see Box 31.1). This commitment was subsequently reaffirmed by the UNSC in 2006 (Resolution 1674) and 2009 (Resolution 1819). Some lauded it as a major breakthrough, while others argued that the ICISS report's findings had been watered down to such an extent that R2P would not, in practice, afford new protections to imperilled peoples.

As a result of doubts held by many states, significant changes had to be made to the draft document to persuade states to adopt the principle of the responsibility to protect. In particular, the proposal to include criteria governing the use of force was dropped and it was agreed that **responsibility to protect intervention**

> ### Box 31.1 Paragraphs 138 and 139 of the 2005 World Summit Outcome Document
>
> 138. Each individual state has the responsibility to protect its populations from genocide, war crimes, ethnic cleansing and crimes against humanity. This responsibility entails the prevention of such crimes, including their incitement, through appropriate and necessary means. We accept that responsibility and will act in accordance with it. The international community should, as appropriate, encourage and help States to exercise this responsibility and support the United Nations in establishing an early warning capability.
>
> 139. The international community, through the United Nations, also has the responsibility to use appropriate diplomatic, humanitarian and other peaceful means, in accordance with Chapters VI and VIII of the Charter of the United Nations, to help protect populations from war crimes, ethnic cleansing and crimes against humanity. In this context, we are prepared to take collective action, in a timely and decisive manner, through the Security Council, in accordance with the Charter, including Chapter VII, on a case-by-case basis and in **cooperation** with relevant regional organizations as appropriate, should peaceful means be inadequate and national authorities are manifestly failing to protect their populations from genocide, war crimes, ethnic cleansing and crimes against humanity.

required express UNSC authorization. This closed down the possibility of appealing to other bodies even if the will of a majority of Council members was blocked by one or more of the P-5 exercising the veto. Although momentous in that this was the first time that the society of states had formally declared that sovereignty might sometimes give way to concerns about human rights, as agreed by member states, the R2P is best understood as a codification of the humanitarian intervention norm that had developed in the 1990s.

As agreed by international society, R2P's primary innovation therefore lay not in what it said about humanitarian intervention but in how it conceptualized intervention as part of a broader international regime for protecting imperilled populations. In a landmark report released in 2009, the UN Secretary General, Ban Ki-moon, argued that R2P comprised three equally weighted and non-sequential pillars (Box 31.2). He also

outlined a range of reforms and strategies that states could use to implement this agenda. These included: signing and implementing international human rights, humanitarian and refugee law; strengthening domestic human rights and rule of law; strengthening the capacity of the UN and regional organizations to utilize diplomacy to prevent crises from escalating; building international society's capacity to give early warning of genocide and mass atrocities; making better use of targeted sanctions; and strengthening the capacity of peace operations to protect civilians. If this agenda were indeed implemented, there is good reason to think that this would help reduce the frequency of genocide and mass atrocities through prevention, increase the measures short of force that international society might use to protect endangered populations, improve international society's ability to save strangers and—possibly—make it easier to forge consensus in cases where all this fails to stem mass killing. At a plenary debate of the General Assembly in July 2009, an overwhelming majority of states endorsed the Secretary-General's approach but it is too early to tell whether rhetorical endorsement will translate into the political will to reform institutions and change behaviour.

Box 31.2 The three pillars of R2P

Pillar one: the responsibility of the state to protect its population from genocide, war crimes, ethnic cleansing and crimes against humanity, and from their incitement. This pillar, the Secretary-General described as the 'bedrock' of the R2P and, in addition to the specific commitments to R2P, derives from the nature of sovereignty itself and the pre-existing legal obligations of states.

Pillar two: the international community's responsibility to assist the state to fulfill its responsibility to protect, particularly by helping them to tackle the causes of genocide and mass atrocities, build the capacity to prevent these crimes, and address problems before they escalate in the commission of the crimes.

Pillar three: in situations where a state has manifestly failed to protect its population from the four crimes, the international community's responsibility to take timely and decisive action through peaceful diplomatic and humanitarian means and, if that fails, other more forceful means in a manner consistent with Chapters VI (pacific measures), VII (enforcement measures) and VIII (regional arrangements) of the UN Charter (para. 139).

(Source: Ban 2009: para 11 (a, b, c))

Key Points

- The 'responsibility to protect' switches the focus from a debate about sovereignty versus human rights to a discussion of how best to protect endangered peoples.
- The ICISS report attempted to move the norm of humanitarian intervention forward by forging a new consensus around the criteria for judging when armed intervention for humanitarian purposes was justifiable.
- There are good reasons to think that criteria alone will not galvanize action or consensus in difficult cases.
- The responsibility to protect was adopted by states at the 2005 World Summit, but in a significantly revised form that builds the principle around three 'pillars'.
- In 2009, states largely endorsed the Secretary-General's approach to implementing R2P, but it remains to be seen whether this will be translated into practice.

Conclusion

Globalization is bringing nearer Kant's vision of moral interconnectedness, but as the Rwandan genocide and global inaction over Darfur so brutally demonstrate, this growth in cosmopolitan sensibilities has not yet

been translated into a global consensus on **forcible humanitarian intervention**. Western publics are increasingly sensitized to the human suffering of others, but this media-nurtured sense of compassion is very selective in its response to human suffering. The media spotlight ensured that governments directed their humanitarian energies to the crises in northern Iraq, Somalia, and Bosnia, but during the same period millions perished in the brutal civil wars in Angola, Liberia, and the Democratic Republic of Congo.

Each case has to be judged on its merits, but as the examples of Somalia and perhaps Kosovo demonstrate, interventions that begin with humanitarian credentials can all too easily degenerate into 'a range of policies and activities which go beyond, or even conflict with, the label "humanitarian"' (Roberts 1993: 448). A further fundamental problem with a strategy of forcible humanitarian intervention concerns the so-called 'body-bag' factor. Is domestic public opinion, especially in Western states, prepared to see their military personnel die in the cause of humanitarian intervention? A striking feature of all post-cold war humanitarian interventions is that no Western government has yet chosen to risk its military personnel in defence of human rights where there was a significant risk of casualties from the outset.

Since 9/11, Western states have expressed humanitarian sentiments in relation to many different types of war. While this indicates the growing power of humanitarianism, the downside of this is that states might abuse humanitarian rationales in justifying their use of force, while only *selectively* responding to humanitarian crises in strategically important areas. For many in the developing world, this is precisely what the USA and the UK have done in Iraq, damaging rather than furthering the humanitarian agenda.

The chapter ended by considering R2P, which has sought to reshape the terms of the debate between supporters and opponents of humanitarian intervention. The concept has certainly helped change the political language used to describe and debate humanitarian intervention, and its adoption at the UN World Summit was an important milestone. Although R2P promises to reconceptualize how international society relates to genocide and mass atrocities, it is a long-term agenda that is unlikely to generate new political will on the part of the major states to incur the costs and risks of saving strangers in the near future.

Questions

1 How far is the use of force the defining characteristic of a humanitarian intervention?
2 How important are motives, intentions, means, and outcomes in judging the humanitarian credentials of an intervention?
3 How persuasive is the counter-restrictionist case for a legal right of humanitarian intervention?
4 Should considerations of international order always be privileged over concerns of individual justice in the society of states?
5 Why has the society of states failed to arrive at a collective consensus on what moral principles should underpin a right of humanitarian intervention?
6 Is there a new norm of legitimate humanitarian intervention?
7 Was the 2003 invasion of Iraq a legitimate humanitarian intervention?
8 To what extent does the 'responsibility to protect' principle resolve some of the political problems associated with humanitarian intervention?
9 Is the UN Secretary-General's approach to implementing R2P likely to strengthen the protection of civilians from genocide and mass atrocities?
10 How far is military force an effective instrument for the promotion of humanitarian values?

Further Reading

Bellamy, A. J. (2009), *Responsibility to Protect: The Global Effort to End Mass Atrocities* (Cambridge: Polity). Provides an assessment of the evolution of R2P, including the debates surrounding its adoption in 2005, and evaluates the implementing of R2P in relation to the prevention of mass atrocities, international reactions to them, and rebuilding afterwards.

Chesterman, S. (2001), *Just War or Just Peace? Humanitarian Intervention in International Law* (Oxford: Oxford University Press). An excellent analysis of the legality of humanitarian intervention that strongly supports the 'restrictionist' view.

Evans, G. (2008), *The Responsibility to Protect: Ending Mass Atrocity Crimes Once and for All* (Washington, DC: The Brookings Institution). A book-length defence of R2P from one of its principal supporters.

Hehir, A. (2009), *Humanitarian Intervention: An Introduction* (Basingstoke: Palgrave Macmillan). A very useful overview of the various debates summarized in this chapter.

Holzgrefe, J. F., and Keohane R. (eds) (2002), *Humanitarian Intervention: Ethical, Legal and Political Dilemmas* (Cambridge: Cambridge University Press). A superb edited collection that explores the practice of humanitarian intervention from the perspectives of moral philosophy, international law, and political practice.

Weiss, T. G. (2007), *Humanitarian Intervention: Ideas in Action* (Cambridge: Polity Press). Provides a compelling introduction to the theory and practice of humanitarian intervention and covers the responsibility to protect.

Welsh, J. (ed.) (2004), *Humanitarian Intervention and International Relations* (Oxford: Oxford University Press). Another first-rate edited volume that brings together International Relations theorists and practitioners who have been involved in intervention in the past decade. It includes a chapter by Wheeler that analyses the development of the humanitarian intervention norm into the twenty-first century.

Wheeler, N. J. (2000), *Saving Strangers: Humanitarian Intervention in International Society* (Oxford: Oxford University Press). Offers a new way of evaluating humanitarian interventions and considers a wide range of interventions in the cold war and post-cold war eras.

Online Resource Centre

Visit the Online Resource Centre that accompanies this book to access more learning resources on this chapter topic at www.oxfordtextbooks.co.uk/orc/baylis5e/

Part Five

Globalization in the future

In this final part of the book we want to offer you some reflections on the impact of globalization for world politics in the new millennium. We thought long and hard about whether the editors should write a conclusion to the previous editions of this book, given that some readers wrote to us to suggest that there should be a concluding section. We eventually decided that it was impossible to do this given all the very different perspectives on globalization found in the preceding chapters. This is an approach we have continued in this edition. Our intention all along has been to show you that there are very distinct ways of looking at globalization, and writing a conclusion would have meant taking sides on which of these we preferred: we think that this is something that you should do. Therefore we asked two scholars to contribute chapters in this part, and, although neither of them is intended as a conclusion, together they outline the main questions concerning the current nature of world politics. Andrew Linklater's chapter examines the forms of political community that are emerging under globalization, while Ian Clark's chapter looks at the question of what kind of order exists in the post-cold war period. We have two main aims for this part of the book: **first**, we want to end by returning to world politics, rather than international politics, by asking about the relationship between political community and globalization; **second**, we want to summarize the main arguments about the nature of world politics since the cold war, to bring the historical story up to date, so to speak. Each of these chapters problematizes the traditional international politics notion of hermetically sealed states acting within a states system. Above all, we want to leave you with a series of deep questions about the effect of globalization both on the state and on world politics. Is the form of political community found in the globalized world different from that found before? Is the state still the unit for political community, or does globalization make cosmopolitan politics more possible? Is there order in the post-cold war world? Is there much difference between the form of order found in the contemporary period and that found in the cold war? Does globalization help or hinder the creation of a more just, or a more equal, world order? We hope that these two chapters will raise a series of questions that will allow you to come to judgements about the overall impact of globalization on politics in the world.

ORC in the spotlight: further reading

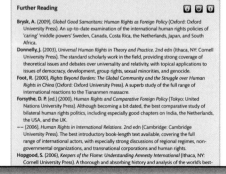

Reading around the subject is essential. Combine the end of chapter further reading suggestions with an online list of journals, weblinks and up to date news from Oxford News Now. Visit www.oxfordtextbooks.co.uk/orc/baylis5e/ for more information.

Chapter 32

Globalization and the transformation of political community

ANDREW LINKLATER

Reader's Guide

Realist approaches to international relations focus on competition and conflict between political communities. They argue that international anarchy leads to unending struggles for security and power. In the main, realists believe that separate states will survive well into the future. Critics maintain that important challenges to traditional conceptions of political community have emerged in recent times. Globalization has led scholars and activists to question the nation-state's capacity to solve global problems such as environmental devastation. It has led many to defend cosmopolitan responses to those problems. Many nation-states are challenged by national or ethnic movements that argue that they possess little more than 'second-class citizenship'. Some of those groups have tried to secede from existing states, while others have aimed to modify existing institutions in order to secure public recognition of group rights. This chapter explains how the nation-state became the dominant political community in modern times. It analyses new conceptions of community and citizenship that have appeared over the last two decades; it asks how far the nation-state is likely to endure as the main object of political loyalty for the foreseeable future, and how far it is likely to change as a result of rising levels of human **interconnectedness**.

Introduction: what is a political community?

Many different types of **community** exist in the modern era: local communities such as neighbourhood groups, associations such as sovereign states, transnational movements such as scientific associations or **international non-governmental organizations** (INGOs), and the 'virtual communities' that have flourished in an age of instant global communication. Each of those communities has its distinctive pattern of **cooperation**. Each depends on a powerful sense of emotional identification with the group and on the willingness to make some personal sacrifices for a more general good. Such dispositions are central to those who see themselves as belonging to a community.

Politics exists in all such communities because members do not have identical views about collective goals or about how to realize them. In modern states, sharp divisions exist between those who think that governments should redistribute wealth and those who believe that unfettered markets should allocate resources. Like **states**, religious communities have their politics, but they may not be political communities according to the definition used here. The desire to worship with others is an essential part of belonging to a religious community, but it is the enthusiasm for self-rule—to be free from the dominion of others—that turns religious and other groups of people into **political communities** (see Ch. 24).

The **loyalty** that binds the members of a political community together marks the outer limits of close cooperation. Members prefer to collaborate with each other and to avoid sharing power and resources with 'outsiders'. Conceptions of a shared past that often highlight memories of suffering in warfare have long been central to political unity. Annual commemorations of **9/11** are an example of how death, threat, and sacrifice shape national histories. Some religious communities ask believers to be martyrs for the cause. But the expectation that members will sacrifice their lives in war for the sake of the larger group has been a central feature of political communities for millennia.

Most people belong to several communities at the same time—to professional or religious groups that may be transnational as well as to **nation-states**. Several regimes, such as Nazi Germany and Stalin's Russia, tried to persuade citizens to forsake loyalties that clashed with the state. Many have failed because citizens attached more importance to their religious or ethnic affiliation than to the state. Liberal democratic communities recognize that citizens value many different loyalties, some directed towards local communities, others towards non-governmental associations such as Greenpeace and Amnesty International. Those states believe that they have moral duties to peoples elsewhere. Most think that they should obey **international law** and promote global

---

Box 32.1 Some political theorists on political community

'The primary good that we distribute to one another is membership in some human community.'
(Michael Walzer)

'What makes a man a citizen [is] the mutual obligation between subject and sovereign.'
(Jean Bodin)

'Individuals are so constituted that they could accomplish but little by themselves and could scarcely get on without the assistance of civil society and its laws. But as soon as a sufficient number have united under a government, they are able to provide for most of their needs, and they find the help of other political societies not so necessary to them as the State is itself to individuals.'
(Emmerich de Vattel)

'Do we want peoples to be virtuous? If so, let us begin by making them love their homeland. But how will they come to love it, if their homeland means nothing more to them than it does to foreigners, and if it grants to them only what it cannot refuse to anyone?'
(Jean-Jacques Rousseau)

'[D]ecisions taken by representatives of nations and nation-states profoundly affect citizens of other nation-states—who in all probability have had no opportunity to signal consent or lack of it—but . . . the international order is structured by agencies and forces over which citizens have minimum, if any, control, and in regard to which they have little basis to signal their [disagreement].'
(David Held)

'I am a citizen of the world.'
(Diogenes)

'I am not a citizen of the world . . . I am not even aware that there is a world such that one could be a citizen of it. No one has ever offered me citizenship, or described the naturalisation process, or enlisted me in the world's institutional structures, or given me an account of its decision procedures . . . or provided me with a list of the benefits and obligations of citizenship, or shown me the world's calendar and the common celebrations and commemorations of its citizens.'
(Michael Walzer)

respect for human rights. Whether **globalization** erodes national loyalties and encourages closer identification with distant peoples is one of the most important questions of the contemporary era.

Whatever the future may hold, there is no doubt that war has had a powerful impact on the evolution of political communities since earliest times. Modern states are no different from their predecessors in trying to ensure that they can count on citizens' loyalty when security and survival are at stake (see Ch. 14). The importance of that demand on citizens is no longer as great in those communities that have been spared major war in recent decades. The period since the end of the Second World War has been described as the longest peace between the great powers since the Treaty of Westphalia in 1648. It is the era in which liberals have argued that globalization—the condition in which many economic, political, cultural and other changes affect all interconnected peoples more or less simultaneously—began to overtake great power rivalry as the primary determinant of the course of world politics (on global interconnectedness, see Mazlish and Iriye 2005). Realists argue that globalization does not have radical consequences. The use of force to oust the Taliban in Afghanistan and to remove Saddam Hussein as part of the so-called **war on**

terror provided a sharp reminder of the continuing centrality of power politics. The proliferation of **weapons of mass destruction** may result in a new era of inter-state rivalries. For those reasons, **cosmopolitanism** may not be the main beneficiary of globalization, and any belief that the current era stands on the threshold of a new era in the history of political community may turn out to be unfounded (see also Chs 22 and 23).

Key Points

- Members of a political community are committed to self-rule.

- Anticipating major war, states have long aimed to persuade citizens that obligations to the 'national community' override duties to other associations.

- Totalitarian powers endeavoured to make the political community absolute. Liberal democratic states recognize that citizens value membership of many communities alongside the nation-state.

- Some have argued that globalization promises a new era of peace between the major industrial powers.

- Realists have argued that the 'war on terror' and the renewed risk of nuclear proliferation show that globalization does not alter the basic features of world politics.

Nationalism and political community

The nation-state has been the dominant form of political community since the French Revolution, but very different forms of community existed in earlier times. The first city-states of Mesopotamia and ancient Greece, the early **empires** of Assyria, Persia, and Rome, and the Ottoman and Chinese Empires were all political communities but they were very different from modern nation-states. Ancient Greek city-states cherished their autonomy but, compared with modern democracies, they had highly exclusionary ideas of community. Rights of political participation were restricted to adult male citizens. Women, resident aliens, and slaves were denied citizenship. Most political systems in human history have been hostile to popular rule. Empires were governed by military elites, not by the people. Ruling strata did not believe that states should represent **nations** or think that each nation should exist as a separate state. Those are recent ideas that have dominated political life for just over two centuries.

European states in the seventeenth century were not nation-states in the modern sense, but **territorial**

states governed by absolutist monarchs. It is important to explain how territorial states differed from earlier states, how they were replaced by nation-states, and how pressures on those relatively new forms of community have arisen in the recent phase of global **interconnectedness**.

Territorial states

The German sociologist Max Weber argued that all states monopolize control of the instruments of violence. But they differ greatly in what they can do with coercive power. Pre-modern states had a limited ability to direct the lives of subjects, whereas modern territorial states have the capacity to regulate (if not control) most aspects of society, including economic activity and relations within the family that were, until recently, beyond their reach. With respect to that difference, Michael Mann (1986: 7–10) argues that modern states enjoy high levels of 'intensive power': **power** that can be projected deep into society. Furthermore, pre-modern states had poorly defined frontiers and a limited ability to control frontier populations. Viable modern states have clearly demarcated borders and the ability to project power across national space—and often well beyond it. Commenting on that difference, Mann (1986) argues that modern states enjoy a high level of 'extensive power': power that can be projected across their territories. The overseas empires that brought non-European peoples under European control demonstrated the modern state's exceptional 'global reach'. That is crucial for understanding the history of globalization. The Spanish and Portuguese conquest of Central and South America in the sixteenth century, and the second wave of European expansion in the late nineteenth century, point to the same conclusion: the **state** was the driving-force behind rising levels of **interconnectedness**.

From territorial states to nation-states

Many territorial states that established the first overseas empires turned into nation-states. As Norbert Elias (2000) argued, the modern state's monopoly control of force largely pacified society, allowing closer economic and social ties to develop. Stronger emotional ties between citizens slowly appeared. There were at least two reasons for that overall development: the rise of industrial **capitalism** and **endemic warfare**. Benedict Anderson (1991) argues that 'print capitalism' prepared the way for national forms of political consciousness. Books, pamphlets, and other mass media disseminated national symbols along with shared narratives about the past and common aspirations. Because of print capitalism, strangers who would never meet could identify with what Anderson calls the 'imagined community' of the nation. The point is that the species is not divided naturally into nations. States played a central role in creating national **identities**, and not least by building national education systems that disseminated shared values.

Modern territorial states emerged in the cauldron of war; indeed, they were largely instruments for waging war. It has been said that successful European states in the sixteenth century were small enough to be governed from a central point, but large enough to resist external threats (Tilly 1992). Warfare was crucial for the transition from the territorial to the national state. Warring states encouraged national solidarity so that citizens would remain loyal in moments of crisis. The turning point was the 1789 **French Revolution**, which created the 'nation in arms' and national conscription. From then

on, **nationalism** has been the ideology with the greatest influence on the evolution of political communities.

To repeat, warfare and capitalist industrialization led to modern societies with powerful nationalist feelings. By claiming to represent the nation, the state increased its ability to mobilize populations for war and for building overseas empires. By the end of the nineteenth century, European nation-states had expanded their worldwide empires, drawing non-European peoples into longer webs of **interconnectedness**. The nation-state was one of the main architects of the economic and political integration of the species; but at the same time, it intensified national differences.

Nationalism was a late eighteenth-century European invention that spread to the rest of the world. **Third World** nationalist movements used European ideas to replace alien government with self-rule. Success in throwing off imperial domination meant that the number of sovereign states more than tripled in three decades after the Second World War, but many of the new political units failed to become viable nation-states. Ethnic rivalries often meant that a sense of identification with the state did not develop. In several regions, divided peoples dismembered the former colonial territories and established their own nation-states. Examples are the separation of India and Pakistan in 1947, and East Pakistan (Bangladesh) and West Pakistan in 1971. As a result of decolonization, the modern state, which was not indigenous to non-European societies, became the dominant form of political community across the world—and the aspiration for many secessionist groups. The globalization of the modern state is one of the main features of increased **interconnectedness**.

Key Points

- Most forms of political community in human history have not represented the nation or the people.

- The idea that the state should represent the nation is a European development that has dominated politics for just over two hundred years.

- War and industrial capitalism are two reasons why the nation-state became the dominant political community.

- The extraordinary power of modern states—the growth of their 'intensive' and 'extensive' power—made global empires possible.

- States have been the main architects of global interconnectedness over the last five centuries.

- The global spread of the European ideas about the state and nationalism are defining features of the modern interconnected era.

Community and citizenship

Modern states acquired an extraordinary ability to wage war and administer overseas empires. It may seem odd that they were also the site for unusual experiments in liberal democratic forms of governance, but there is no paradox here. Modern states created national peoples that could be mobilized for war. Peoples that were formed in that way often resented the state's increased power, as well as its demands to serve in war and to finance it through taxation. They organized to extract **citizenship** rights from the state. Demands for universal citizenship were first heard within the leading European states, but they are now a central part of politics everywhere. Along with the spread of the language of universal human rights, such calls for citizenship reveal that the outlines of a global political culture have developed alongside the increased **interconnectedness** of peoples (see Ch. 25).

Citizenship and rights

Territorial states in early modern Europe were ruled by absolute monarchs who saw the state as their private realm. During the eighteenth and nineteenth centuries, the rising commercial and industrial classes challenged absolutist power; they wanted political rights that were commensurate with their economic importance. Middle classes sought to destroy royal privileges and to promote constitutional government. They demanded the rule of law and representation in politics. They succeeded in winning democratic rights, but refused to grant those rights to the working classes and women. Struggles to extend the suffrage to all adult men and women were central features of modern industrial societies during the late nineteenth and early twentieth centuries.

Demands for welfare rights followed. Labour movements and political parties on the Left argued that because of increasing inequalities of power and wealth the poor lacked full membership of the community. The argument was that legal and political rights mean very little unless people have the power to exercise them. Pressures mounted to deepen the meaning of citizenship by adding social or welfare rights to the legal and political rights that had been won earlier. In the first part of the twentieth century, many Western states introduced national health services, welfare provision for the poor, and more open educational systems in response to such demands from subordinate groups.

T. H. Marshall maintained that ruling groups in societies such as Britain maintained legitimacy by giving all citizens the rights that they had previously monopolized. Many governments in the industrialized West supported that package of citizenship rights in order to defuse social tensions. Some political thinkers in the 1950s and 1960s believed that 'the end of ideology' had arrived in societies such as the USA. What they meant was that Western liberal democracies had largely solved the social conflicts that had threatened political stability.

In the 1950s and 1960s, many Western intellectuals believed that the former colonies would follow the West's path of economic and political development. 'Modernization theorists' spoke about the coming economic and political 'development' of 'traditional' societies. They were confident that new states would undergo the nation-building process that had occurred in Europe. New states would democratize and imitate Western free market economies. In short, increased global connectedness would lead to a broad consensus about the ideal society and government.

Modernization theory was a seriously flawed doctrine. Moreover, civil rights movements, the student revolt, opposition to the Vietnam War, **feminism**, and environmental groups revealed the errors of the 'end of ideology' thesis. Ethnic and religious conflict in new states, the rise of military governments, and economic stagnation demonstrated that modernization theorists underestimated the challenges facing post-colonial societies. But the belief that most societies will come to resemble the West has not disappeared from view. Echoes of modernization theory can be heard in Francis Fukuyama's claim in 1989 that the end of the bipolar era revealed that the global spread of liberal democracy is unstoppable. Its spread was championed on the grounds that liberal states form a unique 'zone of peace', and can reduce conflict elsewhere by exporting democracy. The belief in a rapidly expanding consensus about the good society was rejected by the idea of an impending **clash of civilizations** (Huntington 1993). Recent analyses of the religious revolt against Western secular modernity which has flourished since 9/11 have also argued that globalization produces major cultural cleavages and conflicts rather than an inexorable trend towards a global agreement on core values.

Key Points

- Citizenship rights developed in response to the growing power of modern states.

- The demand to be recognized as a free and equal citizen began with struggles for legal and political rights, to which welfare rights were added in the late nineteenth and early twentieth centuries.

- The stability of modern forms of political community has owed a great deal to the fact that citizens won those rights.

- Modernization theory assumed that Third World societies would emulate Western economic and political development.

- That thesis resurfaced in the West at the end of the bipolar era when it was linked with the idea that liberal democracies form a unique and growing zone of peace. Huntington's notion of an emerging clash of civilizations was one of the main rebuttals of the idea that globalization is leading to a consensus about the superiority of Western institutions and values.

The changing nature of political community

One paradox of modern times is that the globalization of economic and political life has increased, but the national fragmentation of political communities has not declined. Religious and cultural diversity are probably greater than at any time since the end of the Second World War. **Globalization**, the fragmentation of many states—most obviously, the former Soviet Union and the Eastern bloc—and the diversification of belief systems—as in the rise of Christian, Islamic, and other forms of religious fundamentalism—are major forces transforming political communities.

As noted earlier, state fragmentation has occurred in many Third World regions. Novel approaches to precarious Third World states appeared in the early 1990s. The notions of the **quasi-state** or failed state described states that the international community recognized as sovereign although they could not satisfy the basic needs of their populations without external support (Jackson 1990; Helman and Ratner 1992/3). Especially since 9/11, attention has been directed at reconstructing failed states such as Afghanistan that provided a safe haven for 'Islamist' terrorist organizations.

In the 1990s many thinkers asked whether liberal democracies have duties to the peoples of failed states that include intervening to end serious human rights violations (see Ch. 31). In an unforeseen development, the failed state emerged as a problem within Europe itself. The disintegration of the former Yugoslavia was a striking example of a failed state in what was regarded as one of the most liberal and affluent socialist societies in Eastern Europe. Although there were major public disagreements, **NATO** enjoyed substantial popular support for its military intervention in Kosovo in 1999. In that period, many states—but not the USA—also supported the establishment of the International Criminal Court so that human rights violators could be brought to justice.

In Yugoslavia, violent nationalism destroyed a multicultural political community that many observers thought was exemplary in creating harmony between diverse cultural groups. Developments in societies such as Canada, Belgium, Italy, and the United Kingdom illustrate a more general theme that must now be considered. In most societies, some national or ethnic minorities are engaged in a struggle to achieve respect for cultural differences. Those demands are part of a global movement in which minority nations and indigenous peoples learn from each other's experience. Globalization, fragmentation, and diversification are clearly not unrelated phenomena. There is no more dramatic example of the rejection of Western forms of political community than Al Qaeda. That loose movement rejects the Western notion that progress consists in moving towards secular modern societies; it is violently opposed to Western influence in the Islamic world. But it is hostile to Western globalization, and not to globalization as such. Al Qaeda has used the modern banking and communications system to promote its objectives. Disparate and loosely organized, it is a global movement that seeks to win support among the 'faithful' (both within the Islamic world and among alienated Muslims in the West) for a transnational political–religious vision.

The politics of difference

The rise of militant Islam has increased fear among certain socal strata that 'multicultural' government policies result in division and sectarianism. But the difficulties in fostering a consensus about national identity indicate that many societies face major problems in reconciling tensions between demands for preserving what some groups regard as the traditional community and demands for respecting cultural difference.

To understand their predicament, we need to return to the place of war in the formation of modern political communities. In promoting national cultures in Europe, the ruling strata invariably imposed a dominant language and specific standards on subordinate groups. As the British case reveals, the sense of Scottish, Welsh, Irish (and indeed English) identity has survived such efforts to promote an inclusive national identity that binds ethnic or national groups together. Similar differences and divisions are evident in most states.

Ethnic struggles to achieve a level of autonomy, if not total independence, exist in virtually every modern state, but the prospects of success were low when political communities faced the permanent threat of war. The 'long peace' between the great powers has given national movements new opportunities to assert their rights. Core industrial states no longer need to mobilize whole populations for war, and many find it more difficult to construct an idea of the nation that can command widespread support in multicultural societies. The 'war on terror' and the 2003 invasion of Iraq showed that states can still harness popular support for military operations as long as they can persuade major sections of the population that such action is essential to ward off threats to personal and **national security**. On the other hand, public opposition to the Iraq War in the Western democracies indicated that many people regard loyalty to the state as conditional on respect for the UN system and compliance with international law. The conditional nature of loyalty may be one of the most important trends affecting modern political communities, although no state can point to an unbroken history of near total public support. Most have had to deal with periods of social unrest and civil war—including the UK and the USA (Waller and Linklater 2003). However, the modern 'ethnic revolt' provides a reminder that many minority nations and indigenous groups have long displayed qualified or only grudging support to the nation-states that have ruled over them.

Group rights

Claims for **group rights** mark the existence of global changes in attitudes to citizenship (Young 1990). Over the last two centuries, struggles to extend citizenship rights took place without much regard for cultural and other differences. Feminists have argued that they were **gender**-blind: little or no account was taken of the particular needs of women. Exponents of new images of citizenship have argued that public policy, national laws, and social attitudes should display greater sensitivity to differences between citizens—to differences of ethnicity, race, gender, and religion. Minority nations and indigenous peoples in Australia, Canada, and New Zealand, for example, spearheaded claims for group recognition. They sought self-government and 'land rights'. Those are not unrelated 'national' developments that have influenced different nation-states. Representatives of such groups belong to a transnational movement that is trying to promote a global political culture that accords a central place to group rights.

The transborder movement of peoples is one dimension of globalization that feeds into that process. Again, important arguments revolve around the question of how far traditional notions of community should adapt to the multicultural, multi-racial, and multi-denominational nature of society. Recent discussions about wearing 'the veil' in Britain (and about the 'headscarf' in French schools) have produced tensions over the place of group rights. As noted earlier, many fear that concessions to 'difference' will lead to parallel societies and the erosion of shared loyalties. (The fact that 'British Muslims' committed the terrorist acts of 7/7 led some groups to argue for stronger government action to promote socal integration.) Others emphasize that the real challenge is how to promote greater respect for 'difference' (and to solve the interrelated problems of economic inequality, marginalization, and discrimination).

No account of ongoing struggles over the nature of community and citizenship can be complete without discussing feminism. Many feminists have challenged gendered ideas of national culture anchored in the male experience of warfare. They have opposed traditional 'masculinist' notions of community that glorify the national past, often by commemorating success in war. There are tensions within feminism, as within all belief systems. Some feminists have protested against what they see as patriarchal assumptions that underpin, for example, the 'Muslim veil', while many Muslim women respond that the veil expresses their Islamic identity. Western feminism has been accused of seeking to impose a particular conception of 'womanhood' on non-Western peoples. Feminism is therefore entangled in wider global forces. Challenges to patriarchy exist in every society, and stem from global shifts in attitudes to gender. At the same time, many groups attempt to preserve 'traditional' social structures from the influence of Western modernity; they

---

Box 32.2 Contrasting views about the scope of human sympathy

'Whether we can conceive of a way to think of morality that extends some form of sympathy further than our own group remains perhaps the fundamental moral question for contemporary life.'

(Jean Tronto)

'If he was to lose his little finger to-morrow, he would not sleep tonight; but provided he never saw them, he will snore with the most profound security over the ruin of a hundred millions of his brethren, and the destruction of that immense multitude seems plainly an object less interesting to him, than this paltry misfortune of his own.'

(Adam Smith)

'[O]ur sense of solidarity is strongest when those with whom solidarity is expressed are thought of as "one of us", where "us" means something smaller and more local than the human race.'

(Richard Rorty)

'The fact that a person is physically near to us … may make it more likely that we shall assist him, but this does not show that we ought to help him rather than another who happens to be further away.'

(Peter Singer)

'We are nowadays more strongly than ever aware that an enormously large part of humanity live their entire lives on the verge of starvation, that in fact there are always and in many places people dying of hunger. . . . Many members of richer communities feel it to be almost a duty to do something about the misery of other human groups. To avoid misunderstanding on the issue, let it be said that relatively little is done.'

(Norbert Elias)

Do the 'oceans make a community of nations impossible?'

(Immanuel Kant)

---

resist the spread of what they see as atheistic materialism and licentiousness. The varieties of religious **fundamentalism**—Christian, Hindu, Islamic, etc.—are not divorced from each other. Just like the spread of the 'Western values' against which they protest, they are manifestations of rising levels of global **interconnectedness** that produce similar tensions over values in all societies.

Cosmopolitan democracy and transnational citizenship

An intriguing feature of political communities is how they deal with differences of class, gender, sexual identity, religion, ethnicity, and race. No less important is what they make of distinctions between citizens and aliens. Resistance to doctrines that claim that one race, nation, or gender has the right to dominate others has spread to most parts of the world. Modern nation-states have been changed by egalitarian ideas that challenge 'natural' hierarchies between people. A key issue in the study of globalization is whether it will change one of the core assumptions of political communities over many millennia—the belief that members of the same society have few, if any, obligations towards other groups. The question is whether, over the decades and centuries to come, the growing interweaving of peoples' lives will promote identification with humanity as a whole or generate new conflicts and tensions—or, as seems probable, some combination of the two.

Globalization has led many to question the idea that political communities have few responsibilities beyond advancing the interests of citizens. Various global problems that states cannot solve on their own—climate change, for example—have encouraged the proliferation of **non-governmental organizations** (NGOs) concerned with the fate of the earth. Affluent populations are often disturbed by images of suffering caused by state terror, civil conflict, natural disaster, and famine. Support for humanitarian intervention in Somalia in 1993 and Kosovo in 1999, and the largely spontaneous assistance to the victims of the Asian tsunami in 2004, developed in response to images of suffering and distress that the global media can disseminate. Many think that a global **civil society** marks the dawn of a new era of human cooperation. Sceptics stress the continuing appeal of nationalism, the tenacity of the state, and the weakness of cosmopolitan loyalties (see Ch. 24). In their view, interventions in Somalia and Kosovo—and inaction with respect to the 1994 genocide in Rwanda—demonstrate that national populations are unwilling to sacrifice the lives of a significant number of military personnel in conflicts that are regarded as exercises in 'saving strangers' (see Ch. 31). That reluctance is also evident in current unease within Britain about the burden imposed on UK military personnel serving in Afghanistan.

Cosmopolitan democracy

Cosmopolitan approaches to political community have enjoyed a renaissance in recent years. The idea of world citizenship is a concept used by many international non-governmental organizations to promote a stronger sense of responsibility for the global environment and for the future of the species. Proponents of the **cosmopolitan model of democracy** have argued that nation-states have little control over global markets—the recent meltdown of global financial markets illustrates the point—and they have only limited influence on **transnational corporations** whose decisions influence currency values, employment levels, and the prospects for economic growth and successful environmental management. They argue for democratizing international organizations such as the **World Trade Organization**.

Critics argue that such visions are utopian. They maintain that democracy will not flourish at the global level where there is no counterpart to the nation that can engage the emotions of hundreds of millions of people. Democracy, it is argued, requires levels of trust and a commitment to the common good that only exist between people with a shared national identity (Miller 1999). Better then to concentrate on improving exist-ing nation-states than to squander resources pursuing visions of a cosmopolitan political community.

Neo-medievalist approaches

Neo-medievalism is a vision of political community that has attracted attention in recent years. The concept refers to an ideal condition in which people are governed by many overlapping authorities and have loyalties to all of them—which is roughly how life was organized in the Middle Ages before the emergence of the modern state. Globalization and fragmentation have led to renewed interest in a neo-medieval **world order** in which governments transfer some powers to international **institutions** that address global problems while moving others to devolved authorities in regions where the sense of cultural difference is strong (Linklater 1998). In that vision, national governments retain many powers, and citizens stay loyal to the state, which is, however, one level of a multi-tiered system of rule. Loyalties to state would then coexist with strong attachments to sub-state and transnational authorities, none able to dominate the others.

The best prospects for neo-medievalism exist in the European Union where some erosion of sovereign powers has taken place and where traditional conceptions of national interests have lost some of their importance (see Ch. 26). It is no small achievement that the neo-medieval vision enjoys support in a region that was frequently embroiled in major wars. Whether that image of political community will ever appeal beyond Europe is a moot point. No less important is how far organizations such as the EU support a global 'civilizing process' which is concerned, among other things, with promoting respect for such principles as the international legal **norm** prohibiting torture (Linklater 2010).

Key Points

- Globalization and fragmentation are interrelated phenomena that challenge traditional conceptions of community and citizenship.

- Ethnic fragmentation is one reason for failed states in Europe and in the Third World, but demands for the recognition of cultural differences exist in all political communities.

- Some globalization theorists defend cosmopolitan democracy on the grounds that national democracies lack the ability to make global institutions and associations accountable to their citizens.

Case Study Torture and the war on terror

The sociologist Norbert Elias (2000) analysed the forces that led Europeans to think they belonged to a higher civilization. Their 'civilizing process' included growing repugnance towards violence and cruelty. The abolition of public execution and capital punishment in many European societies is an example of changing sensibilities with respect to violence. Related shifts have oc-

curred in global politics. The international community declared its opposition to torture in the 1984 Convention against Torture and Other Cruel, Inhuman or Degrading Treatment or Punishment. Great powers have often ignored human rights violations committed by allies. Nevertheless, the belief that torture is morally unacceptable became a leading global norm after 1945. It was a key element in the distinction between liberal and authoritarian or totalitarian regimes.

The 'war on terror' led the USA and its allies to cooperate with states such as Uzbekistan (which the UN Special Rapporteur on Torture found guilty of serious human rights violations). Security needs displaced human rights. One consequence is that many non-Western regimes have claimed the same entitlement to ignore human rights in the struggle against domestic opposition. Western liberal democracies debated whether certain forms of torture could be justified to extract information from terrorist suspects. 'Extraordinary rendition' referred to the practice of transferring suspects to authoritarian regimes that allegedly use forms of torture outlawed or deemed illegitimate in the West. Western powers have therefore been accused of being complicit in acts of violence that are contrary to international law.

The relaxation of the norm prohibiting torture has raised profound questions about how far liberal restrictions on violence (which grow out of the earlier civilizing process) can alter the course of world politics. Before 9/11, there was a broad global consensus that torture is illegitimate. Most regimes that used torture did not do so openly. Many observers have assumed that the onus is on liberal states and organizations such as the European Union to maintain respect for the global norm against torture. The 'war on terror' may have been a temporary setback to the torture norm, but realists will argue that such principles are among the first to be cast to one side when fears for security run high. The fact that those 'moral compromises' do not pass without challenge provides hope to those who believe that the ideal of eradicating violence may yet make serious headway in world politics (see Foot 2006).

The challenges of global interconnectedness

In recent times, globalization and fragmentation have weakened or destroyed centralized nation-states as different as Indonesia, Yugoslavia, the USSR, and Czechoslovakia. Perhaps new forms of political community that are more respectful of cultural differences and more cosmopolitan than their predecessors will become more widespread in the next phase of globalization.

In many states the apex of violent nationalism was reached in the first half of the twentieth century (see Ch. 3). In 1914, the European ruling classes led willing populations into one of the most destructive wars in

history. Two decades later, a more devastating conflict took place on a global scale. The desire to break with geopolitics and war was a principal motivation for creating a European Community in the early 1950s. War no longer seems likely to engulf the European continent and, for the foreseeable future, it seems unlikely that core industrial powers will use military force against each other. This may be a revolution in world politics, although realists advise against thinking that the current peace will last for ever. It would be foolish to think that future generations are certain to be spared the cocktail of nationalism and totalitarianism that produced the devastation of the Second World War—although in the shorter term globalization seems likely to continue to have a pacifying effect. Certainly, the 'war on terror' revealed how national security politics can eclipse other considerations for largely unforeseen reasons. Viable global financial institutions may be critical for economic **security**, but the state is the political association that many rely on for physical security. During the recent financial crisis, moreover, it was states that rescued failing banks through large injections of capital. For many people—the collapse of the former Yugoslavia illustrates the point—the weakening of state power causes alarm because it is the chief barrier to violent conflict. Of course, many people fear the regime that governs them. For others (the Palestinians, for example), acquiring national sovereignty remains a key aspiration.

Many realists will argue that those points hold the key to understanding the future of political community. In short, most people seem certain to look to the state—whether actual or aspirational—for their security. Does that invalidate efforts to imagine and implement visions of new forms of community and citizenship? There is no agreed answer to that question. Those who subscribe to the tenets of **realism** or **neo-realism** regard visions of alternative forms of political community as a distraction from the permanent challenge of dealing with the problem of force. But many believe that 'post-national' associations are essential if the species is to solve the problem of climate change, reduce global poverty, and manage the whole process of rising levels of human interconnectedness.

There is no reason to choose between those standpoints, but to understand why that is so, it is useful to place the relationship between the state and globalization in a long-term perspective. As noted earlier, European states were the architects of globalization in one sense of that concept, namely the tendency over the last five centuries to create interconnections between societies that had been isolated from each other, or did not know of each other's existence. A second sense of the concept, which stresses that many processes and events affect all peoples more or less simultaneously, is the result of recent technological and communications revolutions. Economic factors play a central role in binding different societies together, but they do not exist in isolation from other forces. High levels of transnational economic activity depend on a stable international system. Without the revolution in technology and communications that has occurred since the Second World War, economic changes

would not affect most societies almost simultaneously, as occurred during the recent global financial crisis.

Higher levels of **interconnectedness**—strategic, economic and so forth—expose societies to forces that they cannot control on their own, although great powers are usually more able than small states to secure the outcomes they desire. Studies of international cooperation within the **functionalist** tradition have argued that, since the latter part of the nineteenth century, states have relied heavily on global institutions to create regulatory frameworks that help them not only to manage the effects of revolutions in military technology, but to control the spread of disease, promote trade and communication, detect and punish transnational criminal organisations, and neutralize or eradicate terrorist groups.

Efforts to coordinate action at the global level do not suspend 'power politics', but they alter it since states have to become skilled at prevailing in diplomatic arenas (through forming coalitions, for example) as against (or as well as) triumphing on the battlefield. They have to recognize that there are often trade-offs between using their power to secure short-term advantages and granting concessions to others that may produce significant benefits for all in the long term. It is conceivable that the challenge of climate change will lead societies to follow the second route, but the future is entirely open, and it is possible that states and other associations will concentrate on short-term gains that compound their collective plight. The point is that globalization creates pressures on states to adapt their interests to each other, and to consider how to manage the patterns of interconnectedness that affect them. But it does not guarantee that they will develop the art of compromise to the point where 'global' interests matter as much as 'national' interests; nor does it ensure that they will conclude, at some future point, that one of their main responsibilities is to promote the sense of belonging to a world community.

Neo-medievalism stresses the necessity under conditions of globalization for combining obligations to fellow nationals with duties to the members of other communities. The key issue is whether modern societies, assisted by transnational and international organizations, can reach the point where multiple loyalties are structured in that way.

Cosmopolitans have been criticized for underestimating the difficulties involved in making that transition, and for failing to appreciate the political dangers that may result from efforts to establish a global community. The so-called communitarian strand of political thought stresses the value that people attach to belonging to a specific community (Miller 1999). Such collectivities have obligations to each other, but those are not as extensive as the duties that fellow citizens have to one another. That state of affairs, the argument continues, is not about to change because of globalization. As a result, efforts to promote the sense of being a citizen of the world will fail because, for most people, citizenship is inextricably linked with the rights and duties that they acquire as inhabitants of particular nation-states (see Walzer 2002).

Poststructuralists have argued that new forms of power and domination may be inherent in cosmopolitan visions and notions of world citizenship. The argument is indebted to Foucault's claim that all forms of knowledge, including those that aim to promote progress or emancipation, are potentially dangerous (see Ch. 10). The contention is that cosmopolitan visions and projects that rest on supposed universal truths run the risk of introducing pernicious distinctions between those who identify with the species and those who stand in the way. The danger is that the cosmopolitan advocates of, say, the universal human rights culture, prepare the ground for new forms of Western power over societies that they believe they should 'liberate'. Unsurprisingly, the idea of **humanitarian intervention** has aroused the suspicion that it functions mainly to elevate 'civilized' Western liberal societies above those who are thought to be unable to escape 'tribal' animosities and to curb the use of force. The implication is that intervention for 'humanitarian' reasons may have less to do with relieving suffering in war-torn areas than with cultivating an image of superiority among those who are able to help. It may be a small step from stressing such divisions between the 'civilized' and the 'barbaric' to using excessive force against those who oppose the 'liberating' force (as in the case of the atrocities at Abu Ghraib).

Neo-medievalism is not immune from that critique. Jacques Derrida (1992) defended a European international community that reduces the monopoly powers of the nation-state and promotes 'post-national' citizenship. But such political designs, he added, are not risk-free. The danger is that new arrangements will reconstitute the divisions between insiders and outsiders that were central to nation-building—for example by promoting a European identity that creates pernicious contrasts with the Islamic world.

Poststructuralists have not restricted their criticisms to cosmopolitans. Their arguments criticize all 'totalizing' identities that rely on divisions between 'self' and 'other'. From that standpoint, the communitarian critics of cosmopolitanism may also be guilty of defending a vision of community that marginalizes specific groups. Representatives of minority nations and indigenous peoples make the same point when they argue that the dominant images of national identity 'screen out' their history and ignore their distinctive position in the wider society. Feminist movements have also argued that large numbers of women suffer exclusion at the hands of 'their' community.

The lesson to draw is that all communities include some people as full members and exclude or marginalize others. The warning is that such dangers will remain whether peoples remain loyal to nations or sovereign states, or identify with specific transnational organizations, or support measures to build a world community. That is not to argue that neo-medieval projects should be avoided or that cosmopolitan programmes are bound to fail. It is to stress that a high level of reflectiveness needs to accompany every effort to transform political community—but also to preserve or improve existing ones.

Higher forms of individual and collective reflectiveness are imperative for managing the social and political effects of rising levels of global interconnectedness. The norms that people acquire in the course of growing up in particular nation-states do not automatically prepare them for the challenge of living with others in a highly interdependent world. Modifying national objectives and changing lifestyles in response to the challenge of climate change are complex matters that may take decades to bring about. Societies are still at an early stage in learning how to adapt to the challenges of global interconnectedness.

It is possible that they will fail. On the other hand, various international organizations exist for the purpose of managing global economic and political problems. Their role in protecting the interests of the most affluent communities has attracted criticism (see Pogge 2002). But the fact that they are judged by cosmopolitan principles of justice should not go unnoticed, and not least because many people in very different societies broadly concur with those philosophical reflections. Since the 1960s, awareness of how global affluence and poverty are interrelated has increased. Knowledge of how the global trading system, agricultural subsidies, and so forth disadvantage vulnerable producers in poor societies is more widespread. Those who spearheaded the fair trade movement can point to success in disseminating a sense of moral responsibility to producers in distant places. Ideas of socially responsible investment represent an advance in highlighting the moral problems that result from profiting from, for example, economic transactions with regimes that violate human rights. Evidence of climate change has promoted a global awareness of how everyday routines in different parts of the world contribute to environmental problems that have caused immense suffering in many regions, and that seem likely to impose unfair burdens on future generations.

In short, as a result of globalization, individuals are linked with 'distant strangers' in unprecedented ways, and cannot avoid difficult questions about the moral principles that should bind them together. It is impossible to know whether globalization will eventually lead to a strong sense of identification with the species as a whole, and to a greater willingness to cooperate with other peoples in building a cosmopolitan community. It is probably unwise to suppose that any single trend will dominate. But there can be no doubt that how communities and individuals should respond to the problems of global interconnectedness is the most important moral and political challenge of the age.

Key Points

- The apex of nationalism in relations between the great powers occurred in the first half of the twentieth century.

- Nationalism remains a powerful force in the modern world, but globalization and fragmentation have led to important debates about the possibility of new forms of political community.

- Cosmopolitan approaches that envisage an international order, in which all individuals are respected as equals, have flourished in the contemporary phase of globalization.

- Communitarian arguments stress that most people value their membership of a specific political community, and are not poised to shift their loyalty from the nation-state to the species.

- Poststructuralists argue that all forms of political community contain dangers of domination or exclusion.

- Globalization has given rise to major debates about the principles that should govern present and future interconnectedness.

Conclusion

The study of international politics has been largely concerned with understanding relations between separate political communities, and particularly relations between the great powers. Realists and neo-realists argue that all states are forced to compete for security and survival in the context of anarchy. They contend that separate states look to their own interests first and foremost. They maintain that the sense of community that exists between the citizens of particular states is unlikely to develop within the world at large. Realists and neo-realists doubt that this will change as long as international anarchy survives.

There is no reason to think that sovereign states are about to be replaced by new forms of political community; but there is no doubt that globalization and fragmentation pose new challenges for nation-states across the world. The most recent phase in the history of global interconnectedness requires a discussion of how far the forms of cooperation that exist within viable states can develop globally. It is difficult to be optimistic

about the immediate future, but it must be remembered that modern forms of globalization are a very recent development in human history, and that species is still learning how to adapt to them (McNeill and McNeill 2003).

A large number of perspectives are relevant to thinking about the future of political community. They include those standpoints that regard the rise of global civil society as evidence that cooperation between different communities is increasing; approaches that hold that political communities may yet evolve together in the direction of neo-medievalism or cosmopolitan democracy; and those positions that maintain that the struggle for power and security is not about to lose its primacy. The differences between those standpoints sharpen the issues that need to be addressed in trying to understand the central issue in the study of globalization: whether it promises to end the kinds of conflict and competition that have dominated international relations for millennia, or will only give them a new form.

Questions

1   What is community, and what makes a community a political community?
2   Why has the modern state been the dominant form of political community?
3   What is the relationship between nationalism, citizenship, and political community?
4   What is the relationship between war and political community?
5   To what extent are globalization and fragmentation transforming political communities?
6   Can one be a citizen of the world?
7   What are the arguments for and against cosmopolitan democracy?
8   What are the main differences between cosmopolitan, communitarian, and post-structuralist understandings of political community?
9   How far did the 'war on terror' reveal that global norms (such as the norm prohibiting torture) lose their power the moment that states and individuals fear for their security?
10 Is globalization promoting an agreement about the moral and political principles that should govern the present phase of human interconnectedness?

Further Reading

General

Linklater, A. (1998), *The Transformation of Political Community: Ethical Foundations of the Post-Westphalian Era* (Cambridge: Polity Press). Provides a more detailed analysis of many themes considered in this chapter.

Communitarian and cosmopolitan arguments

Nussbaum, M. (2002), *In Defence of Country* (Boston, MA: Beacon Press). An excellent collection of essays on patriotism and cosmopolitanism.

The modern state

Elias, N. (2000), *The Civilizing Process: Sociogenetic and Psychogenetic Investigations* (Oxford: Basil Blackwell). A landmark study of the rise of the modern state.

Tilly, C. (1992), *Coercion, Capital and European States: AD 990–1992* (Oxford: Blackwell). An influential account of how the modern state eclipsed other forms of political organization.

Nationalism and group rights

Anderson, B. (1983; revised 1991), *Imagined Communities: Reflections on the Origin and Spread of Nationalism* (London: Verso). A key reference point in discussions about modern nationalism.

Kymlicka, W. (1989), *Liberalism, Community and Culture* (Oxford: Oxford University Press). A pathbreaking study of the significance of the struggle for 'indigenous' rights for liberal democratic communities.

National and world citizenship

Dower, N., and Williams, J. (eds) (2002), *Global Citizenship* (Edinburgh: Edinburgh University Press). A comprehensive collection of essays on world citizenship.

Marshall, T. H. (1973), *Class, Citizenship and Social Development* (Westport, CT: Greenwood Press). A central study of the development of legal, political, and social rights.

Emotional responses to suffering in other societies
Cohen, S. (2001), *States of Denial: Knowing about Atrocities and Suffering* (Cambridge: Polity Press). An excellent sociological study of attitudes to human suffering.

Alternatives to the nation-state
Held, D. (1995), *Democracy and the Global Order: From the Modern State to Global Governance* (Cambridge: Polity Press). An influential defence of cosmopolitan democracy.

Globalization and world history
McNeill, J. R., and McNeill, W. H. (2003), *The Human Web: A Bird's Eye View of World History* (New York: W. W. Norton). A highly accessible overview of how the species has become interconnected over several millennia.
Mazlish, B., and Iriye, A. (eds) (2005), *The Global History Reader* (Abingdon: Routledge). A comprehensive guide to the history of globalization.

Online Resource Centre

 Visit the Online Resource Centre that accompanies this book to access more learning resources on this chapter topic at www.oxfordtextbooks.co.uk/orc/baylis5e/

Chapter 33

Globalization and the post-cold war order

IAN CLARK

Reader's Guide

This chapter explores the nature of the **order** that has developed since the end of the cold war. It asks whether that order is distinctive. It also asks whether globalization is its defining feature. After distinguishing between various types of order—international, world, and global—the chapter sketches the main ingredients of the contemporary order. These extend well beyond the traditional domain of international military security. The argument then addresses globalization as one of the forces that helped to bring the cold war to an end, and investigates the associated trend towards a **post-Westphalian** order. It also explores the ways in which globalization now causes problems and tensions in the present order, especially with regard to its legitimacy. The chapter ends by suggesting that globalization reflects changes within states, not just between them: what is distinctive about the present order is not the imminent demise of the states-system, but the continuation of an **international order**, the constituent units of which are **globalized states**. This analysis is further confirmed by the response to the financial crisis of 2008.

Introduction

Box 33.1 Elements of discontinuity and continuity between cold war and post-cold war orders

Cold war	Discontinuity	Post-cold war
Soviet power in Eastern Europe		Dissolution of the Soviet Union
Bipolar competition		Unipolar peacemaking
Rival ideologies		Supremacy of liberal capitalism
Global security integration		Greater regional autonomy
Military security as high politics		National identity as high politics

Continuity

Some security structures, e.g. NATO
Economic globalization
Human rights
Reaction against secular state
Multiple identities
Environmental agendas
Poverty in the South

This chapter is concerned with three key questions. The first is whether there is now a distinctive pattern of **order** in the post-cold-war world and, if so, what are its principal elements. The second is whether this order should be defined in terms of globalization. The third asks what is now happening to globalization, and what challenges does it face.

Study of the overall character of the post-cold war order remains problematic. While there have been studies aplenty of individual aspects of this present order (ethnicity, identity, religion, peacekeeping, humanitarian intervention, globalization, regionalism, economic transition, democratization, integration, financial instability, terrorism and the war on it, weapons of mass destruction, regime change, etc.), we still lack any grand synthesis of its essential nature.

In analysing the contemporary order, we need to be mindful of how much greater are the demands upon, and the expectations about, the **international order** today than previously. In earlier periods, the interest in the international order was largely 'negative', and lay in prevention of any threats that might emerge from it. The interest is now 'positive' as well, as the international order is a much greater source than hitherto of a range of social goods. It can deliver information, economic resources, human rights, intervention, access to global social movements and international non-governmental organizations (INGOs), and an abundance of cultural artefacts. Many of these 'goods' may be regarded as unwelcome, but they remain highly sought after by some governments, and/or sectors of society, around the world.

Key Points

- The principal characteristics of the contemporary order that give it its distinctive quality are difficult to discern.
- Our understanding of, say, the inter-war period (1919–39) is informed by how it ended, but we do not yet know how our present period will 'end'.
- The international order now delivers a range of international 'goods', but also a wide range of 'bads'.

A typology of order

At the present moment, our ideas about order are being pulled in a number of competing directions. At the one end, they continue to be largely state-centred and retain traditional concerns with the structure of the balance of power, the polarity of the international system, and the current forms of collective security. At the other is a widening agenda that encompasses the relationship between economic and political dimensions, new thinking about human security (see Ch. 29), debates about the distributive consequences of globalization, the role of human rights, the impact of environmentalism, and strategies for human emancipation. Clearly, a number of differing, and potentially competing, conceptions of order are at work.

These draw our attention to a number of important distinctions. Are we to judge the effectiveness of order solely as an aspect of the inter-state system, and thus speak of international order? Or are we to widen the discussion and consider order in terms of its impact on individual human lives and aspirations, and thus talk of a **world order**? Such a distinction is widely noted in the literature, and is replicated in the similar distinction between international society and world society (Clark 2007). However, how does the introduction of the concept of globalization affect the analysis? Does globalized order signify the same as world order or something different? An attempt will be made to answer that question towards the end of this chapter.

The search for the definitive elements of the contemporary order proceeds within quite separate theoretical frameworks (see Introduction). The first is the broadly realist (see Ch. 5). This concentrates upon the structure

of the post-cold war system, especially upon the number of great power actors and the distribution of capabilities among them. It defines order largely in terms of the security structure. It spawned a debate in the early 1990s about the polarity of the post-cold war system, about the possibility of a renewed **concert**, and about the worrisome eventuality that a return to **multipolarity** could herald the erosion of the stability generated by the cold war's bipolarity.

The second is broadly liberal in derivation and focuses upon regimes and institutions, and their associated norms and values (see Ch. 6). Its central claim is that patterns of integration and interdependence had become so deeply embedded in the cold war period, albeit for strategic and geopolitical reasons, that they had by then created a self-sustaining momentum. Since complex systems of **global governance** had been spawned in the interim, these regimes would survive the collapse of the 'realist' conditions that had given rise to them in the first place.

A third line is the one that assesses order in terms of its achievement of individual human emancipation. The mere fact of stability among the major powers, or the institutionalization of relations among the dominant groups of states, tells us little about the quality of life for most inhabitants of the globe. If it is true, as writers like Ken Booth (1999) argue, that governments are the main source of the abuse of human rights, we need to do more than study the international human rights' agreements that these very governments enter into, but look also at what is really happening to people on the ground (see Ch. 30).

Table 33.1 Typologies of order

	Units	Characteristics
Globalized	Global system	End of national polities, societies, and economies
International	States	Concern with agenda of sovereignty and stability
World	Humanity	Concern with agenda of rights, needs, and justice
Globalized international	Globalized states	Agenda of managing relations between states penetrated by global system but still distinguishable within it

A fourth line of exploration is directly via the literature on globalization. This chapter asks simply whether or not globalization may be thought tantamount to a form of order. Must we speak of globalization as an ongoing process without any end-state, or can we instead speak of a globalized order as a distinctive political form? The latter view is clearly set forth in the suggestion that the contemporary Western state conglomerate, collectively, constitutes an 'emergent *global state*' (Shaw 1997: 503–4; 2000). Globalization, on this view, represents an incipient political order in its own right.

Key Points

- When we speak of order, we need to specify order for whom—states, peoples, groups, or individuals.
- International order focuses on stable and peaceful relations between states, often related to the balance of power. It is primarily about military security.
- World order is concerned with other values, such as justice, development, rights, and emancipation.
- A pattern of order may advance some values at the expense of others.

The elements of contemporary order

The 'social-state' system

Initially, there is the basic nature of the contemporary state system itself. The state system is 'social', first, in the sense that states over the past century have performed a range of social functions that distinguish them from earlier phases. The great revival in the political viability of states, from the nadir of the Second World War, is attributable to the largely successful undertaking of this task. While not all states are equal in their ability to deliver these functions, most would now list responsibility for development and economic management, health, welfare, and social planning as essential tasks for the state.

It is 'social' also in the second sense that pressures for emulation tend to reinforce common patterns of behaviour, and similar forms of state institutional structure. Historically, states have emulated each other in developing the social and economic infrastructures of military power. Now this task has broadened as states seek to adopt 'best practice' in terms of economic competitiveness and efficiency. They also face the social pressure to conform to certain standards of human rights, and this has permitted a measure of dilution and delegation of the state's exclusive jurisdiction over its own domestic affairs. In consequence, some of the key rules of the states-system (sovereignty, non-intervention) are undergoing considerable adaptation, and this gives the contemporary order many of its complex and ambivalent qualities.

Identity and the nation-state

A second feature is the multiplicity of issues about identity that have become prevalent since the 1990s. Some of these revolve around contemporary forms of nationalism (see Ch. 24), and are subject to contested assessments as to whether they represent a 'new' nationalism, or a reversion to a pre-existing **primordialism**. The state is both challenged and reinforced by a welter of additional crises of identity—tendencies towards apparently new forms of political community driven by ethnic separatism, regional identities, new transnational projects, new social movements, and the return to culture/religion (see Ch. 25). The key question here is the extent to which these are wholly new tendencies, or represent some kind of historical atavism. The politics of identity at the beginning of the new millennium affects the social nature of the state, as it raises explicit questions about citizenship—who is to count as a citizen, and what is the nature of the contract between state and citizen (see Ch. 32).

It must not, however, be imagined that all such issues of identity have emerged only in the aftermath of the cold war. For example, it could be said that there has been a widespread reaction throughout much of the developing world against what has been seen as the imposition of a modernizing, Westernizing, and secular form of state. The revolution in Iran in 1979 is a case in point, and cautions us not to assume that 'identity politics' were invented simply with the end of the cold war. This is particularly so with regard to the resurgence of religion as a factor in international relations. While it may seem that religion has suddenly been rediscovered, the more plausible account is that it had never gone away, but had simply been less visible under the alternative distractions of the cold war.

Polarity and the collectivization of security

A key area of concern remains the traditional security order. This addresses the present distribution of power, and whether that distribution should be described as **unipolarity**, or as bipolar, multipolar, or some kind of hybrid. This debate has shifted considerably since the early 1990s. At that point, expectations of a resumption of **multipolarity** were widespread, and a US-centred unipolarity thought likely to last for a 'moment', at most. Since then, US predominance has become much more clearly established, so that analysts now routinely refer to American **hegemony**, or some kind of American empire (see Ch. 4). This trend results from US economic successes during the 1990s, coupled with the ongoing difficulties of its other competitors. Japan's economy stagnated over the same period. Russia became embroiled in protracted and deep-seated domestic political and economic transformation. The European Union, although it has both widened and deepened, continues to have difficulty in acting decisively on its own in international crises. China's power remains a long-term prospect, although its economy has certainly grown prodigiously in the early years of the new millennium. In consequence, a key determinant of the present security order remains the role of the USA, and its willingness to become involved in general order-maintenance. This element has been highly variable, with the prominent US role in Kosovo in 1999 and in Iraq in 2003 standing in marked contrast to its unwillingness to become engaged in Rwanda in 1994 or Sudan in 2005–6.

The organization of production and exchange

Another prominent dimension is the political economy of the present order. Central to it is the degree of stability within the international trading and financial systems. The former remains beset by disputes between the world's three great trading groups or **triads**, and their trading relationship with the developing world; the latter shows periodic signs of undergoing meltdown, as during the financial turmoil that afflicted the East Asian economies towards the late 1990s, and the global economy in

2008. This economic order is partially managed by those elements of governance institutionalized in bodies such as the International Monetary Fund (IMF), the World Bank, and the World Trade Organization (WTO). The resulting economic order penetrates deeply: such bodies do not determine just the rules for international trade and borrowing, nor shape exchange rates alone. The full effects of this **internationalization** of production include its impact on those many other things that determine the quality of human lives: production of military equipment, the condition of the environment, social welfare, human (and specifically child) rights in the area of labour, and gender inequalities within the economy and in processes of development.

Multilateral management and governance

One remarkable aspect of the order is the highly dense network of contemporary forms of international governance (regimes, international organizations, and INGOs). These cover most aspects of life, including developments in legal (human rights, war crimes, the International Criminal Court), environmental (Kyoto Protocol), and economic regimes, as well as in the core peacekeeping activities of universal organizations like the United Nations. To what extent can we sensibly refer to globalization as giving rise, in turn, to a system of global governance? What is its potential for further development? Are current international regimes dependent on the underlying power structure of Western dominance and reflective of Western preferences, and how sustainable are they given the cultural diversity of the present world? These issues link the discussion directly to the next element of order, since much of this regime infrastructure is to be found at a regional level.

Regionalism

The development of contemporary regionalism (see Ch. 26) is yet another key to understanding the emerging

---

Box 33.2 Elements of order

Structural elements	Purposive elements
Polarity	Social-state
Multilateralism	Identity
Regionalism	Economic order
Two worlds	Liberal rights

order. This takes various forms, including economic (trading regions), security (such as NATO), and cultural activities. The intensification of regionalism is occasionally viewed as a denial of globalization, but is more plausibly regarded as one aspect of it, rather than as evidence to the contrary. The fact that a number of regions feel the need to develop regional institutions is itself a manifestation of globalization, in the same way that the universal spread of the nation-state, as the principal political form, was an earlier product of globalization. None the less, there are interesting questions about the significance of regionalism for the post-cold war order, such as the seemingly greater degree of autonomy 'enjoyed' by regions since the end of the cold war, and the role of regions in constituting new forms of identity. There is perhaps a paradox that, with the loss of cold war constraints, regions now appear to have greater autonomy—while, at the same time, levels of interpenetration and globalization indicate diminished possibilities for regional insulation.

The liberal rights order

Arguably, this is the feature with the most striking continuities to the cold war period. Human rights had become a conspicuous feature of post-1945 international politics, largely in reaction to the catastrophic experiences of the period before 1945 (see Ch. 30). This theme was a paramount aspect of the cold war period itself and was again highlighted with the collapse of the Soviet bloc, since that event was portrayed as a major step forward in extending the liberal order. In this respect, the focus on **liberal rights** is another element of continuity between the two periods. However, the post-cold war order is paradoxically under pressure precisely because of its seemingly greater promotion of a type of universalism, thought to be evoking forms of religious and cultural resistance.

This relates directly to wider questions about the future of democratization. How this develops is of momentous import for the future stability of the international order and touches on a series of interrelated issues: about the status of democracy as a universal norm; the current variable experience with democratization; the pressures upon democracy arising from globalization (and hence the appeals for cosmopolitan forms of democracy); and the future of democracy as a source of inter-state peace and stability (see Ch. 14).

North–South and the two world orders

Any examination of the contemporary order must give a high profile to the apparent gulf within it, separating the experience of the industrialized North from the increasingly marginalized South. Some see the tensions to which this gives rise as undermining the prospects for longer-term stability (see Ch. 28). Are North–South relations more stable now than in previous eras, or do they remain precariously rooted in inequalities of power, massive gaps in quality of life, and incompatibilities of cultural values? It is also a very moot point, and a key area of disagreement, whether globalization is aggravating these inequalities, or, as its supporters believe, whether it remains the best available means of rectifying them in the longer term. Otherwise expressed, are the problems of the South due to the processes of globalization, or to the South's relative exclusion from them? In any case, does this divide threaten the durability of the post-cold war order, or must we simply recognize it as a key component of that order, and for that reason understand it as an element of structural continuity with its predecessors?

As against this image of two monolithic blocs of North and South, other analysts insist that such a conception is now out of date. The impacts of globalization cut across states and not just between them, yielding complex patterns of stratification that defy easy classification into North and South. There are enormous variations and inequalities within states, and regions, and not just between them. For this reason, it may be too artificial to speak of two such orders, as there is much more diversity than such crude dichotomies tend to imply.

Key Points

- Order is shaped by the changed nature of states and of the tasks they perform.
- Security is increasingly dealt with on a multilateral basis, even when this does not conform to classical 'collective security' models.
- The global economy is primarily shaped by relations between the three key groupings (North America, Western Europe, and East Asia) and is managed by a panoply of Western-dominated institutions.
- Human rights have a much higher profile than in earlier historical periods.
- Are there two separate orders in the North and South, or a more complex diversity of orders?

Box 33.3 Interpretations of globalization and the end of the cold war

'The end of the Cold War division into competing world orders marks a crucial substantive and symbolic transition to single-world economic, cultural and political orders.'

(Shaw 1999: 194)

'America has ceased to be a superpower, because it has met its match: globalization–a globalization which, moreover, it helps to promote despite not managing to master totally its meaning.'

(Laidi 1998: 170)

'Globalization is the most significant development and theme in contemporary life and social theory to emerge since the collapse of Marxist systems.'

(Albrow 1996: 89)

'Globalists continue to maintain that there are big, *fin-de-siècle* transformations under way in the world at large, which can be laid at the door of something called globalization. This new era—popularized as "a world without borders" and symbolized by the dismantling of the Berlin Wall—ostensibly came into its own where the cold war left off.'

(Weiss 1999: 59)

'To talk of 1989 as the beginning of globalisation is very mislead-ing. . . . [G]lobalisation . . . was happening during the Cold War and has continued since. If the Cold War system dominated inter-national politics from 1945 to 1989, then its successor is Ameri-can hegemony, not globalisation.'

(Legrain 2002: 11)

Globalization and the post-Westphalian order

There is a tendency to regard the current high degree of globalization as simply a consequence of the end of the cold war. This view has become coupled to a more general argument about the end of the Westphalian order.

Not surprisingly, many commentators see the post-cold war period as characterized by the intensification of the processes of globalization, particularly with regard to financial integration. The global financial order is now virtually universal in its reach, as is the influence of its principal institutions, such as the World Bank and the International Monetary Fund.

On this reasoning, it is the ending of the cold war that has allowed the further spread of globalization, and we can therefore regard the scope of globalization as a point of difference between the cold war and post-cold war worlds. Unfortunately, there is a danger in such an analysis. The problem is that to regard globalization as simply the consequence of the end of the cold war is to neglect the extent to which globalization also served as a cause of its end. In other words, globalization marks a point of continuity, not simply discontinuity, between the two periods.

In a wider sense, the danger with such a procedure is that it neglects other dimensions of continuity, such as in the construction of a liberal capitalist order (Ikenberry 2001). What is the historical evidence for this type of argument? Its principal element is the view that globalization developed out of the core of Western capitalist states that formed during the cold war. This became such a powerful force that it finally both weakened the other cold war protagonist, namely the Soviet Union, and also made the point of the cold war increasingly irrelevant. As regards the Soviet Union, what damaged and eroded its capacity as a military power was precisely the fact that it had not become integrated into the financial and technological sinews of global capitalism. As regards the logic of the cold war as a whole, the existence of a hostile Soviet bloc was crucial in the initial integration of the Western system. By the 1980s, however, this system was effectively self-sustaining, and no longer required any external enemy to provide its dynamic for growth. In this sense, the Soviet Union had become redundant as far as the needs of the dominant Western system were concerned.

If globalization was both an element of the pre-existing cold war system and also stands out sharply as an element of the contemporary order, it needs to be seen as a point of continuity between the two periods. This logic, in turn, requires us to concede that the present order is not *sui generis*, as it contains within it elements previously present during the cold war. This suggests that the contemporary order should be understood as not wholly distinct from that which preceded it. But if globalization is the element that binds both together, can it be also the key to understanding the present order?

The claim that globalization defines the essential quality of the present order has been denied for a number of reasons. Most generally, if globalization is seen as a long-term historical trend—with various waves—then to interpret the present order in terms of globalization does not say enough about what is specific to the current situation in particular.

Beyond this, globalization has been described as the dystopic absence of order. The general claim is that 'no one seems now to be in control' (Bauman 1998: 58). It is for this reason that globalization has come to be associated with a more general thesis about the demise of the Westphalian order. This system had typified the order since 1648, and its hallmarks were clearly defined states, with hard borders, each enjoying full sovereignty and jurisdiction within its own territory. The rules of the game dictated that states would not intervene in the domestic affairs of each other. Globalization, in contrast, is thought to question the efficacy of borders. This is very much so in the case of the global economy, where it is suggested that borders no longer mean as much as they once did. It also applies to other aspects of political life, such as human rights and humanitarian intervention, where the norms of the Westphalian order have come under increasing pressure.

All these arguments suggest that globalization may be inadequate as the exclusive conceptual basis for understanding the contemporary order because of what globalization *does*. It is too varied in its effects, and so lacking in purpose and goals, so that we cannot visualize a single order constructed on that basis alone.

Indeed, the main theme of these writings is just how disorderly is the process of globalization. But a different form of argument can be made on the basis of what globalization *is*, not just what it does. We need to be more precise about its nature, and not look only at its effects. This will be set out in the final section, after we have reviewed some of the political problems that appear to be attached to globalization today. These arise exactly from that sense of purposelessness and lack of control.

Key Points

- Globalization is often portrayed as an effect of the end of the cold war because this led to its further geographical spread.

- At the same time, globalization needs to be understood as one of the factors that contributed to the end of the cold war. It was the Soviet Union's marginalization from processes of globalization that revealed, and intensified, its weaknesses.

- Accordingly, globalization should be regarded as an element of continuity between the cold war and post-cold-war orders.

- There is reason for scepticism that globalization is the exclusive hallmark of contemporary order.

- Globalization embodies a range of often competing values.

Globalization and legitimacy

On the face of it, globalization potentially creates several problems for the political stability of the current order. Not least is this so with regard to its legitimacy. There is a widely shared view that the emergence of a diffuse protest movement against globalization is symptomatic of a new wave of resistance to it. This creates tensions at several levels. The central problem is understood to be one of the limited effectiveness of democratic practice in present world conditions. At a time when so much emphasis is placed on the virtues of democracy, many question its viability when organized on a purely national basis, given the context of globalization. There are two facets to this issue: representation and accountability. It is all very well for citizens to be represented in national electoral institutions, but what voice does this give them in controlling those very economic, social, and cultural forces that cut across national borders, if

their own governments do not have the capacity to deal with these? Conversely, this creates an issue of accountability. There may be little point in holding national and local politicians accountable through elections if these politicians remain relatively powerless to exercise influence over global corporations, global technology, global environmental changes, or the global financial system. These concerns apply specifically to just how democratic are bodies such as the World Bank and the International Monetary Fund, as well as international organizations such as the United Nations. On a regional level, there has been recurrent anxiety about the so-called legitimacy deficits that afflict the institutions of the European Union (see Ch. 26). The general issue is the lack of congruence between the geographical organization of our various political systems, and the 'deterritorialized' nature of our current economic, social, and political activities.

In the face of these concerns, there has been much debate about the role of an emerging global civil society (Keane 2003). This embraces a variety of cross-national social movements, including anti-globalization activists, as well as a multitude of international non-governmental organizations, such as Greenpeace and Amnesty International. Their proponents see these movements as the only feasible way of directly influencing global policies on such matters as development, environment, human rights, and international security, and hence as the best way of democratizing global governance. Others, however, remain sceptical. There is nothing inherently democratic about global civil society as such, as there is no legitimate basis of representation or accountability to many of these movements (Van Rooy 2003). They may simply represent sectional interests, and make policy hostage to those that are better organized, have greater resources, and are more vocal.

Indeed, from the perspective of many governments in the South, global civil society may aggravate the inequalities between rich and poor. Civil society is resented as an extension of the power of the North, for the reason that such movements have a much more solid basis in the developed world, and are more likely to speak for its interests. This is illustrated, for example, in the tension between the economic development objectives of many governments in the South, and the preferred policies of many environmental movements in the North. The possible objection is that this perpetuates the sense of two contrasting global orders, one for the North (represented both by strong governments and strong civil society movements) as against the South (led by weak governments, and weakly organized civil society). This may contribute to a perceived crisis of legitimacy for the state in the developing world.

Key Points

- Traditional democracy does not offer effective representation in the global order.

- National elections may not make politicians accountable if they cannot control wider global forces.

- There is a heated debate about whether global civil society can help democratize international institutions.

- Some governments in the South remain suspicious of social movements that may be better organized in developed countries.

Box 33.4 The debate about globalization and legitimacy

'The process of globalization has had a mixed impact on the legitimacy of international organizations. The demand for international co-ordination and common action has obviously increased. But at the same time, the effectiveness of IOs has diminished.'

(Junne 2001: 218–19)

'Global structures violate commitments to the politics of consent: there is a global democratic deficit that must be reduced if worldwide arrangements are to be legitimate.'

(Linklater 1999: 477)

'It will be argued that the rising need for enlarged and deepened international cooperation in the age of globalization led to the establishment of new international institutions with specific features. As a result, the intrusiveness of those new international institutions into national societies has increased dramatically.'

(Zurn 2004: 261–2)

'The democratic project is to globalize democracy as we have globalized the economy. '

(Barber 2002: 255)

'Some theorists have pointed to the activity of social movements working beyond state borders as a method of increasing democratic practice. They see a contradiction between the fact that the structures of power . . . are firmly rooted in the global context, but participation, representation and legitimacy are fixed at the state level.'

(O' Brien et al. 2000: 21–2)

'However much individual INGOs and global social movements may have contributed to the extension of democratic politics across the world, they do not currently possess the requisite degree of legitimacy and accountability to be considered as democratic representatives in a globalized political community.'

(Colas 2002: 163)

'Rather than reform, these critics insist that what is required is an alternative system of global governance, privileging people over profits, and the local over the global.'

(Held and McGrew 2002: 64)

Case Study   The crisis of developing state legitimacy

The idea of the two world orders—one applying to the rich and stable North and the other to the poor and unstable South—reinforces the image of a crisis of state legitimacy in the South. Many of these have, since decolonization, been depicted as quasi-states (Jackson 1990), not enjoying the full capacities of strong states. The period since the end of the cold war has reinforced this tendency. It has become commonplace to refer to a number of failed states (e.g. Lebanon, Cambodia, Afghanistan,

Somalia, Rwanda, Zaïre, Zimbabwe), indicating their inability to maintain central order within the state, or to produce at least minimal conditions of social welfare and economic subsistence. In some cases, law and order has broken down into civil war, creating fiefdoms organized by rival warlords.

The deployment by the international community of a number of peacebuilding missions has been implicitly justified on the grounds of the 'failure' of these national authorities to maintain order on their own, especially in the aftermath of international or civil conflict. This has been associated with the revival of doctrines of trusteeship in the international community, charging the strong with some responsibility for protecting the welfare of the weak.

However, there is considerable resentment against this notion of failed states, and it is often suggested that the failures are exactly the outcome of the structural conditions that the Northern powers have themselves created by their economic and political actions. This resentment leads to charges that the instruments of the international community are being used to erode the political legitimacy of Southern governments, thereby making Southern societies more vulnerable to intervention, and more adaptable to the preferences of the rich states. This is further compounded when the most powerful states themselves question the legitimacy of some governments, by designating them as rogue states, or sponsors of terrorism, and questioning their full entitlement to be represented within international negotiations, or to enjoy equal rights with other states. The objection raised is that state failures, and the resulting diminished legitimacy of developing states, are not 'objective' conditions but the products of Northern policies.

1 What causes a state to fail?

2 What responsibility do rich states have for 'failures' in the developing world?

3 Does the international community have a right to administer failed states?

An international order of globalized states?

The chapter now returns to whether globalization can be regarded as the defining element in contemporary order. Globalization could be taken to represent the mainstay of today's order only if it superseded all traditional elements of the international order. But if globalization is an addition to, not a substitute for, the existing international order, then it is not wholly adequate to the task of providing us with the single key to the post-cold war order.

If it can be convincingly held that globalization is not some process over and above the activities of states, but is instead an element within state transformation, we

can develop on this basis a conception of the **globalized state**. Globalization does not make the state disappear, but is a way of thinking about its present form. By extension, globalization does not make redundant the notion of an **international order**, but instead requires us to think about a globalized international order. In short, what is required is a notion of international order composed of globalized states.

Much of the confusion results from the tendency to see globalization as exclusively pertaining to the environment in which states find themselves: globalization

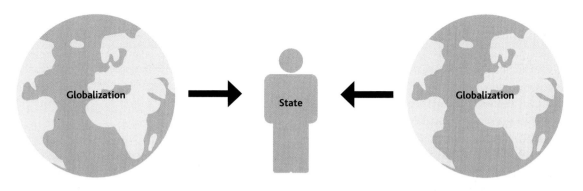

Figure 33.1 Outside-in view of globalization

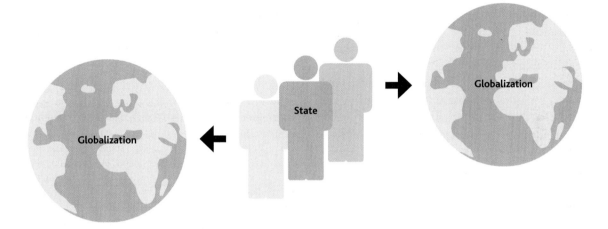

Figure 33.2 Inside-out view of globalization

is a force wholly external to the individual states, and demands an outside-in perspective on the resulting outcomes. On this view, globalization is a claim about the degree of interconnectedness between states, such that the significance of borders, and the reality of separate national actors, is called seriously into question. There is no denying that this is part of what globalization signifies. But what such a one-sided interpretation leaves out is the extent to which globalization refers also to a 'domestic' process of change within states. Regarded in this alternative way, globalization can be understood as an expression of the profound transformations in the nature of the state, and in state–society relations, that have developed in recent decades. This requires an inside-out view of globalization as well. This leads us to think not of the demise or retreat of the state, but about its changing functionality: states still exist but do different things, do some things less well than they used to, and also have taken on new responsibilities in exchange.

Even in an age of globalization, there remain both states and a states-system. We need to face the seeming paradox that there can indeed be an international order of globalized states.

Key Points

- Globalization is often thought of as an extreme form of interdependence. This sees it exclusively as an outside-in development.

- The implication of such analyses is that states are now much weaker as actors. Consequently, they are in retreat or becoming obsolete.

- But if globalization is considered as a transformation in the nature of states themselves, this suggests that states are still central to the discussion of order: they are different but not obsolete. This leads to the idea of a globalized state as a state form, and introduces an inside-out element.

- In this case, there is no contradiction between the norms and rules of a state system operating alongside globalized states.

The global financial crisis

The financial upheaval during 2007–9 lends further support to the core argument of this chapter. On the one hand, it certainly seemed to reaffirm the strong version of the globalization thesis that the world is so powerfully interconnected that no state can isolate itself from harmful impacts. This was demonstrated in the speed with which the sub-prime credit implosion in the USA transmitted itself globally. As the squeeze on international lending affected the real economy, production and trade experienced sharp falls, and even economies such as China's were caught up in its consequences.

On the other hand, the response to the crisis gave the lie to those accounts suggesting that the global economy was no longer embedded in state and political structures, and somehow was able to operate autonomously. The most striking feature of the events of 2008 was the return of state action to underwrite the banking and financial sectors. Leading states, including the USA, had to bail out the banks, either through loans, or effectively through forms of nationalization. Even the USA, the bastion of laissez-faire capitalism, undertook unprecedented levels of governmental intervention in the economy, including the automobile industry. As governments introduced their various stimulus packages to try to push their economies out of recession, there was even a barely concealed attempt to interfere with the market by veiled forms of protectionism.

In short, if the discussion of globalization hitherto had tended to proceed on the basis of a false opposition between globalization and state power—viewed as in a zero-sum relation where more globalization further weakened the role of states—then the financial crunch of 2008 made abundantly clear the extent to which a global economy and global finance remained critically dependent on structural supports from state sources. Indeed, this age of globalization witnessed the return to unusually high levels of **state capitalism** in the so-called market economies.

The major challenge to a business-as-usual model for the future global economy comes from climate change. While responding to this challenge appears particularly difficult during an economic recession, with many competing demands on public finances, the move towards a post-carbon economy is being presented as an opportunity for, not an obstacle to, economic recovery. How far, and how fast, this will go depends on interlocking domestic and international negotiations. Domestically, many governments are trying to enact 'clean energy' legislation to curb emissions. Internationally, much depends on whether an effective post-Kyoto regime can be implemented, and whether it will deliver an acceptable deal between developed and developing states (see Ch. 21). It is no longer possible to talk about the future of globalization without placing responses to climate change at the centre of the discussion.

What all this suggests is that we are not witnessing the end of globalization. More realistically, the financial crisis points towards the beginning of the end of one version of it. That particular model of Anglo-American financial deregulation that has reigned supreme since the 1980s does, indeed, now face major challenges (Gamble 2009). It certainly faces an almost universal crisis of legitimacy, both at the governmental and at the civil society levels. By itself, however, this does not indicate the end of globalization. Levels of interdependence remain very high. While there is, at the moment, a strong desire to insulate national economies from the worst excesses of deregulation, this is unlikely to go as far as policies aimed actively to cut national economies adrift from the global. Virtually all states retain high stakes in this economy. While there is much talk of a burgeoning Chinese economy coming to take the place of the USA as the most powerful influence, there is nothing to suggest that China is about to lead the attack on the international economy, given its own high dependence upon access to it. Had China wished to destroy the liberal project, 2008 presented its best opportunity for doing so. Instead, China played its part in helping to bail out the stricken US economy. We do not yet face the end of globalization, because there is no major state interested in acting as the champion of deglobalization.

Key Points

- Toxic debts rapidly infected the global financial system.
- State intervention was needed to support the system.
- We are seeing the end of one version of globalization, rather than the end of globalization.
- Responses to climate change are now a key driver of future shape of global economy
- Deglobalization has no political champion.

Conclusion

In short, we now face a hybrid situation in which states share a host of responsibilities with both intergovernmental organizations and a multiplicity of non-governmental and transnational actors. This does not, however, mean that the international order has become redundant. It means simply that it needs to be redesigned to take account of the new division of labour between states, global networks, and the rudimentary forms of global governance. As long as states persist as important sources of political agency, they will construct a states-system with its own rules and norms. It is this that we regard as the essential basis of the international order. Currently, the identity of states is undergoing considerable change, to the extent that we can describe them as globalized states. But these globalized states still coexist within an international order, albeit one that now differs from its recent historical forms. This order is currently seeking to develop a set of principles to reflect that transformation. The quest for a post-cold war order is the expression of this uneasy search. There is no reason to assume that recent trends are irreversible, as the revival of the security state after 11 September would seem to indicate. Likewise, the return to forms of **state capitalism** during 2008 was almost wholly unexpected. The globalized state of the late twentieth century is evidently not the only model of likely state development in the future.

Questions

1 Is the post-cold war order still an international order?
2 How important an element in the contemporary order is the condition of globalization?
3 How would you distinguish between an international and a world order, and which is the more important framework for assessing the contemporary situation?
4 In which respects are the 'identities' of states undergoing change?
5 How would you define the polarity of the contemporary international system?
6 Is regionalism a contradiction of globalization?
7 Is the prominence of democracy and liberal rights convincing evidence of the impact of globalization? If so, why is globalization so problematic for democracy?
8 In which ways is globalization creating problems of political legitimacy?
9 Does the 2008 financial crisis point to the end of globalization?
10 Is the idea of an international order of globalized states contradictory?

Further Reading

International order

Bull, H. (1977), *The Anarchical Society: A Study of Order in World Politics* (London: Macmillan), especially Part 1. Provides the standard introduction to this issue from an international society perspective.

Cox, R. (1996), 'Social Forces, States, and World Orders: Beyond International Relations Theory', in R. Cox with T. J. Sinclair, *Approaches to World Order* (Cambridge: Cambridge University Press). An alternative to the 'English School' approach, and steps outside the state-centric framework.

New world orders and the post-cold-war world

Clark, I. (2001), *The Post-Cold War Order: The Spoils of Peace* (Oxford: Oxford University Press). Presents a guide to the debates about the post-cold-war period, viewing the order as the equivalent of a historical peace settlement.

Ikenberry, G. J. (2001), *After Victory: Institutions, Strategic Restraint, and the Rebuilding of Order after Major Wars* (Princeton, NJ: Princeton University Press). Also sets post-cold-war developments in their historical context and argues for the emergence of an increasingly 'constitutional' international order after 1945.

Globalization in the present order

Clark, I. (1999), *Globalization and International Relations Theory* (Oxford: Oxford University Press). Develops a theoretical account of globalization in terms of state transformation.

—— (1997), *Globalization and Fragmentation: International Relations in the Twentieth Century* (Oxford: Oxford University Press). Places the contemporary debates about globalization in historical perspective.

Friedman, T. L. (2006), *The World is Flat: The Globalized World in the Twenty-First Century* (London: Penguin). A detailed journalistic account of the impacts of globalization.

Held, D., and McGrew, A. (eds) (2003), *The Global Transformations Reader: An Introduction to the Globalization Debate*, 2nd edn (Cambridge: Polity Press). A detailed selection of readings about contemporary globalization and its implications.

Wolf, M. (2004), *Why Globalization Works: The Case for the Global Market Economy* (New Haven, CT: Yale University Press). Offers a defence of the economic benefits of globalization.

International legitimacy

Clark, I. (2005), *Legitimacy in International Society* (Oxford: Oxford University Press). Explores the nature of legitimacy within the states system.

—— (2007), *International Legitimacy and World Society* (Oxford: Oxford University Press). Tries to explain how world-society norms are adopted by international society.

The global financial crisis

Gamble, A. (2009), *The Spectre at the Feast: Capitalist Crisis and the Politics of Recession* (Basingstoke: Palgrave Macmillan). An overview of the economic drama of 2007–9.

Online Resource Centre

 Visit the Online Resource Centre that accompanies this book to access more learning resources on this chapter topic at www.oxfordtextbooks.co.uk/orc/baylis5e/

Glossary

Absolute gains: all states seek to gain more power and influence in the system to secure their national interests. This is absolute gain. Offensive neo-realists are also concerned with increasing power relative to other states. One must have enough power to secure interests and more power than any other state in the system—friend or foe.

Abuse: states justify self-interested wars by reference to humanitarian principles.

Agent-structure problem: the problem is how to think about the relationship between agents and structures. One view is that agents are born with already formed identities and interests and then treat other actors and the broad structure that their interactions produce as a constraint on their interests. But this suggests that actors are pre-social to the extent that there is little interest in their identities or possibility that they might change their interests through their interactions with others. Another view is to treat the structure not as a constraint but rather as constituting the actors themselves. Yet this might treat agents as cultural dupes because they are nothing more than artefacts of that structure. The proposed solution to the agent-structure problem is to try and find a way to understand how agents and structures constitute each other.

Anarchic system: the 'ordering principle' of international politics according to realism, and that which defines its structure as lacking any central authority.

Anarchy: a system operating in the absence of any central government. Does not imply chaos, but in realist theory the absence of political authority.

Anti-foundationalist: positions argue that there are never neutral grounds for asserting what is true in any given time or space. Our theories of world define what counts as the facts and so there is no neutral position available to determine between rival claims.

Apartheid: system of racial segregation introduced in South Africa in 1948, designed to ensure white minority domination.

Appeasement: a policy of making concessions to a revanchist (or otherwise territorially acquisitive) state in the hope that settlement of more modest claims will assuage that state's expansionist appetites. Appeasement remains most (in)famously associated with British Prime Minister Neville Chamberlain's acquiescence to Hitler's incursions into Austria and then Czechoslovakia, culminating in the Munich Agreement of September 1938. Since then, appeasement has generally been seen as synonymous with a craven collapse before the demands of dictators—encouraging, not disarming, their aggressive designs.

ASEAN (Association of Southeast Asian Nations): a geopolitical and economic organization of several countries located in Southeast Asia. Initially formed as a display of solidarity against Communism, its aims now have been redefined and broadened to include the acceleration of economic growth and the promotion of regional peace. By 2005 the ASEAN countries had a combined GDP of about $884 billion.

Asian financial crisis: the severe disruption to the economies of Thailand, South Korea, Malaysia, the Philippines and Indonesia in 1997/1998, starting as huge international speculation against the prevailing price of those five countries' currencies and then spreading to intense balance sheet problems for their banking sectors.

Asymmetrical globalization: describes the way in which contemporary globalization is unequally experienced across the world and among different social groups in such a way that it produces a distinctive geography of inclusion in, and exclusion from, the global system.

Axis of evil: phrase deliberately used by George W. Bush in January 2002 to characterize Iran, North Korea, and Iraq.

Balance of power: in realist theory, refers to an equilibrium between states; historical realists regard it as the product of diplomacy (contrived balance) whereas structural realists regard the system as having a tendency towards a natural equilibrium (fortuitous balance). It is a doctrine and an arrangement whereby the power of one state (or group of states) is checked by the countervailing power of other states.

Balance of trade: the difference in monetary value between a country's exports and its imports: if a country is exporting more than it is importing it has a balance of trade surplus; if it is importing more than it is exporting it has a balance of trade deficit.

Bandung Conference: a conference held in 1955 in Bandung Indonesia by representatives of twenty-nine African and Asian countries to encourage decolonization and promote economic and cultural cooperation. The conference led to the establishment of the Non-Aligned Movement of 1961.

Battle of the sexes: a scenario in game theory illustrating the need for a coordination strategy.

Battlespace: in the era of aircraft and satellites, the traditional 'battlefield' has given way to the three-dimensional battlespace.

Biopolitics: concept introduced by Foucault; identifies two forms of intertwined power: the disciplining of the individual body and the regulation of populations.

Breadwinner: a traditionally masculine role of working in the public sphere for wages and providing for the economic needs of the family.

Bretton Woods: the regulatory system introduced at the end of the Second World War in an attempt to bring stability to those elements of the world economy under the US sphere of influence. The underlying objective of Bretton Woods was to provide sufficient policy space within domestic economies for governments to intervene in the interests of ensuring full employment.

Brezhnev doctrine: declaration by Soviet premier Leonid Brezhnev in November 1968 that members of the Warsaw Pact would enjoy only 'limited sovereignty' in their political development. It was associated with the idea of 'limited sovereignty' for Soviet bloc nations, which was used to justify the crushing of the reform movement in Czechoslovakia in 1968.

Brute facts: exist independently of human agreement and will continue to exist even if humans disappear or deny their existence. Constructivists and poststructuralists disagree as to whether brute facts are socially constructed.

Capabilities: the resources that are under an actor's direct control such as population or size of territory, resources, economic strength, military capability, and competence (Waltz 1979: 131).

Capacity building: providing the funds and technical training to allow developing countries to participate in global environmental governance.

Capital controls: formal restrictions on the movement of money from one country to another in an attempt to ensure that finance retains a 'national' rather than a 'global' character. Such restrictions were especially associated with the Bretton Woods system introduced to regulate the western elements of the world economy in the immediate aftermath of the Second World War. They created enhanced policy manoeuvrability for governments seeking to intervene in the economy in an attempt to ensure that the objective of low unemployment was met. Few remnants of the Bretton Woods system of capital controls remain today, and the IMF has created for itself the authority to ensure that they are most unlikely to return.

Capitalism: a system of production in which human labour and its products are commodities that are bought and sold in the market-place. In Marxist analysis, the capitalist mode of production involved a specific set of social relations that were particular to a specific historical period. For Marx there were three main characteristics of capitalism: (1) Everything involved in production (e.g. raw materials, machines, labour involved in the creation of commodities, and the commodities themselves) is given an exchange value, and all can be exchanged, one for the other. In essence, under capitalism everything has its price, including people's working time. (2) Everything that is needed to undertake production (i.e. the factories, and the raw materials) is owned by one class—the capitalists. (3) Workers are 'free', but in order to survive must sell their labour to the capitalist class, and because the capitalist class own the means of production, and control the relations of production, they also control the profit that results from the labour of workers.

Citizenship: the status of having the right to participate in and to be represented in politics.

Civic nationalism: a nationalism which claims the nation is based on commitment to a common set of political values and institutions.

Civil and political rights: one of the two principal groups of internationally recognized human rights. They provide legal protections against abuse by the state and seek to ensure political participation for all citizens. Examples include equality before the law, protection against torture, and freedoms of religion, speech, assembly, and political participation.

Civil society: (1) the totality of all individuals and groups in a society who are not acting as participants in any government institutions, or (2) all individuals and groups who are neither participants in government nor acting in the interests of commercial companies. The two meanings are incompatible and contested. There is a third meaning: the network of social institutions and practices (economic relationships, family and kinship groups, religious, and other social affiliations) which underlie strictly political institutions. For democratic theorists the voluntary character of these associations is taken to be essential to the workings of democratic politics.

Clash of civilizations: controversial idea first used by Samuel Huntington in 1993 to describe the main cultural fault-line of international conflict in a world without communism; the notion has become more popular still since 9/11.

Class: Groups of people in society who share similar characteristics. Used by Marxists in an economic sense to denote people who share the same relationship to the means of production—in capitalist society the bourgeoisie, which owns the means of production, and the proletariat, which do not own the means of production, and in order to subsist, must sell their labour.

Coexistence: the doctrine of live and let live between political communities, or states.

Cold war: extended worldwide conflict between communism and capitalism that is normally taken to have begun in 1947 and concluded in 1989 with the collapse of Soviet power in Europe.

Collaboration: a form of cooperation requiring parties not to defect from a mutually desirable strategy for an individually preferable strategy.

Collective security: refers to an arrangement where 'each state in the system accepts that the security of one is the concern of all, and agrees to join in a collective response to aggression' (Roberts and Kingsbury 1993: 30). It is also the foundational principle of the League of Nations: namely, that member states would take a threat or attack on one member as an assault on them all (and on international norms more generally). The League would accordingly respond in unison to such violations of international law. Appreciating that such concerted action would ensue, putative violators—the League's framers hoped—would be duly deterred from launching aggressive strikes in the first place. As the 1920s and 1930s showed, however, theory and practice diverged wildly, with League members failing to take concerted action against Japanese imperialism in Asia, and German and Italian expansionism in Europe and Africa.

Collectivization of security: the tendency for security to be organized on a multilateral basis, but without the institutional formality of a fully fledged collective security system.

Combating terrorism: consists of anti-terrorism efforts (measures to protect against or mitigate future terrorist attacks) and counterterrorism efforts (proactive actions designed to retaliate against or forestall terrorist actions).

Common humanity: we all have human rights by virtue of our common humanity, and these rights generate correlative moral duties for individuals and states.

Community: a human association in which members share common symbols and wish to cooperate to realize common objectives.

Compliance: if a state is in compliance it is living up to its obligations under a treaty. Many multilateral environmental agreements have some form of 'monitoring and compliance procedures' to help ensure that this happens.

Concert: the directorial role played by a number of great powers, based on norms of mutual consent.

Conditionalities: policy requirements imposed by the IMF or the World Bank – usually with a distinctively neo-liberal character – in return for the disbursement of loans. They are politically controversial insofar as they often nullify domestic electoral mandates.

Consequentialist: For consequentialists, it is the likely consequences of an action that should guide decisions. In international ethics, realism and utilitarianism are the most prominent consequentialist ethics.

Constitutive rules: in contrast to regulative rules, which are rules that regulate already existing activities and thus shape the rules of the game, constitutive rules define the game and its activities, shape the identity and interests of actors, and help define what counts as legitimate action.

Constitutive theories: theories that assume that our theories of the social world help to construct the social world and what we see as the external world. Thus the very concepts we use to think about the world help to make that world what it is. Constitutive theories assume mutually constitutive rather than causal relations among main 'variables'.

Constructivism: an approach to international politics that concerns itself with the centrality of ideas and human consciousness and stresses a holistic and idealist view of structures. As constructivists have examined world politics they have been broadly interested in how the structure constructs the actors' identities and interests, how their interactions are organized and constrained by that structure, and how their very interaction serves to either reproduce or transform that structure.

Containment: American political strategy for resisting perceived Soviet expansion, first publicly espoused by an American diplomat, George Kennan, in 1947. Containment became a powerful factor in American policy towards the Soviet Union for the next forty years, and a self-image of Western policy-makers.

Convention: a type of general treaty between states, often the result of an international conference. A framework convention sets out goals, organizations, scientific research, and review procedures with a view to developing future action to establish and solve environmental problems—in terms of a 'framework convention—adjustable protocol' model.

Cooperation: is required in any situation where parties must act together in order to achieve a mutually acceptable outcome.

Coordination: a form of cooperation requiring parties to pursue a common strategy in order to avoid the mutually undesirable outcome arising from the pursuit of divergent strategies.

CoP: Conference of the Parties to a convention, usually held annually.

Cosmopolitan model of democracy: a condition in which international organizations, transnational corporations, global markets, and so forth are accountable to the peoples of the world. Associated with David Held, Daniele Archibugi, Mary Kaldor, and others, a cosmopolitan model of democracy requires the following: the creation of regional parliaments and the extension of the authority of such regional bodies (like the European Union) which are already in existence; human rights conventions must be entrenched in national parliaments and monitored by a new International Court of Human Rights; the UN must be replaced with a genuinely democratic and accountable global parliament.

Cosmopolitanism: Denoting identification with a community, culture, or idea that transcends borders or particular societies, and implies freedom from local or national conventions/limitations. In the early 21st Century, the dominant cosmopolitanism was that of globalizing capitalism, which promoted a community and culture that was informed by market economics, a concept of universal human rights, and a relatively liberal social culture. The cosmopolitanism of globalizing capitalism fostered a degree of multiculturalism, although it sought to reconcile particular cultures to a common ground of universal political and economic principles.

Counter-restrictionist: international lawyers who argue that there is a legal right of humanitarian intervention in both UN Charter law and customary international law.

Country: a loose general term, which can be used as a synonym for a state. However, it emphasizes the concrete reality of a political community within a geographical boundary. See also the entry for state.

Credit crunch: A term used to describe the global Banking crisis of 2008, which saw the collapse of several banks and consequential global economic downturn.

Critical theory: attempts to challenge the prevailing order by seeking out, analysing, and, where possible, assisting social processes that can potentially lead to emancipatory change.

Culture: The sum of the norms, practices, traditions and genres produced by a community, including the beliefs and practices that characterize social life and indicate how society should be run. Cultures may be constructed in village or city locations, or across family, clan, ethnic, national, religious, and other networks.

Currency markets: otherwise known as, and perhaps strictly-speaking more accurately called, foreign exchange markets. They are purely private sector arrangements for buying and selling currencies, with no public sector oversight of the price at which trades are made or the amount of money that is used to make particular trades.

Decision-making procedures: these identify specific prescriptions for behaviour, the system of voting, for example, which will regularly change as a regime is consolidated and extended. The rules and procedures governing the GATT, for example, underwent substantial modification during its history. Indeed, the purpose of the successive conferences was to change the rules and decisionmaking procedures (Krasner 1985: 4–5).

Decolonization: processes by which colonies become independent of colonial powers and sovereign as states in their own right.

Deconstruction: holds that language is constituted by dichotomies, that one side within a dichotomy is superior to the other and that we should destabilize the hierarchy between inferior and superior terms.

Defensive realism: a structural theory of Realism that views states as security maximizers.

Democracy: a system of government in which the views and interests of the population are represented and promoted through the mechanism of free and fair elections to the political institutions of governance

Democratic peace: a central plank of liberal internationalist thought, the democratic peace thesis makes two claims: first, liberal polities exhibit restraint in their relations with other liberal polities (the so-called separate peace) but are imprudent in relations with authoritarian states. The validity of the democratic peace thesis has been fiercely debated in the IR literature.

Deontological: deontological theories are concerned with the nature of human duty or obligation. They prioritize questions of the 'right' over those of the good. They focus on rules that are always right for everyone to follow, in contrast to rules that might produce a good outcome for an individual, or their society.

Deregulation: the removal of all regulation so that market forces, not government policy, control economic developments.

Détente: relaxation of tension between East and West; Soviet–American détente lasted from the late 1960s to the late 1970s, and was characterized by negotiations and nuclear arms control agreements.

Deterritorialization: a process in which the organization of social activities is increasingly less constrained by geographical proximity and national territorial boundaries. Accelerated by the technological revolution and refers to the diminuition of influence of territorial places, distances, and boundaries over the way people collectively identify themselves or seek political recognition. This permits an expansion of global civil society but equally an expansion of global criminal or terrorist networks.

Development, core ideas, and assumptions: in the orthodox view, the possibility of unlimited economic growth in a free-market system. Economies would reach a 'take-off' point and thereafter wealth would trickle down to those at the bottom. Superiority of the 'Western' model and knowledge. Belief that the process would ultimately benefit everyone. Domination, exploitation of nature. In the alternative view, sufficiency. The inherent value of nature, cultural diversity, and the community-controlled commons (water, land, air, forest). Human activity in balance with nature. Self-reliance. Democratic inclusion, participation, for example, voice for marginalized groups, e.g. women, indigenous groups. Local control.

Diaspora: movement around the world of people who identify themselves racially or through a common ethnic group or history.

Diffusion: concerns how ideas, beliefs, habits, and practices spread across a population.

Diplomacy: in foreign policy it refers to the use of diplomacy as a policy instrument possibly in association with other instruments such as economic or military force to enable an international actor to achieve its policy objectives. Diplomacy in world politics refers to a communications process between international actors that seeks through negotiation to resolve conflict short of war. This process has been refined, institutionalized, and professionalized over many centuries.

Disaggregated state: the tendency for states to become increasingly fragmented actors in global politics as every part of the government machine becomes entangled with its foreign counterparts and others in dealing with global issues through proliferating transgovernmental and global policy networks.

Discourse: a linguistic system that orders statements and concepts. Poststructuralists oppose the distinction between materialism factors and ideas and see the meaning of materiality as constituted through discourse.

DissemiNations: a term coined by Homi Bhabha that refers to the movement or engagement of ideas and knowledge across colonial and postcolonial contexts that defy any easy sense that some cultures adhere to only one set of understandings about how life is and should be led.

Double burden: when women enter the public workforce working for wages, they usually remain responsible for most of the reproductive and caring labour in the private sphere, thus creating a double workload.

Dual moral standard: in realist theory, the idea that there are two principles or standards of right and wrong: one for the individual citizen and a different one for the state.

Ecological footprint: used to demonstrate the load placed upon the Earth's carrying capacity by individuals or nations. It does this by estimating the area of productive land or aqua-system required to sustain a population at its specified standard of living.

Economic, social, and cultural rights: one of the two principal groups of internationally recognized human rights. They guarantee individuals access to essential goods and services and seek to ensure equal social and cultural participation. Examples include rights to food, housing, health care, education, and social insurance.

Emancipation: the achievement of equal political, economic, and social rights.

Embedded liberalism: a term attributed to John Ruggie that refers to market processes and corporate activities backed by a web of social and political constraints and rewards to create a compromise between free trade globally and welfare at home.

Empire: a distinct type of political entity, which may or may not be a state, possessing both a home territory and foreign territories. It is a disputed concept that some have tried to apply to the United States to describe its international reach, huge capabilities, and vital global role of underwriting world order.

Endemic warfare: the condition in which warfare is a recurrent feature of the relations between states not least because they regard it as inevitable.

English School: academic writers who seek to develop the argument that states in interaction with each other constitute an international society.

Enlightenment: associated with rationalist thinkers of the eighteenth century. Key ideas (which some would argue remain mottoes for our age) include: secularism, progress, reason, science, knowledge, and freedom. The motto of the Enlightenment is: 'Sapere aude! Have courage to use your own understanding' (Kant 1991: 54).

Epistemic community: knowledge-based transnational communities of experts and policy activists.

Epistemology: the study of how we can claim to know something. It is about our theories of knowledge.

Equity: also called stock or share; a number of equal portions in the nominal capital of a company; the shareholder thereby owns part of the enterprise.

Ethic of responsibility: for historical realists, an ethic of responsibility is the limits of ethics in international politics; it involves the weighing up of consequences and the realization that positive outcomes may result from amoral actions.

Ethnic nationalism: a nationalism which claims the nation is based on common descent, descent which may be indicated through such characteristics as language, history, way of life, or physical appearance.

Europe: a geographical expression that during the course of the cold war came to be identified with Western Europe, but since 1989 has once again come to be associated with the whole of the European continent.

European Union (EU): the EU was formally created in 1992 following the signing of the Maastricht Treaty. However, the origins of the EU can be traced back to 1951 and the creation of the European Coal and Steel Community, followed in 1957 with a broader customs union (The Treaty of Rome 1958). Originally a grouping of six countries in 1957, 'Europe' grew by adding new members in 1973, 1981, and 1986. Since the fall of the planned economies in Eastern Europe in 1989, the EU has grown and now comprises 27 member states.

Explanatory theories: theories that see the social world as something external to our theories of the social world. On this view, the task of theory is to report on a world that exists independent from the observer and his or her theoretical position. Explanatory theories assume causal relations among main variables.

Extraterritoriality: occurs when one government attempts to exercise its legal authority in the territory of another state. It mainly arises when the US federal government deliberately tries to use domestic law to control the global activities of transnational companies.

Failed state: this is a state that has collapsed and cannot provide for its citizens without substantial external support and where the government of the state has ceased to exist inside the territorial borders of the state.

Feminism: a political project to understand so as to change women's inequality or oppression. For some, aiming to move beyond gender, so that it no longer matters; for others, to validate women's interests, experiences, and choices; for others, to work for more equal and inclusive social relations overall.

Flexible labour: refers to workers who lack job security, benefits, or the right to unionize. It gives companies more flexibility in hiring and firing their workforce.

Forcible humanitarian intervention: military intervention which breaches the principle of state sovereignty where the primary purpose is to alleviate the human suffering of some or all within a state's borders.

Foundationalist: positions assume that all truth claims (about some feature of the world) can be judged objectively true or false.

Fourteen Points: President Woodrow Wilson's vision of international society, first articulated in January 1918, included the principle of self-determination, the conduct of diplomacy on an open (not secret) basis, and the establishment of an association of nations to provide guarantees of independence and territorial integrity. Wilson's ideas exerted an important influence on the Paris Peace Conference, though the principle of self-determination was only selectively pursued when it came to American colonial interests.

Frankfurt School: the Group of theorists associated with the Institute for Social Research, at the University of Frankfurt.

Functionalism: the idea that states can learn to cooperate effectively by beginning with global economic and social issues and then moving towards collaboration in the military and security domain.

Fundamentalism: a strict interpretation of a religious-cultural form drawn from particular understandings—often literal—of basic/fundamental scripture, doctrines, and practices. Fundamentalists typically seek to convert or exclude non-believers from their community.

G20: the Group of Twenty was established in 1999 as a forum in which major advanced and emerging economies discuss global financial and economic matters. Since its inception, it has held annual Finance Ministers and Central Bank Governors Meetings and more recently Summits of Heads of State. G-20 Leaders Summits have been held in Washington in 2008, and in London and Pittsburgh in 2009.

G7: see G8 (Group of Eight).

G77 (Group of 77): established in 1964 by a group of 77 developing countries in the United Nations. Still in existence the G-77 aims to promote collective economic interests, mutual cooperation for development, and negotiating capacity on all major international economic issues within the United Nations system.

G8 (Group of Eight): established in 1975 as the G5 (France, Germany, Japan, the UK, and the USA);

subsequently expanded as the G7 to include Canada and Italy and since 1998 the G8 to include the Russian Federation. The G8 conducts semi-formal collaboration on world economic problems. Government leaders meet in annual G8 Summits, while finance ministers and/or their leading officials periodically hold other consultations. See further www.g8online.org.

Game theory: a branch of mathematics which explores strategic interaction.

GDP: the initials of Gross Domestic Product, which is the monetary value of all goods produced within a country's economy in a year.

Gender: what it means to be male or female in a particular place or time; the social construction of sexual difference.

Gender relations: power relations: the relational construction of masculinity and femininity, in which the masculine is usually privileged but which are contested, and changing.

Gendered division of labour (GDL): the notion of 'women's work', which everywhere includes women's primary responsibility for childcare and housework, and which designates many public and paid forms of work as 'women's' or 'men's', too.

Genealogy: a history of the present that asks what political practices have formed the present and which alternative understandings and discourses have been marginalized and forgotten.

General Agreement on Tariffs and Trade (GATT): the interim measure introduced in 1947 before a permanent institution was established in the form of the World Trade Organization in 1995. It provided a context over a number of negotiating rounds for countries to try to extend bilateral agreements for reducing tariff barriers to trade to multiple third countries.

Genocide: acts committed with the intent to destroy a national, ethnic, racial, or religious group. The United Nations Convention on the Prevention and Punishment of the Crime of Genocide was adopted in 1948.

Glasnost: policy of greater openness pursued by Soviet premier Mikhail Gorbachev from 1985, involving greater toleration of internal dissent and criticism.

Global community: a way to organize governance, authority, and identity that breaks with the sovereign state.

Global environmental governance: usually refers to the corpus of international agreements and organizations but sometimes has a more specialized meaning that stresses governance by private bodies and NGOs.

Global governance: the loose framework of global regulation, both institutional and normative, that constrains conduct. It has many elements: international organizations and law; transnational organizations and frameworks; elements of global civil society; and shared normative principles.

Global network: in a general sense, any network that spans the globe and, in a technical sense, digital networks that allow instant voice and data communication worldwide—the global information highway.

Global policy networks: complexes which bring together the representatives of governments, international organizations, NGOs, and the corporate sector for the formulation and implementation of global public policy.

Global politics: the politics of global social relations in which the pursuit of power, interests, order, and justice transcends regions and continents.

Global polity: the collective structures and processes by which 'interests are articulated and aggregated, decisions are made, values allocated and policies conducted through international or transnational political processes' (Ougaard 2004: 5).

Global responsibility: the idea that states, international institutions, and corporations should take responsibility for issues that do not fall under the rubric of the national interest.

Global South: an imprecise term that refers both to countries once called Third World and to the movement of peoples in the present time within Third World areas of the world and to advanced industrialized countries.

Globalization: a historical process involving a fundamental shift or transformation in the spatial scale of human social organization that links distant communities and expands the reach of power relations across regions and continents. It is also something of a catch-all phrase often used to describe a single world-economy after the collapse of communism, though sometimes employed to define the growing integration of the international capitalist system in the post-war period.

Globalized state: the notion of a particular kind of state that helps sustain globalization, as well as responding to its pressures. The distinctive feature of this concept is that the state is not 'in retreat' but simply behaving differently.

Gold Standard: the late nineteenth- and early twentieth-century system through which all trading relationships were regulated through the movement of gold from importing countries to exporting countries. In theory this was supposed to lead to automatic adjustment in imports and exports, necessarily keeping all countries in trade balance; in practice it did not work this way.

Government: used narrowly to refer to the executive governing a country or more widely to cover the executive, the legislature, the judiciary, the civil service, the armed forces and the police.

Great Depression: a byword for the global economic collapse that ensued following the US Wall Street stock-market crash in October 1929. Economic shockwaves soon rippled around a world already densely interconnected by webs of trade and foreign direct investment with the result that the events of October 1929 were felt in countries as distant as Brazil and Japan.

Group rights: rights that are said to belong to groups such as minority nations or indigenous peoples rather than to individuals.

Harmony of interests: common among nineteenth-century liberals was the idea of a natural order between peoples which had been corrupted by undemocratic state leaders and outdated policies such as the balance of power. If these distortions could be swept away, they believed, we would find that there were no real conflicts between peoples.

Hegemony: a system regulated by a dominant leader, or political (and/or economic) domination of a region, usually by a superpower. In realist theory, the influence a Great Power is able to establish on other states in the system; extent of influence ranges from leadership to dominance. It is also power and control exercised by a leading state over other states.

High politics: the themes highest on the foreign policy agenda, usually those of war, security, and military threats and capabilities.

Holism: the view that structures cannot be decomposed to the individual units and their interactions because structures are more than the sum of their parts and are irreducibly social. The effects of structures, moreover, go beyond merely constraining the actors but also construct them. Constructivism holds that the international structure shapes the identities and interests of the actors.

Holocaust: the term used to describe the attempts by the Nazis to murder the Jewish population of Europe. Some 6 million Jewish people were killed, along with a further million, including Soviet prisoners, gypsies, Poles, communists, gay people, and physically or mentally disabled. The term is also used to describe an obliteration of humanity or an entire group of people.

Horizontal proliferation: means an increase in the number of actors who possess nuclear weapons.

Human development: a capability-oriented approach to development which, in the word of Mahabub ul Haq, seeks to expand the 'range of things that people can do, and what they can be... The most basic capabilities for human development are leading a long and healthy life, being educated and having adequate resources for a decent standard of living... [and] social and political participation in society.'

Human security: the security of people, including their physical safety, their economic and social well-being, respect for their dignity, and the protection of their human rights.

Humanitarian intervention: the principle that the international community has a right/duty to intervene in states which have suffered large-scale loss of life or genocide whether due to deliberate action by its governments or because of the collapse of governance.

Hybrid identity: a term in postcolonial analysis that refers to the dynamic challenges that individuals face in a world presenting multiple options for establishing identities through a combination of often contentious activities of work, migration, group history, ethnicity, class, race, gender, national affiliation, and empathy.

Hybrid international organization: an international organization in which both private transnational actors (NGOs, parties, or companies) and governments or governmental agencies are admitted as members, with each having full rights of participation in policy making, including the right to vote on the final decisions. They are called hybrids to contrast with the common assumption that only intergovernmental organizations (IGOs) and international non-governmental organizations (INGOs) exist. In diplomatic practice they are usually included among the INGOs and so they have sometimes been called hybrid INGOs.

Idealism: holds that ideas have important causal effect on events in international politics, and that ideas can change. Referred to by realists as utopianism since it underestimates the logic of power politics and the constraints this imposes upon political action. Idealism as a substantive theory of international relations is generally associated with the claim that it is possible to create a world of peace. But idealism as a social theory refers to the claim that the most fundamental feature of society is social consciousness. Ideas shape how we see ourselves and our interests, the knowledge that we use to categorize and understand the world, the beliefs we have of others, and the possible and impossible solutions to challenges and threats. The emphasis on ideas does not mean a neglect of material forces such as technology and geography. Instead it is to suggest that the meanings and consequences of these material forces are not given by nature but rather driven by human interpretations and understandings. Idealists seek to apply liberal thinking in domestic politics to international relations, in other words, institutionalize the rule of law. This reasoning is known as the domestic analogy. According to idealists in the early twentieth century, there were two principal requirements for a new world order. First: state leaders, intellectuals, and public opinion had to believe that progress was possible. Second: an international organization had to be created to facilitate peaceful change, disarmament, arbitration, and (where necessary) enforcement. The League of Nations was founded in 1920 but its collective security system failed to prevent the descent into world war in the 1930s.

Identity: the understanding of the self in relationship to an 'other'. Identities are social and thus are always formed in relationship to others. Constructivists generally hold that identities shape interests; we cannot know what we want unless we know who we are. But because identities are social and are produced through interactions, identities can change.

Imperialism: the practice of foreign conquest and rule in the context of global relations of hierarchy and subordination. It can lead to the establishment of an empire.

Individualism: the view that structures can be reduced to the aggregation of individuals and their interactions. International relations theories that ascribe to individualism begin with some assumption of the nature of the units and their interests, usually states and the pursuit of power or wealth, and then examine how the broad structure, usually the distribution of power, constrains how states can act and generates certain patterns in international politics. Individualism stands in contrast to holism.

Influence: the ability of one actor to change the values or the behaviour of another actor.

Institutional isomorphism: observes that actors and organizations that share the same environment will, over time, begin to resemble each other in their attributes and characteristics.

Institutionalization: the degree to which networks or patterns of social interaction are formally constituted as organizations with specific purposes.

Institutions: persistent and having connected sets of rules and practices that prescribe roles, constrain activity, and shape the expectations of actors. Institutions may include organizations, bureaucratic agencies, treaties and agreements, and informal practices that states accept as binding. The balance of power in the international system is an example of an institution. (Adapted from Haas, Keohane, and Levy 1993: 4–5.)

Integration: a process of ever closer union between states, in a regional or international context. The process often begins with cooperation to solve technical problems, referred to by Mitrany (1943) as ramification.

Intellectual property rights: rules that protect the owners of content through copyright, patents, trade marks and trade secrets.

Interconnectedness: the interweaving of human lives so that events in one region of the world have an impact on all or most other people.

Interdependence: a condition where states (or peoples) are affected by decisions taken by others; for example, a decision to raise interest rates in the USA automatically exerts upward pressure on interest rates in other states. Interdependence can be symmetric, i.e. both sets of actors are affected equally, or it can be asymmetric, where the impact varies between actors. A condition where the actions of one state impact upon other states (can be strategic interdependence or economic). Realists equate interdependence with vulnerability.

Intergovernmental organizations (IGOs): an international organization in which full legal membership is officially solely open to states and the decision-making authority lies with representatives from governments.

International community: term used by politicians, the media and non-governmental actors to refer to the states that make up the world, often in the attempt to make the most powerful ones respond to a problem, war, or crisis.

International hierarchy: a structure of authority in which states and other international actors are ranked according to their relative power.

International institutions: organizations such as the European Union, the United Nations, and the World Trade Organization that have become necessary to manage regional or global economic, political and environmental matters. See entry for International organization.

International Law: the formal rules of conduct that states acknowledge or contract between themselves.

International Monetary Fund (IMF): an institution of 186 members as of early 2010, providing extensive technical assistance and short-term flows of stabilization finance to any of those members experiencing temporarily distressed public finances. Since 1978 it has undertaken comprehensive surveillance of the economic performance of individual member states as a precursor to introducing 'corrective' programmes for those countries it deems to have followed the wrong policy course.

International non-governmental organizations (INGOs): an international organization in which membership is open to transnational actors. There are many different types, with membership from 'national' NGOs, local NGOs, companies, political parties, or individual people. A few have other INGOs as members and some have mixed membership structures.

International order: the normative and the institutional pattern in the relationship between states. The elements of this might be thought to include such things as sovereignty, the forms of diplomacy, international law, the role of the great powers, and the codes circumscribing the use of force.

International organization: any institution with formal procedures and formal membership from three or more countries. The minimum number of countries is set at three rather than two, because multilateral relationships have significantly greater complexity than bilateral relationships. There are three types of international organization: see entries for intergovernmental organizations (IGOs), international non-governmental organizations (INGOs) and hybrid international organization.

International regime: defined by Krasner (1983: 2) as a set of 'implicit or explicit principles, norms, rules and decision-making procedures around which actors expectations converge in a given area of international relations'. The concept was developed by neo-realists to analyse the paradox – for them – that international cooperation occurs in some issue areas, despite the struggle for power between states. They assume regimes are created and maintained by a dominant state and/or participation in a regime is the result of a rational cost benefit calculation by each state. In contrast, Pluralists would also stress the independent impact of institutions, the importance of leadership, the involvement of transnational NGOs and companies, and processes of cognitive change, such as growing concern about human rights or the environment.

International society: The concept used to describe a group of sovereign states that recognize, maintain, and develop common norms, rules, and practices that enable them to coexist and cooperate.

International system: a set of interrelated parts connected to form a whole. In Realist theory, systems have defining principles such as hierarchy (in domestic politics) and anarchy (in international politics).

Internationalization: this term is used to denote high levels of international interaction and interdependence, most commonly with regard to the world economy. The term is often used to distinguish this condition from globalization, as the latter implies that there are no longer distinct national economies in a position to interact.

Intertextuality: holds that texts form an 'intertext', so that all texts refer to other texts, but each text is at the same time unique. Shows that meaning changes as texts are quoted by other texts. Calls attention to silences and taken-for-granted assumptions.

Intervention: when there is direct involvement within a state by an outside actor to achieve an outcome preferred by the intervening agency without the consent of the host state.

Intra-firm trade: international trade from one branch of a transnational company to an affiliate of the same company in a different country.

Islam: a religious faith developed by the Prophet Muhammad which in the contemporary period functions as a form of political identity for millions and the inspiration of what some at least now regard as the most important ideological opposition to Western modern values.

Islamic Conference Organization (OIC): The international body of Muslim states, formed following an arson attack on the Al Aqsa mosque in Jerusalem in 1969. The Charter of the OIC was instituted in 1972, and headquarters established in Jeddah, Saudi Arabia. At the beginning of 2010, participants included 57 member states as well as a number of observer states and organizations.

Issue, an: consists of a set of political questions that are seen as being related, because they all invoke the same value conflicts, e.g. the issue of human rights concerns questions that invoke freedom versus order.

Jihad: In Arabic *jihad* simply means struggle. *Jihad* can refer to a purely internal struggle to be a better Muslim, a struggle to make society more closely align with the teachings of the Koran, or a call to arms to wage war in self-defence of an Islamic community under attack. Adding to the confusion are various interpretations of what constitutes 'attack', 'community', and which methods can be used morally and spiritually for self-defence.

Justice: fair or morally defensible treatment for individuals, in the light of human rights standards or standards of economic or social well-being.

Law of nations: literal translation of the ancient Roman term 'jus gentium'. Although today used interchangeably with the term 'international law', or law between nations, its original meaning referred to underlying legal principles common to all nations. This gave it a strongly normative character, which was enhanced when, in the Middle Ages, it came to be closely linked to the ancient Greek concept of Natural Law. Although it retained something of this earlier meaning in Vattel's influential 18th century work, The Law of Nations, the strong emphasis on state sovereignty in Vattel's work may be seen as marking a shift towards the more modern understanding of law between sovereign states.

Liar loans: loans given by banks in the mortgage lending market which provided customers with incentives to deliberately mislead the banks by exaggerating their level of household income in order to qualify for loans to purchase higher-priced houses. No independent verification of household income took place, with bank staff often encouraging customers to bend the truth in the interests of enabling more credit to be sold.

Liberal rights: the agenda of human rights that is driven largely from a Western perspective and derived from classical liberal positions.

Liberalism: according to Doyle (1997: 207), Liberalism includes the following four claims. First, all citizens are juridically equal and have equal rights to education, access to a free press, and religious toleration. Second, the legislative assembly of the state possesses only the authority invested in it by the people, whose basic rights it is not permitted to abuse. Third, a key dimension of the liberty of the individual is the right to own property including productive forces. Fourth, Liberalism contends that the most effective system of economic exchange is one that is largely market driven and not one that is subordinate to bureaucratic regulation and control either domestically or internationally.

Liberalization: describes government policies which reduce the role of the state in the economy such as through the dismantling of trade tariffs and barriers, the deregulation and opening of the financial sector to foreign investors, and the privatization of state enterprises.

Life cycle of norms: is a concept created by Martha Finnemore and Kathryn Sikkink to distinguish the different stages of norm evolution—from emergency to cascade to internalization.

Light industry: industry that requires less capital investment to fund and operate. It is performed with light, rather than heavy, machinery.

Logic of appropriateness: attributes action to whether it is viewed as legitimate and the right thing to do, irrespective of the costs and benefits.

Logic of consequences: attributes action to the anticipated benefits and costs, mindful that other actors are doing the very same thing.

Loyalty: an emotional disposition in which people give institutions (or each other) some degree of unconditional support.

Market failure: results from the inability of the market to produce goods which require collaborative strategies.

Market self-regulation: a system in which financial institutions are allowed to regulate themselves solely on the basis of price signals emerging from markets. Those that interpret price signals successfully will make profits and stay in business; those that interpret them poorly will lose money and be forced into bankruptcy.

Marxism: the view that the most fundamental feature of society is the organization of material forces. Material forces include natural resources, geography, military power, and technology. To understand how the world works, therefore, requires taking these fundamentals into account. For International Relations scholars, this leads to forms of technological determinism or the distribution of military power for understanding the state's foreign policy and patterns of international politics.

Materialism: see Marxism.

Meanings: takes us beyond the description of an object, event, or place and inquires into the significance it has for observers.

Means (or forces) of production: in Marxist theory, these are the elements that combine in the production process. They include labour as well as the tools and technology available during any given historical period.

Microeconomics: the branch of economics studying the behaviour of the firm in a market setting.

Millennium Development Goals: target-based, time-limited commitments in the UN Millennium Declaration 2000 to improve eight areas: poverty and hunger, primary education, gender equality, child mortality, maternal health, tackling diseases such as HIV/AIDS and malaria, environmental sustainability, and partnership working.

MoP: Meeting of the Parties to a protocol.

Mortgage-backed securities: mortgage securitization is a process through which financial institutions can take mortgage debt off their balance sheets by selling contracts to other financial institutions based on claims to future household mortgage repayments. These contracts were traded as securities on global financial markets in the early and mid 2000s without any obvious form of public oversight of how much banks were prepared to get themselves in debt by buying them.

Multilateralism: the tendency for functional aspects of international relations (such as security, trade, or environmental management) to be organized around large numbers of states, or universally, rather than by unilateral state action.

Multinational corporations (MNCs): companies that have operations in more than one country. They will have their headquarters in just one country (the 'home' country) but will either manage production or deliver services in other countries ('host' countries). Multinational corporations will outsource elements of their production where overseas locations give them some sort of economic advantage that they cannot secure at home: this might be a labour cost advantage, a tax advantage, an environmental standards advantage, etc. Also used of a company that has affiliates in a foreign country. These may be branches of the parent company, separately incorporated subsidiaries, or associates, with large minority shareholdings.

Multipolarity: a distribution of power among a number (at least three) of major powers or 'poles'.

Nation: a group of people who recognize each other as sharing a common identity, with a focus on a homeland.

National interest: invoked by realists and state leaders to signify that which is most important to the state—survival being at the top of the list.

National security: a fundamental value in the foreign policy of states.

National self-determination: the right of distinct national groups to become states.

Nationalism: the idea that the world is divided into nations which provide the overriding focus of political identity and loyalty which in turn demands national self-determination. Nationalism also can refer to this idea in the form of a strong sense of identity (sentiment) or organizations and movements seeking to realize this idea (politics).

Nation-state: a political community in which the state claims legitimacy on the grounds that it represents the nation. The nation-state would exist if nearly all the members of a single nation were organized in a single state, without any other national communities being present. Although the term is widely used, no such entities exist.

Natural: a word used to describe socially appropriate gender-role behaviour. When behaviour is seen as natural it is hard to change.

Neoclassical realism: a version of realism that combines both structural factors such as the distribution of power and unit-level factors such as the interests of states (status quo or revisionist).

Neo-colonial: Informal processes that keep former colonies under the power and especially economic influence of former colonial powers and advanced industrial countries.

Neo-medievalism: a condition in which political power is dispersed between local, national, and supranational institutions none of which commands supreme loyalty.

Neo–neo: shorthand for the research agenda that neo-realists and neo-liberals share.

Neo-realism: modification of the realist approach, by recognizing economic resources (in addition to military capabilities) are a basis for exercising influence and also an attempt to make realism 'more scientific' by borrowing models from economics and behavioural social science to explain international politics.

Network: any structure of communication for individuals and/or organizations to exchange information, share experiences, or discuss political goals and tactics. There is no clear boundary between a network and an NGO. A network is less likely than an NGO to become permanent, to have formal membership, to have identifiable leaders or to engage in collective action.

New International Economic Order (NIEO): a twenty-five point manifesto presented to a special session of the United Nations General Assembly in 1974 by the Non-Aligned Movement and the G-77. It aimed to restructure the global economy in ways that would help Third World countries develop and improve their position in the world economy. It was adopted by the General Assembly but was not backed by major economic powers.

9/11: refers specifically to the morning of 11 September 2001 when 19 men highjacked four domestic flights en route to California which were subsequently flown into the World Trade Center and the Pentagon. The fourth plane crashed in Pennsylvania. There were 2,974 fatalities, not including the 19 highjackers, 15 of whom were from Saudi Arabia. The planning and organization for the attack was coordinated in Afghanistan by Osama bin Laden, the leader of Al Qaeda. Approximately a month after the attack the United States and its allies launched an attack against Afghanistan to remove the Taliban from power.

Non-discrimination: a doctrine of equal treatment between states.

Non-governmental organization (NGO): any group of people relating to each other regularly in some formal manner and engaging in collective action, provided that the activities are non-commercial, non-violent and are not on behalf of a government. They are often presumed to be altruistic groups or public interest groups, such as Amnesty International, Oxfam or Greenpeace, but in UN practice they may come from any sector of civil society, including trades unions and faith communities.

Non-intervention: the principle that external powers should not intervene in the domestic affairs of sovereign states.

Non-Nuclear Weapon States: refers to a state that is party to the Treaty on the Non-Proliferation of Nuclear Weapons, meaning it does not possess nuclear weapons.

Non-state actors: a term widely used to mean any actor that is not a government.

Norm entrepreneur: a political actor, whether an individual or an organization, that conceptualises and promotes a new norm, to define an appropriate standard of behaviour for all actors or a defined sub-group of actors in the political system

Normative structure: international relations theory traditionally defines structure in material terms, such as the distribution of power, and then treats structure as a constraint on actors. By identifying a normative structure, Constructivists are noting how structures also are defined by collectively held ideas such as knowledge, rules, beliefs, and norms that not only constrain actors, but also construct categories of meaning, constitute their identities and interests, and define standards of appropriate conduct. Critical here is the concept of a norm, a standard of appropriate behaviour for actors with a given identity. Actors adhere to norms not only because of benefits and costs for doing so but also because they are related to a sense of self.

Normative theory: systematic analyses of the ethical, moral, and political principles which either govern or ought to govern the organization or conduct of global politics. The belief that theories should be concerned with what ought to be, rather than merely diagnosing what is. Norm creation refers to the setting of standards in international relations which governments (and other actors) ought to meet.

Norms: specify general standards of behaviour, and identify the rights and obligations of states. So, in the case of the GATT, the basic norm is that tariffs and non-tariff barriers should be reduced and eventually eliminated. Together, norms and principles define the essential character of a regime and these cannot be changed without transforming the nature of the regime.

North Atlantic Treaty Organization (NATO): organization established by treaty in April 1949 comprising 12 (later 16) countries from Western Europe and North America. The most important aspect of the NATO alliance was the American commitment to the defence of Western Europe.

Nuclear taboo: the idea that a specific international norm has gradually become accepted by the international community that the use of nuclear weapons is unacceptable in warfare.

Nuclear weapons free zone: these are agreements which establish specific environments or geographic regions as nuclear weapons free, although there may be varying requirements between zones.

Offensive realism: a structural theory of realism that views states as security maximizers.

Ontology: the study of what is. It is about the nature of being.

Open war economy: a war which is sustained, not by the combatants primary reliance on their own industrial production, as in the Second World War, but rather by their integration into the world economy, particularly its international criminal dimension.

Order: this may denote any regular or discernible pattern of relationships that are stable over time, or may additionally refer to a condition that allows certain goals to be achieved.

Organization of Petroleum Exporting Countries (OPEC): created in 1960 by the major oil producing countries of Iran, Iraq, Kuwait, Saudi Arabia, and Venezuela, and later expanded in membership to include states like Nigeria, Mexico, and Libya, to coordinate oil production policies in the interest of market stability and profit for producers.

Orientalism: western interpretations of the institutions, cultures, arts, and social life of countries of the East and Middle East. The subject of a major study by Edward Said, Orientalism is associated today with stereotyping and prejudice, often against Islamic societies.

Ostpolitik: the West German government's 'Eastern Policy' of the mid-to-late 1960s, designed to develop relations between West Germany and members of the Warsaw Pact.

Paradigm: theories that share ontological and epistemological assumptions form a paradigm

Patriarchy: a persistent society-wide structure within which gender relations are defined by male dominance and female subordination.

Peace enforcement: designed to bring hostile parties to agreement, which may occur without the consent of the parties.

Peaceful coexistence: the minimal basis for orderly relations between states even when they are in contention with each other, as in the cold war period.

Peacekeeping: the deployment of a UN presence in the field with the consent of all parties (this refers to classical peacekeeping).

Peace of Westphalia: see Treaties of Westphalia.

Perestroika: policy of restructuring, pursued by former Soviet premier, Mikhail Gorbachev in tandem with glasnost, and intended to modernize the Soviet political and economic system.

Pluralism: an umbrella term, borrowed from American political science, used to signify international relations theorists who rejected the realist view of the primacy of the state, the priority of national security, and the assumption that states are unitary actors. It is the theoretical approach that considers all organized groups as being potential political actors and analyses the processes by which actors mobilize support to achieve policy goals. Pluralists can accept that transnational actors and international organizations may influence governments. Equated by some writers with liberalism, but pluralists reject any such link, denying that theory necessarily has a normative component, and holding that liberals are still highly state-centric.

Pluralist international society theory: states are conscious of sharing common interests and common values, but these are limited to norms of sovereignty and non-intervention.

Policy domain: consists of a set of political questions that have to be decided together because they are linked by the political processes in an international organization, e.g. financial policy is resolved in the IMF. A policy domain may cover several issues: financial policy includes development, the environment, and gender issues.

Political community: a community that wishes to govern itself and to be free from alien rule.

Popular culture: those genres and forms of expression that are mass-consumed, including music, film, television, and video games. Popular culture is usually seen as less refined than 'high culture'. The definition of 'high' and 'low'/'popular' culture changes across time and space.

Postcolonial: contemporary international and transnational relations of race, migration, ethnicity, culture, knowledge, power, and identity.

Post-colonial: the study of the interactions between European states and the societies they colonized in the modern period.

Postmodern or 'new' terrorism: Groups and individuals with millennial and apocalyptic ideologies with system level goals. Most value destruction for its own sake, unlike most terrorists in the past who had specific goals usually tied to a territory

Post-Westphalian: an order in which national borders, and the principle of sovereignty, are no longer paramount.

Post-Westphalian War: Intra-state warfare, typical in the post-cold war period, that is aimed neither at the sovereignty of an enemy state, nor at seizing control of the state apparatus of the country in which it is being waged.

Poverty: in the orthodox view, a situation suffered by people who do not have the money to buy food and satisfy other basic material needs. In the alternative view, a situation suffered by people who are not able to meet their material and non-material needs through their own effort.

Power: in the most general sense, the ability of a political actor to achieve its goals. In the realist approach, it is assumed that possession of capabilities will result in influence, so the single word, power, is often used ambiguously to cover both. In the pluralist approach, it is assumed that political interactions can modify the translation of capabilities into influence and therefore it is important to distinguish between the two. Power is defined by most realists in terms of the important resources such as size of armed forces, gross national product, and population that a state possesses. There is the implicit belief that material resources translate into influence. Poststructuralists understand power as productive that is as referring to the constitution of subjectivity in discourse. Knowledge is interwoven with power.

Primordialism: the belief that certain human or social characteristics, such as ethnicity, are deeply embedded in historical conditions.

Principles: in regime theory, they are represented by coherent bodies of theoretical statements about how the world works. The GATT operated on the basis of liberal principles which assert that global welfare will be maximized by free trade.

Prisoners' dilemma: a scenario in game theory illustrating the need for a collaboration strategy.

Programmes and Funds: activities of the UN which are subject to the supervision of the General Assembly and which depend upon voluntary funding by states and other donors.

Protection myth: a popular assumption that male heroes fight wars to protect the vulnerable, primarily women and children. It is used as a justification for states' national security policies, particularly in times of war.

Protocol: a legal instrument that is added to a convention, usually containing detailed rules and undertakings, so that environmental and other problems can be controlled. There can be many protocols to one convention or treaty.

Public bads: the negative consequences which can arise when actors fail to collaborate.

Public goods: goods which can only be produced by a collective decision, and which cannot, therefore, be produced in the market-place.

Quasi-state: a state which has 'negative sovereignty' because other states respect its sovereign independence but lacks 'positive sovereignty' because it does not have the resources or the will to satisfy the needs of its people.

Rapprochement: re-establishment of more friendly relations between the People's Republic of China and the United States in the early 1970s.

Ratification: the procedure by which a state approves a convention or protocol that it has signed. There will be rules in the treaty concerning the number of ratifications required before it can enter into force.

Rational choice: an approach that emphasizes how actors attempt to maximize their interests, how they attempt to select the most efficient means to achieve those interests, and attempts to explain collective outcomes by virtue of the attempt by actors to maximize their preferences under a set of constraints. Deriving largely from economic theorizing, the rational choice to politics and international politics has been immensely influential and applied to a range of issues.

Rationality: reflected in the ability of individuals to place their preferences in rank order and choose the best available preference.

Realism: the theoretical approach that analyzes all international relations as the relation of states engaged in the pursuit of power. Realism cannot accommodate non-state actors within its analysis

Reason of state: the practical application of the doctrine of realism and virtually synonymous with it.

Reciprocity: reflects a 'tit for tat' strategy, only cooperating if others do likewise.

Regime: see also international regime. These are sets of implicit or explicit principles, norms, rules, and decision-making procedures around which actors' expectations converge in a given area of international relations. They are social institutions that are based on agreed rules, norms, principles, and decision-making procedures. These govern the interactions of various state and non-state actors in issue-areas such as the environment or human rights. The global market in coffee, for example, is governed by a variety of treaties, trade agreements, scientific and research protocols, market protocols, and the interests of producers, consumers, and distributors. States organize these interests and consider the practices, rules, and procedures to create a governing arrangement or regime that controls the production of coffee, monitors its distribution, and ultimately determines the price for consumers. (Adapted from Young 1997: 6.)

Regionalism: development of institutionalized cooperation among states and other actors on the basis of regional contiguity as a feature of the international system.

Regionalization: growing interdependence between geographically contiguous states, as in the European Union.

Regulative rules: in contrast to constitutive rules, which define the game and its activities, shape the identity and interests of actors, and help define what counts as legitimate action, regulative rules regulate already existing activities and thus shape the rules of the game.

Regulatory arbitrage: in the world of banking, the process of moving funds or business activity from one country to another, in order to increase profits by escaping the constraints imposed by government regulations. By analogy the term can be applied to any transfer of economic activity by any company in response to government policy.

Relations of production: in Marxist theory, relations of production link and organize the means of production in the production process. They involve both the technical and institutional relationships necessary to allow the production process to proceed, as well as the broader structures that govern the control of the means of production, and control of the end product(s) of that process. Private property and wage labour are two of the key features of the relations of production in capitalist society.

Relative gains: one of the factors that realists argue constrain the willingness of states to cooperate. States are less concerned about whether everyone benefits (absolute gains) and more concerned about whether someone may benefit more than someone else.

Responsibility to protect: states have a responsibility to protect their own citizens, but when they are unable or unwilling to do so this responsibility is transferred to the society of states.

Restrictionists: international lawyers who argue that humanitarian intervention violates Article 2(4) of the UN Charter and is illegal under both UN Charter law and customary international law.

Revolution in military affairs: describes a radical change in the conduct of warfare. This may be driven by technology, but may also result from organizational, doctrinal, or other developments. When the change is of several orders of magnitude, and impacts deeply on wider society, the term 'military revolution' is used to describe it.

Rules: operate at a lower level of generality to principles and norms, and they are often designed to reconcile conflicts which may exist between the principles and norms. Third World states, for example, wanted rules which differentiated between developed and underdeveloped countries.

Second cold war: period of East–West tension in the 1980s compared to the early period of confrontation between 1946 and 1953.

Security: in finance, a contract with a claim to future payments in which (in contrast to bank credits) there is a direct and formally identified relationship between the investor and the borrower; also unlike bank loans, securities are traded in markets.

Security community: 'A group of people which has become "integrated". By integration we mean the attainment, within a territory, of a "sense of community" and of institutions and practices strong enough and widespread enough to assure . . . dependable expectations of "peaceful change" among its population. By a "sense of community" we mean a belief . . . that common social problems must and can be resolved by processes of "peaceful change"' (Karl Deutsch et al. 1957).

Selectivity: an agreed moral principle is at stake in more than one situation, but national interest dictates a divergence of response.

Self-determination: a principle ardently, but selectively, espoused by US President Woodrow Wilson in the peacemaking that followed the First World War: namely that each 'people' should enjoy self-government over its own sovereign nation-state. Wilson pressed for application of this principle to East/Central Europe, but did not believe that other nationalities (in colonized Asia, Africa, the Pacific and Caribbean) were fit for self-rule.

Self-help: in realist theory, in an anarchical environment, states cannot assume other states will come to their defence even if they are allies. Each state must take care of itself.

11 September, 2001 (9/11):   the day when four aircraft were hijacked by Islamic terrorists in the United States—two of which destroyed the World Trade Center in New York, one which partially destroyed the Pentagon, and a fourth which crash-landed in a field in Pennsylvania (see also 9/11).

Sexual relations / power relations: the relational construction of heterosexuality and homosexuality, in which the heterosexual is usually privileged.

Shadow of the future: a metaphor indicating that decision-makers are conscious of the future when making decisions.

Sinatra doctrine: statement by the Soviet foreign ministry in October 1989 that countries of Eastern Europe were 'doing it their way' (a reference to Frank Sinatra's song 'I did it my way') and which marked the end of the Brezhnev doctrine and Soviet hegemony in Eastern Europe.

Single Undertaking: under WTO rules, there is a requirement for members to accept or reject the outcome of multiple multilateral negotiations as one package of reforms, rather than only choosing those parts with which they are most happy.

Skyjacking: the takeover of a commercial airplane for the purpose of seizing hostages and using them hostages to publicize a grievance or bargain for a particular political or economic goal.

Social construction of reality: suggests that reality is a product of human action, interaction, and knowledge. Actors and organizations will interact and develop shared ideas about what exists 'out there', and, once they have agreement about these concepts, this knowledge helps to form their understanding of the world.

Social facts: dependent on human agreement, their existence shapes how we categorize the world and what we do.

Social movement: people with a diffuse sense of collective identity, solidarity, and common purpose that usually leads to collective political behaviour. The concept covers all the different NGOs and networks, plus all their members and all the other individuals who share the common value(s). Thus, the women's movement and the environmental movement are much more than the specific NGOs that provide leadership and focus the desire for social change.

Society of states: an association of sovereign states based on their common interests, values, and norms.

Solidarism: a view that the international society of state is capable of acting together (in solidarity) to uphold or defend shared values. International society is not merely a framework of coexistence but agent for change and humanitarianism.

Sovereign equality: the technical legal equality possessed by sovereign states as expressed in UN General Assembly votes.

Sovereignty: the principle that within its territorial boundaries the state is the supreme political authority, and that outside those boundaries the state recognizes no higher political authority.

Specialized agencies: international institutions which have a special relationship with the central system of the United Nations but which are constitutionally independent, having their own assessed budgets, executive heads and committees, and assemblies of the representatives of all state members.

Stagflation: a situation experienced by many of the world's most advanced industrialized countries in the 1970s, where a period of very limited or even no growth was accompanied by seemingly runaway price increases. The word is a compound of 'stagnation' (indicating the no-growth scenario) and 'inflation' (indicating the large increases in the general price level).

State: the one word is used to refer to three distinct concepts: (1) In international law, a state is an entity that is recognized to exist when a government is in control of a population residing within a defined territory. It is comparable to the idea in domestic law of a company being a legal person. Such entities are seen as possessing sovereignty that is recognised by other states in the international system. (2) In the study of international politics, each state is a country. It is a community of people who interact in the same political system. (3) In philosophy and sociology, the state consists of the apparatus of government, in its broadest sense, covering the executive, the legislature, the administration, the judiciary, the armed forces, and the police. For Weber, the essential domestic feature of a state was a monopoly over the legitimate use of force.

State autonomy: in a more interdependent world, simply to achieve domestic objectives national governments are forced to engage in extensive multilateral collaboration and cooperation. But in becoming more embedded in frameworks of global and regional governance states confront a real dilemma: in return for more effective public policy and meeting their citizens' demands, whether in relation to the drugs trade or employment, their capacity for self-governance—that is state autonomy—is compromised.

State capitalism: an economic system in which state authorities have a financial stake, and degrees of actual control, over the means of production and exchange.

State of war: the conditions (often described by classical realists) where there is no actual conflict, but a permanent cold war that could become a 'hot' war at any time.

State sovereignty: a principle for organizing political space where there is one sovereign authority which governs a given territory. The Treaties of Westphalia is usually defined as the birth of state sovereignty, although it took several hundred years before the principle was fully institutionalized. International Relations theories hold different views of whether state sovereignty has been transformed or even eroded. They also disagree as to whether state sovereignty is a good way of organizing political community that is state sovereignty's normative status.

State system: the regular patterns of interaction between states, but without implying any shared values between them. This is distinguished from the view of a 'society' of states.

Stateless: individuals who do not 'belong' to any state and therefore do not have passports or rights.

State-sponsored terrorism: exists when individual states provide support to terrorist groups including funding, training, and resources including weapons. Claims of state sponsorship of terrorism are difficult to prove. States go to great lengths to ensure that their involvement is as clandestine as possible so that their leaders have a degree of plausible deniability when the respond to such charges. Other claims of state sponsorship are a matter of subjective opinion. In other cases the term confuses 'state terror' (the use of violence by the state to keep its own citizenry fearful, or the original connotation of terrorism) with state-sponsored terrorism.

Statism: in realist theory, the ideology that supports the organization of humankind into particular communities; the values and beliefs of that community are protected and sustained by the state.

Stockholding companies: primarily a seventeenth- and eighteenth-century phenomenon, through which a significant proportion of world trade was conducted by a small number of massive companies. These companies were responsible for opening up trade routes between Europe and Asia, setting up colonial structures in Asia to trade successfully back at home.

Structuration: concerns the relationship between agents and structures, trying to imagine the simultaneous process of the environment shaping actors and actors shaping their environment.

Structure: in the philosophy of the social sciences a structure is something that exists independently of the actor (e.g. social class) but is an important determinant in the nature of the action (e.g. revolution). For contemporary structural realists, the number of Great Powers in the international system constitutes the structure.

Subaltern: social groups at the lowest levels of economic power and esteem who are often excluded from political participation, such as peasants or women. Subaltern Studies, which developed first in India, focuses on the history and culture of subaltern groups.

Sub-prime crisis: the popular expression for the 2007 rupture in mortgage lending markets which exposed banks to bad debts and resulted in a global credit crunch.

Subsistence: Work necessary for basic family survival, such as food production, for which the worker does not receive wages

Summit diplomacy: refers to a direct meeting between heads of government (of the superpowers in particular) to resolve major problems. The 'summit' became a regular mode of contact during the cold war.

Superpower: term used to describe the United States and the Soviet Union after 1945, denoting their global political involvements and military capabilities, including in particular their nuclear arsenals.

Supranationalism: concept in integration theory that implies the creation of common institutions having independent decision-making authority and thus the ability to impose certain decisions and rules on member states.

Survival: the first priority for state leaders, emphasized by historical realists such as Machiavelli, Meinecke, and Weber.

Sustainable development: this has been defined as development that meets the needs of the present without compromising the ability of future generations to meet their own needs.

Technological revolution: refers to the way modern communications (the Internet, satellite communications, high-tech computers) made possible by technological advances have made distance and location less important factors not just for government (including at local and regional levels) but equally in the calculations of other actors such as firms' investment decisions or in the activities of social movements.

Territorial state: a state that has power over the population which resides on its territory but which does not seek to represent the nation or the people as a whole.

Territoriality: borders and territory still remain important, not least for administrative purposes. Under conditions of globalization, however, a new geography of political organization and political power is emerging which transcends territories and borders.

Territory: a portion of the earth's surface appropriated by a political community, or state.

Terrorism: the use of illegitimate violence by sub-state groups to inspire fear, by attacking civilians and/or symbolic targets. This is done for purposes such as drawing widespread attention to a grievance, provoking a severe response, or wearing down their opponent's moral resolve, to affect political change. Determining when the use of violence is legitimate, which is based on contextual morality of the act as opposed to its effects, is the source for disagreement over what constitutes terrorism.

The end of history: famous phrase employed by Francis Fukuyama in 1989; this argued that one phase of history shaped by the antagonism between collectivism and individualism had (two hundred years after the French Revolution) come to an end, leaving Liberalism triumphant.

Theocracy: a state based on religion.

Third World: a notion that was first used in the late 1950s to define both the underdeveloped world and the political and economic project that would help overcome underdevelopment: employed less in the post-cold war era.

Time–space compression: the technologically induced erosion of distance and time giving the appearance of a world that is in communication terms shrinking.

Total war: a term given to the twentieth century's two world wars to denote not only their global scale but also the combatants' pursuit of their opponents' 'unconditional surrender' (a phrase particularly associated with the Western allies in the Second World War). Total war also signifies the mobilization of whole populations—including women into factory work, auxiliary civil defence units, and as paramilitaries and paramedics—as part of the total call-up of all able-bodied citizens in pursuit of victory.

Toxic assets: the name popularly given to the failed investments that most western banks made in mortgage-backed securities in the lead up to the sub-prime crisis.

An important part of the government bailouts that were enacted in many advanced industrialized countries in 2008 and 2009 was an attempt to use public money in order to take the toxic assets off the balance sheets of banks. Western banks had bought large stocks of mortgage-backed securities at often high prices, but when the market for trading these securities completely evaporated in 2008 it revealed huge losses for the banks and unrecoverable short-term debts. Governments typically chose to use the bailouts in order to replace the essentially worthless toxic assets on banks' balance sheets with other assets that continued to have high prices, thus saving the banks from bankruptcy.

Transfer price: the price set by a transnational company for intra-firm trade of goods or services. For accounting purposes, a price must be set for exports, but it need not be related to any market price.

Transition: usually taken to mean the lengthy period between the end of communist planning in the Soviet bloc and the final emergence of a fully functioning democratic capitalist system.

Transnational actor: any civil society actor from one country that has relations with any actor from another country or with an international organization.

Transnational civil society: a political arena in which citizens and private interests collaborate across borders to advance their mutual goals or to bring governments and the formal institutions of global governance to account for their activities.

Transnational company/corporation (TNC): see Multinational corporations (MNCs).

Treaties of Westphalia 1648: the Treaties of Osnabruck and Munster, which together form the 'Peace of Westphalia', ended the Thirty Years War and were crucial in delimiting the political rights and authority of European monarchs. Among other things, the Treaties granted monarchs rights to maintain standing armies, build fortifications, and levy taxes.

Triads: the three economic groupings (North America, Europe, and East Asia).

Triangulation: occurs when trade between two countries is routed indirectly via a third country. For example, in the early 1980s, neither the Argentine Government nor the British Government permitted trade between the two countries, but companies simply sent their exports via Brazil or Western Europe.

Tribal: community defined through family relations or as living in the same local space, usually applied to the non-Western world. When used as a non-academic term it often has the connotations of something that is pre-modern, underdeveloped and inferior to Western societies.

Trilateral Conference: a follow-up meeting to the Bandung Conference in 1966 that was held in Havana Cuba. Five hundred delegates from independent and decolonizing states of Latin America, the Caribbean, Asia and Africa attended. The Conference produced more radical proposals for achieving decolonization and nonaligned power, such as armed struggle.

Truman doctrine: statement made by US President Harry Truman in March 1947 that it 'must be the policy of the United States to support free people who are resisting attempted subjugation by armed minorities or by outside pressures'. Intended to persuade Congress to support limited aid to Turkey and Greece, the doctrine came to underpin the policy of containment and American economic and political support for its allies.

Tyrannical states: states where the sovereign government is massively abusing the human rights of its citizens, engaging in acts of mass killing, ethnic cleansing, and/or genocide.

Unilateral humanitarian intervention: Military intervention for humanitarian purposes which is undertaken without the express authorization of the United Nations Security Council.

Unipolarity: a distribution of power internationally in which there is clearly only one dominant power or 'pole'. Some analysts argue that the international system became unipolar in the 1990s since there was no longer any rival to American power.

United Nations Charter (1945): the Charter of the United Nations is the legal regime that created the United Nations as the world's only 'supranational' organization. The Charter defines the structure of the United Nations, the powers of its constitutive organs, and the rights and obligations of sovereign states party to the Charter. Among other things, the Charter is the key legal document limiting the use of force to instances of self-defence and collective peace enforcement endorsed by the United Nations Security Council. See also Specialized agencies.

Universal Declaration of Human Rights: The principal normative document of the global human rights regime. Adopted by the United Nations General Assembly on 10 December 1948, it provides a comprehensive list of interdependent and indivisible human rights that are accepted as authoritative by most states and other international actors.

Utilitarianism: Utilitarians follow Jeremy Bentham's claim that action should be directed towards producing the 'greatest happiness of the greatest number'. In more recent years the emphasis has been not on happiness, but on welfare or general benefit (happiness being too difficult to achieve). There are also differences between act and rule utilitarians. Act utilitarianism focuses on the impact of actions whereas rule utilitarianism refers to the utility maximization following from universal conformity with a rule or set of rules.

Versailles Peace Treaty: the Treaty of Versailles formally ended the First World War (1914–18). The Treaty established the League of Nations, specified the rights and obligations of the victorious and defeated powers (including the notorious regime of reparations on Germany), and created the 'Mandatories' system under which 'advanced nations' were given legal tutelage over colonial peoples.

Vertical proliferation: refers to the increase in the number of nuclear weapons by those states already in possession of such weapons.

War on terror: an umbrella term coined by the Bush administration and refers to the various military, political, and legal actions taken by the USA and its allies after the attacks on 11 September 2001 to curb the spread of terrorism in general but Islamic-inspired terrorism in particular.

Warsaw Pact: the Warsaw Pact was created in May 1955 in response to West Germany's rearmament and entry into NATO. It comprised the USSR and seven communist states (though Albania withdrew support in 1961). The organization was officially dissolved in July 1991.

Washington Consensus: the belief of key opinion-formers in Washington that global welfare would be maximized by the universal application of neoclassical economic policies which favour a minimalist state and an enhanced role for the market.

Weapons of mass destruction: a category defined by the United Nations in 1948 to include 'atomic explosive weapons, radioactive material weapons, lethal chemical and biological weapons, and any weapons developed in the future which have characteristics comparable in destructive effects to those of the atomic bomb or other weapons mentioned above'.

World Bank Group: a collection of five agencies under the more general rubric of the World Bank, with headquarters in Washington, DC. Its formal objective is to encourage development in low- and medium-income countries with project loans and various advisory services. See further www.worldbank.org.

World government: associated in particular with those Idealists who believe that peace can never be achieved in a world divided into separate sovereign states. Just as governments abolished the state of nature in civil society, the establishment of a world government must end the state of war in international society.

World order: this is a wider category of order than the 'international'. It takes as its units of order, not states, but individual human beings and assesses the degree of order on the basis of the delivery of certain kinds of goods (be it security, human rights, basic needs or justice) for humanity as a whole.

World Trade Organization (WTO):   established in 1995 with headquarters in Geneva, with 153 members as of early 2010. It is a permanent institution covering services, intellectual property and investment issues as well as pure merchandise trade, and it has a disputes settlement mechanism in order to enforce its free trade agenda.

World-travelling: a postcolonial methodology that aims to achieve some mutual understanding between people of different cultures and points of view by finding empathetic ways to enter into the spirit of a different experience and find in it an echo of some part of oneself.

References

Abbott, K., Keohane, R. O., Moravcsik, A., Slaughter, A.-M., and Snidal, D. (2000), 'The Concept of Legalization', *International Organization*, 54(3): 401-20.

Abu-Lughod, J. L. (1989), *Before European Hegemony: The World-System AD 1250-1350* (Oxford: Oxford University Press).

Acharya, A. (2004), 'A Holistic Paradigm', *Security Dialogue*, 35 (September): 355-6.

—— (2007), *Promoting Human Security: Ethical, Normative and Educational Frameworks in South East Asia* (Paris: United Nations Scientific, Cultural and Educational Organization).

Ackerly, B. A., Stern, M., and True, J. (eds) (2006), *Feminist Methodologies for International Relations* (Cambridge: Cambridge University Press).

Adichie, Chimamanda Ngozi (2007), *Half of a Yellow Sun* (London: Harper Perennial).

Adler, E. and Barnett, M. (1998*a*), *Security Communities* (Cambridge: Cambridge University Press).

—— —— (1998*b*), 'A Framework for the Study of Security Communities', in E. Adler and M. Barnett (eds), *Security Communities* (Cambridge: Cambridge University Press): 29-65.

Agnew, J., and Corbridge, S. (1995), *Mastering Space: Hegemony, Territory and International Political Economy* (London: Routledge).

Ahmad, M., and Zartman, W. (1997), 'Political Islam: Can it Become a Loyal Opposition?, *Middle East Policy*, 5(1): 68-84.

Ahmed, A. S. (1992), *Post-Modernism and Islam: Predicament and Promise* (London: Routledge).

—— **and Donnan, Hastings** (eds) (1994), *Islam, Globalization and Postmodernity* (London: Routledge).

Alarcon, N. (1990), 'The Theoretical Subject(s) of This Bridge Called My Back and Anglo-American Feminism', in Gloria Anzaldua (ed.), *Making Face, Making Soul* (San Francisco, CA: Aunt Lute): 356-69.

Albrow, M. (1996), *The Global Age* (Cambridge: Polity Press).

Allison, G. (2000), 'The Impact of Globalization on National and International Security', in J. S. Nye and J. D. Donahue (eds), *Governance in a Globalizing World* (Washington, DC: Brookings Institution): 72-85.

Alperovitz, G. (1965), *Atomic Diplomacy: Hiroshima and Potsdam: The Use of the Atomic Bomb and the American Confrontation with Soviet Power* (New York: Simon & Shuster).

Amstutz, M. R. (1999), *International Ethics* (Lanham, MD: Rowman & Littlefield).

Anderson, B. (1983; revised 1991), *Imagined Communities: Reflections on the Origin and Spread of Nationalism* (London: Verso).

Ang, I. (1995), '"I'm a Feminist But..."', in Barbara Caine and Rosemary Pringle (eds), *Transitions: New Australian Feminisms* (London: Allen & Unwin): 57-73.

Anghie, A. (1996), 'Francisco de Vitoria and the Colonial Origins of International Law', *Social and Legal Studies*, 5(3): 321-36.

Annan, K. (2001), 'Towards a Culture of Peace', available online at http://www.unesco.org/opi2/lettres/TextAnglais/AnnanE.html, last accessed 25 June 2007.

Anzaldua, Gloria (1987), *Borderlands: The Frontera* (San Francisco, CA: Aunt Lute).

Appadurai, Arjun (1996), *Modernization at Large: Cultural Dimensions in Globalization* (Minneapolis, MN: University of Minnesota Press).

Aradau, C. (2008), *Rethinking Trafficking in Women: Politics out of Security* (Basingstoke: Palgrave Macmillan).

Art, R. J., et al. (2002), 'War with Iraq Is Not in America's National Interest', *New York Times* paid advertisement, 26 September.

Ashley, R. K. (1987), 'The Geopolitics of Geopolitical Space: Toward a Critical Social Theory of International Politics', *Alternatives*, 12(4): 403-34.

Association of Southeast Asian Nations (2007), Declaration on the Acceleration of the Establishment of an ASEAN Community by 2015 (12th ASEAN Summit, Cebu, Philippines, 13 January), available online at http://www.12thaseansummit.org.ph/innertemplate3.asp?category=docs&docid=21, last accessed 7 September 2007.

Austin, John (1996), *Lectures in Jurisprudence, Volume One* (Bristol: Thoemmes Press).

Axford, Barrie (1995), *The Global System: Economics, Politics and Culture* (Cambridge: Polity Press)

Bakker, E. (2006), *Jihadi Terrorists in Europe, Their Characteristics and the Circumstances in Which They Joined the Jihad: An Exploratory Study* (Clingendael: Netherlands Institute of International Relations).

Baldwin, D. (ed.) (1993), *Neorealism and Neoliberalism: The Contemporary Debate* (New York: Columbia University Press).

Ban, Ki-moon (2009), *Implementing the Responsibility to Protect*, Report of the UN Secretary-General, A/63/677, 12 January.

Bank for International Settlements (2007), *Triennial Central Bank Survey: Foreign Exchange and Derivatives Market Activity in 2007* (Basel: Bank for International Settlements).

Barber, B. (1996), *Jihad vs. McWorld: How Globalism and Tribalism are Reshaping the World* (New York: Ballantine Books).

—— (2002), *Fear's Empire: War, Terrorism, and Democracy* (New York: W. W. Norton).

Barker, D., and Mander, J. (1999), *Invisible Government: The World Trade Organization: Global Government for the Millennium?* (San Francisco, CA: International Forum on Globalization).

Bauman, Z. (1998), *Globalization: The Human Consequences* (Cambridge: Polity Press).

BBC News (2004), 'Blair terror speech in full', available online at http://news.bbc.co.uk/1/hi/3536131.stm, last accessed 26 January 2009.

Beinin, J. and Stork, J. (eds) (1997), *Political Islam: Essays from Middle East Report* (Los Angeles, CA: University of California Press).

Beitz, C. (1979), *Political Theory and International Relations* (Princeton, NJ: Princeton University Press).

—— (1994), 'Cosmopolitan Liberalism and the States System', in C. Brown (ed.), *Political Restructuring in Europe: Ethical Perspectives* (London: Routledge): 123–36.

Bellamy, A. J. (2002), *Kosovo and International Society* (Basingstoke: Palgrave).

—— (2005), 'Responsibility to Protect or Trojan Horse? The Crisis in Darfur and Humanitarian Intervention After Iraq', *Ethics and International Affairs*, 19(2): 31–54.

—— **and Williams, P. D.** (2009), 'The West and Contemporary Peace Operations', *Journal of Peace Research*, 46(1): 39–57.

Bello, W. (1994), *Dark Victory: The United States, Structural Adjustment and Global Poverty* (London: Pluto).

Bennett, J., and George, S. (1987), *The Hunger Machine* (Cambridge: Polity Press).

Berger, T. (2000), 'Set for Stability? Prospects for Conflict and Cooperation in East Asia', *Review of International Studies*, 26: 427–8.

Bergsten, C. F. (1997), 'Open Regionalism', *The World Economy*, 20: 545–65.

Best, E. (2006), 'Regional Integration and (Good) Regional Governance: Are Common Standards and Indicators Possible?', in P. De Lombaerde (ed.), *Assessment and Measurement of Regional Integration* (London and New York: Routledge): 183–214.

Bethell, L. (1970), *The Abolition of the Brazilian Slave Trade: Britain, Brazil and the Slave Trade Question 1807–1869* (Cambridge: Cambridge University Press).

Beyer, P. (1994), *Religion and Globalization* (London: Sage Publications).

Bhabha, H. (1994), *The Location of Culture* (London and New York: Routledge).

Bhagwati, J. (1991), *The World Trading System at Risk* (Princeton, NJ: Princeton University Press).

Bigelow, R. (1969), *The Dawn Warriors* (London: Scientific Book Club).

Blustein, P. (2001), *The Chastening: Inside the Crisis that Rocked the Global Financial System and Humbled the IMF* (Oxford: Public Affairs).

Bodin, J. (1967), *Six Books of the Commonwealth* (Oxford: Basil Blackwell).

Booth, K. (1991), 'Security and Emancipation', *Review of International Studies*, 17(4): 313–26.

—— (1997), 'Huntington's Homespun Grandeur', *Political Quarterly*, 68(4): 425–8.

—— (1999), 'Three Tyrannies', in T. Dunne and N. J. Wheeler (eds), *Human Rights in Global Politics* (Cambridge: Cambridge University Press).

—— (ed.) (2004), *Critical Security Studies in World Politics* (Boulder, CO: Lynne Rienner).

—— (2007), *Theory of World Security* (Cambridge: Cambridge University Press).

—— **and Dunne, T.** (1999), 'Learning beyond Frontiers', in T. Dunne and N. J. Wheeler (eds), *Human Rights in Global Politics* (Cambridge: Cambridge University Press): 303–28.

—— **and Dunne, T.** (eds) (2002), *World in Collision: Terror and the Future Global Order* (Basingstoke: Palgrave).

Boutros-Ghali, B. (1992), *An Agenda for Peace* (New York: United Nations).

Bloom, M. (2005), *Dying to Win: The Allure of Suicide Terror* (New York: Columbia University Press).

Brass, Paul (1991), *Ethnicity and Nationalism* (London: Sage).

Breitmeier, H., Young, O. R., and Zurn, M. (2007), *Analyzing International Environmental Regimes* (Cambridge, MA: The MIT Press).

Breman, J. G. (2001), 'The Ears of the Hippopotamus: Manifestations, Determinants, and Estimates of the Malaria Burden', *American Journal of Tropical Medicine and Hygiene*, 64(1/2): 1–11, available online at http://www.ajtmh.org/cgi/reprint/64/1_suppl/1-c, last accessed 25 June 2007.

Brewer, A. (1990), *Marxist Theories of Imperialism: A Critical Survey*, 2nd edn (London: Routledge).

Brocklehurst, H. (2007), 'Children and War', in Alan Collins (ed.), *Contemporary Security Studies* (Oxford, Oxford University Press): 367–82.

Broder, J. M. (2009), 'Climate Change Seen as Threat to U.S. Security', *New York Times*, 9.

Brohman, J. (1995), 'Economism and Critical Silences in Development Studies: A Theoretical Critique of Neoliberalism', *Third World Quarterly*, 16(2): 297–318.

Brown, C. (1988), 'Ethics of Coexistence: The International Theory of Terry Nardin', *Review of International Studies*, 14: 213–22.

—— (1999), 'History Ends, Worlds Collide', *Review of International Studies*, 25 (December): 41–57.

—— (2000), 'Cultural Diversity and International Political Theory', *Review of International Studies*, 26(2): 199–213.

Brown, D. (2006), 'Study Claims Iraq's "Excess" Death Toll has Reached 655,000', *Washington Post*, 11 October: A12.

Brown, L. R., and Kane, H. (1995), *Full House: Reassessing the Earth's Population Carrying Capacity* (London: Earthscan).

Brown, M. E., Lynn-Jones, S. M., and Miller, S. E. (1995), 'The Perils of Anarchy, Contemporary Realism, and International Security', *International Security* (Cambridge: MIT Press).

Brown, S. (1992), *International Relations in a Changing Global System* (Boulder, CO: Westview).

—— et al. (1977) *Regimes for the Ocean, Outer Space and the Weather* (Washington, DC: Brookings Institute).

Brownlie, I. (1974), 'Humanitarian Intervention', in J. N. Moore (ed.), *Law and Civil War in the Modern World* (Baltimore, MD: Johns Hopkins University Press): 217–28.

Brundtland, G. H., et al. (1987), *Our Common Future: Report of the World Commission on Environment and Development* (The Brundtland Report) (Oxford: Oxford University Press).

Bull, H. (1977), *The Anarchical Society: A Study of Order in World Politics* (London: Macmillan).

Burke, A. (2004), 'Just War or Ethical Peace? Moral Discourses of Strategic Violence after 9/11', *International Affairs*, 80(2): 329–53.

Burnham, P. (1991), 'Neo-Gramscian Hegemony and International Order', *Capital & Class*, 45: 73–93.

Burtless, G., et al. (1998), *Globalphobia: Confronting Fears about Open Trade* (Washington, DC: Brookings Institution).

Buvinic, M. (1987), 'Women in Poverty: A New Global Underclass', *Foreign Policy* (Fall): 38–53.

Buzan, B. (1983), *People, States and Fear* (London: Harvester).

—— (2001), 'Human Security in International Perspective', in M. C. Anthony and M. J. Hassan (eds), *The Asia Pacific in the New Millennium: Political and Security Challenges* (Kuala Lumpur: Institute of Strategic and International Studies): 583–96.

—— and Gonzalez-Pelaez, A. (eds) (2009), *International Society and the Middle East* (Basingstoke: Palgrave Macmillan).

Byers, M. (1999), *Custom, Power, and the Power of Rules: International Relations and Customary International Law* (Cambridge: Cambridge University Press).

Cammack, P. (2002), 'The Mother of All Governments: The World Bank Matrix for Global Governance', in R. Wilkinson and S. Hughes (eds), *Global Governance: Critical Reflections* (London: Routledge).

Campbell, D. (1992), *Writing Security: United States Foreign Policy and the Politics of Identity* (Manchester: Manchester University Press).

—— (1998), *National Deconstruction: Violence, Identity, and Justice in Bosnia* (Minneapolis, MN: University of Minnesota Press).

—— (2007), 'Poststructuralism', in T. Dunne, M. Kurki, and S. Smith (eds), *International Relations Theories: Discipline and Diversity* (Oxford: Oxford University Press): 203–28.

Caney, S. (1997), 'Human Rights and the Rights of States: Terry Nardin on Non-Intervention', *International Political Science Review*, 18(1): 27–37.

—— (2001), 'International Distributive Justice (review article)', *Political Studies*, 49: 974–97.

Carpenter, C. (2003), '"Women and Children First": Gender, Norms and Humanitarian Evacuation in the Balkans 1991–1995', *International Organization*, 57(4): 66–94.

Carr, E. H. (1939; 2nd edn, 1946), *The Twenty Years' Crisis 1919–1939: An Introduction to the Study of International Relations* (London: Macmillan).

Carson, R. (1962), *Silent Spring* (Harmondsworth: Penguin).

Castells, M. (2000), *The Rise of the Network Society* (Oxford: Blackwell).

Center for Disease Control (2005), 'Fact Sheet: Tuberculosis in the United States', 17 March 2005, available online at http://www.cdc. gov/tb/pubs/TBfactsheets.htm, last accessed 25 June 2007.

Chakrabarty, D. (2000), *Provincializing Europe* (Princeton, NJ: Princeton University Press).

Chalk, P. (1996), *West European Terrorism and Counter-Terrorism: The Evolving Dynamic* (New York: St. Martin's).

Chan, S. (1997), 'Too Neat and Under-thought a Word Order: Huntington and Civilizations', *Millennium: Journal of International Studies*, 26(1): 137–40.

—— (2003), *Robert Mugabe: A Life of Power and Violence* (Ann Arbor, MI: University of Michigan Press).

Chase-Dunn, C. (1994), 'Technology and the Logic of World-Systems', in R. Palan and B. K. Gills (eds), *Transcending the State–Global Divide: A Neostructuralist Agenda in International Relations* (Boulder, CO: Lynne Rienner): 84–105.

—— (1998), *Global Formation: Structures of the World Economy*, updated edn (London: Rowman & Littlefield).

Chetley A. (1986), *The Politics of Baby Foods* (London: Pinter).

Chin, C. (1998), *In Service and Servitude: Foreign Female Domestic Workers and the Malaysia 'Modernity' Project* (New York: Columbia University Press).

Ching, F. (1999), 'Social Impact of the Regional Financial Crisis', in Linda Y. C. Lim, F. Ching, and Bernardo M. Villegas (eds), *The Asian Economic Crisis: Policy Choices, Social Consequences and the Phillipine Case* (New York: Asia Society), available online at http://www.asiasociety.org/publications/update_crisis_ching.html, last accessed 25 June 2007.

Chomsky, N. (1999), *The New Military Humanism: Lessons from Kosovo* (London: Pluto Press).

Chowdhry, G. and Nair, S. (2002), *Power, Postcolonialism and International Relations: Reading Race, Gender, and Class* (London: Routledge).

Christensen, T. (1996), *Useful Adversaries: Grand Strategy, Domestic Mobilization and Sino-American Conflict, 1947–1958* (Princeton, NJ: Princeton University Press).

—— **Jørgensen, K. E., and Wiener, A.** (eds) (2001), *The Social Construction of Europe* (London: Sage).

Clark, I. (1980), *Reform and Resistance in the International Order* (Cambridge: Cambridge University Press).

—— (1989), *The Hierarchy of States: Reform and Resistance in the International Order* (Cambridge: Cambridge University Press).

—— (1999), *Globalization and International Relations Theory* (Oxford: Oxford University Press).

—— (2007), *International Legitimacy and World Society* (Oxford: Oxford University Press).

Coates, A. (1997), *The Ethics of War* (Manchester: Manchester University Press).

Cobban, A. and Hunt, J. W. (1969), translation of Sorel, A. (1888), *Europe and the French Revolution* (London: Fontana).

Cohan, W. (2009), *House of Cards: How Wall Street's Gamblers Broke Capitalism* (London: Allen Lane).

Cohen, B. (1977), *Organizing the World's Money: The Political Economy of International Monetary Relations* (Basingstoke: Macmillan).

Cohn, C. (1993), 'War, Wimps and Women', in M. Cooke and A. Woollacott (eds), *Gendering War Talk* (Princeton, NJ: Princeton University Press): 227–46.

Coker, C. (2001), *Humane Warfare* (London: Routledge).

Colas, A. (2002), *International Civil Society: Social Movements in World Politics* (Cambridge: Polity Press).

Connor, Walker (1994), *Ethno-Nationalism: The Quest for Understanding* (Princeton, NJ: Princeton University Press).

Convention on the Prohibition of the Use, Stockpiling, Production and Transfer of Anti-personnel Mines and on their Destruction, available online at http://www.un.org/Depts/mine/UNDocs/ban_trty.htm, last accessed 15 January 2010.

Cox, M. (2007), 'Hans J. Morgenthau, Realism and the Rise and Fall of the Cold War', in M. C. Williams (ed.), *Realism Reconsidered* (Oxford: Oxford University Press).

Cox, R. (1981), 'Social Forces, States and World Orders: Beyond International Relations Theory', *Millennium* 10(2): 126–55.

Crenshaw, M. (ed.) (1983), *Terrorism, Legitimacy, and Power* (Middletown, CT: Wesleyan University Press).

Cronin, A. K. (2002/2003), 'Behind the Curve: Globalization and International Terrorism', *International Security*, 27(3): 30–58.

Cronin, B. (2003), *Institutions for the Common Good: International Protection Regimes in International Society* (Cambridge: Cambridge University Press).

Crotty, J., and Epstein, G. (1996), 'In Defence of Capital Controls', in L. Panitch (ed.), *Are There Alternatives? Socialist Register 1996* (London: Merlin Press).

Cushman, T. (ed.) (2005), *A Matter of Principle: Humanitarian Arguments for War in Iraq* (Berkeley, CA: University of California Press).

Cusimano, M. K. (ed.) (2000), *Beyond Sovereignty* (New York: St Martin's).

D'Acosta, B. (2006), 'Marginalized Identity: New Frontiers of Research for IR?', in Brooke Ackerly, Maria Stern, and Jacqui True (eds), *Feminist Methodologies for International Relations* (Cambridge: Cambridge University Press): 129–52.

Damrosch, L. F. (ed.) (1993), *Enforcing Restraint: Collective Intervention in Internal Conflicts* (New York: Council on Foreign Relations).

Das, V. (2007), *Life and Words: Violence and the Descent into the Ordinary* (Berkeley, CA: University of California Press).

Deese, D. (2007), *World Trade Politics: Power, Principles, and Leadership* (London: Routledge).

Dekmejian, R. H. (1994), 'The Rise of Political Islamism in Saudi Arabia', *Middle East Journal*, 48(4): 627–43.

Demmers, J., Fernández Jilberto, A., and Hogenboom, B. (eds) (2004), *Good Governance in the Era of Global Neoliberalism: Conflict and Depolitisation in Latin America, Eastern Europe, Asia and Africa* (London: Routledge).

Denemark, R. A., Freidman, J., Gills, B. K., and Modelski, G. (eds) (2000), *World System History* (London: Routledge).

Department for International Development (2005), *Fighting Poverty to Build a Safer World* (London: HMSO), available online at http://www.dfid.gov.uk/pubs/files/securityforall.pdf, last accessed 25 June 2007.

—— (2006), *Eliminating World Poverty: Making Governance Work for the Poor*, Cm 6876 (London: HMSO), available online at http://www.dfid.gov.uk/pubs/files/whitepaper2006/wp2006section3.pdf, last accessed 25 June 2007.

Department of Foreign Affairs and International Trade (Canada) (DFAIT) (1999), *Human Security: Safety for People in a Changing World* (Ottawa: DFAIT).

—— (2000), *Freedom from Fear: Canada's Foreign Policy for Human Security* (Ottawa: DFAIT), available online at http://pubx.dfait-maeci.gc.ca/00_global/Pubs_(at).nsf/4d5c1b5e541f152485256cbb006bb5ff/5615389

3ff8dfda285256bc700653b9f? Open Document, last accessed 25 June 2007.

Der Derian, J. (1992), *Antidiplomacy: Spies, Terror, Speed, and War* (Cambridge, MA and Oxford: Blackwell).

Derrida, J. (1992), *The Other Heading: Reflections on Today's Europe* (Bloomington, IN: Indiana University Press).

Desch, M. (2003), 'The Humanity of American Realism', *Review of International Studies*, 29(3): 415–26.

Deutsch, K. W. (1968), *The Analysis of International Relations* (Englewood Cliffs, NJ: Prentice Hall).

Doyle, M. W. (1986), 'Liberalism and World Politics', *American Political Science Review*, 80(4): 1151–69.

—— (1995), 'On Democratic Peace', *International Security*, 19(4): 164–84.

—— (1997), *Ways of War and Peace: Realism, Liberalism, and Socialism* (New York: W. W. Norton).

Duffield, M. (1998), 'Post-Modern Conflict: Warlords, Post-Adjustment States and Private Protection', *Civil Wars*, 1: 65–102.

Duménil, G., and Lévy, D. (2004), *Capital Resurgent: Roots of the Neoliberal Revolution* (Cambridge, MA: Harvard University Press).

Economic Commission for Africa (ECA) and African Union (AU) (2006), *Assessing Regional Integration in Africa II: Rationalizing Regional Economic Communities* (Addis Abbaba: ECA).

Edwards, M., and Gaventa, J. (2001), *Global Citizen Action: Lessons and Challenges*, (Boulder, CO: Lynne Rienner).

Eichengreen, B. (1996), *Golden Fetters: The Gold Standard and the Great Depression, 1919–1939* (Oxford: Oxford University Press).

Ekins, P. (1992), *A New World Order: Grassroots Movements for Social Change* (London: Routledge).

Elbe, S. (2009), *Virus Alert: Security, Governmentality and the AIDS Pandemic* (New York: Columbia University Press).

Elias, N. (2000), *The Civilizing Process: Sociogenetic and Psychogenetic Investigations* (Oxford: Basil Blackwell).

Enloe, C. (1989), *Bananas, Beaches and Bases: Making Feminist Sense of International Politics* (London: Pandora Books).

—— (2004), *The Curious Feminist: Searching for Women in a New Age of Empire* (Berkeley, CA: University of California Press).

Environmental Degradation and Conflict in Darfur: A Workshop Organized by the University of Peace of the United Nations and the Peace Research Institute,

University of Khartoum, Khartoum, 15/16 December 2004.

Epstein, C. (2007), 'Guilty Bodies, Productive Bodies, Destructive Bodies: Crossing the Biometric Borders', *International Political Sociology*, 1(2): 149-64.

Esposito, J. (1991), *The Straight Path* (Oxford: Oxford University Press).

—— and Piscatori, J. (1991), 'Deomcratization and Islam', *Middle East Journal*, 45(3): 427-40.

—— and Watson, M. (eds) (2000), *Religion and Global Order* (Cardiff: University of Wales Press).

European Union (2003), 'A Secure Europe in a Better World: European Security Strategy', Brussels, 12 December.

Evans, G. (2004), 'When is it Right to Fight?', *Survival*, 46(3): 59-82.

—— (2008), *The Responsibility to Protect: Ending Mass Atrocity Crimes Once and for All* (Washington, DC: The Brookings Institution).

Evans, T. (2005), *The Politics of Human Rights: A Global Perspective* (London: Pluto).

—— (forthcoming), 'The Limits of Tolerance: Islam as Counter-Hegemony', *Review of International Studies*.

Experts Group on Trafficking in Human Beings (2004), *Report of the Experts Group on Trafficking in Human Beings* (Brussels: European Commission, Director-General Justice, Freedom and Security).

Falk, R. (1995a), 'Liberalism at the Global Level: The Last of the Independent Commissions', *Millennium Special Issue: The Globalization of Liberalism?*, 24(3): 563-76.

—— (1995b), *On Humane Governance: Toward a New Global Politics* (Cambridge: Polity Press).

Fandy, M. (1994), 'Egypt's Islamic Group: Regional Revenge?', *Middle East Journal*, 48(4): 607-25.

Fanon, F. (1963), *The Wretched of the Earth* (New York: Grove Press).

—— (1990), *The Wretched of the Earth*, trans. Constance Farrington (London: Penguin).

—— (1952), *Black Skin, White Masks* (London: Pluto).

Farsoun, S. K., and Mashayekhi, M. (1992), *Iran: Political Culture in the Islamic Republic* (London: Routledge).

FBI (1999), *Terrorism in the United States* (Washington, DC: US Government Printing Office for the Federal Bureau of Investigation).

Finnemore, M. (1996), *National Interests in International Society* (Ithaca, NY: Cornell University Press).

—— and Sikkink K. (1998), 'International Norm Dynamics and Political Change', *International Organization*, 52(4): 887-917.

Fischer, F. (1967), *Germany's Aims in the First World War* (New York: W. W. Norton).

Floyd, R. (2007), 'Review of Lene Hansen: *Security as Practice: Discourse Analysis and the Bosnian War*', *Journal of International Relations and Development*, 10(2): 214-17.

Foot, R. (2006), 'Torture: The Struggle over a Peremptory Norm in a Counter-Terrorist Era', *International Relations*, 20(2): 131-51.

Footer, M. (2006), *An Institutional and Normative Analysis of the World Trade Organization* (Leiden: Martinus Nijhoff).

Forsythe, D. P. (1988), 'The United Nations and Human Rights', in L. S. Finkelstein (ed.), *Politics in the United Nations System* (Durham, NC and London: Duke University Press).

Francis, D. (2004), *Rethinking War and Peace* (London: Pluto Press).

Franck, T., and Rodley, N. (1974), 'After Bangladesh: The Law of Humanitarian Intervention by Force', *American Journal of International Law*, 67(2): 275-305.

Foucault, M. (1990), *The History of Sexuality*, Vol. I (London, Penguin).

—— (1996), 'What Our Present Is', in M. Foucault, *Foucault Live: Collected Interviews 1961-1984* (New York: Semiotexte).

Frank, A. G. (1998), *ReORIENT: Global Economy in the Asian Age* (Berkeley, CA: University of California Press).

—— and Gills, B. (eds) (1996), *The World System: Five Hundred Years or Five Thousand?* (London: Routledge).

Freedman, L. (ed.) (1994), *War* (Oxford: Oxford University Press).

—— (1998), *The Revolution in Strategic Affairs*, Adelphi Paper 318 (Oxford: Oxford University Press).

Friedman, T. (2000), *Lexus and the Olive Tree* (New York: Anchor Books).

—— (2005), *The World is Flat: A Brief History of the 21st Century* (New York: Farrar, Straus, Giroux).

Fukuyama, Francis (1989), 'The End of History?', *National Interest* (September): 3-18.

—— (1992), *The End of History and The Last Man* (London: Penguin Books).

Gallagher, P. (2005), *The First Ten Years of the WTO: 1995-2005* (Cambridge: Cambridge University Press).

Gallarotti, G. (1995), *The Anatomy of an International Monetary Regime: The Classical Gold Standard 1880-1914* (New York: Oxford University Press).

Gamble, A. (2009), *The Spectre at the Feast: Capitalist Crisis and the Politics of Recession* (Basingstoke: Palgrave Macmillan).

Gappah, P. (2009), *An Elegy for Easterly* (faber and faber).

Gardiner, S. (2004), 'Ethics and Global Climate Change', *Ethics*, 114: 555-600.

Gardner, R. (1980), *Sterling-Dollar Diplomacy in Current Perspective: The Origins and the Prospects of Our International Economic Order* (New York: Columbia University Press).

Garnett, J. C. (2010), 'The Causes of War and the Conditions of Peace', in J. Baylis, J. Wirtz, and C. S. Gray (eds), *Strategy in the Contemporary World*, 3rd edn (Oxford: Oxford University Press).

Gellner, E. (2006), *Nations and Nationalism*, 2nd edn (Oxford: Blackwell).

Gendering Human Security: From Marginalisation to the Integration of Women in Peace-Building (Oslo: Norwegian Institute of International Affairs and Fafo Forum on Gender Relations in Post-Conflict Transitions, 2001), available online at http://www.fafo.no/pub/rapp/352/352.pdf, last accessed 25 June 2007.

Germain, R., and Kenny, M. (1998), 'Engaging Gramsci: International Relations Theory and the New Gramscians', *Review of International Studies*, 24(1): 3-21.

Giddens, A. (1990), *The Consequences of Modernity: Self and Society in the Late Modern Age* (Cambridge: Polity Press and Stanford, CA: Stanford University Press).

Gill, S. (2008), *Power and Resistance in the New World Order*, 2nd edn (Basingstoke: Palgrave Macmillan).

Gilpin, R. (2001), *Global Political Economy* (Princeton, NJ: Princeton University Press).

—— (2002), *The Challenge of Global Capitalism* (Princeton, NJ: Princeton University Press).

Goldstein, J., Kahler, M., Keohane, R. O., and Slaughter, A.-M. (eds) (2000), 'Legalization in World Politics', *International Organization*, 54(3).

Goodin, R. E. (1988) 'What is So Special About Our Fellow Countrymen?', *Ethics*, 98(4): 663-86.

Goodman, D., and Redclift, M. (1991), *Refashioning Nature: Food, Ecology and Culture* (London: Routledge).

Goodman, J., and Pauly, L. (1993), 'The Obsolescence of Capital Controls? Economic Management in an Age of Global Markets', *World Politics*, 46(1): 50-82.

Government of India, Economic Survey of India 2008-9. 2 July 2009, available online at http://indiabudget.nic.in., last accessed 9 January 2010.

Government of Orissa (2007), 'Orissa: A Perspective' (Bhubaneswar), available online at http://www.teamorissa.org/adv_orissa.asp, last accessed 11 January 2010.

Grabel, I. (2003), 'Averting Crisis? Assessing Measures to Manage Financial Integration in Emerging Economies', *Cambridge Journal of Economics*, 27(3): 317-36.

Gramsci, A. (1971), *Selections from the Prison Notebooks*, ed. and trans. Q. Hoare and G. Nowell Smith (London: Lawrence & Wishart).

Gray, C. (2002), 'World Politics as Usual After September 11: Realism Vindicated', in K. Booth and T. Dunne (eds), *Worlds in Collision: Terror and the Future of Global Order* (Basingstoke: Palgrave Macmillan).

Gray, C. S. (1999), 'Clausewitz Rules, OK? The Future is the Past – with GPS', *Review of International Studies*, 25: 161-82.

—— (2002), *Strategy for Chaos: Revolutions in Military Affairs and the Evidence of History* (London: Frank Cass).

Gray, J. (1995), *Enlightenment's Wake: Politics and Culture at the Close of the Modern Age* (London: Routledge).

Greenwood, B. M., Bojang, K., Whitty, C. J., and Targett, G. A. (2005), 'Malaria', *The Lancet*, 365 (9469): 1487-98.

Grieco, J. (1988a), 'Anarchy and the Limits of Cooperation: A Realist Critique of the Newest Liberal Institutionalism', *International Organization*, 42 (August): 485-507.

—— (1988b), 'Realist Theory and the Problem of International Cooperation', *Journal of Politics*, 50 (August): 600-24.

Grotius, H. (1925), *The Law of War and Peace: De Jure Belli ac Pacis Libri Trea* (New York: Bobbs-Merrill).

Gruber, L. (2000), *Ruling the World: Power Politics and the Rise of Supranational Institutions* (Princeton, NJ: Princeton University Press).

Guazzone, L. (ed.) (1995), *The Islamist Dilemma: The Political Role of Islamist Movements in the Contemporary Arab World* (Reading: Ithaca Press).

Gunaratna, R. (2002), *Inside Al Qaeda: Global Network of Terror* (New York: Columbia University Press).

Haas, P. M., Keohane, R. O., and Levy, M. A. (1993), *Institutions for the Earth: Sources of Effective International Environmental Protection* (Cambridge: MIT Press).

Halliday, F. (1995), *Islam and the Myth of Confrontation* (London: I. B. Tauris).

—— (2001), *The World at 2000: Perils and Promises* (Basingstoke: Palgrave).

Hansen, L. (2006), *Security as Practice: Discourse Analysis and the Bosnian War* (London: Routledge).

Haq, M. (1995), *Reflections on Human Development* (Oxford: Oxford University Press).

Hardin, G. (1968), 'The Tragedy of the Commons', *Science*, 162: 1243–8.

Harvey, D. (1989), *The Condition of Postmodernity: An Enquiry into the Conditions of Cultural Change* (Oxford: Oxford University Press).

—— (2007), *A Brief History of Neoliberalism* (Oxford: Oxford University Press).

Hasenclever, A., Mayer, P., and Rittberger, V. (1997), *Theories of International Regimes* (Cambridge: Cambridge University Press).

Hashemi, S. H. (1996), 'International Society and its Islamic Malcontents', *Fletcher Forum of World Affairs*, 20(2) (Winter/Spring): 13–29.

Hashim, A. S. (2001), 'The World according to Usama Bin Laden', *Naval War College Review*, Autumn: 12–35.

Hastings, A. (1997), *The Construction of Nationhood: Ethnicity, Religion and Nationalism* (Cambridge: Cambridge University Press).

Hay, C. (2000), 'Contemporary Capitalism, Globalization, Regionalization and the Persistence of National Variation', *Review of International Studies*, 26(4): 509–32.

Heazle, M. (2006), *Scientific Uncertainty and the Politics of Whaling* (Washington, DC: University of Washington Press).

Heeren, A. H. L. (1971), *A Manual of the History of the Political System of Europe and its Colonies*, 2 vols (Oxford: Oxford University Press, 1833, repr. New York: Books for Libraries Press).

Held, D. (1993), 'Democracy: From City-states to a Cosmopolitan Order?', in D. Held (ed.), *Prospects for Democracy: North, South, East, West* (Cambridge: Polity Press): 13–52.

—— (1995), *Democracy and the Global Order: From the Modern State to Global Governance* (Cambridge: Polity Press).

—— (2002), 'Cosmopolitanism: Ideas, Realities, Deficits', in D. Held and A. McGrew (eds), *Governing Globalization* (Cambridge: Polity Press): 305–24.

—— **and McGrew, A.** (2002), *Globalization/Anti-Globalization* (Cambridge: Polity Press).

—— —— (2007), *Globalization/Antiglobalization* (Cambridge: Polity Press).

—— —— **et al.** (1999), *Global Transformations: Politics, Economics and Culture* (Cambridge: Polity Press).

Helleiner, E. (1994), *States and the Reemergence of Global Finance: From Bretton Woods to the 1980s* (Ithaca, NY: Cornell University Press).

Helman, G. B., and Ratner, S.R. (1992–93), 'Saving Failed States', *Foreign Policy*, 89: 3–20.

Henkin, Louis (1968), *How Nations Behave: Law and Foreign Policy* (London: Pall Mall Press).

—— (1995), *International Law: Politics and Values* (Dordrecht: Martinus Nijhoff).

Hettne, B. (1999), 'Globalization and the New Regionalism: The Second Great Transformation', in B. Hettne, A. Intoai, and O. Sunkel (eds), *Globalism and the New Regionalism* (Basingstoke: Macmillan): 7–8.

Higgins, R. (1994), *Problems and Process: International Law and How We Use It* (Oxford: Oxford University Press).

Higgott, R. (1995), 'Economic Co-operation in the Asia Pacific: A Theoretical Comparison with the European Union', *Journal of European Public Policy*, 2(3): 361–83.

Hirst, P., and Thompson, G. (1999), *Globalization in Question* (Cambridge: Polity Press).

—— (2003), 'Globalization: A Necessary Myth?', in D. Held and A. McGrew (eds), *The Global Transformations Reader*, 2nd edn (Cambridge: Polity Press): 98–106.

—— **and Bromley, S.** (2009) *Globalization in Question*, 3rd edn (Cambridge: Polity Press).

Hobden, S., and Hobson, J. (2002), *Historical Sociology of International Relations* (Cambridge: Cambridge University Press).

Hobsbawm, E. (1990), *Nations and Nationalism since 1780: Programme, Myth, Reality* (Cambridge: Cambridge University Press)

Hoekman, B., and Kostecki, M. (2009), *The Political Economy of the World Trading System*, 3rd edn (Oxford: Oxford University Press).

Hoffman, S. (1995–96), 'The Politics and Ethics of Military Intervention', *Survival*, 37(4): 29–51.

Homer-Dixon, T. (1991), 'On the Threshold: Environmental Changes as Causes of Acute Conflict', *International Security*, 16: 76–116.

—— (1994), 'Environmental Scarcities and Violent Conflict: Evidence from Cases', *International Security*, 19(1): 5–40.

Hoogvelt, A. (2001), *Globalization and the Post-Colonial World* (Basingstoke: Palgrave).

Hooper, C. (2001), *Manly States* (New York: Columbia University Press).

Hove, C. (1994), *Shebeen Tales: Messages from Harare* (Cape Town: Baobab Books).

Howse, R. (2007), *The WTO System: Law, Politics and Legitimacy* (London: Cameron May).

Hroch, M. (1996), 'From National Movement to the Fully-formed Nation: The Nation-building Process in Europe', in G. Balakrishnan (ed.), *Mapping the Nation* (London: Verso).

Hubert, D. (2004), 'An Idea that Works in Practice', *Security Dialogue*, 35 (September): 351–2.

Human Security Report 2005 (Oxford: Oxford University Press).

Humphreys, M., and Varshney, A. (2004), *Violent Conflict and the Millennium Development: Goals: Diagnosis and Recommendations*, CGSD Working Paper No. 19 (New York: Center on Globalization and Sustainable Development, The Earth Institute at Columbia University), available online at http://www.earthinstitute.columbia.edu/cgsd/documents/humphreys_conflict_and_MDG.pdf, last accessed 25 June 2007.

Huntington, S. (1993a), 'The Clash of Civilizations', *Foreign Affairs*, 72(3): 22–49.

—— (1993b), 'If Not Civilizations, What?', *Foreign Affairs*, 72(4): 22–169.

—— (1996), *The Clash of Civilizations and the Remaking of World Order* (New York: Simon & Schuster and Touchstone).

Hurrell, A. (1995), 'Regionalism in Theoretical Perspective', in L. Fawcett and A. Hurrell (eds), *Regionalism in World Politics: Regional Organization and International Order* (Oxford: Oxford University Press): 37–73.

—— and Woods, N. (1995), 'Globalization and Inequality', *Millennium*, 24(3): 447–70.

Husain, M. Z. (1995), *Global Islamic Politics* (New York: HarperCollins).

—— (1998), 'Non-democratic States and Political Liberalisation in the Middle East: A Structural Analysis', *Third World Quarterly*, 19(1): 63–85.

ICPF (1994), *Uncommon Opportunities: Agenda for Peace and Equitable Development* (London: Zed Books).

Ignatieff, M. (2002), 'Is the Human Rights Era Ending?', *New York Times*, 5 February: A25.

Ikenberry, G. J. (1999), 'Liberal Hegemony and the Future of American Post-war Order', in T. V. Hall and J. A. Hall (eds), *International Order and the Future of World Politics* (Cambridge: Cambridge University Press).

—— (2001), *After Victory: Institutions, Strategic Restraint, and the Rebuilding of Order after Major Wars* (Princeton, NJ: Princeton University Press).

Inayatullah, N., and Blaney, D. (2004) *International Relations and the Problem of Difference* (London: Routledge).

Intergovernmental Panel on Climate Change (IPCC) (2007), *Climate Change 2007: The Physical Science Basis. Contribution of Working Group I to the Fourth Assessment Report of the Intergovernmental Panel on Climate Change*, available online at www.ipcc.ch.

International Commission on Intervention and State Sovereignty (ICISS) (2001), *The Responsibility to Protect* (Ottawa: ICISS).

International Labour Organization (n.d.), 'Facts on Women at Work', available online at www.ilo.org/public/english/region/eurpro/budapest/download/womenwork.pdf.

Jackson, R. H. (1990), *Quasi-States: Sovereignty, International Relations and the Third World* (Cambridge: Cambridge University Press).

—— (2000), *The Global Covenant: Human Conduct in a World of States* (Oxford: Oxford University Press).

—— and Owens, P. (2001), 'The Evolution of International Society', in J. Baylis and S. Smith (eds), *The Globalization of World Politics*, 3rd edn (Oxford: Oxford University Press): 45–62.

Jaquette, J. (2003), 'Feminism and the Challenge of the "Post-Cold War" World', *International Feminist Journal of Politics* 5(3): 331–54.

Jervis, R. (1983), 'Security Regimes', in S. D. Krasner (ed), *International Regimes* (Ithaca, NY: Cornell University Press).

—— (1999), 'Realism, Neoliberalism, and Cooperation: Understanding the Debate', *International Security*, 24 (Summer): 42–63.

Jolly, R., and Ray, D. B. (2006), *National Human Development Reports and the Human Security Framework: A Review of Analysis and Experience* (Brighton: Institute of Development Studies).

Jones, K. (2004), *Who's Afraid of the WTO?* (New York: Oxford University Press).

Junaid, S. (2005), *Terrorism and Global Power Systems* (Oxford: Oxford University Press).

Junne, G. C. A. (2001), 'International Organizations in a Period of Globalization: New (Problems of) Legitimacy', in J.-M. Coicaud and V. Heiskanen (eds), *The Legitimacy of International Organizations* (Tokyo: United Nations University Press).

Kagan, R. (2003), *Paradise and Power: America and Europe in the New World Order* (London: Atlantic Books).

Kaldor, M, (1999), *New and Old Wars: Organised Violence in a Global Era* (Cambridge: Polity Press).

Kant, I. (1991), *Political Writings*, ed. Hans Reiss (Cambridge: Cambridge University Press).

Keane, J. (2003), *Global Civil Society?* (Cambridge: Cambridge University Press).

Keay, J. (1993), *The Honourable Company: A History of the English East India Company* (London: Harper Collins).

Keck, M. E., and Sikkink, K. (1998), *Activists beyond Borders: Transnational Advocacy Networks in International Politics* (Ithaca, NY: Cornell University Press).

Kedourie, Elie (1960), *Nationalism* (London: Hutchinson).

Kegley, C. (ed.) (1995), *Controversies in International Relations Theory: Realism and the Neoliberal Challenge* (New York: St Martin's).

Kelsen, H. (1952), *Principles of International Law* (New York: Rinehart and Company).

Kenen, P. (1996), 'The Feasibility of Taxing Foreign Exchange Transactions', in M. ul Haq, I. Kaul, and I. Grunberg (eds), *The Tobin Tax: Coping with Financial Volatility* (Oxford: Oxford University Press).

Kennan, G. (1986), 'Morality and Foreign Policy', *Foreign Affairs*, 64: 205–18.

—— (1996), 'Diplomacy in the Modern World', in Robert J. Beck, Anthony Clark Arend, and Robert D.Vanger Lugt (eds), *International Rules: Approaches from International Law and International Relations* (Oxford: Oxford University Press): 99–106.

Keohane, R. O. (1984), *After Hegemony: Cooperation and Discord in the World Political Economy* (Princeton, NJ: Princeton University Press).

—— (1986), 'Reflection in Theory of International Politics. A Response to My Critics', in (ed.), *Neorealism and Its Critics* (New York: Columbia University Press):

—— (2002a), 'Institutional Theory in International Relations', in (ed.), *Realism and Institutionalism in*

International Studies (Ann Arbor, MI: University of Michigan Press).

—— (2002b), 'The Globalization of Informal Violence, Theories of World Politics, and the "Liberalism of Fear"', in R. O. Keohane (ed.), *Power and Governance in a Partially Globalized World* (London: Routledge): 272–87.

—— **and Martin, L.** (1995), 'The Promise of Institutionalist Theory', *International Security*, 20(1): 39–51.

—— **and Nye, J. S.** (1972), 'Transnational Relations and World Politics', in *International Organizations* (Cambridge, MA: Harvard University Press).

—— —— (1977), *Power and Interdependence: World Politics in Transition* (Boston: Little, Brown).

—— —— (2003), 'Globalization: What's New? What's not? (And so what?)', in D. Held and A. McGrew (eds), *The Global Transformations Reader* (Cambridge: Polity Press): 75–84.

Keynes, J. M. (1997 [1936]), *The General Theory of Employment, Interest, and Money* (Amherst, NY: Prometheus Books).

—— (2009 [1963]), *Essays in Persuasion*, new edn (London: W. W. Norton).

Khong, Y. F. (2001), 'Human Security: A Shotgun Approach to Alleviating Human Misery', *Global Governance*, 7: 231–37.

Kirkpatrick, J. (1979), 'Dictatorships and Double Standards', *Commentary*, 68.

Kissinger, H. A. (1977), *American Foreign Policy*, 3rd edn (New York: W. W. Norton).

Koehler, S. (2007), 'Professor Explains Continuous Threat from Land Mines', *Ozarks Local News*, 7 February, available online at http://www.banminesusa.org., last accessed 25 June 2007.

Koskenniemi, M. (1989), *From Apology to Utopia: The Structure of International Legal Argument* (Helsinki: Finnish Lawyers Publishing Company).

Koul, A. K. (2005), *A Guide to the WTO and GATT: Economics, Law, and Politics* (The Hague: Kluwer Law International).

Krasner, S. D. (ed.) (1983), *International Regimes* (Ithaca, NY: Cornell University Press).

—— (1985), *Structural Conflict: The Third World Against Global Liberalism* (Berkeley, CA: University of California Press).

—— (1991), 'Global Communications and National Power: Life on the Pareto Frontier', *World Politics*, 43: 336–66.

—— (1993), 'Sovereignty, Regimes and Human Rights', in V. Rittberger (ed.), *Regime Theory and International Relations* (Oxford: Clarendon Press).

—— (1999), *Sovereignty: Organized Hypocrisy* (Princeton, NJ: Princeton University Press).

Kratochwil, F. (1989), *Rules, Norms, and Decisions* (Cambridge: Cambridge University Press).

Krause, K., and Williams, M. C. (eds) (1997), *Critical Security Studies: Concepts and Cases* (London: UCL Press).

Kuperman, A. J. (2005), 'Suicidal Rebellions and the Moral Hazard of Humanitarian Intervention', *Ethnopolitics*, 4(2): 149–73.

—— (2008), 'The Moral Hazard of Humanitarian Intervention: Lessons from the Balkans', *International Studies Quarterly*, 32(1): 49–80.

Laclau, E., and Mouffe, C. (1985), *Hegemony & Socialist Strategy: Towards a Radical Democratic Politics* (London: Verso).

Laidi, Z. (1998), *A World Without Meaning: The Crisis of Meaning in International Politics* (London: Routledge).

Laqueur, W. (1996), 'Postmodern Terrorism', *Foreign Affairs*, 75(5): 24–37.

Layne, C. (2006), 'Impotent Power', *The National Interest*, Sep./Oct.: 41–2.

Legrain, P. (2002), *Open World: The Truth about Globalisation* (London: Abacus).

Lepard, B. D. (2002), *Rethinking Humanitarian Intervention* (University Park, PA: Pennsylvania State University Press).

Lepeska, D. (2008), 'The Perils of Progress: Two Views on Orissa's Future', 8 December 2008, available online at http://www.devex.com/articles/the-perils-of-progress-two-views-on-orissa-s-future, last accessed 11 January 2010.

Levy, M. A., Young, O.R., and Zürn, M. (1995), 'The Study of International Regimes', *European Journal of International Relations*, 1(3): 267–331.

Lewis, B. (1988), *The Political Language of Islam* (Chicago, IL: University of Chicago Press).

Lieven, A., and Hulsman, J. (2006), *Ethical Realism: A View of America's Role in the World* (New York: Pantheon Books).

Lindberg, T. (2005), 'Protect the People', *Washington Times*, 27 September: A19.

Ling, H. L. M. (2002), *Postcolonial International Relations: Conquest and Desire between Asia and the West* (Basingstoke: Palgrave Macmillan).

Linklater, A. (1990), *Men and Citizens in the Theory of International Relations*, 2nd edn (London: Macmillan).

—— (1999), 'The Evolving Spheres of International Justice', *International Affairs*, 75(3).

—— (2002), 'Cosmopolitan Political Communities in International Relations', *International Relations*, 16(1): 135–50.

—— (2005), 'The Harm Principle and Global Ethics', *Global Society*, 20(3): 20.

—— (2010), 'A European Civilizing Process', in C. Hill and M. Smith (eds), *The International Relations of the European Union* (Oxford: Oxford University Press).

Little, R. (1996), 'The Growing Relevance of Pluralism?', in S. Smith, K. Booth, and M. Zalewski (eds), *International Theory: Positivism and Beyond* (Cambridge: Cambridge University Press): 66–86.

Lizza, R. (2007), 'The Invasion of the Alpha Male Democrat', *New York Times*, 7 January.

Lobell, S. E., Ripsman, N. M., and Taliaferro, J. W. (2009), *Neoclassical Realism, the State, and Foreign Policy* (Cambridge: Cambridge University Press).

Lodgaard, S. (2000), 'Human Security: Concept and Operationalization', paper presented to the Expert Seminar on Human Rights and Peace 2000, Palais Wilson, Geneva, 8–9 December.

Luard, E. (ed.) (1992), *Basic Texts in International Relations* (London: Macmillan).

Lugones, M. (1990), 'Playfulness, World-Travelling, and Loving Perception', in Gloria Anzaldua (ed.), *Making Face, Making Soul: Haciendo Caras: Creative and Critical Perspectives by Women of Color* (San Francisco, CA: Aunt Lute Press): 390–402.

Luttwak, E. (1995), 'Towards Post-Heroic Warfare', *Foreign Affairs*, 74: 109–22.

Mabee, B. (2009), *The Globalization of Security* (London: Palgrave).

McCalla, A., and Nash, J. (2008), *Reforming Agricultural Trade for Developing Countries: Key Issues for a Pro-Development Outcome of the Doha Round* (Washington, DC: World Bank Publications).

McClintock, A. (1992), 'The Angel of Progress: Pitfalls of the Term "Post-colonialism"', *Social Text* (Spring): 1–15.

McDougal, M., and Reisman, M. (1983), 'International Law in Policy-Oriented Perspective', in R. MacDonald and D. Johnston (eds), *The Structure and Process of International Law* (The Hague: Martinus Nijhoff).

MacFarlane, N., and Khong, Y. F. (2006), *Human Security and the UN: A Critical History* (Bloomington, IN: Indiana University Press).

McGrew, A. G., Lewis, P. G., et al. (1992), *Global Politics: Globalization and the Nation-state* (Cambridge: Polity Press).

Machiavelli, N. (1988), *The Prince*, ed. Q. Skinner (Cambridge: Cambridge University Press).

McInnes, C., and Lee, K. (2006), 'Health, Security and Foreign Policy', *Review of International Studies*, 32(1).

Mack, A. (2004), 'A Signifier of Shared Values', *Security Dialogue*, 35(3): 366–7.

MacKenzie, M. (2009) 'Empowerment Boom or Bust? Assessing Women's Post-Conflict Empowerment Initiatives', *Cambridge Journal of International Affairs*, 22(2): 199–215.

McLeod, J. (2000), *Beginning Postcolonialism* (Manchester: Manchester University Press).

McNeill, D. (2006), 'Japan and the Whaling Ban: Siege Mentality Fuels "Sustainability" Claims', available online at http://www.japanfocus.org/products/details/2353, last accessed 22 February 2006.

McNeill, J. R., and McNeill, W. H. (2003), *The Human Web: A Bird's Eye View of World History* (New York: W. W. Norton).

Mann, M. (1986; 1993), *The Sources of Social Power, Vol. 1: A History of Power from the Beginning to AD 1760* and *Vol. 2: The Rise of Classes and Nation-States, 1760–1914* (Cambridge: Cambridge University Press).

Mansbach, R. W., Ferguson, Y. H., et al. (1976), *The Web of World Politics: Nonstate Actors in the Global System* (New York: Prentice Hall).

Marchand, M. H., and Runyan, A. S. (eds) (2000), *Gender and Global Restructuring: Sightings, Sites, and Resistances* (New York: Routledge).

Marshall, T. H. (1973), *Class, Citizenship and Social Development* (Westport, CT: Greenwood Press).

Marx, K. (1992), *Capital: Student Edition*, ed. C. J. Arthur (London: Lawrence & Wishart). First published 1867.

—— **and Engels, F.** (1967), *The Communist Manifesto*, with and introduction by A. J. P. Taylor (Harmondsworth: Penguin).

Mattli, W. (1999), *The Logic of Regional Integration: Europe and Beyond* (Cambridge: Cambridge University Press).

—— **and Woods, N.** (eds) (2009), *The Politics of Global Regulation* (Princeton, NJ: Princeton University Press).

Mavroidis, P. (2008), *Trade in Goods: The GATT and the Other Agreements Regulating Trade in Goods* (Oxford: Oxford University Press).

Mazlish, B., and Iriye, A. (eds) (2005), *The Global History Reader* (Abingdon: Routledge).

Mazrui, A. A. (1997), 'Islamic and Western Values', *Foreign Affairs*, 76(5) (September/October): 118–32.

MDG Report (2009), The United Nations Department of Economic and Social Affairs, available online at http://www.un.org/millenniumgoals/pdf/MDG_Report_2009_ENG.pdf, last accessed 12 July 2010.

Mearsheimer, J. (1990), 'Back to the Future: Instability in Europe after the Cold War', *International Security*, 15(1): 5–56.

—— (1994/5), 'The False Promise of International Institutions', *International Security* 19(3): 5–49.

—— (2001), *The Tragedy of Great Power Politics* (New York: W. W. Norton).

—— (2005), 'Hans Morgenthau and the Iraq War: Realism versus Neo-Conservatism', *The National Interest* 81 (Fall): 10.

—— (2006), 'Structural Realism', in Tim Dunne, Milja Kurki, and Steve Smith (eds), *International Relations Theories: Discipline and Diversity* (Oxford: Oxford University Press): 71–88.

—— (2009), 'Another War, Another Defeat', *The American Conservative* (January): 6–8.

—— **and Walt, S.** (2003), 'An Unnecessary War', *Foreign Policy* (Jan.–Feb.): 51–9.

Meinecke, F. (1957), *Machiavellism: The Doctrine of 'Raison d'Etat' and Its Place in Modern History*, trans. D. Scott (London: Routledge).

Mies, M. (1998 [1986]), *Patriarchy and Accumulation on a World Scale: Women in the International Division of Labour* (London: Zed).

—— **et al.** (1988), *Women: The Last Colony* (London: Zed).

Mill, J. S. (1973), 'A Few Words on Non-Intervention', in G. Himmelfarb (ed.), *Essays on Politics and Culture* (Gloucester, MA: Peter Smith): 368–84.

Miller, D. (1998), 'Bounded Citizenship', in K. Hutchings and R. Dannreuther (eds), *The Borders of Citizenship* (Basingstoke: Macmillan).

—— (2000), 'Justice and Inequality', in N. Woods and A. Hurrell (eds), *Inequality, Globalisation and World Politics* (Oxford: Oxford University Press): 187–210.

—— (2002), 'Caney's International Distributive Justice: A Response', *Political Studies*, 50: 974–77.

—— (2004), 'National Responsibility and International Justice', in D. K. Chatterjee (ed.), *The Ethics of Assistance* (Cambridge: Cambridge University Press): 23–143.

Miller, J. (1993), 'The Challenge of Radical Islam', *Foreign Affairs*, 72(2) (Spring): 43–56.

Mingst, K. (2004), *Essentials of International Relations* (New York: W. W. Norton).

Mitrany, D. (1943), *A Working Peace System* (London: RIIA).

Moellendorf, D. (2002), *Cosmopolitan Justice* (Cambridge, MA: Westview Press).

Mohanty, C. (1988), 'Under Western Eyes: Feminist Scholarship and Colonial Discourse', *Feminist Review*, 30: 61–88.

Moon, K. (1997), *Sex Among Allies: Military Prostitution in US–Korea Relations* (New York: Columbia University Press).

Moravcsik, A. (1997), 'Taking Preferences Seriously: A Liberal Theory of International Relations', *International Organization*, 51(4): 513–54.

—— (1998), *The Choice for Europe: Social Purpose and State Power from Messina to Maastricht* (Ithaca, NY: Cornell University Press).

Morgenthau, H. J. (1940), 'Positivism, Functionalism, and International Law', *American Journal of International Law*, 34(2): 260–84.

—— ([1948] 1955, 1962, 1978), *Politics among Nations: The Struggle for Power and Peace*, 2nd edn (New York: Knopf).

—— (1952), *American Foreign Policy: A Critical Examination* (London: Methuen) (also published as *In Defence of the National Interest*).

—— (1985), *Politics among Nations*, 6th edn (New York: McGraw-Hill).

Morton, A. (2007), *Unravelling Gramsci: Hegemony and Passive Revolution in the Global Political Economy* (London: Pluto Press).

Mosse, G. L. (1988), *The Culture of Western Europe: The Nineteenth and Twentieth Centuries* (Boulder, CO: Westview Press).

Mousseau, F., and Mittal, A. (2006), *The Free Market Famine*, Foreign Policy in Focus Commentary, 26 October, available online at www.fpif.org/pdf/gac/0610famine.pdf.

Mueller, J. (1989), *Retreat from Doomsday: The Obsolescence of Major War* (New York: Basic Books).

Munkler, H. (2005), *The New Wars* (Cambridge: Polity).

Munoz, G. M. (ed.) (1999), *Islam, Modernism, and the West: Cultural and Political Relations at the End of the Millennium* (London: I. B. Tauris).

Muolo, P., and Padilla, M. (2008), *Chain of Blame: How Wall Street Caused the Mortgage and Credit Crisis* (Hoboken, NJ: John Wiley and Sons).

Murden, S. (1999), 'Review Article: Huntington and his Critics', *Political Geography*, 18: 1017–22.

—— (2009), 'The Secondary Institutions of the Middle Eastern Regional Interstate Society', in Barry Buzan and Ana Gonzalez-Perry (eds), *International Society and the Middle East* (Basingstoke: Palgrave Macmillan): 117–39.

Murray, A. J. H. (1997), *Reconstructing Realism: Between Power Politics and Cosmopolitan Ethics* (Edinburgh: Keele University Press).

Naimi, M. (2002), 'Post-terror surprises', *Foreign Policy* (September).

Nardin. T. (1983), *Law, Morality and the Relations of States* (Princeton, NJ: Princeton University Press).

—— (2005), 'Humanitarian Imperialism: Response to "Ending Tyranny in Iraq"', *Ethics and International Affairs*, 19(2): 21–6.

Narlikar, A. (2003), *International Trade and Developing Countries: Bargaining Coalitions in the GATT and WTO* (London: Routledge).

National Counter Terrorism Center (2005), *NCTC Fact Sheet and Observations Related to 2005 Terrorist Incidents*, available online at www.NCTC.Gov, last accessed 25 June 2007.

Ngugi wa Thiong' o (1986), *Decolonising the Mind: The Politics of Language in African Literature* (Oxford: James Currey).

Notermans, T. (2007), *Money, Markets, and the State: Social Democratic Economic Policies Since 1918*, new edn (Cambridge: Cambridge University Press).

NSS (2001, 2002), *National Security Strategy of the United States of America* (Washington, DC: US Government Printing Office).

Nussbaum, M. (1996), *For Love of Country: Debating the Limits of Patriotism* (Boston, MA: Beacon Press).

O'Brien, R., Goetz, A. M., et al. (2000), *Contesting Global Governance: Multilateral Economic Institutions and Global Social Movements* (Cambridge: Cambridge University Press).

O'Hagan, J. (1995), 'Civilisational Conflict? Looking for Cultural Enemies', *Third World Quarterly*, 16(1): 19–38.

Office of the Director of National Intelligence (2005), 'Letter from Al-Zawahiri to Al-Zarqawi', 11 October.

Ohmae, K. (1995), *The End of the Nation State* (New York: Free Press).

Olson, J. S. (ed.) (1988), *Dictionary of the Vietnam War* (New York: Greenwood Press).

Olson, M. (1965), *The Logic of Collective Action* (Cambridge, MA: Harvard University Press).

Onwudiwe, I. D. (2001), *The Globalization of Terror* (Burlington, VT: Ashgate).

Ougaard, M. (2004), *Political Globalization: State, Power and Social Forces* (Basingstoke: Palgrave).

Owen, R. (2000), *State, Power and Politics in the Making of the Modern Middle East*, 2nd edn (London: Routledge).

Oxfam (2003), 'Boxing Match in Agricultural Trade', in Briefing Paper 32, available online at www.oxfam.org.

Oye, K. A. (ed.) (1986), *Cooperation Under Anarchy* (Princeton, NJ: Princeton University Press).

Palme Commission (1982), *Common Security: A Programme for Disarmament*, The Report of the Palme Commission (London: Pan Books).

Pape, R. (2005), *Dying to Win: The Strategic Logic of Suicide Terrorism* (New York: Random House).

Parashar, S. (2009), 'Feminist International Relations and Women Militants: Case Studies from Sri Lanka and Kasmir', *Cambridge Journal of International Affairs*, 22(2): 235–56.

Parekh, B. (1997*a*), 'When Religion Meets Politics', *Demos*, 11: 5–7.

—— (1997*b*), 'Rethinking Humanitarian Intervention', *International Political Science Review*, 18(1): 49–70.

Paris, R. (2001), 'Human Security: Paradigm Shift or Hot Air', *International Security*, 26(2): 87–102.

Pearson, R. (2000), 'Rethinking Gender Matters in Development', in T. Allen and A. Thomas (eds), *Poverty and Development in the Twenty-First Century* (Oxford: Oxford University Press): 383–402.

Penttinen, E. (2008), *Globalization, Prostitution and Sex-Trafficking: Corporeal Politics* (London: Routledge).

Peterson, V. S., and Runyan, A. S. (2010), *Global Gender Issues in the New Millennium*, 3rd edn (Boulder, CO: Westview Press).

Pettman, J. J. (1996), *Worlding Women: A Feminist International Politics* (St Leonards: Allen & Unwin).

Petzold-Bradley, E., Carius, A., and Vincze, A. (eds) (2001), *Responding to Environmental Conflicts: Implications for Theory and Practice* (Dordrecht: Kluwer Academic).

Pogge, T. (1989), *Realizing Rawls* (Ithaca, NY: Cornell University Press).

—— (1994), 'Cosmopolitanism and Sovereignty', in C. Brown (ed.), *Political Restructuring in Europe: Ethical Perspectives* (London: Routledge).

—— (2001*a*), 'Priorities of Global Justice', *Metaphilosophy*, 32(1–2).

—— (2001*b*), 'Moral Universalism and Global Economic Justice', *Politics, Philosophy and Economics*, 1(1): 29–58.

—— (2002), *World Poverty and Human Rights: Cosmopolitan Responsibilities and Reforms* (Cambridge: Polity Press).

Polanyi, K. (1957 [1944]), *The Great Transformation: The Social and Political Origins of Our Time* (Boston, MA: Beacon Press).

Porter, P. (2009), *Military Orientalism: Eastern War through Western Eyes* (New York: Columbia University Press).

Porter, T. (2005), *Globalization and Finance* (Cambridge: Polity Press).

Posen, A. (1993), 'Why Central Bank Independence Does Not Cause Low Inflation: There Is No Institutional Fix for Politics', in R. O'Brien (ed.), *Finance and the International Economy, vol. 7* (Oxford: Oxford University Press).

Posen, B. (1993), 'The Security Dilemma and Ethnic Conflict', *Survival*, 35(1): 27–47.

Power and Interest News Report (2006), 'Asia's Coming Water Wars', 22 August, available online at http://www.pinr.com, last accessed 25 June 2007.

PR Newswire Europe (2002), 'London Tuberculosis Rates now at Third World Proportions', 4 December, available online at http://www.prnewswire.co.uk/cgi/news/release?id=95088, last accessed 25 June 2007.

Price, R. (1998), 'Reversing the Gun Sights: Transnational Civil Society Targets Land Mines', *International Organization*, 52(3).

—— (2004), 'Emerging Customary Norms and Anti-Personnel Landmines', in Christian Reus-Smit (ed.), *The Politics of International Law* (Cambridge: Cambridge University Press): 106–30.

Prügl, E. (1999), *The Global Construction of Gender: Home-Based Work in the Political Economy of the 20th Century* (New York: Columbia University Press).

Purvis, N. (1991), 'Critical Legal Studies in Public International Law', *Harvard International Law Journal*, 32(1): 81–127.

Rabasa, A., Chalk, P., et al. (2006), *Beyond al-Qaeda: Part 2, The Outer Rings of the Terrorist Universe* (Santa Monica, CA: RAND).

Ramsey, P. (2002), *The Just War: Force and Political Responsibility* (Lanham, MD: Rowman & Littlefield).

Rapley, J. (1996), *Understanding Development* (Boulder, CO: Lynne Rienner).

Rawls, J. (1971), *A Theory of Justice* (Oxford: Oxford University Press).

—— (1999), *The Law of Peoples* (Cambridge, MA: Harvard University Press).

Reeves, J. (2004), *Culture and International Relations: Natives, Narratives, and Tourists* (London: Routledge).

Rehn, E., and Sirleaf, E. J. (2002), *Women, War, Peace: The Independent Experts' Assessment on the Impact of Armed Conflict on Women and Women's Role in Peace-Building*, available online at http://www.unifem.org/resources/item_detail.php?ProductID=17, last accessed 25 June 2007.

Reisman, W. M. (1985), 'Criteria for the Lawful Use of Force in International Law', *Yale Journal of International Law*, 10(2): 279–85.

Reus-Smit, C. (1999), *The Moral Purpose of the State* (Princeton, NJ: Princeton University Press).

—— (2003), 'Politics and International Legal Obligation', *European Journal of International Relations*, 9(4): 591–625.

Rice, S. (2006), 'The Threat of Global Poverty', *The National Interest* (Spring): 76–82.

Richardson, J. I. (1997), 'Contending Liberalisms: Past and Present', *European Journal of International Relations*, 3(1): 5–33.

Risse-Kappen, T. (ed.) (1995), *Bringing Transnational Relations Back In* (Cambridge: Cambridge University Press).

Rittberger, V. (ed.) (1993), *Regime Theory and International Relations* (Oxford: Clarendon Press).

Roberts, A. (1993), 'Humanitarian War: Military Intervention and Human Rights', *International Affairs*, 69(3): 429–49.

—— and Kingsbury, B. (1993), 'Introduction: The UN's Roles in International Society since 1945', in A. Roberts and B. Kingsbury (eds), *United Nations, Divided World* (Oxford: Clarendon Press).

Roberts, R. (1984), *Questioning Development* (London: Returned Volunteer Action).

Robertson, J. (2008), *US–Asia Economic Relations: A Political Economy of Crisis and the Rise of New Business Actors* (London: Routledge).

Robins, N. (2006), *The Corporation That Changed the World: How the East India Company Shaped the Modern Multinational* (London: Pluto).

Robinson, G. E. (1997), 'Can Islamists be Democrats?: The case of Jordan', *Middle East Journal*, 51(3): 373–87.

Robinson, W. I. (1996), *Promoting Polyarchy: Globalization, US Intervention, and Hegemony* (Cambridge: Cambridge University Press).

—— (2004), *A Theory of Global Capitalism: Production, Class, and State in a Transnational World* (Baltimore, MD: Johns Hopkins University Press).

Rodrik, D. (1997), *Has Globalization Gone Too Far?* (Washington, DC: Institute for International Economics).

Rome Statute of the International Criminal Court, available at http://untreaty.un.org/cod/icc/statute/romefra.htm, last accessed 15 January 2010.

Rosamond, B. (2000), *Theories of European Integration* (Basingstoke: Macmillan).

Rose, G. (1998), 'Neoclassical Realism and Theories of Foreign Policy', *World Politics*, 51(1): 144–72.

Rosenau, J. (1997), *Along the Domestic–Foreign Frontier* (Cambridge: Cambridge University Press).

Rosenberg, J. (1994), *The Empire of Civil Society: A Critique of the Realist Theory of International Relations* (London: Verso).

—— (2000), *The Follies of Globalization Theory: Polemical Essays* (London: Verso).

—— (2006), 'Globalization Theory: A Postmortem', *International Politics* 42(1): 2–74.

Roth, K. (2004), 'The War in Iraq: Justified as Humanitarian Intervention?', Kroc Institute Occasional Paper No. 25 (Notre Dame, IN: The Joan B. Kroc Institute).

Roy, O. (1994), *The Failure of Political Islam* (London: I. B. Tauris, 1994).

Rublee, M. R. (2009), *Non-proliferation Norms: Why States Choose Nuclear Restraint* (Athens, GA: University of Georgia Press).

Ruggie, J. G. (1993), 'Multilateralism: The Anatomy of an Institution', in John Gerard Ruggie (ed.), *Multilateralism Matters* (New York: Columbia University Press): 3–50.

Rupert, M. (1995), *Producing Hegemony: The Politics of Mass Production and American Global Power* (Cambridge: Cambridge University Press).

—— and Solomon, M. S. (2005), *Globalization and International Political Economy: The Politics of Alternative Futures* (Lanham, MD: Rowman & Littlefield).

Sageman, M. (2004), *Understanding Terror Networks* (Philadelphia, PA: University of Pennsylvania Press).

Said, E. (1978), *Orientalism* (London: Penguin).

Salter, M. B. (2006), 'The Global Visa Regime and the Political Technologies of the International Self: Borders, Bodies, Biopolitics', *Alternatives*, 31(2): 167–89.

Schelling, T. C. (1960), *The Strategy of Conflict* (Oxford: Oxford University Press).

Schmidt, B. C. (1998), *The Political Discourse of Anarchy: A Disciplinary History of International Relations* (Albany, NY: State University of New York Press).

—— **and Williams, M. C.** (2008), 'The Bush Doctrine and the Iraq War: Neoconservatives Versus Realists', *Security Studies* 17(2): 191–220.

Scholte, J. A. (2000), *Globalization: A Critical Introduction* (London: Macmillan).

Schwartz, H. (2009), *Subprime Nation: American Power, Global Capital, and the Housing Market* (Ithaca, NY: Cornell University Press).

Schwarz, A. (1999), *A Nation in Waiting: Indonesia's Search for Stability* (Sydney, NSW: Allen & Unwin).

Schweller, R. L. (1996), 'Neo-realism's Status-quo Bias: What Security Dilemma?', *Security Studies*, 5(3): 90–121.

Schweller, R. (1998), *Deadly Imbalances: Tripolarity and Hitler's Strategy of World Conquest* (New York: Columbia University Press).

Scruton, R. (2002), *The West and the Rest: Globalization and the Terrorist Threat* (London: Continuum).

Sen, A. (1981), *Poverty and Famine* (Oxford: Clarendon Press).

—— (1983), 'The Food Problem: Theory and Policy', in A. Gauhar (ed.), *South–South Strategy* (London, Zed Books).

Shapiro, M. J. (1988), *The Politics of Representation: Writing Practices in Biography, Photography and Policy Analysis* (Madison, WI: The University of Wisconsin Press).

—— (1997), *Violent Cartographies: Mapping Culture of War* (Minneapolis, MN: University of Minnesota Press).

Shaw, M. (1997), 'The State of Globalization: Towards a Theory of State Formation', *Review of International Political Economy*, 4 (3).

—— (1999), 'The Global Revolution and the Twenty-first Century: From International Relations to Global Politics', in S. Chan and J. Wiener (eds), *Twentieth Century International History* (London: I. B. Tauris).

—— (2000), *Theory of the Global State: Globality as an Unfinished Revolution* (Cambridge: Cambridge University Press).

Shiller, R. (2008), *The Subprime Solution: How Today's Global Financial Crisis Happened, and What to Do about It* (Princeton, NJ: Princeton University Press).

Shue, H. (1981), 'Exporting Hazards', in P. G. Brown and H. Shue (eds), *Boundaries: National Autonomy and its Limits* (Princeton, NJ: Rowman & Littlefield): 24–40.

Sidahmed, A. S., and Ehteshami, A. (eds) (1996), *Islamic Fundamentalism* (Boulder, CO: Westview Press).

Simes, D. K. (2007), 'End the Crusade', in *The National Interest*, 87 (Jan.–Feb.).

Sinclair, T. (2005), *The New Masters of Capital: American Bond Rating Agencies and the Politics of Creditworthiness* (Ithaca, NY: Cornell University Press).

Singer, P. (1985), 'Famine Affluence, Morality', in C. Beitz (ed.), *International Ethics* (Princeton, NJ: Princeton University Press).

—— (1999), 'The Singer Solution to World Poverty', *New York Times*, 5 July.

—— (2002), *One World: The Ethics of Globalisation* (Melbourne: Text Publishing).

—— **and Gregg, T.** (2004), *How Ethical is Australia? An Examination of a Record of Australia's Record as a Global Citizen* (Melbourne: The Australian Collaboration in conjunction with Black Inc).

Sivan, E. (1989), 'Sunni Radicalism in the Middle East and the Iranian Revolution', *International Journal of Middle Eastern Studies*, 21(1): 1–30.

Skocpol, T. (1979), *States and Social Revolutions: A Comparative Analysis of France, Russia and China* (Cambridge: Cambridge University Press).

Slaughter, A.-M. (1995), 'International Law in a World of Liberal States', *European Journal of International Law*, 6.

—— (2004), *A New World Order* (Princeton, NJ: Princeton University Press).

—— (2000), 'A Liberal Theory of International Law' (unpublished manuscript).

Smith, A. (1986), *The Ethnic Origins of Nations* (Oxford: Blackwell)

Smith, M. (1986), *Realist Thought from Weber to Kissinger* (Baton Rouge, LA: Louisiana State University Press).

Smith, S. (1999), 'The Increasing Insecurity of Security Studies: Conceptualising Security in the Last Twenty Years', *Contemporary Security Policy*, 20(3).

Snyder, J. (1991), *Myths of Empire: Domestic Politics and International Ambition* (Ithaca, NY: Cornell University Press).

Soros, G. (1998), *The Crisis of Global Capitalism: Open Society Endangered* (London: Little, Brown and Company).

Spielmann, P. J. (2009), 'War: Is It Getting More Hellish, Or Less?', *The Guardian*, 12 July, Available at: http://www.guardian.co.uk/world/feedarticle/8604328.

Spivak, G. (1988), 'Can the Subaltern Speak?; in Cary Nelson and Lawrence Grossberg (eds), *Marxism and the Interpretation of Culture* (Chocago, IL: University of Illinois Press): 271–313.

—— (1999), *Critique of Postcolonial Reason: Toward a History of the Vanishing Present* (Harvard University).

Stammers, N. (2009), *Human Rights and Social Movements* (London, Pluto).

Stanlis, P. J. (1953), 'Edmund Burke and the Law of Nations', *American Journal of International Law*, 47(3): 404–5.

Stein, A. (1983), 'Coordination and Collaboration: Regimes in an Anarchic World', in S. D. Krasner (ed.), *International Regimes* (Ithaca, NY: Cornell University Press).

Steiner, H. J., Alston, P., and Goodman, R. (2008), *International Human Rights in Context: Law, Politics, Morals* (3rd edn, Oxford: Oxford University Press).

Stiglitz, J. (2002), *Globalization and Its Discontents* (London: Allen Lane).

Strange, S. (1994), *States and Markets*, 2nd edn (London: Pinter).

Suganami, H. (1989), *The Domestic Analogy and World Order Proposals* (Cambridge: Cambridge University Press).

Suhrke, A. (2004), 'A Stalled Initiative', *Security Dialogue*, 35(3): 365.

Sylvester, C. (1994), *Feminist Theory and International Relations in a Postmodern Era* (Cambridge: Cambridge University Press).

—— (1995), 'African and Western Feminisms: World-Traveling the Tendencies and Possibilities', *Signs: Journal of Women in Culture and Society*, 20 (4): 941–969.

—— (1999), 'Development Studies and Postcolonial Studies: Disparate Tales of the "Third World"', *Third World Quarterly*, 20: 703–21.

—— (2002), *Feminist International Relations: An Unfinished Journey* (Cambridge: Cambridge University Press).

—— (2006), 'Bare Life as a Development/Postcolonial Problematic', *The Geographical Journal*, 172 (1): 66–77.

Tabb, W. (2004), *Economic Governance in the Age of Globalization* (New York: Columbia University Press).

Tahi, M. S. (1995), 'Algeria's Democratisation Process: A Frustrated Hope', *Third World Quarterly*, 16(2): 97–20.

Tal, L. (1995), 'Dealing with Radical Islam: The Case of Jordan', *Survival*, 37(3): 139–56.

Tannenwald, N. (2007), *The Nuclear Taboo: The United States and the Non-Use of Nuclear Weapons since 1945* (Cambridge, Cambridge University Press).

Tarock, A. (1995), 'Civilisational Conflict? Fighting the Enemy under a New Banner', *Third World Quarterly*, 16(1): 5–18.

Taureck, R. (2006), 'Securitisation Theory and Securitisation Studies', *Journal of International Relations and Development*, 9.

Taylor, A. J. P. (1961), *The Origins of the Second World War* (Harmondsworth: Penguin).

Terriff, T., Croft, S., James, L., and Morgan, P. (1999), *Security Studies Today* (Cambridge: Polity Press).

Teschke, B. (2003), *The Myth of 1648: Class, Geopolitics and the Making of International Relations* (London: Verso).

Tesón, F. (2003), 'The Liberal Case for Humanitarian Intervention', in J. L. Holzgrefe and R. O. Keohane (eds.), *Humanitarian Intervention: Ethical, Legal and Political Dilemmas* (Cambridge: Cambridge University Press): 93–129.

—— (2005), 'Ending Tyranny in Iraq', *Ethics and International Affairs*, 19(2): 1–20.

The Economist (2007), 'Special Report on the European Union', 17–23 March.

The Global Fund to Fight AIDS, Tuberculosis and Malaria (n.d.), available at http://www.theglobalfund.org/en/about/aids/, last accessed 15 January 2010.

The Ottawa Citizen (1998), 'Canada, Norway Change their Ways: New Approach Bases Foreign Policy on Human Issues', *The Ottawa Citizen*, 28 May: A18.

Thirkell-White, B. (2005), *The IMF and the Politics of Financial Globalization: From the Asian Crisis to a New International Financial Architecture?* (Basingstoke: Palgrave Macmillan).

Thomas, C. (2000), *Global Governance, Development and Human Security* (London: Pluto).

Thomas, C. and Wilkin, P. (2004), 'Still Waiting After All These Years: The Third World on the Periphery of International Relations', *British Journal of Politics and International Relations*, 6: 223–40.

Thucydides ([1954] 1972), *The Peloponnesian War*, trans. R. Warner (London: Penguin).

Tickner, A. (2003), 'Seeing IR Differently: Notes From the Third World', *Millennium*, 32(2): 295–324.

Tickner, J. A. (1992), *Gender in International Relations: Feminist Perspectives on Achieving Global Security* (New York: Columbia University Press).

—— (2001), *Gendering World Politics: Issues and Approaches in the Post-Cold War Era* (New York: Columbia University Press).

—— (2002), 'Feminist Perspectives on 9/11', *International Studies Perspectives*, 3(4): 333–50.

Tilly, C. (ed.) (1975), *The Formation of Nation States in Western Europe* (Princeton, NJ: Princeton University Press).

—— (1992), *Coercion, Capital and European States, AD 900–1992* (Cambridge, MA: Blackwell).

—— (1995), `States and Nationalism in Europe, 1492–1992', in J. M.Comaroff and P. C. Stern (eds), *Perspectives on Nationalism* (Amsterdam: Gordon and Breach Science Publishers).

Toffler, A., and H. (1993), *War and Anti-War* (Boston, MA: Little Brown).

Tow, W. T., and Trood, R. (2000), 'Linkages between Traditional Security and Human Security', in W. T. Tow, R. Thakur, and In-Taek Hyun (eds), *Asia's Emerging Regional Order* (New York: United Nations University Press): 14.

Trenin, D. (2006), 'Russia Leaves the West', *Foreign Affairs*, 85(4): 95.

Trinh M. (1989), *Woman, Native, Other* (Bloomington, IN: Indiana University Press).

True, J. (2003), 'Mainstreaming Gender in Global Public Policy', *International Feminist Journal of Politics* 5(3): 368–96.

Tucker, R. W. (1977), *The Inequality of Nations* (New York: Basic Books).

Turner, B. S. (1994), *Orientalism, Postmodernism and Globalism* (London: Routledge).

Turner, G. (1993), *National Fictions: Literature, Film and the Construction of Australian Narrative* (London: Allen & Unwin).

UIA (2008), *Yearbook of International Organizations 2008–2009* (Munich: K. G. Saur, five volumes for the Union of International Associations).

UN (1999), *1999 World Survey on the Role of Women in Development: Globalization, Gender and Work* (New York: United Nations).

—— (2002), *Women, Peace and Security: Study Submitted by the Secretary-General Pursuant to Security Council Resolution 1325 (2000)* (New York: United Nations). Available online at: http://www.un.org/womenwatch/feature/wps/, last accessed on 25 June 2007.

—— (2005), *In Larger Freedom: Towards Development, Security and Human Rights for All: Report of the Secretary-General*, March.

—— (2009), *Human Rights in Palestine and Other Occupied Arab Territories: Report of the United Nations Fact Finding Mission on the Gaza Conflict* (http://www2.ohchr.org/english/bodies/hrcouncil/specialsession/9/docs/UNFFMGC_Report.pdf, 15 September 2009).

UNAIDS (2010), 'UN Secretary-General applauds the removal of entry restrictions based on HIV status by United States of America and Republic of Korea', dated 4 January, accessed 7 January 2010, http://www.unaids.org/en/KnowledgeCentre/Resources/FeatureStories/archive/2010/20100104_travelrestrictions.asp

UN Commission on Human Security (2003), *Human Security Now: Protecting and Empowering People* (New York: United Nations): 4. Available online: http://www.humansecurity-chs.org, accessed 8 April 2007.

UNCTAD (2009), *World Investment Report 2009* (Geneva: United Nations Conference on Trade and Development).

UNDP (1994), *United Nations Human Development Report* (New York: Oxford University Press).

—— (1997), *Human Development Report: Human Development to Eradicate Poverty* (New York: United Nations).

—— (2003), *United Nations Development Programme: Human Development Report* (Oxford: OUP/UNDP).

—— (2004), Orissa Human Development Report (Bhubaneswar, Orissa: UNDP, 2004). Available at http://www.orissa.gov.in/p&c/humandevelopment/index.html, accessed 11 January 2010.

—— (2005), *Human Development Report 2005: International Cooperation at a Crossroads* (New York: United Nations Development Programme).

UN, ECOSOC (1950), Economic and Social Council Resolution 288B†(X), 'Arrangements for Consultation with Non-Governmental Organizations', passed on 27 February 1950; amended and replaced by Resolution 1296 (XLIV) of 23 May 1968 and again by Resolution 1996/31 of 25 July 1996.

UNGA Res. 60/1, United Nations General Assembly Resolution 60/1, '2005 World Summit Outcome', passed on 16 September 2005.

Unger, P. (1996), *Living High and Letting Die: Our Illusion of Innocence* (New York: Oxford University Press).

UNHCR (2009), *2008 Global Trends: Refugees, Asylum-seekers, Returnees, Internally Displaced and Stateless Persons.* Available online at: http://www.unhcr.org/4a375c426.html.

UN High-Level Panel on Threats, Challenges and Change (2004), *A More Secure World: Our Shared Responsibility*, A/59/565, December (New York: United Nations).

UN Inter-Agency Committee on Women and Gender Equality (1999), *Final Communiqué: Women's Empowerment in the Context of Human Security* (7–8 December, ESCAP, Bangkok, Thailand), available online at: http://www.un.org/womenwatch/ianwge/collaboration/finalcomm1999.htm, last accessed 25 June 2007.

University of British Columbia, Human Security Center (2006), *The Human Security Brief 2006*, available online at: http://www.humansecuritybrief.info/, last accessed on 25 June 2007.

US Department of State (2003), *Country Reports on Human Rights Practices, Burma*, 31 March 2003, available online at: http://www.state.gov/g/drl/rls/hrrpt/2002/18237.htm, last accessed on 25 June 2007.

US Department of State International Informaion Programmes (2001), 'President Bush announces military strikes in Afghanistan', 7 October, www.usinfo.state.gov/regional/eur/terrorism/bush1007.htm, downloaded on 16 March 2002.

Van Rooy, A. (2003), *The Global Legitimacy Game: Civil Society, Globalization, and Protest* (Basingstoke: Palgrave Macmillan).

Vincent, R. J. (1974), *Nonintervention and International Order* (Princeton, NJ: Princeton University Press).

—— (1986), *Human Rights and International Relations* (Cambridge: Cambridge University Press).

von Martens, G. F. (1795), *Summary of the Law of Nations Founded on the Treaties and Customs of Modern Nations* (Philadelphia, PA: Thomas Bradford).

Wæver, O. (2002), 'Identity, Communities and Foreign Policy: Discourse Analysis as Foreign Policy Theory', in L. Hansen and O. Wæver (eds) (2002), *European Integration and National Identity: The Challenge of the Nordic States* (London: Routledge): 20–49.

Waller, M., and Linklater, A. (eds) (2003), *Political Loyalty and the Nation-State* (London: Routledge).

Wallerstein, I. (1979), *The Capitalist World-Economy* (Cambridge: Cambridge University Press).

—— (1995), *After Liberalism* (New York: New Press).

—— (1998), *Utopistics: Or Historical Choices of the Twenty-First Century* (New York: New Press).

—— (1999), *The End of the World as we Know it: Social Science for the Twenty-first Century* (Minneapolis, MN: University of Minneapolis Press).

—— (2003), *The Decline of American Power: The US in a Chaotic World* (New York: New Press).

—— (2004), *Alternatives: The United States Confronts the World* (London: Paradigm).

—— (2006), *European Universalism: The Rhetoric of Power* (New York: New Press).

Walker, R. B. J. (1990), 'Security, Sovereignty, and the Challenge of World Politics', *Alternatives*, 15(1): 3–27.

—— (1997), 'The Subject of Security', in K. Krause and M. C. Williams (eds), *Critical Security Studies* (Minneapolis, MN: University of Minnesota Press): 61–81.

Walt, S. M. (2002) 'The Enduring Relevance of the Realist Tradition', in I. Katznelson and H. V. Milner (eds), *Political Science: The State of the Discipline* (New York: W. W. Norton).

Waltz, K. (1959), *Man, the State and War* (New York: Columbia University Press).

—— (1979), *Theory of International Politics* (Reading, MA: Addison-Wesley).

—— (1989), 'The Origins of War in Neorealist Theory', in R. I. Rotberg and T. K. Rabb (eds), *The Origin and Prevention of Major Wars* (Cambridge: Cambridge University Press).

—— (2000a), 'Structural Realism after the Cold War', *International Security* 25(1).

—— (2000b), 'Globalization and American Power', *National Interest*, 59: 46–56.

—— (2002), 'The Continuity of International Politics', in K. Booth and T. Dunne (eds), *Worlds in Collision: Terror and the Future of Global Order* (Basingstoke: Palgrave Macmillan).

Walzer, M. (1977), *Just and Unjust Wars: A Moral Argument with Historical Illustration* (Harmondsworth: Penguin and New York: Basic Books).

—— (1983), *The Spheres of Justice: A Defence of Pluralism and Equality* (Oxford: Blackwell).

—— (1994), *Thick and Thin: Moral Argument at Home and Abroad* (Notre Dame, IN: University of Notre Dame Press).

—— (2002), 'Spheres of Affection', in M. Nussbaum (ed.), *In Defence of Country* (Boston, MA: Beacon Press).

Warner, R. (trans.) (1972), Thucydides, *The Peloponnesian War* (Harmondsworth: Penguin).

Watson, M. (2007), *The Political Economy of International Capital Mobility* (Basingstoke: Palgrave Macmillan).

Weber, C. (2006), *Imagining America at War: Morality, Politics, and Film* (London: Routledge).

Weber, H. (2002), 'Global Governance and Poverty Reduction', in S. Hughes and R. Wilkinson (eds), *Global Governance: Critical Perspectives* (Basingstoke: Palgrave): ch .8.

Weiss, L. (1999), 'Globalization and Governance', *Review of International Studies*, 25 (Special Issue).

Weiss, T. G., and Gordenker, L. (eds) (1996), *NGOs, the UN and Global Governance* (Boulder, CO: Lynne Rienner).

Welch, D. (1997), 'The Clash of Civilizations Thesis as an Argument and as a Phenomenon', *Security Studies*, 6(4): 197–216.

Weltman, J. (1995), *World Politics and the Evolution of War* (Baltimore, MD and London: Johns Hopkins University Press).

Wendt, A. (1992), 'Anarchy is What States Make of It: The Social Construction of Power Politics', *International Organization*, 46(2): 391–425.

—— (1999), *Social Theory of International Politics* (Cambridge: Cambridge University Press).

Wessel, I., and Wimhofer, G. (eds) (2001), *Violence in Indonesia* (Hamburg: Abera-Verl).

Western, J. (2005), 'Illusions of Moral Hazard: A Conceptual and Empirical Critique', *Ethnopolitics*, 4(2): 225–36.

Weston, B. H., Falk, R., and D'Amato, A. (1990), *Basic Documents in International Law*, 2nd edn (St Paul, MN: West Publishing).

Wheeler, N. J. (2000), *Saving Strangers: Humanitarian Intervention in International Society* (Oxford: Oxford University Press).

—— (2003), 'Humanitarian Intervention after 9/11', in A. Lang (ed.), *Just Intervention* (Georgetown, Wasshington, DC: Georgetown University Press): 192–216.

—— **and Booth, K.** (1992), 'The Security Dilemma', in J. Baylis and N. J. Rengger (eds), *Dilemmas of World Politics: International Issues in a Changing World* (Oxford: Oxford University Press).

—— **and Dunne, T.** (1998), 'Hedley Bull and the idea of a universal moral community: fictional, primordial or imagined?' in B. A. Roberson (ed.), *International Society and the Development of International Relations Theory* (London: Pinter).

—— **and Morris, J.** (2006), 'Justifying Iraq as a Humanitarian Intervention: The Cure is Worse than the Disease', in R. Thakur and W. P. S. Sidhu (eds), *The Iraq Crisis and World Order: Structural, Institutional and Normative Challenges* (Tokyo: United Nations University Press): 444–63.

Whitworth, S. (1994), *Feminism and International Relations: Towards a Political Economy of Gender in Inter-State and Non-Governmental Institutions* (Basingstoke: Macmillan).

Wiener, A., and Diez, T. (eds) (2004), *European Integration Theory* (Oxford: Oxford University Press).

Whyte, A. F. (1919), *The Practice of Diplomacy*, trans. of François de Callière's *De la manière de négocier avec les souverains* (London: Constable & Co.).

Wight, M. (1977) *Systems of States* (Leicester: Leicester University Press).

Willetts, P. (ed.) (1982), *Pressure Groups in the Global System: The Transnational Relations of Issue-Orientated Non-Governmental Organizations* (London: Pinter).

—— (ed.) (1996), `The Conscience of the World'. The Influence of Non-Governmental Organizations in the UN System* (London: Hurst and Washington, DC: Brookings Institution).

—— (2010), *Non-Governmental Organizations in World Politics. The Construction of Global Governance* (London: Routledge).

Wohlforth, W. (1993), *The Elusive Balance: Power and Perceptions during the Cold War* (Ithaca, NY: Cornell University Press).

World Bank (2005), *Global Economic Prospects 2005: Trade, Regionalism and Development* (Washington, DC: World Bank).

—— (2006), *World Development Indicators, 2006* (Washington, DC: World Bank).

—— (2009), *World Development Report* (Washington, DC: World Bank).

World Commission on Environment and Development (WCED) (1987), *Our Common Future:The World Commission on Environment and Development* (Oxford: Oxford University Press).

World Health Organization (2006), *Avian Influenza ('Bird Flu')—Fact Sheet* (February 2006), www.who.int/mediacentre/factsheets/avian_influenza/en/, last accessed 25 June 2007.

World Trade Organization (2007), *International Trade Statistics 2007* (Geneva: WTO).

—— (2009), *World Trade 2008, Prospects for 2009* (Geneva: WTO).

Wright, Q. (1965), *A Study of War* (Chicago, IL: Chicago University Press).

—— (1968), 'The Study of War', *International Encyclopaedia of the Social Sciences*, Vol. 16.

Wyn Jones, R. (1995), '"Message in a Bottle"—Theory and Praxis in Critical Security Studies', *Contemporary Security Studies*, 16(3): 299–319.

—— (1999), *Security, Strategy and Critical Theory* (Boulder, CO: Lynne Rienner).

Young, I. M. (1990), *Justice and the Politics of Difference* (Princeton, NJ: Princeton University Press).

Zacher, M. W., with B. A. Sutton (1996), *Governing Global Networks: International Regimes for Transportation and Communications* (Cambridge: Cambridge University Press).

Zakaria, F. (1998), *From Wealth to Power: The Unusual Origins of America's World Role* (Princeton, NJ: Princeton University Press).

Zurn, M. (2004), 'Global Governance and Legitimacy Problems', *Government and Opposition*, 39 (2).

Index